CLASSICAL
AND MEDIEVAL
LITERATURE
CRITICISM

Guide to Gale Literary Criticism Series

For criticism on	Consult these Gale series
Authors now living or who died after December 31, 1999	*CONTEMPORARY LITERARY CRITICISM (CLC)*
Authors who died between 1900 and 1999	*TWENTIETH-CENTURY LITERARY CRITICISM (TCLC)*
Authors who died between 1800 and 1899	*NINETEENTH-CENTURY LITERATURE CRITICISM (NCLC)*
Authors who died between 1400 and 1799	*LITERATURE CRITICISM FROM 1400 TO 1800 (LC)* *SHAKESPEAREAN CRITICISM (SC)*
Authors who died before 1400	*CLASSICAL AND MEDIEVAL LITERATURE CRITICISM (CMLC)*
Authors of books for children and young adults	*CHILDREN'S LITERATURE REVIEW (CLR)*
Dramatists	*DRAMA CRITICISM (DC)*
Poets	*POETRY CRITICISM (PC)*
Short story writers	*SHORT STORY CRITICISM (SSC)*
Black writers of the past two hundred years	*BLACK LITERATURE CRITICISM (BLC)* *BLACK LITERATURE CRITICISM SUPPLEMENT (BLCS)*
Hispanic writers of the late nineteenth and twentieth centuries	*HISPANIC LITERATURE CRITICISM (HLC)* *HISPANIC LITERATURE CRITICISM SUPPLEMENT (HLCS)*
Native North American writers and orators of the eighteenth, nineteenth, and twentieth centuries	*NATIVE NORTH AMERICAN LITERATURE (NNAL)*
Major authors from the Renaissance to the present	*WORLD LITERATURE CRITICISM, 1500 TO THE PRESENT (WLC)* *WORLD LITERATURE CRITICISM SUPPLEMENT (WLCS)*

ISSN 0896-0011

Volume 41

CLASSICAL AND MEDIEVAL LITERATURE CRITICISM

Excerpts from Criticism of the Works of World
Authors from Classical Antiquity through the
Fourteenth Century, from the First Appraisals
to Current Evaluations

Jelena O. Krstović
Editor

GALE GROUP

Detroit
New York
San Francisco
London
Boston
Woodbridge, CT

STAFF

Janet Witalec, Lynn M. Spampinato, *Managing Editors, Literature Product*
Kathy D. Darrow, *Product Liaison*
Jelena Krstović, *Editor*
Mark W. Scott, *Publisher, Literature Product*

Elisabeth Gellert, *Associate Editor*
Mary Ruby, Patti A. Tippett, *Technical Training Specialists*
Deborah J. Morad, Kathleen Lopez Nolan, *Managing Editors, Literature Content*
Susan M. Trosky, *Director, Literature Content*

Maria L. Franklin, *Permissions Manager*
Edna Hedblad, *Permissions Specialist*
Sarah Tomasek, *Permissions Assistant*

Victoria B. Cariappa, *Research Manager*
Tracie A. Richardson, *Project Coordinator*
Andrew Guy Malonis, Barbara McNeil, Gary J. Oudersluys, Maureen Richards, Cheryl L. Warnock, *Research Specialists*
Tamara C. Nott, *Research Associate*
Tim Lehnerer, *Research Assistant*

Dorothy Maki, *Manufacturing Manager*
Stacy L. Melson, *Buyer*

Mary Beth Trimper, *Composition and Prepress Manager*
Carolyn Roney, *Composition Specialist*

Randy Bassett, *Image Database Supervisor*
Robert Duncan, *Imaging Specialist*
Mike Logusz, *Graphic Artist*
Pamela A. Reed, *Imaging Coordinator*
Kelly A. Quin, *Imaging Editor*

Library of Congress Catalog Card Number 88-658021
ISBN 0-7876-4383-1
ISSN 0896-0011
Printed in the United States of America

10 9 8 7 6 5 4 3 2 1

Contents

Preface

Since its inception in 1988, *Classical and Medieval Literature Criticism* (*CMLC*) has been a valuable resource for students and librarians seeking critical commentary on the works and authors of antiquity through the fourteenth century. The great poets, prose writers, dramatists, and philosophers of this period form the basis of most humanities curricula, so that virtually every student will encounter many of these works during the course of a high school and college education. Reviewers have found *CMLC* "useful" and "extremely convenient," noting that it "adds to our understanding of the rich legacy left by the ancient period and the Middle Ages," and praising its "general excellence in the presentation of an inherently interesting subject." No other single reference source has surveyed the critical reaction to classical and medieval literature as thoroughly as *CMLC*.

Scope of the Series

CMLC provides an introduction to classical and medieval authors, works, and topics that represent a variety of genres, time periods, and nationalities. By organizing and reprinting an enormous amount of critical commentary written on authors and works of this period in world history, *CMLC* helps students develop valuable insight into literary history, promotes a better understanding of the texts, and sparks ideas for papers and assignments.

Each entry in *CMLC* presents a comprehensive survey of an author's career, an individual work of literature, or a literary topic, and provides the user with a multiplicity of interpretations and assessments. Such variety allows students to pursue their own interests; furthermore, it fosters an awareness that literature is dynamic and responsive to many different opinions. Early commentary is offered to indicate initial responses, later selections document changes in literary reputations, and retrospective analyses provide the reader with modern views. The size of each author entry is a relative reflection of the scope of the criticism available in English.

An author may appear more than once in the series if his or her writings have been the subject of a substantial amount of criticism; in these instances, specific works or groups of works by the author will be covered in separate entries. For example, Homer will be represented by three entries, one devoted to the *Iliad,* one to the *Odyssey,* and one to the Homeric Hymns.

CMLC continues the survey of criticism of world literature begun by Gale's *Contemporary Literary Criticism* (*CLC*), *Twentieth-Century Literary Criticism* (*TCLC*), *Nineteenth-Century Literature Criticism* (*NCLC*), *Literature Criticism from 1400 to 1800* (*LC*), and *Shakespearean Criticism* (*SC*).

Organization of the Book

A *CMLC* entry consists of the following elements:

- The **Author Heading** cites the name under which the author most commonly wrote, followed by birth and death dates. Also located here are any name variations under which an author wrote, including transliterated forms for authors whose native languages use nonroman alphabets. If the author wrote consistently under a pseudonym, the pseudonym will be listed in the author heading and the author's actual name given in parenthesis on the first line of the biographical and critical information. Uncertain birth or death dates are indicated by question marks. Single-work entries are preceded by a heading that consists of the most common form of the title in English translation (if applicable) and the original date of composition.

- The **Introduction** contains background information that introduces the reader to the author, work, or topic that is the subject of the entry.

- A **Portrait of the Author** is included when available.

- The list of **Principal Works** is ordered chronologically by date of first publication and lists the most important works by the author. The genre and publication date of each work is given. In the case of foreign authors whose works have been translated into English, the list will focus primarily on twentieth-century translations, selecting those works most commonly considered the best by critics. Unless otherwise indicated, dramas are dated by first performance, not first publication. Lists of **Representative Works** by different authors appear with topic entries.

- Reprinted **Criticism** is arranged chronologically in each entry to provide a useful perspective on changes in critical evaluation over time. The critic's name and the date of composition or publication of the critical work are given at the beginning of each piece of criticism. Unsigned criticism is preceded by the title of the source in which it appeared. All titles by the author featured in the text are printed in boldface type. Footnotes are reprinted at the end of each essay or excerpt. In the case of excerpted criticism, only those footnotes that pertain to the excerpted texts are included. Criticism in topic entries is arranged chronologically under a variety of subheadings to facilitate the study of different aspects of the topic.

- A complete **Bibliographical Citation** of the original essay or book precedes each piece of criticism.

- Critical essays are prefaced by brief **Annotations** explicating each piece.

- An annotated bibliography of **Further Reading** appears at the end of each entry and suggests resources for additional study. In some cases, significant essays for which the editors could not obtain reprint rights are included here. Boxed material following the further reading list provides references to other biographical and critical sources on the author in series published by Gale.

Cumulative Indexes

A **Cumulative Author Index** lists all of the authors that appear in a wide variety of reference sources published by the Gale Group, including *CMLC*. A complete list of these sources is found facing the first page of the Author Index. The index also includes birth and death dates and cross references between pseudonyms and actual names.

Beginning with the second volume, a **Cumulative Nationality Index** lists all authors featured in *CMLC* by nationality, followed by the number of the *CMLC* volume in which their entry appears.

Beginning with the tenth volume, a **Cumulative Topic Index** lists the literary themes and topics treated in the series as well as in *Nineteenth-Century Literature Criticism, Twentieth-Century Literary Criticism,* and the *Contemporary Literary Criticism* Yearbook, which was discontinued in 1998.

A **Cumulative Title Index** lists in alphabetical order all of the works discussed in the series. Each title listing includes the corresponding volume and page numbers where criticism may be located. Foreign-language titles that have been translated into English are followed by the titles of the translation—for example, *Slovo o polku Igorove (The Song of Igor's Campaign)*. Page numbers following these translated titles refer to all pages on which any form of the titles, either foreign-language or translated, appear. Titles of novels, dramas, nonfiction books, and poetry, short story, or essay collections are printed in italics, while individual poems, short stories, and essays are printed in roman type within quotation marks.

Citing *Classical and Medieval Literature Criticism*

When writing papers, students who quote directly from any volume in the Literary Criticism Series may use the following general format to footnote reprinted criticism. The first example pertains to material drawn from periodicals, the second to material reprinted from books.

T. P. Malnati, "Juvenal and Martial on Social Mobility," *The Classical Journal* 83, no. 2 (December-January 1988): 134-41; reprinted in *Classical and Medieval Literature Criticism,* vol. 35, ed. Jelena Krstović (Farmington Hills, Mich.: The Gale Group, 2000), 366-71.

J. P. Sullivan, "Humanity and Humour; Imagery and Wit," in *Martial: An Unexpected Classic* (Cambridge University Press, 1991), 211-51; excerpted and reprinted in *Classical and Medieval Literature Criticism,* vol. 35, ed. Jelena Krstović (Farmington Hills, Mich.: The Gale Group, 2000), 371-95.

Suggestions are Welcome

Readers who wish to suggest new features, topics, or authors to appear in future volumes, or who have other suggestions or comments are cordially invited to call, write, or fax the Managing Editor:

Managing Editor, Literary Criticism Series
The Gale Group
27500 Drake Road
Farmington Hills, MI 48331-3535
1-800-347-4253 (GALE)
Fax: 248-699-8054

Acknowledgments

The editors wish to thank the copyright holders of the excerpted criticism included in this volume and the permissions managers of many book and magazine publishing companies for assisting us in securing reproduction rights. We are also grateful to the staffs of the Detroit Public Library, the Library of Congress, the University of Detroit Mercy Library, Wayne State University Purdy/Kresge Library Complex, and the University of Michigan Libraries for making their resources available to us. Following is a list of the copyright holders who have granted us permission to reproduce material in this volume of *CMLC*. Every effort has been made to trace copyright, but if omissions have been made, please let us know.

COPYRIGHTED EXCERPTS IN *CMLC*, VOLUME 41, WERE REPRODUCED FROM THE FOLLOWING PERIODICALS:

COPYRIGHTED EXCERPTS IN *CMLC*, VOLUME 41, WERE REPRODUCED FROM THE FOLLOWING BOOKS:

Reproduced by permission.—Lionarons, Joyce Tally. From "The Otherworld and Its Inhabitants in the *Nibelungenlied*," in *A Companion to the "Nibelungenlied."* Edited by Winder McConnell. Camden House, 1998. Copyright © 1998 Winder McConnell. All rights reserved. Reproduced by permission.—McConnell, Winder. From *A Companion to the Nibelungenlied.* Edited by Winder McConnell. Camden House, 1998. Copyright © 1998 Winder McConnell. All rights reserved. Reproduced by permission.—McConnell, Winder. From *The Nibelungenlied.* Twayne Publishers, 1984. Copyright © 1984 by G. K. Hall & Company. All rights reserved. Reproduced with the permission of Macmillan Library Reference USA, a division of Ahsuog, Inc.—Muckle, J.T. From "Clement of Alexandria's Attitude toward Greek Philosophy," in *The Phoenix, Supplementary Vol. 1: Studies in Honor of Gilbert Norway.* Edited by Mary E. White. University of Toronto Press, 1952. Copyright, Canada, 1952. Reproduced by permission.—Robinson, Theodore H. From *The Poetry of the Old Testament.* Duckworth, 1947. Copyright © 1947. Reprinted by permission of Gerald Duckworth and Co. Ltd.

PHOTOGRAPHS APPEARING IN *CMLC*, VOLUME 41, WERE RECEIVED FROM THE FOLLOWING SOURCES:

Clement of Alexandria (seated in chair), woodcut. The Library of Congress.—Kriemheld comforts Gunther, illustration by Johann Heinrich Fussli.—Prophet Jeremiah, print. Archive Photos, Inc. Reproduced by permission.—Siegfried attacking the dragon, illustration by Wilhelm von Kaulbach.—From *Romance of King Orfeo*, title page. The University of Michigan Library. Reproduced by permission.—From *Book of Lamentations of Jeremiah*, manuscript page. The University of Michigan Library. Reproduced by permission.

Clement of Alexandria
c. 150-c. 215

(Full name Titus Flavius Clemens) Greek author and Christian apologist.

INTRODUCTION

The author of numerous theological works, Clement is credited with synthesizing Greek thought, particularly Platonism and Stoicism, with Christian beliefs. His openness to using outside sources familiar to non-Christians helped make Christianity more acceptable to many. Writing and teaching in a time when most Christians were uneducated and even openly hostile to intellectuals, Clement nevertheless was able to make logical and convincing arguments—based on scripture and philosophy—in favor of his adopted religion and against the thriving, learned, Valentinian Gnostics. Clement appropriated the word "gnostic" to describe his notion of the perfect Christian. After Clement's arguments, Gnosticism's appeal to the well-educated diminished. Clement's most famous pupil was the brilliant Origen, who in his own career improved upon many of Clement's initial ideas. Extremely well read, Clement made use of the work of many other writers, including lengthy excerpts of their work in his own; he is thus responsible for the preservation of great portions of ancient literature that would otherwise no longer exist. He was revered as a saint until the seventeenth century, when questions concerning his orthodoxy led to his removal from the church calendar. The great historian Eusebius of Caesarea called Clement an incomparable master of Christian philosophy, and St. Jerome stated that Clement was the most learned of all the Fathers.

BIOGRAPHICAL INFORMATION

Most of what little is known of Clement's life comes from his own writings and from those of Eusebius, who wrote in the fourth century. Clement was born in Athens to parents who were probably pagans. He traveled extensively and was educated in Greece, Southern Italy, Syria, and Egypt. His teacher in Alexandria, then a center of intellectual activity and a base for Gnostics, was Pantaenus, who headed the city's catechetical school. In about 175 he began teaching Clement, who succeeded him as leader of the school around 189. Clement held the position until about 202. It was during this time in Alexandria that he began writing. Sometime after 202, when religious persecution had reached new heights, Clement fled to Caesarea in Cappadocia where he worked with a former pupil, Bishop Alexander. While Alexander was in prison, Clement became head of his church.

MAJOR WORKS

Although the total number of pages of Clement's surviving works rivals that of perhaps any other Christian writer of the second century, scholars point out that his texts are are plagued with corruption. Damaged, mutilated manuscripts, the result of both time and incompetent copyists, would be difficult enough to work with if the author wrote systematically, and Clement's writing has never been described as systematic. He began his career fully devoted to oral instruction and was distrustful of writing—an unease he shared with many Christians of his time. Polished and persuasive writing was even more to be feared, for a winning style is not necessarily a true one, and a reader could be swayed by a clever style, falling prey to a false message. Thus Clement's writings are deliberately digressive and disorderly so that a patient, devoted, and intelligent reader can gain insight here and there while an insincere one will become frustrated and give up. Although many attempts have been made to date his writings, no one has been persuasively successful in narrowing the time frame beyond crediting the majority of it to the latter half of his many years spent in Alexandria. Three of his works are considered his most important, and many scholars view them as constituting a trilogy of sorts. *Protreptikos pros Hellenas* [*Exhortation to the Greeks*] is possibly his first work. It attempts to render the beauty and truth of Christianity in contrast to the errors of paganism. The second main work is *Paidagogus* [*Tutor*], a social history intended to provide students of Christianity with instruction in morality and ethics. Rounding out the three major works is the *Stromateis* [*Miscellanies*], an unsystematic carpetbag of notes on a wide variety of themes. The first book of *Stromateis* was written between 193 and 211 and probably much of the other volumes were written after Clement left Egypt. *Hypotyposes* [*Sketches*] exists only in fragments preserved by other Greek writers but originally encompassed eight volumes devoted to scripture commentary. *Excerpta ex Theodota* [*Excerpts of Theodotus*] is a notebook of quotations and comments believed to have been written by a student of Valentinus and edited and annotated by Clement. One sermon is extant, *Quis Dives Salvetur?* [*Who Is the Rich Man that is being Saved?*], which is based on Mark 10:17-31. It concerns the use of wealth and contends that money is not intrinsically evil. Another notebook, known as the *Prophetic Eclogues* is also extant, as is the discourse *Exhortation to Endurance*, also known as *To the Recently Baptized*. Eusebius mentions several other treatises and discourses of Clement's which are now lost: *Peri Tou Pascha* [*On the Pascha*]; *Peri Nesteias* [*On Fasting*]; *Peri Katalalias* [*On Slander*]; *Peri Anastaseos* [*On Resurrection*]; *Peri Enkrateias* [*On Continence*]; and *Ecclesiastical Canon*, also known as *Against the Judaizers*.

CRITICAL RECEPTION

There has been considerable controversy for at least a century over the nature of the relationship between Clement's three major works, particularly as to whether the *Stromateis* should be considered the third part of a loose trilogy. Basing their arguments on Clement's own statements, many scholars believe the third part would have been a work entitled the *Didaskalos* [*Master*], but there is much disagreement whether the *Stromateis* is actually the *Didaskalos* under a different name, or even whether the *Didaskalos* was indeed ever written. Although Clement makes references to such a work, the critical consensus is that it was never realized. A great deal of scholarly effort has also been devoted to interpreting the message of his work. Most critics agree that it should be viewed in its entirety, for misunderstanding is inevitable if only small portions of it are studied. Many critics suspect that the fact that Clement wrote such discursive works was not so deliberate as he maintained. It is likely that he simply was not up to the task of creating order from his multiplicity of ideas. Fortunately Origen was able to develop a systematic theology and, in interpreting the difficult ideas of Clement, honored the man who taught and influenced him.

PRINCIPAL WORKS

Excerpta ex Theodota [*Excerpts of Theodotus*] (notebook)
Exhortation to Endurance [*To the Recently Baptized*] (essay)
Paidagogus [*Tutor*] (philosophy)
Prophetic Eclogues (notebook)
Protreptikos pros Hellenas [*Exhortation to the Greeks*] (philosophy)
Quis Dives Salvetur? [*Who Is the Rich Man that Is Being Saved?*] (sermon)
Stromateis [*Miscellanies*] (philosophy)

Principal English Translations

Fathers of the Second Century The Ante-Nicene Christian Library (translated by W. Wilson) (philosophy, essays, notebooks, and sermon) 1868
Clement of Alexandria: Quis dives salvetur (translated by P. Mordaunt Barnard) (sermon) 1897
Exhortion to the Greeks, Rich Man's Salvation, To the Newly Baptized (translated by G. W. Butterworth) (essay) 1919
The Excerpta ex Theodoto of Clement of Alexandria (translated by Robert P. Casey) (notebook) 1934
Alexandrian Christianity (contains
Stromateis III & VII) (translated by John Ernest Oulton and Henry Chadwick) (philosophy) 1954
Christ the Educator (translated by Simon P. Wood) (philosophy) 1954

*All Clement's works were composed c. 190–215.

CRITICISM

Charles Bigg (essay date 1886)

SOURCE: "Lecture III" in *The Christian Platonists of Alexandria*, Clarendon Press, 1886, pp. 76-114.

[*In the following excerpt, Bigg provides an overview of many of Clement's beliefs, including those concerning evil, fear, knowledge, and faith.*]

> And now abideth faith, hope, charity, these three: but the greatest of these is charity.—I COR. xiii. 13.

Clement did not admit the pre-existence of the soul or the eternity of Matter,[1] but in other respects followed closely the Philonic view of Creation. God of His goodness and love created the world of Ideas, the invisible heaven and earth, and in accordance with this divine model the Word gave shape and substance to the material universe.[2] The six days are not to be understood literally. They express in an allegory the differing dignity of the things recorded to have been created on each in succession.[3] The pre-eminence of Man is further shown by the fact, that he was not called into existence by a mere command, but moulded, if we may so speak, by the very hands of God,[4] who breathed into his nostrils the 'spirit,' or 'intellect,' the 'sovereign faculty' of the tripartite soul. Thus Man received at birth the 'image,' and may acquire by a virtuous life the 'likeness,' of God, or rather of the Son. The 'image,' the Reason, may be blurred and defaced, but can never be wholly destroyed. It is the 'love-charm,' which makes Man dear to God for his own sake. It is the fountain of that natural yearning, which makes the child always unhappy, when banished from his Father's home. It is by this that he receives, understands, recognises his Father's voice.

But here there arises a difficulty, which had never before been felt in all its force. If God made all things out of nothing, what is the cause of Evil? According to the heathen Platonist, and even in the eyes of Philo, it was Matter. God's purpose was limited and frustrated by the nature of the substance, on which He was compelled to work. The Gnostics carried this view so far as to maintain, that creation was the act of a rebellious spirit, who mingled together things that ought to have been kept apart. But the Christian believed that Matter, as well as Form, was created by God. How then were the imperfections of the universe, pain, sin, waste, inequality, to be accounted for? They can be no part of the intention of Him, who gave all things being because He is Good.

Here again Clement does not grasp the whole range of the problem. He is not affected by the disorder of external Nature, as was the troubled and far-glancing spirit of Origen. To the former all that seems to demand explanation is the existence of Sin, and for this he found an adequate reason in the Freedom of the Human Will.

This conception is as new as the difficulty out of which it sprang. It is to be found in the Apologists, but the Alexandrines were the first to define it and make it the foundation of a system.

St. Paul speaks of Freedom from conflicting motives, but never of Freedom of the Will. There are those who being servants of sin are free from righteousness, those again who being free from sin are servants to God. Between these stand a third class, who are in bondage yet longing to break their fetters—'to will is present with me, but how to perform that which is good I find not.' This is in fact the doctrine of the Platonist, who held that the soul has two instinctive and antagonistic movements, that of Reason towards the Ideal and that of Sense towards Gratification, and that the man is then only truly free, when his sovereign faculty soars freely towards the Good unimpeded by the clamour of Desire. In what sense Will itself is free the Greeks did not attempt to decide. Generally speaking they regarded it as the expression of character, and did not or could not clear up the previous question, how character itself is formed.[5]

Yet precisely at this point, where Plato and St. Paul are in substantial agreement, the Alexandrines broke loose from their allegiance. There were strong reasons for this revolt. They had to account for the Fall of the First Man. This was no mere academical thesis, it was pressed upon them by an active, subtle, and formidable antagonist. If Adam was created perfect, said the Gnostic, he could not have fallen. He was then created imperfect, and in that case the Creator was the cause of his imperfection, and must therefore be imperfect Himself.[6] Closely connected with this argument is the Gnostic Dualism and their peculiar doctrine of predestination. At a later period, when Gnosticism was practically vanquished, Augustine did not hesitate to maintain that, though God predestines, He is yet not the author of evil. But to the Alexandrines this did not seem possible. Determinism in any shape appeared to them to impugn both the divine goodness and the divine right to punish sin, and though they held that in truth God does not punish, they would not acknowledge this in set terms. Hence they were driven to make Will an independent faculty, knowing both good and evil and choosing between them, selecting and in fact creating its own motive. The actual phrase Free Will, *Liberum Arbitrium,* is due to Tertullian, but it expresses with Latin precision what Clement and Origen really mean.

No wise man will attempt to find a precise solution for the eternal antinomy of Freedom and Necessity. It is enough to point out what the Alexandrines did. In their recoil from Gnosticism they abolished Necessity altogether, and gave Freedom a new meaning. We can only judge of their action by its results. It has become possible to ask whether God can do wrong, and almost a heresy to speak of Christ as begotten by the Will of the Father. And already the door is opened for all the barren disputes, that troubled the Church and the Schools from the days of Augustine to those of Pascal.[7]

Evil then in Clement's view is, not a Power, but an Act. It is not the Platonic 'lie in the soul,' nor the Pauline 'law of sin,' not a vicious motive nor a false belief, because these have no constraining force. Vice consists in acting the lie, and we need not act it unless we choose. Clement could not then believe in any inherited depravity of human nature. This follows indeed already from his opinion, that the Reason comes in each case fresh from the hands of its Maker. Adam was created perfect, yet not perfect; perfect inasmuch as every faculty was sound and apt for virtue, not perfect inasmuch as virtue was not yet actualised by obedience. He fell by lust, and so we all fall.[8] There is no entailed necessity between his sin and ours. But though Free Will and Reason, both gifts of God, are enough for guidance in this world, they cannot tell us fully what God is, they cannot bring us into living communion with Him. 'Each of us justifies himself.' 'The true Gnostic creates himself.' Men may 'choose to believe or to disbelieve.'[9] Yet Faith itself is a grace;[10] 'the ball-player cannot catch the ball unless it is thrown to him.' We are created capable of wisdom, goodness, felicity, which yet we can only attain by grasping the Divine Hand outstretched to lift us up. 'Not without special grace does the soul put forth its wings.'[11]

The secrets of this diviner life cannot be expressed in rules and formulas. But there is a point where grace and nature meet, which is the proper field of discipline. Knowledge must be gradually assimilated. Love must creep before it can fly. Christ has revealed to us all truth, but truth is precept before it is conviction. It is by obedience to Authority, that the carpenter and the pilot acquire their skill. So the Christian life begins in Faith,[12] that is belief in the desirability of the End, and willing submission to the Means in their regular progression. But we can learn only within the school, and we must first be cleansed. Hence the gate of the Church is the Baptism of Regeneration. Herein we receive Forgiveness, the only free forgiveness, of all past sins, which leaves the mind like a sheet of blank paper, not good yet 'not bad,' we are brought within the circle of light, within reach of all wholesome sacraments and aids. We have started fairly in the race for the eternal crown.[13]

Beyond this point stretches out the Christian Life, and here begins the most distinctive portion of Clement's teaching. We shall fail to do him justice unless we bear steadily in view the two influences that determined his path—on the one hand the love of St. Paul, on the other the dread of Gnosticism, a dread which did not prevent him from seeing that this peculiar form of error answered to a real and pressing need of the human mind. Gnosticism was in one aspect distorted Paulinism. The cure lay in a full and true presentation of the Apostle's teaching. But Clement only half understood St. Paul, and in his desire to win back the sectaries he draped Christianity in a Gnostic garb.

He saw around him a system little better than the liberal form of Judaism out of which it sprang. The new wine was fermenting in old bottles, the Christian still trembled beneath the handwriting of ordinances. If we read the *Doctrine of the Apostles,* we find there a law which differs from the Mosaic mainly in being more searching and elaborate. The circumstances of the time were such as to confirm and even justify this legalism. Crowds were pressing into the Church, mostly ignorant and undisciplined, some rich and wilful. They brought with them the moral taint, the ingrained prejudices of their old life. We learn from many sources that the same incongruous blending of the Gospel with pagan superstitions, which recurred during the conversion of the Northern Barbarians, existed in some degree in the second and third centuries.[14] Discipline, teaching, supervision, direction, were absolutely necessary to the purity and maintenance of the Faith, and no wise man would attempt to weaken the growing authority of the Priest.

Yet there were those again for whom this atmosphere was not the best, devout souls whose life was hidden with Christ in God, men and women of cultivated thoughtful minds, who fretted under a system of routine and dictation administered, we may suppose, not unfrequently, by ignorant and fanatical officers. Social and personal distinctions were perhaps greater in those days than they have ever been since, and in times of intense religious excitement

these distinctions shape themselves into forms of character, which, though held together by the most powerful of all bands, are yet as different as it is possible for children of the same family to be. Nowhere do we see this more clearly than in the history of the Martyrs. There were those who died, as Polycarp, Perpetua, Blandina, Christlike blessing their persecutors; there were those who brought their fate on their own heads by wild defiance, and went to meet it like Pristinus drugged to insensibility by the fumes of wine; there were others again, like Peregrinus, who found suffering for the Name an easy road to profit, and if the worst happened to notoriety.[15] It was out of this divergence of type that the Gnostic made his gain. What was the Christian teacher to do? How was he to deal with the spirit of discontent and disillusion which he knew to be at work? It was impossible to alter the existing framework of the community. But there might be a life within a life, a Church within a Church, a quiet haven for the spiritually free.

Had Clement written a few years later he would have taken refuge in the distinction between nominal and real Christianity, between the Visible and the Invisible Church. But he lived in a time of transition. As yet the ancient view that all the brethren were in process of salvation, though shaken, was not abandoned. Hence he falls back upon his philosophy, and finds the solution in the Two Lives of Philo, the practical and contemplative Life of Plato and Aristotle, still more exactly in the Stoic distinction between Proficiency and Wisdom.[16] He thought he found the same idea in certain antitheses of St. Paul's—the milk and the solid food—faith and knowledge or mysteries—the spirit of bondage and the spirit of adoption—faith and hope which are less than charity. There were indications in the Roman Clement, in Hermas, in Barnabas,[17] that pointed in the same direction. Other cherished ideas appeared to fit in—the opposition between the servant and the son of God, between God the Lord and God the Father, between the letter and the spirit, between the Human and the Divine Natures of Christ. Gathering all these hints into one, Clement proclaims that the life of the ordinary believer, that is to say of the great body of the Church, is a lower life. Its marks are Faith, Fear and Hope[18]—unquestioning obedience to the letter of Authority, a selfish motive, a morality of abstinence from wrong. It is the sphere of discipline, of repression, of painful effort. Its crown is Holiness,[19] the negative virtue of Self-Control. It is a state of salvation, but not of peace or joy. Above it stands the Higher Life, that of the true Gnostic, the life of Love, Righteousness, Knowledge, of serene and reasonable convictions, of glad and spontaneous moral activity, in which the spirit of man is so closely wedded to the spirit of his Lord that there is no more recalcitrance, and freedom is merged in the *beata necessitas non peccandi.*

Thus Clement insisted as against the Gnostic that purity is the condition of insight, as against the Orthodoxast that law is meant to issue in freedom. On these two piers he built his *Via Media* the Christian Gnosis. It is a compromise between the Church and the world, but the later history of Catholicism is enough to prove how inevitable is such a concession to a body that will govern and yet purify society.

As against the Gnostic, again, Clement protests that the Two Lives are not divided by any law of nature. The one must and should grow out of the other, the one is incomplete without the other. All men, all women are called, as he says, 'to philosophise,' to strive upwards to the highest ideal. Yet the distinction in itself is evil, and Clement has expressed it in such a way as to make not a distinction but a real difference, a breach of principle and continuity. The spiritual life is one because Love, its root, is one. But this Faith, which in the Lower Life leads through Fear and Hope to Love, is itself not Love, but imperfect intellectual apprehension; not personal trust in the Saviour, but a half-persuasion of the desirableness of what the Saviour promises.[20] The belief, the morality, the reward are all external. Fear and Hope are the life, not the outer husk which shields and protects the life till it is strong enough to act by itself. Clement has attempted to seize the Pauline doctrine of Grace without the Pauline doctrine of Faith.[21] He has superposed the Gospel freedom upon the Aristotelian theory of Habit, upon 'reasonable self-love,' upon the legal Christianity of his time, without seeing that between these two an entirely new element must come into play.

This element he has endeavoured to supply by banishing Fear and Hope from the Higher Life. 'Perfect Love casteth out Fear,' which indeed is not a motive but a check. But disinterestedness, which is what Clement wants, does not depend upon the presence or absence of Hope, but on the nature of the thing hoped for. That which was mercenary in its original conception does not become less mercenary because Hope is swallowed up in fruition. In Clement's view the supreme End of all is not Love but Knowledge, and this misplacement of the Ideal involves an egotism which he vainly struggles to escape. He succeeds in placing felicity within the soul, in the fulness of spiritual life, but he has not really advanced beyond the point of view of Philo.

But Fear he has handled in a truly Christian spirit. It is not the fear of the slave who hates his master, it is the reverence of a child for its father, of a citizen for the good magistrate. Tertullian, an African and a lawyer, dwells with fierce satisfaction on terrible visions of torment. The cultivated Greek shrinks not only from the gross materialism of such a picture, but from the idea of retribution which it implies. He is never tired of repeating that Justice is but another name for Mercy. Chastisement is not to be dreaded, but to be embraced. 'The mirror is not evil to the ugly face because it shows it as it is, the physician is not evil to the sick man because he tells him of his fever. For the physician is not the cause of the fever.' Still more evidently true is this of Jesus. 'The Lord who died for us is not our enemy.' Here or hereafter God's desire is not vengeance but correction. In truth it is not He that punishes, but we that draw chastisement on our own heads.[22]

The life of Faith, as he has described it in the later books of the Pedagogue, is in beautiful accordance with these maxims.[23] It is a life, like that of the Puritans in Milton's youth, of severe self-restraint, but built on broad principles, not captious and not gloomy. It should be as the Stoics taught, 'according to Nature,' hence all artificial desires are evil. But Clement condemns on the one hand the self-torture in which some of the Gnostics emulated the Hindoo Fakirs, on the other the Stoic paradox that things external are things indifferent. Here again he is Aristotelian. Innocent pleasure is the salt of life. Wealth rightly used is a blessing. The first requisite is the beauty of virtue, the second the beauty of health; Christ Himself was not beautiful in person.[24] Many thoughts are suggested by this charming and authentic picture of daily Christian life. We see the vulgarity and thinly-veneered barbarism of Roman luxury giving way to true courtesy and refinement. We see the Church, no longer oppressed by instant expectation of the Last Day, settling quietly down to her task of civilising the world. Already her victory is assured.

Those who have been trained in the school of Jesus the Pedagogue are fitted for, are imperatively summoned to a better service. Clement delights to speak of the Higher Life in terms borrowed from Eleusis. It is the Greater Mysteries, of which Christ is the Hierophant and Torch-bearer. Such language is partly conventional and common to all the Platonists of the time.[25] Again it is intended to conciliate the Gnostics and the religious heathen, who had all been initiated, as probably Clement himself had been in his youth. But it is also connected with, and tends to strengthen, the unfortunate doctrine of Reserve.

In the Higher Life Faith gives way to Knowledge, Fear and Hope to Love, while Holiness is merged in Righteousness.

Knowledge, Gnosis, Clement has defined in words taken partly from Philo, partly from the Stoics. From the first he learned that it is the intuitive communion of the intelligence with the Ideas, from the latter that being science it is indefectible. To the Christian doctor Christ is not only the Sum of the Ideas, but the co-equal Son of God, and Gnosis therefore is the 'apprehensive contemplation' of God in the Logos, and not, as in Philo, of God above the Logos.[26] Yet there is a progress in the object of Knowledge, measured by the varying aspect of Christ, who in the Lower Life is manifested chiefly on the human side as Physician, Tutor, and so on, in the Higher chiefly on the divine as Light, Truth, Life. Holiness is the indispensable preliminary of knowledge, which is partly Theology, but still more the experimental knowledge of Christ. The Gnostic is the 'pure in heart' who 'sees God.' 'He that would enter the fragrant shrine,' says Clement, quoting the inscription over the temple gate of Epidaurus, 'must be pure, and purity is to think holy things.[27]' He is the 'approved money-changer,' whose 'practised senses' are the touchstone of truth. His Faith has become Conviction, Authority is superseded by the inner light. To him the deep things of Scripture are revealed. He reads the spirit beneath the letter. In Christ he understands past, present, and future, the theory of Creation, the symbolism of the Law, the inner meaning of the Gospel, the mysteries of the Resurrection.[28] He sees the vital harmony of dogma with dogma, of all dogmas with Reason. In a word, he is an Allegorist. Moral purity and assiduous study of Scripture are the only training that is absolutely necessary.[29] But Clement well knew the importance of mental cultivation. His Gnostic still reads Plato in his leisure moments. 'He is not like the common run of people who fear Greek philosophy as children fear a goblin lest it should run away with them.'[30]

Of Knowledge Love is at once the life-element and the instrument. For 'the more a man loves the more deeply does the penetrate into God.'[31] But here again, most unhappily, Stoicism comes in, and casts the chill shadow of Apathy over the sweetest and simplest of Christian motives. Platonism also helped to mislead. For though the Alexandrines held that Matter is the work of God, they could not wholly divest their minds of the old scholastic dislike of the brute mass and the emotions connected with it. The first thought suggested by the Incarnation is Fear. Love is not of Jesus, but of the Logos, the Ideal. Clement could not bear to think that the rose of Sharon could blossom on common soil.[32] This was the price he paid for his Transcendental Theology.

Love makes man like the beloved. But Christ, like God, was absolutely passionless. So too were the Apostles after their Master's Resurrection. So too must the Gnostic be. Self-control, Holiness, has made the reason absolute master of the brute in the centaur man. He will feel those desires which, like hunger or thirst, are necessary for self-preservation, but not joy nor sorrow nor courage nor indignation nor hatred. He lives in the closest union with the Beloved, so absorbed in the Divine Love that he can no longer be said to love his fellow-creatures in the ordinary sense of the word.[33]

There were many in Clement's own time who shrank from this too ethereal ideal, which, to use his own pharase, 'touches earth with but one foot.' If we take away hope and joy, they urged, will not the Christian be swallowed up by the sorrows of life? And if all union with the Beautiful is preceded by aspiration, how can he be passionless who aspires to the Beautiful?[34] How can we rise without desire, and how can we desire the extinction of desire? It is the argument afterwards pressed with irresistible force by Bossuet and Bourdaloue against Fénelon. Clement replies, 'Love is no more desire but a contented self-appropriation, which restores the Gnostic into oneness with Christ by faith, so that he needs neither time nor place. For by Love he is already in that scene where he will one day dwell. And having anticipated his hope by Gnosis he desires nothing, for he holds in closest possession the very object of desire.' It is the Love which we mortals feel 'in our diviner moments, when Love is satisfied in the completeness of the beloved object.' So absolute is its content, that if it were possible to separate eter-

nal salvation from the knowledge of God, and a choice were given to the Gnostic, he would without hesitation choose the latter. It is the paradox of Mysticism:—

> Be not angry; I resign
> Henceforth all my will to thine:
> I consent that thou depart,
> Though thin absence breaks my heart;
> Go then, and for ever too;
> All is right that thou wilt do.[35]

Of this Ideal (for it is perhaps no more[36]) enough has been said. Clement no doubt overshot the mark. It remains to be seen whether by so doing he encouraged presumption, or led weakness astray. The answer is to be found in the rigour with which he insists upon Holiness as the indispensable condition, on Righteousness as the indispensable fruit of Love.

Like all the early Fathers he attached a very real sense to the word Righteousness. 'Ye were justified by the name of the Lord, ye were made just as He is, and joined in the closest possible union with the Holy Spirit.'[37] It is not mere abstention from evil, which is Holiness, the virtue of the Lower Life, but the free active joyous service of those who are sanctified. It is life which needs no rule. The Gnostic, says Clement in language very like that of Madame de Guyon, has no virtue, because he is virtue. Nature is absorbed by Grace. It is easier to do good than to leave it undone, hence 'good works follow Gnosis as shadow follows substance.'[38] Contemplation is the Gnostic's chief delight, the next is active beneficence, the third is instruction, the work of making others like himself. God gives him an exceeding great reward, the salvation of other men.[39]

Thus Apathy, Detachment, make the sanctified believer not less but more useful to his kind. It is important to add, in view of the objections afterwards urged against the Quietists, that Clement lays great stress upon the observance of the existing Church discipline, the regular use of all the ordinary means of Grace. I will not here dwell upon what he says about Public Worship, the reading of Scripture, the Eucharist, Almsgiving, Fasting.[40] It will be sufficient to state his views on the subject of Prayer,[41] the point on which the Quietists departed most widely from the lines he laid down.

The Gnostic prays without ceasing. He would rather forego the grace of God than enjoy it without prayer. But indeed this is impossible. For our holiness must cooperate with the providence of God, if the blessing is to be perfect. Holiness is a correlative of Providence. For God Himself is a voluntary agent. He does not 'warm like fire' as Plutarch thought, nor can we receive His best gifts involuntarily, even if they be given before we ask.

But God reads the heart, and therefore few words are needed or none. 'Ask,' He says, 'and I will do, think, and I will give.' Good is the prayer which Christians utter in the church, with head and hands uplifted, and foot raised at the Amen, as if to soar above earth. Good is prayer at the three hours,[42] with face turned towards the East, as even pagans use. But better still is the inner colloquy of unspoken supplication for which no place or time is set apart, the praise of him who ploughs, of him who sails upon the sea. The Gnostic's prayer is chiefly Thanksgiving and Intercession, as was that of our Saviour. Beyond this he will ask only for the continuance of the blessings he enjoys, for he desires nothing that he has not, and the Father's Will is enough for him.

The prayer of the Gnostic, even when speechless, is still conscious and active. It is far removed from the blank vacuity of the soul which, as Molinos says, 'lies dead and buried, asleep in Nothingness'[43]—thinking without thought of the Unconditioned. The Silent Prayer of the Quietist is in fact Ecstasy, of which there is not a trace in Clement.

For Clement shrank from his own conclusions. Though the father of all the Mystics he is no Mystic himself. He did not enter the 'enchanted garden' which he opened for others. If he talks of 'flaying the sacrifice,' of leaving sense behind, of Vision, of Epopteia, this is but the parlance of his school. The instrument to which he looks for growth in knowledge is not trance, but the disciplined reason. Hence Gnosis when once attained is indefectible, not like the rapture which Plotinus enjoyed but four times during his acquaintance with Porphyry, which in the experience of Theresa never lasted more than half-an-hour.[44] The Gnostic is no Visionary, no Theurgist, no Antinomian.

These dangers were not far away in the age of Montanus and the Neo-Platonists. The Alexandrines have perhaps too much 'dry light,' but their faith was too closely wedded to reason and the written word to be seduced by these forbidden joys. Mysticism is as yet a Pagan solace. The time for a purely Christian mysticism, which Gerson evolves not from the reason but from the emotions, had not yet arrived. Yet Clement laid the fuel ready for kindling. The spark that was needed was the allegorical interpretation of the Song of Songs. This was supplied, strange to say, by Origen, the least mystical of all divines.

Every baptised Christian, who has not been 'cut off' like a diseased limb by solemn judicial process, is a member of the Church upon earth, is therefore within the pale of salvation. The Church[45] is the Platonic City of God, 'a lovely body and assemblage of men governed by the Word,' 'the company of the Elect.' She is the Bride of Christ, the Virgin Mother, stainless as a Virgin, loving as a Mother. She is One, she is Catholic, because the doctrine and tradition of the Apostles is one; the heretic who has forsaken her fold has 'an assembly devised by man,' 'a school,' but not a Church. One in belief, but not in mechanism. Peter is the first of the Apostles, but the See of Peter is never named. The West is as unknown to Clement as it was to his favourite Homer. Yet in this One Church there is a distinction. There are those who within her fold live as do the Gentiles, these are the flesh of Christ's Mystical Body; there are those who cleave to the Lord and become one spirit

with Him, the Sons of God, the Gnostics; these are the Holy Church, the Spiritual Church; these, and they who are in process to become as these, are the rings which have not dropped from the magnetic chain, but in spiritual union with saints and angels 'wait for the Rest of God.'[46]

The *Stromateis* were written during the Patriarchate of Demetrius amid the bustle and excitement of a revolution. But no echo of the strife penetrated the tranquil seclusion in which Clement lectured and composed. He reflects with calm fidelity the image of the antique times in which he had himself been reared. His heart is with the Republic; he is the Samuel of the new monarchy.

One of the chief pillars of the aggressive theory of Church polity was the claim of the Christian ministry to be regarded as lineal successors of the sacrificial hierarchy of the Jews. But to Clement the true antitype of Levite or Hiereus is the Gnostic, the son or daughter of God, who has been anointed like King, Prophet, or High Priest of the Law, but with the spiritual unction of the Holy Ghost. The Gnostic sacrifice is that of praise, of a contrite spirit, of a soul delivered from carnal lusts; the incense is holy prayer; the altar is the just soul, or the congregation of believers.[47] Beyond this there is no sacrifice except the 'costly,' the 'fireless' Victim once offered upon the Cross.[48] Clement quotes the famous verse of Malachi, but the 'pure offering' is the knowledge of God as Creator derived by the heathen from the light of the universal Word.[49] The much disputed text about the power of the keys he never cites at all, and in the Penance controversy, which was already agitating men's minds, he follows Hermas, allowing but one Absolution for mortal sin after Baptism, a view highly unfavourable to the growing authority of the Bishop.[50] He rarely mentions the three orders of Clergy,[51] and never in connection with the Sacraments. The rich man should have a domestic chaplain or spiritual director, who is to be 'a man of God.'[52] The unlearned brother is not to trust his private judgment, but the interpreter of Scripture is no doubt the Gnostic. The one office assigned to the Presbyter is that of 'making men better,' and this is also the special function of the Gnostic.

It seems most probable that at this time, in the Church of Alexandria, the Eucharist was not yet distinguished in time, ritual, or motive from the primitive Supper of the Lord.[53] Of this, the Agape, the Love-Feast, or Banquet, there were two forms, the public and the private, the first celebrated at a full gathering of the brethren on fixed evenings in the church, the second in private houses.

The first was still disfigured by those excesses and disorders, which St. Paul sharply rebuked, but a century of discipline had not eradicated. It was preceded by reading of the Scriptures, psalms and hymns. After this the Bread and Wine were blessed, and then distributed by the deacons.[54] Viands of every kind, often costly and richly dressed, were provided by the liberality of the wealthier brethren. Clement does not attempt to lay any puritanical restrictions upon social enjoyment. He enforces the rule prohibiting the taste of blood or of meat offered to idols, he explains the code of good manners, and insists upon moderation. The Christian must eat to live, not live to eat. He must not abuse the Father's gifts. He must show by precept and example that the heavenly banquet is not the meat that perisheth, but love, that the believer's true food is Christ.[55]

All that Clement says upon this subject is of the highest value to those who wish to recast for themselves a faithful image of the Church life of the end of the second century. But of all his phrases the most important are those which assure us, that the ordinary evening meal of a Christian household was in a real sense an Agape. It was preceded by the same acts of worship; it was blessed by thanksgiving; it was a true Eucharist. The house father is the house priest. The highest act of Christian devotion is at the same time the simplest and most natural. Husband, wife and child, the house slave, and the invited guest gathered round the domestic board to enjoy with thankfulness the good gifts of God, uplifting their hearts in filial devotion, expanding them in brotherly bounty and kindness. To us the word Eucharist has become a term of ritual, whose proper meaning is all but obsolete. To the Greek it was still a word of common life—thanksgiving, the grateful sense of benefits received, of good gifts showered by the good Father on mind and heart and body. 'He that eateth eateth unto the Lord and keepeth Eucharist to God . . . so that a religious meal is an Eucharist.'[56]

All these good gifts sum themselves up in one, the gift of the Son. In the Eucharist, in its narrower sense, we eat flesh and drink the blood of Christ, 'hallowed food,' of which the bread and wine given by Melchisedech to Abraham was a type.[57] It is 'a mystery passing strange.'[58] 'I will, I will impart to you this grace also, the full and perfect bounty of incorruption. I give to you the knowledge of God. I give to you my perfect Self.' Christ's own Sacrifice, the charter of His High Priesthood, is the condition of His sacramental agency. But what is the special boon that He conveys in that supreme moment, when His sacrifice co-operates with ours, when 'in faith' we partake[59] of the nourishment which He bestows? Not forgiveness— that gift is bestowed in the laver of Regeneration, and if lost must be regained by the stern sacrament of Penance— but incorruption, immortality.[60] The Bread, the Wine mingled with Water, are an allegory. 'The Blood of the Lord is twofold. One is fleshly, whereby we have been ransomed from corruption'—in Baptism—'one is spiritual, with this we have been anointed'—in the Eucharist. The Body is Faith, the Blood is Hope, which is as it were the lifeblood of Faith. 'This is the Flesh and Blood of the Lord, the apprehension of the Divine power and essence.' 'The Blood of His Son cleanseth from all sin. For the doctrine of the Lord which is very strong is called His Blood.'[61]

The elements are 'hallowed food'; 'the meat of babes, that is to say the Lord Jesus, that is to say the Word of God, is spirit made flesh, hallowed flesh from heaven.'[62] These phrases have been interpreted in very different senses. One writer sees in them the doctrine of Transubstantiation, another the doctrine of Zwinglius. Those who read Clement as a whole, who reflect upon his strong antithesis of the letter, the flesh, to the spirit, who take into due account his language on the subject of Priest and Sacrifice, and his emphatic declaration that 'knowledge is our reasonable food,' will be inclined to think that the latter view is far nearer to the truth. Christ is present in the Eucharist as Gnosis, 'in the heart, not in the hand.' The Elements are a symbol, an allegory, perhaps a vehicle, an instrument, inasmuch as they are ordained by Christ Himself, and to substitute any other figure for the one so ordained is heresy. But the veil, though a holy thing because it belongs to the sanctuary, is not the mystery that it shrouds, the allegory is not the truth that it bodies forth.

The chief article of the Christian Gnosis was that of the Future Life. It was as interesting to Pagans as to Christians. 'What will become of the soul after death?' asks Plotinus, as he enters upon this universally fascinating theme. The immortality of the soul was positively denied by none but the 'godless Epicureans.' But the doctrine of the Resurrection was peculiar to the Church, and, while it strengthened her hold upon the masses, was a great stumbling-block in the way of the educated. The Platonist looked upon the body as the 'dungeon of the soul,' and could not understand how any pious man should expect a good God to renew and perpetuate that degrading bondage.

Within the Church itself there was some variety and much confusion of thought. Tertullian and many others held that the soul itself was material.[63] From this followed the terrible belief of Tatian, that it dies with the body, and is raised again with the body, by an act of Divine power, for an eternity of suffering or joy. Others, especially Arabian Christians, held that after dissolution the soul sleeps unconscious, till awakened to life by the restoration of its organism. But the majority believed in an intermediate yet conscious state of existence in Hades or Paradise, extending to the Day of Judgment, when the soul is reunited to the body, from which it has been for a time divorced.

The Resurrection itself they interpreted in the most literal sense. It would be a resurrection of 'this flesh,' of the identical body which had been dissolved by death. The 'change,' spoken of by St. Paul, was strictly limited to the accession of the new attribute of incorruption.[64] Closely allied to this view was the widespread opinion of the Chiliasts, who, resting upon the prophecies of Isaiah and the Apocalypse, believed that after the first Resurrection the saints should reign in the flesh upon earth for a thousand years under the sceptre of Christ. Chiliasm, which in vulgar minds was capable of the most unhappy degradation, was in turn strengthened by the urgent expectation of the End of the World. In the lower strata of Christian society prophecies on this subject were rife. At this very time a calculation, based on the numerical value of the letters composing the word Rome, fixed the downfall of the Empire and the coming of Christ for judgment for the year 195 A.D.[65] The Montanists held that the appointed sign was the appearance of the New Jerusalem in heaven; and this sign was given during the expedition of Severus against the Parthians, when for forty consecutive mornings the vision of a battlemented city hanging in the clouds was beheld by the whole army.[66]

There were differences of opinion again as to the nature, object, duration, of the sufferings that await the wicked in the life to come, especially among the outlying sects. The Valentinians, as we have seen, taught 'conditional immortality,' and regarded the future life as a state of education, of progress through an ascending series of seven heavens. The Clementine *Homilies,* a work composed under strong Judaic influences, expresses different views in different places. In one the sinner is warned that eternal torments await him in the life to come. In another St. Peter proclaims that those who repent, however grievous their offences, will be chastised but for a time, that those who repent not will be tortured for a season and then annihilated.[67] The Church at large believed in an eternity of bliss or of woe. Yet among the Montanists prayers and oblations were offered up on behalf of the departed, and it was thought that these sacrifices could in certain cases quicken the compassion of God towards those who had died in sin. The widow prayed that her lost husband's pangs might be alleviated, and that she might share with him in the First Resurrection. Perpetua, the matron lily of martyrs, in that jail which seemed to be a palace while her baby was at her breast, cried for mercy upon the soul of her little brother, who had died unbaptised.[68]

Clement never composed his promised treatise on the Resurrection, and it is not always easy to attach a definite meaning to his allusive style. But the general outline of his teaching is sufficiently clear. He rejects with scornful brevity the fancies of Chiliasm.[69] The Resurrection body is not 'this flesh,' but, as St. Paul taught, a glorified frame, related to that which we now possess as the grain of corn to the new ear, devoid in particular of the distinctions of sex.[70] The change is wrought by fire. Even Christ rose 'through fire.' Fire is here the agent not of chastisement, but of that mysterious sublimation by which our organism is fitted for existence in a new sphere.

For the sinner the fire burns with a fiercer intensity, because it has a harsher office. It is the pang of unsatisfied lusts that gnaw the soul itself for want of food, the sting of repentance and shame, the sense of loss. It is ministered not by fiends but by good angles,[71] it is alleviated by the prayers of the saints on earth.

There can I think be no doubt (though it has been doubted) that Clement allowed the possibility of repentance and amendment till the Last Day. At that final Assize there will be found those who, like Aridaeus,[72] are incurable, who will still reject, as man always can reject, the proffered grace. But he nowhere expressly limits probation to this brief life. All his theory of punishment, which is strictly Platonic, for he hardly ever quotes Scripture in this connection,[73] points the same way. And many passages might

be adduced which prove how his maxims are to be applied. 'Let them be chastised,' he says of the 'deaf serpents' who refuse to hear the voice of the charmer, 'by God, enduring His paternal correction before the Judgment, till they be ashamed and repent.'[74] In that fiery trial even Sodom and Gomorrha cried unto God and were forgiven. There is no difference between his teaching and that of Origen, except that he generally seems to be thinking of the doom of Christians, that he regards probation as ceasing at the Day of Judgment,[75] and that he does not contemplate the possibility of a fall from grace in the after-life.

Even the just must be purged by the 'wise fire,'[76] before they are fit for the presence of the Most Holy God. Not at once can they see face to face, or enter into possession of those good things which 'eye hath not seen nor ear heard.' When the burden of sin has been laid down, when the angels have taken their appointed 'toll,'[77] the spirit must still grow in knowledge, rising in due course through the seven heavens of the Valentinian, through the three 'mansions' or 'folds' prefigured by the triple hierarchy of the Church.[78] Some—those who have brought forth thirty, or sixty, or a hundredfold, yet have fallen short of what they might have been—mount no higher than this.[79] But the Gnostic, scaling from glory up to glory, will attain at last to the stature of the perfect man, and find rest upon the holy mountain of God, the Church that is above all. There in the changeless Ogdoad, a name borrowed from the Valentinian by the Catholic, as indeed is the greater part of this description, he shall dwell for ever with Christ, the God and Guardian of his faith and love, beholding the Father no longer 'in a glass darkly,' but with the direct unclouded vision of a pure heart, in light that never fades.[80]

Clement speaks of this final consummation as Rest. But it is the rest of God, 'who ceases not from doing good.'[81] There is no absorption, no confusion of subject and object. It is the rest not of unity but of perfect similarity, perfect reciprocity, the polar rest of a soul energising in unimpeded knowledge and love. Farther than this Clement does not dare to pry into the sanctuary of Light. 'I say no more glorifying the Lord.'[82]

Notes

1. The eternity of matter is denied, *Strom.* v. 14. 89. The pre-existence of the soul is rejected, *Strom.* iii. 13. 93; iv. 26. 167; *Eclogae Proph.* § 17. Yet it appears to be implied, *Q.D.S.* 33, 36; *Strom.* vii. 2. 9.

2. *Strom.* v. 6. 39; 14. 93 sq.

3. *Strom.* vi. 16. 142.

4. *Paed.* i. 3.7.

5. The difficulty was felt but not removed by Aristotle. . . .

6. The Gnostics went so far as to assert that he who did not prevent evil is the cause of the evil. The argument is retorted upon them with nnanswerable force in the *Recognitions,* ii. The Demiurge is evil because he tolerates evil. Why then does God tolerate the De-

miurge? The difficulty was strongly felt by Clement, whom it drove to the assertion that Christ's Passion was not ordained by the Father, *Strom.* iv. 12. 86 sq.

7. Origen has formally explained the Alexandrine doctrine of Freedom in the third book of the *De Principiis*. Neither he nor Clement clearly saw what Jeremy Taylor insists upon, that 'in moral things liberty is a direct imperfection, a state of weakness, and supposes weakness of reason and weakness of love.' But practically they admit, as we shall see, that at a certain point in the upward progress Grace absorbs the Will, and that at a certain point in the downward progress evil becomes second nature. Thus the demons have sinned so deeply 'ut revocari nolint magis quam non possint,' *De Princ.* i. 8. 4. But this point of irremediable depravity . . . they refused to fix. This seems to be the essential difference between the Alexandrines on the one hand and the Gnostics and Augustine on the other. Mehlhorn, *Die Lehre von der menschlichen Freiheit nach Or.,* Zeitsch. für Kirch. Gesch. 2 Band, p. 234, is referred to by Dr. Harnack, but I have not seen the article.

8. The soul does not come from the parent, *Strom.* vi. 16. 135. For the original estate of Adam see *Strom.* iv. 23. 150; vi. 12. 96. The Serpent was pleasure, *Protrept.* xi. III, and the precise sin may have been that the first parents anticipated the time fixed by God for their marriage, *Strom.* iii. 17. 103. Compare Philo, *De Mundi Op.* 55 (i. 37) sqq. 'Ita vix alia Adamum primo vixisse conditione noster censet quam posterorum infantes,' Guerike, i. p. 143. Clement does not admit any hereditary guilt. For (i) God punishes only voluntary sins, *Strom.* ii. 14. 60 . . . . (ii) The sins forgiven in Baptism are always spoken of as actual sins. (iii) Infant Baptism, a practice which is very closely connected with the tenet of Original Sin, is never certainly mentioned by Clement . . . . (iv) In *Strom.* iii. 16. 100 Clement replies to the Encratites, who forbade marriage on the ground that the children are accursed . . . . (v) The causes of sin are [discussed in] *Strom.* vii. 3. 16. Yet Adam is the type, though not the source, of sin, *Protrept.* xi. III. So also *Adumb. in Ep. Judae,* p. 1008, 'Sic etiam peccato Adae subjacemus secundum peccati similitudinem,' where the negative is omitted, as by Origen, in the well-known verse, Rom. v. 14. But I doubt very much whether this passage, which goes on to lay down the doctrine of Reprobation is from the hand of Clement.

9. *Strom.* iii. 9. 65: vii. 3. 13: iv. 25. 157.

10. *Strom.* ii. 4. 14: iii. 7. 57.

11. The ball-player, *Strom.* ii. 6. 25. So in *Paed.* i. 6. 28 regeneration is compared to waking or the removal of a cataract; we open our eyes and the light streams in. The words 'no man can come to Me except my Father draw him,' Clement explains differently at different times, *Strom.* iv. 22. 138; v. 13. 83. In the latter passage he quotes with approval the saying of Plato in the *Meno,* that virtue comes to those to whom it comes . . . . Compare also v. I. 7; vi. 6. 45; *Q. D. S.* 10, 21.

12. See especially *Strom.* ii. 2, 3, 4. Clement was very anxious to connect Faith, the Christian watchword, with philosophy . . . .

13. The *locus classicus* on Baptism is *Paed.* i. 6. It carries with it a double grace, Forgiveness and Light . . . .

14. See Münter, *Primordia Ecclesiae Africanae,* pp. 6, 68, 95. The curses on tombstones by which the grave was secured against violation were often copied with slight alterations from the formulas in use among Pagans. See Mr. Ramsay's article, *Cities and Bishoprics of Phrygia,* Journal of Hellenic Studies, Oct. 1883, p. 400.

15. For Pristinus see Tertullian, *De Jej.* 12; Münter, *Prim. Eccl. Afr.* p. 183. The history of Peregrinus will be found in Lucian. He was actually a confessor, and it was not his own fault that he was not a martyr. That these were not isolated instances is clear from the earnestness with which Clement maintains against Heracleon that even those who had denied Christ in their lives washed away their sins by martyrdom; *Strom.* iv. 9. 72 sqq.

16. See the description of . . . Proficiency in Seneca, Ep. 75.

17. Clem. Rom. i. 1. 2; 7. 4; 36. 2; 40. 1; 41. 4; 48. 5; Hermas, *Vis.* i. 2. 1; Barnabas, 1. 5; ii. 2. 3; v. 4; vi. 9; ix. 8; x. 10; xiii. 7. In Hermas and Barnabas the connection of Gnosis with Allegorism is clearly asserted.

18. *Strom.* ii. 12. 55; iv. 7. 53. Sometimes he drops Fear, and speaks of . . . Faith, Hope and Charity, corresponding to the three mansions in the Father's House.

19. *Strom.* iv. 22. 135 . . . .

20. Clement partly realised all this . . . . The spark of knowledge contains the spark of desire, and this is kindled to a flame by better knowledge gained through practice, *Strom.* vi. 17. 150 sqq.

21. How little Clement understood what St. Paul means by Faith will be seen from the following quotations. *Strom.* vi. 13. 108, 'thy faith hath saved thee' was said not to Gentiles, but to Jews who already abounded in good works. vi. 12. 98, Faith is not good in itself, but as leading to Fear and Hope . . . . vi. 12. 103, 'Faith was accounted to Abraham for righteousness when he had advanced to that which is greater and more perfect than faith. For he who merely abstains from wrong is not righteous unless he adds well-doing and knowledge of the reason why he ought to do some things and not do others.' iv. 18. 113, Love is the motive of the Gnostic, Fear that of Faith.

22. *Paed.* i. 8. 62 . . . . For the mirror see *Paed.* i. 9. 88. The same simile is found in Epictetus, ii. 14. 21. It was probably a Stoic commonplace.

23. Clement's doctrine on the subject of Pleasure is to be found in *Paed.* ii, iii; *Strom.* iii. iv. His general aim is to moderate the antique rigour in favour of the wealthier classes . . . . His chief axioms are that pleasure as such is not to be desired by the Christian, and that to be 'according to nature' it must be strictly limited to the end which God intended it to promote. Hence the rule of marital continence, the prohibition of the use of the 'bones of dead animals,' ivory and tortoiseshell, of dyes, and artificial hair. No ring is allowed but a signet. There is a natural and an unnatural use of flowers. 'For in spring-time to walk abroad in meadows dewy and soft and springing fresh with jewelled flowers delights us with a natural and wholesome fragrance, and we suck their sweetness as do the bees. But it is not meet for grave men to carry about in the house a plaited chaplet from meads untrodden.' The stern prohibition of the use of cut flowers is one of the most singular features of primitive Christian discipline. It is hardly necessary to refer to the *De Cor. Mil.* of Tertullian. Art he desparages, but the signet may bear a simple Christian emblem, a dove, a fish, a ship in full sail, a lyre, an anchor, a fisherman. But he was quoted on this account in the Iconoclastic controversy as a favourer of Christian imagery, Photius, *Cod.* 110. Generally speaking, he gives innocent pleasure a liberal scope. 'Wine,' he says, quoting Plato, 'makes a man good-tempered, agreeable to his company, more lenient to his slaves, more complaisant to his friends.' He is much less austere than Origen.

24. *Strom.* iii. 17. 103; vi. 17. 151.

25. It is to be found in Plato himself and Aristotle (see Lobeck, *Aglaophamus,* p. 128), in Philo, and in Plutarch . . . .

26. Gnosis is always *in* Christ; *Strom.* iv. 25. 155; v. 3. 16; vi. 9. 78. Nay, the Saviour *is* our knowledge and spiritual paradise; vi. I. 2.

27. *Strom.* v. I. 13 . . . .

28. *Strom.* vi. 7. 54.

29. The majority of the Christians had not received a regular education and some did not know their letters, *Strom.* i. 20. 99. Erudition is sometimes hurtful to the understanding, as Anaxarchus said, . . . *Strom.* i. 5. 35.

30. *Strom.* vi. 10. 80; 18. 162.

31. *Q. D. S.* 27.

32. The most singular instance of Clement's disparagement of human love is to be found in *Strom.* vii. 12. 70, where married life is regarded as superior to celibacy because it offers so many more temptations to surmount.

33. The leading passages on the subject of Apathy and disinterested Love are *Strom.* iv. 6. 30; 18. 111; 22. 135-146; vi. 9. 71; 12. 100; 16. 138.

34. *Strom.* vi. 9. 73.

35. It was insisted upon by the Quiestists. It is a paradox because the separation is impossible. The Kingdom of Heaven is within you. Milton makes Satan complain, 'Which way I go is hell, myself am hell;' and the converse is true also. But Clement knew this well; cp. *Strom.* v. 10. 63 . . . . Nor did the Quietists think otherwise. Bossuet did not venture directly to deny the mystic paradox, which is in fact admitted in the Articles of Issy. But I must refer my readers to Mr. Vaughan's charming *Hours with the Mystics,* vol. ii. pp. 170, 380, ed. 1856.

36. Clement ascribes Apathy to Christ and to the Apostles after the Resurrection, *Strom.* vi. 9. 71. As regards men he uses sometimes very strong language. The Gnostic becomes a god upon earth, iv. 23. 149; vii. 3. 13 . . . . On the other hand, *Paed.* i. 2. 4; *Strom.* iv. 21. 130; *Q. D. S.* 40, more sober language is employed; Christ is the only perfect man, passion cannot be wholly eradicated in this life, the wise man touches no known sin. It is the *posse non peccare,* not the *non posse peccare.* But Clement is less introspective than Origen. The mere frailty of human nature does not distress him so long as he feels that his heart is safe in Christ.

37. *Strom.* vii. 14. 87. On Righteousness, see especially the fine passage, *Strom.* vi. 12. 102. Origen distinguishes two modes of Righteousness, Innocence, the effect of Baptismal Forgiveness, and the active virtue of Justice. Clement speaks only of the latter. The just man is faithful, but the faithful man is not necessarily just. Faith is salvation, but not righteousness; it gives the will, but not immediately the power to do right. Faith is life, righteousness is health. It would seem then that we might be 'saved' without good works, but Clement never expressly deals with this question. He seems to assert the opposite, *Strom.* v. 1. 7 . . . . On the necessity, the 'merit' of good works, see *Strom.* v. 13. 86; vii. 12. 72; 14. 108.

38. *Strom.* vii. 13. 82.

39. *Strom.* iv. 22. 136 . . . .

40. Public Worship in the morning, *Paed.* ii. 10. 96: Fasting on Wednesday and Friday, *Strom.* vii. 12, 75 . . . .

41. See generally *Strom.* iv. 23. 148; viii. 7. 35 sqq.

42. *Strom.* vii. 7. 40; the Gnostic rose also at intervals during the night to pray, *Paed.* ii. 9. 79; *Strom.* vii. 7. 49.

43. 'Endormie dans le néant,' Molinos, *Guide Spirituelle,* iii. 20. 201. I owe the reference to La Bruyère, *Dialogues sur le Quiétisme,* vol. ff. ed. Servois.

44. Porphyry, *Vita Plotini,* 23, p. 116, ed. Firmin-Didot. For St. Theresa see Barthélemy Saint-Hilaire, *L'École d' Alexandrie,* pp. xlv, lxxix; for Gerson, *ibid.* lxii, xcviii. Vacherot in his third volume traces the connection of the Alexandrines with mediaeval mysticism. Dähne . . . insists that Clement himself was a mystic. It depends upon the meaning which we at-

tach to the word. In one sense all believers in the unseen are Mystics; in another, all believers in whom the emotional element predominates largely over the intellectual. I have taken Mysticism as co-extensive with Ecstasy. Of this again there are several degrees, ranging from the inarticulate communion of the Quietists to pictorial visions. Such visions were regarded with suspicion by Mystics of the higher class, such as St. John of the Cross. See Vaughan, *Hours with the Mystics.*

45. *Strom.* iv. 26. 172; vii. 5. 29; iii. 6. 49; 11. 74; *Paed.* i. 6. 42; *Strom.* vii. 17. 107 (one, true, ancient, catholic), 108 (apostolic).

46. *Strom.* vii. 11. 68: in vii. 14. 87 the Gnostics are the Holy Church, the Spiritual Body of which those who only bear the name of Christian and do not live according to reason are the flesh. Had this point of view been habitual to him Clement must have written very differently about the Lower Life. The Invisible Spiritual Church, the Communion of Saints, is compared to a chain of rings upheld by a magnet, vii. 2. 9. It is the Church of the First Born, *Protrept.* ix. 82 . . . .

47. The sacrifice, *Paed.* iii. 12. 90; *Strom.* ii. 18. 79, 96; v. 11. 67 (immediately after an allusion to the Eucharist); vii. 3. 14; 6. 31, 32. The last cited passage explains the terms altar, incense.

48. *Strom.* v. 11. 66, 70. See also passages quoted in Lecture II.

49. *Strom.* v. 14. 136. The verse had already been applied to the Eucharist in the *Doctrine of the Apostles,* Irenaeus and Justin.

50. *Strom.* ii. 13. 56. Clement follows Hermas, *Mand.* iv. 3, almost verbally, though without naming his authority. He supports this view by Heb. x, 26, 27. Clement nowhere expressly draws a distinction between mortal and venial sins, but it is implied here and in *Strom.* vi. 12. 97 . . . . It is the first, repentance of mortal sin, that could only be repeated once after baptism. It is singular that in *Q. D. S.* he does not enter upon the question . . . .

51. *Strom.* vi. 13. 107. Bishop, Priest, and Deacon symbolise the 'three Mansions,' the three degrees of the Angelic Hierarchy . . . .

52. *Q. D. S.* 41. Probst, *Sakramente,* p. 261, unhesitatingly identifies the Man of God with the Priest. It is just possible that we have here the same admonition as in Origen, *Sel. in Psalmos,* Hom. ii. 6 (Lom. xii. p. 267), 'tantummodo circumspice diligentius, cui debeas confiteri peccatum tuum. Proba prius medicum.' He may mean that the chaplain is to be a priest, but a worthy priest. But were there more than twelve priests in Alexandria, and in any case can there have been enough to supply domestic chaplains to all the rich men who needed them? I do not doubt that the chaplain is to be a Gnostic who is a judge in spiritual matters, *Strom.* vii. 7. 45. Rufinus, before

his ordination, seems to have held such a post in the household of Melania. Compare note above, p. 96. Probst, I may add, endeavours to prove that the Gnostic is the Priest by combining what Clement says of the Gnostic, of Moses, of the Law, and of Christ the Shepherd.

53. This statement, that the Eucharist at Alexandria was not yet separated from the Agape and that both were celebrated together in the evening, may seem doubtful, and indeed I make it with some hesitation. It may be argued, on the other side, (i) That the separation was already made in the West, as we see from Justin and Tertullian, and is found immediately after Clement's time in Palestine, *teste* Origen. (ii) That the word Eucharist is employed by Clement for the Elements, *Strom.* i. 1.5, and for the rite, *Paed.* ii. 2. 20; *Strom.* iv. 25. 161. (iii) That there was a morning service at Alexandria, though we are not told that it included the Eucharist, *Paed.* ii. 10. 96. On the other hand, (i) the Liturgy, so far as we can judge, is not nearly so developed in Clement's church as in that of Origen; (ii) the Agape in both its forms is distinctly mentioned, the Eucharist as a separate office is not; (iii) the word Eucharist is employed of the Agape, *Paed.* ii. 10. 96. (iv) The Agape is mentioned in the Sibylline Oracles—*Or.* viii. 402, 497, *temp.* Trajan or Hadrian; *Or.* v. 265, *temp.* Antoninus Pius—while the Eucharist is not: see Alexandre, ii. 547. It is true that both these authorities are anterior in date to Clement. (v) Dionysius of Alexandria still uses of the rite of Communion the same word. . . which in Clement means the Agape, Eus. *H. E.* vi. 42.5 . . . . (vi) Lastly, I do not know of any passage in an Oriental writer before Clement's time in which the Eucharist appears as a distinct and substantive office. In the *Doctrine of the Apostles* Hilgenfeld observes. . . in chap. 10, 'eucharistia vere coena communis nondum separata ab Agape.' And from Socrates, v. 22, it appears that the Agape lingered on in the churches of Upper Egypt longer than elsewhere. We may infer from this perhaps that Alexandria also had clung to the primitive usage after it had been abandoned by others.

54. Supper followed the Eucharist, see *Paed.* ii. 1. 11 . . . .

55. The description of the Agape will be found at the opening of *Paed.* ii. For a similar and equally graphic account of the coarse vulgarity of Alexandrine luxury, see Philo, *De Vita Cont.* 5 (ii. 477). The contrast between the heathen man of the world and the Christian gentleman as drawn by Clement is most instructive.

56. *Paed.* ii. 1. 10 . . . .

57. *Strom.* iv. 26. 161. The figure is from Philo, and must be interpreted by Philo's light . . . .

58. . . . The chief passages on the subject of the Eucharist are, besides these two, *Paed.* ii. 2. 19 sq.; *Strom.* v. 10. 66. Other notices in *Paed.* i. 5. 15; 6. 38; *Strom.* i. 10. 46; 19. 96; v. 11. 70; vi. 14. 113; *Q.D.S.* 23.

59. *Paed.* ii. 2. 20 . . . .

60. *Paed.* ii. 2. 19; iii. 1. 2.

61. For these four quotations see *Paed.* ii. 2. 19; i. 6. 38; *Strom.* v. 10. 66; *Adumb. in Ep. Joan. I.* p. 1009. I quote the last book always with hesitation.

62. *Strom.* iv. 26. 161; *Paed.* i. 6. 43. The two opposing views are maintained by Döllinger, *Die Eucharistie in den drei ersten Jahrb.*, Mainz, 1826, and Probst, *Liturgie,* on the one hand, and by Höfling, *Die Lehre der ältesten Kirche vom Opfer im Leben und Cultus,* Erlangen, 1851. Upon the whole Höfling's view appears to me to be correct . . . .

63. A Montanist sister in one of her visions saw a soul 'tenera et lucida et aerii coloris et forma per omnia humana,' *De Anima,* 9. Tatian's doctrine in *Oratio ad Graecos,* 13. For the Arabians, Eus. *H. E.* vi. 37; Redepenning, *Origenes,* ii. 105 sqq . . . .

64. See Irenaeus, v. 13; Athenagoras, *De Res.*

65. The four letters composing the word Ρωμη = 948, hence it was supposed the empire would last that number of years, *Or. Sib.* viii. 148. When this expectation was frustrated by the course of events, the authors of the last four Sibylline books struck off 105 years from the Roman Fasti and fixed upon the year 305 in the reign of Diocletian. See much curious information upon similar speculations which recurred again and again from the persecution of Nero downwards, Alexandre, ii. pp. 485 sqq.

66. Tertullian, *Adv. Marc.* iii. 24; Münter, *Primordia Eccl. Afr.* p. 141.

67. Eternal torments in i. 7; xi. 11: the other view in iii. 6.

68. Tertullian, *De Monogamia,* 10, the widow prays for her husband's soul; 'enimvero et pro anima eius orat, et refrigerium interim adpostulat ei et in prima resurrectione consortium, et offert annuis diebus dormitionis eius:' *De Cor. Mil.* 3, 'oblationes pro defunctis, pro natalitiis, annua die facimus' (here he rests the usage on tradition, and not on Scripture: but he may mean only that the oblation is not scriptural as the use of prayer is sanctioned by 2 Tim. i. 18): see also *De Exhort. Cast.* 11. All these treatises are Montanist according to Münter. Montanist also in the opinion of Valesius are the Acta of St. Perpetua. As to the latter it should be observed that the little brother Dinocrates for whom Perpetua intercedes had certainly died unbaptised. For his father was a Pagan—Perpetua herself was baptised in the prison—and the effect of her prayer is that Dinocrates is admitted to the benefits of baptism. 'I saw Dinocrates coming forth from a dark place very hot and thirsty, squalid of face and pallid of hue . . . . And hard by where he stood was a tank full of water, the margin whereof was higher than the stature of the child, and he stood on tiptoe as if he would drink.' Again, 'on the day on which we lay in the stocks,' she prays, and sees Dinocrates cleansed, dressed, and cool, drinking eagerly of the water. 'Then I knew that he was released from pain.' Further, the privilege of intercession is granted to Perpetua by revelation as a special mark of favour. So Clement appears to restrict it to the Gnostic. The practice of prayer for the dead was certainly uncommon at the end of the second century. It is not found in Origen, for *in Rom.* ix. 12 is confessedly from the hand of Rufinus.

69. *Strom.* vii. 12. 74 . . . .

70. *Paed.* i. 4. 10; 6. 46. In this last passage it is said that Christ rose 'through fire,' which changes the natural into the spiritual body, as earthly fire changes wheat into bread. But the resurrection body may still be called flesh, *Paed.* ii. 10. 100; iii. 1. 2.

71. *Strom.* v. 14. 90; vii. 2. 12 . . . .

72. *Strom.* v. 14. 90: in iv. 24. 154 the 'faithless' are as the chaff which the wind driveth away . . . .

73. Isaiah iv. 4 is quoted, *Paed.* iii. 9. 48, and Cor. i. 3. 10-13, *Strom.* v. 4. 26.

74. *Strom.* vii. 16. 102. Repentance is attributed to the dead again in *Strom.* vi. 14. 109. If it be asked *which* repentance Clement speaks of here (see note above, p. 102), the instance of Sodom and Gomorrha, *Adumb. in Ep. Judae,* p. 1008, is very strong. It rests upon Ezekiel xvi. 33, 55, and is employed by Origen in the same way . . . . The question of the orthodoxy or heterodoxy of the Alexandrines in this part of their teaching turns entirely upon the word 'repentance,' to which we shall recur in Lecture VIII.

75. See *Strom.* vii. 2. 12 . . . .

76. *Strom.* vii. 6. 34 . . . . Cp. *Eclogae Proph.* 25. p. 995, and Minucius Felix, xxxv, illic sapiens ignis membra urit et reficit; carpit et nutrit. There is an allusion to Isaiah iv. 4, but the actual phrase 'wise fire' comes from Heraclitus and the Stoics.

77. The Angels who guard the road up to the highest heaven 'take toll' of the passer-by, *Strom.* iv. 18. 117.

78. Clement may have taken the seven heavens from Valentinus or from the Revelation of Sophonias, *Strom.* v. 11. 77. He found allusions to them in Plato's *Timaeus,* p. 31; in Clemens Romanus, i. 20 (of the 'lands' beyond the ocean); in St. Paul, and elsewhere. The same idea is found in the book of Baruch (Origen, *De Princ.* ii. 3. 6), and in Aristo, Fragment iv. in Otto, *Corp. App.* vol. ix. p. 363. See also Hermas, *Vis.* iii. 4, and note there in the ed. of Gebhardt and Harnack. The seven days of purification are a type, *Strom.* iv. 25. 158 . . . .

79. This seems to be clearly meant in *Strom.* iv. 18. 114; vi. 14. 108, 114; cp. also *Ecl. Proph.* 56. But if so, the *poena damni* never wholly ceases, *Strom.* vi. 14. 109.

80. *Strom.* iv. 25. 158; vi. 14. 108; vii. 10. 56, 57.

81. *Strom.* vi. 12. 104.

82. *Strom.* vii. 3. 13.

R. B. Tollinton (essay date 1914)

SOURCE: "Literary Work, " in *Clement of Alexandria: A Study in Christian Liberalism,* Vol. I, Williams and Norgate, 1914, pp. 178-209.

[*In the following excerpt, Tollinton examines difficulties Clement faced in his writing and how he dealt with them—by acting positively instead of defensively, by tailoring his writing to the intelligent reader, and by deliberately disregarding style.*]

During the later years of his residence in Alexandria Clement determined to give his teaching a permanent and written form. It was a natural decision on several grounds. He had lived the life of a student since his early school-days. He had gathered abundant materials. Even within the Church he had the example of many contemporaries who were authors. He had made his home in a city of books and libraries. It is thus no matter for surprise that literary work should have formed a considerable element in the latter half of his career. It is as a writer, not less than as head of the Alexandrian School, that he was afterwards remembered. He was the "Stromatist," the "author," . . . and the like.[1]

Nevertheless, so natural a decision was not reached without a good deal of hesitation. There were considerations against, as well as for, the publication of his teaching in the form of books, and his caution and deliberate care in taking up the pen contrast sharply enough with his freedom and his readiness to follow any train of thought, when once he has started upon the writer's enterprise. It is still possible to see the various lines of argument which occurred to him, as the gains and risks of authorship passed alternately through his mind. It is wholly to Clement's credit that in an age of facile and abundant literary production he treated the question so seriously.

As against writing there was the fact that it would be for him a new departure. Oral instruction was one thing, the written book another.[2] To lecture or preach well was no guarantee of success in writing: indeed, the different qualities demanded by the two modes of expression do not, he suspects, belong to the same nature. There is a certain unrestrained freedom which is the mark of the ready speaker. There is a certain precision and exactitude demanded in the writer, whose words will remain to be questioned and criticised. Even if style does not matter and literary merit forms, as he tells us, no part of his aim, still there is a fundamental difference between the lecture and the treatise. They are distinct modes of spiritual husbandry, not the least among their many diversities being the fact that the lecturer knows his pupils, whereas the author has no knowledge of those who will read his books. So he had to face the question of his personal fitness for a new department of Christian service. His decision was justified by the event.

But there was yet a further difficulty to be faced. To write books was not only to depart from the previous manner of his vocation in the Catechetical School, it was also an innovation on the practice of the teachers he most revered. Those "Elders,"[3] to whom Clement feels himself so greatly indebted, were the recipients and the transmitters of an oral tradition, but they did not write books. He expressly states that this was so,[4] and discusses the reason of their rigid adherence to the oral method. Partly, he thinks, it was because they had not time; partly, because they had not the aptitude. His account of their reasons is obviously inadequate, and even the actual statement that they did not write is open to grave question in the case of his nearest and most influential master, Pantænus.[5] There is no doubt, however, that he regarded oral tradition as the chosen and established method of these earliest teachers whom he does not name. It was a serious matter for him, their pupil, the lesser man of a later day—"few are the equals of our fathers"—to venture on fresh methods, and to impart by writing the truths which wiser and older men had held should only come to fit recipients by the living voice. Clement's regard for the Elders was quite genuine and serious, however difficult it may be to harmonise with his very considerable independence as a teacher. Their example could only be set aside for good and sufficient reasons.

But there were more positive and concrete difficulties yet for him to face, if Clement was to put his teaching into books. So far as the mere question of method, oral or literary, was involved, if he elected to depart from the practice of the Elders, the concern and responsibility were all his own. But wider interests came into account when he considered the possible consequences to his readers. Had it been a question of presenting to the pagan world a simple statement of the Gospel, or of reasserting, from the Christian standpoint, the accepted canons of moral conduct, this further point would hardly have arisen. But Clement had no intention of limiting his published works to these important but preliminary issues. Christianity, as he knew it, had deeper truths and more advanced instruction. There were mysteries and esoteric doctrines and wider views of God's great purpose, which all men were not ready to receive. Among his own pupils he had clearly made distinctions, and some had been led further than others along the road towards perfect vision. A teacher using oral methods could deal in this way with his hearers. He could make selection. A book, on the other hand, must take its chance. The wrong readers might take it up. It would be misunderstood, and criticised by the ignorant; its higher meaning would be subject for ridicule from the uneducated brother, who had established himself on the lower planes of truth. So a dangerous sword would be put into a child's hand or, in another figure, the pearls of truth cast before the unclean swine.

This was likely enough to happen in Alexandria. In Clement's day the Church and the School were not in any close relationship. The School was intellectual, independent, aristocratic, winning its converts successfully from the educated heathen and showing an attitude not wholly unsympathetic to philosophy and even to the better side of

Gnosticism. The rank and file of the Church were men and women of a different order. They were not people of much education. Demetrius, the Bishop, had himself little learning. Even as late as the episcopate of Dionysius A.D. 248-265) there were Elders in Alexandria who thought it wrong to read books which were not orthodox.[6] So culture, philosophy, libraries, and speculation, had slight place in their religion, and for churchmen of this type Gnosticism proved only too clearly the evils of advanced knowledge and the awful conclusions to which inquiry was almost sure to lead.

These sincere and narrow souls appear in Clement's pages as the "Orthodoxasts"; they are the literal, simple believers with whom Origen also was to be acquainted. Their motto was "faith only," and Clement, tender as he was towards these simple brethren as a rule, cannot forbid himself the sarcasm that they "expected to eat the fruit of the vine without taking any pains about its culture."[7] They have their exact counterpart in modern times, and their suspicion of the intellectual attitude towards religion is usually aggressive and irremediable. It was certainly so in Alexandria, and what were such persons likely to say of a book on advanced doctrine with the philosophic and learned Clement as its author? Before he wrote the **Stromateis,** not, it would seem, through earlier publications, but more probably by rumour and gossip which gathered round his lecture-room, he had clearly drawn upon himself a certain amount of ignorant criticism from these unphilosophic brethren. Even if name and reputation were matters of slight account, there was still the possible loss of influence to be considered. Besides, the interests of the Church, and even the spiritual welfare of these simple and nervous brethren, alike demanded that such a project as Clement had in mind should not be rashly undertaken. It was a matter for conscience and right judgment, and Clement faced all the risks before he decided to issue in the form of a book such teaching as, hitherto, had been imparted only to an inner circle of qualified and understanding pupils.

These considerations, more especially the last described, might have led Clement to decline all literary ventures, and our knowledge of him might then have been no more extensive than the scanty information which has survived about Pantænus. Happily the question had two sides, and Clement had owed so much himself to books that he could hardly fail to appreciate the possibilities of literary work in the Church's service. This, indeed, within certain limits, had been already realised. A Christian literature was already in existence, and though the Apostolic and subapostolic fathers were hardly likely to win many converts from Hellenism, more was to be said for the Apologists; and more still for the numerous writers whose works were occasioned by the recent rise of heresies, particularly of Gnosticism. Clement made reference to the *Shepherd of Hermas* to justify his own undertaking, for the mutilated quotation with which the **Stromateis** open is clearly an appeal to precedent and authority. He was also acquainted with the important works of Tatian, Melito, and Irenæus.

Eusebius knew of many other authors who had written books before the **Stromateis** were published.

Thus, if Clement deserted the practice of the Elders, he was at least in harmony with the current habit of the times. The new departure lay not in the actual writing of a book, but in the scale and character of his purpose. Hitherto the Church's literary enterprise had been mainly of a defensive nature. The action of the State or the fanaticism of the crowd called forth the Apologies. The heresies gave rise to many a defence of catholic tradition, so far as this was fixed. Another literature was already forming itself around the Quartodeciman controversy. But for a positive exposition of Christian truth, challenging attention by its use of a secular method and meeting educated readers on ground that was their own, the time had not till now been ripe. Clement realised that the hour for this had come. In Alexandria, at any rate, believers were no longer occupied with the Millennium. Gnostic literature was serious, plentiful, and dangerous, and educated persons were at last beginning to come over in appreciable numbers to Christianity. As against the suspicious multitude of the "simpliciores" were the interests of the thinking minority. The Church—it is possibly to her credit—has always been more tender in her care of the orthodox than in her solicitude for the anxious and unsettled. Clement elected to venture on the less usual course and to write, at the risk of being misinterpreted and criticised, a book which should meet the needs of intelligent and inquiring minds. He hopes to lead his readers into the higher domains of doctrine. He believes he will save some keen spirits from falling into the ways of heresy. He even contemplates the possible recovery for the Church of some who have wandered from the central paths of truth. His books may fall into wrong hands. If so, readers as well as writers have their responsibilities. He can only hope that, as a magnet draws only iron to itself,[8] so his written teaching may attract only those who can claim affinity with its character. It must depend on the reader's conscience; just as even the Eucharist was often so administered that the laity could partake or not, as each should best determine for himself.[9]

On the preparation necessary for the study of higher doctrine he dwells with insistent reiteration. And for himself in his enterprise his standard is not less high. The poorer motives of the author, the desire of profit, the quest of reputation, the temper of the partisan, are all ruled out with a rigour and sincerity that are rare in the world of letters. His one aim is the gain and enlightenment of his readers. He is "foncièrement pédagogue," even in his books, as De Faye remarks with complete justification.[10] So there is an unselfishness in his purpose which does Clement credit: when he wrote, as truly as when he lectured, his main purpose was to hand on to others, who were able to receive them, the truths which he himself had been privileged to see and learn. The aim of religious literature has rarely been discussed from a higher standpoint than in the opening pages of the **Stromateis.** Clement's decision to write books and his whole conception of the responsibilities of the author, are a fine example of the

Church's vocation to minister to intelligence, and a reminder, surely needed in our own time, that unsettled minds, who only hover on the fringe of her membership, are sometimes abundantly deserving of her thought and care.[11]

Such is the central motive of Clement's literary enterprise. There were also subsidiary considerations leading in the same direction. He was getting on in years, and writing would be an aid to memory. The tradition he had received would be more securely conserved in documents than by the living voice alone. If the atheism of Epicurus and the lampoons of Archilochus survived as literature, surely the same methods would not be denied to the herald of the truth. Moreover, books were the offspring of the mind, and to leave behind good offspring was admittedly a noble service to the future. He is keenly concerned to justify on every possible ground the rightful character of his task. And throughout, his appeal is always to good sense and solid reason. Apparently he has no fear of any official censure. There is no hint that he ever thought it possible that Bishop Demetrius would interfere. The Church controlled the School after the appointment of Origen, but not before.

The main interest of Clement's writings lies in the broad lines of their interpretation of Christianity, in the light they throw upon its contact with other tendencies and forces, and in their revelation of his attractive and unusual personality. But their form, not only their content, deserves some consideration, and many questions of a purely literary order arise for all who attempt to acquaint themselves closely with his pages. In the last five and twenty years many competent writers have published books or treatises on Clement and his works. It is worthy of note that a large proportion of this recent literature of the subject is devoted to the discussion of the literary problems that are involved. Reference has already been made to the difficult question of Clement's indebtedness to sources and compilations previously existing. So far as his own writings are concerned, the most important points for consideration are the place of the **Stromateis** in his great tripartite scheme, the order in which his books were written, the aim and nature of some of the incompleted works that are assigned to him. These questions of literary form can to some extent be distinguished from those which concern the substance and content of his writings; yet the distinction is by no means absolute. What he intends to write largely determines the manner of his writing; personal characteristics colour and qualify his style; and his doctrine of reserve has extensive consequences of a literary nature. For convenience the line may be drawn, but it implies no real separation.

The word *Stromateis* has been happily rendered "carpet-bags."[12] Properly, they were the parti-coloured sacks in which blankets and bedding were stowed away. From their variegated appearance they gave the name to a particular class of literature, much in vogue during the second century. A *locus classicus* on the subject is found in the preface to the *Noctes Atticæ* of Aulus Gellius, where the term stands in a list of titles together with *Amalthea's Horn, Honeycombs, Flower-beds,* and similar appellations, all used to denote works in which miscellaneous fragments from different sources and of various character were strung together in unrestricted diversity.[13] Plutarch wrote *Stromateis* of this order. So did Origen. Clement's most important surviving work was so entitled, and amply justified its name. It is not a form of literature which would obviously and naturally suggest itself to a writer who wished to set forth advanced Christian doctrine. The reasons which led Clement to select it so deliberately are curious and interesting.

No doubt he was conscious in using it that he had many various subjects to discuss. A "carpet-bag" is a convenient receptacle for a medley of unclassified articles, and Clement required a form of literature in which he could portray the ideal Gnostic, demonstrate the antiquity of Moses, introduce *bons mots* and occasional good stories, and give wise counsel on the subject of martyrdom. Tedious and irrelevant as his pages often are to the modern reader, they never betray any failure of interest on the part of the writer in his themes. His diversified learning, and his extraordinary delight in the most varied schemes of writing, found their wholly appropriate medium in this avowedly miscellaneous type of literature. He had many seeds to sow, not all of them of Apostolic origin. The result of his husbandry is a "Meadow," a "Paradise," or even more truly a literary "thicket,"[14] where abstract ideas, timely quotations, apt and often amusing incidents, are found growing in profusion side by side.

To some extent Clement must have been conscious of the opportunity such a form of composition would give to his discursive genius. This, however, is not his main reason for selecting it. His choice is not so much determined by his personal bent as by the conditions of the public for whom he writes. In determining to risk the publication of his teaching in the form of a book, we have already seen that he gave precedence to the interests of an intelligent minority over the prejudices and dislike of the suspicious multitude of the believers. But, when the decision had been made, considerations of caution seem again to have possessed him, and partly in regard for simple brethren within the Church, partly, too, with the object of defending the faith from profanation by those who were without, he decides to publish his higher teaching only in a work of cryptic character. There is a long discussion, occupying a third of the Fifth Book of the **Stromateis,**[15] in which he cites instance after instance of such reserve in imparting doctrine. It was not only that the Lord Himself had chosen to teach in Parables. The veil of the Temple, the oracles of the Greeks, the hieroglyphics of Egypt, the symbolism of the Old Testament, the Mysteries of Eleusis, the dark sayings of the Wise, all implied a protection from the common multitude of the secrets revealed and intelligible to the few. Such signs and tokens had their full meaning only for those who could apprehend it. So he thinks it may be possible to scatter seeds of doctrine here and there throughout his pages, in such a fashion that only the wise reader shall discern their true significance. The genuine and patient seeker shall find truth: the quest is to be intentionally difficult, so that the merely inquisitive and the uninstructed may be repelled and kept away. It was a curious and unusual project. We may doubt the entire success of his method for its purpose. No Christian who could read, and either possessed or borrowed a copy of the *Stromateis,* would remain ignorant of Clement's views on Philosophy, Gnosticism, and allegorical exegesis. Still, he was not, so far as we know, actually accused of heresy until a later date, and there is certainly no lack of passages in his writings in which his meaning and the connection of thought are extremely difficult to discover . . . . The modern reader has frequent reason to allow that this intention was fulfilled.

Later writers on the *Stromateis* have not rested content with this account of their character and purpose, as the author gave it. In particular, De Faye believes that they evidence a more serious change in Clement's scheme than the mere employment of the cryptic method would involve. He points out that in the *Pædagogus* Clement speaks in several places of "the **Master**,". . . as though this was to be the title of the third portion of his work. After conversion, which is the office of the "protreptic" Word, after moral training, which is in the charge of the Pædagogue, comes higher teaching, knowledge, initiation into Christian truth, and this the **"Master"** must impart. "And now," he writes, in the closing chapter of the *Pædagogus,* "it is time for me to bring this earlier instruction. . . to an end and for you to listen to the Master."[16] But what follows is, as we know, not a doctrinal work so entitled, but the long drawn miscellany of the *Stromateis.* Even in the Seventh Book the consideration of doctrine is still postponed to "the appropriate season"; in its concluding chapter his project is still regarded as ahead and unattained, and the reader is surprised by the promise of a new start in the very closing sentence of the book.[17]

On this and similar evidence it is argued that the *Stromateis* cannot be the promised *[Didaskalos].* They are rather a work preliminary to the discussion of doctrine, which Clement found necessary, mainly on the grounds of his readers susceptibilities, to insert between the *Pædagogus* and the crowning section of his scheme. When the *Stromateis,* as we possess them, come to an end, they have removed many difficulties and cleared the way, but their purpose has only been preparatory, and the long-expected **"Master"** was destined to remain an unaccomplished project. Such, in outline, is De Faye's interesting solution of this difficult literary question. His interpretation is maintained with great command of the evidence, and with all the clearness of statement for which the best French theological writing is ever remarkable.

But it has not passed unchallenged. The most serious criticism is that of C. Heussi,[18] who argues that the *Stromateis* are the **"Master,"** and contends that no direct statements of Clement prove them to be merely preliminary; that they do not prepare for the "Gnosis," but rather impart it; and

that many expressions of the writer prove them to be the crowning work, to which the opening chapter of the *Pædagogus* looks forward. To these considerations is added the assertion that the first four books of the *Stromateis* must have been written before the *Pædagogus,* since the latter work refers to an already published discussion on marriage, which can be none other than that contained in *Stromateis* II. and III. This last contention, if it could be supported by conclusive evidence, would indeed render De Faye's interpretation untenable, though it would also raise fresh difficulties, if indeed it did not throw the whole problem of Clement's writings into an inextricable confusion. The arguments in favour of this hypothesis are, however, scarcely sufficient to render it a substantial conclusion. The discussion on marriage may have been a lost work of which the fragment quoted in Stählin's edition is all that now survives.[19] Or Clement may have incorporated a previously written monograph in his later work; or possibly the *Pædagogus* may have been revised after the *Stromateis* were written, and the references to the discussion on marriage introduced. On the whole it may be said that there is no sufficient reason to suppose that Clement's great Trilogy was composed in any other order than that in which we possess it.

De Faye seems, then, to have proved that Clement intended to call the third portion of his work *The Master,* and to have also made clear the fact that at the end of the *Stromateis* his main purpose still remains unaccomplished. What is really open to question is the supposition that Clement himself regarded the *Stromateis,* from the first, as a preparatory undertaking and no more. It is difficult to see why he should have introduced a work, merely preliminary, with so serious a preface as stands at the opening of the *Stromateis.* Its whole tone implies that he is on the threshold of his most important task. Moreover, his method of concealing truth, which is sufficiently appropriate on the supposition that he wishes his meaning to be intelligible only to those who have the key of knowledge, would be wholly out of place in a work whose purpose was to remove popular objections. If Clement had intended the *Stromateis* to remove the suspicions of the uneducated, he would naturally have written as plainly as he did in the *Protrepticus,* and invited the attention of every Christian who could read.

A more serious and conclusive consideration is that Clement's language frequently implies that the *Stromateis* do contain, in scattered and fragmentary form, the higher teaching to which the earlier work looks forward. Heussi's quotations seem to show beyond question that the central purpose of the *Stromateis* was doctrinal, however imperfectly this may have been realised. The reader is reminded, in the words of Heraclitus, that we must dig through much earth in order to find a little gold, and that a medley of many seeds must be well shaken in the sieve if we wish to select the wheat.[20] This "gold" and "wheat" can only be identified with those pearls of truth which must not be cast before swine. The author's language here and in many other passages is only intelligible if we suppose that he regarded himself as imparting, in the cryptic method he had selected, that very teaching which was to be the perfect Christian's treasured prize. That this is done secretly, partially, imperfectly; that after the lesser Mysteries initiation into the greater still awaits the reader; that the writer never comes within even tolerable distance of his eventual goal, must be certainly allowed. The *Stromateis* do not accomplish the task of the promised "Master." But neither, on the other hand, is their character purely preliminary. They undertake and commence what it proved beyond the time or power of the writer to accomplish.

In short, Clement started on his enterprise without realising its magnitude and difficulty. It is impossible here to describe in any detail the character of the esoteric teaching[21] he proposed to embody in his completed work, not only because he did not live to accomplish the embodiment, but also because he had never clearly grasped in all its implications the character of his own great purpose. He hopes to advance from a consideration of the genesis of the Cosmos to the contemplation of a reality more ultimate and less material; his purpose is to rise from Cosmogony to Theology.[22] Thus his philosophy of religion is to lead at last to the Ruler of the Universe, "an object difficult to apprehend and capture, ever receding and withdrawing into the distance from him who follows in pursuit."[23] In the important opening chapter of the Fourth Book, where he has set forth his ultimate purpose as clearly as anywhere, he expresses himself with grave hesitation as to its fulfilment. The work will be written, "if God will, and as He may inspire me." Again and again, as he has occasion to refer to this crowning and unachieved portion of his task, his language grows vague, and the implications of his terminology are less assured, and we have hints of a mighty purpose, for which the range of his faculties is hardly adequate. What Clement intended to portray in language can hardly have been anything different from the final vision of the Gnostic soul. For one who has reached this stage, perfect understanding contemplates objects superior to the Cosmos and purely intellectual in their nature, and even moves on to other realms more spiritual still than these. The goal is the conclusive grasp of all reality; the uninterrupted vision of pure Being by the purified intelligence. Now Clement is a true Hellene. He never passes from the intellectual standpoint to mystic rapture. He has his face set towards this transcendent consummation, but he never draws the veil to admit his reader within the shrine. Much as he says about contemplation, the features of the object contemplated are never made manifest in his pages. The truth is, as the mystics knew, that the Beatific Vision lies beyond language; the Prophet's ecstasy, or the symbolism of Art, are less inadequate methods for apprehending the ultimate realities of the Spirit than the cold, clear light of the intelligence.

Thus the fact that Clement chose to write a series of *Stromateis* in the place of the projected **"Master"** must in the main be set down to the character of his public. But that having chosen this type of literature for his medium, he remains, after seven considerable volumes have been writ-

ten, still so remote from the final achievement of his task, is due to the range and magnitude, and still more to the transcendental character, of his undertaking. The repeated and varied plans for future writing; the constant falling back for further discussion upon already considered themes; the apologetic references to the number of preliminary subjects with which he finds it necessary to deal, all evidence a hesitation on the writer's part in approaching the more advanced portions of his subject which is entirely natural when we realise how wide the range of truth, how elevated the point of vision, to which he had originally hoped to show the way. In a word, the *Stromateis* are and yet are not the projected **"Master."** In writing them Clement realised, in part, his purpose of higher teaching. In writing them he also came to recognise that his purpose could never be fully realised at all. J. von Arnim[24] has suggested that Clement was prevented by death from bringing his undertaking to fulfilment. There are difficulties in this suggestion. Is it not at least possible that the *Stromateis* are left unfinished, because Clement became increasingly conscious that the portrayal of complete and final truth lies beyond the achievement of any single human mind?

Clement's activity as a writer was in any case not limited to the great tripartite work, of which the *Stromateis* are the most important section. In all we hear of some twenty treatises which may claim his authorship, though with different degrees of evidence. Beyond the trilogy, only one, the **Quis Dives Salvetur,** has survived intact. Others are known to have existed from mention made of them in ancient authors and from fragments which have been preserved. The earliest evidence for others is as late as the seventh century. With regard to some four or five, while Clement's intention to write on these subjects is clear, we are wholly ignorant as to whether his plans were ever carried into effect. To these considerable uncertainties must be added the further doubt as to the independent character of some of these undertakings. The mention, for example, of a **"Discussion on Marriage"** may, as we have remarked, equally well refer to the Third Book of the *Stromateis* or to a distinct and separate treatise. The whole subject of these fragmentary remains has been very fully dealt with by Zahn in his *Supplementum Clementinum.* For our present purpose it will only be necessary to consider briefly the character and contents of these other writings of our author. Something may also be said on the difficult question of the order of their composition.

Clement's written works appear to have fallen into four classes, when distributed according to the nature of their subject-matter. (1) Some dealt with the Scriptures. (2) Some were controversial. (3) Some again were concerned with the philosophy of doctrine. (4) The fourth class was pastoral in character. Such a division is naturally only tentative. The evidence is in many cases too scanty for certainty, while a book on the Scriptures must clearly to some extent involve doctrine also. But a consideration of his literary work on the lines of this division will at least give some idea of its varied character, and help to dissipate the common misconception of Clement as merely an academic Christian, a second-century professor with few interests outside his library.

(1) The most extensive work on the Scriptures for which Clement was responsible was the ***Hypotyposeis*** or ***Outlines.*** There were eight books of this commentary, so that it was as long as the ***Stromateis.*** Eusebius[25] was familiar with it and quoted it, and so was Photius,[26] who lived in the ninth century and thought the work heretical. The editions[27] give between twenty and thirty fragments of this work in Greek, and there are some longer extracts, from the portion which dealt with the Catholic Epistles, still extant in a Latin translation. The commentary was not a complete one: it only dealt with "certain passages," but apparently no book in either the Old or New Testament was entirely omitted. In many cases the notes are little more than "Scholia"; sometimes also they are of considerable interest, as in their reference to the authorship of the Epistle to the Hebrews, which Saint Luke is said to have translated from a Hebrew original written by Saint Paul; or in their mention of the origin of the fourth or "spiritual" Gospel; or in their statement that Saint John's second Epistle was addressed to a "Babylonian" lady, by name Eclecta. Zahn has reconstructed[28] the table of their probable contents. The surviving fragments are sufficient to afford us many hints on Clement's views of Holy Scripture. They are in this respect a valuable supplement to his more completely extant works. Evidently the work covered too much ground, but it is interesting to know that the master of Origen undertook such a task. Next to the ***Stromateis*** it was probably Clement's most extensive and important book.

It is possible, too, that Clement treated certain parts of Scripture more fully in separate writings. Mention, at any rate, is made of a Commentary on the Prophet Amos,[29] which was apparently distinct from the ***Hypotyposeis.*** Eusebius also states that Clement promised in the ***Stromateis*** to compose a separate work on the Book of Genesis. It is not known whether this was ever accomplished, and even the intention of Clement is doubtful, for Eusebius may have misinterpreted his meaning.[30] Besides these, we have several mentions in the ***Stromateis*** of a projected discussion on **"Prophecy."**[31] This may refer to an intended work on the prophetical books of the Old Testament, or to a treatise on the nature of inspiration, or to some more controversial purpose of dealing with Montanism. There is no reason to suppose that any separate work under this name was ever published by Clement. It is well known that he did not carry out all his plans. It is, however, sufficiently clear that a considerable portion of his literary work, whether accomplished or only projected, had the interpretation of the Holy Scriptures definitely in view. That so much of this has perished is, in the main, due to the fact that greater commentators came after him. In this, as in so many other respects, he was a pioneer, memorable not so much by what he actually achieved as by his recognition of the importance, for the Church's highest interests, of the domain of commentary and exegesis.[32]

(2) A second class of Clement's writings had a controversial purpose. These do not appear to have been numerous, and Clement, though he often opposes Gnostic teaching in the ***Stromateis,*** cared little for controversy on its own account. Towards the end of his stay in Alexandria the Paschal question again came into prominence, and Alexandria sided with Pope Victor against Polycrates and the Quartodecimans of Asia Minor.[33] It seems that Clements was urged by his friends to deal with this debated issue, and his treatise **On the Passover** was mainly directed against an earlier book written by the saintly Quartodeciman, Melito of Sardis.[34] It is clear from a surviving fragment that he adhered to the dates of the Fourth Gospel, as against the Synoptists, and held the Crucifixion, not the Last Supper, to have taken place on the 14th Nisan.[35] The few other quotations we still possess seem to show that, as might be expected, Clement did not confine his argument to historical evidence. More abstract lines of reasoning were evidently employed as well. Possibly they did not greatly contribute to the settlement of a question which was determined in the long run by authority and the growth of uniformity, rather than by *a priori* considerations. But it is significant that even the philosophic Clement was drawn into a discussion of this character. "Ye observe days," wrote Saint Paul reprovingly; yet in such minor issues, when they arise, even the leaders must take their part, and masters of doctrine may not altogether stand aside. Besides, Alexandria had a special interest in points of chronology and the calendar.

A second work of this class was known as the ***Canon Ecclesiasticus,***[36] the alternative title showing that it was written to oppose the "Judaisers," though with what particular portion of their tenets it was concerned the evidence does not enable us to say. Possibly this also was a criticism of the Quartodeciman position. Or, possibly, as the one extant fragment might suggest, the "Judaisers" desired to enforce the literal interpretation of Scripture, and, if that were so, it is quite probable that for once Clement found the task of controversial authorship congenial. An interesting point in connection with this work is that it was dedicated to Alexander, Bishop of Jerusalem, an old pupil and friend of Clement's. No other works of Clement are known to us of a clearly controversial character.

(3) From his interest in the philosophy of Christian doctrine Clement might have been expected to devote much of his literary activity to its consideration. Yet there is no class of his writings in which the evidence is more uncertain, when once we pass beyond the range of his actually existing works. The ***Stromateis*** we possess. And it would be natural to class with them the works ***On the Soul, On the Resurrection, On the Angels, On Principles, On Providence,***[37] supposing these, or any of them, ever to have been written. He intended to write on the Soul and to deal with the Pythagoreans and the doctrine of Transmigration. He intended also to discuss the Lord's Resurrection, and to deal with passages of Scripture in which the general doctrine of the subject is allegorically taught. So, too, he proposed to write about the Angles. Their impor-

tance in Gnostic systems would alone have made this a natural plan. But whether any one of these intentions was ever carried out, we cannot determine. No fragments survive which can with any strong probability be assigned to these proposed discussions on the Soul and on the Angels. Of the treatise **On Providence** several fragments have been preserved, but none of the references or quotations are anterior to the seventh century. If the fragments are genuine, this work seems to have been mainly concerned with the definition of theological terms: it consisted of at least two books, and must have been useful to students of theology. Clement's authorship of it is questionable. Zahn is on the whole disposed to accept it. Stählin is more doubtful.

Finally, there is the work **On Principles.** He proposed a treatise of this kind in the **Stromateis.** And there is some reason to suppose that this was actually written, from the apparent reference to it as already existing, which he makes in the **Quis Dives Salvetur.** Von Arnim[38] has questioned this interpretation of the passage in the last-named work, and it must in any case seem doubtful whether Clement would have gone on to deal with "Principles," if the **Stromateis** were still incomplete. Here, again, nothing can be definitely proved. Thus in the domain of doctrinal philosophy, where Clement might have been expected to write most readily when he had once determined on writing books at all, we are left with nothing beyond the **Stromateis.** The other works mentioned may possibly have existed, but in no case is the evidence more than doubtful. On the whole it is probable that, when Clement found the completion of his great undertaking was beyond his powers, he did not again deal with subjects of this order.

(4) When we come to writings of a pastoral character our information is fuller and more substantial. The office of a teacher may be said to lie midway between the domain of pure theology and that of pastoral care. Clement at any rate managed to combine his special interest in doctrine with no inconsiderable activity in the care of souls. The **Pædagogus,** of course, is concerned with the education of the Christian character; and we breathe as it were the atmosphere of the parish rather than of the lecture-room in his one extant sermon, the **Quis Dives Salvetur.** Eusebius[39] knew of two homilies, one **On Slander,** the other **On Fasting.** An **Address to the Newly Baptised,** exhorting to patience, is mentioned by the same writer; and Clement himself speaks of a treatise **On Continency,** no doubt identical with the **Discussion on Marriage,** to which he refers in the **Pædagogus.**[40] This, as we have seen, is regarded by many authorities as no independent work, but rather that portion of the **Stromateis**[41] in which he deals with the relation of the sexes, and which may have been separately written before the **Stromateis** were commenced. The only evidence, beyond Clement's own statement, is a fragment quoted in the *Sacra Parallela,*[42] which has been wrongly assigned to the Seventh Book of the **Stromateis,** and does not occur in the earlier portions which deal with marriage. This would be naturally assigned to the independent book **On Continency,** if that existed. Zahn[43] inclines to believe

that such a book was written by Clement. Stählin[44] follows Wendland and Heussi in regarding the discussion in the **Stromateis** as being the author's only treatment of this subject. If that is so, this portion of his work hardly falls under the head of "Pastoralia," but we are still left with the four sermons.

A fragment recently discovered by the Rev. P. M. Barnard[45] has been assigned to the **Address to the Newly Baptised.** This fragment may well be an extremely interesting summary of Clement's teaching, but it is difficult, on grounds of style, to regard it as actually coming from his pen. Of the homilies on Slander and Fasting there are no remains. The interest of this portion of Clement's work is the hint it gives us of a period in his career when he was actively engaged in the building up of Christian character. It seems to imply that the teacher of Gnosis and mystery could also deal sympathetically with the minor difficulties of a recent convert. Our slight but suggestive knowledge of this part of Clement's activity may well be connected with the mention of him, already noticed, in Alexander's letter to the Church of Antioch.[46] It accords well with the statement that he had established and increased the flock that was under Alexander's care.

This survey of Clement's literary work would not be complete without some mention of three longer fragments, which are usually attributed to him on the evidence of the manuscripts, but which are extremely puzzling to the critics because of the character of their contents. Of these the first is the so-called Eighth Book of the **Stromateis.** It differs widely from the earlier books, consisting of discussions on logic, such subjects as definition, causality, suspense of judgment being treated, evidently in an incomplete fashion. This is followed by the **Excerpta ex Theodoto,** which the title helps us further to define as a sort of summary or epitome of a phase of teaching recognised as Eastern, and claiming the authority of Valentinus. The extracts are Gnostic in character, with comments added, though the line of separation between the Gnostic teaching and the remarks of the commentator is difficult indeed to draw. Several passages of Scripture are explained, and the heretical terminology is much employed. Finally, these **Excerpta** are followed by the **Ecloga Propheticæ,** which contain fragments of exegesis, one or two interesting mentions of the Elders, and a continuous exposition of the Nineteenth Psalm, which might well have come from the **Hypotyposeis.**

Of these strange and fragmentary relics what can be made? It is Zahn's[47] theory that they are extracts, made by some person other than Clement, from the previously completed Eighth Book of the **Stromateis.** This suggestion has not been generally accepted. It is difficult to believe that even Clement would have united material so heterogeneous as the so-called **Strom.** VIII. and the **Excerpta** in one division of his work. Moreover, the whole series of the extracts would have amounted to at least half the book, and there is no apparent reason in the subject matter for the selection having been made at all. And the title of the second portion, *Excerpta ex Theodoto,* does not harmonise with Zahn's interpretation.

A later theory, suggested in its original form by P. Ruben,[48] adopted and enlarged by von Arnim, and accepted by De Faye, sees in these three different fragments the preparatory notes of Clement for other books which we do not possess.[49] For the full discussion of the whole question the reader must refer to the authorities named above. The balance of probability lies strongly with the more recent suggestion. Clement may well have made notes and extracts from writings with which he did not himself agree. Perhaps there is here an effective answer to those critics of his literary work, who see in him little more than a clever thief of other men's labours. Not as a rule of special interest in themselves, these extracts are still eloquent in their evidence of Clement's laborious thoroughness and of his resolve to understand what others had written, even when it was impossible that he himself should adopt their point of view. Such was the extent and character of Clement's literary work, so far as this may be gathered from the books we possess, and from the scattered fragments and references, which point to others that have not survived. Both in the amount of the work accomplished and in the variety of the subjects on which he wrote, his range of authorship was clearly considerable. It remains to make some reference to the interesting and difficult question of the date and order of his different works.

The evidence on this point is neither abundant nor decisive. Eusebius[50] reckons him among the ecclesiastical writers whose works taught the divinity of Christ before Victor became Bishop of Rome in A.D. 189. If this statement be accepted, Clement was engaged in writing more than twelve years before he left Alexandria. He probably never wholly abandoned work of this character; and this latter supposition, sufficiently probable in itself, is borne out by the dedication of his *Canon Ecclesiasticus* to Bishop Alexander. The Bishop, as we have seen, was Clement's pupil, born, Zahn thinks, about A.D. 170.[51] He became Bishop of Jerusalem after A.D. 211, and appears already to have held this position when the above-named work of Clement was written. Thus there is roughly a period of five and twenty years during which Clement was at least partially occupied in literary work, and it may be inferred from the statement of Eusebius' *Chronicle,*[52] A.D. 204, "Clemens multa et varia conscribit," that his years of greatest activity as a writer were immediately after his departure from Alexandria.

Is it possible, within these limits, to assign more precise dates for the writing of his various books?[53] The most interesting item in such an inquiry arises in connection with the *Stromateis.* Were they written in Alexandria? or were they his latest undertaking, cut short, while still unrevised, by the rude hand of death? Von Arnim[54] and De Faye[55] hold the latter theory. Zahn[56] and Mayor[57] believe other writings followed them. Harnack[58] regards the *Stromateis* as commenced in Alexandria, then interrupted by the writing of the *Pædagogus,* and continued after Clement had

fled before the persecution of Severus. Thus there is a choice of views, and the evidence is very inconclusive. The opening chapter of the *Stromateis* would tend to show that this was Clement's earliest published work. Yet the mention of the death of Commodus[59] clearly places Book I. later than A.D. 192. The references to persecution and martyrdom[60] have been held to suggest the years A.D. 202-3. But the character of the writing, and the entire lack of direct evidence, make the interruption of their composition, either by the writing of the *Pædagogus,* or by Clement's flight from Alexandria, at least improbable. Even with a writer as little interested in concrete facts as Clement, so violent a break in his career, the sudden exile from libraries, and the enforced change from an environment made familiar by twenty years' residence, could hardly fail to have left some trace, had they occurred while the writing of the *Stromateis* was still in process. Moreover, the same suspicious readers whom he had so much in mind when he began writing, are still considered in the Seventh Book,[61] and the quotations and references in the later portions of the work seem to imply that Clement was still within reach of libraries when he wrote them.

It may be frankly admitted that no theory fits all the facts. Somewhere or other each possibility does violence to the evidence. It is not possible to prove, but it is legitimate to suppose, that Clement wrote the *Stromateis* in Alexandria and was cut short by the persecution under Severus in his task. Mainly through recognising the difficulty or impossibility of completing his ambitious scheme, yet partly also because his lot was now cast among a less intellectual public, and partly, it may be, in the hope that he would one day return to his old literary surroundings, he was led first to postpone, and then ultimately to abandon, the great project to which he had set his hand. He turned his attention instead to the exposition of Scripture, to controversy, above all to Pastoralia. So we have, subsequent to the *Stromateis,* the *Outlines,* the tract *Against Judaisers,* the *Address to the Newly Baptised* and that *On Slander.* The "multa *et varia*" of the Eusebian Chronicle gives some support to such a dating of his books. And the difficulties involved are perhaps not greater than those which arise on the theories of von Arnim or of Harnack. If there is a certain element of pathos in the abandonment by Clement in his later years of his great projected scheme, there is also a noble and heroic self-adaptation in his undertaking of lesser tasks, which served their purpose, even though the Christian world has not thought it worth while to preserve more than scanty fragments of their total length. Many men, since the days of good King David, have done useful service, even after they have come to realise that they will never erect the perfect temple of their dreams.

It is difficult to say much in praise of Clement's style from the purely literary point of view. His aims, his ideas, his range of knowledge, deserved indeed a more artistic and graceful medium of expression than the long and involved sentences, the unbalanced diffuseness, the defective taste, which characterise much that he has written. Several causes, no doubt, contributed to this result. The habit of oral instruction, in which he had been occupied for several years before he began to write, would militate against terseness and lucid accuracy of writing. We have already seen how conscious Clement was that the two methods demanded different gifts. His convictions are usually definite, when we reach them, but while his mind moves on the surface of a subject, there is often some lack of clear conception, and this at times is discernible in his style.

But, in addition to this, he disregards style from deliberate intention. It is for him the antithesis of facts and truth. It may please, but it does not profit or instruct. He shares and expresses here the common prejudice of the earlier Christians against Literature and Art as such. That he wrote at all needed some apology: he regards it as almost a virtue to write, if he must write, in any indifferent terminology that occurs and will serve his purpose. If Pantænus were indeed the author of the beautiful *Epistle to Diognetus*,[62] we could wish he had imparted his own power of graceful writing to his pupil, for Clement's disregard of style, however justifiable, has had troublesome consequences for his readers, and has doubtless diminished the influence and popularity of his books.

There is, besides, the further consideration that his purpose to hide the truths he taught from the uninitiated has naturally rendered him obscure, and made doubly doubtful the intention of much that he has written. These causes have contributed to rob his great undertaking of literary attractiveness. It can only be regretted that Clement, who saw so clearly in many other respects how the secular world could minister to faith, did not go on to claim something of Plato's style, as well as of Plato's thought, for the enrichment of his comprehensive task. At times, indeed, he rises above his own principles and his normal level. He is "warmed by the Word,"[63] and when he speaks of the appeal of the Saviour to humanity, or of the wide and disastrous consequences of fair Helen's beauty,[64] or of the higher communion of the Gnostic life, his very subjects give him inspiration and his words have a new life and a closer precision, and we feel that there are other qualities in his nature, which happier literary conditions and ideals might have developed into a greater lucidity and a more perfect grace of words. As it was, he regarded with suspicion some of the best arts of the writer and never sought to acquire their mastery. It should be added that the *Stromateis* were in all probability never revised.

Our principal authority for the text of the ***Protrepticus*** and of the ***Pædagogus*** is a manuscript[65] of the tenth century, now in the National Library in Paris (Paris, Græc., 451, usually referred to as "P"). There are some sixteen other MSS. of these books, but none of them is regarded as independent of P. For the ***Stromateis*** the authority is a manuscript of the eleventh century, now in the Laurentian library in Florence (Laur., V. 3, usually referred to as "L"), of which a sixteenth-century copy exists in Paris. The quotations in Eusebius and other writers are of some service for textual purposes, but it cannot be said, in regard

at any rate to the ***Stromateis,*** that the text of Clement has come down to us in a satisfactory condition. In 1715, John Potter, Regius Professor of Divinity at Oxford and afterwards Bishop of Oxford and Archbishop of Canterbury, published an important edition of Clement. It was a work of very real learning, and many of Potter's notes are still valuable. Dindorf's edition of 1869 was disappointing, but Dr Stählin, in the edition issued under the auspices of the Prussian Academy of Science, has at length given Clement's works to the world in as completely satisfactory a form as the conditions allow. All who feel any serious interest in the old Alexandrine master must welcome with real and merited gratitude the outcome of Dr Stählin's labours. Could Clement but have foreseen that his [notebooks] would one day be thus worthily presented to the Christian students of an age not wholly dissimilar from his own!

Notes

1. See the references in Stählin, I., ix. *sqq.;* III., 224 *sqq.*

2. 320, 996. Both passages are important . . . .

3. *Cp.* De Faye, *Clément d'Alexandrie,* 16 and 28 *sqq.:* Harnack, *Geschichte der altchristlichen Litteratur,* 1. (i.), 291 *sqq.*

4. 996.

5. *Vide supra,* p. 14 . . . .

6. H.E., vii. 7 . . . .

7. 341.

8. 996.

9. 318 . . . .

10. *Op. cit.,* p. 104.

11. On the position and importance of Clement in the literary history of Christianity, see F. Overbeck's article, *Ueber die Anfänge der patristischen Literatur,* in the *Historische Zeitschrift,* 1882, No. 48 (= N.F. 12), especially pp. 444 *sqq.*

12. See Hort and Mayor, *The Seventh Book of the Stromateis,* Introd., chap. i. "On the title Stromateis." "Carpet-bags" is from Bigg.

13. Such works are said to contain "variam et miscellam et quasi confusaneam doctrinam," a description singularly true in the case of Clement's work. *Noct. Att.,* Præfatio, 5 *sqq.*. . .

14. 736, *cp.* 901-2.

15. 656-86 . . . .

16. 309.

17. 867, 901-2.

18. See the important article of this writer, *Die Stromateis des Clemens Alexandrinus und ihr Verhältnis zum Protrepticos und Pædagogos,* Zeitschrift für wissenschaftliche Theologie, Bd. xlv. 1902, pp. 465 sqq . . . .

19. iii. 228.

20. 565-6.

21. Chapters xiv. and xix. give some little further information on this point.

22. 325, *cp.* 564.

23. 431. For the thought see Plato, *Timæus,* 51; Philo, *De Somniis,* i. 11.

24. *De octavo Clementis Stromateorum libro, pp. 7, 13.*

25. *H.E.,* ii. 9; vi. 14.

26. *Bibl. Cod.,* 109 *sqq.*

27. Stählin, iii. 195 *sqq.;* Zahn, *Supplementum Clementinum,* 64 *sqq.. . .*

28. *Op. cit.,* 156.

29. Zahn, *op. cit.,* 45. The authority is the *Lausiac History* of Palladius (c. A.D. 420).

30. Zahn, *loc. cit.*

31. 416, 605, 699.

32. On Clement's relation to Scripture see *infra,* chap. xvii., xviii.

33. *Supra,* p. 110 *Sqq.*

34. *H.E.,* iv. 26; vi. 13; *cp.* v. 24 . . . .

35. . . . Stählin, iii. 217. Zahn, *op. cit.,* 33.

36. *H.E.,* vi. 13 . . . .

37. The first four of these are mentioned by Clement himself: 125, 232, 564, 699, 755, 950 . . . .

38. *Op. cit.,* 13. See, however, Appendix II. of the present work.

39. *H.E.,* vi. 13.

40. 278, *cp.* 199, 226.

41. 502-62.

42. Stählin, iii. 228.

43. *Op. cit., 37 sqq.*

44. III., lxiii., lxx. 228.

45. *Ib.,* p. 221.

46. *Supra,* p. 24.

47. *Op. cit.,* 104 *sqq.*

48. *Clem. Al. Exc. ex Theod. Dissertatio philologica,* Leipzig, 1892.

49. *Op. cit.* Von Arnim rightly points out that on this hypothesis *Strom.* VIII., the *Excerpta,* and the *Eclogæ* would all possess a similar character, being extracts from other writings made by Clement in preparation for another work: "una eademque simplici ratione explicatam habebitis trium illorum quæ Stromateum VII. secuntur corporum conformationem," p. 9. See De Faye, pp. 332-3; also C. Barth, *Die Interpretation des neuen Testaments in der Valentinianischen Gnosis* (Texte und Untersuchungen, R. III., Bd. vii.), p. I:

where the *Excerpta* are said to have been put together, "wohlzu künftiger Verarbeitung für eine Streitschrift."

50. *H.E.,* v. 28.

51. *Op. cit.,* p. 171, "spätestens um 170."

52. Migne, *Pat. Gr.,* xix. 568.

53. On this subject see also Appendix II.

54. *Op. cit.,* 7, 13.

55. P. 120.

56. Pp. 173 *sqq.*

57. xviii.-xix.

58. *Geschichte der altchr. Lit.,* II. (ii), 9 *sqq.*

59. 402-3.

60. 494, etc. See also Appendix I.

61. 829, 894 . . . .

62. Lightfoot, *Apostolic Fathers,* Ed. Harmer, suggests this, p. 488.

63. 263.

64. 259-60.

65. Facsimiles are given in Stählin's edition, vol. iii., *ad fin.,* and also at the commencement of this chapter.

E. F. Osborn (essay date 1916)

SOURCE: "Teaching and Writing in the First Chapter of the *Stromateis* of Clement of Alexandria," in *The Journal of Theological Studies,* Vol. XVII, No. 66, January, 1916, pp. 335-43.

[*In the following excerpt, Osborn explains Clement's justifications for writing: to spread the word of God, to carry on tradition, and to battle heresy. Additionally, Osborn advances arguments that the* Stromateis *is actually the* Didaskalos.]

I. THE ARGUMENT

The prejudice against writing was strong in the Church of the second century. The living voice was the best medium for the communication of Christian truth.[1] Writings were public and it was wrong to cast pearls before swine. To write implied that one was inspired by the Holy Spirit and this was a presumptuous claim.[2] If one must write, it were better that one should write badly. The heretics had shown that a clever style could mislead and corrupt. The first chapter of the **Stromateis** presents the most extensive treatment of this question. Here Clement argues that it is right to teach through written notes. Writing, says Clement, shares wisdom which must be shared, proclaims the word which must be proclaimed, hands on tradition which must be handed on, and fights heresy which must be fought. It does all these things not haphazardly, but under definite conditions and restrictions.

(i) *Wisdom must be shared*

The second page of the **Stromateis** (the first page is missing from the manuscript) begins with a quotation from the *Visions* of Hermas. The Shepherd, the angel of repentance, commands Hermas to write. The full sentence reads: "'For this reason,' he says, "I command you first to write down the commandments and parables, that you may read them again and again and be able to keep them."'[3] The latter half of the sentence begins the second page of the manuscript. We may assume that the first half was on the first page.

This quotation is followed by an argument concerning the use of writing itself. Is it a good thing to write? If it is not, then why do we have letters and an alphabet? No one would want writing to be abolished. Who then should write? It would be ridiculous to allow the atheists and immoral people to write while the Christians cannot do so. It is a good thing to leave good children behind us and our words are the children of our souls. [Wisdom]. . .must be shared and is inspired by a love for man and a desire to benefit man. The teacher who is the father, the sower, the steward of God's riches,[4] can beget the gift of knowledge and sow the seed and lend out truth effectively through written works. Writings will be as useful to the ignorant as a lyre to an ass. The Lord taught in parables by which he revealed but did not cause the ignorance of his hearers.[5] He will judge the unprofitable servant who keeps the truth to himself and does not hand it on.[6]

Elsewhere Clement says that his true gnostic is never jealous of others. He does not begrudge them what he has. He would rather give tradition to the unworthy than not give it to the worthy. Through his great love he takes the risk. 'There are those who call themselves gnostics who are more jealous of their own people than of those outside.'[7]

(ii) *Writing proclaims the word*

Both writer and speaker are heralds of God,. . . as with pen and voice they make faith active through love.[8] The hearer or reader chooses for or against the truth. God is not to blame.[9] He sends the proclamation, whether written or spoken, which gives the basis of faith, the zeal for disciplined living, the urge for truth, the impulse to inquiry, and the trace of knowledge. So the writer is the benefactor of those to whom he brings the saving truth.[10] He has the solemn responsibility of the distribution of the word which requires a clean hand and a clean heart as does the distribution of the bread of the Eucharist.[11] Presumption or jealousy must not be his motive. He must seek only the salvation of his hearers. Here the teacher who writes is safer from blame than the teacher who speaks. He is less liable to flattery and corruption because his audience is not present to him. The writer has here a clear advantage over the speaker.[12] Because labourers are few and the harvest is plentiful we should pray for more writers and speakers.[13] Such work is all under God. For those who receive the word are God's cultivation and God's building.[14]

It had been objected that the writing of the truths of the Gospel in their simple form would mean that the Sophists could ridicule them.[15] But the teacher who writes has no intention of giving his writing to those who do not believe. Only the believer can choose rightly and can learn. We must have a new heart and new spirit before we hear the words of God.[16] While the writer cannot test his pupils directly as can the speaker, yet he can better test himself. He can make sure that he has no desire for gain or glory and that he always does the will of the Father, receiving freely and giving freely.[17] The pupil's co-operation is more essential for the writer. The eye of the reader's soul must be free from obstructions and his mind must be emptied of all preconceptions. What is written will kindle the spark of his soul and turn the eye of his soul to vision. As soon as something is placed within this soul, like the graft in a fruit tree, it springs into life through being joined to what is already there. Christians must examine themselves lest they fall under judgement.[18]

(iii) *Writing hands on tradition*

Clement records in writing the clear and living words which he had been privileged to hear. He writes not with skill, but seeks with simplicity to set out what had been said to him by his teachers. There was an Ionian in Greece and two others in Magna Graecia—one from Syria and the other from Egypt. There were two more in the east—an Assyrian and a Hebrew in Palestine. His last and greatest teacher was in Egypt. He remained with this man who, like a bee,[19] gathered from the flowers of the prophetic and apostolic meadow and begot pure knowledge in the souls of his hearers. The Ionian teacher may have been Melito of Sardis. The Syrian may have been Bardesan or Tatian. The Jew could have been Theophilus of Caesarea or Theodotus the Gnostic. The last was Pantaenus.[20]

The greatness of these men lay in their ability to hand on 'the true tradition of the blessed teaching' straight from Peter, James, John, and Paul, the holy apostles. This tradition they received as a child from a father, and it was their privilege to deposit in the souls of their hearers the seed of their spiritual fore-fathers.[21] They will be glad that what they said is being recorded. The fact, not the form, of the expression will please them. For wisdom must be passed on. Tradition must be handed down. A father rejoices when his son shows love for wisdom. A cannot be kept clear except by constant emptying. Iron cannot be kept bright except by use. A light is not to be put under a bushel. What is the use of wisdom if it does not make people wise? The Saviour always saving and working as he looks to the Father. When on earth a man teaches and another learns they both learn, because there is one Master. There is one Teacher of the speaker and of the hearer and he is the cause of understanding and of speech.[22] The Lord encouraged the doing of good on the Sabbath day. (This offended some, just as writing does.) The divine mysteries are to be shared by those who can receive them. Some things are entrusted to speech rather than to writing. Within the Church the divine mysteries[23] are handed down.[24]

Written notes will be feeble compared to the original discourses; but they will revive the memory of what they record. 'To him who has it shall be added.'[25] They will prevent further loss through forgetfulness. Some things have already been lost before this record has been made. Some things are omitted on purpose because it would be wrong and dangerous to put them on paper. Clement does not begrudge these things; but they could be misunderstood and he would be 'giving a sword to a child'.[26]

(iv) *Writing combats heresy*

Clement will set out the opinions of the great heresies and will place beside them the highest gnosis which is 'according to the glorious and holy rule of tradition'.[27] He will be a Hebrew to the Hebrews and a Greek to the Greeks. He will teach every man in all wisdom so that he may present him perfect in Christ.[28] Classical texts will add spice to the writing and will relax the tension of thought. They will bridge the gap between the tradition and those who must be reached. Just as people use a herald as a mediator, so Clement uses many ideas and words which are familiar and attractive to his readers. There is no danger in this for the one truth will stand out from the many opinions.[29] The bare seeds of truth are guarded by the farmers of faith. Timorous souls will complain that one should not waste time on things which do not bring one nearer one's goal. They think that philosophy is an evil thing; but it will be shown that philosophy is the work of God's providence. All things, including pagan culture, are a preparation for the truth.[30]

The *Stromateis* expose the heresies in written form and so fortify the pupil against their seductive influence. Irenaeus wrote to give similar evidence because the heretics by their clever writing confuse and mislead their readers. 'They talk like we do, but think quite differently.'[31] The Stromateis combat heresy in a positive way by building up the Christian culturally and spiritually. He who has the true gnosis will not want a false one. He needs the gnostic word about the Father, Son, and Holy Spirit and about his soul.[32] He should not be ignorant of what heretics and pagans regard as articles of faith.[33]

II. TEACHING AND TRADITION

The unity of the tradition derives from its origin as a gift of God to the Church. The aim of the writer is to preserve not his own ideas but the blessed tradition which is handed down from spiritual father to son. Tradition is the source of truth because it comes from God and God alone can teach truth. At the end of Book VI of the *Stromateis* Clement speaks of the inability of men to teach about God and of the ephemeral quality of their teaching. The teaching which is from God is alone trustworthy and is strong in the face of opposition. 'For no gift of God is weak.'[34]

The unity of the tradition is spread over a wide geographical extent. Clement had not always lived in Alexandria. His teachers were scattered in different parts of the Mediterranean world. Yet he gained from them a knowledge which was a unity, for the tradition was one tradition. 'But the word of our Teacher did not stay in Judaea alone, as philosophy stayed in Greece, but was poured out over all the world.'[35] Irenaeus had written of the diffusion and unity of the Christian tradition[36] and this unity is borne out in the writings of Clement and Irenaeus. Clement has been regarded as the Hellenistic philosopher and Irenaeus as the biblical theologian. Yet Clement is for ever drawing his material from the Bible and Irenaeus uses lengthy philosophical argument against the heretics.

The unity of holy scripture and tradition is shown in this chapter. Pantaenus is the preserver of the apostolic tradition. He is the Sicilian bee who gathers from the prophetic and apostolic meadow to beget pure knowledge in the souls of his hearers. This means that his teaching is drawn from scripture and at the same time is the true tradition of the blessed teaching. Scripture and tradition are not set against one another. Each is expressed in the other.[37]

The tradition has been unwritten. The elders did not write because they were occupied in teaching. They could not afford the distraction nor the time which writing must entail. They saw that writing and teaching were of a different nature. The words of the teacher flow rapidly; but the words of the writer are subject to careful examination and must be carefully chosen.[38] Papias preferred the 'voice which lives and abides' to the reading of books.[39] Irenaeus spoke of the unwritten tradition given by the apostles to their successors and of those who cannot read but who have salvation written by the Spirit on their hearts.[40]

Yet, says Clement, the time has come when tradition should be written down. Much has been forgotten and unless what he now remembers is written down all may be lost. Elsewhere he says: 'For the sacred trust of the elders speaks through writing and uses the help of the writer for the handing down of tradition for the salvation of those who will read it.'[41] At this crucial stage Clement feels himself to be the link between the apostolic past and the Church of the future. The urgency of the crisis makes him write.[42]

There is another reason why tradition should now be written. The heretics have claimed that they have the true tradition.[43] So long as apostolic tradition is unwritten, they cannot be openly disproved. Their claim for an oral tradition which is superior to Scripture is based on St. Paul's words: 'We *speak* wisdom among the perfect, but not the wisdom of this world.' Clement and Papias claim the one virtue of accuracy for their account of tradition.[44]

The concept of tradition in Clement has been disquieting to some because of the esoteric flavour of much of his language. Nevertheless, it is clear from the argument of the first chapter that Clement does not regard tradition as a secret which cannot be divulged. Some things cannot in fact be written and it would be misleading and dangerous to try to write them. But they are not withheld. It is wrong to begrudge such things to others through envy or jealousy. The whole tenor of Clement's argument and the direction of his thought is to the spreading of the gospel tradition to all who are able to receive it. There is an esoteric attitude in much that he says and this attitude has its roots in the New Testament; but there is no esoteric doctrine.[45]

The description of the Christian teacher is of intrinsic value. The teacher is a father to the pupil, a sower of seed, a messenger of God, a nourisher of souls, and a link in a living tradition. He requires faith and holiness from his pupils. As he teaches, he himself is taught, for there is one Teacher who gives speech to the speaker and understanding to the hearer. There are some echoes of Clement in the Panegyric of Gregory Thaumaturgus to Origen.[46] There were teachers throughout the Christian world who attracted learners from other countries. The teachers to whom Clement refers were all Christians, who handed on the true tradition of the blessed teaching. Each, however, had something special and one could move with profit from one to the other.[47]

III. THE DIDASKALOS

At the beginning of the *Paidagogos* Clement makes it clear that the Logos performs a threefold function: as *protreptikos* he exhorts pagans to come to salvation, as *paidagogos* he trains the believer and cures his passions, and as *didaskalos* he leads the believer on to knowledge. The same Logos exhorts, trains, and finally teaches.[48]

Again at the end of the *Paidagogos,* Clement writes: "'But it is not my place", says the Paidagogos, "to go on to teach these things; but we need a 'didaskalos' to expound those holy words, and to him we must now move on. Indeed it is now time that I had stopped my 'paidagogia', and time for you to be listening to the Didaskalos.'"[49]

For a long time it appears to have been generally accepted that the three activities of the Logos were mirrored in the three great works of Clement—*Protreptikos*, *Paidagogos*, and *Stromateis*. The *Stromateis* were the third great work which gave to the Christian the knowledge of God. In 1898 de Faye[50] challenged the traditional view, insisting that the *Stromateis* could not be the *Didaskalos* because they had the wrong title and contents. They were too incoherent and unsystematic. The *Didaskalos* was to be an exposition of Christian doctrine based on scripture and developed along the lines of Greek thought. Before Clement went on to this work, he realized that he must in some way soften the opposition of the Church to the use of Greek culture. So he wrote the *Stromateis* which profess in the first book to set out the grounds for using pagan culture in the expression of Christian truth.

Since de Faye wrote, many others have contributed to the controversy. These include Wendland, Heussi, Collomp, Bousset, Prat, Munck, Lazzati, Pohlenz, and Quatember. More than one set of three works has been postulated and a variety of explanation has been offered. There is no agreement on the issue.[51]

From the analysis of the first chapter certain points arise which would strengthen the claim of the *Stromateis* to be reconsidered as the work of the Logos who is Didaskalos.

1. The argument of the first chapter is designed to show that written notes are a suitable method for the communication of Christian truth. This communication is called teaching, instructing, and proclaiming. The relationship at the basis of the argument is always that of a teacher to a pupil rather than that of a preacher to a congregation . . . . There is no point whatever in filling the first chapter of the *Stromateis* with intricate argument in favour of written teaching if the *Stromateis* are not going to teach.[52]

2. The *Stromateis* are not merely notes which teach. They are also notes which have taught. They are the record of what Clement heard from his teachers. Shaped and expressed by Clement, they owe their substance, he claims, not to his ingenuity and skill but to his memory of powerful teaching. The *Stromateis* are a record of teaching.

3. The teaching which the notes record and preserve is not simply what certain illustrious people have said. It is the teaching which comes from God through scripture and tradition. It is 'the true tradition of the blessed teaching'. The *Stromateis* are to preserve this tradition of divine teaching, to revive the recollection of it and to prevent it from being lost.

4. The first chapter of the *Stromateis* is concerned with the justification of the remainder of the work. 'Should this work be written? Should one write at all?' Clement, after having written the *Protreptikos,* . . . feels argument to be necessary before he can write the *Stromateis*. No argument was needed to justify the writing of the *Protreptikos* and the *Paidagogos*. Clearly the *Stromateis* must be a different kind of discourse. The only other kind of discourse which Clement has envisaged is that of the Logos who is Didaskalos.

5. What Clement has predicted of the *Didaskalos* is fulfilled by the *Stromateis*. The first chapter indicates that the work will show and reveal the opinions of the philosophers, the heretics, and of the true philosophy and gnosis.[53] It also makes clear that its supreme concern is with the true gnosis. This concern is also indicated by the title of the work and by the contents of the work as a whole.[54] The *Didaskalos* was to show and reveal opinions and to lead the believer to knowledge.

6. There is nothing contrary to the plan and method of Christian teaching in the studied disorder of the *Stromateis*. In fact it is for Clement the appropriate manner.[55] The writing seeks to kindle a spark, to sow a seed, or to be the bait to catch a fish. It does not aim to prove things in the manner of a geometrical problem. Clement's view of teaching has something of the impressionist about it. The *Stromateis* are written in a literary form appropriate to Clement's understanding of teaching.

7. There is also a negative reason for the disorder of the *Stromateis*. They are, as Clement indicates in this first

chapter and elsewhere, designed for concealment. Why does Clement go to such trouble to mystify and mislead the enemy? If the **Stromateis** are not the **Didaskalos,** they have nothing to hide.

Notes

1. Papias in Eusebius, *H.E.* iii. 39. 3, 4 . . . .

2. 2 Tim. iii. 16. The gospels were limited to four: Irenaeus, *Adv. Haer.* iii. 11.

3. Hermas, *Vis.* v. 5.

4. *Strom.* i. 1. 3.

5. *Strom.* i. 1. 2.

6. *Strom.* i. 1. 3.

7. *Ecl. Proph.* 28. 1.

8. *Strom.* i. 1. 4; Gal. v. 6.

9. cp. Plato, *Rep.* 617E.

10. *Strom.* i. 1. 4.

11. *Strom.* i. 1. 5.

12. *Strom.* i. 1. 6; 1 Thess. ii. 5-7.

13. *Strom.* i. 1. 7; Matt. ix. 37; Luke x. 2.

14. *Strom.* i. 1. 7; 1 Cor. iii. 8, 9.

15. Philosophers would speak to their own initiates but would not write: cp. *Strom.* i. 1. 14 and v. 10. 65; Origen, *Contra Celsum,* i. 7; Cadiou, *La jeunesse d'Origène,* p. 185.

16. *Strom.* i. 1. 8.

17. *Strom.* i. 1. 9; Matt. x. 8. Cp. Harnack, *The Origin of the New Testament,* p. 138.

18. *Strom.* i. 1. 10; 1 Cor. xi. 30, 31. For the main point of section (ii) cp. Irenaeus, *Adv. Haer.* iii. 1, where the origin of the written gospels in the preached word is described. The four gospels record the preaching of Matthew, Peter, Paul, and John respectively.

19. See 'Bees in Clement of Alexandria' by W. Telfer, *F.T.S.* xxviii (1927), p. 167.

20. See *Stromate I,* Sources Chrétiennes (Paris, 1951), p. 51; G. Bardy, *Recherches de science religieuse,* xxvii (1937), pp. 71 ff.

21. *Strom.* i. 1. 11.

22. *Strom.* i. 1. 12. The whole argument springs from the vitality of Clement's Logos doctrine.

23. See H. G. Marsh in *J.T.S.* xxxvii (1936), pp. 64 ff. See also Mondésert, *Clément d' Alexandrie* (1944), chap. 2.

24. *Strom.* i. 1. 13.

25. *Strom.* i. 1. 14; Matt. xiii. 12.

26. *Strom.* i. 1. 14.

27. *Strom.* i. 1. 15; Clement of Rome, *Ep. Ad. Cor.* vii. 2.

28. *Strom.* i. 1. 15; Coloss. 1. 28.

29. *Strom.* i. 1. 16.

30. Cp. *Strom.* vi. 11. 91. Other education is useful. The Scriptures of the Lord are essential.

31. Irenaeus, *Adv. Haer.* Praef.

32. *Ecl. Proph.* 29. 1. Cp. Augustine, *Solil.* 1. 2, 7.

33. *Ecl. Proph.* 29. 3.

34. *Strom.* vi. 18. 165-7.

35. *Strom.* vi. 18. 167.

36. *Adv. Haer.* i. 10; iii. 1-2.

37. Cp. Harnack, *The Origin of the New Testament,* p. 43: 'When we speak today of the antagonism and conflict between Scripture and Tradition, the tradition in question is a second tradition.' Cp. G. W. H. Lampe in *Scripture and Tradition,* ed. Dillistone (1955), pp. 41, 50-51. The unity of scripture and tradition was maintained against the gnostics.

38. *Ecl. Proph.* 27. 4.

39. Eusebius, *H.E.* iii. 39. 3, 4.

40. *Adv. Haer.* iii. 4.

41. *Ecl. Proph.* 27. 4.

42. Bousset sees in Clement the beginning of a proper Christian literature: *Jüdisch-christlicher Schulbetrieb in Alexandrien und Rom* (1915), p. 155.

43. Cp. Lampe, op. cit., p. 41.

44. Papias: 'I learnt well and remembered well' (Eus. *H.E.* iii. 39. 3).

45. Cp. Mondésert, op. cit., p. 61: 'Chez Clément point d'autre secret que la sublimité de la connaissance des mystéres divins, qu'il s'efforce lui-même d'atteindre, dans la méditation et la prière et qu'il tâche, au contraire, de faire entrevoir à ses lecteurs, s'ils en sont dignes, en les exprimant du mieux qu'il peut, à l'aide de la dialectique platonicienne et des plus hautes expressions de l'Ecriture.'

46. Note especially vi, ix, xv, and xvii. The style of the work is a contrast to Clement's compact style.

47. Clement's account of teaching and teachers is biblical in substance. Rengstorf, in Kittel, *T.W.N.T.,* bd. ii, pp. 150-65, shows that a teacher is one who from the Torah points the way of God, that the teaching is biblical revelation and is classed with reading and exhortation (1 Tim. iv. 13) and that all scripture is divinely inspired and profitable for teaching (2 Tim. iii. 16).

48. *Paid.* i. 1. 1-3.

49. *Paid.* iii. 12. 97.

50. *Clément d'Alexandrie* (Paris, 1898), pp. 45 ff., 78-111, 126-48.

51. The controversy is outlined in the introduction to *Stromate I,* Sources Chrétiennes (Paris, 1951), and also in my book, *The Philosophy of Clement of Alexandria* (Cambridge, 1957), pp. 5-7.

52. It is possible that the lost first page had explicit references to the Logos who teaches. The references in the *Paidagogos* occur at the beginning and end of the work.

53. Cp. *Paid.* i. 1, 2.

54. Cp. *Paid.* i. 1. 3 and *Paid.* iii. 12. 98.

55. See *The Philosophy of Clement of Alexandria* (Cambridge, 1957), pp. 7-12, for a fuller discussion of this point.

G. W. Butterworth (essay date 1916)

SOURCE: "The Deification of Man in Clement of Alexandria," in *The Journal of Theological Studies,* Vol. XVII, No. 66, January, 1916, pp. 157-69.

[*In the following excerpt, Butterworth explores the influence of Greek thought on Clement's teachings concerning the process of man achieving union with God both on earth and after death.*]

I

The possibility of man being deified, or becoming a god, is asserted by many Christian Fathers from the middle of the second century onwards, but by none more frequently or unreservedly than by Clement of Alexandria. In the following pages all the passages of Clement which bear upon this subject will be examined, and an attempt made (i) to fix his meaning with certainty; and (ii) to trace his thought to its origins.

II

Deification, according to Clement, is a process that begins on earth. It is made possible by the fact that man contains within himself a spark of the divine nature, and is therefore in the highest part of his being akin to God. God is Mind. . .[1] 'and the image of Mind is seen in man alone; so that the good man is, so far as his soul goes, in the form and likeness of God, while God in His turn is in the form of man: for the form of each is Mind.'[2] Elsewhere the common element is said to be reason, or the Word, present with God in the character of the Son and with man in the character of the Saviour.[3] This union of man with God is fostered and developed by the practice of virtue and by progress in knowledge. Each advance in virtue is a step towards the divine life. Here is must be remembered that Clement's idea of the divine life is negative rather than positive; for he thinks of it chiefly as an absence of all human activities and corporeal limitations.[4] God is without needs. . . and without feelings or passions. . .[5] Consequently we find the 'gods' of Psalm lxxxi 6 interpreted to mean those who throw off as far as possible all that is merely human. . .[6] Virtue is thus regarded as a divesting process, an approach to the passionless life of God, rather than as an unceasing activity for good.[7] Since God and man are alike Mind, God in His entire being and man in his innermost essence, it follows that man has only to set aside, as far as possible, the temporary encumbrance of body and senses to become something very much like what God is. Again, a marked characteristic of the divine life is unity, and unity is acquired by man when he attains to the condition. . .when he is no longer disturbed and divided by warring passions. So from this point of view also man is said to become deified even on earth.[8] Sometimes Clement speaks of this life as being a preparation for the god-like life to come. Christians 'practise here on earth the heavenly way of life by which we are deified'.[9] Or again, the soul, becoming virtuous in thought, word, and deed through the Lord's power, practises being a god.[10] Deification also follows upon discipleship; as Ischomachus makes his pupils farmers, Demosthenes orators, Aristotle scientists, Plato philosophers, and so forth, in the same way the Lord makes those who learn from Him and obey Him gods while still in the flesh.[11] The disciple will strive to become passionless like his teacher.[12]

The second means of reaching the condition of deification is by knowledge; for Clement is in full accord with the Socratic doctrine that knowledge is equivalent to virtue and ignorance to vice.[13] Man, he says, is deified by 'heavenly teaching'.[14] The perfect Christian (i.e. the gnostic) will know 'what is fitting both in theory and in life, as to how one should live who will some day become a god, and is even now being made like to God'.[15] In explaining the fifth commandment, Clement says that our 'Father' means God; so 'the commandment speaks of those who know God as sons and gods'.[16] This 'knowledge' is not a mere intellectual knowledge, in which the knower stands outside and indifferent to the thing known. It is the gradual realization of the bond that exists between God and man. It leads therefore to a union of love wherein God is related to man as friend to friend; and such a relationship may possibly bring a man into the angelic state. . . here on earth.[17] The true life is, in fact, a continual ascent, just as its opposite is a descent. Those who reject the Church tradition and rush into heretical opinions are, like Circe's victims, changed into beasts, because they have lost the power to become 'men of God'; but when one returns, hears the Scriptures, and attends to the truth, it is 'as if a god is produced out of a man'.[18] The highest stage of the ascent through knowledge is contemplation, or the vision of God,[19] and he who contemplates the unseen God is said to 'live as a god among men'.[20]

III

So far we have considered deification as applied by Clement to man upon earth. What his hyperbolical language means is simply this, that the divine element in man is gradually brought into closer and more conscious union with God from whom in the beginning it came. This element is by nature purely spiritual, i.e. opposed to matter. It can only reach its full developement, therefore, when by the practice of virtue it is freed from material associations, from the needs and affections of sense; and when at the same time it is used for its proper purpose, viz. the contemplation of ideas or, in other words, the vision of God.[21] One in whom this developement takes place is lifted far above the level of ordinary men, since he has parted with most of what is merely human in his nature. So great is the difference, that Clement feels no hesitation in calling him no longer a man, but a god.

There are, however, a number of passages which speak of deification as occurring after death. These deserve separate consideration. First of all we notice a passage that stands in an intermediate position, inasmuch as it describes the stages in the process of deification, stretching over from this life into the next. These stages are: (i) Baptism, (ii) enlightenment, (iii) sonship, (iv) perfection, (v) immortality. Clement illustrates the final result of this developement by a reference to Ps. lxxxi 6 (Sept.) 'I said, ye are gods', &c.;[22] that is to say, he asserts that men become gods when to the gnostic perfection attained on earth there is added that immortality which can be fully possessed only after death. Perfection and immortality are of course two prominent characteristics of God, and when man attains them he becomes like God. Accordingly Clement applies the term 'god' to angels and spirits of the blest, who are conceived of as dwelling above in the 'super-celestial place'.[23] Here are the 'blessed abodes of the gods',[24] whence the great company of 'angels and gods' look down upon the Christian athlete as, while yet upon earth, he struggles in the spiritual conflict.[25] One day, when the lusts of the flesh have left him, he too will ascend to that heavenly sphere and be immortalized with the divine beings.[26] Of this life the gnostic training gives a foretaste, since it teaches us 'the nature of the life we shall hereafter live with gods. . .according to the will of God. . .'.[27] To those who reach this stage, Clement goes on to say, 'the name of gods is given, for they will be enthroned along with the other gods, who are set first in order under the Saviour'.[28]

This last remark will shew how careful Clement is to distinguish between the most exalted of men or angels and Christ. 'The whole army of angels and gods has been subjected to the Word.'[29] The prophets are called 'children of God', but Christ is the 'true Son'.[30] The title 'god' is therefore never applied by him to angels or men in the same sense as to Christ. In a like manner he guards against any confusion of the human and divine natures which might be imagined to arise from the presence of the Holy Spirit in man; for he asserts expressly that 'it is not as a portion of God that the Spirit is in each one of us'.[31]

IV

Before we consider the sources of Clement's teaching as here outlined, it will be useful to notice certain similar expressions which occur in other Christian writings of earlier or contemporary date. The deification of man is mentioned by Justin Martyr, Theophilus of Antioch, Irenaeus, and Hippolytus. Speaking of Ganymede and other characters of Greek mythology who were taken up to heaven, Justin contrasts the Christian belief that 'only those are immortalized who live near to God in holiness and virtue'.[32]

Again, the Word 'by his instruction makes mortals immortal, makes men gods'.[33] Theophilus of Antioch discusses whether God made man by nature mortal or immortal. Not immortal, he says, for in that case 'God would have made him a god'. Man was, in fact, made neither mortal nor immortal, but capable of either state, so that if he kept the commandments of God he should receive immortality as a reward and should become a god.[34] Irenaeus and Hippolytus write in the same way; the Christian is at length 'to become a god', or in other words to be 'begotten unto immortality'.[35] It is plain that neither of these writers understands 'deification' to be anything but another and rather more forcible expression for the immortalizing of Christians after death. We have already shewn that this is substantially what Clement means by it. The only difference is, perhaps, that Clement lays stress upon the earthly preparation for immortality as being itself the first stage in the process of deification. This, however, is a natural consequence of his division of Christians into 'simple believers' and 'gnostics', a distinction unknown to his predecessors at any rate outside Alexandria. The 'gnostic', by detachment from the things of sense, coupled with unceasing contemplation, gains for himself while still on earth the essentials of the divine life, in a manner not possible to ordinary men. Allowing for this difference, we may say that Clement's thought on the subject of deification does not go beyond that of most second and early third century Greek Christian writers.

V

We can now ask, 'What was the influence that led the earliest Greek Fathers, and Clement in particular, to use language expressing deification, when all they had in mind was the simple Christian doctrine of the future life?' Certainly it was not the Scriptures. There is nothing in either the Old or the New Testament which by itself could even faintly suggest that man might practise being a god in this world and actually become one in the next. In the Old Testament the bare question of a future life is scarcely raised at all.[36] Later on, in the Apocryphal and Apocalyptic literature, it is brought into prominence in connexion with the kindred doctrines of a Resurrection and Worldjudgement. But no Jewish writer, whether Palestinian or Hellenistic, was likely to obscure his firm belief in the unity of God by applying to men the terminology of deification. As for the New Testament, we can imagine how vigorously such language would have been repudiated by, let us say, St Paul, in whose eyes 'gods many and lords many' could never have seemed anything but the distinctive mark of false religion. A Scriptural origin being therefore out of the question, we must turn to Greek thought as the influence responsible for this element in Clement's theology. It is no exaggeration to say that Clement views every Christian doctrine through the medium of Greek ideas and a Greek temperament. In the case in hand the medium has exercised a plainly discernible effect upon the doctrine, as will be seen from the following considerations.

(i) Greek philosophy, depending largely upon Plato, tended to regard the future life of the virtuous man as an ascent of his spiritual nature, after death, towards the divine.[37] This is opposed to the purely Christian view, as taught in the New Testament; for there the new life is essentially a 'resurrection life', i.e. one which follows upon a divine intervention and judgement. The New Testament doctrine has kinship with Jewish Apocalyptic, but shews little, if any, trace of Greek influence. In Clement, however, the Greek idea of gradual ascent is dominant.[38] The root difference between these two conceptions may be thus stated. The one postulates a common judgement, equally necessary for all, because all have sinned. This is followed, in those who believe on Christ, by exaltation to an eternal life with God. The stress being laid upon God's goodness and Christ's redemption, there is little room left for inequalities among believing men. The other view represents the future life as beginning immediately after death,[39] without any judgement other than what may be called a self-acting one. If a man has in this life despised all bodily things and devoted himself to contemplation, death is a manifest gain, for it rids him of a useless encumbrance. But such men are rare; and therefore wide differences appear, a few choice spirits ascending at once to high places, while the majority keep close to the earth they have loved. In this scheme God is hardly needed at all, except as an object of contemplation. Clement's extant works prove that his mind dwelt naturally in this Greek atmosphere; for he rarely mentions either the Resurrection or the Judgement (in their objective Christian forms) or the Second Advent,[40] whereas the spiritual 'life after death' meets us, one might almost say, on every page. It was this which allowed the higher souls, such as those of gnostics and martyrs,[41] to ascend at once into the very presence of God, an exaltation so great that it seemed to warrant their being called divine, or even gods.[42]

(ii) A second influence is to be found in the idea of the universe as a series of spheres circling above the earth. We do not begin to understand the thought of the ancient world in regard to such matters as the conception of a future life until we put away all modern notions of astronomy. It would seem that Clement accepted the current theory of seven heavens rising one above the other, followed by the fixed sphere which bordered on the 'intellectual world'[43] These heavens varied in degree of grossness according to their distance from the earth; but not even the highest of them was what we should call incorporeal. The soul of man was thought of as rising in a spatial sense through these spheres,[44] until it reached the abode. . . for which it was fitted. We cannot set down any consistent account of Clement's opinions on this subject,[45] nor is it necessary for the present purpose. The general outlines of the system are enough to prove how naturally titles of divinity would attach themselves to souls who had reached the highest possible heaven, when that heaven is believed to be spatially above us. Much of the majesty of God to a child's mind is due to the fact that He dwells 'above the bright blue sky': and the decay of this belief accounts to some extent for the confusion in which the average man finds himself to-day with regard to the existence of God; he has ceased to look for Him in the sky,[46] and has not yet discovered where else to turn his eyes.

The belief in a series of heavens is not of course exclusively Greek. It is found also among the Jews, and clear signs of it appear in the New Testament. St Paul speaks of 'the heavenly places',[47] and he himself was caught up into the 'third heaven'.[48] Christ the great high priest has 'passed through the heavens', and is now made 'higher than the heavens', according to the Epistle to the Hebrews.[49] But the New Testament, while accepting this belief (for no other was open to that age), does not use it to explain the exaltation of saints after death.[50] Clement's thought must therefore be held to come ultimately from Greek and not from purely Christian sources.[51]

VI

Clement was in no way conscious that his ideas were not quite on a line with the Scriptures taken in their original meaning. He lived in a Greek world, among people who, whether themselves Greek or Jewish or Christian by birth and religion, breathed Greek ideas as inevitably as they breathed the common air. When Clement examined the Scriptures he had no eyes to see them as they really were, but only as they appeared through this peculiar mental atmosphere. Under such circumstances he could find in them support and authority for ways of thinking which had their true source elsewhere. In regard to the deification of man there are two Scriptural passages which furnished him with proof for his statements: Ps. lxxxi 6 (Sept.)[52] and St Luke xx 36 . . . . The first of these passages derives special importance from the fact that it is appealed to in St John x 34-35 as bearing some sort of witness to the truth of Christ's divinity. The original sense is difficult to determine. Probably the passage does not refer to princes or judges of Israel, but to subordinate deities or angels who ruled over heathen nations under the chief sovereignty of Jahweh.[53] In St John x 34, however, it seems to be interpreted as applying to princes: 'those to whom the word of God came.' Clement does not mention this New Testament use of the passage, nor does he attempt to investigate its context or literal meaning. He takes the words as a simple prophecy of what Christians may become both now and hereafter.[54]

The other passage (St Luke xx 36), or rather the single word ισάγγελος is quoted three times in the Seventh Book of the *Stromateis,* while the parallel from St Matthew xxii 30 is referred to in the Fourth Book. The Jewish and Christian doctrine of angels could without much difficulty be merged into the Greek idea of subsidiary gods; and this is what Clement does, for we find his thoughts travelling from Homer to Plato, and again from Plato to the New Testament, with no consciousness of a break in the connexion. It will help to make this plain if the passage from the Fourth Book is quoted in full.[55]

'Plato says with reason that he who contemplates the ideas will live as a god among men. Now Mind is the place of ideas, and God is Mind. The man therefore who contemplates the unseen God is living as a god among men, according to Plato; and Socrates in the *Sophist* called the Eleatic stranger, who was a dialectician, a god, of the same kind as the gods who, "in the guise of strangers",[56] visit the cities of men.[57]. . . For when a soul has once risen above the sphere of generation, and exists by itself and in company with the ideas, like the *coryphaeus* in the *Theaetetus*,[58] such an one, having now become "as an angel", will be with Christ, rapt in contemplation, ever observing the will of God. That is the real man who "alone is wise, while others flit as shadows".'[59]

Here Clement lays his thought as bare as he can. It is fundamentally Greek, and the Scriptural reference is brought in to illustrate opinions already formed; though probably Clement would have felt and declared that the Scriptures were his sole authority.

None the less we must admit that the two passages here mentioned, and more especially Ps. lxxxi, exercised in their way a powerful influence on Christian thought. Had they been absent from the Scriptures, Clement's allegorism was no doubt capable of finding others to support his views; and yet it is hard to think of anything that could have quite filled the place of the unmistakeable 'I said, ye are gods'. These words come to him instinctively whenever the perfection of man is in question; and the same is true of Origen. Though in order of thought they are not a prime authority, it is certain that they helped materially to keep alive the idea and language of deification.

VII

Two other points may be mentioned. The language of deification must have had, one would think, great disadvantages at a time when the Church was struggling to secure her position in a world dominated by polytheism. To simple men, who pay more regard to words than to the meaning which may be hidden behind them, it might well have seemed that Clement, and some of the Apologists who preceded him, were in danger of giving away the Christian case by their loose employment of [theós] and cognate terms, in the current Greek fashion, to designate immortalized men. Plainly, however, this view of things never affected Clement; for, as we have seen, he calls men 'gods' without any reserve or hesitation. This mode of speech was, moreover, continued long after his day, as the writings of subsequent Greek Fathers testify.[60] But we do notice, I think, in Origen, a tendency to be more restrained and careful than Clement is in the use of such terms. It is true that the *loci classici* of Ps. lxxxi 6 and St Luke xx 36 mean practically the same for him as they do for Clement. He admits, for instance, on the strength of Ps. lxxxi 1, that the angelic powers are called 'gods';[61] but when, in another place, he interprets the same verse of human judges 'who, on account of the superhuman purity of their character, were said to be gods', he adds the qualification, 'in accordance with an ancient Jewish mode of speech'.[62] Angels, again, because of their divine nature, are sometimes called 'gods' in the Scriptures; but not, Origen hastens to say, in

order that we may worship them in place of God.[63] When speaking of men made perfect he uses such expressions as the following: 'equal to the angels';[64] 'taken up into the order of angels'[65] to behold the 'holy and blessed life';[66] placed 'in the assembly of righteous and blessed beings'.[67] With Clement the last of these phrases would in all likelihood have read, 'the assembly of angels and gods'.[68] In his commentary on St John, Origen has occasion to notice the phrase 'every man is a liar'. 'So', he continues, 'every man must be said not to stand in the truth. For if anyone is no longer a liar, and does stand in the truth, such an one is not a man; so that to him and to his like God can say, "I said, ye are gods".'[69] Even here Origen is careful to leave the words to God. The difference between Clement and Origen on this point is not great; but these passages give at the least some reason for thinking that Origen hesitated to reproduce his master's expressions in their more unguarded forms.

Secondly, the whole argument of this paper shews that, wherever in Clement the word [theós] occurs in reference to man (exclusive of Christ), the true English equivalent is not 'God', nor 'god', but 'a god'. In the plural of course there is no difficulty. The *Ante-Nicene Christian Library*, which contains the only translation into English of Clement's complete works, frequently mars the sense by rendering [theós] as 'God'.[70] In every case 'a god' will give as nearly as possible the meaning that Clement intended; i.e. one of a number of spiritualized and exalted beings, endowed with immortality, free from bodily passions, and devoted solely to the contemplation of God . . . .

Notes

1. See i 71[25] (78), where the Word is called 'a true Son of the Mind.' . . . Also ii 331[10] (648) . . . . And ii 320[19] (638), where Schwartz's conjecture is rendered almost a certainty by the two parallels here adduced. See again ii 317[11] (634). The references in this paper are to volume, page, and line in Stählin's edition of Clement. The bracketed figures indicate Potter's pages.

2. ii 468[5-7] (776) . . . .

3. i 236[28]-237[1] (251) . . . .

4. iii 61 (831). . . ('free from all limitations'—Dr Mayor's translation). See also ii 374[7-15] (689), where Clement says that by abstracting length, breadth, depth, and position, you arrive at a conception of unity. If you then take away all that pertains to bodies or to things called bodiless, you can reach some sort of conception of God, learning, however, not what He is, but what He is not.

5. We must not take these expressions too literally, or God would be reduced to a mere idea. The truth is, Clement has failed to combine the various elements of his thought.

6. ii 181[8-10] (494). Explaining Ps. lxxxi 6 (Sept.) 'I said, ye are gods; and ye are all sons of the Highest.'. . .

7. iii 10$^{23\text{-}25}$ (836) . . . . Good works . . . are mentioned in i 68$^{25\text{-}26}$ (75). See also ii 484^{27} (792), 'What is the use of a good that does not do good?' Still, Clement's general thought tends towards a repression, rather than a judicious use, of our full human nature. One who followed out his principles to their logical extreme would be more likely to become a contemplative hermit than, let us say, a missionary to lepers . . . .

8. ii 315$^{25\text{-}26}$ (633) . . . .

9. i 149$^{4\text{-}5}$ (156) . . . .

10. ii 488$^{26\text{-}27}$ (797) . . . .

11. iii 71$^{14\text{-}21}$ (894) . . . .

12. ii 468$^{3\text{-}4}$ (776) . . . .

13. ii 488$^{27\text{-}29}$ (797) . . . . In iii 71$^{24\text{-}25}$ (894) Clement admits that sin is due to 'weakness' as well as to ignorance . . . .

14. i 81^{1} (88-89) . . . .

15. iii 5$^{1\text{-}3}$ (830) . . . .

16. ii 507$^{1\text{-}2}$ (816) . . . .

17. iii 42$^{8\text{-}11}$ (866) . . . . See also iii 60$^{6\text{-}8}$ (883).

18. iii 67$^{15\text{-}16}$ (890) . . . .

19. iii 49$^{15\text{-}16}$ (873) . . . .

20. ii 317$^{11\text{-}12}$ (634) . . . .

21. ii 317$^{10\text{-}12}$ (634) . . . .

22. i 105$^{20\text{-}22}$ (113) . . . .

23. ii 42^{15} (355) . . . .

24. iii 10$^{8\text{-}9}$ (835) . . . .

25. iii 14$^{26\text{-}28}$ (839) . . . .

26. i 120$^{30\text{-}31}$ (128) . . . .

27. iii 41$^{16\text{-}17}$ (865) . . . .

28. iii 41$^{23\text{-}25}$ (865) . . . . Compare Milton *Comus* 9-11:

'the crown that Virtue gives,
After this mortal change, to her true servants,
Amongst the enthroned gods on sainted seats'.

29. iii 6$^{3\text{-}4}$ (831) . . . .

30. ii 382$^{7\text{-}9}$ (697) . . . .

31. ii 384$^{10\text{-}11}$ (699) . . . . This statement may be intended primarily to deny that the Holy Spirits is a material body, able to be distributed in portions to many people. (See Origen *Contra Celsum* vi 70; *De Principiis* i 1. 3.) The above argument would not be invalidated if this were the case. On the contrary, it would be strengthened, since the Spirit's presence would tend to dwindle into a vague power or influence.

32. Justin Martyr *Apol.* i 21 . . . .

33. Justin Martyr *Oratio ad Graecos* 5 . . . .

34. Theophilus *ad Autolycum* ii 27 . . . .

35. Irenaeus iv 38. 4 'non ab initio dii facti sumus, sed primo quidem homines, tunc demum dii' . . . .

36. Certain aspirations after immortality find expression in the later Psalms. Cf. Ps. xvi 10, xlix 15. Dan. xii 2-3 belongs of course to the Apocalyptic writings.

37. See Plato *Phaedo* 80 D-81 D.

38. He speaks, for instance, of the various dwelling-places that are allotted to believers in accordance with their deserts. See ii 264$^{12\text{-}13}$ (579) . . . . Also ii 489^{6} (797) . . . . Clement's constant use of the phrase 'assimilation to God' (from Plato, cf. *Theaetetus* 176 B) also shews his belief that man's progress is throughout a gradual one. For example see i 64^{31} (71), and everywhere.

39. . . . See i 67$^{7\text{-}8}$ (74), i 107$^{19\text{-}20}$ (115), i 112^{7} (120), ii 409^{9} (722), and elsewhere.

40. The Resurrection in a spiritual sense is mentioned several times. See i 61^{19} (68) . . . . Clement twice promises a treatise on the Resurrection—i 118$^{2\text{-}3}$ (125) and i 219^{28} (232)—but apparently he never wrote it. He makes three casual allusions to the Second Advent: iii 152^{21} (1002), iii 213^{20} (1010), and iii 223$^{19\text{-}20}$ ('Address to the Newly Baptized', not found in Potter).

41. ii 254^{27}-255^{1} (570) . . . .

42. In this paragraph it is not maintained that the two views of the future life are irreconcileable; but only that Clement leans, both in thought and in expression, almost entirely towards the Greek view. The contrast between these two is presented from another point of view in R. H. Charles's *Eschatology* pp. 80 (note) and 155 sq.

43. ii 318$^{30\text{-}31}$ (636) . . . . Also the lines following these: ii 318^{31}-319^{1} (636) . . . . See, too, ii 377$^{19\text{-}24}$ (692), an Apocalyptic quotation; and ii 503$^{8\text{-}9}$ (811-812) . . . .

44. Just as daemons, who, according to Clement, are foul and earth-loving spirits, cannot ascend at all, but remain fixed to earth. See i 45$^{25\text{-}30}$ (49) and Plato *Phaedo* 81 C D.

45. Origen is more explicit. The 'heaven' of God's people is either in the 'fixed sphere', or above it; it is not incorporeal (*mundum incorporeum*), only invisible to us; nor is it a world of 'pure ideas', as the Greeks thought . . ., but in its way substantial: *De Principiis* ii 3. 6-7. There are also super-celestial abodes, in which dwell higher beings still; *De Principiis* ii 9. 3.

46. For old-world ideas, in which Clement heartily concurs, see i 56$^{1\text{-}3}$ (53). . . from Euripides; and a quotation of similar import from Democritus in i 52$^{17\text{-}20}$ (59).

47. Eph. i 20 and elsewhere . . . .

48. 2 Cor. xii 2.

49. Heb. iv 14; vii 26.

50. In I Thess. iv 17, for instance, where a progress through the air is spoken of, this is mentioned in connexion with the Second Advent and the General Resurrection, just those doctrines which Greek thought was inclined to leave out of sight.

51. The ideas of deification current in Orphic and Pythagorean circles, or those connected with the Stoic theory of the divine immanence cannot be regarded as having materially influenced Clement, on account of their essentially pantheistic character. Clement certainly never believed that the spirit of any man became merged in the Deity. Indeed, so strongly is he averse from this doctrine, that he vigorously denies the identity of human and divine virtue, which the Stoics taught. See iii 63$^{10-11}$ (886); also his complete denial of pantheistic ideas in ii 384$^{1-17}$ (698-699) . . . .

52. . . . The first verse of the Psalm is also quoted in ii 181^5 (494) . . . .

53. The Psalm seems to be a complaint about the oppression of Israel by the heathen . . . . See Hastings *Dictionary of the Bible,* extra volume p. 724^b . . . .

54. See i 86$^{17-18}$ (94), where the words are attributed to 'the prophet'. Other quotations of this passage occur in i 105^{22} (113), ii 181$^{5-9}$ (494), and ii 314$^{23-24}$ (632) . . . .

55. ii 317$^{10-19}$ (634-635). The text of the important parts of this passage is given on p. 160 *supra* notes 1 and 2.

56. Homer *Odyssey* xvii 485.

57. Stählin suspects a break in the text here.

58. Plato *Theaetetus* 173 c.

59. Homer *Odyssey* x 495 . . . .

60. Harnack says that 'after Theophilus, Irenaeus, Hippolytus, and Origen, it is found in all the Fathers of the ancient Church'. *Hist. Dogma,* Eng. trans., iii p. 164 note.

61. Origen *Contra Celsum* viii 3-4; also iv 29.

62. *Contra Celsum* iv 31 ελεέγοντο ειναι θεοι] πατρίίω τινι Ἰονδαίων εθει.

63. *Contra Celsum* v 4; also v 5.

64. *De Principiis* iv 1. 29 (iv 4. 2); also *Contra Celsum* iv 29.

65. *De Principiis* i 8. 4.

66. *Ibid.* i 3. 8.

67. *Contra Celsum* vi 61.

68. Compare Clement iii 6$^{3-4}$ (831):. . .iii 14^{26} (839). . . : and iii 41$^{16-17}$ (865).

69. Origen *Comm. on St John* xx 27 (xx 241-242). Other references to this subject in Origen are: *Comm. on St John* xx 29 (xx 266); *Homilies on Jeremiah* xv 6; also a quotation from him in Pamphilus *Apol. pro Orig.* 5.

70. See *Ante-Nicene Library,* 'Clement of Alexandria', i 24, i 274, ii 209, ii 370, ii 408 ('divine', which avoids the difficulty, but is not a correct translation), ii 477 ('a God', which seems to be unmeaning). Dr Mayor's translation of *Stromateis* vii gives 'a god' except in one instance (p. 7 of Hort and Mayor's edition), where 'god' stands without the article . . . .

Robert P. Casey (essay date 1925)

SOURCE: "Clement of Alexandria and the Beginnings of Christian Platonism," in *Harvard Theological Review,* Vol. 18, No. 1, January, 1925, pp. 39-101.

[*In the following essay, Casey examines the effect of Platonism and Stoicism on Clement's theology and summarizes the "great trilogy."*]

One of the most fruitful branches of recent patristic study has been the effort to determine the relation between early Christian theology and Greek philosophy. Starting from the assumption that the affinities between the two were many and close, scholars have found themselves able to draw detailed inferences of literary and intellectual dependence, and in the case of many Christian authors to discover the exact sources from which they drew their philosophic ideas, or at least to assign these to some contemporary school. Without such work an accurate estimate of the fathers' views and ways of thinking is impossible, but it must be remembered that an author is not explained, or even fairly represented, by showing how much he may have derived from others, for in the last analysis his finished thought is his own, however extensive the foreign material employed in its construction. It is not, therefore, at the end but at the beginning of his work that the historian of thought can expect most help from the investigation of sources, since even an author who differs from his contemporaries in his answers to current problems must usually begin by seeing them as they do. The background of an author's thought must have supplied the starting point for many of his ideas.

Clement of Alexandria is one of those writers in whose works the search for sources has met with greatest success. A glance at the elaborate notes in Stählin's edition will show how often it is possible to identify his quotations from pagan authors, and in the religious and philosophic literature current at his time to find parallels to his ideas. In describing his conception of God it is frequently necessary to indicate these borrowings and to elucidate obscure ideas by a reference to contexts hinted at but not expressly mentioned. The value of this is undeniable, but it is on the whole less important than the knowledge thus obtained of the way in which Clement regarded the fundamental problems of theology, and particularly those of the being of God and the knowledge of God.

A characteristic of Greek philosophic theology was its lively interest in ontology. The early differences between the Ionians and Eleatics were prophetic of conflicting tendencies in Greek thought which were destined to determine the structure of its whole history. This conflict first becomes of great importance for theology in the writings of Plato.

In the discussion concerning being and non-being between Theaetetus and the Stranger in the Sophist, the Stranger says that two main views about the nature of reality are held by contemporary philosophers:

> Some drag everything to earth from heaven and the unseen, clumsily seizing rocks and oaks with their hands. For they lay hold of all such things and insist that only that exists which can be perceived and touched, and they define reality and body as identical . . . . But if any of their opponents shall say that something exists that has no body, they altogether despise him and will not listen to anything else.
>
> *Theaetetus.* These are terrible fellows you speak of and I have already met many of them.
>
> *Stranger.* Therefore those who oppose them cautiously defend themselves from above, maintaining that intellectual essences and immaterial ideas constitute the true reality . . . . And by arguments they break into small bits the 'bodies' of these other men and their alleged truth, insisting that these are becoming rather than being . . . . And on this subject, Theaetetus, there has always been an endless war, between these two parties.[1]

The importance of this distinction for a general conception of the universe is made clear by Plato in the Timaeus, where Timaeus prefaces his exposition of cosmology by saying:

> First, then, in my opinion, this distinction must be made: what is that which always exists but is never in process of becoming, and what is that which has always been in process of becoming but never has real existence? The former is comprehensible by thought with the help of reason, the latter is to be grasped by opinion with the aid of irrational sensation, since it is in the process of becoming or perishing and thus never really exists.[2]

He goes on to argue that since the Creator must have selected a beautiful model for his work and only Reality is beautiful, it must be that eternal Reality is the pattern, of which the material world is but the imperfect image. The place of the Creator in the scheme of things Plato admits is difficult to determine, but it is clear that he is to be included in eternal Reality, for it is later stated that God supplies not only the energy but also the pattern of creation, so that the world can be described as "the image of the Creator, a god which can be perceived, the greatest and most excellent and most beautiful and most perfect."[3]

The philosophic materialism to which Plato refers received its first great development in Stoicism, and his description of those who "define reality and body as identical, and if anyone says that something exists that has no body, they altogether despise him and will not listen to anything else," is equally applicable to Zeno and Chrysippus. These philosophers maintained that all reality was material, and that the only four things which were immaterial—empty space, time, place, and *[ta lekta]*—were strictly unreal.[4] In the category of material things they placed God, whose nature was the physical element *[pneuma]*. *[Pneuma]* was both substantial and rational, and being the subtlest form of existence, it permeated the whole universe, endowing the cosmos with its own rational properties.[5]

On the principle of affinity so potent in ancient thought, Plato's immaterial Reality could only be known by an immaterial mind, whose nature shared in that of the objects of its knowledge. Reality could be described ontologically as *[asōmatos]*,[6] or epistemologically as *[noetos]*. In Stoicism material reality could only be known by material means, so that the mind of the individual was conceived also as *[pneuma]*, a fragment of the ultimate existence which made the universe an ordered and intelligible whole.

In the third century B.C. these two systems were in open rivalry. Platonism had yielded something to the criticism of Aristotle but had lost none of its radical immaterialism, for in spite of his objections to Plato's formulation of the doctrine of ideas, Aristotle was in no sense a materialist. Stoicism was at the height of its classical development in the system of Chrysippus, who not only systematized but enormously enlarged the substance of Zeno's thought. One of his most important contributions was the substantial support he gave to the materialism of his predecessor by an elaborate epistemology, unequalled in ingenuity in the succeeding history of materialistic philosophy. Yet no sooner was this splendid structure completed than it was subjected to the sharpest criticism. Carneades, a pupil of Chrysippus and a former Stoic, came out against the system he had earlier accepted, and conducted an attack on the very citadel which Chrysippus felt he had made most sure, the Stoic theory of knowledge.

The two main supports of this theory were sensation, which provided the materials of thought, and comprehension, which arranged the materials in proper order and made knowledge possible. A direct contact of the mind with reality was thus secured, and the problem of error was solved by an appeal to the experience of certainty accompanying some ideas and to the common assent given to some notions, both of which served as the norm for determining truth. Carneades proceeded to abolish all these criteria. He showed first of all that sensation was the least reliable of witnesses, and that, so far from connecting us with reality, it constantly deceives us in the most ordinary experiences of everyday life. Against the experience of certainty he pointed to the profound conviction with which error was often maintained, and against the argument from general consent he objected that such assent could never be shown to exist, and in any case could only be a multiplicity of fallible judgments, the validity of which in each case could never be proved.

These objections to the possibility of knowledge in general were urged with special force against Stoic theology.

The ground was cut from under theological belief, but more than this, all the implications of the problem of evil were developed in telling opposition to the Stoic theory of a universal purpose animating the world and favorable to man.

Roused by these objections, the Stoics were not slow to make spirited replies, but in reality their position was much weakened; and their appreciation of this fact is witnessed in the revision of the older systems by the philosophers of the Middle Stoa. Chrysippus believed that he had made sure of the contact of mind with reality from the premises of a thorough-going materialism; but Carneades' polemic aimed to show that this supposed contact was an illusion, and that there was no assurance of the mind's relations with a reality outside itself. To avoid this difficulty and to gain once more the certainty of truth, the Stoics turned for help to their old opponent Plato. Posidonius, who led in this movement, abandoned Chrysippus' assumption that the mind was both functionally and substantially a unit, and substituted for it Plato's trichotomy, intending thereby to avoid the objections raised against the old Stoic sensationalism. Reason, he maintained, was above sensation and akin to the nature of the Universe and God. In determining truth reason was dependent on sensation only for the raw stuff of knowledge; the truth of its judgments proceeded from its own inherent capacity for determining the right relations of things. Truth thus came to be a function of the mind and only indirectly a property of judgments.[7]

In spite of the concessions made to Platonism, Posidonius remained a materialist as did his successors in the Stoic school. He identified the rational principle, God, with the ether, the finest and most remote of the elements . . . .In the rise of Neo-pythagoreanism a similar attempt to reconcile Stoicism and Platonism was made, but this time from the premises of Platonic immaterialism. The movement in its earliest stage is difficult to follow, but it probably began in Alexandria, where it received its most elaborate and successful development. The influence of Posidonius on the early Neo-pythagoreans was apparently considerable,[8] but unlike him the latter freely admitted the existence of immaterial reality, and took as their principal metaphysical problem the relations between the material and immaterial worlds.

One of the ablest of this new school was Philo of Alexandria. In his treatise *De opificio mundi,* he follows Plato in assuming an immaterial pattern invented by the divine mind and realized so far as possible by the divine energy in creation, but he lays much more emphasis than Plato on the continued activity of God in the world. By a brilliant stroke he identified the immanent and active Reason of Stoicism with the transcendent divine Mind of Platonism, and making the necessary accommodations to Platonic anthropology and epistemology obtained the advantages of the two rival systems.

Whether this solution of the ancient problem was completely satisfactory may be questioned, but of its historical importance there can be no doubt. The history of later Stoicism shows no striking advance in thought, and for the early enthusiasm for speculative issues is substituted an earnest desire to find comfort and reconciliation with the divine in a world of discomforting change and sadness. Neo-pythagoreanism, however, led straight to Neo-platonism and to a revival on a grand scale of the philosophy of immaterialism. The climax came with the school of Ammonius Saccas[9] at Alexandria and the writings of Plotinus.

The period in which this revival of Platonism took place saw also the beginnings of Christianity, and in the second century it became apparent that Christian theology, if it were to survive, must justify itself philosophically. In doing so it had to make its choice between the materialism of the Stoa and the immaterialism of Plato. That it ultimately chose the latter may in part be attributed to the influence of men like Philo and Numenius,[10] who had shown the possibility of interpreting Jewish theology by Platonic metaphysics; but two other factors must also be considered. In the first place Platonism had the vigor of a renewed youth, which attracted to it the keenest minds of that generation; but more than this a certain natural affinity existed between Christianity and Platonism. It can be no accident that the early Christian Platonists were men on whom the genius of Paul and John had made the deepest impression. The Christian philosophy developed in Alexandria by Clement and Origen, contemporaries of Plotinus, was associated with a Christian mysticism to which Paul, John, and Plato all contributed. In rejecting under its impulse the Christian Stoicism of Tertullian in favor of the Alexandrine philosophy, the church fell heir to the last great product of Greek thought.

Clement's writings are a clear indication of his wide interests and of his insight into theological problems.[11] Apart from sermons and treatises on various theological topics and questions of the day, fragments of correspondence, and reading notes for forthcoming works, there remain portions of his great exegetical work, the *Hypotyposes,* which include commentaries on the Catholic and Johannine Epistles, and his "great trilogy," which comprises the *Protrepticus, Paedagogus,* and *Stromateis.* The *Protrepticus* appeared shortly after his appointment to the catechetical School, and contains a refutation of paganism and a proof of the superiority of Christianity over other religions and philosophies. Some years later the *Paedagogus* was issued as a manual of Christian morals and ethics, and this was followed by the *Stromateis,* most of which was written after he left Egypt. This work can best be described as prolegomena to the study of systematic theology. In these three works Clement traced the work of the Logos, both in leading men from paganism to Christianity and in training them in the hard practice of Christian life.

In his original plan for the great trilogy is apparent the outline of Clement's life and of the lives of converts he had known. Its execution, however, did not wholly fulfill his own program, which was to end the series by a real system of dogmatic and speculative theology. It is his great merit that he saw the possibility and urgent necessity of such a system, but his mind was naturally unsystematic, and though he could keep himself in hand when discussing pagan errors and Christian morals, the organization of Christian philosophy proved too interesting in its details, too bewildering in its complexity, to be accomplished in a closely written volume of exposition and debate. The passage in **Strom.** vi. 1, where he asserts the sufficiency of the rambling treatment of great themes for those who are really capable of understanding, must be taken partly as an admission of defeat. As he proceeded in his task, its magnitude grew upon him and new questions arose which had to be settled before he could take up the great issues which still beckoned him from a distance. In the prefaces to the **Paedagogus** and to Books iv and vi of the **Stromateis** can be seen how the perspective changed as he advanced, and how little any one of his programmatic statements can be taken as sure prophecies of his actual results.[12] At the end of the seventh book he promises more **Stromateis** . . . .

Though Clement's goal was never reached by the path which he had determined, the main outlines of his thought are clear enough to his reader. In discussing his idea of God it will be well to follow his own course of exposition, taking the **Protrepticus, Paedagogus,** and **Stromateis** in order and introducing relevant passages from his other works as they serve to illustrate points raised by the three major treatises.

The idea of God forms the centre of discussion in the **Protrepticus.** Clement, like Aristides, makes it the touchstone of true religion, and shows that to disparage paganism and glorify Christianity all that is needed is a comparison of the ideas of deity which each professes. Clement's objections to the pagan gods are those which had become familiar in Christian apologetic in the second century. The imperfect nature of the gods is inconsistent with the perfect divine nature; their motives and behavior as described in mythology are unworthy of the character of God. His originality in dealing with the defects of paganism does not, therefore, lie in new motives of polemic but in the elaboration with which he develops familiar themes. Earlier apologists had been content with casual references to the most flagrant and familiar of the scandals of Jove's court, but Clement adorns his attack on the old religion with a wealth of detail and heaps count upon count in his indictment of the gods.[13]

A considerable portion of his material is drawn from Greek literature, with which he was more familiar than most of his pagan contemporaries. A comparison of the **Protrepticus** with Plutarch's *De audiendis poetis* or *De superstitione* is favorable to Clement's erudition. He knows the attacks of philosophers on popular theology, and cites with approval those who risked the charge of atheism by their attacks on the gods.

> Therefore I cannot conceal how it surprises me that they called atheists Euhemerus of Agrigentum and

Nicanor of Cyprus and Diogenes and Hippo the Milesian and besides these that Cyrenian, Theodorus by name, and many more who lived soberly and perceived more clearly than other men the error about the gods. For if they did not know the truth, they at least suspected error, which is no small seed and grows up as a spark of wisdom unto truth.[14]

In one passage he reproduces the Stoic theory of the sevenfold origin of the gods which is found also in Cicero's *De natura deorum* and in the Epitome of Pseudo-Plutarch.[15]

More important than these literary allusions is his treatment of the mysteries. He says:

> I will not mockingly betray them, as they say Alcibiades did,[16] but I will lay bare the witchcraft concealed in them and expose your so-called gods to whom belong the mystic rites; I will display them as on the stage of life to the spectators of the truth.[17]

What follows is particularly interesting to us because much of it cannot be paralleled in other extant literary sources, but its interest to his earliest readers was of a different order. The attack on mythology was a familiar theme of the philosophers and popular preachers and no longer produced the shock that Xenophanes' verses had once done, but the polemic against the mysteries was an assault on a living faith. The Phrygian rites still had their devotees, the worship of Dionysus was widespread and popular, the wails of Osiris' mourners could be heard each year in the streets of Alexandria, and the Serapeion was frequented by pious worshippers. The criticism of Zeus also was aimed at an existing religion, for his name was often used to reconcile popular religion and philosophy, and in connection with Serapis and other deities Zeus still held a place in popular devotion.[18]

From the religion of the multitude Clement passes to the religion of educated men. His objection to philosophy is the common Christian one that it involved God in matter and led its adherents to worship Creation instead of the Creator. According to him not only the Milesian physicists and the Stoics but even Theophrastus[19] was a materialist and advocated opinions unworthy of God's nature, though some others, Anaximander, Anaxagoras, and Archelaus, were led by speculation to views much nearer the truth. Plato, Cleanthes, the Pythagoreans, and some of the poets give evidence of real inspiration, and their utterances, like those of the prophets, can be taken as true statements of the doctrine of God.

Clement's selection of quotations from poets and philosophers is significant as showing what he believed they reflected of his own thought. For the most part they are eloquent statements of universal theism, like the passage from Plato's epistle, "Around the King of all are all things, and he is the cause of all things good,"[20] with which Clement compares Deut. 25, 13-15, or the Pythagorean dictum, "God is one and is not, as some suppose, outside creation but in it, existing wholly in the whole cycle, cause and guardian of all, the blending of the universe[21] and fashioner of his own power and of all his works, the giver of light in heaven, and father of the universe, mind and animating principle of the whole cycle, mover of all."[22] The verses from Cleanthes are notable, for although Clement quotes them as a statement of Cleanthes' theology, he is almost certainly wrong. They really contain a definition of the notion of good, and Clement's use of them shows that he, not Cleanthes, identified God with the idea of the Good.

This treatment of paganism was much more forceful than any provided by previous apologists of Christianity. The polemic was not aimed at a man of straw but at contemporary pagan customs and ideas. It compares favorably both in substance and strategy not only with Christian writings of the same type but with apologetic works of pagans like Celsus and Porphyry. It could command, as no other Christian writing had done, the attention and respect of educated men. Its polemic was, however, only a means to a greater end, the preparation for his principal task, which was to expound in a convincing way the truth about God that Christianity offered in place of the pagan errors.

Clement begins his exposition with a chapter on the Old Testament. The inspiration of the poets and philosophers is real, but limited, and is sometimes obscured by interest in literary form and style. The prophetic writings are "the short cut to salvation."[23] "With unadorned simplicity they present us with the clearest possible ideas as the starting-point for piety, and lay the foundations of truth."[24] The passages from the Old Testament which follow are selected by the same principle that determined the choice of quotations from the philosophers and poets. They are not obscure utterances of the prophetic spirit which must be interpreted by allegory, but are general statements of monotheism and protests against idolatry. The relevance of Jewish sayings for gentile readers is explained by the universality of all wisdom which has its ground in God and is the content of his reason . . . . Upon the foundation of prophetic revelation Clement erects his Christian edifice.

In his later works Clement deals objectively with the idea of God, defining and describing ultimate Reality in terms of epistemology and metaphysics; but, in the **Protrepticus** the idea of God is built up from religious and moral experience. Man is in a fallen state, having lost the vision of truth by his own fault. To achieve salvation he must regain that vision by his own efforts and by the help which God freely gives to those who willingly turn to him.[25] The goal of salvation is the Truth and the Truth is God, but truth is moral as well as intellectual and its possession can never be gained without piety.[26] Truth and piety therefore are complementary in experience, as truth and goodness are inseparable aspects of the nature of God. In the struggle for salvation various stages can be distinguished, and various elements indicated which contribute to success. In all these stages and elements God is present. In them his purpose, his character, and certain aspects of his nature are revealed. Clement's description of these is unsystematic,

not to say confused, but the reader can see beneath the disorder of enthusiasm the beginnings of a brilliant and coherent doctrine of God.

The moral of his polemic against paganism is the same as Paul's in Rom. 1, 18 ff. Man is without excuse, for he has heard the "preaching of justification." The Logos has unfolded the truth, and has shown to men the height of salvation, how by repentance they may be saved or by disobedience they will be judged. Repentance and obedience are the first condition of salvation.[27] Clement is emphatic in his insistence that man's fault is the result of his own free will and thought,[28] and like Paul he will admit no ultimate distinction between these two faculties. When the mind errs, the will follows; when the will transgresses, the mind turns from truth. The fallen stage can be described indifferently as one of ignorance[29] or of disobedience,[30] since each term includes the other, and the process of redemption begins with a change of mind. . .,[31] which is inevitably accompanied by a response of will.

In the conversion from good to evil, from ignorance to knowledge, man is helped by the grace of God. Grace, however, is not conceived by Clement as a special force which is instituted by God to repair the weakness brought in by sin. The grace of God is a natural grace, and its activity is a part of the normal functioning of man's spiritual organism.[32] Without the grace of God man is not truly himself, and when in conversion he again feels the surge of new power, it is the thrill of normal health regained.[33] The beginnings of the cure may be painful. Clement does not hesitate to admit with Augustine that fear is a powerful tonic,[34] but the artificial stimulus is not needed for long and is soon followed by the normal activity of grace in faith, knowledge, and love.

By means of grace and in the exercise of faith man arrives at both truth and piety and finds himself in the presence of God. Faith like truth is a complex experience involving the mind, will, and affections. It expresses in dynamic terms man's attitude to the truth, and indicates his normal capacity for receiving and holding it.[35] Clement's idea of truth is unintelligible unless it be understood that it is for him not a concept, but an aspect of the nature of God; like John he thinks of it not as a picture of reality but as reality itself.[36] Its content is invariable and exhaustive, but faith grasps only those of its infinite forms and aspects which the believer is fitted to appreciate and use. As truth demands a volitional as well as an intellectual response, so it is revealed through moral as well as through intellectual channels. In the practice of Christian virtue and in obedience to the commandments, the believer's faith is expressed and at the same time truth is impressed upon him.

The natural capacity of man to receive truth and so to gain direct access to God is the basis of Clement's universalism.[37] It is God's constant purpose to save mankind, and if they only will to believe and repent they can be saved.[38] This fixed intention on God's part is the sure proof of his friendly concern for man . . . .It is displayed in the means and opportunities offered to men for salvation; and since, as we have seen, these belong to man's natural state, God's benevolence is rooted and grounded in the order of things. "The Lord, since he is man's friend, summons all men to the knowledge of the truth and sends forth the Paraclete."[39] Man has the promise, has God's friendship; his only task is to receive the grace offered.[40] When this is done he immediately comes into his natural state as one of God's children.

> Those who are still faithless are called children of wrath, being inclined to error. But we who have laid error aside are no longer nurslings of wrath, but are turning eagerly to the truth. Therefore we who were once sons of lawlessness have now through the benevolence of the Logos become sons of God.[41]

> Oh supreme benevolence! Not as a teacher to pupils, not as a master to his slaves, not as a God to men, but as a kind father he admonishes his sons.[42]

In the interval between Paul and Clement, 'father,' as a divine title, usually indicated either that God was the benevolent creator of the universe or that he stood in a special relation to Christ.[43] Clement is familiar with these usages, but he also emphasizes the Pauline conception that God is the father of Christ and Christians in virtue of their common possession of his Spirit. In the *Protrepticus* 'father' is used in an overwhelming majority of cases in connection with the process of salvation.[44] It is the function of the Logos to reconcile disobedient sons to the Father.[45] . . . "Thou art a man in thy generic nature, seek him who created thee; thou art a son in thine individual character, recognize thy father."[46] In a significant passage Clement says that God wishes to be called father only by Christians.

> It is true for us to say that only the pious Christian is rich and prudent and well born, and therefore to say and believe that he is an image of God with his likeness who has by Christ Jesus become righteous, holy with prudence, and in so far forth is now like unto God. Indeed the prophet does not conceal the favor when he says, "I say that ye all are gods and sons of the Highest." For it is we, even we, whom he has adopted, and he wishes to be called 'father' only by us and not by the disobedient.[47]

Here, as elsewhere, God's will must not be taken in too anthropomorphic a sense. It describes not God's arbitrary choice but the nature of things, which are ultimately the expression of his being.[48] God wishes to be called father by Christians only because by them alone has that natural relationship between God and man been resumed which the metaphor of 'father' and 'son' expresses. God is their 'real father' . . . ,[49] just as he is the only real God. Behind the relations which are dependent upon the circumstances of the phenomenal world is the eternal relation between humanity and the God-head, and in this consists the fatherhood of God and the sonship of man.[50]

These descriptions of salvation operate inevitably with analogies from human experience. The relations of friend-

ship and sonship approximate as well as any can do to the conditions of redemption, but they imply a duality which is eliminated from the clearer expressions of Clement's thought on the subject. It is true, humanly speaking, that man's experience of God is comparable to these high moments of earthly life, but in reality the analogy is reversed, and the relation of God to man is the fundamental one, from which the truth and beauty of its human counterparts are derived. In *Protrept.* i. 8, 4, Clement defines his thought more accurately. The kenosis of Phil. 2, 6-7 is due to God's eagerness to save man.

> And now the Logos himself clearly speaks to you, putting faithlessness to shame. Yea, I say, the Logos of God became man that henceforth you might learn from a man how man may become divine.[51]

Similar expressions occur in the Epistola Apostolorum, in Irenaeus, and in Athanasius . . . .

The lesson of the Incarnation is that it reveals the significance of man's highest intellectual powers. It teaches man to become fully himself and in doing so to become divine.

This doctrine is the key to Clement's whole conception of the relation of God to man. It is the explanation of his views of faith, truth, and piety, and makes clear his thought on the divine benevolence. It is the foundation of that intellectual mysticism which he first developed to grand proportions in a form consistent with the premises of Christian theology.

> Hear now ye that are afar off and hear ye that are nigh. The Logos has not been hidden from any. He is a common light and shines upon all men. None is a Cimmerian in reason. Let us hasten to salvation, to rebirth. Let us who are many hasten to be gathered unto one love in the unity of the monadic essence. Since we do good, let us in like manner pursue unity, searching for the good monad. And the unity of many, arising out of a multitude of separate voices, takes on a divine harmony, and becomes one concordant sound following one director and teacher, the Logos, and coming to rest at the same Truth, saying, "Abba, Father." God welcomes this true utterance, receiving it as the first fruits from his children.[52]

Clement's doctrine of God as Creator is in agreement with the thought of his time, though it is relatively less prominent in his writings than in those of the other apologists of the second century. It is stated in its most general terms in *Protrept.* iv. 63, where he contrasts the creative power of the Greek artists, who make only images, with God, who has created the heavens and everything in them:

> Therefore some are deceived, I know not how, and worship the divine creation, the sun and the moon and the rest of the starry host, irrationally assuming that these, the instruments of time, are gods. For by his word were they established and by the breath of his mouth is all their power. Now human art creates houses and ships and cities and writings, but how shall I say what God makes? Surely the whole world! It is his

work. Heaven and sun and angels and men are the works of his fingers. How great is God's power! Creation is only his will. For God alone created, since he alone is really divine. He fashions by his mere will, and creation follows him at his simple wish. Here is where the band of philosophers is led astray, for they admit that man was nobly created for the contemplation of the heaven, but they worship the heavenly bodies and objects which can be grasped by sight. For although the heavenly bodies are not human creations, they have been indeed fashioned for men. And let not any of you worship the sun, but let him desire the Maker of the sun; nor let him deify the cosmos, but let him seek the Creator of the cosmos. For it seems that the only refuge left for him who is to reach the gates of salvation is divine wisdom. There, as from a sacred refuge, the man who is pressing on to salvation can no longer be torn away by any of the demons.

It is possible to see latent in this general exposition the outline of Clement's more precise thought. In a more technical statement of his doctrine of creation a theory of the Logos would appear, and in this passage it is clearly assumed. It lurks behind the 'word' . . . and 'breath' . . . of Ps. 23, 6 and in the expressions 'his will' and 'divine wisdom.' Yet it is characteristic of Clement's apologetic method that he does not confuse the readers of his *Exhortation* by an abstruse metaphysical theory, and it is symptomatic of his sensitiveness to the fundamental unity of the divine nature that he does not always sharply distinguish between God and his Logos either in the creation or government of the world. When such distinctions become necessary for a clear theory, he draws them with a firm hand, but ordinarily he assumes them and lays his emphasis on the divine unity which embraces all the modes and activities of the Godhead and in which man himself may be included.

The biblical elements in Clement's doctrine of God are frequently a source of difficulty to the student of his thought, for their vivid expressions of God's personality and their lively anthropomorphism are strangely unsuited to express Clement's conception of the divine nature.[53] This problem is discussed formally in later works, but even in the *Protrepticus* Clement gives a clue to his position. He describes the stages of progress in theology by saying, "Faith will lead the way, experience will teach, Scripture will instruct,"[54] and in this aphorism his theological method is summarized. By faith truth is perceived and appropriated; by experience it is tested and used; with the help of Scripture it is formulated and expressed. Clement comes to the Bible for the authoritative statement of a truth already perceived. Its lessons are not the substitute for faith or experience, but complement both by adding to their substance and aiding their expression. In its pages he could find much that was congenial to his spirit and temper, and where its thought was not his own, the allegorical exegesis learned from Philo extracted new meanings by which the unity of all Christian knowledge was maintained.

The premise of all Clement's thought was that God is Reality, and by this he did not mean only that God actu-

ally exists or that he is responsible for the whole of creation.[55] With Plato and Plotinus he took the phenomenal world more or less for granted, and felt the problem of reality to lie deeper as he sought for meaning and value in the swirl and confusion of sensible existence. But while the minds of Plato and Plotinus roamed at large through the universe, trying eagerly and hopefully every road and by-path that might lead them to their goal, Clement's interest was concentrated on the religious and moral experience of Christianity, which seemed to offer the surest proof, the closest analogy, or better the finest realization, of the divine unity in all things. The unity of Christians with each other, with Christ, and with God, the opportunity for which lay in the divine character of the enlightened human *[nous]*, could be described with equal correctness as one of love or of the primary substance. Inge says of Plotinus that it was for him "a matter of faith that the hierarchies of existence and of value must ultimately be found to correspond";[56] for Clement such a correspondence was a clearcut conviction.

The confident appeal to philosophic ideas in the *Protrepticus* and the ready use of philosophic terms indicate even more clearly than does the apologetic value attached to Greek philosophy a new departure for Christian theology. This becomes more striking in the *Paedagogus,* which is addressed to Christian and not to pagan readers, for, with the exception of Tertullian, the apologists used philosophy as little more than a common meeting-ground with pagans, and they leave the impression that their real affinities are with such exponents of uninstructed piety as Clement of Rome and Hermas. Clement's philosophy is a natural and inevitable part of his religion, and he assumes that it is, or may become, so to many of his readers. The *Paedagogus* and the *Stromateis* are thus the first pieces of early Christian literature that assume the existence of an educated Christian public.

The greater part of the *Paedagogus* is devoted to a detailed exposition of Christian life, which is treated not as obedience to a prescribed law, but as the fulfilment of the purpose of the Logos. The goal of morality is to live according to reason . . . . The life of perfect virtue is an instance of the principle stated in the *Protrepticus* that God became man that man might become divine, for the educative influence of God's own reason can be detected in all rational human behavior.

The first book of the *Paedagogus* is a general discussion of the Logos and his educative work. The treatment is topical and discursive, but as a whole contains a fair exposition of the ethic upon which the practical moral instruction of the later books is based. Its bearing on the doctrine of God is close, since Clement's interest in Providence is keenest when it is concerned with the inner life and dispositions of mankind, and it is a significant part of his contribution to the Christian idea of God that he extended its application to so many individual aspects of human life.

The book opens with a chapter on the functions of the Logos. It is constructed upon an elaborate pun on the word *[logos]*, in which various types of discourse *[logos]*, distinguished by Stoic rhetoricians are taken over to describe the activity of the divine reason *[logos]*. A passage in one of Seneca's letters says that Posidonius considered it necessary for a rhetorician to have mastered not only the art of instruction (*praeceptio*) but also persuasion (*suasio*), consolation (*consolatio*), and exhortation (*exhortatio*).[57] Each of these genres had its special function. Clement says that exhortation . . . dealt with habits and customs. . . and that similarly it is the office of the divine Logos to lead men from their old habits and opinions to the new and better ones of Christianity. Persuasive discourse . . . is concerned with a man's conscious acts, the products of his deliberate choice . . . and the divine Logos also presides over the voluntary behavior of Christians. Consolation. . . heals the wounds of passion and grief . . . , and the divine Logos also acts as a physician settling the emotional disturbances which threaten the healthy calm of man's soul. Instruction . . . , too, has its counterpart in the revelation of doctrine made by the Logos . . . .

The main thesis of [*Paed.* i. 13] is that "everything which is contrary to sound reason is sin, and that virtue is a disposition of the soul in agreement with reason throughout the whole of life." When man does not live according to reason, he becomes an irrational animal and is like one of the beasts. His salvation therefore lies in obedience to reason, which for a Christian is the equivalent of obedience to the commandments. Christian life is defined as a system of rational behavior, the continuous active fulfilment of the teachings of reason. 'Reason' in this connection is ambiguous, since it may refer either to the mind of man or to the divine Logos, but it is probable that both are intended and that the Logos is conceived as guiding men by the natural processes of their thought and by the commandments he has issued in Scripture for them to obey.

The goal of Christian life, which is reached by the performance of its appropriate duties and requirements, is that rest in God which comes from a perfect unity of divine and human wills. The immediate purposes of these obligations are various, since some relate to the ordinary conduct of life, some to the art of living well, some only concern life here, and others pertain to future happiness after death. All, however, have one ultimate goal, to make life rational and so divine, for the reason of man and the reason of God are fundamentally one.

The other kind of sin is emotional and to this the Logos is especially attentive. Clement is a sufficiently good psychologist to see that this is the easier and more dangerous type of sin, and that it is quite different in character from the other. The sin which is contrary to reason is the product of deliberate but misguided choice, while the sins of passion are due to an inability to control the sudden inrush of feeling which allows no time for consideration or reflection on its direction and consequences. This type of sin Clement rightly terms 'involuntary'[58] for though it is in flagrant violation of the will of God, it involves the will

of man as little as it does his reason. The harmful emotions which cause it are in Clement's view contrary to human nature, so that when affected by them the soul becomes sick and is in need of a physician.[59] At these times the friendly Tutor abandons his preceptive discourse and offers consolation. He turns physician, and applies the necessary remedies to cure the illness, so that by his ministrations the soul becomes again well and strong.

As a wise physician the Logos not only cures the present malady but teaches his patient how to avoid the moral diseases which constantly threaten his health. Perfect sinlessness is the prerogative of God alone, but all Christians can seek to avoid voluntary sins and he who is well trained learns to overcome involuntary sins and to achieve the ideal state . . . .[60]

The similarity of this ethic to that of the Stoa is apparent, and accounts for the liberal use of Stoic material in the literary composition of the *Paedagogus*. What distinguishes Clement's ethic from Stoicism is the place assigned to the incarnation. The Stoics had been content to prove that the universe was by nature rational, and that man, though often misled by unreasoning impulses, could turn at will to a life guided by intelligence and good sense. Clement agreed to this, but as a convert to Christianity he knew the difference which the new religion had made in his own life, and was prepared with Paul to find a similar change reflected on a grander scale in history. To him, therefore, the incarnation marked a definite historical turning-point in the moral education of humanity. To the sporadic manifestations of divine truth and power in pre-christian times had finally succeeded a perfect example of all that humanity was able either to attain or to receive of the divine life.

Clement's conception of the incarnation has much in common with the Stoic notion of the perfect Sage. The substance of this was that the nature of things provided the possibility that all might truly be wise, but that in practice few, if any, were likely to become so.[61] The main function of this ideal figure, therefore, was to mark out the far limits of human moral capacity, and to show men what they might be if only they tried hard enough. The weakness of the Stoic teaching lay in its lack of examples, for the philosophers were modest in claiming such a distinction for themselves and skeptical as to recognizing it in others. Several noted ancients were thought to have reached the goal, but it was not certain, and little practical use was made of their supposed achievement.[62] For Clement, the sage was not only an ever present possibility, but an accomplished fact in the life of Jesus Christ, and this fact guaranteed to all Christians the practicability of the ideal. The soul of Jesus had been really 'impassible', and he alone had gone sinless through life, which proved his right to be our judge, and constituted an obligation to make our souls as much like his as possible.[63] That complete sinlessness was a prerogative of godhead Clement admits, but he says that the Christian sage can at least avoid all conscious misdemeanors.[64]

In spite of their similarity the Stoics' idea of the sage and Clement's idea of Christ were significantly different, for the sage had no other business than to be his own impassible self, while it was the nature of Christ to impart to others his unique characteristics in proportion as they were able to receive them and unite themselves with him. This difference is indicative of a corresponding distinction in the idea of God. In Stoicism even divine benevolence was a passive virtue, a component of individual perfection, but in Christianity God shared his very life with humanity and sealed his love by a miracle of self-surrender. The purpose of the incarnation was not only to demonstrate the divine possibilities in human nature, but also to reaffirm a quality of God's character already expressed in creation.

The creation of man was only partly an end in itself; he was made in the image and likeness of God that God might appropriately love him. God was all goodness, and man must share in his nature, for God could only love what was good.[65] The incarnation reaffirmed God's love, since it was designed to recreate the divine element in man which sin and neglect had been allowed to cripple. It also manifested God's goodness, for his love is simply his goodness in action; in Clement's words, "As there is no light which does not shine, no mover which does not set in motion, and no friend who is not friendly, so there is no goodness which does not help or guide to salvation."[66]

It was a characteristic tenet of Valentinian theology that not all who were saved had the same status and enjoyed an equal measure of divine favor. This distinction in rank was referred back to a primary difference in native capacity which allowed some men to grasp more of the truth and thus to assimilate more of the divine nature than others . . . . In this there was much that was attractive for one who was impressed by the widely different types of achievement produced by the same divine grace. Paul had seen something of the problem when dealing with the variety of spiritual gifts in 1 Cor. 12, and had given his answer in the metaphor of Christ's body with its many members. Clement rejected the Valentinian view,[67] for he felt that it implied a fundamental injustice in God's dealing with men; and his own solution was a development of Paul's which nevertheless reckoned with the facts that Valentinus had wrongly explained.

In *Paed.* i. 6 Clement shows that all Christians are in reality equal and perfected in the sight of God. His starting point is baptism.

> Now when we were reborn, we received straightway that perfect thing . . . for which we were striving. For we are enlightened, which is to know God . . . ,[68] hence he cannot be imperfect who has known that which is perfect. And do not be offended with me when I profess to have known God, for this manner of speech was pleasing to the Logos and he is free. When the Lord was baptized, a voice called out of heaven to him, a witness of the Beloved, saying, "Thou art my beloved Son, this day have I begotten thee." Let us therefore ask the wise whether Christ who is reborn to-day is now perfect or—monstrous thought!—imperfect. If he is imperfect, there is still something he must learn, but

that he should learn anything more is most unlikely, since he is one with God and no one could be greater than the Logos nor a teacher of the only Teacher. Will they not then unwillingly admit that the Logos, begotten perfect from the perfect Father, is reborn perfectly according to the plan of the dispensation. And if he were perfect, why was the perfect one baptized? They say it was necessary in order to complete the announcement to humanity. Very good, I admit that. Did he therefore become perfect when he was baptized by John? Clearly. Therefore he learned nothing from him? Nothing at all. And was he made perfect merely by the washing, and sanctified by the descent of the Holy Spirit? Exactly.[69]

And the same thing happens also in our case, for the Lord has become our example. When we are baptized we are enlightened, when perfected we are made immortal. "I say," he says, "ye are all gods and sons of the Most High." And this act is called by various names, favor. . .and illumination. . . and perfection . . . and washing . . . . We call it a washing because we are cleansed thoroughly from our sins; a favor because the penalties of our sins are remitted; an illumination because that holy saving light is directly seen, that is, because we clearly see God; perfection since it lacks nothing, for what is lacking to one who has known God? Besides, it would be absurd that anything which has not been completed should be truly called a favor of God. Now he who is perfect will presumably bestow perfect gifts, and as all things occur at his command, so the fulfilment of his favor follows upon his mere desire to bestow it, for the future is anticipated by the power of his will. Furthermore release from evil is the beginning of salvation, and only we who have reached the frontiers of life are now perfect, and we being separated from death now live.

Moreover salvation is following Christ. "For in him was life." "Verily, verily, I say unto you," he says, "he who hearkens to my word and believes on him that sent me, *has* eternal life and comes not into judgment, but has passed from death to life." Thus perfection consists only in having faith and being born again. For God is never weak. For as his will is deed and this deed is called the world, so also his will is the salvation of men and this has been called the church. Therefore he knows whom he has called, and whom he has called he has saved. And he has called and saved at the same moment. "For ye are taught of God," the Apostle says. It is not then permissible for us to regard what we have been taught by him as imperfect, but the lesson is the eternal salvation of an eternal Saviour, to whom be thanks for ever and ever, Amen. And he who has only been reborn, since he has the Name, has been enlightened, has been released from darkness, and has straightway received the light.

In this passage Clement avoids the defect of Valentinian theology, that God might be considered a respecter of persons,[70] and leaves no room for favoritism in the plan of salvation. He also gives a fresh statement of that intellectual and moral mysticism which is the culminating point of his idea of God. In the *Protrepticus* he was concerned with pointing out to all men the universal opportunity of faith. The strength of his appeal lay for pagans in the possibility open to them of sharing in the divine Nature by receiving and absorbing Christian truth; its proof was the incarnation, in which God became man that man might become divine by realizing his own divine potentialities. In the *Paedagogus* a different audience is addressed. The readers are now baptized Christians, whose business is to know the dignity of their calling and the responsibilities implicit in the opportunity they have embraced. Clement tells them that they are all children of God, since all know him, possess his Spirit, and share in his life. In baptism their minds were enlightened, and this experience was both the seal and instrument of their salvation. By it they came to know God, who is perfect, and in their knowledge to share in his perfection.

Both the knowledge and the perfection which are the products of baptismal illumination deserve special attention. To know God is not to know about God but to have that direct vision of his Being which in the Johannine phrase is itself 'eternal life.' Such knowledge is a divine favor, bestowed through the intellect, but its effects are not only intellectual, for they permeate the whole moral nature of the believer, and Christians become not only "taught of God" but "gods and sons of the Most High." The finest example of this process is in the incarnation, for, like Christians, Jesus Christ became perfect at his baptism. The notion of this perfection is one of Clement's subtlest thoughts, for in spite of the assertion that Christians share in the perfection of Christ, the meaning is not that Christ and Christians are exactly alike . . . . The "equality of salvation" does not exclude important differences between Christ and the believers and between one believer and another, for their equality and perfection are estimated from the point of view of God's purpose, which varies in different cases. Christians are alike perfect, not because they all have the same capacities and functions, but because in knowing God they have equally realized his will and can fulfil with equal acceptability his purpose for them. Such perfection excludes false pride and a mistaken sense of inferiority. Against both is set the consciousness that in the life of every saved Christian, whatever may be its circumstances, pulses a divine energy which is the living expression of God's will and character.

Clement finds it necessary to make one qualification of his notion of perfection in view of the improved state of Christians after death. Although from the point of view of God's will they may be perfect here, it is certain that when they are rid of the encumbrances of the flesh and dwell as pure spirit, they will have attained a higher stage of perfection. How then can a state be called perfect which is only the first of an ascending series? Clement's answer is that the future blessedness is contained potentially in the present life, so that it can now be possessed and even enjoyed, though it has not been fully realized.[71] This power of effective anticipation is a property of faith, which from this point of view may be defined as the perfection of learning, for in it the matter of instruction is transmuted into the living experience of the believer.[72] Nothing is lacking in faith, and those who possess it share either directly or through a lively expectancy the security and joy which it promises. Since salvation, whether present or future, is always conceived by Clement in terms of participation in the divine nature, this theory may be taken as a further explanation of the activity of God in man.

Chapter VIII-XII of the first book of the *Paedagogus* deal with a problem in theodicy. In Chapter VII the work of the *Paedagogus* has been described, and the means and aim of his instruction outlined. The goal of this education is the vision of God; its mark is the persistent endeavor to lead a holy life. Since the Logos is the guide of humanity, he must train all men in his régime and to do this different pedagogic methods are required, for though some men will listen to the gentle voice of persuasion, others must be sternly threatened and inspired with fear and awe before they can be led to repentance and faith.[73] To this second course objections have been raised, and it is maintained, in manifest disregard of the wholesome influence of fear in conversion, that the disciplinary measures of the Logos are really signs of God's anger and dislike.[74] Clement insists that such a view is founded on a complete misunderstanding of God's nature and motives. The nature of God is love, and every act of his will is an expression of this fundamental aspect of his character. All existence, being the product of his design, is also the manifestation of his love, so that the bare fact that anything exists is a proof that God loves it. God hates nothing, for hatred is contradictory to his nature.[75]

Of all creation man is the most loved of God, partly because he is its noblest work, partly because he is able to respond to the affection God so lavishly showers upon him.[76] Since, therefore, God is goodness itself and goodness issues inevitably in love, and since God's love for man is doubly sure, it follows that all his dealings with man must be actuated by a supreme benevolence in which no drop of malice could possibly be mingled.[77] Thus God's seeming anger is in reality an expression of his love, and his wrathful acts are all designed to cure men of sin and are signs not of ill will but of good will. What we regard as our punishment is either necessary to our moral education or incidental to the realization of God's moral purpose, which works against us only because we have set ourselves against it in deliberate disregard of its sovereign rights.

Clement is particularly concerned to defend God from the charge of petty vengeance. He admits that divine punishment visits the disobedient; for such punishment is a corrective and of great benefit to its recipient, but this is not revenge, which is, on the contrary, a return for evil advantageous to him who has been wronged.[78] It is evident how far Clement is removed from the Old Testament, where God's wrath is regularly considered to be his natural and righteous attitude toward all who offend against his majesty.[79] Clement sees in the wrath of God hardly more than a metaphor, useful in distinguishing an important aspect of divine love but open to grave misunderstanding and often in need of qualification.[80] Like all analogies from personality it must be used cautiously, as the only human attribute which can be assigned to God with perfect confidence is love. In him "the passion of wrath—if indeed it is right to call his admonishing 'wrath'—is friendly to man . . . since God condescends to emotion for man's sake, for whom also God's Reason became man."[81]

From the literary point of view the *Stromateis* is the weakest of all Clement's works, but in its thought it is the most important one. Its public was to be a limited and select one, composed of those whose soundness in faith was assured and whose special capabilities and training had shown them ready for advanced instruction in speculative theology. One might think that in addressing such an audience, Clement would have had no difficulty in plainly speaking his mind. Yet even in such congenial company he was obsessed with nervous caution lest his book fall into the hands of some uninstructed person and serve as a cause of downfall to one unprepared to grasp its real meaning.[82] To lessen this danger he proposed to develop his material in a deliberately unsystematic way, confident that such a method would prove wearisome and confusing to the uninitiated, but would stimulate those who desired knowledge to search the more diligently in the labyrinth of his pages for the truth concealed therein.[83] That he had some native talent for such a procedure he had made clear in his previous writings, but the *Stromateis* is easily his masterpiece of rambling obscurity. The value of the book, therefore, lies in its ideas, and these appear especially significant when considered from the point of view of the people to whom, with some trepidation, they were addressed.

These differed from the mass of Christians in that they had learned the lessons of their Tutor and were ambitious candidates for the higher education which he could give them . . . . They had faith and could translate their faith into virtuous conduct, but in doing so they had discovered that this medium was inadequate to render all that demanded expression in their souls. Clement realized that the knowledge which their faith called for was of a different variety from that which seemed adequate to most Christians. He saw in their demand for wider learning and deeper understanding the capacity for a perfection markedly different from that of the average pious Christian. From the premises of his own intellectual mysticism, the greater knowledge of God to which they aspired involved not only a better comprehension but also a more complete assimilation of the divine life, so that these gnostics in achieving their goal would become a kind of divine aristocracy, representing the maximum degree of divinity which man was capable of absorbing, and entering therefore into a relation with God peculiar to their own special talents and attainments.[84]

At first sight the existence of such a group might seem to imperil Clement's theory of the equality of salvation, and to reopen all those difficult problems in theodicy which he had seen latent in Valentinus's explanations of the inequalities of men's spiritual lives. Surely, if man's faith was the god-given measure of his capacity to receive truth, and if

in faith he came to a knowledge of God and to the perfection of that purpose which God had ordained in him, then these men, more perfect than the perfect, possessing a knowledge better than their fellows, constituted a grave anomaly in God's absolutely just economy.

The difficulty is a real one, and from Clement's premises strictly insuperable, since he could not deny the superiority of the gnostic over the average Christian, and had to admit that what distinguished him was a difference in the structure of his faith for which God was ultimately responsible.[85] Clement's only course was to evade the difficulty, and he does this with such skill that his system betrays hardly a sign of the danger to which it had been exposed. His method is time-honored in theology; he uses the same words in different senses. In the *Paedagogus* all faithful believers are said to be perfect and to know God; but, as we have seen, that perfection is a relative, or rather functional, concept and qualifies human life only from the point of view of its particular destiny, that is, the specific purpose which God had intended for it. Thus all men who acted by the faith that was in them were perfect instruments of the divine will. In the *Stromateis* a different perfection is considered. The standard here is not God's purpose in individual human lives but the ultimate capacity of the human [phúsis] to participate in the divine life. When this ultimate capacity has been realized—the conditions of the individual subject including the structure of his faith being favorable—then perfection has been attained.[86] There are then two kinds of perfection, measured by different standards; and whereas all faithful Christians possess the one, only the Christian gnostic attains the other.

The case of knowledge is similar. All the faithful have the knowledge of God which is given to them in baptism. Since that knowledge is of perfection, it is from one point of view impious to say that one Christian's knowledge is better or greater than another's. Nevertheless there are various ways of knowing God. The average man knows him chiefly through his will, which he lovingly obeys and makes his own. It is possible, however, to know him intellectually, and since God is himself an intellectual Substance, such knowledge is purer, freer, and more direct than that which is mediated through the material complexity of moral struggle . . . .

Since the gnostic vision affords the best knowledge of God which man can achieve, it is in this vision that Clement's conception of deity must be sought. It must not be forgotten, however, that in arriving at contemplation the gnostic has travelled far, and that each step of the way has brought fresh revelation of the true character and nature of God. First had been the recognition of faith, and of the divine possibilities in man which its new discovery of personal worth and power revealed; then followed a period of discipline, when that power, conformed to the will of God, had to be used to redeem and renew the soul; finally, and this only in the case of the true gnostic, faith might take the subordinate, almost mechanical, place of an adjustment to the accepted duties of existence, while life's best vigor passed into the intellect, glowingly absorbed in fresh visions of the divine Being.

It is now time to ask what is the content of the gnostic's heavenly vision and how he conceived the object of his contemplation. Early in the **Stromateis** Clement warns his readers that they must prepare to learn philosophy if they would follow the gnostic path,[87] and though he is careful not to attach too much importance to what he considers only an instrument of knowledge, it is nevertheless clear that the tasks of the gnostic and of the philosopher have much in common.[88] Yet the gnostic differs from the philosopher in having his goal already fixed. Any philosophy will not do, he is not free to pick and choose, since philosophy comes at a late, not at an early stage of his pilgrim's progress and must lead him straight and true to the desired end. Even in the **Protrepticus** Clement leaves his readers in no doubt about the kind of metaphysics to which he is addicted, for Platonism is written large on every page of that treatise. It is less apparent in the **Paedagogus,** where speculation plays a minor rôle, though one passage gives the most extreme of all his definitions of divine transcendence. It is in the **Stromateis** that the doctrine of God rests solidly upon a philosophic foundation, for here it is intelligible and significant only from the premises of Platonic immaterialism and in contrast to the materialist philosophy of religion held by the Stoics or by Christian Stoics like Tertullian.

Clement's conception of God's transcendence is from the historical point of view probably the most significant portion of his theology. It appears in its most extreme form in **Paed.** i. 8, 71, 1, where, commenting on John 17, 21 ff., Clement says: . . .

> But God is one and beyond the One and beyond the Monad itself. Therefore also the 'thou' (17, 21), a particle having demonstrative force, indicates the only really existent God, who was and is and shall be, to which three tenses the single expression ϛων (cf. Exod. 3, 14) applies.

Inge, in his *Philosophy of Plotinus,* says that "Clement of Alexandria, as a Christian, feels the same objection [as Philo] to saying that God is 'beyond Reality.' . . . [He] outdoes the Platonists by saying that He is 'beyond the One and above the Monad,' a phrase which seems to have no meaning;"[89] but a comparison of this passage with other statements of Clement about divine transcendence shows the idea expressed here to be a consistent and necessary part of Clement's doctrine. In **Protrept.** ix. 88, 2-3 it is said that reason is a common light which shines on all men, by which they should press on to rebirth: . . .

> Let us who are many hasten to be gathered unto one love according to the unity of the monadic essence. Since we do good, let us in like manner pursue unity by seeking the good Monad. But the unity of many arising out of a multitude of separate voices takes on a divine harmony and becomes one concordant sound, following one director and teacher, the Logos, and com-

ing to rest at the Truth itself saying "Abba, Father." God welcomes this true utterance, receiving it as the first fruits from his children.

It is clear from this passage that the cry 'Abba, Father' mounts up to God from those united to the Monad itself, so that whatever may be its nature the Monad certainly does not embrace the entire godhead.[90] What it does include is the Logos and those who are united with him in the perfect realization of his presence in their own reason. This unity is an organic unity, dynamic and energetic rather than natural or substantial. It is not alienated from God and is truly divine, but it is not the whole of divinity, for beyond this celestial unity of reason and love are still the lofty heights of God, which even the gaze of the true gnostic can only vaguely distinguish.

The matter is stated more clearly in **Strom.** v. 11, 71, 2-3, where Clement compares the gnostic faith with the mysteries. These require purification and instruction in the minor mysteries before culminating in the great mysteries, in which learning is abandoned for the contemplation and immediate apprehension of reality . . . . He continues:

> And we should take the way of purification by confession but that of vision by analysis; advancing to the primary act of intelligence, we obtain our first principle by analysis from the elements that underlie this way, abstracting from body its physical properties and removing the dimensions of depth, then of width, and then, after these, that of thickness. Now what is left is a point, a monad so to speak, having position, but if we remove its position, it is conceived simply as a monad. If we should then abstract all the material properties and those called immaterial, we should cast ourselves on the greatness of Christ and thence advance by holiness into Immensity, and we should approach in some way the conception of the Omnipotent, understanding not what he is but what he is not . . . .

A comparison of this passage with Plotinus, *Ennead.* v. 3, 17, is instructive. For Plotinus the goal is the One, which since it is shared by all reality without sharing in anything other than itself, he does not hesitate to place beyond existence. To reach the One it is necessary to transcend both the senses and the discursive reason, where the distinction between subject and object is still possible. When it comes to the description of the union with the One, Plotinus, like Clement, abandons metaphysics for metaphor: . . .

> And at the moment when the soul is suddenly illuminated, then it is proper to believe that it has the vision, for this is indeed the light, is from God, and is God. And you must know that He is present when, like any other god, as some one calls him into a house, He comes and illuminates it, or does not come and does not illuminate it and so the soul is unilluminated and godless so far as he is concerned. But when the soul is illuminated, it possesses what it sought, and this is the true end of the soul, to come into contact with that light and to see it by the light itself; beholding it not by another light but by the very light by which also it sees. For the light that illuminated it is the very one it

must see, for neither is the sun beheld by the light of another. How can this come to pass? Abstract everything . . . .

. . . . .

In the chapter following various points are taken up for discussion . . . .

(1) There are some who maintain that God is material (*deum corpus esse*) on scriptural grounds. They quote "God is a consuming fire" (Deut. 4, 24); "God is (a) Spirit and those who worship him must worship in spirit and in truth" (John 4, 24).[91] But the Scriptures say, "God is light, and there is no darkness in him" (John 1, 5). The light referred to is not physical light, like that of the sun, but intellectual light, as is shown by "In thy light we see light" (Ps. 35, 10).[92]

(2) A similar reasoning applies to "God is a consuming fire." God consumes the evil thoughts of our minds and the evil desires of our souls by his (immaterial) influence. So with "God is spirit"; in Scripture 'spirit' is the antithesis to matter (*aliquid contrarium corpori huic crassiori et solidiori*), and in the text, "The letter kills, the spirit makes alive" (2 Cor. 3, 6), 'letter' is equivalent to material things, 'spirit' to intellectual reality (*per litteram corporalia significat, per spiritum intellectualia, quae et spiritalia dicimus*).

(3) The Holy Spirit must not be thought to be material because all the saints share in it, as if it could be divided up into material parts and distributed. That would be as foolish as to suppose that people who took part in the medical profession did so by having particles of medicine in their possession. What they have in common is an understanding of their science (*intellectum artis ipsius disciplinaeque percipiunt*).[93]

(4) The point of Jesus' reply to the Samaritan woman was that the worship of God does not depend on the prerogatives of material places (*recedendum esse a praesumptione corporalium locorum huic qui vult deum sequi*).

(5) Then the argument apparently takes a new turn. Having refuted the materialist argument, he now maintains that God is incomprehensible and inconceivable (*incomprehensibilem inaestimabilem*); but after a brief discussion of the superiority of thought over sensation, because the objects of thought are immaterial, he concludes:

> What in the whole world of reason, that is of *immaterial reality*, is so superior to everything else, so ineffably and inconceivably excellent as God? (*Quid autem in omnibus intellectualibus, id est incorporeis, tam praestans omnibus, tam ineffabiliter atque inaestimabiliter praecellens quam deus?*)

(6) Just as the eye knows the sun by the splendor of its rays and not by direct vision, so the mind knows God by contemplation of the works of nature and providence, without being able to know God as He is. *Therefore* God

is in no way material but simple, rational nature admitting no foreign admixture . . . .

As mind requires no bodily place or form, so the nature of God consists in absolute unity and simplicity, devoid of all material admixture.

Sea-sickness is no argument against the mind's independence of space, for when a man goes on the water he is transgressing the natural conditions of his existence, and his body through which the mind works is disturbed. Least of all does such an objection apply to God, who is not, as we are, composite by nature, made up of body and soul.

The mind is not like the body in requiring material growth to increase its effectiveness. The mind grows by intellectual exercises. (*Indiget sane mens magnitudine intelligibile, quia non corporaliter, sed intelligibiliter crescit*).

(7) Let those who hold the mind to be material explain how it understands difficult and subtle arguments, whence its powers of memory, of observing invisible and understanding immaterial reality, and of comprehending the divine teachings which are clearly immaterial.

Underlying every bodily sense is some corresponding reality, as color corresponds to sight, sound to hearing, etc. Is it then possible that mind, which is so superior to sense, has no such reality and is only an accident of matter (*non videtur absurdum. . . esse intellectualis naturae virtutem, corporibus accidentem vel consequentem*)? Those who speak in this way doubtless wrong the higher power within themselves, but they also cast an insult on God in thinking that he can be understood by a bodily nature. For according to them that which can be understood by matter is material. They will not understand that there is a kinship between the minds of men and God, whose rational image the mind is, and that through this something of the nature of the Godhead can be perceived, especially if the mind be purified and isolated from matter.

(8) For those who require scriptural proof to believe that the nature of God transcends matter there are the texts, "Who is the image of the invisible God" (Col. 1, 15), and "No one hath seen God at any time." If any one should urge that the Only Begotten, though an image of the invisible God, might himself be material, there is the text, "No one knoweth the Father but the Son and the Son but the Father." The relations between Father and Son are shown here to consist in the power of thought (*per virtutem scientiae, non per visibilitatis fragilitatem*). The word 'know' instead of 'see' is chosen in order to show that immaterial, not material, natures are in question.

(9) The text, "Blessed are the pure in heart for they shall see God" (Matt. 5, 8), only strengthens the position, since it is not physical sight but intellectual vision which is meant.[94]

In all this, system and development are due to Origen, but the multiplication of texts and the addition of arguments only substantiate Clement's main ideas, namely that God is immaterial intellectual reality . . . .

An important undercurrent in Origen's development of the idea of God is his opposition both to the supporters of a biblical anthropomorphism and to those theological materialists who stood for a Christian Stoicism rather than for a Christian Platonism.[95] Similar polemic is to be found in Clement's work.

Anthropomorphism was a particularly difficult problem, for it was one of the chief objections raised against Christianity by philosophers[96] but was strongly supported by a large number of pious and simple believers in the church. In their view the authority of Scripturee involved the acceptance of its plain sense, so that when the Bible refers to God's hands and feet and eyes and to his throne and footstool, they regarded these terms as literal descriptions of the being of God, arguing from Gen. 1, 26 that as man was made in the image of God, the divine Creator must closely resemble the noblest of his creatures.[97] So extreme a position was apparently not encouraged by theologians of the church, but there is evidence to show that it was common among the uninstructed.[98]

As a Platonist Clement found such crudities intolerable, and he rejects them summarily. Even though the Bible appears to ascribe human characteristics to the Godhead it must not be so understood. Beneath the words which to the ignorant suggest such impieties, lie hidden meanings consistent with the true philosophic doctrine of God's nature.[99]

An example of this, adapted from Aristobulus, is given from the story of God's appearance on Mt. Sinai. The truth which this story presents in allegorical form is the coming into the world of the divine power which pervades the universe and proclaims the inaccessible light. The enormous multitude and the size of their encampment about Sinai indicate that God's presence is not confined to one locality, for he is everywhere.[100] . . .

For Clement the imitation of God is essentially intellectual; the truth of Gen. 1, 26 is realized when the mind of man has become the clear reflection of the divine Logos.[101] It is true that this reflection is visible in behavior as well as in thought,[102] but it is not fundamentally a matter of behavior or even of moral motive, but proceeds from man's natural capacity to become divine and so to be like God. Philo, however, distinguishes in this connection between the transcendent God and the intelligible Logos, and says that only the latter can be imitated by man,[103] and Clement would have agreed to this qualification. Man becomes like God when he enters into the divine life by the presence of the Logos in his own reason.[104] Unlike Philo, Clement has in Jesus Christ a living example of man's power to resemble God, and can encourage his gnostic to become by contemplation and moral effort that which Christ was by nature.[105]

Against Stoic materialism Clement raises an uncompromising front.[106] Much that he says of the incompatibility of this philosophy with the true concenption of God's nature had been said before by the apologists, but he sees the issues involved more clearly than they, and his more consistent Platonism gives an added point to his remarks. He does not develop his antagonism into a systematic polemic like Origen's, but the seeds are present of the conflict which in the next generation made forever impossible the union of Stoic physics and Christian theology.

One instance will suffice to show the effect of Clement's Platonic theology on his religion, for in his doctrine of prayer the religious implications of his immaterialist philosophy clearly appear. The essence of prayer he believes not to lie in external acts, or even in petitions for good of any kind, but rather to be a special aspect of that perfect companionship with God which is realized in the life of the Christian gnostic. Ritual and petitionary prayers are too limited in their application to be satisfactory, and tend, by their emphasis on the time and place of worship and the specific objects desired, to misrepresent the true nature of God and the character of his providence. Since God needs nothing, being absolutely sufficient, and since he is everywhere, the only prayer which is worthy of him is a quality of life which penetrates all thought, feeling, and behavior, endowing it with a divine purpose and directing its every motion towards God.

> Wherefore it is neither in a definite place or special shrine, nor yet at certain feasts and days set apart that the gnostic honors God, returning thanks to him for knowledge bestowed and the gifts of the (heavenly) citizenship; but he will do this all his life in every place, whether he be alone by himself or have with him some who share his belief.[107] And if the presence of some good man always moulds for the better one who converses with him, by reason of the respect and reverence which he inspires, with much more reason must he who is always in the uninterrupted presence of God by means of his knowledge and his life and his thankful spirit be raised above himself on every occasion, both in regard to his actions and his words and his temper. Such is he who believes that God is everywhere present, and does not suppose him to be shut up in definite places, so as to be tempted to incontinence by the imagination, forsooth, that he could ever be apart from God whether by day or night. Accordingly all our life is a festival; being persuaded that God is everywhere present on all sides, we praise Him as we till the ground, we sing hymns as we sail the sea, we feel this inspiration in all that we do. And the gnostic enjoys a still closer intimacy with God, being at once serious and cheerful in everything, serious because his thoughts are turned towards heaven, and cheerful as he reckons up the blessings with which God has enriched our human life.[108]

The gnostic's life is thus a continuous prayer and thanksgiving, not only when he turns his thoughts to transcendent realities, but even in the common tasks of daily routine.

Nevertheless it is in contemplation that the ultimate significance of prayer is realized. Although Clement is always careful to indicate the practical consequences of his mysticism, and to show that the life of God is revealed no less in simple duty than in rapt ecstasy, he must in the end explain the lower by the higher and so resort to that closest contact of mind with Mind in which the human experience of God culminates.

> Every place then and every time at which we entertain the thought of God is truly hallowed; but when he who is at once right-minded and thankful makes his request in prayer, he in a way contributes to the granting of his petition, receiving with joy the desired object through the instrumentality of his prayer. For when the Giver of all good meets with readiness on our part, all good things follow at once on the mere conception in the mind. Certainly prayer is a test of the attitude of the character towards what is fitting. And if voice and speech are given to us with a view to understanding, how can God help hearing the soul and the mind by itself, seeing that soul already apprehends soul, and mind apprehends mind. Wherefore God has no need to learn various tongues, as human interpreters have, but understands at once the minds of all men, and what the voice signifies to us, that our thought utters to God, since even before the creation he knew that it would come into our mind. It is permitted to man therefore to speed his prayer even without a voice, if he only concentrates all his spiritual energy upon the inner voice of the mind by his undistracted turning to God.[109]

With all this Clement does not deny the legitimacy of corporate worship or the desirability of praying with set objects in view. He accepts these data of religious life, desiring only to interpret them in the light of what he believes to be the true theology. Behind the acts of ritual must lie the persistent effort of the soul to abandon the sensible world for the world of intellectual reality, where it may contemplate God with direct vision; and in setting fixed hours for prayer, it must not be forgotten that all life is a prayerful effort toward fellowship with God. The example of Jesus shows the desirability of praying with specific intentions,[110] but this must not be thought to imply that God is ignorant of our needs or requires encouragement for his benevolence. The essence of this kind of prayer is that it fixes the mind on objects the qualities of which are transmitted in contemplation to the soul of the believer. Prayer is thus a matter of grave importance in the formation of character, since it exposes the most sensitive portions of the soul to influences which determine its ultimate quality and its permanent relations with God. When the objects of prayer are good, their excellence is gradually assimilated into the habits of the supplicant and eventually become an integral part of his nature, but when they are bad, havoc is wrought in the soul.[111] The prayer of the Christian gnostic is directed toward a more complete knowledge of God, and results in a fuller participation in the divine life. This participation . . . does not produce quiescence, for divine Reality is instinct with the inexhaustible energy of infinite love, and this energy is communicated without diminution to all those who share in the vision of truth. The measure of participation, and therefore of communicated energy, depends on the capacity of the worshipper, and as he advances along the path of

perfection, he constantly grows in both the knowledge and the power of God.[112]

The importance of Clement's idea of God may be estimated from the point of view either of its originality or of its influence on posterity, and a sound judgment of his achievement must take account of both these factors. It may be paradoxical to claim a high degree of originality for a doctrine which has been shown to consist very largely of fragments of Greek philosophy combined with some of the traditional elements of ancient Catholic Christianity. It is nevertheless true that Clement's dependence on previous thought is only a necessary condition of his work, which, so far from detracting from its merit, accentuates it by revealing some of its main difficulties.[113] In a comparison of Clement's theology with that of his predecessors, what is remarkable is not only his superior understanding of philosophy, but also his profound appreciation of the peculiar genius of Christianity. Clement is an eclectic in all his thinking,[114] but his eclecticism is guided by a fine instinct for religious as well as intellectual values, and he is drawn irresistibly to the original sources of inspiration. Among the philosophers it is Plato whom he knows best and from whose thought and writing he most frequently borrows.[115] Of Christian literature he is most at home in the New Testament,[116] and he has a broader appreciation of Paul and John than any of his predecessors.[117] With all this he has a sense of what is logically possible, and makes a real effort to unite within a single system the carefully wrought ideas of philosophy and the spontaneous notions of religion. The result is a real philosophy of religion, controlled by the ontological and epistemological premises of Platonism, but also inspired by the less formal mysticism of early Christians like Paul and John.

If Clement's combinations of philosophy and tradition are more satisfactory than many current in his time, it is because he was able to see the affinities between the authors whom he used. By adopting the allegorical method of exegesis he was dispensed from taking into account many of the Jewish elements in Christianity that were fundamentally irreconcilable with his view of ultimate reality, and he could thus concentrate his attention on aspects of Pauline and Johannine thought which could easily be harmonized with his own system and made to enrich it. A modern critic would undoubtedly quarrel with his assumption that all that was valuable in Platonism was implied in the New Testament, yet it must be admitted that apart from formal expression there are real affinities between Paul, John, and Plato which Clement was the first to see and to make use of.[118] Of these related elements, which were due to a common experience of religion, a common conception of its functions, and a similar estimate of life as a whole, Platonism offered a possible philosophic interpretation, and Clement was the first to take full advantage of the offer.[119] In doing so he became the founder of Christian Platonism and the father of Christian intellectual mysticism.

In making this claim it is necessary to stop for a moment and ask what distinguishes Christian Platonism from its two parents, and particularly in what way its idea of God differs from traditional Christian conceptions and from the thought of Platonists who were not influenced by Christianity. It is easy to see what Platonism brought into the partnership, for it supplied Christianity with an immaterialist philosophy that sustained and clarified its finest moral and religious aspirations, interpreting them in the light of a general view of the universe. Christianity's contribution was more subtle, and consisted fundamentally in a modification and extended application of the Platonic conception of divine love. Dean Inge believes the difference between Neoplatonic and Christian philosophy to be concentrated in the doctrine of the incarnation,[120] but this doctrine is only an instance of a general tendency, in which the influence of Pauline and Johannine mysticism is apparent, the tendency to make the divine love real and concrete in the lives of all sorts and conditions of men.

In non-christian circles the difficulty in which philosophic religion, then as always, was involved was conflict with popular religion. It was clear to the philosophers that current notions of the gods were altogether inconsistent with the perfection of the divine nature, but it was no less plain to the mass of believers that their primitive theology was adequate to their needs, so that while religion persisted among the masses and was cultivated by philosophers, it took two different and scarcely related forms.[121] . . . But in the church Christian Platonism succeeded in bridging a similar gap between the religion of uninstructed and educated men, and in bringing home to the simple believer and to the theologian the perception that what united them was a common bond of divine knowledge and love, which expressed and communicated itself in different ways but proceeded ultimately from the same source.

Clement's influence on posterity is difficult to estimate, for it was for the most part indirect. He was apparently little read throughout the Middle Ages, and it was not until the sixteenth century that interest in his writings revived.[122] Grabmann attributes his lack of popularity to the fact that his works were early put on the Index,[123] but a deeper reason is the difficulty to minds trained in systematic theology offered by the peculiar discipline required for understanding Clement's thought and by the mazes of careless writing through which his winding ideas have to be followed. Catholic theology has in the main shown sharp outlines, easily reflected from the thinker's mind to the poet's imagination, lightly transferred from the scholar's page to the artist's canvas; and to such sharp outlines Clement's mystical spirit was opposed. To be understood by many, Clement from the first needed interpretation, and this interpretation was the task of Origen.

It is singular that the difference between these two men, who had so much in common, should be so great. Though both were philosophic theologians, theology for Clement was only the direct way to the vision of truth, while with Origen it entered upon a new stage as a science *suo jure* possessing a method and rationale of its own. The

systematizing genius of Origen profoundly affected the way in which he reproduced Clement's thought. Clement's ideas can be recognized in many of Origen's pages, but the image is not absolutely true; the medium of reflection has contributed too much for perfect accuracy . . . .

In this treatise Origen maintains with Clement that the principal benefit of prayer is communion with God,[124] that petitionary prayer for earthly goods is inappropriate, since the true Christian accepts all life as God's gift,[125] and that prayer in the best sense is a fixed habit of mind giving a single direction to all behavior.[126] With Clement also he insists that love and charity are the best preparation for prayer,[127] that its most precious result is the divine power communicated from God to man in moments of contemplation and ecstasy,[128] and that those are in error who say that since God's will is fixed and the order of nature unchangeable, prayer is therefore superfluous.[129] What is not to be found in Clement is anything corresponding to Origen's . . . his careful exegesis of the Lord's prayer,[130] his long discussion of the times for prayer and the postures appropriate to it,[131] and his classification of prayers into four types based on 1 Tim. *2, 1*.[132] Here Origen is the systematic theologian finishing and retouching Clement's bold, free sketch.

The motive of Clement's theology is an irresistible impulse to seek God in every aspect of experience and to recognize his presence and love in that unity of goodness which embraces all things. Origen, on the other hand, in the *De principiis* explains his conception of his task by pointing to the quarrels of his contemporaries and affirming the necessity for a definition of the faith which will take due account of the functions of revelation and rational inquiry: *"propter hoc necessarium videtur prius de his singulis certam lineam manifestamque reguiam ponere, tum deinde etiam de ceteris quaerere."*[133] The bloom of Clement's enthusiasm tends to wither in this pedantic atmosphere of the schoolroom, and the divine unity of all thought, to him so certain, seems broken by this *certa linea manifestaque regula* within which Origen would confine the mysteries of revelation; yet it must be admitted that without some such modification, Clement's philosophic conception of God would never have found a place in official Christian theology. Not only did Origen's influence and prestige give Clement's doctrine a currency otherwise unattainable, but his adaptation of the doctrine to the nascent scholastic system made possible its survival within the church. Henceforward Christian Platonism with its idea of God as an immaterial, intellectual substance, its characteristic piety, and its fine mysticism was a permanent element in Christian theology, exercising a refining influence which neither the crushing weight of traditional conservatism nor the disintegrating forces of speculative radicalism have succeeded in destroying.[134] In the century which followed Origen's death his teachings became the centre of a storm of theological debate, the echoes of which were heard even in the anathemas of mediaeval councils. Many of his views, such as the periodic conflagration of the world and the impossibility of the fleshly resurrection, were condemned, but his belief about the divine nature emerged triumphant. While the anthropomorphists fought earnestly against the banishment of their material God whose piercing gaze no act of theirs escaped, whose throne was the heavens, and upon whose glorious form their eyes would one day be permitted to rest, the Christian doctrine of God was becoming inextricably involved in a trinitarian theory, the substance and form of which would have been impossible but for Clement and Origen, whose immaterialist teaching it presupposed. In the East Athanasius and Eusebius of Nicomedia represent divergent tendencies within the Origenist school, while in the West the thought of Augustine followed paths suggested by classical Neoplatonist works which drew their inspiration from Alexandrine sources. Even in the Scholastic period, when the philosophy of Aristotle gave new directions to Christian theology, the doctrine of God did not lose the Platonic stamp first deeply impressed upon it by Clement of Alexandria.[135]

Notes

1. Cf. Plato, Sophist, pp. 246-247. Aristotle used this distinction as a principle of classification of the philosophers who went before him. Cf. De anima, 404b, 30-405a, 7 (Simplicius, Comm. pp. 30-31), Meta. A, 7-8, p. 988; he was followed in this by the later doxographers, e.g. Galen, Hist. Phil. 14 (Diels, Dox. Graeci, 608, 18).

2. Timaeus, pp. 27D-28A

3. Timaeus, p. 92C.

4. 'Unreal' but not 'non-existent', cf. Zeller, Phil. der Griechen, 4te Aufl. iii. 1, pp. 89, n. 1, 119, 125.

5. Cf. Hans Leisegang, Der heilige Geist, i. Berlin, 1919.

6. *[Asōmatos]* came to be the catchword of Platonic metaphysics. A history of the word and the ideas lying behind it is much needed. Something of its importance can be seen from the following passages: Plato, Soph. pp. 246-257; Polit. 286A; Phileb. 64B; Phaedo 85E; Aristotle, De anima 404b, 30-405a, 7; 405a, 7; 405a, 27; 405b, 11; 409b, 21; Meta. A, 7,988a, 25; A, 8, 988b, 25; De gen. et corr. 5, 320a, 30; Topica vi. 12, 149b, 1; Nat. Auscult. iv, 1, 209a, 16; idem iv. 4, 212a, 16; idem iv. 4, 212a, 12; idem iv, 8, 215b, 5, 10; Plutarch, Moralia, pp. 1073e, 424e, 424e, 926a-b, 718 f., 1014b-c, 1029d, 1085c, 894c, 602f, 905b, 1074a-c, 1073e, 1080-1081, 960c, 1002c, 1086a, 63c; Vitae, Marcelluls c. 14, p. 305e; Seneca, Ad Helviam viii, 3; Epistulae 90. 29; 89. 16; 58. 11-15; Cicero de nat. deor. 1, 12, 30; Diels, Doxographi Graeci, pp. 606 6, 13.12, 615, 387.10, 409.26, 308, 288, 449, 395, 608.18, 305, 460.27.

7. Schmekel, Philosophie der mittleren Stoa, pp. 353 ff.

8. The question of Posidonius's influence has been much discussed. Cf. K. Gronau. Poseidonius und die jüdisch-christliche Genesis-exegese (1914); K. Reinhardt, Poseidonios, Munich, 1921.

9. The figure of Ammonius Saccas remains in the same obscurity as that of Pantaenus. The relations of Clement to Pantaenus were similar to those of Plotinus to Ammonius. Origen is supposed to have been a pupil of Ammonius; cf. Zeller, Kleine Schriften, ii. pp. 91 ff.

10. Cf. Euseb., Praep. ev. ix. 7; xi. 9-10; Nemesius, De natura humana ii.

11. Cf. Bardenhewer, Geschichte der altkirchl. Literatur, II. 2te Aufl. 1914, pp. 43 ff.

12. The loss of the prefaces to Strom. Bk. i. prevents us from knowing exactly his intentions when he began to write it. How difficult he found it to stop can be seen from Protrept. xii, 123 . . . .

13. Clement's treatment of paganism may be compared in this respect with Irenaeus's treatment of Gnosticism.

14. Protrept. ii. 24.

15. Protrept. ii. 26 . . . .

16. The reference is to a famous incident recorded in Plutarch's Alcibiades 19 . . . .

17. Protrept. ii. 12, 1.

18. On the place which these deities held in the world to which Clement addressed his writings, cf. J. Geffcken, Der Ausgang des griechisch-römischen Heidentums, Heidelberg, 1920, chaps. 1-2.

19. Protrept. v-viii . . . .

20. Plato, Epist. ii. p. 312 E.

21. . . . cf. Exc. ex. Theod. § 17, von Arnim, Fragm. vet. Stoic. ii. 145, 151. Cornutus, De nat. deor. c. 3. Zeller, Phil. der Griech. 4te Aufl. iii. 1, p. 129.

22. Protrept. vi. 72, 4-5.

23. . . . Protrept. viii. 77, 1; cf. Paed. i. 3, 9.

24. Protrept. viii. 77, 1.

25. Protrept. xi. 117.

26. The definition of piety is given in Protrept. ix. 86, 2 . . . .

27. Protrept. xi. 116, 1.

28. Protrept. x. 99, 4.

29. Protrept. x. 100, 2; 103, 4; xi, 113, 3; 114, 1; ii. 23, 1; ii. 10, 3; v. 65, 4.

30. Protrept. i. 9, 5; ix. 85, 1; x. 95, 2-3; i. 8, 3; cf. Paed. i. 4, 10, 1.

31. Protrept. i. 4, 3; x. 92, 2; x. 104, 3.

32. Protrept. i. 6, 3; i. 8, 1; i. 8, 3; x. 95, 1.

33. The metaphor of the physician was a favorite one with Clement as with the Stoics: Protrept. x. 91, 3; cf. Paed. i. 2, 6, 1; i. 1, 3, 1-3.

34. Protrept. i. 8, 2; i. 8, 3; ix. 87, 3; x. 95, 1-2; Ecl. proph. 9, 1-3; 20, 4; Strom. ii. 7.

35. This aspect of Clement's idea of faith appears clearly in Protrept. x. 95, 3.

36. Clement's idea of truth can be studied in the following passages: Protrept. i. 2, 1-2; i. 4, 2; i. 6, 2-3; ii. 10, 1; ii. 12, 1; ii. 24, 2; vi. 68, 2; vi. 69, 1; vi. 71, 1; vii. 74-77; viii. 77, 1; viii. 80, 4; ix. 85, 3; x. 89, 2; x. 95, 2; x. 109, 1; xi. 114, 3; xii. 121, 3.

37. Clement, like Jesus and unlike most Christian thinkers in the interval, held that salvation was open to all but achieved by few. This type of pessimism held no implications unfavorable either to the justice or to the mercy of God; cf. Exc. ex Theod. 27, 4-7.

38. Protrept. xi. 116, 1.

39. Protrept. ix. 85, 3.

40. Protrept. i. 6, 3.

41. Protrept. ii. 27, 2.

42. Protrept. ix. 82, 2.

43. The classic example of this is in the Apostles' Creed.

44. Protrept. i. 6, 1; viii. 82, 2; x. 89, 2; x. 91, 3; x. 94, 1; x. 95, 2; x. 99, 3; xi. 113-114; xi. 115, 4; xii. 123, 1; Paed. i. 5, 21, 2. Clement does not hesitate to attribute maternal as well as paternal care to God; Protrept. x. 91, 3; Quis dives salv. 37 . . . .

45. The care of the Logos is said to be paternal . . . . Protrept. x. 95, 2.

46. Ibid.

47. Protrept. xii. 122, 4-123, 1.

48. Cf. Strom. iv. 6, 27, 2 . . . .

49. Cf. Protrept. x. 89, 2, ii. 25, 2.

50. Conversion is, strictly speaking, a return to sonship, the resumption of a previous relation temporarily severed; cf. Protrept. ii. 27, 2-3; i. 6, 4; ii. 25, 3; x. 91, 3; 92, 2.

51. Cf. Protrept. i. 5, 2-4; i. 6, 4; ii. 25, 3 . . . .

52. Protrept. ix. 88, 2-3; cf. i. 6, 3; i. 8, 3; iv. 56, 2.

53. This difficulty, which is common to all Christian Platonists, was made easier by the pioneer work of Philo in showing how by the allegorical method of exegesis biblical verses could be given a meaning appropriate to any theological context. On Clement's indebtedness to Philo in this respect, see C. Siegfried, Philo v. Alex. als Ausleger des Alten Testaments, Jena, 1875, pp. 343-351, and Stählin's notes passim.

54. Protrept. ix. 88, 1.

55. Protrept. ii. 23, 1; ii. 25, 2; iv. 51, 6; iv. 63, 3; vi. 68, 3; iv. 69, 1-3; vi. 71, 1; cf. i. 7, 3.

56. Philosophy of Plotinus, i. p. 132. A striking example of this in Clement is Ecl. proph. 25, 3.

57. Epist. moral. 95, 65.

58. Paed. i. 2, 5, 1 . . . .

59. . . . It is intersting to find in Clement this term 'sick soul' which has had such vogue among psychologists of religion since James's Varieties of Religious Experience; cf. Eclog. proph. 11, 2. In Strom. i. 7, 3 there is a reference to healthy-mindedness.

60. Paed. i. 2, 4, 2-3.

61. Zeller, Gesch. der Phil., 4te Aufl. iii. 1. pp. 254 ff.

62. Ibid., pp. 259-260; Strom. vii. 2, 7, 4-5.

63. Paed. i. 2, 4, 1-2.

64. Paed. i. 2, 4, 3.

65. Paed. i. 3, 7, 1-2.

66. Paed. i. 3, 9, 3.

67. Paed. i. 6, 31, 2; i. 6, 52, 2 . . . .

68. Cf. Harnack, Die Terminologie der Wiedergeburt und verwandter Erlebnisse in der ältesten Kirche (T. U. xlii), pp. 127-128.

69. Cf. C. Gore, Dissertations, pp. 113-114 . . . .

70. Whether this was a legitimate criticism of the Valentinian position is another question . . . .

71. Paed. i. 6, 28, 3-5.

72. Paed. i. 6, 29 . . . .

73. Paed. i, 8, 66, 5 ff.

74. Paed. i. 8, 64, 3.

75. Paed. i. 8, 62-65.

76. Paed. i. 8, 63, 1.

77. Paed. i. 8, 70, 1.

78. Paed. i. 8, 70, 3.

79. In Clement's view God is above taking personal offence, partly because he is essentially above the category of personality. Neither Jehovah's outbursts of fury nor that colder resentment which Anselm conceived to be God's response to man's violation of his honor is consistent with Clement's conception of the divine nature.

80. Paed. i. 8, 68, 3.

81. Paed. i. 8, 74, 4, cf. 62, 2 . . . .

82. Strom. i. 1.

83. Strom. iv. 2, 4, 1 ff.

84. This is clear from Strom. vi. 12 and vi. 14, 109, 1-2 . . . .

85. Clement sees a similar difficulty in the system of Basilides (Strom. ii. 3), but is unable to escape entirely from sharing it.

86. This thesis is developed, Strom. iv. 21-23; cf. especially iv. 21, 130, 1 ff.; iv. 23, 150, 2 ff . . . .

87. Strom. i. 1, 18.

88. Strom. 1, 2.

89. Philosophy of Plotinus, 2d ed., ii, p. 111.

90. Cf. Strom. iv. 25, 156, 1-2 . . . .

91. Cf. Comm. on John xiii, 21, ed. Preuschen, p. 244.

92. Cf. Origin, Comm. on John i, 26, ed. Preuschen, p. 31 . . . . Cf. Origen, Comm. on John xiii, 22, p. 246.

93. For the view which Origen combats, cf. Tertullian, De baptismo 4.

94. Cf. Clem. Alex., Strom. v. 1, 7.

95. It is the latter that is prominent in the De principiis; cf. Comm. on John xiii, 21; Contra Cels. vi. 70-71; iii. 47; Comm. on Rom. iii, 1, ed. Lommatzsch, pp. 168-171 (cf. Harnack, Der kirchengeschichtliche Ertrag der exegetischen Arbeiten des Origenes (T. U. xlii), pp. 93-94); for the former cf. Sel. in Genesim on Gen. 1, 26, Migne P. G. xii. 93-95; Hom. in Gen. i. 13-15, ed. Baehrens, pp. 15-19; iii. 1 ff., pp. 39 ff.; Contra Cels. vii. 27; iv. 5, may have been based on popular Christian ideas (Loofs, Dogmengeschichte, 4te Aufl., p. 125, n. 1).

96. Origen, Contra Cels. vii. 27 and 36 ff . . . .

97. Anthropomorphism of this kind was current at the time of Celsus (177-178 A.D.), who took it to be common Christian belief (loc. cit.). It must have been known to Irenaeus (Adv. haer. ii. 13, 3-4), who treats it with his usual caution, and to Tertullian, who made dangerous concessions to it. The first whom we know to have defended this position was Melito (Origen, Selecta in Gen. 1, 26; Jerome, De viris illustr. c. 24; Gennadius, De dogm. eccles. c. 4; cf. Harnack, Überlieferung der griechischen Apologeten (T. U. i), pp. 243 ff.), and the first to conduct a sustained attack upon it was Origen, although Clement also condemned it in strong terms. Anthropomorphism became a menance in the 4th century. The Egyptian monks found Origen's immaterialism one of the most objectionable parts of his teaching. Socrates relates an amusing incident about Theophilus of Alexandria. A mob of fanatical ascetics stormed his residence, threatening his life because he maintained that God was immaterial and man not made in God's physical image. The tactful bishop found no difficulty in condemning Origen, and dodged the theological issue by a graceful compliment . . . . The incident is significant in showing that among the educated clergy the influence of Origen's immaterialism was paramount. Socr. H. E. vi. 7, Migne P. G. 67, 684; cf. Epiphan., Haer. 70; Aug., Conf. vi. 3; Aug., Epist. cxix; cf. Harnack, Dogmengesch., 4te Aufl., ii. p. 122, n. 2.

98. Harnack, Dogmengesch., 4te Aufl., ii. p. 122, n. 2.

99. Strom. vi. 16, 136, 3; v. 11, 71, 4-5; ii. 16, 72, 1-3; ii. 19, 102, 6.

100. Strom. vi. 3, 32, 3-34, 3 . . . .

101. Strom. ii. 19, 102, 6; cf. Paed. iii, 1, 1, 5; Protrept. x. 98, 3; xii. 121, 1.

102. Strom. ii. 19, 102, 2.

103. Euseb., Praep. evang. vii. 1, ed. Gifford iii. p. 349. Abrahams, Studies, ii. p. 158.

104. Strom. ii. 19, 97, 1. . . cf. Protrept. iv. 59, 2-3; Paed. i. 3, 9. 1-2.

105. Paed. i. 12, 98, 1 ff.

106. Strom. i. 11, 51, 1 . . . . Cf. Protrept. v. 66, 3; Strom. vii. 7, 37, 1-2; Cf. Mayor and Hort, Clement of Alexandria, Book VII of the Stromateis, pp. 254-255. My exposition of Clement's doctrine of prayer is based chiefly on Stromateis vii. 7. I have therefore omitted references to special points except in the case of quotations.

107. Cf. Strom. vii. 5, 29, 3-8: "And if the word holy is taken in two senses, as applied to God himself and also to the building raised in his honor, surely we should be right in giving to the church, which was instituted to the honor of God in accordance with sanctified wisdom, the name of a holy temple of God, that precious temple built by no mechanic art, nay, not embellished even by an angel's hand, but made into a shrine by the will of God himself. I use the name of the church now not of the place but of the congregation of saints. This is the shrine that is best fitted for the reception of the greatness of the dignity of God. For to Him who is all-worthy, or rather in comparison with whom all else is worthless, there is consecrated that creature which is of great worth owing to its pre-eminent holiness. And such would be the gnostic who is of great worth and precious in the sight of God, he in whom God is enshrined, i.e., in whom the knowledge of God is consecrated. Here too we should find the likeness. . . the divine and sanctified image . . . —here in the righteous soul, after it has been itself blessed as having been already purified and now performing blessed deeds. Here we find both that which is enshrined and that which is in process of enshrinement, the former in the case of those who are already gnostics, the latter in those who are capable of becoming so, though they may not yet be worthy to receive the knowledge of God. For all that is destined to believe is already faithful in the eye of God and consecrated to honor, an image of virtue dedicated to God."

108. Strom. vii. 7, 35, 3-7.

109. Strom. vii. 7, 43, 1-5.

110. "Yet the petition is not superfluous, even though good things be granted without petition made. For instance, thanksgiving and prayer for the conversion of his neighbors are the duty of the gnostic. Thus the Lord also prayed, returning thanks for the 'accomplishment' of his ministry and praying that 'as many as possible might share in knowledge' in order that God 'who alone is good,' alone is the Saviour, 'may be glorified through his Son' in those who are being saved through the salvation which is according to knowledge, and that the knowledge of him may grow from age to age. Howbeit the mere faith that one will receive is itself also a kind of prayer stored up in a gnostic spirit." Strom. vii. 7, 41, 6-8.

111. Strom. vii. 7, 38, 1 f. and 7,34 f.

112. Cf. Strom. vii. 3, 13, 1 ff.: "As to the rest I keep silent, giving glory to God: only I say that these

gnostic souls are so carried away by the magnificence of the vision . . . that they cannot confine themselves within the lines of the constitution by which each holy degree is assigned and in accordance with which the blessed abodes of the gods have been marked out and allotted; but being counted as 'holy among the holy' and translated absolutely and entirely to another sphere, they keep on always moving to higher and yet higher regions, until they no longer greet the divine vision in, or by means of, mirrors, but with loving hearts feast forever on the uncloying never-ending sight, radiant in its transparent clearness, while throughout the endless ages they taste a never-wearying delight and thus continue, all alike honored with an identity of pre-eminence. This is the apprehensive 'vision of the pure in heart.' This, therefore, is the life-work of the perfected gnostic, viz., to hold communion with God through the great High Priest, being made like the Lord; as far as may be . . . by means of all his service towards God, a service which extends to the salvation of men by his solicitous goodness towards us, and also by public worship and by teaching and by active kindness. Aye, and in being thus assimilated to God . . . the gnostic is making and fashioning himself and also forming those who hear him, while, so far as may be, he assimilates to that which is by nature free from passion that which has been subdued by training to a passionless state: and this he effects by 'undisturbed intercourse' and communion 'with the Lord.' Of this gnostic assimilation the canons, as it appears to me, are gentleness, kindness, and a noble devoutness." Cf. Strom. vi. 12, 102, 1 ff.

113. Christian philosophy can never be wholly free from the restraint of Christian history and tradition, and is in constant danger either of breaking too definitely with them, as the Gnostics did, or of allowing itself to be oppressively bound by them. Some of these difficulties are made admirably clear by Lebreton, 'Le désaccord de la foi populaire et de la théologie savante dans l'Église chrétienne du IIIe siècle, Revue d'histoire ecclésiastique, 1923, pp. 481 ff., 1924, pp. 5 ff.; and Batiffol, Primitive Catholicism, pp. 246 ff.

114. Cf. Strom. i. 7, 37, 6 and de Faye's comment, Clément d'Alexandrie, Paris, 1906, pp. 153-154.

115. A brief study of Stählin's critical notes shows this. I have verified a considerable number of Clement's quotations from Plato, and have found that he quotes with that same facile inaccuracy that characterizes his use of the New Testament, though in occasional instances a real difference in text is possible.

116. It must be remembered that whereas in the exegesis of the Old Testament Clement is sometimes dependent on Philo, in the New he is often breaking fresh ground.

117. This seems to me certain, though the proof would require a long discussion. In spite of the beautiful rendering of 1 Cor. 13 in I Clem. 49-50 and oc-casional passages in Ignatius and Hermas, Paul's mysticism was as little understood as his theory of justification. In Irenaeus he receives more attention, but Irenaeus is no mystic, and uses Paul chiefly to support his "physische Erlösungslehre" (Loofs, Leitfaden, 4te Aufl., pp. 146 ff.). John fared even worse. A measure of the popular understanding of his gospel can be taken from the Epistola Apostolorum; Irenaeus understands him no better than Paul, and Ignatius turned John's thought into an emotional, not an intellectual, mysticism. Of Justin, who is probably nearest to Clement in his conception of Christianity, it cannot be certain that he knew the Fourth Gospel.

118. The following passages illustrate this, though of course it is not maintained that Clement gives the correct exegesis in each case: Protrept. ix. 84, 6-85, 1; ix. 88, 2-3; x. 92, 4-93, 1; x. 98, 3; x. 100, 4; 101, 2; xi. 112, 2-113, 1; xi. 115, 4-5; Paed. ii. 1, 5-6; iii. 1, 2-3; Strom. ii. 4, 12, 1; vi. 13, 107, 3-14; 108, 5; vi. 12, 102, 1-2; i. 1, 4, 1-4; i. 1, 7, 1-4; i. 5, 32, 4; i. 8, 41, 6-42, 4; i. 9, 45, 1-6; i. 11, 53, 4-54, 4; ii. 5, 21, 1; ii. 5, 22, 5-8; ii. 22, 136, 1-6; iv. 7, 42, 3; vii. 2, 9, 4-11, 3; vii. 3, 16, 6; vii. 7, 46, 3; iv. 18, 111, 1-4; iv. 7, 52; iv. 21, 132-133.

119. For instance, Clement's insistence that the value of salvation is inherent and absolute; Strom. iv. 6, 29, 3-4 and iv. 22, 136-138; iv. 23, 147, 4 ff.

120. Philosophy of Plotinus, 2d ed., ii. pp. 206-209 . . . .

121. Cf. S. Dill, Roman Society from Nero to Marcus Aurelius, pp. 289-626; J. Geffcken, Der Ausgang des griechisch-römischen Heidentums, Heidelberg, 1920, pp. 4-89 . . . .

122. Early mentions of Clement given by Stählin, i. pp. ix-xvi. The first printed edition of Clement's work was a product of the revival of patristic learning inspired by Marcellus Cervinus, librarian of the Vactican and later Pope Marcellus II. Petrus Victorius who undertook the work at Marcellus's suggestion and under Cosmo de'Medici's patronage, intimates that it was not carried through without opposition. "Haec igitur sunt, quae praesidio fuerunt optime auctori pereunti ac pene jam e manibus elapso: in quo certe ut dolendum est tam utilem gravemque scriptorem tam diulatuisse: accusandi, qui tam egregios ac fructuosos veterum labores supprimunt, ita magnopere laetandum ipsum in vitam rediisse, atque omnem impetum fortunae evasisse; amandique ac toto pectore celebrandi, qui hujuscemodi monimenta, magna superiorum hominum cura, beneficioque Deorum e tot incendiis bellorum tempestatibusque, erepta, pervulgant, et ab anni huiuscemodi iniuria in perpetuum vindicant," ed. Victorius, Florence, 1500, p. 4. On the succeeding editions of Clement's works see Stählin, i. pp. ixv ff. The question of Clement's orthodoxy was much discussed in the sixteenth century, when his name was dropped from the Roman martyrology on the recommendation of Baronius. In meeting a protest against the act Benedict XIV treated the

question of Clement's status and theological position with discretion and impartiality, though he was probably as much influenced by moderns like Petavius and Berbeirac as by Photius and Cassiodorus. In spite of this undercurrent of suspicion Clement has continued to have many admirers within the church.

123. The Index contains the following item: "Opuscula alterius Clementis Alexandrini apocrypha," which has often been taken to refer to the author of the Stromateis. That this is far from certain has been shown by Cognat, Clément d' Alexandrie, pp. 464-466, and Bigg, Christian Platonists, 2d ed., p. 317, n. 1.

124. De oratione 8.

125. Ibid., 11, 13, 19.

126. Ibid., 12.

127. Ibid., 9, 1; 11.

128. Ibid., 8, 13.

129. Ibid., 5-7. These skeptics are probably the followers of Prodicus mentioned by Clement, Strom. vii. 7, 41

. . . .

130. Ibid., 18-30.

131. Ibid., 31-32.

132. Ibid., 14, 31.

133. De principiis i, Praef. 2.

134. The influence of Christian Platonism can be seen in such studies as Inge's Christian Mysticism (Bampton Lectures), 1899, and Dom Cuthbert Butler's Western Mysticism, London, 1922.

135. Cf. Aquinas, Summa Theol. i. 3, 1-2; i. 6, 1-2; i. 89, 1; ii. 1, 4. Even in Protestant scholasticism its influence survived; cf. E. Troeltsch, Vernunft und Offenbarung, pp. 15 ff.

W. C. de Pauley (essay date 1925)

SOURCE: "The Image of God: A Study in Clement of Alexandria," in *The Church Quarterly Review*, Vol. C, April-July, 1925, pp. 96-121.

[*In the following essay, de Pauley summarizes Clement's views on God the Father and explores the difficulties involved with his use of the word "spirit" in analyzing man's psychic elements.*]

Religion, mysticism, and idealist philosophy, even when their careers have run along different roads, have always made the problem of man's relation to God a central problem; for right thinking and right living presuppose that man is aware, more or less clearly, of his place in the order of things. The Alexandrian Fathers, though acquainted with the wealth of Greek speculation, did not pass by the simple intuitive insight of the Hebrew seer who conceived this mysterious relation after the analogy of a reality and an image of it. It will be the object of this

study to describe as accurately as possible what Clement read into this metaphor. Before attempting to collect his teaching from his rambling and sometimes tedious chapters, we shall do well to remind ourselves what he thought about the Original, in whose image man was made, namely, God.

The references to the First Person of the Trinity may be said to fall into three groups: God as He is in Himself; God as He transcends His creation; and God as He is immanent in His creation.

First, like Philo his predecessor, and Plotinus his successor, both of them non-Christians, he would disentangle the Deity from all relationships with men and things. He who inhabits eternity must in His essence and existence be independent of the space and time relations of our changing world; and, by a method of analysis and elimination, Clement strips God of all the predicates of finite thinking. If we were to predicate any quality whatsoever of God, no matter how great or good, we should only be classifying Him under the categories of our own limited experience. We move in a world of life and death; we are creatures of appetite; how can we find a word in our vocabulary which may express the Unbegotten and Eternal? 'Everything that falls under a name is begotten.'[1] When we have analyzed our concept of God, and then proceeded to think away in succession each of the elements, we are left with 'God is one, and beyond the one, and above the monad itself.'[2] 'If, then, abstracting all that belongs to bodies and the properties of things, we cast ourselves into the greatness of Christ, and thence go forward through holiness into immensity, we may attain somehow to the conception of the Almighty, not knowing what He is, but what He is not . . . . The First Cause is not, then, in a place, but above place, and time, and name, and conception.'[3] God's existence cannot be demonstrated.[4] His moral nature cannot be conceived after the analogy of human virtue. If He is self-sufficient, He needs nothing; if He is aloof from our fleeting sphere, He is not subject to perturbation, and, therefore, He does not practise self-control.[5]

In the sequel, we shall see the central place assigned to the idea of man as God's image in Clement's loosely organized system of doctrine; but, at the outset, it is important to observe that God's path is in the great waters and His footsteps are not known. In contrast with Stoicism, which allows God to be lost in the world, the Scriptural teaching of God's *apartness* had to be maintained, even though it is expressed in terms of Greek thought.[6]

Considered in relation to the world, God, in the first place, is First Cause. From the nature of the case, there can be only one First Principle, and, therefore, matter is not eternal.[7] It is not quite clear whether Clement thought of creation as the ordering of a disorderly material, after the idea of Plato's doctrine in the *Timaeus*;[8] but at least he holds that matter is no evil and recalcitrant power existing independently of God. One passage suggests a creation *ex nihilo*. He asks, 'But how shall I tell what God makes?' The reply is: 'Behold the whole universe; it is His work:

and the heaven, and the sun, and angels, and men, are the works of His fingers. How great is the power of God! His bare volition was the creation of the universe. For God alone made it, because He alone is truly God. By the bare exercise of volition He creates; His mere willing was followed by the springing into being of what He willed.'[9] But whether Clement would subscribe to St. Augustine's belief on this point or not, he anticipated him in saying that the world is created not *in* time, but *with* time.[10]

As First Principle and Cause of all things, God is good, and His goodness is inseparable from His essence. 'For God did not make a beginning of being Lord and Good, being always what He is. Nor will He ever cease to do good, although He bring all things to an end.'[11] Here again he avoids the extreme immanence of Stoicism, and tells us that good does not flow from God of necessity, and apart from His willing it. Fire emits heat, because it must: God is the source of good, because He wills good.[12] This world is the best of all possible worlds, as far as its constitution and nature are concerned, and God must not be charged with the evil which we experience in it.[13] Thus while Clement almost equates sin with ignorance, he is careful to avoid that shallow optimism which would reduce evil to illusion by looking at it *sub specie aeternitatis*. There is evil in the world, and when we have agreed that it is not to be laid at the Gate of the Eternal, we shall be free to believe in God's providence. Even natural religion, when it is not warped by ungodly living, teaches God's providential rule;[14] and revealed religion goes so far as to see particular providences in special cases, wrought within the general sphere of providence.[15]

Finally, God is immanent in His creation as a whole, and more particularly in its finest flower, man, who is created in His image. 'The same One who is very far off has come very near—an unspeakable wonder. I am a God near at hand, says the Lord. He is far off in respect of essence—for how can that which is created apprehend the Uncreated?—but He is very near by His power in which all things have been embraced. Yes, the power of God is always present, laying hold of us by that power which sees, and is beneficent and disciplinary.'[16] God lives in the world as well as above it.

In passing from Clement's beliefs about God the Father to his doctrine of man, we shall do well to remember that here also philosophy and religion are inseparable if not identical and mutually inclusive. He admits that there is much bad philosophy, but he maintains that Christianity is the true philosophy. The ancients, unless when blinded by wilful ignorance and enfeebled mentally by immoral living, were able to catch some broken lights of Truth.[17] In the Christian religion, Truth in its totality is revealed, or, more exactly, it is evealed as fully as man of finite, mental capacity, limited by conditions of the body, can grasp it. Heraclitus, Anaxagoras, and the rest, often talked very excellent sense, and Plato, above all others, has much to pass on to the Christian. Philosophy, as expounded in his pages, Clement tells us, is to be treated as a nut: part of it you

eat, and part of it you throw away. The edible kernel apparently contains good psychology, for in the *Paedagogus* Clement takes over the Platonic trichotomy, with the important difference that the spirited element, which, in his model, was the natural ally of reason, is now given a psychic value on a level with the appetites. 'The irascible part, being brutal, dwells near to insanity.'[18] Apparently the Stoic model of the wise man, notorious for cultivated apathy, is preferred to the more natural, and it must be said more Christian, virtue of moral enthusiasm.

Now while it is natural for a man who has not been within the sphere of Christian influence to search for God, and with some degree of certainty to attain his quest, he can reach only that knowledge of Him which will teach him to order his life here on earth. Virtue is the ability to order the affairs of this life after that harmony which is written so large in the conscience that all who run may read; but preparation for the life to come, when the portals of death are crossed, demands a fuller revelation, the revelation of Christ, the Divine Word. 'The commandments issued with respect to natural life are published to the multitude; but those which are suited for living well, and from which eternal life springs, we have to consider, as in a sketch, as we read them out of the Scriptures.'[19] In later times St. Thomas Aquinas was faced with the same difficulty. The virtues of Platonism—justice, wisdom, courage, and temperance—could not be gainsaid: there were men of old, even outside Israel, whose counsels and lives must be given a place in the *Summa*. These cardinal virtues, therefore, Thomas assigns to *lex naturalis,* and limits their scope to the life below, and the Christian virtues of faith, hope, and love, he derives from *lex divina.* These three prepare the Christian for the immortality of the beatific vision.[20]

The Platonic trichotomy, which may be reduced to a dichotomy of rational and irrational elements, is not an exclusive model: for an eclectic thinker must needs make room for the teaching of the Stoics, to say nothing of the difficulty of harmonizing these several and partial truths with the doctrine of the soul revealed in the Old and New Dispensations. A number of questions suggest themselves. What did Clement mean by the rational soul? How does he conceive its relation to God? What connexion has it with the 'spirit' of St. Paul? Is there a sharp line of distinction between the two main soul elements, the rational and irrational, introducing a fundamental cleft into the soul's unity?

In itself, the irrational and lower soul, the part which has not 'logos,' presents no difficulty: it is similar to the vital principle which animates sub-human forms of life. The chief passages in which it is treated shew that by the irrational soul Clement understands the five senses—sight, hearing, smell, touch, and taste, which, taken together, are the basis of experience; the power of speech; the power of reproduction; the power of motion; the power of nutrition; the power of growth. All pleasure-pain and emotional reactions are within it. Clement regards these powers and functions as united and made coherent by what he calls the carnal spirit, the 'pneuma sarkikon or somatikon.'[21]

The rational soul, or mind ('nous'), is the ruling, 'hegemonic,' faculty; by it we reason, and exercise the powers of choice, investigation, study, knowledge and judgement. It is a ruling faculty, because it is adapted to rule the desires and emotions. In one passage the ruling faculty is distinguished from a spiritual principle, which is communicated to man at his creation, and said to be quite distinct from the manifestation of activity on the part of the Holy Spirit in a Christian;[22] whereas, in another passage the two are identified, namely, 'the intellectual or spiritual faculty, the "dianoetic" or "pneumatic," or whatever you choose to call it.'[23] The possession of this rational soul, whose essence is purer than that of the animals, raises man above all other forms of animate life, in that it endows him with the capacity to know God, and invests him with the quality of being valuable in himself as an end, and not simply as a mere means to something outside himself.[24] As a merely irrational creature, man is said to be earth-born: as rational, he is a heavenly plant.[25]

Now although this soul-complex of irrational and rational elements is a union of diverse elements, Clement believes that the two, in a very real sense, are one. Man's soul has a God-ward and a world-ward look; he has both the power to gaze at the stars and the power to search for the Principle who guides and sustains their movements. Perhaps the clearest statement is that 'spirit is joined to the soul, which is inspired by it.'[26] Man's spirit, or reason, dwells in his irrational soul, in which it is a tenant with extraordinary rights. Ideally, spirit has complete control of its psychic habitat. Thus the rational man 'rises up against the corporeal soul, putting a bit in the mouth of the irrational spirit when it breaks loose, because the flesh lusteth against the spirit.'[27] Plotinus afterwards taught that in the processions of soul from the One, the higher grades contain their emanations within them, while at the same time remaining outside them, so that in the case of man, there is always an element which does not 'come down' and mingle in sense-life. The difference here is that, in contrast with both Stoicism and Neo-Platonism, the higher and the lower elements are different in kind, and not simply in degree. The rational soul is in essence higher than the irrational soul in which it takes up its abode. Nor can the rational soul be regarded as an emanation from the One, in that its essence is distinct from and inferior to the essence of God. Thus the element which constitutes man a man, as distinct from an animal and distinct from God, is something *sui generis,* not capable of a *decrescendo* or *crescendo* into anything else. So Clement tells us that 'the mercy of God is rich towards us, who are in no respect related to Him; I say either in essence or nature, or in the peculiar energy of our essence, but only in our being the work of His will.'[28] But just as the relation of man's rational soul to God is a real relation, so is its relation to his own irrational soul. The two are necessary to his earth existence. No doubt God tests us and values us after the quality of our higher nature, but His canon is rational

control of the irrational soul. 'For we men,' he tells us, 'hear the voice and see the bodily form, but the Lord searcheth the spirit, from which both speech and sight proceed. In like manner whether disease or accident befall the gnostic, ay, or even death the most terrible of all things, he continues unchanged in soul, knowing that all such things are a necessary result of creation but that, even so, they are made by the power of God a medicine of salvation.'[29] The body is animated by the irrational soul or corporeal spirit, but that spirit is under the control of the rational spirit proper. Sense impressions may be copied in the rational soul or mind, and sensations classified and interpreted there,[30] but it is in the motives of the rational soul that the source of bodily activity properly arises. Man is not constituted to react to sense stimuli; he can initiate action by the innate power of the rational soul.[31] Thus he says that the corporeal spirit, under the influence of the rational spirit, moves the body to good actions.[32] For this reason, all man's activities are placed in a relation of subordination to the rule of the rational soul.[33] If, from one point of view, as we have seen, spirit resides in the irrational soul, controlling, through it, the body, so, from another point of view, the irrational element is part of the rational. 'We . . . assert that rational and ruling power is the cause of the constitution of the living creature; also this, the irrational part, is animated, and is part of it.'[34] Strictly speaking, human activity arises in the higher element, but since it is manifested in bodily action, the Decalogue may be said to be applicable to the twofold spirits, and to issue in clean hands as well as in pure hearts.[35]

The term 'spirit' has two distinct ancestries, Greek and Hebrew, and Clement does not hesitate to confuse us by adopting both. In Stoic literature, 'spirit' is applied to any and every phase of what we should call soul activity. It is a material substance, conceived of as fire or warm air, akin to its ultimate origin, the Primal Fire or Spirit, which appears first in Greek thought in the fragments of Heraclitus, who conceives it to be the monistic principle of reality. In its different levels of manifestation, it is distinguished by what is called tension ('tonos'), which is less intense in the lower than in the higher forms. First, it is said to appear as the principle of cohesion ('hexis') in what we call inanimate matter; second, it is growth ('physis') when we see it in the stratum represented by plants; third, it is soul ('psyche') in animals; and, finally, in man it is reason ('nous'), where its peculiar tension makes him akin to the Deity. Relying on the spirit common to God and men, Cleanthes addresses God in this strain:

> Thee it is meet that mortals should invoke,
> For we thine offspring are, and sole of all
> Created things that live and move on earth
> Receive from Thee the image of the One.

Stoic psychology in this way deals with psychic elements as gradations or degrees of reality in which one and the same reality is active throughout, and attempts to keep this principle to the fore by using the term 'spirit' to cover each grade. Thus, although Stoicism makes use of reason or the ruling (hegemonic) power to mark off man's peculiar activity, the Platonic distinction between the rational and irrational elements, as differing in kind, is set aside. It is to Platonism that Clement reverts, though his terminology is Stoical, when he places the rational 'spirit' in the irrational 'spirit.' The ruling element, in Clement's view, ought to rule, because it is something *sui generis,* and more noble in essence than the 'spirit' in which it takes up its dwelling. His preference for the Platonic teaching is determined by Holy Scripture, where he learns that the Lord God breathed into man's nostrils 'the breath of life; and man became a living soul,' quite distinct in nature from the animals.[36] The Stoic might say that all things, whether inanimate, animate, or human, were images of God: Clement holds that nothing in the whole creation save man's divine soul is an image of God. He tells us that 'it were wrong for what is mortal to be made like what is immortal.'[37] Perhaps his diatribe on image-worship may suggest the reason why he could not, like St. Augustine and St. Thomas Aquinas, both steeped in Greek traditions, see a trace of the Creator in the things of nature. 'Let none of you worship the sun, but set his desires on the Maker of the sun; nor deify the universe, but seek after the Creator of the universe.'[38]

We have remarked that Clement drew on Hebrew thought also in his use of the term 'spirit.' What has just been said in the last paragraphs applies to all men alike, whether pagan or Christian: it is an analysis of the 'natural' man of St. Paul. St. Paul treats the 'natural' man as a union of body and soul ('psyche'), mind ('nous') being an element of the latter.[39] The *differentia* of the Christian he finds in the development of the Hebrew idea of 'spirit,' as witnessed in the experience of himself and of others who were transformed by the descent of the Holy Spirit into their souls. The Christian man, in his view, by virtue of baptism, is reconstituted or re-created, and receives a new element, 'spirit,' by which he becomes a 'spiritual' man. Something not his by nature takes possession of him and moulds him afresh. Similarly, Clement speaks of a new gift of the Holy Spirit, by which a man is perfected. Of the baptism of Jesus Christ by John the Baptist, he asks, 'He is perfected by the washing—of baptism—alone, and is sanctified by the descent of the Spirit?' and replies, 'Such is the case. The same also takes place in our case whose exemplar Christ became. Being baptized, we are illuminated; illuminated, we become sons; being made sons, we are made perfect; being made perfect, we are made immortal . . . '[40] More explicitly, in another passage, he ascribes the growth of moral and spiritual life to this transcendent element: 'He Himself formed man of the dust, and regenerated him by water; and made him grow by His Spirit; and trained him by His word to adoption and salvation; in order that, transforming earth-born man into a holy and heavenly plant by His advent, He might fulfil to the utmost that divine utterance, "Let us make man in our image and likeness."'[41]

If the Stoics and Clement, in assigning to man the ability to know the morally good, appear to stand on common ground, the agreement is one about effects rather than about causes. The 'innate ideas' of the Stoics belong merely to a higher stratum in a series of strata rising from lower to higher by degrees of functioning, whereas to Clement the 'witness inborn and competent, viz. faith, which of itself, and from its own resources, chooses at once what is best' is the activity of a faculty transcendently higher than all other psychic elements, because it is inbreathed into man by God.[42] And yet a further difference appears when we relate the effect to the cause: the Stoics say that senseexperience draws the innate ideas of morality into the clearer light of consciousness; Clement adds that the grace of the Divine Teacher, Jesus Christ, is an element of experience. 'The heavenly and true divine love comes to men thus, when in the soul itself the spark of true goodness, kindled in the soul by the Divine Word, is able to burst into flame . . . '[43] Education and self-discipline can do much, but apart from grace, they may not do all. 'The thoughts of virtuous men are produced by the inspiration of God.'[44]

The duty of man, in the light of this psychology, will be to apprehend God's will and to perform it, and to bring the irrational elements of his soul into obedience to truth. 'Christian conduct is the operation of the rational soul in accordance with a correct judgement and aspiration after the truth, which attains its destined end through the body, the soul's consort and ally.'[45] The task of living is, before all else, to gain insight into the principles of living, and, secondly, to gain control of the appetites in such a way that each is given its due in an ordered and balanced life. All men are born with this capacity for mental and spiritual growth; but, like Adam, all men have failed to live up to the light that is in them. Sin may be said to be either disobedience to the heavenly vision, or the deliberate failure to catch that vision at all.[46] In each case it is really preference for pleasure in place of the good. 'The first man when in Paradise sported free, because he was the child of God; but when he succumbed to pleasure (for the serpent allegorically signifies pleasure crawling on its belly, earthly wickedness nourished for fuel to the flames) was as a child seduced by lusts, and grew old in disobedience; and by disobeying his Father, dishonoured God.'[47] Each man falls of himself, and must not trace his weakness to Adam, who is merely the type of all sinners.[48] He himself alone is responsible for his fall, and bears his own punishment, which, like his sin, is two-fold, being, first, ignorance, and second, the triumph of the irrational animal over the rational human. His two-fold penalty may be summed up in the single word death, which is not the separation of soul from body, but rather the separation of the rational soul from truth, on the one hand, and, on the other hand, its alliance with the desires of the irrational soul.[49]

It is clear from the foregoing analysis of man's psychic elements, that the image of God is predicable only of man's rational soul, or more exactly, of man's rational soul as 'informed' by the Holy Spirit or the Divine Word. Mind only reaches its fullest expression when it is indwelt by Spirit, as Dr. Temple puts it in *Christus Veritas*. But mind is a higher stage of reality than mere life and mere matter, and it is only in the *milieu* of matter as 'informed' by life, or soul, that mind develops and reaches its fulness. We have been given a potential nature, which develops within the influence of a medium lower than itself, through the power of the Divine. We stand between the infinitely great and the infinitely little: the infinitely little is within us, and the more we permit it to influence us, the less shall we be in touch with the infinitely great. History is a perpetual witness to the conflict of the sense element, which clamours for the indulgence of passion and pleasure, with the higher element which refuses to be satisfied with less than fellowship with God. The potential element remains at a low level of potentiality: the image of God is blurred. In this light, Clement conceives the Incarnation as the revelation of our potential nature raised to the highest possible degree of actuality. The life which we were intended to live, a life of contemplation issuing in good conduct, was lived by Jesus Christ, who, at all times, was a perfect Image of God. Both the Hebrews and the Greeks caught some flashes of the ideal life, but in Jesus Christ we have the Light in all its radiance. No doubt, Clement's Christology is seriously defective, and refuses to give an adequate place to the body and the human soul of Jesus Christ; but, at least, he is convinced that the life of the Word on earth was a perfect reflexion of the life of God, and of the ideal human life, in terms which human mentality could grasp. 'He ate not for the sake of His body, which was sustained by a holy energy, but that the false idea might not arise in the minds of His companions that He had been manifested only in semblance. He was altogether incapable of suffering: there entered into Him from without no emotion of pleasure or of pain.'[50] Thus Jesus Christ is not only without the evil consequences which attend life in contact with a human body but He lacks even the consequences which are not in themselves sinful. He is incapable of passion, and, therefore, passionless. St. Augustine was just as good a Platonist as Clement, but he was one of the 'twice-born' souls who came to Christ through great tribulation, and the ideal of impassibility did not attract him, as it did not the writer of the 'spiritual gospel,' who tells us that Jesus wept. He, however, belonged to the days when eye could see and hands could handle 'concerning the Word of life.' But, on the other hand, we must not imagine that the Word is a cold intellectual unit, for the final cause of the Incarnation is love.

'The Saviour then could never be a hater of men, seeing that it was owing to His abounding love for man that He scorned not the weakness of human flesh, but having clothed Himself with it, has come into the world for the common salvation of men.'[51] He asks, 'What, then, does this instrument—the Word of God, the Lord, the New Song—desire? To open the eyes of the blind, and unstop the ears of the deaf, and to lead the lame or the erring to righteousness, to exhibit God to the foolish, to put a stop to corruption, to conquer death, to reconcile disobedient children to their father. The instrument of God loves mankind. The Lord pities, instructs, exhorts, admonishes, saves, shields, and of His bounty promises us the kingdom of heaven as a reward for learning; and the only advantage He reaps is, that we are saved.'[52] His mission is one of 'admonishing, upbraiding, blaming, chiding, reproving threatening, healing, promising, favouring,'[53] and when men are constrained to repent, 'He rejoices, without suffering change.'[54]

Into the drama of human history, which is being enacted by the blurred images of God, there bursts the Perfect Image, who, working outside them, reveals to them what they might be, and working within them, with their cooperation, removes the tarnish and cleanses them from corruption. By His work God's favoured handiwork may fulfil its destiny and reveal His glory. By His mediating grace men may become intelligent agents who know and do the good, and be images of the Image of Him whom none hath seen at any time. Christ is 'in truth the Onlybegotten, the express image of the glory of the universal King and almighty Father, stamping on the mind of the gnostic the perfect vision after His own image, so that the divine image is now beheld in a third embodiment, assimilated as far as possible to the Second Cause, to Him, namely, who is the Life indeed, owing to whom we live the true life, copying the example of Him who is made to us knowledge, while we converse with the things which are stable and altogether unchangeable.'[55] We may, therefore, speak of individual men,[56] and of the Church which they compose, as indwelt by God. 'The earthly Church is the image of the heavenly.'[57] Clement goes so far as to speak of men who have already attained to the perfection of the image as being 'gods,' meaning, most probably, that they share in immortality with God.[58]

There are many allusions to, and some descriptions of, the human image of God as Clement pictures it. Sometimes he would appear to believe that here and now man may put on immortality,[59] but more often he limits human perfection by the Platonic qualification 'as far as possible.' Like all theologians, he is faced with the antinomy of man earning freedom in conflict with elements which reside in him, and from which he cannot completely free himself. The very impediments in the way to the attainment of self-mastery remain as conditions of self-mastery, even when it is won. Our only solace lies in the fact that we shall still continue to develop the image when the body has been laid aside.[60]

The image, as we have seen, is the rational soul, and it is perfected when it is free from all attendant influences of the irrational soul to which it is united. The rational soul, to use a modern term, is the Ego, as it is in Stoicism. The influences which retard its development and expression are passions and emotions, because they introduce an unbalancing factor which clouds the judgements of reason Passion gives a bias to sanity and reduces its victim to the level of opinion. We halt between many opinions, and become vacillating creatures, unless we have accustomed ourselves to see things in the clear light of reason.[61] Passions are described as 'an abscess of the truth.'[62] Men fear, are proud, lust, hate, because they have not learned to control the animal within.[63] If we could but learn to control bodily impulses, which, in themselves, are not evil, we should deal with them as a book-keeper deals with figures. The maxim, 'Know thyself,' Plato pointed out, really means 'Know God,' and Clement gives it a more comprehensive interpretation, as 'to know for what we were born.'[64] We were born to be saved, to be impregnated with the Divine life, to be perfect and immortal replicas of our Creator, and the body with which we have been endowed is suited admirably to forward these ends. 'Those, then, who vilify the body are wrong; not considering that the frame of man was formed erect for the contemplation of heaven, and that the organization of the senses tends to knowledge; and that the members and parts are arranged for good, not for pleasure. Whence this abode becomes receptive of the soul which is most precious to God; and is dignified with the Holy Spirit through the sanctification of soul and body, perfected with the perfection of the Saviour.'[65] Again, he tells us that 'the harmonious mechanism of the body contributes to the understanding which leads to goodness of nature.'[66] If it be true that we become like the objects which we permit the mind to dwell upon, it is obvious that absorption in the many-coloured delights of sense-perception will disturb the unity of the mind; but if the body, through our control, is an organized system, with its activities directed to the service of the mind, we shall be at peace with ourselves, and in harmony with the Image on whom our attention is fixed. 'Instruction harmonizes man, and by harmonizing makes him natural.'[67] The rational soul is akin to the Truth which it grasps, and provided that its grasp is enduring and perpetual, it is identified with the Truth.[68]

The real or inner man is a rational being, who rules his appetites by preserving a studied aloofness from their delights. But Clement is a mystic, and it would be erroneous to suppose that the gnostic is devoid of all emotional tone. Plato's cold science of dialectic with its cope-stone of articulated and systematized knowledge is only an aspect of the Platonic good, for, in the *Symposium,* we learn that Philosophy and Love are identical.[69] 'The simple truth is, that men love the good.' Even Kant allowed himself to be moved by the starry heavens without, and the moral law within. Stoicism approves of three good affections ('eupatheiai'), and 'for the much derided "apathy" of the school is substituted the doctrine of "eupathy."'[70] It obliges us to approximate to the state of Caution, which is subdivided into Shame and Sanctity, the latter being a disposition to avoid offences against the gods. Second, there is Readiness, that 'reasonable stretching out after future advantage'; and, finally, Joy, 'the reasonable appreciation of present advantages.'[71] So also, we find that Clement's asceticism is tempered with delights such as pass the understanding of the man who lives after the flesh. Thus fear is commended, provided that it is balanced by reverence, and is quite distinct from fear accompanied by hate for the object feared.[72] We ought to fear God.[73] Modesty is good.[74] Faith, Knowledge, and Peace delight the good man.[75] The motive of his actions is love.[76] He hopes, because his look

is always to the future.[77] Nevertheless there is a difficulty in that courage, joy, desire are disapproved, even though they are produced rationally, on the ground that there is no object capable of arousing these states in the perfect man. Clement himself solves the difficulty by telling us that such a man loves God, and that from that love nothing can possibly dislodge him. If it is objected that the perfect man desires God, the reply is that he already possesses God, and, therefore, cannot be said to desire Him. In the same strain, Plato describes love as 'the love of the everlasting possession of the good.'[78] Clement says that to exercise the love which is a gift from God is to be in one unvarying state.[79] And if the unvarying state is defined in strictly intellectual terms in such a passage as the following, 'The perpetual exercise of the intellect is the essence of an intelligent being, which results from an uninterrupted process of admixture, and remains eternal contemplation, a living substance ("hypostasis")',[80] there is recognition of a desire which is in itself intellectual.[81] True immortality is impassibility, and, in a sense, we can attain it here and now, because the rational soul has the power to abstract itself from its mundane partner for periods of time, and to retire into the Presence within.[82]

The gnostic is spiritually alive, and carnally dead. His unbroken habit has been severance of soul from body, and when the final severance comes, he bears it with ease and without fear.[83] Simple Christians and ordinary folk, unskilled in the inner mysteries of the truth, cannot part from the body with gnostic resignation; it is not so clear to them that, in God's economy, dissolution of soul and body naturally follows upon their union.[84] In any event, whatever the soul's character may be, it passes as a more or less developed image of God into the great Beyond.[85] What has been, is. The disembodied soul, certain of its capacities of knowledge developed, and certain undeveloped, enters upon a fresh field of experience. It sets out on a new life with the advantages and disadvantages of its anterior life, as the case may be, and its future will be conditioned by its past. One additional advantage the disembodied soul will have over its incarnate state: 'souls, although darkened by passions, when released from their bodies, are able to perceive more clearly, because of their being no longer obscured by the paltry flesh.'[86]

Clement has not given us a detailed account of the life of the disembodied soul. It would appear that gnostics, who have won impassibility, and who are already immortal, when still in the flesh pass without any period of preparation into the presence of Jesus Christ. 'No sooner does (the gnostic) hear the Master's call to depart, than he follows it; nay, owing to his good conscience even leads the way so to speak, hastening to offer his sacrifice of thanksgiving, and being joined with Christ there, to make himself worthy from his purity to receive by inward union the power of God which is supplied by Christ.'[87] That the gnostic enters immediately upon his inheritance is confirmed, as Dr Patrick points out, by the fact that he is said to 'pity those who undergo discipline after death.'[88] Clement does say that the martyr is welcomed by the Saviour and conducted by Him to the Father's bosom.[89] Both the gnostic and the martyr appear to pass from glory to glory, until they reach the stage of the perfect man.[90] All other souls come under a purifying discipline, which is spoken of figuratively as fire, and is part of the same healing ministry of the Word which is exercised here on earth. It is sometimes said that Clement accepts the reformative and deterrent theories of punishment, and that retribution finds no place in his thoughts about Divine providence. Thus he tells us that 'God does not take vengeance, for vengeance is a retaliation for evil, but He corrects with a view to the good, both public and private, of those who are corrected.'[91] But Clement was too good a Platonist to drop retribution *in toto*. We are told that 'God dispenses to all according to desert, His distribution being righteous,'[92] and that 'the Word will not pass over their transgressions in silence.'[93] Unlike St. Augustine, he had no sympathy with Marcionism, and he saw that God's love is just as active when He punishes as when He constrains. Clement lays it down as the truest of all truths, that 'the good and godly shall obtain the good reward . . . ; while, on the other hand, the wicked shall receive meet punishment,' and the sufferings which evil souls endure are self-caused rather than God-caused.[94] This tendency to attribute Divine punishments to God's economy rather than to God Himself directly is an expedient which has often been adopted in order to lay the onus of the suffering on the sinner. Archbishop King wrote: 'As to Punishments which God has affix'd by way of Sanction to Positive Laws, we must affirm, that they are to be esteem'd as Admonitions and Notices of the Mischiefs consequent upon evil elections, rather than that God Himself will immediately inflict them.'[95] If there is a God whose good providence has adapted creation to the moral and spiritual development of men, we must believe that creation takes sides with moral and spiritual, and that it sets its face against them that do evil. Penalty both here and hereafter is designed to lead to sinners' repentance. Clement believes that in the cleansing power of the Word imperfect souls may have removed from them those passions which still continue to taint the image, because even though they are out of the body, and the irrational soul is removed, the irrational effects of the latter still continue to glow in the rational soul. Or, to put the same thing positively, and from the side of the sinner, repentance is possible when death is past.[96]

Purification and repentance, as mutual accompaniments, gradually work the imperfect soul up to a higher stage of perfection, and it passes from mansion to mansion, until it learns to become a better reflexion of the impassibility of Him whose image it is. While it pays the penalty of its misdeeds, it is aware of what might have been. St. Augustine combined with the doctrine of a literal fire this psychological truth that consciousness of failure to reach the ideal life constitutes the nature of punishment in the hereafter; whereas Clement more sanely identifies the two by treating fire as the symbol of the mental distress which may lead to repentance. 'We say that fire sanctifies not flesh but sinful souls, and by fire, we mean not that which is all-devouring and common, but the fire which penetrates the soul which walks through the fire.'[97] Whether these imperfect souls, even when purified, ever reach to the full perfection of the image, the evidence in Clement's writings does not permit us to say. One passage suggests that they remain in mansions lower than those which the gnostic and the martyr inhabit. 'The man of faith (the simple believer) is distressed yet further, either because he has not yet attained, or not fully attained, what he sees that others have shared. And, moreover, he is ashamed because of the transgressions which he had committed, which in truth are the greatest punishments to the man of faith. And although the punishments cease, as a matter of fact, at the completion of the full penalty, and the purification of each, those who have been deemed worthy of the "other fold" have the greatest abiding sorrow, the sorrow of not being along with those who have been glorified because of righteousness.'[98] However sinful, ignorant, foolish, imperfect the soul may be, it is a divine thing, and the possession of free will always leaves open the way to repentance and spiritual progress. Even the devil can repent.[99] On the other hand, the possession of freedom leaves open also the possibility of resistance to the influences of the Word, and Clement mentions 'everlasting death' as possible.[100] Farrar claimed the support of Clement for the idea of universal hope, but the passages adduced by him cannot bear this interpretation.[101] One passage definitely excludes it: 'God bestows life freely; . . . evil custom, after our departure from this world, brings on the sinner unavailing remorse with punishment.'[102] But whatever Clement's considered judgement about the state of the impenitent may have been, if his optimism allowed him to face the problem at all, his great contribution to Christian theology may be said to be his belief in the power of the soul to grow more and more like Christ, the Divine Image of God.

If we peruse Clement's pages with a view to discerning his beliefs about the Resurrection and the nature of the Resurrection body, we shall look in vain. His projected treatise on the subject, if ever it was written, is not extant; and when he refers to the Resurrection the language is generally mystical. In one fragment, a comment on 2 Cor. v 16, he would seem to countenance the thought of the return of our Lord in a physical integument. 'Christ . . . ceased to live after the flesh. How? Not by putting off the body? Far be it! For with it as His own He shall come, the Judge of all. But by divesting Himself of physical affections, such as hunger, and thirst, and sleep, and weariness. For now He has a body incapable of suffering and of injury.'[103] In the same strain, he speaks of our flesh as incorruptible. 'Paul says, speaking of the Lord, "Because He emptied Himself, taking the form of a servant," calling the outward man servant, previous to the Lord becoming a servant and wearing flesh. But the compassionate God Himself set the flesh free, and releasing it from destruction, and from bitter and deadly bondage, endowed it with incorruptibility, arraying the flesh in this, the holy embellishment of eternity—immortality.'[104] But it is doubtful whether the context, which disapproves of adorning the body in an extravagant fashion, does not deal with the gnostic's body in this life. A few lines further, in commenting on Is. liii 2, 3, he asks, 'Yet who was more admirable than the Lord?' and answers, 'But it was not the beauty of the flesh visible to the eye, but the true beauty of both soul and body, which He exhibited, which in the former is beneficence; in the latter—that is, the flesh—immortality.' It is just possible that he may mean that a body perfectly controlled by a perfect soul is a visible impassible symbol of the real and invisible impassibility.

Whatever the nature of the Resurrection body may be, there is no doubt about an actual Resurrection. By 'I will raise him up at the last day,' he understands, I will raise up the man who apprehends Me by faith now in this world. This spiritual Resurrection is followed by another, when the world has come to an end, at which end the believer enters upon the actual realization of those joys already present within him in anticipation. 'But faith is not lame in any respect; nor after our departure from this world does it make us who have believed, and received without distinction the earnest of future good, wait; but having in anticipation grasped by faith that which is future, after the Resurrection we receive it as present, in order that that may be fulfilled which was spoken, "Be it according to thy faith."'[105] Elsewhere he speaks of the mystical Resurrection which the gnostic celebrates on the occasions when he resists temptation: 'The gnostic carries out the evangelical command and makes that the Lord's day on which he puts away an evil thought and assumes one suited to the gnostic, doing honour to the Lord's Resurrection in himself.'[106] After the Resurrection at the end, of which this one is the prelude, he will not be a composite creature, for there is no composite thing, or creature endowed with sensation in heaven.[107]

At this stage we may set about making a summary of this teaching, and by throwing the main features of the whole into different terminology, attempt to make it more vivid to the modern eye.

As we survey the wonderful expanse of creation, teeming as it is with variety and richness, which man's observation and reason cannot fully classify and explain, we see that it falls into three clearly marked divisions. First, there is the inanimate division, that group of lifeless earth, and rock, and planet, and sea, which does not grow, and is insensible to the influence of man's will. The chemist and the physicist can give us the formula for almost anything we care to name in this group, for its objects are simply collections of atoms combined in specific ways. The second division is the world of living things, and in it we have the first division raised to life. This second division is higher than the first, because in it we can see atoms organized by life, and more or less controlled by life in purposive directions. It may be possible to state the exact elements which go to make up the body of a dog; but the dog, as he stands before us, responding to his master's approach with wagging tail and welcoming bark, is a living unit, which can, to some extent, give direction to his body. A rock cannot hurl itself at me: but a dog may dislike me and bite me. The third division, to which we as men belong, is the world of spirit, or reason, or will. It includes the two lower divisions, the inanimate and animate, and gives them a definitely purposive direction. Man sets before himself deliberately a rational and spiritual end, and uses his body to reach it. The dog may have a rudimentary sense of duty; but he is not under the obligation we know, when conscience says 'Thou shalt not.' Man can use his organic collection of atoms to carry out the will of God, whom he may know, in conscience, in prayer, and in sacrament.

But if, instead of working up in this way, from the inanimate, through the animate, to the spiritual, we were to work down, we can see just what it is that gives to man his peculiar value. Working down from God, the Eternal who inhabits eternity, we start from One who is Infinite Wisdom, Infinite Power, Infinite Love, Infinite Life, we first come to men who are said, in the Book of Genesis, to be in His image. Whatever God is, man is in a less degree. Man has something of wisdom, something of power, something of love, something of life. If we want to know what God really is, Genesis says, Look at man.

We all know what happened. We do not require to go to Genesis to find out. We look at history, and we look at ourselves, and we see a blurred image. Man has preferred foolishness to wisdom, his own power to God's power, hate to love, death to life. Man defaced the image; man sinned. We all know what happened next. A new Image appeared on earth, who was the 'express image of the Father,' and by His manner of life, revealed the nature of God, and the nature of man. Before He passed to His death on the cross, He could say that He preserved the Image of God unblurred, without spot and without wrinkle. 'I have glorified thee on the earth, having accomplished the work which thou hast given me to do.'

What did Jesus Christ do that marked Him out at all times as the Image of God? What is it that makes us say when we look at Him that we see God? He knew God. The particular gift given to man at his creation was the ability to know God. The man who knows God is His image. A mirror may give an image by reflexion. The face in the mirror is merely on the surface of the mirror. Remove the image, and the mirror is as it was. The image is external to the mirror, and does not affect it. The inanimate creation catches the glory of God on the surface, and is not adapted to reveal Him, so to speak, from the inside.[108] The next level of reality, the animate, in its higher forms, can be an image only by way of imitation.[109] The dog can imitate a man, by copying his movements; but it cannot be man-like in its soul. True it is that a man may sink to the brute level, and become brutish, but the brute cannot rise above its definitely fixed limitations. But at the spiritual level, we have a stratum of reality, which can, after a fashion, lead the kind of life that God lives. Man has something of God's wisdom, something of His power, something of His love, something of His life. Thus Christ is an expression of the nature of God in the highest possible human terms. He does not reflect God from the outside; He does not imitate God; but He lives, in the limitations of human nature, the kind of life which God lives outside our world of space and time. That kind of life He lived, because He knew, in the depths of His consciousness, the principles of living.

If to be like God is to live, as nearly as we may, the life which God lives, it must be true that ours will be an eternal life. If our thoughts are as God's, and our interests are as His, we too are eternal. 'And this is life eternal, that they should know thee the only true God, and him whom thou thoudidst send, even Jesus Christ.' Our destiny is not a future to be ended when the atoms of our bodies are separated, but an eternal future, when our souls shall live, because they have learned to know God, and in the process of learning, have become like Him.

It is our task to cultivate the image of God within us, given to us at birth, and studying His Perfect Image in the Gospel pages, and approaching Him in prayer and sacrament, to know Him, and in knowing Him, to become like Him, eternal. Only that which is like Him can enter into His presence, and live with Him; and in this world of time we are called upon by Christ to learn of Him, and to build up a knowledge of Him such as cannot fail to render us capable of seeing Him as He is.

Notes

1. *Str.* v 13, 83.
2. *Paed.* i 8, 71.
3. *Str.* v 11, 71.
4. *Str.* iv 25, 156.
5. *Str.* ii 18, 81; *cf.* iv 23, 151.
6. *Str.* v 14, 89.
7. *Str.* v 14, 89; *ib.* 115.
8. *Str.* vi 14, 142.
9. *Prot.* iv 63.
10. *Str.* vi 16, 142. *Cf. Confess.* xi 20; *de Civ.Dei,* xi 4.
11. *Str.* v 14, 141.
12. *Str.* vii 7, 42.
13. *Str.* vii 2, 8; i 17, 84; *Pead.* viii 63.
14. *Str.* v 13, 87; *Prot.* x 103.
15. *Str.* i 11, 52; vii 2, 12.
16. *Str.* ii 1, 5; *cf. Prot.* vi 68; x 91.
17. *Prot.* vii 74.
18. *Paed.* iii 1, 1; *Str.* vii 10, 59.
19. *Paed.* i 13, 103.
20. *Summa* i 2, q. 91, 2; q, 51, 1; q, 91, 4.
21. *Str.* vi 16, 134-136; *cf.* ii 11, 50.
22. *Str.* vi 16, 134.
23. *Str.* ii 11, 50.
24. *Prot.* x 100; *Paed.* i 3, 7; *Str.* v 13, 87.
25. *Prot.* x 98; *Paed.* i 12, 98; *Prot.* ii 25.
26. *Str.* ii 2, 20.
27. *Str.* vii 12, 79.
28. *Str.* ii 16, 75.
29. *Str.* vii 11, 61; *cf. Str.* i 24, 159; *Paed.* i 12, 102.
30. *Str.* vii 7, 36.
31. *Str.* ii 11, 50; vi 16, 136; v 3.
32. *Str.* vi 16, 136.
33. *Str.* vi 16, 135.
34. *Ibid.*
35. *Str.* vi 16, 136.
36. *Gen.* ii 7.
37. *Str.* ii 19, 20; *cf.* 16, 74; 16, 136.
38. *Prot.* iv 63.
39. *Rom.* vii 23.
40. *Paed.* i 6, 25.
41. *Ibid.* i 12, 98.
42. *Prot.* x 95.
43. *Ibid.* xi 117.
44. *Str.* vi 17, 157.
45. *Paed.* i 13, 102.
46. *Str.* vii 16, 101.
47. *Prot.* xi III.
48. *Str.* ii 19, 98.
49. *Prot.* xi 115; *Str.* ii 7, 34; iv 3, 12.
50. *Str.* vi 9, 71. *Cf.* C. E. Raven, *Apollinarianism,* p. 15.
51. *Str.* vii 2, 8.
52. *Prot.* i 6.
53. *Paed.* i 9, 75.
54. *Str.* ii 16, 73.
55. *Str.* vii 3, 16.
56. *Str.* vii 3, 16.
57. *Str.* iv 8, 66.
58. W. R. Inge, *Philosophy of Plotinus,* i p. 100. 'The Gnostic "trains himself to be God"; a phrase which was not shocking to Greek theology, since "god" meant an immortal being.' *Cf.* J. B. Mayor, *Str.* vii 16, 101. Clement's position is safeguarded by *Str.* ii 16, 75, quoted above.
59. *Str.* vii 9, 56.
60. *Str.* vii 2, 12.
61. *Str.* ii 11, 52.
62. *Paed.* i 8, 64.
63. *Str.* vi 15, 115; *cf. Quis dives salvetur?* iv 25.
64. *Str.* vii 3, 20.

65. *Str.* iv 26, 163.

66. *Str.* iv 4, 17.

67. *Str.* iv 23, 149.

68. *Str.* i 28, 178; ii 2, 9.

69. *Symp.* 20ID ff.

70. E. V. Arnold, *Roman Stoicism,* p. 323.

71. *Cf.* Seneca, *Ep.* 23, 4.

72. *Paed.* i 9, 87.

73. *Str.* i 27, 173.

74. *Paed.* ii 10, 100.

75. *Str.* ii 11, 51; *cf.* iv 23, 149.

76. *Str.* iv 22, 135.

77. *Str.* v 3, 16.

78. *Symp.* 201D ff.

79. *Str.* vi 9, 71, 72.

80. *Str.* iv 22, 136; *cf.* vi 1, 3.

81. *Str.* ii 2, 9 . . .

82. *Str.* v 14, 133; *Paed.* ii 9, 82.

83. *Str.* iv 3, 12.

84. *Str.* iii 9, 64.

85. *Str.* vi 14, 109.

86. *Str.* vi 6, 46.

87. *Str.* vii 12, 79; *cf.* vi 13, 105.

88. *Str.* vii 12, 79. See *Clement of Alexandria,* p. 136. On this point C. Bigg, *The Christian Platonists of Alexandria,* p. 149, would appear to be incorrect, when he interprets Clement as of the opinion that *all* souls are disciplined.

89. *Quis dives,* 42; *Str.* iv 4, 14.

90. *Str.* vi 13, 107.

91. *Str.* vii 16, 102.

92. *Str.* iv 6, 29.

93. *Paed.* i 7, 58.

94. *Prot.* x 90.

95. *An Essay on the Origin of Evil,* 1731, p. 304.

96. *Str.* iv 6, 37.

97. *Str.* vii 6, 34.

98. *Str.* vi 14, 109. *Cf.* Patrick, *Clement of Alexandria,* p. 137.

99. *Str.* i 17, 83.

100. *Paed.* i 8, 74.

101. *Cf.* E. B. Pusey, *What is of Faith as to Everlasting Punishment,* p. 190.

102. On this passage R. B. Tollington, *Clement of Alexandria,* ii, p. 252, says, 'Once indeed he speaks of fruitless repentance and requital in another state, but even in this passage he adds a reference to the knowledge that comes by pain . . . ' But what the child is said to learn through suffering is that 'superstition destroys . . . and piety saves.' *Prot.* x. 90.

103. J. A. Cramer's *Catenae* (Oxford, 1840) vol. iii.

104. *Paed.* iii 1, 2.

105. *Paed.* i 6, 29.

106. *Str.* vii 12, 76.

107. *Str.* v 3.

108. *Str.* i 19, 94.

109. *Str.* iv 6, 30.

Works Cited

1. *Clementis Alexandrini Opera omnia.* Edidit R. Klotz. (Lipsiae. 1831-2.)

2. *Clement of Alexandria, Miscellanies Book VII.* The Greek Text, with Introduction, Translation, Notes, Dissertations and Indices. By the late F. J. A. Hort, D.D., D.C.L., LL.D., and Joseph B. Mayor. (London: Macmillan and Co. Ltd. 1902.)

3. *Clement of Alexandria: Quis Dives Salvetur.* Re-edited together with an Introduction on the MSS of Clement's Works. By P. M. Barnard. 'Texts and Studies,' V 2. (Cambridge: at the University Press. 1897.)

4. *Clemens Alexandrinus.* Herausgegeben von Dr. Otto Stählin. (Leipzig: Hinrichs. 1905-9.)

5. *Clement of Alexandria.* By R. B. Tollinton, B.D. Two volumes. (London: Williams and Norgate. 1914.)

And other works.

J. T. Muckle (essay date 1952)

SOURCE: "Clement of Alexandria's Attitude toward Greek Philosophy," in *The Phoenix,* Supplementary Vol. I, 1952, pp. 139-46.

[*In the following essay, Muckle discusses Clement's view that philosophy enabled the Greeks to begin the assent to the truth of the Gospel.*]

It is uncertain where Titus Flavius Clemens (*ca.*150-*ca.*216) was born. It is generally considered by scholars today that he was a native[1] of Athens and that he received his early education in that city. After his conversion to Christianity, he travelled considerably, like St. Justin Martyr, seeking a teacher to give him higher instruction. His journeys took him from Greece to Southern Italy, to Palestine, and finally to Egypt, where at Alexandria he found the greatest teacher, likely Pantaenus.[2]

Clement remained at Alexandria as student and teacher for over twenty years (*ca.*180-*ca.*202). Although he himself makes no reference to it, Eusebius[3] and St. Jerome[4] say that he became head of the catechetical school upon the death of Pantaenus.[5]

Alexandria had long been a great commercial centre and a cosmopolitan city. In a sense it was the New York of the East. There was a large Greek population, probably an even greater Jewish element, besides a native group of considerable size. It was a centre of letters marked by a tendency to attempt to harmonize the various schools of thought.[6] About two centuries before, Philo had tried to adapt Platonism to his interpretation of the Old Testament. Clement was likely following a tradition received from Pantaenus in using Greek philosophy, especially that of Plato and the Stoics, in building up a structure of Christian thought and practice which, to his mind, would lead a Christian to the acme of perfection. He does not write primarily as a philosopher or as a dogmatic theologian. His chief work, the **Stromata,** connected series of chapters in seven[7] Books in which he would point the way for the Christian who is properly disposed to reach the perfection of a Christian gnostic.[8] He expounded dogma only in so far as his general purpose required. He was a man of wide learning and apparently of deep piety. Although there is more than one doctrinal error in his gnosticism, his devotion to the cause of Christ and to the salvation of men stands out in all his writings.[9]

To Clement the Incarnation is the central fact in the history of man.[10] All previous human thought, in so far as it was true, all revelation before Christ had been a preparation for the acceptance of Christ and His Gospel. The two great forces in this process were the Old Testament and Greek philosophy. To Clement they disposed and prepared the Jews and the Pagans respectively for belief in Christ and His Gospel.

> Just as at the opportune time came the preaching (of the Gospel), so also at the opportune time were the Law and the prophets given to the barbarians and philosophy to the Greeks to fit their ears for the Gospel.[11]

Clement even speaks of philosophy as leading the Greeks to justification before the advent of Christ.

> Philosophy, then, before the coming of the Lord was necessary to the Greeks for justification.[12]

By this he does not mean that philosophy is the efficient cause of justification. It predisposed the Greek mind to recognize and penetrate truths and to formulate a rational ethic. Relative to the attainment of justification, philosophy was like the first step or two of a stairway or as the study of grammar for one who is to pursue philosophy.

> Philosophy by itself formerly justified the Greeks—not justification in the full sense to the attainment of which it helps, but as the first and second steps of a stairway which leads to an upper story, or as the grammarian is of assistance to the philosopher.[13] . . . The same God Who as the sponsor . . . for both the covenants (the Old and the New) was the giver of Greek philosophy

to the Greeks through which the Almighty is glorified among them . . . accordingly, from the Greek discipline . . . as also from that of the Law, men are gathered into one race of the saved . . . trained in different covenant.[14] . . . The philosophy of the Greeks was given to them as their own covenant, which was a stepping stone to the philosophy which is according to Christ.[15]

But for Clement philosophy alone was not enough to conduct the Greeks into heaven. Faith was necessary, which is the mark of free will on the part of one well disposed and aided by grace. The Gentiles who through a special attribute of their nature lived according to reason led a true life even as the Jews who lived according to the Law. But they reached their ultimate goal, heaven, only after they made an act of faith in Christ and His Gospel.

> If to live well is to live lawfully, and to live rationally is to live according to law, if those who lived uprightly before the Law were considered men of faith and judged just, then it is manifest that those of old, who being outside the Law had lived uprightly because of their special character . . . , reaching the ward of Limbo . . . , were straightway converted and believed on hearing the voice of the Lord . . . through His apostles.[16] . . . For those who were justified by philosophy not only faith in the Lord but also turning away from idolatry was lacking.[17]

By the term Greek philosophy Clement does not mean that of any particular school. Although, in a general sense, he is a pronounced Platonist, he chooses from the tenets of each school[18] what he considers true, at least in part, and capable of adaptation to the teachings of Christ.

> And by philosophy, I do not mean the Stoic or Platonic or the Epicurean or Aristotelian, but whatever has been well put by any of those sects, teaching righteousness along with knowledge pervaded by piety . . . : all this assortment . . . I call philosophy.[19]

Using the words of Socrates,[20] he calls those philosophers who have philosophized right; he also adopts the words of Plato.[21]

> Philosophers are those who delight in seeing the truth . . .[22]

He justifies his position by citing Holy Scripture,[23] stating that certain chosen men, wise of heart, God filled with the spirit of insight . . . which is nothing else than understanding . . . , a faculty of the soul capable of contemplating realities, and this power extends not only to the arts but also to philosophy itself.[24]

> Philosophy "partaking of a more exquisite perfection. . . participates in wisdom."[25] It is a gift of divine Providence to the Greeks to prepare and dispose the Greek mind for true faith (i.e. belief in Christ's Gospel). So there is no absurdity in philosophy's having been given by Divine Providence to the Greeks as a preparatory discipline for the perfection which is through Christ.[26]

Clement holds then that certain men were gifted by God to enable them to reach a partial truth. The Word . . . was in them to the extent that they discovered truth:[27] a doctrine much like that of St. Justin Martyr.

In drawing upon Greek thought, Clement does not confine himself to philosophers. He quotes from the poets;[28] more than any other early ecclesiastical writer. Some parts of his works, e.g. *Stromata* 5.14; 6.2, are but tissues of quotations from them. Clement holds that they too were taught by the prophets and utter truth in a veiled manner . . .[29] Like all the Fathers of the Church, he does not try to bring out the beauty of their style; he is not a humanist in that sense.[30] He gleans from their works passages which contain thought that supports the truths of revelation. He quotes not only from works extant today, but also from many Greek poems now lost. Stählin lists over seven hundred passages from the poets.[31] Clement must have known the *Iliad* almost by heart. Of the tragedians, Euripides is his favourite . . .

Clement does not describe in detail how Greek thought was a preparation for the Gospel, but it is possible from his writings to glean texts besides those already given, which show his mind fairly well. According to him, the object of Greek philosophers and poets alike was to pursue truth.[32] The doctrines that there is one first cause, that God is without beginning or end, that He is the searcher of hearts, that for man the highest purpose in life is to become like unto Him, that the world was created, that there are angels, good and bad, all this and more Clement professes to find in Greek thought. He goes so far as to say that the Greeks reached God in the sense that they learned truth about Him. They see God as He is reflected in man himself, as we see images and reflections in water.[33] The truth reached by Greek philosophy is partial and elementary in regard both to its content and its degree of certitude. But faith rests on the voice of God Himself and so presents truth absolute which cannot be impugned; it is authentic and unassailable. It is self-sufficient and perfect in its own right and needs nothing for its defence, not even philosophy. Most of the faithful who have never learned philosophy have been trained by Wisdom and have received the Word of God through faith. Philosophy does, nevertheless, touch on the truth and so can fit the mind, as the rain does the soil, and dispose it to assent to God's Word, but it is not a *conditio sine qua non* for the faith, much less the efficient cause.[34] At most it can be called a concurrent or contributing cause; as many men launching a ship all concur in the task, yet it can be accomplished if any one of them drops out.[35]

It is the content of faith which is the criterion of philosophical truth, not *vice versa*.[36] But philosophy, as well as all other erudition, purges, ennobles, trains, and predisposes the mind towards truth.[37] Just as the grammarian is of assistance to one who is to devote himself to philosophy,[38] so is philosophy the servant of its queen, the truth of faith which is wisdom. Clement repeats the thought and almost the words of Philo[39] when he says:

> As the general studies . . . contribute to philosophy, their mistres . . . , so also does philosophy to the

acquisition of wisdom. For philosophy is the pursuit of wisdom, and wisdom is the knowledge of things human and divine and of their causes. Wisdom is then the queen . . . of philosophy as the latter is of the preparatory studies . . . .[40]

Philosophy prepared the Greeks for the Gospel also by training their minds and raising them up to intellectual subjects. It purified the Greek mind from mundane things and gave it clearness of vision, effects which contributed to the apprehension of truth. It trained it, aroused its intelligence, and produced in it an inquiring shrewdness.[41] Philosophy gave the Greeks the "feel" for truth wherever found; trained by the Spirit of Wisdom to a high degree of understanding, they came to recognize and embrace the truth even when it was presented to them in the Hebrew Scriptures.

> The philosophers, severally trained to a proper power of discernment[42] under the Spirit of discernment, whenever they carefully investigated not philosophy in part but philosophy absolute bore witness to the truth in a truth-loving and humble manner, even in the case of truths well put by those not of their school, and advanced to understanding under the divine ministration of the ineffable Goodness which regularly leads creatures on to what is better according to their capacity. And further, having come into contact not only with Greeks but also with barbarians (i.e. the Hebrews), they were led on to the Faith in virtue of a discipline they had undergone together for an individual comprehension. And, once having embraced the foundation of truth, they received in addition the power of advancing to investigation and, loving to be learners and reaching for knowledge, they hastened on to salvation.[43]

Philosophy enabled the Greek mind to rid itself to some extent of false ideas. For dialectics especially enables one to detect error and to defend onself against it.[44] Borrowing the terminology of the mysteries of Greek religion, Clement says that Baptism is an initiation into a mystery which is preceded by a mental discipline.[45]

With Clement, as with Plato, philosophical thought has a moral aspect; it is the knowledge of goodness as well as of truth. "It makes men virtuous," and the true philosopher is the thinker whose life conforms to his true and noble teaching.[46] But Clement does not press the point to the extent that he claims that the moral precepts of the Greeks sanctified them. At most, he asserts that philosophy prepared them for justification through faith in Christ and His Gospel. But the moral effect of Greek philosophy, if not expressed, shines through nearly all the texts quoted above regarding philosophy as a preparation for the Gospel.

Perhaps Clement's attitude towards Greek philosophy is best illustrated by his application of the parable of the five barley loaves and two fish with which Christ fed the multitude.[47] Both the barley loaves and the fish represent the preparatory training of man for the wheat bread of the Gospel. The loaves represent the Jewish Law and the two fish "signify the Hellenic philosophy . . . given as food for those lying on the ground."[48]

Although Clement was not much quoted by subsequent Greek ecclesiastical writers, yet he made a contribution to the establishment of the Christian attitude in the East towards classical culture. He counteracted the extreme position of Tatian, who, like Tertullian in the West, looked with pronounced disfavour on all classical culture. Both were extremists who ended up in heresy and their attitude towards the classics is not representative of early ecclesiastical writers. Clement's position was somewhat modified by Origen who like him was a Platonist with eclectic tendencies. But it was especially St. Basil who established the true place of classical thought in Christian education in the East.

Notes

1. Epiphanius *Haereses* 32.6 says that in his day some thought he was a native of Athens, others of Alexandria.

2. *Stromata* 1.1.11. O. Stählin's *Clemens Alexandrinus* 2 (Leipzig 1906) 8 in *Die griechischen christlichen Schriftsteller der ersten drei Fahrhunderte* is a critical edition in four volumes, the last of which is made up of indices: vol. 1 (Leipzig 1905); 2 (Leipzig 1906); 3 (Leipzig 1909); 4 (Leipzig 1936). In this paper all references to the works of Clement relate to this edition. I give the title of the work, the book (if more than one), the chapter and paragraph, followed by a semicolon; then the volume and page of Stählin's edition.

3. *Historia Ecclesiastica* 6.6.

4. *De Viris illustribus* 38 (*P L*.23.686).

5. For a discussion of the historical value of this statement of Eusebius and St. Jerome, see G. Bardy, "Aux Origines de l'école d'Alexandrie," *Recherches de science religieuse* 27 (1937) 65-90.

6. For a description of the Alexandria of Clement's time, see R. B. Tollington, *Clement of Alexandria* 1 (London 1914) chapters 2 and 3; Claude Mondésert, *Clément d' Alexandrie* (Paris 1944) chapter 1.

7. The eighth Book is not considered an integral part of the *Stromata; cf.* A. Puech, *Histoire de la littérature chrétienne* 1 (Paris 1928) 345; Stählin 1.xli.

8. An exposition of Clement's gnosticism does not come within the limits of this paper. Suffice it to say that for him it is a scientific knowledge of the full content of faith culminating in love, achieved by comparatively few of the faithful. It is a knowledge not only of the Scriptures but also of a so-called secret tradition handed down orally from Christ through Saints Peter, James, John, and Paul. This tradition is not at all that of Catholic Doctrine contained within the *magisterium* of the Church. Clement tried to establish a Christian to counteract the heretical gnosticism of his day, but he does not escape entirely from the errors of the latter . . .

9. See e.g. his appraisal of the role of Christ and his exhortation to men to embrace His Gospel in the last two chapters of his *Protrepticus.*

10. Although Clement expressly describes the role of Christ as redeemer, yet His role as teacher finds greater emphasis in his works. The Incarnate Word is the Saviour; "The Word . . . who was with God and by whom all things were created, has appeared, our Teacher" (*Protrepticus* 1.7; 1.7). The Word Incarnate is "The Lord who from the beginning gave revelations by prophecy but now is plainly calling to salvation" (*op. cit.* [see n. 2] 1.7; 1.8). "The Word is in the heart of each man as the seed of truth." See *Strom.* 6.7.57; 2.460. For the role of the Word see also *Strom.* 5.5.41-43; 2.452-453: 7.2.6; 3.6 *et passim* in the *Protrepticus, Paedagogus,* and *Stromata.* See also J. Lebreton, "La théorie de la connaissance religieuse chez Clément d'Alexandrie," *Recherches de science religieuse* 18 (1928) 465-469; C. Mondésert *op. cit.* (see n. 6) 187, "Histoire religieuse de l'humanité"; also A. de la Barre, "Clément d'Alexandrie," *Dictionnaire de théologie catholique* 3. cols. 158-163, 188-190. For a discussion of the statement in Photius, *Bibliotheca Cod.* 109 ascribing a doctrine of two *Logoi* to Clement see R. P. Casey, "Clement and the two divine *Logoi,*" *FTS* 25 (Oct. 1923) 42-56.

11. *Strom.* 6.6.44; 2.453. Clement often uses the term, "barbarians," to denote the Jews; also "barbarian philosophy" to denote the Old Testament, sometimes both Old and New; and he even includes in *Strom.* 6.4.35; 2.448 Egyptian and Eastern thought, i.e. non-Greek. Of course he makes no reference to that of the Latin West.

12. *Strom.* 1.5.28; 2.17. See also *Strom.* 6.17.153; 2.510.

13. *Strom.* 1.20.99; 2.63.

14. *Strom.* 6.5.42; 2.452.

15. *Strom.* 6.8.67; 2.465. See *Strom.* 1.7.37; 2.24.

16. *Strom.* 6.6.47; 2.455.

17. *Strom.* 6.6.44; 2.454. See also *Strom.* 2.9.44; 2.136. Clement holds that after their death Christ and His apostles descended into Limbo to preach the Gospel to those of good will who were detained there; Christ preached to the Jews, the apostles to the Gentiles. Those of the latter who made an act of faith in Christ and His Gospel and rejected idolatry were taken to heaven.

18. Clement draws from all the schools but is most indebted to the Platonists and Stoics. Stählin *op. cit.* (see n. 2) 4.30ff. lists the references to his quotations. Those from Plato fill ten columns, those from Chrysippus (fragments) five columns. Plato is the lover of truth, . . . *Strom.* 5.10.66; 2.370; as one inspired: . . . *Strom.* 1.8.42; 2.28.

19. *Strom.* 1.7.37; 2.24; 6.7.55; 2.459.

20. *Phaedo* 69C. *Strom.* 1.19.92; 2.59.

21. *Rep.* 5.475E.

22. *Strom.* 1.19.93; 2.60.

23. Exodus 28.3 (*Septuagint*); 31.2-6 . . .

24. See *Strom.* 6.17.154; 2.511: 1.4.25-26; 2.16.

25. *Strom.* 6.17.156; 2.512.

26. *Strom.* 6.17.153; 2.510.

27. *Strom.* 1.19.94-95; 2.61. In other places, Clement accepts the Judaeo-Alexandrine doctrine that the philosophers borrowed most if not all their basic truths from the Old Law. *Cf. Strom.* 5.4.19; 2.338, and many other passages. Clement is not always consistent. He is striving to win over numerous Christians in Alexandria who held that revealed truth contained all that was needed to become perfect. His varying positions on this and other topics may be due largely to circumstances of time, place, and persons he hoped to reach. The composition of his *Stromata* probably extended over a span of about ten years; *cf.* O. Bardenhewer, *Geschichte der altkirchlichen Literatur* 2 (Freiburg im Br. 1914) 66-67. For the "anticlassical" section at Alexandria, see J. Lebreton, "Le désaccord de la foi populaire et de la théologie savante dans l'église chrétienne du IIIe siécle," *Rev. hist. ecclés.* 19 (1923) 492ff; M. de Faye, *Clément d'Alexandrie* (Paris 1906) 137.

28. Stählin *op. cit.* (see n. 2) 4.30ff. lists the references for his quotations from the poets.

29. *Strom.* 5.4.24; 2.340.

30. Christians are to pay no heed to the rhythm and melody of Greek poetry but should stop their ears to it, passing by its aesthetic appeal. For they know that, once Greek literature has captured their ears, they will never afterwards be able to retrace their steps. But he who is to instruct Greek catechumens should not refrain from the pursuit of learning (φιλομαθιας). He should not linger over it, but dwell upon it only long enough to get what is useful to his hearers. *Cf. Strom.* 6.11.89; 2.476.

31. For Clement's use of Greek poetry see P. Camelot, "Les idées de Clément d'Alexandrie sur l'utilisation des sciences et de la littérature profane," *Recherches de science religieuse* 21 (1931) 38-66.

32. See *Strom.* 1.19.93; 2.60: 5.3.16; 2.336: 5.4.24; 2.340.

33. *Strom.* 5.14.99ff; 2.392ff: 1.19.94ff; 2.60-62.

34. *Strom.* 1.20.97ff; 2.62ff. See also *Strom.* 6.8.68; 2.465: 1.7.37; 2.24-25: 2.2.4ff; 2.114ff.

35. *Strom.* 1.20.99; 2.63.

36. *Strom.* 2.4.15; 2.120.

37. *Strom.* 1.6.33-35; 2.21-22.

38. *Strom.* 1.20.99; 2.63.

39. *De Congressu quaerendae Eruditionis gratia* 79.

40. *Strom.* 1.5.30; 2.19. The main theme of the *Stromata* is an exposition of Christian gnosticism and a description of the process whereby a Christian who is well disposed arrives at it . . . His view of the role of philosophy in preparing the Greek world for the Gospel is a preliminary step to establish his point that philosophy is a useful gift of Providence working through chosen men.

41. *Strom.* 1.5.32; 2.21. See also *Strom.* 1.16.80; 2.52: 7.3.20; 3.14.

42. *Cf.* Exodus 28.3. (*Septuagint*); 31.2-6.

43. *Strom.* 6.17.154; 2.511.

44. *Strom.* 1.9.43; 2.29: See also *Strom.* 1.20.99-100; 2.63-64: 6.10.82-83; 2.173.

45. Not only philosophy proper but also the Liberal Arts, especially mathematics and dialectics, contributed to this. *Strom.* 6.11.90; 2.477: 5.2.70; 2.373-374. See Plotinus *Enneads* 1.3.3 for a similar idea: mathematics and dialectics as a discipline towards mysticism.

46. *Strom.* 6.17.159; 2.513: 1.18.93; 2.60: 1.7.55; 2.459.

47. Matt. 14.15; John 6.9.

48. *Strom.* 6.11.94; 2.479.

John R. Donahue (essay date 1963)

SOURCE: "Stoic Indifferents and Christian Indifference in Clement of Alexandria," in *Traditio*, Vol. 19, 1963, pp. 438-46.

[*In the following essay, Donahue explains how Clement's usage of the term "indifferent" was influenced by Stoic notions of indifference; he also cites it as an example of how Clement adapted the thoughts of others into his own teachings of a practical Christian morality.*]

Throughout the **Paedagogos,** the **Stromata,** and the **Quis dives salvetur?** Clement of Alexandria uses the term 'indifferent' . . . or one of its derivatives. In all of these instances except three, the term is found in the moral sense redolent of Stoic usage.[1] The present study attempts to treat by a comprehensive analysis of the term the meaning of 'indifferent' in Clement, its significance for his moral *ascesis,* and certain problems that arise from its use. Because of the marked similarity between Clement's usage of this term and that of the Stoics a brief discussion of the Stoic of indifference is necessary as a background to Clement's teaching.[2] It is hoped that such a study will provide a concrete example of the adaptation of Stoic morality to practical Christian asceticism.

According to the Stoics the wise man alone is truly happy, for he lives in harmony with nature and with his reason conformed to universal reason.[3] In the attainment of happiness he should make himself immune to the influence of external goods; to him virtue alone is good and vice evil, as Seneca says: 'Nec malum esse ullum nisi turpe, nec bonum nisi honestum.'[4] External goods have no influence on his happiness and cannot sway him toward good or evil; for all being except virtue and vice falls into the category of the 'indifferent,' defined as that which makes no contribution either to happiness or to ill fortune.[5] Diogenes Laertius, writing of Zeno, says that among the indifferents one must include things such as wealth, fame, health, and strength.[6] Indifferents . . . are, therefore, those external things which, having no bearing on the happiness of the wise man nor in any way disturbing his emotional equilibrium, are in the category of neither good nor bad.

The rigoristic statements of the dichotomy of virtue and vice, with all else purely indifferent, did not exist unmodified in the Stoic school. Cicero, writing of Aristo, who proposed the rigoristic scheme, states that, if this doctrine were followed, 'all life would be thrown into confusion, since there would be no distinction between the things that pertain to the conduct of life, and no choice need be exercised among them.'[7] Zeno himself foresaw the difficulty with the rigoristic position and distinguished within the indifferents 'things preferred' and 'things rejected' . . . and qualified the things preferred as those which have some worth.[8] Worth or value is described as that which contributes to harmonious living and will contribute positively to happiness.[9] In effect, the wise man can be happy without good health or a good family, but these things are aids to happiness. This assumption does not negate the previous assertion that all external things are indifferent, since the preferred are helps to happiness, but not absolutely necessary, therefore in the category of indifferent, though qualified by having some worth. Though opinion on the nature of the indifferents was to be developed and modified by later Stoic writers, most notably Panaetius, the doctrine of the interior self-sufficiency of the wise man and the indifference of external things to his happiness or virtue was to remain fundamentally unchanged.[10]

With these focal notions of Stoic teaching in mind, we may now analyze Clement's usage of the term. Inasmuch as Clement freely adopts the language of Greek philosophy to his scriptural exegesis it is not surprising to find indifference mentioned early in his works in a scriptural context.[11] In narrating St. Peter's vision in Acts 10.9-17, Clement remarks:' . . . the use of foods is a matter of indifference for us too,' and he qualifies this statement by a reference to Mt.15.11,' . . . not that which goes into the mouth defiles man.'[12] Later, writing to the Christians of Alexandria who were faced with the problem of adapting the austere Gospel morality to the social exigencies of their society, Clement advises: 'We need not abstain from rich foods . . . since we should consider the rich variety of foods a matter of indifference.'[13] This statement is expanded to include the opinion that not only are rich foods indifferent, but the 'use of food is a matter of indifference.'[14] The Christian need not abstain from the rich banquets of Alexandria, for the food and the use of it is indifferent, that is, it has no bearing on the morality of his actions. Clement explicitly links his use of the category of indifference to the Stoics by stating that the Stoics are admirable because they affirm that the soul's pursuit of virtue is not affected by health or disease since these are indifferent.[15]

In his long homily on the story of the rich man in Mk. 10.17-31, and the impediment that riches pose to salvation, Clement, after distinguishing riches within the soul and without, remarks that a man who casts away his worldly possessions can still be rich in passions. This distinction is based on the nature of riches, which are neither good nor evil, but indifferent, while the important thing for a life of true poverty, in fulfillment of the Gospel admonition, is the proper use of things.[16] From the texts cited it is clear that Clement paralleled the Stoic teaching rather closely by categorizing external goods, e.g. riches, health, food and drink, as indifferent.

In two of the citations above the word 'use' was joined to the concept of indifference.[17] In these texts 'use' was viewed objectively and passively; now the discussion will center about those texts where it has an active connotation. In the second book of the **Stromata** we find the admonition:

> There is need of a man who shall use in a discriminating and undisturbed way those things from which passions arise, for example, wealth and poverty, honor and dishonor, health and sickness, life and death, toil and pleasure: for in order that we may use with indifference indifferent things, there must be a great difference in us who have been previously afflicted with much weakness and in distortion of bad training ignorantly indulged ourselves.[18]

At first sight there seems to be a contradiction in the above sentiments between the admission that passions arise from external goods, such as wealth and health, and the recommendation that we use these same things indifferently. The solution is found in the traditional teaching of the Stoa that there are two kinds of indifferents: one so called because it has no bearing on happiness; and the other, indiffernet because it cannot excite passions.[19] Diogenes Laertius states that it is obviously not in the latter sense that health, wealth, and fame are considered indifferent.[20] It seems clear that Clement adopts this classification and distinction.

Also, in the above passage, Clement's affirmation that we should 'use with indifference indifferent things' . . . appears tautological, since he has already classed certain goods as indifferent and affirmed that their use is indifferent. The statement that we should use indifferent things indifferently explicitly affirms what was contained in his prior affirmation that things are indifferent and so too their use. In the above text indifference has been transferred from an objective quality of beings and a modality of their use to a subjective mental disposition and principle of moral activity. Again, writing on the rich man, Clement states:

> . . . yet it was not impossible even amid this [the allurements of wealth] to lay hold of salvation, if one would but transfer himself from sensible wealth to that which belongs to the mind and is taught by God, and would learn to make good and proper use of things indifferent and how to set out for eternal life.[21]

In this passage the proper use of indifferent things is not a condition for right moral action resulting from the nature of objects, but a subjective disposition resulting from a conversion . . . to a new way of thinking. The man who will be saved is the one whose mental riches consist in the ability to put to proper use the indifferent things. Indifference is a quality of external things placing them of their nature outside the sphere of morality; to this quality corresponds a mental attitude which man should cultivate and a moral disposition which results from indifferent use.

In the survey of Stoic teaching it was seen that, although external goods as indifferent contribute nothing to happiness or misery, some of the external goods are preferable . . . in the quest for happiness.[22] Though it would not be surprising to find this same qualification in Clement's teaching on indifference, actually, the opposite is true . . . [In] the fourth book of the *Stromata,* where, in describing how the true gnostic should view corporeal reality, he says:

> . . . for the soul is not good by nature, nor the body bad, nor does it follow that whatever is not good is immediately claimed as bad. There are certain mediate things . . . and within these mediate things certain ones are preferable and others rejected.[23]

. . . Potter evidently holds a direct correspondence between the means and the indifferents. Critical opinion is, however, divided on this equation. W. Capitaine (1903) agreed to the substitution of indifferents for mediate things in this passage, while K. Ernesti (1900) and M. Spanneut (1957), in commenting on the same text, hold that the above statement refers to the degrees of knowledge and that the means are morally good but called mediate because they are actions of the 'simple believer' who is *in via* to perfect knowledge.[24] They hold that the text from *Strom.* 4.26 must be taken in conjunction with *Strom.* 6.14 which reads:

> As, then, to be simply saved is the result of medium action, but to be saved rightly and becomingly is right action, so all action of the gnostic is right action; that of the simple believer is intermediate action . . . and that not yet perfected according to reason, nor made right according to knowledge; but every action of the heathen is sinful.[25]

Thus Clement distinguishes three states: that of the perfect man, the simple believer, and the sinner. To these states correspond right action, intermediate action, and sinful action. In another instance Clement uses the term 'mediate actions' where one would expect 'indifferent action.' He writes that man gains true virtue by keeping his eyes on God, the First Cause of all things, and by so doing he will make true judgements about' . . . what are his virtues and what his vices; and about things good, bad, and intermediate.'[26] W. Wilson renders the last phrase of the above citation 'good, bad, and *indifferent.*'[27] . . .

In light of these conflicting opinions on the identification of the means and the indifferents, what conclusions can be drawn regarding the interpretation of the above texts? Ernesti and Spanneut are certainly correct in holding that when Clement speaks of intermediate action as action of the simple believer, he does not mean indifferent action. On the other hand, their argumentation that when he speaks of means preferred and rejected, Clement could not well substitute indifferents, is not too cogent. Certainly the weight of traditional usage argues for the substitution of indifferents for mediate things in *Strom.* 4.26. Clement also states that some of the indifferents are preferable . . . Though it may be granted that intermediate actions, as actions of the simple believer, are not the same as indifferents, it need not be likewise affirmed that actions mediate between good and evil cannot be called indifferents. The intermediate actions of *Strom.* 6.14 are not intermediate between good and evil, but between the pure virtue of the saved and the sinful action of the heathen. Indifferents, on the other hand, are mediate between good and evil, so that the simple believer, making right use of an indifferent object, may place an action which is no longer indifferent because in the sphere of objective religious values it is mediate between true virtue and sin, but still indifferent as regards the object of his choice, which was an indifferent object. Therefore, in the text where Clement speaks of means as preferred and rejected, one could substitute indifferents for means, but this substitution need not be applied in those texts where mediate action is discussed.

In several other passages we find the conjunction of the indifferents with some form of the verb 'to live.' In *Strom.* 3.5-6, Clement takes great pains to refute two opinions. The first denies the need for any sexual self-control, while the second demands a continence which is too rigorous. The proponents of the first opinion cite Gal. 5.13: 'You have been called to freedom,' as an excuse for license. Clement says of their interpretation:

> But if passion must be gratified and the shameful life is to be preferred as indifferent, then either all passions must be obeyed, and if so, the most unholy practices must be adopted as a result of those things which seduce us, or we can turn away from these pleasures and no longer is life lived indifferently.[28]

Writing earlier of the same group, Clement proposes the same conclusion:

> . . . for they either teach you should live indifferently or are excessively ashamed and praise self-control through ill-will or contentiousness.[29]

At the end of the same section we find the statement that for the Christian to whom the Logos will show the true life through the Scriptures, life is not to be lived indifferently.[30] Allied to these statements is a condemnation of those 'who abuse the flesh and live indifferently.'[31]

Preliminary examination of the above texts seems to indicate a concept of indifference opposed to that thus far discussed. Previously indifference was praised as an attitude commendable to the Christian, and action and use joined to indifference recommended. Now life lived indifferently is censured and equated with sexual license. Clement's doctrine would seem to be in contradiction or, at best, seriously lacking in accurate terminology.

A basis for a solution to this problem is suggested by a random statement Clement makes while discussing the opinions of various schools on the end of man. In the catalogue of opinions we find the statement: 'Why should I mention Aristo, for he says that the end is indifference . . . ?' Clement then adds his criticism of this doctrine in the cryptic statement: 'For what is indifferent simply abandons the indifferent'.[32]. . .

This criticism of Aristo uttered by Clement must be understood in the light of two other ancient criticisms of this doctrine. Cicero criticizes Aristo on the ground that if his doctrine were carried to its logical conclusion life would be meaningless and there would be no place for wisdom or human choices, since everything would be absolutely indifferent.[33] Now to say that everything is absolutely indifferent is to say that the end of life is indifferent. Later in the same work Cicero repeats Chrysippus' objections to Aristo by saying that the doctrine so proposed would do away with all moral worth.[34] Diogenes Laertius, writing of Aristo, says that his doctrine would result in abandoning logic and physics and would result in a concentration upon ethics.[35]

Therefore, when Clement censures indifference and living indifferently, he is not denying his previous doctrine. He is rejecting a philosophy which would hold that the end of life is indifferent and has indicated the basis of his rejection in the succinct statement that such an end would preclude any real doctrine of indifference. Indifference is not an end, but a quality of external goods and an interior disposition which helps to ward off the influence of passion in moral choices. If the end of life is indifferent or life is lived indifferently, there is no moral choice and no right use. Clement is also seen to be within the Stoic tradition in his rejection of Aristo by following closely the objections of Chrysippus against the doctrine of absolute indifference. There exists, then, no contradiction between the two groups of statements on indifference.

From a comprehensive study of the uses of the term [indifferent] in the writings of Clement of Alexandria, the following conclusions may be adduced by way of a summary. That external objects such as wealth or poverty, health or sickness, life or death, are neither good nor bad in themselves and hence indifferent is clearly affirmed in Clement's writings. The close similarity of his thought and language to Stoicism argues for a direct influence. Clement is forceful in stating that 'indifferent use of indifferent things' is necessary for the Christian and by this affirmation makes of indifference a moral habit. While censuring a life lived indifferent to any end or purpose, he maintains his fundamental positions on the indifference of exterior things and on its interiorization as a principle governing choice. His teaching is modified by contact with other

schools, as is shown by the close relationship between the 'means' and the 'indifferents.' Clement does not intend a theoretical study of indifference; indifference is primarily a norm for moral action and a help in making judgements free from the influence of passion.[36]

The teaching on the indifferents, in its practical aspect, is seen most clearly in the selections from the ***Quis dives salvetur?*** where the notion of riches as indifferent, and the cultivation of an attitude of indifference toward them and their possession, provide the key to the dilemma posed by the Gospel story of the rich young man. Though it would be improper to speak of the teaching on the indifferents as integral to Clement's theological speculation, it is quite valid to emphasize its importance in the realm of practical Christian morality and asceticism.

Notes

1. The text of Clement used throughout is the edition of O. Stählin, GCS (4 vols. Leipzig 1905-36). The three instances of [indifferent] used in a non-moral sense are: *Paed.* 2.12.123 (GCS 1.231.9); *Strom.* 5.12.79 (GCS 2.378.25) and *Strom.* 6.2.5 (GCS 2.424.20). In these passages Clement uses 'indifferent' in the sense of 'making no difference' or of having no logical consequence in a discussion.

2. Because of the complexity of Clement's work many proximate sources have been adduced for his Stoic notions. P. Wendland, *Quaestiones Musonianae* (Berlin 1886), whom C. P. Parker 'Musonius in Clement,' *Harvard Studies in Classical Philology* 12 (1901) 191-200, followed, finds a lost treatise of Musonius in the *Paedagogos* of Clement. A. Scheck, O.S.B., *De fontibus Clementis Alexandrini* (Augsburg 1888) 49, holds that in philosophical matters Clement (along with Diogenes Laertius) depends on Favorinus. Despite the difficulty of discovering the actual sources used by Clement, a strong influence of the Stoa on the school of Alexandria is certain. Cf. M. Pohlenz, *Die Stoa* (Göttingen 1959) 1416-418, and J. Stelzenberger, *Die Beziehungen der früchristlichen Sittenlehre zur Ethik der Stoa* (Munich 1933) 166-170; 226-231.

3. E. Zeller, *The Stoics, Epicureans and Sceptics* (London 1880) 223-242. M. Pohlenz, *op. cit.* I 110-143.

4. Seneca, *De beneficiis* 7.2.2.

5. Sextus Empiricus, *Outlines of Pyrrhonism* 3.177 . . . Sextus distinguishes the indifferents in three senses: the first, that which is an object of neither inclination nor disinclination; the second, that which is an object of inclination or disinclination, but not toward any definite object; and a third sense as that which contributes to neither happiness nor unhappiness. Zeller, *op. cit.* 232 n. 3, dismisses the first two senses as irrelevant. It is the third sense that will be considered in Clement.

6. Diogenes Laertius, *Vitae* 7.104-105. Diogenes testifies to two senses of indifferent, but holds that the

proper sense is 'that which contributes to neither happiness nor unhappiness.'

7. Cicero, *De finibus* 3.50:' . . . confunderetur omnis vita . . . cum inter ea quae ad vitam degendam pertinerent nihil omnino interesset neque ullum dilectum adhiberi oporteret.'

8. *Stoicorum Veterum Fragmenta* 1.192 (ed. J. von Arnim, Leipzig 1921); Pohlenz, *Die Stoa,* II 69.

9. Diogenes Laertius, *Vitae* 7.105.

10. For a detailed and complete treatment of the indifferents in Stoic thought, cf. M. Reesor, 'The "Indifferents" in the Old and Middle Stoa,' *Transactions and Proceedings of the American Philological Association* 82 (1951) 102-110. The author here very clearly discusses the doctrine as propounded by the Old Stoa and the changes it underwent under the influence of later writers, especially Panaetius. For an example of the substantial identity of doctrine between the older and later Stoic writers, cf. Epictetus, *Discourses* 2.16.19; 4.1.

11. On this adaptation of Clement, cf. C. Mondésert, S.J., *Clément d'Alexandrie: Introduction à l'étude de sa pensée religieuse à partir de l'écriture* (Paris 1944) 221-227.

12. *Paed.* 2.16.3 (GCS 1.165.21-24) . . .

13. *Paed.* 2.10.1 (GCS 1.160.20-24) . . .

14. *Paed.* 2.9.1 (GCS 1.159.24) . . .

15. *Strom.* 4.15.19 (GCS 2.256.33) . . .

16. *Quis dives* 15.3 (GCS 3.169.20) . . .

17. Cf. nn. 12 and 14 *supra*.

18. *Strom.* 2.20.109 (GCS 2.173.4) . . .

19. Diogenes Laertius, *Vitae* 7.105.

20. *Loc. cit.*

21. *Quis dives* 20.2 (GCS 3.172.26-30) . . .

22. Cf. nn. 8 and 9 *supra;* Reesor, *art. cit.* (n. 10 *supra*) 103-104.

23. *Strom.* 4.26.164 (GCS 2.321.17-20) . . .

24. Wilhelm Capitaine, *Die Moral des Clemens von Alexandrien* (Paderborn 1903) 192, describes the mediate things as those which are neither good nor bad and, for a definition of these *Mitteldinge,* refers to *Strom.* 4.26.164. Cf. n.23 *supra* and *Strom.* 2.7.34 (GCS 2.130.26), where τα μεταξη αρετης are listed as poverty, illness, lack of honor, and a poor family background—things which are also classed as indifferent. Konrad Ernesti, *Die Ethik des Titus Flavius Clemens von Alexandrien* (Paderborn 1900) 20. Michel Spanneut, *Le stoïcisme des Pères de l' Église* (Paris 1957) 245.

25. *Strom.* 6.14.111 (GCS 2.487.25) . . .

26. *Strom.* 7.3.17 (GCS 3.13.6) . . .

27. W. Wilson, *op. cit.* (n. 18 *supra*) II 418.

28. *Strom.* 3.5.41 (GCS 2.214.30) . . .

29. *Strom.* 3.4.40 (GCS 2.214.10) . . .

30. *Strom.* 3.5.42 (GCS 2.215.19) . . .

31. *Strom.* 3.10.70 (GCS 2.228.5) . . . Cf. also *Strom.* 3.8.61 (GCS 2.224.10).

32. *Strom.* 2.21.129 (GCS 2.183.14) . . . Cf. W. Wilson, *op. cit.* II 73 . . .

33. Cicero, *De finibus* 3.50.

34. Cicero, *De finibus* 4.69: 'Quod enim sapientia pedem ubi poneret non habebat sublatis officiis omnibus, officia autem tollebantur delectu omni et discrimine remoto, quae esse non poterant rebus omnibus sic exaequatis ut inter eas nihil interesset . . .'

35. Diogenes Laertius, *Vitae* 7.160.

36. Spanneut, *Le stoícisme des Pères* 266. 'Enfin, dans le domaine moral, son influence est primordiale et se laisse préciser. Le Stoïcisme antique a fourni au christianisme une série de concepts et de théories; l stoïcisme contemporain lui a dicté—et jusque dans les mots—sa morale pratique. Ces données sont parfois adaptées ou transposées, mais le stoïcisme est partout reconnaissable et sa place, au total, est bien grande aux premiers siècles de l'Église dans toutes les questions qui concernent l'homme.'

Walter Wagner (essay date 1968)

SOURCE: "Another Look at the Literary Problem in Clement of Alexandria's Major Writings," in *Church History,* Vol. XXXVII, No. 3, September, 1986, pp. 251-60.

[*In the following essay, Wagner surveys the history of the theses concerning the controversial relationship between Clement's three major works.*]

The relationship among Clement of Alexandria's three major works, ***Protreptikos, Paidagōgos*** and ***Stromateis,*** has vexed scholars for almost a century. Present state of the question reflects the condition of Clement studies as a whole: a welter of promising insights, ingenious theories, many contradictions and frustrating confusion. Recent attempts to approach the Alexandrine through historical-exegetical procedures have reopened Clement studies and have suggested that re-examination and re-evaluation of his theology are in order.[1]

The literary question is important to an understanding of Clement's thought, for the relationship of the three works may furnish insight into the structure of his theology. The variety of theories about the relationship indicates that the history of the interpretation of the Church Father is one of disagreements. To clarify the questions involved, the various theses will be surveyed and then another thesis offered.

The traditional position holds the three works to be a trilogy in which the ***Protreptikos*** and ***Paidagōgos*** serve as exhortation and instruction for converts and the 'simple faithful,'' while the ***Stromateis*** is esoteric teaching for the gnostic. The main text for this and other theses is Paid. I, 3, 3

> But eagerly desiring, then, to perfect us by a gradation for salvation in an effective discipline, a beautiful *oikonomia* is joined by the all-philanthropic Logos, first exhorting (*protrepōn*), then training (*paidagōgōn*) and finally, teaching (*ekdidaskōn*).

In the light of earlier statements, Clement clearly depicted the Logos as functioning in three ways. The first two dealt with *praktikē*, while the last with *methodikē*. When the Logos acted in the former manner, He assumed the roles of *protreptikos* and *paidagōgos*. In dispensing advanced and presumably esoteric guidance, He took the part of *didaskalos*.

Proponents of the traditional thesis noted that two of the three works were titled ***Protreptikos*** and ***Paidagōgos,*** that the ***Stromateis*** was obviously related to these, and that Clement indicated that blossoms of gnosis could be discerned in the ***Stromateis***. They concluded that the ***Stromateis*** should be considered under the title ***Didaskalos***. On the basis of the opening chapter of the *paidagōgos* they held that Clement not only depicted three functions of the Logos, but also wrote a trilogy which corresponded to those functions.[2]

The position had two major drawbacks. First, Clement neither called the ***Stromateis*** *"Didaskalos,"* nor is there any reference in his extant works that he projected such a work, nor is any such work mentioned by those who claimed familiarity with his writings. Eusebius and Photius did not connect the ***Stromateis*** to the other works and did not indicate that Clement had a well-defined literary plan. Second, Bardenhewer pointed out the disconcerting fact that the ***Stromateis*** failed to live up to the expectation of being a discourse on the Logos's role as *didaskalos* of esoteric gnosis, for it repeatedly lapsed into ethical matters discussed in the previous two works.[3] In short, in both title and content the ***Stromateis*** did not fit the role scholars expected of the ***Didaskalos***.

Eugene De Faye advanced the view that Clement projected a trilogy, but after completing two-thirds of it was forced into a digression.[4] The ***Didaskalos*** would have made extensive use of philosophy. Because the *orthodoxoi* and "simple faithful" distrusted philosophy on account of pagan and heretical distortions, Clement undertook a defense of philosophy in God's plan which was to serve as a preface to the ***Didaskalos***. De Faye further suggested that the defense-preface was the ***Stromateis*** and that either Clement never wrote the ***Didaskalos*** or it is no longer extant. The thesis recognized the lengthy sections, chiefly in ***Strom***. I-IV, which treated philosophy in the context of the Logos's pre and post-*parousia* activities to justify men. De

Faye, however, did not deal as fully with the closing books which were concerned with the character of the true gnostics.

Paul Wendland immediately but incompletely criticized De Faye's thesis and Carl Heussi developed the criticisms and Wendland's suggestions.[5] The Wendland-Heussi thesis, based on inadequate pre-Stählin texts, examined verb tenses at particular points and came to startling conclusions.[6] Specifically, they held that ***Strom***. I-IV was written prior to both the ***Protreptikos*** and the ***Paidagōgos,*** and that after writing the ***Protreptikos,*** Clement conceived the idea of a trilogy with the ***Protreptikos*** as the first member. The completed trilogy then consisted of the ***Protreptikos, Paidagōgos*** and ***Strom***. V-VIII; the ***Paidagōgos*** contained the promised writing on marriage, while ***Strom***. V-VII dealt with the passions.[7]

The thesis explained the distracting opening of the ***Stromateis,*** preserved the traditional view that the works form a trilogy, and took into account the nature of the material in the closing books of the ***Stromateis***. ***Stromateis*** V-VIII, then, was the ***Didaskalos***. But Otto Stählin questioned the thesis's basic assumptions by suggesting that there were references to the ***Protreptikos*** and ***Paidagōgos*** in the ***Stromateis*** prior to Book V.[8]

Next Johannes Munck struck at the logic and psychology of the thesis and then demolished it by demonstrating passages in ***Strom***. I and III reflected and were dependent upon the ***Paidgōgos***.[9] He then put forward the theory that Clement had planned two necessarily unrelated trilogies. The first, intended for simple believers, was to consist of the ***Protreptikos, Paidagōgos*** and ***Didaskalos***. The second, intended solely for gnostics, was to be ***Strom***. I-III, ***Strom***. IV-VII and ***Physiologia***.[10] According to Munck Clement did not write the final members of the trilogies. Stählin gave the view qualified support, and Lazzati, although he accused Munck of rigidly systematizing Clement's thought, agreed that Clement wrote exoteric and esoteric works.[11]

Friedrick Quatember, frustrated by the proliferation of theories, held that previous scholars consistently misinterpreted the crucial passage in the *paidagōgos*.[12] He argued that Clement was not proposing a trilogy but was setting forth three forms of the Logos's teaching-drawing men to salvation. Clement described the Logos's dynamic activity and did not want to write three treatises which isolated the instruction proper to each form of that educational activity. On the basis of careful exegesis Quatember claimed that the search for a trilogy, a search which centered on the ***Stromateis,*** misunderstood and distorted Clement's purpose and ethical teaching. Thus Clement set forth not a literary plan but a *Heilsplan*.

Quatember noted that the purpose of the Logos-*didaskalos* was to lead men into the depths of gnosis. Clement considered attempts to write of such revelation as dangerous and open to misunderstanding, and it is therefore highly doubtful that he intended to write a work which purported to present such a *didaskalia*.

Because of wartime and post-war conditions and the limited publications of doctoral dissertations, Quatember's work did not come to the attention of other scholars. Walther Völker, who had not seen it, independently attacked Munck's double trilogy thesis and wrecked the assumption that the **Stromateis** was unrelated to the other two major works.[13] Exasperated with the multiplication of complex theories, he termed the whole debate a word quarrel which did not contribute to understanding Clement. Yet Völker took a stand on the issue. He returned to the traditional thesis but adopted the qualification of the earlier English scholar, R. E. Tollinton:

> In short Clement started on his enterprise without realizing the magnitude and difficulty . . . he did not live to accomplish the embodiment (and) he had never clearly grasped in all its implications the character of his own great purpose . . . . Thus the fact that Clement chose to write a series of Stromateis in place of the projected "Master" must in the main be set down to the character of his public . . . . In a word, the Stromateis are and yet are not the projected "Master." In writing them Clement realized in part his purpose of higher teaching. In writing them he also came to recognize that his own purpose could never be fully realized at all.[14]

In the twenty years since Quatember's too-little known work and Völker's strictures, nothing has been done with the issue of the literary relationship. Quatember's break with the customary interpretation of the key passages, however, opened the way for at least one more attempt to examine the problem.

II

An historical-exegetical study gives full attention both to the writings and the *Sitz im Leben* in which they were written. The basis for a new view is the recognition of Clement's knowledge and use of contemporary ethical literary forms. It has been recognized that the opening of the **Paidagōgos** reflects concerns also present in Stoic ethics, but there have been no attempts to delineate these and related aspects in reference to Clement.[15] The suggested thesis acknowledges its debt to the forms of Stoic ethics but holds these forms were in common use, even by Philo. In order to develop the thesis Zeno, Posidonius, Cicero, Seneca and Philo must be cited.

Zeno and many who followed him divided philosophy into three branches: logic, ethics and physics (*physiologia*). He subdivided ethics into more than eight sections, two of which were *aretai* and *kathēkonta*. *Aretai* consisted of primary virtues (the same as Plato's innate *aretai*) and particular virtues (magnaminity, self control or *egkrateia*, endurance, good counsel and presence of mind).[16] *Kathēkonta* were further defined as all actions which *logos* would have a man do. These were split into absolute and conditional duties. The former were always incumbent

upon a man, while the latter were binding only under particular circumstances. Presence of mind was the *aretē* which found what was *kathēkon*.

Stoic emphasis on *kathēkonta* was expressed in literature. Zeno, Cleanthes, Panaetius and Posidonius wrote treatises basically titled *Peri Kathēkontōn*.[17] It is also clear that philosophical teachers attracted and encouraged new students through a rhetorically ornate work called *Protreptikos*.[18] Aristotle, Cleanthes, Marcus Brutus and Posidonius all wrote such works.[19]

Posidonius held that only man's soul had the rational faculty, although it shared the willing and appetitive faculties with animals.[20] The rational faculty increased in greatness and strength by means of proper *paideia*. Men went through three stages of development, each with its proper form of teaching. In the first, *phaulos* or low-ranking beginner, threats, promises, compulsion and encouragement were used. The second, *prokopos* or progressing learner, was based on lessons, arguments, encouragement, praise and admonitions. The final stage, *sophos* or wiseman, was not dealt with extensively in the extant works, but involved initiation into the *dogmata* of philosophical-religious truths.

Posidonius retained the three-fold division of philosophy and the subdivision of duties into absolute and conditional. Ethics itself was composed of only two branches, *theōretikē* and *praktikē*. The former involved thorough knowledge of the absolute duties or general principles, which were termed *Kathorthōmata*. *Praktikē* was the area of conditional duties for which he used the expression *kathēkontōn protropōn te kai apotropōn*.[21] In order to be roused to rational ethical conduct, the soul needed precept-giving, persuasion, consolation, exhortation and investigation of causes (*kathēkonta, hypothetikē, paramathetikē, aitologia.*)[22]

Posidonius's division of ethics into *theōretikē* which dealt with *katorthōmata*, and *praktikē*, which dealt with *kathēkonta* (now restricted to particular duties) kept the sense of initiation into the mysteries of ethics. *Protreptikos* and *Peri Kathēkontōn* therefore were directed chiefly toward *praktikē*.[23]

This two-fold division of ethics was reflected in Posidonius's independently yet syncretistically minded pupil, Cicero. The orator-statesman opened *De Officiis* by noting that moral treatises were traditionally separated into two parts which correspond to a *Peri Kathēkontōn* and a *Peri Katorthōmatōn*.[24] *De Officiis* is Cicero's *Peri Kathēkontōn*. He defined *katorthōmata* as the fulfillment or goal of all human actions, while *kathēkonta* were the practical common duties.

Seneca held to the three-fold division of philosophy and concentrated on ethics.[25] He indicated there was debate over the relative merits of *Katorthōmata* and *Kathēkonta*.[26] Common duties, he maintained, were in the realm of *prak-*

tikē or *phronēsis*, while general principles were properly included in *Sophia* or *Theōretikē*. Seneca took a mediating position in the debate, writing that it was impossible to separate the two and that elements of *katorthōmata-theōretikē* were mingled with *kathēkonta-praktikē* so as to excite the student to press on to fulfillment. The student passed through the three stages of beginner, learner and wiseman.[27] During the ascent to fulfillment the individual increasingly was brought closer to *katorthōmata- theōre-tikē* until he became a *sophos*. Ethics entailed an esoteric tradition. In discussing the *katorthōmata* Seneca employed terms from the mysteries. Only the adept knew the *katorthōmata* fully, while the uninitiated knew the *kathēkonta* in the *phaulos* and *prokopos* stages.[28]

Philo of Alexandria accepted the three-fold division of philosophy and the two-part sub-division of ethics, but held that the ineffable mysteries of God transcended philosophy.[29] Philosophy was only the loving search for wisdom, while wisdom herself led men to initiation into the mystery. He also kept the distinction between *katorthōmata-theōretikē* and *kathēkonta-praktikē*. In the Eden garden-soul the trees which were beautiful to see (*theōretike*) were the *aretai katorthōmata*, while those good to eat (*praktikē*) of *kathēkonta*.[30] Philo thereby equated the primary virtues with *kathorthōmata* or absolute duties, and the particular virtues with *kathēkonta* or conditional duties.

In summary, the *Sitz im Leben* shows that a tri-partite division of philosophy with ethics as one part was commonly accepted. Ethics was split into two portions, one being practical and concerned with specific duties and the other having an esoteric portion and dealing with *katorthōmata*. Traces of the esoteric portion could be discerned in the elementary practical instruction. Also common was a three-fold view of man's progress, in which man was depicted as coming into greater knowledge of the esoteric foundations and goals of ethics. Philosophy's fulfillment was not attained in ethics but in *physiologia*. The goal of ethics was *aretē*, but man's goal was full initiation by wisdom into the gnosis of nature and God. This structure of ethics tended to be expressed in literary form as *protreptikoi* and two-part ethical treatises. One part of the latter literary form was a *Peri Kathēkontōn*, while the other discussed *katorthōmata* more fully. While *Protreptikoi* and *Peri kathēkontōn* contained elements of *katorthōmata-theōretikē*, they were concerned with particular duties and *praktikē*.

Clement accepted this three part view of philosophy. He considered ethics the gateway to cosmogony (*kosmogonia*), apparently another term he employed for *physiologia*. Philosophy in turn led to the highest form of knowledge, *Epopteia* or initiation into the great mysteries of theology. *Epopteia* transcended philosophy.[31] Ethics was fulfilled in the lesser mysteries of *katorthōmata*, which in turn served as the transition to *physiologia-kosmogonia*. The supreme mysteries were in the crowing realm of initiation-vision, *Epopteia*.[32]

Clement divided the human career into four stages but actually maintained the basic three-fold structure.[33] He halved the *phaulos* stage into those who were disobedient (pagans and unconverted Jews) and those who were legal slaves to God (catechumens, i.e., those formally enrolled in the Church for preparation to be enlightened by baptism). The baptized or legal slaves were the *prokopoi*, the faithful servants of God who were engaged in the ascent of becoming complete men in the image and likeness of the Logos. The *sophos* or gnostic was the adopted son of God. He was in the Logos's image and likeness as much as was humanly possible.[34]

The Logos addressed Himself to men in these stages in three ways. To the *phauloi* of both classes He spoke as *protreptikos*, while to the *prokopoi* as *paidagōgos* and to the *sophoi* as *didaskalos*. Such an arrangement was integral to God's loving *oikonomia* in which the Logos philanthropically improved the soul so that it was drawn willingly to consummation in true manhood.[35]

This understanding of man and God's plan allows insight into the relationships among the three works. Almost all the extant works are best understood as belonging to the ethical division of philosophy. The **Stromateis** is clearly an ethical treatise.[36] In discussing the nature and title of the **Stromateis** Clement remarked that the work was properly named, for it contained the seeds of generative doctrine.[37]

This is the same view which Seneca and Philo had of *katorthōmata* prior to initiation. Clement indicated that the reader was to make progress not only in the preliminary teaching of the **Protreptikos** and **Paidagōgos,** but also in the garden of the **Stromateis**. The **Stromateis** contributed to the reader's advance in becoming a gnostic, yet it did not end that advance.[38]

The three works are ethical treatises and were to be used in the individual's ethical training within the Church with the Logos as healer and guide. Each work had the seeds of *katorthōmata-theoretikē* planted in *kathēkonta-praktikē*. To be saved in the proper manner was to know the foundations and goals of the specific duties, i.e., to know the *katorthōmata* from which the *katheokonta* came and to which they directed the student.[39] The **Stromateis** dealt more fully with the *katorthōmata* than the other two works. Clement suggested that the Logos led His children in three general ways: what was useful and advisable, what was praiseworthy, and what was blessed.[40]

The first way involved actions which were to be encouraged (*protreptikos*) and discouraged (*apotreptikos*), and the second indicated what was commendable (*epainetikos*) and worthy of recrimination (*psketikos*). These two forms were carefully developed in the **Paidagōgos** and can be seen in an undeveloped manner in the **Protreptikos**. The third form, *makarios*, was not handled in those treatises, but the **Stromateis** discussed the blessed state of the gnostic and his responsibility. The tones of the **Stromateis** suggest that it may serve as the transition between the Logos's *paidagōgia* on what is praiseworthy, useful and advisable to what was blessed. It is clear, however, that the work was part neither of *physiologia* nor *epopteia*, but of ethics. The **Stromateis** indicated something of the lesser mysteries of the ethical branch of philosophy, but was not an exposition of the greater mysteries.

In light of the accepted ethically oriented literary practice, therefore, the **Protreptikos** and the **Paidagōgos** can be termed Clement's expositions on particular duties with traces of *kathorthōmata*. Broadly, these two works cover the field of *kathēkonta* and were aimed at the first two classes of men. More narrowly construed, the **Proptreptikos** was designed for the two groups in the *phaulos* stage. The tone, often abusive, threatening and mocking, became ultimately encouraging and hopeful, for it was intended to jab and exhort the *phauli* to their next stage in God's beautiful *oikonomia*. Intended for baptized Christians, God's servant-children, the **Paidagōgos**'s tone was pointed but re-assuring and guiding. Particular duties (*kathēkonta*) dominated the work, although these were preceded and followed by important discussions of God's action and man's responsibility.

Book I supplied the general framework by considering man's habits, actions and passions which were addressed by the Logos's protreptic, hypothetic and paramythetic actions.[41] The theme of the Christ-Logos leading His new children to salvation dominated the whole work. Books II and III handled the specific manners of that leading in terms of *kathēkonta*. In regard to literary form the **Paidagōgos** can be considered Clement's *Peri Kathēkontōn*. The **Protreptikos** and **Paidagōgos** together meet the concerns of the branch of ethics called *praktikē*.

The **Stromateis**, as Bardenhewer discerned, returned constantly to ethical themes. The work can be seen as Clement's attempt to write the second part of a total ethical discourse, the equivalent of a *Peri Katorthōmata*. He worked within the limits of the distinctions among ethics, *physiologia* and *epopteia*. The treatise is a more fully developed exposition of the religious-ethical foundations of God's plan and man's action. The **Stromateis** was not a **Didaskalos**; indeed it is improbable that Clement would have considered writing a work which boasted putting *epopteia*-revelation into written form.

The **Stromateis** is instead exactly what Clement said it was—a sheaf of notes, artfully planned, through which the reader could continue his advance in soul-improvement. It was for those already sufficiently trained in *kathēkonta* and who had the ability to gain from exposure to the *kathorthōmata* which undergirded the specific duties. Yet the work was open to all readers, even non-Christians, but only those subject to the Logos could gain fully from it. The **Stromateis** was meaningful to the highly trained *prokopos*, the man whose actions, habits and passions were strengthened and admost completely healed by the Logos. It led him to the fullness of *aretē* so that he could look forward

to advancement in *physiologia* and then ultimate rest (*anapausis*) in *Epopteia*.

The major works, then, are best understood as ethical treatises which respect the traditional divisions of philosophy. Seen from the perspective of those divisions, the treaties fulfill the *praktikē* portion and direct the reader to the completion of the *theoretikē* portion of ethics. The **Protreptikos** and **Paidagōgos** deal chiefly with *kathēkonta*, presenting the Logos as *praktikē* in liberating and healing sinful men. The **Stromateis** indicates more clearly, but not completely, the *katorthōmata-theōretikē* of the Logos. Seen from the perspective of the internal relationships, it is clear that the three works are arranged so that the discerning, capable reader ought to move from *phaulos* to the brink of *sophos* with their assistance. Since Clement related the three, they actually form one total work. The movement from one to another is similar to the ethical-paidagogical progress man makes in the Church under the gentle guidance of the one Logos in His several roles.

The three works are consequently not a trilogy in the sense of the traditional thesis but are best viewed as ethical treatises which, considered as a whole, satisfy the requirements of writings on particular and absolute duties. The major writings are a thoughtful, fundamentally complete and consistent attempt to present an ethic in Christ.

Notes

1. One noteworthy historical-exegetical study is Georg Kretschmar's unpublished PhD. thesis (University of Heidelberg, 1950), *Jesus Christus in der Theologie des Klemens von Alexandrien*. The writer is grateful to Dr. Kretschmar for sending a copy to him and for allowing Drew University, Madison, N. J., to microfilm his work.

2. Among the older exponents of the traditional view are John Kaye, *Some Account of the Writings and Opinions of Clement of Alexandria* (London, 1835) and William Wilson, *The Writings of Clement of Alexandria* (Edinburgh, 1901).

3. Otto Bardenhewer, *Patrologie,* 2nd edition (Freiburg im Breisgau) p. 114.

4. Eugene De Faye, *Clément d' Alexandrie* (Paris, 1898).

5. Paul Wendland, review of De Faye's book in *Theologische Literaturzeitung,* XXIII, (Dec. 10, 1898) 653f. Carl Heussi, "Die Stromateis des Clemens Alexandrinus und ihr Verhältnis zum Protreptikos und Paedagogos," *Zeitschrift für wissenschaftliche Theologie,* XLV, (1902), 465-512.

6. Adolph Harnack, Theodore Zahn and Otto Bardenhewer readily accepted the view as did Francis Havey ("Clement of Alexandria" in the *Catholic Encyclopedia,* New York, 1908, p. 12) and Simon Wood (*Clement of Alexandria. Christ the Educator,* New York 1954).

7. They recognized that present Book VIII was not original to the work but considerations on logic.

8. Otto Stählin, *Bibliothek der Kirchenvlater . . . Clemens von Alexandreia,* I (Munich, 1934 ed.), 32.

9. Johannes Munck, *Untersuchungen über Klemens von Alexandrien* (Stuttgart, 1933).

10. Among the treatises Clement proposed to write but which he did not or which are not extant were a *Physiologia* as well as a *Peri Archön.*

11. Stählin, I, 33-35. G. Lazzati, *Introduzione allo studio di Clemente Alessandrino* (Milan, 1939).

12. Friedrich Quatember, S.J., *Die christliche Lebenshaltung des Klemens von Alexandreia.* Originally a PhD. thesis for the Gregorian University (Rome, 1942), it was published in Vienna in 1947.

13. Walther Völker, *Der wahre Gnostiker nach Clemens Alexandrinus* (Leipzig, 1952). It was completed during World War II but not published due to production problems.

14. R. B. Tollinton, *Clement of Alexandria. A Study in Christian Liebralism.* I (London, 1914), 192f. *Völker,* p. 32, nt. 1.

15. *Stählin* I, 204, nt. 1; Karl Reinhardt, *Posidonius* (Munich, 1921), p. 56; *Wood,* p. 3, nt. 2.

16. Diogenes Laertius (*Lives of the Eminent Philosophers,* VII, 108) stressed that Zeno was the first to use *Kathēkonta* (that which is fitting and proper) in ethics.

17. *Diogenes Laertius,* VII, 4, 91, 92, 166. Cicero, *De Officiis* I, 7f.

18. Seneca, *Epistle* XCV, 65 noted *protreptikos* as one of five things needed to rouse the soul to rational conduct. The literary style and use of *protreptikoi* is considered by Wilhelm Gehäusser, *Der Protreptikos des Posidonius* (Munich, 1912) and Ingemar During, *Aristotle's Protrepticos. An attempt at Reconstruction* (Goteborg, 1961). Helpful considerations are given by G. Pire, *Stoïcisme et Pédàgogie* (Paris, 1958).

19. *Diogenes Laertius,* VIII. Seneca, *Epistle* XCV, 45. Aristotle, *Fragment 51.*

20. Much debate surrounds Posidonius. *Diogenes Laertius* XII, 39f. has the bulk of his known views and there are also comments in Sextus Epiricus's *Against the Dagmatists,* Cicero, Seneca and Galen (*De Placitis Hippocrates et Platonis*). In addition to Gerhäusser and Reinhardt Posidonius was dealt with by Werner Jaeger, *Nemesius von Emessa* (Berlin, 1914); J. Dobson, "The Posidonius Myth," *Classical Quarterly* (1918) XII, pp. 179-195; Paul Schubert, *Die Eschatologie des Posidonius* (Leipzig, 1927); Ludwig Edelstein, "The Philosophical System of Posidonius," *The American Journal of Philology* (1936) LI, pp. 286-325; and B. Hijmans's "Posidonius' Ethics," *Acta Classica* (1959), pp. 27-42. This study is endebted to Hijmans's work.

21. *Diogenes Laertius,* VII, 84.

22. Seneca, *Epistle* XCV, 65.

23. *Diogenes Laertius,* VII, 84.

24. Cicero, *De Officiis,* 1, 7-8.

25. Seneca's *Epistle* LXXXIX dealt with the parts of philosophy and mentioned the *paedagogus* of humanity was the philosopher. The moral portion of philosophy had three parts: speculation (*thōretikē*), impulse (*hormētikē*) and action (*praktikē*).

26. Seneca's *Epistle* XCIV defended *kathēkonta,* while XCV took up the cause of *katorthōmata.*

27. Seneca, *Epistle* LII, 3-4.

28. Seneca, *Epistle* XCV, 64. Plutarch (*On the Education of Children,* 10) described those who fulfilled their *paideia* as "hierophants of the gods and torch-bearers of wisdom."

29. Philo, *Legum Allegoria* I, 57; *De Congressu* 14; *De Decalogo* 20; De Cherubim 12-20; *De Virtutibus* 3; *De Vita Mosis* 11; *De Posteriatate Caini* 6, 38, 42; *De Ebrietate* 21-22, 39; *Quod Ominis Probus* 2; *De Sacrificii* 5, 10, 22-25; *De Agricultura* 3. Philo also called Deuteronomy Moses's *Protreptikos (De Agricultura* 17, 39).

   Clement's use of Philo was noted by De Faye, Völker, Wilhelm Boussett (*Jüdisch-Christliche Schulbetrieb in Alexandrien und Rom,* Göttingen, 1915). Albert Outler ("The 'Platonism' of Clement of Alexandria," *Journal of Religion,* 1940, XX, 217-240) and Erich Osborn (*The Philosophy of Clement of Alexandria,* Cambridge, 1957).

30. Philo, *Legum Allegoria* I, 56-66.

31. *Strom.* I. 30; 97, 1; 176, 1-3; IV. 104; VI. 84; VII. 4. Clement probably considered logic as prefatory to ethics. Present *Strom.* VIII may be a portion of his logic.

32. *Prot.* 118.
    Paid. I. 102-103
    Strom. I. 176; IV. 155; V. 70; VI. 54; 108.

33. *Prot.* 5; 8; 85; 95.
    Paid. I. 1; 18; 26; 53; 98; III. 37.
    Strom. I. 2; 173; VI. 102.

34. *Prot.* 117
    Paid. I. 1-3; 98-99; III. 86-101.
    Strom. II. 97.

35. *Paid.* I. 87. *Strom.* IV. 3; VI. 50; 78.

36. *Strom.* IV. 3; VI. 1

37. *Strom.* IV. 6. Eusebius (*Ecclesiastical History* VI. 13) felt he called it *Stromateis* because it contained a variety of pagan opinions, history and specimens of learning.

38. *Strom.* VI. 1-4; IV. 1.

39. *Strom.* VI. 111.

40. *Paid.* I. 75-95.

41. *Paid.* I. 1f.

John Ferguson (essay date 1974)

SOURCE: "Clement's Achievement," *in Clement of Alexandria,* Twayne Publishers, 1974, pp. 192-94.

[*In the following essay, Ferguson summarizes Clement's ideas and his importance, crediting him with being the "real founder of a Christian philosophy of religion."*]

In his masterly book *Christ and Culture* H. Richard Niebuhr identified five main attitudes which Christians have taken towards secular culture. The first emphasizes the opposition between Christ and culture. The second claims a fundamental agreement between Christ and culture. In the third ("Christ above culture"), Christ is seen as the fulfillment of cultural aspirations, at once continuous and discontinuous with the culture that has gone before. The fourth sees "Christ and Culture in Paradox," a dualist view in which man lives in two worlds and has responsibilities to both. The final attitude is conversionist; Christ is seen as the transformer of culture. In this debate Clement clearly belongs to the third group, of which he is the supreme representative. "There is only one river of truth, but a lot of streams disgorge their waters into it" (*Str.* 1,5,29).

He has, as Montdésert says, an "audacious optimism, his confidence in the power and authority of truth." But the Logos, who reveals truth, also "loves concealment." Hence, allegorical interpretation. Yet this, alien to our temper, springs from the assumption that there is a pattern in the universe, and that if you cut through the universe at different points you will find the same pattern. So too with Clement's rich use of imagery; it comes from a total view of life. Even his characteristic wordplay is linked to a belief that word and object are part of a single pattern.

Clement in his use of language appears at his most modern and at his most profound. He insists that we cannot speak of God as he is (*Str.* 2,16; 5,17). We can speak about God; we are not naming him, but pointing the mind in the right direction; we may think of One, or light, or reality—and go beyond that. A whole philosophy of religious language might be built on Clement's assertion that essential discourse is to say "God is the Lord of all" (*Str.* 6,17).

Clement's philosophy of life centers on God, who is one and beyond one (*Paed.* 1,8,71); it looks backward to the Middle Platonism of Maximus of Tyre and Albinus, and forward to the Neo-Platonism of Plotinus. His theology is based firmly on the Logos, as the revelation of God. He found in Philo woven together the Jewish Memra, the Word by which God speaks and it is done, and the Greek teaching of the Reason behind the universe, and he Christianized Philo; he declared that the Logos was revealed in Jesus (*Protr.* 1,7). It is astonishing that Clement was accused of denigrating the Son; it was a juster charge that he

identified the Son too closely with the Father. But Clement's theology is not a systematic construct; it is an expression of experience.

The world is good; Clement will have nothing of Gnostic dualism; evil is not a substance. But man is fallen, and God becomes man so that man may become God (*Protr.* 8,4; *Str.* 7,101,4). Clement has a warm, joyous, healthy picture of human life as he portrays the Christian gentleman in the last two books of *The Tutor* and the fragment from *To the Newly Baptized.* From faith to fulfillment there are two roads, one moral and one intellectual, love and knowledge. Ultimately they are one; knowledge is the perfection of love (*Str.* 4,7,54), love the perfection of knowledge. The ultimate aim is knowledge of God. To know oneself is to know God; to know God is to become like God (*Paed.* 3,1). The true Gnostic has his fulfillment in the eternal vision of God.

As a man Clement's sanity attracts us. For many this was an age of anxiety. Already in the reign of Marcus Aurelius the frontier dams of empire were leaking, straining. The emperor himself had been a pensive, wistful, ineffective agnostic. Contrast the warm humanity of Clement with his insistence that joy is the keynote of the church and gladness of the Christian gnostic (*Str.* 7,101). Charles Bigg said of him: "No later writer has so serene and hopeful a view of human nature."

Clement is the real founder of a Christian philosophy of religion. The Neo-Platonists were to come to their philosophical commitment in three stages—purification, initiation, vision. The Christian Platonist before them offers a parallel scheme. It was a remarkable achievement to conceive it, still more to go so far towards executing it. Adolf Harnack assessed it justly. He called it "the boldest literary experiment in the history of the church," "the first attempt to use Holy Scripture and the church tradition—together with the assumption that Christ, as the Reason of the world, is the source of all truth—as the basis of a presentation of Christianity, which at once addresses itself to the cultured by satisfying the scientific demand for a philosophical ethic and theory of the world, and at the same time reveals to the believer the rich content of his faith."

James E. Davison (essay date 1983)

SOURCE: "Structural Similarities and Dissimilarities in the Thought of Clement of Alexandria and the Valentinians," in *The Second Century: A Journal of Early Christian Studies,* Vol. 3, No. 4, Winter, 1983, pp. 201-17.

[*In the following essay, Davison compares and contrasts the stances of the Valentinians and of Clement in four areas: the doctrine of God; creation and humanity; salvation; and eschatology.*]

Even a cursory reading of selections from the work of Clement of Alexandria suggests that there are characteristic motifs at work that set him somewhat apart from the general trend of developing orthodoxy in the late second and early third centuries.[1] These motifs bear resemblances to features that are well known from Gnosticism. When we bear in mind that Clement sometimes quotes Valentinus and the Valentinians approvingly,[2] we are led to wonder how close Clement's thought in fact is to that of Gnosticism and, more particularly, to that of the Valentinians.

A comparison of the basic structure of Clement's theology to that found in the Valentinians is the more interesting due to the special affinities of Valentinus to Christianity. He and his followers appear to have developed as a "small offshoot from an orthodox main body."[3] Born in Egypt and educated in Alexandria, he made his way to Rome around 140, nearly becoming bishop of the church there.[4] His teaching was continued—with modifications—by his followers at Alexandria; hence, Clement, living there later in the century, knew the basic Valentinian viewpoints well. This can be seen most readily from his *Excerpts from Theodotus*.

The present comparison will be restricted to the general structural features of Valentinianism and to the source material found in Clement himself—almost exclusively in the *Stromateis* and the *Excerpts*—with occasional references to material in Irenaeus's *Against Heresies*.[5] Four headings will be examined: the doctrine of God, creation and man, salvation, and eschatology. In each case the Valentinian view will be outlined; then Clement's position will be set out and, finally, comparisons and contrasts will be made. I will then draw some conclusions regarding the relationship of Clement to Valentinianism in general.

I

THE DOCTRINE OF GOD

The starting point for the Valentinian doctrine of God is the absolute transcendence of the deity. He is the "unknown Father" (*Exc.* 7,1), the "Depth" that is inexpressible and incomprehensible (*Exc.* 29). He is so completely other that he can be spoken of only in terms of negation. There seems to have been some divergence among Valentinians regarding the question of whether the Father is to be regarded originally as paired with a syzygy or as existing alone. Valentinus himself and the "Oriental School," of which Theodotus was a member, appear to have held the former view, while Ptolemaeus and the "Italic School" leaned toward the latter.[6] In any case, the Father is understood as at some point paired with another Aeon, *Sigē,* Silence (also called *Ennoia*)—"the Mother of all who were put forward by Depth" (*Exc.* 29). The pairing of Aeons is typical of Valentinianism, and it is the reason offered for a distinction between "pleromata" and "images": "whatever come out of a syzygia are complete in themselves (pleromas) and whatever come out of one are images" (*Exc.* 32,1; cf. *Strom.* IV. xiii). It would be a mistake to conceive of those pairs dualistically. Sagnard is probably correct that the female element of the pair is intended to express a quality which is inherent in the male element.[7]

The various paired Aeons of the Pleroma originated as emanations from the Father. They represent in hypostatized form various aspects of his fullness, and they are arranged in a hierarchical order. There is therefore a scale of being from superior to inferior in the Pleroma, and each Aeon-pair has its proper place within it. The basic Valentinian Ogdoad is composed of four syzygies: Father and Silence; Monogenes and Truth; Logos and Life; and Man and Church (Irenaeus, *Adv. haer.* I.i.1). Valentinian exegesis found support for this differentiation in John 1. The first verse of the Gospel, "In the *Archē* was the Logos, and the Logos was with God, and the Logos was God," substantiates the first three male elements of the pairs: the Father (God); the Nous (*Archē*); and the Logos.[8] It should be noted that, taking this verse with John 1:18 ("The Only-begotten God who is in the bosom of the Father"), the Valentinians stressed that both the Logos and the Monogenes Son are rightfully called "God."

First on the scale of emanations stands Monogenes, also called Nous and Son. He was first put forth when the Father, totally unknown, wished to be known: through his own thought . . . the Father caused Monogenes to emanate as a "spirit of Knowledge" arising from Knowledge: "So he too who came forth from Knowledge, that is, from the Father's thought, became Knowledge, that is, the Son" (*Exc.* 7,1). Notice that the same emphasis on the divinity of Monogenes as seen in the interpretation of John 1 is repeated here. The Son is Knowledge proceeding from Knowledge. Casey comments that this is simply "a complicated way of saying that Monogenes, even when projected, remained consubstantial with the Father."[9] Monogenes knows the Father, since he is Knowledge; but he is the only Aeon who can know the Father, and this limitation upon the Aeons sets up the conditions that led to crisis in the Pleroma.

At this point we encounter an extremely important feature of the Valentinian doctrine of God. While some forms of Gnosticism locate evil in an external source, Gnosticism in general and Valentinianism in particular placed the origin of evil squarely within the Godhead itself.[10] Error and fallibility are possible within the Pleroma. A fall is most likely to occur at the weakest point, of course, and that is precisely where tragedy occurred. Sophia, the last of the emanations, developed a passion to know the Father (*Exc.* 30,2). In her wish to "grasp that which is beyond knowledge," she ended in "ignorance and formlessness" (31,3; cf. *Adv. haer.* I.ii-iii). The fall is not just a harmless lapse, but a tragedy: it carries with it unavoidable consequences that result in the formation of the material world and the concomitant need for salvation from it.

Clement's doctrine of God, like that of the Valentinians, takes as its point of departure the utter transcendence of God. He is "above all speech, all conception, all thought" (*Strom.* V.x). Appealing to the same passage as the Gnostics, John 1:18, Clement says that here the apostle identifies invisibility and ineffability with the "bosom of God" (V.xii). "Hence," he writes elsewhere, "some have called it the Depth, as containing and embosoming all things, inaccessible and boundless." The reference to "the Depth" appears to indicate the Gnostics; Clement accepts it as a fitting description of the One who ultimately is beyond description.[11]

Clement, too, affirms strongly a negative theology. It is necessary to abstract from all corporeal properties and afterwards from all incorporeal properties, in order that "we may reach somehow to the conception of the Almighty, knowing not what He is, but what He is not" (V.xi). This does not mean that no terms may be applied to God. Names like "the Depth," "the One," "the Good," "Absolute Being," "Father," and "Lord" are all acceptable so long as it is remembered that they are not used "properly" (V.xii). None of them alone can express God, but "all together are indicative of the power of the Omnipotent."[12]

While Clement employs an emanationist model of the Godhead,[13] he does not maintain an original syzygy at the foundation of divine reality; nor does he hold that the deity is composed of a series of paired Aeons. Rather, his standpoint is trinitarian. References to the Father, Son, and Spirit are to be found throughout his works, although it seems that Clement is more concerned with the status of the Son than the Spirit.[14] Accordingly, this discussion is limited to his comments regarding the Son.

The Son is the eternal image of the invisible God (**Strom.** V.vi), and it is through Him that we are to learn the "Remoter Cause," the Father (VII.i). The Son is the αρχη (V.vi; VII.i; *Exc.* 19,1-2); the Word and Wisdom (VII.ii); or the Word, Wisdom, and Power of God (V.i). Clement especially likes to describe the Son not only as God's image, but also as the "face of God."[15] Notice that, for Clement, the Son is a single hypostasis, embracing in himself a number of titles and functions that the Valentinians dispersed among a variety of Aeons. With regard to the term "Monogenes," for example, Clement specifically affirms that the Jesus who appeared on earth is "one and the same" as the Onlybegotten.[16] Elsewhere Clement comments that it is one and the same Logos who is the Son, who is the Creator of everything, who spoke through the prophets, and who was manifested in the Savior (*Exc.* 19,1ff.; cf. 8,1).

Although Clement is opposed to the Valentinian doctrine of God, there is a clear structural similarity between the two concepts of God. Both concepts employ an emanationist model, and in both the emanated beings—however many or few—are all of divine status. In both, the original, ultimate Godhead is unlimited and beyond comprehension. Therefore, he can be known only by the Revealer, his Nous.

The major difference in Clement's conception from that of the Valentinians seems to reside in the fact that he strictly limits the number of aspects of the Father which may be hypostatized. Obviously, the principle for Clement's limitation is the church's tradition (**Strom.** VII.xvi; cf. xvii).

The Valentinians too could speak of Father, Son, and Spirit, but that did not hinder them from identifying a number of other beings in the divine hierarchy as well.

We must note one other difference: while Son and Spirit are subordinate to the Father for Clement, their divine attributes are not thereby lessened. Consequently, there can be no suggestion of failure or weakness in the Godhead. Sin is due either to ignorance or inability and, Clement comments, "both depend on ourselves" (VII.xvi). God is wholly good, and so too is his Son (**Paed.** I.viii). This contrast finds almost symbolic expression in the fact that the name of the Aeon to whom the Valentinians attribute evil in the Pleroma, Sophia, is attributed emphatically by Clement to the Son: He is not only God's Word, but also his Wisdom!

II

CREATION AND HUMANITY

For the Valentinians, creation is a negative concept: matter has arisen only because of failure in the Pleroma. Sophia's fall resulted in the production of some sort of formless substance that the Christ shaped into Achamoth, or lower Sophia. From the passions of Lower Sophia emerged the four elements and the soul. At length she formed the Demiurge, an inferior, harsh being (*Exc.* 33,4), who in turn created the world.[17] By his activity the material and psychic substances were fashioned into a world. The pneumatic element, however, was placed in man without his knowledge (*Exc.* 50,1-53,5).

In accordance with the three basic substances, the Valentinians distinguished three kinds of people—material (hylic), animal (psychic), and spiritual (pneumatic). The differences among them are absolute. There is no hope for members of the first class; they are purely material and are destined by nature for utter destruction at the end (81,1). Between the other two classes, the all-important difference is that some were implanted imperceptibly with spiritual seed by Sophia (53,2) or, alternatively, by the Logos (2,1). These are the pneumatics; they are the best of mankind (21,1), for they contain an element of the Pleroma within themselves and are thus destined, ineluctably, to return to the Pleroma at the end.

According to the Valentinians the pneumatics possess salvation by nature (56,3). The psychics, in contrast, possess free will and face an uncertain destiny. Salvation, albeit on a lower plane, is possible for them, but only if they live moral, continent lives (*Adv. haer.* I.vi.4). The Valentinians designated the psychics as the "called" and identified them with the "orthodox" in the Church, while they saw themselves as the "elect."[18]

While the human situation in the world is one of darkness and death (*Exc.* 22,2; 80,1), human beings are not really responsible for their tragic state. The fall must be characterized as tragedy and fate, not as guilt. That the elect should be saved from this state, therefore, is due not so much to God's goodness as to a kind of moral necessity: it is incumbent upon the Pleroma to rectify its failure.

For Clement, on the other hand, the creation is not negative, but positive. He argues that the docetic rejection of human birth as unholy is a "blasphemy against the will of God and the mystery of creation" (**Strom.** III.xvii). Creation must be good, for the Creator is God himself (II.viii). Clement rejects any attempt, either Gnostic or Marcionite, to attribute the creation to a Demiurge distinct from the Good God himself (V.i). Wishing to avoid any suggestion of docetism, he rebukes Valentinus for claiming that Christ's body was not really material, but psychic (III.xvii).

Clement, too, makes a triple division among men: Gnostics, believers, and the hard of heart (VII.ii). While this distinction is significant, it is not based on the inherent nature of man. According to Clement, "Salvation is from a change due to obedience, but not from nature" (II.xx). All men, since they possess mind, also possess free will. Thus, "we are born to obey the commandments, if we choose to be willing to be saved" (VII.iii).

Man's present situation in the world, Clement says, is in darkness, delusion (**Protr.** 1), bondage, ignorance (10), and error (9). Attracted by pleasure, the first man disobeyed God and became "fettered to sins" (11). Thus humans are responsible for the situation in which they live, and God's redemption is an act of pure kindness and love. Jonas suggests that for the Valentinians the world actually exists for the sake of salvation, so that the real object of salvation is the godhead itself.[19] This is not true of Clement.

III

SALVATION

As has often been remarked, soteriology is the basic interest of all Gnostic theology. Since the overriding problem for human beings is ignorance—ignorance of their origin and destiny—it is essential that the Pleroma impart knowledge to people. At baptism complete gnosis is made available.

> But it is not only the washing that is liberating, but the knowledge of who we were, and what we have become, where we were or where we were placed, whither we hasten, from what we are redeemed, what birth is and what rebirth. (**Exc.** 78,1f.)

Sagnard remarks that this knowledge is in fact the *raison d' être* for Valentinianism.[20] With knowledge in his possession, a person is freed from fate (78,1) and enters into salvation.

While knowledge had been imparted gradually throughout history, the process culminated with the human Jesus. At his own baptism the powers of the Pleroma descended upon him, accompanying him throughout his earthly ministry and departing only at his passion. After his resurrection he remains at the right hand of the Demiurge until

the end.[21] The way to salvation has been made available fully in Jesus Christ; hence, he is given the name Savior. Obviously, this term is virtually equivalent to "revealer."

The knowledge thus revealed has an esoteric character. The Valentinians saw such knowledge as containing great "mysteries" (*Adv. haer.* I.i.3) understandable only by those who are spiritual, that is, the Gnostics themselves. These mysteries run much deeper than the common, public teachings of the mass of Christian believers; in fact, they encompass "the perfect knowledge of God" (I.vi.1; cf. III.ii.2). Ptolemaeus argues that this secret tradition is just as firm as is the tradition claimed by orthodoxy, for it has been passed down orally by succession from the apostles.[22]

How should the enlightened pneumatic live in the world? Two opposing lifestyles could be based on Gnostic principles: libertinism or asceticism.[23] Clearly, Valentinus cannot be classed as a libertine. Clement quotes him as arguing that only through the Son "can the heart become pure, by the expulsion of every evil spirit from the heart." After commenting on the unclean spirits that cause the heart to perform lustful deeds, Valentinus remarks that "when the only good Father visits it, it is sanctified, and gleams with light" (**Strom.** II.xx). Of the positive comments that Clement makes about Valentinus and the Valentinians, all have to do with ethics.[24] For instance, Clement quotes Valentinus's view that Jesus was continent with regard to food and drink to illustrate the fact that continence must be applied more broadly than to sexuality alone (**Strom.** III.vii).

Although Valentinus cannot be classed as a libertine, the term "ascetic" would hardly fit either. Clement also remarks that, since the Valentinians hold that the union of man and woman "is derived from the divine emanation in heaven above," they approve of marriage (III.i) and speak of sexual intercourse as a "spiritual union" (III.iv).

No less than the Valentinians, Clement's major concern is soteriology. Human beings are in an unhappy situation and need redemption. Due to Adam's fall into disobedience, humans are captive to ignorance and error. Hence, gnosis is needed, and gnosis is what, ultimately, Jesus Christ has come to bring. Jesus' role as Savior, therefore, as with the Gnostics, especially involves revelation. While the Valentinians could speak at the most of a readying of pneumatic seed for the coming of the Savior,[25] Clement holds to continuous, significant revelation to all human beings throughout the course of history. The basis of this view is his overarching concept of the Son as Logos (cf. **Exc.** 19,1ff.). The Logos, who became incarnate in Christ, had already been active among both Jews and Gentiles . . . . Clement maintains that the revelations of the Old Testament prophets as well as the truths of Gentile philosophy and poetry derive from the Logos. Hence, while he argues at times that the truths of philosophy were stolen from Moses and the prophets, his more characteristic view is that the Greeks, too, have been inspired by God.[26]

The full revelation has come, nevertheless, in Jesus Christ. He is frequently called the "Teacher" (as in **Strom.** V.i;

VII.ii). The second work in Clement's trilogy, the **Paedagogus,** derives its title from the office of the Logos as Tutor (**Paed.** I.i). In Jesus Christ God himself is made known (**Paed.** I.vii). By this revelation, human beings discover how they can be deified: "The Word of God became man, that thou mayest learn from man how man may become God" (**Protrep.** 1).

Like the Valentinians, Clement holds to the existence of a secret tradition within the church. As with the general tradition proclaimed to the mass of believers, this tradition derives from the apostles (**Strom.** VI. viii), but it is taught only to those who are worthy (I.xii), that is, to those who are "capable of receiving and being molded" by such secret teachings (I.i). Clement likes to call such teachings "mysteries."[27]

The contrast between a simple teaching offered to the multitudes and a secret teaching reserved for initiates corresponds to Clement's major distinction between faith and knowledge. This distinction is so great that he can describe the movement from faith to knowledge in the same terms as the conversion from nonbelief to belief: "And, in my view, the first saving change is that from heathenism to faith . . . and the second, that from faith to knowledge" (**Strom.** VII.x). However, Clement stresses that, in spite of the great difference, there is continuity between the two states. Belief, he writes,

> is the foundation of knowledge. But Christ is both the foundation and the superstructure, by whom are both the beginning and the ends. And the extreme points, the beginning and the end—I mean faith and love—are not taught. But knowledge, conveyed by tradition according to the grace of God as a deposit, is entrusted to those who show themselves worthy of it;. . .For it is said, "to him that hath shall be given": to faith, knowledge; and to knowledge, love; and to love, the inheritance.[28]

Notice that Clement does not distinguish faith and knowledge absolutely. There is no substantial dichotomy among human beings; and, although knowledge is a higher stage than faith, it is not separate from faith (V.i). In the Valentinian view, pneumatics and psychics are forever distinguished; for Clement, the Gnostic is something the believer can—and should—become.

Further, Clement considers knowledge and love almost interchangeable here. Camelot points out that Clement offers two ways to attain perfection, or to become a true Gnostic. The one is moral; the other, intellectual. The one is concerned with virtue and love; the other, with an intellectual ascent.[29] However, as the above quotation indicates, the two ways are not mutually exclusive. Gnosis is not purely intellectual; love is perfected by knowledge and knowledge is perfected by love.[30]

Concretely, Clement's ethical thinking incorporates the Stoic virtue of impassibility, or passionlessness. As God, who is purely noncorporeal, is "impassible, free of anger,

destitute of desire" (IV.xxiii), man too must strive to attain the same condition (VII.iii) . . . . According to Clement Jesus ate food only to avoid giving any grounds for a docetic interpretation of his nature (VI.ix). In fact, his body did not need food at all, since it was maintained by a "holy energy." Clement asserts that "He was entirely impassible; inaccessible to any movement of feeling— either pleasure or pain." This explains the fact that Clement quotes Valentinus approvingly to the effect that Jesus

> ate and drank in a manner peculiar to himself, and the food did not pass out of his body. Such was the power of his continence that food was not corrupted within him; for he himself was not subject to the process of corruption. (III.vii)

Valentinus and Clement are not making precisely the same point, for Valentinus intends his comment in the sense that Christ's body was psychical; that is, it was not corporeal at all (III.xvii). Clement, in contrast, means to affirm the real, physical character of the Lord's body. Still, at best we can say that Clement just barely avoids docetism himself. While Christ's body was real, all bodily needs are eliminated and his human soul loses all significance.[31]

Unlike Jesus, Clement's Gnostic can never live in this world without passion as regards his physical existence. Bodily necessities continue to affect him. However, he can attempt to imitate the Savior as regards passions of the soul, and Clement is convinced that the apostles, after Christ's resurrection, were indeed successful at living in such a state . . . (VI.ix).

In harmony with the Valentinians, then, Clement conceives of salvation as consisting especially in the gaining of knowledge that drives away ignorance and allows humans to achieve union with God. For both, the role of the Savior, Jesus Christ, is essentially that of providing the revelation of the knowledge necessary for this redemption. Both also affirm strongly a secret tradition available only to a select group of initiates. A strong distinction is made by both the Valentinians and Clement between this small circle of the truly spiritual and the rest of those who belong to the church. The ideal mode of life of this higher class seems to be essentially the same in both schemes—witness the docetic view, to some degree at least, of the Savior's nature.

Nevertheless, there are important differences between the conceptions of Clement and the Valentinians. The distinction in levels within the church, while significant for Clement, is conceived not as an unbridgeable gap between different natures, but as a difference of lower and higher stages that he hopes is temporary. The goal of all, not just some, is union with God. There is also a significant difference between the two conceptions regarding the relation of ethics to the gnosis which is revealed by the Savior. For the Valentinians, the moral life in this world does not appear to be a central theme.[32] For Clement, in contrast, ethics is a primary concern: love is an essential element in the constitution of the true Gnostic; thus, love and knowledge belong together.

IV

ESCHATOLOGY

For the Valentinians, at the end Jesus will assemble the elect seed and enter into the Pleroma with Sophia. This indicates a substantial union of the elect with the Godhead; they return from whence they came, so that the Pleroma is finally reunited and brought to repose. The Valentinians can speak of resurrection in this context, but it is obviously not to be understood as in any sense physical; matter is destined only for utter destruction.

The Demiurge and the psychics advance to the position Sophia has held; they enter only the intermediate Ogdoad, the place of Repose near—but outside—the Pleroma (**Exc.** 63). The substantial dichotomy within humanity—between pneumatics and psychics—is thus continued into eternity. Material souls, which constitute a third class within mankind, are of course destroyed in the fire. When all of this has occurred, the whole process of salvation will be complete. But the restoration will not in fact return everything precisely to its former condition. Originally, all that existed was the Pleroma in a state of pure Repose.

Now, not only is there the Pleroma, but there is also a nondivine, perfected "creation" as well. The good psychic elements, an inevitable product of Sophia's fall, cannot enter into the full Repose of the Pleroma, but neither would it be just, apparently, to annihilate them completely, since they have lived morally. Hence, a heaven is created for them to make their existence as blessed as possible.

For Clement, the consummation means the completion of the advancement[33] that has already begun on earth in the life of the Gnostic. The soul ascends through the seven heavens until it reaches a state of perfect contemplation. There, together with the seven archangels, the elect will behold the face of God, that is, the Son (**Exc.** 11,1; 15,2; 23,4-5). Clement conceives of this ascent as a gradual one, so that a purgation by fire is necessary in the afterlife (**Strom.** VII.vi). The fire will purify believers and cause most nonbelievers to repent, so that only those who are incurable due to their perseverance in rejection will themselves be rejected.[34]

The perfected Gnostic will be deified (**Protr.** 9; 11). This does not mean that humans will become divine; they continue to remain creatures, but now they have become as much like God as possible.[35] The soul has become pure, and it is "now no longer distinguished by . . . the body, being bound to it like an oyster to its shell" (**Strom.** V.xiv).

Both the Valentinians and Clement thus maintain a distinction within humanity extending into the eschaton, although the conceptions of the distinction vary. Clement allows for a much larger group to participate in salvation, and he holds that the differences between humans are due to their actions, not to their natures. Both the Valentinians and Clement, further, articulate the eschatological existence as an ascent into the divine realm, with the material reality of this world being annihilated. But the Valentinians picture the eschaton as an escape from a bad existence, while Clement sees it rather in terms of passing from one stage—which, in itself and by nature, is not bad—to a better one. In addition, Clement continues to affirm a distinction in natures between the Creator and his creatures, instead of a reunion of the divine nature with itself. The ascending soul is deified, that is, it becomes as much like God as possible, but it remains a creature.[36]

V

SUMMARY

As we have seen, there are impressive parallels between Clement's viewpoint and that of the Valentinians. The most significant similarities may be summarized in the following points:

(1) *The Emanationist View of the Godhead.* In both schemes God the Father is understood first and foremost as an unlimited, incomprehensible being, beyond all conception. The Godhead is pictured in terms of an emanationist model. Later emanations, while fully divine, are more limited and consequently in some sense subordinate. The primary emanation is the Nous, and only he can comprehend the Father. At the same time, because of his diminished transcendence, he can reveal the otherwise unknowable Father.

(2) *Salvation as Knowledge.* For both Clement and the Valentinians, human beings are bound in darkness and ignorance and are in need of salvation. Salvation, conceived of essentially as knowledge, is the central concern of both systems. Consequently, the Savior-figure is understood particularly as a Revealer. Further, this revealed knowledge is seen as the prerogative of a select few: it is withheld from the majority in the church, but is available to initiates by secret, oral tradition.

(3) *The Dichotomy within the Church.* Both schemes thus view salvation as involving two levels within the Church—those with and those without knowledge. There is thus a broader class which has a lesser salvation as well as a smaller, "elite" group that participates in full salvation. The latter group enjoys a relationship to God which is not shared by the larger group of common believers.

(4) *The Ideal for Life in the World.* Life in this world means a mode of existence that is provisional at best; hence both Clement and the Valentinians view the ideal life-style in terms of what we may characterize as a moderate asceticism. Both advocate a limited, cautious use of the material realities of the world.[37]

(5) *Eschatological Ascent.* Ultimate salvation for both signifies a transcendence of the empirical realm. Matter will be destroyed, and the saved will ascend to the realm of the divine.

From these parallels it is clear that there are some very basic structural similarities between the thought of Clement and that of the Valentinians. Thus Clement's comparatively positive reaction to Valentinus, which might seem unexpected at first glance, is not surprising. The affinities between Clement and Valentinus are due to their common roots in the philosophical currents of the time, especially in Philo, Middle Platonism, and Numenius.

Nevertheless, along with these similarities, there are also some basic points where Clement diverges from the conceptions of the Valentinians. These can be summarized as follows:

(1) *The Infallible Godhead.* For the Valentinians, weakness and liability to error are conceivable qualities of the Godhead. The myths of the emanations of the Aeons and the fall of Sophia recount the divine prehistory and explain how the present deplorable situation came into being. Curiously, starting from the utter illimitability and total otherness of God, the Valentinian system ends with a fallible Godhead.[38] Clement, in contrast, denies any possibility of divine limitation and error. Thus, the responsibility for evil must be set squarely within the created realm.

(2) *A Universal Inclusive Outlook.* In the Valentinian conception, the world is a cosmic mistake which stands in opposition to God. As God has limited his relationship to this unwilled universe to the placing of pneumatic seed within it, his activity within the world is also confined within a very narrow range. Divine activity is exhausted in redeeming the "elect." For Clement, however, the world is good; it is the product of the divine will. Clement's outlook on the world is correspondingly broader. Three instances will clarify this. First, the Logos is active in all of human history, inspiring not only the prophets of Israel, but active in the poetry and philosophy of the Greeks as well.[39] Second, God is concerned with all human beings, not just with an exclusive class. Since all humans have the same nature, all can be saved. The guilt is purely one's own if anyone does not come to be among the "elect." Third and finally, all the elements of creation—even matter—must be judged positively. While matter is certainly an inferior reality, it has its proper place in serving God's ultimate intentions for the perfection of human beings.

(3) *The Expectation of a Perfected Creation.* When the eschaton arrives, according to the Valentinians, the elect seed will be taken up into the Pleroma from which it came. All reality will return to its original, placid state, and—with one exception—created reality will be destroyed. The exception is that a place of repose will be left for the Demiurge and the psychics. However, this appears to be a concession to the "orthodox" rather than a consistent part of Valentinian theory.[40] At best, it is an afterthought on the part of the Father, not an aspect of the pretemporal, divine plan for creation. Clement views the matter very differently. For him, a perfected creation in which humans progress from a lower to a higher existence was God's original intention. Yet the ascent to God does not entail a radical break with the past: there is continuity throughout. Consequently, not only does the person perfectly united to God remain substantially human, but he also remains substantially one with the person who has not (yet) ascended so far. For Clement, then, creation was originally intended for—and is destined ultimately to receive—completion, not annihilation.

There is no question that the concerns of Clement and Valentinus are the same and that the doctrines of God and salvation betray obvious similarities. However, the dissimilarities appear to be the more decisive. Jonas claims that there are elements of rebellion, protest, and extremism at the heart of Gnostic thought, and that its characteristic mood is very pessimistic.[41] Interestingly, Harnack isolated optimism as a characteristic feature of Clement's thought and, thus, as one of the elements that distinguish him from Gnosticism.[42] In terms of this psychological feature, Clement and the Valentinians would appear to be worlds apart.

Underlying the divergences between Clement and Valentinus is Clement's affirmation of the Judeo-Christian tradition that God is one, good, and Creator of heaven and earth. The Valentinians rejected the God of Genesis, demoting him to the status of a Demiurge; they reversed Jewish belief about this God as the One, true, and good God; and they denied the concomitant Old Testament assertions of the goodness of creation and the responsibility of mankind for sin in the world. In addition, they did not hold to any difference in essence between God and those whom he redeems. Now these are all characteristic assertions not only of Jewish belief but also of the "orthodox" *regula fidei* as well, and Clement adheres to these beliefs.

Thus, for all of his speculative, ascetic leanings, Clement's loyalty to basic tenets of Jewish tradition and of developing orthodoxy in the church places him in fundamental opposition to Valentinianism. Clement's relatively favorable reaction to Valentinus is due partly to Valentinus's own inclination to a "moderate" Gnosticism, partly to Clement's own stance markedly to the left in the orthodox spectrum, and—not the least important point—partly to one of Clement's own characteristic traits, an unusual openness to the ideas and thoughts of others.[43]

Notes

1. In general, quotations from Clement will follow the translation in *The Ante-Nicene Fathers,* Vol. II, ed. Alexander Roberts and James Donaldson (Grand Rapids, 1971²). It should be noted that there is a significant number of inaccuracies in the English translation. *Stromateis* III, which is presented in Latin in the *ANF,* will be quoted from John Oulton and Henry Chadwick, *Alexandrian Christianity, Library of Christian Classics,* Vol. III (Philadelphia, 1954). Quotations from the *Excerpta ex Theodoto* will follow the translation of Robert Pierce Casey, *The Excerpta ex Theodoto of Clement of Alexandria, Studies and Documents,* Vol. I (London, 1934).

2. Cf. *Strom.* III.i.iv,vii; VI.vi.

3. James F. McCue, "Orthodoxy and Heresy: Walter Bauer and the Valentinians," *Vig. Chr.* 33 (1979) 130.

4. Tertullian, *Adv. Valent.* 4.

5. Elaine Pagels, "Conflicting Versions of Valentinian Eschatology: Irenaeus and the *Excerpta ex Theodoto,*" *HTR* 67 (1974) 35-53, questions the accuracy of Irenaeus's picture of the Valentinians, but her argument is unconvincing. Cf. James F. McCue, "Conflicting Versions of Valentinianism? Irenaeus and the *EXCERPTA EX THEODOTO,*" in Bentley Layton, ed., *The Rediscovery of Gnosticism,* I: *The School of Valentinus* (Leiden, 1979) 404-416.

6. Gilles Quispel, "The Original Doctrine of Valentinus," in *Gnostic Studies,* Vol. I (Leiden, 1974) 28.

7. F. Sagnard, ed., *Clément d'Alexandrie: Extraits de Théodote* (Paris, 1948) 21-22.

8. *Exc.* 6,1-4; Iren., *Adv. haer.* I.viii.5. This identification of Monogenes with *Archē* is made also by Clement (as in *Strom.* VI.vii), as it is by numerous other early Christian writers. Cf. refs. in Sagnard, *Clément d'Alexandrie,* 65.

9. Casey, *Excerpta,* p. 102.

10. Hans Jonas, "Delimitation of the Gnostic Phenomenon," in U. Bianchi, ed., *Le Origini dello Gnosticismo* (Leiden, 1967) 96.

11. G. W.H. Lampe, ed., *A Patristic Greek Lexicon* (Oxford, 1961) 306, does not list any places where the term is applied to God by the Greek Fathers. Unfortunately, however, the present reference is not listed either.

12. See A. H. Armstrong's comments on this negative theology in "The Self-Definition of Christianity in Relation to Later Platonism," in E. P. Sanders, ed., *Jewish and Christian Self-Definition,* I: *The Shaping of Christianity in the Second and Third Centuries* (Philadelphia, 1980) 92-97. See also S. R. C. Lilla, *Clement of Alexandria: A Study in Christian Platonism and Gnosticism* (Oxford, 1971) 217-226.

13. It is generally agreed that Clement's concept originates most directly from Philo's concept of the Logos as emanating from God. For details of Clement's doctrine of the Logos and its connections not only with Philo but also with Platonic currents of thought, see Lilla, ibid., 199-212.

14. This, of course, is not particularly different from other Christian writings of the era. See Origen, *de Princ.* I. Pref.: "it is not yet clearly known whether he (the Spirit) is to be thought of as begotten or unbegotten, or as being himself also a Son of God or not."

15. Cf., for example, VII.x. Clement emphasizes this idea in the *Excerpta,* pointing out that God is unknown except as he is visible in the Son (cf. 10,5-12,1; 23,5).

16. *Exc.* 7,3c. Casey attributes this to the Valentinians. But see *Exc.* 4,2, where the same thought is present: the Light that is manifest on earth is the same Light that is on High.

17. For a systematic account of the details of these events, see Hans Jonas, *The Gnostic Religion* (Boston, 1958) 182-190.

18. Cf. Clement's somewhat resentful comment in *Strom.* IV. xiii: "Let not the above-mentioned people [Valentinus and Basilides], then, call us, by way of reproach, 'natural men.'"

19. Jonas, *Gnostic Religion,* 196.

20. Sagnard, *Clément d' Alexandrie,* 203. Sagnard has a useful appendix on baptism on pp. 229-239.

21. *Exc.* 62,1. This accords with the relatively positive view of the Demiurge offered by Ptolemaeus; see *Letter to Flora. Exc.* 38,1-3 suggests a more antagonistic relationship between Jesus and the Demiurge.

22. *Letter to Flora,* in Epiphanius, *Panarion haeresium* 33,7.

23. See the summary in Jonas, *Gnostic Religion,* 266-278.

24. The passages that are in some sense positive are: II.xx; III.i; III.iv; III.vii; VI.vi.

25. Jonas, *Gnostic Religion,* 195; see Elaine Pagels, "The Valentinian Claim to Esoteric Exegesis of Romans as Basis for Anthropological Theory," *Vig. Chr.* 26 (1972) 241-258.

26. Adolf von Harnack, *History of Dogma,* Vol. II (New York, 1958) 326. Cf. for example, *Protr.* 6, where both conceptions appear side by side.

27. Lilla, *Clement of Alexandria,* pp. 146-148. For Clement's conception of secret tradition in general, see pp. 144-158. See also P. Th. Camelot, *Foi et gnose: Introduction à l'étude de la connaissance mystique chez Clément d'Alexandrie* (Paris, 1945) 90-95.

28. *Strom.* VII.x. For a detailed discussion of faith and gnosis, see Lilla, op.cit., 118-189.

29. Camelot, *Foi et gnose,* 50ff.

30. Ibid., 123-128.

31. Cf. Aloys Grillmeier, *Christ in Christian Tradition* (Atlanta, 1975) 136-138. In *Strom.* VI.ix, Clement says that while Jesus partook of food in order to avoid the danger of docetism, food and drink were not really necessary for him: his body was maintained by "holy energy."

32. As illustration, note the lack of any ethical questions among those that Valentinian gnosis is intended to answer in the quotation at the beginning of this section. Plotinus sees this as a major objection against the Gnostics (*Ennead* II.9.15).

33. Προχπη is the technical term for this process. Cf. *Exc.* 4,1;10,4;11,1;12,2;15,1;17,3;19,3.

34. Charles Bigg, *The Christian Platonists of Alexandria* (Oxford, 1886) 111ff.

35. Recall that according to the *Excerpta* the elect reach the same plane as the seven Archangels, the highest creations (10,1ff.). George M. Schurr, "On the Logic of Ante-Nicene Affirmations of the 'Deification' of the Christian," *ATR* 51 (1969) 99, points out that Clement rejects pagan religion for its claims regarding the "deification" of humans, while at the same time employing the term to describe the ultimate status of Christians.

36. That the ascending soul is not consubstantial with the object of vision is similar to Jewish apocalyptic rather than Greek and Gnostic views of ascent. See John D. Turner, "The Gnostic Threefold Path to Enlightenment: The Ascent of Mind and Descent of Wisdom," *NovT* 22 (1980) 324-351, especially 341ff.

37. See Chadwick's discussion of Clement's and the Valentinians' view of marriage (*Alexandrian Christianity*, pp. 30-39).

38. Jacques E. Ménard, in his article, "Normative Self-Definition in Gnosticism" (in Sanders, *Jewish and Christian Self-Definition*, pp. 134-150), sees the myth of the fall as essential to all Gnostic systems (pp. 140-41).

39. Raoul Mortley, "The Past in Clement of Alexandria: A Study of an Attempt to Define Christianity in Socio-Cultural Terms," in Sanders, ibid., pp. 186-200, thinks that interest in the past is an orthodox, as opposed to a Gnostic, concern (p. 190).

40. Given the strongly negative concept of created reality and the fact that the real concern of Gnostic mythology is to describe the return of the pneumatic seed to a restored Pleroma, there is no logical place for the admission that one of the elements of the created reality continues to exist through all eternity.

41. Jonas, "Delimitation of the Gnostic Phenomenon," p. 100.

42. Harnack, p. 327. It is noteworthy that Paul Henry ("The Place of Plotinus in the History of Thought," in Plotinus, *The Enneads*, trans. Stephen MacKenna [London, 1956] xxxv-lxx) characterizes Plotinus's view as a "fundamental optimism" too (p. lvii).

43. See Lilla's comprehensive inquiry into the sources of Clement's thought and his conclusion that Clement's system combines three distinct streams of thought: Jewish-Alexandrine philosophy, the broad Platonic tradition, and Gnosticism (*Clement of Alexandria*, 227ff.).

Donald Kinder (essay date 1989-90)

SOURCE: "Clement of Alexandria: Conflicting Views on Women," in *The Second Century: A Journal of Early Christian Studies*, Vol. 7, No. 4, Winter 1989-90, pp. 213-20.

[*In the following essay, Kinder contends that Clement believed that while women should be subservient to men in daily life, they could ultimately be equal before God.*]

In his introduction to the *Library of Christian Classics* translation of **Stromata** III, Henry Chadwick pronounced Clement of Alexandria's views on marriage as "curiously confused."[1] One might also regard Clement's views on women as equally so. Clement grants to women equal capacity with men for attaining virtue and perfection.[2] He even acknowledges for them the possibility of training in the Christian philosophy.[3] However, all that Clement grants to women he appears to take away when he asserts that women succumb more easily to temptation,[4] that their place is in the home, waiting on their husbands,[5] and that by their seductive wiles they pose a constant threat to men.[6] Is there some way of connecting these apparently contradictory positions? Moreover, when one examines the role Clement ascribes to women in marriage, one wonders how, in fact, women can be men's equals when Clement maintains that they are so unequal in authority and in the allotted roles of the household. Do these tensions in Clement's views on women reflect the tensions already present in his culture and sources? Finally, is there any way to make any sense at all of what appears to be in Clement so incoherent?

Clement asserts in **Stromata** IV. 8.59.3 that both men and women are obligated to pursue virtue.[7] From the **Paedagogus** especially, it is seen that Clement enjoins both sexes to emulate the life of the Instructor, keeping themselves as free from all voluntary transgressions as possible.[8] Indeed, Clement claims in the **Stromata** that this capacity for virtue is innate in women as well as men.[9] Clement goes so far as to reject any view that posits different natures for women and men, saying that if such a position were true, then only men would be required to practice virtue, and women would be free to do whatever they wished.[10] Thus, in his opinion, women must seek after all the major virtues usually attributed to men, i.e. self-control, righteousness, and temperance.[11]

Clement's reasoning behind these assertions is that women share with men in all the common traits of *anthropos*. Not only do women share in the common physiological traits of the human species (such as respiration, sight, and hearing),[12] but they also participate in the goodness of human creation in general. Clement refers to the human individual as the highest and most beautiful of God's creatures.[13] Humankind is also unique due to the fact that the breath of deity resides in every individual.[14] Clement claims that the reason God gave life to humankind in the first place was that every person, male and female, might be permitted to know God.[15]

Clement's optimistic view of the human race, therefore, informs his belief that women as well as men should seek their highest potential. This higher path of spirituality, to which Clement refers as the way of the true gnostic, is open to both sexes. Women, too, must not only combat desire, but attempt to be completely above it.[16] Even in the area of sexual relations, Clement recommends that both marriage partners engage in relations only with the predetermined purpose of having children.[17] Here Clement argues that motivation by passion is not only part of the lower way, but also is not living according to nature. This Stoic *apatheia* is also required when, on occasion, women are faced with persecution and possible martyrdom.[18] Clement commends many women who have given their lives with such impassibility.[19]

Clement regards the study of philosophy as preerequisite to attaining this higher life, and again he envisions women included in such training.[20] For him, philosophy teaches righteousness and virtue, and thus whatever contributes to such an end is appropriate, even if it is derived from Stoic, Platonic, Epicurean, Aristotelian, or any other school.[21] Clement contends that philosophizing is necessary for the gnostic to be able to endure any circumstance, whether martyrdom or, for a woman, life with a difficult husband.[22] Clement feels that divine providence, therefore, gave philosophy to the whole human race for its benefit and instruction, and to overlook such an aid is to overlook the chief means for acquiring virtue.[23]

But in spite of Clement's remarks that women as well as men share in the capacity for virtue and are equally obligated to achieve it, it is clear that for Clement major differences do, in fact, separate the sexes. Chief among these is the obvious difference in physical construction. He states that women's bodies are softer than men's; therefore, he concedes to women the wearing of softer apparel.[24] Of greater importance, Clement believes that difference in physical design necessitates difference in temporal activity. He claims that women's bodies are suitable for giving birth to children and, in his mind, the corollary, to housekeeping. On the other hand, men are physically superior and should be involved in more active pursuits.[25]

In marriage, the obvious difference between the sexes is seen in their allotted roles and in who leads the relationship. From Clement's perspective, the divinely appointed head is the husband.[26] The wife is to be subject and subservient to him. The list of household duties which Clement provides in *Paedagogus* III. 10 definitely confirms his refusal to allow women to go beyond the traditional role of housekeeper. For him, the good wife must remain indoors most of the time to keep house, and when the husband is home she should provide for his every need.[27] The husband, however, while the wife is busily exercising by cooking or making clothes, is told to keep himself physically fit by taking walks, playing ball, or going fishing.[28]

With regard to the procreation of children, for Clement the goal of marriage, although both mother and father contribute to the conception of the child, it is clear that Clement thinks the father provides the more significant part. The wife seems designed only as the receptor of the husband's seed, which in Clement's eyes is already the whole person.[29]

Even when life with the husband seemingly becomes unbearable for the wife (some might think that Clement's depiction of the wife in constant servitude to her husband is just that), Clement does not give the wife the option of leaving. Any divorce proceedings must be initiated by the husband.[30] Instead, the wife must continue to "never do anything against his will, with the exception of what is contributing to virtue and salvation."[31] She may quietly attempt to persuade him toward greater virtue, but if she is unsuccessful, she must be content in realizing that God is "her helper and associate" and that her real aim in life is to please the Lord.[32]

Clement's outlook, in which women are granted equal natures with men but in actuality are relegated to be men's servants, has strong similarities with that of many Stoic philosophers. Several Stoics had been known for their promotion of women's equality with men. Yet, like Clement, they retained positions which definitely portray women as the weaker sex, in need of domination by men, and best suited for housework. Antipater, in the second century B.C., describes marriage as the full union of men and women. He states:

> Other friendships are like platefuls of beans or mixtures of juxtaposition, but the union of man and wife is like the mixing of wine and water, or any case of penetration; for they are united not only by the ties of substance and soul and the dearest bond of children, but also in body.[33]

Later, Plutarch[34] wrote that "marriage is a source of friendship, for it is a common participation in the mysteries," and within it there is a "daily growth between man and wife of mutual respect, kindness, affection and confidence."[35] In his treatise *Bravery of Women* he stated that "man's virtues and woman's virtues are one and the same."[36] Likewise, Musonius argued that women as well as men possess a natural inclination to virtue, and "That Women Too Should Study Philosophy."[37] In discussing "Should Daughters Receive the Same Education as Sons?" he asserts that virtue is "equally appropriate to the nature of both" sexes.[38]

Upon closer examination, however, even though these Stoics argue theoretically for the equality of the sexes, they contend that women are inferior and therefore should be subordinate to their husbands. Antipater's treatise *Concerning Marriage* is addressed to men who wonder if marriage might be a burden to their freedom. To these men he writes:

> Life with a wife seems to appear troublesome to some men because of their inability to rule . . . . Certain things they willingly and corruptly surrender to a wife, and do not teach her anything concerning household management.[39]

It should also be noted that Antipater states that if a man desires a life of leisure devoted to reason or politics, he should find a wife who will manage the house for him, and thus free him for more important things.[40] In practice, therefore, Antipater was not an advocate of equality of the sexes.

Plutarch, though lauding the virtue of women, enumerates for new brides tasks which are clearly subservient. He writes that a wife should have no feeling of her own. Neither should she have preferences, friends, property, or even her own religion, but should follow the husband in everything.[41] He suggests, "A woman ought to do her talking either to her husband or through her husband." Moreover, Plutarch advises the husband to control the wife as "the soul controls the body."[42] It appears that Plutarch praises the ideal of marriage only when the wife is willing to forfeit her mind and personality to her husband.

Also, Musonius demonstrates the distance between the theoretical affirmations of women and the prescriptions he recommends for them. While he claims that women indeed have the same capacity for virtue, he is aware that some may object to this theory and say that women will abandon their household duties.[43] Musonius responds by discussing the four cardinal virtues which a woman learns in her study of philosophy. He explains all four from a practical perspective and argues, "In the first place a woman must be a good housekeeper."[44] Later, he refers to women's education:

> I do not mean that women should possess technical skill and acuteness in argument. It would be quite superfluous, since they will use philosophy for the ends of their life as women.[45]

Musonius states clearly the ends of a woman's life:

> Prepared to nourish her children at her own breast, and to serve her husband with her own hands, and willing to do things which some would consider no better than a slave's work. Would not such a woman be a great help to the man who married her?[46]

To the objection that his theory on equality will cause men to take up spinning and women to exercise in the gymnasium, he states that indoor work is still more suitable for women, and outdoor work for men. Occasionally, if need arises, Musonius admits that this arrangement might be varied, but this appears the exceptional case.[47] Thus, even though Musonius seems to reject the theory of women *always* inside the home and men outside, he still largely retains it in practice.

Furthermore, Musonius employs the typical Greek distinction between men and women as stronger-weaker, ruler-ruled, and better-worse. In his contention that neither husband nor wife should commit adultery, he argues as follows:

> And yet surely one will not expect men to be less moral than women, nor less capable of disciplining their desire, thereby revealing the stronger in judgment inferior to the weaker, the ruler to the ruled. In fact, it behooves men to be much better if they expect to be superior to women, for surely if they appear to be less self-controlled they will also be baser characters.[48]

Clement, too, believes that women are inferior morally, and in his argumentation seems closer to the Musonian

Stoic tradition than to certain Christian writers of his period. For example, while he agrees with Tertullian that women need to be veiled, unlike Tertullian, he fails to root this advice in the original sin of Eve.[49] For Clement, women's present weakness is not attributable to an ongoing defect which the first woman placed upon womankind. He states that each person sins by individual choice.[50] Admittedly, in Clement's view, women choose wrongly more than men, but for Clement this seems due to women's basic character, not to any continuing "sentence of God" upon them.[51] Clement merely assumes women's weakness without discussion. He is therefore more like Musonius in remaining in the philosophic tradition which had long viewed women as men's inferior in every way.[52]

For Clement and for the Stoics, it is clear that what one considers virtue determines what day-to-day roles are recommended for women. For Musonius, as has been noted, the virtue for women is in the demonstration of their ability to be good housekeepers. For Clement, one of the chief virtues for women is chaste behavior. He seems to think that this virtue is best met when women remain at home. He states:

> Not to deck and adorn herself beyond what is becoming, renders a wife free of calumnious suspicion, while she devotes herself assiduously to prayers and supplications; avoiding frequent departures from the house, and shutting herself up as far as possible from the view of all not related to her, and deeming housekeeping of more consequence than impertinent trifling.[53]

Clement apparently believes that such behavior serves as the best preventative against adultery.[54]

In the practical sphere, therefore, it appears that for both Clement and Musonius, women must pursue virtue by seeking to fill the domestic mold according to the status-quo. Moreover, the study of philosophy, which both Musonius and Clement recommend for women, serves as instruction to reinforce such service. While Clement argues that philosophy can benefit those men or women who must occasionally face persecution, it is apparent that philosophy's major benefits lie in the day-to-day guidelines for life at home.[55] Nonetheless, one wonders how a woman, in Clement's view, might even have time for philosophizing since she is constantly assumed to be keeping house and serving her husband. Thus Clement, along with the Stoics, is not bothered by a distinction between the equality of one's ultimate nature and the unequal distribution of physical and moral strength which, in their minds, must necessarily lead to a distinction in roles.[56] In their opinion, it is entirely possible for women to share equality with men before God, while still being directed to the traditional role of the husband's subservient housekeeper and mother of his children.

Notes

1. *Alexandrian Christianity,* ed. Henry Chadwick and J. E. L. Oulton (Philadelphia: Westminster Press, 1954) 33.

2. *Strom.* IV. 859.1-3; cf. *Paedagogus* I.4.1.

3. *Strom.* IV. 8.62.4-63.1; 8.67.1-3; 1.1.1.

4. *Paed.* II. 10.107.2; 2.33.2.

5. *Paed.* III. 11.58.1; 10.49.3-5.

6. Ibid. II. 2.33.4; *Strom.* III. 12.93.1-3; *Paed.* III. 11.83.3-4.

7. Cf. IV. 8.59.1.

8. *Paed.* I. 3.9.1.

9. *Strom.* IV. 8.59.1.

10. Ibid. IV. 8.19.2.

11. *Paed.* I. 4.10.2.

12. Ibid.

13. Ibid. I. 8.63.1.

14. Ibid. I. 3.7.1; cf. Genesis 1:26; 2:7.

15. *Strom.* III. 9.64.3.

16. Ibid. III. 7.57-58.

17. *Paed.* II. 10.90.3; 10.98.2; *Strom.* III. 7.58.2; et al.

18. *Strom.* IV. 1.1; cf. IV. 8.58.3.

19. Ibid. IV. 8.58.2.

20. Ibid. IV. 8.62.4-63.1.

21. Ibid. I. 7.37.6.

22. Ibid. IV. 8.67.1-3.

23. Ibid. VI. 17.159.6.

24. *Paed.* II. 10.107.3.

25. Ibid. III. 3.19.1-2. The same passage states that women are assigned "passivity."

26. *Strom.* IV. 8.63.5.

27. Ibid. III. 10.49.3-5; cf. II. 23.146.1.

28. *Paed.* III. 10.50.1-50.2.

29. Ibid. II. 10.94.4.

30. *Strom.* II. 23.145.3.

31. Ibid. IV. 19.123.2.

32. Ibid. 20.127.2.

33. Antipater, *Concerning Marriage.* Frag. in H. F. A. von Arnim, *Stoicorum veterum fragmenta* (Leipzig, 1903-1924) III. 254ff. Trans. in E. V. Arnold, *Roman Stoicism* (Cambridge, 1911), p. 319. Cancik-Lindemaier speaks of Antipater's making possible the equality of men and women: Hildegard Cancik-Lindemaier, "Ehe und Liebe. Entwürfe griechischen Philosophen und römischer Dichter," in *Zum Thema Frau in Kirche und Gesellschaft. Zur Unmundigkeit verurteilt?* ed. Hubert Cancik, et al. (Stuttgart: Katholisches Bibelwerk, 1972) 62. Cf. Albrecht Oepke, "GUNE," *Theological Dictionary of the New Testament,* vol. 1, ed. by Geoffrey Bromiley (Grand Rapids: Eerdmans, 1964) 779.

34. Actually a Middle Platonist, but he had appropriated many views of the Middle Stoa.

35. Plutarch, *Erotikos* 769A.

36. *Bravery of Women* 242F.

37. *Oration* III.

38. P. 46, 32, Lutz. Cora Lutz provides an English translation of Musonius in "Musonius Rufus: The Roman Socrates," *Yale Classical Studies* 10 (1947): 38-49. Oepke states that with Musonius the estimation of women and marriage reaches its climax; op. cit., p. 780.

39. Antipater, *Concerning Marriage* 256.2-9. Trans. by David Balch in *Let Wives Be Submissive; the Domestic Code in 1 Peter* (Chico, Ca.: Scholars Press, 1981) 145.

40. *Concerning Marriage* 256.33—257.10.

41. *Advice to Bride and Groom* 138B-146A.

42. Ibid. 140A-D, 142D-E, 145C-E.

43. P. 42.11-15, Lutz.

44. Ibid. 40.10-12, 17, Lutz.

45. P. 19, 8-14, Lutz.

46. *Orat.* III, Lutz.

47. Ibid. 46.13-31, Lutz.

48. P. 86.38-88.4, Lutz.

49. *Paed.* II. 10.114.3; cf. Tertullian, *De Cultu Feminarum* 1.1. Tertullian sees women's covering as part of their garb of penitence.

50. *Strom.* III. 9.65.1.

51. Tertullian, *De Cultu Feminarum* 1.1.

52. The Alexandria of Clement's time had for a century or more been experiencing a revival of Greek philosophy of an eclectic nature, whose principal ingredients were Pythagoreanism, Platonism, and especially Stoicism. For philosophy's influence on Clement, see Simon Wood's introduction to *Christ the Educator* (New York: Fathers of the Church, 1954) vii, x-xvi; as well as the important study by S. R. C. Lilla, *Clement of Alexandria: A Study in Christian Platonism and Gnosticism* (Oxford, 1971). Lilla says Clement's overall system "represents the meeting point of three distinct streams: the Jewish Alexandrine philosophy, the Platonic tradition, and Gnosticism" (p. 227). Also informative is Eric Osborn, "Clement of Alexandria: A Review of Research, 1958-1982," *Second Century* 3 (1983): 219-244.

53. *Strom.* II. 23.146.1.

54. The quoted passage occurs in the context of Clement's discussion on divorce and adultery.

55. In the passage where Clement states that women are to "philosophize equally with men" (*Strom.* IV. 8.62.4), the context concerns who is rulling the home.

56. Manning argues cogently that to talk of a Stoic concept of the "equality" of the sexes requires so many reservations that it is best to dispense with the term altogether. C. E. Manning, "Seneca and the Stoics on the Equality of the Sexes," *Mnemosyne* 26 (1973): 176.

David Dawson (essay date 1992)

SOURCE: "Clement: The New Song of the *Logos*," in *Allegorical Readers and Cultural Revision in Ancient Alexandria,* University of California Press, 1992, pp. 183-234.

[*In the following excerpt, Dawson describes Justin of Flavia Neapolis's method of interpreting allegorically the word of God in Biblical and non-Biblical texts, and contends that Clement applied Justin's ideas in his own reading.*]

Like Valentinus, Clement (Titus Flavius Clemens) was an independent Christian intellectual and teacher in second-century Alexandria. He was born around 150 C.E. of pagan parents, probably in Athens. Following a *topos* of Hellenistic intellectual autobiography, he tells us that after travels to Italy, Syria, and Palestine in search of teachers, he finally discovered the finest teacher of all in Egypt.[1] Upon arriving in Alexandria around 180 C.E., Clement began a vigorous teaching and writing career in the city that lasted until 202/203 C.E., when the violent persecution of Christians by the emperor Septimius Severus forced him to leave Egypt. He fled to Cappadocia, where he joined a certain Alexander, who later became bishop of Jerusalem. Clement died in Cappadocia before 215 C.E., without seeing Egypt again.[2]

Clement was a prolific author, and a good portion of his literary production has survived.[3] His major extant works are often referred to as a trilogy, though only the first two treatises are clearly related to one another. There is first an appeal to pagans to embrace the new Christian philosophy (**Exhortation to the Greeks; Protreptikos pros Hellēnas**), then a handbook of social and personal ethics (**The Tutor; Paidagōgos**), and (apparently in place of a projected, but unwritten, third component of the trilogy that would have been entitled **The Teacher,** or **Didaskalos**) a lengthy, rambling series of obscurely arranged ruminations on Christianity as the true *gnōsis* (**The Carpets** or **Miscellanies; Strōmateis**). The other complete extant work is a homily on Mark 10.17-31 entitled **Who Is the Rich Man Who Is Being Saved?** (**Quis dives salvetur; Tis ho sōzomenos plousios**). We also have considerable portions of two collections of Clement's quotations from other writings and notes: extracts from the work of Valentinus's student Theodotus (**Excerpta ex Theodoto**) and comments on selected passages from Hebrew scripture (**Eclogae propheticae**). The rest of Clement's works have perished, except for a few fragments.[4]

We have now examined in some detail two strikingly different forms of allegorical reading for the sake of cultural

revision. Philo read scripture allegorically on the assumption that Moses was an original author who had re-inscribed cultural and philosophical wisdom in the form of the Pentateuch. Valentinus read his precursors (especially Gnostic myth) allegorically, expressing his revision of culture in the form of his own creative allegorical composition. Clement illustrates yet a third mode of allegorical reading and cultural revision. He specialized in what he called the traditions of the "elders"—teachers who were thought to have transmitted by word of mouth the inner secrets of the Christian gospel, derived ultimately from Jesus himself. Following earlier Christian traditions, Clement identified Jesus as the divine Word or *logos*—a divine entity that, according to the Middle Platonic philosophy prevalent in Clement's day, mediated between the transcendent God and the material world. The first part of this chapter examines the distinctive hermeneutical application of this Middle Platonic concept of *logos* by Clement's immediate predecessor, Justin of Flavia Neapolis (Justin Martyr). Justin claimed that this *logos* or preexistent Christ was the voice of God, to be discovered in the pages of Hebrew scripture and certain works of pagan philosophy. With Justin as his model, Clement reads his precursor texts and traditions allegorically to discover beneath the surface of the words an original Word or divine voice.

In the second part of the chapter, I turn to a discussion of Clement's various applications of this voice-based hermeneutic. Prior in time and authority to all other sources of meaning and truth, this divine voice "speaks" wisdom through all sorts of writings, including, but not limited to, the texts that Christians call "scripture." Just as a ventriloquist "throws" his or her voice, making it appear as though any number of other objects are speaking, so Clement construes scripture and other texts as expressions of a single divine voice, the discourse of God's own speech. The *logos* speaks the allegorical "other" meanings of scripture and pagan classics, and the clarity and intensity of that voice determine the relative authority of those texts. Clement's mode of reading consequently relativizes all texts—whether classical literature, the Septuagint, or the New Testament—by subordinating them to an underlying divine discourse. Because he discovers the same speaker everywhere, he is able to relate very different texts to one another as he sees fit, avoiding when necessary or convenient their lexical details or historical interrelations. Clement's appeal to a divine voice allows him to relate diverse texts as "scripture" and "canon" in a bewildering variety of ways.

Although I have used the terms "scripture" and "New Testament" throughout this study, we must always bear in mind that in the second century C.E. the boundaries of both were not clearly defined, but fluctuating and permeable. Unlike Valentinus, Clement holds a conception of the New Testament as a literary category, but that category does not match contemporary or later collections denoted by the same label. Furthermore, works such as the "prophetic and poetic" Sibylline oracles stand somewhere on the vague borderline between "scripture" and nonscriptural Greek literature. Rather than trying to decide on "independent" grounds which texts are part of Clement's "scripture" and which are not or—and this is a different question—which texts are "canonical" and which are not, I have taken a broadly pragmatic and functional approach that relates the revisionary capacity of "scripture" to existing texts that are treated as though canonical. When one text is subordinated to a second in an interpretative reading, the subordinated text may be said to have a certain functional "canonicity" because it has sufficient authority to attract commentary. The subordinating text may in turn be said to function as "scripture" in the sense that—at least for that moment—it exercises hermeneutical authority over the first, canonical text. Of course, this labeling does not decide whether the subordinated "canonical" text also functions as "scripture" in other interpretative contexts; on other occasions, it may indeed exercise authority over another "canonical" text, in which case it too "functions scripturally." "Canonicity," then, simply denotes the role of being the object of revisionary interpretation, while "scriptural" status denotes a measure of interpretative authority exercised over canonical texts. Neither category has any necessary relation to collections of texts later gathered together under the title New Testament. Only by broadening traditional categories in this way—which in fact is what Clement's *logos*-based allegorical revision demands—will we be able to appreciate the nature of the hermeneutical struggle in which Clement was engaged.

Finally, Clement's allegorical readings of classical, Jewish, and Christian texts also serve a number of social purposes. In the third part of the chapter, I examine Clement's hermeneutic as part of his social role as a theological teacher and ecclesiastical advocate in Alexandria. In particular, I analyze his use of allegorical interpretation to define the character and limits of his own Christian community in relation to a number of alternative Christian groups. This process of communal self-definition and social boundary maintenance grows directly out of Clement's own ambivalent sensibility; attentive to the authoritative claims of an emerging Christian "orthodoxy," he is equally responsive to the appeals of an esoteric and speculative Christian *gnōsis*. However, in the end, the desire for orthodoxy gains the upper hand, and Clement offers readers a domesticated version of the radical Christian *gnōsis* represented by Valentinus.

LOGOS THEOLOGY AS ALLEGORICAL HERMENEUTIC

Even though both Philo and Valentinus drew on current speculation about the divine *logos*, neither gave it the sort of thoroughgoing hermeneutical emphasis that Clement did. Clement's consistent emphasis on a theology of divine voice distinguishes his allegorical hermeneutic from both Philo's and Valentinus's. Because Clement understands scripture as a kind of tape recording of divine speech, he tends to characterize Moses as a divine spokesperson, rather than as Philo's divine scribe.[5] Through Moses and the rest of the prophets, the *logos* as the divine pedagogue speaks (**Paed.** 1.2.5.1; 3.11.75.3), and the vari-

eties of that speech result in a wide range of rhetorical tones and modes of speech in the Septuagint. New Testament writings also display varied rhetorical modes. For example, Paul's declaration in 1 Corinthians 3.2 "I have given you milk to drink" is not simply a straight forward statement; the rhetorical scenario is more subtle—these words are spoken "mystically" by "the Holy Spirit in the apostle, using the voice of the Lord" (**Paed.** 1.6.49.2).

Just as scripture is the recorded speech of God, so faith—as both goal and presupposition of scripture reading—comes from hearing rather than reading:

> But as the proclamation [*kērygma*] [i.e., of the gospel] has come now at the fit time, so also at the fit time were the law and the prophets given to the barbarians, and philosophy to the Greeks, to fit their ears for the proclamation [*kērygma*]. (**Strom.** 6.6.44.1)

Thus Abraham at the oak of Mamre "through hearing believed the voice" (**Strom.** 5.1.4.1). "We ought not to surrender our ears to all who speak and write rashly," writes Clement,

> for cups also, which are taken hold of by many by the ears, are dirtied, and lose the ears; and besides, when they fall they are broken. In the same way also, those, who have polluted the pure hearing of faith by many trifles, at last becoming deaf to the truth, become useless and fall to the earth. (**Strom.** 5.1.12.4)

In a passage stressing the unity of a God who makes the same promises to Christians as to Hebrew patriarchs, Clement insists that Christians, as the seed of Abraham, are Israelites "convinced not by signs, but by hearing" (**Strom.** 2.6.28.4). He then quotes Isaiah 54.1 (= Gal. 4.27) as evidence for the application of Hebrew prophecy to Christians. However, Clement did not invent this notion of a divine voice speaking through the texts of both Christian and non-Christian literature. Before we turn to an examination of Clement's distinctive use of this voice-based hermeneutic, it will be helpful to consider his principal Christian hermeneutical model.

The notion of a divine voice speaking through scripture and other texts was the basis for the two "apologies" of Justin (ca. 100-ca. 165 C.E.), a Christian Platonist active in Rome in the middle of the second century C.E.[6] Justin combined a Christianized interpretation of the biblical concept of the "Word of God" with Middle Platonic speculation about the *logos* as an entity that "mediated" the relationship between the transcendent high God and the material world. This synthesis resulted in a conception of the *logos* as a divine voice that spoke through the mouths of Hebrew prophets like Moses and Greek philosophers like Socrates, and that through a paradoxical act of incarnation finally became physically embodied as the teacher Jesus of Nazareth. Upon the death, resurrection, and ascension of Jesus, the divine voice reappeared as the spirit of the risen Jesus in the preaching of the apostles. Justin's first apology, written about 156 C.E., was addressed to the Roman emperor Antoninus Pius and his adopted sons, Marcus Aurelius and Lucius Verus. The second apology (perhaps originally part of the first) was written about 161 C.E. and though addressed to the Roman Senate in the extant manuscript, was probably originally addressed to several emperors.[7] We have no indication that these works were read by any of the addressees, but they were widely read in Christian circles and became extremely influential in subsequent Christian theology.

Although Clement does not refer to Justin by name, it is virtually certain that he was familiar with Justin's writings.[8] Even in the unlikely event that Clement had not read Justin's works directly, he could have learned about Justin's ideas from the writings of Irenaeus, bishop of Lyons. In his work *Against Heresies* (ca. 180 C.E.), Irenaeus had adopted and transformed Justin's theology as it had been expressed in Justin's earlier work of the same title (now lost). Clement was familiar with Irenaeus's *Against Heresies,* which, as a papyrus fragment of the second century C.E. attests, was available in Alexandria soon after it was written.[9] He also had access to many of the same examples of early Christian biblical interpretation and Middle Platonic philosophy with which Justin was familiar. Indeed, if one were a philosophically literate person in the second century C.E. and lived in any of the major centers of the empire, such as Rome, Athens, or Alexandria, Middle Platonism would be virtually inescapable. It was especially easy for Clement to assimilate this philosophical tradition, for it was well represented both in Athens, where he grew up and was educated, and in Alexandria, where he later wrote and taught. The Middle Platonists Calvenus Taurus and Atticus were active in Athens, and the shadowy Eudorus as well as Philo (who was as much a Middle Platonist as he was an allegorical exegete) were based in Alexandria.[10] Clement also preserves a fragment from a work by the Middle Platonist Numenius of Apamea, a pagan contemporary of Justin who will be important in our analysis of Justin's hermeneutic. Numenius flourished in the mid-second century and provides a very close philosophical parallel to Justin.

Clement set aside or minimized many of Justin's cruder formulations (in particular his demonology) and, unlike Justin, drew extensively on Aristotelian logic (especially in his discussions of the nature of faith). But he followed Justin's basic model of a hermeneutic of the divine voice.[11] Consequently, just as it proved useful to examine the works of Aristeas and Aristobulus as precursors of Philo's more far-reaching interpretation of scripture, so Justin's two brief apologies provide a helpful introduction to the sort of revisionary hermeneutical perspective that Clement was to extend to a much wider range of literature. We will begin our investigation of Justin's *logos* theology by commenting first on its biblical and philosophical roots. We will then examine his transformation of this essentially philosophical and theological formulation into a hermeneutical principle. In particular, we will want to observe in some detail how Justin turns a concept representing a divine being into one representing the meaning and interpretation of texts.

In the Hebrew Bible, the "Word of God" generally refers to divine agency in all its forms: speech, action, and other modes of self-revelation. For the most part, this "Word" does not become a distinct entity or hypostasis of its own but remains a metaphor for expressing the deity's self-extension into the nondivine realm. But in later Jewish speculation, the category "wisdom," functioning virtually as a synonym for "Word," did begin to assume a quasi-distinct status of its own. In the Book of Proverbs, for example, wisdom says of itself: "The Lord created me at the beginning of his work/the first of his acts of old./Ages ago I was set up,/at the first, before the beginning of/the earth" (Prov. 8.22-23). In some circles of Jewish speculation, wisdom was even identified with the preexistent Torah itself, and both were understood to represent God's plan for, and instrument of, creation.[12] In early Christian literature, especially the Pauline epistles and the Gospel of John, the "Word" and/or "wisdom" was sometimes identified with the preexistent Son of God, who became incarnate, taking the form of Jesus of Nazareth (see, for example, 1 Cor. 1.18ff., 2.6ff.; Phil. 2; John 1.1-18).

Philo had already combined elements of Jewish speculation about the divine Word or wisdom with Middle Platonic ideas about the *logos*. In fact, he used Proverbs 8 as biblical support for his belief in an intermediary *logos* with quasi-independent status.[13] Providing a similar, but specifically Christian, variant of Philo's interpretation, Justin brought together reflection on the Word of God as Christ with aspects of Middle Platonic *logos* conceptions.[14] He too appealed to Proverbs 8, in this case to prove the preexistence of Christ (*Dial.* 61.3). This assimilation by Hellenistic Jews and Christians of the biblical discussion of the divine "Word" with philosophical conceptions of the *logos* was facilitated by the Septuagint's translation of "Word of God" as *logos theou*.

Justin also drew extensively on prevailing philosophical ideas about a divine *logos*. By the second century C.E., Middle Platonism had largely displaced Stoicism as the dominant philosophical world view in the Greco-Roman world. Middle Platonism was a form of Platonic philosophy that drew upon other philosophical systems in order to address questions that Plato had left unanswered, to explore further ideas that he had suggested, and, in general, to make Platonism an attractive philosophy for the contemporary era. On the basis of an essentially Platonic philosophical framework and vocabulary, Middle Platonists embraced certain features of Stoic ethics and physics, Aristotelian logic, and Pythagorean metaphysics and number speculation as ways of giving fuller and more accurate expression to their understanding of Plato.[15] Middle Platonists were especially preoccupied with the nature and activity of the supreme principle or highest divine being. Despite having significant differences among themselves regarding the characterization of this being, most Middle

Platonists emphasized its utter transcendence. They were convinced that the ultimate realm of true being could never come into direct contact with the ordinary realm of becoming. The realm of being was atemporal, immutable, and imperishable; the realm of becoming was subject to time, change, and decay. In order for such a transcendent God to have relevance for the world and human beings, the relationship between God and the world needed to be "mediated" by another entity. This entity would provide a "buffer zone," connecting God with, while protecting God from, the world. Various entities played this role, sometimes Plato's demiurge, sometimes his world soul; the principal mediator was often aided by a host of lesser intermediaries, including angels, demons, and disembodied souls.

Many Middle Platonists added to this mediating figure features characteristic of the Stoic *logos*. We have already seen that *logos* was the term used by Stoic philosophers to refer to God, that is, the divine, physical energy that permeated reality in the form of a fiery ether. By Philo's time, some Middle Platonists had taken up this Stoic notion of the *logos* and integrated it in their system. This integration naturally required the elimination of the materialistic features of the Stoic idea. The Middle Platonists reinterpreted the material energy of the Stoic *logos* as an immaterial force, which they then identified with the mediating entity, sometimes referred to as the "second" god. Meanwhile, they continued to speak of a first or high God, who remained uninvolved with the world and whose only act was the self-reflection that gave rise to the second, mediating god. The result, despite a variety of terminology, is essentially a two-tiered system: a first God, completely transcendent and unknowable, and a second god (the *logos*), responsible for all divine contact with, and action upon, the material realm.[16] Sometimes the second god was further divided, producing a third divine entity. In such cases, the second god was characterized by closer association with the first God, while the third god (or "lower" dimension of the second god) concerned itself more directly with the material realm.

Both the Christian Middle Platonist Justin and the Pythagorizing Middle Platonist Numenius reflect many of these Middle Platonic ideas.[17] While a detailed comparative analysis of the two figures would exceed the scope of this book, a few observations of similarities and differences will give some idea of just how much these two Platonists share. Justin speaks of a first God who is eternal, immovable, unchanging, nameless and unbegotten, utterly detached from the material realm. As a result,

> you must not imagine that the unbegotten God himself came down or went up from any place. For the ineffable Father and Lord of all neither has come to any place, nor walks, nor sleeps, nor rises up, but remains in his own place, wherever that is. (*Dial.* 127; cf. *Dial.* 56)

There is also a second god or *logos*, who mediates between the high God and the world, and a "spirit" that oc-cupies the third place.[18] Numenius also spoke of three divine entities: a first God, who exists in himself and is devoid of agency, a second god or demiurge responsible for all motion, and a third entity (which Proclus mistakenly identifies as creation—"what was fashioned"—but which almost certainly refers to a lower aspect of the second god).[19] There are, however, differences: Justin's high God is both Father and creator, while Numenius restricts creation to the second god or demiurge.[20] This difference probably reflects Justin's basic monotheism, as well as his identification of Plato's father and maker (Pl. *Tim.* 28C) with biblical descriptions of the creative action of God. Justin goes on to stress the close association between the first God and the second: the second god is emitted without any diminution in the being of the first God, as one fire is generated from another. Numenius uses the same analogy to stress the participation of the second god in the first.[21]

Both Justin and Numenius use a passage from an alleged Platonic epistle to endorse their views of multiple divine entities. In the *Second Epistle*, the author writes: "All things are about the King of all and exist for him, and he is the cause of all is good. The second things are about the Second and the third about the Third."[22] Justin quotes the second sentence, interpreting Plato as referring to the Father, Son, and Holy Spirit (*Ap.* 1.60.7).[23] Numenius used the same passage as a warrant for the three gods of his system.[24] And just as Justin equated the Holy Spirit with the spirit hovering over the waters in Genesis 1.2 (*Ap.* 1.60.6), so Numenius allegorized the same verse for his own purposes.[25] Thus we see that Justin and Numenius share much the same Middle Platonic theology, especially the distinction between a first God and a second.

The Middle Platonist first God had one further characteristic: it was "generative" or "productive" (*spermatikos*). This idea was taken from the Stoics. Although in borrowing this Stoic idea, Middle Platonists necessarily eliminated its materialistic aspects, they preserved its generative character. According to the Stoics, the divine *logos* had fragmented itself into the *logoi* that constituted human minds; the human mind was literally part of the divine ether that pervaded the cosmos. Like that cosmic fire, the *logos* of human reason was productive: it was able to generate "seeds," which were the principles and concepts of human thought. Hence, the Stoics called the *logos* the *logos spermatikos* or "generative *logos*." Middle Platonists preserved this link between the second god (or *logos*) and human reason by thinking of the *logos* as a kind of cosmic mind in which human minds were now said to "participate." Through its illumination of the human mind, the Middle Platonic *logos* was thus the ultimate source of human thoughts.

This Middle Platonic notion of an immaterial, productive second god or *logos* was well in place by Justin's time; versions of it were prevalent in both Hellenistic Jewish and pagan metaphysical speculation. For example, in the preceding century, Philo had spoken of the *logos* as a divine hypostasis, separated from the divine intellect, and he had given it various names: Power, Second God, First Born of God, Son of God, Angel, and Apostle.[26] In two instances, Philo refers explicitly to the *logos spermatikos*—once as the transcendent creator of physical and spiritual life and once as human reason.[27] Justin may well have drawn on Philo's works and certainly drew on New Testament texts in formulating his own version of the *logos spermatikos*.[28] But it is also likely that he was familiar with Numenius's use of the conception. Numenius had described the relation of the first God to the second god or demiurge by drawing on an analogous relation between a farm owner and farm laborer. The farmer himself is responsible for the initial sowing of the crops, but the laborer then takes over the cultivation of the field. Numenius writes:

> Just as there is a relation between the farmer and the one that plants, so in just the same way is the first God related to the demiurge. The former, as farmer, sows [*speirein*] the seed [*sperma*] of every soul into all the things which partake of it; while the lawgiver plants and distributes and transplants what has been sown from that source into each one of us. (Frag. 13)[29]

As we shall see, Justin holds a similar view of a divine *logos* mediating the productive activity of God vis-à-vis individual human souls. Although Justin's notion of the *logos spermatikos* owes something to Philo and Numenius, he goes his own way by following the Gospel of John and other Christian literature in identifying this *logos* with Christ alone.[30] For the Christian Middle Platonist Justin, the divine, generative *logos* was Christ or the preexistent Son of God, as well as the incarnate Son, Jesus of Nazareth. Such an assertion of the divine demiurge's direct association with matter would have been totally unacceptable, not to say repugnant, to Numenius.[31]

According to Justin, this divine *logos* was the single source of prophetic revelation (*Ap.* 1.12.7-10) and philosophical illumination (*Ap.* 1.5 and passim); it was also the essence of the words, and, finally, the person, of Jesus (*Ap.* 1.14ff.). Justin's hermeneutical application of the *logos* concept appears in three interrelated themes that dominate his writings: the *logos*'s spermatic or generative character, the battle between the *logos* and the demons, and the plagiarism of scripture by pagan philosophers. All three themes appear in Philo, and all three (especially the first and third) were developed by Clement as part of his own allegorical revision of pagan and Christian competitors.

Justin's basic claim is that Hebrew scripture is a transcription of divine speech. When scripture is properly read, one hears the voice of God: "When you hear the utterances of the prophets spoken as it were personally, you must not suppose that they are spoken by the inspired themselves, but by the divine *logos* who moves them" (*Ap.* 1.36.1). Understanding what the divine voice is saying requires a certain hermeneutical sophistication, however, for the voice adopts different points of view, depending on the character through which and the circumstance in which it speaks:

> For sometimes he [the divine *logos*] declares things that are to come to pass, in the manner of one who foretells the future; sometimes he speaks as from the person of God the Lord and Father of all; sometimes as from the person of Christ; sometimes as from the person of the people answering the Lord or his father, just as you can see even in your own writers, one person being the writer of the whole, but introducing the persons [*prosōpa*] who converse. (*Ap.* 1.36.2)

The prophetic voice of Hebrew scripture continues in the person of Jesus: when Jesus opens his mouth to teach, the divine *logos* speaks. This divine speech endures even after Jesus' death, in the preaching of the apostles: "by the power of God," the apostles "proclaimed to every race of human beings that were sent by Christ to teach all the *logos* of God" (*Ap.* 1.39.3). The apostles are able to express the *logos* of God precisely because that *logos,* in the form of the risen spirit of Jesus, entered into them and enabled them to interpret Hebrew prophecy: through the apostles, the *logos* has become the authoritative interpreter of its own message (*Ap.* 1.50.12).

It is interesting to note that Numenius seems to have held a similar view of the way literature could be designed to convey a message through various rhetorical modes of speech.[32] In a fragment from his lost work *On the Secrets in Plato,* he observes that Plato has intentionally conveyed certain points of view through the construction of the dramatic dialogue of the *Euthyphro.* In particular, Numenius notes that Plato dramatizes his criticism of Athenian religious orthodoxy by using Euthyphro as his spokesperson:

> Since speaking the truth was more important to him than life itself, he saw that there was a way he could both live *and* speak the truth without risk: he made Euthyphro play the part of the Athenians—an arrogant twit and a remarkably bad theologian—and set Socrates against him in his usual character, confronting everyone he met just as he was accustomed to do. (Frag. 23.12-18)[33]

It seems that Numenius, like Justin, was as much a hermeneutician as a philosopher. Like Justin, he seems to have been attentive to the way the basic message of a single author could be conveyed in various dramatic and rhetorical forms. And according to Origen, Numenius also did not refrain from "using in his own writings the words of the [Jewish] prophets and treating them allegorically [*tropologein*]" (Frag. 1b.6-8).[34] It seems likely, then, that Numenius, as a Platonist interpreter of literature, brought to his own work a hermeneutical sensibility similar to Justin's.

For Justin, the divine voice that speaks in Hebrew scripture, in the teaching of Jesus, and in the *kērygma* of the apostles also speaks in at least some pagan philosophy. He makes this clear when responding to the pagan challenge that Christian revelation had irresponsibly neglected the fates of those who lived before Jesus:

> We have been taught that Christ is the firstborn of God, and we have declared above that he is the *logos* of

whom every race of human beings partook [*metechein*]; and those who lived with *logos* [*meta logou*] are Christians, even though they have been thought atheists; as, among the Greeks, Socrates and Heraclitus, and those like them; and among the barbarians, Abraham, and Ananias, and Azarias, and Misael, and Elias, and many others whose actions and names we now decline to recount, because we know it would be tedious. (*Ap.* 1.46.2-3)

Such persons who lived before Christ but who nevertheless shared in the *logos* (*meta logou*) are de facto Christians (*Ap.* 1.46.4).

By the same token, those who lived before Christ but who did not share in the *logos* (*aneu logou*) are de facto persecutors of Christ (*Ap.* 1.46.4). The presence of the persecutors of the *logos*/Christ indicates that history was not a divine monologue; from the outset (i.e., from the fall of those angels who became demons), divine speech had to assert itself in the face of stringent opposition from demonic forces. According to Justin, the demons were originally angels, who subsequently turned against God. His account of this angelic fall assimilates Genesis 6, which describes the attack on the "daughters of men" by the "sons of God," to contemporary Middle Platonic speculation about demons:

> God, when he had made the whole world . . . committed the care of human beings and of all things under heaven to angels whom he appointed over them. But the angels transgressed this appointment, and were captivated by love of women, and begat children who are those that are called demons. (*Ap.* 2.4[5].2-3)

The demons, who coerced human beings into worshiping them, are responsible for "murders, wars, adulteries, intemperate deeds, and all wickedness" (*Ap.* 2.4[5].4). The mythmakers became the unwitting tools of demonic self-expression, and the poets became equally deluded accomplices of the mythmakers. Both attributed demonic activity to deities and their offspring:

> Whence also the poets and mythmakers, not knowing that it was the angels and those demons who had been begotten by them that did these things to men, and women, and cities, and nations, which they related, ascribed them to God himself, and to those who were accounted to be his very offspring, and to the offspring of those who were called his brothers, Neptune and Pluto, and to the children again of these their offspring. For whatever name each of the angels had given to himself and his children, by that name they called them. (*Ap.* 2.4[5].5-6)

Whether before or after the appearance of the *logos* in the person of Jesus, the demons constantly opposed its voice, wherever it appeared. This demonic opposition could take direct, violent forms, such as the persecution of Socrates, the crucifixion of Jesus, or the attacks on Justin and his Christian contemporaries. But the demons could also attack indirectly, through subversive literary representations and the willful misinterpretation of scripture. They were able to gain power over human minds through the images of themselves that they created; in effect, the demons personified themselves and generated mythical narratives in which they took leading roles. Those accounts frightened human beings into calling them "gods":

> Since of old these evil demons, effecting apparitions [*epiphaneiai*] of themselves, both defiled women and corrupted boys, and showed such fearful sights to men, that those who did not judge with *logos* [*logōi*] the actions that were done, were struck with terror; and being carried away by fear, and not knowing that these were evil demons, they called them gods, and gave to each the name which each of the demons chose for himself. (*Ap.* 1.5.2)

But demonic mythology does not consist in wholly novel literary productions. On the contrary, demons are essentially parasitic—they create myths that distort or parody scripture in order to neutralize its effect:

> Before he [the *logos*] became a human being among human beings, some [mythmakers] under the influence of the evil demons just mentioned, told through the poets as having already occurred the myths they had invented, just as now they are responsible for the slanders and godless deeds alleged against us, of which there is neither witness nor demonstration. (*Ap.* 1.23.3)

Here Justin explains that the demons first corrupted the original makers of myths, and then the poets simply compounded the problem by incorporating those myths into their poetry. It is interesting to compare Justin with Cornutus. Both writers have a view of the corruption of original theological wisdom, but Cornutus holds a much more sanguine view of the mythmakers than Justin, for he has no theory of demonic corruption at the very origin. But for Justin, the demons corrupted truth and generated falsehood from the outset, and the poets who use pagan mythology only pass along the deciet.[35] Unlike Cornutus, Justin does not recommend the separation of pure original myth from contaminating additions: at their worst, the myths are entirely corrupt; at best, they are perversions of the true accounts of scripture that should entirely displace them.

When properly read, scripture prophesies the coming full appearance of the *logos* that will destroy the demons. But in a preemptive strike, the demons seek to erode the credibility of scripture and its proper interpretation by creating myths that look like scripture. The idea is that when the pagan myths are then criticized as fiction by Christians or other devotees of the *logos,* scripture itself will fall under the same critique of being fiction because of its similar mythical appearance:

> But those who hand down the myths which the poets have made adduce no proof to the youths who learn them; and we proceed to demonstrate that they have been uttered by the influence of wicked demons, to deceive and lead astray the human race. For having heard it proclaimed through the prophets that the Christ was to come, and that the ungodly among human beings were to be punished by fire, they put forward many to

be called sons of Zeus, under the impression that they would be able to produce in human beings the idea that things which were said with regard to Christ were marvellous tales [*teratologiai*], like the things which were said by the poets.

(*Ap.* 1.54.1-2)

Justin insists that the Jews, like the demons, also misread Hebrew scripture. Either they fail to recognize the messianic prophecies or, having recognized them, fail to refer them to Jesus as the true Messiah. In particular, the Jews did not understand the theory of multiple speakers that Justin presents: consequently, "although the Jews possessed the books of the prophets," they "did not . . . recognize Christ even when he came" (*Ap.* 1.36.3). The Jews are not directly to blame, however; for like the Greek mythmakers and poets, they too were the unwitting instruments by which the demons continued their assault on the *logos*. Consequently, Justin can link Jewish hermeneutical failure (in this example, Jewish failure to see that the *logos*, not the ineffable high God, appears to Moses in the burning bush) and their persecution of Christ by associating both with the work of the demons:

> [Theophanies like the burning bush] are written for the sake of proving that Jesus the Christ is the Son of God and his apostle, being of old the *logos* [*proteron logos ōn*], and appearing sometimes in the form of fire, and sometimes in a bodiless image; but now, by the will of God, having become a human being for the human race, he endured all the sufferings which the demons instigated the senseless [*anoētoi*] Jews to inflict upon him; who, though they have it expressly [*rhētōs*] affirmed in the writings of Moses, "And an angel of God spoke to Moses in a flame of fire in a bush, and said, I am that I am, the God of Abraham, and the God of Isaac, and the God of Jacob," yet maintain that he who said this was the father and maker [*dēmiourgos*] of the universe. (*Ap.* 1.63.10-11)

For Justin, then, the proper interpretation of scripture and all other literature requires attending to the authentic divine speech in the text and resisting a variety of distorting interpretations and competing literary alternatives promulgated by the demons.

From time to time, those who lived with a share of the *logos* did seek to resist the mythology of the demons, but the demons were quick to fight back; this cosmic battle lies behind the career of Socrates. Socrates deserves the admiration of Christians because he

> cast out from the state both Homer and the rest of the poets, and taught human beings to reject the evil demons and those who did the things which the poets related; and he exhorted them to become acquainted with God who was to them unknown, by means of rational investigation [*dia logou zētēseōs*], saying "that it is neither easy to find the father and maker [*dēmiourgos*] of all, nor, having found him, is it safe to declare him to all." (Pl. *Tim.* 28C, altered, in *Ap.* 2.10.6)

But the demons quickly counterattacked:

> When Socrates skillfully endeavored, by true reason [*logōi alēthei*], to bring these things to light, and deliver

human beings from the demons, then the demons themselves, by means of those who rejoiced in iniquity, brought about his death, as an atheist and an impious person, on the charge that "he was introducing new divinities." (Pl. *Ap.* 24B in *Ap.* 1.5.3)

Justin argues that he and his Christian contemporaries are suffering the same attacks because they are simply carrying on the Socratic protest in a more intense form (more intense since, unlike Socrates, they enjoy the full presence of the *logos* in the form of Christ):

> For not only among the Greeks were these things condemned by *logos* [*hypo logou*] through Socrates [*dia Sōcratous*], but also among the barbarians by the *logos* himself [*hyp' autou tou logou*], who took shape, and became man, and was called Jesus Christ. (*Ap.* 1.5.4)

Whenever one detects similarity between pagan and biblical descriptions, there are, then, only a few possible explanations: we have already discussed two of them—either pagans who have been enlightened by their share of the *logos* have expressed an insight similar to scripture's or the evil demons have produced a distorted version of scripture. There is, however, a third possibility, which Justin probably took from Philo: that pagans have simply plagiarized the Bible directly. Justin argues, for example, that Plato takes his account of creation in the *Timaeus* from the opening verses of Moses' Genesis and that Hesiod derives his discussion of Erebus from Moses as well (*Ap.* 1.59.1-6). Similarly, Plato's idea in the *Timaeus* that the power of the high God was placed "crosswise" in the universe was in fact a misinterpretation of a biblical prophecy of Christ in Numbers 21 (*Ap.* 1.60). Like Philo, Justin is sure that Moses lived and wrote long before any of the Greek philosophers, but he is also sure that the *logos* existed before Moses. The key point, of course, is not that Christians "hold the same opinions as others," but that all others who share the *logos* "speak in imitation of ours" (*Ap.* 1.60.10)—or, as Justin more audaciously announces, "whatever things were rightly said among all persons, are the property of us Christians" (*Ap.* 2.13.4).[36]

Despite the fact that his use of *logos* theology as a hermeneutical principle enables him to bring together biblical revelation and philosophical illumination as a single act of divine self-manifestation and production of textual meaning, Justin firmly maintains the distinctiveness and superiority of the specifically Christian revelation. Even with his share of the *logos*, Socrates does not attain to the fullness of Christian insight. Justin tells his readers that he himself turned from Platonic philosophy to Christianity "not because the teachings of Plato are different from those of Christ, but because they are not in all respects similar, as neither are those of the others—Stoics, and poets, and historians" (*Ap.* 2.13.2).[37] It is true that "each one, by having portions of the divine generative *logos* [*apo merous tou spermatikou theiou logou*], spoke well, whenever he saw what was congruent with it" (*Ap.* 2.13.3) and that "all the writers were able to see realities [*ta onta*] dimly [*amydrōs*] through the spore of the implanted *logos* that was in them [*dia tēs enousēs emphytou tou logou sporas*]" (*Ap.* 2.13.5). But Justin immediately spells out the implication of his qualifications (i.e., "a share" and "dimly"). There is, he insists, a vital distinction to be made between "the seed and the ability to imitate it by one's own capacity" *(sperma tinos kai mimēma kata dynamin dothen)* and "the thing itself, of which there is participation and imitation by virtue of its own favor [*kata charin tēn ap' ekeinou*]" (*Ap.* 2.13.6).

Justin thus makes it clear that Christians, not pagans, enjoy the full presence, and, indeed, possession, of the *logos* itself. Socrates, we saw, performed his critique "by rational investigation" (*dia logou zētēseōs*) (*Ap.* 2.10.6), but Christ performs the same critique "through his own power" (*dia tēs heautou dynameōs*) (*Ap.* 2.10.7). Justin claims that this qualitative, not quantitative, distinction was well recognized by persons from all walks of life and of all degrees of education:

> For no one trusted in Socrates so as to die for this doctrine, but in Christ, who was partially known even by Socrates [*hypo Sōcratous apo merous gnōsthenti*]— for he was and is the *logos* who is in every person, and who foretold the things that were to come to pass both through the prophets and in his own person [*di' heautou*] when he was made of like passions, and taught these things—not only philosophers and philologians believed, but also artisans and people entirely uneducated, despising both glory, and fear, and death: since he [or it—i.e., either Christ or his doctrine] is a power [*dynamis*] of the ineffable Father, and not the mere instrument of human reason [*anthrōpeiou logou kataskeuē*]. (*Ap.* 2.10.8)

In the end, Justin's voice of the *logos* drowns out the voices of all cultural competitors by absorbing them into its own divine fullness. This voice is the original voice of truth. As Justin points out, truth at its origin was one, and religious sects developed only because human beings turned away from the one truth to cultivate their own idiosyncratic opinions (*Dial.* 2.1-2). Thus Justin provided a chronological account of heresy in his lost work *Against Heresies,* in which heretical error was portrayed as a progressive deviation from original, single religious truth, handed down from misguided teachers to misguided pupils. Justin's notion of heresy as deviance from original truth set the pattern not only for Irenaeus's *Against Heresies,* but for most subsequent Christian heresiologists. Once again, Numenius provides a parallel idea, in his work *on the Infidelity of the Academy toward Plato.* Just as Justin insists that heretics corrupt the pure divine truth, so Numenius contends that Plato's successors fell away from the teaching of the master into sectarian division because they "did not hold to the primitive heritage but rapidly divided, intentionally or not" (frag. 24: cf. frags. 25-28).[38] Hence the pagan Middle Platonist, no less than his Christian contemporary, sought to recover an ancient and original wisdom, which was still spoken forth in the pages of ancient literature, despite the efforts of heretics and sectarians to corrupt it.

Notes

1. Cf. Justin *Dialogue with Trypho, a Jew* 2 (in *Ante-Nicene Fathers,* vol. 1, ed. Roberts and Donaldson).

2. Johannes Quasten, *Patrology,* vol. 2: *The Ante-Nicene Literature after Irenaeus* (1953; reprint, Utrecht-Antwerp: Spectrum, 1975), 5-6.

3. I have used the standard critical Greek text, Otto Stählin, ed., *Die griechischen christlichen Schriftsteller der ersten drei Jahrhunderte,* 4 vols. (Berlin: Akademie-Verlag, 1905-36). In general, English translations are from Roberts and Donaldson, *Ante-Nicene Fathers,* vol. 2: *Fathers of the Second Century* (1884; reprint, Grand Rapids, Mich.: Eerdmans, 1979). When necessary, however, I have modified this translation or simply retranslated the text. I quote also from Henry Chadwick's translation of *Strōmateis* 3 and 7 in John Ernest Leonard Oulton and Henry Chadwick, *Alexandrian Christianity: Selected Translations of Clement and Origen with Introductions and Notes* (Philadelphia: Westminster, 1955) and from Clement of Alexandria, *Christ the Educator,* trans. Simon P. Wood (New York: Fathers of the Church, 1954). Quotations from the *Eclogae propheticae* are based on an unpublished translation by Alan Scott. References to Clement's works will be to treatise, book (when applicable), and chapter. Paragraph and sentence numbers as given in Stählin's right-hand margin are included as well, thus *Strom.* 1.10.22.4-5. This system of reference has been used instead of the more customary volume, page, and line of the Stählin edition in order to provide easy access to the English translations as well as to the standard Greek text.

4. The lost works include a lengthy commentary on Hebrew and Christian scripture (*The Outlines* or *Sketches; Hypotypōseis*) as well as the following titles: *On the Pasch, Ecclesiastical Canon or Against the Judaizers, On Providence* (Clementine authorship uncertain), *Exhortation to Endurance or To the Recently Baptized, Discourse on Fasting, On Slander, On the Prophet Amos* (Clementine authorship uncertain) (from Quasten, *Patrology,* vol. 2, 6-19).

5. Moses, writes Clement, "who was after the law . . . foretold that it was necessary to hear in order that we might, according to the apostle, receive Christ, the fullness of the law" (*Strom.* 4.21.130.3). Clement takes the proclamation of Deuteronomy 18.18, "I will put my words in his mouth, and he shall speak to them all that I will command him," as a clear indication of Moses' prophetic (and decidedly oral) role.

6. I have used the Greek texts in A. W. F. Blunt, ed., *The Apologies of Justin Martyr,* Cambridge Patristic Texts, ed. A. J. Mason (Cambridge: Cambridge Univ. Press, 1911). I have largely followed the English translation in Roberts and Donaldson, *Ante-Nicene Fathers,* vol. 1, though I have also made modifications, especially in light of Edward Rochie Hardy's

translation, "The First Apology of Justin, the Martyr," in *Early Christian Fathers,* ed. Cyril C. Richardson, The Library of Christian Classics 1 (New York: Macmillan, 1970), 242-89, as well as Blunt's suggestions. I will designate the first apology by *Ap.* 1 and the second by *Ap.* 2. References to the second apology will give both the chapter numbers of the original manuscript (preserved by Blunt) and, in brackets, the chapter numbers according to the reordering adopted by the *Ante-Nicene Fathers* translators.

7. Robert M. Grant, *Greek Apologists of the Second Century* (Philadelphia: Westminster, 1988), 55.

8. Henry Chadwick, *Early Christian Thought and the Classical Tradition: Studies in Justin, Clement, and Origen* (New York: Oxford Univ. Press, 1966), 40; also "Clement of Alexandria," in *The Cambridge History of Later Greek and Early Medieval Philosophy,* ed. A. H. Armstrong (Cambridge: Cambridge Univ. Press, 1967), 170-71. Clement does refer to Justin's pupil Tatian: see *Strom.* 1.21.101.1-2 for Clement's appeal to Tatian to prove the antiquity of Moses and *Strom.* 3.12.81 for his rejection of Tatian's encratism.

9. *POxy.* iii. 405, cited by Roberts, *Early Christian Egypt,* 14.

10. The standard discussion of Middle Platonism, which has the virtue of resisting generalizations and describing the specific systems of individual philosophers, is John Dillon, *The Middle Platonists: 80 B.C. to A.D. 220* (Ithaca, N. Y.: Cornell Univ. Press, 1977). I have also made use of the summary discussions in R. A. Norris, Jr., *God and World in Early Christian Theology: A Study in Justin Martyr, Irenaeus, Tertullian, and Origen* (New York: Seabury, 1965), 41-68, especially 52-53. Clement draws upon Philo's exegetical works frequently, often in the form of direct quotation and without attribution. My discussion of Justin's apologies in the context of Middle Platonism draws on the detailed studies of Carl Andresen, "Justin und der mittlere Platonismus," *Zeitschrift für die Neutestamentliche Wissenschaft und die Kunde der Älternen Kirche* 44 (1952-53): 157-95; Ragnar Holte, "Logos Spermatikos: Christianity and Ancient Philosophy According to St. Justin's Apologies," *Studia Theologica* 12 (1958): 109-68.

11. Chadwick, *Early Christian Thought,* 40-41.

12. Holte, "Logos Spermatikos," 122-23.

13. Ibid., 123.

14. Justin himself reports that he studied with Epicurean, Stoic, Aristotelian, and Platonic teachers, though this autobiographical account may be shaped according to his general claim for the absorption of all useful pagan philosophy by Christianity (see *Dial.* 1-9).

15. Dillon, *Middle Platonists,* xiv-xv, points out that what is commonly, but misleadingly, referred to as Middle Platonism's "eclecticism" is an anachronism.

These philosophers saw themselves not as eclectics, but as drawing on the insights of competing philosophical systems to help give coherent expression to their own unified and systematic vision of Plato's "authentic" philosophy.

16. Dillon, *Middle Platonists,* 367, notes that this distinction between the supreme God and the demiurge may be found in Numenius and all other Pythagoreans, as well as in Albinus. He adds that Platonists who do not make a complete separation between the two gods nevertheless make a very strong distinction, which is functionally equivalent.

17. I have used Numenius, *Fragments,* ed. and trans. Édouard Des Places (Paris: "Les Belles Lettres" [Budé], 1973). See the discussion of the relevant fragments of Numenius in Dillon, *Middle Platonists,* 367ff.

18. Cf. *Ap.* 1.13.3:

Our teacher of these things is Jesus Christ, who also was born for this purpose, and was crucified under Pontius Pilate, procurator of Judea, in the time of Tiberius Caesar; and that we reasonably worship him, having learned that he is the Son of the true God himself, and holding him in the second place, and the prophetic spirit in the third, we will prove.

19. Cf. frags. 11, 12, 15, 21. At one point, Justin also conflates the second god or *logos* with the third entity, the spirit: "It is wrong, therefore, to understand the spirit and the power of God as anything else than the Word, who is also the first-born of God" (*Ap.* 1.33.6).

20. See Dillon, *Middle Platonists,* 367-69.

21. *Dial.* 61:

For he [the *logos*] can be called by all those names [Holy Spirit, Glory of the Lord, Son, Wisdom, Angel, God, Lord, *Logos,* Captain] since he ministers to the Father's will, and since he was begotten of the Father by an act of will; just as we see happening among ourselves: for when we give out some word, we beget the word; yet not by abscission, so as to lessen the word [which remains] in us, when we give it out: and just as we see also happening in the case of a fire, which is not lessened when it has kindled [another], but remains the same; and that which has been kindled by it likewise appears to exist by itself, not diminishing that from which it was kindled.

Compare the same analogy used by Justin's pupil, Tatian (*Oration* 5) and by Numenius (frag. 14).

22. Pl. *Ep.* 2.312E (quoted by Grant, *Greek Apologists,* 62).

23. Grant, *Greek Apologists,* 215 n. 46, records other early uses of the Plato passage: Athenagoras *Leg. pro Christ.* 23.7; Clement *Strom.* 5.14.103.1; Celsus in Origen *c. Cels.* 6.18. Hippolytus charged that Valentinus used the passage in his invention of the *plērōma* (*Haer.* 6.37.5-6).

24. Frag. 15.

25. Frag. 30.

26. Holte, "Logos Spermatikos," 123.

27. Cf. *Her.* 119: *aoratos kai spermatikos kai technikos logos; L.A.* 3.150: *ho spermatikos kai gennētikos tōn kalōn logos orthos* (cited by Holte, "Logos Spermatikos," 124 n. 54).

28. Holte, "Logos Spermatikos," 128, suggests that he may have been especially influenced by Matthew 13.3ff., Jesus' parable of the sower who sows the word of God.

29. See Dillon, *Middle Platonists,* 368, for discussion of this passage. He observes that this notion of a divine sowing is similar to Nicomachus's description of the Monad being "seminally (*spermatikos*) all things in Nature" and is reminiscent of Plato *Timaeus* 41E, where the demiurge sows souls into the various "organs of Time," as well as of *Republic* 10.597D, which describes God as a "planter" (*phytourgos*) of physical objects. Dillon discusses the transformation of Stoic *spermatikoi logoi* into the generative, but immaterial, "ideas of God" in Antiochus, Seneca (*Ep* 58, which preserves a Platonic source), Philo, and Albinus (95, 137, 159, and 285, respectively).

30. Holte, "Logos Spermatikos," 127.

31. Cf. *Ap.* 1.13.4:

    For they proclaim our madness to consist in this, that we give to a crucified man a place second to the unchangeable and eternal God, the creator of all; for they do not discern the mystery that is herein, to which, as we make it plain to you, we pray you to give heed.

    See Dillon, *Middle Platonists,* 369, 373ff., on Numenius's negative evaluation of matter.

32. The following discussion of Numenius as literary interpreter is drawn entirely from Lamberton's discussion in *Homer the Theologian,* 64-70.

33. Lamberton's translation, *Homer the Theologian,* 63.

34. Lamberton, *Homer the Theologian,* 62, concludes that Numenius almost certainly used allegorically interpreted passages from the Christian New Testament as well as the Hebrew Bible.

35. Little can be said about Numenius's views on demons. Dillon, *Middle Platonists,* 378, points to Numenius's allegorical interpretation of the battle between the Athenians and the Atlantians in the *Timaeus* as a conflict between "more noble souls who are nurslings of Athena, and others who are agents of generation (*genesiourgoi*), who are in the service of the god who presides over generation (Poseidon)" (frag. 37). Dillon speculates further that the category "servants of Poseidon" might represent material demons who were "engaged in snaring souls into incarnation."

36. Cf. *Ap.* 1.23.1:

Whatever we assert in conformity with what has been taught us by Christ, and by the prophets who preceded him, are alone true, and are older than all the writers who have existed . . . we claim to be acknowledged, not because we say the same things as these writers said, but because we say true things.

37. Cf. *Ap.* 1.20.1-3:

    And the Sibyl and Hystaspes said that there should be a dissolution through fire by God of things corruptible. And the philosophers called Stoics teach that even God himself shall be resolved into fire, and they say that the world is to be formed anew by this revolution; but we understand that God, the creator of all things, is superior to the things that are changed. If, therefore, on some points we teach the same things as the poets and philosophers whom you honor, and on other points are fuller and more divine in our teaching, and if we alone afford proof of what we assert, why are we unjustly hated more than all others?

38. See Lamberton's discussion in *Homer the Theologian,* 54-59 . . . .

Eric Osborn (essay date 1994)

SOURCE: "Arguments for Faith in Clement of Alexandria," in *Vigiliae Christianae,* Vol. 48, No. 1, 1994, pp. 1-24.

[*In the following essay, Osborn examines in turn each of Clement's eight arguments for faith and the resulting philosophical problems.*]

In the history of ideas, the defence of faith, which is offered by Clement of Alexandria, ranks beside that of Paul who, in Romans 4, sought to prove the primacy of the faith of Abraham over the law of Moses. Paul was supported by the Letter to the Hebrews, which claimed that not only Abraham, but all the notables of Jewish scripture were persons of faith. Yet faith found its first principle and perfection in Jesus. For Clement, just as the law was a *paidagogos* to the Jews, so philosophy was a *paidagogos* to the Greeks to bring them to Christ. In the second century, both *paidagogoi* were unhappy at their compulsory retirement, especially since they were required to leave their books behind for use by their younger replacement. Justin made it clear that the scriptures now belonged to Christians; Tertullian warned all that the scriptures were Christian property.

In philosophy, Justin and Clement used an identical formula to assert that whatever had been well said, belonged to Christians. Justin's *logos spermatikos* claimed Socrates and Heraclitus as Christians before Christ. Clement, in his **Stromateis,** claimed that the Greek schools had torn the limbs of truth apart; Christ brought them all together. The need for philosophical argument was self-evident for it would have to be used to prove itself unnecessary. The protest against the Christian acquisition of Greek philosophy was strong and found its centre exactly where Jewish protest against Paul was fixed—the inadequacy of faith. Clement's reply defended faith with philosophical arguments which he connected to the arguments which Paul and the Epistle to the Hebrews had used against a different opponent.

The move from the New Testament to Christian theology through the joining of New Testament ideas to Greek philosophy was, I think, the beginning of European thought, and the argument about faith stands in the centre of that development. Faith became an object of attack from philosophers because it claimed too much and from Gnostics because it achieved too little. Clement of Alexandria's plea for the faith, which he had learned from his much-quoted Paul, is pervasive and of many strands. These strands have sometimes been separated between bible and philosophy[1] and subjected to limited scrutiny. My concern is to let the two sources speak together, to look at them in the light of recent discussion concerning Greek philosophy, and to solve a long-standing problem of false attribution, where Zeno is supplanted by Aristotle.

Christians were, according to the Platonist Celsus, always saying, 'Only believe', and never offering rational grounds for the acceptance of their creeds. Origen replied that not everyone could be a full-time philosopher, and that the scriptures were studied with logical rigour. Further, most people had neither time nor ability for rational inquiry and they must be helped (*Cels.* 1.9). Indeed, philosophers choose their school of philosophy on non-rational impulse, either because they have met a certain teacher or believe one school to be better than the rest (*Cels.* 1.10). Faith in the supreme God is a commendable thing, the writers of the Gospels were plainly honest men and Christian doctrines are coherent with the common notions of human reason (*Cels.* 3.39f.).

Clement's reply to the same criticism had been more complex. He needed more argument to meet the objections of Gnostics as well as philosophers to the high place which Christians gave to faith in their preaching, worship and discipline. He drew his account of faith from Paul (to whom he attributed the Epistle to the Hebrews), John, Plato, Aristotle, Theophrastus, Stoics, Epicurus and others. The philosophy of Clement's day, Middle Platonism, mixed Plato with Aristotle and the Stoics.

Faith was anticipation, assent, perception, hearing God in scripture, intuition of the unproved first-principle, discernment by criterion, dialectic and divine wisdom, unity with God.

Despite diversity of origin, all these moves in ancient epistemology had served a common end, that of finding a basis for knowledge and avoiding 'infinite regress'.

Clement was a Stromatist, not simply to hide things from unthinking Sophists, but because he wanted his different readers to learn from the similarities between their own ideas and Christian faith. 'To those who ask for the wisdom which is in us, we must present what is familiar to them so that, as easily as possible, through their own ideas . . . they may reasonably arrive at faith in the truth' (*str* 5.3.18).

For Clement, as he begins the discussion in ***Stromateis*** 2 and takes it up again in ***Stromateis*** 5, argument and faith are necessary to one another. Argument for faith is still argument. His introduction indicates his approach. Philosophical proof is a benefit to minds rather than to tongues (*str.* 2.1.3). Just as fowls which scratch vigorously for their own food have the best flesh, so there is need for pain and effort by those who search for truth (*str.* 2.1.3). We need wisdom in all our ways (Prov. 3:5f.). Faith is the way and the fear of God is foremost (*str.* 2.2.4). The barbarian or biblical philosophy is perfect and true. Wisdom is the unerring knowledge of reality, of virtues and of the roots of things (Wisd. 7:17ff.; *str.* 2.2.5). Clement begins from the fear of the lord, as extolled in the Wisdom literature, which had already joined the faith of the Old Testament to Hellenistic philosophy (*str.* 2.2.4).

Divine wisdom is the universal guide. She requires rejection of earthly wisdom, conformity to reason, discriminating use of secular culture, departure from evil and, supremely, the fear of God (Prov. 3:5,6,7,12,23). Through wisdom God gives true understanding of existing things: 'a knowledge of the structure of the world and the operation of the elements; the beginning and end of epochs and their middle course; the alternating solstices and the changing seasons; the cycles of the years and the constellations; the nature of living creatures and behaviour of wild beasts; the violent force of winds and the thoughts of men; the varieties of plants and the virtues of roots. I learnt it all, hidden or manifest, for I was taught by her whose skill made all things, wisdom' (Wisd. 7:17-21). With these verses, Clement summarises 'barbarian philosophy' and the wisdom which leads to God who, although remote in essence, has come near to men (Jer. 23:23).[2] The riddles of divine utterance and the deep things of the spirit, he says, are secrets which exclude the unworthy. What is holy must be kept from the dogs. Heraclitus limited understanding to the few and seems to rebuke the many who do not believe; the prophets tell us that the righteous live by faith and without faith there can be no understanding. Without faith, said the writer to Hebrews, it is impossible to please God (*str.* 2.2.4-8).

Clement's eight arguments are the following:

First, *faith is preconception,* the substance of things hoped for.

Second, *faith is assent or decision,* and never a natural possession.

Third, *faith is hearing and seeing,* as the definition and narrative of Hebrews 11 make clear.

Fourth, *faith is listening to God in the scriptures.*

Fifth, a first principle *is to be unproved and unprovable.* To avoid infinite regress, there has to be a starting point which is grasped by faith.[3]

Sixth, *faith is the criterion* which judges that something was true or false.

Seventh, *faith is always on the move, from faith to faith,* moving up the ladder of dialectic. It is the grain of mustard seed which stimulates the soul to grow.

Eighth, *faith is fixed on God and in some way divine,* a source of *power and stability.* From the shifting sands of error, it moves to the firm ground of truth and there it remains.

All these arguments raise problems which show that they never were without ambiguity. In order to use them Clement had to decide what they meant; their close examination shows how many questions had to be faced in order to give an account of faith. The eight points also show how intricately scripture and philosophy are joined. Today it seems natural to divide the language of philosophy and the language of the bible.[4] For Clement the bible was the barbarian philosophy and logos linked the text of scripture to human reason. It was not possible to pluck instant fruit from the vines; there had to be planting, weeding, watering and all sorts of farming. It is a mistake, in the elucidation of Clement's complex ideas, to isolate philosophical argument from evangelical exhortation. Clement quotes Plato 600 times and Paul 1200 times; frequently they are quoted together.

1. PRECONCEPTION AND HOPE

Faith, says Clement, is denigrated by the Greeks but it is what they recognise as a deliberate preconception or anticipation. Hebrews 11 has offered the same defence of faith: faith gives substance to our hopes (*str.* 2.2.8).

'Epicurus supposes faith to be a preconception of the mind, He explains this preconception as attention directed to something clear and a clear concept of something. He declares that no one can make an inquiry, confront a problem, have an opinion and indeed make a refutation without a preconception' (*str.* 2.4.16). Epicurus saw that without an anticipation one cannot inquire, doubt, judge. Isaiah insisted that there could be no understanding without faith (7:9) and Heraclitus wrote 'Except one hopes for what is beyond hope, he will not find it, for it will remain impossible to examine and to understand' (Diels 18). This means that the blessed and happy man must be from the beginning a partaker of truth, believing and trustworthy (Plato, *Laws* 730bc). The *apistos* is hopeless in the arena of truth and is a fool (*str.* 2.4.16).

Hope depends on faith. Even Basilides, the Gnostic, saw that faith is the assent of the soul to things which are not present to the senses (*str.* 2.6.17). Basilides went wrong

when he denied the freedom of faith and the decision which it involved. Faith is a wise preconception prior to comprehension. It is an expectation and confidence in the only and all-sufficient God, whose beneficence and kindness are turned to us (*str.* 2.6.28).

The *function* of Epicurean preconceptions is to make knowledge possible, when the perceiver is confronted by a mass of sensations.[5] Preconceptions are . . . distinguished from other mental visions by their generic content.'[6] They claim to generate universals from streams of phenomena. By means of preconception we recognise different kinds of things. The mind selects from streams of atomic images to form the preconception which enlarges the act of perception.[7] Preconceptions become indispensable starting points. 'It is as a matter of fact, from Epicurus on, a philosophical commonplace that preconceptions are what make inquiry possible'.[8] Regrettably, they were no more impregnable against Skeptics than were other starting points, for the Skeptic simply claimed that he had different preconceptions and could not choose between them.[9]

There are three different theories concerning the *origin* of preconceptions. In the first account they are due to repeated sensation, in the second they are innate, and in the third they are ingrained.

(i) Preconceptions come from what has frequently been evident to the sense (D.L. 10.33). Each word brings to the mind a clear delineation which is a self-evident starting point, and which removes the danger of infinite regress (cf. *Ep.Hdt.* 37f.). We do not inquire about anything of which we have no prior knowledge. Sensations are marked off from one another and classified by means of preconceptions, which have been gained through repeated experiences of particular objects (D.L. 10.33). Other concepts may also be derived from preconceptions; even the gods are objects of refined perception.[10]

(ii) The late Stoicizing Academy speaks of innate preconceptions. For example, every race of men possesses, in its untaught state, a preconception of the gods. 'Epicurus' word for this is *prolepsis,* that is what we may call a delineation of a thing, preconceived by the mind, without which understanding, inquiry and discussion are impossible' (Cicero, *ND* 1.44).[11] These preconceptions are *insitae* and *innatae.*

(iii) In between these positions is that of the Old Stoa. Chrysippus considered preconceptions to be ingrained rather than innate, and was credited with clearing up confusion between preconceptions and conceptions (Plutarch, *Comm. not.* 1059C). 'There is no other "evidence" in the Old Stoic writers for a theory of any kind of "inborn" belief; their philosophy needs no such beliefs and should not be saddled with them.'[12]

Attempts to harmonise the different accounts of origin have been unsuccessful.[13] The first belongs to Epicurus, the second to the late Stoicizing Academy and the third to the Old Stoa. For the Epicurean, the world is perceived as divided into natural kinds which we recognise, for the Stoic, definition is a prerequisite for any inquiry. The Stoic idea aims to represent the world. The Epicurean idea simply responds to a stimulus in the world. The scholarly consensus that Stoics merely took over Epicurean preconception is seriously wrong.[14] We have no Epicurean text which sets out exactly the nature of preconception; but the empiricist, materialist position of the Epicureans should prevent them being assimilated by Stoicizing commentators. *Prolepseis* are concerned, not with mental states, but with states of affairs in the world.[15] *Prolepseis* organise *phainomena* either into natural kinds or into persistent conditions.[16] Anything more must be a conceptual invention. There is a difference between recognizing something in the world and conceiving something which represents it.[17]

The 'substance of things hoped for' in Hebrews 11 is a simple development from Pauline theology. Just as Abraham was justified by faith, so all Old Testament notables are heroes of faith.[18] The notion of anticipation (*vorauseilen, vorangehen, vorausnehmen*) is stressed by Bultmann in his sermons. 'To be a Christian, to believe, means to have hurried on ahead of the time of this world. It means to stand already at the end of this world.'[19] In this way faith becomes that victory which overcomes the world (1Jn 5:4).[20] As so often for Clement, Heraclitus, for whom hope is essential to understanding,[21] provided the link between philosophy and the bible.

Clement's adoption of *prolepsis* is not a blind appropriation, because there are different theories between which he must choose. For his own reasons, Clement gives Epicurus a more Stoic doctrine than he had propounded; but he cannot (for anti-Gnostic reasons) concede that preconceptions are innate. Faith is *hekousios* and it is a clear vision of the future which links faith and hope. These claims lead on to the next two arguments.

2. ASSENT AND CHOICE

The preconception of faith is chosen. It is the assent of godliness, or saying 'yes' to God . . . (*str.* 2.2.8). Faith (*str.* 2.2.9). is an assent which unites[22] the believer to God. Faith provides a foundation by rational anticipatory choice. The decision to follow what is better is the beginning of understanding. Unswerving anticipatory choice . . . provides the movement towards knowledge (*str.* 2.2.9). Choice and decision had been important for Plato and especially for Aristotle (*Nic.Eth.* 1139a 31ff.).[23] Here Clement is concerned both to attack Gnostics and to convince philosophers. For Basilides, faith is innate and, as for Valentinus, inferior to knowledge. Both deny that faith is a matter of free choice (*str.* 2.3.10). For Clement, faith must be voluntary (*str.* 2.3.11).

The scriptures tell of free choice, and the scriptural command to believe is an invitation to assent or choose. With a willing spirit we choose life and believe God through his

voice (*str.* 2.4.12). Following Hebrews 11, the faith of Abel, Enoch, Noah, Abraham, Isaac, Jacob, Sarah, is celebrated. Clement continues with Joseph and Moses who also chose God's way of faith. Faith is in our power and shows its effects in a repentance which is freely chosen (*str.* 2.6.27). Both Platonists and Stoics say that assent is in our power (Chrysippus *frag.phys.* 992) (*str.* 2.12.54). Indeed all opinion, judgement, conjecture and learning is assent, which is faith. Unbelief shows that its opposite (faith) is possible, while it remains a mere privation and has no real existence (*str.* 2.12.55). Faith as the voluntary assent of the soul produces good works and right action (*str.* 5.13.86). We may note, in contrast (*str.* 5.5.28), that David says 'Be angry and sin not' (Ps. 4:5). This means, says Clement, that we should not give our assent to the impression of anger or confirm it by action.

Confession (*homologia*) to God is martyrdom (*marturia*). The soul which has lived purely, known God and obeyed his commandments is a *martus* by life and word. It sheds blood all along the way of life until it goes from earth to be with God (*str.* 4.4.15). However, those (Marcionites or others) who choose martyrdom out of hatred for their creator, do not qualify as 'believing martyrs'. They have not known the only true God and die in futility. Nor are words enough. The true confession of martyrs is not what their voice utters, but the deeds and actions which correspond to faith (*str.* 4.9.71).

Knowledge, for Zeno (SVF i 68), is a form of grasping or comprehension, a *katalepsis* which cannot be overthrown by any argument. External objects produce impressions, which reach the governing-principle of the perceiver (SVF ii 56), who *assents* or judges that his impression corresponds to fact. Then, he grasps the impression and finally he knows. Zeno described the four stages, by extending his open hand which received the impression, then partly closing his hand to show assent, then clenching his fist to show cognition and finally grasping his fist with his other hand to show what knowledge was like (Cic.*Acad.* 2.145). Many things may be grasped and known by the senses, but never without assent, which we may give or withhold. Yet the living mind must admit what is self-evident as surely as scales sink under weights (Cic.*Acad.* 2.37f.). Some impressions are immediately certain; these cognitive or recognizable impressions virtually take us by the hair and drag us to assent (Sextus, *Adv.math.*, vii, 257).

Sense perceptions are like blows from outside to which the assent of the mind must be given from within (Cic.*Acad.* 1.40f.). The senses send their impressions to the mind which assesses their testimony. The wise man gives assent only to impressions which are cognitive and consequently he does not err. Ignorance is changeable and weak assent. While the wise man supposes nothing weakly, but securely and firmly . . . the inferior man is precipitate and gives assent without cognition.[24]

Assent is given by the ruling faculty of the soul (Aetius 4.21) mediating between impressions and impulses.

'Without assent there is neither action nor impulsion'.[25] Such assent means 'going along with' or 'committing oneself to' the truth of an impression. For the New Academy, assent was not an acceptable theory. Carneades had driven it as a wild and savage monster from their minds (*Acad.* 2.108). Arcesilaus denied the propriety of assent to any truth (*Acad.* 1.43-6). Assents are bad; suspension of judgement is good (Sext.Emp.*Pyrr.* 1.232-4). As well as assent, Clement gives an account of faith as choice, when reason fails. We do not inquire into questions which are obvious, opaque, ambivalent, or which have one irrefutable side. If the cause for inquiry is removed in any of these ways, then faith is established . . . (*str.* 5.1.5).

3. Perception, hearing, seeing and believing

Faith needs to perceive that to which its assent may be given. Faith is the scrutiny of things not seen (Heb. 11:1). Moses endured as seeing him who is invisible (Heb. 11:27). He who hopes, as he who believes, says Clement, sees with his mind both mental objects and future things. What is just, good, true is seen with the mind and not with the eyes (*str.* 5.3.16). Faith is prior to argument, and may be considered as a form of perception. For Theophrastus, Clement tells us, *aisthesis* is the *arche* of faith. From perception the *archai* come to our *logos* and *dianoia* (*str.* 2.2.9). While truth is found in *aisthesis, nous, episteme* and *hupolepsis, nous* is first by nature, even if for us *aisthesis* is first in the order of our experience. Sensation and *nous* are the essence of knowledge, sharing what is *enarges*. Sensation is the ladder to knowledge. Faith advances through things which are perceived, leaves assumptions. . . behind and comes to rest in truth (*str.* 2.3.13). While materialists grasp rocks and oaks in their hands to argue with idealists (*Sophist* 246a), faith provides a new eye, new ear and new heart which apprehend what eye has not seen nor ear heard nor has entered in to the heart of man (1 Cor. 2:9; Is. 64:4). By faith comes the quick comprehension of the disciples of the lord. They discern the false from the genuine, like money changers, who tell others what is counterfeit but who do not try to explain why, because only they have learnt the difference (*str.* 2.4.15).[26] Those who have ears to hear should hear. Epicharmus explains further that it is mind which sees and hears, while all else is deaf and blind. Heraclitus describes unbelievers as ignorant of how to hear or to speak, while Solomon (Sir. 6:33) links hearing with comprehension and wisdom (*str.* 2.5.24).

Such hearing comes from the son of God through the word of the lord and the preaching of the apostles; it ends in faith (Is. 53:1; Rom. 10:17, 14, 15). Word and preaching need cooperation. As in a game of ball the thrower must have someone to catch, so faith catches what it hears and is a cooperating cause in the gaining of truth (*str.* 2.6.25).

Faith is the ear of the soul, whereby he who has ears to hear may hear, and comprehend what the lord says.[27] Faith of teacher and of hearer work together to the one end of salvation. Paul speaks of the mutual faith which he shares with the Romans (Rom. 1:11f.).

Faith directs the sight of the soul to discovery. Obstacles like jealousy and greed must be cleared away (*str.* 5.1.11). So there are to be no pearls cast before swine; the natural man does not receive the things of God (*str.* 1.12.56 also 5.4.25). All, both barbarians and Greeks, who have spoken of divine things, have veiled their account of first principles in riddles, symbols, allegories, and metaphors (*str.* 5.4.21). The common crowd will stay with their five senses; but we must go within the veil. Plato excluded the uninitiated who thought that all existence could be grasped by their hands. God cannot be known by those who are limited to their five senses. The son revealed the father in the flesh but he is known only in the spirit. We walk by faith, not by sight (*str.* 5.6.34) . . . .

. . . In scripture the language of seeing and hearing is present on every side. Paul speaks of the new eye and ear, of looking to things unseen and eternal, even of visions in the third heaven. Hebrews 11 is full of the evidence of what is unseen. Blindness and deafness are the epistemological illnesses of the Gospels. At the last judgment, condemnation is pronounced on those who did not see, in the hungry, thirsty, lonely, naked, sick and prisoner, the presence of their lord.[28]

4. Faith and scripture

Perception leaves us with the question: where is God to be seen and heard? God is the first object of faith and the arguments for faith only work because God has spoken in scripture. Here we receive the voice of God as irrefutable proof. The strength of scripture is, like the call of the Sirens, greater than human power; it disposes hearers, almost against their wills, to receive its words (*str.* 2.2.9).

Plato (*Tim* 40de), says Clement, claims that it is possible to learn the truth only from God or from the offspring of God. We are confident in the divine oracles which we possess and the truth we learn from the son of God, a truth which was first prophesied and then made clear (*str.* 6.15.123).

The disciples of Pythagoras found. . . a sufficient ground for faith. Therefore the lovers of truth will not refuse faith to a master worthy of faith, the only saviour and God (*str.* 2.5.24). From him come the word of the lord, the preaching of the apostles, and the hearing which turns to faith (Is. 53:1; Rom. 10:17,14,15) (*str.* 2.6.25).

In general, faith and proof may depend on either knowledge or opinion. From the scriptures we have proof based on knowledge in an obedience which is faith in God (*str.* 2.11.48). Even the simplest faith has this knowledge or rationality. The highest proof produces *episteme* through scriptures and leads on to *gnosis* (*str.* 2.11.49). Faith cannot be overthrown because God comes to our help in scripture (*str.* 5.1.5). It would be wrong further to disbelieve God and ask for proofs from him (*str.* 5.1.6).

Clement's strong claims for scripture might be assisted in two ways. First, it was common in the ancient world to look to literature as a source of all knowledge.[29] Secondly, Christians (notably Justin) took over Jewish scriptures which were studied as the oracles of God, a complex totality of truth. These had ceased to belong to the Jews and had become Christian property. Irenaeus, Clement and Tertullian saw them as crowned by the writings of the New Testament. The central problem, which Clement raises with striking clarity, is the relation between divine oracle and the philosophy, which for him means argument. Plato, he shows, had established the conjunction. In Philo, oracle almost swallows philosophy, and in the Gnostics there is nothing but oracle. Clement stays close to Plato and insists that we should follow the wind of the argument wherever it leads. Philosophical argument is never optional: we should have to argue in order to show it to be unnecessary (*str.* 6.18.162).

For Clement the divine oracles are alive. His enthusiasm for scripture is enhanced by its novelty. He writes with the wonder of the poet John Keats, 'On first looking into Chapman's Homer'. Faith, says Clement, is active through love in writing or speaking the word (*str.* 1.1.4). The prophets and disciples of the spirit knew by faith (*str.* 1.9.45). We are taught by God, instructed by the son of God in the truly 'sacred letters which are the scriptures' (*str.* 1.20.98). Faith in Christ and the knowledge of the gospel provide explanation and fulfilment of the law. As Isaiah says, unless we believe, we do not understand. We must believe what the law prophesies and delivers in oracles in order to understand the Old Testament, which Christ, by his coming, expounded. Indeed faith in Christ and the knowledge of the gospel are the exegesis of the law and its fulfilment (*str.* 4.21.134).

At the same time philosophy is at least as important as oracle. The scriptures provide the real philosophy and true theology if we read them often, put them to the test by faith and practise them in the whole of our lives (*str.* 5.9.56). He who believes scripture and the voice of the lord may be trusted. Scripture is the criterion and first principle, and not subject to criticism. It is reasonable to grasp by faith the unprovable first principle and to receive from it demonstrations about the first principle. In this way we are trained to know truth by the voice of the lord (*str.* 7.16.95). We have already arrived at the next argument.[30]

5. FAITH AND PROOF

Scripture makes claims about God and salvation. How can these be rationally accepted? The faith of Abraham points to one cause and principle of all things, to the self-existent God, who justifies the ungodly, raises the dead and creates out of nothing. God, says Clement, who is remote in his being, has come near to us (Jer. 23:23f.). Moses, on the mountain, entered into the darkness, into the inaccessible ideas about existence (*str.* 2.2.6). Hiddent truth may now be learnt (Prov. 1:2-6; *str.* 2.2.6). With the Holy Spirit, it is possible to search the deep things of God (1 Cor 2:10). That which is holy is not for dogs (*str.* 2.2.7). Understanding follows faith (Is. 7:9).[31]

For the first-principles of things are not proved or provable. They are not known by practical *techne* or by *phronesis* which handles changeable things: the first principle or cause of all things is known by faith alone.[32] All knowledge may be taught, and what is taught is based on previous knowledge. The first principle was not known to Greeks like Thales or Anaxagoras. Since no one can know and teach first principles, we must call no man our master on earth (*str.* 2.3.13). Wisdom, which begins from the fear of the Lord, the grace and word of God, is faith.

God, we are told later, in **Stromateis** 5, gave us life and reason; he wished that our life be both reasonable and good. From Justin's *logos spermatikos* onwards, this was the dominant theme of early Christian thought: reason and goodness stand together. The logos of the father of all things is not just a spoken word but his wisdom and transparent goodness, his divine and sovereign power, his almighty will, conceivable even for those who do not confess him (*str.* 5.1.6). Man's own rational power is limited. Paul declared God's judgement on the fragile wisdom of the disputers of this world. In similar vein Numa, king of the Romans, rightly built a temple to faith and peace, which are the opposites of the worldly debate. Abram was justified by faith, recognised God as superior to creation and scored an extra Alpha to be called Abraham. He had always been interested in the heavens; when he grasped the simplicity and unity of God, he received a second Alpha and a new name. The link of justification and the indemonstrable first principle is an important clue to the meaning of faith (*str.* 5.1.8). While Empedocles claimed truth in his myths, he declared that the inclination to faith . . . is resisted by the mind (*str.* 5.1.9). So Paul put his faith not in the wisdom of men, but in the power of God, which alone and without proofs can save.

In his logic note-book of **Stromateis** 8, Clement expands his claim that first principles cannot be proved or else they would not be first principles but dependent on something prior to them. This is the simplest argument for faith. It is not a proof of God's existence, but a proof that God, because he is God and ultimate first principle, is only accessible to faith (*str.* 8.3.6f.). An account of unprovable firstprinciples had been central to the logic of Aristotle, as stated in the Metaphysics. 'There cannot be demonstration of everything alike: the process would go on to infinity so that there would still be no demonstration'(*Met* 1006a6), and elaborated in *Posterior Analytics* 2.19.100a,[33] where it is insisted that there must be unproved first-principles. These are of two kinds: principles on which reasoning works (non-contradiction and excluded middle) and axioms (mathematical and ethical).

The final chapter of *Posterior Analytics* bases all knowledge on *sensation*, which is an 'innate discriminatory capacity', distinguishing one thing from another. From memory and experience, we come to know the 'whole universal that has come to rest in the soul (the one apart from the many, whatever is one and the same in all those things)'(*Post. an.* 2.19.100a); beginning from particulars, we perceive universals, then categories which are 'the ultimate first principles of all that exists, *qua* existing'(*Met* 1005b10). In the end 'Now besides *episteme* only *nous* infallibly gives truth, therefore *nous* is the source of all knowledge, the *arche* of the *archai*'.[34]

Aristotle's account of dialectic and first principles has been explored in a recent study.[35] Dialectic cannot find the first principles of science, which must be self-evident, and be grasped as true and necessary in themselves. First principles are grasped by *nous* (*Post.An.* 100b5-17). The self-evident will not seem self-evident to us before we grasp it. Empirical inquiry, induction, dialectic are ways to first principles; but they do not make a first principle self-evident. They may serve as stimuli or occasions for intuition. For Plato, dialectic, through its coherence, could justify first principles;[36] Aristotle denies this because dialectic is shaped by the common beliefs from which it starts and these beliefs are always open to challenge. 'Aristotle's assumptions about knowledge and justification do not seem to yield a solution to the problems he has raised for himself; either the sort of intuition he advocates is indefensible or (if the right defence is found) it is superfluous'.[37]

However Aristotle seems to take a new direction in *Metaphysics* 4. In his account of first philosophy he uses a new method, which may be described as 'strong dialectic' and 'which differs from pure dialectic in so far as it selects only some of the premises that pure dialectic allows'.[38] Strong dialectic considers that the right kind of coherence can justify the truth of a belief and will explain the kind of argument which Aristotle assigns to first philosophy. While Aristotle never explicitly renounces his early foundationalism (which is inconsistent with strong dialectic), 'the anti-sceptical arguments in *Metaphysics* IV show that at any rate he does not consistently adhere to the foundationalism of the *Analytics*'.[39] His practice of strong dialectic may be defended on the ground that his first principles and methods provide a basis for the criticism of his own conclusions. However the problem remains for us today: if we have no alternative to dialectic as a method, we face his difficulties about first principles.[40] Clement is close to the central puzzle, since together with faith and dialectic, he states the need for 'true dialectic, which is philosophy mixed with truth's(*str.* 1.27.177).

By argument and faith, Clement continues, we reach the first principle of all things (*str.* 2.4.14); the errors of Thales show that there is no other way. Faith is a grace which goes beyond the indemonstrable principle to what is entirely simple, and in no way material. The point of Clement's argument is that it shows how faith and God are correlative. For Paul, faith depends on the God who justifies the ungodly (Rom 4:5), raises the dead and creates out of nothing (Rom 4:17). Such a God is the ultimate first principle and not accessible except by faith.

6. JUDGEMENT AND CRITERION

The first principles which faith grasps are the elements of truth. They may therefore be used to test other claims to truth. The faith which holds them becomes the criterion for which Hellenistic philosophy sought.[41]

Aristotle, according to Clement, says[42] that the *krima* which follows the knowledge of a thing and affirms it to be true is faith. Faith, then, is the criterion of knowledge and greater than knowledge because it determines whether knowledge is true or false (*str.* 2.4.15). The only possible reference in Aristotle seems to be in *Top.* 4.5,126b: 'Similarly also the belief will be present in the opinion since it is the intensification of the opinion; so the opinion will believe. Further the result of making an assertion of this kind will be to call intensification intensified and excess excessive. For the belief is intensified; if therefore, belief is intensification, intensification would be intensified'.[43] This is an unlikely source for Clement's simple claim.

There remain four possibilities behind Clement's account. First, it may refer to a lost text of Aristotle. Secondly, it may be a development from what Aristotle said about the importance of a canon. When speaking of the construction of the soul, he talks of the carpenter's straight rule which can test both straight and curved lines, while a curved rule can test nothing (*anima* 1.5,411a). Thirdly, the claim may come from a rhetorical source. When an orator offers an argument, we call it a *pistis,* because we are intended to *pisteuein* the conclusion after being convinced by the argument. It is from our *pistis* that we judge the strength of the argument and the *episteme* of its author.[44] Finally, because the argument is strongly Stoic, it is probable that a Stoic argument has simply been attributed to Aristotle in error. Inaccurate citation was common in Clement's day.[45]

The Stoic origin of the argument can now be asserted with confidence.[46] The same argument, in an extended form, is attributed by Cicero to Zeno (*Acad.* 1.41f.) and set out in these terms:

1. Assent is a voluntary act.

2. Not all sensible presentations are worthy of faith (*fides*).

3. Only those, which possess clarity and are recognisable presentations, are worthy of faith.

4. Sensation, firmly grasped or recognisable, is knowledge (*scientia*), irremoveable by reasoning. All other sensation is ignorance (*inscientia*).

5. The stage between knowledge and ignorance is *comprehensio,* and it alone is credible '*sed solum ei credendum esse credebat*' (*Acad.* 1.42).

6. Hence Zeno granted *fides* also to the senses, because it let go nothing which was capable of being its object, and because nature had given a *canon* (or *criterion*) and a first principle of itself from which the first principle of a thing might be impressed on the mind.

Finally, Cicero, following Antiochus, remarks that 'the Stoic system should be considered a correction of the Old

Academy rather than another new teaching' (*Acad.* 1.43). This makes the attribution to Aristotle easy to understand.

Clement's summary of this argument, which he would have learnt from a Greek source similar to that of Cicero, is brief: the judgement concerning the truth of a presentation judges whether it is faithful and this verdict is reached by faith, using its own criterion. Here the argument from assent seems to be repeated . . . .

Canon and *criterion* dominated Hellenistic philosophy, for they indicated the way in which objective truth might be tested.[47] The canon of Epicurus set out criteria to test truth and falsity. Clement speaks similarly of the canon of the church which is the confession of the essential articles of faith (*str.* 7.15.90). For example, the criterion of faith works at scripture to present a coherent account which follows from faith's first principle. The lover of truth must exercise strength of soul, strict adherence to faith's rule, critical discrimination between true and false, and a sense of what is essential. Heretics do not follow logical rules and plain argument. The believer will not abandon the truth to which the Word has appointed him, but stands firm, grows old in the scriptures, lives by the gospel and finds proofs in the law and the prophets. He must never defile the truth or canon of the church. Heretics do not enter by the main door of the church, the tradition of Christ, but cut a side door through the wall (*str.* 7.17.106). The pious forger of the 'Secret Gospel of Mark' took this reference to a hole in the wall literally and one modern writer has tumbled in after him.[48] The failure of the heretic is a twofold logical error, through failure to use a true criterion and failure to observe simple rules of argument.[49]

7. FAITH, KNOWLEDGE AND LOVE

Faith as criterion could have a negative function. For Clement, its use was primarily positive. Faith was needed as the beginning of exuberant growth, strenuous thought and virtuous living. Clement attacks those who want bare faith alone, who are not prepared to cultivate and farm the vines they plant, but wish to harvest fruit immediately (*str.* 1.9.43). In contrast, the true dialectic, which is philosophy mixed with truth, ascends and descends (*str.* 1.28.177).

(i) Faith and dialectic

Faith becomes knowledge (*gnosis*) for which it has provided a good foundation. It moves on towards knowledge by a process of dialectic. Clement has been well known for his account of the way in which faith grows to knowledge in his Christian savant, the true gnostic. Intellectual progress comes through dialectic and scripture. For Justin and Clement, scripture is the mind and will of God (*dial.* 68); it replaces the Platonic forms.

We have noted differences between Plato and Aristotle on the use of dialectic. Plato believed that dialectic could reach the highest first principle; Aristotle did not. Yet for both, intuition was needed at the top of the logical ladder, so Clement used both Plato and Aristotle. Plato took him

to the unknown and ineffable God who, according to Acts 17, was declared in Jesus Christ (*str.* 5.12.81f.); in another place the via negativa is taken to the monad, then to the dimension of Christ, then to the void, and then to a perception of the Almighty (*str.* 5.11.71).

For later Platonism, dialectic is concerned with the upward movement of the *Republic,* where hypotheses are destroyed to be replaced by more ultimate principles.[50] This is what Clement means when he speaks of the true dialectic, which is applied to scripture: universal principles like the Sermon on the Mount and the love commandment would stand at the top, while particular injunctions would stand at the bottom. Yet at the same time there is downward movement to particular points, as in the demolition of Gnostic *koinonia* (*str.* 3.5.42). In *Phaedrus, Politicus, Sophist,* and elsewhere, dialectic is also concerned with dividing and joining specific kinds. Definitions are ladders which proceed downwards to these kinds.

(ii) Faith as a virtue

As indicated earlier, the theme of early Christian thought was that God required both reason and goodness. Faith is the royal wisdom described by Plato.[51] Those who have believed in Christ are *chrestoi,* as those cared for by the true king are kingly. What is right is lawful because the law is right reason. Law is the king of all (Pindar, fr. 169). For Plato and the Stoics, only the wise man is king and ruler (*str.* 2.4.18).

Plato (*Laws* 630bc and *Rep* 475bc) commends faithfulness. Faith is the mother of virtues (*str.* 2.5.23). Faith is divine and cannot be eroded by worldly friendship or fear. Love makes men believers, and faith is the foundation of love (*str.* 2.6.30). Faith is the first movement to salvation. It is followed by fear, hope, repentance, temperance, patience and finally love and knowledge (*str.* 2.6.31). The sequence of the virtues may also be seen as faith hoping through repentance, fear through faith: patience and practice lead on to love (*str.* 2.9.45). Both faith and gnosis look to the past in memory and to the future in hope (*str.* 2.12.53).

Hermas (*Vis.* 3.8.roughly), Clement continues, describes faith as the virtue by which the elect are saved; it is followed by continence, simplicity, knowledge, innocence, modesty, love, all of which are the daughters of faith (*str.* 2.12.55).

God (*str.* 5.1.13) is love, and known to those who love; he is faithful and known to those who are faithful. We are joined to him by divine love, so that by like we may see like. God's temple is built on the threefold foundation of faith, hope and love (*str.* 5.1.13).

After having presented testimonies from the Greeks about faith Clement adds only a few about hope and love. Plato speaks of hope about life after death in several places:

Crito 48b, *Phaedrus* 248f, *Symp.* 206c-208b; *Theaet.* 150bc (*str.* 5.2.14).

(iii) Faith to faith

Faith and knowledge are inseparable, as are the father and the son (*str.* 5.1.1). Faith is twofold, for Paul speaks of righteousness which is revealed from faith to faith (Rom. 1:17). A common faith, says Clement, is the foundation; this is indeed what Paul is saying. Paul is concerned with unbroken continuity and the dimensions of a new world,[52] rather than with two separate stages of development. The perfection of faith comes from instruction and logos. Faith saves men and removes mountains (*str.* 5.2.1). Faith stimulates the soul like a grain of mustard and grows to greatness in it, so that the words about things above rest on it (*str.* 5.2.1). Faith (*str.* 5.1.11) is not inactive and alone. It seeks and finds. Sophocles says that what is sought may be captured but what is neglected escapes. The sight of the soul must be directed towards discovery and freed from the obstacles in its way (*str.* 2.2.9).

The just live by faith. We must not hold back, but believe so that our souls are saved (Heb. 10:32-9). The endurance of faith (Heb. 11:36-40; 12:1,2) looks to Jesus the pioneer and perfecter of faith (*str.* 4.16.103). The faith which by love ascends to knowledge is desirable for its own sake. If we had to choose between the knowledge of God and eternal salvation we should choose knowledge. The soul never sleeps. The constant exertion of the intelligence is the essence of an intelligent being (*str.* 4.22.136); this is the divine perfection to which we are called.

(iv) Perfection of faith (*paid.* 1.6.25-52)

Faith brings life and is perfect in itself. For the believer after death there is no waiting, since, through the pledge of life eternal, he has anticipated the future by faith. Faith goes from promise to enlightened knowledge to final rest. Instruction leads to faith, which goes on to baptism, and then to the training of the holy spirit. Faith is the one salvation of all men and guarantees equality in communion with God. As Paul says, we had the law as our *paidagogos* until faith came; now as God's children through faith, we are all one in Christ. There is no distinction between those who are enlightened and those who are at an animal or psychic level. All who have abandoned carnal desires are equal and spiritual in the presence of their lord. They have been baptised by one spirit into one body (1 Cor. 12:13). Paul explained Christian maturity when he told us to be children in wickedness, but men in understanding (1 Cor. 14:20). The childish things which he has put away (1 Cor. 13:11) are not smallness of stature or age. Because he is no longer under the law (Gal. 4:1-5), he has lost the fear of childish phantoms of the mind. To be a grown man is to be obedient to the word, master of oneself, to believe and be saved by voluntary choice, to be free from irrational fear, to be a son and not a servant (Gal. 4:7). Childhood in Christ is full maturity, instead of infancy under the law. The infant milk of children in Christ (1 Cor 3:2) is dif-

ficult to relate to the perfection of milk and honey (*paid.* 1.6.24f.). Clement finally goes into physiology to explain the link. The Christian life in which we are being trained is a system of rational[53] actions and an unceasing energy which is faith.

Greek philosophy cleanses and prepares the soul for faith. Then truth builds knowledge on the foundation of faith (*str.* 7.3.20). Faith does not search for God, but confesses and glorifies him. Knowledge starts from faith and goes on to love, the inheritance and the endless end (*str.* 7.10.55). Faith is a comprehensive knowledge of the essentials; knowledge proves what it receives from faith and goes on to certainty (*str.* 7.10.57). Yet faith remains supreme, although some have deviated from the truth in their zeal to surpass common faith (*str.* 7.16.97).

8. STRENGTH AND STABILITY

For critics like Celsus, faith was a weaker thing and the affliction of feeble minds.

(i) Power of God.

Faith is the power of God (cf. 1 Cor. 2:5) and the strength of truth. It moves mountains and determines what we receive. According to our faith, we receive (*str.* 2.11.48). Paul, says Clement, pointed faith away from the wisdom of men to the power of God, which alone and without proofs, can save (*str.* 5.1.9).

(ii) Stability and blood.

The mature Christian (the true 'gnostic') is fixed firmly by faith . . . (*str.* 2.11.51) while the man who thinks that he is wise and does not willingly attach himself to truth, is moved by uncertain and capricious impulses (*str.* 2.11.51). While faith and knowledge make the soul constant and uniform, error brings instability and change. Knowledge brings tranquillity, rest and peace (*str.* 2.11.52). 'Therefore also to believe in him and through him is to become a unit, being indivisibly made one in him; but to disbelieve means separation, estrangement, and division' (*str.* 4.25.157). Here the drive to unity with the One has clear Platonic overtones. To those who believe and obey, grace will overflow and abound (*prot.* 9.85). 'Your faith has saved you' was said to Jews who had kept the law; those who lived blamelessly needed only faith in the lord (*str.* 6.14.108). Faith is the *stasis* of the soul concerning what is (*str.* 4.22.143). Yet it is a strange stability. The crown of thorns which the lord wore is a type of our faith, of life because of the tree, of joy because it is a crown, of danger because of thorns. No one can approach the word without blood (*paed.* 2.8.73).

(iii) God in us

The aim of faith is assimilation to God, as required by Plato, and the end is the restitution of the promise effected by faith (*str.* 2.22.136). Faith grants divinity to the believer. Those, who are taught by the son of God, possess the truth, for he is the person of truth (*str.* 6.15.122). On the believer rests the head of the universe (we have the mind of Christ, 1 Cor. 2:16), the kind and gentle word who subverts the craftiness and empty thoughts of the wise (*str.* 1.3.23; 1 Cor. 3:19f.).

CONCLUSION

The concept of faith aims at simplicity. Hope, assent, perception, hearing, testing, and the mustard seed which grows—all these seem straightforward ideas. Yet the concept is tied at every point to interesting philosophical problems and there is always a variety of interpretations between which Clement has made a rational choice. To these Clement adds his own contemporary controversy with Basilides, who wants faith to be a natural endowment, and Gnostics, who divide faith from knowledge. It is not the case, as some *Quellenforschung* has suggested, that Clement has collected unambiguous arguments from different sources. Clement's arguments make at least one good point. Preconception is a proper part of epistemology. Assent or choice is essential to Christian faith, which is always a matter of confession. Perception of God is a part of faith. There is a tension between the claim that faith is concerned with what is not seem but anticipated and the claim that God is indeed heard and perceived; this is inescapable if the Christian message of both present and future eschatology be understood. Scripture stands as the rational link with God; yet as divine oracle it has symbolic content. The argument to an unproved *arche* does not prove God, but shows why Pauline faith and God go together. Faith serves as a criterion to discern true from false. The growth of faith follows the word where it leads. The final link of faith and God guards against triumphalism and preserves the dialectic of Christian existence which lives by dying. Clement has no trouble joining the faith of the scriptures with the faith of philosophers. A unity had already been achieved within the Wisdom literature; he added, to the concept of the bible as the barbarian philosophy, the theology of Paul, the wisdom of Christ crucified. Like all second century theologians, Clement thought that a God, who had become incarnate in Jesus, was more credible than a creator who had not cared enough to redeem the world he had made. Hellenistic philosophers were concerned to find arguable alternatives to the negative arguments which Skeptics produced and the rivers of words which flowed from Sophists. Epistemology had a continuing urgency in their studies. Their several proposals were taken up by Clement, fortified by Plato and Aristotle, linked with scripture and turned into arguments for faith. Faith remained central to Clement in his deep dependence on Paul. 'Faith is strength to salvation and power to eternal life' (*str.* 2.12.53). Abraham's faith, as Paul indicated, was in the only God who showed his absolute sovereignty in the justification of the ungodly, creation out of nothing and the resurrection of the dead. This God is the first cause of all that exists, the ultimate first principle. Faith is not inferior to other ways of knowing, but the only way to know the sovereign God.[54]

Notes

1. As in my *The philosophy of Clement of Alexandria* (Cambridge, 1957) and S.R.C. Lilla's *Clement of Alexandria, A study of Christian Platonism and Gnosticism* (Oxford, 1971).

2. While drawing on Philo, his main point (on the coming near of the unapproachable God) is not from Philo.

3. Much ancient theory of knowledge was deductive and took geometry as its model. There had to be axioms.

4. Herein lies the limitation of K. Prümm's useful study, Glaube und Erkenntnis im zweiten Buch der Stromata des Klemens von Alexandrien, *Scholastik* 12 (1937), 17-57. The same weakness in other work has already been noted above.

5. A. Manuwald, *Die Prolepsislehre Epikurs* (Bonn, 1972), 103.

6. D.K. Glidden, *Epicurean prolepsis,* Oxford studies in ancient philosophy, III, (Oxford, 1985), 194.

7. Ibid., 205.

8. Long and Sedley, *The Hellenistic philosophers,* 1, 89.

9. Sextus Empiricus, *adv. math.,* 8.331f. See Long and Sedley, 1, 249.

10. A.A. Long, *Hellenistic philosophy* (London, 1974), 25.

11. Translation, Long and Sedley, *Hellenistic philosophers,* 1, 141.

12. J.M. Rist, *Stoic philosophy* (Cambridge, 1969), 139 . . . .

13. A. Manuwald, *Die Prolepsislehre Epikurs* (Bonn, 1972), 39.

14. D.K. Glidden, *Epicurean prolepsis,* 179f.

15. Ibid., 201.

16. Ibid., 210.

17. Ibid., 212.

18. They were not made perfect, nor did they receive the promise. The new situation of Christian hope is set out in 2 Cor. 3.1-18. Paul's hope belongs to a minister of the new covenant which is marked by freedom, boldness and boasting. See R. Bultmann, *TWNT,* 2, 528.

19. R. Bultmann, *Marburger Predigten* (Tübingen, 1956), 170f.

20. Anticipation is also the theme of J. Moltmann, *Theologie der Hoffnung* (München, 1964), 9-30.

21. The influence of Heraclitus on Clement is strong. See for an introductory statement P. Valentin, Héraclite et Clément d'Alexandrie, *RSR,* 46 (1958). Heraclitus was important for, and transmitted by, the Stoics.

22. ενωτιηχ ςνγχατάθεςις. Declining Stählin's emendation εννοητιχη, as do Mondésert and Prümm.

23. Prümm, Glaube 23.

24. Stob. 2.111f., Long and Sedley, *The Hellenistic philosophers,* 1, 256.

25. Plutarch, *Stoic. Repug.* 1057A, Long and Sedley, *The Hellenistic philosophers* 1, 317.

26. 'The artist makes us see what is, in a sense manifestly and edifyingly *there* (real), but unseen before, and the metaphysician does this too'. I. Murdoch, *Metaphysics as a guide to morals* (London, 1992), 433.

27. Homer, says Clement, uses 'hear' instead of 'perceive', a specific form of perception instead of the generic concept.

28. A useful philosophical treatment of this kind of perception is found in, William P. Alston, *Perceiving God, the epistemology of religious experience* (Cornell University Press, Ithaca and London, 1991).

29. Poetry was 'a massive repository of useful knowledge, a sort of encyclopedia of ethics, politics, history and technology'. E.A. Havelock, *Preface to Plato* (Oxford, 1963), 27, cited by R. Bambrough, *Reason, truth and God,* 122. While this might not help strict followers of Plato, who banished poets from his city, Clement quotes poets incessantly.

30. Before moving on, we should note that the distinction between divine oracle and true philosophy was and remains central to the Christian use of scripture.

31. Clement turns the virtue of faith into a necessity for knowledge. God is not to be found except by abstraction from earthly things and by entering the abyss of faith and the dimension of Christ (*str.* 5.11.71).

32. For Aristotle, a first principle is also a cause. See Guthrie, *History,* 6, 178. Prümm does not see why for Clement, as a Platonist, the ground of knowledge has to be the ground of being. See Prümm, *Glaube,* 28.

33. 'The last chapter of the *Posterior Analytics* is . . . a confession of his epistemological faith, a statement of the source from which in the last resort all knowledge springs.' W.K.C. Guthrie, *A history of Greek philosophy,* 6, *Aristotle, an encounter* (Cambridge, 1981), 179.

34. Guthrie, *Aristotle,* 184.

35. T.H. Irwin, *Aristotle's first principles* (Oxford, 1988).

36. Plato's dialectic had gone on to the form of the good; but Aristotle would not do this (*EN* 1095 a 26-28).

37. Irwin, *First principles,* 149.

38. Ibid., 476. Aristotle, says Irwin, gives an inversely proportional amount of space to problems which he regards as important.

39. Ibid., 482.

40. Ibid., 484.

41. See Sext. Emp. 7.29 and J.M. Rist, *Stoic Philosophy* (Cambridge, 1969), 133-51.

42. Theodoret attributes this formula to Aristotle (*Graec.affect.cur.* 1, 90). Stählin points out that it cannot be found in the text. Mondésert suggests *Top.,* IV, 5, 126b.

43. Loeb translation.

44. I owe this comment to Prof. H.A.S. Tarrant. See on this point Frances Young, *The art of performance* (London, 1990), 123ff., and 131; also see J.L. Kinneavy, *Greek rhetorical origins and Christian faith* (Oxford, 1987), 26-53.

45. See C. Collard, Athenaeus, the Epitome, Eustathius and quotations from tragedy, *RFIC* (1969), 157; also E. Osborn, Philo and Clement: Citation and influence, in *Lebendige Überlieferung* (Beirut and Ostfildern, 1992), FS H.-J. Vogt, ed. N. El-Khoury et al., 231.

46. For the place of the criterion in Stoic epistemology see J.M. Rist, *Stoic Philosophy* (Cambridge, 1969), 138-42.

47. See Osborn, Reason and the rule of faith, in the second century AD, in *The Making of Orthodoxy,* FS H. Chadwick (Cambridge, 1989), 40-61.

48. Morton Smith, *Clement of Alexandria and a secret Gospel of Mark* (Cambridge, Mass., 1973). See my rejection of this hypothesis in an article, Clement of Alexandria: a review of research, 1958-1982, *The Second Century,* 1985, 219-24, especially pages 223-5.

49. Osborn, Reason and the rule of faith, 51-53.

50. Albinus (*Did.* 5) describes three types of analysis: (i) the upward movement from sensible things to 'primary intelligibles' (as in *Symp.* 210a ff.), (ii) the upward move from demonstrable to indemonstrable propositions (as in *Phaedrus* 245c ff.), (iii) the move from hypothetical to non-hypothetical principles (as in *Rep.* 6, 510b ff.). We cannot be sure when this organisation of Plato's ideas took place; but it probably occurred in the Old Academy and was taken over by Albinus. See John Dillon, *The Middle Platonists* (London, 1977), 277f.

51. In *Euthydemus* 291D and *Politicus* 259AB.

52. E. Käsemann, *Commentary on Romans* (Grand Rapids, 1980), 31.

53. Taught by the logos.

54. I wish to thank Dr. Robin Jackson of Ormond College and the University of Melbourne for discussion and help at several points of ancient Greek and Hellenistic philosophy.

Annewies van den Hoek (essay date 1996)

SOURCE: "Techniques of Quotation in Clement of Alexandria: A View of Ancient Literary Working Methods," in *Vigiliae Christianae,* Vol. 50, No. 3, 1996, pp. 223-43.

[In the following excerpt, van den Hoek examines Clement's use of borrowed and quoted passages, including his accuracy, his method of giving credit, and his characteristic way of incorporating the material.]

INTRODUCTION

Borrowed material embedded in the flow of a writer's text is a common phenomenon in Antiquity. Since Clement's writings have so many borrowings, his case is of almost emblematic significance for this aspect of ancient literary technique. The problem has many facets. The way he accumulated his borrowed material deserves attention, and there the testimony of other ancient writers can be of great value. The sources that Clement quotes should be investigated, as well as how accurately he uses them, and how often and in what way he credits them. Turning the issue of accuracy on its head, the way he subtly or unsubtly transforms his borrowed material should also be explored.

NATURE OF CLEMENT'S WRITINGS

Clement of Alexandria is known to the modern reader as a difficult author. The stigma of being difficult is earned in part because of the "obscure" ways,[1] in which he expresses himself and also because of his numerous digressive references to other writers, which often tend to obstruct rather than to clarify his thoughts. This unclear style may be intentional. Clement warns the reader that knowledge of the ultimate truth is not to be obtained easily.[2] His obscurity may even have a pedagogical implication; the faithful need to grow spiritually, and the road toward knowledge can be travelled only by dint of hard labour.[3] Obscurity may also be connected with the literary genre that Clement prefered: "Stromateis," literary weavings.[4] Loose and digressive structure is especially evident in his massive work, the **Stromateis,** but it is not totally absent from his other works either.

Much has been written about Clement's borrowings in general, especially around the turn of the century, and it is unnecessary here to repeat all the different theories that have been advanced; a few, however, should be mentioned.[5] Some scholars have maintained that Clement was essentially copying his works from anthologies, epitomes and handbooks.[6] Others have suggested that he in part transcribed oral traditions derived from his teachers.[7] Unfortunately, neither of these speculations, interesting as they are, can be proven: the written words of anthologies and handbooks have largely been lost, and the oral traditions of Clement's teachers are equally impossible to retrace. Research during this century has generally taken a more productive course and has analyzed and has come to value Clement's literary creativity in its own right. Scholars have grown more interested in the organization of his material, including the borrowings and their placement in the flow of his verbiage.[8]

As is often the case with theories (even if they are ultimately discarded), something useful can be learned from them. The theory that handbooks and anthologies were important for Clement, for example, remains intriguing and cannot be dismissed lightly. It cannot be coincidental, for example, that some of Clement's selections of poetry can be paralleled in the work of later anthologists such as Johannes Stobaeus.[9] Even though Clement does not seem to have been a slavish copyist as once was suggested, a part of his material must have come from other compilations. It remains to be seen whether these compilations were anthologies that provided abridged selections collected around specific topics or whether they were writings of single authors whose works already contained much borrowed material, such as Dio Chrysostomus,[10] or Plutarch[11] a century earlier. Using compilations and creating new ones was certainly in the air, as can be seen from contemporaries of Clement, such as Sextus,[12] Athenaeus,[13] or Diogenes Laertius.[14]

Some borrowings certainly came in a more direct way, namely through first-hand acquaintance with individual authors. Some may initially have come through memory; Clement was highly literate and belonged to a time when memorization was much valued. On the other hand, not all of these "first-hand borrowings" could have been memorized; it would seem impossible for a human mind to have retained such masses of material, and it is clear, as will be shown later on, that Clement consulted sources directly or else took notes while reading them. The technique of note-taking is itself of interest in this context and deserves some attention in its own right.

TECHNIQUES OF NOTE-TAKING IN ANTIQUITY

. . . Literature provides us with examples of how notes were made and how they were used. Pliny the Younger in his well-known letter to Baebius Macer explains how his uncle managed to write so many books in spite of his busy life in public affairs.[15] He reports that books were read to his uncle at various moments of the day, during meals, during spare time, during travel, in short, on all possible occasions. During such readings, the elder Pliny used to make notes and excerpts.[16] He kept a secretary at his side with book and notebook, and the two might exchange the roles of reader and note-taker.[17] At his death, Pliny left his nephew one hundred sixty notebooks of selected passages, densely written in a minute hand on both sides of scrolls. An interesting detail is that reading was done from scrolls and final notes were written on scrolls, but the secretary's initial notes were compiled on tablets, which he calls "pugillares."[18]

An example of notes in the form of excerpts, as described by Pliny has come to light in modern times. The papyrus of Toura[19] discovered in 1946 contains a collection of excerpts from several works of Origen, some of which stem from his *Contra Celsum.* It is not known what the reason for this "Readers Digest" version was, but it dates from around the time that Origen's works were being condemned officially.[20] Since the full text of *Contra Celsum* is extant, the technique of excerpting can be closely observed. Jean Scherer notes many interesting details. The length of the fragments is variable; it can cover a word, some lines or several pages. The excerpts become shorter and more "hurried" towards the end of a book. The excerptor seems to have had a particular interest in biblical quotations, these, of course, being readily available throughout Origen's works. The process is one of constant abbreviation, and sometimes the text does not seem to contain more than simple reading notes.[21]

For both Pliny and the papyrus of Toura the concept of "notes" is equivalent to "excerpts made from other works." Other reports do not spell out what kind of notes are meant. Lucian, for example, writes that every historian should take notes before composing and writing a book.[22] Notes seem also to have been important for the composition of the Gospels. The *Ecclesiastical History* of Eusebius informs us that Papias refered to notes as a first phase in the composition of the gospel of Mark.[23] If one accepts the authenticity of the fragmentary letter of Clement to Theodorus, yet another report can be added; Clement says that Mark carried with himself both his own notes and those of Peter, which he used for his first Gospel and for another more spiritual Gospel.[24]

Notes could also circulate, as is mentioned in connection with a Greek Hellenistic author, Apollonius of Perge.[25] Apollonius, who was a mathematician, reportedly sent out notes that formed the first draft of one of his books to be reviewed and commented on by friends.[26] Passing around such provisional texts without the author's name attached, as Devreesse points out, was not without its risks in those days (as perhaps in our times as well); sometimes manuscripts managed to get lost and could end up in the wrong hands or even reappear under the wrong name.[27]

Yet another variety of note-taking can be identified from early Byzantine sources, as Marcel Richard has shown.[28] He discusses in great detail the Greek words . . . which have survived in the titles (or also sometimes at the end) of manuscripts, and which mean "according to the teaching of" or "taken during the course of," preceding the name of the lecturer.[29] This kind of note-taking reflects a custom that existed much earlier. In his *Church History* Eusebius tells how late in his life Origen permitted shorthand writers to take down his public discourses, a practice that he had not allowed in his earlier days.[30]

It would be interesting to know more about such lecture notes, which were apparently intended for circulation. Was the text produced from the notes also edited by the note-taker, and was it sent back for approval to the lecturer?[31] Unfortunately, these details are almost never explicitly described. Apparently much depended on the scrupulousness or carelessness of a particular lecturer. Some authors have been quite conscientious about their written production, but others simply handed over the organization and the editing to a trusted pupil. Arrian took notes on and published the lectures of his teacher, Epictetus.[32] Amelius did the same for his teacher, Plotinus.[33] Hermotimos, according to Lucian, was an eternal student who spent his time editing the lectures of his teachers.[34] There apparently were other celebrated but even less responsible intellectuals who just left behind them a messy bunch of raw notes.[35]

To summarize these observations on note-taking, an author or his/her entourage could take notes in the form of excerpts from other manuscripts as material to be incorporated in future learned books, as did Pliny the Elder. Notes could also be made systematically to produce an abridged version of a manuscript, as in the papyrus of Toura. Lucian, Papias and Clement mention notes that were taken before the composition of a book; they do not specify whether these notes were excerpts from other works or different kinds of notes. Notes could form the text of a book in statu nascendi, as in the case of Apollonius. Finally, notes could be taken during lectures and then written down not by the lecturer himself but by someone in the audience. Most relevant for understanding the background to Clement's borrowed quotations is the first and second example of notetaking, the cases of Pliny and the papyrus of Toura, where notes were equivalent to excerpts.

DEFINING A QUOTATION

Clement borrows passages from numerous sources that reflect not only biblical and early Christian writings but also the whole span of Greek literature from Homer to his own time.[36] Material from Philo, analyzed previously by this author, will form the backbone of the discussion of techniques of quotation, but a few words should be said about some of Clement's other sources to avoid giving the misleading impression that Philo was Clement's main focus of attention. Philo is, indeed, prominently represented in the columns of Stählin's index,[37] but Plato is even more so.[38] Among the poets Homer is the most frequently cited,[39] followed by Euripides.[40] The champion in terms of popularity, however, is not to be found among the likes of Plato, the Stoics,[41] Homer, Hesiod,[42] Euripides, or Herodotus,[43] but is, by quite a wide margin, good old Saint Paul.[44]

In his selection of non-Christian and non-Jewish sources, Clement is a typical representative of the Hellenistic-Roman tradition. The same sources are cited in about the same proportions by other authors, whether pagan or Christian.[45] Clement compares closely with other "bookworms" such as Plutarch and Eusebius, both separated from Clement (in opposite directions) by a century; they too were writers who reportedly loved books and libraries and planted many borrowings throughout their works.

Up to this point the neutral term "borrowing" has been used, because not all material taken from other writers is a clear-cut quotation. This problem is well-known to anyone who works with quotations in authors of almost any period of the past. At some point terminologies must be formulated for these varying kinds of "recycled materials," and a definition of the word "quotation" must be included. Whether dealing with Antiquity, the Middle Ages, or the Enlightenment, it must be determined how close the correspondance is with our twentieth century definition of a quotation. General handbooks of Greek literature and language do not give much help, but general linguistic studies have contributed to the theoretical framework for the study of quotations.[46]

Individual scholars in the classical area have tried to create their own classifications. Some need to be mentioned. Particularly useful is a compact monograph on Plutarch's quotations by William C. Helmbold and Edward N. O'Neil.[47] The booklet consists primarily of an alphabetical list of quotations beginning with Acesander and ending with Zopyrus (both previously unknown to this writer). There are another 495 names in between. Without counting the exact number of quotations, it was estimated that there was a total of 6840, not including the places where Plutarch quotes himself.[48] The book has a small introduction of barely four pages, in which the authors address the problems of identification, classification and terminology. They do not offer a definite solution, but only pose the problem. Nonetheless, their separation of borrowed material into quotations, reminiscences, references and paraphrases is very helpful. They do not, however, define the borders between these terms.

Other studies create their own classifications.[49] Some of them were so detailed that they became too complicated for the purposes aimed at here. In analyzing Clement's borrowings from Philo, a scheme was required that would do justice to Clement's various techniques but that would not result in too many distinctions. The forest of quotations should not be hidden by the trees of classification. The simple distinctions offered by Helmbold and O'Neil therefore proved to be the most serviceable.

As has been shown elsewhere,[50] the distinctions in Clement's Philonic borrowings can be considered threefold on one level and fourfold on another. First, the various borrowings can be usefully separated into quotations, paraphrases and reminiscences. Quotations should be defined as having a considerable degree of literality. They need not be verbatim in a modern sense, but they should follow the source to a considerable extent. A paraphrase distinguishes itself from a quotation in that only a few words of the original source (sometimes only one or two) are present. Reminiscences, in turn, are different from allusions by having no literal correspondences but merely resemblences in theme or thought.

There are, however, some vaguely Philonic bits in Clement that do not fit into any of these three categories. A large number of passages are philosophical or literary commonplaces, and a new approach seems necessary to assess them and put them in relation to the other borrowings. To deal with the loose ends, all putative borrowings were reclassified from a slightly different angle: namely, according to their degree of dependence on Philo. This second method of classification consisted of four categories, rating from A to D.[51] Again, not too many options were permitted since that would obstruct the clarity of the

system. *A* meant a certain dependence (which in the other terminology was a quotation or paraphrase); *B* was probable dependence (paraphrase or reminiscence); *C* unprovable dependence (reminiscence); *D* no dependence. The two classifications were then brought together, partly overlapping and partly supplementing one another. The advantage of the second system is that it also reflects the uncertainties in the relationship between two authors, about which there had been so much speculation over the centuries.

Much could be said about why quotations were used, what function they had for an author, whether they added something to the argument or if they were primarily embellishments, and what effect they had on the reader.[52] These are important considerations in the study of borrowings, but they can only be mentioned here, since they do not directly relate to the technique of borrowing itself.

CLEMENT'S TECHNIQUES OF QUOTING

Quotations are, of course, most identifiable when the ancient authors themselves inform us that they are quoting. It would be a good subject for a dissertation to investigate the practice of indicating quotations by name and/or book. It has often been said that in ancient rhetorical traditions, citing by name was not customary or even polite, because the educated audience was supposed to know their classics. In the same way that educated audiences are—or rather were—supposed to know their Shakespeare, Molière, or Vondel, depending on the country involved.

Let us, therefore, have a closer look again at some of the Shakespeares of Antiquity to whom Clement refers and try to analyze how regularly he does or does not name them when he quotes them. As already mentioned, Paul, Plato, Homer and Euripides are the most frequently used, and therefore will be our primary subjects. For this kind of analysis a quatitative method can be extremely helpful. Via Stählin's index and the assemblage of Greek literature on computer, the *Thesaurus Linguae Graecae*, it is possible to gain some numerical insight into the relationship between borrowings and citations of the name. A preliminary caveat: the computer index of the *TLG* is a wonderful and accurate means to gain a quick insight into words in their context; the index of Stählin, however, is less accurate since it is a vast vessel of very diverse materials that were collected over the centuries. Experience suggests that it contains too many parallels, not all of which are valid. Weeding out Stählin's index systematically, however, would be a thesis-like job for every author involved, and has not been attempted here. Since all the numbers were used in the same way, namely the index versus the *TLG*, it seemed a legitimate method, since the relative deviation factor is (presumably) the same for most authors, although the absolute numbers may not be totally reliable.[53] The results of this "census" are tabulated at the end of the article.

According to Stählin's index, there are 1273 Pauline borrowings in Clement . . . . 296 are connected with borrowings, and in the other 13 cases, Clement just mentions Paul's name without borrowing anything: in other words, it was just namedropping. Thus 24% of the references to Paul in Stählin's index are clearly identified by a mention of his name, and the majority of these 296 references so distinguished represent distinct quotations,[54] namely 269. On only 28 occasions the letter from which a quotation was taken was also named, which represents 9% of the explicit references to the apostle.[55] Seven of Paul's letters were cited.

Stählin's index lists 618 borrowings from Plato. In 139 cases Plato's name is mentioned . . .[56] that is, in almost 22% of the passages, a figure quite close to Paul's 24%. Plato's name, however, was merely dropped more frequently than Paul's was: on 41 occasions. On 98 of the occasions when Plato was cited by name, a particular thought or text was brought into Clement's discussion, and 70 of these passages were direct quotations. Occasionally Plato is quoted verbatim without his name being mentioned—how often, however, still remains to be seen. Also remarkable was the high frequency with which the source of the Platonic borrowing was specified. A particular book, dialogue or letter was cited 39 times: that is, almost 29% of the times that Plato's name comes up,[57] in contrast to only 9% in Paul's case. As it turns out, 17 different writings of Plato are involved, and on six occasions Clement even refers to an individual volume, particularly when he quotes from the *Politeia*.

Among the poets cited by Clement, Homer is the most popular.[58] According to Stählin's index, Homer is the source for 243 passages, 143 drawn from the Iliad and 100 from the Odyssey. Homer's name or a reference to "the poet" . . . turns up on 82 occasions, which is 34% of the total number. Of these 82 mentions of the poet's name, 69 are connected with borrowings, and 54 of them are word-for-word. The proportion of literal quotations is relatively high, as can be expected in borrowings from poetry. As with Plato, some literal quotations occur without Homer's name being mentioned. Homer's name was mentioned unaccompanied by a borrowing 13 times; this occurs, for example, in the context of chronologies or linked to Hesiod. Very rarely does Clement refer to the specific source of his borrowings from Homer.[59]

The second most-popular poet for Clement is Euripides.[60] Stählin attributes 117 passages to him, and the *TLG* provides 59 occurrences of his name . . . . Sometimes Euripides' name is placed between two quotations from his works, and therefore there are fewer "unacknowledged" borrowings than appears at first glance. In this quick survey, two such cases turned up, and there must be some more. Thus, there are 61 acknowledged borrowings for Euripides (so far), which is 52% of Stählin's references: a figure higher than for Homer and more than double the percentages for Paul or Plato. Almost all the borrowings from Euripides were literal quotations, namely 58 out of 61.[61] Clement cites the source within Euripides 16 times, and mentions a strikingly large number of writings:

namely, 13 different plays.[62] If one counts the total number of Euripidean works, including the ones that Clement does not identify, he quotes from an even higher number: namely 31 different plays, 12 of which have survived in complete form. That means that a large part of Clement's quotations come from lost plays, some of which could be identified either because Clement mentioned them by name or because they are identified by other authors who preserve parallels; 14 fragments remain unidentified, and some of them are of dubious origin.

Much Philonic material appears in Clement. Stählin lists 279 references: more than Euripides or Homer, though less than half of the number for Plato. Strangely, Philo himself is mentioned only four times (only 1.5% of the total). Philo certainly does not fit into the general pattern, and scholars have rightly been puzzled by the rare occurrence of his name.[63] There may be a specific reason for this silence, but for the moment we only can guess what it was. On the other hand, if one uses a different method of calculation, the silence may be somewhat more apparent than real. As with Euripides, one citation of the name may be coupled with numerous borrowings. In the case of Philo, there are long sequences of borrowings from one book, and one citation of the name may have been deemed sufficient by Clement. Thus his name is mentioned in three of the four long sequences and left out in one of the sequences and the four short sequences of borrowings. Thus, it can be argued that Philo is credited as much as 38% of the time, if one looks only at the coherent passages. None of the disconnected scraps that Stählin connects with Philo are, however, associated with a name. The figure, thus, can drop back substantially.

Various explanations have been advanced for Clement's unwillingness to acknowledge his debt to Philo. Eric Osborn sees it in terms of a duel with the Marcionites; Clement found it prudent to downplay his Jewish sources to avoid loosing adherents to a group well known for its hostile attitude towards the teachings of Moses.[64] David Runia approaches the problem from a different angle. Philo may not have been mentioned explicitly because Clement saw himself in the same theological tradition.[65]

There are other authors that Clement does, indeed, credit rarely. Tatian is mentioned only three times, and not always where one would expect it;[66] his name is, for example, left out in one of the extensive borrowings in book one of the **Stromateis**. It has been suggested that Tatian was one of Clement's teachers before he came to Alexandria. Something similar may have happened to another teacher, Pantaenus, of whom we know very little.[67] Pantaenus' name is mentioned only once by Clement: namely, in his **Eclogae Propheticae**.[68] In his **Stromateis** Clement professes to be greatly indebted to him, but he does not refer to Pantaenus by name but in metaphoric terms only;[69] on other occasions he brings up the authority of an "elder," . . . which may refer to Pantaenus as well.[70] Eusebius informs us that Clement mentions his teacher by name in his **Hypotyposes** and that he refers to Pantaenus' interpretations of Scripture.[71] Unfortunately, the *Hypotyposes* are mostly lost so that Eusebius' remarks cannot be verified. Even if we include the *Hypotyposes,* the name of Pantaenus comes up very rarely.[72]

In her recent dissertation, Denise Buell notes the special rhetorical function that omitting his teachers' names could have had for Clement.[73] Not the individual identities of the teachers, but their roles as mediators between the apostles and Clement's own time would have been important. To put the names of his teachers in the foreground would have overemphasized "their importance as individuals, a charge that Clement makes against the followers of Marcion, Basilides, and Valentinus (see *Strom.* VII 108,1)." Logically then, omitting Philo's name can be seen as placing him in the ranks of Clement's direct mentors.

To return to the subject of techniques, there are many ways to introduce a quotation; the most obvious examples are: "so and so said" or "according to so and so," and all the possible variants of this model. Writers can address themselves also to their source in a more direct way, for example, through the vocative: "O Paul," or "O Homer," which is a good rhetorical device found in many ancient authors. Sometimes literal quotations can be identified by introductory expressions . . . .

Only a small fraction of Clement's very numerous quotations, however, are highlighted by *katà léxin* (only 24), but it is interesting that in every instance Clement also accurately identifies the author and the work from which he quotes.[74] He seems to use the phrase *katà léxin* for quotations from any kind of work except for the O.T. Most often it occurs in quotations from gnostic writers (12 times), various Greek authors in general (8 times, 3 from Plato), a few times from the Lucan Acts or Pseudo-Apostolic writings (3 times), and once from the Jewish author Aristobulos. It is particularly striking that Clement acknowledges the works of his gnostic adversaries in such an accurate way, naming author and book. This scrupulousness stands in sharp contrast to his practice in borrowing from authors to whom he apparently felt a kinship, such as Philo, Tatian, and Pantaenus.

Another introduction to a quotation is formed by the words ōdé pōs.[75] The phrase could be translated as "thus," or "in this way," and sometimes it need not be translated at all and can simply be rendered by a colon before the quotation. The adverb pōs apparently loses its indefinite flavor when it functions as an introduction to a quotation and becomes a kind of technical device.[76] The proof of this usage can be found in *Str.* III 9, 2, where Clement surprisingly introduces his quotation with . . . "(Epiphanes) thus goes on literally" . . . Although the expression ōdé pōs may also occur without being connected with a quotation, this happens only rarely (6 times). In the other 69 occasions it is linked to a quotation. This time the O.T. is well represented, particularly the Psalms and Proverbs,[77] but only a few gnostic authors are so addressed.[78] Some logia and apostolic writings are introduced with the phrase,[79] but

hte majority of quotations distinguished in this way comes from Greek literature.[80]

A third word that often occurs in connection with a quotation is the adverb αντικρυς, "straight on" or "openly." It can be found either before or after a quotation. It serves to emphasize a particular interpretation or admonition. It occurs 60 times, 7 of which are unrelated to a borrowing. Of the remaining 53 occurrences, 43 are related to direct quotations. Greek literature, again, is prominent (23 times), followed by the O.T. (14); in this biblical group, books of wisdom stand out (*Psalms* 5; *Prov.* 2; *Sap.* 2). Of the N.T. (16 references in total), a remarkably high number (8) are from the Sermon on the Mount, and 7 are from the letters of Paul.

The adverb . . . "expressly" or "explicitly" is also frequent in this context. It occurs 21 times, 18 of which in combination with a quotation and 3 referring to a general opinion of a philosopher or prophet. The divisions are not clearly defined; of the 18 occurrences, 5 are related to Greek literature, 5 to the O.T. (2 of which to the deuterocanonical Sirach) and 8 to the N.T.

Finally, there are some characteristic ways in which Clement incorporates his borrowings, whether they are literal quotations or freer transpositions. These peculiarities emerged during the course of close comparisons between Philo and Clement.[81] It was a great advantage, of course, that most of the works of Philo have survived, making them available for comparison; so many of the quotations in Clement and other authors can not be fully analyzed, since nothing remains to compare them with. Also the large volume of material represented by Clement's Philonic borrowings offers an advantage, since their sheer quantity makes it easier to discover recurring techniques. Results suggested by authors represented in only a few borrowings must be viewed with greater caution. As in all statistical surveys the accuracy of the findings correlate directly to the numbers involved.

Clement often quotes in sequential order; that means that the borrowings stay in the sequence in which they occurred in the original source.[82] This pattern appears not only in the borrowings from Philo, but in biblical material, as Claude Mondésert has pointed out[83] and in other quotations as well, such as those from the *First letter of Clement to the Corinthians* incorporated into book IV of the *Stromateis.*[84]

In some sequences, a peculiar phenomenon could be observed. Clement did not always start from the earliest point within the source he was using; he would begin with a reminiscence and then leap back to the beginning of his source and restart with quotations in a sequence, selecting a few lines from each column until he had run through the whole scroll.[85] The practice could be explained in a visual way; the author first cited from memory and then looked for the specific text; leafing through the manuscript, or rather, unrolling the scroll, he became more and more interested in it and read through the whole work. This method could be observed several times. On one occasion the process was reversed; instead of rolling the scroll forward, from beginning to end, Clement rolled it backwards.[86] It is quite possible that while reading through the manuscripts the author would have taken notes or would have had them taken for use in his final text.

The sequences tend to have a certain inner rationale; they often started out with relatively literal quotations and would subsequently decline to a less literal and more abbreviated rendition of his source.[87] After some transitional and introductory phrasing of his own, Clement would then turn to his source again, repeating the process of moving from literal to loose. This phenomenon suggests the use of notes as a basis for composition in a way that is similar to what we heard earlier from the letter of Pliny the Younger.

Without exception, all borrowings are heavily abbreviated and condensed, which again indicates the use of notes. Clement tends to draw on some authors, such as Philo, Barnabas and Hermas, for their quotations from the O.T. His technique is to focus on a biblical passage but to include phrases of the author he is consulting as a kind of wrapping material, so that some of their words remain attached to the biblical quotation.[88] This is also how the source could be recognized; the shreds of alien wrapping supplied by Philo, Hermas or Barnabas make it clear that the O.T. was not consulted directly.[89] Sometimes, however, when a quotation within a quotation occurs, Clement extends the biblical component from his own memory; the biblical passage becomes longer than it had been in his intermediary source.[90]

When one compares a truncated "chunk" of borrowing to the text of Clement's source, as can be done with the treatises of Philo or the *Letter of Clement to the Corinthians,* it is striking how abruptly the material is sometimes presented.[91] Abbreviations, discontinuities and modifications can give sentences a strange twist or an illogical turn. Repeatedly, confusion and disorder are created; words are altered in strange ways, and sentences are chopped into cryptic fragments. The development of Clement's thought at times would be incomprehensible if the original text was not at hand.[92]

In spite of his rather brutal cut-paste-and-twist technique, his illogical insertions and his abrupt transitions, Clement is also capable of clever and ingenious inventions.[93] At times, he subtly turns the words of his source to serve his own purposes. Thus material is transformed by conversion and rearrangement. An impressive ability to vary and juggle is persistently manifest.[94]

As was already noticed, Clement makes use of another technique: that of addressing himself to his source. He sets up an implied dialogue that makes it clear that he questions his model and uses it critically.[95] The implied dialogue may be created by the addition of a conjunction or an adverb that turns the borrowed material into a hypoth-

esis rather than an assertion; Clement may also frame quotations in interrogative sentences. All these additions, have, of course, a considerable effect on the meaning and intention of the borrowed words.

Another distinctive technique is the process of accumulation.[96] This process, which is characteristic of Clement's working method in general, occurs with particular evidence in quotations. Accumulation is often a product of his associative way of thinking; one word, as it were, evokes another without the support of a logical connection; various layers of imaginative thought are piled on each other. The technique is particularly common in the construction of allegories. Schematically described, Clement departs from a biblical starting point; he introduces a first layer of allegories, derived from one source, and then follows with more interpretations taken from other sources or that he invents himself. He usually closes with a distinctly Christian allegory. At other times the development of a theme and not an allegory is involved. He seems to be working toward a biblical text, which he cites at the end, and he chooses his quotations from Greek authors in the light of the biblical text.

CONCLUDING REMARKS

It can be seen how a consideration of general problems involving borrowing in Antiquity can be a helpful background for viewing techniques of individual authors. It is, in fact, difficult to understand how an author like Clement of Alexandria worked without being aware of the interaction of memory, intermediate sources, direct consultation of texts, and notetaking. Other authors provide helpful models to reconstruct how Clement balanced these elements. In turn, classifying Clement's borrowings can throw light on other authors. Key issues for his method of work are his variable way of acknowledging his sources, which leaves strange gaps in the credits to authors that seem to have been dear to his heart. His way of introducing quotations also varies, with contrasting techniques for introducing apostles and philosophers, poets and prophets, friends and foes. His tendency to work in terms of sequences from a single work while still producing a discontinuous effect is also characteristic. The very abundance of borrowings in Clement makes him an especially useful subject for this kind of analysis.[97]

Notes

1. Jaap Mansfeld has pointed out that speaking or writing in unclear and hidden ways has a long tradition in Antiquity; he cites Galen as his main example but refers to many others, including early Christian authors. Mansfeld argues that "obscurity" in philosophical or poetic texts justifies, as it were, methods of exegesis used by the interpreters of these texts. Mansfeld calls these interpretive methods "creative" and includes allegorical interpretations among them, see Jaap Mansfeld, *Prolegomena. Questions to be settled before the study of an author, or a text,* (Leiden, 1994), 155-161.

2. See, for example, *Str.* I 2,2: 20,4; 56,2.

3. See, for example, *Str.* VI 2,3-4; 96,4.

4. On the meaning of the word see, André Méhat, *Étude sur les "Stromates" de Clément d'Alexandrie* (Patristica Sorbonensia 7, Paris 1966), 96-98.

5. For a historical survey, see Otto Stählin, *Clemens von Alexandreia,* Bibliothek der Kirchenväter Bd VII/1 (München, 1938), Introduction 47ff.

6. See A. Elter, *De gnomologiorum Graecorum historia atque origine* (Bonn, 1893-1895); H. Diels, *Doxographi Graeci* (Berlin, 1897). Others argued that Clement copied one particular source, see, P. Wendland, *Quaestiones Musonianae* (Berlin, 1886); J. Gabrielsson, *Über die Quellen des Clemens Alexandrinus,* 2 vols. (Upsala, 1907 and 1909).

7. See W. Bousset, *Jüdisch-Christlicher Schulbetrieb in Alexandria und Rom* (Göttingen, 1915).

8. For a bibliography, see my *Clement of Alexandria and his Use of Philo in the Stromateis* (Leiden, 1988), 3-4.

9. For some examples, see Henry Chadwick, art. "Florilegium," *RAC* 7 (1969), 1131-1160, esp. 1144.

10. 40-(after) 112 C.E.

11. 50-(after) 120 C.E.

12. Floruit circa 200 C.E.

13. Floruit circa 200 C.E.

14. First half of the third century C.E. For his working technique, see Jørgen Mejer, *Diogenes Laertius and His Hellenistic Background* (Hermes Einzelschriften 40, Wiesbaden, 1978), 16-29 . . . .

15. Pliny the Younger, *Epistulae,* III 5,7 ff., see also Colin H. Roberts, "The Codex," *Proceedings of the British Academy* vol. XL (1954), 169-204; Colin H. Roberts and T.C. Skeat, *The Birth of the Codex* (London, 1983).

16. Dorandi, "Den Autoren," 14-15, points out that Pliny's sequence of "legere," "adnotare" and "excerpere" reflects a variety of working techniques. Thus "adnotare" would refer to making marks in the text of parts that had to be excerpted later on.

17. As an illustration of how serious he was about study, he made sure that his secretary was protected from the cold of winter by long sleeves so that no working time would be lost (*Ep.* III 5, 15). On another occasion, one of the guests asked the reader to go back and repeat a word that he had mispronounced. When Pliny the Elder asked, "could you not understand him?" the friend admitted that he could. Pliny then said, "then why make him go back; your interruption has cost us at least ten lines (*Ep.* III 5, 12)."

18. Small enough to hold in the hand, see the word "pugillus": "what can be held in the fist." For a discussion of the use, see Joseph van Haelst, "Les origines du codex," in *Les débuts du codex* (Alain Blanchard, ed., Turnhout 1989), 13-35; Horst Blanck, *Das Buch,* 48-52. Tiziano Dorandi, "Die Authoren," 14. 32.

19. Museum of Cairo, papyrus no. 88747; the excerpts from *Contra Celsum* have been published by Jean Scherer, *Extraits des livres I et II du Contre Celse d'Origène d'aprés le papyrus no 88747 du Musée du Caire* (Institut français d'Archéologie Orientale, Bibliothéque d'étude, XXVIII, Cairo, 1956), 26-29.

20. Early seventh century, see Jean Scherer, *Extraits,* 1-2.

21. Jean Scherer, *Extraits,* 26-27.

22. Lucian, *Quomodo historia conscribenda sit,* 47-48.

23. Eusebius, *HE* III 39, 15-16, cited by Wayne Meeks, "Hypomnemata from an Untamed Sceptic: A Response to George Kennedy," in *The Relationships Among the Gospels. An Interdisciplinary Dialogue,* William O. Walker ed. (San Antonio, 1978), 157-172.

24. Clement, *Letter to Theodorus,* GCS Clement IV/1, XVII-XVIII.

25. Second half of the third century B.C.E.

26. Cf. Apollonius of Perge, *Conica,* book I, 2-4 (ed. J.L. Heiberg, Teubner, 1891). For the preview of books by friends, see also Horst Blanck, *Das Buch,* 118 ff.

27. Robert Devreesse, *Introduction á l'étude des manuscrits grecs* (Paris, 1954), 77. There are various reports about authors whose writings circulated without their consent; see Cicero, *Letter to Atticus* (3,12,2). Origen received a request from alarmed friends to publish the "authentic" version of some debates he had had with opponents, since inaccurate reports apparently were in circulation; see Jean Scherer, *Entretiens d'Origéne avec Héraclide et les évêques, ses collégues sur le Pére, le Fils et l'âme* (Cairo, 1949), 50-51. H. Marrou calls attention to a case concerning Augustin (*Retractationes* II 13 [39]) in which his personal notes had been surreptitiously brought out against his wishes, see H.I. Marrou, "La technique de l'édition á l'époque patristique," *VigChr* 3 (1949), 208-224, 209.

28. Marcel Richard, "ἀπὸ φωνης," *Byzantion* 20 (1950), 191-222 . . . .

29. This meaning of the phrase ἀπὸ φωνης is connected with a particular period, namely from the end of the fifth until the seventh century, thereafter the words continue to occur in manuscripts but without the addition of a name so that the meaning of the words changes.

30. See Eusebius, *HE* VI 36. Earlier in Origen's career we also hear about shorthand writers, but, that was slightly different, since he intentionally dictated to them, see Eusebius, *HE* VI 23.

31. At times this was not possible since the author had died, see Epictetus, *Dissertationes* 5 (ed. Schenkl, Teubner, 1894).

32. Epictetus, _Dissertationes_ 5.

33. Porphyry, _Vita Plotini_ 3,46-47; 4,5; see also, Marie-Odille Goulet-Cazé, "Lécole de Plotin," in _Porphyre, la vie de Plotin_ I (Luc Brisson, Marie-Odille Goulet-Cazé, Richard Goulet and Denis O'Brien eds., Paris, 1982), 231-257.

34. Lucian, _Hermotimus_ 2.

35. See Robert Devreesse, _Introduction,_ 78, who refers to Pamphila (Photius, cod. 175).

36. In the indices of Stählin (_BKV_ 7 and 20) 462 sources are listed: O.T. (42); N.T. (25); early Christian (32); non-Christian 363. Tollinton counts 348 sources, see R.B. Tollinton, _Clement of Alexandria. A study in Christian Liberalism,_ 2 vols. (London, 1914), 157; he refers to a study of P.A. Scheck, _De Fontibus Clementis Alexandrini_ (Augsburg, 1889), 15. Tollinton was unable to consult the index by Stählin, which appeared only in 1936 _(GCS);_ 1933-36 _(BKV)._

37. 279 putative references; 9 columns in the _BKV_ editions, which are more complete than Stählin's original Index in the _GCS;_ one column in the _BKV_ contains an average of 40 quotations.

38. 618 possible references and 15.5 columns.

39. 243 possible references and 6 columns.

40. 117 possible references and 3,5 columns.

41. Chrysippus is represented by 4 columns.

42. Hesiod is represented by 1 column.

43. Herodotus is represented by 2 columns.

44. 1273 possible references and 27 columns, pseudo-Pauline letters included; only followed at a large distance by Matthew 11 columns; Luke 7.5 columns; John 5 columns; Mark 3 columns; Acts 1.5 columns.

45. See, for example, Plutarch. For poetry quotations in Early Christian authors, see Nicole Zeegers-vander Vorst, _Les citations des poètes grecs chez les apologètes chrétiens du IIe siècle_ (Louvain, 1972), 31-44.

46. For further bibliography, see Antoine Compagnon, _La seconde main ou le travail de la citation_ (Paris, 1979); also Wilhelm Krause, _Die Stellung der frühchristlichen Autoren zur heidnischen Literatur_ (Wien, 1958), 51-58, esp. note 1, in which (primarily German) literature is cited.

47. William C. Helmbold and Edward N. O'Neil, _Plutarch's Quotations_ (Phiological Monographs XIX, APA, 1959).

48. There are an average of 45 quotations per column and two columns per page, which makes a total of 76 x 90 = 6840. Stählin's index of Clement contains approximately 7300 references; O.T. (1600); N.T. (2100); Early Christian authors (380); Greek literature (3180). From the numbers for Philo it turned out that of the 279 references 125 (45%) were true borrowings, of which 93 (33%) were clearcut quota-

tions. Even if we apply the percentages for Philo (45% and 33%) to the total numbers of Stählin's index, the outcome is impressive: 3285 borrowings, of which 2409 are quotations. Compared to Plutarch's number Clement is overshadowed, but Plutarch's oeuvre is after all much more extensive than that of Clement.

49. Cf. P.J.G. Gussen, _Het leven in Alexandrïe volgens cultuurhistorische gegevens in de Paedagogus (boke I en III) van Clemens Alexandrinus_ (Assen, 1955); Wilhelm Krause, _Die Stellung_ (see note 53 above). André Méhat, _Kephalaia; Recherches sur les matériaux des "Stromates" de Clément d'Alexandrie et leur utilisation_ (thèse dact., 1966). Nicole Zeegers-vander Vorst, _Les citations_ (see note 52 above); F. Castincaud, _Les citations d'auteurs grecs profanes dans le Pédagogue de Clément d'Alexandrie_ (mémoire pour la maîtrise, Poitiers, 1976).

50. See my _Clement of Alexandria,_ 20-21.

51. See my _Clement of Alexandria,_ 22.

52. For these questions, see also the studies of Compagnon and Krause mentioned above, (note 53).

53. Stählin's index may be more reliable for poetry than for prose.

54. How many quotations are hidden among the remaining 76% of Stählin's references is uncertain; this survey was primarily concerned with the occurrence of Paul's name and writings.

55. A negligible 2% of the total number.

56. The claim that Plato's philosophy originates from the teachings of the Hebrews and in particular of Moses fits into a general apologetic argument; for an extensive documentation of this subject, see Heinrich Dörrie, _Der hellenistische Rahmen des kaiserzeitlichen Platonismus_ (Der Platonismus in der Antike, Bd. II H. Dörrie and M. Baltes eds., Stuttgart, 1990), 190-219, nos. 69-71 (texts), 480-505 (commentary).

57. 6% of the total occurrences.

58. 38% of all poetic references are to Homer.

59. On only one occasion was a reference to the Odyssey found, see _Protr._ II 35,2.

60. 18% of all poetic references are to Euripides. Hesiod represents 5%, and all others are less than 5%.

61. On only one occasion the name was dropped without quotation.

62. In 26% of the passages with the name a source also is mentioned, which represents 14% of the total.

63. For a discussion of the issue, see Eric Osborn, "Philo and Clement," _Prudentia_ 19 (1987), 35-49; most recently David T. Runia, _Philo in Early Christian Literature. A Survey,_ Assen, 1993.

64. Osborn, "Philo," 35 ff.

65. Personal communication.

66. Out of 13 occasions (which still results in 23%); for a portrait of Tatian in Clement, see Alain Le Boulluec, *La notion d'hérésie dans la littérature grecque IIe-IIIe siècles*, 2 vols. (Paris, 1985), II 346-348.

67. See Pierre Nautin, "Pantène," *Tome commémoratif du Millénaire de la Bibliothéque d'Alexandrie* (Alexandria, 1953), 145-152.

68. In connection with a quotation, see *Ecl.* 56,2.

69. In *Str.* I 11,2 (the true Sicilian bee).

70. *Protr.* 113,1; *Ecl.* 50,1; *Fragm.* 22 (III 201,26); *Fr.* in I Joh. 1,1 (III 210,1).

71. Eusebius, *HE* V 11,2; VI 13,2. Pierre Nautin, "Fin," 296. 281, suggests that the *Eclogae Propheticae* (and also the *Excerpta*) are a part of the *Hypotyposes,* and that Eusebius is actually referring to *Ecl.* 56,2. Nautin maintains that a scribe excerpted and abbreviated the writings that occur after book VII of the *Stromateis* as preserved in the Codex Laurentianus V 3; these writings are: book VIII of the *Stromateis,* the *Excerpta,* and the *Eclogae.* A majority of scholars, such as J. Munck, R.P. Casey, G. Lazzati, Cl. Mondésert, F. Sagnard, O. Stählin and A. Méhat consider these writings, however, as Clement's reading notes for later works. Since the character of these writings seems to correspond with his technique of note-taking, there is ample reason to attribute them to Clement himself and not to a later scribe.

72. Monique Alexandre (personal communication) calls attention to a similar situation in the *Pedagogue,* where Clement is very close to the first century author Musonius Rufus, whose name, however, is never spelled out.

73. Denise Kimber Buell, *Procreative Language in Clement of Alexandria* (Ph.D. Dissertation, Harvard University, 1995), 108-109 . . . .

74. On the accuracy of these quotations, see also William C. Helmbold and Edward N. O'Neill, *Plutarch's Quotations,* p. IX . . . .

75. Variants. . . occur similarly.

76. This observation is also made by Liddell and Scott s. v. πως: "sometimes merely to qualify their force, when it cannot be always rendered by any one English equivalent."

77. A total of 13 times, of which are 4 from the Psalms and 4 from Proverbs.

78. Only 3 times.

79. A total of 12 times.

80. A total of 37 times, including Plato 6, Euripides 4 and Homer 1.

81. See my *Clement of Alexandria,* 214-217.

82. The most clear example of this technique can be observed in *Str.* II 78-100 where Clement quotes extensively from Philo's *De Virtutibus.* Similar patterns have been observed in the working techniques of Diogenes Laertius, see Jørgen Mejer, *Diogenes,* 18.

83. See Claude Mondésert, *Clément d'Alexandrie; introduction á l'étude de sa pensée religieuse á partir de l'Écriture* (Paris 1944); also André Méhat, *Kephalaia; Recherches sur les matériaux des "Stromates" de Clément d'Alexandrie et leur utilisation* (thése dactyl.), 1966.

84. *Str.* IV 105-119.

85. See, for example, *Str.* II 78,2-3 and 81,1-2; V 32,2 and 32,3; I 29,10 and 30,3; II 51,3 and 51,4.

86. See *Str.* II 5,3-6,4.

87. This characteristic was also observed in the papyrus of Toura, see above note 25.

88. Similarly in the papyrus of Toura, see above note 25.

89. See, for example, for Philo, *Str.* II 5-6; for Hermas, *Paed.* II 83,4-5 for Barnabas, *Str.* II 67,2-3; also Annewies van den Hoek, "Clement and Origen as Sources on 'Noncanonical' Scriptural Traditions," *Origeniana Sexta* (Gilles Dorival and Alain Le Boulluec eds., Leuven, 1995), 100-101.

90. See *Str.* II 5-6; 94,1; 96,3.

91. Especially the quotations from Philo's *De Virtutibus* fall into this category (*Str.* II 81,3; 83,3; 85,3; 94,3; 95,1). Philo had already offered disconnected precepts from the Pentateuch, which become even more chunky through Clement's treatment; for a detailed description, see my *Clement of Alexandria,* 69-115.

92. For example, when Clement mistakenly or absent-mindedly takes one word from a following sentence of his source and connects it with the previous sentence, see, for example *Str.* II 90,2 (in a quotation from Philo); *Str.* VI 131,2 (in a quotation from Hermas).

93. See, for example, in *Str.* II 81,1-3 where two disconnected sentences are used to project a different viewpoint. Philo had stated that a "true" man has to behave in a manly fashion. Clement alters: the man who devotes himself to the "truth" behaves in a manly way; also *Str.* II 97,2 where two fragmentary sentences are combined ingeniously.

94. See, for example, *Str.* II 78,2-3; 80-81; 94,3-5.

95. See, for example, in borrowings from Philo *Str.* II 81, 3 92,2 94, 4. On occasion he also rejects the interpretation of his source, as in *Paed.* II 83,4-5 (in a quotation from Barnabas).

96. This technique can be observed throughout Clement's works.

97. Many thanks go to Alain Le Boulluec and Jean-Daniel Dubois, at whose seminar at the ÉPHÉ (1994) in Paris an earlier version of this paper was presented. Similarly the Boston Area Patristic Group and the seminar of Richard Thomas and Greg Nagy at the Harvard Classics Department helped to define

some of the questions; at Harvard the response by Sarolta Takács was very helpful. David Runia gave constructive advice and provided important bibliography. Finally, thanks go to François Bovon, Brian Daley and John Herrmann for their support and their critical eye(s).

Peter (Panayiotis) Karavites (essay date 1999)

SOURCE: "Clement's Gnostic," in *Evil, Freedom, and the Road to Perfection in Clement of Alexandria*, Brill, 1999, pp. 139-74.

[*In the following excerpt, Karavites describes Clement's ideas concerning the perfect Christian and contrasts them with the views of the Gnostics.*]

It is certain that Clement's basic purpose in writing his various treatises was to sketch the picture of the perfect Christian, the *gnostic*, as he visualized him. Clement's picture differs fundamentally from that offered by the Gnostics who, in his view, diverted from the true apostolic tradition, ending up with a caricature of the perfect Christian. Had they grasped the true spirit of the Law and adhered to the teachings of Christ, of his apostles, and of the actual Christian tradition, they might not have strayed so far from the truth. References to the perfect Christian are scattered throughout Clement's writings, but makes an effort to develop the topic more systematically in Book Seven. It has been left to modern scholars to cull the scattered evidence and present a picture of the truly Christian man as sketched by him. This chapter has not been written with the aim of duplicating or improving upon what other scholars have said, nor is it an attempt to give a systematic view of Clement's theory of the gnostic. It has only been added here because I did not think that an essay on Clement's conception of evil could be complete without mention, no matter how brief, of his notion of the perfect Christian, his gnostic.

It should be made clear that adhesion to the Mosaic Law, though commendable, was not sufficient for the achievement of that spiritual state Clement identified with the gnostic. Conformance to the ordinances of the law, any law, is useful socially and not infrequently a personal source of satisfaction and contentment. But as it has already been pointed out the truth of the Law denotes something much more than a legal instruction. It expresses a reality which is richer and deeper.[1] An analogy closer to the truth would be a comparison of the Torah with the artist's conception of the laws of artistic creation, or of musical composition. The artist who wants to express beauty through colors must go beyond the rules of color and harmony in order to discover and to express the relations that constitute the beauty of the subjects he is treating. The Biblical Law is closer to this conception. This is how Christ viewed the Law and why He intermittently leveled His vehement criticism against the Scribes and the Pharisees. Not that they did not fulfill the regulations of the Law or that that such a fulfillment was not a major accomplishment. The Pharisee in the parable of the Publican and the Pharisee fasted twice a week and tithed his revenue. This tithing was in itself a major feat. How many of us, how many Christians can today boast as he did that they tithe their revenues. Yet that was not what the spirit of the Law required. Fasting and tithing, important regulations of the Law though they might have been were not enough. The person who remained limited to these parameters of the Law had failed to penetrate its true meaning, since the Law consisted of more that rigid regulations.

The Mosaic Law is a revelation of God Himself, a gift of His grace, not a legalistic statute. It is an invitation to the people of Israel to become the receiver and carrier of the name of God, to become the reflection of that truth which is God Himself. The revelation of God's name denotes His communion and relationship with the person to whom He is revealing His name, and a possibility of that person's substantive acquaintance with the revealer. For this reason Moses, when he assumed the mission God gave him, asked that God reveal His name to him (Ex. 3.13). It was in this sense that the Israelites perceived the Law as having established a special relationship with them, a compact, a covenant, revealed by the commandment in Leviticus: "you shall be holy; as I, the Lord your God, am Holy" (19.2).

Thus, even in the Old Testament adherence to the Law did not simply mean compliance with some objective legislation designed to secure the social order or individual virtue. Maintenance of the Law instead elevated each Israelite to membership in the people of God. The Israelite ought to adhere to the Law not to secure for himself some special reward, but to secure his belonging to the people of God on whom God's promise had been bestowed. Adherence to the Law did not aim at private justification but at the revelation of the truth of the living God through the covenant of God with His people. It is through such an understanding of the Law, through such a dynamic revelation and unfolding of God to man that one can also understand the saying of Christ that He came not to abolish but to fulfill the Law (Matt. 5.17).

From this standpoint Christ's admonition to the rich young man to sell his possessions and to distribute them to the poor shows the extent of the young man's misunderstanding of the Law he claimed to have so faithfully respected. Respect for the Law as a sort of training for the real thing was good, and Christ was the first to admit it. But respect of the Law had not made yet the young man perfect in terms of eternal life. He, like the priest and the Levite in the parable (Luk. 10.31-32) was in reality a "doer" of the Law but idle . . . in regard to the true life.[2] If the young man wished to be perfect he should have freed himself from the passions that bound him to the weakness of this life. Consequently, the "if you wish" denotes the freedom the individual has and the choice he has to make as a free agent. But even that choice is not sufficient because the achievement of perfection depends on God, Who gives it to those who are willing and are exceeding earnest . . . as the young man was obviously not. Man's willingness and God's grace were necessary for the accomplishment of man's perfection. In this sense God does not compel; compulsion is repulsive to God. On the other hand, God supplies grace to those who seek it and bestows it on those who ask for it (*QDS* 10.1). Those who earnestly seek it and acquire it achieve what is above the Law and its gifts.[3]

The way for men to acquire God's grace is to follow Christ's example. Christ became perfect and sanctified in His humanity through His baptism and the descent of the Holy Spirit.[4] The same takes place in our case, according to Clement.[5] So, when we are baptized we are illuminated and acquire the potential to become sons of God. We are made perfect, and being made perfect we become immortal.[6] The acquisition of perfection is thus partly but significantly the result of the grace of God.[7] Washing and illumination are the means by which the Christians cleanse their sins and by which the penalties accruing for transgression are remitted.[8] It is called illumination because by it that holy light of salvation is beheld; that is, we clearly see God. Through baptism man dies with Christ and is resurrected with Him in the life of the new time. Man at first dead in sin enters into the life of grace, which is offered to him through the seal of the gift of the Holy Spirit. By this granting of the seal of the gift of God the baptized obtains the ability to achieve deification, something that had become impossible after his fall. The baptism as a new birth of man bestowed by the Holy Spirit supersedes his natural birth. The baptized becomes a spiritual being since he was baptized in the Spirit. The father of the baptized is Christ Himself. Thus all those baptized in Christ, while physically children of various fathers, become supernaturally children of Christ, in supersession of all physical relations. It is for this reason that Christ calls His disciples not only "friends" but also "little children" (John, 13, 33). The rehabilitation of the soul has its beginning in baptism and its completion through the vision of God in the future time . . . . The period of man's life after his baptism affords him the possibility of maturation in the life according to Christ and the development of communion with God through the cooperation of God's gift. This life in Christ must be witnessed in the daily conduct of the baptized.

FAITH AS A PREREQUISITE OF PERFECTION

Though baptism is so essential for man's advancement to the state of perfection, baptism itself does not automatically guarantee its attainment without certain indispensable spiritual requisites and the constant effort to maintain this state of grace and perfection. One basic prerequisite for baptism, also necessary in the struggle for deification, is faith. Faith is that internal good . . . that inward power that leads man to confess and glorify God's existence. Man has to start with faith and develop it with the help of the grace of God (*Str.* 7.55.2-3). Faith is the property of

the wise man who is not wise according to the world but according to God, and who is taught without training in the usual texts which represent the wisdom of men but rather through the spiritual texts (*Paed.* 3.78.2). The truth of this process is demonstrated by the fact that though many faithful are ill-disposed to any formal form of training they nonetheless attain spiritual excellence, while others whose natural disposition toward education is good do not attain the excellence adverted to by Clement, because through neglect or indifference they do not free themselves from evil.[9] A man of faith is perfect, according to Clement, because nothing is wanting to faith since it is perfect and complete in itself. If ought is wanting to it, then it is not wholly perfect.[10] Faith then is that experience of the presence of God which brings man into personal communion with God and makes him a communicant of His goodness (*Str.* 4.143.3). When this personal element is absent faith becomes empty, a formal convention, which objectifies God and makes Him into an indifferent object of worship. This object becomes eventually surrounded by other objectified values which in the end are not related to God and make communion with God a matter of indifference. Piety, prayer, fasting, alms-giving, sacrificing easily become independent values not simply means of communion with God. Something like it had happened to the Pharisee of the parable who boasted about his compliance with the Law. Those accomplishments of his had not succeeded in bringing him into communication with God, because they were perceived by him as self-values. Something similar had happened to Euthyphro in the corresponding Platonic dialogue when he confused external formalities with piety. It took a Socrates to disabuse him of his error.

The external world constitutes a reference to God, and the observation of our surrounding world leads us to the search of God. Yet faith in God should not be viewed as an imposition by external necessity but should remain an expression of freedom. Without faith in God man becomes alienated from this world; on the other hand, the simple recognition of God as creator does not save man either. Man's salvation requires his personal encounter and communion with God. Though faith as a personal relation and communion with God is not identified with the social conventions, it nevertheless possesses a social dimension since man's faith in God is connected directly with man's relation to his fellow-man.

Man by himself has no power to acquire faith unless God bestows it on him (*Str.* 1.38.5). The believer therefore depends largely on God. If God withdrew His grace even for a minute, man's faith would cease. The question that naturally arises is why God does not bestow faith on everybody, not just on the few. This question is difficult to answer and Clement comes up with various responses. First, that if some believe and others do not this is not due to God but to those who do not believe. The second answer relates to the first, that not everybody seeks out God and that only those who seek receive faith (*Str.* 5.12.1-2). Thirdly, even among those who seek out God not all will find him, but only those who go about it rightly.

Clement does not seem to confront the question of how man is moved to seek out God, especially seek him out rightly, since by himself man does not have this ability. If there are certain presuppositions and qualifications for seeking out God is the grace of God fundamental or simply ancillary? Clement does not answer this question satisfactorily. He simply states that faith is a divine gift and a human propensity or ability but which he does not say how it originates. He simply states that faith is a divine gift that thus becomes a human propensity or ability but does not say how it originates in man except by the power of God. Thus the question becomes circuitous (*Str.* 5.9.2). He adds only that when the urge for the development of faith appears, it has to be cultivated by listening to the catechism or that it can, on occasion, be grasped without knowledge (*Ecl. Proph.* 28.3). By introducing the element of knowledge Clement reverts to Greek philosophy wherein character improvement depends on intellectual discipline and training. However, realizing the insufficiency of his answers to the question of faith, he tries to escape from the difficulties by adding that faith is a gift of God and hence different from knowledge (*Str.* 7.55.1-3)

Clement persists that the essential characteristic of Christian faith is that it permeates man's whole being and becomes a way of life. It is not a simple learning . . . of some teaching which requires only the approval of reason but a way of life. And although it is not an inherent virtue, it nevertheless saturates the whole being of the believer, thereby becoming an "internal good" which admits God's existence and glorifies Him. Whereas elsewhere he makes faith the product of a divine gift which is the sine qua non for the origin of faith, he at the same time describes it as if this gift were something secondary (*Str.* 7.55. 2-3). It becomes easier for him when he explains that the object of faith is God, though again he gets into trouble when he maintains that the believer does not arrive at faith by a deductive process but accepts it as something given. His assertion that faith is a relationship or way to approach God does not shed much more light on the question. What, apparently, Clement has in mind is the Judeo-Christian God as He has been revealed through the prophets and Christ, not just a form of deism.[11]

Faith is essentially acquired by the knowledge of Christ's teachings (*Str.* 4.159.1) which connect the believer with God and with himself. This relationship established by faith is unique to the Christian man and Clement implicitly denies that faith in other Gods connects the believer to the believed. For Clement to have made such a statement would have been absurd since the believed was viewed by him as the one perfect reality. What Clement refuses to admit here is that the faith of the pagan believer engendered a relation analogous to the Christian faith, and that the pagan believer accepted the believed as much of a reality as the Christian accepted his God.

Furthermore, Clement views the Christian faith as "born in time," perhaps for two reasons: first, because the incarnation of Christ and His teachings took place in time, and,

secondly, because the of faith of most Christians at his time was born at a certain time, this being the time of their conversion (most of the Christians in Clement's time were converts) which can be seen as new birth and new life. This new life is not easy; on the contrary, like the life of Christ it is full of suffering and sacrifice because belief is not simply faith in some abstract philosophical theory but a living and active faith (*Theod. Extr.* 86.2). Clement seems to think that faith in some abstract philosophical theory is easy compared to the Christian faith, something that might have been preponderantly but not absolutely true if we look at the life of Socrates and others who chose to live consistently with their philosophical beliefs.

FAITH AND JUSTICE

Though many may disagree with his assessment of the difficulties stemming from living a life consistent with the ideals of Christian faith most would agree with him that the end of such a life is perfection . . . to be accomplished by the Christian's strict compliance with the will of God (*Paed.* 3.101.1-2). Clement adds that faith and justice are often identical because the non-believer cannot really be just, a view that again may not be true (*Protr.* 104.2). He qualifies his statement by saying that justice is not the "common" faith but the special all-inclusive faith which is knowledge of God (*Paed.* 1.103.1-5). Justice and faith are similar because faith, like justice, expresses a relationship to God (*Str.* 7.78.7). In a sense, faith can be seen as the foundation of justice (*Ecl. Proph.* 37.2) while justice is the end of faith (*Paed.* 2.103.2-3). Faith ends with life's existence whereas justice partakes of the divine presence with its knowledge of God (*Str.* 6.78.1 and unknown fr. 48). Those who died in Christ are not called believers any longer but righteous. Faith is thus temporal leading to justice and eternal life, while justice is participation in the divine life, that is, the constant vision of God. At the end, despite the distinction between the two concepts Clement concludes that neither faith can exist without justice nor justice without faith (*Protr.* 116.3) The just is just when he has faith in God and His will (*Ecl. Proph.* 60.1).

KNOWLEDGE

While Clement thus seems to place faith above knowledge, he did not mean to downgrade the importance of knowledge as an element conducive to the perfection of the Christian man. As in the case of the Law, so knowledge for Clement is something much more than what we consider formal education. It is the understanding of things present, future, and past, things which are certain and reliable because imparted and revealed by the Son of God. But Clement warns that those whose purpose in life is contemplation toward perfection can reach it only by learning the prophetic utterances by which they will grasp the present, the future, and the past.[12] Thus true knowledge . . . deals with intellectual objects which are beyond the sphere of the world, and with objects more spiritual than those which the eye can see, and the ear can hear. The gnostic learns of these things from the teacher who unveils the holy of holies in an ascending order to those who are truly recipient of the Lord's adoption.[13] The things the gnostics learn are contained in the prophecies which are full of knowledge as it has been given by the Lord. This knowledge is an attribute of the rational soul which trains itself so that by knowledge it may become entitled to immortality. For Clement learning is the beginning of all rational action since learning is older than the action that follows it.[14]

In his discussion of knowledge Clement tries to differentiate between what men regard as knowledge and what he considers knowledge from the Christian standpoint. In this sense knowledge is not simply a field of education in which someone has specialized. It is not even just the knowledge of good and evil, the ethical intellectualism suggested by Socrates. It is that but also more than that. It is that knowledge which provides an irrefragable comprehension of things divine and human, of those that Christ has taught men through the prophets and through His advent. It is irrefragable because it has been revealed to us by him. This knowledge is not acquired through reason . . . trained by that education through which the latent powers of man are developed and self-perfection is accomplished.[15] True, Clement admits that the realization of God in man begins through the function of the mind (*Str.* 5.73.2; 7.5). The next step is meeting God and remaining obedient to His will (*QDS* 18.7). Part of this obedience is expressed not as compliance with humanistic action but as a conviction of anthropognosy and autognosy, that is, the "know thyself." Through this self-knowledge we acquire the right relationship to God. Thus the knowledge that springs from logical inquiry is related to the knowledge that comes through faith and illumination. Both are interdependent things conducive to the accomplishment of the same goal. But the first is not sufficient. Man needs also God's gift, His light. Without this light we cannot know God as perfectly as possible. In that state of imperfection we may know God as others did, which implies that Clement is aware that pagans also knew of the direct relation of light to the knowledge of God. True philosophy, according to the Sibyl, is that which is deposited in the heart of people and which is the knowledge of God Who is likened to the light and the sun, an agent opposed to the darkness and ignorance (*Protr.* 77.2-3). This knowledge the believer receives through revelation by the Holy Spirit (*Protr.* 78.1). The light, which Clement identifies with God, Who is the creator of light, can help man disperse the darkness and ignorance of his life.[16] Whereas the Greeks had knowledge of the God, their knowledge was imperfect. Even such a great genius as Plato merely touched the truth about God without really grasping it perfectly.[17] Only God's grace is a sure means to know the truth about God and the salvation that comes from Him.[18] The knowledge of God Clement refers to is knowledge as through a mirror . . . that is, this knowledge is not of His substance but of His activity through revelation.[19] That is why the knowledge of God and His truth differs in the Bible from that of the Greek philosophy as much as a dream from reality (*Protr.* 64.1).

The human body is also instrumental in the knowledge of God because by virtue of our being alive we posses knowledge and through living we learn and achieve the good (*Str.* 4.18. 1-2). Here Clement seems to follow again in the footsteps of Plato who speaks of the harmony between body and soul, an idea Clement adapts to the Christian message.[20] He reasons that the loving God appears in the Church as activity . . . which has manifested itself in human form thought live agents, such as the apostles, who continued His teaching after His coming, as He had also manifested Himself through the prophets and through His own incarnation. The physical element is useful because God in human form was most suitable to serve the humanity of man (*Ecl. Proph.* 23.1-2). Owing to His saving activity our spiritual way of life and our body have been sanctified and Christ is glorified through our body.[21]

Clement consequently rejects the ancient notion that the body was evil and that it served as the tomb of the soul, an idea quite different from his concept of harmony.[22] In rejecting this ancient theory he combats the similar Gnostic ideas about the body, claiming that in essence the body is a thing indifferent . . . , a theory propounded earlier by the Stoics.[23] But whereas the Stoics spoke of the body as an indifferent thing, Clement went a step further by asserting that the body can be sanctified and that the importance of the body should be seen in Christ's incarnation by which He saved humanity. He also stresses that God is glorified through our physical nature and that man can attain moral progress through his physical being.[24]

Clement equally reminded us that the knowledge of God begins with the aid of our senses and our reason, provided that sensory preception is combined with prudence. In this way the individual is led gradually to sound . . . knowledge, though he agrees with Philo that the process is difficult, making the object difficult to attain, . . .[25] Clement draws from Aristoboulos, who seemed to have had similar ideas about the knowledge of God, which he had purportedly borrowed from Plato.[26] He mentions with approbation Plato's and Aristoboulos' theory that wonder is the first step of philosophical inquiry and that man should start with the intelligible things if he were to understand the causes of the visible order (*Str.* 5.8.6).[27]

The knowledge of God has its beginnings in the knowledge of ourselves. By this statement Clement gives to the Socratic apophthegm a Christian twist. When one knows himself he learns that he is a child of God and is thereby led to the attainment of the knowledge of the Father by seeking to liken himself to God.[28] He learns that Christ's church is a school, and that Christ is the only true teacher who bestows the sacred and saving knowledge.[29] Through self-knowledge he comes to know his purpose in life which is none other than the fulfilment of the commandments, which obtain his adoption as child of God and his salvation.[30] For Clement the purpose of the creation of man's soul is knowledge which in the end is the knowledge of our sinful nature that leads us to repentance, from which springs the finding of our soul and our salvation.[31] Clement's idea of the importance of self-knowledge as a means of finding ourselves is substantially different from

Philo's theory where self-knowledge is the awareness of our smallness, the knowledge of the nothingness of our mortal nature.[32] Such an awareness of our nothingness is primarily a help in the attainment of the knowledge of God since only when the creature recognizes its own nothingness is it ready to encounter the creator.

Self-knowledge is a topic to which Clement frequently returns. The study of ourselves begins with the knowledge of our body and what happens to our nature. From there it proceeds to more intellectual things whose guide is reason. When the individual cleanses his flesh and his spirit, he is freed from those influences that keep him earth-bound and nothing else is left but for him to get on the road that leads to the understanding of God.[33] Though Clement here never loses sight of the role of revelation in knowledge, he nonetheless seems to adhere closely to philosophy as the road that brings to God. True, knowledge of God through philosophic inquiry alone is impossible, but Clement inclines to believe that the best road to knowledge includes philosophy, provided one does not mistake this road as the desired terminal.[34] The guide in the discovery of knowledge should be Christ, the Logos of God.[35] After he has said that, Clement does not hesitate to voice his difference to philosophy. The knowledge of God through self-knowledge is not a theoretical knowledge of the road to God nor is it the simple knowledge of either the simple or difficult concepts of revelation. Nor is it the knowledge of the works of God. It is knowledge and participation in the divine will and activity, especially that activity which was unknown to philosophy but which relates to the salvation of man. Self-knowledge is also found in the Gnostic texts except that there it concerns the knowledge of the former state of the soul and not participation in the will of God or man's salvation.[36] True knowledge provides an irrefragable comprehension of things divine and human, and of everything that Christ has taught men through the prophets and through His advent. It is irrefragable because it has been revealed to us by Him. This knowledge is what produces true wisdom.[37] Only by the acquisition of this knowledge which does not puff up and does not work conceit can man acquire trust in the truth and so live in accordance with the gospel and discover the proofs for which he has searched in the Law.[38]

Clement's emphasis on knowledge carries the mystical implication that God is not only inaccessible and invisible but also accessible and visible. The possibility of communion with God and the seeing of His glory depends on the accessibility and understanding of His divinity. Invisible and inaccessible in His substance God becomes visible and accessible in His activity. This distinction between the substance and activity of God is already known to Clement from Athenagoras.[39]

The vision of God is of course granted as a divine gift but also as a recompense for human effort towards spiritual advancement and perfection. One must labor constantly, however, to be granted this vision. This effort is seen as a constant human exercise of cleansing and return to himself

and God. Attachment to the carnal desires and the deceitful pleasures removes man from God. Sinlessness is not understood here as a negative situation limited to the abstinence from sin but is something active, directly connected with the exercise of virtue and especially love.[40] Love exemplifies the superseding character of virtue over sin. Sin is a later product of man's disobedience while virtue is without beginning since it stems eternally from God and is granted by him to the spirit of man. This does not reduce man's responsibility nor the importance of his cooperation with God. But before man can "see" God, he has to find the truth and orient his existence toward God while at the same time converting his passionate tendency for himself and the world into a selfless and "divine" love.[41]

Knowledge and Truth

Closely associated with knowledge is the issue of truth and how to find it. Clement here tackles the problem arising from the attempt to interpret the true tradition as handed down by the apostles and by the teachings of Christ. His solution is an awkwardly axiomatic but reasonable statement that what is subject to interpretation and criticism cannot be a first principle (*Str.* 7.95.5-6). This is an irreducible and self-evident fact to him. He then advances to the inevitable conclusion that we can grasp by faith the indemonstrable first principle which he equates with truth and God.

Truth for Clement is a reality that resides outside of the world. The present world is subject to change and corruption (*Str.* 7.30.2). Truth is eternal and changeless, identified with God. Truth is the real being; it is God. All truth has as its criterion and measure God (*Protr.* 1.69.1). Truth being God does not stay in itself but comes into the world. Truth is "eternal food" (*Str.* 5.70.1) and he who attains to it and distinguishes himself in good works shall gain the prize of everlasting life (*QDS.* 1.4). Doubting truth ends up in the opposite, that is, death and destruction (*Str.* 4.8.3-4). Because God did not wish to abandon man after his fall, He allowed him to have some truth. This kindness on the part of God explains the traces of truth to be found in Greek philosophy. Since philosophy is a search for the truth and the nature of things, it is not totally ignorant of truth (*Str.* 1.32.4). In philosophy itself there is truth, and true beauty (*Str.* 6.150.6). The truth of philosophy is not only the product of investigation "from below" by man; it is also divine grace given to the Greeks from above.[42] But this truth in philosophy is mixed with many lies and much error. Philosophy contains a part of truth; it is not itself the truth (*Str.* 1.87.1). How can we distinguish the truth from the lies in philosophy? Clement's answer needs no great elaboration: through the revealed truth by Christ Who is the only true philosophy (*Str.* 6.58.2). When one realizes that Christ as the Son of God is our true teacher, he is convinced that Christ's teaching is truth (*Str.* 5.85.2). Thus Clement answers a difficult problem without the need to analyze it thoroughly. Without Christ's revelation there cannot be full knowledge of truth, and without the full knowledge of truth there can be no knowledge. The Greek philosophers themselves are intellectually infants if they have not been made men by Christ (*Str.* 1.53.1-2).

On the other hand, those who are afraid of philosophy and avoid it resemble children who are afraid that phantoms may abduct them (*Str.* 6.80.5). Here Clement attempts to combine his admiration for Greek education with the newly revealed truth. Philosophy, according to him, is not only the method for the development and understanding of the Christian truth but it also contains truth. Philosophy thus becomes necessary for the better understanding of truth because it serves as the underpinning of Christian theory (*Str.* 6. 62.1). Clement's view constitutes a scathing criticism of the opponents of Greek education. If one can know the truth about Christ, he feels, he can more readily grasp it with the knowledge of Greek philosophy (*Str.* 1.178.1). The dialectician proceeds with his ascent to the hierarchy of essences, forms, or powers until he climbs, as Plato did, to the highest essence of all, the ultimate reality which is the Good or God. To this Platonic dialectic process Clement added the element of faith. Faith and dialectic joined together and led to knowledge of reality and to the real God, although not the God of Platonic intellectualism. Thus Clement does not stray too far from Greek philosophy which seeks to know God through human effort, relying on an innate original communion between man and heaven (*Protr.* 25.3). We can say that as Christ came to fulfill the Law so Clement sought to fulfill Greek philosophy with revelation. In this respect he saw no antithesis between the two, despite his occasional protests about philosophy, and contrary to the many reservations and fears expressed by many of his contemporaries.[43] In essence, Clement reemphasized the "likeness" between God and the world and the continuity between creation and redemption. Greek philosophy therefore accomplished two most important tasks: first it prepared its students for the reception of the Christian message, the true philosophy, Truth itself. In a typical Heracleitean fashion Clement again reminds us that this truth can be known only by a select few and is the object of esoteric knowledge. The teacher of this knowledge is the historical Christ, the incarnation of the Divine Logos. Those who want to become gnostics must study and take into account philosophy (*Str.* 2.45.6). Granted that even without philosophy a person can become a gnostic, but philosophy makes it easier to achieve this goal since it provides the background for the right interpretation of the Scriptures. This leads to the second task philosophy performs: it becomes the key to the disclosure of the inner meaning of the Scriptures.[44]

Those who accept the bond between philosophy and revelation become trained to the knowledge of truth (*Str.* 7.95.6). Truth which is accepted as knowledge is not a simple statement which may also recognize ignorance; that type of truth is simply an opinion. What is stated by men must be proved by the voice of God, the only demonstration Clement accepts as valid. The voice of God is in the Bible and in the tradition passed onto us by the apostles and their disciples. This tradition was a body of sayings

and doings ascribed to the apostles which was universally accepted by the Christians of Clement's time. Living in the sub-apostolic era, so close to the founders of the new religion, Clement realized that Bible and tradition were the only interpretations of truth he held as authentic (*Str.* 7.95.3). Those who had merely tasted . . . the Scriptures he classified as believers, whereas those who had advanced further and had become correct expounders of the truth were the gnostics. As in life craftsmen are superior to ordinary people and can model beyond the common man's ability, so those who give a complete proof of the Scriptures based on their faith in the Scriptural writings themselves can best persuade with their demonstrations the common man (*Str.* 7.96.1).

Beyond the definition of truth and knowledge as the scientific possession of what is good and unchangeable, things divine and human (*Paed.* 2.25.3; *Str.* 7.70), truth and knowledge are also described as the rational guide that leads the spirit away from the passions and death and into the path of good-doing.[45] This type of knowledge pilots to the infinite and perfect end, showing men the future life they will lead according to God "among other Gods," by which he means among other gnostics (*Str.* 7.56.4). Knowledge is quick in purifying and transforming a person. With ease it removes the soul to what is akin to the soul and by its own light conveys man through mystic stages until he can gaze on God face to face . . . with understanding and comprehension (*Str.* 7.57.1). In this understanding consists the perfection of the gnostic soul, because this understanding means that the soul is with the Lord, and so the soul is also in immediate subjection to him (*Str.* 7.57.1-2). While faith is a comprehensive knowledge of the essentials, knowledge itself is the strong and sure demonstration of what is received by faith from God's teaching, conveying the soul on to infallibility, science, and comprehension (*Str.* 7.56.2-3). This knowledge terminates in love-giving and in turning the loved from that which is unknown to that which is known, making the knowing one a creature equal to angels, . . .[46]

It is therefore impossible for those who are still under the direction of passions to receive true knowledge of God, and if they have no true knowledge of God they do not have any final hope. The person who fails to attain this end is liable to the charge of ignorance of God, an ignorance which is displayed by one's way of living (*Str.* 3.43.1). The conduct of one's life reveals him who knows and follows the commandments, the very light that is in us.[47] Knowledge is a form of divine understanding and light, engendered in the soul from obedience to the commandments, which makes everything clear and enables man to know himself and God. For knowledge stands to the mind as the eye to the body.[48] That is the reason Clement considered faith "cultivated" by knowledge as worth more than "simple" faith (*Str.* 1.43.1-3). His distinction between cultivated and simple faith seems to concern those Christians who in reacting against the rationalism of heterodoxists went to the extreme in underlining only simple faith as the basic ingredient of salvation and perfection. They rejected the learning of philosophy and natural science . . . to the chagrin of Clement who, though himself critical of the pagan beliefs of the Greeks, found their education nonetheless conducive to the better understanding of the Christian truths. Hence his intriguing comment that to demand faith alone without knowledge is as if one wished to gather grapes immediately, without bestowing care on the vine (*Str.* 1.43.1) But he who directs everything towards an upright life, procuring examples from the Greeks and barbarians, is an experienced searcher after the truth and a man of wisdom possessing the qualities of the Lydian stone which was believed to have the power of distinguishing the spurious from the genuine gold. The true and knowledgeable gnostic can distinguish sophistry from philosophy, rhetoric from dialectic, truth from a lie.[49]

Clement considers the ability to distinguish among these intellectual differences as well as between expressions of double meaning whether in philosophy or in the Bible as very important. Even Christ, when questioned, sought to answer occasionally by expressions of double meanings. Consequently, knowledge of philosophy is important because it enables a person to avoid deception by ambiguity and helps him attain to the supreme knowledge that frees him from restrictions; it metamorphoses him into a perfect moral entity.[50] What Clement wishes for the Christian here is the achievement of the Christian ethos and of personal distinctiveness and freedom. This can be realized if only man can effect a change in his mode of existence, the end-result of the realization of the Christian message. Clement's gnostic must free himself from the oppressive claims of his individual nature which binds him to the weaknesses and the impersonal survival of the species. Only through this liberation from natural necessity can the Christian man exist as a distinctive personality in a life with Christ, a life of love. Only by this road of freedom can man achieve his likeness to God and become a gnostic. And only by becoming a gnostic will man achieve the reality of unity with the good that will free him from corruption and death. Essential to the achievement of this goal is that the Christian understand fully the prophets and apostles, especially since some of their sayings have a hidden meaning which demands skill in understanding (*Str.* 1.45.1).

Clement realizes at this point that he may be falling into the trap of contradiction because the apostles and prophets were demonstrably lacking in formal education. He seeks to escape from this predicament by pointing out that the prophets and the apostles knew infallibly the meaning of what the spirit had said in a way that others cannot easily know it. Hence, he concludes that it is not for those without knowledge to explain casually the prophets and the apostles (*Str.* 1.45.2). Knowledge will also help the gnostic to identify what is safe and good with what seems dreadful in appearance, though not necessarily in reality. This identification enables him to know what is truly to be dreaded and that which is dreaded because of a false opinion rather than its truth. So he discriminates intelligently what the Word intimates to him as requisite and necessary, and really safe for him: that is, what is good

from what appears to be so.[51] Pursuing Plato's thought, Clement avers that it is from ignorance of what is and what is not to be dreaded that man acts. Therefore, the only man of courage is the gnostic who knows present and future good things and the things to be dreaded. Since the gnostic knows that vice . . . is alone hateful and destructive, he makes war against it.[52] Clement's distinction between of dreaded and non-dreaded things provides him with the opportunity to express his reservation about those "martyrs" who precipitously exposed themselves to danger and to praise those, who when called by God, surrendered themselves promptly to martyrdom in the exercise of rational fortitude, simply obeying the call from a love of God.[53]

VIRTUE, KNOWLEDGE AND THEOSIS

In a way Clement seems to believe that virtue is the inclination to hunt for the best and the disposition of the soul to regard everything in life in the light of reason.[54] To a limited degree virtue is inherent because every man by nature possesses the ability to perfectibility. Even though we do not originally possess virtue we have the propensity for it (*Str.* 6.95.5). This natural propensity man must develop through training and learning, turning it into an activity that dominates the passions (*Paed.* 1.16.1-3). When man becomes the master of his passions he becomes virtuous. Clement inclines to believe that once an individual has achieved virtue he is not very likely to lose it, though he recognizes that the maintenance of virtue requires constant vigilance. The theory that a person can become perfect in virtue is wrong since virtue is the voluntary and conscious effort toward the perfect (*Paed.* 1.34. 1-2). If nature affords us the possibility of near perfection in virtue, it is only as an act of will developed through learning and training, which is achieved in a different degree by different persons.[55] Clement does not forget to add, however, that the most essential part in the achievement of virtue is God's grace and help. The propensity to virtue is the objective factor while the perfection through training is the subjective element. Without these two factors there is no attainment of virtue. Yet the two factors are not enough for the development of virtue because both factors are of this world. If they were sufficient man would not need God's help. He could achieve virtue by himself. Thus virtue is not only moral perfection, it is also to a great extent a divine contribution. Here again Clement's thinking remains consistent with the Christian theory as he distances himself from the Greek ideal of virtue which emphasized primarily the human element. Clement does not deny man's freedom of the will in the accomplishment of virtue, but points out that this accomplishment is not possible without God.[56]

In a similar vein, Clement stresses that growth in virtue is not something done because of the perfectible hopes to acquire something in this world, though there might be beneficial offshoots from this attainment. Neither happiness nor worldly goods are the object of the virtuous person, as they are in Greek philosophy. The ultimate aim of this perfection is being with God which produces the real happiness.[57] This happiness of the gnostic obtains even when external conditions for him are not so fortunate. The virtuous is internally calm and lives at peace with God; consequently, he is in peace with the world and himself. Virtue thus leads to likeness with God (*Str.* 6.114.6). The gnostic becomes similar to God, to paraphrase Heracleitus, because he wills what God wills.[58]

That it is Greek philosophical thought that Clement paraphrases in Christian terms becomes obvious from a quick survey of Plato's treatment of the subject and from the very fact that Clement himself does not hesitate to refer occasionally to Plato's theory of man's perfection. A brief discussion of Plato's religious ideas will sufficiently demonstrate the dependence of Clement gnostic model on Plato's theory of the "ideal" person. The teachings of Plato (no distinction between Socratic and Platonic ideas is made here; this is not a study on Plato) can be summarized in three quick propositions: his description of the perfection; man's moral autonomy and self-sufficiency; and man's self-knowledge which unmistakably leads to the inner understanding of the basic principles of the good. Plato believed that virtue was knowledge (Lach. 194 D) and that when one possesses the knowledge of good, he will try to follow it in his life.[59] Evil for Plato is not part of human nature (he will modify this view in some of his later works) but of human ignorance. In opposition, human nature is not voluntarily evil.[60] His conviction was that reason is capable of perfecting humanity. He thus presents Socrates as adhering to this proposition and as dedicating his life to it.

Plato's conviction has a rationalist basis, though the mystic, the religous, element is not absent from it. Yet Plato's rationalism should not be confused with the ideal of the Enlightenment. His idea was not the possession of knowledge as the proponents of the Enlightenment presented rational knowledge but a total development of one's personality under the guidance of reason, by which he means the spirit as a superior, guiding principle. This coinherence of reason and spirit is what Plato calls the "true harmony" (Lach. 188 D), the pairing of words and deeds, which Plato so admired in the character of Socrates (Apol. 33 A).

The program in the life of Socrates, Socrates' own perfection, the perfection of his fellow citizens he so ardently pursued, his zeal in the accomplishment of this ideal have a missionary, religious tinge about them. His steady faith in the idea that a divine reason governs the world and puts order and shape to all points to the fact that Socrates was a person of a deeply religious nature who believed that only when man surrenders voluntarily his own self to reason and its dictates he allows the divine proclivities in him to reveal themselves.[61] How is this religiosity reconciled with Socrates' rationalism? Socrates lived the "feeling of mystery." He realized that the human ability for knowledge was not unlimited.[62] This side of his character is evinced by his faith in . . . that strange inner voice which turned him away from doing something at

crucial moments of his life.[63] He believed that this voice was the command of the divine. He could not rationally explain it and concluded that it must have been of divine origin. The assumption led him also to the belief in the prophetic meaning of dreams.[64] His belief in the prophetic character of dreams is the "revenge of mysticism against rationalism."[65]

The philosopher pays no attention to beauty, riches, bodily rigor, political power, and glory, things that the common people admire. He disdains such possessions because they are not conducive to the improvement of his soul.[66] He preoccupies himself only with spiritual things that motivate the soul to look upwards and preaches the gospel of "refuge" from the world which he understands as "likeness to God." (Plat. Theaet. 176 A-B). He is possessed by a burning desire for the paternal home, that is the divine kingdom. He feels as stranger in the visible world of evil and desires to elevate himself to the divine eternal kingdom. The fundamental presupposition for the accomplishment of this task is for him to deny decisively the body with its senses and to fly with the wings of spirit to our heavenly country. When man accomplishes this goal, he will come close to God.

This incessant struggle that Plato felt was also felt later by another religious personality (Rom. 7.22-25). The Pauline struggle between the law of his body and mind Plato ascribes to two different worlds. On the one hand is the kingdom of God and eternal being; on the other, the world of nature and sinfulness. The soul belongs to the first, the body to the second. The soul strives to elevate itself to heavens; the body ties it to the earth. The difference between the Platonic and Pauline view lies in the fact that Paul expected redemption from the grace of God, while Plato expected man to fight for his own salvation. Both, however, agree that man should try his best not to allow the enslavement of the soul by the body. Both concur that the destiny of our life is to leave this life.

Only through death of the body the soul manages to live its own life. Conversely, the soul dies when human corporeality grows. For man to partake of the eternal life, which only befits the soul, man must die as to the body; he must free himself of his earthly life. Death is the freeing of the soul from the body and its physical demands (Phaed. 64 C; 67 D). This happens only when the body's physical demise is achieved, and the soul is freed from the body. This is indeed the liberation from the body that the philosopher anticipates since it frees him from sensual pleasures and deadens his desires (Phaed. 64 D; 65 B). In the former case, death is not an evil, as people commonly believe but the desired goal (Phaed. 68 D; 65 B; 83 A). Philosophy then can be defined as the study and the exercise of death.[67]

Plato therefore stresses the nostalgic expectations of death that characterizes people of strong religious propensities. It is a feature of the deeply religious natures of all times and in all sorts of civilizations that they are not terrified by death. On the contrary, they make it the center of their life's theory. Death not only as physical dissipation of the body, but also death in life, that is the moral mortality of the sinful body, opens up the road to another life where the troubles of earthly life are not counted, and where eternal happïness always shines. An understanding God, full of love and kindness has destined and invited man to this happiness. Man will reach this destiny if he makes it the main objective of his life by acting in accordance of the philosophical ideals.[68] This ideal has no relation to earthly happiness; it supervenes it. It is man's perfection, his likeness to God.[69] Man's guide towards this goal is not only the measure set by himself, but the measure also set by God for man's thought and action (Plat. Laws 4. 716 C), a position contrary to that of Protagoras. The true philosopher who stands closer to God lives as if in a cloud that passes over the earth, Plato says quoting Pindar.[70] Pluto, Plato continues, must be honored of all gods because it bestows upon man the most wishful thing: death (Rep. 8.828 D). Coward and slave is he who is afraid of death. The accomplished philosopher does not consider death fearful . . . . On the contrary, it is life that is fearful (Gorg. 492 E).

It was mentioned above that Plato intimates that man cannot understand the divine solely with the aid of reason, a position with which Clement wholeheartedly would later concur. Reason cannot go that far. This leap can be made only by him who has been given divine inspiration . . . and grace. Only he can experience such a *contemplatio sui generis*. One could call this leap upwards "divine logos" or theory, . . .[71] What one feels inside him is impossible to explain in human terms (Rep. 6. 509 A). This feeling which amounts to the possession of the soul by the divine, creates in the possessed an ineffable state that Plato understood when he called it "divine madness," created by the gods.[72] Only few are given this privilege to divine madness (Phaedr. 69 C-D). For this reason the many consider the philosopher who is possessed by this ecstatic mania a fool. (Phaedr. 249 D). But this "fool" experiences directly the miracle of the power that possessed him and lifts him from earth to heaven. In this heaven he lives the indescribable sensation of internal transformation. He feels that wings grow in his soul. His soul finds itself in a flood of passion and is filled with joy, throbbing like a fevered pulse (Phaedr. 252 D). She tastes a pleasure which is sweet beyond compare (Phaedr. 252 D).

By the use of this simile Plato endeavors to describe the erotic suffering of the philosopher's soul for the divine and to define what he means by divine madness, which he identifies with the religious experience. This experience produces pain and happiness. Pain is caused by the realization of one's imperfections, while happiness is caused when he finally attains that which he dreams of, the saturation of his soul by the holy and its emotional wrenching by a superhuman force that makes man similar to God. All these characteristics of the mystical religious experience Plato portrays symbolically with the madness, the divine eros.

The soul is redeemed through eros, because through it it tastes happiness; through it it plunges in the "ocean of the good" (Symp. 210 D). Through eros it attains the direct view of the eternal, pure, and beautiful (Symp. 211 A) which is also the Supreme Good, the Pure Truth, God Himself (Phaedr. 249 D). Thus it is freed from its pain; enjoys the decorous pleasure; and finds at last life worth living.[73]

Clement, like Plato above, affirms that the few are the chosen, the bacchoi, who are initiated in the divine mystery of virtue and knowledge; they are those inspired by God, the true philosophers. In contrast, most of the people do not enter into the sacred mysteries of philosophy. They are those who stay at the entrance . . . and, like the plain worshippers of Dionysus, carry only the external symbols of worship, like the rod from the plant narthex.[74] This difference between the many and the few in regard to philosophy Clement relates to the saying of the gospel that those invited are many but the chosen are few.

The same selectivity pertains to faith which is also the privilege of the few. This is logical since faith is the base on which knowledge is built.[75] It is not far fetched to conclude from Clement's observations that he is here also critical of the Gnostics, or some of them at least. His description of the elect as those who abandoned evil habits may be an indirect criticism of those sects of Gnostics who resorted to all sorts of immoral activities on the premise that being elect they could not be touched by evil. Clement clearly implies that the adherents of immorality, Gnostics or not, are neither elect nor gnostics in his sense of the word.[76] He rejects unreservedly the Gnostic theory that man is saved by nature. He considers this theory false from the Christian standpoint and contradictory to the Gnostics' own theories.[77] Because the true Christian gnostic believes that the world is the creation of the good God, he uses the world's goods as a means of his moral improvement. In contrast, many of the "elect" of Gnosticism believed that the world is the creation of a lower divinity, hostile to their nature. This misconception led them to two extremes. Some of these Gnostics avoided the goods of the world owing to their extreme continence, whereas others over utilized the material goods in complete disregard of morality.[78] By taking this position they felt they showed contempt for the creator god, his creatures and his laws (*Str.* 3.34.1-4). Clement's gnostic shows disregard for the material goods only when they become an impediment to his salvation. His attitude to material goods springs from his knowledge of God's commands recognizing that through this knowledge he partakes of the divine will and becomes a child of God, οι κειος, (*Str.* 7.78.4-5). The Gnostic elect stands apart of the world not through the knowledge of the commands of God and his respect for them but through his natural choice for salvation.

In a somewhat over optimistic fashion Clement believes that all the Christian wise men know that there exist many unintelligible things in the world but that the gnostic understands them whereas the non-gnostic does not. The difference is owing to God's assistance. It would have been incongruous for him who suffered for man out of love to hide anything which is conducive to man's knowledge, a statement contradictory to his criticism of the Gnostic sects (*Str.* 7.68.1). Such a statement can be justified only on the premise that Clement relied more on faith for the acquisition of that knowledge than the Gnostics who spoke of illumination (*Str.* 6.68.2; 8.5.4). He relies on his conviction that knowledge stems from the belief that Christ's revelation given to the apostles is complete, and that the apostles, versed as they were in this complete knowledge, are the first gnostics. The same is true of those who followed them and who interpret the Scriptures as authentically as the apostles.[79] The inference is again that Christ could not have concealed anything from his disciples, or they from theirs. The practical outcome of this knowledge is good works, a conclusion with which neither Plato, nor Aristotle, or other Greek philosophers would have disagreed, their emphasis on knowledge notwithstanding.[80] The accent on knowledge by Clement may be due to his effort to balance his former emphasis on faith in opposition to the Gnostic who underrated faith in comparison to knowledge. What Clement may be trying to show here is that the true Christians accepted faith as the cornerstone of their belief, without ignoring the importance of knowledge. No doubt Clement is also influenced by or reacting to Plato and Philo here. The first viewed knowledge of God as the aim and end of life without any reference to faith; the second underrated faith in relation to knowledge.[81] Philosophy in general emphasized the importance of knowledge and its beneficial effects.[82] Clement himself recognized the significance of Greek education, and would not have wished to leave the impression that he was casting aspersion on its value, because of his concern for faith. After all, the purpose for which we were created, says Clement, is to reach the knowledge of God (*Paed.* 2.14.6). The knowledge of God is in accord with the divine will and becomes "communion with immortality".[83]

KNOWLEDGE, THE FEW, AND THE MANY

The Greeks believed that knowledge and truth were the privilege of the few.[84] Clement, as we have already seen, agrees with this notion, but he proceeds to say that the knowledge of God is impossible in this life and that only the pure in heart will see God when they reach perfection. He who lives in ignorance is sinning, but he who lives in knowledge of the truth is equal to God because he is spiritualized, therefore elect (*Str.* 4.168.2). Knowledge becomes a light which when used properly by man disperses the darkness of lies and ignorance (*Protr.* 77.3). With the weapons of true knowledge the gnostic fights off the force of evil (*Str.* 2.111. 2-3). By this knowledge the gnostic begets strength which enables him to work his own salvation and that of others.[85] The knowledge of Christ, renders the gnostic close to God and makes him a partner of the divine power and nature.[86]

Once again Clement does not reject the pagan knowledge, but taking his cue from Heracleitus who said that the philosophers must be knowledgeable of many things and mindful of Protagoras for whom a logical argument should always be opposed by another logical argument, he concludes that the gnostic Christian should be well grounded in everything to answer properly and at all times.[87] Christian knowledge is thus a mixture of the Scriptures and pagan philosophy, a mixture whose aim is the realization of the will of God and one's salvation thereby. Thus, knowledge has also a practical end.[88] Knowledge and experience are associated with virtuous life since they help us distinguish between correct and false life and know the past and foresee the future as it relates to our salvation. A man's virtue demonstrates his relation to goodness and since goodness is God virtue denotes a relationship of man to God. Virtue then is the participation of man in the goodness of God. Beyond this type of virtue there is not true virtue. The autonomous virtue is false because it is alienated from its source, which is God. The pursuit of virtue has as its result the transfiguration of life, not merely a change in external behavior, "except a man be born again, he cannot see the Kingdom of God" (John 3.3). The rebirth of man requires a mode of existence wherein life is realized as communion in love and relationship. Christianity then as well as pagan education became for Clement the sources from which he drew for the formulation of his own ideas about the wise man whom he contrasted to the wise man of the philosophers (*Str.* 1.37.6). Understandably, Clement's gnostic is the perfect type of man since this gnostic conducts himself according to human reason and more particularly according to the Logos revealed to us by God. Clement also contrasts his gnostic to the ideal man of the Gnostic system. His gnostic is the knower and participant of the divine activities and qualities whose aim is the perfection and salvation of man (*Paed.* 3.101.1-2). Such perfection is accomplished by the study of the divine way of life and conduct, that is, by doing what is pleasant to God. This divine activity is the outgrowth of the knowledge of God, which is likened to the sun and light in contrast to the darkness of ignorance (*Protr.* 77. 2-3). This knowledge of God the Christian receives through the revelation of the Holy Spirit, the agent that spoke to the prophets (*Protr.* 78.1).

There is another way in which knowledge of philosophy is useful. That is because by it one can comprehend natural science which treats all phenomena in the world of sense. This knowledge constitutes the first step by which the spirit elevates itself to the knowledge of God.[89] For those who are really interested in the truth, knowledge is the purification of the soul (*Str.* 4.39.1).

He who trained himself to the summit of knowledge and the elevated height of the perfect man obviously made it his choice to live infallibly and to subject himself to constant training for the attainment of the steadfastness of knowledge (*Str.* 7.46.7). By this attainment his habit of doing good has become nature (virtue) and through the exercise of the will by the force of reason and care, virtue is incapable of being lost (*Str.* 7.47.3) Knowledge also teaches us to perceive all things that are capable of contributing to the permanence of virtue. The highest contributor is the knowledge of God. And he who knows God is holy and pious (. . . *Str.* 7.47. 2-3) and is in command of himself and what belongs to him. Since he has a firm grasp of divine science . . . he makes a genuine approach to the truth (*Str.* 7.17.1). The knowledge and apprehension of intellectual objects must be called firm scientific knowledge whose divine function is to consider the First Cause, namely God, by "Whom all things were made, and without Whom nothing was made" and to further consider what is joined and what is disjoined, and the position each object holds and what power and service each contributes.[90] He who has no knowledge of good is wicked . . . . There is only one good, the Father, and to be ignorant of the Father is death, whereas to know Him is eternal life.[91] Paraphrasing Plato, Clement points out that knowledge is the "eating" and "drinking" of the divine Word.[92]

For Clement there is a distinction between wisdom acquired through learning and the wisdom which comes from some kind of natural disposition . . . . He does not belabor the degree to which the natural disposition benefits from the learning experiences in life outside of formal education. He does not evaluate the extent of natural wisdom as against the acquired . . . . He seems to incline toward the view that the acquisition of virtues is a combination of knowledge and training which ends up in a kind of habit-forming disposition toward the good. Knowledge is not innate in men but it is acquired, that is, attained by a process which requires long training, application, and progress (*Str.* 6.78. 3). Then through incessant practice it passes into the habit of virtue. When perfected, virtue becomes infallible inasmuch as its possessor has apprehended the First Cause and what is produced by it, and is sure about them. He also knows what is good and evil and has learned from his apprehension of the truth, which is God, the most exact truth from the beginning of the world to the end (*Str.* 6.78. 4).

While Clement says that faith is indispensable and nothing is above it, elsewhere he intimates that knowledge is the highest good (*Str.* 6.109.2). Not simply the believer but the gnostic believer is the righteous man. After a circuitous argument Clement ends up admitting the interdependence of knowledge and faith. Real faith cannot exist without knowledge and knowledge without faith. On this premise, Clement concludes that the nature of the beneficent is to do good and a good person will not do evil as evil cannot result in aught virtuous. Philosophy is not the product of vice since it makes men virtuous (*Str.* 6.159.6; 1.80.5). It follows then that philosophy is the work of God, whose work is solely to do good by making men virtuous. Further proof of the beneficent character of philosophy is that its practice does not belong to the wicked but was accorded to the best of the Greeks and that it was bestowed upon them manifestly from Providence which assigns to each what is befitting in accordance with his deserts (*Str.* 6.159.8).

By a similar, somewhat circuitous argument, Clement intends to answer the question posed to the Christians by the Gnostics as to whether Adam was created perfect or imperfect. The question really shows how overriding to the Gnostics was the issue of the real creator of this universe. For if Adam was created imperfect how can he be the work of a perfect God? If perfect, how then did this perfect being transgress God's commandments? (*Str.* 6.96.1).

Clement tries to escape the dilemma by counter-proposing that Adam was not perfect in his creation, but adapted to the reception of virtue. He considers it of great importance in regard to virtue for men to be made fit for its attainment (*Str.* 6.92.2-3). Here knowledge helps since we are rational beings and philosophy is a rational study. Therefore we have some strong affinity to education by which we improve ourselves to the point of attaining the perfection Clement visualized for the gnostic person. It is true that some men are more apt to attain perfect virtue and others some kind of it, particularly since some of them apply themselves more and others less to training in virtue.[93]

Exercise in virtue leads to perfection, but this perfection, which is assumed to be the most desirable and highest thing, is not identical with God. Clement rejects the theory of the Stoics that virtue in God and man is the same.[94] Such a theory is impious because it presents man as God, thereby reducing the uniqueness of the unattainability of God's perfection. Though the gnostic may be perfect, his perfection should not be equated with the perfection of God as it is impossible for any one to become as perfect as God.[95] Human perfection is relative and is understood as a blameless living in full compliance with the gospel. Certainly one could argue that there might be a logical error on the part of Clement here since perfection is an absolute, but Clement tried his best to express in human terms the perfection of the Christian man vis-à-vis the perfection of God. The relativity of human perfection leads Clement to the discussion of still another facet of the gnostic concept of human affections.

AFFECTIONS OR PASSIONS

Clement considers the gnostic qua human as subject to human affections such as hunger and thirst, which are necessary for the maintenance of the body. Somehow Clement is trying to draw a distinction between human needs and the spiritual status of the gnostic on earth, but his views at this point get him in muddled waters and even the Church later refused to entertain the implications of his argument. Clement rejects as ludicrous the supposition that Christ's body qua flesh required the necessary aids for its maintenance. He thus concludes that Christ did not in reality need to eat, being a God, but that he ate not for the sake of the body, which was kept together by a holy energy, but in order to avoid creating the impression on those who were with Him that He was not also human. According to Clement Christ on the earth was entirely impassible . . . and impervious to feelings of pleasure and pain (*Str.* 6.71.2). In contrast, the apostles originally were subject to such human feelings, but through the Lord's teachings, a steady conditioning of their minds and unvarying exercise, they achieved that gnostic state, after Christ's resurrection, that rendered them impervious to human passion and affections (*Str.* 6.71.1-3).

Even if it should be granted that human affections such as courage, joy, desire, zeal and so on when ruled by reason are good, they are irrelevant in the case of the gnostic. For instance, the gnostic does not do what inspires fear, since he regards none of the things that occur in life as things to be dreaded. The only affection that possesses him is the love towards God, and nothing can dislodge him from that love. He does not need cheerfulness because he does not fall into pain; not that he does not feel pain, but that he knows that even pain happens for the good. Consequently, he does not allow pain to trouble him. Nor does he get angry since there is nothing to move him to anger, inasmuch as his love of God makes him feel no anger toward any of God's creatures. Nor does he envy, for nothing is wanting to him, once he has reached the gnostic stage (*Str.* 6.71.4-5). The good man then is Godlike in form and semblance as these concern his soul (*Str.* 6.72.2)

Someone may argue that the gnostic may still be subject to desires and passions by pointing out that love is a desire. Clement does not accept this type of love as desire on the part of him who loves but calls it affection. He who by virtue of love is already in the midst of that which he is destined to be, does not desire anything, inasmuch as he has, as far as possible, the very thing that is desired, love. And he who has reached the state of perfection has gained the exceptional light and has no need to revert to the "delights" of the world. Anything beyond the necessary is viewed as luxury and luxury is an excess that leads man away from the truth.[96] The gnostic has freed his soul from passions no longer making use of the body, but allowing the body only the use of necessities so that he may not give it cause for dissolution.[97] It was this love of unnecessary luxury that prevented the rich young man of the parable from winning the everlasting life, in spite of his attention to the commandments of the Law (Luk. 16. 19-23).

In essence Clement does not seem to mind the possession of luxuries he condemns, provided men did not make them the aim of their lives and ipso facto a hindrance to their perfection. For a person who has achieved excellence and is good luxury becomes incidental and valueless, or valuable only as a means to the exercise of the good. Here Clement seems to agree with the Gnostics who had argued in a similar manner on other occasions, and with Plato.[98] Clement once again here advises use not abuse of what God has bestowed on mankind, since he who has learned to rein in his passions, to train himself to impassibility, to develop the beneficence of gnostic perfection has become like God and equal to the angels.[99] The attainment of excellence is for Clement reflected in the Platonic and Stoic tetradic virtues of righteousness, temperance, manliness, Godliness. Of these virtues righteousness is square, equal on all sides and alike in word, in deed, in abstinence from evil, and in beneficence, forming gnostic perfection, nowhere and in no respect halting, so that the righteous never appear unjust and unequal.[100] The righteous are believers but not every believer is necessarily righteous.

Clement visualizes a progression to perfection according to which only he who attains perfection is righteous (*Str.* 6.102.5). The believer who merely abstains from evil conduct is not righteous unless he also attained beneficence and knowledge, and the work of righteousness, i.e. the activity of doing good in every circumstance (*Str.* 6.103.1-2). This righteousness of the gnostic does not rest on civil contracts or on the prohibitions and commandments of the Law but flows from the gnostic's spontaneous action and his love for God.[101] The ethics of the gnostic has nothing to do with good and evil whose conclusions and developments cannot be other than conventional. It precludes relativity in values which would permit objective valuations and judicial calculations. The good man's ethics measure man by revealing the image of God in the person. The good man's ethics aim at that morality that restores him to the fullness of life, transcending the limitations created by his nature. This is accomplished only if he undergoes a change in his mode of existence. To do so he must free himself from the claims of his individual nature which binds him to the impersonal survival of the species.[102] No doubt the change which is the goal of the Christian can sometimes be measured by social criteria and objective ethics, with the evaluation categories of good and virtue. But it is not identified with them. Clement does not reject these evaluative criteria but in no way does he confine them within the limits of social behavior and the conventional obligations that govern such behavior. The rightous will maintain prudence and exercise moderation in the calmness of his soul, and he will also be receptive to what is commanded, with aversion to what is base as alien to him.[103] He is decorous and supramundane and he will do everything in an orderly fashion, while he will never do what he is not allowed to do.[104] He is rich in the highest degree in desiring nothing. He has a few elementary wants, and yet he is in the midst of an abudance of all good through the knowledge of the good. The first consequence of his righteousness is to love and to associate with those of his own kind both on this earth and in heaven.[105] He is liberal of what he possesses, a philanthropist, and a hater of the wicked, entertaining a perfect aversion to all villainy. He is the true servant of God and spontaneously subjects himself to His command, pure in heart not through the commandments but through the knowledge of God. As such he is the friend of God.[106] Things which are really to be dreaded are foreign to him and what is contrary to good cannot be sheltered by him because it is impossible for contraries to meet in the same person at the same time. The gnostic acts well the drama of life which God has given him to play and knows both what is to be done and what is to be endured.[107] Day and night, doing and reciting the Lord's commands, the gnostic rejoices exceedingly not only in resisting villainy, in the morning and at noon, but also when walking about, when asleep, when dressing and undressing. He is even giving thanks to God like Job who resigned himself to God's love throughout his suffering.[108]

Like Paul, Clement makes love . . . a concept superior to righteousness . . . . Love is the most sacred and sovereign of all concepts and makes the gnostic the perfect individual that he is. Because the gnostic, by virtue of being a lover . . . of the one true God, he is the really perfect man and friend of God placed in the rank of a son. He is crowned as one judged worthy to behold the everlasting God Almighty face to face.[109] His whole life is a holy festival.[110] His soul is a holy statue similar to God. He is the truly begotten of God, the express image of the universal king and almighty Father, Who impresses on him as a gnostic the seal of perfect contemplation.[111] His function is to have converse with God through the Great and High Priest (Hebr. 4.14), up to the measure of his capacity.[112] Each person who is admitted to this state of holiness is illuminated . . . and in an indissoluble union with God.[113] He who contemplates the unseen God lives as a God among men. The soul of the gnostic, rising above the sphere of generation, is by itself apart and dwells among ideas, and like the Coryphaeus in Plato's Theaetetus becomes an angel rapt in contemplation, forever keeping in view the will of God, "Alone wise, while these flit like shadows".[114]

The attainment of perfection is possible equally for men and women, but for both Clement underscores the importance of education, application, and training, thereby clarifying that perfection is not an objective matter but a subjective one, depending on the individual's effort (*Str.* 4.118. 1; 124.1). Equally, the way to the attainment of that perfection may not be one-sided but many-sided. One thing is, however, certain: the gnostic, though stretched on the rack, his eyes gouged and brutally tormented, or submitted to what is most terrible of all, death, will remain happy. The gnostic will never have the ultimate end placed in this world and he will never be wrenched from his freedom and his signal love of God.[115]

From this very brief exposition of Clement's idea of Christian perfection some important generalizations can be gathered. To begin with, the common and unquenched thirst of the Christian man is for his salvation, not for conventional improvements of one's character and conduct. For this reason, the basic moral problem for man is the realization of the freedom of ethos far from any conventional evaluation or utilitarian prearrangements.[116] In Clement's works ethos is associated with the description of the essence of truth about man. We start that is, with the ontological question, What is Being? What does it mean to be a man and what is the relationship of the biological being to itself? The creation of man as an image of God is to be located in this unity of ethos and being.

Man is created afterm then image of God and this image is identical in nature to God's, though many-sided in the particular persons (*Protr.* 120.3-5). Man's being symbolizes God's presence which makes man participant in true being. Man is the image of God not because he has common physical characteristics with him, but because he has the capacity to be free from space and physical necessities since, though a human being subjec to limitations, as a personal being he is capable of superseding his physical

limitations. In other words, man is created to become a communicant of the qualities of God, especially God's love which is the real life.

Though fallen once from God's grace man does not cease to be a creature of God. His nature is created with a natural individuality that is mortal and perishable. But on this created and mortal nature God impressed His image and His likeness (Gen. 2.7), opening the possibility of real life. The "image and "likeness" of man are directly connected to the knowledge of God by the constant effort of man to convert the assertion "in the image of God" to the "likeness of God".[117] Clement's idea about the "image" and "likeness" may be following the biblical model but is also affected by Clement's other favorite source, Greek philosophy. He uses the statement of the Pythagorean Eurysus contained in his treatise *About Fate* where God used Himself as model for the creation of man.[118] In other places he borrows several expressions by the Greeks which to him allude to the idea of "in the image and likeness" of God (*Str.* 4.171.3-4). He sees no contradiction in so doing since the Greeks "copied" these ideas from the Bible, according to a misconception popular at his time among Christian writers.[119] Elsewhere he identifies "in the image and likeness" with mind . . . as Pythagoras, Plato and Aristotle did when they considered nous as coming from God.[120] Clement adds to the philosophical interpretations the notion that the Holy Spirit acts on the nous by bestowing its gift . . . to guide man's spiritual qualities toward his perfection, since the perfection of man consists in the activation of the potential powers in man through self-knowledge, a process by which God also becomes known. The gnostic arrives by the unalterable custom of good-doing to the "likeness" of God inasmuch as good-doing is a facet of man's likeness to God.[121] The good cannot be looked on as an idea because it must be a reality, since only as a reality can it be connected with human life. If it were only an idea it could not have been associated with the reality of life. If it is a reality, then it can be connected with man's life and be defined accordingly. Good must be sought both within the world and within man, for if it existed only in the world and was not attainable by man, it would not have been a true and real good. According to Clement's teaching then the good is not an idea but a personal present; it is God himself. Clement, who used the Old Testament text of the Septuagint, explain that the "in the image" description denotes the spirit in which God created man while "in the likeness" denotes man's dynamic potential. When man who was created "in the image" of God becomes a consummate human being he approaches the likeness of God. Behind both these pictures, the "image" and "likeness," are for Clement a mystery, similar to the incarnation of God.[122] Consequently, the biological individuality of every person does not exhaust his being. What makes a person a true being is man's privilege in the freedom of choice and in his personal distinctiveness which is realized and revealed in the act of his communion and relationship with God and his fellow-men. Unlike the animals that are subject to the activity of nature, man is the dynamic revelation of the image of

God, and a being of personal uniqueness with the potential of being free from all prearranged limitations on his spiritual side. Through his free will man can accept or reject the purpose of his being; he can refuse the freedom of love and personal communion and reject God's invitation and by so doing, he can exclude himself from real life, that is, his union with God. By saying yes to God he can exercise that privilege to become almost equal to God. But by saying no to God he can lose his privileged status as distinctive person, by which is meant something that has its face (sight) turned towards something other than itself, namely God.[123]

Person . . . represents a way of life which presupposes natural existence but is also distinct from the way of other persons, though not in its basic spiritual potential. The elements of the image of God are the spiritual elements of man: his reason and his freedom. His reason and freedom provide man with the possibility of superseding his nature and becoming equal to God (Gen. 3.5). Man partakes of true being to the extent that he controls the autonomy of his nature. He partakes in the true life to the degree that he supersedes his natural limitations and his mortality. From the moment he rejects God's invitation and seeks to assert his independence by separating himself from God, he jeopardizes his true being and alienates himself from his destiny in life. The physical necessities of his individual nature become his real purpose in life; they master him and end up as "passions" and causes of pain and ultimate death instead of useful tools towards his final end of theosis. It is unfortunate that we, after the fashion of the prodigal son in the gospel, abuse God's gifts.[124] We should use them as their masters without undue attachment. We are enjoined to rule over them and not to be slaves to them. We should raise our eyes aloft to what is true and fill ourselves with the divine food, thereby enjoying that certain and lasting and pure pleasure. This way of partaking of food manifests the love for Christ. Conversely, those who live fattening themselves like beasts feed themselves irrationally to spiritual death, looking downwards towards the earth and bending continuously over tables, in pursuit of a life of gluttony. They bury in the earth what is good in order to pursue a life without future, courting voracity alone.[125]

Clement's concern should not be taken to mean that he ever wanted to remove man's social intercourse; only that he simply regarded with suspicion the slippery customs of man which he considered a potential for spiritual calamity. Man should partake of the necessities and avoid daintiness.[126] The natural needs for survival should not compete with that personal freedom and distinctiveness of man which can only be realized as love beyond any natural necessity. Freedom of the individual is never lifted; it only changes to antithetical rivalry with nature. It becomes a tragic division of the human being (Rom. 7.23). That is the reason Clement insists on the interpretation of sin as failure, the missing of the real target of life which is for human beings the supersession of their nature and the attainment of personal freedom and individual uniqueness.

Failure of the individual to realize his essential aim is tantamount to failing to maintain the uniqueness of his existence through love. Thus the moral dilemma which stems from Clement's interpretation of sin as failure or missing the mark is not the conventional idea of good and evil, of merit or social conventions. It is that and more; it is the dilemma between life and death, between purity or existential indigence and corruption.[127] Thus Clement's morality goes beyond good and evil; it refers to ontological realities not to meritorious conventions.

After the fall of man his personal uniqueness and his freedom could not have superseded the physical necessity of his biological autonomy. But with the incarnation of God, the natural distance between man and God, created after man's fall, was removed. The union of the human with the divine nature in the person of the Second Adam freed human nature from its imprisonment within the limits of its individuality.[128] What this Second Adam made now possible was the possibility for man to participate in the "new" way of life, in the new ethos, enabling man to resist his instincts and impulses and to live loving and being loved.

In the first Adam the natural desire for subsistence became the driving force which condemned his race to alienation and concern with the survival of mortal individuality. With the coming of Christ this process is reversed: the divine and human natures are brought together in Christ, the second Adam. This bringing together of the two natures frees humanity from its self-imposed bondage within the limits of mortal individuality. Now human nature subsists as a personal hypostasis of communion with the divine. The second Adam became responsible for a new creation and a new humanity which exists in communion with God. He became the visible archetype of the Christian gnostic to whom he now gave a concrete example for his eyes to follow.

What this regeneration of man through the Second Adam requires is the cooperation of man's freedom, the supersession of his natural limitations, his ascent to God's love, his becoming a person. What God asks of man is an effort, however small, to reject his individual weaknesses, to resist his deleterious impulses and to will to live as a loving being and a loved one. He asks him to empty himself. . . of every element of individual autonomy for the sake of a life of love and communion with his fellow man and God. Man's compliance with this ethos defines his practical piety. This practical piety is the effort that assures the freedom and the volition of man to deny the rebellion of the individual will, and to imitate the obedience of the Second Adam. This obedience consists not in subjection to any conventions of a legal order but in faithfulness to the image and likeness of God.

Compliance with this ethos aims at the regeneration of one's whole life, not simply at the change of one's external conduct (*Str.* 1.26.1-4). The external forms, the objectified criteria of individual virtue, are not identified with the truth of salvation. On the contrary, it is possible that they mislead man inasmuch as they distance him from salvation because they tend to bewitch him to the glory and praise of men. The change of the Christian may sometimes be measured by the criteria of the objectified social morality, with the evaluative categories of good and evil. But they are not identical with them and are essentially different. The individual virtue does not always imply a true change that can lead to salvation. If man is to imitate God's picture he cannot remain within the bounds of the socially good conduct and conventional obligations. He must supersede them. It is to such a superssion that Clement points the way in his scattered exhortations throughout his work. All the evangelical admonitions have as their goal love, that potent element that overcomes human egocentrism and individuality for the sake of the realization of the image of God. The attainment of this love is the true fulfillment of the Law, making the aims of the Law become reality provided that this reality is not to be interpreted as an altruistic end. It does not aim simply at the improvement of social conduct but at that union whose end is God (*Str.* 4.52.1-2). In this sense, love is not an easy beginning, but the uninterruptedly searched for end, the "never fulfilled perfection" or satisfaction of the moral journey of man. The beginning is the realization of man's inadequacy and hence his search for the grace of God, which will convert man's isolated life to one of communion and relationship.

This type of relationship and union was expressed by those Christians whose biological relations were often superseded by devotion to Christ in the transfer to the Church of the terms that belonged to the family relationship. For the new ecclesiastical order "father" was not necessarily the natural person but the Father in heaven, while brothers were the members of the Church. Equally, a Christian's mother was not only the person that gave him natural birth but the spiritual institution that gave him a new birth and made him member of a new complex of relations that superseded all exclusivity.[129] He wanted to be a friend and son of Christ and aspired to become worthy and be called brother of the Lord. The early Christians' removal of the distinction between male and female is a fact that refers to the eschatological fullness of existence. This eschatological fullness abolishes the separation between men and women because this differentiation is a natural not a spiritual one. It is a necessity of nature that secures its survival. It has no place in the kingdom of God. The distinction into sexes does not reflect an ontological distinction, nor does it refer to the manner of existence or to the image God impressed upon man. For this reason it is removed at the end of life.[130] No wonder Clement, like Paul, exhorted the man to treat his wife as a sister and not as sexual object.

Notes

1. Walter Gutbrod, *Das Gesetz im Alten Testament* in the *Theologisches Wörterbuch zum Neuen Testament*, G. Kittel, ed., vol. 4, p. 1029 ff.; also Walter Eichrodt, *Theologie des Alten Testaments,* part I (Berlin, 1948) 31 ff.; Str. 7, 14.3; Chr. Giannaras, *The Freedom of Morality* (Athens, 1982) 72. This is the new title of

the translation of this book which came to my attention belatedly. Hereafter I will refer to it with this title.

2. QDS 9. 1-2; Str. 4.29.3; Rom. 7.12; 10.4; 8.14-17; Gal.3.24.

3. QDS 10.3; 12.1; Mark, 19.21; Mark, 10.21; Stählin points to the similarity between Str. 7. 6.3 and Hebr. 6.18. See also Str.3.83. 1-5; Völker, *Der Wahre Gnostiker,* 254-56. Plato seems to think that *nomos* is not the source from which one should expect salvation. He may well conceive of a political order in which positive laws are of but small importance. In fact they may even be outright detrimental. In the Republic the value of laws as stabilizing element in the proposed state is decidedly inferior to that of education, 4.425.A-C. Even in the Laws itself there are passages, as in book nine where it is said that if true knowledge and reason are present laws may be dispensed with, since written laws with their rigid and dogmatic regulations have inevitable shortcomings. In the Statesman the same view is developed at greater length. Polit. 293 E ff.; and Laws 9.875 C-D; 6.769 D with Shorey's note, Paul Shorey, *What Plato Said* (University. of Chicago, 1933) 635. For Plato laws are but poor imitation of the right type of law and the origin or status of the right law must never be confused with that of imitations. True law is the manifestation of the perfected individual who has achieved the Platonic justice, Friedrich Solmsen, *Plato's Theology* (Cornell University Press, 1942) 163-64.

4. Paed. 1.25. 3 and SC ad loc. n. 2.

5. Paed. 1.26.1 . . . . see also Introduction to *Paedagogos,* in SC, p. 81. . .

6. Ps. 82.6; Paed. 1.26.1; SC Introduction to Paed. pp. 39-41 and ad loc. p. 158, n. 4; Ps 72.6.

7. Paed. 1.26.2; SC ad loc. n.5; Rom. 6.23.

8. Paed. 1.26. 2; SC ad loc. n. 7 ff.; Rom. 6.23; I Cor. 4.4; Tit. 3.5; James. 1.17.

9. Str. 1.34.4; Str. 4.8.5; SC ad loc., n. 1; Paed. 1.26. 3-27. 1; Plat. Gorg. 478 C-D.

10. Paed. 1.26.2; 29.2

11. M. Farantos, *Peri Dikaiosynês, Systematic Ereuna eis to Ergon Klementos Alexandreôs* (Athens, 1971) 163-64.

12. Str. 6. 61.1-2; Gal. 5.19.23.

13. Str. 6.68.1; I. Cor. 2.6

14. Str. 6.68.2-3; 69.2; SVF 3. 462.

15. Str. 6.137.1; 2.50.1-2; Philo, *De Mutat. Nom.* 111; W. Jaeger, *Paideia* (Oxford, Univ. Press, 1965) 286-331.

16. Protr. 67.2; 7; 84.2; Str. 6.148. 1-2; 5.100. 4; SVF 2.1134.

17. To support his view he refers to Greek philosophy in several places, Str. 1.98.4; Plat. Phaedr. 246 C-D.

18. Protr. 79.1-2; Str. 2.6.1.

19. Protr. 79.3; Str. 2.6.1; I Cor. 13.2 . . . .

20. Plat. Rep. 410 C; 591 D.

21. Str. 3.59.4; 62.1; 65.2.

22. Str. 3.17.1-18.5; Plat. Phaedr. 64 A; 69.C;.

23. Str. 4. 164.2-4; SVF 3. 122; Diog. Laert. 7. 104-5.

24. Ecl. Proph. 23.2-3; Str. 7.61.1-2; SC ad loc. ns. 1 and 2; Str. 8.23.2; 7.53.3; SC ad loc. n.3; Ps. 93.11.

25. Philo De Som. 1.62-65; Str. 2.5.3; 5.73.3; Comm ad loc.; Plat. Phaedr. 509 D; 517 B.

26. Str. 6.137. 5-138.4; Eus. PE 13.12-13; Paed. 2.25.3; Plat. Theaet. 155 D;

27. Aristl. Met. I 2 (892b); Plat. Rep. 511 C-E.

28. Paed. 3.1.1; 2.1.2; I John 3.2;

29. Paed. 3.98.1; I John 2.2; Str. 6.2.4.

30. Str. 7. 20.7-8; SC ad loc. ns 2-4; Plat. Rep. 10.617 E; 620 E-621 A; 2.75.2.

31. Str. 4.27.3; 7.79.7.

32. Hans Jonas, *The Gnostic Religion* (Boston, 1963) 280; Philo, Mut. Non.54; Matt. 10.39.

33. Paed. 2.1.2-3; Str. 4.18.1-2; 32.1-2.

34. Str. 5.49.1; Protr. 80.1; Str.1.93.3-4; SC ad loc.; Plat. Rep. 7. 534 B-C.

35. Str. 2.18.1; SC ad loc. ns.2-4; Str. 2.9.4; 6.61.1; Plat. Euthyd. 291 D; Polit. 259 A-B.

36. J. M. Robinson, *The Nag Hammadi Library,* 3rd ed., (San Francisco, 1990) 126-34.

37. Str. 6.54. 1; Str. 1.24. ff.; 177. 1; Str. 2.9.4; 6.61.1; Paed. 2.25.3.

38. Str. 7. 104.1-2; SC ad loc. ns.1-2; II Tim. 2.15; I. Cor. 4.19

39. Athenagoras, *On the Resurrection of the Dead,* 1. Irenaeus fr. 5, PG 7, 1232B. This distinction between substance and activity is thereafter well made among the Fathers of the Eastern Church, most probably because of the Christological controversies that followed the second century A.D.

40. QDS 28-29.6.

41. Str. 4.113.4; 5.13.2; Völker, *Der Wahre Gnostiker,* 489, n. 1.

42. Str. 1.20.1; 6.67.1; 7.12.4-5. That philosophy is a gift of God to the Greeks as preparation to higher knowledge is a new idea in Christian theology, Stählin, *Einleitung* 558-59.

43. Str. 6.80.5; Farantos, *Peri Dykaiosynés,* 30.

44. Lilla Salvatore, *Clement of Alexandreia, A Study in Christian Platonism and Gnosticism* (Oxford Univ. Press) 57

45. Str. 7.71.3; SC ad loc. n.2; Plat. Phaed. 67 D. Clement uses here Plato's reference and gives it a Christian twist.

46. Str. 7.78.6; SC ad loc. n. 1;I Thess. 4.17.

47. Str. 3.44.2; Ferguson *Stromateis* ad. loc.

48. Str. 3.44. 3; Aristl. Nic. Eth. 1.4. 1096 b.

49. Str. 1.44.2. Clement here clearly alludes to the celebrated passage of Plat. Gorg. 465 C . . . .

50. Str. 1.44.4; Matt. 4.4.

51. Str. 7.65.1-3. SC ad loc. ns 5-6; SVF 3.117; Plat. Lach. 198 B-199 D; Prot. 359 D - 360 E; Clement follows here Plat. Menex. 247 E; Rep. 436 B.

52. Str. 7.65.6; SC ad loc n. 5; CAF Adesp. 245; Plat. Prot. 360 C; . . . Plat. Lach. 197 A-B.

53. Str. 7.66.4; SC ad loc. n.5; Plat. 68 D. Since even those who endure punishment for the sake of delight and reward may be blessed after death, a concession on the part of Clement to the idea that Christians should not do things for the sake of reward. Gnostics live for the love of God, not for the expectation of rewards. Love is to be chosen for itself not for anything else, Str. 7.67.1; SC ad loc. ns 4-7; Plat. Phaed. 68 D.

54. Protr. 61.4; Paed. 1.101.2; SVF 3.293 which relates to 262; SVF 2.36 and note; Plat. Rep. 4.444 D-E; Phaed. 279 B-C; Phil. 52. B. Virtue for Plato is not the impeccable conduct of citizen in his private or public life nor the avoidance of extremes in the Aristotelian meaning. The essence of virtue goes deeper. In Plato's view important is man's beauty and power of soul (Rep. 4.444 D-E) and likeness to God. These must be the primary targets of the good man's efforts and of the responsible political leader. All other values are judged from their contribution to the moral betterment of man (Phaedr. 279 B-C). Only the salvation of the soul, the providential preservation of that treasure which lies hidden inside man, must be the aim of life. In this resides the true happiness and pleasure which only the few, the eclectic are in a position to taste (Phil. 52.B).

55. Str. 6.96.3; Plat. Phaed. 69 C; F. J. Winter, *Die Ethic des Clements von Alexandrien* (Leipzig, 1882) 127.

56. Str. 4.124. 2-3; 6.157.4.

57. Paed. 2. 121. 2-3; Str. 5.95.4. Clement seems to respond here to the Hellenic idea that the good person should also be looking good in his outside from, i. e. fortunate in life.

58. E. F. Osborn, *The Philosophy of Clement of Alexandreia* (Cambridge, 1957) 93-94.

59. Plat. Meno 77 B; Prot. 352 C; Gorg. 440 B.

60. Plat. Prot. 345 E; Laws 5.731 C; 9.860 D.

61. Plat. Apol. 41 C-D; Phaed. 62 D.

62. Eduard Meyer, *Geschichte des Altertums,* vol. 4 (Berlin, 1901) 453.

63. Apol. 40 B; Phaedr. 242 B-C; Theaet. 151 A.

64. Crito 44 A-C; Phaed. 60 C.

65. K. Joel, *Geschichte der antiquen Philosophy* (Tübingen, 1921) 817.

66. Plat. Rep. 6. 491 C; 7. 519 B; 9.591 D.

67. Phaed. 80 C - 81 A; 67 E; Rep. 6. 488 B; 492 E.

68. Tim. 90 A; Rep. 6.490 B; 10.611 E; Laws 10.899 D.

69. Phaed. 82. B-C; Rep. 2.383 C; 6. 498 E; 10.613 B; Theaet. 176 B; Tim. 41 C; 69 A-C; 71 D-E; 90 C.

70. Theaet. 173 E . . . *Pindari Carmina*, OCT, fr. 302a; Rep. 1.500. B-C; Soph. 216 C.

71. Phaed. 85 D; Rep. 7. 517 D; Tim. 28 C.

72. Phaedr. 244 A-D; 245 B; 256 B.

73. Symp. 211 D; Phaedr. 249 C; 245 B-C; R. Lagersborg, *Die Platonische Liebe* (Leipzig, 1926) 115 for the mystical, religious significance in Plato.

74. Str. 1.92.3-4; Plat. Phaed. 69.C-D; Str.5.17.4-5.

75. Str. 6.126.2; 7.57.2-4; SC ad loc ns. 8 and 1-7; Matt. 5.8; I Cor. 13.12; I Thess. 4.17.

76. Jonas, *Gnostic Religion*, 270; K. Rudolf, *Gnosis, The Nature and History of Gnosticism* (New York, 1987) 249-50.

77. Str. 2.113. 1-114.6;2.115.1-2; Str. 7.40.1; SC ad loc. ns. 5-6 and 1-2.

78. Str. 3.8.1-2; 9.2-3; 12.1-3; 54.1; 45.1-2; 7.78.1-3; SC ad loc. ns. 1-3.

79. Str. 4.75.1-4; Str. 7.52.1-2; SC ad loc. ns. 3-6.

80. Str. 6.99.5; QDS 19.3-5; Plat. Rep. 2. 362 E; Gorg. 500 D; 501 A; Aristl. Met. 983b 12-28.

81. Str. 1.100.3-4; Plat. Phaedr. 266 B; Theaet. 176 B; Philo De Vit. Mos. 7.22.

82. Str. 6.99.1-3; Paed. 2.15.4; Plat. Soph.230 E.

83. Str. 4.27.3; John 17.3.

84. Str. 5.7.6; 5.17.4-6; Plat. Rep. 6. 494 D; Epim. 973C; Phaed. 69 C.

85. Str. 2.122.1; 3.42.6-43.1.

86. Str. 7.44.5; SC ad loc. ns 5 and 1; Str. 2.96.4-97.2; R. Casey, *The Excerpta ex Theodoto of Clement of Alexandria* (Clement, 1934) 10 on exc. 17.3-4.

87. Str. 7.46.9 - 47.1; SC ad loc. ns. 4-5; Plat. Rep. 2, 361 C-D; Phil. 64.C; Apol. 30 C-D; Epict. *Enchir.* 53; Disc. 2.23. 42.

88. Str. 2.97; 4.147.1; 7.86.1-6; SC ad loc. ns.2-8; I Cor. 6.9; Gal. 3.24; I Cor. 6. 11; Matt. 5.45.

89. Str. 7.17.1-3; SC ad loc ns 6-8 and 1-3; John 1.3; Origen, *Contr. Celsus* 6.71; Prot. 66.3 with note in SC; Str. 1.51.1-52.3; 5.14.1-8; SVF 2.1039.

90. Str. 7. 17.2; SC ad loc. ns. 7-8.

91. Str. 5. 63.8; Rom. 1.11. Perhaps there is an anti-Gnostic thrust in this passage, see Comm. to Clement's reference above.

92. Str. 1.43.1-4; 5.66.2-4 (βρωμα δεη εποπτικη Φεωρια); Plat. Letter 7. 341 C 6-D 2; Rep.II, 378 A 5-6. Plato speaks of the searcher for God as the great and invaluable victim. Similarly Paul says that in our Pascha Christ sacrificed Himself for us, thus becoming the invaluable victim, I Cor. 5-6; John 17.19. See also SC comm. ad 5.66.2 ff.

93. Str. 6.96.3; 2.5.1-4; Plut. Mor. 2; Aristl. *De part. anim.* 1.1. 13, 642 a 27; Met. 5.1.8 (1025b 17).

94. Str. 7.88.5; SC ad loc. n.3; SVF 3. 250; 2.135.3; 6.114.4-5.

95. Elsewhere Paed. 3.1.5 Clement comes closer to stating that man becomes God, but again he qualifies it by adding only because God so wills it, Diognetus, 10.4; SC ad Paed. 3.1.5 . . . .

96. Str. 6.75.1-2; I Tim. 6.16; Paed. 2.102.2.

97. Str. 6.75.3; 7.17.4; SC ad loc. n. 4; Plat. Rep. 3. 413 B.

98. Paed. 2.120.4; SC ad loc; reminds us of Plat. Phaedr. 279 C; Laws 5. 739 C cited in Protr. 122. 2; CAF 3. p. 486 no. 412; Epict. 3. 1.6. The community of goods is a Stoic idea.

99. Str. 6.105.1; I. Bywater, *The Journal of Philology* 4 (1872) 210 . . . .

100. Str. 6.102. 4; SC ad loc.; Plat. Prot. 339 B; 344 A; Aristl. Nic. Eth. 1.10 (1100b 21);

101. Str. 6.125.5-6 . . . .

102. Giannaras, *The Freedom*, 37.

103. Str. 7.18.2; Plat. Crat. 411 E; Aristl. Nic. Eth. 6.5 (1140b 11 ff.).

104. Str. 7.18.2; SC ad loc. ns. 2-5; Paed. 2.39.4 with SC note . . . .

105. Str. 7.18.3; SC ad loc. n.6; Andronicus, *Peri Pathon*, Part II, Karl Schuchhardt (ed.), (Heidelberg, 1883) 25 ff.

106. Str. 4.39.5; Matt. 5.8; James 2. 23

107. Str. 7.16.5; SC ad loc. ns.5-6; Plat. Rep. 4. 436 B; TGF *Adesp.* 117; Epict. *Enchir.* 17; Diog. Laert. 7.160; Suet. Octav. 99; Seneca, Epistl. 77.20; Plat. Phil. 50 B; Marc. Aur. 12.36; p. 167. 6.

108. Str. 7.80.3-4; SC ad loc. ns 2-4; 7.36.2-37; SC ad loc.ns. 2-7 and 1-5; 1-4; Plat. Theaet. 173 D; Plat. Phaed. 84 B; The passage is reminiscent of Epict. 8.12 by whom no doubt, Clement is here strongly influenced, Str. 7.78.5-6. SC ad loc. ns. 5 and 1.

109. Str. 1.94.6; 6.102.2; 7.57.1; SC ad loc. n.8; Plat. Phaed. 84 B; Paed. 1.58.1; Str. 7.68.4; SC ad loc. ns. 5-6; 6.108.1; Str. 2.88.2; 7.57.1; SC ad loc. ns. 8 and 1-3; Plat. Phaed. 84 B; Matt. 5.8; I. Cor. 13.12 He does everything by means of which he shall be able to acquire the knowledge of what he desires, Str. 7.60. 2-61.1-6; SC ad loc. 3-6; 1-8; 1-2; 1.65.5.

110. Str. 7.35.6; SC ad loc. ns. 7 and 1; 7. 48.3; SC ad loc. n.2; Plat. Phaedr. 247 A; Matt. 6.7; 9-13

111. Str. 7.16.6; SC ad loc. ns. 1-5; Kannicht, Bruno, Snell (eds.), TGF, vol. 2 (Göttingen, 1981) fr 117.

112. Str. 7.13.2; SC ad loc. ns. 7 and 1; Plat. Rep. 10. 613 B.

113. Str. 7.14.1; SC ad loc. n.6; 7.103.1; SC ad loc. n.6; II Cor. 10.5; Matt. 16.25; Eph. 4. 22-24. Clement recognizes that the Greek intellectuals preceded the Christians in deifying the "gnostic" life, without the knowledge Christ Whom they could not have known, Str. 5.68.4 and Comm in SC; 5.69.6; Isocr. Paneg. 30-32; CAF 3. p.490; D. L. Page, *Hellenistic Epigrams*, vol. 2 (Cambr. Univ. Press, 1968) 157. Plato rightly comments (Str. 4.155. 3) that he who devotes himself to the contemplation of ideas will live as a God among men. He further says that he who contemplates the unseen God lives as a God among men. Stählin believes that there are at least three such references to Plato in the Sophist, but fails to give the exact references. One certainly is in the beginning, 216 A-C. See also Phaedr. 247 C; Rep. 6. 509 D; 7.517 B; Str. 5.73.3 and Comm. in SC.

114. Str. 4.155.4; Plat. Theaet. 173 C; Aristl. De Anim. 429a 27; Od. 10. 495

115. Str. 7.61.5; SC ad loc. ns 6-8; 4.32.1-2; Str. 5.108.2-4; SC ad loc. in comm.; Plat. Rep. 2. 361 E;

116. Str. 4.35.1-2; Plat. Phaed. 114 B-C; P. Chantraine, *Dictionnaire Etymologique de la lange Grecque,* vol. 3 (Paris, 1974) 942; H. Frisk, *Griechisches Etymologisches Wörterbuch* (Heidelberg, 1960) 602.

117. Gen. 1.26; Protr. 120.3-5; Str. 2.131.2-6-132.2; 7.86.5; SC ad loc. n.4; I Cor. 6.11; Matt. 5.45; 7.101.4-5; SC ad loc. ns. 2-5; Str. 2.134.2; 2.97.1-98.3; 7.13.3; SC ad loc. ns. 2-4.

118. Mullach, FPG 2, P.112; Str. 5.29.1; SC ad loc. comm.

119. Str. 5.29.3 SC ad loc. comm.; H. Chadwick, *Early Christian Thought* (New York, 1962) 44 something that Celsus reverses, see Lilla, *Clement of Alex.* 30-40.

120. Str. 4.139.4; Plat. Theaet. 176 B; Str. 2. 136.6; Protr. 98.4; Str.6.72.2.

121. Str. 6.166.1-4; I Cor. 2.10-14; Paed. 98.2; Plat. Laws 777 B.

122. Str. 6.65.6; 7.13.3; SC ad loc. ns. 1-2; Paed. 3.1.1; Str. 6.60.3; Plat. Meno 97 ff.; Phaedr. 266 B; Od. 5.193; SVF 3. 264; Paed. 2.83.2-3; Str. 7.52.3; Str. 6. 72.1-2; Aristl. Met. 1072b 24-30; Politics 1325b 1721 where theory is more praxis than any other activity. Protr. 120.3-4; Paed. 1.4.2; Col. 1.15; II Cor. 4.4.

123. Protr. 3.1-4; Str. 6.48.3; Deut. 30.15-19; Str. 7.56.2; SC ad loc. n.2; 57.1; SC ns. 8 and 1-3; I. Thess. 4.17; Protr. 120.1.

124. Paed. 2.9.2-4; SC ad loc. n.4; Luk. 15.11; Ps. Justin, *Léttre*, 12; Plat. Rep. 9.586 A.

125. Paed. 2.9.4. Some expressions are probably borrowed from Musonius 18 A, p. p.97. 5 H; 18 B, p. 104.1-2.

126. Paed. 2.9.3; SC ad loc.; Ps. Justin, *Léttre* 13; Aesch. Eum. 285.

127. Str. 4.27. 3; SVF 3.221; Plat. Rep. 8.521 C.

128. Str. 2.98.2-3 and SC ad loc. n.1, an extremely important note explaining the unique significance of the idea of freedom among the Greek Fathers of the Early Church; Irenaeus, Ad Haer. 4.27.1.4. Also Paed. 1.31.1-2; P. Th. Camelot, *Foi et Gnose* (Paris, 1945) 30; Theod. Extr. 45, 1-3.

129. Str. 2.100.1-3. This idea comes from Philo, *De Nobil.* 3-4

130. John Zezioulas, *Apo to Prosôpeion eis to Prosôpon* (Thessalonike, 1977) 315-16; Giannaras, *The Freedom,* 62, n.7.

ABBREVIATIONS

BEP: *Bibliothêkê Hellênôn Paterôn,* Constantine Bonis (ed.) (Athens, no date).

BKV: *Bibliothek der Kirchenväter,* O. Bardenhwer, T. Schermann, C. Weyman, Kempten, (eds.) (München 1911—)

CSEL: *Corpus Scriptorum Ecclesiasticorum Latinorum* (Vienna, 1866-)

CAF: *Comicorum Atticorum Fragmenta,* Theodore Koch, 3 vols. (Leipzing, 1883).

Diels: *Die Fragmente der vorsokratiker,* Diels H. and Kranz (Weidmann, 1974).

FHG: *Fragmenta Historicorum Graecorum,* Müller, Karl (ed.) 4 vols. (Paris, 1851).

FPhGr: *Fragmenta Philosophorum Graecorum,* Mullach, F.G.A. (ed.), (Paris, 1881).

GCS: Die *greichischen Christlichen Schrifsteller der estern Jahrhunderte* (Berlin, 1897—).

Die Fragmente zur Dialektik der Stoiker, Husler, Karlheinz, 4 vols. (Stuttgart, 1987).

HSCP: *Harvard Studies in Classical Philology*

JHS: *Journal of Hellenic Studies.*

Long and Sedley: A.A. Long and D.N. Sedley, *The Hellenistic Philosophers* (Cambridge Univ. Press, 1987) 2 vols.

SC: *Sources Chrétiennes* (Paris, 1942 —).

Stählin, O., *Die griechischen christlichen Schriftsteller der esten drei Jahrhunderte,* vols, 12, 52 (15), 17, 39 (Leipzig, 1905-60), referred to also in abbreviated form as GCS.

Stählin, O., *Des Clements von Alexandreia ausgewehlte Schriften aus den griechischen übersetzt* (Münich, 1934).

SVF: *Stoicorum Veterum Fragmenta,* repr. of the Teubner ed. In Dubuque, Iowa, no year.

TGF: *Tragicorum Graecorum Fragmenta,* Nauck, Augustus (ed.) (Hildesheim, 1964).

TGF: *Tragicorum Graecorum Fragmenta,* Richard Kannich, Stefan Radt, Bruno, Snell (eds.) (Göttingen, 1981) . . . .

TWNT: *Theologisches Wörterbuch zum Neuen Testament*

ZNTW: *Zeitschrift für die neutestamentliche Wissenschaft und die Kunde der älteren Kirche.*

FURTHER READING

Criticism

Buckley, Jorunn Jabobsen. "Females, Males, and Angels in Clement of Alexandria's *Excerpta ex Theodoto.*" In *Female Fault and Fulfilment in Gnosticism,* pp. 61–83. Chapel Hill: The University of North Carolina Press, 1986.

    Analysis of Clement's use of the terms "female," "male," and "angel."

Buell, Denise Kimber. "Producing Descent/Dissent: Clement of Alexandria's Use of Filial Metaphors as IntraChristian Polemic." *Harvard Theological Review* 90, No. 1 (January 1997): 89-104.

    Study of Clement's use of procreative and kinship imagery to legitimatize certain Christians as heirs.

Bywater, I. "Critical Notes on Clement of Alexandria." *The Journal of Philology* IV (1872): 203-18.

    Corrections to and explanations for many textual errors perpetrated upon Clement's manuscripts.

Casey, R. P. "Clement and the Two Divine Logoi." *The Journal of Theological Studies* XXV (1924): 43-56.

    Analysis of the distinctions Clement made regarding the nature of the Logos.

Chadwick, Henry. "The Liberal Puritan." In *Early Christian Thought and the Classical Tradition: Studies in Justin, Clement, and Origen,* pp. 31–65. Oxford: Clarendon Press, 1966.

    Examination of Clement's philosophies.

Clark, Elizabeth A. *Clement's Use of Aristotle: The Aristotelian Contribution to Clement of Alexandria's Refutation of Gnosticism..* Lewiston, N.Y.: E. Mellen Press, 1977, 182p.

    Study of the role Aristotelian elements in Clement's polemic against Gnosticism.

Floyd, W. E. G. *Clement of Alexandria's Treatment of the Problem of Evil.* London: Oxford University Press, 1971, 107p.

    Investigation of Clement's theodicy and how he fundamentally altered Christian study of the nature of evil.

Lilla, Salvatore R. C. *Clement of Alexandria: A Study in Christian Platonism and Gnosticism.* London: Oxford University Press, 1971, 266p.

    Examination of how Clement attempted to reconcile and synthesize Christianity and Hellenism.

Maier, Harry O. "Clement of Alexandria and the Care of the Self." *Journal of the American Academy of Religion* LXII, No. 3 (Fall 1994): 719-45.

    Analysis of Clement's notions concerning the care of the self as an example of how his philosophy both overlapped with and modified pagan ideas.

Murphy, Mable Gant. *Nature Allusions in the Works of Clement of Alexandria.* Washington, D.C.: The Catholic University of America Press, 1941, 124p.

    Classification and assessment of allusions to nature found in Clement's works.

Osborn, E. F. *The Philosophy of Clement of Alexandria.* Cambridge: University Press, 1957, 206p.

    Analysis of Clement's understanding of simple and complex unities concerning God, Goodness, and Truth.

Parker, Charles Pomeroy. "Musonius in Clement." *Harvard Studies in Classical Philology* XII (1901): 191-200.

    Consideration of the problem of disentangling a lost treatise of Musonius from Paedagogus. Includes the conjectured Greek text.

Paulsen, David. "Ethical Individualism in Clement of Alexandria." *Concordia Theological Monthly* XLIII, No. 1 (January 1972): 3-20.

    Explanation for Clement's emphasis on individual perfection above communal concerns.

Ritter, A. M. "Clement of Alexandria and the Problem of Christian Norms." *Studia Patristica* XVIII, No. 3 (1983): 421-36.

    Consideration of where Clement's theology fits in the framework of early Catholicism.

Timothy, H. B. "Clement of Alexandria." In *The Early Christian Apologists and Greek Philosophy.* Assen, pp. 59–80. The Netherlands: Van Gorcum, 1972.

    Overview of Clement's teachings.

Tollinton, R. B. *Clement of Alexandria: A Study in Christian Liberalism.* 2 vols. London: Williams and Norgate, 1914.

    Presentation of Clement's life, knowledge, teachings, and work in the context of his own period but with relevance to modern times.

Van de Bunt, Annewies. "Milk and Honey in the Theology of Clement of Alexandria." In *Fides Sacramenti Sacra-*

mentum Fidei, pp. 27–39. Assen, The Netherlands: Van Gorcum, 1981.

    Demonstration of how Clement entertains opposing theological interpretations simultaneously.

Van den Hoek, Annewies. "How Alexandrian was Clement of Alexandria? Reflections on Clement and His Alexandrian Background." *The Heythrop Journal* XXXI, No. 2 (April 1990): 179-94.

    Investigation of Alexandrian influences on Clement's writings.

————."The 'Catechetical' School of Early Christian Alexandria and Its Philonic Heritage." *Harvard Theological Review* 90, No. 1 (January 1997): 59-87.

    Examination of Clement's views on the relationship between school and church.

Van Eijk, A. H. C. "The Gospel of Philip and Clement of Alexandria: Gnostic and Ecclesiastical Theology on the Resurrection and the Eucharist." *Vigiliae Christianae* 25, No. 2 (June 1971): 94-120.

    Study of parallels between saying 23 of the Gospel of Philip and three passages from Paedagogus.

Das Nibelungenlied
c. 1190-c. 1204.

(Also known as *Der Nibelunge Nôt* and *Lay of the Nibelungen*) German poem. For further information on *Das Nibelungenlied*, see *CMLC*, Volume 1.

INTRODUCTION

The *Nibelungenlied* is the most celebrated heroic epic of German Medieval literature. In its home country, the tale of honor, murder, and revenge is still read by the general public as well as students. A favorite of critics, the *Nibelungenlied* is praised for its symmetrical form and its mingling of fiction and history, encompassing Germany's ancient heroic songs, the fall of the Burgundian Empire in 437, and the courtly romance tradition of twelfth- and thirteenth-century Europe. Scholars have been unable to identify its author but linguistic studies and historical references date the poem's composition to sometime between 1190 and 1204, with the year 1203 being cited traditionally. Its literary roots reach back to the Vikings and Scandinavia, possibly to the ninth century, but some scholars believe that the ultimate source was Germany and that the tale spread northward before it came back home in altered form. The message of the *Nibelungenlied*—if indeed there is a message—is hotly debated by critics. Some of the poem's wide modern appeal is likely due to the fact that it fits equally well with many different interpretations.

PLOT AND MAJOR CHARACTERS

The *Nibelungenlied* is neatly divided into two parts by most critics. The first focuses on the mythic hero Siegfried and his murder, while the second part, largely historical, concerns the fall of the Burgundians, a tribe residing in the southern part of Germany. The poem opens in Worms, at the Burgundian court of three royal brothers—Gunther, Gernôt, and Gîselher—and their sister Kriemhild. Siegfried, a prince from the Netherlands, travels to Worms with the intention of marrying Kriemhild but must wait a year before seeing her. In the meantime, he distinguishes himself in numerous battles, partly through his own strength and partly through magic. He conquers the Nibelungs (a name meaning "inhabitants of the mist") and wins their treasure—a sword, and a cloak that makes its wearer invisible. Gunther wishes to marry Brunhild, who is an Icelandic queen of fantastic strength, and persuades Siegfried to wear the magic cloak on his behalf and win Brunhild through a series of duplicitous physical contests in which the invisible Siegfried actually performs the feats that appear to be accomplished by Gunther. For his help,

Siegfried is given Kriemhild's hand in a double wedding ceremony that includes the exchange of vows between Gunther and Brunhild. Once Brunhild realizes she has been tricked into marrying Gunther she employs Hagen, Gunther's vassal, to murder Siegfried. On a hunting trip, Hagen stabs Siegfried in the back and kills him, after which he sinks the treasure of the Nibelungs in the Rhine, significantly decreasing Kriemhild's power and influence. The second part of the *Nibelungenlied* begins ten years later. Kriemhild marries Etzel (Attila the Hun) on the promise of his vassal, Rüdiger, that he will defend her against her enemies. Years pass and Kriemhild invites her brothers and their party to Etzel's court with the intention of avenging Siegfried's death. Kriemhild persuades some of Etzel's lords to attack the Burgundians and, after a bloody battle, all the Burgundians are slain save for Gunther and Hagen, who are brought to the Queen by Dietrich of Bern. When Hagen refuses to tell Kriemhild where he has sunk the Nibelung treasure, she has Gunther beheaded. Hagen still refuses to divulge the location and Kriemhild, furious, cuts off his head with Siegfried's sword. Hildebrand, Dietrich's vassal, is outraged by the Queen's ruthlessness and kills her.

MAJOR THEMES

Kriemhild provides a theme for the *Nibelungenlied* when she states that "all joy must end in sorrow." By no means is this accepted by everyone as the main theme, however. Some scholars read the poem in terms of the code of chivalry, represented by Siegfried, or in terms of Christianity, exemplified by Rüdiger. Still others interpret the poem as a tragedy of godless self-will, a revival of Germanic spirit, or a warning against pride. Certainly, elements of fatalism, heroism, guilt, honor, faithfulness, and justice abound in the epic. Many modern critics decry what they perceive as a tendency towards over-analysis, arguing that there may not be a hidden purpose—or any purpose—in the *Nibelungenlied* beyond the telling of a simple yet exciting tale.

CRITICAL RECEPTION

Popular in Medieval times, the *Nibelungenlied* gradually lost favor with readers until it was rediscovered in 1755 in a castle in Tirol by J. H. Obereit, and translated from Middle High German into German in 1757. In the early 1800s, the *Nibelungenlied* was embraced by the German Romantics as part of their national legacy and often favorably compared with the *Iliad*. Scholars have also debated whether or not the poem truly is distinctively German; many feel that concentration on the *Nibelungenlied* as a national work is misguided. The *Nibelungenlied* has inspired diverse areas of study. Examining the structure of the poem involves oral formulism, semantics, and syntactic analysis. Through this type of work, much has been learned about the development of the oral tale which served as the basis for the written version. Another popular field of study is comparing and contrasting the *Nibelungenlied* with its Norse versions and studying its mythic elements. Scholars find little argument that the impetus for the second half of the tale was the defeat of the Burgundians by the Huns, but many critics believe that taking a historical approach in analysis is too limiting, and they prefer to study the *Nibelungenlied* purely as literature. The nature of the poem lends itself to various interpretations since the author incorporates little commentary beyond stock phrases, simply letting the tale unfold without clarifying the motives of the characters. The individual reader is thus left to decide whether or not Hagen is a hero or a villain, for example, or whether the tale promotes honor or warns against it. Frank G. Ryder states the poem is "a true work of world literature, faithful to its time but not bound by it, comprehensible and of significance to an audience centuries removed."

PRINCIPAL WORKS

Principal English Translations

The Nibelungenlied (translated by Daniel B. Shumway) (poetry) 1909

"Song of the Nibelungs:" A Verse Translation from the Middle High German "Nibelungenlied" (translated by Frank G. Ryder) (poetry) 1962

The Nibelungenlied (translated by A. T. Hatto) (poetry) 1965

The Nibelungenlied (translated by D. G. Mowatt) (poetry) 1965

The Nibelungenlied (translated by William Nanson Lettsom) (poetry) 1977

The Nibelungenlied (translated by Robert Lichtenstein) (poetry) 1991

German Epic Poetry: "The Nibelungenlied," the "Older Lay of Hildebrand," and Other Works (edited by Francis G. Gentry et al.) (poetry) 1995

CRITICISM

Otto L. Jiriczek (essay date 1902)

SOURCE: "The Saga of the Niblungs" in *Northern Hero Legends*, J. M. Dent & Co., 1902, pp. 10-61.

[*In the following excerpt, Jiriczek discusses the historical and mythical foundations of the* Nibelungenlied, *and the development, continuance, and extinction of the saga.*]

. . . III. THE HISTORICAL FOUNDATION OF THE SAGA.

In German and Norse sources mention is made of a Burgundian king Gibich, Norse Gjuki [in the **Nibelunlied** his name is Dancrât] who is said to have three sons, Gunther, Gernot, Giselher; in Norse, Gunnar, Guthormr, Hogni [Hagen stands for Giselher in the Seyfriedslied also]. The historical origin of some of these names may be proved. In the Lex Burgundionum, which was proclaimed at the beginning of the sixth century, King Gundobad enumerates his ancestors and predecessors: Gibica, Godomar, Gislaharius and Gundaharius. These four alliterative names are therefore an historical genealogy of ancient Burgundian kings. The list of names affords indeed no clue as to the relationship or the chronological order of the persons mentioned. Whether the four succeeded each other in the above order, or whether we must assume the three last (as in the saga) to have been brothers and co-rulers—a state of things which is not unknown in Germanic history—must remain an open question. In Norse tradition the name Godomar became corrupted to Guthormr, in German sagas it was replaced by Gernot. Hagen was substituted for Giselher in Norse tradition, and in the Seyfriedslied.

Other historical sources afford further evidence bearing on King Gundaharl. From the year 413 the Burgundians, an East Germanic tribe related to the Goths, whose oldest known home was between the Oder and the Vistula, dwelt in Germania prima, on the left bank of the Rhine, roughly speaking, in the district of the present Palatinate. But their power was short-lived. As early as the year 435 they were defeated by Aëtius, and in 437 King Gundicarius, with his whole clan and people, fell by the sword of the Huns. The remnant of the Burgundians settled in Savoy and soon became Romanized. After barely a century's existence this Burgundian kingdom perished at the hands of the Franks. The second king of these Burgundians of Savoy was the Gundobad mentioned above. Our information concerning the destruction of the Rhenish Burgundians is scanty. We do not hear whence these Huns came, whether they were allies of Aëtius, and whether Gundahari's tragic fate was brought about by a surprise, or, as seems probable, by treachery. But we know enough to realize that the saga of the destruction of the Burgundian kings by the Huns rests upon an historical foundation. *Attila* himself, who, together with his brother Bleda, had ruled the Huns of the Theiss valley since 433, was not engaged in this battle, but it seemed so natural to assume that the celebrated ruler of the Huns must have played a part in this Hunnish victory that not only the saga, but later historians also, attributed the destruction of the Burgundians to him.

Etzel-Attila is not the only historical character among the Huns immortalized by the saga: Bloedelin is Attila's brother Bleda, and Helche is known in history as Attila's wife. . . . The connection between Theodoric and Attila reflects the historical connection of the Ostrogoths (before Theodoric) with Attila (cf. for further details the Dietrich cycle). The death of Attila (in the Norse form of the saga) is also founded on history. In the year 453 Attila married a Germanic princess, named Hildico. On the morning after his wedding his servants discovered him weltering in his blood. He had died from an attack of hæmorrhage. Naturally a report that he had been murdered by Hildico began to spread, and before long this rumour was accepted by historians as an historical fact, a *motif* for which was not long wanting. The murder was said to be an act of vengeance on the part of the Germanic princess for the murder of her father (her kinsmen) by Attila. Thus the development of an historical saga may be traced in historical sources. The saga underwent yet further changes in the epic, and connected the vengeance of Hildico with the destruction of the Burgundians, by making Hildico a sister of the Burgundian kings.

We find the saga in this older form in Norse tradition, where Gudrun avenges the death of her brothers on Atli. The German saga has undergone considerable changes, the result of the fusion of the Burgundian saga with the Siegfried myth. The identity of the avenging Kriemhild (it was only in Norse tradition that the name of Gudrun was substituted) with the historical character of Hildico, is proved by the name. Hildico is a pet name formed from Hilde, which is the second element in the compound Kriemhild.

But there is no further historical evidence for the saga. Important features of it, such as the connection of the Burgundian kings with Siegfried, and some of the chief characters, such as Siegfried, Hagen and Brunhild, have no prototypes in history. Hagen is said to have been Aëtius.[1]

Various historical characters have been traced in the person of Siegfried, for instance, the Austrasian King Sigibert, husband of Brunihildis, who was murdered in 575 at the instigation of the notorious Fredegunde. He has even been taken to be Arminius, but none of these hypotheses are tenable. Siegfried and the other characters of the saga mentioned above are not historical, but have originated in poetry and myth.

IV. THE MYTHICAL FOUNDATION OF THE SAGA.

A hero of superhuman strength and beauty was brought up by a demonic smith in the forest. He slew a dragon, and thereby acquired an immense treasure. He penetrated the magic flames which encircled a rock, and awakened a walkyrie from her charmed sleep. He wedded her, but forgot her in consequence of a draught of oblivion, which brought him into the power of the King of the Niblungs, whose sister he married. He surrendered his own bride to the Niblungs, who won his treasure by treacherously slaying him. This is, in brief outline, the story of Siegfried, which, though lacking any historical basis, appears in our sources in connection with the historical saga of the Burgundians.

If, on the one hand, the second part of the Saga of the Niblungs, the destruction of the Burgundian kings by Attila, is clearly recognizable as historical, and, on the other, the story of Siegfried's youth up to his arrival at the court of Burgundy is as clearly mythical in character, the fact that the rest of the story of Siegfried is only preserved in combination with the Saga of the Gjukings renders the differentiation of the two elements and the reconstruction of the Siegfried myth extremely difficult.

The difficulty is enhanced by the discrepancies and inconsistencies of the authorities—on the one hand by the divergence of the German version from the Norse, on the other by the incompatibility of the one with the other. In Norse tradition the acquisition of the hoard is combined with the struggle against the dragon, whilst in the *Nibelungenlied* these are independent features. But the Seyfriedslied proves that in Germany also these two elements of the saga were originally united, and that the version of the *Nibelungenlied* is a deviation from the original saga. The story of how Siegfried was to divide the hoard between the two brothers who had quarrelled, and how he then slew them both, is a widespread, originally Indian *motif* which has no connection with the ancient Siegfried myth.

No German versions relate the awakening of the Walkyrie by Siegfried and his marriage with her. Obscure allusions in the *Nibelungenlied* and somewhat more distinct ones in the Seyfriedslied, corrupt though it be, indicate, however, that this portion of the Siegfried saga was also current in Germany. The authorities are not agreed as to the identity of the walkyrie whom Siegfried awakens from sleep, and the one whom he wins for Gunther (for further details cf. the remarks sub. Sketch of the Saga).

Such divergencies afford scope for the greatest possible diversity of opinion as to the reconstruction of the original poem on Siegfried, and yet more as to the mythological interpretation of the original form of the saga. It is impossible to enter more closely into these diverse opinions in this connection, and it must suffice to have indicated in some measure the partially hypothetical character of the reconstruction and mythological interpretations of the saga.

The justification for a mythological interpretation of the Siegfried saga may be deduced from a whole series of features which in other connections also are proved to be undoubtedly mythical. The slaying of a dragon by a hero, and his consequent acquisition of a treasure, are a well-known form of the heroization of an elemental process of nature common to all Arian mythologies. A thunderstorm in spring is the destruction by a Light-God of a cloud-dragon, from whose downfall proceeds the fertilizing rain that begets vegetation; in this form the vegetation of summer is the hoard. The deliverance of a maiden by a hero who presses through the flames is an achievement attributed even to gods. Thus Skirnir wins Gerda for Freyr, thus Svipdag wins Menglöd. The latter name, which signifies her 'who rejoices in the necklet,' is a distinct allusion to the old Germanic Sun-goddess Frija (Norse Frigg) who is in possession of the Brisingamen.[2]

So far it is clear that the Siegfried myth is originally a nature-myth: a Light-Hero (as in related myths a Light-God) wins the sun-maiden. Whether it be founded upon a season-myth or a day-and-night-myth—both conceptions are closely allied and both probably contributed to the formation of the myth—the result is in either case the tragic issue of the myth in its heroic form. The sun sets in the darkness whence it rose, and the earth that blossoms in summer lapses into the bondage of winter, whence a new summer will deliver her; or, in the heroic form of the saga: the Light-Hero or Summer-Hero succumbs after a brief existence to the Powers of Darkness who slay him. These Powers of Darkness are the Niblungs (Norse, Niflungar), the children of the mist, whose very name marks them as the demonic powers of death. Niflheimr, Niflhel, and 'Nebulo' is the Scandinavian Hades, and 'Nebulo' is translated in Old High German glosses by 'magic being,' 'fiend,' 'spectre.' The epic symbol for the surrender of the hero to the gloomy powers of death is the allurement of a fair demonic maiden who presents him with the draught of oblivion. This elf-myth survives to the present day in songs and sagas in Norway and the Faröe Islands and is supported by the evidence of Saxo Grammaticus and of Icelandic sagas, in which young men succumb to powers of the nether world, the 'hulder,' *i.e.* veiled, invisible ones; cf. the names Niblungs, Grimhild (*i.e.* the masked, veiled one), when a wondrously fair hulder-maiden tenders them a draught of oblivion, whereupon they are drawn into the subterranean realm of the demons in the mountains, to stay there for ever, or to suffer mutilation and death. Thus Siegfried succumbs to the Niblungs, and is by them deprived of bride, treasure and life.

The epic form in which this myth is conveyed, the deeply tragic touch which represents Siegfried as winning his own bride for the Niblungs in the form of another, a deed which brings about both his and his bride's death, must be looked upon as a purely poetic-epic elaboration of the myth, influenced, however, probably by a deep undercurrent of nature-symbolism: 'The maiden slumbering upon the lonely peak is the sun, the wall of flame which encircles her is the red glow of dawn, Siegfried is the young day. He ascends the peak, the glow of dawn fades before his splendour, radiant the sun rises from her couch, and bestows her glad greeting upon the whole expanse of nature. But light and shade are indissolubly linked; by its own inexorable advance, day must needs turn to night. When in the evening the sun sinks to rest, and is again surrounded by a rampart of flame, the glow of evening, day again approaches, but no longer in the youthful form of morning to arouse the maiden from sleep, but in the gloomy shape of Gunther to lie down beside her. Day has turned to night (saga-transformation), the rampart of flame fades away, the day and the sun glide into the realm of darkness.' [Wilmanns.]

The demonic Niblungs were replaced by the Burgundian kings who belong to the historical saga. How and why this substitution was accomplished, we are now unable to say, but through this younger stratum of the saga we get distinct glimpses of the older mythical foundation. Hagen, who appears by the side of the Burgundian kings, is a purely mythical demonic being, borrowed from the previous period. The name Grimhild (bellona larvata) also belongs, apparently by virtue of its significance, to the older mythical stratum. Its resemblance to the name of the historical Hildico may perhaps be one of the points which have produced a coalescence of the Saga of the Niblungs with the Saga of the Burgundians. But the original connection is most plainly indicated by the application of the name Niblungs (Norse, Niflungar) to the Burgundian kings. In German and Norse tradition the name is applied to the G jukings only in the second part of the saga (after Siegfried's death), and this circumstance, for which no adequate explanation has so far been found, has been taken to imply that the name was attributed to the Burgundian kings, only in so far as they were the possessors of the treasure of the Niblungs. But if that were the case, Siegfried would have the foremost claim to the name, and yet he is never called Niblung. This interpretation must therefore be rejected in favour of the assumption that the older mythical name of Siegfried's opponents has penetrated into the younger historical period of the saga. On the other hand, the coalescence of the two forms has, in some respects, considerably modified the character of the mythical saga. The fact that human beings have taken the place of the demonic adversaries of Siegfried has lifted the veil of gloomy twilight in which the saga was wrapped. The demonic traits of the bewitching elf-maiden have faded. Kriemhild is no longer a baleful demon in the semblance of a woman, but a loving wife. Nor is the relation of her brothers to Siegfried one of natural antagonism. It is only the disastrous blows of an unkindly fate which turn it to Siegfried's destruction. Further variations in the subject-matter resulting from the treatment of the saga in epic poetry will be discussed in the following paragraph.

Parallels which may be traced in myths of the gods do not justify the assumption that Siegfried is the incarnation of some god, perhaps Wodan or Freyr; they only prove that such myths were the result of the same nature-symbolism. Locations of the Siegfried-Brunhild saga, such as the above-mentioned 'Bed of Brunhild,' have been looked upon as shrines of the heroes who were worshipped there as gods. We have, however, no evidence for the divine worship of Siegfried, nor do these locations imply such worship. But the term 'Bed of Brunhild' indicates that the location was determined in part by a reminiscence of the nature-myth according to which the sun-maiden was asleep upon the mountain.

The credibility of this assumption is increased by a second location in the Rhenish Palatinate.[3] A rock in the forest near Dürkheim is known as 'Brummholzstuhl,' which turns out to be a corrupt form of 'Brinholdestul' (Brunhild's seat), which is mentioned in a charter of 1360. Until recently fires were kindled there in spring, and inscriptions and tokens dating from the Roman occupation which imply the worship of the gods [Mercurius Cisustius Deus is mentioned] and of the spring [sun-wheels] prove the spot to have been a shrine. The fact that the Siegfried-Brunhild saga, which must be far older than the date of the charter quoted above, was subsequently localized there, proves that the consciousness of its having originally been a nature-myth had survived.

V. Development of the Saga.

The historical events upon which the second part of the saga is founded took place on the banks of the Rhine, which also provide the background for the saga, and Norse tradition also points to Germany and the districts along the Rhine as having been its home. It is 'into the Rhine' that Sigurd dips his sword when testing it against the flock of wool; he is slain 'to the south of the Rhine'; the treasure of the Niblungs is buried 'in the Rhine'; Sigmund holds sway over 'the land of the Franks'; Sigurd is riding towards 'the land of the Franks' when he comes upon the flame-encircled mountain of the Walkyrie; he is called 'the Southern, the German (inn húnski) hero.' The Saga of the Niblungs originated among the Rhine-Franks, the immediate successors of the Burgundians in Germania prima, and travelled thence northwards, though how and in what form remains an unsolved problem.

No literary document has preserved any account of the saga in its original German form. A mere name now and again (cf. p. 19) proves its existence, and not until the 13th century do songs afford information in greater detail. Norse tradition has preserved the saga at an earlier stage in lays which were composed in Norway, Iceland and Greenland between the 9th and 11th centuries. This Norse tradition being older than the German, has preserved the saga in a form which is in many respects purer. For instance, Kriemhild-Gudrun takes vengeance on Atli for her brothers' death, a touch which corresponds more closely than the German version to the original historical saga. Norse heathendom preserved the mythical elements for a longer period of time and in a purer form than would have been possible in Christianized Germany.

But the Norse version must not in every respect be credited with greater purity and originality. The intimate connection of Odin with the fate of the Volsungs, at least to the extent related in the Saga of the Volsungs, is certainly a subsequent Norse addition. The names Kriemhild and Sieglind have been correctly preserved in the German version, as proved in the first case by the connection between Kriemhild and Hildico, and, in the second, by the alliteration. The Norse version has replaced them by Gudrun and Hjördis. In Scandinavia, moreover, the saga became corrupted by the arbitrary introduction of other characters—Atli, for instance, is represented as Kriemhild's brother—and it has become confused by contamination with Norse sagas. Thus the Norse hero Helgi Hundingsbane is made out to be a son of Sigmund. It is, moreover, only in Scandinavia that the Ermanarich-saga is linked with the Saga of the Niblungs by the introduction of Svanhild as the daughter of Gudrun and Sigurd (cf. p. 89). The genealogical ambition of Norse dynasties, which manifested itself in a desire to prove their descent from the most eminent legendary heroes, led to the creation of Aslaug, the ostensible daughter of Sigurd and Brynhild, who was made the ancestress of famous kings.

The most important transformation which the German form of the saga underwent, is the change in the relation of Kriemhild to Etzel and her brothers. Without Etzel's consent, in fact against his express desire, she dooms her brothers to destruction. In the old saga Siegfried's death remained unavenged. Ethical feeling demanded that the Burgundian kings should perish in retaliation and atonement for Siegfried's murder. This change in the saga is due to a change in ethical principles. From the Germanic point of view the bond of kinship is stronger than the bond of wedlock. An altered moral conception, in consequence of which marriage was held to constitute a higher and more sacred claim, laid upon Kriemhild the obligation of exacting blood-vengeance for her husband.

In the further development of the saga various characters were added which were absent from the older form—Dietrich von Bern, for instance, who lived as an exile at the court of Etzel. Older Norse tradition does not mention him. His introduction is due to the cultivation of the saga in Austria and Bavaria, where Etzel's character also underwent a complete change.[4] The cruelty and avarice of Etzel's character as it appears in Norse tradition, reflect the impression produced by the 'Scourge of God' upon his adversaries, and represent the original Franconian conception of the saga. Etzel in the *Nibelungenlied* is the figure of a wise, gentle and high-minded king, such as the imagination of the Ostrogoths, his faithful, favoured and honoured allies, painted him, a conception which passed over into the Austro-Bavarian hero-saga of Etzel and Dietrich.

In Austria, too, the figure of the generous Margrave Rüdiger was linked with the saga. He is mentioned as early as the 12th century as a hero famous in song. So far no historical or mythical interpretation of this legendary character has been discovered. But the saga underwent poetic treatment and cultivation in other lands besides Austria, and, in consequence, yet further characters were added.

The introduction of Volker of Alzei is due to Rhenish minstrels who perhaps borrowed the type of minstrel and hero—a combination which does not occur elsewhere in German saga—from old French epics, in which it is not unusual.

Irnfried and Iring are characters taken from the Saxon saga. Irnfried is the historical king of the Thuringians who in the year 530 lost throne and life in a struggle against the allied Franks and Saxons. Iring, however, whom the Saxon historian Widukind introduces into the Irmenfried saga, is a mythical being of whose original significance we know no more than that the Milky Way was called 'Iring's Way' after him. The two Margraves Gero and Eckewart are apparently also Saxons, namely, the historical Margrave Gero of East Saxony (+ 965) and Eckewart of Meissen (+ 1002). But whether Saxon or Franconian minstrels introduced these semi-mythical, semi-historical Saxon heroes into the saga cannot be determined. The Thidrekssaga mentions only Iring, which seems to militate against the assumption that these characters were added by Saxon minstrels, though the fact that the Thidrekssaga is a later version must also be taken into consideration. An originally mythical character is incorporated with the historical figure of Eckewart, namely the faithful warner Eckehart, who appears in the *Nibelungenlied* as the guardian of Rüdiger's march. His legendary significance has been almost entirely lost sight of, which renders the whole scene in Rüdiger's marches enigmatic and obscure.

The most far-reaching changes in the German saga, as contained in the *Nibelungenlied*, are produced by the gradual disappearance of the mythical portions of the saga. This may in part be due to the gradual fading of heathen reminiscences in Christian times, but in a large measure it is the outcome of the poet's own æsthetic principles and literary taste. The Seyfriedslied and several other authorities prove that Siegfried's training in the forest by a smith, his struggle with the dragon, the rescue of a maiden, are by no means unknown to the German saga. The absence of these features, or their gradual disappearance, from the *Nibelungenlied* must therefore be regarded as an act of deliberate and personal elimination on the part of a poet conforming to a canon of courtly æstheticism. For instance, Siegfried is bred at his father's court in pomp and honour and all chivalrous accomplishments. The ancient saga of his having been brought up as an orphan by a smith in the forest would have struck the poet as unseemly and lacking in 'courtoisie.'[5]

VI. CONTINUANCE AND EXTINCTION OF THE SAGA.

A considerable number of extant MSS. dating from the thirteenth to the sixteenth centuries prove the extreme popularity of the *Nibelungenlied*. The Seyfriedslied appeared in print as late as the sixteenth century, and it was dramatized by Hans Sachs in 1557. Allusions in Fischart and other sixteenth-century authors presuppose a knowledge of the saga, and a chap-book of the 'hürnen Seyfried,' the Horny Siegfried, which is founded upon the Seyfriedslied (earliest printed edition 1726), appeared in numerous successive editions in the course of the eighteenth and nineteenth centuries, and may still be found on book-stalls at wakes and fairs.

These testimonies are, however, merely proofs of the perpetuation of the saga in literary tradition. Others tend to show that the saga itself was current among the people until the end of the Middle Ages. Der Marner, an itinerant Swabian minstrel, who as a blind old man was murdered towards the end of the thirteenth century, enumerates among the songs favoured by his audience 'The Death of Siegfried,' and 'Kriemhild's Treachery,' and in Hugo von Trimberg's *Renner*, a didactic poem belonging to the fourteenth century, Siegfried's fight with the dragon, Kriemhild's treachery, and the hoard of the Niblungs are quoted as being popular subjects of the minstrelsy of the day. Local tradition survived for a considerable period at Worms (due, of course, to a late localization of the saga). In the year 1188 the grave of the 'hürnen Seyfried,' a giant, was shown to the Emperor Frederick III. As late as the beginning of the seventeenth century, the trunk of a huge fir-tree was exhibited in a church at Worms, as having been the shaft of the horn-clad giant Seyfried.

Moreover, though in the numerous examples of folk-songs which go to prove the survival of popular poetry in the Middle Ages, Dietrich von Bern is the favourite figure, yet Seyfried is now and again mentioned side by side with him. The terrors of the Thirty Years' War, which swept over the national life of Germany like a devastating fire, destroyed the last surviving traces of the hero-saga, as well as almost every other popular mediæval tradition. Since then the memory of Siegfried, as of all other legendary heroes, has been extinct among the people. Only in fairy lore the ancient hero may perchance survive, though nameless. This is almost certainly the case in the tale of Dornröschen, the Sleeping Beauty in the Wood, which, oddly enough, perpetuates a portion of the pure Siegfried myth, namely, the hero's awakening of a maiden out of the bonds of a death-like sleep. But a hedge of thorns has taken the place of the original rampart of flames.

Scandinavian popular tradition is more abundant and longer-lived. In Denmark so-called Kæmpeviser (heroic ballads) concerning the Lady Grimild, Siward and Brynhild were sung down to modern times, and the *Chronicle of Hven*, which was written in Latin in the sixteenth century (a version which is unfortunately lost), and translated into Danish in the seventeenth century, proves that the Saga of the Niblungs was localized upon the island of Hven in the Sound between Seeland and Schonen.[6] Fragments of the saga survive to this day among the inhabitants of Hven.

The great abundance of Norwegian folk-songs dealing with Siegfried, even towards the end of the Middle Ages, is proved by the songs and fragments of songs which have been collected from current popular tradition, even in our day, and which probably still survive in remote districts. Though the greater number of these Danish and Norwegian songs may trace back to literary sources, they afford valuable evidence for the reintroduction and survival of the saga among the people.

Sweden supplies only one Kæmpevise bearing on this subject, the Swedish origin of which is, moreover, not above suspicion. But a few scenes from the Sigurd saga scratched on stones found in Södermannsland, Upland and other Swedish districts, prove that in heathen and early Christian times the saga was as extensively known in Sweden as in other Scandinavian countries. For instance, on the curious Ramsundsberg stone, which also bears a Runic inscription, we may see 'the otter in the Andvara-waterfall, also the anvil, the tongs, the hammer and the bellows of Regin the dwarf, and, further, Sigurd slaying the grim dragon, and roasting its heart on the coals. There is also a picture of Sigurd's horse Grani, laden with Fafnir's hoard, and of the two birds perched upon a tree, whose twittering revealed to Sigurd Regin's intended treachery, and of the headless trunk of Regin, slain by Sigurd.'[7]

The tradition of the saga is most varied upon the Faröe Islands. But the songs sung there as an accompaniment to the dance,[8] are no more proofs of the survival of the saga from the Old Norse period than the Danish-Norwegian Kæmpeviser. Both have sprung from later literary sources, yet they are fully five hundred years old, and have become so thoroughly popularized that to this day Sigurd and Brunhild may be said to survive in the folk-song of a Germanic tribe.

Notes

1. In ancient documents Hagen bears the appellation 'von Troja,' 'von Tronje.' In this case the semi-classical fable of the Trojan origin of all the Franks has been applied to the person of a famous hero celebrated in song by the Franks, and probably also claimed as a Frank. The *Nibelungenlied* and other sources, misled by the resemblance in name, then represented him as being a native of Tronje = Kirchberg in the north of Alsatia, and thus produced a local connection between him and the kings of Worms.

2. For further details cf. the Hilde-Gudrun saga, and North. Mythology sub. 'Freyr' and 'Brisingamen.'

3. The following information was supplied by Fr. Vogt.

4. After Vogt. Cf. the sketch of the Dietrich saga.

5. Cf. Samml. Göschen: Nibelungen and Kudrun. Introduction to the *Nibelungenlied*.

6. Translated by Rassmann, vol. II. p. 188 ff

7. Montelius after Säve.

8. Translated by Rassmann, I. 306 ff.; 'Regin the Smith,' I. 313 ff.; Brunhild, II. 134 ff.; 'Högni.'

Frances E. Sandbach (essay date 1903)

SOURCE: "Influence on English Literature" in *The Nibelungenlied and Gudrun in England and America*, David Nutt, 1903, pp. 118-35.

[In the following excerpt, Sandbach explores Middle English and Modern English literary works that may have been influenced by or adapted from the Nibelungenlied.*]*

. . .—In the literature of the Middle English period there is, so far as I know, only one reference to the Nibelungen story that can be looked upon as at all certain. This was pointed out by Professor W. P. Ker in *Folk Lore,* ix. 372, and occurs in the metrical romance of "Sir Degravant," in the following passage (vv. 525 *ff.*):—

Y hade leve she were myne | Thane alle the gold in the Reyne | ffausoned one florene, | She is myne so dere.

(MS. *drere*)

Whatever the third of these lines means, the second clearly contains a reference to the Nibelungen Hoard. But such an expression may be only proverbial, and point to an earlier rather than a contemporary knowledge of the story.

Worth noticing here is one other passage in Middle English literature first remarked by Weber in the "Illustrations of Northern Antiquities," (*cf.* p. 82). It consists of an interesting parallel to Gunther and Brunhild's wedding-night scene, and occurs in the metrical romance of "Sir Bevis of Hampton," the Auchinleck MS. of which dates from the first quarter of the fourteenth century. The English versions are derived from a French source, similar to the Anglo-Norman *Boeve de Haumtone,* but Bevis was originally an English hero.

After an adventurous career in the East, Sir Bevis brings back to Europe a lady, Josian, who is to become his wife. Leaving her at Cologne, he proceeds to his home in the Isle of Wight for the purpose of driving out his villainous old stepfather, and thus gives a certain unscrupulous Earl Miles an opportunity of wooing Josian. Eventually forced into marrying him, she determines at all costs to remain faithful to her betrothed; on retiring for the night she persuades Miles to dismiss the attendants, attacks him unawares, and strangles him with her girdle. According to the Anglo-Norman poem (ed. A. Stimming, *Der anglonormannische Boeve de Haumtone:* Halle, 1899), she throws the girdle over his head, pulls, and breaks his neck (vv. 2110-2116). In the English versions, however, the parallel to the scene in the *Nibelungenlied* is closer, for Josian carries the girdle over a curtain pole (or, as one MS. has it, a beam), and leaves the corpse hanging all night (*cf.* E. Kölbing's edition, "The Romance of Sir Beues of Hamtoun" (London, 1894); vv. 3219-3224). Summaries of the poem are to be found in J. Ashton's "Romances of Chivalry" (London, [2]1890), and G. Ellis's "Early English Metrical Romances" (London, [2]1848).

Although it is safer to assume that this parallel is accidental, or that the motive was in existence before its application in the two poems, the faint possibility remains, that either the author or the translator of "Sir Bevis" borrowed it from a version of the Nibelungen tradition. It is to be observed, too, that a reminiscence of Germanic saga appears in another part of the romance (Auchinleck MS., 2605) where Wade, presumably the fierce old Wate of *Gudrun,* is mentioned.

. . .—All knowledge of the Nibelungen saga having died out, as may fairly be assumed, early in the Middle English, or even in the Old English period, the story remained unknown in this country until its reimportation by Weber in his "Northern Antiquities." His book was known and appreciated probably by only a select few, on whom, however, its influence was considerable, not least, as we have seen, on Carlyle. The general tendency of this influence was, however, scientific and scholarly. Weber's readers developed an interest which led them to study the *Nibelungenlied* and other Old German poems in the original, or in translation, and in some cases to communicate the results of their study to the public in essays and articles. This has, indeed, been the tendency even up to the present; a purely literary use of the saga material, or of any part of it, has been quite exceptional.

The earliest adaptation of the story in this sense is in the anonymous *Popular Tales and Romances of the Northern Nations*[1] (London, 1823), one of which is entitled, *The Hoard of the Nibelungen,* vol. iii. 199-250). The whole book is of the ghostly romantic type so much in vogue early in the last century, and the tales are written in a style suggestive of winter evenings and bated breath. The opening of *The Hoard of the Nibelungen* affords a good illustration:—

> "It was a gloomy autumnal night, as the moon, sinking amidst dark clouds, cast a fearful light upon the ruins of the fortress of Worms on the Adda, before which two sentinels were pacing to and fro, being stationed there in order to prevent the approach of any one towards the treasures which were supposed to be concealed within the vaults of the ancient castle."

Soon after the ghost of Monk Ilsan[2] appears and rides away, whereupon one of the sentinels relates how the monk is doomed to watch over the Hoard, and explains that no mortal hands can remove it, except in the ghost's absence. This leads up to an extraordinarily garbled version of the Nibelungen story, in which we recognise as characters King Gibich of Rhetia and his daughter Grimhilda; Brunilda, the betrothed of Gundachar; also Rudiger, the minstrel Volcker, Hagen of Troy, Ezzel, Dietrich of Bern, and Hildebrand. Siegfried's place is taken by Fradolfo, brother of Brunilda and possessor of the Hoard in virtue of his descent from the kings of the Netherlands.

The plot of the story may be summed up thus: Grimhilda is jealous of Brunilda's jewels, and proceeds to scheme for the treasure, which she eventually obtains by marrying Fradolfo, who murders Gibich and seizes Rhetia. The Burgundians, incensed, attack Grimhilda's castle after Fradolfo has been slain by Hagen, but without success. By magic spells she makes herself appear very beautiful, and convinces them for a time of her innocence. She now prepares an enchanted garden (here we see the influence of the *Rosengarten zu Worms*), into which she entices most of the characters, including Ezzel, who falls in love with and marries her. At a banquet she accuses Hagen of having murdered Fradolfo and stolen the Hoard; the guests take sides and fight, Grimhilda urging them on; but Hildebrand suddenly appears and kills her, whereupon the enchantment is removed, and the survivors stop fighting. Ilsan only, who had been Grimhilda's accomplice throughout, was put to death.

In conclusion, the sentinels descend to the vaults in search of the treasure, and soon after exchange their service for a life of opulence.

The next work influenced by the *Nibelungenlied* is one on a much higher literary level, the Hon. and Rev. William Herbert's *Attila, King of the Huns* (London, 1838), consisting of two parts; *I. Attila, or the Triumph of Christianity: a poem;* and *II., Attila and his Predecessors: an Historical Treatise.*

The second part does not properly belong to this section, and, moreover, contains nothing of interest beyond a few references to the *Nibelungenlied,* and theories as to the identity of Attila with Siegfried and the British King Arthur (pp. 518, 523-526, 535). Some passages in the poem, however, are based on the Norse and German versions of the Nibelungen saga. "The history of Hilda," Herbert says in his preface, "is conformable with the accounts given in the Scandinavian and Teutonic legends, reconciling their differences. The name of Escam, the daughter and wife of Attila, mentioned in the history of Priscus, is applied to the legends concerning the younger Hilda, who was his daughter and wife." Considering Attila identical with Siegfried, Hilda thus takes the *rôle* of Brunhild (Siegfried's first betrothed, according to the Eddas), Escam that of Kriemhild, who is supposed to be identical with (H)ildico, Attila's last wife and reputed murderess.

The first part of Book vii. (the whole consists of twelve books and a "Farewell," and comprises some 7500 lines of blank verse) relates how Hilda is divorced by Attila in favour of Escam, and handed over, drugged, to Gunther of Burgundy. In Book xi., having learned by her magic arts that Attila's fall is at hand, she induces Gunther to plot his murder with the help of Hagen. She herself pays an apparently friendly visit to the Hunnish court, but Escam, becoming jealous and suspicious, tells three dreams of ill omen she has had: that Attila had been slain by two wild boars, that he had been overwhelmed by the fall of two mountains,[3] and that he had been stung by two snakes. Hilda betrays herself by changing colour, but at this moment Gunther and Hagen appear. She contrives to warn them by passing them a ring wrapped in wolf skin, whereupon Hagen springs up, resolved to sell his life dearly. After his sword has broken, he is overpowered; his heart is cut out and carried to Gunther, who is left to die in a vault infested by snakes. Book xii. tells of Hilda's revenge more or less in accordance with the Norse tradition.

Herbert's numerous translations of Scandinavian poems testify to his knowledge of that literature, but the extent of his acquaintance with the *Nibelungenlied* is doubtful, for he states in a footnote to p. 242 that it, as well as the Edda, relates the device by which Hilda warned her husband. He first read the Upper German version in Weber's "Illustrations of Northern Antiquities," to which he referred the year after its appearance in his notes to a poem on *Brynhilda,* printed in "Helga: a Poem" (London, 1815).

The lines containing the speech in which Hilda incites her husband to murder Attila will provide a favourable example of his style (xi. 336-366):—

> She sought the loathed abode
> Of Gunther, to whose bed by treason given

She dwelt estranged from love, with might and scorn
Denying his approach. "Arise," she cried,
"If ever love within thee, or bold hopes
Have lit a generous spark. The heaven-sent plague
Vexes e'en now the Hun, and with poised wing
Destruction hovers o'er his host. Arise,
And be the minister of deadly hate!
Revenge must blot the treason out, that soil'd
My wedded couch with shame. I brook not, I,
Two husbands; nor divide to mortal man
Or bland endearments, or the power which makes
Man higher than the angels. Choose thou scorn
And hatred that shall wither all thine hopes
Now and hereafter, or the long-sought meed
Which I unwilling to revenge assign.
Gentle acceptance; and therewith, the might
That springs from Scandian magic, and the old lore
Of that dark cabbala, to Gozan brought
By Shalmanezar's captives, or the signs
Symbolic, borne to utmost Orient
By Manes, wisest of the sons of earth.
Arise, and seal with sacramental blood
Our hymeneals, and supremely blest
With Hilda reign!" This said, on him she bent
A smile so full of witchery, it stole
His senses, and o'er all his thoughts enthrall'd
Such blandishment and soft persuasion threw,
That life seem'd nothing worth, without the love
Of that pernicious matron, won by guilt.

In 1848 an anonymous author produced for the especial delectation of children, "The Heroic Life and Exploits of Siegfried the Dragon Slayer: an Old German Story" (London, 1848), with eight illustrations, designed by Kaulbach, and very crudely coloured. The material of this work seems to have been collected from a variety of sources, among which the *Nibelungenlied, Hürnen Seyfrid,* and some of the *Heldenbuch* romances are readily distinguishable; at the same time the author's imagination has also had free play. The contents are divided into fourteen "Adventures," as follows (the observations in brackets are mine):—

1. Of King Siegmund, and of Heroes, Dwarfs, Giants, and Dragons of Ancient Times. (Introductory.)

2. Of Siegfried the Swift, how he grew up to be a Hero, and of his throwing the Spear. (Marvellous record of youthful prowess.)

3. Of the Emperor Otnit and Wolfdietrich, and how Siegfried asked permission to go out into the World. (From the *Heldenbuch* romances: *Otnit* and *Hugdietrich und Wolfdietrich.*)

4. How Siegfried the Swift went through the Wilderness, and what he encountered there. (He catches a stag with a golden crown, finds an underground smithy, and frightens the dwarfs into politeness.)

5. Mimer relates the Adventures of Wieland, the best of all Smiths and Armourers.

6. How Siegfried brings an Urochs to the Smiths. (Imitation of the bear scene in the *Nibelungenlied.*)

7. How Siegfried learns to be a Smith, and how he was sent by the treacherous Mimer to the Dragon. (Norse version.)

8. How Siegfried fights with the Dragon, and bathes himself in his blood. (As in the *Thidrekssaga* and the *Nibelungenlied.*)

9. How Siegfried comes again to the Smithy, and settles accounts with Mimer. (Norse.)

10. Siegfried sees the great Dragon, and meets a King of the Dwarfs.

11. Siegfried's fight with the faithless Giants under the Drachenstein.

12. Of the great Wonders which Siegfried saw in the Dragon's Rock.

13. How Siegfried first sees the King's Daughter, and is received by her.

14. Siegfried's fight with the Dragon.

Adventures 10-14 are based on the *Hürnen Seyfrid*. In conclusion, it is remarked that the sequel is told in other songs and legends, the "Rose-garden of Worms" is mentioned, and some old Worms customs connected with the tradition are referred to.

We now come to a work which stands in the first rank of modern adaptations of the old sagas, William Morris's "The Story of Sigurd the Völsung, and the Fall of the Niblungs[4] (London, 1877; Kelmscott Press, 1898). Though the poem follows in general the Scandinavian version of the story, the influence of the Old German poem is noticeable in two ways. In the first place, as F. Hueffer pointed out in his review in the *Gentleman's Magazine,* xix. (N.S.) 46 *ff.,* Morris's metre is practically that of the *Nibelungenlied.* Each line contains six stresses, after the third of which follows usually a syllable without stress, then the cæsura. As a rule the feet are iambic, but anapæsts are frequent, especially at the beginning of the line and after the cæsura. The rime, too, is masculine, but there is no division into strophes.

As regards the contents, Morris adhered for the most part more or less closely to the Norse tradition, but the influence of the *Nibelungenlied* is sometimes discernible in details as well as in one important motive. Gudrun does not warn her brothers of the intended treachery; on the contrary she is bent on avenging Sigurd's death, and with this end arouses Atli's desire for the Nibelungen treasure. Among the lesser traces of the influence of the German poem are the constant use of the phrases, "the need of the Niblungs," and "The Niblungs' need" towards the end of the poem; the substitution of the *falcon* for the *hawk* in

Gudrun's dream (p. 176); Hogni's advice to his comrades to throw out the corpses from the hall after the first conflict (p. 363); his ruse of allowing some of the Huns to enter, that they may be the more easily slain (p. 364); and the drinking of the blood of the slain (p. 366).

The third of these occurs in the following passage, as also an addition which seems to have been suggested by the *Nibelungenlied* scene where Volker plays the weary Burgundians to sleep (pp. 363 *f.*):—

> Then biddeth the heart-wise Hogni, and men to the windows climb,
> And uplift the war-grey corpses, dead drift of the stormy time,
> And cast them adown to their people: thence they come aback and say
> That scarce shall ye see the houses, and no whit the wheel-worn way
> For the spears and shields of the Eastlands that the merchant city throng;
> And back to the Niblung burg-gate the way seemed weary-long.
>
> Yet passeth hour on hour, and the doors they watch and ward
> But a long while hear no mail-clash, nor the ringing of the sword;
> Then droop the Niblung children, and their wounds are waxen chill,
> And they think of the Burg by the river, and the builded holy hill,
> And their eyes are set on Gudrun as of men who would beseech;
> But unlearned are they in craving and know not dastard's speech.
> Then doth Giuki's first-begotten a deed most fair to be told,
> For his fair harp Gunnar taketh, and the warp of silver and gold;
> With the hand of a cunning harper he dealeth with the strings,
> And his voice in their midst goeth upward, as of ancient days he sings
> Of the days before the Niblungs, and the days that shall be yet;
> Till the hour of toil and smiting the warrior hearts forget,
> Nor hear the gathering foemen, nor the sound of swords aloof:
> Then clear the song of Gunnar goes up to the dusky roof,
> And the coming spear-host tarries, and the bearers of the woe
> Through the cloisters of King Atli with lingering footsteps go.

Although "Sigurd the Völsung" is the only work by Morris in which the influence of the *Nibelungenlied* is strongly marked, he was acquainted with the old epic at least as early as 1856. In that year he contributed to the *Oxford and Cambridge Magazine* (started by himself and a few friends in January 1856, but discontinued after twelve months), a tale entitled, "The Hollow Land," and headed by a quotation from the *Nibelungenlied.*[5] It was probably due to Morris's influence that Burne-Jones, who was associated with him in bringing out the magazine referred to, painted in the same year "a city background to a picture of the *Nibelungenlied.*"[6]

One book remains to be noticed: J. Baldwin's "The Story of Siegfried" (London, undated; acquired by the British Museum, 1883).

The materials for this story, told especially for young people, are gathered from nearly all the numerous versions of the saga. In some parts the *Nibelungenlied* is followed, in others the Eddas or the Völsungasaga, and occasionally the minor poems. Episodes from Teutonic mythology are also woven into the story, but the details are largely products of Baldwin's imagination.

The whole is divided into twenty "Adventures," of which the first eight (pp. 1-114) are chiefly concerned with Siegfried's early fortunes, *i.e.* those prior to the point at which the *Nibelungenlied* takes up the story. Adventure ix. relates "The Journey to Burgundy-Land," making Siegfried arrive there unawares, and contrary to his father's advice. Kriemhild's dream appears in x., but xi., "How the Springtime came," contains the story of Idun and her apples. The remaining Adventures continue the story up to Siegfried's death, and the bringing of the Hoard to Burgundy. Interruptions occur, however, in xiii. (the story of Balder), xv. (containing "Alberich's Story"), and xvii. (the story of Loki). Apart from these digressions, the latter part of the book is based mainly on the *Nibelungenlied.* Some useful notes occupy pp. 294-306, with a number of quotations from and references to other works, among them: Carlyle's Essay, Morris's "Sigurd the Volsung," Weber's "Northern Antiquities," and the translations of Auber Forestier and Lettsom.

The tone of the book is thoroughly healthy and breezy, as well as imaginative and poetical. To the student it would be of little value, but it is eminently fitted for its purpose as a book for young people.

Notes

1. There is a copy in the British Museum.
2. A prominent character in the *Rosengarten zu Worms,* where he represents the ex-warrior who has entered a monastery but lost none of his pugnacity.
3. In the footnote to p. 240, four lines of the *Nibelungenlied* are translated as testimony to the source from which these two dreams are taken.
4. *Cf.* Gustav Gruener's "The Nibelungenlied and Sage in Modern Poetry," *M.L.A.A.,* xi. 220 *ff.* Noticed on p. 112.
5. M'Kail, "Life of W. Morris," vol. i. p. 98.
6. Bell, "Edward Burne-Jones," p. 26.

George Fenwick Jones (essay date 1960)

SOURCE: "Rüdiger's Dilemma," *Studies in Philology,* Vol. LVII, No. 1, January, 1960, pp. 7-21.

[*In the following essay, Jones explains how the Germanic ethics of the* Nibelungenlied *differ from modern values, and urges that the reader be aware of these differences in trying to understand the motivation of the characters in the work.*]

We smile at jousts before the walls of Troy in medieval epics and at cannons in early illustrations of Old Testament battlefields; yet we tend to be less critical of modern thoughts and sentiments attributed to historical characters by recent novelists and even by historians and literary critics. Restricted as we are to our own culture, we find it hard to realize that people can experience reality through a completely different set of terms and values, unless by chance we have read anthropological studies of primitive civilizations. Unfortunately, it is a difficult task to enter the spirit of a past time, as Goethe's Faust complains to Wagner. Bygone days are a book with seven seals, and what we call the spirit of the times is basically our own spirit, in which the times are reflected.

To illustrate the difficulty of correctly interpreting ancient literature, I have selected Rüdiger's dilemma in the thirty-seventh canto of the **Lay of the Nibelungs,** because it is well known and has often been interpreted from a modern point of view. Margrave Rüdiger was a vassal of the Hunnish king Attila, or Etzel as he was known in German legends. A penniless exile when he arrived at the Hunnish court, he soon won the king's favor through loyal service and became his most trusted liege-man. After the death of Etzel's wife, Rüdiger was chosen to woo another for him, namely Kriemhild, Siegfried's widow. Kriemhild, who yearned to avenge the murder of her husband, accepted Etzel's suit only after Rüdiger promised to serve her faithfully in whatever thing she commanded.

Later, when Kriemhild lures her brothers, the Burgundian kings, to Etzel's court, Rüdiger entertains them en route in his castles at Bechlarn, gives them rich gifts, affiances his daughter to one of them, and conducts them, in all innocence, to Etzel's court. Then, after Kriemhild has started hostilities between the Burgundians and the Huns, she commands Rüdiger to fight against the Burgundians, even though they are now his friends and kinsmen.

Modern critics have explained Rüdigers's quandary as a conflict of duties, or else as a struggle of contradictory loyalties, or even as the struggle of duty against inclination, that is, of *Pflicht* versus *Neigung*. Gustav Ehrismann, whose history of medieval German literature remains the most influential handbook on the subject, says that Rüdiger "falls in the conflict of two duties: through duty to his liege-lady he must fight to the death against his friends; fealty is stronger than friendship."[1] Ehrismann believed Rüdiger more concerned with his inner integrity than with public opinion concerning it. This is not surprising, in view of his equation of the word *êre* with Ciceronian *honestum,*[2] an equation which has since been discredited.[3]

A quarter of a century later, in what is perhaps the most penetrating interpretation of this episode, Friedrich Panzer describes a "grave spiritual conflict, into which a deeply moral and basically good man sees himself placed. He must choose between two conflicting duties, the violation of which no matter which he decides to follow, will bring him the contempt and reproach of the world."[4] Although Panzer mentions the hero's concern for his good name, he nevertheless stresses his basic morality and seems to attribute it to his innate moral goodness.

In a popular literary history of the same year, Helmut de Boor finds Rüdiger more "modern" than Dietrich von Bern, another protagonist in the poem. Only in his case is the tragedy "a spiritual conflict without resolution. He is not, like Dietrich, above the parties; he feels himself crushed between them. Any decision he makes will destroy his moral personality (str. 2134). He alone feels a threat to his soul and its salvation, and he alone can truly turn to and appeal to God. Also, his certainty of death is unlike that of the others: it emanates from the morally broken man's awareness that his salvation has been destroyed by his own decision. It lacks the exaltation of victory. Yet the poet finally leads him back into the heroic sphere. Rüdiger is morally justified in the incomparable scene in which he exchanges shields with Hagen. This is not through divine guidance or grace. The confirmation of his moral integrity through the magnanimous gesture of the friendly enemy is the restoration of his honor, a restoration formed in accord with the heroic view of life. Therefore his final struggle and death are not unlike the heroic fates of the others."[5]

As we shall see, these modern interpretations are correct only if the words "moral" (*sittlich*), "duty" (*Pflicht*), and "honor" (*Ehre*) are related to old Germanic ethics, rather than to modern Christian-Stoic values. This is difficult to do. Jan de Vries thus explains a modern German's difficulty in understanding the thoughts of his Germanic forefathers: "He speaks the same language, even if at another stage of its development; but it seems that strangers are talking with each other. Even if we say faith, honor, holiness, gift, or marriage, we mean something essentially different by these words from that which our heathen ancestors meant. In any case, their concept has an entirely different nuance. We must even be ready to expect that the similarity of the language will sometimes hinder us more than help us, because we are much too inclined to overlook the gulf between the old and the new meanings of the words."[6]

If this task is difficult for a German, it is perhaps even more difficult for an American. When reading Ehrismann, Panzer, or de Boor, a young American will tend to translate *Treue* and *Ehre* as "loyalty" and "honor," which are worlds apart from the original concepts of *triuwe* and *êre*.[7] The word "duty" (*Pflicht*) has no counterpart in the **Lay of the Nibelungs,** unless it is thought to be included in the word *triuwe*. Likewise, the much used term "moral" or "ethical" (*sittlich*), which also lacks a counterpart in the poem, must be related to Germanic ethics, which was based on social custom rather than divine sanction.[8]

Ehrismann, Panzer, and de Boor do not indicate that good deeds in a heroic shame-culture are motivated differently from those in modern Christian civilization. By saying nothing to the contrary, these scholars imply that this struggle, which nearly all call a *Seelenkampf,* is in the same category as the internal struggles experienced by the protagonists of nineteenth-century, that is to say post-Kantian, dramas. But is the problem the same? Before deciding this question, perhaps we should quickly survey the cultural origins of Rüdiger's difficult decision.

As most critics agree, the **Lay of the Nibelungs** is firmly rooted in ancient Germanic folkways. In order to survive, every society must inculcate into its members those attitudes and behavior patterns necessary for its own maintenance. Because the ancient Teutons were constantly at war, they extolled the martial virtues of courage and loyalty to one's leader. In order to foster such virtues, Germanic society praised those men who practiced them and scorned those who did not. According to Tacitus's *Germania,* cowards were drowned in quagmires (c. 12) and anyone who threw away his shield in battle was barred from sacrifice and council (c. 6); and therefore it is not surprising that survivors of lost battles often hanged themselves (c. 6).

To be esteemed a man of honor, a warrior had to fulfill his promise to fight for his leader. The bond between Germanic chieftains and their followers was often designated by the word *triuwe,* a word that originally denoted a contract or agreement.[9] Such a bond or contract was inviolable once hostilities had begun. As Caesar relates in his *Gallic War* (IV, 23), if a warrior failed to fight after promising his services, he was scorned and never again trusted. The fate of such shirkers is vividly portrayed near the end of *Beowulf,* when Wiglaf reviles the faithless retainers who failed their leader in battle. It is to be noted that *triuwe,* being a contract, could be terminated at will by either party, provided he gave due notice and returned the gifts he had received. Whereas *triuwe* was voluntary between leader and follower, it was automatic and obligatory between kinsmen, even between those joined only by marriage; and it was also binding between host and guest.[10]

The purpose of being brave and loyal was to win honor and avoid shame; for lasting fame was man's only hope of immortality.[11] In contrast to this shame-culture, the Christian missionaries introduced a guilt-culture: they taught that men should do good works in return for heavenly rewards and should avoid evil in order to escape hell's fire. Many pagan virtues, such as keeping faith, were felt to be pleasing to God and were therefore endorsed by the Church. Others, such as greed for fame and desire for revenge, were believed displeasing to God and therefore damned as sins.

In addition to these easily understood teachings about divine reward and punishment, the Christian missionaries also introduced some ideas from the Greek Stoics, whose philosophy had begun to reach Rome at about the time the Teutons first tried to cross the Roman frontiers. The Stoics, who were interested in the individual rather than in society, felt that a man's true value lay in himself rather than in the judgment of other people. Consequently honor, in the sense of public esteem and renown, had no value, except in so far as its absence might be harmful.

Stoic scorn for fame was transmitted to medieval Churchmen through Cicero's *De Officiis,* which argues that *honestum,* or moral rectitude, is more desirable than public acclaim. Nevertheless, even though such an attitude is occasionally reflected in clerical writings,[12] it had little influence on secular literature, which continued to recognize public opinion and worldly fame as the highest values. The old Germanic views about honor and fame prevailed not only in *Beowulf* and the Norse sagas but even in the French *chansons de geste* and the German court poetry of the High Middle Ages. Except for the introduction of moderation as an ideal in courtly poetry, Stoic influences are at a minimum, especially with regard to fame and honor.[13]

The Germanic ethos of the **Lay of the Nibelungs** is apparent at first glance. To be sure, God is often invoked; yet these invocations are extraneous and merely an ingredient of the courtly veneer that has been superimposed on the basic work. In fact the pagan Etzel invokes God as often as the Christian warriors do. The church at Worms serves only as a setting for two queens to squabble over precedence, an action more worthy of Germanic than Christian conduct; and a chaplain accompanies the Burgundians on their fatal trip to Etzel's land so that Hagen can throw him into the Danube and thus test the mermaids' dire prophecy. Courage and *triuwe* are the chief virtues in the **Lay of the Nibelungs,** just as they had been in ancient Germanic epics. Except for the Huns, everyone in the poem is immensely brave. *Triuwe* is illustrated often, best in Hagen's loyalty to his lords and in their refusal to turn him over to Kriemhild to save their own lives. The Germanic virtue of largess (*milte*) is mentioned constantly in the poem, but mostly in connection with its practical function of earning honor. Typical are the statements that Siegfried's parents were liberal at their festival in order to win honor with wealth[14] and that Gunther serves his guests good food to avoid disgrace.[15] When Gunther rewards the emissaries from his Saxon and Danish enemies, he does so through a will to superiority, as is shown by their fear to refuse.[16]

The Burgundians put honor above all other considerations, and desire for honor motivates all their actions. Kriemhild desires revenge in order to reinstate her honor; and, even though they know of her treacherous designs, the Burgundians must accept her fatal invitation rather than be considered cowards. When Siegfried is betrayed, he reminds his murderers that even their descendants will be reproached, like those of Beowulf's faithless vassals.[17]

If we except Rüdiger, it is clear that no character in the **Lay of the Nibelungs** does good works for disinterested reasons. To use Kantian terminology, no one obeys the categorical imperative. When the Burgundians attack the Saxons, they do so not out of patriotism, or even out of an inner sense of duty, but rather to win honor.[18] Gernot tells his brothers that they should be loyal to Kriemhild because it will bring them honor,[19] and Gunther seconds him by saying that he wishes to maintain his *triuwe* and not act shamefully.[20] When Irinc insists on fighting alone with Hagen, he does so to win honor,[21] and twelve heroes join Rüdiger in order to win renown.[22] When Dietrich thinks that Hildebrand has broken the truce, he says that he would take his life if he would not suffer disgrace because of it,[23] and later he refuses to kill Hagen because it would bring him little honor to kill an exhausted man.[24] No one tries to appeal to anyone's sense of right and wrong, but only to his desire for honor. When Gernot asks Etzel to let the Burgundians fight in the open, he assures him that it will bring him honor.[25] Dietrich reminds Kriemhild that she will suffer dishonor if she attacks her kinsmen, especially since they have come trustingly.[26]

But is Rüdiger really an exception? He could be, because, as Friedrich Panzer has proved,[27] he was a late importation from France, a character created at the time of the *Moralium Dogma*. Moreover, he is frequently called *der guote* and he asks God for guidance. Yet, if Rüdiger were an exception, then the **Lay of the Nibelungs** would be an inconsistent work, and this is certainly not the case. Rüdiger's epithet of *der guote* is probably due to the fact that Ogier, his prototype in the French epic *Renaus de Montauban*, was often called *le bon*. Besides that, the epithet *der guote* did not necessarily imply moral goodness, in our sense of the word. Gunther is so designated even though he acts treacherously towards Siegfried.[28] Today, the term "a good man" suggests moral excellence, whereas "a good boxer" merely suggests skill, courage, and endurance. In MHG literature *guot*, when attributed to men, most often suggested power, wealth, and majesty; and it was also the antonym of the word *bœse*, in its sense of weak or cowardly. Perhaps God was invoked so often in the Rüdiger episode because He had been invoked often in the *chanson de geste* on which it was based, but even there such invocations were largely an extraneous adornment. As in the **Lay of the Nibelungs,** the heroes of *Renaus de Montauban* seem motivated largely by concern for their good names.[29]

Much mention is made of Rüdiger's exceptional *milte;* but there is no proof that it is performed disinterestedly. When Rüdiger persuades the Burgundians to accept his hospitality for four days, the poet adds, "that was spoken of far and wide"; and, because of such lavish entertainment, Rüdiger could live liberally with great honors.[30] We should remember that, in the case of a man of honor, liberality was performed in order to win praise, as many courtly poets have attested.

But rather than conjecture about Rüdiger's true motivation, why don't we ask him? Then we will see that he, like his ancient pagan ancestors, is concerned more with his good name as a warrior and a vassal than with Divine Law or categorical imperatives. When Rüdiger swears his fatal oath to Kriemhild, he assures her that, when she reminds him of it, he will never disgrace himself by breaking it.[31] When Etzel offers Rüdiger extra funds for his trip

to Worms, Rüdiger refuses them on the grounds that it would be *unlobelîch* to desire them.[32] De Boor, the editor of the most popular text, explains *unlobelîch* to mean *unangemessen,* or improper.[33] But why not say "unpraiseworthy," as the Nibelung poet did? As we have seen, medieval men judged the value of an act by public opinion, not by subjective evaluation. Before going to Worms, Rüdiger sees to the weapons and clothes of his retainers so they will enjoy honor before the princes.[34] When Etzel and Kriemhild insist that he fight the Burgundians, he is afraid that if he kills one of them the world will hate him.[35] When the Burgundians remind him of the gifts he has given them, he tells them that he wishes he could continue to give to them so that he could thereby avoid reproach.[36] He then apologizes to the Burgundians and says that he wishes they were back on the Rhine and he were dead with honors.[37] When he finally enters the fray, the poet calls him a "fame-thirsting man,"[38] and rightfully so, since he is driven to his doom by his desire for an untarnished reputation.

As Etzel's vassal, Rüdiger must prove his *triuwe* by defending his liege-lord's honor against his enemies. In addition, he has also made a solemn oath, along with all his men, to serve Kriemhild personally and preserve her honor.[39] Therefore, according to ancient yet still valid Germanic law, failure to fulfill his obligation will make him *triuwelôs,* and therefore both *rehtelôs* and *erlôs.*[40] As we have seen, this would have been a fate worse than death.

Although Rüdiger is deterred from his fealty by legal and emotional ties to the Burgundians, he knows that people will call him a coward if he does not fight. In the *Lay of Hildebrand,* the father must kill his own son rather than be called a coward.[41] So too Rüdiger must fight his new kinsmen rather than suffer such ignominy. The kind of insult he would suffer had been indicated by Volker's denunciation of the timid Huns: "Those who eat the prince's bread here so shamefully and now refuse him in his need, I see many of them standing around most cravenly, although they would like to be brave. They shall always suffer disgrace because of it."[42] Rüdiger is right in fearing such reproach; for a Hun soon sees him hesitating and remarks that, although he has enjoyed Etzel's favors, he has not yet struck a praiseworthy stroke;[43] and Rüdiger must vindicate his honor by striking the Hun dead with his fist. Even after Rüdiger has died in honoring his obligation, Kriemhild reviles him as a troth-breaker because she thinks he is negotiating to conduct the Burgundians back to Worms in spite of her gifts.[44]

Both Volker and the Hun allude to material gifts, for it was these that made feudal obligations binding. Consequently, Rüdiger begs Kriemhild and Etzel to take back all the castles and lands they have given him and to let him leave as he came, a penniless exile.[45] This was a noble gesture, for exile was a fearful existence for an other-directed man; and it is not by chance that the MHG word for exile has become the NHG word for misery (*Elend*).

However, the battle has begun, and it is now too late for Rüdiger to serve notice without loss of honor. On the other hand, it is also too late for him to break honorably with the Burgundians, as Gunther reminds him.[46] According to Germanic law and ethics, he could have terminated his *triuwe* to them unilaterally, provided that he had given due notice, returned all gifts, and broken off his daughter's engagement. In his case, he would probably have had to conduct them safely out of Etzel's land too, since he was responsible for having brought them there.

Rüdiger's true motivation is perhaps best revealed in the two strophes in which he deplores having to renounce all the *êren, triuwen,* and *zuhten* that God has granted him because, no matter which choice he makes, he will have acted *bœslîche* and very *übele*.[47] If he does neither, it will be even worse: all people will reproach him. In reading these strophes we are subconsciously influenced by the meaning of the modern words *Ehre, Treue, Zucht, böslich,* and *übel,* which naturally lead us astray.

In her dissertation on the words *triuwe* and *stæte,* Vera Vollmer remarks that "nothing makes the understanding of Middle High German poets more difficult for the modern reader than the numerous abstract words like *güete, kiusche, êre, riuwe, genade, zuht, mâze, triuwe, stæte,* and *reine, valsch, sælic.* To be sure, most of these expressions still exist in the language of today; but the difficulty lies precisely therein. Instead of investigating the meaning of the expressions in Middle High German thoroughly in order to find the New High German word corresponding most closely (as one would do if the words no longer existed today), one is tempted merely to use the present linguistic form."[48] It will be noted that she expressly mentions the three important nouns in Rüdiger's famous declamation.

No doubt Rüdiger's abstract words already had strong moral overtones; yet they suit this context best in their older meanings: *êren,* honors; *triuwen,* fealty; *zuhten,* decorum; *bœslîche,* cowardly; *übele,* nocuously. Since the *triuwen* and *zuhten* are gifts of God that Rüdiger can lose, they can best be understood as his reputation for practicing these virtues;[49] for, as we have seen, other-directed men cannot distinguish between intrinsic values and their social recognition. But regardless of Rüdiger's conscious meaning, we can see that, in good rhetorical style, he has put the most important factor last: "All people will reproach me."

As Friedrich Panzer has observed, the language of these two strophes seems to have been influenced by a passage in Hartmann of Aue's *Iwein,* in which the Arthurian knight Iwein must make a similar choice.[50] Iwein is obligated to defend an old knight from a giant because the old knight is his host and also the brother-in-law of his friend Gawein. Unfortunately the giant is scheduled to appear on the very day that Iwein has promised to defend Lunete in a trial by combat many miles away. When the giant is late in arriving, Iwein fears that all his honor will be lost. The host promises him money to remain and reminds him that both his friend Gawein and God will be indebted to him if

he does. Iwein at first agrees to remain, but then he wavers. He will be dishonored if he rides away; yet he will be disgraced if he remains.[51] If he does not help his hosts, he will be considered a coward.[52] In his quandary he, like Rüdiger, calls upon God for guidance. Unlike Rüdiger, however, his problem is solved happily; for the giant arrives in time for Iwein to defeat him and hurry on to his next commitment and thus save his good name.

Like Ogier, but unlike Iwein, Rüdiger at first regrets having to jeopardize his soul; for he seems to believe that God damns those who violate their promise of safe-conduct,[53] although it was the heathen Teutons rather than the Christians who scorned this practice. In spite of this much-mentioned concern for his soul, Rüdiger nevertheless decides in favor of his worldly reputation and thus shows that, even in his case, pagan values outweighed Christian ones. As mentioned, he feared that the *world* (not God!) would hate him if he killed one of the Burgundians.

As mentioned earlier, the ancient Germans had an anthropocentric value code and strove for the recognition and praise of their peers; for both the criterion and the reward of good behavior was the opinion of mankind. The theocentric code introduced by the Church taught that good deeds should be performed in exchange for heavenly rewards; and churchmen formulated a pattern of behavior believed to be pleasing to God. Naturally this behavior pattern prevailed as an ideal as long as the Church dominated society and convinced people of the reality of heavenly rewards.

With the Enlightenment, however, many people began to question the reality of heavenly rewards. Nevertheless, the values and behavior patterns introduced by the Church had been so long accepted that they were felt to have intrinsic value even without divine authority. Deprived of divine sanction, they had to stand on their own merits. That is to say, they were credited with absolute value. As Cicero had stated so many centuries before, moral rectitude was of value for its own sake, not because it was pleasing to men or to the gods.

Since the age of Kant, this philosophic view has steadily spread at the cost of the theological view. In the dramas of Schiller and Hebbel, for example, the more admirable protagonists care more for absolute right and wrong than for public opinion or even divine rewards. Hebbel's Duke Ernst is concerned with helping his subjects, not with winning their praise. On the other hand, Hebbel's petty family tyrant, Meister Anton, is primarily concerned with what the neighbors will think; and he treasures his honor above his daughter's life.

In Wedekind's *Der Kammersänger,* the opera singer Gerardo says, "The measure for a man's importance is the world and not the inner conviction that he acquires through years of brooding."[54] Later, when his mistress commits suicide in his room, his only concern is that he will miss the train to Brussels and thus break his contract, for no one will engage an artist who is *kontraktbrüchig*. It is apparent that Wedekind, as a modern man with Stoic views about inner and outer values, considers Gerardo contemptible; yet Gerardo's motivation would have been quite worthy of a Germanic hero, who would have also respected the world's opinion and heroically sacrificed all, even the lives of his friends, rather than break a contract.

But such observations do not mean that other-directed motivation cannot furnish great tragedy. To the contrary, the other-directed hero is the stuff of great drama. Because we have recently been taught that outer values are less noble than inner ones, we are reluctant to attribute them to the heroes of old. We are like the little boy who asked the preacher about the joys of Heaven, and if they are like eating ice cream. When the preacher assured him that they are not like eating ice cream, but are a thousand times greater, the little boy was disillusioned and lost his faith in God, because he could not believe that anything else could be so good as eating ice cream.

Actually, the loss of honor by an other-directed man is the most tragic fate imaginable. The Christian martyr or the inner-directed man who perishes in a good cause has the inner satisfaction of knowing that he is right. The other-directed man who loses the world's esteem loses his self-esteem too, since he has no inner resources to fall back on. Rüdiger must lose his honor, the treasure he values above all else. Should he be defeated, he will lose his honor, as all defeated warriors do. If he survives, he will be publicly scorned for betraying his guests and kinsmen. If he refuses to fight them, he will be called a coward as well as troth-breaker and will be shunned by honorable society. When he finally enters the fight, he does so in hope of finding death, not because death will vindicate his honor, but rather it will save him from living to see his shame. He does not know that poetic justice will let him slay his slayer and thus remove one small item of his disgrace by letting him be killed without being defeated.

If anyone doubts that loss of public esteem is fitting stuff for tragedy, let him ask Shakespeare, the greatest dramatist of all. In *Richard II,* when Norfolk is accused of breaking his fealty to his kings, he begs permission to fight a duel with his slanderer in order to regain his honor. He says:

> The purest treasure mortal times afford
> Is spotless reputation. That away,
> Men are but guilded loam or painted clay.
> A jewel in a ten times barr'd-up chest
> Is a bold spirit in a loyal breast.
> Mine honour is my life. Both grow in one:
> Take honour from me, and my life is done.
> Then, dear my liege, mine honour let me try;
> In that I live, and for that I will die.

Obviously Norfolk is using "honour" in the sense of "reputation"; for, as philosophers have long taught, no one can take away a man's inner integrity. Rüdiger, who was created fully four centuries before Norfolk, was also con-

cerned with his good name more than with the fulfillment of any categorical imperative, as a nineteenth-century hero might have been. And, like Norfolk, he was ready to die for his reputation.

Notes

1. "Mannentreue geht vor Freundestreue" (*Geschichte der deutohen Literatur,* München, 1935, II, *Sohlussband,* p. 136). He summarizes this episode as: "Kriemhild mahnt Rüedeger an seinen Treueid, und nach schwerem Seelenkampfe folgt er seiner Dienstpflicht" (p. 134).

2. "Die Grundlagen des ritterlichen Tugendsystems," *Zeitschrift für deutsches Altertum,* 56, 1919, pp. 137-215; and throughout his *Geschichte der deuischen Literatur.*

3. See E. R. Curtius, "Des 'ritterliche Tugensystem'," *Deutsche Viertel-Jahrsschrift,* 21, 1943, pp. 343 ff. Reprinted in *Europäische Literatur und lateinisches Mittelalter,* Bern, 1948, *Exkurs* 18, 508-523. See also Friedrich Maurer, "Das ritterliche Tugendsystem," *Deutsche Vierteljahrsschrift,* 23, 1949, pp. 274-285, and "Tugend und Ehre," *Wirkendes Wort,* 1951-52, *Heft* 2, pp. 72-80.

4. *Das Nibelungenlied,* Stuttgart, 1955, p. 421. See pp. 256-261, 421-424. In describing Rüdiger's unlimited liberality, he attributes it to his goodness of heart (p. 257) and does not mention, as the poet so frankly does, that gifts are given in exchange for praise.

5. H. de Boor and R. Newald, *Geschichte der deutschen Literatur,* München, 1955, II, p. 166.

6. *Die geistige Welt der Germanen,* Halle, 1945, pp. 2-3.

7. A typical American definition of "honor" is that in *Morrow's Wordfinder,* ed. P. Hugon, N. Y. 1927, p. 157: "A high excellence of character tending particularly to respect of the unprotected rights of others; (honesty, respect for the property rights of others.)" An informal poll of Princeton students produced impromptu definitions such as "an inner sense of right and wrong," "a character trait causing one to do what he thinks is right," etc. Not a single student referred to objective honor as a possible meaning. It is not surprising that many students erroneously write their honor pledge as "I pledge *on* my honour . . ." instead of "I pledge my honor . . ."

8. Hans Kuhn states: "Sittlichkeit und Religion haben bei den heidnischen Germanen nicht viel miteinander zu tun gehabt. Ihre sittlichen Forderungen waren keine göttlichen Gebote" (*Germanische Altertumskunde,* ed. H. Schneider, München, 1951, p. 177).

9. Jan de Vries, p. 20.

10. When Tacitus says the Teutons considered it *nefas* to refuse to give hospitality to a stranger (*Germania,* c. 21), *nefas* should be interpreted as "shameful." This attitude lasted for centuries. In *Lamprechts Alex-*

ander (ed. K. Kinzel, Halle, 1884, vv. 6355-6358) Queen Candacis warns her sons: "woldet ir an einen gaste tûn uher laster, des wurde after lande gebreitet uher scande." Her appeal is not made to their sense of right but only to their concern for their reputations.

11. "Der Ruhm, die 'gute Nachrede nach dem Tode,' ist dem Heiden, was dem Christen die ewige Seligkeit: das höchste gute" (Andreas Heusler, *Germanentum*, p. 103); "Der höchste Besitz des Germanen und der entscheidende Massstab für alles, was er tat und liess, war seine Ehre und de Ruhum, der ihn überleben sollte" (Hans Kuhn in *Germanische Altertumskunde*, p. 215).

12. Stoic views on honor were readily available in Boethius' *De Consolatione Philosophiae* and St. Martin of Braga's *Formula Vitae Honestae*.

13. Thirteenth-century poets were frank in saying that men did good works in order to win praise: "Darumb tut ein pider man guten dinch daz man in preis" (*Die Gedichte Heinrichs des Teichners*, ed. H. Niewöhner, Berlin, 1953, 1, pp. 10-11).

14. "Die mohten wol bejagen mit guote michel êre" (*NL*, 29, 2-3. All references to *Das Nibelungenlied*, ed. H. de Boor, Leipzig, 1949, *Deutsche Klassiker des Mittelalters*, Vol. III).

15. "aller slahte schande" (*NL*, 309).

16. "dine torsten niht versprechen" (*NL*, 166, 3).

17. "Die sint dâ von bescholten, swaz ir wirt geborn her nâch disen zîten" (990, 1); "mit laster ir gescheiden sult von guoten recken sîn" (990, 4).

18. "sus wurben nâch den êren" (*NL*, 203, 4); "die stolzen Burgunden habent sô gevarn, daz si vor allen scanden ir êre kunnen wol bewarn" (232, 3-4).

19. "wir suln ir sîn getriuwe, daz ist zen êren uns gewant" (*NL*, 1211, 4).

20. "wir suln doch niht alle meinlîchen tuon" (*NL*, 1213, 2).

21. "er warp nâch êren" (*NL*, 2036, 3).

22. "die wolden prîs erwerben" (*NL*, 2169, 3).

23. "het ihs niht immer schande" (*NL*, 2312, 4).

24. "ich hâns lützel êre" (*NL*, 2351, 2).

25. "daz ist iu êre getân" (*NL*, 2096, 4).

26. Diu bete dich lützel êret (*NL*, 1902, 1). See note 10.

27. *Studien zum Nibelungenlied*, Frankfurt, 1943, pp. 58-72; also in *Das Nibelungenlied*, Stuttgart, 1955, pp. 421-24.

28. *NL*, 141, 1; 1148. 1. Gunther is called *ungetriuwe* (*NL*, 887, 3).

29. In the few verses quoted by Panzer (*Studien*, pp. 62-67) we find: v. 8222, "Bien me doit tot li mons et blamer et honnir"; vv. 7421-22, "Se tu nous lais morir, ce sera mesprison: Reprochié te sera mais en

tres toutes corts"; vv. 10039-40, "Jamais honor n'auroie nul jor en nul pais, Ains seroie honis, dolereus et mendis."

30. "dô wart dâ getân von des wirtes milte daz vere wart geseit (*NL*, 1691, 2-3); er konde mileclîche mit grôzen êren leben (1694, 3). Spervogel alluded to the fame that Rüdiger acquired through his hospitality by saying of a generous man, "Dô der guote Wernhart an dise werlt geborn wart, dô begonde er teilen al sîn guot. dô gewan der Rüedegeres muot, der saz ze Bechelæren und pflac der marke mangen tac; der wart von sîner frümkeit sô mære." (*Minnesanges Rrühling*, 25, 34-26, 5).

31. "ich tuon iu selbe alsam, swenne ir mich mant der mære, daz ich michs nimmer gescham" (*NL*, 1266, 3-4). This verse seems to have been misunderstood by Simrock and many other translators.

32. "gerte ich dînes guotes, daz wære unlobelîch" (*NL*, 1153, 2).

33. Footnote to *NL*, 1153,2. Likewise, when Kriemhild's uncle advises her to buy honor as Helche has done, de Boor explains *koufen* to mean "acquire" or "earn" (*erwerben, verdienen*, note to 1330, 3), although it was clearly a business transaction.

34. "alsô daz wir's êre vor fürsten mügen hân" (*NL*, 1155, 3). See also 339, 2; 334, 4; 345, 4; 360, 4, *et passim*.

35. "vil sêre vorhte er daz, ob er ir einen slüege, daz im diu werlt trüege haz" (*NL*, 2156, 3-4).

36. "sone wurde mir dar umbe nimmer schelten gatân" (*NL*, 2181, 4).

37. "Das wolde got . . . daz ir ze Rîne wæret unde ich wære tôt mit etelichen êren" (*NL*, 2183, 1-3).

38. "êre gernde man" (*NL*, 2218, 3). In inciting him into action, Kriemhild reminds him that she has heard many heroes speak well of him: "ich hôrt'iu vil der recken den prîs vil grœzlîchen geben" (*NL*, 2148, 4).

39. "des sî êre haben solde, des sichert'ir Rüedegêres hant" (*NL*, 1258, 4). See 1266.

40. Rudolf von Ems lets Alexander say of his vassals, "brechen die ir triuwe an mir, daz laster und die schande ist ir" (*Alexander*, vv. 14, 553-54). The hero of his *Wilhelm von Orlens* (vv. 9496-98) says, "Brichet er denne die warheit, So muos er iemere Triuwelos sin unde ane ere."

41. W. Braune, *Althochdeuisches Lesebuch*, Halle, 1949, XXVIII, vv. 58 ff.

42. "Die hie sô lasterlîchen ezzent des fürsten brôt unde im nu geswîchent in der græzesten nôt, der siche ich hie manigen vil zagelîche stân, unt wellent dôch sîn küene: si müezens immer schande hân" (*NL*, 2027).

43. *NL*, 2139.

44. *NL*, 2228, 2229.

45. *NL*, 2157.

46. "Ir widersagt uns nu ze spâte" (*NL*, 2179, 1).

47. "Owê mir gotes armen, daz ich ditz gelebet hân. aller mîner êren der muoz ich abe stân, triuwen unde zühte, der got an mir gebôt. owê got von himele, daz mihs niht wendet der tôt! (*NL*, 2153). Swelhez ich nu lâze unt daz ander begân, sô hân ich bœslîche und vil übele getân: lâze aber ich si beide, mich schiltet elliu diet. nu ruoche mich bewîsen der mir ze lebene geriet." (*NL*, 2154).

48. *Die Begriffe der Triuwe und der Stæte in der höfischen Minnedichtung,* Diss. Tübingen, 1914, p. 1.

49. After Rüdiger has given him his shield, Hagen says: "got sol daz gebieten daz iuwer tugent immer lebe" (*NL*, 2199). Here *tugent* probably means "fame of your virtue." See strophes 2151, 2161. According to Werner Bopp, *Die Geschichte des Wortes 'tugent,'* Dissertation Heidelberg, 1935, p. 33, the word *tugent* could be used to mean praise or the public recognition of praiseworthy behavior.

50. *Hartmann von Aue, Ereo Iwein,* ed. H. Naumann, Leipzig, 1933, vv. 4870-4913.

51. "ich bin, als ez mir nû stât, guněret ob ich rîte und geschendet ob "ch bîte" (vv. 4885-86).

52. "sô hânt sî des iemer wân daz ich des lîbes sî ein zage" (*NL*, 4911-12).

53. "daz ich die sêle vliese, des enhân ich niht gesworn. zuo dirre hôhgesîte brâht'ich die fürsten wol geborn" (*NL*, 2150, 3-4).

54. "Der Maszstab für die Bedeutung eines Menschen ist die Welt und nicht die innere Überzeugung, die man sich durch jahrelanges Hinbrüten aneignet" (Sc. 7).

D. G. Mowatt (essay date 1961)

SOURCE: "Studies Towards an Interpretation of the *Nibelungenlied*," *German Life & Letters*, New Series Vol. XIV, No. 4, July, 1961, pp. 257-70.

[*In the following essay, Mowatt explains why taking a historical approach in analyzing the* Nibelungenlied *is unsatisfactory; Mowatt then offers suggestions for studying it using a structural approach.*]

A. The Historical Approach; Its Use and Its Limitations

The **Nibelungenlied** is a work of medieval literature, and is usually interpreted historically. There are good reasons why this has been, and will no doubt continue to be so. The Court Epic and Lyric are not easily accessible to a present-day audience, and even students of German are sometimes reluctant to make the effort of understanding which they require. The research of medievalists has succeeded in lessening the gap between the modern and medieval mind, and in giving us at least some idea of what Middle High German authors were trying to do. We can

feel for them as they struggle to turn Celtic mythology into Christian fable, or heroic saga into courtly entertainment. Their efforts to disembody sex, however salutary they may have been at the time, are not so well received; but even *Minnesang* invites respect for the sheer impossibility of the task it sets itself.

Nevertheless, the historical approach, however useful, is only one among many. There are other correctives to a first, uninformed, common-sense reaction, and realization of this fact has gradually gained ground. Anything written since the eighteenth century is felt now to be, at least in theory, accessible to a modern audience on its own merits. The reader who states that he can see nothing in Goethe's *Faust* is no longer certain to be referred firmly to its eighteenth-century background and Goethe's biography. He will now often be referred instead to certain aspects of the work itself which may have escaped his notice. This second alternative has always existed, and indeed came naturally to men like Goethe and Herder; but during the dark ages of nineteenth-century historicism it was obscured. It is only recently that it has come into its own, achieving a well-argued body of theory, and a noticeable influence on practising critics and scholars, even in Germany.

All this applies, unfortunately, to 'Modern Literature' only. The Middle Ages, as everyone knows, were different. They were, for example, deficient in 'historical sense'. To the nineteenth century, with its own hypertrophied organ, this was enough to condemn them to the most historical of interpretations. An age which could cheerfully shuffle historical events, or advocate in the same breath Germanic and courtly ethics, Christian and Celtic mythology, individual license and social restraint, was obviously inaccessible. Its productions could only be explained, never understood. This defeatist attitude to courtly literature has its linguistic analogue in 'Germanic Philology'. Both are unhappily still with us.

But this is not to say that the Medievalists, in their historical stronghold, are unaware of what is going on outside. They know of it, and they deal with it in one of two ways: with boiling oil, or more recently, with the kiss of death. The boiling oil technique involves a withdrawal into an expertise so profound that medieval literature becomes meaningless to everyone but a medievalist, and the stronghold is preserved. The kiss of death usually takes the form of a generous rejection of historicism, followed by a rigidly historical interpretation. The intruder sees his weapons borrowed and blunted, all to no purpose, and the stronghold is again preserved. The **Nibelungenlied** has suffered much from the first of these defences, so that common-sense rejection by most readers, and historical dismemberment in Germany have been the rule. The second defence appears in an article by B. Nagel.[1] After some opening remarks about the advisability of interpreting a poem in its own right, he sets to work with a primitive concept of structural symmetry in one hand, and the Intentional Fallacy in the other. His results are not noticeably different from those of more thorough-going historicists. The same approach, at second hand, is found in a review of Professor Panzer's book: *Das Nibelungenlied*. The reviewer is able to say:[2]

> Methodisch befindet sich der Verfasser übrigens ganz auf der Linie der modernsten literaturwissenschaftlichen Forschung.

In support, he quotes the chapter-headings and the author's preface. Professor Panzer's 'method' is thus equated with his intention, and his achievement, which is nothing if not historical, is overlooked in the process. A more honest attempt at a genuinely ahistorical interpretation was made by W. J. Schröder,[3] but he too misled himself by fixing his structural insights on to a historical time-scale inherited from previous research.

In practice, then, German scholars still hold to the distinction between medieval literature, which needs to be protected from 'neuzeitliche poetischästhetische Wertungen oder gar moderne Impressionen',[4] and modern literature, which can look after itself. Apparently this is no longer the case in English studies, or at least not entirely. Henry Bosley Wolf, reviewing a book on Beowulf, could say in 1954:[5]

> (The) . . . study . . . is a valuable addition to the growing corpus of literature treating this Old English poem as a work of art.

Whether true or not, this is a breathtaking thought for a Germanist, and it is comforting to turn to Tolkien's description of the situation eighteen years earlier. In tones reminiscent of Quiller-Couch on History of Literature, he summarizes previous research as follows:[6]

> *Beowulf* is a half-baked native epic the development of which was killed by Latin learning; it was inspired by the emulation of Virgil, and is a product of the education that came in with Christianity; it is feeble and incompetent as narrative; the rules of narrative are cleverly observed in the manner of the learned epic; it is the confused product of a committee of muddle-headed and probably beer-bemused Anglo-Saxons (this is a Gallic voice); it is a string of pagan lays edited by monks; it is the work of a learned but inaccurate Christian antiquarian; it is a work of genius, rare and surprising in the period, though the genius seems to have been shown principally in doing something much better left undone . . . ; it is a wild folk-tale (general chorus); it is a poem of an aristocratic and courtly tradition (same voices); it is a hotch-potch; it is a sociological, anthropological, archaeological document; it is a mythical allegory . . . ; it is rude and rough; it is a masterpiece of metrical art; it has no shape at all; it is singularly weak in construction; it is a clever allegory of contemporary politics . . . ; its architecture is solid; it is thin and cheap (a solemn voice); it is undeniably weighty (the same voice); it is a national epic; it is a translation from the Danish; it was imported by Frisian traders; it is a burden to English syllabuses; and (final universal chorus of all voices) it is worth studying.

Most of this, and certainly the last unison could apply equally well to the *Nibelungenlied* literature. The discord in the inner parts is ascribed by Tolkien to the historical bias of Beowulf studies. Speculation about origins, he points out, is no help in interpretation. The fact that all scholars nevertheless approve of the poem merely shows that they are all reacting to the same thing, and that this thing is not the object of their divergent researches. The *Nibelungenlied* also excites an admiration in scholars which their utterance does nothing to explain, and both works have been made to carry the blame for this contradiction. The disunity is projected into *Beowulf* as a discrepancy between lofty style and ignoble theme; into the *Nibelungenlied* as a contrast between heroic matter and courtly treatment. The real disunity lies of course in the conflict between true appreciation and irrelevant research. The excellence of both works can only be dependent on their whole structure. Occupation with the text, for whatever extraneous reason, brings increasing familiarity with this structure, and even enthusiasm for the works. And this has nothing to do with the pallid admiration we profess for the poet's skill in welding disparate elements together, or in making the two halves of the *Nibelungenlied* roughly equal in size. Such condescending glances over the poet's shoulder are out of place. It is the final result of his labours which makes its impact on us, and this is what we should analyse.

As with most great works of literature, the common-sense reaction is defensive. It is more comfortable to reject, or laugh at a structure than to submit to it. All one needs is a firm and unquestioned absolute, such as 'how people behave', or 'what I expect from a work of art'. Since the traditional interpretation of the *Nibelungenlied* is essentially a relativistic counter-blast to such smugness, it seemed advisable to list some of these common-sense reactions before suggesting a different corrective. The relativism to be offered in this case is not, of course, historical, but aesthetic. A view is put forward of the basic structure of the poem, and an attempt is made to show how some of the traditional objections can be resolved in the light of this suggestion.

Two standards frequently applied by common sense are those of psychological credibility in the characters, and logical consistency in the plot. The *Nibelungenlied* is peculiarly vulnerable to such an assault. There is, for instance, a notable discrepancy between what we are told of the characters, and what they in fact do. Thus: Siegfried is said to be strong, beautiful, kind, considerate, accomplished, an exemplary and fabulously rich king. But what are we to make of his callous and deceitful treatment of Brünhilt? His wife-beating? All this nonsense about dwarves and dragons? And if he is going to be so polite and patient in his wooing of Kriemhilt, why does he turn up as a landless knight and offer to fight her brother? There is also something highly disreputable about his past. He knows more about Brünhilt than one would expect from his upbringing, and one wonders sometimes exactly what went on at Xanten. We read, for instance:

er begunde mit sinnen   werben scoeniu wîp,
di trûten wol mit êren   des küenen Sîvrides lîp

(26, 3-4)

De Boor[7] tries hard to make this sound innocent, by translating *trûten* as 'hätten geliebt'; but it could equally well mean 'liebten' in the lowest sense, and indeed Gunther seems to suspect Siegfried's tendencies in this direction when he warns him off Brünhilt:

'Âne daz du iht triutest'   sprach der künec dô
'die mîne lieben frouwen   anders bin ich es vrô.'

(655, 1-2)

Gunther is supposed to be a great and powerful king, and a loving brother. But he does very little to deserve this description. He dithers, and is often over-ruled by his vassal. He says he loves his sister, but he connives in her humiliation, removing first her husband, and then her fortune. He is apparently something of a warrior at the end, but it is not at all clear whether he survives so long through his own prowess, or merely because Hagen and the others have looked after him so carefully. In the Saxon War, Siegfried leaves him safely at home, saying with benevolent contempt:

'Her künec sît hie heime',   sprach dô Sîvrit,
'sît daz iuwer recken   mir wellent volgen mit.
belîbet bî den frouwen   und traget hôhen muot.
ich trouwe iu wol behüeten   beidiu êre unde guot.'

(174)

He does take one firm step, on his own decision, against Siegfried's advice; and that is to go after Brünhilt. But the whole thing is a dismal failure, and he commands no more respect as a lover than as a king. *Hagen* is described as strong, loyal, and terrible. In a sense, his actions bear this out, especially in the second part, but we are forced to condemn him for his barbarity and deceit. This reaction is not indeed particularly modern, and seems to have started in the thirteenth century with the author of MS.C. Furthermore, the means he uses are disproportionate to his ends. Why *murder* Siegfried after all? Gunther shows no such feverish concern for his wife's honour. Apologies are made (861), the crime of 'sich rüemen' is denied on oath (858), and everyone (including Hagen!) is prepared to gloss over the awkward matter of the ring and the girdle. 'We had better keep our wives in order in future' is Siegfried's conclusion. Brünhilt, admittedly, remains unhappy, and her tears move Hagen to swear revenge (863-4); but Gunther, who is after all her husband, seems quite unperturbed. Perhaps he is wondering whether he should hit her himself, or stand down in favour of Siegfried again. At all events, his thoughts are the reverse of homicidal.

er ist uns ze saelden   unt ze êren geborn

(872, 2)

he says, with some emotion. In order to persuade him that his guide and protector needs murdering, Hagen has to

introduce a new sin for Siegfried, that of standing in the way of Gunther's territorial expansion (870). He blends this with the rabble-rousing slogan 'suln wir gouche ziehen?' (867), at the same time insisting that it is Brünhilt's public humiliation that is the real issue (867; 873). And yet, if it had not been for Siegfried, there would have been no Brünhilt for him to insult, and Gunther's own territory would already have been appropriated by the Saxons. Can it be that Hagen is jealous? And what had poor Kriemhilt done to deserve the treatment she gets from Hagen after her husband's death?

Brünhilt as a character is impossible. No one could be so 'vreislîch' and so 'minneclîch' at the same time. There is something peculiarly distasteful about the thought of this shot-putting amazon dissolving into tears in order to get Siegfried murdered. We can only agree with her husband, who remarks after their first night together:

want ich hân den übeln tiuvel   heim ze hûse geladen.

(649, 2)

Kriemhilt presents difficulties only to the initiated. Common sense accepts readily her progression from sweet maiden, via proud wife, to embittered widow. She is a little mercenary, but then so is everyone else.

The historical answer to these objections is well known. The details are still in dispute, but there is a common, all-purpose hypothesis underlying all such solutions, namely that the poet was courtly, and his 'Stoff' was not. Thus the magical, superhuman attributes of Siegfried, Brünhilt, and to a lesser extent Hagen, were traditional; the rest were his own contribution. Similarly, the fate of the Burgundians and Kriemhilt's revenge were supplied by legend or pseudo-history, whereas the details of their behaviour were taken from contemporary customs. All inconsistencies can be explained from this postulate. Either the poet would have liked to change his 'Stoff', but did not dare; or he tried to, but did not succeed. The other sort of question, such as 'Why does Hagen kill Siegfried? Why are the Burgundians so obstinate at the end? Why is everyone so mercenary?' is ruled out as being anachronistic, and resolved by reference to Germanic or medieval ethical principles, such as 'Sippentreue', or 'milte'.

As far as the causal explanations of inconsistencies are concerned, it is clear that they are quite irrelevant to our understanding of the *Nibelungenlied* itself. They deal exclusively with its genesis, and cannot be invoked to veto its interpretation. The unmistakable relationship between Siegfried and Brünhilt,[8] for instance, cannot be dismissed from the *Nibelungenlied* simply because it is also found elsewhere. The historical explanations of morals and motives, on the other hand, are not so much irrelevant, as limiting. If we confine ourselves to them, then we are assuming that the differences between the Middle High Germans and ourselves are more fundamental than the similarities.

Some such improbable assumption is at the root of any attempt to substitute 'Geistesgeschichte' for literary interpretation. Social forms and symbols are only the raw material of literature. The Middle High German poet does not just hold up a succession of banners issued by the Zeitgeist, and marked 'minne, thirteenth century', or 'triuwe, Germanic'. He selects from the ones available to him, and arranges them in patterns. In doing so, he refines and qualifies his ready-made symbols by juxtaposing and opposing them to others. The structure which results is not the one which was already available to all medieval thinkers. Nor is it necessarily inaccessible to us. Relations can be meaningful, even when the units related are unidentified. If it were not so, there would be no algebra. It follows that unfamiliar symbols need present no obstacle to understanding, as long as we direct our attention to the relationships the poet has established between them. There is a knight-errant in John Osborne's *Look back in Anger,* and the audience is not mystified. Conversely, no amount of familiarity, acquired or inherited, will supply the precise meaning of a symbol in any particular work. We have learnt, for instance, that *walt* for the medieval mind had quite different associations from those we have inherited from the Romantics. It was a terrifying place, something to be run from, rather than sat in. And yet, when we read of Erec and Enîte:

> und als si kâmen in den walt
> ûz der sorgen gewalt
> wider ûf ir kunden wec,
>
>   (lines 6760-63)

we realize that this generalized information is not enough. A wood, for Hartman as for Eichendorff, is wild, as opposed to cultivated country, and its precise function in *Êrec* has still to be worked out. At all events, it seems to be preferable to Limors, and even to Penefrec (lines 7239-41).

B. STRUCTURAL APPROACH AND ANALYSIS

There is still room, then, for a structural approach to the *Nibelungenlied.* The common-sense objections may be due not to lack of historical information about the pieces, but to lack of insight into the pattern. In looking for such a pattern, the main characters provide the most obvious and convenient units to start with. The fact that they are the focus of common-sense incredulity is not due to chance. Even when this lay reaction is discounted, it remains true that Siegfried, Brünhilt and the Court at Worms are presented as discrete entities. As W. J. Schröder[9] has observed, they are delineated before they are brought together. With the partial absorption of these two strange characters, the smooth facade of the Court itself begins to split; distinct and warring units appear in the shape of Gunther, Hagen and Kriemhilt, so that we wonder what can have held them together in the first place. In any case, their emergence as individuals is essentially a by-product of the impact of Siegfried and Brünhilt on Gunther's court. If the nature of this impact is to be understood, a reasonable first step would be to examine closely the delineation of these three entities, Brünhilt, Siegfried and the Burgundian Court, as offered by the text.

Brünhilt is the strong silent virgin. She lives a long way from everybody. Everybody has heard of her. Only the strongest and bravest man can win her. Unsuccessful suitors get killed. The symbol is not very hard to interpret. It is a challenge to the male principle to assert itself. Sexual conquest is equated with physical prowess, and the best man is equated with the strongest. The second-best man is warned to keep off; if he ignores the warning, he is punished by death.

If we disregard causal explanations of how this symbol found its way into the *Nibelungenlied,* and look instead for its nearest relation within the work, we cannot help thinking of Siegfried. Nor, indeed, can Brünhilt,[10] for he is the obvious candidate;—strong, beautiful, proud, and with a youthful eagerness to try out his strength. One thinks of his challenge to Gunther when he arrives at Worms. He openly equates kingship with conquest, and the right to rule with physical strength. Furthermore, as Hagen and Gunther are well aware, he is the only man who knows the way to Îsenstein, or what to do when he gets there. He alone is strong enough to overthrow Brünhilt, both in the contest, and in the bed. But he not only knows how to deal with Brünhilt; he also embodies, in his own right, a set of hyperbolic qualities which are complementary to hers. She is strongest in defence; he is strongest in attack. She is impenetrable; he is impervious. Both are misused by Gunther, but whereas she is mistaken, he is misled. They are in fact extreme versions of female (unassailable) and male (irresistible), with a strong tendency to make contact.

In the world where Siegfried and Brünhilt belong together, there are no rules for civilized and sophisticated behaviour. It is often said that theirs is an 'uncourtly' world, and from the point of view of the thirteenth century this is no doubt true. But what is far more important is that it is essentially an anti-social, uncompromising world, where only absolutes and superlatives apply.

Nothing could be more different from this than the court at Worms, where a respect for traditional forms and loyalties serves to inhibit all response to a new situation, such as the arrival of Siegfried, or the Saxon War. Gunther is the symbol of this formal excellence; on his own ground (politics, keeping the peace), he is admirable; it is only when he steps outside this that his limitations become apparent. Gunther's world is of course 'courtly',[11] but again the actual medieval details are not the interesting thing. The interesting thing about Gunther's world is that it is carefully regulated, with a set procedure for every event. It is in fact 'society', as against 'nature', the harmonious group as against the identified pair.

So far, we have considered only the ready-made symbols. The structure of the *Nibelungenlied* lies in the way in which they are brought together, and the inevitable results. Thus Siegfried and Brünhilt are both brought to Worms, and rather uncomfortably acclimatized to law and order. Brünhilt's difficulties are well known, but Siegfried is also reluctant in a more unobtrusive way: he makes several attempts to leave the court, only to be held back by the hope of Kriemhilt.[12] Gunther, on the other hand, takes it into his head to go after Brünhilt. In order to do this, he has to call in Siegfried, and ask him to take over something that every man should really do for himself. His scheme works, after a fashion, but it is all based on trickery and deceit; Siegfried doesn't make a very good vassal, and Gunther makes a very poor Siegfried. It is only a matter of time before he meets the fate of all second-rate suitors, and is killed. Since he stands for a whole way of life at Worms, the whole homogeneous society has to perish with him. In this sense, the quarrel between Gunther and Kriemhilt in the second part is seen as an internal struggle in a society that has lost its bearings. Their mistake was to introduce the disruptive force of Brünhilt and Siegfried into their nicely balanced world; and in this, Kriemhilt is just as culpable and tenacious as the others. Once they have tried brute strength, their established forms cease to work. Even when they have removed Siegfried, the immediate embarrassment, and Brünhilt has faded away, they still cannot agree, and they go on squabbling over the treasure, which is all that is left, until they wipe each other out.

It could be said, then, that we are presented with two pairs of characters, adapted to very different environments, and showing correspondingly dissimilar behaviour patterns. The pairs are brought together and reshuffled, after the manner of the molecules in Goethe's chemical analogy. But, as in the *Wahlverwandtschaften,* the uncomplicated fortunes of inorganic compounds can only be a starting-point. In both works, the natural (or elective) affinities are confused, qualified and complicated out of existence by the demands of social organization. The pairs: Siegfried-Brünhilt and Eduard-Ottilie are never completely realized. The process is inhibited in the *Wahlverwandtschaften* by the inertia of the pairing already accomplished. In the *Nibelungenlied,* it is wilfully pushed in another direction, and the compounds which actually result are highly unstable. The pairs Siegfried-Kriemhilt and Gunther-Brünhilt embody tensions which cannot be ignored indefinitely.

If we examine the *Nibelungenlied* with this working hypothesis in mind, many of the apparent flaws in the work are seen to be features of the overall structure. Gunther the great warrior and Gunther on the bedroom wall is a direct result of his two incompatible functions: king at Worms, and husband to Brünhilt. Siegfried the courtly gentleman and Siegfried the supernatural strongman is similarly structural. He arrives at Worms like something from another world, and consciously represses his natural instincts in order to fit in. His one motive, in arriving and in staying, is the acquisition of Kriemhilt. The others, after their first fright, use him, with disastrous results for themselves. He uses them, or better, he manipulates their set of conventions (in his subordination to Gunther, in the Saxon War,

and in his very correct courtship of Kriemhilt), with equally disastrous results. Having created this impossible situation, he blandly assumes that everything will be all right. On two occasions he relaxes so much that he forgets the courtly rules he has adopted. His advice to Gunther on keeping one's wife in order, for instance, is quite monstrously inapplicable, both to Gunther's marriage, and his own.

> 'Man sol sô vrouwen ziehen'   sprach Sîfrit der de-gen,
> 'daz si üppecliche sprüche   lâzen under wegen.
> verbiut ez dînem wîbe,   der mînen tuon ich sam.
> ir grôzen ungefüege   ich mich waerlichen scham'.
>
> (862)

This applies to a quite different world where a Siegfried might have married a Brünhilt, and having won her by force, would continue to keep her in order by force. But in fact it is the courtly Kriemhilt he has married, and her reaction to her good hiding is to tell Hagen, with the best of wifely intentions, how to kill her husband. Gunther's reaction to the advice is not recorded. The subject must have been painful, and a suitable reply hard to find. It is hardly surprising, in the circumstances, that only twelve stanzas later he agrees to have Siegfried murdered. Siegfried's other indiscretion comes, appropriately enough, just before his final removal from the scene. He catches a bear, and terrorizes all the courtly hunters by letting it loose in the middle of their meal. This is the last fling.[13]

Hagen's inconsistencies follow a similar pattern. He is loyal and efficient, according to his lights, but his lights do not go quite far enough. His murder of Siegfried, and his victimization of Kriemhilt are part of this limited vision. He feels that they are foreign bodies in his world, and wants to get rid of them. But the whole situation is really beyond him by this time. He knows enough about Siegfried and the supernatural to be wary of them. But he thinks he can control them, and indeed advises Gunther to use Siegfried for his Brünhilt-escapade. It is not until they arrive at Îsenstein, that he finds himself immediately out of his depth. He wants the Burgundians to hold on to their weapons, being convinced that Gunther has bitten off more than he can chew (438). But he does not realize the extent of Gunther's dependence on Siegfried. Gunther is not really in any immediate danger, and even if he were, Hagen would not be much help. This is Siegfried's world, and different rules apply.

> Dô sprach ein kameraere: 'ir sult uns geben diu swert
> unt ouch die liehten brünne'.   'des sît ir ungewert'
> sprach von Tronege Hagene: 'wir wellens selbe tragen'.
> dô begonde im Sîfrit   da von diu rehten maere sagen.
>
> 'Man pfliget in dirre bürge,   daz wil ich iu sagen,
> daz neheine geste   hie wâfen sulen tragen.

nu lât si tragen hinnen,   daz ist wol getân.'
des volgete vil ungerne   Hagene Guntheres man.

(406-7)

Hagen also warns against the fatal journey to Etzel's court. Again he senses danger, without knowing how to ward if off. But this time, when his advice is ignored, he finds himself back in a world he understands. Organization of troop-movements, keeping up morale, and of course fighting, are things he can manage. We can and often do say that Hagen 'grows in stature' in the second part, but there is no inconsistency in the change. It is essentially the same figure in an entirely different situation.

Like Siegfried and Gunther, so too does Kriemhilt saddle herself with two irreconcilable functions: sister to Gunther and wife to Siegfried. The Kriemhilt of Part I is firmly embedded in the sterile courtly society of Worms. She and Gunther have everything in common, even to the extent of sharing a disastrous disposition to marry outside their capabilities. Gunther pretends to be a child of nature; Kriemhilt allows Siegfried to go through the motions of a lovesick Minnesinger. Between them they manage to split up the Siegfried-Brünhilt entity, acquiring roughly equal shares, and it is in this sense that their death-struggle in Part II can be called an internal squabble over the remains of Siegfried's power. But in the process, both become something else. Gunther becomes the husband of Brünhilt; Kriemhilt becomes the wife of Siegfried. The positions are precarious, ill-fitting and untenable in the long run. But the patriarchal Hagen sees it more simply. Gunther has acquired Brünhilt; Siegfried has acquired Kriemhilt. And this is how he can accept Brünhilt unquestioningly as his Queen, while resenting both Siegfried and Kriemhilt as foreign bodies at Worms.

The impossibility of Kriemhilt's position does not become clear at once. She removes, with Siegfried, to Xanten, accepting her new function, and relinquishing her old one with apparent whole-heartedness. Indeed, the separation of the two courts might have provided a permanent solution—if it had not been for Brünhilt. She is still stuck, quite incongruously, at Worms. Once deprived of her virginity, she is nothing in her own right; but this would not matter in the natural order of things, since only the best and strongest man on earth is capable of winning and marrying her. In the natural order of things, she would happily give up her virginal independence for marriage to this man; sacrifice her own power in order to harness an even greater one. On the face of it, this is what has happened; logically, Gunther is the best and strongest man on earth. Unfortunately, she cannot really believe this. She cannot convince herself that Siegfried is subordinate to Gunther, whatever anyone says. He does not behave like a vassal, not indeed look like a second-rate suitor. And so she brings the two pairs together again, and the peaceful interlude is over. The result, as one might expect, is that the real nature of the situation is made intolerably apparent, and Siegfried is murdered. It is often remarked that Brünhilt now fades out of the picture. But what else could she do?

She only exists as a counterpart to Siegfried. Her duty is to preserve herself until the right man comes to claim her. For recognition of this man, she relies on the objective trial of strength, much as Kleist's characters rely, less symbolically, on their unerring 'Gefühl'. But unlike that of Kleist's characters, her 'Gefühl' is in the event utterly reliable. She has played her part correctly, the right man, Siegfried, has come to claim her, she has recognized him, and given herself to him. But instead of taking possession, he immediately hands over to Gunther. She has discovered, in fact that the other half of the symbol no longer believes in it, and is quite happy to turn it into meaningless play-acting, in order to embroil himself somewhere else where he does not belong, namely with Kriemhilt. He is, evidently, too well-educated to take her seriously; as she would have known earlier, if she could have heard his knowing and detached description of her to Gunther:

'ja hât diu küneginne   so vreislîche sit'.

(330, 2)

His betrayal of her is similar to Faust's betrayal of Mephistopheles, but much more final. Mephisto could presumably turn his attentions elsewhere after losing his prize; Brünhilt has only one bolt, and having shot it, she ceases to exist as a significant figure.

With Siegfried and Brünhilt out of the way, there is no reason why the court at Worms should not settle down again, with Gunther and Hagen in their traditional rôles, and Kriemhilt still dispensing 'hôhen muot'; or so, at least, Gunther seems to think when he makes friends with Kriemhilt. Hagen, being more practical, has his doubts, but he also tries to patch things up by throwing away the treasure, and warning against Kriemhilt's marriage to Etzel. He evidently thinks that if only Kriemhilt could stop being Siegfried's wife, and go back to being Gunther's sister, the court at Worms would still be manageable.

Kriemhilt herself, at the end of Part I, and even in Part II, is rather a pathetic figure. Having once experienced Siegfried, she cannot accept Hagen's and Gunther's solution. But neither can she go on being Siegfried's wife. The marriage was impossible in the first place, and it is no accident that she is personally responsible for his death. She evidently has no idea of what she has married. How else could she conceive of Hagen as Siegfried's protector in battle? This sort of relationship is relevant to the society at Worms, but Siegfried, after all, has a 'hurnîn hût'. From the front, to his enemies in battle, he is impervious. He is only vulnerable from behind, to his wife. His possession of this one soft spot shows that his self-reliance is not absolute. He needs, or at least is capable of taking a mate, and in this sense he is human. But the continued efficacy of his thick skin after marriage depends on complete withdrawal from social inter-dependence. Brünhilt, one feels, would have understood this. Kriemhilt does not. It was she who detached him from his context in the first place; and now, by trying to fit him into the values of Worms, she kills him.

After his death, she persists in her confusion. She refuses to go back with Sigemunt, because she feels the ties of home and family too strongly (1081). On the other hand, she refuses to take up her old place at the court, first living apart, then marrying Etzel, and all the time grieving for Siegfried. No wonder Hagen turns his suspicions to her; but in doing so, he interprets her and her treasure in the same practical terms as he had Siegfried. To him, the treasure means political power for Kriemhilt, and political danger for Worms. To Kriemhilt, it just means Siegfried, something she had once possessed, never understood, and unwittingly destroyed.[14] Sinking the treasure no more solves the real problem than killing Siegfried had done. It merely drives Kriemhilt to accept a substitute for both, in the shape of Etzel, and the process grinds on to its grisly conclusion.

It is Hagen's triumph when he dies, that he has wiped away all trace of Siegfried and his treasure. It is Siegfried's and, in a way, Brünhilt's triumph that they have utterly destroyed this cosy little Burgundian society. It is Kriemhilt's tragedy, that she has helped towards both these ends; the death of her husband, and the extinction of her family. Her personal achievement is nil. It is customary to talk of Kriemhilt's revenge; but what use is revenge, when it is Siegfried that she wants? She lost him, because she was too much attached to her own society. In her efforts to get him back, she destroys that society. In destroying its last representative, Hagen, she severs her last connexion with Siegfried and his treasure. All she is left with is his sword, which is not much use against Hildebrant.[15]

C. Result

One might say, then, that the *Nibelungenlied* is one of those works which explore some of the consequences of a confusion between two levels of organization. It shows us what happens when an individual, anti-social ideal of behaviour tries to adopt a set of conventions it does not understand, and a highly formalized society invokes forces which it cannot control. This is not a very improbable suggestion. The essential limitations of courtly rules and regulations are exposed, but the exposure has a positive side. To recognize the limitations is to understand the true function of society; and this last theme runs right through the Courtly Epic of the time. Êrec, Îwein, Parzival, Tristan, all have to forget, break or abandon the rules before they can begin to understand the point of them. Gunther, Arthur, Mark, are all variants of the same king-figure. They preside, spur on, hold back, regulate, reward and punish. All are strangely incapable of action, and depend largely on their subjects. They are, in fact, the conventions of the society over which they preside. When these conventions have positive value, they become noble figures, like Mark after the love-grotto, or Gunther in the final battle; where the rules are out of place, they become ridiculous, like Mark most of the time, Gunther in love, or Arthur with his marriage difficulties. Siegfried's nearest relation in the Court Epic is, of course, Tristan-Riwalîn. Both are adopted by model kings, and used as tools. Both are rather too ef-

ficient at their tasks, and find themselves in conflict with the Court as a result. Both kings find themselves wholly or partly alienated first from their sister, and then from their wife. The essential difference lies in the way the Court reacts to this situation. Tintagel may be moribund, but it manages to expel the two sets of lovers, and to survive.[16] Worms tries to absorb them, and fails.

Like all brief accounts of structure, this one is schematic in the extreme, and leaves large areas of the work untouched. It is impossible to exhaust a complex work of literature in one, or indeed in twenty articles. It is, however, possible to suggest a tentative hypothesis as to the essential structure, based on a close study of the text. Much of the detailed evidence has been withheld, for reasons of clarity and space. Much more has not yet been considered. Both these defects are to be remedied to some extent in a following article by H. D. Sacker, in which he examines some aspects of the formal texture.[17] The hypothesis itself is of practical value only. It is hoped that scholars will find it worth modifying.

Notes

1. B. Nagel, 'Die künstlerische Eigenleistung des Nibelungendichters', *Wolfram-Jahrbuch* (1953), pp. 23-47.

2. In *Moderna Språk,* vol. LI (1957), p. 377.

3. W. J. Schröder, *Das Nibelungenlied* (Halle/Saale, 1954), (reprinted from *PBB,* vol. LXXVI). [Illegible Text] Tonnelat, in his introduction to *La Chanson des Nibelungen* (translated into French), and his critical work of the same name (Bibliothèque de Philologie Germanique, vol VI (1944), and (Paris, 1916), is admittedly unhistorical, but confines himself to plot-mechanics.

4. B. Nagel, loc. cit., p. 26.

5. In *MLQ,* vol. XV (1954), p. 182.

6. J. R. R. Tolkien, *Beowulf; the Monsters and the Critics* (Sir Israel Gollancz Memorial Lecture, 1936); reprinted from *The Proceedings of the British Academy,* vol. XXII, p. 7.

7. In his edition (Deutsche Klassiker des Mittelalters), F. A. Brockhaus (Wiesbaden, 1956); note to line 26, 4. All quotations are also from this edition.

8. The function of this relationship is discussed below, pp. 8ff.

9. B. Mergell, *Euphorion,* vol. LXV (1950), pp. 305ff., 'Nibelungenlied und höfischer Roman', contains a similar insight, though concerned with other questions.

10. She expects him to come and claim her (419-420), and is never reconciled to the fact that he does not. See p. 267, below.

11. The evidence is collected, and compared with the picture offered in the Court Epics, by N. Dürrenmatt, *Das Nibelungenlied im Kreise der höfischen Dichtung,* Diss. Bern, 1945.

12. cf. 123, 4; 126, 3; 132, 2; 136; 258; 289.

13. The whole hunt scene is a miniature reflection of Siegfried's changing fortunes and position at Worms. It is hoped to discuss it in a later article.

14. The relevant passages are: 1739; 1743; 1789; 2367; 2372. The symbol of the *hort* is also due for extensive discussion.

15. The whole passage, from 2367, 4 (*welt ir mir geben widere waz ir mir habt genomen*), to 2372, 4 turns on personal loss and repayment, rather than on revenge.

16. There is, however, nothing positive about its survival, as W. Schwarz has shown in his inaugural lecture: *Gottfrieds von Strassburg Tristan und Isolde* (Groningen, Djakarta, 1955).

17. For the distinction between 'structure' and 'texture', see E. M. Wilkinson, '"Form" and "Content" in the Aesthetics of German Classicism', *Still- und Formprobleme in der Literatur,* pp. 18-27 (1959).

18. Since the final revision of this article, a certain amount of work on the structure of the *Nibelungenlied* has appeared. Some of this is mentioned in my review of Walchinger's *Studien zum Nibelungenlied* (p. 304 of this number). Details of the rest are contained in Walchinger's bibliography.

Hugh Sacker (essay date 1961)

SOURCE: "On Irony and Symbolism in the *Nibelunglied*: Two Preliminary Notes," *German Life & Letters*, New Series Vol. XIV, No. 4, July, 1961, pp. 271-81.

[*In the following essay, Sacker examines examples of irony in the* Nibelungenlied *and points out some previously overlooked uses of symbolism.*]

I. IRONY

It has always been recognized that irony plays some part in the *Nibelungenlied,*[1] but so far as I know attention has been concentrated on those instances which make the person or deed appear more heroic and not upon those which tend to undermine the heroic appearance. That this latter possibility also exists is perhaps most easily proved from an incident in the second half, where Kriemhilt tries to persuade her knights to attack the two men Hagen and Volker. Four hundred of them arm themselves and accompany her in threatening fashion; they see and hear their queen defied and insulted, and she calls upon them to attack. The narrator at this point describes them as 'die übermüeten degene' and, as 'übermüete' is normally used by him of people too proud and rash to count the cost of what they do,[2] the reader expects a clash—but no, the phrase has been used ironically:

Si sprach: 'nu hoert, ir recken,　　wa er mir lougent niht

aller miner leide.　　swaz im da von geschiht,
daz ist mir vil unmaere,　　ir Etzelen man.'
die übermüeten degene　　ein ander sahen si an.

(1792)

The anti-climax is neat: they look at each other in dismay and then retire without a blow being struck. More specifically still, a few stanzas later the fiddler Volker says with reference to the Huns: 'ez heizent allez degene und sint geliche niht gemuot' (1821, 4). All are called warriors, but not all, one may perhaps paraphrase, reveal in their actions a warrior's heart.

This open statement of Volker's that things are not always what they seem is without parallel in the *Nibelungenlied,* but there are many parallels to the implicit irony of the narrator's description of the cowardly Huns as 'übermüete'. Where these have been noticed by scholars in the past, they have usually been regretted as unintended by the poet—which, as we have no external evidence of the poet's intention, is a diplomatic way of saying that they do not fit in with the scholar's own interpretation. My intention here is to reconsider a few particular examples, and to suggest the place they occupy in the total pattern; whether this pattern is the one intended by the poet need not concern us, if we take as our object of study not his intention, but his achievement.

One of the more obvious features of the work is the stock adjective, of the type of 'übermüete', which so frequently accompanies any reference to any character whatsoever. It has been studied in detail in a dissertation,[3] and more recently has received a couple of pages in Friedrich Panzer's stimulating review of all matters concerning the *Nibelungenlied.*[4] Sometimes the adjective appears appropriate to the particular situation or character, more often it does not. Panzer writes regretfully:

Aber überwiegend sind die Beiwörter starr und formelhaft und nehmen dadurch den Personen das Individuelle, statt sie zu kennzeichnen . . . Form und Gehalt befinden sich danach vielfach nicht in vollkommenem Einklang . . . Es begreift sich das aus der weitgehenden Idealisierung, die unserer Dichtung eignet (p. 134).

The argument is, I think, that the poet saw his characters as types, and applied to them the adjectives appropriate to ideal representatives of these types—regardless of the individual character or situation. This may very well be true—but it need not be regretted if, as I believe, the resultant relationship between the typical, idealized comment and the circumstances of the particular case is both enjoyable in itself and consonant with what the poet achieved in other respects.

To take an example. When the Amazonian Brünhilt hears from Siegfried that Gunther has come to woo her, she replies threateningly that he must then compete with her in certain games and that he and all his company will forfeit their lives if he loses. Some such adjective as 'vreislich', which has been applied to her in anticipation (330, 2), would be appropriate here; but instead a 'stock' feminine adjective is used to round off Brünhilt's challenging speech:

> 'Den stein sol er werfen unt springen dar nach,
> den ger mit mir schiezen. lat iu niht sin ze gach.
> ir muget wol hie verliesen die ere und ouch den lip.
> des bedenket iuch vil ebene,' sprach daz minnecliche wip.
>
> (425)

The context of *minneclich* may be regarded here as twofold. There is the 'vertical' thread of comment running the whole length of the work, according to which all noble ladies are lovable, and there is the 'horizontal' block of the particular episode, which shows Brünhilt as rather fearsome. 'Minneclich' is appropriate to the one, but not obviously to the other: one wonders if Brünhilt is presented as attractive even though (or precisely because?) she is threatening her suitors with death, or if the narrator is mocking at the very idea of finding such a she-devil attractive. Either way he is drawing attention to the contrast between the two aspects of the context, between the conventional approach to courtly ladies in general and the behaviour of this particular one; either way he is supported by the situation, since on the one hand Gunther evidently had been attracted by the fearsomeness of Brünhilt (cf. 328f.), while on the other her actual appearance does now put him off:

> Er dahte in sinem muote: 'waz sol diz wesen?
> der tiuvel uz der helle wie kunder da vor genesen?
> waer ich ze Burgonden mit dem lebene min,
> si müeste hie vil lange vri vor miner minne sin.'
>
> (442)

In view of this support from the situation, the ambiguities and ironic possibilities in the adjective should, I suggest, be accepted—and enjoyed. It is mistaken to uphold the claims of the 'vertical' context at the expense of the 'horizontal' when the complex relationship between the two is relevant to the main course of the plot.[5]

This main course of the plot has usually been taken absolutely seriously—apparently on the assumption that the heroic code did not allow of any questioning (let alone of any mockery) in the Middle Ages. The crucial episode here touched on proves otherwise, for the very fact that Gunther, knowing himself unequal to the task, should yet seek to win Brünhilt is not simply somewhat discreditable but essentially *farcical*—and the farce of the bedroom scene to which it leads is therefore not, as almost all critics seem to think, a regrettable lapse on the author's part (to be explained away by reference to the vulgarity of source and audience), but an artistically necessary revelation of the falsity of Gunther's position. Gunther has confused the increase of public power which Siegfried's help has brought with an increase of personal strength, and

has won a wife by trickery; before the world his public honour may be maintained, but in the privacy of the bedroom his private shame is ludicrously exposed.

The narrator ostensibly supports Gunther's honour, throughout saying only 'nice' things about him; but as his actions do not always bear out these comments, there are many occasions on which an alert reader feels the need to raise an eyebrow. For the moment I will omit the stock adjectives, and indicate other types of implicit irony. For instance there is the comment on Gunther's final success with Brünhilt. In the preceding stanzas we have seen Gunther fail to force his will on Brünhilt, get ignominiously tied up to a nail on the wall—and call in Siegfried. We have seen Siegfried struggle for his life with Brünhilt, just win—and leave her to Gunther to deflower. This Gunther accomplishes:

> Done was ouch si niht sterker dann ein ander wip.
> er trute minnecliche den ir vil schoenen lip.
> ob siz versuochte mere, waz kunde daz vervan?
> daz het ir allez Gunther mit sinen minnen getan.
>
> (682)

It is true that with her virginity Brünhilt loses her great strength, and it is true that Gunther's desire to marry her has eventually brought about her loss of virginity—but to sum the whole episode up in terms of Gunther accomplishing all this with his love is to exaggerate so blatantly, to disregard so sublimely Gunther's total dependence on Siegfried (which has just been illustrated so drastically) that a smile is unavoidable. Once again the two contexts, of the ideal commentary and the real situation, have coincided to produce an ironic effect. Literally, and ideally, it was Gunther who reduced Brünhilt, essentially, however, it was Siegfried.

If the irony here depends on stressing the literal at the expense of the essential, elsewhere it is the incidental which is used for ironical emphasis. For instance the competition with Brünhilt in Islant reveals almost as effectively as the wedding night Gunther's personal weakness. Carried along under Siegfried's arm, he appears a ludicrous enough figure to the reader, though Brünhilt's followers, who cannot see Siegfried, are of course deceived: '*si* wanden daz er hete diu spil mit siner kraft getan' (467,4). This is not so; but as the very next line points out, if Gunther lacks the strength which alone is necessary to win Brünhilt, he possesses other qualities such as courtesy, and knows how to acknowledge the homage Brünhilt's followers proceed to offer him in gracious fashion: 'Er gruoztes' minnecliche, ja was er tugende rich' (468, 1). This second half-line is unnecessary and is phrased emphatically; coming where it does, it implicitly invites comparison between the qualities Gunther possesses and those he lacks: he needs Siegfried to win Brünhilt, but he can exchange courtesies on his own account.

The ironies I have been considering arise from apparent discrepancies between the commentary and the action; what is the effect when these are in accord? One possibility can be seen from a further investigation of 'minneclich'; this seems inappropriate in Islant, especially when applied to Brünhilt herself, but it is appropriate to Gunther, who greets Brünhilt's followers 'minnecliche', appropriate altogether indeed at Worms, and especially so to Kriemhilt, who appears in her youth as 'diu minnecliche' *par excellence.* She is thus indirectly contrasted with Brünhilt; and since it is the aggressiveness with which Brünhilt reacts to the approach of any male that makes the description of her as 'minneclich' somewhat strange, it is worth considering if 'minneclich' seems so appropriate to Kriemhilt precisely because her outstanding characteristic as a maiden is her utter passivity. She is subject to her brothers in all ways; for a whole year Siegfried is never even allowed to see her—a state of affairs not obligatory at the time or in the work, as a comparison with Rüedeger's daughter Gotelint shows—and when she does appear she is demure beyond belief. One wonders if it is this very passivity which attracts the mighty Siegfried, just as it is the challenge of Brünhilt which attracts the weaker Gunther. Neither man sees the lady of his choice before choosing her; of both it might be said that they merely seek out a certain type of feminine reaction. Their ability to choose at a distance, according to the general reputation of the ladies concerned, is explained if the ladies merely represent, at least before their marriage, the two men's different ideals of maidenhood. The grotesqueness of Gunther's ideal can scarcely be ignored and is, as argued above, emphasized by the odd use of 'minneclich'; but is not Siegfried's ideal equally strange, and does not the very appropriateness of the repetitive and wishy-washy 'minneclich' suggest this? Then, however, the question would arise: is some element of irony always present when a stock adjective is used?

This short exploratory study is not the place to investigate this problem at length; nor do I wish to indulge in a long terminological discussion on what does and what does not deserve the name of irony. My impression is that the stock adjective plays a more vital part in the *Nibelungenlied* than has generally been recognized, and that recognition of this fact has been hampered by an undue respect on the part of modern desk-bound scholars both for heroism—which has blinded them to those elements in the works of an earlier age which expose the weaknesses of the heroic code—and for commentaries, which has led them to disregard those elements in the plot which clash with the statements of the narrator. Not of course that one should expect the stock adjective to be always exciting, always distressingly right or grotesquely wrong; much of the time its importance may be minimal. All I would suggest is that where one finds an idealistic commentary interwoven with a realistic plot, an interplay of meaning is likely to result which may be described as irony, and that where this is found it should not be ignored.

In the light of these considerations I should like finally to consider the opening twelve stanzas of the work as found in the version we usually read today. When here the three Burgundian kings are introduced as exceedingly powerful rulers, possessed of great personal courage and bravery,

who enjoy happiness and high honour all their days, the reader who already knows the story is surely compelled to raise an eyebrow. Are these the kings who are afraid to fight the Saxons themselves but leave it to Siegfried? Who reward him for his constant help and trusting nature by murdering him? At the very best, if one takes these stanzas at their face value, one is compelled to feel a little patronizing towards a poet who repeats a phrase like 'ein uz erwelter degen' three times in twelve stanzas. At the worst one abandons all attempt at understanding or appreciating the work as it stands, and begins to hack it about, to make it conform on one pretext or another to a preconceived idea of what it *ought* to be. It is for instance common to disregard most of these opening stanzas altogether because they are missing from some manuscripts and may not have belonged to the earliest version. But they are present in other manuscripts and, no matter who invented them, the effect of their presence may still be profitably investigated.

Thus we may notice that in the light of subsequent events the opening twelve stanzas appear ironic, and once this is recognized the very fatuity of repetitions like 'ein uz erwelter degen' may be enjoyed. So also may the narrator's not necessarily innocuous 'als ich gesaget han' (8, 1): after all, the contrast that has been emphasized throughout this study is between what the narrator *says* of his characters and what their actions reveal. Indeed I think that almost every phrase in these first twelve stanzas appears highly ambiguous if examined closely, not least the bland formula with which they close:

> Von des hoves krefte   und von ir witen kraft,
> von ir vil hohen werdekeit   und von ir ritterschaft,
> der die herren pflagen   mit vröuden al ir leben,
> des enkunde iu zeware   niemen gar ein ende geben.
>
> (12)

This is of course to suggest that irony is not just a minor and occasional but from the very first a major and everpresent element in the B text of the *Nibelungenlied* (as edited by de Boor). The characters who appear in it are human and reveal very human failings: Gunther is a rather vicious weakling, Hagen proud, pig-headed and ruthless, Siegfried brash, self-centred and stupid, while Kriemhilt—'diu minnecliche!'—never becomes a person in her own right at all: content to be shut up by her brothers as a girl, she hero-worships her husband in his lifetime and disintegrates into a spiteful memory on his death.

But of course this is not all the truth about these people; the work contains a considerable element of irony but is not a satire. That is perhaps one reason why it is so elusive and yet so satisfying.

II. SYMBOLISM

The suggestion put forward in the preceding study, that the narrator's comments furnish no direct guide to the significance of events related in the *Nibelungenlied,* happily does not mean that the poet has left us without guidance of any kind: on the contrary, as has always been known, he provides fingerposts in the form of symbols. Some of these are interpreted, at least in part, within the work, for example Kriemhilt's dream in the opening *aventiure;* others, such as the ring and the girdle Siegfried takes from Brünhilt, play their own part in the development of the plot. But I want to suggest that even such universally acknowledged symbols have not been given their full weight by scholars, and that there are others equally important which have been ignored altogether. In doing so I shall group together as symbolic a variety of incidents which might profitably be separated into different categories. They have, however, in my opinion, one thing in common: their small individual structure resembles the general overall structure of the work. Because it is this resemblance which I want to emphasize, I group them all together and (loosely) label them all symbolic; more precise terminological distinction would simply blur their common feature.

One interesting thing about Kriemhilt's dream is that on closer inspection it clearly supports the interpretation of Siegfried's position in the work suggested by Mr Mowatt in a separate study in this issue. After the twelve stanzas describing the perfection of the Burgundian court comes this one:

In disen hoheu eren   troumte Kriemhilde,
wie si züge einen valken   starc scoen und wilde,
den ir zwene arn erkrummen.   daz si daz muoste
                   sehen:
ir enkunde in dirre werlde   leider nimmer gesce-
                   hen.

                      (13)

In the following stanzas it is indicated that the falcon symbolizes Siegfried, and there can be no doubt that the two adjectives 'starc' and 'scoene' are peculiarly appropriate to him. One may therefore well ask if 'wilde' is not appropriate too, and if Siegfried is not by nature wild, uncivilized. If that is so, the verb 'ziehen' will have a special significance, for it means in this context to tame and train (a wild bird to behave as one wishes). The Siegfried who arrives at Worms so wildly is in fact outwardly tamed by Kriemhilt—it is his desire to win her hand which makes him conform to the conventions of the Burgundian court (123, 4)—and yet, as he remains to the end of his life the lord of the Nibelungen, an elemental figure beyond all morality, tragedy results. This unresolved tension, which exists both within Siegfried and between him and the court of Worms, may be regarded as one of the primary sources of conflict in the work; yet it is never made explicit by the narrator, only indicated in this one stanza introducing the falcon symbol.

The ring and the girdle which Siegfried takes from Brünhilt, when given their full weight, provide the chief evidence that the obvious reason for Siegfried's murder is the true one: no matter how complex the immediate motivation may be, he is ultimately murdered for his vital and

peculiarly high-handed part in the conquest of Brünhilt. Siegfried overcomes Brünhilt—on Gunther's behalf—in order to win Kriemhilt. Gunther, weak and vicious as he is, may well be content with the way Siegfried hands Brünhilt over intact at the crucial moment; it is easy for him to accept Siegfried's word that he never boasted to Kriemhilt of having deflowered Brünhilt, but the ring and the girdle which Kriemhilt wears—that she wears them is as significant as that Siegfried took them—reveal to one and all that, however the details have been managed, the essential fact remains: Brünhilt's virginity was sacrificed by Siegfried to Kriemhilt. The subsidiary fact, that Siegfried kept his promise to Gunther and did not actually deflower Brünhilt, is no more consolation to the latter than is his willingness to swear that he did not boast to Kriemhilt of doing so. Indeed precisely what has gone wrong for Brünhilt is that the one man who was her master did *not* in the least desire her. (Had Siegfried first claimed her body, she might in some sense have been his, might to some extent have found fulfilment. As it is, she is permanently degraded, and revenge alone remains.) Siegfried dies for the real injury he does Brünhilt, and not (primarily) because of any curious notion of honour we may attribute to medieval society.

The symbolic nature of the falcon, as of the ring and the girdle, is indicated by the poet; what I now wish to suggest is that certain other episodes in the work are also symbolic, even though their symbolism is not so indicated. It is indeed perfectly possible, though not necessary, that the poet himself did not consciously recognize them as symbols at all. But if it is axiomatic that the work of all artists, even medieval ones, is more complex than they consciously realize, then I would suggest that when we find, at a crucial point in the story, a small but striking incident reflecting in miniature the main course of events, we should describe this too as symbolic, ponder its significance, and enjoy its position and its character.

Siegfried is murdered while drinking from a 'brunne' (I use the Middle High German word because English lacks an equivalent embracing both concepts of 'spring' and 'well'); near the 'brunne' is a lime tree against which he rests his weapons. Now this combination of a single lime tree and a 'brunne' is surprising here; for although it is a common combination in Middle High German literature, it is normally, as for instance in *Iwein,* the setting for a love-affair. Professor Hatto has investigated the association of the lime tree with love;[6] it may, I think, briefly be classed as a phallic symbol, and the spring or, particularly clearly in *Iwein,* the well which goes with it is its complement, a vaginal symbol. Trees and wells commonly have these associations even outside Middle High German literature: the question is whether such an association here would add to or detract from the function and significance of the episode.

Siegfried arrives first at the 'brunne'; but although he has been behaving particularly brashly the moment before (965-970), now he is so courteous that he does not drink until Gunther has done so. And the narrator says: 'do engalt er siner zühte' (980, 1), although it is not clear how he thus paid for his courtesy. One may perhaps suppose that had Siegfried drunk straight away, Hagen would not by then have reached the 'brunne', but does it not still remain something of a mystery why the narrator bothered to introduce this complication—unless, as I would suggest, it was to draw attention to the larger implications of the episode? Siegfried is killed as a result of the unwonted courtesy he shows in wooing Kriemhilt; he dies for the service he has rendered Gunther, dies that is, in the language of symbol, because he allowed Gunther to 'drink at the well'. It is this fact, I think, which the circumstances of his death suggest.

Incidentally there may also be significance in the apparently trivial detail that it is—of all things—a lime leaf which prevents the dragon's blood from rendering Siegfried totally impregnable. Not only is this a leaf from the tree of love, it is itself heart-shaped, and it falls between Siegfried's shoulder-blades so that Hagen's spear pierces his very heart. And of course Hagen had learnt the secret of it from Kriemhilt. Does it not seem as though Siegfried's love for Kriemhilt were his one weak point?

What I next propose is an additional significance for an episode whose apparent symbolism has always been recognized. In accordance with Siegfried's pretence to be Gunther's vassal during the wooing of Brünhilt, a pretence designed to elevate Gunther in her eyes, Siegfried leads out and holds Gunther's horse upon arrival in Islant. The symbolic act is certainly meant to deceive Brünhilt, but rather strangely fails of its purpose, for she and her company still regard Siegfried as the leader a few stanzas later. This small discrepancy has so far as I know disturbed no modern scholar, nor has anyone wondered at the poet's bothering to mention that Siegfried leads out his own horse after he has led out Gunther's. Yet these apparently trivial details may be significant. Horses, in medieval literature as elsewhere, function frequently as symbols of virility, and the acceptance of such a function here adds immediately to the depth of the scene: the actions of Siegfried as Gunther's groom may be considered as an appropriate symbolization of the services Siegfried renders Gunther both in the tournament with Brünhilt and later in the bedroom scene; only when Gunther is safely in the saddle can he manage by himself. Thus the episode not only indicates the apparent dependence of Siegfried on Gunther, but also the real dependence of Gunther on Siegfried—and it appears to be this latter dependence to which Brünhilt and her ladies instinctively react.—On the other hand there is a real sense in which Siegfried is dependent on Gunther, for he early resolved not to try to win Kriemhilt by force but to serve her brother in the hope of being rewarded by her hand; and this dependence is I think indicated by the fact that Siegfried only leads out his own horse *after* he has seen Gunther safely mounted. The small but crucial scene thus symbolizes, not just one element in the relationship of the two men, but the essential basis of the whole relationship between Siegfried, Gunther, Brünhilt and Kriemhilt.

The last symbol to which I want to draw attention is Hagen's super-heroic feat in ferrying the entire Burgundian army across the Danube single-handed:

> Zem ersten braht' er über   tusent ritter her,
> dar nach die sinen recken.   dannoch was ir mer.
> niun tusent knehte   die fuort' er an daz lant.
> des tages was unmüezec   des küenen Tronegaeres
>   hant.
>
>   (1573)

The presumably deliberate understatement in this last line—the bold Tronegaere's hand was busy that day—makes Heusler's assumption, that the poet himself would have joined in the modern reader's mild amusement at so exaggerated an episode, probable.[7] But the physical impossibility of Hagen's act surely underlines its symbolic importance. Hagen and Hagen alone, the narrator insists, gets the Burgundians across this river, which in the story is the only major obstacle on the road from Burgundy to Austria. In view of the fuss the narrator makes about the crossing one may wonder whether they become different people in Austria—and the answer provides an otherwise missing key to our understanding of the main course of the story. For the Burgundians who in Austria destroy such a vast horde of peoples before they themselves finally perish are barely recognizable as those who were so utterly afraid to take up the Saxon challenge at Worms. At last their deeds vindicate the claims the narrator has continually made for them, at last they really behave something like heroes, Gunther and Hagen being second only to Dietrich and Hildebrant. And, moreover, the fifth stanza of the work may suggest such a contrast:

> Die herren waren milte,   von arde hoh erborn,
> mit kraft unmazen küene,   di recken uz erkorn.
> da zen Burgonden   so was ir lant genant.
> si frumten starkiu wunder   sit in Etzelen lant.

The crossing of the Danube symbolizes this transformation; but the Burgundians do not row themselves over, Hagen does it for them.

Hagen's one other decisive action is the killing of Siegfried (the very action which led the Burgundians to their present plight), and it is significant that he behaves on this occasion in a manner reminiscent of that earlier one. For if one asks for the immediate reason why Hagen has to ferry the Burgundians across, one must answer: because he has killed the ferryman. And does this ferryman not recall Siegfried, who piloted Gunther to Islant?—It is an assumption which would explain many of the details of the scene between Hagen and the ferryman, details which otherwise seem unnecessarily full and strangely puzzling. The ferryman, like Siegfried, is too rich and too powerful to need to serve others: 'der verge was so riche, daz im niht dienen zam' (1551, 1). He is in fact not really a ferryman at all, yet he comes across to fetch Hagen—when the latter offers him payment in the form of a single gold ring. The symbolic implications of this ring recall how Siegfried was rewarded for his services with Kriemhilt, and the reference to the ferryman's recent marriage helps to complete the picture. Moreover the ferryman, like Siegfried, is tricked by Hagen, who turns out to be no relative but an enemy, and who kills him.

The Burgundians then are different people once they have crossed the Danube, and it is Hagen's murder of Siegfried, reflected in his murder of the ferryman, which leads to their transformation. The psychological basis of their transformed behaviour, of their new-found heroism, seems to be the acceptance of probable death: if survival is impossible one has nothing to lose by being defiant. From this aspect too Hagen appears as the one responsible person, for he alone has anticipated death in Austria (1461), and no one else hears of the prophecy of the Danube maidens until the crossing is complete. But then, when all the others are across, Hagen tests out the prophecy by flinging the chaplain into the water; and finally, after destroying the unmistakably symbolical boat, by which alone, we are asked to believe, the army could have returned, he informs the others of their fate. His dominant rôle in the events that lead to the (interrelated) heroism and destruction of the Burgundians in the second half of the **Nibelungenlied** could scarcely be indicated more clearly.[8]

Here then, once again, the main course of the story is reflected in a single incident. In this incident, as in the others I have mentioned, there are details which may not seem to tally. On the one hand I would maintain that this does not affect the argument, for of course these episodes exist independently in their own right as well as for the symbolic meaning they contain. Yet divergent details should not be dismissed too lightly: they may illuminate the main story if allowed to do so. And this I would make as my final point: whenever we find an apparent discrepancy in the **Nibelungenlied,** let us not disregard it as a fault too easily: for whatever the origin—and it may of course indicate the disparity of the various sources at the poet's disposal—the poet arranged it consciously or unconsciously as it is—and he was surely a greater poet than has often been allowed.[9]

Notes

1. Quoted throughout from the 13th ed. by Karl Bartsch and Helmut de Boor, Wiesbaden, 1956.

2. This and other linguistic points can easily be checked from Karl Bartsch, *Der Nibelunge Not,* vol. II, 2 *Wörterbuch,* Leipzig, 1880.

3. Gottlieb Stopz, *Epitheta ornantia im Kudrunlied, im Biterolf und im Nibelungenlied,* Diss. Tübingen, 1930.

4. Friedrich Panzer, *Das Nibelungenlied, Entstehung und Gestalt,* Stuttgart, 1955.

5. It may be noticed that the intriguing 'minnecliche' occurs in the last half-line of the stanza. Such occurrences have frequently been dismissed as padding by bored scholars. But the last half-line remains an important one, whether used for climax or anti-climax,

for positive, negative or ironic statement, for action or for comment. The multiplicity of use may indeed be taken as testimony to the greatness of the work; if all its nuances are enjoyed, it will not be found boring.

6. A. T. Hatto, 'The lime-tree and early German, Goliard and English lyric poetry', *Modern Language Review,* vol. XLIX (1954).

7. Andreas Heusler, *Nibelungensage und Nibelungenlied,* 5th ed., Dortmund, 1955, p. 68.

8. Dr F. J. Stopp has suggested to me that in Hagen's ability to ferry vast numbers across the Danube, there is an echo of Charon. Do the doomed Burgundians not weigh more than the shades who cross the Styx?

9. I should like to thank Professor Helena M. Gamer for helping me to get these notes, whose origins lie several years back, into some sort of shape. They remain, however, only preliminary gropings towards a new understanding of the *Nibelungenlied.* Subsequent work by D. G. Mowatt and myself has led to an interpretative commentary on the whole work, which will we hope appear in about eighteen months.

Werner A. Mueller (essay date 1962)

SOURCE: "The Essence" and "The Significance" in *The Nibelungenlied Today: Its Substance, Essence, and Significance*, The University of North Carolina Press, 1962, pp. 59-92.

[*In the following excerpt, Mueller explains that the* Nibelungenlied's *main theme is man himself, particularly how he responds to a dilemma. Mueller also explores the poet's concerns and his relation to his work and contends that the poem, without promoting specific religious values, nevertheless affirms man's need for faith.*]

"Die Kunst ist eine Vermittlerin des Unaussprechlichen; darum scheint es eine Torheit, sie wieder durch Worte vermitteln zu wollen. Doch indem wir uns darum bemühen, findet sich für den Verstand so mancher Gewinn, der dem ausübenden Vermögen auch wieder zugute kommt." GOETHE

The *Nibelungen* story fails to represent a dominant idea that can be clearly grasped. As a work of art embracing the reflections of infinity rather than of material limitations, although its subject matter is stark reality, the song defies a verbal statement as to its special message, a schoolbook explanation of its intent that can be catalogued as factual truth, yet in reality prevents the reader from experiencing its full, spiritual validity. The story takes the reader from the court of Worms to Xanten, Isenstein, through Austria and Hungary, covering scores of years characterized by actions and events that cause the death of countless men, the boldest and the noblest under drastic circumstances, while whole tribes are virtually annihilated. Although distant historical events have given substance to the story, passed on as legends or as myths, it is not history we read about. In the absence of the idea of a nation or a country as a moral force and romantically extolled, the work can also not be labeled a national epic, as Virgil's Aeneid constituted for the Romans, and as which it is occasionally proclaimed by modern patriots. Regardless of their nationality or their Teutonic heritage, the people of the song appeal to us chiefly as they are human beings of flesh and blood, of greatness and of folly, psychologically convincing both in their strength and in their failings. Now tasting earthly pleasures and delights, now suffering the opposites, they find themselves involved in struggle and intrigues concerning dubious precepts like honor and prestige, in the pursuit of which they reach grandeur as well as infamy. The greatness of their will and tragic end, their struggle for assertion of their personalities and for self-preservation in a world of human conflicts arising from within and from without, arouse a definite response in us who are beset by similar complexities. Kindness, refinement, lofty thoughts, developing to dubious ideologies or crushed by violence and primitive brutality, have left a greater stain upon our age than witnessed by the *Nibelungen*. Although the tragic story of their greatness and their failure is narrated with epic objectivity and as the literary theme *per se,* causing the reader to reflect as he is moved by its inherent truth, the search for tangible ideas imbedded in the song has occupied the critics up to our time.

1

Stirred by the collective doom of friend and foe, of guilty and of innocent, the author of the *"Klage"* was the first to add elaborate comments to the **Nibelungenlied** soon after it was circulated.[1] Praising the faithfulness of Kriemhild, who revenged her murdered husband, the author cleanses her from any guilt of which the reader might accuse her, replying in particular to those who claim that she is suffering well deserved torments of hell. As Hagen is declared the villain who caused it all, *"der vâlant der ez allez riet"* (1250), Kriemhild is said to be in heaven, living in the love of God. The *Klage* author is convinced that God's eternal order is upheld and that justice prevails in the end, according to his personal concepts of right and wrong, of guilt and punishment, and in accordance to his knowledge of God's will. This moralistic attitude of judging and ascribing guilt and innocence, contrasting Siegfried as the man of light with Hagen as a character of darkness, the former good, the latter evil, has found its followers up to our time. While Josef Weinheber reflects: *"Immer entsteht dem lichten / Siegfried ein Tronje im Nu . . . ,"* Wilhelm Dilthey speaks of the demonic quality of Hagen, symbolizing the powers of darkness that destroy the one who walks in the light.[2] Also Gustav Ehrismann considers guilt and punishment leading ideas of the epic; experienced by the heroes as their fate, both categories are particularly applicable to Brunhild and to Kriemhild, each of whom contracts a guilt for which she finds her proper punishment.[3] As outcome of such thinking in terms of right and wrong, of black and white, and in accordance to the dubious quality of justice as proclaimed by man, Hagen is now condemned as a ruthless murderer by one, now extolled or

considered expiated by another commentator; similarly, Kriemhild is declared guilty and a true *vâlandinne* or praised as revenger "immaculate."[4] Werner Fechter even sees in Hagen both, the envious intriguer who sows evil and finds pleasure in destroying and the very tool of God, assassinating Siegfried, the truly guilty one.[5] As Siegfried's guilt or innocence is likewise subject to controversial appraisals, Katharina Bollinger finds him implicated not merely by a moral and objective guilt as Fechter states, but also by a *Seins-Schuld"*, a kind of existential guilt.[6] Andreas Heusler, on the other hand, speaks of Siegfried's *"Kindesunschuld,"* a naive and childlike innocence whose victim he becomes,[7] while Dietrich von Kralik considers him the innocent victim of Brunhild, who is the really guilty person of the song.[8] These contradictory interpretations of moral guilt in modern days present interesting parallels to man's confusion and dilemma not unlike those which are reflected in the work itself. In the absence of moral absolutes, however, and in consideration of man's ambiguous views on glory, honesty, or honor, on right and wrong, subject to personal evaluation at any age, this moralistic attitude of judging the heroes of our song fails to exert persuasive force and to do justice to the total implications of the work.

Some of the very critics who think in terms of light and dark, of glorious and inglorious deeds, of strong and weak, seem also influenced by patriotic or national concern, seeing in the song an idealization of their German ancestors. For some of them the faithfulness of Kriemhild, a Germanic heroine of exemplary traits, is the essential theme; others dwell upon the heroic attitude that is extolled in the song as its primary merit. The bold acceptance of a higher fate, now with defiance, now with enthusiasm; the unflinching resistance to unconquerable circumstances as man's greatest achievement; the blind obedience to the commands of loyalty and leadership; the readiness to die heroically in the pursuit and in the name of honor—all these are stressed as the leading ideas of the Germanic epic, which were particularly suited to endorse nationalistic ideologies in vogue when these interpretations were popular. These commentators do not write about the great futility of which the story tells; they praise the spirit of the men who rise above their fate by either bravely killing others or by dying in heroic battle without tears, and they presume man's greatness has been proved, his victory affirmed, a catharsis achieved.

Another group of modern interpreters is guided by psychological theories, enabling them to crystalize a variety of themes that seem embedded in the story. Thus Arnold H. Price declares the modern idea that man carries the seed of his destruction as psychological necessity within himself, the possible theme of the epic.[9] Without assuming that the poet himself was aware of such a theory, Price describes the brilliant insight of the author in respect to his characterizations. Thus the poet deliberately stresses Kriemhild's "violent streak" early in our epic when she voices her intent to stay beautiful and happy and never to suffer man's love. Kriemhild's very horror of marriage significantly exerts a special attraction to Siegfried, indicating a negative tendency in his nature, too. Eventually both are married and very much in love with each other, which "the author does not consider inconsistent with Kriemhild's previous dislike of marriage," as Price states.[10] But due to the devious depth of Kriemhild's personality she subconsciously maneuvers her husband into an impossible situation when she announces that Brunhild has been his mistress; as further indication of the true violence and fierceness inherent in her character, Kriemhild makes Siegfried's death possible by revealing his vulnerable spot to his enemy. As Price concludes: "The author's attempt to provide the major figures of the epic with an entirely new characterization not only supplies a coherent and realistic motivation, but also the theme for the epic, i.e. that man carries the seed of his destruction in his character."[11] Acceptance of the logic and the power of such psychic drives in man as a dominating force, taking the place of moral principles, as Price seems to imply, would reduce man to the world of instincts, appetites and hidden urges, precluding moral choice; this world is further complicated by man's ability to rationalize and to idealize his destructive drives to which he submits. Not unlike the vague idea of fate, this view fails to give due credit to man's spiritual potentialities, to his moral strength, to his sense of truth, and to his free will. As the creative process of man's artistic inspiration and expression has escaped scientific explanation, also man's spiritual experiences of God and of infinity as well as of himself as free-willed participant in the great stream of life, the basis for his moral consciousness, reflect far greater forces than psychological approaches can identify.

An outgrowth of this modern probing and explaining of human behavior are the speculative theories imposed upon the song that try to state some natural laws involved, upheld or violated, which are declared the causes for its tragic course. Thus Werner Fechter advances the thought that the **Nibelungenlied** describes the guilt of Siegfried who stepped out of his order when he, the *"Sonnenheros mit dem strahlenden Blick,"* failed to take Brunhild for his wife, *"die ihm Bestimmte, Gleichartige."*[12] Failing to fulfill his superhuman possibilities, Siegfried was faithless to himself, that means to his own character, by marrying *"ein blosses Menschenweib,"* while he helped Gunther to wed with impudence a superhuman being to whom he had no claim. These violations are Siegfried's guilt; everything else develops in consequence of it, as Fechter concludes, and Siegfried's murder as well as the outcome of the struggle confirm the existence of a higher justice.[13] Also Bert Nagel considers Siegfried and Brunhild predestined to be mates and sees in their failure to find the way to each other the cause for the ensuing catastrophe that makes the tragedy complete.[14] The guilt, however, is less Siegfried's than Gunther's, with whose wooing the tragic complexities begin. The contradictions of Siegfried's and Brunhild's relationship constitute the important psychological background of the story, maintaining a constant condition of tension which is increased by the paradoxical state of life as found in the personality of Siegfried, *"des starken Schwachen,"* strong in his heroic qualities, yet weak in his

desire for Kriemhild's love.[15] Nagel calls the song a tragedy of guilt, ending with catharsis as symbolized by tears rather than by expressions of despair.[16]

Next to this motive of Brunhild's love and jealousy of Siegfried, which mostly seems inferred by the critics from the existing or re-constructed, literary sources of the **Nibelungenlied,** but which appear neglected, if not entirely unused by the poet himself, the theme of power likewise has found a number of new supporters recently. Thus Siegfried Beyschlag analyzes the idea of a realistic struggle for power as the essential topic of the song;[17] since political realities are the foremost concern of the ruling kings, rating higher than personal relationships and loyalties, Siegfried's assassination is necessary due to the threat to the security of the court of Worms which he poses.[18] As even Ruediger is guided by political necessities (!), Gunther and his brothers, too, must decide in favor of the regal power against their kin and friends. Also Kriemhild's revenge is conceived not merely as a retribution for the murder of her husband, but for the restoration of the power which Siegfried represented for her. As political considerations are the dominating forces effective in the story, as Beyschlag maintains, its tragedy is really Siegfried's murder since it constitutes a gross political blunder, whose consequences are pitilessly described.[19] Also W. J. Schroeder sees in the struggle of the *Nibelungen* chiefly a fight for power that finds its logical conclusion in the murderous battle at the end.[20] Declaring the possession of the treasure a symbol of power, which the *Nibelungen* had to take, as also Friedrich Neuman does, Schroeder characterizes Kriemhild's actions in the second part of the story as chiefly directed to regain the treasure.[21] There is no antithesis of good and evil in the song, but merely of strength and weakness in the sense of Nietzsche.[22] The law of nature that the best, i.e. the strongest, must be the first also prevails in human society. Worldly power not supported by strength must decline.[23] Kriemhild and Gunther do not act from strength, but from fear of lacking power; thus they fight for mere survival and no longer strive to enlarge their power. Weakness, however, is guilt, and death is the price for weakness, for the hybrid claim of power, and for arrogance.[24] Hagen realizes his master's weakness and tries to keep an outside appearance of Gunter's strength alive. The *Nibelungen* are driven by natural necessities as compelling as Homer's αναγκη; man's acceptance of nature's will as his fate constitutes his wisdom and heroic greatness.[25]

Dated or absurd as some of these interpretations may seem today, they constitute a serious effort to verbalize the implications, the message, and the idea of this great work of art that exerts such stirring impact upon the reader. Although the moralistic, the patriotic, the psychological, and the philosophic-speculative approaches may illuminate some special aspects of the epic, they fail to realize its complex totality or to reflect its wider scope. Some analytical investigations of the text, however, stand out for sober observations which seem beyond dispute. After his life-long occupation with the **Nibelungenlied,** Friedrich Panzer comes to the conclusion that its deepest concern have never been events of our material world, but *"die geistigen-sittlichen Vorgänge im Innenleben des Menschen"* and his *"Bewährung in den Konflikten",* man's spiritual and moral sense and his behavior in adversities, a statement which we like.[26] Friedrich Neumann sees in the story of the *Nibelungen* a conglomerate of literary sources as it is *"echtes Schicksal in eine . . . schwer deutbare Handlung des Leides hinüberentwickelt;"*[27] what once was accepted as genuine fate has changed for the poet of *"Der Nibelunge Not"* to experiences of suffering and sorrow which he, not in affinity with the Germanic concept of blind fate, found difficult to assimilate. *"Leid"* as the primary theme of the work is also stressed by Friedrich Maurer, who defines it as the very opposite of honor, namely as the consciousness of insults and dishonor suffered, as *"Beleidigung"* rather than grief, as which Neumann sees it.[28] For Maurer *leid* and honor are the motivating forces in Kriemhild, Hagen, Ruediger, and Hildebrand. Kriemhild's revenge is not inspired by her faithfulness, but signifies her quest for restoration of her injured honor; Hagen is driven by concern about the honor of his masters, of Brunhild, of the Burgundian realm, and of himself. The treasure thus becomes the symbol of honor rather than of power; who has the treasure also has the honor. Although Maurer considers *"das furchtbare Leid, . . . das schicksalshaft über den Menschen in der Welt kommt,"* the essential subject of the song, it does not signify to him its deepest meaning, which, as he likewise realizes, has not been clearly formulated by the artist.[29] The silence of the poet as to his intent can be interpreted in several ways, as Maurer believes: it can imply a silent condemnation of man's way who, without reference to God, yields to his human passions and to the ideas of honor and revenge; it also might suggest the poet's *"stumme Frage nach dem Sinn solchen Geschehens,"* the question of the meaning of the tragic events which he could not truly comprehend, as Neumann suggests, or to which he did not know the answer, as Maurer states.[30]

2

What constitutes the essence of this elusive work that has no definite idea advanced to which its various critics could agree? What is its central topic with which the poet seems chiefly concerned? The song is not the story of Siegfried and of Brunhild, of Kriemhild and of Hagen, of Ruediger or Giselher, of Ihring, Wolfhart, Gunther, or Dietrich and of Etzel. They all take merely a part in it, they move and act, they are involved in a very complex interrelationship as they are poised partly against each other and partly with each other; all are eventually the victims of events which they themselves collectively were active to beget. Thousands of brave men additionally, good vassals all, share in the fortunes and misfortunes of the leading principals, while thousands more, bereft of husbands, kin and friends, stand mute around the scene, silent and unidentified. Greater than the sum of singular events, of tales of individuals, of groups, or relatives and foes, the epic of the *Nibelungen* relates man's greatest, universal theme, the story of himself; as it specifically depicts, the *Nibelungen's "Not,"* it stresses man in his dilemma, without the

comfort of his pondering the precarious state in which he finds himself, soliciting our sympathy and leading us to contemplation in regard to ourselves.

At the very beginning of the song a tragic chord is struck, alluring, ominous, of sad grandeur as it develops further on. Yet in dramatic contrast to its notes, foreboding woe and sadness, melodious happy chords abound, enthralling by their beauty. These lusty melodies reflect man's joy of life, as we have seen, his sensitivities and his refinement, his lofty spirit and his honorable bearing; the tragic chords remind us of man's basic vanity and weakness, of his dangerous potentialities that make him stumble in the end, destroying prematurely his happiness, his very joys, his earthly life. Without a special message, the epic gains its greatest actuality from its valid reflection of man's realities as the poet experienced them and passed them on to us in the symbolic story of the *Nibelungen,* symbolic for the ways of man, both for his strength and for his failures. Two obstacles that man encounters in his life determine his dilemma, his futility, and his tragic end: the one is the duality within himself, a part of his existence; the other is the paradox that he encounters chiefly as experience from without. With both he has to cope, yet both defy his reason and his command, preventing him from finding or maintaining completion, lasting harmony, and final peace. In everything he wills, he values, and pursues, there are the possibilities of either harming or advancing him, with parallel effects, sometimes reversed, upon his fellowmen. There is potential good and evil inherent in his values, in his convictions and emotions which he upholds with various strength at different times. Not any of these forces are ever fully realized or are pursued with single-mindedness, but each concept is colored by some other one and fused to a conglomerate of contradictory ingredients; each might now dominate, now yield, now be abandoned, now again prevail.

Even the *Nibelungen's* very joy of life, a basic and essential trait for a happy existence, embraces the potentials of happiness and failure. Characterized by noble, generous behavior, by loftiness of aims and fearlessness, it sometimes ends in disregard of ethics. It is the *hohe muot,* the joyous, spirited acceptance of life, so characteristic of the heroes of our story, which leads to carefreeness, to arrogance and recklessness, even to violence. The *"hohe muot"* (680) of Siegfried entices him to boisterous deeds such as the stripping of the ring from Brunhild's finger and as the taking of her belt as souvenir and an eventual gift to his own bride, actions that some consider a part of Siegfried's guilt, which means his doom. Kriemhild clearly realizes the danger for her spouse to be carried away by his *"'übermuot'"* (896, 3), which she describes to Hagen, this "charming carefreeness," as K. Bollinger calls it,[31] which is so typical of Siegfried's disposition and of which he is the victim. Yet this high, excessive spirit can also collapse with equal speed as it arises. Setting out to Worms with unquestioned assurance of winning Kriemhild for his wife, exhibiting to Gunther and his men nothing but *"'starkez ubermüeten'"* (117, 4), as Ortwin correctly states, he succumbs to doubt and diffidence when he eventually meets the maiden of his choice. He is ready even to give up his heart's desire, to admit defeat, and to return to Xanten before Giselher persuades him to stay on. The decision to journey to Isenstein is another example of a high-spirited, courageous disposition that inspires the four men who partake in it. But soon this *hohe muot* leads to deception, which is morally not objectionable on the level of the fairy tale to which this episode belongs, but to which the keen participants agree in their *"übermüete"* (387, 2); in the spirit of great self-assurance they are unconcerned about the danger of the fraud to which they agree and are completely unaware of the tragic complications which it is to have for them. A similarly reckless disposition characterizes the Burgundians at their arrival at Etzel's court when none of them deigns it advisable to inform the guileless king of Kriemhild's threatening designs:

> *Swie grimme und wie starke*   *si in vîent wære,*
> *het iemen gesaget Etzeln*   *diu rehten mære,*
> *er het' wol understanden*   *daz doch sît dâ geschach.*
> *durch ir vil starken übermuot*   *ir deheiner ims verjach.*
>
>   (1865)

The following disaster might well have been stalled by Etzel if arrogance and pride would not have prevented the *Nibelungen* from speaking to the king, as the poet states. But Hagen's short and untrue answer: *"'uns hât niemen niht getân'"* (1863, 1), with which he brushes Etzel's worried question aside, sets the tone for all the *Nibelungen*. Since Kriemhild is present when Hagen lies to Etzel, stating that the Burgundians were accustomed to go around in arms during the first three days of any festivities, which the queen knows not to be true, this statement underscores his reckless spirit as it indicates his obvious unconcern about her hostile disposition, but at the same time conveys to her that the Nibelungen are ready to fight.

Perhaps this tendency of man to be carried from a wholesome disposition of joy and self-assurance to the extremes of pride and recklessness, of arrogance and violence, can be described as lack of self-restraint, i.e. a lack of *mâze* and self-discipline. The question then would be how far this lack is due to ignorance, to education, to unwillingness, or due to emotions, to folly, to beliefs, or even to ideals of strength and other precepts of behavior which man proclaims as values. The fact remains that man is just one step away from turning what seems sound and great to a provocative, ignoble thing, as the *Nibelungen* well exemplify. Volker stains the record of his courageous fighting spirit by deliberately killing his opponent in a tournament; in his eagerness to fight he also advocates disobedience to one's leader as he lures Wolfhart into battle against the strict orders of the latter's master:

> *Dô sprach der videlære:*   *"der vorhte ist gar ze vil,*
> *swaz man im verbiutet,*   *derz allez lâzen wil.*
> *daz kan ich niht geheizen*   *rehten heldes muot".*
>
>   (2268, 1-3)

Hagen approves of Volker's bold suggestion not to obey one's master in everything: *"diu rede dûhte Hagenen von sînem hergesellen guot"* (2268, 4). Wolfhart is ready to attack, heeding Volker's challenge, but he is held back by Hildebrand, who correctly calls his nephew's rashness a mad and foolish anger: *"'ich wæne du woldeste wüeten durch dînen tumben zorn'"* (2271, 3). Upon Volker's further taunts, however, the hot-headed, youthful Wolfhart leaps against the *videlære*, tearing the older Hildebrand and all the Amelungians into the wanton fight that was useless and unpremeditated and brought death to all, Hagen, Gunther and Hildebrand being the sole survivors.

The coexistence of kindness and brutality, of gentleness and violence in man is a further aspect of his duality. Even the kindest and most generous of all, the marcgrave Ruediger, can strike a fellowman to death merely because he casts suspicion on the other's integrity. Ruediger's deed is done in anger, aggravated by his inner disquietude, yet it is not followed by regret as if kindness had never touched his heart. Reversely, a most brutal man like Hagen can be filled with sudden kindness and extend his sympathy and lasting friendship to a man like Ruediger who comes to fight with him. None of the heroes of the song fails to reveal inherent kindness at some time and violence, if not outright brutality, at another time. Volker, whose gentler traits are echoed by his music, by his refined behavior at Bechelaren, and by his warmth of friendship with Hagen, does not only substitute his fiddler's bow, with which he lulls his wearied comrades to their last sleep, by a sword of violent intent and force, used in a noble fight; he also kills quite brutally an unnamed marcgrave who tries to aid a wounded comrade, still living on the pile of seven thousand dead, during a lull in the battle. Incidentally, it is at the advice of Giselher, a hero *"getriuwe unde guot"* (1099, 4) and *"sô rehte tugentlîch gemuot"* (2161, 4) that these dead and wounded are tossed from the landing of the stairs into the court before the hall.

As the poet narrates how his heroes now pray to God or ask for His advice, now fall victim to the devil's promptings, he reminds us drastically of another, perhaps most fundamental conflict in man's nature. It is the contrast of his knowledge and awareness of God, of man's possibility of pleasing Him and finding peace in his direction toward Him, and of his vain, if not devilish pursuits in life which are in disregard of God. The sorry end of Ruediger, a man bemoaned by all, appears of special sad significance not just because he is so generous and kind, the father of all virtues, but because he is a man, torn and impelled by inner contrasts, victim of his duality. Troubled by both, the inner voice of God and outside appeals in conflict with his conscience, he choses to heed the call of man and to fulfill what one expects of him. Thus he sacrifices a state of harmony with God, trying to preserve his state of worldly honor in the eyes of men.

The tragedy of Kriemhild likewise is her complete surrender of peace and grace in God while yielding to the forces of human passions and desires that lead to her devilish revenge. At the beginning of the song Kriemhild is pictured as a truly gentle woman, restrained, refined, modest in all her *"magtlîchen zühten"* (615, 1). Her beautiful renown, the beauty of her bearing, of her composure and appearance are corresponding to the beauty of her soul, a soul that knows itself in harmony with God.[32] The happy years as Siegfried's wife have altered her but little; they have added more self-assurance to her personality, some worldliness and vanity. The sudden death of Siegfried brings forth passionate grief as well as furious thoughts in her, intensified perhaps by the awareness that she herself has been a factor in the betrayal of her husband, though unsuspecting and unknowing. After four days of frantic grief she enters an existence of seclusion in complete retreat from the realities of life; she takes her lonely residence next to the church where she can pray to God to have mercy on Siegfried's soul, whose grave she visits daily; *"si alle zît dar gie"* (1103, 2). She has abandoned the common joys of life, even the vanities of special dress, as she has lost all interest in further happiness on earth. But her life of mourning, praying, and remembering in seclusion does not prevail for many years; eventually the world intrudes both form without and from within. She is urged and persuaded to agree to a reconciliation with her brother, the ruling king and secret partner in her husband's murder. Then she is forced to a decision in regard to her wealth, once Siegfried's gold, of which she has been totally oblivious ever since his death more than three years ago. The treasure is taken from the custody of Alberich and brought to Worms, where Kriemhild now begins to use it freely, making new friends by means of it. Hagen, however, soon insists that it is taken away from her in hostile violation of her rights, which not only renews old wounds but also adds to her awareness of the dishonor and the wrongs that she has suffered for so long without any defense. After a further period of sadness and of passive mourning, extending over many years, a second marriage is proposed to her which she is urged by friends and kin to accept although it is entirely against the inclinations of her heart. The promise of new happiness has no appeal to her. Had she not known that love must end in grief and happiness in sorrow? Did she not taste the greatest happiness that can be found as long as she was Siegfried's wife? Now the grief is hers which once she had foreseen would follow married happiness. Also the possibilities of new prestige and wealth have lost their lure for her. The consciousness, however, of being the victim of brutal violence and fraud, of hateful and dishonoring actions, and the latent wish to right and revenge the wrongs which she and Siegfried had to suffer from Hagen's hand especially, have never been entirely extinguished in her troubled mind since that very moment when she first called to God in her despair, asking that He might assist her friends in punishing the murderers of her husband. Thus she agrees to a new marriage merely as it renews the latent hope for possible revenge, a thought that gradually increases to such compelling urge that her entire personality seems totally reversed as it is saturated by that single wish; the mourning, passive widow leaves her solitude of praying to grow into a scheming woman, dishonest, heartless, cruel, eventually a vâlandinne. This latter term suggests no longer a human, God-inspired person, but a fiendish subject of the devil, devoid of love and pity, a creature without a soul, a mockery of God. No greater contrast in one person seems imaginable, dramatically revealing his dual nature and conflicting potentialities, than Kriemhild represents. First the gentle maiden, modest, refined, withdrawn, watching Siegfried from a distance and keeping her love virtuously in her heart; eventually a blushing, tender bride and a devoted wife; later a lonely widow, a recluse in her residence, going to church devoutly to pray for Siegfried's soul, scorning all joys of life. Then Kriemhild, the revenger, kneeling before one of her vassals or pleading for assistance in spite of stern rebukes from those who are obliged to serve her; offering vessels filled with gold to buy and bribe her men for treachery, for murder and for arson; and finally wielding a sword against her hated enemy, defenseless yet relentless as he is, beheading him with her own hands. Kriemhild, the leading person of the song, emerges as the greatest example of man's conflicting potentialities, of either seeking and preserving a state of peace in God, of which man can experience an acute awareness as part of his existence at moments of grace and quiet surrender; or of upholding concepts of vain and dubious substance without contact with God, in the pursuit of which he yields to his anxieties and easily neglects his soul. While Ruediger is briefly conscious of his contrary directions and his predicament in consequence of man's duality, at least for one enlightened moment, Kriemhild fails to realize the tragic contrasts of her being as she slowly descends to be the tool of crude emotions and ambitions that prompt her vile designs, the victim of her dual nature.

Even to Kriemhild's great opponent, wanton and ruthless Hagen, a final state of harmony with God has been attributed. Bodo Mergell, as we have seen, declares him acting in regard to Ruediger in God's behalf, thus rising from the level of trachery and guilt to fulfillment *"im Angesicht Gottes,"* in a pronounced contrast to Kriemhild's path that ends in darkness and despair.[33] Although this interpretation of Hagen's kindness toward Ruediger goes too far when it suggests redemption in the eyes of God, the sudden rise of true humanity even in a man like him can serve as a further example of man's contrasting inclinations in terms of his direction, toward his spiritual potentialities or toward the appeals of his earthly existence, worsened by atavistic instincts. In Hagen's case, however, the latter influences clearly predominate, exemplified particularly by his unChristian, unforgiving, and provoking actions toward Kriemhild, for whose sufferings he showed not only complete dicsoncern, but true delight up to the last. Where man seems determined in his actions by one of his divers potentials, he does not necessarily accomplish the extremes. When Ruediger turns deaf to the appeal of God, he does not change into a devilish person; or when Hagen shows kindness instead of grim intent, he still does not attain the status of a pious man. Only the central figure of the song, Kriemhild, embraces the extremes most drastically, winning our affection as child of God, gaining our sympathy in her distress and conflict of emotions, arousing pity and

Kriemhild holding Gunther's head, from an 1805 edition of the Nibelungenlied.

compassion as she descends, distorted in her fall, bereft of any soul, as she appears.

One might add to the list of man's conflicting possibilities his potentials of love and hate as were described above, or of reason and emotion as they appear in conflict with each other. There are also contrasting wishes and beliefs, upheld with various strength at different times, and there are ideologies and values which now appear important, now of no consequence, now even fully contradictory. By whatever terms man's double and unsteady nature is characterized, the *Nibelungen* dramatically exemplify how man is harboring the opposites within his dual nature, how he is oscillating between his potentialities, how he is likely to succumb, to stumble, and even to destroy himself.

3

Though mostly unaware of their duality, the *Nibelungen* experience the paradox as a reality which they clearly perceive, accepting it as part of their existence, dumbfounded, yet without reflection or demur. When man in his contrasting drives has concentrated his intent upon a certain aim which he pursues, he frequently accomplishes the very opposite of what he planned. Kriemhild merely hastens Siegfried's death while she is anxious to protect him, giving away the secret of his vulnerable spot and even marking it for the betrayer whose help she anxiously solicits. Ruedi-

ger's oath to Kriemhild, rendered without suspicion of any future complications, obliges him eventually to partake in an ignoble deed that is in conflict with his conscience and utterly contrary to the spirit with which the oath was offered. His welcome guests and friends whom Ruediger accompanies as loyal guide to days of joy as he believes, he really leads into a trap to grief and death; he even is compelled to help in their destruction. While Giselher avoids an open clash with Ruediger, whose enemy he paradoxically has become, Gernot accepts the grim reality and slays the marcgrave without further hesitation, using the very sword that Ruediger had given him as a token of good will. The sword that Gernot lifts for honor's sake against the man who merely fights to save his honor; the sword that once belonged to Ruediger's own son; the gift of which the widow of the giver had heartily approved while he was still alive; and most dramatically, the gift that kills the giver—all these round up the paradoxes that mark the final moments of troubled Ruediger. Staying away from the hostilities that turned the planned festivities of Etzel into an ugly farce, he might have pondered his own eagerness with which he once persuaded Kriemhild to accept his master's hand; what he had hoped would bring new happiness to both, also enhancing Etzel's glory, has turned to grief and shame, disgracing the reputation of his noble king.

Also Hagen's endeavors to perpetuate the power and the honor of his masters beget the very opposite of what he intends, involving his king in great dishonesty that causes Gunther's death and the annihilation of his brothers and his loyal subjects. The treasure of Siegfried, too, brought to Worms upon Hagen's initiative, is of no advantage to the Burgundians but merely detrimental. When Kriemhild gains new friends by means of this gold, it is sunk into the Rhine where nobody benefits from it. This stealing of the treasure, however, arouses new resentment in Kriemhild and strengthens her hate and her desire for eventual revenge, whose victims all the *Nibelungen* eventually become. But Kriemhild, too, accomplishes merely the opposite of what she desperately wants; she neither stills her grief, nor does she restore her honor or prestige by her disgraceful plots, but she only increases her dishonor, her humiliation, and her frustration on earth which are at their highest when she finally kills Hagen who still can sneer at her. Unable even to enjoy the briefest momentary satisfaction, her grief and hate slightly relieved by her impetuous act of killing the cause of all her turmoil, she herself becomes the screaming victim of Hildebrand's violent blows with which he slays her instantly. The fact that Kriemhild is killed by one of her own subjects while her husband king stands idly by, presents perhaps another paradox, unless one is inclined to judge Hildebrand's spontaneous deed an act of mercy rather than of angry retribution, of which he himself, however, is scarcely aware.

While most of these reversals defy man's purpose from without, resulting from realities beyond the individual's perception or control, man also must experience the paradox within himself. Thus Kriemhild's final hate engulfs her favorite brother for whom she longs and whom she loves, making her pitiless to his requests for mercy and causing his death. Also Gunther betrays his sister against his emotional inclinations and brotherly affections when he allows the stealing of the gold; "'*si ist diu swester mîn*'" (1131, 3), he weakly argues before he agrees to Hagen's plan. Etzel, too, must have encountered a painful change of heart when he condoned the slaying of his wife whose wishes and desires he called his greatest joy only shortly ago. Hagen's faithfulness to Brunhild and to his masters' court makes him faithless to Kriemhild and to Siegfried regardless of his previous feelings toward them and in spite of the fact that the one is his master's sister, the other his master's best and most faithful friend. Gernot feels compelled to challenge Ruediger, seeing him slay so many of the *Nibelungen:* "'*daz müet mich âne mâze: ich'n kans niht an gesehen mêr*'" (2216, 4), killing his friend and former host as he is killed in turn by him.

The poem underscores the paradox which man encounters in his will and actions as it dramatically describes the vicissitudes that grace or cloud his daily life. These are the alternating happy chords accompanying his realities, as Volker's gentle melodies insert an element of beauty and of peace into the grimness of the hour; his weary comrades put their premonitions aside and go to sleep although danger is imminent. The luxury with which the visitors are housed, their beds covered with foreign silk and fur as rarely have been offered to kings before, is contradictory to both the melancholy mood that haunts the weary guests, and the hostess' devious designs to have them murdered in their sleep. Siegfried rides through the woods in his most carefree mood, the lustiest of the hunters, a radiant child of nature and a very prince of men, shortly before he is mortally pierced, the greatest quarry of the hunt. The peaceful place where he is slain, the forest with its mysteries, the spring that gives cool water, the grass, the tender flowers now stained by his warm blood, all these present a gripping contrast to the act of murder, a foul, ignoble deed pursued with ruthlessness. The imminence and power of the paradox, shaping the *Nibelungen's* realities and defying their intent, are thus persuasively intensified as feast and *hôchgezît* are carefully described as background to the struggles that ensue, and as man's hopes and pleasures are vividly narrated before disaster strikes.

Oblivious or aware of those threatening reversals that foil their will, the *Nibelungen* accept the resulting reality as part of their existence that cannot be disputed or averted. There are almost no accusations or complaints against a higher power, nor are there any elevating thoughts expressed, praising divine authority when man has been frustrated or dies forlorn. While to the modern reader the adversities encountered present inducement to religious speculations in regard to providence or justice, the *Nibelungen* fail to engage in such reflections of their realities. Dietrich and Ruediger alone appear spiritually disturbed as they briefly ponder their conflicting situations. They feel forsaken by God rather than victims of reality as they experience their dilemmas; they sadly realize their paradoxi-

cal position that they engage in doing what is against their moral conscience, fighting against their friends, upholding worldly concepts that are in contrast to the promptings of their Christian souls. Dietrich enters the fight against the last surviving *Nibelungen,* with whom he sympathizes, in conflict with his inclinations and his spiritual convictions, adhering to the manners that are expected from a warrior of his reputation, not unlike Ruediger who threw himself into the final battle against his very friends, both of them vaguely haunted by a sense of moral despair.

4

Endowed with the potentials of opposites, foiled in their efforts by the paradox, the *Nibelungen* fail to achieve a victory that is commensurate with their struggle and their will. Now in compliance with their moral values and traditions, vague and conflicting as they often are, now following expediency or simply driven by emotions, they rarely satisfy more than one momentary urge by their spontaneous decisions in their reactions to reality. Neglecting their spiritual potentialities, they also fail to reach a state of inner peace and harmony that could endure or carry them above adversities. Their aims and values are ambiguous, confused, and contradictory as they initiate aggressive actions or engage in violent hostilities; their course becomes erratic and their intent subject to frequent change as they experience the paradox which distorts their will. Eventually they die as victims of their earthly values and realities not less than of themselves, suffering total defeat.

Being without a reconciliatory turn, the story ends in sadness and in failure as its last major characters are slain. Thousands have lost their lives before, dying in consequence of various aspects of their ethics, their emotions, and their will. Fighters of great renown, Gunther and Hagen do not lose their lives in wild and lusty battle, but are infamously beheaded as prisoners; they are not victims merely of Kriemhild's hatred and frustration, but also of their own convictions, errors, and anxieties; beginning with the murder of Siegfried, for which they were unwilling to make amends or show regret, they pursue a course of action detrimental to themselves. Having initiated the inglorious death of Gunther, first by involving him in Siegfried's death, then by referring to the oath of silence as long as his last king was still alive, Hagen dies as an utter failure. When all his kings are dead and nothing is left for which he still might fight, he dies with unforgiving hatred of his greatest enemy, clinging in proud defiance to the spectre of heroic poise while unconvincingly evoking God:

> "Nu ist von Burgonden   der edel künec tôt,
> Gîselher der junge,   und ouch her Gêrnôt.
> den schaz den weiz nu niemen   wan got unde mîn:
> der sol dich, vâlandinne,   immer wol verholn sîn".
>
> (2371)

Kriemhild's *leid* unstilled and her revenge short of its goal unless atonement for the death of Siegfried was her chief aim and moral purpose, she herself is slain partly in consequence of honor which she has violated by her last, desperate deed, partly in revenge of Hagen, who was "'*der aller beste degen, / der ie kom ze sturme oder ie schilt getruoc*'" (2374, 2-3), as Etzel says of him. Bemoaning the fact that such a hero had to die from the hand of a woman, and regardless of the mockery, contempt and violence which he suffered from him, the king allows his own wife to be miserably slain by the impetuous old Hildebrand. As all the active members of the strife lie dead, the house of the Burgundians virtually destroyed, no victory gained by anyone, Dietrich and Etzel weep in mourning for the thousands who have died. Countless others far and near join in their tears as sadness spreads. Thus ends the song, the final chapter of the *Nibelungen,* without offering consoling thoughts, without affirming justice, mercy, grace, a gripping story of man's ways.

As joy has given way to sorrow and only tears remain, as all in which man gloried has found a gloomy end, the reader is aware of man's forlorn and tragic state. The *Nibelungen,* however, do not consider themselves partakers in a tragedy. Stunned by Siegfried's death as Kriemhild is, steeped in moral conflict or God-forsaken, as Ruediger and Dietrich briefly feel, the *Nibelungen* experience only a temporary consciousness of tragic circumstances that mark their lives; they neither reflect upon the nature or significance of these, nor do they share a tragic view of life as such. Thus in the absence of pronounced spiritual doubt, of moral qualms, or of a lingering sense of failure, they do not gain the stature of tragic characters, regardless of the greatness of their struggle and of their final fall.

. . . . .

> "Das Tragische ist nicht Transzendenz, nicht im Grunde des Seins, sondern in der Erscheinung der Zeit." KARL JASPERS

Does the *Nibelungen* epic suggest the hopelessness of man's existence and of his strife? Is it a eulogy glorifying man's greatness in defying his realities, his "fate," in living dangerously, with spirit and with courage? Does it present a nihilistic point of view, believing that man's joys and pleasures, his aims and his ideals are mere illusions without worth? The very silence of the poet as well as his creative effort, poetically recording the *Nibelungen's* "*Not,*" suggest a twofold answer to the significance of his elusive epic. In order to substantiate a final statement, consideration must be given to the poet in connection with his work, both as an artist and as a man.

1

A work of art as a bare minimum can be the medium of the artist by which he voices an experience, a bit of wisdom, or a truth he found. If he succeeds in expressing his intelligence in a neatly condensed and balanced form, his work will affect others according to the weight, the freshness and validity of his experiences as well as to the beauty it contains. Eventually the artist and his work are linked, a profile of the author is established, his message and intent are analyzed, interpreted, and classified. A work of art as

complex in its scope as the *Nibelungenlied,* however, ceases to be the mouthpiece of its maker, by which he voices individual emotions or experiences as such. No longer is his work the medium of the artist alone, but he himself has now become the subject of impelling forces that reveal unrealized experiences to him, perhaps a pre-existent knowledge of which he only now, and sometimes very fleeting, grows aware. Engrossed in shaping his material, the artist might encounter flashes of sudden insight, suggesting that his hand is guided by an outside intelligence which is greater than he; no longer is his work the total sum of various strands of thoughts, no longer a mere blend of individual emotions. Instead of a personal statement rendered with clarity of purpose and individual force, his work in its complexity reveals an absolute above the artist's insight, perhaps even beyond his comprehension, as a truth emerges independently from his original conception and intent; the artist as the medium of forces greater than himself stands now in the shadow of his own work to which he was inspired. To his audience the poet might become a myth, a legend, or he might be forgotten behind his work, as happened to the writer of the *Nibelungenlied.* Nevertheless, a valid appraisal of a special work of art must probe the mind of its creator to gain as full a comprehension of its totality as possible. Evaluating certain aspects which the poet stresses or elaborates upon, appraising direct statements or omissions, we might detect his purpose, his true intent, perhaps even a message he wanted to convey. What can we glean about the unknown artist as is reflected in his work, particularly in relation to his subject and to his own concern in reference to it?

The poet's work embraces a complex entity of human strife and passions, of sorrow and of joy, of paradoxes and extremes, an ever changing spectrum of man's varied existence as valid and as actual today as at the author's time. The poet is a shrewd *observer* of man in his conflicting drives as he presents each individual in his special attempt of life, each life unique as one of countless possibilities. He knows how strength and weakness can be found within one character as in Gunther, morally weak and full of pretense, yet fighting with unflinching courage at the side of his men; or as in Giselher, basically strong and true, yet shrinking from preventing obvious wrongs where moral courage might have helped. The poet knows how man will go to church now with devotion and humility, now with anger and hatred in his heart. He has observed how worship often means adherence mainly to customary form rather than faith and piety, or seeking comfort for a heart that only hears the promptings of its anguish mainly and yields to them with doubled force as soon as mass is over, while God is left behind. The poet is acquainted with the good and happy life of married men and women, devoted to each other and also to their children, as Siegmund and Sieglind, or Ruediger and Gotelind. He knows the feelings of a father toward his son, the premonitions of king Siegmund while Siegfried is slain, the thoughts of dying Siegfried going to his son, the pride of Etzel in regard to Ortlieb, his and Krimehild's child. More than this, however, the poet understands the joys and arrogance of man, his pride and his anxieties, the conflicts of his dual nature; of all he gives a vivid picture that shows him as a man of penetrating observation and sensitivity. As master of characterization he lends reality and freshness to those of his descriptions that deal with universal traits of man rather than with everyday events like feasts, receptions, tournament or battle, which he describes more generally.

The poet's strength of *empathy* is great, revealing his affinity with all that is human and his own dualistic potentialities that make him truly understand the feelings of his heroes. Except where treachery is involved, from which he recoils, the poet rarely sets himself apart from those whose story he relates. Thus he rides high with them in feasts and tournaments, he cheers them on in contests, he takes part in their lusty fighting as in the Saxon War; likewise he shares their weariness, their agonies, the tears of Kriemhild or the grief of Etzel, whose voice sounds like a wounded lion's when the blood-spattered body of Ruediger is shown to him. At times the poet seems enthralled by the dramatic scenes, which he himself designs, although as artist and a man of faith, as we shall see, his inclination is not merely to satisfy some latent want for spectacles of human passion, for the display of naked instincts, or for blood and violence, but to depict the various aspects of man's life. Emotionally, however, not disengaged nor morally aloof, he presents pitiless reality with such impassioned glow that it attracts, and thrills, and also frightens by its daring imagery: the spear protruding from the back of Siegfried who leaps up from the fountain to seize his shield, his only weapon left, to smash it over his assailant that its jewels scatter from their burst settings; the dangling javelin in Ihring's head that must be broken off before the helmet can be taken from the dying man; the tired warriors, trapped within the burning hall, drinking the blood of their own dead to quench the thirst and to renew their strength; Gunther hanging from a peg during his wedding night, his monstrous bride enjoying the comforts of their bed; perhaps even the wails of Werbel, possibly tragic-comic: *"'wie klenke ich nu die dœne . . .'"* (1964, 4), after Hagen has neatly severed his right hand, brutally unconcerned whether the minstrel ever plucks the strings again.

The artist's own potentials, controlled as they might be, are of such range that he experiences his heroes in their drives and their spontaneous reactions from within themselves, as one might say; he deeply understands these men of whom he actually had only read or learned from various sources and whose mentality, rooted in prehistoric past, is not identical with his. As the ambiguous expression of the heroes, referring to *"die veigen,"* does not express a categorical belief in fate, as we have seen, also the poet uses a similar pattern of speech in his concluding lines, likewise without convincing force: *"Dô was gelegen aller dâ der veigen lîp"* (2377, 1). Such a statement could suggest a fatalistic view that fate has moved its victims like puppets to their final destination, a predetermined death, if he restricts this phrase to its original, limited sense which it no longer carried at his time. Not far before

this final passage our narrator conveys poetically the dying of scores of knights by conjuring up the image of death looking for his men: *"der tôt der suochte sêre dâ sîn gesinde was"* (2224, 3), while Giselher complains: *"'Der tôt uns sêre roubet'"* (2226, 1), both statements referring to Ruediger's death and to the furious struggle that followed it. It is doubtful that this figure of death as a person is more than a mere metaphor, like death stalking as reaper or as skeleton with scythe, poetical expressions to symbolize his grandeur and his force. The artist's final phrase, *"der veigen lîp,"* appears to be of similar poetic quality, deliberately chosen for its archaic overtones appropriate to the heroic past of which his story told. While its restricted meaning does not seem compelling to the poet, it faintly echoes Giselher's premonitions when everything looked hopeless, and Hagen's final statement, still ringing in the writer's ear: *"'und ist ouch rehte ergangen als ich mir hête gedâht'"* (2370, 4), vaguely implying the idea, perhaps, that fate rather than realistic causes might be the reason for the dire end of the Burgundians. The possibility, however, cannot be denied that the poet, too, may momentarily yield to hidden half-beliefs and to some latent urge to tie man's lot to forces that arrange his destiny as his heroes have done under stress and at certain occasions. As reality and fiction readily fuse in a work of art, its author may well toy in his creative make-believe with the alluring thoughts that dreams really foretell the future, that fate or fortune teller's wisdom are actual facts and forces in man's life, without, however, stating definitely his rational convictions or his true and deepest faith.

The poet obviously does not share a fatalistic, but a *tragic view of life* which drew him to the story of man's distress, the topic of the *Nibelungenlied,* ending in man's untimely death. This tragic knowledge means awareness of man's precarious state, of his afflictions and resulting failures, initiating his own sorrows in spite of the potentials of greatness, happiness, and innocence. The poet recognizes the temptations of worldly treasures, large as Siegfried's gold, or small as an armlet, which can bring man to fall, exemplified by the unlucky ferryman; he is acquainted with the transitoriness of power and prestige to which man is subjected; he also is aware that man is likely to destroy himself not less than his fellowmen in the pursuit of honor at any cost; he states that joy will end in sorrow. The ancient sources for his epic story reflected the Germanic concepts of strife, misfortune, death as fate and as man's true realities which he must meet with courage and defiance to triumph over them. The poet of the *Nibelungenlied,* however, no longer draws his heroes as objects of blind fate or guided by a narrow, traditional behavior code of prehistoric days, but as victims of their anxieties, their inner conflicts, and their own choices and decisions. Failing to gain what they pursue, destroying whom they want to save or whom they love, they act against themselves as they are torn by their conflicting inclinations. The failures of the *Nibelungen,* resulting from their conflicts, echo the poet's tragic view of life as he considers them common to man, aspects that rob him of a state of peace in spite of his potentials of greatness and of happiness. He leaves no doubt that his story is not a happy one as he states early that the quarrel of two women will cause a miserable end to many a proud knight, worthy of fame and honor: *"vil stolziu ritterscaft / mit lobelîchen êren . . . / si sturben sît jæmerliche von zweier edelen frouwen nît"* (6, 2-4); likewise he summarizes after the hostile outbursts of the arguing queens: *"von zweier vrouwen bâgen wart vil manic helt verlorn"* (876, 4). These summary statements tend to suggest that such quarrel is not merely a singular historical event of which the poet tells, but rather in the nature of man himself: pride, quarrels, envy, jealousy, not more than *nît* and *bâge* suffice to unleash human conflicts of such proportions that they will cause the death of all involved. Strengthened by further references to the ensuing grief in consequence of human actions, these introductory remarks clearly indicate the poet's melancholy outlook upon the ways of men, his tragic view of life.

Although some heroes of the song epitomize the concept of heroic death as glory and fulfillment, the poet does not dwell upon the triumph which they voice; instead, we are reminded of the tragic aspects of their death and of the sorrow of their surviving friends and king. The poet does not share in Wolfhart's boast that he has sold his life one-hundredfold and dies a glorious death, slain by a king; he draws our thoughts to Hildebrand who never suffered greater grief in all his life than by his nephew's death:

> *Hildebrant der alte*   *Wolfharten vallen sach;*
> *im wæne vor sînem tôde*   *sô rehte leide nie ge-*
> *schach;*
>
> (2298, 3-4)

the aged Hildebrand embraces Wolfhart's bleeding body and pathetically tries to carry him out of the hall, but finds his weight too heavy and has to leave him behind. Dietrich likewise bemoans the death of this young and noble warrior with desperate emphasis: *"'Owê, lieber Wolfhart, sol ich dich hân verlorn, / sô mac mich balde riuwen daz ich ie wart geborn'"* (2322, 1-2)! It is the sadness which the poet stresses rather than the glory which his heroes claim. At the death of Ihring, *weinen, klagen, nôt* and *leit genuoc* abound when the dying hero warns his countrymen not to be lured by Kriemhild's gold and not to repeat his vain, useless attack on Hagen, who would slay them, too. Also Hagen's final show of courage and defiance of Dietrich and of Kriemhild in the face of death elicits no comment of awe or admiration from the poet. While Etzel praises Hagen for his quality as a fighter, Hildebrand's impetuous action of leaping at the queen, who screams in deadly panic as she is struck, presents such a tragic and dramatic climax that no exaltation can arise. Indeed, after the death of all who perished in this fight—the severed head of Gunther, likewise the head and corpse of Hagen as well as Kriemhild's mutilated body liyng where they fell before the stunned survivors—, sadness and tears prevail as Dietrich and Etzel freely weep and loudly bewail the death of *"mâge unde man"* (2377, 4). Thus with the poet's full intent the story ends as tragedy, in *"jâmer unde nôt"* (2378, 2), in woe and misery.

The frequent references of the writer to the grief and sorrow of his people denote his *sympathy* with them. In contrast to his epic objectivity which he preserves in his descriptions of their strifes and actions, he writes with warm compassion when their hearts are involved, in friendship or in love, in sadness or in suffering. This human sympathy, coupled with tolerance, is particularly apparent in the character of Dietrich von Berne, a figure of the poet's choice and individual characterization, not necessarily an integrated part of the literary sources for the *Nibelungen* which he used; like Ruediger, also Dietrich is introduced into this tale as the artist's own creation in connection with the *Nibelungen's* final stand. Dietrich is delineated as a man of heart and reason, of moral courage equal to his fighting strength, a man of impartiality, of kindness toward friend and foe. Subject to the deepest grief himself, stating in utter desolation: *"'owê daz vor leide niemen sterben nemac'"* (2323, 4), when he mourns the death of his own men, he still can feel compassion for the two survivors in the other camp who were responsible for the slaying of Dietrich's men. Thus he addresses Gunther:

> *"Gedenket an iuch selben*   *unde an iuwer leit,*
> *tôt der iuwern vriunde*   *und ouch diu arbeit,*
> *ob ez iu guoten recken*   *beswæret iht den muot."*
>
> (2331, 1-3)

He speaks of the afflictions suffered by both of them; was not the sacrifice of Ruediger, their common friend, enough? There was no enmity existing that justified a fight. How could Gunther and Hagen have failed to consider the tragic consequences of their wanton fight against his men:

> *"'Ez geschach ze dirre werlde*   *nie leider manne*
> *mêr.*
> *ir gedâhtet übele*   *an mîn und iuwer sêr'"*.
>
> (2332, 1-2)

Offering a peaceful settlement, as we have seen, and merely asking for atonement which he feels is fair, Dietrich addresses them, the slayers of his men, not as an enemy, but as a friend, aware of their distress not less than of his own. Rejected by Hagen, he continues to plead without any vindictiveness, pledging his honor and his life to lead them safely home. When also this last offer is refused, he accepts the challenge of a fight with them in which he overpowers both, battling with each of them in turn. Although Hagen, wounded by Dietrich's blows, is still a dangerous opponent, armed with Siegfried's famous sword, Dietrich nevertheless drops his protecting shield to capture his opponent with bare arms and thus to spare his life, and does the same with Gunther after Hagen has become his prisoner. Dietrich's thoughts and sentiments: *"'ich hâns lützel êre, soltu tôt vor mir geligen'"* (2351, 2), do not reflect honor from the heroic point of view as in regard to the ensuing glory of a victorious fight, nor from the viewpoint which the world might take; it is the Christian concept of kindness and compassion toward one's fellow-man, honoring the dignity in others, even in an enemy, by which Dietrich is guided. When he gives up his shield to make Hagen his prisoner instead of killing him, he does so *"mit sorgen"* (2351, 4), as he is still in danger of Hagen's formidable strength and wary of Siegfried's sword. When Hagen and Gunther are overcome, Dietrich has to bind them as otherwise they still could bring death to anyone they encounter, as the poet explains. Delivering his prisoners to the triumphant queen, Dietrich pleads in their behalf for mercy and sheds tears of compassion for these heroes whom he did not care to overpower and to humiliate by binding them, whose lifes he spared, and whom he rather would have taken home to Worms than deliver them to Kriemhild. Even though it might be granted that the poet felt compelled to follow his existing sources according to which Hagen had to die from the revenging hand of Kriemhild, whose victim also Gunther had to be, Dietrich's pronounced expressions of genuine compassion and regret clearly echo the poet's sentiments and are deliberately introduced. Regardless of the motives for their fighting-will or of their previous falsehood, the poet sympathizes with his heroes in their tragic state, even with Hagen and with Gunther, the last survivors of the battle that saw the death of all their friends and kin, upholding their conviction of heroic honor to the last.

A ware of human tragedy, a man of sympathy und understanding, the poet is *forgiving* rather than accusing; as he rarely condemns an action of which he disapproves, he also neither incriminates his fellowmen, nor passes any final judgment on anyone of them. He recognizes human greatness and praises courage, kindness, and loyalty in man. Epithets like bold, keen, good, kind, generous, high-spirited, or faithful greatly outnumber negatives like evil, faithless, false, or murderous in the characterizations of individual actions of his heroes. Only where he speaks of falsehood and of treachery, he momentarily breaks his reserve and voices condemnation of such acts. Although he might have favorites among his characters like Siegfried, Giselher, or Ruediger, who seem to be the victims of special circumstances that lead them to decisions of tragic consequences, he does not state a preference for them, nor a dislike of others. He even refrains from judging Hagen, the ruthless plotter and assassin, and from condemning Kriemhild, the *vâlandinne*, as which she is pictured in the end. The poet knows that man can be the subject of God and of the devil as he can listen to the voice of each, being exposed to both. Thus he underlines the good and noble features particularly in the characters of those in whom the evil inclinations seem to predominate. Gunther's and Hagen's falsehood is pronounced, yet the poet dwells upon their loyalty and praises their indomitable spirit; the picture of Kriemhild which he draws, first in her gentility and state of grace, then in her role as primitive revenger, is just and balanced, apt to stress the tragedy of her dilemma and to arous our pity with her fall rather than our final condemnation. To the dismay of theorists and moralists, the poet does not think in terms of guilt and innocence, or black and white, although he mentions causes and effects, now merely hinted at, now identified, determining man's morality.

To understand, however, the poet's personal, *moral concern* in spite of his reluctance of passing judgment on his fellowman, we must again consider Dietrich who speaks most eloquently for the author himself. Aware of Kriemhild's treacherous intent, aroused by her display of anger and aggressive hate when she discovers that her guests are warned, Dietrich calls her a "'vâlandinne'" (1748, 4), a reprimand and challenge made by a man whose moral courage and integrity cannot be weakened even by a queen with all her worldly power; the poet adds in Kriemhild's favor that she left the scene very much ashamed, her conscience stirred, her hate, however, unabated. The last defiant curse of Hagen, "'vâlandinne'" (2371, 4), with which he triumphs over Kriemhild, possibly taken by the author from his immediate sources, is here anticipated and put into the mouth of Dietrich with great significance, as we believe. Helmut de Boor considers the early introduction of this term, coming from the lips of Dietrich, a blunder of our poet and a weakening of its weight.[34] For sheer drama and effect, Hagen's curse is more impressive in the final scene, spiked with hate and passion, than Dietrich's earlier reprimand. Yet coming from the murderer of Siegfried, the violator and betrayer of her trust and rights, a man who was most instrumental in making Kriemhild what he calls her now, Hagen's violent remark, meant to insult the queen once more, has no moral significance. Dietrich's use of this term, however, reveals his and the poet's great concern about Kriemhild's dishonest attitude which both of them condemn. What Kriemhild has initiated and what she now pursues up to the bitter end, is here deliberately characterized as evil, devilish, and morally unworthy. Dietrich repeats his disapproval of Kriemhild's course when he rejects her pleas for help, stating that it honors her little to betray her kin: "'*diu bete dich lützel êret, vil edeles fürsten wîp*'" (1902, 1); also here Dietrich considers honor more in a Christian, moral sense than as a concept of glory and prestige, particularly as he points out to her that her friends and relatives have come in good faith, "'*ûf genâde*'" (1902, 3), trusting in her kindness and honesty. This moral reprimand of Kriemhild's schemes, however, does not imply pronouncement of a final judgment by the poet or by Dietrich, nor does it constitute an outright condemnation of the queen with any finality; it is mainly directed at her faithless plans which she pursues, as it also denotes her evil potentialities to which she yields. We must remember that Dietrich later protects the queen, the faithless instigator of Bloedelin's attack, when he leads her safely from the banquet hall to where the fight had spread, although peaceful retreat was granted only to his and Ruediger's men. When Hagen and Gunther are overcome by Dietrich, who was compelled to fight them, he faithfully delivers them to Kriemhild, appealing to her better nature in which he trusts and still believes; and most significantly, his tears after the death of all are also shed over her mutilated body as she lies before him on the ground as the final victim of the tragedy.

Also Hagen's faithlessness is similarly reprimanded not only by the poet's direct condemnation of the murderer's *"grôze mussewende"* (981, 4) or by Giselher's reference to the latter's deceitfulness, but also by Dietrich. When Hagen flippantly refers to the dead and buried Siegfried who will never come back, the venerable king rebukes him tersely: "*'Die Sîfrides wunden lâzen wir nu stên'*" (1726, 1), demanding to leave Siegfried's death undiscussed; Dietrich does not merely voice his acquiescence in a regrettable act of many years ago, but he expresses his moral indignation at Hagen's remark, if not at his murder. Here as well as later in his various talks with Kriemhild or with the leading *Nibelungen* Dietrich clearly shows his disapproval while he avoids vindictiveness; in the spirit of the poet, he points his finger at a moral wrong and professes where he stands, but he refrains from condemning the other person, leaving the question of guilt undiscussed and undisputed.

The poet's moral concern can also be deduced from his frequent praises. Father of all virtues is the final tribute given to Ruediger whose kindliness and generous hospitality he describes with special emphasis, as he has Eckewart say of Ruediger: "*'sîn herze tugende birt'*" (1639, 2), considering the marcgrave's heart and soul the source and basis of his moral virtues. The poet also praises Gunther's generosity as a redeeming feature of his character where it occurs. On greed, however, or on the lust for worldly riches our author frowns, realizing the evil consequences; "*diu gir nâch grôzem guote vil bœsez ende gît*" (1554, 2), he states. Paying tribute to the *hohe muot* of his heroes of the past, the poet lauds their courage that seems to him greater than it prevails at his own time. Friedrich Panzer suggests that the heroic age appealed more strongly to the poet than his own, basing his proposition upon the praise given to Etzel who wants to throw himself into the fight, as kings at the poet's time seldom do:

> *Der künec der was sô küene,* *er wold' erwinden niht,*
> *daz von sô rîchem fürsten* *selten nu geschiht.*
> *man muose in bî dem vezzel* *ziehen wider dan.*[35]
>
> (2022, 1-3)

Panzer also sees a possible preference for the past implied in the author's following comment: "*si vâhten alsô grimme daz man ez nimmer mêr getuot*" (2212, 4), which, however, seems counteracted by a reference in favor of the present: "*sô grôze missewende ein helt nu nimmer mêr begât*" (981, 4). It is rather dubious and little born out by the poet's general attitude that he should have shown partiality to the past of which he reports. There is the possibility of deliberate criticism of those who are in power at the writer's age and actively responsible for war, but stay away from battle in contrast to former times; the poet also might merely intend to stress the incomparable fury of the battle in which his noblest hero falls, Ruediger, a warrior par excellence, "*vil küene unt ouch vil lobelîch*" (2213, 4), a man without any equal. The author's statements, however, clearly confirm his recognition of the moral fibre that is inherent in any strong and gallant fighter. A distinction between moral courage, as is particularly apparent in Dietrich von Berne, and physical courage, as evident in all the heroes, is not specifically made; their defiant attitude at the threat of death, however, upholding the ideal of fearlessness, has ingredients similar to those in moral courage. Where noble spirit changes to haughtiness and where the *hohe muot* grows into *übermüete,* the poet is concerned. Thus he modifies the splendid picture of the court of Worms by early references to the arrogance prevailing there, which is likely to cause trouble. It is this reckless spirit that characterizes the actions of the heroes at Isenstein and later at their arrival at Etzel's court when none of them informs the king of Kriemhild's treacherous designs that mean a threat to all of them.

As far as pride and honor are concerned, the glory of his heroes, the poet seems rather *skeptical.* He understands the proud emotions of his men as he describes the values which they cherish, but he abstains from special praise as he does not attach moral significance to them. As he does not linger on the glories of their victories when their courageous fighting has come to an end, but draws our attention to the victims who paid the price, he likewise does not glory in their aims which they proudly pursue. With barely a comment or praise he relates Sigfried's bold intent to win Kriemhild, relying on his strength alone, and Gunther's decision to challenge Brunhild's superhuman strength, as well as the joyful departure of the *Nibelungen* on their risky journey to the court of Etzel, defying all the warnings given. As he knows the pitfalls of pride, leading now to envy, now to arrogance, he also recognizes the transitoriness of glory and of honor whose worldly glamour he objectively describes without extolling it. When he commends the honor of the court of Worms where Kriemhild grows up with modesty and poise, protected by her brothers and secure in a realm served by noble knights, he considers moral qualities like generosity and kindness, manly courage, and brotherly affection parts of the renown that constitute this honor and repute. Yet significantly he ends even this description of "*lobelîchen êren*" (6, 3) of the men at Worms with the somber reminder that all die miserably in the end. He recognizes honor as Ihring's sole motive for his daring attack on Hagen, as he likewise characterizes Ruediger and Gernot in their final, tragic encounter as "*die êre gernde man*" (2218, 3), men who live for honor, men who die for honor, friends who even slay each other in the name of honor. When finally all joys of life, all pride and courage of the *Nibelungen* are dissipated in merciless and suicidal fighting, the poet soberly concludes:

> "*diu vil michel êre* *was dâ gelegen tôt;*
> *diu liute heten alle* *jâmer unde nôt*".
>
> (2378, 1-2)

Of all the honor and magnificence that once prevailed nothing is left; "*hie hât daz mære ein ende: daz ist der Nibelunge nôt*" (2379, 4). Thus the poet ends in a skeptical and rather melancholy mood; he does not truly condemn the aspects of worldly honor which his heroes cherish nor does he suggest that the honor for which they are willing to die is of immortal quality, or that honor for the sake of

honor has any moral value as such. He sees the transitoriness of it, its dangers and temptations, and he is conscious
of its worldly limitations.

2

"In der ursprünglichen tragischen Anschauung, wenn
sie rein bewahrt wird, liegt schon, was eigentlich Philosophie ist: Bewegung, Frage, Offenheit,—Ergriffen-
heit, Staunen,—Wahrhaftigkeit, Illusionslosigkeit." KARL
JASPERS

In recognition of the author's sober attitude and of his
moral and compassionate concern, we have to stay with
him, the unknown and inspired poet, in our attempt to find
an answer to the significance of his great work in which
no definite idea seems developed, no thought deliberately
pursued, no final message given. Telling a story without a
moral, embracing history and legends, yet not concerned
with history as such, the poet delineates aspects of man
that show his greatness and his failures, his vulnerability
and weakness as we have seen. As he specifically relates
man's *"Nôt,"* man's sufferings and dilemma against the
background of his honors and his joys, the end of all is
grief and tears. With sympathetic objectivity the poet has
presented to the reader from his chariot of epic art this
special segment of human strife and failure, without attempting to predispose the thinking of his guest. The journey finished now, the chariot driver silent, the reader's
heart is stirred as he is left alone, while no judgment has
been pronounced, no victory claimed, no worldly or divine
order invoked. The weeping and the mourning that filled
the final scene precluded any statement by the poet to his
guest; a thoughtful melancholy mood persists while no
true catharsis has been obtained. What is the reason for the
poet's leaving without an answer, without concluding message, without apotheosis?

Not a philosopher, developing a system of reason and conjecture, the poet is a man of contemplative disposition
who shares with us his knowledge of human tragedy. He
does not want to preach or to reform, to moralize or merely
entertain. His work is not an allegory or an example for
some theories he holds; no religious dogma is advanced
pronouncing truth κατ εξοχήν. As form of art and symbol, however, his work is truth as such and a reflection of
an absolute, yet only of significance if grasped and re-
experienced by human minds, if weighted in probing contemplation. This then is the significance of this great work
and of the poet's silence in regard to his intent: *inviting
man to contemplation, specifically to contemplation of
himself.*

Leaving the thoughtful reader in a suspended state of mind,
the poet has not placed him at the brink of grim despair,
nor landed him on fields of comfort and of harmonies unmitigated, but he has left him on a rock of sorrow, a place
of sad awareness where he can shed consoling tears, reflect the lot of man, and contemplate his ways. It is the
very nature of such tragic knowledge, as the poet's, not to
seek dogmatic, dialectic confirmation of its existential

necessity, but rather to arouse man's thoughts to questions
which possibly defy his reason and a finite answer, to
arouse astonishment and awe, a sense of inwardness; leading man closer to the basis of himself, such contemplation
might provide redemption and relief to him in his dilemma
as it opens the way to faith. As reflection does not aim at
reason or at explanations, it seeks a comprehension of
man's totality, of his realities and of his potentialities, not
to pronounce a truth, but to experience truth.

Having witnessed the struggle of the *Nibelungen,* the
reader is beset by riddles, by uncertainties and by the adversities as they are part of man's existence. Beginning
with the most immediate, the reader might reflect: Is man
doomed to a tragic state of life, to self-destruction, to violent, untimely death of which our story tells? Are courage
and defiance man's only means to keep his self-respect
and to maintain his dignity on earth? Are power, riches,
worldly honor man's truest comforts and rewards? What
are the aspects of this honor, eagerly sought and self-
proclaimed, defended with his life sometimes slyly obtained? Are joys that end in sorrow his greatest and his
only joys? Is man's collective thinking in terms of earthly
values, as our heroes share, a sufficient substitute for lone-
liness, for individual faith? The *Nibelungen* die for honor,
in loyalty to others, and they prefer the risks of action and
adventure to a sheltered and passive life as Rumolt advocates. Does such a disposition reveal idealistic concepts
and possibilities of human greatness, or is it merely linked
to honor and prestige, to worldly vanities of little moral
significance? What constitutes their victories or their defeat, what their successes and their failures? Does Hagen
or Kriemhild come close to victory over the other? Does
none of them? Do both? Is Kriemhild ever driven by inevitable necessity, is any of the heroes at any time without
a choice, a helpless pawn on a predetermined course?
Must one assume, deny, or prove a higher will at work,
can one confirm divine intelligence taking an active part?

Does Kriemhild really open up her heart when she addresses God in prayer, asking for His advice? Is Ruediger's decision the only one that he can make? Is it beyond
his reach to take the leap to God, as Kierkegaard later advocated, a step which in the marcgrave's age the hermit
Trevrizent has taken? The *Nibelungen* share many aspects
ot the Christian culture of the Staufian knights; Giselher
and Gernot, young Kriemhild, the families at Xanten and
at Bechelaren, Dietrich, and even Etzel show very strongly
the ennobling influences of their faith. Yet none of those
who die lift up their eyes to heaven as none affirms infinity; while each proves man's tenacity to uphold human
ideologies, none dies as witness of his faith, but all as victims of their limited and self-proclaimed ideals.

Does our author present realities of man beyond the segment of his story? Is there a basic difference between the
Nibelungen and modern man? Are human conflicts in better balance now as man reflects more thoroughly upon the
aspects of his life? Or does collective thinking in questionable terms of human values, of ideologies, or of expedi-

ency provide the standard answers for a bewildered individual, establishing the code for his behavior? Does faith prevail? When one looks at the failures of modern man in recent times, considering his sense of guilt, of shame, or of forlornness, the violent story of the *Nibelungen,* unwilling or inept to contemplate upon themselves, presents perhaps a tame comparison to modern violence and ills. Yet to the stunned contemporary, partaker in events beyond the scope of individual comprehension, the **Nibelungenlied** attains special significance. As it describes man in his glory and defeat, in kindness and brutality, in suicidal struggle, its actuality appears unparalleled. The contemplative attitude which it demands, the valid questions which it poses, timeless in terms of man, can lead the modern reader to experiences of truth that give him greater understanding of himself, of the conflicting values of his age, and of the state of man on earth.

3

Will the reader formulate a final judgement where the poet stays reserved as he maintains an attitude of sympathetic understanding? Can guilt be ascertained for any of the *Nibelungen* beyond a moral doubt? The overt acts of murder, certainly, as the assassination of Siegfried, of Ortlieb, of the unnamed Hun who rode in the tournament, and finally Gunther's beheading upon commands of Kriemhild, deliberate, base, and hateful slayings, will be condoned by none and morally condemned by all. Beyond these individual transgressions of moral laws, however, that stain the murderer's character and involve collectively a host of others, the contemplative reader will be reluctant to pronounce a final verdict of guilt upon his fellowman who did what he considered right according to his moral code. As the poet mourns the death of all, as he reflects the grief of the survivors, the sorrows to which the joys of man have changed, and finally the end of all the honor and magnificence which they had shared, there is no exultation, no claim that justice has been wrought according to a higher will, no assertion of faith. Will the reader, on the contrary, leave the scene with the conviction that all is well with man, that right has won a victory and justice is pronounced while punishment is meted out? While Walther Joh. Schroeder presumes that for the poet of the song a transcendental plane, a possible existence beyond his earthly one, had no validity,[36] Hugo Kuhn suggests that Kriemhild's death, more than mere penalty for the slaying of Hagen, took place *"im Dienste eines höheren Rechtes oder vielleicht Gottes,"* accepting divine authority as a likely possibility.[37]

Shall we then consider the **Nibelungenlied** a nihilistic statement of man's spiritual and existential forlornness within his earthly limitations as his only reality, or can we declare it a manifest of transcendental faith in spite of the poet's reluctance to verbalize his faith? When Sophocles revealed to man his tragic state, he stressed his helplessness against the whims of various Gods as well as the greatness of suffering humanity; the poet of the *Nibelungen,* however, does not invoke the will of God as he describes man's misery in spite of his potentials. When kind-

ness, happiness, good will are swept aside by violence and disaster, as friends turn foes, and when eventually the *Nibelungen* destroy themselves, no God or supernatural forces seem involved. The tragical events develop logically and psychologically convincing, subject to causes and effects, provoked by man himself; no God is named as shaper of events or final judge, revealing His force or will. Nevertheless, the writer of the *Nibelungen* is a man of *faith* as is *reflected in his work.*

Of immaterial substance and not for material satisfaction, art is not bound by earthly limitations or explainable by reason. As it affirms intangible realities, it is of transcendental nature. As such it symbolizes faith as well as truth as pure as man can grasp. Reflecting man spiritually, *sub specie aeternitatis,* in every aspect of his being and in his widest potentialities, it addresses itself to the soul of man, his only medium to experience the existence of infinity. While the nihilist, blocked by mental doubts and reason, merely derives some intellectual diversion or entertainment from a work of art, the faithful attains a mystic union with the powers of infinitude which art reflects and which imparted inspiration to the artist as it infused his consciousness with unsubstantial and spiritual realities, the core of any faith. Art can be degraded by the esthetic pleasure seeker and become a shallow form as faith can be reviled by dialectic tricksters, for both are paradoxical, art to physical nature and faith to material reality. While the contented man will not reflect upon his life nor feel inclined to look beyond his happy spot, despair and dread will nourish faith and art. A probing of man's ways and potentialities, a yearning for redemption from his troubled state within material limits, as well as genuine compassion will lead man to experience spiritual realms of which he is a living part. Yet only by compassion and surrender, leaving reason behind, by awe and contemplation to which the poet of the **Nibelungenlied** is beckoning his readers, will man experience art and faith as symbols of infinity, his true realities.

The poet's sympathy with man, sharing the joys and woes of others who were fictitious or historical, but not related to himself, raised him above his own existence. Concerned with man's spiritual values, his failures and his strifes, and expressing his awareness of human tragedy and greatness through the symbolic form of art, he revealed his basic faith. Yet unlike his two great contemporaries, Wolfram von Eschenbach and Hartmann von Aue, the poet of the **Nibelungenlied** did not suggest solutions of man's duality by religious precepts, *"wie man zer werlde solde leben",* trying to serve harmoniously the world of God and man. As his main character is not a pondering individual like Parzival, *"'. . . ein man der sünde hat'",* or like Gregorius or Erec, but man collectively reflected by the *Nibelungen,* he does not partake in the religious discussion of his time that centered around the individual and speculated about the nature of his sins, showing the possibilities of penance, mercy, and atonement. In fact, compared to *Iwein* and to *Parzival,* the **Nibelungenlied** resembles an "erratic boulder," as Hugo Kuhn has phrased it.[38] This metaphor, however, might not only be applicable in reference to the unbridled, surging strength which is apparent in the song and makes it look uncouth next to the highly polished, phantastic, and romantic epics of knightly elegance that blossomed at this time; the "erratic boulder" might be man himself as pictured in our work, unique in his discord and adversities, disproportioned in a harmonious universe, inept, misguided, or unwilling to contemplate his attitudes, reluctant to embrace and live his faith. The poet clearly indicates that man is able to communicate with God, that he will pray to Him particularly in distress, and that he can experience His voice within himself; he also confirms that men can be guided by spiritual forces greater than the earthly values which he proclaims. Thus Ruediger gives his shield away, while Hagen and Volker place sympathy and friendship above political and vassal obligations; Giselher avoids a clash with Ruediger in spite of his initial threats; Dietrich, deprived of his mysterious luck, places the principles of mercy and forgiveness above the concept of total revenge, sparing his weary, still defiant, dangerous opponents; also Etzel seems guided by spiritual commands, swallowing his pride when insults are hurled into his face and overlooking Volker's killing in order to preserve the peace and to protect his guests; eventually, Etzel even weeps over the body of his hateful foe, the slayer of his child, honoring what was great in his opponent. Although the poem stresses the weakness of man's faith, it neither indicates a complete absence of faith or a disbelief in it, nor does it prove futility of faith except where it is merely superstitious belief. The validity of trust in magic forces like special strength or luck, a magic sword or treasure, is ostensively disproved as all these powers lose their alleged advantages, deserting their prophets and their owners or being essential causes for their fall.

4

The *Nibelungenlied* does not constitute a galmorous account of a heroic life which man should emulate. It does not extol the values of glory and of honor, of strength and of defiance, although it recognizes basic and potential greatness that causes man to turn to them. It does not make a nihilistic statement that man is doomed, a pawn of fate, living a hopeless life; it gains significance, however, by the tragic undertone accompanying the story of man's glamour and man's strife, of his frustrations and his failures. Stressing man's *"Not,"* the song invites the reader to contemplate, to re-appraise man's values, to probe into himself. As work of art, projecting man into infinity, it symbolizes faith, admitting man's potential of spirituality, yet leaving God, His power and His will subject to individual experience, to individual search. A grandiose statement of man's limitless potentials for better and for worse, for heaven, earth, and hell, the poet's work significantly affirms *the possibility of faith—man's need of faith.*

Notes

1. Karl Bartsch, *Die Klage* (Leipzig, 1875).

2. Wilhelm Dilthey, *Von Deutscher Dichtung und Musik* (Leipzig, 1933), p. 179: "Der unbefangene, ver-trauensvolle, heroische Jugendmut Siegfried's auf der Jagd ist begleitet von den düsteren, mächtigen Grundakkorden, die aus der dämonischen Natur Hagens und aus dem dunklen Mordplan stammen. . . . Die Zerstörung der Lichtgestalt, des *lichten* Helden durch das *Dunkle, Böse, heimlich Zerstörende* . . ." (italics added).

3. Gustav Ehrismann, *Geschichte der Deutschen Literatur bis zum Ausgang des Mittelalters, 2. Teil, Mittelhochdeutsche Literatur, Schlussband* (Munich, 1935), p. 35: "Folgerichtig und schicksalsgemäss entwickeln sich die Taten und Ereignisse . . . Das Schicksal als führende Idee des Gedichtes tritt deutlich in Gestalt von Schuld und Sühne hervor; die Schuld der Burgunder liegt im Mord Sigfrids, die Sühne in ihrem Untergang, die Schuld Kriemhilds in der Vernichtung des eigenen Geschlechtes und ihre Sühne in ihrem Tod."

4. Friedrich Ranke, *Deutsche Literaturgeschichte in Grundzügen,* ed. B. Boesch (Bern, 1946), p. 53: ". . . nur noch ihr [Kriemhild's] eigener Tod lässt die Grässlichkeit der Szene ertragen; und doch steht *das Bild der Rächerin Kriemhild* dem Hörer *unbefleckt* in der Erinnerung: eine Vorzeitheldin, die, anstatt in Witwentrauer zu versinken, mit hartem, zuletzt fast versteinertem Willen das Schicksal zu dem von ihr gewollten Ziele zwingt." (Italics added). Cf. Ehrismann, op. cit., p. 136: "Hagen vollbringt den Mord aus Treue zu seiner beleidigten Königin, und durch seine . . . Mannentreue tritt er uns auch menschlich näher . . . In anderer Form tritt die Treue bei Kriemhild als Treubund und damit als ethisches Grundmotiv des ganzen Liedes auf."—J. Schwietering, *Deutsche Dichtung des Mittelalters* (Munich, 1938), p. 204: "Der Schmerz um Siegfried hat durchaus die Oberhand . . . Kriemhilds Treue lässt sich erst . . . an ihrem Leid voll ermessen." Max Mell, *Der Nibelunge Not* (Salzburg, 1951, pp. 144-145, has Kriemhild say:

"Denn nicht Hagen allein hat Siegfried gemordet.
Es muss heissen: Hagen und Kriemhild habens getan.
Sein letzter Gedanke konnte sein:
Mein Weib hat mich verraten . . ."

5. Werner Fechter, *Siegfrieds Schuld und das Weltbild des Nibelungenliedes* (Hamburg, 1948), p. 43: "Hagen bleibt *der schwarze Neider,* . . . der niederträchtige Intrigant, der Böses sät, Zwietracht sucht und seine Lust am Verderben hat. Aber er ist, indem er Siegfried mordet, *zugleich der Arm des strafenden Richters*" (italics added). "Ebenso bleibt Siegfried der leuchtende Held . . ., aber zugleich ist er der Verneiner der Ordnung, der sich seiner Bestimmung widersetzt, der die Grenze seiner Art frevelhaft überschreitet und der so wenig Achtung vor der gleichartigen Genossin hat, dass er, nur an sich selbst denkend, ihr Leben zerstört und sie als Tauschgut behandelt."

6. Katharina Bollinger, *Das Tragische im höfischen Epos* (Würzburg, 1939) pp. 4-6, 10, 12 et al.

7. Andreas Heusler, *Germanistische Abhandlungen, Festschrift für Hermann Paul* (1902), p. 93.

8. Dietrich Kralik, *Das Nibelungenlied*, trans. Karl Simrock (Stuttgart, 1954), p. xxx (introduction): "Die ganze Schuld an den späteren tragischen Konsequenzen wird so der Brünhild aufgebürdet, die ja überhaupt als ein ihre Freier . . . mordendes fürchterliches Kraftweib in ein recht ungünstiges Licht gerückt erscheint . . . Brünhild ist die Schuldige, Sigfried ist ihr unschuldiges Opfer."

9. Arnold H. Price, "Characterization in the Nibelungenlied," *Monatshefte,* LI (December 1959), 341-350.

10. Price, p. 344.

11. Price, p. 349.

12. Fechter, p. 35; see also p. 40: "Wer nicht in Treue sein will, der er ist, kann überhaupt nicht sein. Die Ordnung hat das Bestreben, sich zu erhalten. Wer sie stört, vernichtet sie. So vollzieht sich auch in Siegfrieds Tod ein Naturgesetz."

13. Fechter, p. 35: "Darüber hinaus überschreitet er in der Ehe mit Kriemhild die Grenze seiner Art und ermöglicht Gunther den Frevel, sich ein übermenschliches Wesen zu gatten. Hier liegt *Siegfrieds Schuld;. Alles andere fliesst aus dieser Quelle*" (italics added). p. 45: ". . . über allem lebt der starke Glaube, dass nicht ein blindes Schicksal den Lauf der Welt bestimmt sondern die Gerechtigkeit . . ."

14. Bert Nagel, "Die Künstlerische Eigenleistung des Nibelungendichters," *Wolfram Jahrbuch,* ed. Wolfg. Stammler, (1953), 23-47.

15. Nagel, p. 43.

16. Nagel, p. 40: [the poet super-imposes upon the] "*Verhängnistragik,* dass zwei zur Partnerschaft prädestinierte Menschen sich nicht . . . ergreifen; . . . eine die Katastrophe auslösende *Schuldtragik,* der Siegfried und Kriemhild . . . auch Brünhild und . . . alle Personen der Handlung zum Opfer fallen." (italics added).—Nagel ends his observations with the following statement, p. 47: "Am Ende steht nicht die Verzweiflung vor dem Nichts, sondern nur die lindernde Träne, nicht die ausweglose Verhärtung, sondern die Lösung ins Menschliche. Über das Chaos der Zerstörung erheben sich, als Neues und Zukunftweisendes, die heiligen Kräfte des Mitfühlens und Mitleidens."

17. Siegfried Beyschlag, "Das Motiv der Macht bei Siegfrieds Tod," *German.-Roman. Monatsschrift,* XXXIII (1952).

18. Beyschlag, p. 99: ". . . es geht nicht um eine Vergeltung für den Freiertrug . . ., sondern ausschliesslich um die Beseitigung des Mannes, der . . . einen bedrohlichen Anspruch auf Vorrang, Land und Reich erhoben hat." p. 105: "Das oberste Gesetz des Handelns für die Brüder ebenso wie für den regierenden König: die Wahrung und Einheit und Unversehrtheit

des Reiches . . ." p. 106: "Auch Gunther und seine Brüder . . . entscheiden . . . wie Rüdiger: *für die staatliche Notwendigkeit,* wie sie sie sehen. *Selbst bei Kriemhilds Rache liegt Gleiches vor*" (italics added).

19. Beyschlag, p. 107: ". . . gemäss der Darstellung des Dichters, Siegfried ist nie eine Bedrohung für Gunther, die Beseitigung . . . ein Fehlschluss, ein beklagenswertes, tragisches Verhängnis, dem Motto der Dichtung vom *leit* als . . . Ende der *liebe* . . . ein-und untergeordnet."

20. Walther Joh. Schröder, *Das Nibelungenlied,* Sonderdruck (Halle, 1954), p. 38: "Man versteht dies mörderische Wüten nur, wenn man den ganzen Kampf als *Machtkampf* auffasst, der hier in seiner letzten nackten Brutalität ausgespielt wird" (italics added).

21. Schröder, p. 35: "Im Hort wird die Macht konkret. In ihm lebt Siegfried weiter. Wer den Hort hat, hat auch die Macht in Worms." p. 36: "Als Hagen . . . schweigt, enthauptet sie [Kriemhild] ihn selbst. Alles, was sie tut, tut sie nur, um den Hort zu gewinnen."

22. Schröder, p. 63.

23. Schröder, p. 40: "Mit Hilfe des eigentümlichen Motivs der Doppelheirat und Aufweisung ihrer Folgen bringt der Dichter den Leitgedanken seines Werkes heraus, den man in kürzester Form folgendermassen formulieren könnte: eine Herrschaft, die nicht auf Stärke gegründet ist, muss zerfallen. Natur und Gesellschaft stehen nur dann im Einklang miteinander, wenn der Beste auch der Erste ist. Allgemeiner: Die Rangordnung einer echten Gesellschaft muss Naturordnung sein."

24. Schröder, p. 63: "Der Tod ist der Schwäche Sold; . . . Hochmut rächt sich, da der Hochmütige alle . . . Auswege verschmäht, ja, nicht einmal erwägt."

25. Schröder, p. 64: "Das Heroische liegt in der Einheit von Wollen und Müssen, und die Weisheit des Menschen ist das Wissen um das Notwendige."

26. Friedrich Panzer, *Das Nibelungenlied* (Stuttgart, 1955), p. 455.

27. Friedrich Neumann, "Nibelungenlied und Klage," *Die Deutsche Literatur des Mittelalters,* ed. Wolfg. Stammler (Berlin, 1940), p. 558.

28. Friedrich Maurer, *Leid* (Bern & Munich, 1951).

29. Maurer, p. 37.

30. Maurer, p. 38.

31. Bollinger, p. 6: Siegfried's "liebenswürdige Verantwortungslosigkeit."

32. Dürrenmatt, pp. 181-221, pays tribute to Kriemhilds' potentialities of attaining the highest forms of womanhood possible at her time; but destructive forces prevented her from complete fulfillment. Her boast and the ensuing quarrel came from her finest characteristic: her love of Siegfried; thus a special tragic

note is introduced, suggesting "dass die Tugenden eines Menschen seine grösste Gefahr . . . bedeuten" (p. 193).

33. Mergell, p. 318: ". . . nicht nur das menschliche Mitgefühl, auch das religiöse Empfinden des Hörers und Lesers auf Seiten Hagens und der im Tod vollendeten Burgunder; Hagen ist es, der sterbend den Gedanken auf Gott richten, den Namen Gottes nennen darf, während Kriemhild umgekehrt vor Gott und Menschen als Verdammte erscheint." cf. above nn. 8, 9, 16.

34. de Boor, *Nibelungenlied,* p. 276, n. 1748, 4: "Teufelin . . . ist (2371, 4) das letzte Trutzwort Hagens gegen Kriemhild. So früh und im Munde Dietrichs verliert es sein Gewicht und ist, gleich der ganzen Zeile, ein *Stilfehler* des jüngsten Dichters" (italics added).

35. Panzer, p. 210.

36. Schröder, p. 87: "Die Wendung zum Höheren, die Erhebung der Basis menschlicher Existenz auf eine neue, geistige, transzendente Ebene war dem Heldenepos nicht möglich. Es gibt für den Verfasser des Nibelungenliedes keine Existenz jenseits unserer. . . . Zwar weiss er um die Möglichkeit; aber sie wird ihm nicht zur Wirklichkeit."

37. Hugo Kuhn, "Brunhilds und Kriemhilds Tod," *Zeitschrift für das deutsche Altertum,* 82, (1950), 191-199.

38. Hugo Kuhn, "Das Rittertum in der Stauferzeit," *Annalen der deutschen Literatur* (1952), 152-157.

Hugo Bekker (essay date 1971)

SOURCE: "Conclusion: Structural Devices and Their Consequences" in The *"Nibelungenlied": A Literary Analysis,* University of Toronto Press, 1971, pp. 149-65.

[*In the following excerpt, Bekker examines the function of the* Nibelungenlied*'s imagery and symbolism and discusses the epic's abundant symmetry and varied pace.*]

The previous chapters have attempted to draw attention to some of the building materials used in the *Nibelungenlied,* and to the nature of their distribution. What the total structure amounts to is a different matter. In order to attempt an evaluation of the epic as a whole, it is necessary to deal with some devices that are akin to that of parallelism, which so far has provided the base from which to view isolated motifs, events, or the functions of individual characters. The task involved demands a survey of the imagery in the epic, of the nature of the symmetry in it, and of pace and action.

The *Nibelungenlied* does little or nothing to meet a demand for "pure" poetry; its integrated structure offers a foursquare resistance to such a search. This does not mean, however, that there is no symbolism in the epic. If we look, as we have done, into the technique of its composition, it becomes apparent that much of the value to be gleaned from it is conveyed by series of parallel images. Some of this imagery is as obvious as the moon similes applied to Kriemhild (283) and Siegfried (817) respectively (chapter 111, pp. 60 ff.); some of it is more recondite, and its significance strikes us only when we have immersed ourselves for a time in the epic and begun to notice things which at first may have escaped us in the swift succession of events. Such significance is not so much a matter of the images or symbols themselves as of their placing. It may be compared to the composition of a picture in which a number of objects, more or less significant in themselves, subtly gain added importance from the interrelations of balance and perspective.

A typical example may be mentioned once again to show how the consequences of the poet's arrangements at times hold the key to a correct understanding of the developments. Consider Kriemhild's function in the tailor scene, her statement about Brunhild's having been Siegfried's *Kebse,* and her role in bringing Hagen up to date about Siegfried's vulnerable spot. The interrelation between these scenes provides one of the many examples of how the poet sets his images—whether verbal, pictorial, or otherwise—squarely before the reader and allows them to do their own work.

We have seen how intricate the patterns of parallel motifs can become; the first instance of Kriemhild's "helping" Hagen links with the gem motif which itself occurs in a series and shows a movement that parallels the course of the events. With this way of working with imagery, it is often impossible to strip off the imagery and to present the naked content, for with natural imagery the images *are* the content. It is this phenomenon, the use of natural images, that explains the poet's ease and freedom in shifting from the plane of the narrative flow to that of symbolic significance, and back again. For though the symbolism in the epic seldom interferes with its narrative environment, at times it is more significant than the environment itself. A typical example is encountered when Gotelind gives Nudung's shield to Hagen (chapter VII, pp. 143 ff.). An occasional lapse may occur, as in Rüdeger's shield scene. The inconsistency here (cf. chapter VIII, p. 145) is so striking that it is tempting to interpret it as a deliberate device to draw attention to the symbolic rather than the narrative consequence of the scene.

To put it differently: the imagery and symbolism in the *Nibelungenlied* tend to be strictly functional, even when most pictorial. For it is pictorial: the poet has the eye of a painter and a lightning facility for unforgettably fixing a scene, a look, a movement, in a few words only. For instance, there is Brunhild's look over the shoulder, her ordering that the Burgundians be given their weapons back (477); there is the woman's hauteur and self-assurance, and the insult that look over the shoulder spells for Hagen, who looks even darker than usual, not being accustomed to being put in his place—and by a woman at that! There is the insensitivity of young Dankwart, who is happy to have his weapons back (448) and does not notice the anger of his elder brother. Compare to this another look over the shoulder (1788): Hagen striding across the courtyard, the grouping of the waiting Burgundians, the charged atmosphere. The poet does not tell us all this; he simply shows us and lets his picture produce its own effect. We "see" the slant of Brunhild's or Hagen's face in relief. And by way of another example there is the priest leaning over the church utensils (1575), his hands grasping the gunwale, his capacious habit filled with airpockets that in a moment will help him to stay afloat and gain the shore. Over and over again in such pithy details the poet displays his power to catch and fix a visual impression. And whether he is working on the grand scale or on the small, his images are not only clear, but also consistent; or rather, they are clear because they are consistent. No deviation into philosophy, no express preoccupation with symbolic values seduces him for a moment into taking his eye off its object.

But though the pictorial manner of portrayal is an essential mark of the epic's style, the formation of the materials does not rely solely or even mainly on the poet's "eye." It is his mind that orders the materials, and the mind is reflective rather than speculative. The poet is not philosophically oriented. His reflections do not seek depth; they remain on the surface of things, but they interrelate and refer. This procedure does not suggest a lack of erudition; it merely reflects the poet's psychological make-up.

If the poet requires something useful to his story—some theatrical property, as one might say—he does not falsify the picture by suddenly introducing a strange implement from nowhere. He makes do with what he has. When, for instance, Brunhild's belt is mentioned for the first time (636), it is because something is needed, something detachable, that Brunhild would have at hand as a matter of course to bind Gunther.[1] The belt is the very thing. But look what the poet gains by thus introducing a natural symbol in the most off-hand manner. It is with this belt that Gunther is bridled. Does not the dominance of the allegorical lady Chastity over the allegorical figure Lust come to mind? The narrative thus manages to avoid introducing something totally incongruous, without substituting the symbolic for the pictorial image.

The poet of the *Nibelungenlied,* then, is not interested in making his own imagery and symbols. His interest lies in working with natural ones, those that are ready-made.[2] These symbols are themselves instances of what they symbolize. By simply being what they are, they tell us something about the nature of the greater thing, as protection and safety are greater than the shield symbolizing them, or as the belt is but a visible sign of something more important than itself. The poet arranges such devices in order to add to the richness of his delivery. He does not *make* them meaningful, universal, or always recognizable; they *are* all that. Though they may be old, they are ever new and fresh. The symbolism is therefore not private symbolism, and it

resists being called medieval or modern or whatever; such symbolism is of all times and places, and it begs to communicate.[3]

The imagery based on such symbolism displays its universal, because natural, pattern at all levels and in all circumstances, whether or not the poet is or could be conscious of these possible values. We therefore have the right to read from the arrangement of the imagery all the significance we can find, provided, of course, that our interpretation does not involve a degradation of the imagery. With this in mind, we could take any example, great or small, and detect its occasional subtlety and—once we had surrendered to it—its fascination; for instance, the imagery of hands.

Whereas the hand imagery discussed previously (chapter 11, pp. 33 f.) pertains to the many instances in which hands are said or implied to carry war gear, five times hands are said to be white; each time the mention of the white hand occurs in "courtly" situations.[4] But this courtly aura does not mean that such hands—in contrast to those engaged in warfare—are "reflective." Kriemhild's holding hands with Siegfried, for instance (cf. 294 and 661), is hardly proof that now hand and reason are in harmony. Whether her former unwillingness to welcome a man's love was reasonable or not—her mother thought it was not—Kriemhild's decision was at least based on a type of reasoning, whatever its soundness. Now her gesture of intimacy in holding hands with Siegfried is proof that her determination to remain uninvolved with love was but a "wint" (47), and the mention of her white hand, while suggesting a little idyll, is proof that reason has been suspended. So also when Kriemhild's white hands lift the head of the dead Siegfried to give him a last kiss (1069): her sorrow is measureless, "*unmaezlichen* groz" (1066).[5]

In Bechlaren, Giselher's white hands embrace Rüdeger's daughter (1685). The idyllic aspect of this scene remains superficial, and Giselher himself comes to repudiate the note of tenderness which the mention of his white hands helped to convey (cf. 2819). In another instance of the motif—Gotelind's taking the shield off the wall of Bechlaren—the hand has not only a life, but also a culture of its own. As when Kriemhild and Siegfried hold hands, this is a moment "wenn die Hände sprechen." The white hands of Gotelind speak a pithier and more communicative language than language as such. Here, too, however, the hands seem detached from the waking personality. Gotelind acts as though in trance. Her hands are like independent agents, acting without the benefit of reason to give away the shield, the symbol of protection.

And so, whenever hands are said to be doing something, they fail to acquire power by association with their owners. Precisely because of the courtly value suggested by the whiteness of hands, their unexpected *under*-the-surface value—or rather, the very lack of it—becomes more portentous in alluding to the discrepancies between hands and minds than in those instances in which the hand is said to handle the sword, shield, or spear.

The hand imagery in the *Nibelungenlied* tells more about the characters. Together with the motifs of battle anger (chapter II, pp. 31 ff.) and of acquiescence (chapter I, pp. 21 ff.), it suggests a lack of inner substance. The poet does not spell this out, he merely shows us its effects. Though aware of the unconscious—witness Kriemhild's endeavor to keep Siegfried from going to meet the allegedly renewed hostilities of the Saxons (921 ff.)—the poet is not greatly interested in exploiting it. He is interested in some of its manifestations—dreams, for instance, and the way in which hands act independently. But while leaving untouched the dark recesses of his characters' minds, he reveals some of their thoughts nevertheless, by juxtaposition or otherwise, as when he uses the window motif to show that only Kriemhild leaves a window to destroy (chapter I, pp. 20 f.).

It is this lack of inner substance that makes the characters in the *Nibelungenlied* rely on appearances. This fact also accounts for the importance of public opinion. Insults are as bad as they are taken to be, as though whatever they say is thereby made true. Honor thus comes to rely on the opinion of others. At every juncture of the narrative it also inevitably provides impetus to the ever increasing forces of annihilation, precisely because the enhancement and vindication of honor is a central commitment of all the characters. For instance, in the exchanges between Gunther, Hagen, Giselher, and Ortwin after the queens' quarrel, the question of whether Siegfried must die revolves around honor (cf. 866 ff.). The defense of Brunhild's honor as Hagen pretends to understand it (cf. chapter VI, pp. 127 ff.) becomes for Tronje a *Tarnkappe* under whose protection he can strike down Siegfried with impunity. Hagen, for that matter, is a master in the manipulation of honor.

Honor in the *Nibelungenlied,* it should be noted, is exclusively a *diesseits* value, its importance in conjunction with the deity being of little consequence. True, at Siegfried's *Schwertleite* the poet tells how a mass was sung: "got man do ze eren eine messe sanc" (33), but this and other periodic processions to the minster are little more than backdrops adding to the honor and aura of the court. When Siegfried is in church, the poet does not say that he thanks God for Kriemhild, but "er mohte sinen saelden des immer sagen danc" / *"He would always thank his good fortune"* (301). Even Rüdeger's anguished appeals to God are lamentations for the unavoidable loss of honor, not God's but his own (2153). Rüdeger's courtly life as based on honor may be at God's behest, but his bitterness towards God for now despoiling him of his honor—"'nu ruoche mich bewisen der mir ze lebene geriet'" / *"'Let him who called me to life advise me'"* (2154)—is far from any Christian acquiescence in the greater glory of God.[6]

The adherence or nonadherence to court etiquette in so far as it centers around honor may be a two-edged sword, capable of exalting on the one hand or of insulting on the other (cf. chapter I, p. 14). The potency of this weapon derives from the deadly seriousness with which the forms are adhered to. Every departure from the code is fraught with consequences. Gunther is angry when Etzel's minstrels refuse the gifts he offers (1490). When he and the other Burgundians arrive in Gran, Kriemhild departs from the norm by kissing Giselher only. Hagen reacts immediately, and he immediately draws his conclusions (1737 f.).

Various forms of honor, then, are often at cross purposes with each other, and thus one of the main principles of order and cohesion turns into a principle of division and destruction. Honor sets individuals against each other, and the poet can only stand aghast at the carnage. The closed, self-referential world of the *Nibelungenlied,* with no point of reference outside itself, has no answer to its self-generated destruction. It is "eine selbstmahlende Mühle," an existential plight.[7]

An important feature of the structure of the *Nibelungenlied* is that of symmetry. Such symmetry—Panzer calls it mere repetition[8]—is akin to parallelism, but the significant difference lies in the fact that parallelism participates in the self-referential and self-revealing patterns, whereas symmetry lends regularity and order. With this difference in mind, we can speak of the "Parallelität der Rollen und Schicksale zwischen Sifrit und Rüdiger,"[9] but also of points of symmetry between them. Whereas Wachinger's reference to parallelism hinges on the events taking place, the symmetry in the roles of these two figures depends on details that in themselves are not significant. Both Siegfried and Rüdeger are killed with their own weapons; Siegfried is killed from behind by his own spear, and Rüdeger is felled in a face-to-face battle by the sword he has given to Gernot. The difference in this similarity reflects on Hagen's function, or lack of it (cf. chapter VII, pp. 144 f.). Furthermore, Siegfried as well as Rüdeger travels with twelve companions to Worms (64, 2170), and both are separated from their own shields when they receive the mortal spear thrust or sword blow. For that matter, Siegfried sparks gems off his shield when he beats Hagen with it (985); Rüdeger also forces gems off shields in the battle ending in his death (2212). As we have seen, the poet has made good use of this parallelistic motif (cf. chapter I, pp. 10 ff.). Before their deaths, Siegfried and Rüdeger commend (996, 2164) the care of wife and child to the King—who is less responsible for those deaths than is his queen in each instance.

It is not the individual instances of symmetry that are of consequence, but their very abundance. The following enumeration stands by itself. Twice a king decides to woo on hearsay (44 and 329). Twice Siegfried is recognized through a window (84, 411); twice he asks Gunther why he is downcast (153, 883); and twice he is told that the Saxons have announced war (143, 880). Twice Siegfried fights with Alberich (96, 497); twice mention is made of talks between husband and wife in the intimacy of the bedroom (1168, 1400); and twice a queen makes a pretence in order to have relatives invited for a visit (726 ff., 1401 ff.). There are two engagement scenes (614, 1683), and twice we are told that couples to be married are not in a position to consummate their intended union (528, 1358). Twice a queen about to leave her country tries to settle her inheritance (522, 691 ff.); in each instance she is less than completely successful. Twice Gunther is warned not to go abroad (330, 1458 ff.); in each instance he goes anyway. Both Kriemhild (1248) and Rüdeger (2154 ff.) find themselves in a quandary and see no way out of the difficulty besetting them. Both finally choose the world's—that is, their own—rather than God's honor. In the first two *Aventiure* the poet divides his attention between Kriemhild and Siegfried; the portraits reflect each other in alternate descriptions. Symmetry occurs also when two sets of brothers fight each other in the dark of Bavaria (1608 ff.). When Siegfried gets a son, Gunther does also; each child is his uncle's namesake.

Of a rather different order are those cases of symmetry that involve groupings. In strophes 583 and 590 we find companies of ladies and knights going hand in hand. The same happens in strophe 1395, and later in Bechlaren (1667 ff.). In the latter instance there is an explicit indication that protocol is observed: Gotelind goes with the most important guest, Gunther; Rüdeger goes with Gernot; his daughter leads Giselher. Also in Gran we see knights going hand in hand (1804 f.): Dietrich goes with Gunther, Irnfrit with Gernot, Rüdeger with Giselher; Hawart holds Iring's hand; Dankwart goes with Wolfhart. Here, too, rules of protocol and rank are observed, Hagen and Volker being the only two who adhere to their own set of values.

Order of rank also makes for symmetry when large groups are involved. In these, the kings are the focal points towards whom and around whom the entourage is grouped and from which it derives its significance. Instances of such groupings occur during the double wedding ceremony (cf. 617, 626 f.). Official encounters are also full of regulated pomp: when Brunhild arrives in Worms (tenth *Aventiure*) and when Kriemhild arrives in Santen (eleventh *Aventiure*) or meets Etzel (twenty-second *Aventiure*), dignity and circumstance give these encounters the quality of colorful processions meeting each other. These are but a few of the indications that social occasions are formal and never fail to observe strict decorum.[10]

When festivities are threatened or are disrupted by enmity, we have the kings above the groupings. The function of these kings is to be normative; throughout the epic they are, or attempt to be, the centers of authority.[11] If need be, they conciliate, or seek to do so. It is their duty to have order and "fröude" prevail. Elsewhere, kings acquiesce or hide their worries so that harmony and joy may remain unmarred.

Insistence on order and symmetry is also applied in geography: it takes twelve days to travel from Worms to Islant (382), from Bechlaren to the Rhine (1175), from Gran to Worms (1430), and from Worms to the Danube (1515). Time lapses are synchronized also: a decade passes between Kriemhild's departure from and her return to Worms; another ten years pass between her departure for Gran and the visit of the Burgundians.

The order evoked in these symmetrical configurations significantly reflects the principle of order to which the society is committed. Thus seen, the principle of symmetry that lies deeply embedded in the structure of the *Nibelungenlied* cannot be viewed as so many instances of repetitiousness, but constitutes a compelling maturity. The importance of this orderly principle is supported by the considerations that deal with the pace of the *Nibelungenlied*.

The epic is at one moment deliberately slow and majestic, then again fast and turbulent. The references to periods of time support this alternation between slackening and quickening of the pace. The two ten-year periods make the epic as a whole chronologically slow. Elsewhere, important events take place within the space of a few days or even less. Towards the end the pace becomes downright furious, the space narrower. The poet frequently resorts to foreshortening devices to indicate coming events. But in contrast to this is the large amount of direct description which slows the narrative. Descriptions of timeconsuming preparations are often detailed, though they do not further the plot, and they are placed so as to give the impression that we are present. They thus appear to consume the full number of days or weeks allotted to the operations themselves. The passages describing the preparations for various festivities or departures, with a richness of detail far in excess of the demands of the story, are typical examples of the poet's method. At first glance, at any rate, many passages seem irrelevant and detachable. To take a well known example, some ten strophes are devoted to Kriemhild's dressing scene in the quarrel episode, but our discussion of it (cf. chapter III, pp. 53 ff.) made it clear that its true significance as a source of insight into Kriemhild's and Brunhild's manner of thinking is not readily apparent.[12] As far as the *action* of the epic is concerned, the passage adds little. Similarly, strophes dealing with festivities and courtly occasions in general seem to add little or nothing to the development of the plot, and provide a slowing effect. On a somewhat different plane, the poet's "I heard" and "I was told" cooperate to the same effect.

Unlike these descriptions and the narrator's comments, the direct discourse contributes to speed. Panzer speaks of "handelnde Reden in den Gipfeln der Fabel."[13] These dialogues are rapid and dynamic because they tend to use verbs of action and because they often allude to the hand as the doer of deeds. In fact, rapidity of dialogue often obscures the course of these interchanges. As a consequence, the characters tend to talk past each other. Misunderstanding is their common failure.[14] Warnings go unheeded and advice is scorned. Only once is this failure to communicate adequately recognized (2333), but the insight comes too late to do any good. What with the tendency of words to go their own stubborn way, it is small wonder that kings seek to impose silence and that the would-be retainers of harmony acquiesce.

Kriemhild and Ute fail to communicate because they fail to define their terms. It is as if each is so introverted in her own thoughts and mold of thinking about love that it does not occur to either of them that the other may be thinking of something else. These misunderstandings are allowed to continue and to warp relationships. Such a failure to clarify lies at the base of the crucial quarrel between the queens.

As Bumke has shown,[15] the participants in the council meeting after the queens' quarrel also talk past each other. They have ears only for their own assumptions and opinions, and it is a bit of an accident that they end with a decision at all. Bumke explains the "vagueness" of the dialogue as due to the various sources with which the poet is working, but viewed from *within* the epic the conversation is but another example of the inability of the characters to explain themselves.

In this connection, Bumke's suggestion that Ortwin's offer to kill Siegfried (869) is perhaps in one of the sources mentioned by Gernot[16] may be true as far as the sources are concerned, but from the present line of reasoning we can only say that Ortwin was also the more belligerent in the encounter scene (cf. chapter VII, p. 121). During that meeting Ortwin had good reason to feel offended by Siegfried, who taunted him in no vague terms. Stopped by Gernot's command to be silent, Ortwin was at the time unable to make Siegfried pay for his insult. Now, in the council meeting, he seizes the opportunity to square the old account.

These remarks on the pace in the epic show that the poet's art does not fail him when he wants to call upon the reader's capacity to experience things with him. We may think that he works by overt statement rather than by suggestion, yet in the end we find that he has suggested more than the content of his statements. The effect of these statements is cumulative; for instance, as we read from one *Aventiure* to the next, the sense of everything closing and rushing in upon us produces finally a profound claustrophobia. Looking back, we see the beginning of the "maere," colorful and gay with its festivals and *buhurts*. The disappearance of ornament, of clothes and other colorful materials, contributes to this effect by negative suggestion. In the end all that is left of color is the red of blood, and the yellow of gold streaming out of Kriemhild's coffers (cf. 2130).

It could be said that the modification of the poet's sources confirmed this pull in two opposite directions. By selection and addition he has produced a story much more symmetrical than his sources, and he has regularized time and distance to a higher degree than his sources ever warranted. Further instances of symmetry could be cited, but they would not alter our conclusions.

These observations suggest a way of approaching the epic. The symmetry of scene, action, or characterization, the pace of the narrative—now slow and now quickening, the abundance of generalizing details contrasted with pithy concrete descriptions, the predominantly dramatic discourse, all indicate that the *Nibelungenlied* is not the best work in which to look for delicate characterization. For full delineation of character is not called for in the design; nor is it possible, though this does not prevent our appreciating the many subtle hints which give us insight into the various characters.[17]

To suggest, however, that the element of characterization is minor in the epic does not justify turning to the plot and making it the focus of interest. For the epic depends only in part on the virtues that make a good story: swift pace, suspense, variety, intrigue. We encounter all these, but not in all the episodes. The swift pace of one *Aventiure* may slow down to a crawl in the next; suspense as often as not is toned down by predictory elements liberally sprinkled throughout the many hundreds of strophes; variety, too, often bows out to the repetitive device of parallelism and symmetry; intrigue appears in the actions of some of the characters but not in the poet's method of presentation; the main events are forecast long before they occur. Thus the structure of the epic works against story interest.

If, then, because of the variance between speed and slowness, brevity and length, dialogues and descriptions, pithiness and elaboration, neither characterization nor plot can supply the basis on which the *Nibelungenlied* is to be read, it seems reasonable to conclude, on the principle that a literary monument should be approached on the basis of its own assumptions, that the epic is centered neither on character nor on plot. We can neither examine nor evaluate it according to canons by which it was not written and which it cannot satisfy. Its very texture, its characters and its action, rather than existing for any great interest in themselves, point to a "representational," a "metaphorical" method. There is in the epic a close correlation among the elements on this level that gives support to such an approach.

I suggest, then, that the *Nibelungenlied* presents a poetic pageant,[18] and that its materials are organized in such a way as to contribute to the complex design expressing the nature of the noble life or, in sharp contrast to it, to show how this life can be threatened and is in fact brought to destruction by counter forces. Hagen and Kriemhild may seem to be the embodiments of these counter forces, but actually they work through all the characters. We thus can speak of the *Nibelungenlied* as the story of a pageant destroyed. It is immediately concerned with noble activities, with pomp, ceremony, dignity, power, love, and chivalry, and with the attempts by the exponents of nobility to invoke perpetually the principle of form and order and *fröude*. The disruption of this order lies at the heart of the epic. The society depicted in it is one in which form is full of significance. Life here is conducted at a dignified, processional pace, and is itself perhaps a reflection—or rather a reproduction—of the order of the universe. What gives this conception of life its perspective, its depth, and its sometimes frenetic seriousness (see 1893 ff.) is its awareness of a formidable, antagonistic element, an ever threatening danger, even in the moments of supreme assuredness. When the arrival of Siegfried in Worms seems to threaten this mode of life, Gunther refutes his claims by referring to orderly inheritance. This counterforce—not to be identified with any specific individual or individuals[19]—falls across the pattern of order, and is exemplified in the sudden turns of plot such as Kriemhild's falcon dream, the bedroom episode, the bear scene,[20] or Volker's killing the Hun at Gran's joust.

The descriptive passages support this interpretation of a pageant destroyed, not only in the parts dealing with knighthood in general, but also in the manner in which the antagonistic destructive forces in this life, no matter how represented or suggested, interrupt the leisure of the narrative. At first the interruptions are only momentary—insignificant clouds on the horizon, as in Siegmund's warning to Siegfried not to go to Worms. Then, presently, they become longer and more momentous with Siegfried's frist arrival in Worms and, later, the Saxon war. Ultimately the waves of antagonism follow each other with diminishing intervals, rising higher and higher, until in the end they sweep along all that stands for order and pattern and harmony.

The "hochgeziten" in the epic contribute to the rich texture in the fabric of noble life that the poem presents. That is also the reason why details relating to strength, beauty, and magnificence are in the superlative: they contribute to knightly splendor in all its forms:

> Do stuont so minnecliche   daz Sigmundes kint,
> sam er entworfen waere   an ein permint
> von guotes meisters listen,   als man im jach,
> daz man helt deheinen   nie so scoenen gesach.

> *There stood the child of Sieglind, handsome as though drawn on parchment by the cunning hand of a master; indeed, it was said that no handsomer hero was ever seen.*

In a strophe like this, for example, the description of Siegfried is more than surface ornamentation. It is linked with a score of other passages as an expression of Siegfried's pre-eminence. Beginning with the second *Aventiure,* all the descriptions of him serve to widen and perpetuate our notion of him as variously the ruler, conqueror, judge, lover, or hunter. Among other details, whether subsequent or not, the splendor of the hoard and the wealth of Santen are directly associated with Siegfried's role.

The establishment of Siegfried's pre-eminence is essential to the meaning of the epic, and it is carried out on the multiple levels characteristic of the poet's whole method of working. There is an obvious correspondence between the quality of these descriptions and Siegfried's position as a central figure. From this vantage point it will not do to suggest that the poet's sympathy lies with the "Germanic" rather than the "courtly" qualities in the epic, or vice versa. The distinction is a false one and works havoc with the endeavor to consider the epic as a homogeneous unit. Attention might be drawn, for instance, to Hildebrand's role in the closing *Aventiure.* It has been said that his killing of

Kriemhild issues from his adherence to "ere" and "triuwe" in the Germanic-heroic sense of those terms. But considering the way Kriemhild has debased kingship by laying waste entire realms, in defiance of her royal obligation to preserve and enhance order, peace, and harmony, Hildebrand's action may be regarded as an act of justice. Seen in this manner, the last *Aventiure* is to an important degree to be appreciated for its symbolic value.

Similarly, there is no indication that the poet prefers the courtly life as exemplified in love to the courtly life as exemplified in other knightly activities. Siegfried's position suggests that the worship of Mars is no less an important facet of the orderly noble life than is the worship of Venus. To Siegfried goes the honor in the Saxon war as well as the honor in love, and for a while at any rate he comes out on top in a work in which superlatives are used freely, and *is* the ideal lover, king, judge, warrior, hunter, strong man, and rich man. There is no overt indication that the poet takes a dark view of this hyperbolic Siegfried. Nor, for that matter, does he draw overt moral conclusions about the force that brings Siegfried to destruction. In a literature where death is one of the most powerful instruments of moral exemplum, the poet goes out of his way to stifle any fixing of blame. Here, too, he tries to retain balance.

Love in this society is taken for granted; it is never in debate. We simply discover how faithfully experience in love exemplifies the partial blindness of all earthly experience. Love, we find, can create dissension between relatives, and can make otherwise active men abject. This kind of balance regarding love, if it precludes satire, does not rule out irony. Indeed, irony is fully consonant with the dignified view. No moral preference is expressed or implied in the many views of love that we encounter: Brunhild's, Kriemhild's, Ute's, Siegfried's, Gunther's, Etzel's,[21] Volker's; Hagen is the only figure who has none. All we can glean from these various types of love is that they create tensions in the very structure of the epic; there is no indication that one type is superior to another. Nor is there indication that a tragic attitude is to be adopted towards any of these loves. The tragedy, if such it may be called, stems from the fact that these loves clash and cause hatreds, and that the hatreds can work themselves out on a gigantic scale because of the power the haters command.

With these views, it becomes possible to suggest that Siegfried and Hagen, Brunhild and Kriemhild, each in his or her way exemplifies legitimate attitudes of equal "value," and that they balance and supplement each other in providing not moral conflict but variety. To find the real issue in the ***Nibelungenlied*** we must therefore look not so much at the relationships between them, but at their common position in relation to the world in which they have their being, that is, the wouldbe orderly and dignified world. And the poet expresses this issue not only through a tension between the ordered structure and the violent ups and downs of the surface narrative—too plainly to be seen to require elaborate analysis—but also through a complication of texture. The impressive patterned edifice of the noble life, its dignity and richness, its regard for law and decorum, its perpetual concern that harmony and "fröude" be retained, all are bulwarks against the ever threatening forces of chaos, and are in constant collision with them. And perhaps the crowning nobility—despite the *diesseits* orientation of the characters—is situated beyond the grasp of social order, and beyond magnificence in any earthly sense. For in the final strophes of the **Nibelungenlied** there may lie hidden a perception of order beyond chaos. When the earthly designs have totally crumbled, types of nobility yet remain: Etzel, still the representative of kingship in so far as he sought to avert chaos, and still capable of seeing the justice of his queen's death; Dietrich von Bern, the representative of nobility in its widest sense;[22] and Hildebrand, the representative of justice.

Notes

1. Whereas the B* text speaks of the belt "den [Brünhilt] umb ir siten truoc" (636), the C* version changes this to "den si alle zite truoc," perhaps to make acceptable the notion that Brunhild would wear the belt in bed. Under the circumstances prevailing, Brunhild would indeed be wise to keep the belt on. Regardless of the difference between the versions, the belt would be close at hand, off or on.

2. Mowatt, "Studies," p. 262.

3. Perhaps Mowatt and Sacker, *The Nibelungenlied*, p. 27, mean the same thing when they say that "the literary masterpieces of the Middle Ages . . . arrange historically conditioned elements in patterns of universal validity." Even so, symbolism as defined here has little in common with symbolism as understood by Mowatt and Sacker. Witness, for instance, their comment on strophe 909: "In one sense, the bear is Brünnhilde, caught by Sifrid, set loose in Burgundian society, captured a second time by Sifrid, and finally rendered harmless. But whereas Brünnhilde was spared penetration and death (see note 459-461), the bear is less gently treated. In another sense, the bear is Sifrid himself, an uncomfortable guest in Burgundian society, a well-meaning disaster (the bear is only trying to run away), and finally a ritual murder victim. And in so far as Sifrid and Brünnhilde are one composite symbol, the bear is the spark in their relationship that Sifrid stamped out." By definition, of course, natural symbolism cannot be as equivocal as this. In retrospect it may be fair to say that the difference between the thrust of the *Commentary* and that of the present work lies to an important degree in the different definitions of symbolism.

4. To quote Schwarze, "Die Frau," 389, note 6: "Diese Formel kehrt in der Poesie jener Zeit häufig wieder; vgl. *Sanct Oskars Leben,* 577; *Tristan,* 484, 36; *Aucassin und Nicolete,* 26, 11: 'ses blances mains'; *Tristan,* 256, 10 findet sich auch 'liehte hende.'"

5. The adjective "wise" in 1069 may be simply to fill out the meter.

6. On Christianity in the epic, see, e.g., A. Schönbach, "Die Nibelungen," in: *Das Christentum in der altdeutschen Heldendichtung* (Graz, 1897); Nagel, "Heidentum und Christentum," *Der Horizont,* II (1957), 27-37; *idem,* "Heidnisches und Christliches im *Nibelungenlied,*" *Ruperto-Carola,* x (1958), XXIV, 61-81; Hans Kuhn, "Heldensage und Christentum," [*Studies in Philology*] (1960), 515-24; Weber, *Das Nibelungenlied,* pp. 125 ff.; Nagel, *Das Nibelungenlied,* pp. 208 ff.

7. On honor in the epic, see, e.g., Jones, "Rüdiger's Dilemma"; Mueller, *The Nibelungenlied Today,* pp. 9 ff.; H. Naumann, "Die Ritter-Ehre der Stauferzeit," *Euphorion,* XLII (1947).

8. Panzer, *Das Nibelungenlied,* p. 131.

9. Wachinger, *Studien,* p. 95.

10. Dürrenmatt, *Das Nibelungenlied,* p. 93.

11. Not necessarily in contradiction to this, Weber, *Das Nibelungenlied,* p. 83, speaks of the obvious "Abwertung der Königsgestalten."

12. This can also be said of the hunt in the sixteenth *Aventiure.* But see Singer, "The Hunting Contest."

13. Panzer, *Das Nibelungenlied,* p. 132.

14. *If* the *Nibelungenlied* were a story centering around the delineation of character, this perpetual misunderstanding and the habitual inadequacy of language as a tool of communication would lead to the Kafkaesque conclusion that each individual stands in isolation. Mowatt and Sacker, *The Nibelungenlied,* p. 7, speak of "a whole series of unperceptive characters in the work."

15. Bumke, "Quellen," pp. 18 ff.

16. *Ibid.,* p. 20. Incidentally, there is little Germanic about Ortwin's—or Kriemhild's—long nurtured thirst for revenge.

17. Weber, *Das Nibelungenlied,* p. 195: "Es geht nicht um einzelne konkrete Gestalten, sondern um viel mehr: um Schicksale und Mächte als die in der Tiefe herrschenden Gewalten, und noch mehr: es geht weiterhin um das geistige Objekt dieser Schicksale und dieser Mächte des Untergründigen. Dieses geistige Objekt aber, dessen sich die Finsternis bemächtigt, ist das Rittertum."

18. Singer, "The Hunting Contest," p. 167, finds that the term "pageant" suggests itself for the hunting scene, and on p. 169 he makes a statement which this chapter suggests to be applicable to the epic as a whole: "The . . . pageant is constantly subject to abrupt termination."

19. Mergell, *Nibelungenlied,* p. 321, for one, thinks that "es dem Dichter darauf ankommt . . . den Endkampf nicht als Anstiftung eines einzelnen (sei er Hunne oder Burgunder, Heide oder Christ, König oder Mann), sondern mit der zwingenden Gewalt des Naturereignisses hereinbrechen zu lassen." It would

seem, however, in contrast to Mergell that Hagen is also a victim of this "Gewalt des Naturereignisses."

20. This suggestion does not contradict the statements made on this scene by Singer in "The Hunting Contest."

21. Nagel, *Das Nibelungenlied*, pp. 84 ff., sees no difference between Gunther's love for Brunhild and Etzel's for Kriemhild. Many critics share this opinion. Mowatt and Sacker, for instance, throughout their *Commentary* see Etzel as a figure whose sexual drive, and little else, determines his relation to Kriemhild. It would seem, however, that Etzel comes to achieve a type of *maze*. The thought whether he "'sol . . . Kriemhild immer geligen bi'" / "*'should ever be loved by Kriemhild'*" (1151) plays a role as well as the question "'ob si in [sinem] lande krone solde tragen'" / "*'whether she should wear a crown in [his] land'*" (1149). Elsewhere we read that "si was im als sin lip" / "*he loved her as his own life*" (1400) and that "getriuwe was sin muot" / "*his mind was faithful*" (1402)—statements that are not applied to Gunther. And verses like these:

> 1869:
> Kriemhilt mit ir vrouwen   in diu venster gesaz
> zuo Etzel dem richen;   vil liep was im daz.
>
> *Kriemhild with her ladies sat in the windows beside the mighty Etzel; this pleased him much.*

convey Etzel's balanced orientation, in which there is room for warmth as well as satisfaction in Kriemhild's ability to be a consort.

22. See Nagel, "Dietrichbild," parts I and II.

Bibliography

Bumke, Joachim. "Die Quellen der Brünhildfabel im *Nibelungenlied*," *Euphorion*, LIV (1960), 1-38

Dürrenmatt, Nelly. *Das Nibelungenlied im Kreis der höfischen Dichtung,* Bern, 1944

Mergell, Bodo. "*Nibelungenlied* und höfischer Roman," *Euphorion*, XLV (1950), 305-36

Mowatt, D. G. "Studies towards an Interpretation of the *Nibelungenlied*," *GLL*, XIV (1960/61), 257-70

———*The Nibelungenlied: Translated,* London/New York, 1962

Mowatt, D. G. and Sacker, Hugh. *The Nibelungenlied: An Interpretative Commentary,* Toronto, 1967

Nagel, Bert. "Heldentum und Christentum," *Der Horizont,* 11 (1957), 27-37

———"Heidnisches und Christliches im *Nibelungenlied*," *Ruperto-Carola,* 24. Bd. (1958), 61-81

———"Das Dietrichbild im *Nibelungenlied*," 1. Teil, *ZfdP,* LXXVIII (1959), 258-68; 11. Teil, *ZfdP,* LXXIX (1960), 28-57

Panzer, Friedrich. *Das Nibelungenlied: Entstehung und Gestalt,* Stuttgart, 1955

Schönbach, Anton. "Die Nibelungen," in: *Das Christentum in der Altdeutschen Heldendichtung,* Graz, 1897, pp. 1-56

Schwarze, M. "Die Frau in dem *Nibelungenliede* und in der *Kudrun*," *ZfdP,* XVI (1884), 384-470

Singer, C. S. "The Hunting Contest: An Interpretation of the Sixteenth *Aventiure* of the *Nibelungenlied*," *GR,* XLII (1967)

Wachinger, Burghart. *Studien zum Nibelungenlied: Vorausdeutung, Aufbau, Motivierung,* Tübingen, 1960

Weber, Gottfried. *Das Nibelungenlied: Problem und Idee,* Stuttgart, 1963

Harold D. Dickerson, Jr. (essay date 1975)

SOURCE: "Hagen: A Negative View," *Semasia,* Vol. 2, 1975, pp. 43-59.

[*In the following essay, Dickerson argues against viewing Hagen as heroic, contending instead that he should be regarded as an evil character.*]

Much progress has been made in recent years toward a modern and comprehensive view of the ***Nibelungenlied.*** The pioneering studies of D. W. Mowatt,[1] Hugh Sacker[2] and Hugo Bekkar[3]—to choose only three—have suggested new solutions to the problem of the work's inconsistencies which up to now have either been left unexplained or attributed to the "postulate" that the poet was courtly but his subject matter was not.[4] The new discoveries that the poem deals with entire social groups rather than individuals,[5] that it depicts a world fragmented by the intrusion of foreign elements,[6] that irony[7] and "self-referential patterns"[8] play an important role in structure have made it possible to view these inconsistencies in a new light, to see them no longer as lapses and defects but as integral parts of the poet's method. The apparent inconsistency in the figure of Hagen von Tronege is a case in point.

Of all the inhabitants of Worms, Hagen is the most problematic. We have no choice, it seems, but to accept the idea of two Hagens: the murderer of the first part who stabs Siegfried in the back and the hero of the second who singlehandedly becomes "der trôst der Nibelunge" (1726,4).[9] But if the ***Nibelungenlied*** is as great as we think it is, "a literary monument worthy to be read for its own sake,"[10] then the idea of two Hagens or two Kriemhilds is unacceptable and requires a better explanation than simply the poet's inability to "unite two stories which once were separate."[11]

With Hagen one of the chief difficulties is that almost any interpretation of his personality, even those which are diametrically opposed, contain an element of truth. He certainly is "over-weening"[12] and endowed "mit einem beson-deren Sinn für die Nachtseiten des Daseins;"[13] and a case *can*be made for him as a "responsible statesman"[14] who shows "intelligent initiative"[15] in his political decisions. But then Hagen also has the earmarks of a megalomaniac, "[ein] ichbesessener Außenseiter"[16] but one, it seems, with "rare qualities"[17] who in that emotional shield scene with Rüdeger appears truly to undergo "eine sittliche Vertief-ung."[18]

The main reason for these contradictory assessments is that traditionally scholars have attempted to find some-thing positive in Hagen. This is due, no doubt, to the posi-tion of the *Nibelungenlied* as a national epic where ideo-logues from Felix Dahn to Hermann Goering have seen in Hagen the archetype of Teutonic virtue and loyalty.[19] For the poet's contemporaries, however, this was not the case. In the *C version, for example, Hagen is referred to ex-plicitly as "der mordaer Hagene" and "ir morder ungetriu-wer;"[20] and in the *Klage,* he is condemned outright: "[Hagen] ist nu komen an die stat / dâ uns sîn übermuot / nu vil kleinen schaden tuot."[21] The point is that scholars should not automatically assume that the author of the *Klage,* because of his moralizing tone, failed to appreciate hagen's significance in the *Nibelungenlied.* As many have pointed out,[22] the opinions of the times must be taken into consideration. Thus to make a hero out of Hagen, this drinker of human blood, who leads an entire people to de-struction, is, as Helmut Brackert points out, "[eine] Ver-fälschung der Dichtung,"[23] a good example of what Sacker calls forcing the poem to conform to a "preconceived idea of what it *ought* to be."[24]

One preliminary observation to be made about Hagen is that his true protagonist is not Siegfried, with whom he has been too closely linked,[25] but Kriemhild. Even a cur-sory reading reveals that their roles are both parallel and complementary. Despite the importance of Brunhild, it is Kriemhild who dominates the first part while Hagen re-mains in the background only to emerge later when he kills Siegfried and sinks the hoard into the Rhine. In the second part it is Hagen who has center stage while Kriem-hild remains behind the scenes until she kills Hagen and in turn is killed by Hildebrant. This is not to say that the other figures are not important; but if the action of the poem is reduced to its simplest terms, it turns out to be primarily the story of Hagen and Kriemhild. Kriemhild, however, is the less problematic of the two.

The "minneclîche meit" (3) at the beginning of the poem who becomes the "vâlandinne" (1748/2371) at the end cer-tainly has more than her share of human faults. Spoiled, egoistic and possessive, she is, like the other characters of the *Nibelungenlied,* best "viewed from a distance."[26] But it is precisely because of these faults that she is credible and, as Schröder says, a human being of "flesh and blood"[27] who truly becomes a tragic figure. She has, after all, un-wittingly helped to kill the only person she has ever loved. And there is no need to doubt, I think, that Kriemhild loved Siegfried for his person and not for his power and

prestige.[28] The fact that she retreated from her original re-solve never to fall in love (15) shows that she must have had a change of heart when Siegfried appeared on the scene. As Hugo Bekker suggests, her situation is like Isol-de's and she might just as well "have drunk a love po-tion."[29]

Kriemhild is a woman so in love, so smitten with Sieg-fried, that, give her limitations as a human being, she goes completely insane when Siegfried is murdered. We cannot expect from a medieval poet a clinical analysis of her mental collapse; what we get instead is a moving account of her grief which culminates in her tears of blood (1069). The "sacramental" significance of this phenomenon has been treated elsewhere;[30] but it is also possible to see in these tears, by the very intensity of the image they evoke, the precise moment when Kriemhild's mind snaps under the strain of her grief. The brutal murder, the discovery of the body thrown callously before the door, the tears of blood, the final opening of the casket—all this was in-tended by the poet to move his courtly audience and to demonstrate, as Schröder aptly puts it, that Kriemhild's grief hat "einen wahren, innerseelischen Charakter."[31] If the story of Kriemhild is the story of a woman gone mad, then there is no inconsistency in her development. The murderous psychopath we see at the end is the same self-ish young woman we saw at the beginning of the poem who thought she could avoid both *liebe* and *leit* (15). To use Schröder's words, "daß die Rächende eine Leidende war und ist, daß die Leidende eine Liebende war und ist, konstituiert die Einheit der Person wie der Dichtung."[32] The cause of all this grief and madness is Hagen von Tro-nege; and *his* case requires more explanation.

. . . . .

To begin, Hagen is both uncourtly and an outsider at Worms. I say this not because of his origins in the Ger-manic legends, but because of the chasm that separates him from such courtly types as Siegfried and Gunther. Siegfried, despite his pre-courtly beginnings, is the courtly hero *par excellence* whose every move is "an interesting game," an "elaborate frolic."[33] For Hagen however, courtly appearances mean nothing. The mere fact that he can kill Siegfried in a way reserved for animals[34] and then throw the body unceremoniously in front of Kriemhild's door re-veals, to say the least, a total disregard for courtly conven-tion. This is not to say that Hagen never plays the courtly role,[35] but when he does, it is always with an ulterior mo-tive as, for example, in Island where he prefers to stay with the ladies (531) while Siegfried goes to Worms as a messenger. The idyllc scene at Bechelaren, usually consid-ered a high point in Hagen's humanity and courtliness,[36] is a case in point. His seemingly well intended suggestion that Rüdeger's daughter and Giselher marry conceals a darker motive than merely his knowledge that such a mar-riage involving Kriemhild's favorite brother would work to the advantage of the Burgundians.[37] On the contrary, the exact opposite is the case: by effecting an alliance between Worms and Bechelaren, Hagen makes it impossible for Rüdeger to break his oath of layalty to Kriemhild (1265ff.), thus assuring the destruction not only of the Burgundians but of Rüdeger and his men as well. In that agonizing scene where Rüdeger pleads with Kriemhild to be released from his oath, he uses the planned marriage of his daughter and Giselher as his trump card but to not avail (2161). Hagen has seen to it that his "saving clause"[38] about his honor (1266,4) is of no use to him. This is not to say that Hagen had in mind Rüdeger's oath to Kriemhild when he made the marriage proposal at Bechelaren. The truth of the matter is that we never know what Hagen is thinking. We can only agree with Bekker that the poet's "allusion to the girl's fate [1680] suggests that Hagen with his proposal is the agent who brings about the fulfillment of what the poet calls inevitable."[39]

Even when Hagen lies, he does so for reason entirely different from the others at Worms. When Gunther, for example, deceives Siegfried about the Saxon war (884), he has in mind only the preservation of worldly values, in this case, courtly appearances and his reputation as a king. Like Siegfried, when for some unknown reason he gave Brunhild's ring and belt to Kriemhild, Gunther has no idea of the consequences of his acts. The possible ramifications of a murdered Siegfried simply never enter his mind. This is not the case with Hagen: his lies and deceptions lead paradoxically to a truth that points far beyond the exigencies of daily life at court.[40] When he denies killing the fairy man (1568), for example, this lie heads to the higher truth that no one will return alive to Worms (1580,4/1587), a truth made all the more concrete by Hagen's destruction of the boat (1581). The point is that Hagen, regardless of the consequences, inevitably tells the truth while his courtly masters, who are ignorant of the consequences, inevitably lie for the sake of their reputations. Thus while Gunther is spreading his absurd story about the "robbers" (1045,4) who supposedly killed Siegfried, Hagen is standing by Siegfried's body whose wounds bleed profusely in the presence of his murderer.

Hagen's willingness to admit openly his deed, his "unbedingte Offenheit," as one critic calls it,[41] is often seen as a heroic trait, the hallmark of Teutonic virtue.[42] But as Josef Körner pointed out more than fifty years ago, Hagen is loyal and truthful to no one.[43] When, for example, Hagen flaunts his guilt in Kriemhild's face (1790), he is being sadistically cruel, not honest; and when he confesses openly about killing the fairy man (1604) and later to Gunther (1626) about the death of Gelfrat, he is acting the hypocrite and not the brave hero. After all, he himself had destroyed the boat (1581) so that there was no reason to conceal the facts. Had Hagen really been loyal, he would never have kept silent about the river fairies' prophecy of doom (1542). But he does, claiming that his kings would never believe him: "daz waere mînen herren müelîch ze sagene, / daz wir zen Hiunen solden vliesen alle den lîp" (1543). Though the poet does not say, it is probable that the quite opposite was the case, that Gunther, had he known the truth, would have called off the entire expedition. If this is true, then Hagen's famous answer to Kriemhild's question (nu saget, het Hagene, wer hât nâch iu ge-

sant? [1787,1]) is only empty talk, the utterance of a supremely cynical mind:

> "Nâch mir sande niemen," sprach dô Hagene.
> "man ladete her ze lande drîe degene:
> die heizent mine herren, sô bin ich ir man.
> deheiner hovereise bin ich selten hinder in be- stân."[44]
>
> (1788)

To be sure, the words are true. He has in fact never allowed his masters to journey alone; but as their *man,* he should have had their best interests at heart. Whatever Hagen's reasons for leaving Worms, they have little to do with loyalty[45] and nothing to do with respect for "the established order."[46]

D. G. Mowatt suggests that the *Nibelungenlied* is the tragedy of courtly Worms whose "smooth façade" splits apart "with the partial absorption of . . . two strange characters."[47] This is not the place to dispute this idea, but I should like to add that without Hagen this "absorption" could very well have taken place. But Hagen, with his antisocial nature and his irrational insistence that Siegfried must die (870), is the one person who stands in the way of any reconcilitation between what Mowatt calls "the harmonious group" (Worms) and the "identified pair" (Siegfried and Brunhild).[48] Hagen, by his very nature, is "ein absolut Einsamer"[49] whose inability to compromise places him well beyond the pale of any rational conception of social organization. If this is true, then Hagen is as much of a foreign element in Worms as Brunhild and Siegfried. But he is more than just an outsider: he is the *enemy within,* a demonic presence, as it were, in the midst of courtly society.

Gottfried Weber, who sees in Hagen "diesen Abgrund der Dämonie,"[50] has already provided valuable insights into the demonic quality of Hagen's character. It is Carl S. Singer, however, who takes Weber's findings to their logical conclusion when he compares Hagen with Iago, thus offering us in his masterful interpretatation of the sixteenth Aventiure an accurate assessment of Hagen's role in the poem. The poet, he writes, "would . . . have us see throughout the spectacle of [the hunting contest] that Hagen must be the victor, that there can indeed be no contest between Siegfried, who knows and thinks only life, and Hagen, who is sworn to, and possessed by, the powers that control life."[51] There can be no doubt that Hagen is somehow attuned with those perverse foces that run counter to everything positive in life, those same forces that turn *liebe* into *leit.* It is thus no accident that his role is that of "der Voraussagende" and "der Wissende"[52] and that he alone is the only one who *knows* the way to Etzel's court (1524), who *knows* the journey will mean the destruction of all (1210/1458) and who *knows* in advance how other people will act.[53] Thus Hagen's existence is inexplicable and best understood against the background of man's existential plight. To analyze his acts individually, to separate and classify them, leads to a dead end because there is no rational basis underlying anything he does. Siegfried's murder is a case in point.

The traditional reasons that he had to avenge Brunhild's honor, that he envied and hated Siegfried, that he wanted to increase the political power of Worms, are not fully convincing. There is no reason to assume that Hagen cares about Brunhild's honor, this "tiuvels brût" (450,4), as he himself calls her, whose honor he alludes to only twice (864/1790) and who once even insulted him (447). Nor is there any logical basis for Hagen's hatred for Siegfried. On the contrary, Hagen behaves with considerable constraint when Siegfried first arrives upon the scene and even welcomes his assistance in the Saxon war (151). In a similar vein, there is no hard evidence to support Siegfried Beyschlag's contention that Siegfried, through Kriemhild, was making "einen bedrohlichen Anspruch auf Vorrang"[54] or for Bostock's comment that Hagen acts as the "responsible statesman" when he "liquidates" Siegfried.[55] In reality, Siegfried is a harmless fellow[56] who retires to his own lands after his marriage and would have stayed there forever had it not been for Brunhild's ill conceived invitation. Furthermore, Hagen's claim that Gunther would acquire more territory with Siegfried out of the way is both "vague and irrelevant."[57] In fact, Hagen's scheme to avenge Brunhild's honor is, as Körner has already suggested, "nur Deckmotiv für eine tiefer gehende Feindschaft."[58] But this hostility is not directed toward Siegfried, as Körner believes,[59] but toward *anything,* in my view, that runs counter to Hagen's wishes. The point I want to make is that we simply do not know why Hagen kills Siegfried.[60] The act is irrational and inexplicable. And the reason the plan makes no sense is because Hagen, as Singer points out,[61] "simply does not care" about anything.[62] Brunhild's honor, the fate of his kings, his friend Volker,[63] the hoard which he himself sinks into the Rhine[64]— all this means nothing to him. The only thing that matters to Hagen, it seems, is defiance for its own sake. Gottfried Weber suggests that Hagen makes his rebellious attitude into something absolute, "[die] Verabsolutierung heldisch-kraftgeschwellten Trotzes."[65] This is true, but for Weber's *heldisch* I would substitute *pervers;* for it is also possible to see Hagen's much vaunted courage as nothing less than a perverted urge to destroy, an expression of violence for its own sake.[66] Hagen admits as much to Gunther *before* crossing the Danube while the Burgundians are still under the impression that the visit in Gran will be one of peace.

> "Jan' ist mir," sprach Hagene,   "mîn leben niht sô leit,
> daz ich mich welle ertrenken   in disen ünden breit.
> ê sol von mînen handen   ersterben manic man
> in Etzelen landen: des ich vil guoten   willen hân."
>
>   (1530)

There can be little doubt that the prospect of bloodshed is a pleasing one to Hagen.

Indeed, it would not be farfetched to say that the disaster at Gran is Hagen's own creation. To be sure, there were many causes leading up to it: Siegfried's theft of the ring and the belt, Brunhild's jealousy of Kriemhild, Rüdeger's oath, Kriemhild's madness, to name the most important. But these are only isolated links in a long chain of events. It is Hagen who fuses these links together, thus bestowing upon the poem the unity and logic of its action; namely, the gradual and progressive destruction of an entire people. Schröder's interpretation of Hagen's final words to Kriemhild comes to mind: "du hâst iz nâch dinem willen z'einem ende brâht, / und ist ouch rehte ergangen als ich mir hête gedâht." (2370). In Schröder's view, Hagen could just as well have said *nach minen* instead of *dinen willen:* "Denn [Hagen] selbst hat diesen Ausgang herbeiführen helfen und das Seine dazu beigetragen, daß keiner zurückkehrte, wie die Meerfrauen prophezeit hatten."[67] It is Hagen who destroys the boat (1581), who withholds information (1620), who deliberately provokes Kriemhild's wrath (1760ff.) and who conceives (1918) Ortlieb's murder long before it actually happens (1962). From this it would seem that Hagen is intent upon making his own prophecy—"ir habt iu selben widerseit" (1458)—as well as that of the river fairies come true. It is as if he had said: Since you will not listen to me (1458) and since you think I am afraid of Kriemhild's wrath (1463), I shall go with you anyway and prove that you will not come back alive." And this is exactly what Hagen does. From the moment he takes the Burgundians "singlehanded"[68] across the Danube, their fate is sealed and the way is paved for the fulfillment of Hagen's prophecy. The events leading up to the death of Rüdeger will bear this out.

The shield scene is usually interpreted as a grand gesture on Hagen's part, his "überlegenster und schönster Freundesdienst,"[69] which allows Rüdeger to retain both his honor and the salvation of his soul.[70] The truth of the matter is that Rüdeger is at the end of his tether. He had always followed the courtly code and lead an exemplary life. But now for the first time the system fails him. Regardless of whether he helps Kriemhild or the Burgundians, he will violate that Christian and courtly code of ethics that had always been his infallible guide. Friedrich Maurer sums it up nicely: "sein Wollen und seine Pflicht" are no longer one.[71] As Maurer further points out, there is no divine order and harmony in the *Nibelungenlied:* "es gibt nur den Tod, der die Entehrung, das Leid beendet oder verhindert."[72] What this means, though Maurer does not say so, is that there is only one option left to Rüdeger—suicide. When he offers his shield to Hagen, he has already made this decision and establishes a symbolic bond between himself and the one person in the poem who truly understands the nature of the void. Maurer is correct in pointing out that Rüdeger does not die a Christian death; but in place of his suggestion that his death was "Germanic" and "heroic,"[73] I would seize upon his own phrase—"der Abgrund tut sich vor [Rüdeger] auf"—[74] and say that Rüdeger's death is that of a man at the edge of the abyss. In those final moments, before charging into the fray like a raging animal, Rüdeger has become what Hagen is: an irrational and destructive force. Rüdeger's death is Hagen's personal triumph, the triumph of a spirit that always denies.

And with this we come to the true significance of Hagen: he is a destroyer of values, a creator of voids. Kriemhild's love for Siegfried is a case in point. Their marriage should have been the ultimate realization of *êre* and *minne*. But their marriage was also a colossal mismatch, doomed, as Bekker points out,[75] from the moment of its inception. That its failure would mean the death of thousands, is proof enough that the thread that holds man in check from his baser impulses is a slender one. It is Hagen who breaks this thread when he deprives Kriemhild of Siegfried, the one thing in her life which she had raised to an absolute. That this is so, we need only witness the depth of her grief:

> Dô seic si zuo der erden,   daz si niht ensprach.
> die schoenen vreudelôsen   ligen man dô sach.
> Kriemhilde jâmer   wart unmâzen grôz:
> do erschrê si nâch unkrefte   daz al diu kemenâte erdôz
>
> (1009)

Bereft of Siegfried, Kriemhild is at an absolute dead end, "ez ist an sîme lîbe al min vreude gelegen" (1055,4). Her only other link to Siegfried is the hoard; but Hagen even robs her of this. To borrow Bekker's phrase, the hoard for Kriemhild "is. . . . a piece of Siegfried,"[76] an extension of his person, which, if used against Hagen, would be tantamount to a living Siegfried avenging his own murder. The point to be made is that when Hagen robs Kriemhild of both Siegfried *and* the hoard, he creates in her a void so great that she is driven into a madness as black and hopeless as that of King Lear. And because Kriemhild is not only a powerful queen, but a powerful queen gone *mad,* it is a void that swallows up an entire civilization.

. . . . .

By focusing on Hagen and on the fullscale destruction at the end of the poem, it becomes clear that the *Nibelungenlied,* among other things, is a document of man's existential plight. It is Kriemhild who states the central issue of this plight when she proposes to Hagen, "welt ir mir geben widere daz ir mir genomen, / so muget ir noch wol lebende heim zen Burgonden komen" (2367). But Hagen knows what crazed and demented Kriemhild does not: that the irretrievable cannot be retrieved, that nothing lost can be regained. With Gunther's death, which he himself, incidentally, arranges (2368), Hagen is ready for his final triumph: "der [hort] sol dich, vâlandinne, immer wol verholen sîn" (2371,4). Both Siegfried and the hoard, everything that had given meaning to Kriemhild's life, is irrevocably lost;[77] and whatever sanity she still might possess vanishes under the weight of this horrible truth. She kills Hagen with Siegfried's sword, the final link between herself and him; and when she does, the poem has come full circle. The void that Hagen created has taken its due and everything and everyone involved is lost forever in its

depths. Hagen's triumph is to have reduced a once proud and confident queen to a subhuman level of creatural pain and suffering. Like a wounded animal, her cries and shouts of pain are to no avail when Hildebrant finally turns on her. "waz mohte si gehelfen daz si sô groezlîchen schrê?" (2376,4).

Thus to look for anything positive or heroic in Hagen is, in my reading of the poem, to search for something that is not there. Hagen is living proof that a perversity dwells in all things. This is not to say that he is an agent of the devil or a creature of another world. On the contrary, it is a total lack of supernatural qualities that makes him the elusive and fascinating character he is. Hagen is simply Hagen; that is to say, this human being of flesh and blood is as real as the perversity he represents. As J. Stout points out, the compilers of the *Nibelungenlied* "haben [in ihm] das Böse, das Teuflische, den Antichristen personifiziert."[78] Taken to its logical conclusion, Hagen is the living presence of evil in what Bekker calls the "closed self-referential world of the *Nibelungenlied*" which has "no point of reference outside itself" and "no answer to its self-generated destruction".[79]

The poet of the *Nibelungenlied* must have been disillusioned with the optimism and the complacency of his times. To paraphrase Singer, the poem seems to be saying that the man-created values of the courtly world are of no value to man in his "inevitable conflict" with the powers that control and delimit human life. I would add to this that these delimiting powers are God-given *absolutes;* and against them, the pseudo absolutes of *êre* and *minne,* as they are depicted in the courtly figures of the *Nibelungenlied,* are nothing. And yet with all its blood and carnage, the poem can hardly be called a document of nihilism. Grim as it is, there is a degree of justice in the end: Hagen, this negative spirit, gets his just desserts; and in the person of Dietrich von Bern who, in Weber's view, represents "[eine] höhere Geistigkeit,"[80] courtly life seems destined to go on. To be sure, there is no "transcendental superstructure by which the characters can orient themselves and resolve their struggles."[81] But this, I think, was an integral part of the author's method and had nothing to do with his religious convictions. Instead of moralizing, he offered his courtly audience an exaggerated but realistic picture of the terror that lurked beneath the calm surface of courtly life. And, in turn, his courtly listeners were expected to supply the missing "superstructure" and pass judgment in God's name. This, of course, is precisely what happsns in the *Klage* where Kriemhild is saved and Hagen condemned. As R. Pérennec convincingly argues, the *Nibelungenlied* is a secular poem which makes use of "un schéma familier et efficace" to demonstrate more vividly than "la littérature d'inspiration chrétienne" an inescapable fact of existence: "la mort est dans la vie, la force est faiblesse, la sécurité danger."[82]

What the poem seems to be saying—at least in my reading of it—is that the enemy is within man himself, that in every society there is a Hagen or Hagen-like force that threatens to destroy it. The fact that the poem deals with the courtly world of the thirteenth century does not make it any less universal. To paraphrase Robert Frost, there is "something" that does not "love a wall" and there is also something that does not love man's aspirations to success and happiness. The ***Nibelungenlied*** is a "humble and religious"[83] demonstration of this "something." Let us not forget that Kriemhild was once a charming girl who was hated by no one (3,1), who planned to stay beautiful forever (15,3) and who intended to avoid both joy and sorrow (17,3). The poem stands as a warning that despite man's institutions, his cultures and his best intentions, there is yet a higher force that directs his life. As all things must die, so too must joy inevitably turn to sorrow. Why this is so is "something" that no one understands. Indeed, Hagen's final words to Kriemhild (2371), "den schatz den weiz zu niemen wan got unde mîn: / der sol dich, vâlandinne, immer wol verholen sîn" have the same awesome finality as those of Iago when Othello asks him *why* he did it:

Demand me nothing; what you know, you know:
From this time forth I never will speak word.

(Act V, ii)

Notes

1. D. G. Mowatt, "Studies toward an Interpretation of the 'Nibelungenlied,'" *GLL,* 14 (1960/61), 257-270.

2. Hugh Sacker, "On Irony in the *Nibelungenlied:* Two Preliminary Notes," Ibid., 271-281.

3. Hugo Bekker, *The Nibelungenlied: A Literary Analysis* (Toronto: Univ. of Toronto Press, 1971).

4. Mowatt, pp. 261/262.

5. Siegfried Beyschlag, "Das Motiv der Macht bei Siegfrieds Tod," *GRM,* 33 (1951/52), 96-108. Here, p. 105.

6. Mowatt, p. 263 f.

7. Sacker, passim.

8. Bekker, p. 6 et passim.

9. All quotations are from *Das Nibelungelied,* nach der Ausgabe von Karl Bartsch, ed. Helmut de Boor, 17th ed. (Wiesbaden: F. A. Brockhaus, 1963).

10. Bekker, p. x.

11. K. C. King, "The Message of the 'Nibelungenlied'—A Reply," *MLR,* 57 (1962), 541-550. Here, p. 547.

12. P. B. Salmon, "Why does Hagen die?" *GLL,* 18 (1963), 3-13. Here p. 12.

13. Gottfried Weber, *Das Nibelungenlied: Problem und Idee* (Stuttgart: J. B. Metzler, 1963), p. 43.

14. J. K. Bostock, "The Message of the 'Nibelungenlied,'" *MLR,* 55 (1960), 200-212. Here, p. 207.

15. Ursula R. Mahlendorf and Frank J. Tobin, "Hagen: A Reappraisal," *Monatshefte,* 63 (1971), 125-140. Here, p. 130.

16. Rolf Endres, *Einführung in die mittelhochdeutsche Literatur* (Frankfurt am Main: ein Ullstein Buch, No. 2811, 1971), p. 154.

17. *The Nibelungenlied,* trans. A. T. Hatto (Baltimore: Penguin Books, No. L137, 1964), p. 323.

18. Julius Schwietering, *Die deutsche Dichtung des Mittelalters* (Darmstadt, 1957), p. 205.

19. See Helmut Brackert, "Nibelungenlied und Nationalgedanke," *Mediaevalia litteraria: Festschrift für Helmut de Boor zum 80. Geburtstag,* eds. Ursala Henning und Herbert Kolb (Munich: C. HBeck Verlag), 343-364. Here, p. 356. See also *Literatur in der Schule. Band I: Mittelalterliche Texte im Unterricht,* eds. Helmut Brackert, Hannelore Christ, Horst Holzschuh (Munich: C. H. Beck Verlag, 1973), p. 72ff.

20. *Das Nibelungenlied,* ed. Friedrich Zarncke (Leipzig, 1894), stanzas 1282/1681. Quoted after Werner Schröder, "Die Tragödie Kriemhilds im Nibelungenlied," *Nibelungen-Studien* (Stuttgart: J. B. Metzler, 1968), 48-156. Here, p. 156.

21. *Diu Klage,* ed. Karl Bartsch (Darmstadt, 1964), v. 3524ff. Quoted after Endres, p. 164.

22. Schröder, "Tragödie," p. 156; King, p. 543; Endres, p. 147ff.

23. Brackert, p. 349.

24. Sacker, p. 275.

25. For many scholars, the events of the poem can be traced back to Hagen's jealousy of Siegfried. In Weber's view, for example, Hagen envies the "unermeßliche Macht" (p. 44) that Sigfried derives from the hoard (7774); Beyschlag (p. 99) identifies stanza 122f. as the beginning of hostilities between Hagen and Siegfried. See also Werner Hoffman, *Das Nibelungenlied* (Munich: R Oldenbourg Verlag, 1969), p. 75: ". . . Sigfrids Ankunft [hat] seine [Hagens] Stellung in Worms insofern verändert, als hier fortan nicht mehr er, sondern Sigfrid der körperlich stärkste Mann ist (s. schon 130,2-4)."

26. Hatto, p. 323.

27. Schröder, "Tragödie," p. 93.

28. Cf. stanza 294.

29. Bekker, p. 62.

30. See H. B. Willson, "Blood and Wounds in the 'Nibelungenlied,'" *MLR,* 55, (1960), 40-50. Here, p. 42.

31. Schröder, "Tragödie," p. 122.

32. *Ibid.,* p. 112.

33. Carl S. Singer, "The Hunting Contest: An Interpretation of the Sixteenth Aventiure of the *Nibelungenlied, GR,*" 42 (1967), 163-183. Here, p. 170.

34. *Ibid.,* p. 183.

35. Cf. stanza 598.

36. For example, Weber (p. 49) talks of ". . . die Todesahnung, die ihn [Hagen] mild macht für seine Freunde—ins Granitene aber verhärtet für seine Gegenspielerin."

37. See Mahlendorf and Tobin, p. 133.

38. Hatto, p. 162 (note).

39. Bekker, p. 146.

40. This is not to say that Hagen never plays the courtly games when he lies. Cf. stanza 473 where Hagen lies to Brunhild about the whereabouts of Siegfried during the Island contests.

41. Friedrich Panzer, *Das Nibelungenlied: Entstehung und Gestalt* (Stuttgart: W. Kohlhammer, 1955), p. 240.

42. See Hermann Schneider, *Heldendichtung, Geistlichendichtung, Ritterdichtung* (Heidelberg, 1943), p. 381: "Er ist der gute Gefolgsmann, der die Beschimpfung seiner Königin, seines Könighauses rächt; heimtückische Züge fehlen nicht, aber von dem kleinlichen Bösewichte, dem schlechten Kerl, den spätere Bearbeiter aus ihm machen wollten, rückt er ab."

43. Jose Körner, *Das Nibelungenlied* (Leipzig, (1921), p. 82.

44. But see Mahlendorf and Tobin (p. 129) for whom stanza 1788 represents the directness and simplicity of Hagen's concept of duty.

45. See Endres, p. 147ff.

46. Mahlendorf and Tobin, p. 128.

47. Mowatt, p. 263.

48. *Ibid.,* p. 264.

49. Weber, p. 56.

50. *Ibid.,* p. 45.

51. Singer, pp. 179/183.

52. Burghart Wachinger, *Studien zum Nibelungenlied* (Tübingen: Max Niemeyer Verlag, 1960), p. 36.

53. Mahlendorf and Tobin (p. 132) talk of "Hagen's uncanny ability to predict people's reactions. . . ."

54. Beyschlag, p. 100.

55. Bostock, p. 207.

56. Bostock (p. 205) refers to Siegfried as "the simpleminded Sivrit."

57. See D. G. Mowatt & Hugh Sacker, *The Nibelungenlied: An Interpretative Commentary* (Toronto: Univ. of Toronto Press, 1967), p. 86.

58. Körner, p. 77.

59. Cf. Körner's interpretation (p. 77) of stanza 993: "Wer mir [Hagen] überlegen ist, den hasse ich."

60. But see Bakker (p. 134): "And so we must conclude that Brunhild's and Hagen's reasons for wishing Siegfried dead, though very different, issue from the same discovery: each of them sees Siegfried as a king whose error is his love for Kriemhild and his consequent failure to assert his status as the strongest king."

61. Singer, p. 179.

62. Bekker (p. 130) develops this same theme further.

63. Körner (p. 80) compares Hagen's friendship for Volker with "Wallen-steins Liebe zu Max Piccolomini." For an opposite view, see Bekker (p. 143) who sees "no particularly warm personal feelings" for Volker "on Hagen's part."

64. Bekker (p. 131) suspects that Hagen fully intended to use the hoard (1137). In my view, however, Hagen sank the hoard in the Rhine so that no one would ever use it. It is thus quite probable that Hagen, as Bekker suggests (p. 131), was prepared to break the oath he made to the kings in stanza 1140.

65. Weber, p. 56.

66. Endres (p. 146f.) talks of Hagen's "destruktive Komplexe."

67. Schröder, "Zum Problem der Hortfrage im Nibelungenlied," *Nibelungenlied-Studien* (Stuttgart: J. B. Metzler, 1968), p. 178.

68. Sacker, p. 279.

69. Hans Naumann, Höfische Symbolik: Rüdegers Tod," *DVjs,* 10 (1932), 387-403. Here, p. 393.

70. *Ibid.*

71. Friedrich Maurer, *Leid* (Bern and Munich: Francke Verlag, 1951), p. 34.

72. *Ibid.,* p. 37.

73. *Ibid.*

74. *Ibid.,* p. 34.

75. See Bekker's chapters "Brunhild: the Kingship Motif" (p. 69ff) and "Brunhild: the *Eigenmann* Motif" (p. 84ff.).

76. Bekker, p. 68.

77. Cf. Schröder, "Hortfrage," p. 173: "Nicht das ihr geraubte Gold, sondern den ermordeten Sivrit fordert sie zurück, nicht etwas theoretisch Mögliches, sondern etwas absolut Unmögliches."

78. J. Stout, *Und ouch Hagene* (Groningen: J. B. Wolters, 1963), p. 325.

79. Bekker, p. 155.

80. Weber, p. 55.

81. Mahlendorf and Tobin, p. 139.

82. R. Pérennec, "Remarques sur la seizième aventure de la Chanson des Nibelungen, *Etudes Germaniques,* 28 (1973), 153-166. Here, p. 164.

83. Bostock, p. 201.

Francis G. Gentry (essay date 1976)

SOURCE: "Hagen and the Problem of Individuality in the *Nibelungenlied,*" *Monatshefte,* Vol. 68, No. 1, 1976, pp. 5-12.

[*In the following essay, Gentry maintains that the* Nibelungenlied *explores the issue of feudal bonds while it instructs its audience that an individual moral decision can override law and custom.*]

I

The history of *Nibelungenlied** scholarship is a fascinating chapter within the larger scope of Germanic philology.[1] More than any other work of the *Blütezeit* the *Nibelungenlied* has attracted researchers for reasons other than purely aesthetic. Only in the last thirty years has the emphasis of research been shifted to an evaluation of the epic as a literary work.[2] One of the main problems of this modern criticism has been to disentangle the *Nibelungenlied* from its contemporary epic companions, the Arthurian romances, most notably those of Hartmann and Wolfram. As a result the *Nibelungenlied* is compared either expressly or tacitly with the romances and is evaluated in their terms. For many the *Nibelungenlied* is a Christian/courtly work, while for others it is Germanic/heroic, depending upon how many common features the epic is seen by the individual scholar to share with the Arthurian tales.[3] Although these views do not necessarily bring any greater clarification of the meaning of the *Nibelungenlied,* their presence is quite understandable. The Arthurian society, with its emphasis on youth, harmony, and idealized knighthood as well as on deeds of great nobility and compassion, has a far greater attraction for the researcher than the Nibelungen society which is a heady mixture of violence, barbarity, and cruelty, relieved only occasionally by lighter moments of beauty and joy. Further, the resolution of the moral conflicts in the *Nibelungenlied* does not take place in an atmosphere of joy and reconciliation, but rather in one of tragedy and tears.

Faced with this state of affairs, it is small wonder that the epic often suffers by comparison with the optimistic Arthurian romance. Since the idealistic ambience of the romance is taken as the norm, it is difficult not to view the *Nibelungenlied* as being antithetical to the beauty of these other works and their central theme, the dignity of the individual. Such a view, however, imposes upon the work a mode of thought which is alien to the matter of the *Nibelungenlied* in that it emanates from critical reflection not so much upon the *Nibelungenlied* itself but upon other works. This process tends to obscure the intention of the poet and the meaning of his work. If the *Nibelungenlied* does have points in common with the Arthurian romances, they should be elicited by an analysis of the epic itself. Thus the starting point of the investigation should not be the question how does the *Nibelungenlied* reflect the mode of the Arthurian romance, but rather why did some unknown person around 1200 take up a tale which had its ultimate roots in events which took place several hundred years previous and fashion an epic *apparently* so completely out of place, when compared with the creations of his contemporaries.

In recent years one critical approach has appeared which seems best suited to answer this question. It postulates that the poet is making a statement about the social and political conditions of his age, namely about the dominant structure of feudalism.[4] Feudalism is a system of relationships in which individuals are bound together by solemn oaths of loyalty. In different countries it manifested itself in various ways, but the fundamental principle of a pledge of service to someone of a higher station and the acceptance of this pledge is the most common feature.[5] Mixed in with feudal theory of political relationships are also the ancient communal ties of the Germanic tribes described by Tacitus, so that by 1200 the feudal system in Germany had a complex structure influencing all aspects of social and political life. And, as Walter Ullmann has pointed out, it was a system in which the individual was an important factor:

> One thing seems clear, and that is that the feudal arrangement, at whatever level it was practiced, of necessity presupposed the responsibility of the individual. It was not just a matter of receiving a command or a law, but it was necessary to employ one's own critical faculties.[6]

To determine if the Nibelungen poet is addressing himself to problems connected with the feudal bond and the roles of the individuals who comprise it, the two major scenes of discord within the *Nibelungenlied,* Siegfried's murder and the combat between Rüdeger and the Burgundians, will be singled out for consideration. In both episodes the conflict between that which is seen to be legal and personal obligation is given prominence and is commented on by the poet. In order to view this conflict at close hand and thereby get a glimpse of the possible purpose of the poet and the meaning of his work, the actions and motives of the major protagonist in both scenes, Hagen, will be analyzed.

This task is somewhat complicated because few figures in German literature have managed to arouse such strong passions in scholars as Hagen of Tronje. Indeed it is not even possible to say that scholarly opinion about Hagen is divided; it is fragmented. Gottfried Weber views Hagen as "dämoniegeladen".[7] Bert Nagel sees in Hagen the Germanic hero, the absolute opposite of the Christian knight.[8] For Hugo Bekker, Hagen remains the reprehensible traitor, all of whose actions originate from his treachery.[9] Bodo Mergell, on the other hand, believes to glimpse Hagen in his final scene with Kriemhild as standing "stellvertretend vor Gott," while David G. Mowatt and Hugh Sacker suggest the possibility that Hagen is a latent homosexual.[10] If, however, the thesis that the poet wishes to examine the feudal problematic and, further, to comment on his characters' conception of their responsibilities within this relationship is used as the starting point, a less sensational evaluation of Hagen and his actions can be achieved.[11]

II

At the Burgundian court Hagen functions as the chief vassal of the king, a position which he zealously fulfills. His one concern is to uphold and preserve the honor and integrity of his lord, regardless of the consequences. Hagen has responsibility toward Siegfried only insofar as the latter is a friend and ally of the Burgundians. For Hagen Siegfried is simply a means to an end, that end being the greater honor of his king. Until the quarrel of the queens there is no indication of personal feelings on his part toward Siegfried, neither friendship nor enmity. In all the adventures which the Burgundians undertake until Siegfried's marriage, namely the Saxon War and the wooing expedition to Island, Hagen consistently manipulates to include Siegfried in the plans, ostensibly to insure that nothing goes awry. Once Kriemhild has publicly insulted Brunhild, however, Hagen feels compelled to intervene directly because through this insult the honor of his king has been attacked, and he must act decisively to erase this blot.

It is primarily the murder of Siegfried which has earned Hagen the opprobrium of most critics. Most recently Ursula Mahlendorf and Frank Tobin have attempted to view the problem free of emotional excess and in the light of medieval law.[12] Their basic argument is that the characters of the **Nibelungenlied,** but especially Gunther and Hagen, violate principles both of form and law. Gunther does so by not adhering to proper legal formality when Brunhild lodges her complaint against Kriemhild and later by not convening a court after the *Bahrprobe* (pp. 230-232). Hagen, through his actions, violates the spirit of the law, even if he does abide by the form (pp. 233-235). Gunther, by his support of Hagen both in the murder and the subsequent theft of the treasure, places the entire Burgundian society outside of the law and proper form (pp. 234-235). The authors' view that Siegfried's death and the events leading up to it should be considered as a legal problem is quite correct. However, by concentrating on the expected form surrounding a legal case and by reliance on a later written code of law (*Sachsenspiegel*) they neglect the possibility that according to the law which had force at the time of the **Nibelungenlied**-namely that which the *audience* would consider to have validity-Siegfried's murder was *legal*. Further the poet is not saying that Gunther and Hagen are *ungereht* but rather *ungetriuwe*. The law which had validity at this time, and indeed for centuries thereafter, in spite of written codes, is customary law.[13] Therefore, the question should not concern matters of form but rather should be: was Hagen justified, according to customary law, to take the life of Siegfried? The answer must be yes. The ancient concept of *Blutrache* was a 'legitimate' and viable force throughout the Middle Ages.[14] Although the *treuga dei* initiated by the Church and the various proclamations of *Landfrieden* by the emperors attempted to curtail the taking of blood revenge, their general lack of effectiveness is attested to by the fact that the taking of revenge was banned absolutely under all circumstances only in 1495.[15] Also because *Blutrache* is part of Germanic customary law and had, therefore, the force of tradition and communal consensus behind it, it would be favored over any written edict.[16] Further, by feudal times an insult was considered to be a blood offense (Zacharias) so that the legal basis for Hagen's action is apparently sound. Grotesque as it may seem, it appears that Hagen acts from the noblest of motives, to avenge the insult done to his queen and, by extension, his king. Indeed Hagen, himself, states the above as the sole reason for his murderous attack on Siegfried on several occasions (864; 873), and most emphatically during his confrontation with Kriemhild when the Burgundians arrive at Etzel's court:

> Er sprach: "waz sol des mêre?   der rede is nû genuoc.
> ich binz aber Hagene   der Sîfriden sluoc,
> den helt ze sînen handen.   wie sêre er des engalt
> daz diu vrouwe Kriemhilt   die schoenen Prünhilden schalt! . . .
>
> (1790)

But in spite of the authority of custom Hagen is castigated by the poet for faithfully discharging his duties. The murder is decried in the strongest possible terms, as *untriuwe*.[17] By so doing the poet is denying unconditional validity to this feudal practice and is unequivocally saying that the ancient principle of *Blutrache* which had been assimilated within the feudal system is wrong. For although custom demanded Siegfried's death, conscience did not, a fact which Gunther recognized earlier when pressed by Hagen to take revenge:

> Dô sprach der künic selbe: "er'n hât uns niht getân
> niwan guot und êre;   man sol in leben lân.
> was tuoc ob ich dem recken   waere nu gehaz?
> er was uns ie getriuwe   und tet vil weclîche daz."
>
> (868)

Here Gunther has the opportunity to act in accordance with a more humane ethos of peace and reconciliation. He has already accepted Siegfried's explanation of innocence (860) and is willing to let matters stand. In the face of his chief advisor, however, Gunther is not strong enough to prevail, to do that which he knows to be right. He sacrifices his friend and ally to the dictates of the law and thereby abdicates his individual responsibilities toward him. While the matter is legally defensible, it is morally wrong. By slaying Siegfried Hagen has fulfilled his obligations to Gunther, yet in the arena of morality he has committed an unjust act, as has Gunther for assenting to the deed. In the murder of Siegfried the poet is not lamenting improper legal procedures but rather an improper moral action permissible within the existing legal and social structure To stress his view of what the correct behavior in such a situation should be, the poet returns to the conflict between that which is legally admissable and that which is morally right in "âventiure 37."

III

Just as Hagen has managed to win the disfavor of most critics of the **Nibelungenlied,** Rüdeger of Bechlarn in like measure has won their sympathy.[18] No other character in the work is so universally loved and respected. Rüdeger is the gentle surrogate for Etzel with Kriemhild, and he naively believes that the noble love of his lord will help

Siegfried's widow forget her sorrow (1234). His probity is so well known that Gunther allows him to state the purpose of his visit immediately, even though that is not the proper form within the feudal system (1192). Rüdeger is the friend of the Burgundians and especially of Hagen whom he knew when Hagen was a hostage at Etzel's court. He is the gracious host and giftgiver when the Burgundians remain at Bechlarn on their journey to Gran. He is also the proud father who gives his daughter in marriage to Giselher. Thus before the climactic battle Rüdeger stands in close personal bonds with the Burgundians. Added to his later difficulty but not qualitatively altering his relationship is the fact that he also escorts the Burgundians to Gran, imposing the further obligation of safe conduct on him. Completing the picture of Rüdeger's obligations to all parties are his feudal ties to Etzel and Kriemhild, supplemented by the formal oath of protection he swore to Kriemhild while he was at Worms (1258).

Even after the battle has started, Rüdeger, seeking to uphold his feelings of responsibility toward the Burgundians, attempts to remain neutral. Only upon the pleading of Etzel and Kriemhild does he succumb and agree to abide by his feudal duties, in spite of the fact that he knows he will be doing wrong. He will lose his soul (2150), and all his virtues such as *êre, triuwe,* and *zuht* will be gone (2153). Rüdeger feels himself torn between two opposing loyalties. Legally, however, Rüdeger should experience no conflict since by entering the battle he is only doing that which is required of him under law, the defense of his lord. Etzel certainly has the right to call on Rüdeger for assistance since, in his view, he has been unjustly attacked. Rüdeger's attempt to renounce his obligations to Etzel through the *diffidatio* (2157) must be viewed as a final desperate act.[19] Etzel refuses to release him from his bond, and Rüdeger cannot now abandon his lord in this moment of gravity. To do so would be to his everlasting dishonor. In like manner are his later statements concerning his obligations to the Burgundians as his guests and relations through marriage (2159-2161) to be seen, feeble attempts to avoid the inevitable. For in such a case his feudal responsibilities override any others he may have, even according to one source, blood kin, something the Burgundians were not.[20]

Rüdeger is clearly in an impossible situation, morally. His king holds him to his feudal obligations, and the Burgundians refuse to reliquish him from their ties of friendship (2179). Like Gunther in Part I, Rüdeger here recognizes that his adherence to law is questionable, and also like Gunther he is unable to assert his individuality and make the correct moral decision. What the proper mode of behavior should have been is to be shown by what appears to be the most unlikely of persons, Hagen. For as Rüdeger sorrowfully prepares to do battle, Hagen calls to him and bids that they should talk some more (2193). Further he complains that the shield which Gotelind gave him has been destroyed and he appeals to Rüdeger to give him his own shield (2195). Rüdeger willingly does so with the wish that Hagen return with it to Worms (2196). This simple exchange has given Rüdeger one last chance to

evidence his noble nature, and the effect it has on Hagen is striking. For after he has received the shield from Rüdeger, he laments:

> "Sô wê mir dirre maere",   sprach aber Hagene.
> "wir heten ander swaere   sô vil ze tragene:
> sul wir mit friunden strîten,   daz sî got gekleit."
>
> (2200, 1-3)

He goes on to say:

> "Nu lôn'ich iu der gâbe,   vil edel Rüedegêr
> swie halt gein iu gebâren   dise recken hêr,
> daz nimmer iuch gerüeret   in strîte hie mîn hant,
> ob ir si alle slüeget   die von Burgonden lant."
>
> (2201)

With this statement Hagen has discarded, for this encounter, his feudal *triuwe* to his lords.[21] In essence, then, Hagen is being *ungetriuwe* toward his kings, and can no longer be considered the perfect vassal. Hagen, who killed Siegfried to preserve the honor of his lord, now chooses to disregard his feudal obligation in favor of his personal one to Rüdeger when the threat of physical danger is much more immediate than in the previous episode. Astonishing as this turn in events may seem at first glance, the Nibelungen poet has been slowly preparing the way for the replacement of *der grimme Hagene* by Hagen, *trôst der Nibelunge.*[22] This process of "rehabilitation" begins as the Burgundians are riding out from Worms toward Gran. The poet says of him, "er was den Nibelungen ein helflîcher trôst" (1526, 2). This appelation is later repeated by Dietrich von Bern as the warriors arrive at Etzel's court (1726, 4). He has been specially greeted by Rüdeger and his wife, and Etzel, once he recognizes his old friend, cannot see anything sinister about him (1754). Clearly, then, the poet wishes to move away from Hagen, the slayer of Siegfried, and his *untriuwe* and emphasize now his good qualities. For it is precisely this new side of Hagen, his noble nature, which the poet chooses to accent when he has Hagen discard his vassal loyalty in favor of his friendship with Rüdeger.

In this scene the poet has utilized the character of Hagen to the best possible advantage. For by having Hagen make the decision to do what, under the circumstances, is morally right but legally improper, he has left no doubt as to his attitude toward the responsibilities of individuals within the feudal system. The bond of friendship which united Gunther and Siegfried and Rüdeger and the Burgundians has more moral weight than the legal considerations in those instances when the cause to break the former is unjust. In the eyes of the poet no provocation is sufficient for blood revenge. Thus Hagen's insistence that Siegfried be killed and that the law be followed leads to his condemnation. In "âventiure 37" when he acts in an unlawful manner he is not criticized by the poet, not even by his king! Rüdeger, on the other hand, expresses his certain knowledge that what he is doing goes against morality to the extent that his soul will be lost. In both instances the individuals who had the possibility to avert tragedy, Gunther and Rüdeger, were not strong enough to assert their individuality. Hagen, on the one occasion on which he experiences this conflict, betrays no uncertainty and acts without hesitation. His action is not enough to undo all the forces which have been set in motion, but it is sufficient to give Rüdeger a chance to engage in the battle with some measure of honor and, more importantly, shows the members of the feudal audience that in instances of moral conflict it is possible to go against law and custom and still retain one's honor and worth as an individual.

The stress on individual moral decision leads to a new evaluation of the *Nibelungenlied* and illustrates that the epic is not such an anomaly within the courtly period, but rather has the great theme of the individual in common with the Arthurian romances. But unlike the romances in which the individual is set apart from his society and achieves his own higher, more intimate calling, the individual in the *Nibelungenlied* is seen as an integral part of his society. And for that society to function, to be considered a just and moral organization, it is the duty of each member to behave in a moral and responsible manner, not merely for his own good but for that of society as a whole. The poet is not working within an idealized atmosphere with ideal heroes, but rather he operates within a definable political structure which threatens, in his view, to hinder the moral decision-making ability of the individual on occasions. His goal is to allow the feudal system and its adherents the opportunity to achieve their potential. By taking the matter of the ancient legends of Siegfried and the Nibelungen and by restructuring it to apply to the contemporary situation of the feudal system, the Nibelungen poet has presented his audience not with an antiquarian conceit but either consciously or unconsciously follows in the tradition of the ancient singers who sought not only to entertain but also to edify their listeners with their songs.

Notes

The basis of this study is ms. B. All quotations and stanza numbers are taken from the Karl Bartsch edition of *Das Nibelungenlied,* ed. Helmut deBoor, 17th ed. (Wiesbaden: Brockhaus Verlag, 1963).

1. Most recently presented in: Werner Hoffmann, *Mittelhochdeutsche Heldendichtung* (Berlin: Erich Schmidt Verlag, 1974), pp. 69-76.

2. See: Francis G. Gentry, "Trends in *Nibelungenlied* Research since 1949: A Critical Review," *Amsterdamer Beiträge zur älteren Germanistik,* 7 (1974), 125-139.

3. See among others: Friedrich Maurer, *Leid, Studien zur Bedeutungs- und Problemgeschichte besonders in den großen Epen der staufischen Zeit,* 3rd ed. (Bern & München: Francke Verlag, 1964), pp. 13-38; Bodo Mergell, "*Nibelungenlied* und höfischer Roman," *Euphorion,* 45 (1950), 305-336; Bert Nagel, *Das Nibelungenlied. Stoff, Form, Ethos* (Frankfurt/M: Hirschgraben Verlag, 1965); Walter Johannes Schröder,

"*Das Nibelungenlied.* Versuch einer Deutung," *PBB* (Halle), 76 (1954/55), 56-156; Gottfried Weber, *Das Nibelungenlied. Problem und Idee* (Stuttgart: Metzler Verlag, 1963).

Of the above Maurer and Schröder view the *Nibelungenlied* as being basically Germanic/heroic, while Nagel and Mergell lean toward the Christian/courtly interpretation. Weber believes that the Nibelungen poet was seeking a new concept "eines germanisch-heldisch-christlichen Gott-Mensch-Welt-Bildes." (p. 194).

4. See Gentry, 136-139.

5. Marc Bloch, *Feudal Society,* trans. L. A. Manyon (Chicago: University of Chicago Press, 1964), I, pp. 145-162; F. L. Ganshof, *Feudalism,* 3d ed., trans. Philip Grierson (New York & Evanston: Harper & Row, 1964), pp. 72-75.

6. Walter Ullmann, *The Individual and Society in the Middle Ages* (Baltimore: The Johns Hopkins Press, 1966), p. 65.

7. Weber, p. 58.

8. Nagel, p. 268.

9. Hugo Bekker, *Das Nibelungenlied: A Literary Analysis* (Toronto: University of Toronto Press, 1971), pp. 124-126, 133, 135-136.

10. Mergell, pp. 322-323; David Mowatt & Hugh Sacker, *The Nibelungenlied: An Interpretative Commentary* (Toronto: University of Toronto Press, 1967), p. 92.

11. Hoffmann, pp. 84-85.

12. Ursula Mahlendorf & Frank Tobin, "Legality and Formality in the *Nibelungenlied,*" *Monatshefte,* 66 (1974), pp. 225-238.

13. Ullmann, pp. 59-60; Fritz Kern, *Recht und Verfassung im Mittelalter* (Darmstadt: Wissenschaftliche Buchgesellschaft, 1965), p. 32; Heinrich Brunner, *Grundzüge der deutschen Rechtsgeschichte,* 3d ed. (Leipzig: Duncker & Humblot, 1908), p. 97.

14. Rainer Zacharias, "Die Blutrache im deutschen Mittelalter," *ZfdA,* 91 (1962), 167-201, here, 182-188.

15. Brunner, pp. 164-165.

16. Ullmann, pp. 59-60; Kern, p. 32.

17. Stanzas: 876, 1-2; 915, 4; 988, 3-4; 1074, 1-2; 971, 4; 887, 3; 911, 4; 916, 1-2.

18. The literature on Rüdeger and his dilemma generally accepts the fact that the poet wished to portray Rüdeger as a decent honorable man. The reader is directed to a recent study by Jochen Splett in which the various theories about Rüdeger are critically treated: *Rüdiger von Bechlarn* (Heidelberg: Winter Verlag, 1968). A less charitable view of Rüdeger is held by Weber who refers to him as a "höfischer Ehrgeizling" (p. 99) and a "Kulturchrist" (p. 94). A similar, but less radical, view has been recently of-

fered by Hugo Bekker, "Rüdeger von Bechlarn and Dietrich von Bern," *Monatshefte,* 66 (1974), pp. 239-253.

19. deBoor, FN 2157; Peter Wapnewski, "Rüdigers Schild: Zur 37. Aventiure des *Nibelungenliedes,*" *Euphorion,* 54 (1960), 380-410, here, 390.

20. Bloch, I, p. 234.

21. The significance of this action has been passed over by scholars with the exception of Peter Wapnewski, pp. 396-398 and Hoffmann, pp. 84-85.

22. For a fuller presentation of the change in Hagen's character see: Francis G. Gentry, *Triuwe and Vriunt in the Nibelungenlied* (Amsterdam: Rodopi Verlag, 1975), pp. 77-79.

Michael Curschmann (essay date 1977)

SOURCE: "The Concept of the Oral Formula as an Impediment to Our Understanding of Medieval Oral Poetry," *Medievalia et Humanistica,* No. 8, 1977, pp. 63-76.

[*In the following essay, Curschmann contends that dogmatic advocates of the theory of oral-formulaic composition have rendered a disservice to* Nibelungenlied *studies by, among other things, relying too much on scientific analysis and failing to take proper notice of the nature of literature in the Middle Ages.*]

Over the past quarter-century or so, the Theory of Oral-Formulaic Composition has exerted the most profound influence in several disciplines that have to do with epic literature and related genres—living, ancient, medieval, European, Asian, African.[1] It has set in motion and continues to inform a truly international and interdisciplinary process of re-evaluation of traditional critical norms. In view of this it may seem odd at first that Germanic—more specifically, German—studies have been rather slow to respond. Or, to put it differently and a little more precisely, why is it that, while a fair number of Germanists from this side of the Atlantic have done their best to promote the cause of this theory, there has, until recently, been only the faintest echo from the other side?

Up to a point, American scholars are justified in chastising their German counterparts for a certain lack of past comprehension and present interest. But the situation is not quite as simple as Ruth Hartzell Firestone makes it sound when she says that "German scholarship could neither understand nor accept the implications of [John] Meier's observations [on the nature of oral traditions] at that time [1909]" or that even Theodor Frings and Maximilian Braun, his Slavist colleague, failed "to comprehend fully the nature of oral composition."[2] Notions such as Meier's have, at least in some areas (e.g., the ballad, and folksong in general), played an important role in twentieth-century German scholarship; the work of Frings and Braun, practically contemporaneous with Parry's, resulted in a differ-

ent, not less valid, theory of oral composition;[3] at least in one case, which will be discussed later, the concept of multiple authorship of a traditional text was arrived at without recourse to any particular theory; and as a result of all this, German Germanists might, in turn, be justified in regarding as an exercise in single-minded quantification much of what goes on in the relentless pursuit of the Theory of Oral-Formulaic Composition.

Useful as it is, *The Haymes Bibliography of the Oral Theory* (1973) also raises a clear warning signal. Undertakings of this type are a sure sign that their subject is becoming academic, frozen in its own original premises. The Oral Theory, or, for short, the Theory, deserves a better fate, and it is particularly in this context of critical discussion of some fundamental questions that recent developments in medieval German studies merit attention and comment.

For medieval studies, in general, the most fundamental of these questions has, of course, always been whether it is legitimate at all to apply a theory developed pragmatically in the field of a living tradition to medieval literary production. Before turning to the text that was bound to become the *pièce de résistance* in any systematic discussion of basic issues, the **Nibelungenlied,** I should therefore like to illustrate, with three concrete examples, the general spectrum of attitudes that have been taken in this regard. (1) Armin Wishard's call for a "revaluation of the *Spielmannsepen*" provides an example of unquestioning acceptance, including the acceptance of Milman Parry's original definition of the formula which quite a few recent studies in other fields have found in need of modification.[4] (2) Ruth Hartzell Firestone has investigated a different *corpus,* texts from the thirteenth-century Dietrich cycle. Tempered by several reservations regarding the direct applicability of the Theory in such cases, for example, the question of end rhyme versus assonance, her initial research produced statistics which she judged to be inconclusive, although three of the five poems revealed a formula density exceeding the accepted minimum requirement for orally composed texts (p. 3). Submitting to this verdict, she attempts to clarify the picture through an application of Vladimir Propp's descriptive method of folktale analysis, thereby replacing one extraneous theory by another, rather than meeting the texts on their own ground. (3) Lars Lönnroth, on the other hand, to quote an example from Scandinavian studies, has taken full account of the special living conditions of his sources, that is, the specifically North-Germanic combination of poetry and prose in the Sagas. In this context the Eddic lays appear to him as "carefully polished products of poetic craftsmanship, as rhetorical and dramatic showpieces meticulously preserved from one performance to the next, where they would be the especially esteemed highlights of a legendary and, presumably, highly variable prose story." That does not exclude the possibility "that a certain *element* of oral-formulaic improvisation sometimes entered the performance when the performer's memorization was less than perfect" (Lönnroth's emphasis).[5] The Theory has provided the incentive to take another close look at specifically medieval conditions of delivery and transmission, and it remains extremely useful in matters of detail as well, precisely because it is being introduced with critical restraint.

For anyone who is at all inclined to consider certain medieval texts in terms of oral traditions that produce them, the *Nibelungenlied* is probably the most interesting (and challenging) German text, and, conversely, it is also the text which stands to gain most from such attention. The main point at issue is, naturally, the mode of composition of that work which has been preserved in over thirty manuscripts and manuscript fragments representing, basically, three versions, which are, in turn, represented by three thirteenth-century manuscripts, A, B, and C. However, this question is inextricably bound up with two other considerations: How and in what form did the material develop from the late Migration Period to the time around 1200, and how do we explain the considerable textual diversity which exists between A, B, and C, as well as within each of these groups? Several recent studies have attempted to clarify this picture in one way or another and from different points of view.[6]

The first of these, by Helmut Brackert, looks primarily at the history of the text after its codification, without advancing any firm conclusions as to what exactly accounts for this diversity. Brackert's meticulous investigation of manuscript readings directly challenges the basic assumption underlying the classical stemma established by Wilhelm Braune: that the three main branches of the tradition can be subsumed under one archetype and, beyond that, one original. One must assume some form of oral interference throughout the thirteenth century, second injections of "genuine" Nibelungen material, and at the beginning of the written tradition known to us stand several oral versions. The existence of one poet who "was greater than all the others" (Brackert, p. 170) and to whom the text owes its high degree of internal cohesiveness can be acknowledged, but his version has no higher claim to authenticity than any of the other oral productions that were in use concurrently during, as well as after, the period of incipient codification of the material.

Based as it is on simple, if highly imaginative and trenchant, textual criticism, and not on any particular theory of poetic diction, Brackert's analysis has indeed yielded the most persuasive evidence so far of the presence of a strong oral element in the *Nibelungenlied* tradition well into the thirteenth century. It is in the area of manuscript diffusion and all its aspects, the specifically medieval condition of distribution, that any further explication of the *Nibelungenlied* in terms of its oral past and present should have begun or, at the very least, looked for support or corrective evidence.

But that would have meant giving up the criterion of formulaic usage as the chief, if not sole, determinant and characteristic of oral tradition, and in this respect advocates of the Theory in the context of medieval literature are entirely dogmatic. It never even occurred to Edward Haymes, who of course knew Brackert's study, to weave this notion of multiple authorship at least into his overall conclusion, which consistently speaks of "the" *Nibelungenlied* (p. 107). Haymes's own approach is essentially synchronic, and he simply gives statistics based on the vulgate—statistics for two formulaic systems, with a view not only to demonstrating formulaic content but also to relating formulaic usage to metrical structure.[7] Comparing these to similar statistics obtained from a contemporary example of highly literate narrative, Gotfrid's *Tristan,* he concludes that the *Nibelungenlied* is an orally composed work.

Franz Baeuml's approach is more explicitly past-oriented, at least in his first paper, written in collaboration with Donald Ward. He has analysed some fifty stanzas from various segments of the poem, which show a particularly high degree of formulaic density, and which he uses to counter the methodological premises underlying Andreas Heusler's classical reconstruction of the poem's genesis. This verse material is, Baeuml and Ward say, obviously of an oral tradition, and this, in turn, means that a) many details that Heusler attributed to the last master are, in fact, much older and b) no precise description of earlier stages in the development of the material can be given, since oral traditions do not produce fixed texts.

In general terms, at least, Haymes and Baeuml are in agreement by viewing the *Nibelungenlied* as a poem with an exclusively oral past. This may be conceded as a matter of heuristic principle, despite the fact that, as I shall discuss later, the formulaic diction of the extant text is no doubt multiple in origin.

Regarding the manner in which the extant text was *composed,* Baeuml and Haymes are in agreement only insofar as they, unlike Brackert, recognize only one text, which must, by definition, have been written. Beyond that, their views differ substantially. For Haymes, the *Nibelungenlied,* as we have it, is a dictated (or self-dictated) oral composition (p. 104), in line with his *dictum* that "as long as a text displays all the characteristics of traditional language, it is, if only in the technical sense, an 'oral' text" (p. 37). For Baeuml, the transposition of the narrative from oral into written form was "not the work of an oral but that of an educated, courtly poet" (p. 362).

In the context of his first article this statement came as an abrupt aside open to misunderstanding, but Baeuml has since clarified his position in a paper written in collaboration with Agnes Bruno. In the earlier instance stanzas were selected for their value in the argument against Heusler. Taken as a whole, the poem is actually very uneven in formulaic density per stanza (from 85 to 25 percent), and this means that we have here a learned, literate poet who, in turn, worked from a dictated text.[8] Of the latter, Baeuml and Bruno say that, as long as we have the technique (means) of composition in mind and the text is predominantly formulaic, "it belongs to the oral tradition, even if it was composed on the typewriter" (p. 485).

Two comments are in order at this point. It is remarkable—and revealing—that two studies for which formulaic usage is the common critical denominator can come to such different conclusions regarding the status of the work under examination. Moreover, the formulations used by both scholars to characterize as oral the dictated text assumed by both in effect dispose of the Theory as a meaningful tool of literary criticism, for they actually blur the theoretical distinction between written and oral without realizing its critical potential.

While Baeuml and Bruno concede, in fact, that the formulation quoted above might be taken as an exaggeration "of the concepts of 'oral' and 'written' to the point of meaninglessness" (p. 485, n. 17), they already construct a new dichotomy. The new argument in this second paper fulfills a dual function. It is meant to support the application of the Theory on socio-anthropological grounds and to illuminate further the categorical difference between written and oral in the light of yet another parallel between twentieth-century Yugoslavia and late twelfth-century Germany. According to Baeuml and Bruno, the parallel consists in the fact that an analphabetic, and therefore oral, culture exists within (or below) a dominant literate, written culture. What once was the prevalent mode of literary communication also among the members of the upper class has now become the hallmark of the literature of the disadvantaged, and the step from oral to written therefore entails a drastic "change of perception" of the same narrative material (p. 481). The man who re-worked the dictated text of the *Nibelungenlied* worked for a literate society with a new "perceptual orientation," as Baeuml and his collaborator Edda Spielmann say in the latest published continuation of the argument. It is beginning to look as though the chief purpose of these investigations into the oral character of the *Nibelungenlied* has been, after all, to stress the literary character of the extant text, where this literate perception permits oral formulas to be used (and appreciated) as "ironic" statements reflecting conscious distance from the tradition (see especially p. 254 ff.). All this seems to be based on the unevenness in formula density discovered by the computer.

Few would deny that the *Nibelungenlied* frequently reflects upon itself, that is, its traditional subject matter—the same could be said of *Beowulf*. But does this presuppose an absolute juxtaposition of analphabetic and literate cultures? Brackert's findings completely undermine this view as far as the *Nibelungenlied* is concerned, and Hans Fromm calls it anachronistic on general grounds. The analphabetic lay culture of the late twelfth century, he says, occupied a position that was, if anything, above that of the school-educated clergy and its (few) lay pupils: Literacy did not confer social status (Fromm, p. 58ff.). Although this broadside misses a couple of fine points in Baeuml's argument and could not take into account the elaborations advanced in his latest paper, it is essentially on target. One might, in fact, add that for centuries the literate culture of the monasteries and, later, the episcopal courts seems to have been quite happily—if mischievously and, for the most part, unproductively—wedded to the "subculture" of indigenous oral tradition. Indirect testimony abounds: from the Fulda monks who slipped the text of the *Hildebrandslied* into a Latin theological codex to one of the most conspicuous church dignitaries of his time, Bishop Gunther of Bamberg, who preferred listening to stories about Attila and Theodoric to reading Augustin and Gregory. *Fabulas curiales* his irate friend Meinhard calls them![9] And let us not forget the British scribe Lucas who, in 1170, revived the spirits of a defeated Danish army with recitals of *memoratis ueterum uirtutibus,* a semi-learned man who behaves in a way highly reminiscent of the earliest accounts of how (oral) heroic lays were used (and composed).[10] As opposed to the recording of a text that would never have been written down, had not the modern scholar been on the spot and brought about an abrupt media transfer, medieval written traditions of originally oral material are the eventual outcome of a process of gradual cultural amalgamation.

Fromm himself has described the situation of around 1200 in terms of a symbiotic relationship between written and oral and attempted, on this basis, to reconcile Brackert's findings with the positive results of the debate on the oral composition of the *Nibelungenlied.* A "symbiotic culture" in which the institution of public oral recitation before aristocratic lay audiences constantly mediates between oral and written (p. 60) creates "intermediate types" of epic composition (not to be confused with "transitional texts"!) (p. 60). Even the courtly romance becomes part of this concept: In subject matter it looks towards the aristocratic, illiterate lay culture, but it has no oral past and depends on literacy for its existence.

Another of these intermediate types is represented by the *Nibelungenlied* and its branches. Here, Fromm, in addition to recalling Parry's and Lord's experiences, draw on his own extensive experience with the Finnokarelian material and his field work in the Faroes. His conclusion is that the textual congruity among the *Nibelungenlied* manuscripts is much too extensive not to reflect a written original. This written version existed side by side with oral ones but was separated from them by the "higher degree of linguistic and compositional consciousness" of one particularly gifted individual. At the same time, this individual was prevented from excessive innovation by his audience's knowledge of these concurrent oral versions. In the process of further transmission of his text this "symbiotic competition" makes itself felt in two ways: the continuing influence of the oral tradition and the demands of modern taste that bring about amelioration and refinement (pp. 61-63).

One need not agree with every detail of this analysis to accept the principle that, rather than exclude each other—be it as a matter of technical procedure in composition or of a radical perceptual change—the oral and the literary are closely intertwined in a case such as this. Beyond that, and along with the discussion that preceded it, the idea of a symbiotic culture leads to several general conclusions regarding the applicability of the Theory to medieval situations.

The first is elementary but bears re-stating: Any such attempt must be preceded by careful study of the living conditions and cultural ambience of the document in question. Only in this way can we learn whether, where, and how to apply.

Second, the chief obstacle in the path of this seemingly self-evident approach is the concept of the poetic formula itself and the way in which it is linked to the concept of "oral." That is to say, whether we are "for" or "against" application, we have become obsessed with a definition of formulaic usage that is bound to be at variance with what is formulaic in medieval poetic usage. This conclusion is re-enforced by the work of Hans Dieter Lutz, who has addressed himself to this problem with a brief (and rather abstract) critique of the Theory and its application by Baeuml and his collaborators and with a book which seeks to develop a method of describing (medieval) formulaic usage in precise quantitative terms.[11]

In spite of the counterarguments advanced by Haymes in the new foreword to his dissertation (p. VII ff.), Lutz seems to me to be essentially correct in stating that the Theory provides a descriptive, not an explanatory or analytical model: It "knows" that what it describes is oral narrative, and hence it cannot be used, except with a great deal of reservation and caution, to answer such questions as "Why is a medieval text formulaic or non-formulaic?" Nevertheless, Lutz's proposals for a future "Ersatztheorie" seem to me more to the point. Among the things that this new theory would have to take into account, according to Lutz, is the fact that in German epic verse the relation between metre and formula is not as one-sided as it is in Serbocroatian verse, according to Lord. In view of Haymes's remark that the example from *Dukus Horant* used by Lutz ("Zur Formelhaftigkeit," p. 444) is an isolated aberration on the part of the author or the scribe (p. IX), I should like to state quite emphatically what everyone with some experience in the thirteenth-century heroic epic and similar epic forms knows only too well: Formulas, formula systems, and stereotyped diction can at any time supersede metrical regularity as the ordering principle of the text.[12] At least as high on my own list of major factors to be considered is the use of end rhyme, or, more specifically, the conventional use of a small number of trivial rhymes which creates its own "system" of formulaic response, producing equivalences that are indistinguishable from what the Theory would designate as correspondences resulting from the process of oral composition.

Of course, beneath all this still lurk two questions which have bothered critics, as well as thoughtful adherents, of the Theory almost from the beginning: Given the assumption that a certain formula density denotes an orally composed text, how can this density be established in exact statistical terms; and how can formulaic usage be defined in a way which makes it susceptible to such scientific

analysis? The methods and procedures which Lutz has used to provide at least a preliminary answer derive from information and communication theory, and for this first test of their applicability he has confined himself to one, the most simple, type of formula, the noun-adjective combination. The analysis is based on four carefully chosen epic texts representing different literary backgrounds and trends between 1150 and 1250.

To describe Lutz's computer-aided operation in sufficient detail to do justice to its complexity would fill several pages. I shall confine myself to a few general observations. In line with Lutz's overall position, his "operational definition" of the formula seeks to ascertain the presence or absence of formulaic diction, not to interpret the results. The immediate goal is to identify formulas, irrespective of their provenance and function, and the resulting concept of the formula is bound to be at variance with all definitions advanced within the general framework of the Theory. It allows not only for varying relative position of article, adjective, and noun in what amounts to six phenotypes of the basic model but also for the injection of various kinds of lexical qualifiers into this basic model. Thus *der haiden werc vil spaehe* can, if other conditions are met, be considered a formulaic variant of *daz spaehe werc*.

The operation itself is relational and seems to work—at least in the sense that the statistical results take into account every factor that could conceivably be of significance, for example, the total numbers of adjectives, nouns, and noun-adjective combinations in the text under investigation, the length of that text, and the relation between the absolute frequency of a given noun-adjective combination and the average frequency of the respective adjective in combination with other nouns. This system also permits comparison between different texts and distinguishes between word sequence whose formulaic character is evident from the text which is the primary target of the investigation ("Formel qua Text") and phrases which turn out to be formulaic only after consideration of other texts, as well ("Formel qua Tradition"). Finally, it opens up the prospect of a general typology of formulaic language in quantitative, functional, sociogeographic, as well as socio-literary terms (diagram on p. 131), recognizing that a theory which seeks to explain the phenomenon of formulaic usage for this period cannot possibly exclude the notion of multiple origin and purpose.

It remains to be seen whether Lutz or anyone else will ever find the time and muster the energy required to expand this model and advance the investigation to a point where the results become sufficiently clear to warrant a systematic re-appraisal of the relationship between formulaic diction and orality in Middle High German or other medieval texts.

This brings me to my third conclusion. We have become so mesmerized by the specificity of the claim made by the Theory—absolute distinction between written and oral creation—that we have forgotten all the other aspects of oral culture which pertain to the production and dissemination of vernacular literature in the Middle Ages—aspects that in many cases are just as or more important than that of how, exactly, the text was composed. We have forgotten, in other words, that in a culture which is still predominantly oral, in the general sense, there is no room for an absolute juxtaposition of oral and written, in a specific sense, and that when we use the term "oral" in speaking about the Middle Ages we are of necessity speaking of a cultural phenomenon that is infinitely more varied and complex than that from which the Theory derives.

How does the institution of oral performance influence the external proportions (and internal cohesion) of written texts? Examples and questions range from the major works of Wolfram and their subdivision into "books" to a fifteenth-century redaction of the thirteenth-century *Wolfdietrich* which concludes with the statement that the narrative has been condensed from 700 to 333 stanzas so that it can be presented in one session (*auf einem sitzen*). Oral proportions are not the concern of oral singers alone. What are the sources and what is the ultimate purpose behind the directness of address and repartee with which a poet like Wolfram communicates with his audience? He is the only one among the German writers of courtly romance working around 1200 who makes direct reference to the traditional heroic poetry current at the same time and in the same circles. It is quite possible that his own stance of public oral communication has something to do with his predilection for or, at least, close acquaintance with this genre. However this may be, his style reflects the same symbiotic culture in which the *Nibelungenlied* surfaced as a written document, only this time we are looking at it from the viewpoint of a literate poet who reacts to an oral environment.

But I want to return to the *Nibelungenlied* for a concrete example that may show in which direction the more relaxed attitude advocated by Fromm and implicit in Brackert's analysis may develop new perspectives (although it may at the same time revive old issues). Chapters six through eleven, some four hundred stanzas in the vulgate version, relate Gunther's courtship of Brünhild, an episode which is firmly intertwined with Sigfrid's courtship of Krimhild: Krimhild's hand is the price for Sigfrid's assistance in the matter; the whole affair culminates in a double wedding; and the manner in which Sigfrid assists Gunther becomes the root cause of the following quarrel of the queens and Sigfrid's death. Hence, when modern scholars speak of a hypothetical *Lay of Brünhild* as one, if not the chief, source of the first part of the poem, they usually mean a poem which went considerably beyond the limited narrative framework of Gunther's courtship. If one looks at the manuscript tradition with heightened awareness of the potential presence of oral "interference," one detects something else as well: the existence and continuous influence of a (probably oral) lay of Brünhild which told the story of Gunther's courtship more or less on its own and which I shall call *The Short Lay of Brünhild.*

Branches A, B, and C disagree as to where exactly chapter six begins, and they do so in a way which rather isolates the stanza which appears as no. 325 in the Bartsch-de Boor edition. Here are the three versions of this text (from Batt's synoptic, diplomatic reprint):

Iteniwiv maere   sich hůben vber Rin.
man seite daz da were   manich magedin.
der dahte imeine werben   des kunich Gvnthers
                                        mvt
daz dvhte sine rechen   vn die heeren alle gůt.

                                        A (324)

Itniwe maere   sich hvben vber Rin.
man sagte daz da waere   manech scone magedin.
der gedaht im eine erwerben   Gvnther der kvnech
                                        gvt.
da von begvnde dem rechen   vil sere hohen der
                                        mvt.

                                        B (323)

Iteniwe maere   sich hvben vmben vmben Rin.
ez sprachen zv dem kunige   die hosten mage sin,
warvmbe er niht ennaeme   ein wip zv siner ê.
da sprach der chunic riche: "ine wil niht langer
                                        biten me."

                                        C (327)

In A this stanza opens the sixth chapter, in B it concludes the fifth, and in C it forms a different kind of conclusion to chapter five, with the help of an additional stanza, C 328. The editors of the standard text have in this case followed A, instead of B, and stanza 324 of the Bartsch-de Boor edition does indeed provide the most logical conclusion for chapter five, at least as far as A and B are concerned: It foreshadows things to come, as do many stanzas in this position, and, along with 323, it responds quite pointedly to the end of chapter three (137; 138). On the other hand, stanza 326, rather than 325, is the logical opening for chapter six in all three versions: The phrase *ez was ein küneginne gesezzen über se* (326,1) marks the beginning of a new story or major episode in highly typical, stereotyped fashion (echoing, by the way, the introductions of Krimhild and Sigfrid in chapters one and two, respectively), and what follows immediately—description of Brünhild's activities and re-introduction of Gunther *as ein riter wolgetan* and *vogt von Rine,* her potential suitor (326-329)—is completely in keeping with this style.

With its announcement of "tidings never heard before" that prompt Gunther to think of winning one of the many lovely maidens across the Rhine—the reading of AB—stanza 325 is not only redundant but completely undermines the effect of the following introduction. Indeed, all three branches of the manuscript tradition seem to treat it as a kind of foreign body that has to be neutralized somehow. Does it represent an attempt, made at the stage of a common archetype, and not very successfully as it turns out, to provide a smoother transition after the "master" had opened chapter six rather abruptly by adhering closely to another, independent version of the episode? Or is it this stanza 325 which records or paraphrases the beginning of another popular version? The redactor may have wanted to provide the reciter with an alternative introduction closer to the way in which the audience was accustomed to hearing the story told, and it may even have been a marginal entry at first.

Version C gives a substantially different context, including a substantially different wording of stanza 325 which is elaborated in C 328 and, early in chapter six, C 332. This arrangement in C leads into chapter six in a way which parallels most closely the standard introduction to such courtship tales: The "tidings never heard before" are that Gunther's relatives urge him to take a wife, he agrees to take counsel in the matter, and his choice of Brünhild is indeed made during such a meeting. This different narrative patterning is not entirely confined to C, though. In essential agreement with the spirit of C and in contrast to B, which at this point comments on Gunther's elation at the thought of marriage, version A says in 325,4 (A 324,4) that his intentions were welcomed by his men.[13] It seems highly likely, then, that A and C reflect, in different degrees and independently, the motivation for Gunther's courtship as *The Short Lay of Brünhild* conceived it, in line with one of the standard variants of the popular courtship pattern.

Unlike C, which is not only longer but also gives a fairly consistent alternative interpretation of the material, A as a whole is quite close to B. However, there is one important exception which, when seen in conjunction with what has just been discussed, provides the most telling clue to *The Short Lay of Brünhild:* It is 61 stanzas shorter. In this connection it has often been noted, but I know of no attempt to interpret the fact, that no less than 55 of these stanzas concern the Brünhild episode, from chapter six to the end of chapter eleven.[14] Moreover, this tendency toward a more concise rendering is most evident, by far, in chapters six and seven, the core of the Brünhild story, if it is viewed mainly as a story of (successful) courtship. It is hard to believe that this two-fold concentration is pure coincidence: A is, in this case, closer than B or C, at least in format, to a type of narrative which told the story in sketchier fashion, with primary emphasis on the theme of courtship, as such, and less (probably much less) attention to the wider context.

This hypothetical *Short Lay of Brünhild* probably fit the description of a poem which Wolfgang Mohr, as early as 1942, postulated as one of the sources of the **Nibelungenlied** on purely stylistic grounds, that is, the close stylistic affinity between the Brünhild episode and the so-called "Spielmannsepen." He called it a poem which had taken as its subject "one sector of the well-known Sigfrid legend and given it colour and a life of its own in an independent poetic production.[15] Beyond that, we can now say that the relationship between this lay and the **Nibelungenlied** was not confined to one moment of contact. The *Short Lay of Brünhild* and the evolving written versions of the great epic are very likely to have crossed paths more than once.

We may never understand the details fully, but in general the picture is reasonably clear: What we observe here is part of a constant debate between competing versions and even types of narrative dealing with the same material in either written or oral form. I have little doubt that the *Nibelungenklage,* the poem which, purporting to be the authentic conclusion of the story of the Nibelungen, follows the *Lied* from the beginning of the known manuscript tradition but is now generally regarded as a secondary commentary on one or the other of the written versions, is, in fact, the record of the situation in which a written tradition begins serious competition with oral ones.[16] The *Klage* "quotes" from a tradition that is still very much in flux: This is apparent in its rendering of individual incidents, such as the murder of young Ortlieb, as well as in the way in which its anonymous author toys continuously (and inconsistently) with questions of source, transmission, and previous knowledge on the part of the audience. A closer re-examination may well show that this poem, which accommodates much of the substance of the story in indirect presentation, as it were, is an early literary experiment that actually paves the way for the process of poeticization and codification that produces the *Lied* as a text through which poet and audience finally face the old tales on their own generic terms. At any rate, it is this phenomenon of active interdependence of the two cultures that we must make part of the critical apparatus we use to interpret the **Nibelungenlied** as a work of art.

Notes

1. For a recent survey see A. B. Lord, "Perspectives on Recent Work on Oral Literature," *FMLS,* 10 (1974), 187-210. A first version of my article served, along with others, as the basis for discussion at a seminar on oral poetry at the eighty-ninth Annual Meeting of the MLA in 1974 in New York; it has been thoroughly revised and updated.

2. Ruth R. Hartzell Firestone, *Elements of Traditional Structure in the Couplet Epics of the Late MHG Dietrich Cycle,* Göppinger Arbeiten zur Germanistik, No. 170 (Göppingen: A. Kümmerle, 1975), p. 26, and ibid., note 9. Cf. John Meier, *Werden und Wesen des Volksepos,* 1909; rpt. in *Das deutsche Versepos,* ed. Walter J. Schröder (Darmstadt: Wissenschaftliche Buchgesellschaft, 1969), pp. 143-181.

3. See my article, "Oral Poetry in Medieval English, French, and German Literature: Some Notes on Recent Research," *Speculum,* 42 (1967), pp. 36-52. An important study of traditional composition following in Th. Frings's footsteps is by Hinrich Siefken, *Überindividuelle Formen und der Aufbau des Kudrunepos, Medium Aevum,* No. 11 (München: Fink, 1967). Manfred Caliebe has made an attempt to combine the two approaches in his study, *Dukus Horant: Studien zu seiner literarischen Tradition,* Philologische Studien und Quellen, No. 70 (Berlin: Schmidt, 1973), esp. p. 87ff. (cf. my review, *Speculum,* 51 [1976], pp. 715-717).

4. A. Wishard, "Formulaic Composition in the *Spielmannsepik," PLL,* 8 (1972), 243-251, esp. 251: The

article is based on the author's unpublished dissertation, "Composition by Formula and Theme in the Middle High German *Spielmannsepik*," University of Oregon 1970.

5. Lars Lönnroth, "Hjalmar's Death-Song and the Delivery of Eddic Poetry," *Speculum, 46* (1971), 1-20, pp. 10 and 18, respectively. Regarding the compositional technique behind the sagas as such, Carol J. Clover has written an astute analysis of narration in "tripartite scenes arranged paratactically in sequence" as "a fundamental point of contact with oral tale-telling." "Scene in Saga Composition," *ANF, 89* (1974), 57-83, esp. p. 82.

6. Helmut Brackert, *Beiträge zur Handschriftenkritik des Nibelungenliedes,* Quellen und Forschungen, N.S. No. 11 (Berlin: de Gruyter, 1963). Franz H. Baeuml and Donald J. Ward, "Zur mündlichen Überlieferung des Nibelungenliedes," *DVLG,* 41 (1967), 351-390. Edward Haymes, *Mündliches Epos in mittelhoch-deustcher Zeit,* Dissertation, Erlangen, 1969; re-issued, with a new foreword, as Göppinger Arbeiten zur Germanistik, No 164 (Göppingen: A. Kümmerle, 1975). Franz H. Baeuml and Agnes M. Bruno, "Weiteres zur mündlichen Überlieferung des Nibelungenliedes," *DVLG,* 46 (1972), 479-493. Hans Fromm, *Der oder die Dichter des Nibelungenliedes?* in *Acta: IV. Congresso Latino-Americano de Estudos Germanisticos* (São Paulo, 1974), 51-66. Franz H. Baeuml and Edda Spielmann, "From Illiteracy to Literacy: Prolegomena to a Study of the *Nibelungenlied*," *FMLS,* 10 (1974), 248-259. See also my comments in *"Spielmannsepik," Wege und Ergebnisse der Forschung von 1907-1965. Mit Ergänzungen und Nachträgen bis 1967* (Stuttgart: Metzler, 1968), esp. pp. 102-108. A voluminous study of Germanic formulicity, which devotes some 250 of its over 600 pages specifically to the *Nibelungenlied,* unfortunately appeared too late to be incorporated into the following discussion: Teresa Pàroli, *Sull' elemento formulare nella poesia Germanica antica,* Biblioteca di ricerche linguistiche e filologiche, No. 4 (Rome: Istituto di Glottologia, 1975). Unless otherwise stated, *Nibelungenlied* references are to the critical edition of B, closest to the so-called vulgate text: *Das Nibelungenlied,* ed. Karl Bartsch-Helmut de Boor (Wiesbaden: F. A. Brockhaus, 1972). A synoptic view of all three versions is provided by Michael S. Batts (ed.), *Das Nibelungenlied* (Tübingen: M. Niemeyer, 1971).

7. From a purely methodological point of view this approach seems superior to that followed by Franz Baeuml, although it did apparently prevent Haymes from spotting substantial variations in formulaic density.

8. Baeuml-Bruno, p. 487, n. 20, and Baeuml-Spielmann, p. 249. It is in this methodological context, although not with the aim of proving this particular theory, that Agnes M. Bruno has carried out her computer analysis of the style of the *Nibelungenlied* (*Toward a Quantitative Methodology for Stylistic Analyses,* Uni-

versity of California Publications in Modern Philology, No. 109 [Berkeley: University of California Press, 1974]), and the great concordance published more recently by Baeuml in association with Eva-Maria Fallone (Compendia, No. 7. Leeds: W. S. Maney and Son, 1976) also contains indices designed especially "to serve research in the area of formulaic composition" (p. IX). For a voice against these kinds of quantification cf. Otto Holzapfel, "Homer—Nibelungenlied—Novalis: zur Diskussion um die Formelhaftigkeit epischer Dichtung," *Fabula,* 15 (1974), 34-46; a more positive survey is by N. T. J. Voorwinden, "De dichter van het Nibelungenlied: zanger of schrijver?" in *Literatuur en samenleving in de middeleeuwen* (1976) 63-81.

9. On the overall significance of Meinhard's remarks, see Carl Erdmann, "Fabulae Curiales," *ZfdA,* 73 (1936), 87-98.

10. *Saxonis Grammatici "Gesta Danorum,"* ed. Alfred Holder (Strassburg: Karl J. Trübner, 1886), p. 583.

11. H. D. Lutz, "Zur Formelhaftigkeit mittelhochdeutscher Texte und zur 'theory of oral-formulaic composition,'" *DVLG,* 48 (1974), 432-447; *Zur Formelhaftigkeit der Adjektiv-Substantiv-Verbindung im Mittelhochdeutschen: Struktur-Statistik-Semantik* Münchener Texte und Untersuchungen zur deutschen Literatur des Mittelalters, No. 52 (Munich: C. H. Beck, 1975).

12. Lutz's example is, in turn, taken from the article by Werner Schwarz, which constitutes the first full-scale attempt at applying the Theory to a German (in this case Judeo-German) text: "Die weltliche Volksliteratur der Juden im Mittelalter," in *Judentum im Mittelalter,* ed. P. Wilpert (Berlin: de Gruyter, 1965), pp. 72-91.

13. On the difference between the readings of A and B, with regard to the relative courtliness of the response, see Brackert.

14. For a general discussion of this material, see Brackert, p. 55ff. and 155ff.

15. W. Mohr, Review of Dietrich von Kralik, *Die Sigfridtrilogie im Nibelungenlied und in der Thidrekssaga,* in *Dichtung und Volkstum,* 42 (1942), 83-123, esp. p. 122.

16. See Karl Bertau, *Deutsche Literatur im europäischen Mittelater,* I: 800-1197 (München: C. H. Beck, 1972), esp. p. 744ff. Bertau's aphoristic comments on the problem point in the right direction, but a good deal of further investigation is needed, which I hope to carry out in the not-too-distant future.

D. R. McLintock (essay date 1977)

SOURCE: "The Reconciliation in the *Nibelungenlied*," *German Life and Letters*, Vol. XXX, No. 2, January, 1997, pp. 138-49.

[*In the following essay, McLintock explains that the* Nibelungenlied *is best approached aesthetically, for its literary qualities.*]

Recent years have seen numerous interpretations of the **Nibelungenlied.** Scholars have sought to elicit its 'meaning' or 'message' and imagined they could divine the author's 'intention': he was contrasting 'pagan' and 'Christian' values, deploring revenge, finding fault with old-style 'demonic' heroism, or demonstrating the baleful effects of lay arrogance. Some of these readings, one suspects, would have been incomprehensible to the poet and his audience; others perhaps capture attitudes that they would have shared. Most tend to reduce the work to an exemplum; the epic, however, refuses to be compassed by neat interpretative schemes.[1] The poet was an artist, not a thinker, and if we wish to appreciate his poem we must approach it aesthetically. Admittedly we must beware of investing the word 'poet' with anachronistic connotations: the composer of the **Nibelungenlied** arranged and presented stories that belonged to his public; he did not appropriate them as a modern poet appropriates his material, or, indeed, as Gottfried or Wolfram appropriated theirs.[2]

What we admire in the epic is not its moral, social, or psychological insights, but its literary qualities—the power of its individual scenes and the grandeur of the total architecture to which they contribute. An essential feature of this architecture, obvious even to a reader who knows nothing of source-study, is the balance between the two main parts of the work, the first treating of Sivrit's death, the second of 'der Nibelunge nôt'. Each half deals with a breach of faith; in the first it is that of Gunther with his friend Sivrit, in the second that of Kriemhilt with her brothers. The persecutors of the first part become the persecuted of the second. Yet the work is not a simple story of crime and punishment. Right and wrong, justice and criminality, are equally distributed, at least in version B, which is commonly believed to be closest to the work of the Last Poet. The Burgundian kings, who assented to the treacherous murder of Sivrit, defend themselves with dazzling heroism against a treachery equal to that of which they themselves had been guilty, displaying exemplary loyalty to each other and to their vassal Hagen.

The poet achieves this balance between the two halves, not allowing the work to degenerate into a mere story of revenge, partly by means of an important bridge-passage, *Aventiure* 19. In this section Kriemhilt is reconciled with her brothers, in particular Gunther; her perfidy in the second part arises from her violationg this solemn reconciliation, as the poet clearly states later (str. 1394). From now on she is justified only in pursuing Hagen for the murder of Sivrit. The same *âventiure* tells also of the theft of Kriemhilt's Hoard, to which Gunther gives his assent, and of its sinking in the Rhine. Not until str. 1742 does Kriemhilt learn of her brothers' complicity in the sinking of the Hoard, and from then on she has a new grievance against them, though hardly one commensurate with the vengeance she exacts. The two halves are thus kept discrete, but

linked. Kriemhilt's grievance against Gunther over his part in her husband's murder is formally set aside, to be replaced by another, over the theft of the Hoard, at a later stage. It may be said that Gunther dies for the Hoard, as he had done in the earliest version of the story, though the final defiant refusal to reveal its whereabouts has passed to Hagen. Kriemhilt is never reconciled with Hagen. To her grievance against him for the murder of Sivrit is added another, for the stealing of the Hoard, which she is led to believe to be Hagen's work alone. These two grievances she herself links in her final confrontation with him. We may say, then, that each half is concerned with a wrong done to Kriemhilt by her brothers, and that the second half tells of her perfidy towards them. The two halves are linked by the Hoard, which comes to Burgundy as a consequence of the reconciliation, the *suone,* and is immediately stolen, ostensibly by Hagen; the whole work is unified by the enduring enmity between Kriemhilt and Hagen.

Such a reading of the work, based upon its structure, is of course open to objection. It might be held that Gunther is relatively unimportant by comparison with Hagen, and that our analysis accords him undue prominence.[3] True, he is apparently indecisive, manipulated at will by Hagen, and he does follow Hagen's advice over the murder of Sivrit and the theft of the Hoard. However, he alone resolves upon the two momentous journeys which determine the action—the journey to Prünhilt and the journey to Etzel. Indeed, the latter is undertaken against Hagen's advice. Gunther also disregards Hagen's advice when he allows Kriemhilt to marry Etzel. Ductile though he appears, nothing can be done without his assent. The killing of Sivrit is planned and executed by Hagen, but the plan cannot go ahead until the King has dropped his opposition and shown interest in its feasibility (str. 874). It is true that Hagen proposes the reconciliation in order to get the Treasure to Burgundy, and that he subsequently steals it and sinks it in the Rhine, but Gunther arranges the reconciliation and later agrees to the robbery, while the proposal to sink the Treasure in the Rhine comes from his brother Gernot.

Hagen appears throughout as a ruthless man of action, manipulating others, untroubled by moral scruples, scornful of dissimulation (except for practical ends), clear-sighted in his assessment of political and military situations. An admirer of his type might call him 'ein Realpolitiker mit dem Mut zum Verbrechen'. Gunther, by contrast, is afflicted by conscience whenever he is tempted to ignoble or criminal action, and he does not enjoy the triumph such action brings him. He begins to sorrow (str. 870) when Hagen holds out the prospect of aggrandizement through the liquidation of Sivrit, and he weeps (str. 991 f) together with those 'die iht triuwe heten' over the dying friend whom he has betrayed. With Gunther's tears we may contrast Hagen's exultation and his incomprehension of the general grief (str. 993). When Hagen suggests depriving Kriemhilt of the Hoard, the King has an access of squeamishness, but the vassal, knowing his master, is ready with the well-tried specific: 'Lât mich den schuldigen sîn' (str. 1131).

Hagen is Gunther's chief counsellor and chief executive; and we are inclined, since his counsel is so often heeded and its execution invariably efficient, to assign to him the principal blame for the crimes he commits. Yet, while he must bear the guilt for murdering the ferryman and the infant Ortliep as well as for trying to murder the chaplain, one might dispute the extent of his culpability in the two crimes for which Kriemhilt pursues him. Even if we were to regard Gunther and Hagen as equal partners in the murder of Sivrit, as is suggested by the two eagles, the two boars and the two mountains of Kriemhilt's dreams, it is arguable that less blame attaches to the man who, without thought of right and wrong, devised and executed the crime than to the one who gave the signal in full knowledge of the guilt that he was thereby incurring. The narrator (str. 876) seems to view the murder as Gunther's crime, implying that, by following his vassal in a course of monstrous treachery, he was violating a principle of kingship; and the dying Sivrit upbraids Gunther (str. 992) as the one who has done the harm. There is no exculpation for a king who is capable of resolute action but chooses to follow immoral advice. U. R. Mahlendorf and F. J. Tobin are surely right to insist that he is 'by law a criminal and a murderer',[4] and Roswitha Wisniewski to see in him an example of the *dominus sine virtute* or the *rex iniquus*.[5]

Yet such a view of the morality of the work, it might be objected, is legalistic and facile. To say that after the *suone* there is no *casus belli* until Kriemhilt learns that her brothers ordered the sinking of the Hoard is to ignore the fact that they deny her justice by shielding her arch-enemy. Moreover, the audience is not kept in ignorance of their machinations and is bound to sympathize with her. Gunther fatuously believes in the efficacy of the reconciliation,[6] and only Hagen seems to know how things really stand (str. 1457-64). On the other side too there are mitigating circumstances. The killing of Sivrit, while undoubtedly an act of treachery, is a response to a gross scandal resulting from a public insult to the Burgundian queen. How else can Gunther restore the honour of his house but by punishing the man who, however uncalculatingly, has brought it into disrepute? Certainly not, as Sivrit unhelpfully suggests, by chastising his wife. Should Gunther preside over the dissolution of his power, or should he follow Hagen in what may be the only practical course open to him? And should be stand by while Kriemhilt suborns his subjects, as she later suborns those of her second husand, or should he deprive her of the mean to suborn? Kriemhilt is not the woman to forgo her legitimate vengeance, nor Gunther the man to abdicate his legitimate power. Kriemhilt can secure justice only through perfidy; Gunther can vindicate his kingship only through treachery. Both are forced by circumstances to forsake the one virtue that all endorse, *triuwe*. Both are guilty, but avoidance of guilt would have meant abject surrender. One might say that the ***Nibelungenlied*** illustrates the impracticability of any code of behaviour in the real world except that of ruthless self-assertion—but let us not be tempted to foist yet another 'intention' upon the poet.

The effect of the *suone* in *Aventiure* 19 is, as we have seen, to put Kriemhilt in the wrong vis-à-vis her brothers, while the theft of the Hoard, also recounted in *Aventiure* 19, once more puts them in the wrong in relation to her. This section has two further important effects: first, it safeguards the role of the Hoard in the structure of the epic, since its theft furnishes Kriemhilt with a new grievance against her brothers as well as an additional ground for pursuing Hagen; secondly, it preserves the heroic integrity of the older of the two legends, the Fall of the Burgundians. Without it the Kings would be facing simple vengeance for the murder of their brother-in-law; with it they can still appear as victims of *notissima perfidia Grimildae,* enjoying the sympathy of Rüdiger and Dietrich and—at least to some extent—of the audience.

Norse tradition too knows of a reconciliation between brother and sister three-and-a-half years after the murder.[7] This involves compensation and is effected with the aid of a draught brewed by their mother. While this brew is no doubt a Norse invention, the reconciliation itself is hardly likely to have arisen independently, though its function is different in the north, which preserved the old version of the Fall of the Burgundians. While in the south it ensures that the brothers face a perfidious Kriemhilt, in the north it assures them of a loyal Guðrun. Nor is the south alone in making the Fall of the Burgundians into a consequence of the murder of their first brother-in-law: the north too saw it partly as an act of revenge by their second brother-in-law for the death of his sister Brynhild[8] (though this motive is hardly developed) and as a consequence of their having deprived themelves of the protection of Siguro[9] It is an over-simplification to speak of the vengeance-motive's supplanting the treasure-motive. Both are present in both branches of the tradition, the south emphasizing the former, the north the latter.

It is difficult to imagine a cyclic treatment of the two legends (which have three principal characters in common) without an intervening reconciliation. It seems likely that this bridge was constructed when the legends were first linked. If the story of Sigfrid's death never stood alone, we may surmise that from the beginning there was a reconciliation between his widow and her brother three-and-a-half years after the murder. The north chose to make the reconciliation irrevocable and thereby to preserve the old Fall of the Burgundians, while the south made it violable and thereby ensured the widow's revenge. In both branches of the tradition, however, the principal effect was the same: the Burgundians went bravely to their deaths, dying heroically as victims of treachery.

Yet how did the Kings retain the sympathy of poets and audiences in spite of their having done to death a man whom we are accustomed to call 'der strahlende Held'? If Heusler is right in accrediting the second version of the Fall of the Burgundians to a Bavarian poet,[10] we may surmise that the audience would have had little time for a foreign queen who ruined the generous Etzel, sacrificed his son, suborned his brother and violated the rules of Hunnish hospitality. If, with Hugo Kuhn, we see the reshaping of the legend as a Merovingian invention designed to accommodate the later career of the historical Brunhild, renamed Kriemhild,[11] we may ascribe the continued sympathy with the murderers to a Frankish ambience in which the Visigothic Brunhild was regarded as the enemy of legitimacy. The reason may have been simple literary conservatism: it was one thing to make the Kings fall victim to their sister's vengeance rather than to Attila's cupidity, but quite another to deprive them of their stature as heroes.

Yet there may be a literary cause other than mere conservatism. According to Heusler, the death of Sigfrid remained a preamble to the Fall of the Burgundians in both the second and third postulated stages. Perhaps *Aventiure* 20 of our epic contains all that earlier Bavarian audiences knew of the wrongs suffered by Kriemhilt. None of these reasons, however, seems sufficient to explain how centuries could pass without, apparently, any attempt to justify her revenge. Perhaps the answer lies in the state of the Sigfrid material throughout these centuries. In Heusler's scheme, the story of his death, related in the Frankish Lay of Brunhild, remained constant from the sixth century to the twelfth, when a 'spielmännisch' Lay of Sigfrid was composed. In the earlier lay the heroine suffered an irremediable wrong at the hands of Sigfrid, who was acting in the interest of his friend Gunther. She took vengeance on both by making Gunther have Sigfrid killed, thus ridding herself of the author of her indignity and depriving her unworthy husband of his powerful friend. Heusler believed that the Norse versions told substantially the original story: the change of shape, the ride through the flame, the chaste nuptial nights with the dividing sword. These, he thought, were replaced in the eleventh-century poem by the cloak of invisibility, the athletic contests and the conquest in the bed-chamber. This view has been powerfully challenged by Klaus von See,[12] who surmises that the wall of flame was a characteristically Norse motif presupposing a famous horse (which only Sigurð, not Sivrit, possesses). He argues too that the quarrel of the Queens was not original: its absence from the *Edda* is not, he thinks, due to a gap in the Codex Regius; from the occurrence of unusual vocabulary in the account of the quarrel both in the *Volsunga Saga* and in the corresponding passage of the *Þidriks Saga* he concludes that the quarrel entered the former work from Germany by way of the latter. The dividing sword, however, he regards as a blind motif surviving from the original fable, and he interprets it, on very slender evidence, as part of the ritual of a 'Prokurationsheirat' once performed by Sigfrid on behalf of Gunther.

We may suspend judgment on von See's arguments about the quarrel and the sword, but his criticism of Heusler's reliance on Norse sources as evidence of the earliest version is cogent. He suggests that the German and the Norse accounts of the wooing of Brunhild replace something much simpler (for him a 'Prokurations heirat'), and he believes that this early simplicity is preserved in the *Þidriks Saga* (This would make North Germany a kind of legend-

ary 'Reliktgebiet' between two centres of innovation, South Germany and Scandinavia.) In both branches of the tradition Brunhild is tricked into marrying Gunther with Sigfrid's (Sigurð's) help, given freely in the south, obtained by ruse (the philtre of oblivion) in the north. Since the philtre of oblivion is usually taken to be a Norse accretion to the story, we must presume that in the original lay, as in the epic, Sigfrid was a willing accomplice in deceit. How he won Brunhild for Gunther we do not know and, not knowing the means he used, we can do no more than guess at the nature of his offence against her. Perhaps he tricked her—but how? Perhaps he used *force majeure*. Perhaps he had promised her marriage, as apparently Sigurð had in the *Þidriks Saga,* and then abandoned her for a better match. Perhaps she loved him and was spurned. Whatever the precise nature of his role, it clearly involved inflicting on Brunhild a gross indignity which made him, in her eyes, deserving of death; and at the heroic stage of the legend, when Brunhild had not yet become *des tiuveles wîp* but was still a heroic human figure, this role must have been at least ambivalent, if not positively distasteful. The original Sigfrid was probably not unlike the callous, self-seeking Sigurð of the *Þidriks Saga.* To say, with Heusler, that deceit practised against 'the foreign woman' was not offensive to the Germanic world,[13] or, with Neumann, that the defloration of a friend's wife at the friend's request attracted no opprobrium,[14] is to imply that the Germanic warrior caste had little respect for the women their kings took to wife. Can we believe this?

The late K. C. King came very close to the view of Sigfrid that we have just advanced when he said that 'he dies for a deed which at its best is questionable, at its worst little more than procuring'.[15] King did not pursue this point, but he did emphasize the passive nature of Sigfrid's role in the wooing of Brunhild, saying: 'The only active function he performs is to be called upon to act as the catspaw.'[16] He distinguished between 'stories about Siegfried', in which the hero played an active role, and the account of his death, which in its early form was a 'story about Brunhild'. King did not discuss the relative chronology of the Young Sigfrid material and the Lay of Brunhild and contented himself with the surmise that Sigfrid the dragon-killer and the 'mysterious man of courage' who won Brunhild were originally separate figures. It is conceivable that the Lay of Brunhild belongs to an earlier legendary stratum than the 'stories about Siegfried'; the hero may have acquired his role as a dragon-killer from Sigmund, whose feats were known to the poet of *Beowulf.* King makes a striking comparison between Sigfrid and Dietrich, around whom similar fantastic stories grew up.[17] Now, since Dietrich was originally a historical figure, we may be certain that he was fleeing from Otacher's spite for some time before he began to fight with dwarfs and giants. What gives us pause in the case of Sigfrid is our uncertainty about his origin. If he was not a historical figure at all, but, as Panzer thought, 'eine heroisierte Märchengestalt',[18] he must have had supernatural attributes from the beginning. On the whole, however, a historical origin seems probable for both him and Brunhild, especially in view of the persuasive arguments of Hugo Kuhn. This would allow us to regard the undoubted fairy-tale elements in the extant versions as later accretions.

Let us assume—we can do no more—that the fairy-tale elements in the Sigfrid material are not original. If we strip them away from the story of his death, we arrive at a fable which Neumann has summarized as follows:

> Ein starker Fremdling, mächtiger Besitzer eines Hortes (Siegfried), hat sich am Hofe des Königs festgesetzt und dessen Schwester geheiratet. In einem zwielichtigen Vorgang hilft er mit Erfolg, daß der König eine fremdartige Königin (eine Hild) erringt. Ohnehin wegen seiner Macht beargwöhnt, wird er nichtsahnend Anlaß zu einem Streit der beiden Frauen, bei dem es um die Frage geht, wer den mächtigsten Mann hat. Die Königin, in der Tiefe ihrer Ehre und damit ihres Seins getroffen, rächt sich, indem sie den Mann der Gegnerin, den Hortbesitzer, dessen Überlegenheit einen Zustand des Gleichgewichts verhindert, durch Meuchelmord beseitigen läßt. Was folgt, liegt für uns im Dunkeln; in jedem Falle endet das Geschehen in der inneren Niederlage des Königs, der sich zum Mord aufreizen ließ.[19]

In the heroic world trickery is allied with treachery, justifiable perhaps against a treacherous foe, contemptible if employed against the unsuspecting or vulnerable. In the world of fairy-tale it is associated with magic and is used by men to prevail over malevolent supernatural forces. In order to prevail they must learn a magic secret or secure the aid of a benevolent superhuman being. The ascendancy of human beings is short-lived, and the natural order soon reasserts itself. When the superhuman Sigfrid befriends Gunther and employs his magic to win the malevolent Brunhild for him, he incurs no blame, since he is siding with humans against the supernatural. When Brunhild, bereft of her supernatural strength, uses human trickery to avenge herself, the sympathy is not with her, but with her victim, whose human friends have turned false under her malevolent persuasion. The irruption of fairy-tale motivation into the Sigfrid-Brunhild material resulted in something like the following fable:

> Sigfrid, a benevolent stranger well-known for his superhuman strength but with a 'conditioned life', comes to Gunther's court and makes friends with him. Desiring to marry Gunther's sister Kriemhild, he undertakes, in return for her hand, to help him win the beautiful but malevolent Brunhild, a distant queen endowed with superhuman strength which is conditional upon her remaining a virgin. The hero employs magic in order to win her for Gunther, both in the athletic contests which she stipulates and (probably) in the bedchamber, where she loses her virginity and her strength. Later Kriemhild insultingly reveals the trickery to Brunhild, who then incites her husband or one of his men to kill the hero. Kriemhild is tricked into revealing the secret of Sigfrid's conditioned life, and he is murdered. Brunhild lives on, triumphant, but reduced to the status of a mere human being.

This story is far removed from the mood of the heroic world, where men and women drew their strength from their own will. One may, if one wishes, call it 'spielmännisch', implying an affinity with such works as *Salman und Morolf*. Its author and his audience clearly delighted in astonishing feats of strength and had a taste for the burlesque (can the scene in the bed-chamber ever have been other than farcical?). The hero is portrayed as 'der listige man', acting on Gunther's behalf much as Morolf does on Salman's errands—though unlike Morolf he does not kill the queen, despite having Gunther's permission to do so (*Nibelungenlied* str. 655). Such a story can have posed little danger to the still heroic Fall of the Burgundians.

Nevertheless, the callous trickster has been transformed into a hero of sorts, whose death is regrettable and might justify his widow in seeking revenge. The ground has been laid for the re-heroicizing of the Brunhild-Sigfrid story, but now with Sigfrid as the tragic figure, since the object of his deceit has become a deserving victim. This was the task to which the Last Poet addressed himself. As far as he could, he played down the supernatural attributes of Sigfrid, transforming him into a courtly prince, an exemplary knight, a generous victor, a wise counsellor, a trusting friend, and a tender lover. Needless to say, this Sivrit (as we may now call him) does not eclipse the cunning helper or the dangerous outsider of previous stages; the stratification of the epic is nowhere more obvious than in the figure of Sivrit.

A similar up-grading of the Sigfrid figure (Sigurð) had taken place in the north, which had its own stock of fairy-tale motifs associated with the world of gods and demi-gods. Sigurð was endowed with superhuman strength and courage, but the trickery passed to the sorceress Grimhild, the mother of the Gjukungs. The philtre of oblivion brewed by her exculpates Sigurð from the deceit practised against Brynhild, and these two become a pair of doomed lovers, cheated of their happiness by fate and false friends. It may be that in both north and south a greater guilt was felt to lie with the king who betrayed his friend and helper than with the helper who acted, however deceitfully, out of friendship. The transformation of the helper into a tragic victim of treachery in both branches of the tradition should not deceive us into regarding the original Sigfrid as an unequivocally radiant hero. Remove the magic from both versions and he appears as K. C. King described him.

If Heusler was right in believing that the first version of the Sigfrid-Brunhild material was current long after it had been loosely linked with the Fall of the Burgundians, we may imagine that Sigfrid's death was viewed as the regrettable outcome of an unfortunate imbroglio, something that the Burgundians might take in their stride in the spirit of *þaes oferēode, þisses swā maeg*. It did not inevitably cast a shadow on the bravery with which they faced death later among the Huns, whether their adversary was a covetous brother-in-law or a vengeful sister. They rode to the Huns because to fail to do so would have been cowardly, believing themselves—and believed by the audience—to be in the right. After the Last Poet had made Sivrit into a true hero and his death into a monstrous act of disloyalty, there was a danger that the audience's sympathy might veer over to the side of his widow and that the Kings would be regarded merely as criminals overtaken by justice. It was here that the *suone* came to the poet's aid: by freely agreeing to make up her quarrel with Gunther, Kriemhilt forfeited her right to prosecute her vengeance against him. Even so, the heroism of the Burgundians in this last 'Nibelunge Not' was equivocal: the audience might admire their magnificent defiance and their steadfast loyalty to each other, but it could not fail to recall the reasons for their predicament. We might say—if we wanted to offer another interpretation of the work (one, incidentally, which would be close to Weber's)—that the poet was depicting a heroism emptied of all moral content but the martial virtues.

What we have said about the **Nibelungenlied** applies to version B. It is clear from the manuscript tradition, however, that many members of the public preferred version C, which goes a long way towards exculpating Kriemhilt and denigrating Hagen.[20] The differences between the two versions have often been discussed, and we will concentrate here on the one feature of the story, the *suone*, which posed the biggest obstacle to any redistribution of right and wrong. In version B we are not told whether Gunther shared Hagen's desire to get the Hoard to Burgundy and engineered the reconciliation to that end. When the narrator comments on the propriety of Gunther's seeking a reconciliation, he apparently refers only to past harm that had come to Kriemhilt *von sînem râte* (str. 1114). Version C refers to Gunther's ulterior motive (str. 1127 C)—

durch des hordes liebe   was der rât getân:
dar umbe riet die suone   der vil ungetriuwe man

—and while 'der vil ungetriuwe man' is probably Hagen, it could possibly be Gunther (depending on the sense of *riet*). In B we are told that no more tearful reconciliation was ever effected *under vriunden* (str. 1115); in C (str. 1128) this phrase is replaced by *mit valsche*. Kriemhilt's attitude too is different in the later version. In B (str. 1112) she rejects Gernot's request that she should receive Gunther, but to Giselher's pleading she at once responds with the words 'Ich wil den künec grüezen' (str. 1113). In C (str. 1124) she makes it clear that she enters into the *suone* under duress, and she reproaches her brothers for constraining her:

Sie sprach 'ich muoz in grüezen: irn welts mich
                                     niht erlân.
des habt ir grôze sünde.   der künec hât mir getân
sô vil der herzen swære   gar âne mîne scholt.
mîn munt im giht der suone,   im wirt daz herze
                                     nimmer holt.'

To which she adds, at the end of an additional strophe in which the brothers surmise that Gunther might still be able to win her over by some unspecified compensation: 'seht, nû tuon ich swaz ir welt' (1125 C). Kriemhilt appears to be keeping her options open, refusing to go back on her earlier declaration (1112 B; 1123 C) 'holt wird ich in nim-

mer, die ez dâ hânt getân'. The *suone* has in C become a formality on both sides: for Gunther it is a device, for Kriemhilt a meaningless ritual. It is not surprising, therefore, that the redactor should have rewritten the first three lines of str. 1394 B (1421 C) and removed from it the suggestion that the devil counselled Kriemhilt to go back on her solemn reconciliation with one of her brothers (Giselher in MSS A, B and M, Gunther in D, I, d and h).

The changes we have just discussed have the effect of lightening, if not removing, the burden of guilt that Kriemhilt bears for her perfidy towards her brothers. They do not change the reader's assessment of the martial bravery which they and Hagen display in their last stand. His assessment of Hagen's motives, however, is affected by other changes in *Aventiure* 19. In B the only hint of his having private designs on the Hoard is contained in the words 'er wânde er sold in niezen' (1137), where *niezen* need not imply that Hagen expected to be its sole beneficiary. (No more need be implied than that he expected to administer it on behalf of his kings.) In C his selfish designs are clear: the phrase is modified to 'er wânde in niezen eine' (str. 1152), and this is repeated in an additional strophe, containing an imputation of *untriuwe*. It is indeed but a short step from a covetous Hagen to a disloyal Hagen, and this step is taken by the redactor. At the end of the work Hagen, 'knowing' that Kriemhilt will not spare him and fearing that after his death she will release Gunther, withholds the secret of the Hoard in order to make sure that Gunther dies with him. Thus the mutual loyalty of master and man, which alone of all loyalties remains intact in version B, is violated in C by the man. In *Aventiure* 36 his masters had been prepared to face death rather than surrender him to Kriemhilt, but he is ready to seal Gunther's fate by manipulating Kriemhilt for the last time. (It has been suggested that Hagen's silence in *Aventiure* 36, when he could have saved his Kings by giving himself up, is reprehensible.[21] This is dubious: the heroic code required a man, when called upon, to fight to the death beside his lord, but it contained no clause enjoining self-surrender. If Hagen knew the text 'Greater love hath no man . . .' he had no reason to apply it to himself.)

The occurrence of the *suone* in both the German and the Scandinavian tradition suggests that it was an ancient feature dating from the epoch when the Sigfrid-Brunhild material was first grafted on to the older legend of the Fall of the Burgundians. As we have seen, its function in the north was to keep their sister loyal; in the south it made her perfidious. In both branches of the tradition it helped to preserve the heroic mood of the older legend, both in its original and in its revised form. However, the Last Poet's transformation of Sigfrid into a figure of full heroic stature posed a danger. By taking in hand the task of uniting (or, if there really was a Merovingian *Kriemhildlied*, of re-uniting) the two fables as equipollent parts of one epic, the poet incurred a literary challenge. How was he to describe the death of Sivrit at the hands of false friends and yet withhold enough sympathy from his widow to allow these friends to enjoy the audience's admiration when it was their turn to die? By skilful management of his material and reliance on the *suone* he was able to establish a fine balance between right and wrong, sympathy and revulsion. This was an artistic achievement; if we are inclined to read a moral message into it, this is our business, not the poet's. The redactor who made version C and whom Professor Hatto has aptly called 'a rationalist, who, like many a person in the audience, required an explicit statement of motives and general clarity, whatever the cost,'[22] did what the Last Poet had studiously avoided doing: he disturbed the balance, seeking to exculpate Kriemhilt and to denigrate her principal adversary Hagen. We must concede that he went about his task with some skill, a skill which is nowhere more evident than in *Aventiure* 19. Whether or not version C is the most 'German' version of the epic (as Salmon suggests),[23] it is in some ways a reassuring work, to be recommended to those who wish to be convinced that there is something like simple justice in the world. Version B, on the other hand, is a disturbing work, for, like the *Hildebrandslied* before it, it offers no such reassurance.

Notes

1. A notable exception is the work of D. G. Mowatt and Hugh Sacker, *The Nibelungenlied. An Interpretative Commentary* (Toronto, 1967), which provides a 'running commentary' on the text and, despite some idiosyncratic judgements, at least attempts to let it speak for itself.

2. F. Neumann, in his perceptive work *Das Nibelungenlied in seiner Zeit* (Göttingen, 1967), is prepared to acknowledge that the composer of the basic text was a great artist, but reluctant to use the term 'Dichter', lest this should confer upon the work 'einen Charakter des Allzupersönlichen, betont Genialischen im Sinne des Einzelgängerischen'. He characterizes the poet's skill as 'handwerklich' (p. 165) and prefers to call him 'der Nibelungenmeister' (p. 139).

3. This judgment, so natural to the modern reader, has been most recently expressed by P. B. Salmon, 'The German-ness of the *Nibelungenlied*', *New German Studies,* 4 (1976), 3, where he asserts that 'Gunther is on some occasions little more than a royal figurehead'. Later (p. 9) he writes: 'In the *Nibelungenlied* only three of the principal characters are present throughout: Kriemhilt, Gunther and Hagen. Of these Gunther is relatively unimportant: he is directly responsible neither for the death of Sîvrit nor for the theft of the treasure . . . , much as he may have been involved in the conspiracy on both occasions . . .' The key-phrases in these statements are 'on some occasions' and 'directly'.

4. Ursula R. Mahlendorf and Frank J. Tobin, 'Legality and Formality in the *Nibelungenlied'*, *Monatshefte,* 66 (1974), 225-37. This study attempts to provide the contemporary legal context for the epic, chiefly by invoking the *Sachsenspiegel*.

5. R. Wisniewski, 'Das Versagen des Königs. Zur Interpretation des Nibelungenliedes', *Beitr.* (Tübingen), 95 Sonderheft (1973), 170-86.

6. Mowatt and Sacker, *op. cit.,* p. 100, aptly contrast Hagen's realism with Gunther's 'fatuous faith in convention at all costs'. Gunther's fatuity consists in his assumption that Kriemhilt will be bound by an agreement that he himself has breached. Mahlendorf and Tobin (*op. cit.*) stress the Burgundians' reliance on formality, contrasting it with Sivrit's total disregard of form.

7. The fullest account is in *Volsunga Saga* 34 (paralleled in *Gudrúnar kviða II*), adumbrated by Brynhild's words, ibid. 32, 'sættask munu þit Guðrún brátt' (paralleled in *Sigurðar kviða in skamma* 54, 'Sátt munoð ip Guðrún, snemr, enn þú hyggir'. (*Volsunga Saga* is here quoted according to R. G. Finch's edition, the Eddic poems according to G. Neckel's.)

8. In the *Volsunga Saga* 38 Atli claims the Hoard as his wife's property and presents himself as Sigurð's avenger. In the prose section of the *Edda* headed *Dráp Niflunga* we read: Ófriðr var þá milli Giúcunga oc Atla. Kendi hann Giúcungom vold um andlát Brynhildar'.

9. In *Volsunga Saga* 32 Guðrun prophesies: 'Nú munu þér riðdí her fyrst, ok er þér komid til bardaga, þá munu þér finna at Sigurðr er eigi á aðra hond yðr, ok munu þér þá sjá at Sigurðr var yður gæfa ok styrkr'.

10. A. Heusler, *Nibelungensage und Nibelungenlied* (2nd edition, Dortmund, 1922).

11. Brunhild und das Kriemhildlied', in K. Wais, *Frühe Epik Westeuropas und die Vorgeschichte des Nibelungenliedes* I (Tübingen, 1953), pp. 9-29.

12. 'Die Werbung um Brünhild', *ZfdA,* 88 (1957-58), 1-20.

13. *Op. cit.,* p. 16.

14. 'Das Weib muß auch im sexuellen Kampf erliegen, durch den Eroberer seine Jungfräulichkeit verlieren . . . Auch da ist an Siegfried nichts zu tadeln.' (From an early essay 'Schichten der Ethik im Nibelungenliede', reprinted in the work cited in note 2 above, p. 11.)

15. K. C. King (ed.), *Das Lied vom hürnen Seyfrid,* Manchester, 1958, p. 44.

16. *Ibid.,* p. 45.

17. *Ibid.,* p. 43.

18. F. Panzer, *Das Nibelungenlied. Entste hung und Gestalt,* Stuttgart, 1955, pp. 285 ff, reiterates this view, first advanced in 1912. He writes: 'Wer der Erzählung des NL von Siegfried, seinem Tun und Leiden eine befriedigende sagen- und literargeschichtliche Deutung geben will, muß sich zu der Einsicht durchringen, daß wir es in Siegfried nicht mit einer historischen, sondern einer Märchenfigur zu tun haben'.

19. *Op. cit.,* pp. 171 f.

20. The B and C texts are here quoted according to the edition of Karl Bartsch, *Der Nibelunge Not. Mit den Abweichungen von der Nibelunge Liet* (Leipzig, 1870).

21. In the 'Introduction to a Second Reading' which accompanies his English translation (*The Nibelungenlied*. A new translation by A. T. Hatto, Harmondsworth, revised ed., 1969) our gratuland writes (p. 319): '. . . the only thing that is needed to avoid the destruction of the house whose faithful guardian he claims to be is for him to walk out of the hall and die fighting.' Salmon, op. cit., p. 10, cites F. Genzmer's judgment (from the introduction to a translation of the epic based on version C) that 'Hagen gar nicht daran dachte, sich selbst zu opfern, um seine Könige und Freunde zu retten'.

22. *Op. cit.*, p. 363.

23. *Op. cit.*, pp. 20 f.

Berta Lösel-Wieland-Engelmann (essay date 1980)

SOURCE: "Feminist Repercussions of a Literary Research Project," *Atlantis*, Vol. 6, No. 1, Fall, 1980, pp. 84-90.

[*In the following essay, Lösel-Wieland-Engelmann provides a personal account of her experiences in promoting the idea of female authorship for the* Nibelunglied.]

The following experiences may show how a woman who never was much involved in feminism can suddenly be made aware of a multiplicity of problems that are peculiar to women.

Up to a quiet day in August 1977 I fulfilled my usual duties as a middle-aged part-time secretary to a small number of professors of German. Then I was given some lecture notes to type, the contents of which I found rather strange. They dealt with the **Nibelungenlied**[1] **(NL)**, an extremely well-known medieval epic that had been meticulously studied for over 200 years, and about which large library shelves had already been filled. And yet the lecture notes stressed again and again that nobody really knew anything definite about the work in question. Not only was the author unknown but it was even impossible to categorize him. He could not very well have been a knight because the epic showed little familiarity with details of war and hunting; he could not have been a minstrel because he was far too well educated, and he could not have been a cleric because he did not show enough concern about theological or philosophical subjects. He clearly did not belong to any of the three groups from which the poets of that time emerged. He also showed a strange mixture of Christianity and "paganism" and gave a highly uneven characterization of the most important male figure (Hagen), so that there was never much agreement about that man. Some critics declared him to be a superhero while others saw in him some cowardly traits or even designated him

as a criminal. In addition the epic lacked any discernible "message" to its readers, since no firm opinions on anything could be abstracted. Obviously the author did not have any "Weltanschauung" to speak of.

Of all those "problems" and "enigmas" I found the last one hardest to believe. How could anybody write close to 10,000 lines and never divulge his likes and dislikes? Did the poet really never indicate what delighted him and what annoyed him?

I had become curious and soon read an English and a German version of the poem, as well as a considerable number of commentaries in both languages. My confusion and surprise grew with every page. There seemed to be an enormous gap between the things that I had noticed in the poem and the things that the commentators had discovered in it. Even in such cases where the experts disagreed among themselves, they hardly ever came close to expressing the thoughts and feelings which the epic had aroused in me. That huge difference in opinion worried me and made me unsure of my ability to comprehend what I had read. More and more I got the eerie feeling that something was profoundly wrong somewhere: either I was crazy or everybody else was. My boss was certainly right to some degree: there are lots of "enigmas" around the *NL*. In my view, however, the "enigmatic" things did not come from the ancient masterpiece itself—which I found simple and straight-forward—but rather from the responses which it had generated in 98% of all German professors who had studied it in depth during the last two centuries. It amazed me that they could not feel the same sympathy for the heroine which I felt, and could not share my understanding of her thoughts and reactions and aspirations. Just why were nearly all their comments so strangely warped and twisted and upside-down?

It is very easy to sum up the main story: in a very underhanded and sneaky manner a woman (Kriemhild) gets tricked by a man (Hagen) to give away a secret which is instrumental in facilitating the subsequent murder of her beloved husband (Siegfried). Afterwards Hagen, the murderer, proceeds to rob the widow of her immense personal fortune and to sink it into the Rhine. Quite naturally, such treatment makes Kriemhild furious and bitter and resentful and thirsty for revenge. Since she does not have any way of doing Hagen any harm, she remarries in the hope that her new husband—the powerful and immensely rich Hunnish king Etzel—might later supply her with the necessary means for getting even with her archenemy. When Kriemhild's endeavours—after many years of waiting and many futile attempts—lead to success, this results in an extensive bloodbath, because too many men are on Hagen's side and wish to protect and help him in thwarting justice.

This main plot is preceded by a sub-plot. A woman (Brunhild) gets tricked by a man (Siegfried) into giving up her original resolution of marrying only a man who is stronger than herself. Under a guise Siegfried subdues the strong Brunhild and then turns her over to his buddy, a weakling named Gunter. When Brunhild later finds out about this dirty deal she also becomes furious and bitter and resentful and thirsty for revenge. With the cunning help of Hagen she succeeds in getting Siegfried killed.

As can be seen from the above short synopsis, in each case a woman is terribly wronged and decides not to put up meekly with the outrageous treatment given to her but instead tries to make the guilty man pay for his crime. In the case of the main heroine, Kriemhild, this takes many years and an unusual amount of ingenuity and persistence.

The foregoing summary is completely my own and is probably the only one of its type. If a person reads one thousand descriptions of the contents of the *NL,* none will stress what I have stressed, i.e., the wrongs inflicted on the two women. As a rule, those incidents are either treated as minor matters or even as comic interludes. The women's hatred and desire to strike back get treated as abnormal and as some strange and freakish aberrations. As the commentators see it, revenge is a "man's business," and women should suffer in silence whatever is being done to them. This type of thinking leads the critics to condemnations of Kriemhild and Brunhild as being "inhuman" monsters.

Parallel to this critical assessment of the two main female figures goes a continuous attempt by the professors of German to upgrade the real monster, the male protagonist Hagen. That man not only kills an unsuspecting and unarmed Siegfried but also a child and the child's tutor and he tries to drown a defenseless priest. Yet a great number of "heroic" qualities are still discovered. And when this "hero" taunts and mocks the poor Kriemhild in a most unchivalrous manner, Hagen gets one round of applause after the other from the male research community. Even for a non-feminist like me this glaring partiality was easy to recognize as male chauvinism. I consider it as an especially dangerous type since it is surrounded by the aura of academic research and professorial competence, and those circumstances have a strange after-effect: even female professors join the men in praising Hagen and trampling on the heroine. They do not seem to be able to resist a certain "brainwashing" effect to which they are subjected during their studies.

After a few weeks of reading I was in the mood of writing a scathing attack on male bias in literary research, illustrating it with the most glaring examples I have found in the secondary literature about the *NL.* It was, for instance, most illuminating to see how a murder was assessed. In the case of Hagen—who murdered a man who had not done anything to wrong him—the murderer was patted on the back as a far-sighted elder statesman and "realpolitiker" who wisely did away with a man that might possibly at a later time have become a danger to his king (a statement which is not supported by the text of the poem). In the case of Kriemhild—who selected as her target the man who had destroyed her happiness by murdering her husband and subsequently taking away her fortune—her

desire to kill made the commentators paint her as a depraved and despicable monster who had "lost her humanity." "Human" women are probably imagined as the willing and uncomplaining recipients of as many blows as the men wish to inflict.

My planned attack on male chauvinism in literary research, however, never got off the ground because I was severely sidetracked. It had bothered me all along that I seemed to be the only person who understood the poet and I did not relish the exclusivity and arrogance which was contained in such an assumption. Thus I kept asking further questions: why should I be singled out for having a better understanding of the poet's intentions than anybody else had obtained in two centuries? How could I lay claim to knowing more about the *NL* than the thousands of professors who had made it their main object of studies, some of them devoting literally their entire life to getting a peek behind its "mysteries"?

Then one day, out of the blue, an idea hit me like a tone of bricks: that poem must have been written by a woman! That would explain everything! How natural it would be that the poem refused to "make sense" to the male research community. When they tried to find out what that man was saying to them, it was actually a woman who was talking all along! And since the poet and the audience always operated on a different "wavelength," no clear "message" ever came across! It was, of course, different with me. Not only was I a woman, but in addition I had formed my first opinions about the poem before any professor was able to give me his "introduction" and to precondition me towards the things which I was to find in the epic.

My suddenly-aroused suspicion about female authorship gave me a great initial euphoria and I marvelled about all the unusual and even comic aspects of my possible discovery. But where should I go from here? How would the experts like it if one of their greatest problems was solved single-handedly for them by a woman—who was not even a professor—and how would they like it if the solution meant heaping tremendous glory on another woman? After all, the *NL* is not some unimportant or recent work but holds a privileged position in the esteem of all educated German-speaking people. Its place is somewhat comparable to that of the *Iliad* for the Greeks, the *Beowulf* for the English, the *Song of Roland* for the French or *El Cid* for the Spanish. This epic is one of those lengthy works which sometimes appear early in a nation's life and are something like a "start-up signal" for a national literature.

And other questions popped up: what were my money and time requirements? Was it at all possible for an inexperienced person to attack a huge body of previous "scientific" evidence? No doubt, this project was a few sizes too large for me. Finally, how would my husband take it, if I wasted time and money and energy on a hopeless cause?

Despite all the doubts I did start because it was already too late to turn back. The project had somehow a life of its own that had taken hold of me.

Around the year 1200 the most literate ladies were to be found in convents. Already the Germany of the tenth century boasted a well-known female writer, a nun of the Benedictine order. If I wanted a solid foundation for my idea I needed a very old convent in the town of Passau in Bavaria (since Passau is believed to have been the locale for writing the *NL*). This basic requirement was soon met. Not only does the poem refer to a convent at the confluence of the three Passau rivers but such a convent stands there to this very day (in 1200 it was already over 400 years old). Subsequently I obtained a little brochure about the history of that place from the Bishop's administration. In that booklet I found amazing parallels between the female protagonist of the epic on the one hand and a much-venerated abbess of the convent on the other hand.

Each of the two women belonged to the Burgundian royal family and each married a king who reigned in Hungary. On the way to Hungary each of them was counselled be a Passau bishop named Pilgrim. Each woman went through terrible heart-break when a hunt ended with the death of a person who was very dear to her (in the case of the real Hungarian queen it was her only living son whom she lost in a hunting accident and in the case of the fictitious character Kriemhild it was her husband who was murdered during a hunt.) Each woman went through nasty hierarchy struggles with another woman: the widowed Hungarian queen Gisela had to yield her place to the mother of her husband's nephew, and Kriemhild was expected to yield it to the wife of her brother. After the husband's death each woman was robbed of a considerable fortune.

Another remarkable point surfaced. During the years from about 1000 to 1161 the convent (consisting of about 30-40 noble ladies, mostly widows) owned a huge tract of valuable land and they also had important toll privileges. They were not only very rich but also had extreme independence, since they were accountable to nobody but the Emperor himself. For over 150 years this situation was a constant annoyance and challenge to the Bishop of Passau who wished to expropriate the nuns' lands and to get their toll concessions, and wanted them under his overall jurisdiction. Finally one of them, who happened to be the nephew of the Emperor Barbarossa, succeeded in 1161 to get the changes effected, and the proud and independent inhabitants of the convent were deprived of all their sources of income. It goes without saying that this transition from wealth and freedom to poverty and subservience will have aroused a lot of violent and unkind feelings, with the main antagonism being strictly along sexist lines. After all, the parties on both sides belonged to the same nation (Bavarian-German), to the same religion (Catholic) and to the same class (members of the nobility). The only conceivable reason for reducing the income and the influence of the nuns was the fact that they were women and, therefore, considered easy to handle, and had to put up with this type of land-switching. If there ever was any group of women being rudely made aware of the meaning of being "only" female, it was this group of nuns at Passau-Niedernburg in 1161.

I had thus collected already three points in favour of my hypothesis, before I had even begun to look closely at the text. Not only had I pinpointed a group of women from whose midst could easily have come a great writer but I had also found a "model" for the heroine and had uncovered the fact that those women had been very drastically jolted into a new consciousness of their inferior position in matters of property and self-determination.

After having delineated the possible environment for the creation of the epic I turned by attention again to the text. Where did it contain indications of female thinking? Was there enough internal evidence to strengthen my hypothesis? There certainly was, and it was, moreover, easy to find. My research often was nothing more than scanning the comments of experts for things which were supposedly "unusual" or "strange" or "peculiar." In nine cases out of ten that designation did not apply any more as soon as the epic was seen as having been written by a woman. I found quite a number of such things but will give here only three examples of a sex-related viewpoint.

The German knights of 1200 were—like knights everywhere in medieval Europe—eager to prove themselves in all sorts of skirmishes and battles for their overlord or country or the advancement of Christianity. If no real battles were available they played games which were mock-battles, and they clearly enjoyed what they were doing. Fighting with weapons in their hands was more or less a normal state of affairs for a certain class during that time, and gave those men a sense of worth and fulfillment. Strangely enough the German *NL* is mostly devoid of any hurrahs in favour of fighting. Whenever the poet describes such scenes she puts considerable emphasis on the negative aspects. Instead of hailing the victors the narrator glumly reminds us that soon women and girls will again be shedding tears. Since the convents of that time were mainly inhabited by widows, this negative attitude towards battles does most likely indicate a female point of view.

Another much-discussed peculiarity of the *NL* consists of a considerable number of stanzas devoted to the sewing of clothes (that part even got the nickname "the tailor stanzas"). It is a well-known fact that the nuns of that time were not only famous for creating beautiful tapestries but also luxurious vestments for the higher clergy and much-adorned clothes for festive occasions.

While the poet pays a lot of attention to the production of clothes, he/she never goes into any details about the production of weapons, and he/she has very little to say about horses. Whenever he/she describes such all-male excursions like a hunting party or a battle, he/she is rather fuzzy or makes factual mistakes. A knight would have had a better knowledge of such matters, and clerics and minstrels were close enough to their overlords so that they had access to second-hand information. Only a woman who was cut off from asking knowledgeable persons could make the blunders that appear in the *NL.*

There is another, rather amusing hint towards female authorship of Germany's one and only national (and so-called "heroic") epic: it is the way in which a man is sometimes named in a strictly matriarchal manner. If we, in our days, would treat Nixon or Kissinger or Carter or Trudeau in such a manner, we would have to refer to them as "Pat's husband," "Nancy's husband," "Rosalynn's husband" and "Margaret's husband." It is rather strange to hear when a famous super-hero is sometimes called "Sieglinde's child (Sieglinde having been his mother) and later "Kriemhild's husband."

These examples must suffice since another item remains to be listed. It is quite hard to explain (being highly technical) but is very suspicious.

Like many medieval works the *NL* has come down to us in several manuscripts. Although there is a considerable number of them, they fall into only two main groups, which are called the B-group and the C-group. There are various differences between the two versions but one stands out: in the C-group the heroine Kriemhild is shown in the best possible light and her enemy is painted pitch-black. This character assessment has been changed in B, where Hagen has been morally "upgraded" while Kriemhild is provided with as many moral blemishes as could be added without touching the poem's overall structure. In other worlds, some time in the thirteenth century a thorough rewriting of the epic took place along sexist lines. The aim was to change the poem to such a degree that the poet's assessment of "good" and "bad" was weakened to a considerable degree. This does, of course, lead to the question: which one is the original version and which is the falsification?

I took the existence of the two versions as a further proof for my suspicion. In my view the C-version had come first (where the woman was good and the man terribly wicked). Since that version, admittedly, is rather biased in favour of the woman, and since this probably did not agree with the taste of the male audience, the story was obviously changed.

The experts do, however, say something different. On and off during the nineteenth century there were researchers who were sure that C was the early version, but somehow they got shouted down by the overwhelming majority of those scholars that were irresistibly drawn to the B-version. Without really bothering about the scientific basis for their decision, the scholars simply "knew" that the B-version was the original. Today that male-oriented version is the only one used and all teaching and research (and translations) are based on it. The existence of the C-version was explained as follows:

Only a few months after the B-version had been written, a tenderhearted scribe who could not bear seeing a woman maligned—super-knight in brilliantly-shining armour that he was—came to her rescue by beautifying her picture. The story of this unspeakably lofty example of male gallantry has been passed on from generation to generation, and today everybody believes it. Except me. I do admit

that there are kind men in existence and that some of them come to the help of women in need. But that type of men would most probably help some real-life woman and not waste an extreme amount of energy and many years of his life on the "rescue" of a paper-woman, a mere figure in a story. Even the most gallant and unselfish man likes to get a "thank-you" nod from his adored lady, and no fictitious heroine is able to grant even that much.

The first version of my article went to two journals. One editor—who happened to be a *NL*-scholar—stated in eight lines that I was wrong and did not bother to tell me where and why or to offer alternative explanations for the many details that I had observed. The editor of the second journal (also an *NL*-scholar) and his referees had another trick up their sleeves by pretending that they could not read.

The purpose of my article had been plainly stated: I wished that the previous question "Was the *NL* written by a knight, a minstrel or a cleric?" should henceforth be changed to read "Was the *NL* written by a knight, a minstrel, a cleric or a nun?" All that I wished was to include the woman in the *question*. I now was treated as if I had proclaimed a new unassailable dogma and, in the kind and paternalistic manner, I was told that such *statements* needed documentary proof. As soon as I had the documents together (has the Vatican a copy of the nun's invoice??) my article would certainly be printed. A really nice and neat way of turning me down and one which, moreover, sounded so extremely responsible on a scientific level. That decision, however, raised a number of immediate questions: what "documentary evidence" had all those previous scholars offered when they advanced their ideas about the poet having been a knight, a minstrel or a cleric? Why did they get into print if everything needs to be proven first beyond any doubt? How come that those three hypotheses had enjoyed a very long life of active discussion and all of a sudden the discussion was to be closed? Do century-old rules of the game have to be changed as soon as a woman appears on the horizon?

Fortunately for me not all editors of journals on German literature have written books about the *NL* or are specialists on the Middle Ages, and so I did find one who was willing to take a risk with my very controversial subject.

Meanwhile a few other persons believe that my question should not be asked. A female graduate student in Germany with whom I exchanged letters wished to write her Ph.D. thesis on the subject of the author of the *NL,* with a view to investigating further my hypothesis about a woman. Her intended work was declared to be "irresponsible" from a scientific point of view. Since grants are not given for the pursuit of irresponsible topics, the young lady in question is now looking for a more acceptable subject which does not pose a threat to her professors. Maybe they are afraid that they cannot sell their books any more if they are invalidated by some new development.

In addition they probably do not cherish the idea that a poem which they always praised and venerated as a na-

CLASSICAL AND MEDIEVAL LITERATURE CRITICISM, Vol. 41

tional monument could possibly be unveiled as nothing more than a well-disguised feminist manifesto which was intent on exposing men's injustice and meanness, stone-heartedness and greed, solidarity and conspiracies in their dealings with women.

Notes

1. This article is not annotated in the usual manner since it is only a report about the genesis of another article that was published in a scholarly journal and has 57 footnotes (Berta Lösel-Wieland-Engelmann, "Verdanken wir das *Nibelungenlied* einer Niedern-burger Nonne?" in: *Monatshefte,* Spring 1980, University of Wisconsin Press, pp. 5-25). The article appeared in German and relies heavily on German sources. An English-speakingperson who wishes to acquaint herself/himself with the *NL,* can do so by reading A. T. Hatto's *The Nibelungenlied: A New Translation* (Harmondsworth, 1969). A good example for a prejudiced commentary on the *NL* is provided by Werner A. Mueller's *The Nibelungenlied Today: Its Substance, Essence and Significance* (Chapel Hill, 1962). No person with whom I had personal dealings is named in this paper since I, for the time being, wish to protect the guilty.

Winder McConnell (essay date 1984)

SOURCE: "The Reception of the *Nibelungenlied* in Germany from the *Klage* to the Twentieth Century" in *The Nibelungenlied*, Twayne Publishers, 1984, pp. 84-101.

[*In the following essay, McConnell offers an overview of the* Nibelungenlied's *influence on German literature.*]

If the number of popular and artistic works based on the *Nibelungenlied* may be considered evidence of the attraction the epic held for subsequent generations of readers and theatergoers, then we may certainly conclude that the poem has proved to be one of the most inspiring "sources" in the history of German literature. I have already considered in the Introduction the extent to which the *Nibelungenlied* has captured scholarly interest from the time of Obereit and Bodmer to the present. But what of the influence the work exerted in the literary sphere subsequent to its genesis in the form known to us from the turn of the thirteenth century? Actually, it is more appropriate to speak of the influence of the *Nibelungen* tradition per se, although this is not meant to diminish the significance of the *Nibelungenlied* for the later creative process. The scores of dramas written during the nineteenth and twentieth centuries, for example, are almost entirely based on the epic. However, the popular *Lied vom Hürnen Seyfrid* (The lay of Seyfrid, the Dragon-Slayer) together with its analogues, the play by Hans Sachs and the folk book, is more indebted to the Nordic sources which relate *in extenso* of Siegfried's youth. The same is true of Wagner's *Ring des Nibelungen, (Ring of the Nibelungen)* the mythological el-

ements of which hark back to the *Edda* and the *Völsunga Saga.* The *Nibelungenlied* is part of a remarkably rich tradition which spans centuries in terms of its literary expression.

Within the framework of the present monograph, it is impossible to provide more than a basic overview of the subsequent literary treatment of the *Nibelungen* tradition and the *Nibelungenlied* itself. For the most part, I have not considered the nonliterary manifestations of the subject matter (film, postcards, art, etc.). The number of dramas, poems, and novels based on the *Nibelungenlied* alone is legion, and while I have felt it appropriate to linger for a while in some instances and offer the reader a more intimate glimpse of the intentions of a particular author (thereby exposing my own prejudices), I have made no attempt to treat systematically every literary work which uses the epic as a base. For the reception of the *Nibelungenlied* in Germany during the nineteenth and twentieth centuries, I have to acknowledge a heavy debt to the studies of Holger Schulz,[1] Otfrid Ehrismann,[2] and Werner Wunderlich,[3] works which may accurately be designated as indispensable for anyone who wishes to gain insight into the great proclivity of *Nibelungen* materials produced over the past two hundred years.

Diu Klage

Diu Klage (The lament) is "a brief inferior sequel"[4] to the *Nibelungenlied,* an elegiac commentary of 4,360 verses in rhyming couplets, appended to all of the major manuscripts of its great predecessor.[5] The *Klage* is, at one and the same time, a commentary on events which transpire in the *Nibelungenlied,* a defense of Kriemhild as well as a condemnation of Hagen, and a narration of the course of events subsequent to the mass slaughter in the Great Hall of Attila. Above all, it is an elegy addressed to the prominent figures who are no more, as well as to the masses of Burgundians and Huns slain during the fray.

On the question of Siegfried's "guilt," the anonymous poet is unambiguous in assigning the hero a share of the responsibility for bringing about his death: "unt daz er selbe den tôt / gewan von sîner übermuot" ("Until he himself was killed as a result of his haughtiness," 38-39). No details of the actual murder are provided, although the blame for the deed is placed on Gunther (103), Hagen (104), and Brünhild (104) respectively. The poet also emphasizes the excessive lamenting of Kriemhild (95-96), but, unlike the author of the *Nibelungenlied,* who is inclined to consider such a lack of moderation as unnatural and destructive, and who, at least in manuscript B, paints a most uncomplimentary picture of the queen as a she-devil, the *Klage* poet takes Kriemhild's side and praises her actions. No one, he asserts, should condemn her for wishing to avenge Siegfried's death (139), a less than veiled criticism, perhaps, of those before him who have portrayed Kriemhild from a decidedly negative point of view. His response to such criticism is summed up in verses 154-58:

> swer ditze maere merken kan,
> der sagt unschuldic gar ir lîp,

wan daz daz vil edel werde wîp
taete nâch ir triuwe
ir râche in grôzer riuwe.

(Whoever can take note of this tale will declare that the queen was guiltless. For the noble lady acted out of loyalty, exacting her revenge in great sorrow.)

It is, in fact, her loyalty which, the poet proclaims, will assure her a place in heaven (571-76). Earlier, however, when considering the loss of forty thousand men prior to the death of Hagen (236-37), the author had explicitly stated that Kriemhild's decision to let matters run their course had emanated "von krankem sinne" ("from a sick mind," 243), which hardly seems to accord with his later defense of the queen. Moreover, to associate Kriemhild's loyalty and the deeds she has committed as a result of it with her right to a place in Heaven gives us cause to wonder if the poet was aware of the basic tenets of Christianity. He (or she?) was caught between justifying Kriemhild's quest for revenge on the one hand, and the horror perceived at the extent of the catastrophe on the other. Hildebrand's killing of Kriemhild is condemned (732-33). Hildebrand had hewn Kriemhild to pieces because she had cut down a defenseless Hagen. In the *Klage,* however, Hildebrand soundly condemns the late Hagen for all that has transpired, according him, in fact, the appellation *vâlant* so poignantly used to depict a demonic Kriemhild in the *Nibelungenlied* (note *Klage,* 1250). The Burgundians, as a whole, allowed their *übermuot* to prevent them from telling Attila about the true state of affairs at a time when the monarch might well have taken measures to circumvent the mass slaughter which later ensued (284-89). Hildebrand also refers to this *übermuot* in 1277 and sees it as the reason for the fact that the Burgundians have been afflicted by "den gotes slac" ("God's wrath," 1276).

The *Klage* utilizes four major geographical locations: Attila's court, Bechelaren, Passau, and Worms. Rüdeger, the "vater aller tugende" ("epitome of virtue," 2133), is particularly mourned, the poet claiming that "an dem was mit wârheit / verlorn der werlde wünne" ("With him was lost, in truth, the joy of the world," 1962-63). In Passau, Bishop Pilgrim puts the blame for all that has happened exclusively on Hagen, maintaining that one should rue the day that he was born (3420). In Worms, Rumold refers to "Hagenen übermuot" (4031) as well as to his "grôzen untriuwen" ("great treachery," 4035). The intention is clear: the poet is attempting to absolve Kriemhild as much as possible of guilt for the catastrophe, and Hagen, a totally dark figure, is to bear the blame, or at least the major part of it. There are frequent references to the wrath of God, and in general we may say that Christian overtones (as confused as they may be) are more conspicuous in the *Klage* than in the *Nibelungenlied.*[6] In an attempt to provide a more optimistic outlook on the future, the poet refers to the impending coronation of young Siegfried, Brünhild's son, in Worms. The land cannot remain without a king, and both Brünhild and the surviving Burgundian nobility find consolation in the forthcoming ceremony.

As a defense of Kriemhild and a condemnation of Hagen, the *Klage* leaves us unconvinced. The black and white attitude of the poet in no way accords with the text of the *Nibelungenlied* or the intention of its author. The author lacked the depth and perspective of his forerunner and clearly had little sympathy with the ambivalent disposition of the latter toward his main characters. The weak attempt to provide some sort of happy ending to the tragedy stands in blatant contrast to the conclusion of the *Nibelungenlied.* The final section of the *Klage* (4323-60) adds some (probably unintentional) levity to the predominant atmosphere of despair, as the poet expresses his regret at not being able to inform us of the fate of Attila, whether he was taken up into the air, buried alive, brought to Heaven, whether he climbed out of his skin, scurried away into a hole in the wall, or went to hell and was consumed by the devil.

LATE MEDIEVAL AND EARLY BAROQUE RENDITIONS OF THE YOUNG SIEGFRIED STORY

Working from ten of eleven extant prints of the *Lied vom Hürnen Seyfrid (The lay of Seyfrid, the Dragon-Slayer),* K. C. King published, in 1958, a critical edition of this early New High German poem, dating from the late fifteenth century.[7] The work consists of 179 eight-line stanzas with the rhyme scheme A B C B D E F E. The *Lied* harks back to a source with which the *Nibelungenlied* poet was probably familiar, but which he did not exploit to full advantage. It is primarily concerned with Seyfrid's (Siegfried's) adventures as a young man, his fight with a dragon, his almost total invulnerability acquired by bathing in the slain dragon's blood, and his love of Kriemhild, daughter of King Gybich. Seyfrid subsequently rescues the princess from the lair of a dragon and undergoes a series of adventures culminating in his slaying of the giant Kuperan with the aid of a dwarf. The poem closes with a reference to the growing jealousy of Hagen and Gyrnot, and the later death of Seyfrid at the hands of Hagen.

Noteworthy in the *Lied* is the fact that, from the outset, Seyfrid is portrayed as a brash young man who is self-assertive and physically strong, but not given to listening to others:

> Der knab was so můtwillig
> Darzů starck und auch gross
> Das seyn vatter und můter
> Der ding gar seer verdross
> Er wolt nie keynem menschen
> Seyn tag seyn underthon
> Im stund seyn syn und můte
> Das er nur zůg daruon.
>
> (Stanza 2)

(The boy was strong and tall but also so headstrong that his father and mother became quite concerned about him. He never wanted to be subordinated to anyone, and all he could ever think of was getting away.)

The tendency to assert himself and to ignore the status of others is reflected in stanzas 173 through 176, as Seyfrid arouses animosity in King Gunther and his brothers, leading to his subsequent murder by Hagen in the "Otten waldt" (Odenwald, 177.8).[8]

Das Lied vom Hürnen Seyfrid, which Eugen Mogk, in his inaugural lecture at the University of Leipzig in 1895, had referred to as a "Bänkelsängerlied" ("balladmonger's tune"), can scarcely be compared with the *Nibelungenlied* in terms of literary merit. Scholars are not at all sure whether the poem is actually a combination of several independent lays, as Wilhelm Grimm suggested,[9] or the work of one author. Its importance, however, within the literary tradition of the *Nibelungen* is summed up by King in the excellent introduction to his edition:

> However one looks at the poem it is undeniable that it tells us things about Siegfried which the other sources we know do not tell us; and these things are of interest whether they can be traced back to Germanic antiquity or not, for it is just as important for the history of literature to know whether an ancient popular hero remained merely an ancient popular hero or whether he continued to occupy a significant position in the creative literature of later times.[10]

Relying to a large degree on *Das Lied vom Hürnen Seyfrid* as a base, Hans Sachs completed, in 1557, his tragedy in seven acts, *Der Hürnen Seufrid* (Sewfrid, the Dragon-Slayer), and thus became the first writer to adapt a segment of the *Nibelungen* tradition for the stage. The *Lied* serves as a basis for the first five acts of the play, while the preparations for the fight between Sewfrid and Dietrich, as well as the actual combat (acts 6 and 7), appear to be based on a work from the late thirteenth century, *Der grosse Rosengarten.* It is impossible to ascertain whether Hans Sachs knew the *Nibelungenlied,* although most scholars are inclined to doubt that this was the case.

As in the *Lied,* Sewfrid, son of Sigmund, is not given to courtly mores and, from the outset, demonstrates a high degree of haughtiness. He is "gar vnadelicher art" ("certainly not noble in bearing"),[11] "frech, verwegen vnd muetwillig" ("haughty, daring, and headstrong").[12] Acts 3 through 5 deal with the abduction of Crimhilt by the dragon and Sewfrid's adventures in the process of rescuing her. When, in act 5, Sewfrid learns from the dwarf that he will only be granted eight years together with Crimhilt, he accepts it as "God's will" (747; note also 900!). Acts 6 and 7 are of particular interest to us. In the former, Crimhilt is depicted as an ambitious woman, eager to see how Sewfrid would fare in battle against Dietrich, and quite conscious of the universal fame he will attain should he prove triumphant (note 896f.). Significantly, *vbermuet (Übermut,* "haughtiness," "arrogance") is singled out in 870 as a trait from which nothing good can come. In the contest which follows, Dietrich eventually proves to be too formidable for Sewfrid, who flees to Crimhilt and seeks refuge in her lap! This is a very different image of the hero as compared to the way Siegfried was portrayed in earlier sources, as well as in later works. The final act of Sachs's tragedy relates the murder of Sewfrid by Hagen who, in 1068f, gives some idea of the motivation behing

Sigfried and the dragon, from an 1883 edition of the Nibelungenlied.

the deed: "Nun hat auch ain ent dein hochmuet, / Der vns fort nit mer irren thuet" ("Now your arrogance has come to an end, and will no longer give us cause to worry"; compare strophe 993 in the *Nibelungenlied!*).[13]

The *Wunderschöne Historia von dem gehörnten Siegfried* (The marvelous story of Siegfried, the Dragon-Slayer), commonly dated from 1726,[14] the year of the earliest surviving edition, had its origins as a printed folk book almost seventy years earlier, as Harold Jantz has shown in his delightful and informative essay, "The Last Branch of the Nibelungen Tree."[15] Like its poetic forerunner, the prose *Historia* relates the story of Siegfried, here the son of King Sieghardus of the Netherlands, a tall, muscular young man, whose urge for independence causes his parents some anxiety. Even though the king's advisers suggest that the prince be allowed to make his way in the world, Siegfried takes his leave unannounced. After a brief encounter with a smith, whom he antagonizes with his arrogance and brute strength, Siegfried slays a dragon in a nearby forest and burns him, using the fat which is produced to toughen *(hürnen)* his skin. The greater part of the folk book is devoted to the story of Siegfried's rescue of Florigunda, daughter of King Gilbaldus of Worms, from a dragon. As in the *Lied* and the play, prince and princess wed, but Siegfried incurs the jealousy of his three brothers-in-law because he consistently wins the prizes offered in tournaments. He is eventually killed by one of the trio,

Hagenwald, and is avenged by his father, Sieghardus. The folk book closes with an allusion to Löwhardus, Siegfried's son, who, it is said, grew up to be a fine hero.[16]

In many respects, the *Historia* is simply a prose rendition of the late-fifteenth-century *Lied*. Siegfried is portrayed, however, as a Christian knight; and, as in the *Lied,* there is no attempt to depict the heroine, Florigunda, as the avenging she-devil, an image which would scarcely have found much sympathetic reception in the early seventeenth century.

THE NINETEENTH CENTURY

Throughout the remainder of the seventeenth and most of the eighteenth century, the subject matter of the *Nibelungen* provided no incentive for further literary productions among German authors. With the advent of romanticism and the national fervor which swept through the country at the time of the Napoleonic Wars, enthusiasm for the German past in general and the Middle Ages in particular increased among poets as well as scholars. The effort to free Germany and Europe from Napoleon's armies was complemented by the attempt to use the *Nibelungenlied* for political purposes. Siegfried, the dragon-slayer, came to be regarded as a national hero, the German Achilles. Ludwig Tieck's ballads, "Siegfrieds Jugend" (Siegfried's Youth) and "Siegfried der Drachentödter" (Siegfried the Dragon-Slayer, 1804), concentrate on the early life of the hero, although the second poem also alludes to his death. Tieck does not ignore Siegfried's *übermuot,* but in "Siegfried der Drachentödter" that word assumes a more positive quality than is the case in either the *Nibelungenlied* or the *Lied vom Hürnen Seyfrid.* Ludwig Uhland composed a poem in rhyming couplets with Siegfried as the central figure, "Siegfrieds Schwert" (Siegfried's sword, 1812), and the prominent translator of the *Nibelungenlied,* Karl Simrock, produced a ballad entitled "Der Nibelungen-Hort" (The treasure of the Nibelungs, 1827). The popularity of lyric and epic renditions of the *Nibelungen* theme was extraordinary throughout the nineteenth century,[17] but it was in drama where, more than anywhere else, the extent to which the material had captured the imagination of contemporary authors was demonstrated.

In particular, one witnesses a veritable proliferation of *Nibelungenlied* dramas which reflect, in chronological sequence, the spirit of the Wars of Liberation against Napoleon, the national movements of the mid-nineteenth century (especially the Revolution of 1848), and the nationalistic tendencies prevalent at the time of the founding of the Second Reich by Bismarck (1871). In his dissertation, *Der Nibelungenstoff auf dem deutschen Theater* (The *Nibelungen* theme on the German stage),[18] Holger Schulz lists no fewer than fourteen dramas which were produced between 1810 and 1861, including works by such noted authors as Ludwig Uhland, Geibel, Ibsen, and Hebbel.[19] Hebbel's trilogy (*Der gehörnte Siegfried* (Siegfried, the Dragon-Slayer), *Siegfrieds Tod* (Siegfried's death), *Kriemhilds Rache* (Kriemhild's Revenge), which I shall examine more

closely, enjoyed considerable popularity on the German stage in the nineteenth and early twentieth centuries, but failed to exercise much influence on subsequent dramas. It was probably not fully understood, despite the number of successful productions it enjoyed.[20] Between 1866 and 1951, Schulz lists a further twenty *Nibelungenlied* dramas, many of which, however, he designates as amateurish ("dilettantische Stücke").[21] Apart from dramas concerned with the theme of the *Nibelungenlied* in general, Schulz also cites a number of works dealing with individual figures (Rüdeger, Attila, Kudrun, Dietrich), as well as a few "Merovingian dramas," which accord with the efforts to link Merovingian history to the events depicted in the epic.

Although there was no lack of *Nibelungen* dramas throughout the nineteenth century, few managed to gain any lasting recognition. Gottfried Weber states: "Regardless of the reason, none of them ever attained the poetic stature of the medieval work."[22] Many were not received well on the stage, and, of the dozens which appeared in print, only Hebbel's *Nibelungen* is still read with any frequency today (the readers being primarily Germanists and their students). In his poem, "Sigurd unter den Gänsen" (Sigurd among the geese, 1839), Friedrich Rückert poked fun at the dilettantism inherent in many of the plays which used the *Nibelungenlied* as a source, falling over it "wie jugendliche Leser / oder wie ein Heer von Recensenten" ("like youthful readers or an army of critics").[23] In Heine's "Deutschland," Germany was compared to the brash, temperamental Siegfried whom we find in the *Lied vom Hürnen Seyfrid.* Felix Dahn's "Der Bundestag" (The federal parliament) utilized the treasure of the Nibelungs as a symbol of unity. In his "Deutsche Lieder" (German songs) Dahn compared the envisioned destruction of Germany at the hands of a Russian, French, and Italian coalition to the heroic demise of the Nibelungs in Attila's Great Hall.

Let us return for a while to Friedrich Hebbel's *Die Nibelungen: Ein deutsches Trauerspiel in drei Abteilungen /* (The Nibelungs: A German tragedy in three parts), for of all the plays produced during the nineteenth and twentieth centuries on this theme, it is the one that deserves more than fleeting mention. Hebbel's diary entry of 18 February 1857 alludes to a visit the dramatist paid to the home of Amalia Schoppen in Hamburg, at which time he became acquainted with the *Nibelungenlied* and was particularly impressed by the figures. In Vienna, Hebbel attended a performance of Ernst Raupach's *Der Nibelungenhort* (The treasure of the Nibelungs, published 1834) and, in a letter to Charlotte Rousseau, he expressed his delight with Christine Enghaus (whom he later married) in the role of Chriemhild. Hebbel's drama was conceived over a period of five years, from 1855 to 1860, during which time he familiarized himself with the renditions of previous authors. He was aware of the difficulties inherent in such a project, the most prominent being the transposing of epic figures onto the stage,[24] but he believed that the *Nibelungenlied* poet had been a "dramatist from his head to his toes."[25]

The *Nibelungen* consists of three parts: *Der gehörnte Sieg-fried: Vorspiel in einem Akt, Siegfrieds Tod,* and *Kriem-hilds Rache.* Under the influence of Friedrich Theodor Vis-cher, Hebbel attempted to produce a drama in conformity with the latter's call for a logical justification of every ac-tion undertaken by psychologically unified characters. Members of human society (in contrast to those figures whose origins lay in the supernatural sphere) were to be depicted as acting from a position of complete independ-ence and would bear full responsibility for their actions.[26] In *Der gehörnte Siegfried,* Hebbel retains much of the ar-rogance we associate with Siegfried upon his arrival in Worms: "Ich grüss dich, König Gunther von Burgund!— / Du staunst, dass du den Siegfried bei dir siehst? / Er ko-mmt, mit dir zu kämpfen um dein Reich!" ("I greet you, King Gunther of Burgundy. You are amazed to see Sieg-fried here before you? I have come to fight you for your empire.")[27] We are also made aware of Gunther's overesti-mation of his talents. Upon hearing of the danger for Brün-hild's suitors and the fate of those who have hitherto at-tempted to woo her, the king exclaims that this can only prove that she is intended for him. As in the *Nibelungen-lied,* a deal is fashioned whereby Siegfried agrees to pro-cure Brünhild (who, he maintains, has not touched his heart) for Gunther if he can wed Kriemhild in return. Sieg-fried has thus been clearly identified with a world set far apart from that of the court at Worms. The ominous pre-dictions regarding the outcome of the wooing mission are delivered by Volker: "Nein, König, bleib daheim / Es en-det schlecht" ("No, my king, remain at home. This will turn out badly").[28] Volker recognizes the deeper signifi-cance in what is proposed, and maintains that "falsche Künste" ("magic") are not appropriate to the Burgundians.

In *Siegfrieds Tod,* Hebbel places Brünhild squarely into the foreground and, in a scene reminiscent of the arrival of the Burgundians in Iceland in the *Nibelungenlied,* allows her to address Siegfried first in the assumption that it is he who has come to woo her. He devotes no time to the ac-tual ordeals in which Gunther-Siegfried must prove victo-rious in order to obtain Brünhild, but quickly moves the scene from Isenland and Brünhild's castle to Worms and Gunther's palace. It is Hagen who makes the initial sug-gestion that Siegfried "tame" Brünhild in bed, claiming that the honor of the king is at stake. In contrast to the situation in the *Nibelungenlied,* Siegfried is less than will-ing to comply with the request. His eventual acquiescence, coupled with his indiscretion in taking Brünhild's girdle, leads to the subsequent confrontation between Brünhild, conscious of her status as queen of the Burgundians, and Kriemhild, to whom Siegfried is "the strongest man in the world." When Hagen states that Siegfried must die, his motives go beyond those of his counterpart in the *Nibel-ungenlied.* It is not just a question of jealousy and dislike or, for that matter, fear of the hero. Siegfried is not simply the "Schwätzer" ("prattler"). Hagen recognizes that there is more than hate perceived by Brünhild toward Siegfried. They are of the same world, inescapably drawn to one an-other by their very nature; theirs is a magical bond that can only be dissolved by death:

> "Ein Zauber ists,
> Durch den sich ihr Geschlecht erhalten will,
> Und der die letzte Riesin ohne Lust
> Wie ohne Wahl zum letzten Riesen treibt."

(act 4, scene 9)

("It is magic, by means of which their race attempts to survive, and which draws the last giantess—neither by choice, nor by desire—to the last giant.")

Kriemhild is modeled closely on her counterpart in the *Ni-belungenlied,* and, in *Kriemhilds Rache,* Hebbel also al-lows her to degenerate into a dark figure who would "cut down a hundred brothers" (act 4, scene 4) in order to get Hagen's head. As in the medieval forerunner, the Burgun-dian kings are in no way inclined to give in to Kriemhild's offer that they may leave Attila's court unharmed after turning over Hagen. Lifted from the *Nibelungenlied* as well are Rüdeger's plight (act 5, scene 11) and the final confrontation between Hagen and Kriemhild, including a contemporary version of the original appellative hurled at Kriemhild by Hagen, "Unhold" ("devil," act 5, scene 14). Similarly, Hagen dies by Kriemhild's hand, and the queen is struck down by Hildebrand, who refers to her as a devil. In contrast to the *Nibelungenlied,* however, Hebbel's drama concludes with Attila's abdication and Dietrich's acceptance of his crown "in the name of the one who died on the cross" (act 5, scene 14).

What had Hebbel intended with the *Nibelungen?* In a short essay entitled "An den geneigten Leser" (To the sympa-thetic reader), he expressed his desire to adapt "the dra-matic treasure of the *Nibelungenlied*"[29] for the stage. The actions of the characters were to be their own, that is, in-dependent of the influence of superhuman beings. While Hebbel urged his readers to seek nothing more than the "Nibelungen Not" behind this tragedy, he clearly offered a three-phrase development from the mythical, through the heathen, to the Christian era. In marked contrast to the *Ni-belungenlied,* where no future is envisioned, Hebbel's *Ni-belungen,* while not conveying in the final words of Di-etrich (who represents the antithesis of the demonic Hagen) the idea of a "crawling to the cross,"[30] offers an affirma-tion of a new life, a new beginning, and thus endows the work with a very different spirit when compared with that of its medieval forerunner.

The patriotic fervor engendered by the Franco-Prussian War of 1870-71 led to a glorification of conflict and lent emphasis to the concepts of unity, strength, and loyalty. Emanuel Geibel's poem, "An Deutschland. Januar 1871" (To Germany, January, 1871) contained a reference to the "marrow of the Nibelungs," and Julius Rodenberg's "Die Heimkehr" (The homecoming, 1872), a tribute to Wilhelm I, referred to the Kaiser as the "Sieg-Fried" of the German people. All of Germany became a "Nibelungenland" (Adolf Bartels, 1896) in the last years of the nineteenth century, and the Germans themselves were depicted as the "Nibel-ungenstamm," "the Nibelungen clan." Bismarck, the "Iron Chancellor" and engineer of German unity in the last half of the nineteenth century, was also compared to Siegfried in Felix Dahn's poems "Jung-Bismarck" (Young Bismarck) and "Bei Bismarcks Tod" (On Bismarck's death). This symbolism became even more pronounced in Hermann Hoffmeister's "Der eiserne Siegfried" (Iron Siegfried), where Bismarck was compared to the hero of Xanten, and Fafnir, the slain dragon, to the threatening "Sozial-demokratismus" which was becoming more and more noticeable throughout the land.

The *Nibelungen* theme inspired not only literary productions in the nineteenth century. Vischer, whose influence on Hebbel has been noted above, was the first to attempt the production of an opera based on the subject ("Vorschlag zu einer Oper" [Suggestion for an opera, 1844]), and he was followed by Louise Otto (*Die Nibelungen als Oper,* [The Nibelungen as opera, 1845]), the Dane Nils Wilhelm Gade (*Siegfried und Brynhilde,* 1847, a fragment), and Heinrich Dorn (*Die Nibelungen,* 1854). In 1874, Richard Wagner completed his tetralogy, *Der Ring des Nibelungen (The Ring of the Nibelungen),* consisting of the *Vorabend, Das Rheingold (Prelude, Rhine Gold,* 1854), and the three music dramas, *Die Walküre (The Valkyries,* 1856), *Siegfried* (1871), and *Götterdämmerung (Twilight of the Gods,* 1874). The first complete performance of the *Ring* was given in August 1876 in Bayreuth. In a letter to Franz Müller in Weimar, dated 9 January 1855, Wagner referred to the sources he had consulted, ranging from Lachmann's *Nibelungen Noth und Klage,* through the *Edda, Völsunga Saga, Wilkina-* and *Niflunga Saga,* to secondary literature such as F. Joseph Mone's *Untersuchungen zur deutschen Heldensage* (Studies on German heroic poetry), which he considered to be very important. Wagner was not concerned about remaining "true" to the sources; he used them freely, deriving most of his material from the *Edda* and the *Völsunga Saga.* His chief interest lay in the mythical aspects of the material, and he did not bother with the destruction of the Burgundians. The *Rheingold,* in fact, is devoid of purely human characters. Brünhild is a central figure while Gutrune (Kriemhild) is reduced to fulfilling a necessary dramatic function. The *Ring* also betrays the influence of classical tragedy and myth, and the tetralogy may be described as a veritable potpourri of Germanic motifs, Christianity, Greek myth, and humanism.

Wagner also emphasizes the animosity perceived by Hagen toward Siegfried and Brünhild. He is jealous of the former and also despises him. Hagen deliberates; Siegfried acts. Hagen is conscious of the significance of events transpiring around him; Siegfried, although free, remains naive, oblivious to the ultimate meaning of his actions. Unlike Siegfried, who openly admits that he often forgets the ring of the Nibelungs and the treasure, Hagen's aim in life is directed toward procuring the former.

Vischer maintained that, owing to the stature and archaism of its figures, a dramatization of the *Nibelungen* theme was impossible. Wagner contradicted Vischer in a most impressive manner, although in his own time, it was by no means certain that his tetralogy would enjoy the critical acclaim it does today. Writing of the first English performance of the *Ring* in the *Era* of 13 May 1882, the music critic concluded: "That the *Nibelungen Ring,* in spite of its occasional power and beauty, can ever be popular, is more than we expect and certainly more than we hope for."[31]

THE TWENTIETH CENTURY

There is no radical break with tradition in *Nibelungenlied* reception during the early twentieth century. According to Werner Wunderlich,[32] three basic "types of reception" can be discerned: (1) Siegfried is portrayed as the young, carefree hero, whose foremost attributes are courage and loyalty; (2) the work and its figures are regarded from a mythical perspective, with Siegfried depicted as a symbol of "light" in contrast to his antagonists, who represent the "dark" side of existence; (3) the work is cited as an attempt to convey the image of "higher man," with both Siegfried and Brünhild regarded as exemplary. Intrinsic to this third type was the existential necessity of the hero's demise. In 1909, Paul Ernst, whom Ernst Alker has described as the "most important representative of neoclassicism,"[33] produced his demonic drama, *Brunhild* (followed, in 1918, by *Chriemhild*), in which he attempted through the use of expressionistic devices to move away from a Hebbel-like "Psychologisierung" ("psychologizing") of the characters and present the myth of the "higher man" and the ultimate tragedy of an existence which attained perfection only through its own demise. Ernst's drama had yet another function to fulfill, however, as the author himself indicated in his "Nachwort zu Chriemhild": "If something of the pride of the German has been expressed in my work, pride which he may now be accorded at the time of his great humiliation, then I shall be happy, for I will thus have fulfilled my obligation as a poet."[34] Siegfried and Brünhild are portrayed as "outsiders," as beings set apart from the rest of society, "higher entities," whose very nature cannot help but bring them into conflict with the world about them. Although they ideally should serve as models for "lower men," such as Gunther and Kriemhild, the manner in which they are abused by the latter leads to their tragic demise.[35] The question of guilt is not pertinent in Ernst's dramas. Fate is decisive, and it lies in the nature of the hero to behave as a demigod, trapped by his insistence on coming to terms with the world of "lower men," with release possible only in death. When Ernst's Hagen, whom the author viewed as a "figure of depth, strength, greatness, and tragedy,"[36] decides that Siegfried must die, he acts from higher necessity, knowing full well that Gunther and Khriemhild are the "cancer" in society.[37]

World War I produced a further utilization of the *Nibelungenlied* in the service of the country, an identification of main characters in the medieval epic with specific German traits or institutions. Siegfried was viewed as a symbol of military strength and was compared to both Germany and the German army. At the beginning of the war this was also true for Hagen, although he later became associated with the "stab-in-the-back" theory advanced by many in the postwar period.[38] Wilhelm Scherer ("Nibelungentreue:

Kriegsgesänge" [Nibelung loyalty: war songs, 1916]) conjured up the image of a reincarnated Siegfried representing strength and loyalty, and Werner Jansen dedicated his novel *Das Buch Treue: Nibelungenroman* (The book of loyalty: A Nibelung novel, 1921) to the German war dead, the memory of whose heroism and loyalty had given him the courage to bring his work to its conclusion. When the war was lost and the Weimar Republic founded, conservative opponents of the regime turned to the **Nibelungenlied** as a model in their call for Germany's renewal, for, if models were indeed to be found, one need look no further than to the "national epic." Friedrich Vogt, in a reference to "Nibelungentreue" ("Nibelung loyalty"), compared the endurance demonstrated by the Burgundians in the burning palace of Attila to Germany's will to resist the enemy coalitions of World War I (*Französischer und deutscher Nationalgeist im Rolandslied und im Nibelungenlied* [French and German national spirit in the lay of Roland and the Nibelungenlied, 1922]).

The *Nibelungen* theme found warm reception in National Socialist Germany between 1933 and 1945. Wunderlich contrasts the different perspectives from which the material was viewed. During the Weimar Republic, the themes and motifs of the **Nibelungenlied** had been employed by authors of antirepublican persuasion to express optimism for Germany's future, but poets and dramatists sympathetic to the Third Reich spoke in terms of the present. Siegfried was seen by some as the prototype of Nordic man, as the embodiment of the Nordic spirit. His fate was compared with that of the Germanic race. In "Das Lied von Siegfried" (The lay of Siegfried, 1934), Hans Henning von Grote portrayed Siegfried, the dragon-slayer, as the destroyer of dark forces, the personification of loyalty and the ever-recurring hero in times of peril. The identification of Siegfried with Arminius was revitalized by Bodo Ernst in his *Siegfried-Armin: Der Mythos vom deutschen Menschen* (Siegfried-Arminius: The myth of the German, 1935) and Paul Albrecht in *Arminius-Sigurfrid: Ein Roman des deutschen Volkes* (Arminius-Siegfried: A novel of the German people, 1935). Ernst Huttig's *Siegfried: Festliches Spiel in drei dramatischen Szenen und zwei Bühnenbildern* (Siegfried: A festive play in three dramatic scenes and two stage scenes, 1934) depicts the hero as a selfless warrior in the service of others, comparable to Germany and the role of its soldiers in foreign service throughout the world in previous centuries. Similar thoughts were echoed by Karl Busch in *Das Nibelungenlied in deutscher Geschichte und Kunst* (The Nibelungenlied in German history and art, 1934). Josef Weinheber's poem "Siegfried-Hagen" (1936) compares the perilous situation of the "blond-haired hero," murdered among his "friends," with that of the Reich, which the poet considers in danger of collapsing as a result of inner strife and lack of harmony. But Hagen, too, could be portrayed as the "personification of the Nordic type,"[39] as in Wulf Bley's play *Die Gibichunge* (The Gibechs, 1934), in which the hero of Troneck maintains that it was his destiny to kill Siegfried.[40] Throughout this period in Germany, the **Nibelungenlied** was regarded as a work which reflected "the historical mission of the German people and the natural and necessary battle for existence of the individual as well as the race, or the people.[41] The Nibelungs were considered the epitome of courage, prowess in battle, and, above all, loyalty, both to the people and its leader. With the outbreak of World War II, the bellicose tendencies of individuals and peoples in the **Nibelungenlied,** the spirit of the warrior, became prime models for a new generation of soldiers.[42] As the military victories of the years 1939 to 1942 gave way to the defeats of 1943 to 1945, the emphasis was placed more on the fatalistic acceptance of catastrophe, of defiance in the face of death and total destruction. To die was not important; to die with honor in a heroic struggle, as the Nibelungs had done, was paramount. War was considered the test of heroic man, that which ultimately gave meaning to one's existence, a theme which was prominent in Hans Baumann's *Rüdiger von Bechelaren: Das Passauer Nibelungenspiel* (Rüdeger of Bechelaren: Passau's Nibelung play, 1939).

The postwar period evinced two major phases in the reception of the **Nibelungenlied** in Germany.[43] On the one hand, there was a concerted effort to move away from the trends of earlier periods, while, on the other, some of the old concepts and interpretations continued to be propagated. In 1944, the production of the first part of Max Mell's drama, *Der Nibelunge Not* (The tragedy of the Nibelungs), took place in Vienna. The second part, *Kriemhilds Rache,* was performed six years later. Mell attempted to move away from titanic concepts and, while accentuating Christian ethnics in his work, depicted the Nibelungs as human beings. In two tragedies, *Siegfried* and *Grimhild* (1948), Wilhelm Hildebrand Schäfer depicted the world as a stage on which Siegfried, the visionary, a superior man, is destroyed by the narrow-mindedness of society and its pragmatic outlook. Reinhold Schneider's play, *Tarnkappe* (The magic cloak, 1951), is rooted in the Christian-humanistic tradition and portrays the constant struggle faced by the individual to realize a Christian existence in this life.

In the 1950s, the theme of the *Nibelungen* fell prey to *Trivialliteratur* and pornography. In the comic series, *Sigurd,* Siegfried appears as a German Tarzan or Superman, and the figure was sexually exploited in the 1969 film *Siegfried und das sagenhafte Liebesleben der Nibelungen* (Siegfried and the fabulous love life of the Nibelungs). (Compare, however, the skill with which the subject had been treated in the 1920s in the expressionistic films of Fritz Lang.) Crude sexual symbolism also characterized the 1961 novel by Martin Beheim-Schwarzbach, *Der Stern von Burgund: Roman der Nibelungen* (The star of Burgundy: A novel of the Nibelungs). What has appeared over the past twenty-five years in the Federal Republic of Germany utilizing the *Nibelungen* theme has been almost exclusively satirical in nature.[44] Robert Neumann's *Sperrfeuer um Deutschland* (Germany under Siege, 1950) and *Das Buch Treue: Ein Domelanen-Roman* (The book of loyalty: A novel of the Domelans, 1962) parodied both the concept of *Nibelungentreue* as well as the works of prior generations of authors who had adapted the theme.

Joachim Fernau's *Disteln für Hagen: Bestandsaufnahme der deutschen Seele* (third edition, 1966) is a satirical retelling of the **Nibelungenlied** with the ambitious goal of determining the essence of the German mind. Axel Plogsted's play, *Die Nibelungen* (1975), and Beda Odemann's *Alles bebt vor Onkel Hagen: Ein Verhohnepiepel der deutschen "Heldensage"* (Everyone's frightened of Uncle Hagen: A satire on German heroic poetry) demonstrate that few contemporary authors who deal with the *Nibelungen* topic are as concerned with the aesthetics of their "literary" products as they are with parodying the concepts (particularly loyalty and heroism) which are of major significance in the medieval work. In this respect, they have become rather predictable, and, unfortunately, often tedious. In contrast, Franz Fühmann (German Democratic Republic) has regarded the **Nibelungenlied** as a "novel about feudal society and its power structures,"[45] and has attempted in his poem "Der Nibelunge Not" (1956) to explain recent German history and provide a vision for the future. The optimistic tenor of the concluding strophes of Fühmann's poem stands in marked contrast to the apocalyptic conclusion of the medieval epic.

We shall close this chapter with an allusion to the popular interest demonstrated over the past few years in determining the historical and geographical background of the epic. Helmut Berndt's *Das 40. Abenteuer: Auf den Spuren der Nibelungen* (The Fortieth Adventure: Tracking the Nibelungs, 1964, with numerous subsequent editions) still adhered to the "traditional" route of the Burgundians from Worms on the Rhine through Bavaria and Austria to Hungary. In the summer of 1981, two new works appeared disputing the hitherto prevailing view that the Burgundians had actually journeyed to Hungary, or that the Nibelung treasure was sunk in the Rhine near Worms. The titles of both books in themselves betray the "new" direction of historically oriented lay studies: Heinz Ritter Schaumburg, *Die Nibelungen zogen nordwärts* (The Nibelungs went north), and Walter Böckmann, *Der Nibelungen Tod in Soest* (The demise of the Nibelungs in Soest). Well might we query with Werner Wunderlich: "The beginnings of a new myth?"[46]

Notes

1. Holger Schulz, *Der Nibelungenstoff auf dem deutschen Theater* (Cologne: F. Hansen, 1972).

2. Otfrid Ehrismann, *Das Nibelungenlied in Deutschland: Studien zur Rezeption des Nibelungenlieds von der Mitte des 18. Jahrhunderts bis zum Ersten Weltkrieg,* Münchner Universitäts-Schriften, Philosophische Fakultät, vol. 14 (Munich, 1975).

3. Werner Wunderlich, ed., *Der Schatz des Drachentödters: Materialien zur Wirkungsgeschichte des Nibelungenliedes,* Literaturwissenschaft, Gesellschaftswissenschaft, no. 30 (Stuttgart, 1977).

4. Henry and Mary Garland, *The Oxford Companion to German Literature* (Oxford: Clarendon Press, 1976), p. 635, s. v. *Nibelungenlied.*

5. *Diu Klage: Mit den Lesarten sämtlicher Handschriften,* ed. Karl Bartsch (1875; reprint ed., Darmstadt, 1964). Quotations in my text are based on this edition.

6. Despite his words in praise of Kriemhild's *triuwe,* it is difficult to imagine how the *Klage* poet could possibly have felt a reconciliation possible between the queen's obsession with revenge and her absolutism on the one hand, and Christian principles on the other.

7. K. C. King, ed., *Das Lied vom Hürnen Seyfrid,* with introduction and notes (Manchester: University of Manchester Press, 1958). Quotations in my text are based on this edition.

8. It should be noted that while in the *Lied* Seyfrid dies in a forest, this is not the case in the *Nibelungenlied.* The murder takes place by a stream in a grove on the periphery of the forest. Common to both works is Siegfried's tendency to be overbearing, a source of *sorge,* and hence *leit,* to those around him.

9. Wilhelm Grimm, *Die deutsche Heldensage,* 4th ed. (1889; reprint ed., Darmstadt: Wissenschaftliche Buchgesellschaft, 1957), p. 284.

10. King, ed., *Das Lied vom Hürnen Seyfrid,* p. 40.

11. Hans Sachs, *Der Hürnen Seufrid: Tragoedie in sieben Acten,* ed. Edmund Goetze, 2d ed., Neudrucke deutscher Literaturwerke, Neue Folge, vol. 19 (Tübingen: Niemeyer, 1967), act 1, verse 56.

12. Ibid., act 1, verse 58.

13. An excellent review of the reception of *Der Hürnen Seyfrid* (as well as heroic themes in general) in sixteenth-century Nuremberg is provided by Helmut Weinacht, "Das Motiv vom Hürnen Seyfrid im Nürnberg des 16. Jahrhunderts: Zum Problem der bürgerlichen Rezeption heldenepischer Stoffe," in *Hans Sachs und Nürnberg: Bedingungen und Probleme reichsstädtischer Literatur: Hans Sachs zum 400. Todestag am 19. Januar 1976,* ed. Horst Brunner, Gerhard Hirschmann, and Fritz Schnelbögl, Nürnberger Forschungen, vol. 19 (Nuremberg: Selbstverein des Verlags für Geschichte, 1976), pp. 137-81.

14. See, for example, Henry and Mary Garland, *The Oxford Companion to German Literature,* p. 412, s.v. *Hürnen Seyfrid, Der.* Weinacht, however, acknowledges the fact that 1726 is simply the date of the latest extant edition, and refers to the article by Jantz noted below in n. 15.

15. Harold Jantz, "The Last Branch of the Nibelungen Tree," *MLN* 80 (1965):433-40.

16. Scholars had long assumed that this was probably an allusion to a fictitious tale, but the work did, in fact, exist, and a copy of it may be found in the Harold Jantz Collection at Duke University.

17. See the selection provided by Werner Wunderlich in *Der Schatz des Drachentödters,* p. 21.

18. See above, n. 1. This is the best survey in print of dramatizations of the *Nibelungenlied* on the German stage during the nineteenth and twentieth centuries.

19. Werner Wunderlich lists a total of thirty-three dramatic productions between 1821 and 1918. It is worth noting that the first attempt since Hans Sachs to dramatize the *Nibelungen* theme, the trilogy, *Der Held des Nordens* (The hero of the north), by Friedrich Baron de la Motte Fouqué (dedicated to J. G. Fichte), is based on the Eddic lays and the first two parts of the *Völsunga Saga,* as well as the *Ragnar Saga.*

20. For a discussion of thirty-four performances of Hebbel's *Nibelungen* (or individual parts of the trilogy) between 31 January 1861, when it premiered at the Grossherzogliches Hoftheater in Weimar, and 21 May 1925, see Walther Landgrebe, *Hebbels Dichtungen auf der Bühne,* Forschungen zur Literatur-, Theater- und Zeitungswissenschaft, vol. 1 (Oldenburg: Schulz, 1927).

21. Schulz, *Der Nibelungenstoff auf dem deutschen Theater,* p. 95.

22. Weber, *Nibelungenlied,* p. 88.

23. Friedrich Rückert, "Sigurd unter den Gänsen," in *Friedrich Rükkerts gesammelte Poetische Werke,* vol. 7 (Frankfurt am Main: Sauerländer, 1868), p. 57.

24. In this regard, note the letter written to Hebbel by Georg Gottfried Gervinus in which the latter stated: "I have always considered it something of an impossibility to bring the figures of the old epics onto the stage" (Friedrich Hebbel, *Sämtliche Werke,* ed. Richard Maria Weber, vol. 7, *Briefe,* appendix [Berlin: B. Behr, 1901-7], p. 410).

25. Friedrich Hebbel, "An den geneigten Leser," posthumously published foreword to the *Nibelungen,* in *Hebbels Werke,* ed. Theodor Poppe (Berlin: Bong & Co., 1923), 5:12. A fine introduction to Hebbel's *Nibelungen* is offered by Sten G. Flygt, *Friedrich Hebbel,* Twayne's World Authors Series, no. 56 (New York: Twayne Publishers, 1968), pp. 132-41. Note also Wilhelm Emrich, *Hebbels Nibelungen: Götzen und Götter der Moderne,* Akademie der Wissenschaften und der Literatur, Jahrgang 1973-74, no. 6 (Mainz: Akademie der Wissenschaften und der Literatur, 1974).

26. See Schulz, *Der Nibelungenstoff auf dem deutschen Theater,* p. 84.

27. Friedrich Hebbel, *Die Nibelungen,* in *Hebbels Werke in zwei Bänden,* ed. Walther Vontin, vol. 2, *Dramen und Prosa* (Hamburg: Hoffmann and Campe Verlag, n.d.), pp. 14-15 (*Vorspiel,* scene 2).

28. Ibid., p. 28 (*Vorspiel,* scene 4). Quotes in text are based on the Vontin edition.

29. Ibid., p. 203.

30. See Jost Hermand, "Hebbels 'Nibelungen'—Ein deutsches Trauerspiel," in *Hebbel in neuer Sicht,* ed. Helmut Kreuzer, 2d ed., Sprache und Literatur, vol. 9 (Stuttgart: Kohlhammer, 1969), p. 330. See, however, Sten G. Flygt, *Friedrich Hebbel,* p. 134: "The inexorable duty to exact vengence is, of course, the feature of heathendom which brings about its collapse. The chaplain, Rüdeger, and Dietrich von Bern represent the new form of the Idea, Christianity, with its ethical norms of self-control, humility, and readiness to forgive."

31. Quoted by Raymond Mander and Joe Mitchenson, *The Wagner Companion* (New York: Hawthorn Books, 1977), p. 159.

32. Wunderlich, *Der Schatz des Drachentödters,* p. 51.

33. Ernst Alker, *Die deutsche Literatur im 19. Jahrhundert* (Stuttgart: A. Kröner, 1961), p. 734.

34. Paul Ernst, "Nachwort zu Chriemhild," in *Gesammelte Dramen,* vol. 2, pt. 1 (Munich: Georg Müller, 1922), p. 325. It is worth noting that Ernst considered Hagen to be the "personification of the idea of the German people" (p. 324).

35. See Karl Hunger, "Paul Ernsts 'Brunhild' and 'Chriemhild,'" *Zeitschrift für deutsche Bildung* 2 (1941):33.

36. Paul Ernst, "Die Nibelungen: Stoff, Epos und Drama," in *Weg zur Form,* 3d ed. (Munich: G. Müller, 1928), p. 171.

37. Note Ernst, *Brunhild: Trauerspiel in drei Aufzügen,* in *Gesammelte Dramen,* vol. 2, pt. 1 (Munich: Georg Müller, 1922), act 1 (p. 203):

    "Ihr zwei seid das Geschwür in unserm Leib,

    Und Selbstvernichtungswut ist euer Leben. . . .

    Wär' ich dein Mann nicht: dich wollt' ich ermorden,

    Chriemhild und dich. Dann wäre alles gut."

    ("You two are the cancer in our body and you are possessed by a death-wish. If I were not your vassal, I would kill both you and Kriemhild. Then everything would be fine.")

38. See, for example, Adolf Hitler, *Mein Kampf,* 72d ed. (Munich: Franz Eher, 1933), p. 707: "the struggling Siegfried fell victim to the stab in the back."

39. Werner Wunderlich, *Der Schatz des Drachentödters,* p. 86.

40. This attempt to acknowledge positive attributes in Hagen sometimes led to contradictions among authors of the period as to how, precisely, the figure ought to be interpreted. Wilhelm Helmich, for example, referred to the manner in which children loved the "fairy-tale hero" Siegfried, and hated his antagonist, Hagen ("Deutsch," in Ernst Dobbers and Kurt Higelke, eds., *Rassenpolitische Unterrichtspraxis: Der Rassengedanke in der Unterrichtsgestaltung der Volksschulfächer* [Leipzig: Julius Klinkhardt, 1939], p. 34). Note, on the other hand, the positive portrayal of Hagen at the conclusion of Friedrich Schreyvogel's novel, *Die Nibelungen* (1940).

41. Wunderlich, *Der Schatz des Drachentödters*, p. 90.

42. The last division formed in the Waffen-SS (Combat SS) in March and April 1945, consisting in large part of recruits from the SS-Junkerschule (SS Officer Training School) at Bad Tölz, was the 38th SS-Panzer Grenadier Division, designated "Nibelungen." The heavily fortified defense network built along the French-German border between 1933 and 1938 was known as both the *Westwall* and the *Siegfriedlinie*.

43. Note Wunderlich, *Der Schatz des Drachentödters*, p. 97.

44. However, a considerable number of translations of the *Nibelungenlied* into New High German have appeared from the late fifties through to the seventies, including those of Helmut de Boor (1959), Felix Genzmer (1961), Horst Wolfram Geissler (1966), Helmut Brackert (1970), and Ulrich Pretzel (1973).

45. "Neu erzählen—neu gewinnen," Arbeitsgespräch mit Franz Fühmann, in *Neue deutsche Literatur* 18, no. 2 (1970):68.

46. Werner Wunderlich, *Der Schatz des Drachentödters*, p. 118. Schaumburg's earlier remarks on the subject should be noted: "Etzels Ende," *Der Spiegel* 29, no. 40 (1975):222-25. The suggestion that Soest may have actually been the "location" of the Nibelungs' demise is not new. See ten Doornkaat Koolmann, *Soest, die Stätte des Nibelungenunterganges?* (Soest: Rocholsche Buchdruckerei W. Jahn, 1935).

Abbreviations

ANF: Arkiv för nordisk filologi

CG:Colloquia Germanica

DU: Der Deutschunterricht

DVjs: Deutsche Vierteljahrsschrift für Literaturwissenschaft und Geistesgeschichte

GRM: Germanisch-Romanische Monatsschrift

MLN: Modern Language Notes

MLR: Modern Language Review

PBB: Beiträge zur Geschichte der deutschen Sprache und Literatur (Halle and Tübingen)

WW: Wirkendes Wort

ZfdA: Zeitschrift für deutsches Altertum

ZfdPh: Zeitschrift für deutsche Philologie

ZfvLg: Zeitschrift für vergleichende Literaturgeschichte

Edward R. Haymes (essay date 1986)

SOURCE: "Conclusion: The Alternative to Heroism" in *The "Nibelungenlied": History and Interpretation*, University of Illinois Press, 1992, pp. 101-14.

[*In the following excerpt, Haymes explores the conflicts between the heroic, the courtly, and the diplomatic in the* Nibelungenlied *and contends that the tale serves as a warning against the abuse of new values.*]

The **Nibelungenlied** presents us with two fatally flawed heroes, Siegfried and Hagen, representing two sharply contrasted literary and ethical patterns. The first half of the poem demonstrates the problems that arise when social order becomes blurred and the false ideals of chivalric courtliness are followed. Siegfried is led astray by the power of *minne* and he eventually dies because of his error. He pretends to a social status that is not his in order to gain his goal. He follows the pattern of the ideal knight of the new generation, the king who performs service in order to gain the love of his lady. Brünhild serves as something of a social arbiter in the Siegfried story and it is her conviction that the social order is awry that leads directly to the confrontation with Kriemhild and thus to Siegfried's death. The poet accentuates the foreign elements in Siegfried's makeup by putting them into the framework of the Nibelung tradition and writing his poem both with and against that tradition. If we compare the version of Siegfried's story in our poem with the other surviving sources, we see that the vast majority of the additions by our poet have to do with service on the one hand and *minne* on the other. The two are combined in a form of *minnedienst* surrounding first the Saxon war and then, more importantly, the deluding of Brünhild. In each of these service episodes we have the service and reward cycle basic to *Minnesang*. Siegfried lays the groundwork for his own destruction through his thoughtless adherence to these two foreign ideals and his blithe indifference to the stabilizing structures of his own society. This is almost certainly the point in Siegfried's puzzling challenge to Gunther upon his arrival in Worms.

Gunther is, at least initially, better in tune with this world of stable structures and traditional values. He bases his claim to power on heredity and not on the strength of his right arm. He seeks to preserve his power through persuasion and the following of good advice. Only when his desire to win Brünhild enters the picture does he begin to leave this secure foundation behind. The wooing expedition to Isenstein is a repetition of Siegfried's wooing expedition to Worms and thus an entry into the behavior pattern represented by Siegfried, a pattern that is diametrically opposed to the foundation of social and political stability upon which Gunther's power initially rests. The new pattern is essentially the fairy-tale-like pattern of bride-winning represented in contemporary courtly literature as the pattern followed by the knighterrant. A concurrent motif to this is the fact that the king who imitates the romance hero places his political and social power at risk. He can be called upon to defend his power by anyone at any time. Gunther thus leaves behind the stable position he claimed in the arrival scene. Hartmann demonstrates this continual jeopardy of the romance hero clearly in the case of Iwein and his duty to protect the fountain, the symbol of his newly won power. Following the pattern of the romance hero, Siegfried must demonstrate continually through his physical prowess and his readiness for adventure that he is indeed worthy of his kingship. From the standpoint of traditional values, Siegfried represents chaos. His position at home is factually based—as is Gunther's—on heredity, but he is willing to place all of it at risk to prove his fitness for kingship according to the ethic of the romances. His silly challenge of his own castle guards in Nibelungenland (Str. 482-502) is understandable within the aventiure pattern of the Arthurian romance.

The Nibelung poet presents the contrast between the two world views, the traditionally based and the chaotic, by a contrast of two literary traditions. The oral tradition of the transmitted Nibelung stories is associated with the stability of the Burgundian and Netherlandic courts before the introduction of the new chivalric values represented by Siegfried's knight-errantry and his courtly love relationship to Kriemhild. The work is cast in the form of the traditional epic, within which the elements of French chivalric literature had to stand out as foreign bodies. The poet's generic stratagem thus leads the audience into a position of expecting one set of ethical values and finding another, a new set of values that could only be considered dangerous in its disruptive force. We are told from the beginning that the beauty worship (and by association the other characteristics) of chivalric-courtly style would bring about the death of many knights. The poet provides numerous signposts to an understanding of his literary technique, a technique that involved the citation of one literary style within the framework of another.

The second half of the poem was apparently a given from the start of work on the first half on. We know that the Fall of the Burgundians looms on the horizon of the Siegfried story like a dark cloud. It seems highly probable that our poet had a more or less complete picture of the final catastrophe to draw on as he worked out his version of the Siegfried story. The version of the Fall our poet had available to him was, as we have seen, probably a purely heroic story in which Hagen played the central role his structural position in the epic would seem to demand. Our poet subtly rearranged the materials of his source to provide a sort of anti-Siegfried, a hero whose ethical patterns were tied to a past that was no longer viable in the feudal world of the twelfth century.

Hagen dies because he is too proud to call the peacemaking forces of his society into operation. He is most afraid of appearing to be afraid. His concept of honor is too narrow to permit the sort of compromise required in a world full of political conflict. In a manner reminiscent of his combination of literary techniques in the Siegfried story, our poet throws the hero role of the traditional Hagen into question by reducing his actual deeds and by making him overly concerned with appearances. The poet was not able to draw on established literary genres to make this point, but he was able to combine the established shape of the heroic Hagen story with a number of damning details to produce a new, fatally flawed Hagen. His flaw is not to be sought in his apparent villainy toward Siegfried and Kriemhild, but in his adherence to a destructive, atavistic notion of heroic honor. The fact that it was atavistic did not keep it from being an important part of the thinking and behavior of our poet's contemporaries. By demonstrating the worst possible outcome, the *Nibelungenlied* calls for an examination of the flawed ethical patterns that lead to destruction.

Since both major heroes of the epic represent untenable positions, it would be well to turn to the figures that seem to represent positive values to the poet.

Whole books have been written about Rüedeger. He seems to embody all of the virtues we could admire in that period. He is the one figure who seems most "modern" within the archaic framework of the Fall of the Burgundians. Because of his openness and guilelessness he is drawn into an insoluble dilemma that involves personal, even familial ties on the one hand and feudal obligation on the other. After the battle begins, he is doomed no matter which side he chooses. It is thus important to note that he follows the demands of feudal obligation and enters the battle against his friends, among them the intended husband for his daughter.

It is a commonplace of *Nibelungenlied* criticism that Rüedeger represents a "courtly" ethic opposed to the more heroic one represented by Hagen. The refined atmosphere at his castle in Bechelaren and the brief reminiscence of *Minnesang* language in connection with the betrothal of his daughter to Giselher both point in this direction. He is not, however, a representative of the newly imported chivalry represented by Siegfried and his adoption of the knight-errant ethic of the Arthurian romances. He is more closely associated with the feudal sense of order and stability represented by Gunther at the beginning of the epic. The few pointers we have in this direction have to do with Rüedeger's concern about the class difference between his daughter and Giselher, who is betrothed to her during the Burgundians' visit. He is acutely aware of the differences, as the following passage makes clear:

> Dô sprach der marcgrâve: "wie möchte daz gesîn,
> daz immer künec gerte   der lieben tohter mîn?
> wir sîn hie ellende,   beide ich und mîn wîp:
> waz hilfet grôziu schoene   der guoten juncvrou-
>   wen lîp?"
>
> (1676)[1]

The Burgundians are willing to overlook the status differences. Given the stress on status problems in the first half of the poem, we can perhaps be pardoned for seeing a repetition of the pattern of breakdown in established feudal relationships in this uneven match. Rüedeger's status will be brought home to him and the Burgundians in the final battle. His daughter may be married to a king, but he is still a vassal to Etzel.

The main purpose of this connection within the narrative is, of course, to strengthen the bonding between Rüedeger and the Burgundians and thus to sharpen and add a certain poignancy to the conflict that comes later, but the Nibelungen poet's concern with social status should make us pay special attention to any question concerning a person's rank.

Rüedeger plays no significant role until the outbreak of hostilities. He is among those who are allowed safe conduct to leave the hall after the actual fighting has broken out. He requests a truce from the Burgundians and it is gladly given. Ironically he closes his statement with the line: "sô sol ouch vride staete guoten vriunden gezemen." ("So should steadfast peace be appropriate to good friends.") (1996,4) He takes five hundred men with him. Later he wishes fervently that the battle could be stopped and even calls on Dietrich to help stop it. A Hun sees him standing in tears and complains that the man who has the most from Etzel is not coming to his aid. Thus begins the tragic conflict in which Rüedeger offers to give up his feudal holdings if the king will free him from the obligation of fighting against his friends. Etzel cannot do this and Rüedeger is forced to take up arms against the Burgundians.

This decision is a recognition of the greater force of feudal obligation in the new society reflected in our epic. Ties based on blood relationships were the strongest in the society that produced the original Nibelungen story. Following close behind these were obligations to inlaws and the duty to protect one's guests. In our late medieval epic, however, Etzel argues from a position that assumes that the artificial relationship represented by the feudal bond was more powerful than the older obligation represented by the rights of guests and in-law relatives.

Barbarossa is supposed to have kneeled before Henry the Lion at Chiavenna in order to cause the latter to fulfill his feudal obligation of *auxilium*. Henry refused and it eventually led to his downfall. Etzel and Kriemhild kneel together in front of Rüedeger in the hope of gaining his support against the Nibelungs. After hearing all of their pleading, Rüedeger offers to dissolve the feudal relationship to escape from his dilemma. Only after Etzel refuses this offer does Rüedeger agree to go into battle. He is bound by his duty as a vassal to violate the older human ties of friendship, hospitality and in-law relationship.

In some ways Hagen and Rüedeger occupy symmetrical positions on their respective sides. They are both chief vassal and major advisor to the kings. Each is forced into the conflict against his better judgment. Each becomes a powerful and destructive force in battle. The difference lies in the attitude toward feudal order. Hagen acts totally on his own and brings about his lords' destruction as well as his own. The order of the feudal hierarchy is disturbed when a powerful vassal assumes the leadership in place of a weak king. Hagen is such a powerful figure that he attracts "vassals" of his own (such as Volker). Rüedeger is painted in absolutely positive colors throughout and there is never any question of his being a flawed tragic hero in

the sense of Hagen or Siegfried. He is a victim of powerful forces beyond his power to change them. He dies the exemplary vassal at the same time Hagen is in effect violating his own fidelity to his lords by letting an enemy kill them without entering the battle.

Like so many scenes in the *Nibelungenlied,* the confrontation between Hagen and Rüedeger is ironic in its double meaning. On the one hand there is an affecting show of magnanimity in the request for the shield and Rüedeger's giving of it. We are drawn into the moving scene and it heightens our sense of the tragedy involved in the slaughter all around, but it also involves two vassals restricting the extent of their obedience to their respective lords, a sort of mini-treason that is intimately tied up with the problems of feudal society reflected in the epic as a whole. Rüedeger's attack leaves Gernot and numberless Burgundian knights dead. He dies in the process of killing his son-in-law's brother.

In many respects Rüedeger is more victim than protagonist. He does not have the political freedom to break free from the situation created by Hagen and Kriemhild. This freedom of action is reserved for the man who would be peacemaker, Dietrich von Bern. We must observe at the outset that Dietrich is unsuccessful, that his peacemaking efforts are doomed to be foiled by a pig-headed devotion to a very limited concept of honor on the part of the combatants, particularly Hagen. If the text did not insist again and again on this role for Dietrich, we would have to decide that we were reading modern notions of pacifism into the character. However, when we observe how many new and untraditional passages in our epic deal specifically with the possibility of preventing the bloodshed, or at least of mitigating it, we can no longer ignore this aspect. It is as new and surprising as Siegfried's appearing in the role of a *minneritter;* perhaps more so, since there were no established secular literary models for peacemakers.

As we have seen, Dietrich makes his first attempt at peacemaking as the Nibelungs (Burgundians) arrive before Etzel's castle. He warns them of Kriemhild's continued grief for Siegfried and then withdraws to play a minor role in the proceedings. Etzel also plays a brief role as potential peacemaker. In the midst of one of the covert struggles between Kriemhild and Hagen, we are told outright:

> Swie grimme und swie starke   si in vîent waere,
> het iemen gesaget Etzeln   diu rehten maere,
> er het' wol understanden,   daz doch sît dâ geschach,
> durch ir vil starken übermuot   ir deheiner ims verjach.
>
> (1865)[2]

The arrogant ones of the last line are, of course, Hagen and the Burgundians. They are unwilling to jeopardize their honor by exposing the true state of affairs to Etzel. Later in the story, Etzel is unable to return to this role because of the mortal injury done to him in the murder of his son and because of the unrelenting pressure exercised by Kriemhild. His potential role is, in any case, far less active than Dietrich's. The poet mentions the possibility to indicate that the machinery for peace exists and that it is not being used.

Dietrich returns to his active role as peacemaker in the scene following the death of Etzel's son and the open outbreak of hostilities. He uses his authority with the guests to take Etzel and Kriemhild (along with Rüedeger and his men) out of the hall. In doing this, he is not only protecting his host, but also holding back the forces of chaos, if only for a moment. Etzel is, after all, still king and his is the only power that should be able to have any effect on the succeeding violence. The fact that it doesn't only serves to point up further the breakdown of order that has taken place.

Dietrich himself later realizes that Etzel is a barrier to peace. This realization is made clear when Rüedeger seeks his help in bringing the bloodshed to an end.

> Do enbôt im der von Berne   "wer möht' iz under-
>   stân?
> ez enwil der künec Etzel   niemen scheiden lân."[3]

Immediately after receiving this message, Rüedeger is drawn into the conflict himself.

We next see Dietrich after Rüedeger's death. His men hear the noise of lamentation and rush to their lord wondering who might have fallen now. They guess that it might even be the king or Kriemhilt. Dietrich warns against hasty guesses and bids his men "unde lât si des geniezen, daz ich in mînen fride bôt." ("and let them enjoy the fact that I gave them my truce." (2238,4). Wolfhart asks to be sent to find out what has gone on, but Dietrich knows better than to send him for fear that his "ungefüege vrâge" ("impolite questions") might cause warriors to lose their good sense. He sends Helpfrich instead, who brings back the unwelcome news that Rüedeger has been killed.

This is unbelievable, since Dietrich knows of the close relationship between Rüedeger and the Burgundians. He decides to send Hildebrand after more information. The old *wafenmeister* sets out on his errand armed only in his "zühten" ("good breeding") on his errand when he encounters his nephew Wolfhart, who chides him and suggests that he will have to return in shame if he does not arm himself. The narrative here amounts almost to commentary:

> Dô garte sich der wîse   durch des tumben rât.
> ê daz ers innen wurde,   dô wâren in ir wât
> alle Dietrîches recken   unt truogen swert enhant.
> dem helde was ez leide,   vil gerne hêt erz erwant.[4]

They say they want to keep Hagen from ridiculing him. When they arrive before the hall, the inevitable flyting between the hotheads on both sides begins. We are told several times that the fighting would have broken out sooner

if the men had not been afraid of losing their lord's good will, "wand' er uns strîten hie verbôt." ("Because he forbade us to fight here.") (2267,4b) After two reminders of this injunction, the fight finally breaks out and all of Dietrich's men but Hildebrand are killed.

When Hildebrand appears wounded and bloody before him, Dietrich is at first unwilling to believe the catastrophe that has befallen his men. He then breaks out in a loud lament for the men he has lost and finally, recovering his "rehte heldes muot" ("true heroic courage"), he arms himself and sets out grimly to meet the two remaining Burgundians.

Dietrich appears before Gunther and Hagen with as much justification for killing as anyone has had in the whole epic, since the Burgundians have killed all but one of his vassals. Both the damage to his power base and his obligation to his slain vassals would call for vengeance, but he still holds to the idea of a reasonable solution. He offers them safe conduct if they will surrender:

> "Ergib dich mir ze gîsel,   du und ouch dîn man.
> So wil ich behüeten,   so ich aller beste kan,
> daz dir hie zen Hiunen   niemen niht entuot,
> dune solt an mir niht vinden   niwan triuwe unde
>   guot."
>
>   (2337)[1]

Hagen rudely rejects the offer (although it was specifically made to Gunther) and Dietrich is forced to do battle. Since the two men are weak and wounded, Dietrich is able to take both captive; Hagen first and then Gunther. He does not realize that Kriemhild's thirst for revenge is so great that she will kill even unarmed captives.

The episode of Dietrich's vassals is quite unnecessary in terms of the tradition. Tradition did require that Gunther and Hagen be delievered bound before Kriemhild, but it was unnecessary to have Dietrich do it. The involvement of Dietrich's men serves only to highlight Dietrich's role as an apostle of peace and reason.

Later heroic epic parodied this image of Dietrich. In the *Rosengarten* Dietrich holds back from his climactic battle with Siegfried until Hildebrand accuses him of cowardice. Dietrich then explodes into a superhuman rage comparable perhaps to the *berserkr* state of Norse warriors. In this condition he is able to defeat Siegfried. Apparently the peace-seeking Dietrich of the **Nibelungenlied** was such a strange animal that the later poet of the *Rosengarten* was only able to understand his behavior as cowardice.

If the peacemaker Dietrich was such a strange phenomenon in the literature of the period, is it possible that we are reading something into the figure that even the Nibelungen poet never dreamed of? A comparison of the version in our Nibelungen epic and that in the *Thidrekssaga* shows that this characterization is unique to our epic. In the saga it is Rodingeir's (Rüedeger's) wife who warns the Burgundians that Kriemhild is still weeping for Siegfried.

In the scene in which Dietrich's warriors enter the fray, it is Thidrek (Dietrich) himself who calls on his men to arm themselves: "Now is my best friend dead, Markgraf Rodingeir. Now I can no longer sit idly by. Arm yourselves, my vassals! I must now do battle with the Niflungs." The contrast could not be greater. The Nibelungen poet carefully builds up a situation in which Dietrich can send his men to the Burgundians to ask for Rüedeger's body, a peaceful mission. It is only the hotheadedness of Wolfhart that draws them into the battle. In the *Thidrekssaga* Thidrek simply reaches a breaking point and finally enters the battle to avenge Rodingeir. In the saga his action is somewhat similar to that of the Dietrich of the *Rosengarten*. The final battle with Hagen is not an attempt to capture him (there is also no offer of safe conduct) and the battle comes to an end when Dietrich gets tired of the equally matched battle and begins to breathe fire (a typical ability of Dietrich's in the saga and the German Dietrich stories). The fire makes Hagen's chain mail so hot that he has to submit. (Hagen later dies of his wounds so that there is no final scene with Kriemhild.) If the saga represents an earlier epic version of the Fall of the Burgundians, the "ältere Not," then much of the unique quality of the surviving Nibelungen epic was totally missing there. Dietrich's role as unsuccessful peacemaker is one of the special qualities of our epic.

It is difficult to find a medieval German parallel to this role. The so-called "peace movement" of the period was something quite different, although there are points of contact. The concern of the *pax Dei* and the *Landfrieden* of the period was more the protection of civil peace among the subjects of a king. The *pax Dei* was concerned with the prevention of minor feuds, but it did not involve in most cases the sort of national catastrophe described in the *Nibelungenlied.* The uses of the word "vride" (peace) in the poem refer, almost without exception, to a brief truce or to the assurance of one fighter to another that he will not attack him, such as the *vride* given Rüedeger by Hagen as the former enters the battle. The more global notion of preventing war and of trying to end it once it has come into being is apparently quite foreign to the legal vocabulary of the Middle Ages, but the concept is present in numerous literary works. In the Icelandic sagas there is often the suggestion that the killing that goes on could have been prevented if men of good will could only have prevailed. This feeling is particularly strong in *Njal's Saga,* in which the object of most lawsuits is the arrival at a settlement that will prevent bloodshed. The peace so arrived at only breaks down when the parties are unwilling to recognize the validity of the settlement or when someone breaks the conditions imposed. (In the saga, it is, significantly enough, the women who drive their men to seek vengeance even after a settlement has been reached.) In the *Nebelungenlied* there is also a settlement of sorts, arrived at between Kriemhild and her brothers (but specifically excluding Hagen) following Siegfried's murder. The settlement is broken when Gunther allows Hagen to take Kriemhild's dowry, the Nibelungen treasure, and sink it in the Rhine.

The peacemaking role of Dietrich is a different matter, though. He is somehow the personification of the feeling that the catastrophe could have been prevented if there had been more reason and less pride among the principal actors in the story.

The poet of the *Nibelungenlied* portrays his figures as being caught up in ethical patterns from which they are unable to escape. Kriemhild is caught up in the revenge ethic—an atavistic pattern that has survived until the present day. Hagen represents the traditional heroic warrior ethic, an ideal that had not yet died out in spite of attempts to replace it with more humane models. Rüedeger and Dietrich in particular represent attempts to demonstrate an ethic of restraint combined with personal bravery and heroism. Rüedeger dies because of his willingness to place feudal obligation above his own superior moral point of view. Dietrich does not do this (he is, of course, in a different feudal situation) and is thus partially successful where no one else has been. His one entry into the battle is the result of his last attempt to make peace. In the *Nibelungenlied* the motors for destruction are destroyed at a stupendous price, but the pattern of reasonable pacification is clearly established as a "might have been" alternative.

Thus it is Dietrich von Bern who combines the virtues the Nibelungen poet wished to propagate. He is not the chivalric *minneritter* we find in Siegfried nor is he the proud hero of Germanic tradition exemplified by Hagen. We are apparently meant to admire Hagen while we condemn his arrogance and inflexibility. Dietrich never really has a chance to demonstrate the positive results of diplomacy, reasonableness, and the appropriate use of strength, but it is clear from the "editorial" comments of the poet that this alternative could have prevented the carnage and frustrated Kriemhild's desire for revenge.

The ethical position represented by Dietrich is prefigured in the first half by Gunther's younger brothers, Gernot and Giselher. Gernot is the leader of the reconciliation party after Siegfried's challenge to Gunther upon his arrival in Worms. He is opposed by hotheads like Ortwin, but he prevails. Later it is Giselher who opposes the Hagen party in their desire to see Siegfried die. (Gernot's position is not made clear.) After having remained aloof from the murder plot, Giselher is also the leader of the peace and reconciliation party during the years of Kriemhild's mourning. Like the Dietrich of the "Fall," Giselher and Gernot represent peaceful alternatives to the violent actions that do take place.

The two doomed heroes imply different, but complementary ethical models. The two kinds of failure represented by Siegfried and Hagen point through negative example toward an ethos of feudal behavior that is based on traditional values, but is able to apply reason and forebearance in conflict siuations. It has long been recognized that the *Nibelungenlied* does not glorify the violence it retells, but the implications of this refusal have never been fully thought out. Perhaps the model of feudal stability, forebearance and diplomacy sketched above indicates in what direction these implications lead.

As the chapter on social and political history indicated, the *Nibelungenlied* was the product of a period in which there was much gratuitous violence and considerable insecurity about individual roles and social values. The readiness with which the foreign model of chivalry was adopted shows the receptiveness of a society whose members were unsure of themselves and desirous of new directions. The Nibelungen poet saw clearly that this new model was as dangerous as the old one and that it contributed to a breakdown of the stabilizing values within society. Within the framework of our modern understanding of the Middle Ages we have been used to seeing the adoption of "courtly" values as a step forward, a mitigation of the often barbaric behavior of the men of that time. But the almost totally negative impact of the chivalric ethos in the Siegfried story should make us aware that our positive view of the ethical implications of chivalry during this period was not universally accepted by its contemporaries.

If there is any validity to the view that sees the adoption of chivalric values as a justification and legitimization of social mobility through service, then the chivalric ethos as a whole could well have been viewed as a danger by those whose interests were endangered by the combination of territorialization and the rise in status of the *ministeriales*. What better way, then, of combatting this danger than by retelling a traditional story in such a way that the hero's downfall is directly attributable to his adoption of values held in highest esteem by the literature of chivalry, *minne* and service. Siegfried's adoption of these as his guiding values led him to bend the structure of feudal society to his own ends and eventually doomed him. We can read in his doom a warning to those who would use the new values to justify their own violation of traditional rights and privileges.

We began this investigation by looking at the *Nibelungenlied* within its literary and historical horizon of expectations and trying to read the signs toward which the "deviations from the accepted modes of intelligibility" pointed. The great attention paid to Siegfried's service and his performance as a *minneritter* made it clear that something of importance was being set forth here. In the case of Hagen we have a different kind of dialectic. Hagen is like Siegfried in that he is a traditional type. He is the implacable hero, the warrior fighting like Roland against impossible odds. Like Roland he is also caught between his sense of honor and the reasonable demands of an advisor, in this case Dietrich von Bern. The dialectic between the doomed hero and the survivor diplomat is complementary to the tension in Gunther's court as it moved away from a government by tradition, heredity, and reason at the beginning of our epic. The ethical stance of the Nibelungen poet is clearly on the side of hereditary authority and diplomatic solutions to conflict.

The ethical strata implied by the *Nibelungenlied* cannot be limited to the two traditionally associated with the poem, the heroic and the courtly. As we have seen, that which earlier critics have called courtly must be divided into at least two very different levels. I see a three-tiered set of patterns in the poem. At the extremes are the atavistic heroic stance embodied by Hagen and such minor figures as Ortwin and Wolfhart and the chivalric complex represented by Siegfried and his relationship to Kriemhild. Between the two is the stable world of hereditary nobility in which conflicts are first submitted to a diplomatic solution. Gunther and his younger brothers represent this world at the beginning of the epic and Dietrich von Bern represents it at the end. Diplomacy and stability fail because of the power of the extreme positions represented by the two flawed heroes, but they are always clearly present in the actions of peacemaker figures like Giselher and Dietrich.

This ethical position is precisely the position we would expect from a member of the court of Wolfger of Passau. The bishop was a diplomat of great skill and the representative of a dynasty that based its claim to the German throne as much on heredity as on its own virtues. In addition to this, there are, as I mentioned earlier, internal indications that the poem arose within Wolfger's sphere of influence.

One of the few elements in the poem extraneous to the plot is the obligatory mention of Passau in the course of every journey up and down the Danube. Nor does there seem to be any narrative necessity for the introduction of Bishop Pilgrim as a member of the royal family of Worms (he is a maternal uncle of Kriemhild and her brothers). His court is always a point of brief repose for the travelers and he is always very happy to see the Burgundians. Even the messengers Wärbel and Swemmel stop and inform him of the impending visit of his nephews and their knights. There might be a reason for a point of repose halfway between Worms and Etzelnburg were it not for Rüedeger's court at Bechelaren, which fulfills that function to a far greater extent than Passau. The most reasonable explanation for this continual reference to Passau is that these passages were meant to link up the ancient story with the court at which it was told. The references to Pilgrim are thus veiled compliments to the patron of the epic's composition, Bishop Wolfger. I realize that in suggesting this explanation I am violating my promise to avoid positivistic interpretation of the poem, but I feel that the evidence is strong enough to link the poem to Wolfger's court and that we gain more than we lose by adopting this as a working hypothesis. If the poem was not composed at Wolfger's court, then it was written by someone with concerns recognizably similar to those of the great diplomat.

The *Nibelungenlied* is thus a very political poem, almost certainly composed at a very political court. The horizon of historical expectations sketched above in Chapter Two gives us a number of points of departure for an understanding of the political and social concerns of the poem. We have seen the possible connection between Siegfried and the problem of territorialization and the probable echo of Philip of Swabia's lack of leadership in the Gunther of the first half of our poem. Corollary to this is the concern for the stability of political structures, for the recognition of traditionally accepted claims to power. A king who claims to be a vassal can be as dangerous in his way as a vassal who claims to be (or hopes to become) a king. Siegfried Beyschlag recognized the implications of such violations of feudal order in an important essay on "Das Nibelungenlied als aktuelle Dichtung seiner Zeit." Although many of Beyschlag's examples differ from mine, his recognition of the fundamental message of the poem has accompanied me throughout the work on this book. His concluding remarks make an apt conclusion to this discussion:

> That which is called into question in the epic and through which the doom of this world is shown is the reversal of these [the feudal] relationships and along with them the order of the human community as a result of human fallibility due to the original sin of the destruction of established order. Such reversal is: that the free lord of royal birth enmeshes himself in the appearance of servility, that the vassal acts on his own in place of his lords and thereby nullifies their function of *pax* and *justitia*. Fateful *disturbatio* with a distortion of values, with injustice and suffering is the result. In these images we find the nagging questions of contemporary society. Where does the way lead when the functions of order are turned around? The Nibelungen epic answers: to destruction.

. . . . .

Since [this] chapter reiterates points that have been made earlier, I shall not repeat the documentation. One point that had not been stressed is the repeated attempts of the Staufer to establish heredity as the principle of succession for the German kingship. There can be little doubt that the Staufer party considered heredity a guarantee of stability. Their efforts on behalf of their own successors and the importance given to succession in the *privilegium minus* illustrate their viewpoint. Engels discusses this point on p. 105f.

The major treatment of Rüedeger is by Jochen Splett. He is also the subject of chapters in almost all of the book-length treatments. See especially Weber, Ihlenburg and Nagel. Considerable light is thrown on the episode in which Hagen asks Rüedeger for his shield in the article by Wapnewski "Rüdigers Schild."

The treatment of Dietrich in this section owes much to reflection on Ihlenburg's presentation of Dietrich as the man who "overcomes that which brings about the end of Hagen and Ruedeger." He is seen as the man who recognizes the rottenness of the feudal ethos and rejects it. I would disagree with Ihlenburg's conclusion by pointing out that the poet of our *Nibelungenlied* actually sought to stabilize feudal structures and that Dietrich's variance from established practice was calculated to salvage the social order, not to call it into question. Ihlenburg deserves a great deal of credit, however, for recognizing Dietrich's role and presenting him as an exemplary figure. Heinzle (pp. 188-190) discusses the motif of Dietrich's supposed reluctance to fight in the later Dietrich epics.

The quotes from Ihlenburg are from p. 129. In the original the sentence reads "Scheitert Hagen leztlich an seinem einseitig starren Ehrbegriff, so scheitert Rüdiger an einem einseitig starren Pflichtbegriff."

The locus classicus for the two-tiered ethical model is the article by Friedrich Neumann "Schichten der Ethik," which has been reprinted in Neumann's book of Nibelungen essays *Das Nibelungenlied in seiner Zeit*.

The role of Passau in the epic has been explored most fully by Heuwieser. Panzer gives a brief resume of the arguments in favor of a Passau origin on pp. 369-374. Heger provides supporting evidence in her study of Wulfger (*Lebenszeugnis Walthers von der Vogelweide*).

The concluding quote is from Siegfried Beyschlag, "Das Nibelungenlied als aktuelle Dichtung seiner Zeit," p. 230.

Notes

1. Then spoke the margrave: "how could that be,
   that a king could ever desire my dear daughter?
   We are exiles here, both my wife and I:
   What good does the good maiden's great beauty do?

2. As grimly and strongly she hated them,
   if anyone had told Etzel the true situation,
   he would have prevented that which happened there later.
   Because of their great arrogance no one told him.

3. Then the man from Bern had him told "who can stop it?
   King Etzel doesn't want to have it ended by anyone."

4. Then the experienced man armed himself
   because of the inexperienced man's advice.
   before he was aware of it, there were armored there

Theodore M. Andersson (essay date 1987)

SOURCE: "Interpretations" in *A Preface to the "Nibelungenlied"*, Stanford: Stanford University Press, 1987, pp. 144-66.

[*In the following excerpt, Andersson summarizes the new approaches taken in critical analyses of the* Nibelungenlied *during the last half of the twentieth century.*]

Two publications by Nelly Dürrenmatt and Friedrich Panzer in 1945 marked a turning point in the analysis of the **Nibelungenlied** and ushered in a period of postwar criticism that differed distinctly from the work done during the forty years before the war.[1] These earlier years were dominated by Andreas Heusler, whose pertinent studies appeared from 1902 to 1941.[2] Heusler's project was to comprehend the **Nibelungenlied** against the background of the earlier forms of the legend. Much of his work was therefore devoted to a reconstruction of these forms through a painstaking comparison of the surviving versions. After the war scholars came to believe that his approach was too backward-looking, and strenuous efforts were made to find a new method that would integrate the *Nibelungenlied* more decisively into the literary scene around 1200. This was the underlying rationale in both Dürrenmatt's and Panzer's books.

Panzer proceeded from the observation that German literature in the second half of the twelfth century was revolutionized by French impulses. He set out to show that French literature was no less crucial for the *Nibelungenlied* than for courtly romance and sought to demonstrate a series of borrowings from the *chansons de geste,* notably *Daurel et Beton, Renaus de Montauban,* and the *Song of Roland.* In addition, he believed that he could isolate occasional Virgilian echoes and derive certain scenes in the *Nibelungenlied* from contemporary political events. For example, he associated the idyll at Pöchlarn in Adventure 27 with Frederick Barbarossa's visit to the court of King Bela of Hungary in 1189, during which the emperor betrothed his youngest son to Bela's daughter. In other words, Panzer argued both a more elevated literary culture for the poet and a greater freedom in devising new episodes. Occasionally his derivation of the narrative from French sources or current events ran counter to Heusler's location of the same episodes in the native "Brünhildenlied" or the "Ältere Not." In order to argue that the idyll at Pöchlarn originated in the state visit of 1189 he was obliged, for example, to demonstrate that the poet did not find the episode in the "Ältere Not," as Heusler assumed. This constraint led to a long chapter in which he argued that the "Ältere Not" in fact never existed. Instead, Panzer reasoned, the relationship between the *Nibelungenlied* and *þiðreks saga* should be explained not from a common source but from the Norwegian compiler's extensive reworking of the *Nibelungenlied* itself.

Panzer's book is a curious example of the wrong solution put forward at the right historical moment. His new source proposals have enjoyed little favor, and the direct derivation of the account in *þiðreks saga* from the *Nibelungenlied* has never been credited by the scholars most competent to judge the issue.[3] Nevertheless, his book had a liberating effect because it offered release from Heusler's constructions. Scholars who had not performed the source operations themselves were inclined to believe Panzer, at least to the extent that Heusler's system now appeared to be more fragile than they had previously imagined. Even where Panzer's book is not directly mentioned in the critical literature, the reader senses that it lies beneath a new skepticism toward source study and a new eagerness to evaluate the *Nibelungenlied* on its own terms, as an autonomous creation comparable to the works of Hartmann, Wolfram, and Gottfried.

Whereas Panzer's book followed tradition by dealing almost exclusively with source questions, Nelly Dürrenmatt broke more clearly with the past. She made a considerably juster estimate of Heusler's achievements than Panzer but argued that he had isolated the *Nibelungenlied* too programmatically from courtly epic.[4] She therefore set herself the task of identifying the courtly elements. This labor is carried out in the form of a somewhat mechanical comparison of ritual scenes: reception and leave-taking formalities, forms of hospitality, gift-giving, festive arrangements, mourning practices, knighting and marriage ceremonies. Her conclusion is that the *Nibelungenlied* poet is in fact more interested and prodigal in these ritual matters than the writers of precourtly or courtly epic. He therefore emerges as an almost hypercourtly figure rather than a nostalgic re-creator of heroic antiquity.

Like Panzer's book, Dürrenmatt's had an impact not quite commensurate with its real accomplishment. The ceremonial elements she singles out are not a characteristic feature of German courtly epic, so that the comparison does not so much establish an analogy as point up a difference. Moreover, in the second section of the book, on some of the more important characters in the poem, she distinguishes carefully between those features already present in the sources as posited by Heusler and new features not anticipated by the sources. She does not therefore disallow Heusler's findings but merely tries to focus the extant redaction more clearly. In the heat of a new critical day, however, her book lent itself to a more far-reaching interpretation. It was read as a reorientation of the *Nibelungenlied* away from earlier literature and into closer apposition with the latest fashions. Though still grounded in Heusler's work, it offered an alternative context that encouraged the abandonment of Heusler's system.

One of the criticisms leveled at Heusler, especially by Panzer, was the origin of his science in Germanic or even Scandinavian studies. Not only Heusler but also the other important Nibelung scholars of the 1920's and 1930's (Neckel, Schneider, de Boor, Hempel) belonged to this tradition. Dürrenmatt's shift of focus to classical Middle High German literature allowed scholars in this latter field to turn their attention to the *Nibelungenlied* less hesitantly than before. Wolfram and Gottfried scholars figured prominently in the new generation (Mergell, W. J. Schröder, W. Schröder, Weber, Wapnewski, Bumke). The *Nibelungenlied* had now been recruited for their literature, and they were free to approach it unencumbered by the legendary apparatus that Panzer had declared irrelevant.

This trend was of course promoted in no small measure by the New Critical methods that prevailed in German literary studies just after World War II. Close reading was the order of the day, and Panzer's abolition of legendary history extended this critical license to the *Nibelungenlied.* The first result was a series of intense interpretations of the poem without regard to possible sources.

TEXTUAL INTERPRETATIONS (1950-65)

Three studies by Bodo Mergell, Walter Johannes Schröder, and Werner Schröder, the last two of monograph size, may serve as samples of the new approach. They appeared in

1950, 1955, and 1960 and have in common a concern with the structure of the poem and the capacity of that structure to communicate the poet's intention. They assume that the structure is coherent and meaningful, thus departing from an earlier view that the poet recast an inherited story, making piecemeal modifications without strict regard for the overall plan of the poem and without necessarily imputing a consistent meaning to the whole.

Mergell attaches his study explicitly to Dürrenmatt's precedent, but is more interested in the governing idea of the poem than in the outer trappings.[5] He discovers a set of counterbalancing tensions. Siegfried stands in significant opposition to the court at Worms, in which he represents a new dynamic vitality in the context of an older petrified culture. The relationship is dialectical because Gunther needs the primitive strength of a Siegfried for his bridal quest, and Siegfried needs the courtly polish of a Gunther for his wooing. Mergell sees Siegfried's entry into the life at Worms as analogous to Parzival's entry into the world in search of renewal. Kriemhild and Hagen form a similar polarity; she is gradually reduced from loving wife and grieving widow to avenging demon, while Hagen experiences a countervalent rise from traitor to triumphant guardian. This contrast dominates the poem as a whole and describes a religious arc culminating in a final confrontation with God. Hagen, however, stands alone with God in his victorious preservation of the hidden gold,[6] whereas Kriemhild is condemned as a "vâlandinne" (she-devil). Mergell compares this structural chiasmus to the rise of the Grail hero and the counterbalancing fall of the neutral angels in *Parzival*.

A second preoccupation of Mergell's article is the formal patterning of the poem as a whole. He divides it into eight pentads, each comprising five adventures, with the centerpiece (Adventure 20) doing service in both the fourth and fifth pentad. More interestingly, he notes that the ***Nibelungenlied*** shares its two-part structure with courtly romance. As in courtly romance, the bipartition is not arbitrary or meaningless but a contrastive design revealing different degrees of religious awareness.

W. J. Schröder's analysis is also structural in nature, but it attempts a more encompassing interpretation.[7] He takes note of Heusler's caution against the imposition of a didactic principle on heroic stories, but advocates a search not so much for a didactic principle as for a coherent plot.[8] He begins with an analysis of the characters, urging that they are not to be confused with real people, whose actions are motivated by individual responses to a given situation. Heroic poetry does not motivate action psychologically but through the manipulation of motifs. The characters are comparable to chess pieces, each limited to a particular type of move. Thus a queen will make only moves that are inherent in her nature as a queen. The drastic changes in such characters as Kriemhild and Siegfried (maiden becomes maenad, aggressor becomes ally) would appear to contradict this principle, but the changes are only apparent. Kriemhild merely becomes what she already is; she realizes her latent queenliness. Siegfried, on the other hand, merely takes on the deceptive appearance of a different being. Corresponding to these split-level characters is a splitlevel stage: a courtly contemporary scene (Worms) and a mythic past (Nibelungenland, Islant, Hunland).

Within this divided realm each man seeks out the matching woman. Siegfried (strength) woos Kriemhild (beauty), while Gunther (king) woos Brünhild (queen). They achieve their goals not by virtue of what they are but by assuming opposite characteristics. Siegfried becomes a courtier, and Gunther borrows Siegfried's strength. Reality is traded for appearance. Thus the ground is laid for deceived expectations. Kriemhild, who desires the strongest man, must be reassured that it was actually Siegfried, not Gunther, who subdued Brünhild, but Brünhild, who desires to be a queen, must be reassured that Siegfried is in truth a vassal. Their insistence precipitates the revelations of the queens' quarrel and makes Siegfried's presence in Worms a threat to the status quo.

The underlying problem in the poem is the survival of the court at Worms. It stands in jeopardy because Kriemhild and her brothers represent two different spheres; she is a creature of nature, but the outlook of her brothers is determined by their social milieu. It is the function of the plot to bring this latent conflict to the surface. Siegfried is the catalyst. He lays claim to Worms by virtue of his inherent strength. Gunther, on the other hand, maintains his claim by virtue of his legitimacy. The strain is further exacerbated by the subsequent marriages, which aim at joining compatible partners. These partners achieve their ends, however, only by resorting to a mode of existence contradictory to their inherent mode. Siegfried, the quintessence of natural strength, must subordinate himself to the artificial demands of society and become dependent on it. Gunther, the quintessential king, must put himself under Siegfried's tutelage. Thus, when the contract is fulfilled, both discover that in the process they have betrayed themselves and compromised their very existence.

The upshot of the inherent differences between Kriemhild's nature and that of her brothers is a deadly conflict. First the men, Gunther and Siegfried, act to set the conflict aside, but then the women, Kriemhild and Brünhild, act to ensure that it will assert itself with full force. Gunther triumphs at the end of Part I and Kriemhild at the end of Part II, but both triumph only in appearance, because both are powerless without the outsider Siegfried. Society, in the person of Gunther, enlists nature (Siegfried's strength) in Part I, while nature (Kriemhild) enlists the festive forms of society in Part II. Nature succumbs in Part I, society in Part II. In this drama the strong characters (Siegfried and Brünhild) play the secondary roles, while the weak characters (Gunther and Kriemhild) play the lead roles. The implication is that catastrophe ensues from weakness.

Not content with these largely structural and functional collocations, Schröder goes on to speculate on the historical theme of the *Nibelungenlied,* that is, the extent to which it transposes the past into the present. Reversing Heusler's dictum that heroic poetry is personalized history, Schröder proposes to penetrate the historical layer by depersonalizing and thereby repoliticizing the action of the *Nibelungenlied.* Gunther's personal weakness is tantamount to political incompetence; the courtly culture of Worms is no more than an empty form. Siegfried's strength is therefore a prerequisite for political security. In this way the poet plays off "old" strength against "new" culture, nature against society. In the process Siegfried and Brünhild are modernized at Worms, while Kriemhild and Gunther are transported back into mythic time in Nibelungenland and Islant. Schröder suggests that this pattern reflects the discrepancy between real power and nominal rule that led to the downfall of the Merovingian dynasty. Seen in this way, the primitive narrative material of the *Nibelungenlied,* generally taken to betray the poet's inability to adjust the old story to his new purposes, becomes meaningful. The poet's intention was to redramatize the basic thought of the old story, the incongruence of political power and political rule.

Like Mergell, Schröder comes to the study of the *Nibelungenlied* from Wolfram's *Parzival.* Unlike Mergell, he is intent on drawing a distinction. After reviewing the broad similarities and dissimilarities between the *Nibelungenlied* and *Parzival,* he concludes that they pose the same question but provide different answers. They ask how the weak individual can assume power. The *Nibelungenlied* judges that he cannot. Wolfram judges that he can if he undergoes a transformation. Parzival obeys an ethical imperative to seek the truth. The figures in the *Nibelungenlied* follow no such imperative and are trapped in a static existence. The two-part narrative structures contrast correspondingly; in the first part of each the king establishes himself, but in the second part Gunther loses his life whereas Parzival is guided *volens nolens* by God. In other words, *Parzival* is predicated on the model of salvation, but death in the *Nibelungenlied* is unredeemed. Where Wolfram constructs teleologically, the *Nibelungenlied* merely observes the human state.

In a final section Schröder urges the importance of the *Klage* as the first interpretation of the *Nibelungenlied* and a key to the contemporary understanding of the work. It exculpates Kriemhild but condemns Hagen and Gunther, attributing the catastrophe to their arrogance (vv. 3,434-38). By implication their guilt lies in an excessive self-reliance without regard for a higher truth. This critique bears out Schröder's comparison between the *Nibelungenlied* and *Parzival.*

Although Werner Schröder places his study under the auspices of the title "Das Buoch Chreimhilden" found in MS Munich 341 (D), just as Heusler had done forty years earlier, he begins with the rejection of Heusler's method that had by now become a new exordial topic.[9] He held that Heusler's approach was not so different from Lachmann's; Heusler merely made his slices vertically rather than hori-

zontally, assigning much of the flavor to the bottom layers of the cake. According to Schröder any concession of literary qualities to the earlier forms of the story necessarily detracted from the final confection. Another part of the exordial topic, this one borrowed from Panzer, is the overestimation of a book by the French scholar Ernest Tonnelat, which German scholars espoused after the war because it adhered faithfully to the text of the *Nibelungenlied* without undertaking excursions into textual prehistory.[10]

W. Schröder too was intent on a precise understanding of the text as it stands, but on the basis of a much more cautious reading than the one put forward by W. J. Schröder, with whom he takes strong issue, particularly on the symbolic interpretation of characters. As a consequence, much of the study is devoted to lexical tallies and the gauging of shades of meaning, particularly in the word *leit* (sorrow, injury, etc.), which Friedrich Maurer had placed at the center of his interpretation.[11] Whereas W. J. Schröder probably made the *Nibelungenlied* more interesting than it really is, W. Schröder's recapitulations make it decidedly less interesting than it is.

Schröder's aim is not only to vindicate Kriemhild's place at the center of the poet's design but also to rehabilitate her, to rescue her on the one hand from symbolic reductionism (p. 93) and on the other hand from the suspicion of mixed motives. Maurer had interpreted her desire for the Nibelung treasure as a real desire for reparation of the wrong committed against her and a symbolic restoration of her honor.[12] Schröder argues repeatedly that the treasure is not a real issue.[13] The poet would not have lavished so much attention on the love relationship if that were not the sole motive for her revenge. Kriemhild thus grieves only for her husband, not for the power or prestige that he conferred. When she demands the treasure from Hagen, her wish is only to triumph over her husband's killer. Her interest in the treasure only masks her longing for Siegfried. Like W. J. Schröder, W. Schröder concludes with an appeal to the *Klage* (and redaction C), which authenticate his reading by emphasizing Kriemhild's fidelity and guiltlessness.

The rethinking of the *Nibelungenlied* apparent in these German studies was echoed in a group of articles by three British scholars in 1960 and 1961. J. K. Bostock's contribution was temperamentally in line with Werner Schröder's close reading.[14] It interprets the poem in terms of church teaching and attributes the final catastrophe to moral flaws, notably *übermuot,* or arrogance, a sin of which virtually everyone in the poem is convicted.[15] The strength of the article is that it locates a unified moral principle supported by the frequent occurrence of a particular word. The weakness is that it reads rather like a critical penitential, in which the sins of the various characters are tallied up and penance duly prescribed.

D. G. Mowatt's article is more in keeping with W. J. Schröder's symbolical reading, but it is theoretically uncompromising.[16] Mowatt categorically declares the principles of New Criticism applicable to medieval literature in general and the *Nibelungenlied* in particular, decrying only the tendency of German scholars to make occasional concessions to historical thinking. He finds it unnecessary to invoke different narrative layers in explaining apparent contradictions. With W. J. Schröder he locates a meaningful design in the fateful bringing together of dissimilar natures (Brünhild/Gunther, Kriemhild/Siegfried), and uses the Goethean analogy of elective affinities. The incompatibility of social and individualistic instincts is the theme of the *Nibelungenlied,* just as it is of other courtly epics.

Hugh Sacker credits the poet not only with thematic structures but with ironic and symbolic effects as well.[17] He resists the idea that epithets are merely stereotypical and urges cases in which adjectives such as *übermüete* (bold) or *minneclîch* (lovely) signal quite the opposite. Indeed, he finds the first twelve stanzas of the poem thoroughly shot through with irony. In the area of symbolism he offers not only the sexually significant ring and belt taken from Brünhild and a plausible analogy between the wild falcon of Kriemhild's dream and the wild suitor who materializes at Worms, but also some rather unexpected sexual symbolism in Siegfried's death scene. Such imputations represent a real leap in our estimate of the poet, since they imply his ability both to create intricate meanings and to undermine them at the same time. If true, Sacker's observations would not so much clarify as complicate our understanding of the poem.[18]

The postwar attempts to come to terms with the *Nibelungenlied* in more text-oriented studies culminated in a series of books published between 1955 and 1965. The first was Friedrich Panzer's volume of almost five hundred pages.[19] Those sections devoted to the form of the *Nibelungenlied* remain an indispensable compendium of tabulations relating to such matters as metrics, style, vocabulary, formulas, rhetorical devices, numerical predilections, ceremonial effects, descriptive modes, sententious expressions, inner chronology, contradictions, and so forth. The long chapter of 165 pages on sources is flawed, however, by Panzer's misconstruction of the textual relationships. It is symptomatic that he cites approvingly the work on French heroic epic by Joseph Bédier, whose inventionism was swept away just four years later by Ramón Menéndez Pidal.[20] Panzer conceded Heusler's "Brünhildenlied" but abolished the "Ältere Not," emphasizing instead the role of French borrowings and contemporary history. All these pages must now be read with a grain of salt. Panzer does not offer an interpretation as such, only a brief chapter of general assessment (pp. 454-69), which serves as a summation of the poetic qualities of the *Nibelungenlied* and its position between heroic poetry and chivalric literature. A concluding comparison with Homer notes the great distance between the parochialism of the German poem and Homer's Hellenic panorama, but suggests that the *Nibelungenlied* offers some compensation in making the inner life of its characters transparent.

Whereas Panzer's book attempts to consolidate the revolution against traditional source studies, Burghart Wach-

inger's sober monograph both participates in and tempers the revolution.[21] His book consists of discrete sections on anticipations, structure, and motivation. The first two in particular reflect the preoccupations of the postwar descriptivists, but Wachinger refrains from the temptation to impose ideal proportions in his calculation of the structural divisions. He sees the macrostructure in terms of the major temporal intervals at the end of Adventure 11 (eleven years), the beginning and end of Adventure 19 (three and a half and nine years), and the beginning of Adventure 23 (twelve years), thus singling out an objective criterion for his divisions. The most interesting section of the book is the last, which is an exercise in ascertaining whether the motivations of the action may be grasped without reference to underlying versions that the *Nibelungenlied* poet failed to integrate convincingly into his final elaboration. In the course of this examination three cruxes are subjected to careful analysis: the motivation of Siegfried's death, the reconciliation of Kriemhild with her brothers at the end of Adventure 19, and her demand for the treasure at the end of the poem. Siegfried's tragedy is interpreted as a result of his subordination to the service of love and hence to Gunther, a sham service with dire consequences. Wachinger thus proposes ill-fated love as the cause of Siegfried's death, but confesses that the motivation is overgrown by other issues to the point of mystification.

The peculiarity that in Adventure 19 the seizure of Kriemhild's treasure comes directly on the heels of her reconciliation is explained by the rigors of the story, which required that the reconciliation take place in order to make Kriemhild's new marriage and the subsequent invitation possible, while at the same time allowing scope for the unresolved hostilities. Kriemhild's loss of her treasure effectively, though not ostensibly, cancels the reconciliation, thus allowing the antagonism to persist unabated below the surface of the action. The difficulties involved in a clear reading of the passage are illustrated by a particularly massive intervention of the C redactor at this point in the story. Finally, Wachinger turns to Kriemhild's last-minute demand for the restoration of her treasure, the motif that so preoccupied Werner Schröder in the same year. Wachinger suggests that she commits herself not to kill Hagen when Dietrich delivers him bound and helpless into her hands. She at first honors the commitment by demanding only satisfaction, but Hagen seizes the opportunity by contriving Gunther's death. Kriemhild now goes back on her commitment, kills Hagen, and thereby justifies her own death.

Unlike other more impetuous apologists, Wachinger formulates his explanations with great caution. In a concluding statement (pp. 139-45) he warns against the dangers of positive overinterpretation along either psychological or symbolical lines (in the manner of W. J. Schröder). At the same time, a reduction of the *Nibelungenlied* to mere dramatic vitality seems to him less than adequate. He suggests that the interest of the poem may finally lie in the unresolved tension between the parts and the whole, between psychological portrayal and the unintegrated narrative facts. His book is admirable in its reserve, but it offers the student relatively little encouragement. It confirms that the *Nibelungenlied* is indeed very difficult to explain and hints that its charm may lie in its very uninterpretability.

Other critics were not ready for Wachinger's resignation. In 1963 Gottfried Weber published a general interpretation as ambitious in scope as W. J. Schröder's.[22] It pursues the reaction against Heusler (and the compensatory elevation of Tonnelat) in decisive terms, arguing that "attention to the sources perforce obscures the clear recognition of the literary work" (p. 2). Accordingly, about half the book is devoted to a step-by-step retracing of the roles played by the major characters. In the process the heroic figures emerge in the same questionable light that Bostock's brief essay had thrown on them. Siegfried is judged to have succumbed to hubris and a misguided subservience to love. He is flawed by the split between outward courtliness and inner arrogance. Hagen betrays his own better vision when, in vain concern for his honor, he agrees to the journey to Hunland though he knows it is fatal. The Burgundian and Hunnish kings are feeble enough to suggest that the poet had had some unedifying experience of kingship (p. 83). Rüdeger too is a victim of his own chivalric ambition and lack of internalized Christianity.

In all these figures Weber detects a deep-seated pride, which breeds hate, which in turn breeds vengeance and deception. They have in common an inability to transcend their egocentric interests. As a result the formal requirements of chivalry are transformed into a demonic preoccupation with honor, unmitigated by religious faith. The unfulfilled knights of the *Nibelungenlied* are driven to take refuge in heroic action. In terms of intellectual history, the poet was suspended between heroic nostalgia and the false optimism of chivalric culture. He portrayed a disillusionment with the latter and a reversion to the former. He thus associated himself with the more conservative and less intellectual impulses of Austro-Bavarian writers in opposition to the cultivation of chivalric and courtly values in the West.[23]

Bert Nagel's contributions to the study of the *Nibelungenlied* span more than twenty-five years from 1953 to 1979. One of the earliest and perhaps the best dates from 1954 and is remarkable for its delicate application of textual analysis and keen aesthetic observations.[24] Whereas other critics urged a reformulation of doctrine, Nagel was more eager to promote a greater appreciation of the poetic qualities, not least of all the particular effects of the *Nibelungenlied* stanza. His comments are there fore difficult to summarize. Fundamentally he is concerned with the poet's difficult position between old and new literary conventions, and the skill with which he navigates the shoals. He suggests how the poet mediates between the "old lore" of the Nibelung legend and the new biographical incorporation of Kriemhild, how Kriemhild and Hagen function both as exemplary victims of dark drama and individual personalities, how the dissonant intimations of doom merge

with scenes of courtly splendor from the outset to unify the poem as a whole, how the obvious difficulty of maintaining a clear epic flow is offset by dramatic scenes, how the archaic bridal-quest pattern is modernized in terms of courtly love, and how the poet capitalizes on the discrepancy between traditional energy and new refinement to create a feeling of "realism" and vitality in a figure such as Siegfried.

Nagel does not dispute the importance of earlier versions and the residue of discrepancies, but he believes that the poet's Janus position could be an opportunity as well as a dilemma. This does not mean that characters speak and act according to a perfectly consistent idea of their personalities. They can speak "out of character," as the poet's mouthpiece, for example when Hagen urges church attendance on his companions (stanzas 1,855-56). Nor does it mean that the poem is faultlessly composed, but Nagel asks us to bear in mind that it was intended to be read aloud in installments and that under these circumstances the power of individual scenes would have overshadowed defects in the narrative as a whole.

The undeniable contradictions in the text lend themselves to an analysis in terms of active renovations as well as passive reception. Kriemhild is in some sense two persons, but in the poet's new design she also grows organically from courtly maiden to demonic avenger. In the invitation sequence Nagel accepts the confusing indices of her real longing to see her brothers and her mania for revenge as psychologically comprehensible (stanzas 1,391-1,405). Even the notorious chronological difficulties that enable Kriemhild to give birth to Ortlieb in her fifties can be justified to the extent that they convey the timelessness of the vengeance imperative. Similarly, Siegfried's knowledge of Brünhild and his familiarity with Isenstein may be understood symbolically as evidence of an inner affinity. Hence Siegfried's tragedy grows out of his failure to realize his natural destiny with Brünhild and his formation of an unnatural bond with Kriemhild. Brünhild, correspondingly deprived of her destiny, sheds tears in stanza 618, alleging the injustice done Kriemhild in marrying her to a vassal, but this allegation is a pretext designed at once to mask and reveal her own bitter disappointment.

The early phase in Nagel's work culminated in his book of 1965.[25] Where the early monograph succeeds in its suggestive impressionism, the book fails because it attempts, but does not attain, comprehensiveness. It is the true heir of the period between 1950 and 1965 in its emphasis on formal criteria. The first section, on history, is half the length of the following sections on *Form* and *Ethos,* and "history" turns out to mean only contemporary history, not the literary history of the poem. Like Panzer's book, Nagel's tends to become a repertory of rhetorical features, for example structural schemes, parallelisms, and motival repetitions.[26] No summation or theory emerges from these pages, which offer something more like a running commentary. Nagel's book marked the end of a period. Formal analysis was for the moment exhausted in Germany and gave way to other trends. Only in England and the United States did it survive as a brief aftermath.[27]

BETWEEN THE TRENDS (1960-75)

Even before 1960 there was an uneasy stirring that may be understood as a reaction against the freewheeling surface interpretations of the postwar years. Klaus von See published two traditional source studies in 1957 and 1958, proposing a legal-historical background for Siegfried's role as delegate wooer.[28] Joachim Bumke published three source studies in 1958 and 1960, one constructing a source for Adventure 8, one exploring the relationship between the *Nibelungenlied* and *Daurel et Beton,* and one outlining dual sources for Part I of the *Nibelungenlied.*[29] As we saw in the previous chapter, Wapnewski's article of 1960 set Rüdeger's dilemma in a legal-historical context and took conscientious account of the source problems.[30] In 1959 Gerhart Lohse returned to the relationship between the *Nibelungenlied* and *þiðreks saga,* and in 1961 Roswitha Wisniewski published an elaborate study of the sources of Part II, vindicating Heusler's "Ältere Not" despite the persistent doubts of the previous decade.[31] That the field was not yet ready for such a reaction is indicated by the unbroken silence surrounding Lohse's study and the belated acceptance of Wisniewski's conclusions by Werner Hoffmann in 1982.[32] An analogous English reaction against descriptivism was expressed by K. C. King in 1962; he too reclaimed a role for source study.[33]

The intermediate period between text interpretation and historical interpretation also saw the appearance of two books by Friedrich Neumann (1967) and Walter Falk (1974). One looks backward in time, the other forward. Neumann's volume is not a unified study but a reprinting and refurbishing of earlier articles.[34] The collection is of interest because it shows a scholar of the older school coming to grips with the formalist revolution. His first article originally appeared in 1924.[35] It analyzes various characters with attention to the discrepancy between traditional roles in earlier versions of the legend and the more refined manners of the *Nibelungenlied:* Siegfried's old role as uncouth interloper at Worms and his new role as courtly prince, Brünhild's old role as powerful princess and her new role as comic amazon, Kriemhild's old role as merciless avenger and her new role as courtly lady. According to Neumann such characters were not conceived as living individuals but as exemplary figures embodying particular functions. When ideals and social functions changed, the characters remained suspended between two times. The poet failed to modernize in consistent detail. Neumann agrees with Heusler that the refrain on "love and sorrow" is not adequate to thematize the epic, and he is content to see the poet's achievement in his presentation of dramatic events and colorful scenes.[36] By prefacing his book with this essay, Neumann clearly declares his skepticism toward attempts to interpret the poem from a purely contemporary stance and without reference to the residue of older layers.

His chief essay nonetheless makes a real effort to absorb the descriptivist approach by rehearsing the action in painstaking detail, not once but twice.[37] These summaries are followed by a critique of Mergell, Maurer, Beyschlag, W. Schröder, and Weber. Mergell receives particularly harsh criticism for remaining on the surface of the text, ignoring problems, and arriving at an interpretation on the basis of a few passages randomly selected and arbitrarily connected. Neumann's criticism achieves its effect through an appeal to sound common sense, but it is not sophisticated and fails to do much damage to the descriptivist hypothesis. The interpretation of all epic depends, after all, on the selection and combination of significant moments. Neumann does not show why the *Nibelungenlied* should constitute a special exception to this procedure and why disharmonies caused by the retention of old motifs in a new context should be disabling for the interpreter who seeks to establish an ideological framework.

To assign as recent a book as Walter Falk's to the intermediate period is stretching a point, but the author explains in his preface that the central Chapters 5-9 go back to 1961-63, that is, to what we might call the high interpretive period.[38] Falk espouses two fundamental doctrines of this period, the "crime and punishment hypothesis" most clearly formulated by Bostock, and the "two-world hypothesis," which we have encountered in the work of Mergell, W. J. Schröder, Weber, and, in subdued form, Wachinger.[39] The "crime and punishment hypothesis" observes that the poem culminates in disaster and posits moral guilt to explain it; the attractiveness of such an interpretation to the postwar generation is obvious. The "two-world hypothesis" holds that two incongruent spheres are brought together with disastrous consequences (e.g., Siegfried or Brünhild in the courtly world of Worms), or that natural affinities (most commonly the bond between Siegfried and Brünhild) are ignored to the detriment of all.

Falk's book has perhaps most in common with Weber's because it advances a religious interpretation. The point of departure is Walther von der Vogelweide's "Ich saz ûf eime steine" and the idea that "guot und weltlîch êre" (wealth and worldly honor) cannot be reconciled with "gotes hulde" (God's grace). Falk explains Walther's view as the result of an inner crisis precipitated by a disillusionment with *Minnedienst* (love service), and suggests that the characters in the *Nibelungenlied* also strive for *guot* and *êre* without being able to reconcile them with *gotes hulde.* Siegfried belongs by nature to an "inner world," but he enters the artificial world of Worms and therefore finds himself straddling two opposed existences. Because he belongs to the same world as Brünhild, he is able to win her for the "world of honor" in Worms. In so doing, he tricks Gunther by drawing him out of the "world of honor," thus realizing his boast to conquer Worms.

At the same time, however, Siegfried succumbs to the "world of honor" for the sake of love. By winning Kriemhild with *Minnedienst* he transforms himself from a servant of love into its master; *Minnedienst* is revealed in its true light as an instrument for achieving power. As a result of his *Minnedienst* Siegfried makes the transition from challenger and conqueror to a new existence as representative and defender of the "world of honor," but Kriemhild, out of arrogance, wishes to free him from this restrictive existence. Hence the quarrel of the queens. But ultimately she too is trapped; in appealing to Hagen to protect Siegfried, she submits to the prime representative of the "world of honor." We are led to understand that an allegiance to courtly love has also undermined her natural principles. Love is thus the root cause of Siegfried's death, but he is love's accomplice; having fulfilled his boast to subdue the Burgundians, he has become a threat to them and thus motivates his own death. As in Walther's "Ich saz ûf eime steine," *untriuwe* and *gewalt* (faithlessness and violence) lurk in the *Nibelungenlied,* which is an epic counterpart to Walther's lyric.

HISTORICAL INTERPRETATIONS (1965-80)

Falk's structural principles look back to the analytical methods of the 1960's, but his attempt to locate the *Nibelungenlied* in the political crisis that inspired Walther belongs to the following period of historical interpretations. The latter preoccupation is perhaps already implicit in Panzer's emphasis on contemporary events underlying certain episodes in the *Nibelungenlied,* but the first explicitly political interpretation was put forward in an essay of 1952 by Siegfried Beyschlag.[40]

Beyschlag begins by pointing out a passage in *þiðreks saga* (2:262.17-26) suggesting that Sigurd's presence challenges Gunnar's status as king and that Grimhild poses a similar threat to Brynhild. The same threat is hinted at in the *Nibelungenlied* when Kriemhild blandly states that the whole realm should be subject to Seigfried (stanza 815) and then demands precedence before the court. Beyschlag assembles indications of a court party in opposition to Siegfried and in favor of his elimination, concluding that political issues are a significant factor in the motivation of his death. According to Beyschlag, it could scarcely be coincidental that such a theme surfaced in a literary work during the interregnum years after 1197, and he anticipates Falk with a reference to Walther's political poetry.

Wapnewski's essay of 1960 also made use of political facts to illumine Rüdeger's options in Adventure 37, but the period of systematic historical interpretations was ushered in with a brief article by Josef Szövérffy in 1965.[41] Szövérffy points out that the disaster of Part I is conditioned by Siegfried's quasi-feudal subordination to Gunther in the hope of winning Kriemhild, and that the disaster of Part II is predicated on Rüdeger's similarly quasi-feudal oath to support Kriemhild in Hunland. Feudal allegiances of a questionable nature are therefore the motor of tragedy, and Szövérffy suggests that such skepticism must have been a feature of the years following the quarrel between pope and emperor over the investiture of bishops; the excommunication of emperors and the release of vassals from feudal bonds during these years had destabilized the system of obligations. Szövérffy's proposal is too general to have much explanatory force, but it was the first to es-

tablish itself as a clear alternative to legendary analysis in Heusler's tradition or to the more recent textual interpretations.

As we saw in Chapter 5, Karl Heinz Ihlenburg also adduced the problematical character of feudal structures in a full-scale study from 1969.[42] He projected the *Nibelungenlied* against the background of the troubled political scene after the death of Henry VI in 1197, but more broadly against the efforts of the aristocracy to assert itself against imperial authority in the twelfth century. The pattern of weak kings (Gunther and Etzel) and powerful vassals (Hagen and Rüdeger) suggested to him the inherent frailty of political institutions.

In an important article from 1974, Jan-Dirk Müller focuses the social forces in a somewhat different light, as a contest not between royalty and aristocracy but between competing elements within the aristocracy.[43] Departing from earlier efforts to thematize the action of the *Nibelungenlied* allegorically, Müller undertakes only to identify certain tensions in the text that mirror contemporary social conditions.

Müller begins with Siegfried's brash claim at Worms, which cannot succeed because it is a challenge to legitimate authority. In the context of political realities such a demonstration of knightly prowess is illusory. Gunther, contrary to Ihlenburg's view, is not to be seen as a weak king but as the bearer of royal authority, charged with the maintenance of peace and able to contain Siegfried's challenge. Siegfried becomes socialized when he relinquishes the idea of individual combat and enters the world of service, love service for Kriemhild's hand and political service on Gunther's behalf. But the idea of service is ambiguous because it is associated both with the voluntary service undertaken by the free hereditary nobility and the obligatory service performed by the unfree *eigenman* or *ministerialis.* In Islant, where, in distinction to Worms, strength and status are the same thing, Siegfried must impersonate an *eigenman* and feign social inferiority not to be mistaken for the suitor himself. Brünhild is therefore confronted with confusing indices, and her confusion determines the sequel.

This confusion is the substance of the queens' quarrel, which is designed to clarify whether Siegfried is Gunther's "genôz" (equal—stanza 819) or his "man" (stanza 821). The word *man* can mean free vassal, but it can also mean unfree *ministerialis,* and this is the sense in which Brünhild understands it. The semantic ambiguity reflects a historical development in which unfree *ministeriales* were rising into positions previously reserved for free nobles, and in which these nobles were themselves losing traditional prerogatives. Class friction ensued, and the question whether a particular man in royal service was a *man* (free vassal) or *eigenholt* (*ministerialis*) was socially crucial. The calamity of Part I thus grows out of Brünhild's misconstruction of Siegfried's voluntary service as obligatory service. Müller points out that the class tension between old and new nobility seems to have been prevalent in southeastern Germany, where the hereditary nobility lost ground in the last third of the twelfth century but in some cases vigorously resisted the trend. This situation may have been particularly pronounced around Passau, where the *Nibelungenlied* is most likely to have been written.

Two rather more impressionistic historical studies appeared in a volume of essays on medieval Austrian literature published in 1977. Helmut Birkhan concentrates on the broader literary and political context and suggests that the *Nibelungenlied* may have represented a compromise between the historically oriented Welf literature of the East and the courtly Hohenstaufen literature of the West.[44] Passau, with its Hohenstaufen sympathies but Welf location in Bavaria, would have been conducive to this double vision, and the period after Henry the Lion's fall in 1180 and the submission of his Danish ally Valdemar in 1181 would have been the right moment for the poet's barbs against the Bavarian and Saxon targets of Hohenstaufen animosity. Birkhan doubts that Rüdeger was conceived as a fictional reflection of a Babenberg duke, such as Leopold VI, because a duke would scarcely have been flattered to see himself counterfeited as a count. Birkhan suggests instead that Rüdeger may have been intended as an idealized antitype to Barbarossa's faithless vassal Henry the Lion.

In the same volume Sylvia Konecny draws attention to King Sigemund's abdication in Siegfried's favor (stanza 713) and explains it on the basis of a Frankish practice that precluded an uncrowned prince from having a binding marriage or legitimate heirs.[45] Sigemund's abdication may therefore be understood as an effort to maximize Siegfried's value as a marriage partner for Kriemhild. Of particular interest in this line of argument is Konecny's further assumption of a hypothetical earlier version of the tale incorporating the abdication motif. Thus the old practice of basing interpretations on genetic deductions is reversed, and historical considerations lead to the positing of new sources. In more general terms Konecny urges the thematic contrast between a weak monarchy at Worms, where Gunther allows himself to become Hagen's instrument, and a strong monarchy at Xanten, where there is no visible sign of aristocratic encroachment.

A contrast between Xanten and Worms is also the point of departure for Peter Czerwinski, who understands the former as a primitive culture predicated on force and the latter as a more advanced bureaucratic culture.[46] Siegfried, the exponent of primitive culture, must validate himself by an exercise of strength at Worms, but the challenge is averted and his energy is translated into formal service in the new hierarchy. The relations between Siegfried and Gunther are regulated by subordinating one to the other. Siegfried then takes over the Saxon campaign because Gunther can maintain his position only as long as he is exempt from the exercise of force. Love also works to socialize natural impulses, and Kriemhild's beauty is placed in the service of the court's larger interests.

The upshot of the wooing on Islant dramatizes the conflict between a primitive and a more advanced from of culture.

When representatives of the primitive culture (Siegfried and Brünhild) are installed at Worms, they incite violence and jeopardize the hierarchical structure. Hagen's contradictory role in this situation is that he is technically a vassal in the hierarchical model, but refuses to subordinate himself and acts on his own initiative. The catastrophe in Hunland also proceeds from a disintegration of the new order in the face of uncontrolled violence. What Czerwinski proposes is another version of the "two-world hypothesis," but despite his references to twelfth-century territorialization, his reading is more in keeping with W. J. Schröder's symbolical interpretation than with the more recent historical interpretations.

A summary by Gert Kaiser may serve as the final example in this group.[47] It combines sociohistorical and reception analysis by seeking to identify a socially distinct readership. Following Jan-Dirk Müller, Kaiser argues that the trouble arises because Brünhild misunderstands Siegfried's service as that of an unfree *ministerialis,* but he goes on to suggest that the view of service in the *Nibelungenlied* stands in direct opposition to the approval of service in Arthurian epic and the *romans d'antiquite'.* The *Nibelungenlied* poet rejects the idea of service precisely because it is tainted by association with the class of *ministeriales.* Part II is in effect a conservative celebration of voluntary loyalty in opposition to obligatory service, but the ideological message is esthetically rescued by Hagen's private pact with Rüdeger in defiance of strict feudal loyalty. Kaiser thus goes a step further than Müller, who suggested only involuntary echoes of social tensions. Kaiser assigns these tensions to the thematic fabric of the poem.

CONCLUSION

The status of *Nibelungenlied* research at the end of our period is conveniently represented by fourteen articles from a conference held in Hohenems in September of 1979 and published the following year.[48] These papers are remarkable for the lack of continuity they display. None pursues the text-interpretive model prevalent in the period 1950-65, and only one attaches to the sociohistorical tradition of 1965-80. Significantly, the one exception, an important essay by Ursula Hennig, levels some telling criticism at such proponents of historical interpretation as Szöverffy, Ihlenburg, and Jan-Dirk Müller.[49] Against Müller she argues that *eigenholt* does not mean *ministerialis* but rather 'bondsman'. Brünhild's description of Siegfried as *eigenholt* in stanzas 620 and 803 does not therefore constitute a subtle misunderstanding of feudal distinctions; it is a deliberately exaggerated provocation. Henning denies that feudal concepts have motivating force in the *Nibelungenlied* and reasserts the importance of literary comprehension. By virtue of its exclusions, then, the Hohenems conference would seem to mark the end of an era.

Equally remarkable is the conference's thematic consistency in another area. No fewer than six of the fourteen contributions are connected in some way with oral-formulaic composition.[50] Some make positive use of the theory, but others are cautious about it. In a paper independent of similar suggestions made a year earlier by Michael Curschmann, Norbert Voorwinden arrives at the conclusion that the *Klage* was composed chiefly on the basis of a preliterary transmission of the Nibelung story.[51] Burghart Wachinger, this time with explicit reference to Curschmann, comes to the opposite conclusion, that the *Klage* is based on a definite text of the *Nibelungenlied,* although it may in turn have contributed to the final shape of that epic as we know it.[52] Both agree that the transmission of these texts was more open to oral alteration than has traditionally been assumed. Achim Masser solidifies the evidence for oral transmission by identifying oral doublets inserted at different points in the written text of the *Nibelungenlied.*[53] Peter K. Stein, on the other hand, reduces the significance of oral-formulaic analysis by showing that the formulism in a text of *Orendel* is literary in nature.[54]

The period of oral-formulaic analysis as applied to the *Nibelungenlied* corresponds roughly to the period of sociohistorical analysis; Franz Bäuml's first relevant study appeared in 1967 and his latest in the Hohenems volume of 1980.[55] On the other hand, the theory as it pertains to Germanic belongs more generally speaking to the preceding period of textual study, which began with the *Beowulf* article by Francis P. Magoun, Jr., in 1953.[56] Oral-formulaic analysis occupies an ambiguous position in both periods. It is both textual and nontextual, historical and nonhistorical. It is textual because it adheres closely to the phrasing of the poem and seeks to account precisely for that phrasing, but it is non-textual because it causes the reader to retreat quickly into the obscurity of textlessness. It is historical because it provides a genetic explanation of the poem and probes the context of literacy, but it is nonhistorical because it posits earlier versions that are not readily distinguishable from the extant ones. It does not, for example, provide an instrument for measuring the differences between the *Nibelungenlied* of 1200, the "Ältere Not" of 1160-70, and Saxo's *carmen* of Grimhild's perfidy from 1131. It is in any event noninterpretive because the art of preliterary criticism has yet to be evolved. That nearly half the contributions in the Hohenems volume grow out of the oral-formulaic debate in itself signals a retreat from the interpretive efforts of the previous decades.

Subtracting a study by Stefan Sonderegger on conversational language in the *Nibelungenlied* and a plenary address by Werner Schröder, we are left with five papers on various topics. Werner Hoffmann provides a helpful review of discussions in the literary histories from Gervinus to Bertau.[57] Walter Haug, in the tradition of Kurt Wais, undertakes a comparison with a bridal-quest story in the *Mabinogion.*[58] Alois Wolf revives Panzer's problem of French sources and suggests motival and scenic similarities, especially to the cycle of Guillaume d'Orange.[59] Uwe Meves returns to the Passau archives and suggests that the literary patronage of *König Rother* may underlie the acknowledgment of Wolfger's patronage in the *Nibelungen-*

lied.[60] Otfrid Ehrismann adopts a psychological angle in contrasting Parts I and II and locating the superior appeal of the latter in its therapeutic exorcism of death.[61] What these contributions have in common is an attempt to extract new perspectives from traditional approaches. A reading of the volume as a whole suggests a temporary lack of consensus on the direction *Nibelungenlied* studies should take and hence an open prospect.

This sense of equilibrium, in contrast to the decisive critical initiatives of 1950-65 and 1965-80, also emerges from the most important recent contribution to *Nibelungenlied* studies, Werner Hoffmann's fifth revised edition of the Metzler volume *Das Nibelungenlied* (1982), originally published in collaboration with Gottfried Weber in 1961.[62] In its latest form this book has undergone not only a great development in coverage, which makes it the indispensable guide, but also a shift in emphasis. The first edition, presumably under Weber's influence, largely accepted Friedrich Panzer's revolution (e.g., pp. 13-16) and participated in the ensuing descriptivist redefinition of the task (e.g., pp. 63-64). Hoffmann's revision of 1982 rejects Panzer's philological conclusions (pp. 53-54), provides an ample review of the Norse texts and the relevant source questions (pp. 47-56), and allows cautiously for the usefulness of diachronic study in the interpretive project (p. 61).[63]

It is not the task of this chapter to propose yet another interpretation of the *Nibelungenlied* but rather to suggest a strategy and outline the parameters of interpretation. Clearly a close reading of the text is as fundamental now as it was in 1950, and the sociohistorical studies of 1965-80 have just as clearly widened our perspective on the text. But both these approaches, which undertook to root the *Nibelungenlied* more firmly in the contemporary scene, have failed to fulfill that promise. The literary readings of 1950-65 limited the context too exclusively to courtly romance, particularly to *Parzival,* all or large parts of which were written later. The sociohistorical analyses disregarded the literary context altogether. The *Nibelungenlied* has therefore remained in the isolation about which Dürrenmatt, Panzer, and later critics complained.

The strategy proposed in Chapters 5-7 aims to anchor the poem not only in contemporary Arthurian epic but also in the more general context of German literature during the period 1150-1200, including the immediate sources, the "Ältere Not" and the "Brünhildenlied." These poems were also a part of twelfth-century German literature and contributed to the literary framework in which the author of the *Nibelungenlied* worked. Just as the historical critics have taught us to hear institutional echoes in the text, so too we should learn to identify literary echoes. Perhaps most neglected in its formative role is the minstrel epic, especially *König Rother.* A glance at this tradition reveals a series of literary ironies. We may see in Rüdeger the subverted delegate wooer, the trickster tricked, the comic figure of tradition recast in a tragic role. Similarly, Siegfried inherits both the roles of wooer and of delegate wooer from bridal-quest romance. The conventions of this form shed light on a number of traditionally difficult scenes: the puzzling apprehension of Siegfried's parents when he declares his intention to woo Kriemhild, the obsession with finery, his journey "in recken wîse," Kriemhild's reluctance, the discordant hostility between the suitor and the bride's family in the notorious confrontation of Adventure 3, the magic cloak and extravagant trickery in Islant, Siegfried's fictitious identity as Gunther's vassal, his rescue force from Nibelungenland, and the comic doubling of his role as both suitor and delegate in Adventure 9. When the listeners around 1200 heard these scenes, they recognized the literary background, and when the happy-go-lucky wooer was transformed into the tragic victim of Adventure 16, they appreciated the discrepancy between the old convention and the new creation.

More than a few listeners would have been familiar with Heinrich von Veldeke's *Eneide* and would have pondered the distance between marital comedy and marital tragedy. They would have been acquainted with the new idealization of marriage, if not in *Guillaume d'Angleterre,* at least in Hartmann's epics. In some form they would have known the Hellenistic tradition of family fidelity and domestic reintegration, for example the stories of Faustinianus and Crescentia in the *Kaiserchronik.* The family disintegrations of the *Nibelungenlied* would have echoed harshly against this happier legacy.

More learned listeners would have known something of the tradition of universal history reflected in the *Annolied* and *Kaiserchronik.* If they knew of Franko's foundation at Xanten, they were in a position to connect Siegfried's preeminence with the idea of national emergence. The anti-Roman story of Adelger in the *Kaiserchronik* and the anti-Byzantine barbs in *König Rother* would have promoted such an understanding. Franco-German competition was no less a part of the political scene than the disparagement of Rome and Constantinople. The elevation of Siegfried could very well have been perceived as an epic counter-thrust to the French Roland, well known from the *Rolandslied,* as well as to the Greek Alexander and the Roman Aeneas. Regional politics was also a factor in contemporary literature, as the *Annolied,* Heinrich von Veldeke's *Servatius,* and the Soest claim to the Nibelung catastrophe illustrate. Regionalism clarifies the Austro-Hohenstaufen bias against Bavarians and Saxons, as well as Passau's counterclaim to possession of the true transmission of the legend.

These general considerations can be further refined by measuring the *Nibelungenlied* against the immediate sources. Part II in particular lends itself to such comparison and permits us to isolate the poet's concerns. He rehabilitates Hagen in no fewer than five new adventures designed to vindicate his standing among the Burgundians. Breeding, candor, loyalty, kinship, and friendship are the values the poet espouses. Ferdinand Urbanek produced interesting evidence for advocacy of family loyalty and fast friendship, connected with contemporary Austro-Bavarian

tensions, underlying *König Rother,* and some analogous political background might be surmised for the *Nibelungenlied.*[64] Rüdeger's dilemma in Adventure 37 could be making an immediate political point. In any event, the resurrection of Hagen from his treachery in Part I and the reintegration of kith and kin in Part II are evident when our knowledge of the "Ältere Not" is brought to bear.

Siegfried is also promoted from a lesser role in the "Brünhildenlied" to more heroic dimensions in the *Nibelungenlied.* In his case as well as Hagen's, a study of the text's development from earlier versions produces evidence against the descriptivist hypotheses. These hypotheses (e.g., W. J. Schröder, Weber, Falk) have suggested a pattern of weakness, falseness, and prevarication subtending the catastrophe of the *Nibelungenlied.* They subscribe to what I have called the "crime and punishment" interpretation, the idea that Siegfried, Hagen, and the others contract a guilt that they must ultimately expiate. A historical reading against the sources suggests rather that they are heroic figures caught in the traditional impasse of heroic action. They must die, for that is the generic law of heroic literature, but they transcend their fate with a display of personal qualities. They do so in different ways. Siegfried's display is limited to an exhibition of matchless strength; he has the surplus vitality but also the unconsciousness of youth. Hagen is older, more experienced, more vulnerable, but completely aware of the world around him. His heroism is the triumph of consciousness. In this sense, perhaps, the *Nibelungenlied* fits into the structure of contemporary Arthurian romance, in which the two-part structure cultivated by both Hartmann and Wolfram marks out a growth from innocence to knowledge. In the Arthurian epics the trajectory is constructive and optimistic. In the *Nibelungenlied* it is tragic, but not necessarily pessimistic. The moral qualities displayed in Part II are no less triumphant for being ill-fated.

Kriemhild too appears in a somewhat different light if she is viewed in the mirror of the sources. Critics have frequently remarked on her rehabilitation in redaction C and the *Klage,* compared to the standard redaction B, and have argued a difference in interpretation. But if we in turn compare the Kriemhild of B to her ancestor in the "Ältere Not," we may find reasons to moderate our judgment. The poets of the "Ältere Not" and the *Nibelungenlied* were both heir to the idea of Kriemhild's unequivocal "perfidy against her brothers." The poet of the "Ältere Not" does not appear to have deviated from this image. Kriemhild cajoles Etzel into the treacherous invitation of her relatives and personally dispatches a letter with false promises. She confronts Hagen directly on his arrival then undertakes machinations behind Etzel's back to instigate an attack on the guests. When all else fails, she incites her young son to strike Hagen in the face in order to precipitate the fray. Without a preface telling of Siegfried's death, these actions appear in a clearly negative light.

But the *Nibelungenlied* poet altered the portrait completely by adding Kriemhild's youthful love story, her betrayal by

Hagen and her brothers, her four and a half years of widowed grief cut off from her family in Worms, and the seizure of her bride price. In this version her action is amply motivated. It is no longer a question of perfidy but of marital fidelity of the sort encouraged by ecclesiastical emphasis on the permanent union of hearts and by such models of marital faith as Hartmann's Enîta or Wolfram's Sigûne. A historical perspective on Kriemhild suggests not that the B and C poets had substantially different views of her character but that there was a consistent and linear unburdening of her, undertaken first by the B poet and then pursued logically by the C poet.

After a prolonged period of reaction against source criticism and literary-historical analysis the time may be ripe to experiment once again with these traditional approaches. The *Nibelungenlied* should indeed be integrated more decisively into the period in which it was written, but this procedure stands to profit no less from the study of contemporary literature than from the study of contemporary history. Only a small part of that literature has been touched on here. The rest remains to be explored.

Notes

1. Dürrenmatt, *Das Nibelungenlied im Kreis der höfischen Dichtung;* Panzer, *Studien zum Nibelungenliede.*

2. Heusler, "Die Lieder der Lücke im Codex Regius" and *Die altgermanische Dichtung,* 2d rev. ed.

3. See note 6 to Chapter 6.

4. Compare Dürrenmatt, p. 7, with Panzer, *Studien zum Nibelungenliede,* p. 3, and *Das Nibelungenlied,* pp. 11-13.

5. Mergell, "Nibelungenlied und höfischer Roman." On Dürrenmatt see pp. 5-6.

6. Mergell bases his view of Hagen on stanza 2,371, but cf. W. J. Schröder, "Das Nibelungenlied: Versuch einer Deutung," p. 125, note 1; rpt. p. 127, note 1. Also Gentry, "Trends in 'Nibelungenlied' Research since 1949," p. 128.

7. W. J. Schröder, "Das *Nibelungenlied,"* p. 58; rpt. p. 60.

8. Heusler, *Nibelungensage und Nibelungenlied,* p. 58: "Heroische Geschichten bequemen sich ungern einem lehrhaften Leitsatz."

9. W. Schröder, "Die Tragödie Kriemhilts," pp. 41-43; rpt. pp. 49-51.

10. Tonnelat, *La Chanson des Nibelungen.*

11. Maurer, *Leid.*

12. Ibid., pp. 21 and 31.

13. W. Schröder, "Die Tragödie" rpt. pp. 73, 80, 86, 93, 98-99, 149.

14. Bostock, "The Message of the 'Nibelungenlied.'"

15. On the often meaningless use of *übermuot* in the *Nibelungenlied* see Wachinger, *Studien zum Nibelun-* *genlied,* p. 105, and Sacker, "On Irony and Symbolism," pp. 271-72.

16. Mowatt, "Studies towards an Interpretation of the 'Nibelungenlied.'"

17. Sacker, "On Irony and Symbolism."

18. In general see Hoffmann's just assessment of the Anglo-American contributions in "Die englische und amerikanische Nibelungenforschung 1959-62."

19. Panzer, *Das Nibelungenlied: Entstehung und Gestalt.*

20. Menéndez Pidal, *La Chanson de Roland y el neotradicionalismo.*

21. Wachinger, *Studien zum Nibelungenlied.*

22. Weber, *Das Nibelungenlied: Problem und Idee.*

23. A similar suggestion had already been made by W. J. Schröder, "Das Nibelungenlied: Versuch einer Deutung," pp. 142-43; rpt. pp. 144-45.

24. Nagel, "Zur Interpretation und Wertung des Nibelungenliedes."

25. Nagel, *Das Nibelungenlied: Stoff—Form—Ethos.*

26. Ibid., e.g., pp. 81, 97, 118, 128.

27. Representative of this aftermath are Mowatt and Sacker, *The Nibelungenlied: An Interpretative Commentary;* Bekker, *The Nibelungenlied: A Literary Analysis;* Gentry, *Triuwe and vriunt in the Nibelungenlied.* It might be noted, however, that Mowatt's and Sacker's *Commentary* grew out of their articles from 1961 and that Bekker's book built on articles from 1966 and 1967: "Kingship in the *Nibelungenlied*" and "The 'Eigenmann'-Motif in the *Nibelungenlied.*"

28. Von See, "Die Werbung um Brünhild" and "Freierprobe und Königinnenzank."

29. Bumke, "Sigfrids Fahrt ins Nibelungenland"; "Die Eberjagd im Daurel und in der Nibelungendichtung"; "Die Quellen der Brünhildfabel im Nibelungenlied."

30. Wapnewski, "Rüdigers Schild."

31. Lohse, "Die Beziehungen zwischen der Thidrekssaga und den Handschriften des Nibelungenliedes"; Wisniewski, *Die Darstellung des Niflungenun-terganges in der Thidrekssaga.*

32. Hoffmann, *Das Nibelungenlied,* p. 54.

33. King, "The Message of the 'Nibelungenlied.'"

34. Neumann, *Das Nibelungenlied in seiner Zeit.*

35. Neumann, "Schichten der Ethik im Nibelungenliede." Cf. Nagel's essay "Stoffzwang der Uberlieferung in mittelhochdeutscher Dichtung."

36. Heusler, *Nibelungensage und Nibelungenlied,* p. 57; Neumann, *Das Nibelungenlied in seiner Zeit,* p. 29.

37. Neumann, *Das Nibelungenlied in seiner Zeit,* pp. 65-105 and 109-21.

38. Falk, *Das Nibelungenlied in seiner Epoche,* p. 20.

39. A briefer example of the "crime and punishment hypothesis" from this period is Wisniewski's "Das Versagen des Königs." Wisniewski concentrates on the disastrous consequences of Gunther's weakness, which she places in the context of medieval *speculum regale* literature.

40. Beyschlag, "Das Motiv der Macht bei Siegfrieds Tod."

41. Szövérffy, "Das Nibelungenlied: Strukturelle Beobachtungen und Zeitgeschichte."

42. Ihlenburg, *Das Nibelungenlied: Problem und Gehalt.*

43. Müller, "Sivrit: *künec—man—eigenholt.*" Müller criticizes Ihlenburg on p. 116.

44. Birkhan, "Zur Entstehung und Absicht des Nibelungenliedes."

45. Konecny, "Das Sozialgefüge am Burgundenhof." A more likely source for Sigemund's abdication would seem to be King Latinus' abdication in favor of Aeneas in Veldeke's *Eneide*, vv. 13,287-91.

46. Czerwinski, "Das Nibelungenlied: Widersprüche höfischer Gewaltreglementierung."

47. Kaiser, "Deutsche Heldenepik."

48. "Hohenemser Studien zum Nibelungenlied" in *Montfort: Vierteljahresschrift für Geschichte und Gegenwart Vorarlbergs,* 32 (1980), 181-381 (7-207).

49. Henning, "Herr und Mann: Zur Ständegliederung im Nibelungenlied."

50. For earlier reactions to the oral-formulaic theory in Germany see Fromm, "Der oder die Dichter des Nibelungenliedes?"; W. Hoffmann, *Mittelhochdeutsche Heldendichtung,* pp. 53-59; Heinzle, *Mittelhochdeutsche Dietrichepik,* pp. 67-92; von See, "Was ist Heldendichtung?," esp. rpt. pp. 168-76.

51. Curschmann, "'Nibelungenlied' und 'Nibelungenklage'"; Voorwinden, "Nibelungenklage und Nibelungenlied."

52. Wachinger, "Die 'Klage' und das Nibelungenlied."

53. Masser, "Von Alternativstrophen und Vortragsvarianten im Nibelungenlied."

54. Stein, "Orendel 1512: Probleme und Möglichkeiten der Anwendung der *theory of oral-formulaic poetry* bei der literaturhistorischen Interpretation eines mittelhochdeutschen Textes."

55. Bäuml and Ward, "Zur mündlichen Überlieferung des Nibelungenliedes," and Bäuml, "Zum Verständnis mittelalterlicher Mitteilungen." Since the writing of this report Bäuml has contributed a further article, "Medieval Texts and the Two Theories of Oral-Formulaic Composition."

56. For a history and critique of the oral-formulaic theory as applied to the *Nibelungenlied* see Sperberg-McQueen, "An Analysis of Recent Work on *Nibelungenlied* Poetics."

57. Hoffmann, "Das Nibelungenlied in der Literaturgeschichtsschreibung von Gervinus bis Bertau."

58. Haug, "Normatives Modell oder hermeneutisches Experiment."

59. Wolf, "Die Verschriftlichung der Nibelungensage und die französischdeutschen Literaturbeziehungen im Mittelalter."

60. Meves, "Bischof Wolfger von Passau, *sîn schrîber, meister Kuonrât* und die Nibelungenüberlieferung."

61. Ehrismann, "Archaisches und Modernes im Nibelungenlied: Pathos und Abwehr."

62. Hoffmann, *Heldendichtung II: Nibelungenlied* (1961; rpt. 1964 and 1968; rev. 1974).

63. A similar shift away from the *Nibelungenlied* as sole arbiter of the tradition and toward greater consideration of other testimony is apparent in Nagel's essay "Noch einmal Nibelungenlied." The same trend is visible in the Anglo-Saxon world in Hatto's "Medieval German" in *Traditions of Heroic and Epic Poetry,* 1:177, where he writes, "But it seems to the present writer that studies of Nibelung tradition which assume Heusler's theories to be passé, condemn themselves to swift oblivion."

64. Urbanek, *Kaiser, Grafen und Mäzene im König Rother,* pp. 73-82.

Abbreviations

The following abbreviations are used in the Notes and the Works Cited:

ABäG: Amsterdamer Beiträge zur älteren Germanistik.

BGDSL: Beiträge zur Geschichte der deutschen Sprache und Literatur.

GLL: German Life and Letters.

GR: Germanic Review.

GRM: Germanisch-romanische Monatsschrift. "Hohenemser Studien": "Hohenemser Studien zum Nibelungenlied." In *Montfort: Vierteljahresschrift für Geschichte und Gegenwart Vorarlbergs,* 32 (1980), 181-381 [7-207].

JIG: Jahrbuch für internationale Germanistik.

MGH: Monumenta Germaniae Historica

MLR: Modern Language Review.

MTU: Münchener Texte und Untersuchungen zur deutschen Literatur des Mittelalters

WW: Wirkendes Wort.

ZDA: Zeitschrift für deutsches Altertum und deutsche Literatur.

Works Cited

Bäuml, Franz H. "Medieval Texts and the Two Theories of Oral-Formulaic Composition: A Proposal for a Third Theory." *New Literary History,* 16 (1984), 31-49.

Bäuml, Franz H., and Donald J. Ward. "Zur mündlichen Überlieferung des Nibelungenliedes." *DVLG*, 41 (1967), 351-90.

Bekker, Hugo. "The 'Eigenmann'-Motif in the *Nibelungenlied*." *GR*, 42 (1967), 5-15.

———. "Kingship in the *Nibelungenlied*." *GR*, 41 (1966), 251-63.

———. *The Nibelungenlied: A Literary Analysis.* Toronto, 1971.

Beyschlag, Siegfried. "Das Motiv der Macht bei Siegfrieds Tod." *GRM*, 33 (1952), 95-108. Rpt. in *Zur germanisch-deutschen Heldensage: Sechzehn Aufsätze zum neuen Forschungsstand*, ed. Karl Hauck, pp. 195-213. Wege der Forschung, 14. Darmstadt, 1965.

Birkhan, Helmut. "Zur Entstehung und Absicht des Nibelungenliedes." In *Österreichische Literatur zur Zeit der Babenberger: Vorträge der Lilienfelder Tagung 1976*, ed. Alfred Ebenbauer, Fritz Peter Knapp, and Ingrid Strasser, pp. 1-24. Vienna, 1977.

Bostock, J. Knight. "The Message of the 'Nibelungenlied.'" *MLR* 55 (1960), 200-212. Trans. as "Der Sinn des Nibelungenlieds" in Rupp, pp. 84-109.

Bumke, Joachim. "Die Eberjagd im Daurel und in der Nibelungendichtung." *GRM*, 41 (1960), 105-11.

———. "Die Quellen der Brünhildfabel im Nibelungenlied." *Euphorion*, 54 (1960), 1-38.

———. "Sigfrids Fahrt ins Nibelungenland: Zur achten aventiure des Nibelungenliedes." *BGDSL* (Tübingen), 80 (1958), 253-68.

Curschmann, Michael. "'Nibelungenlied' und 'Nibelungenklage': "Über Mündlichkeit und Schriftlichkeit im Prozess der Episierung." In *Deutsche Literatur im Mittelalter: Kontakte und Perspektiven. Hugo Kuhn zum Gedenken*, ed. Christoph Cormeau, pp. 85-119. Stuttgart, 1979.

Czerwinski, Peter. "Das Nibelungenlied: Widersprüche höfischer Gewaltreglementierung." In *Einführung in die deutsche Literatur des 12. bis 16. Jahrhunderts*, vol. 1: *Adel und Hof—12./13. Jahrhundert*, ed. Winfried Frey, Walter Raitz, and Dieter Seitz, pp. 49-87. Opladen, 1979.

Dürrenmatt, Nelly. *Das Nibelungenlied im Kreis der höfischen Dichtung*. Bern, 1945.

Ehrismann, Otfrid. "Archaisches und Modernes im Nibelungenlied: Pathos und Abwehr." In the "Hohenemser Studien," pp. 338-48 [164-74].

Falk, Walter. *Das Nibelungenlied in seiner Epoche: Revision eines romantischen Mythos*. Heidelberg, 1974.

Fromm, Hans. "Der oder die Dichter des Nibelungenliedes?" In *Colloquio italo-germanico sul tema: I Nibelunghi*. Atti dei Convegni Lincei, 1:63-74. Rome, 1974. Also appeared in *Acta: IV. Congresso Latino-Americano de Estudios Germanísticos* (São Paulo, 1974), pp. 51-66.

Gentry, Francis G. "Trends in 'Nibelungenlied' Research since 1949: A Critical Review." *ABäG*, 7 (1974), 125-39.

Hatto, A. T. "Medieval German." In *Traditions of Heroic and Epic Poetry*, vol. 1: *The Traditions*, ed. A. T. Hatto, pp. 165-95. London, 1980.

Haug, Walter. "Normatives Modell oder hermeneutisches Experiment: Überlegungen zu einer grundsätzlichen Revision des Heuslerschen Nibelungen-Modells." In the "Hohenemser Studien," pp. 212-26 [38-52].

Heinzle, Joachim. *Mittelhochdeutsche Dietrichepik: Untersuchungen zur Tradierungsweise, Überlieferungskritik und Gattungsgeschichte später Heldendichtung*. MTU, 62. Munich, 1978.

Hennig, Ursula. "Herr und Mann: Zur Ständegliederung im Nibelungenlied." In the "Hohenemser Studien," pp. 349-59 [175-85].

Heusler, Andreas. *Die altgermanische Dichtung*. 2d rev. ed. Potsdam, 1941; rpt. Darmstadt, 1957.

———. "Die Lieder der Lücke im Codex Regius der Edda." In *Germanistische Abhandlungen, Hermann Paul dargebracht*, pp. 1-98. Strasbourg, 1902. Rpt. in his *Kleine Schriften*, vol. 2, ed. Stefan Sonderegger, pp. 223-91.

———. *Nibelungensage und Nibelungenlied: Die Stoffgeschichte des deutschen Heldenepos*. 6th ed. Dortmund, 1965.

Hoffmann, Werner. *Mittelhochdeutsche Heldendichtung*. Grundlagen der Germanistik, 14. Berlin, 1974.

"Das Nibelungenlied in der Literaturgeschichtsschreibung von Gervinus bis Bertau." In the "Hohenemser Studien," pp. 193-211 [19-37].

Ihlenburg, Karl Heinz. *Das Nibelungenlied: Problem und Gehalt*. Berlin, 1969.

Kaiser, Gert. "Deutsche Heldenepik." In *Neues Handbuch der Literaturwissenschaft*, vol. 7: *Europäisches Hochmittelalter*, ed. Henning Krauss, pp. 181-205. Wiesbaden, 1981.

King, K. C. "The Message of the 'Nibelungenlied'—A Reply." *MLR*, 57 (1962), 541-50. Trans. as "Der Sinn des Nibelungenlieds—Eine Entgegnung" in Rupp, pp. 218-36.

Konecny, Sylvia. "Das Sozialgefüge am Burgundenhof." In *Österreichische Literatur zur Zeit der Babenberger: Vorträge der Lilienfelder Tagung 1976*, ed. Alfred Ebenbauer, Fritz Peter Knapp, and Ingrid Strasser, pp. 97-116. Vienna, 1977.

Lohse, Gerhart. "Die Beziehungen zwischen der Thidrekssaga und den Handschriften des Nibelungenliedes." *BGDSL* (Tübingen), 81 (1959), 295-347.

Masser, Achim. "Von Alternativstrophen und Vortragsvarianten im Nibelungenlied." In the "Hohenemser Studien," pp. 299-311 [125-37].

Maurer, Friedrich. *Leid: Studien zur Bedeutungs- und Problemgeschichte besonders in den grossen Epen der staufischen Zeit.* Bern, 1951; 4th ed. 1969.

Menéndez Pidal, Ramón. *La Chanson de Roland y el neotradicionalismo: Orígenes de la épica románica.* Madrid, 1959. Rev. by the author with René Louis and trans. by Irénée-Marcel Cluzel as *La Chanson de Roland et la tradition épique des Francs* (Paris, 1960).

Mergell, Bodo. "Nibelungenlied und höfischer Roman." *Euphorion,* 45 (1950), 305-36. Rpt. in Rupp, pp. 3-39.

Meves, Uwe. "Bischof Wolfger von Passau, *sîn schrîber, meister Kuonrât* und die Nibelungenüberlieferung." In the "Hohenemser Studien," pp. 246-63 [72-89].

Mowatt, D. G. "Studies Towards an Interpretation of the 'Nibelungenlied.'" *GLL,* 14 (1961), 257-70. Trans. as "Zur Interpretation des Nibelungenlieds" in Rupp, pp. 179-200.

Müller, Jan-Dirk. "Sivrit: *künec—man—eigenholt.* Zur sozialen Problematik des Nibelungenliedes." *ABäG,* 7 (1974), 85-124.

Nagel, Bert. "Zur Interpretation und Wertung des Nibelungenliedes." *Neue Heidelberger Jahrbücher* (1954), pp. 1-89. Rev. and rpt. as "Widersprüche im Nibelungenlied" in Rupp, pp. 367-431.

———. *Das Nibelungenlied: Stoff—Form—Ethos.* Frankfurt am Main, 1965.

———. "Noch einmal Nibelungenlied." In *Studien zur deutschen Literatur des Mittelalters,* ed. Rudolf Schützeichel with Ulrich Fellmann, pp. 264-318. Bonn, 1979. [This volume is sometimes referred to as *Festgabe für Gerhart Lohse* but is so identified only in an editor's note on p. 773.] Rpt. in his *Kleine Schriften zur deutschen Literatur,* Göppinger Arbeiten zur Germanistik, 310 (Göppingen, 1981), pp. 129-96.

Neumann, Friedrich. *Das Nibelungenlied in seiner Zeit.* Göttingen, 1967.

———. "Schichten der Ethik im Nibelungenliede." In *Festschrift Eugen Mogk zum 70. Geburtstag, 19. Juli 1924,* pp.119-45. Halle, 1924. Rpt. in his *Das Nibelungenlied in seiner Zeit,* pp. 9-34.

Panzer, Friedrich. *Das Nibelungenlied: Entstehung und Gestalt.* Stuttgart, 1955.

———. *Studien zum Nibelungenliede.* Frankfurt am Main, 1945. Paul the Deacon. *Historia Langobardorum.* Ed. L. Bethmann and G. Waitz. MGH: *Scriptores rerum Langobardicarum et Italicarum saec. VI-IX.* Hannover, 1878.

Sacker, Hugh. "On Irony and Symbolism in the Nibelungenlied: Two Preliminary Notes." *GLL,* 14 (1961), 271-81. Trans. as "Über Ironie und Symbolismus im Nibelungenlied: Zwei vorläufige Studien" in Rupp, pp. 201-17.

Schröder, Walter Johannes. "Das Nibelungenlied: Versuch einer Deutung." *BGDSL* (Halle), 76 (1954-55), 56-143. Rpt. in his *rede und meine: Aufsätze und Vorträge zur deutschen Literatur des Mittelalters* (Cologne, 1978), pp. 58-145.

Schröder, Werner. "Die Tragödie Kriemhilts im Nibelungenlied." *ZDA,* 90 (1960-61), 41-80 and 123-60. Rpt. in his *Nibelungenlied-Studien,* pp. 48-156.

See, Klaus von. "Der Germane als Barbar." *JIG,* 13 (1981), 42-72.

———. "Was ist Heldendichtung?" In *Europäische Heldendichtung,* ed. Klaus von See, pp. 1-38. Wege der Forschung, 500. Darmstadt, 1978. Rpt. in his *Edda, Saga, Skaldendichtung,* pp. 154-93.

Sperberg-McQueen, Christopher Michael. "An Analysis of Recent Work on *Nibelungenlied* Poetics." Diss. Stanford, 1985.

Stein, Peter K. "Orendel 1512: Probleme und Möglichkeiten der Anwendung der *theory of oral-formulaic poetry* bei der literaturhistorischen Interpretation eines mittelhochdeutschen Textes." In the "Hohenemser Studien," pp. 322-37 [148-63].

Szövérffy, Josef. "Das Nibelungenlied: Strukturelle Beobachtungen und Zeitgeschichte." *WW,* 15 (1965), 233-38. Rpt. in Rupp, pp. 322-32.

Tonnelat, Ernest. *La Chanson des Nibelungen: Etude sur la composition et la formation du poème épique.* Publications de la Faculté des Lettres de l'Université de Strasbourg, 30. Paris, 1926.

Urbanek, Ferdinand. *Kaiser, Grafen und Mäzene im König Rother.* Philologische Studien und Quellen, 71. Berlin, 1976.

Voorwinden, Norbert. "Nibelungenklage und Nibelungenlied." In the "Hohenemser Studien," pp. 276-87 [102-13].

Wachinger, Burghart. "Die 'Klage' und das Nibelungenlied." In the "Hohenemser Studien," pp. 264-75 [90-101].

———. *Studien zum Nibelungenlied: Vorausdeutungen, Aufbau, Motivierung.* Tübingen, 1960.

Wapnewski, Peter. "Rüdigers Schild: Zur 37. Aventiure des 'Nibelungenliedes.'" *Euphorion,* 54 (1960), 380-410. Rpt. in Rupp, pp. 134-78.

Weber, Gottfried, with Werner Hoffmann. *Das Nibelungenlied: Problem und Idee.* Stuttgart, 1963.

Wisniewski, Roswitha. "Das Versagen des Königs: Zur Interpretation des Nibelungenliedes." In *Festschrift für Ingeborg Schröbler zum 65. Geburtstag,* ed. Dietrich

Schmidtke and Helga Schüppert [= *BGDSL,* 95, (1973)], pp. 170-86. Tübingen, 1973.

Wolf, Alois. "Die Verschriftlichung der Nibelungensage und die französisch-deutschen Literaturbeziehungen im Mittelalter." In the "Hohenemser Studien," pp. 227-45 [53-71].

Joyce Tally Lionarons (essay date 1998)

SOURCE: "The Otherworld and Its Inhabitants in the *Nibelungenlied*" in *A Companion to the "Nibelungenlied",* edited by Winder McConnell, Camden House, 1998, pp. 153-71.

[*In the following essay, Lionarons explores the relationship between mythical characters and humans in the* Nibelungenlied.]

Every reader of the *Nibelungenlied* soon recognizes that there are at least two different worlds, and perhaps two different times, coexisting within the poem. The first is the "real," historically conceived society of Worms and Xanten: this is a chivalric, courtly world in which normal human beings—albeit sometimes kings and princesses—are born, live, marry, compete for influence and political power, and finally die. The second may be termed the "Otherworld."[1] Not all its inhabitants are human, and those who are seem preternaturally strong, with knowledge and power far surpassing the denizens of the "real" world. The non-human inhabitants of the Otherworld come straight from myth and *Märchen:* there are giants and dwarfs, dangerous dragons, and beautiful elf-like women inhabiting rivers and springs. The Otherworld is a place of essences, in which appearance and reality, intrinsic worth and external status coincide; it has neither politics nor political intrigue, but a hero, if he is both strong and lucky enough to prevail over his adversaries, may win treasures there: gold, land, a specially wrought sword or a magical talisman. And yet the Otherworld is not simply a place for fairytales: its depiction in the poem repeatedly sounds a somber and somewhat disturbing note in suggestions that the Otherworld may in fact be a manifestation of the Underworld, the land of the dead.

Precisely how to characterize the relationship between the two worlds has caused some critical dispute. Many scholars see the dividing line as one of ethos: a "heroic" or "mythic" world is contrasted to the everyday historical world. Walter Johannes Schröder states the opposition clearly: "Dem mythisch-märchenhaften Norden steht der geschichtliche Süden gegenüber."[2] Some also emphasize a difference in time, finding the Otherworld to represent a more archaic age than that of its courtly counterpart. Jan de Vries argues that the Otherworld "seems to belong to the remotest past."[3] Still others see the difference as primarily psychological: Walter Falk, for example, draws a distinction between an external world of physical reality and "eine traumhafte, psychische Innenwelt,"[4] where all

the supernatural events of the poem occur. Despite their differences, however, most contemporary students of the *Nibelungenlied* would probably agree with Otfrid Ehrismann's assessment of the situation: "Die neue Welt ist politischer, und sie macht den alten Zauber symbolfähig."[5] This essay will examine the poem's "old magic" and its practitioners, both as they relate to the mythic and folkloric contexts from which they arise, and as they function, symbolically or otherwise, within the textual world(s) of the *Nibelungenlied* as a whole.

The primary point at which the Otherworld intersects with the historical world is in the character of Siegfried.[6] Siegfried belongs equally to both worlds, and in fact, he seems to have had two different upbringings, one in each. In Xanten, he is a courtly young prince ("eins edelen küneges kint," 20,1b), educated in the mannered and diplomatic customs of an idealized medieval German society.[7] He is not allowed to ride out alone, being always in the company of his tutors or other wise counselors who are conscious of protecting his honor (. . . 25,3). He is initiated into knighthood at a spectacularly lavish *Schwertleite,* at which he gives away land and cities to others but refuses the crown of the Netherlands for himself because his parents, Siegmund and Sieglind, are still alive (29-43). Yet as Hagen's description of Siegfried's youthful adventures in *Âventiure* 3 makes clear, at this point he has already undergone another sort of heroic initiation in the Otherworld. There Siegfried does ride out alone (. . . 88,1a) to find two princes, Schilbung and Nibelung, engaged in dividing their treasure (91). The princes offer him Nibelung's sword Balmung as a reward for his help (93), and although we are given no explicit account of what follows, it is clear that when Siegfried fails to divide the treasure to their satisfaction, a violent conflict erupts and the young hero must fight for his life against the princes, twelve giants, seven hundred warriors, and the dwarf Alberich (93-96). By the end Siegfried has won the land, the hoard, and Alberich's cloak (or literally "hood") of invisibility, the *tarnkappe* (97,3a). Moreover, in a seemingly unrelated incident, Siegfried kills a dragon ("einen lintrachen," 100,2a) and bathes in its blood, acquiring horn-hard skin and thus virtual invulnerability in battle. Later, Kriemhild reveals to Hagen that his invulnerability is not total: a leaf fell onto the hero's back, shielding one spot from the dragon's blood (902) and leaving him unprotected against anyone who knows the secret.

Both incidents have ample precedent in Germanic myth and legend, and it is important to examine their motifs individually. When Siegfried first finds the two princes, they have brought the treasure, called "Nibelung's hoard" ("Hort der Nibelunges," 89,1a) out from its resting place in a hollow mountain (. . . 89,2a). This would seem to indicate that the treasure once belonged to an earlier King Nibelung, most likely the father of Schilbung and Nibelung II, who has died and been buried with his treasure in a mountain cavern. "Hollow hills" of this kind have a long history in Germanic legend, where they are most often represented as habitations of the dead, either as burial mounds or as entrances to the underworld; thus, a hero's entry into such a hill or mound, or his winning of a hoard associated with a hollow hill, can be interpreted as a symbolic journey into the world of the dead. Ancient Scandinavian folk beliefs, for example, include the idea of "dying into the mountain" to be welcomed by one's departed friends and ancestors, and there are mountains in southern Sweden that were once believed to be the homes of the dead and therefore given the name *Valholl* (Valhalla), "hall of the slain."[8] Moreover, in *Njals saga,* after the Icelander Svan dies during a storm on a fishing expedition, it is reported that . . . ("some fishermen at Kaldbak thought they had seen Svan being warmly welcomed into the innermost depths of Kaldbakhorn Mountain").[9] Closer and perhaps more relevant to the specifically German context of the **Nibelungenlied** may be South and West Germanic stories of buried and entranced kings waiting inside mountain caverns for the day on which they will be called upon to save the world: both Friedrich Barbarossa and Charlemagne are reputed to be inside the Untersberg in Austria, while Friedrich II is in the Kyffhäuser in Germany, and King Arthur in Cadbury Hill in Somerset.[10]

Those beings who dwell inside actual burial mounds are neither so heroic nor so well-intentioned. In the Northern tradition such mounds can be inhabited by the corporeal ghosts of their buried occupants—called *draugar* in Old Norse—who at certain times, generally at midwinter, leave their barrows to ravage the countryside. Even mounds that appear outwardly peaceful can turn out quite otherwise, for some *draugar* remain quiescent as long as the gold and weapons they are buried with are untouched. Nevertheless, anyone entering a mound to steal its treasure will find the *draugr* more than able to fight viciously if disturbed. Stories of *draugr*-quellings are found throughout the Scandinavian saga tradition, with notable examples occurring in *Grettis saga,* and in the story of Þórstein Uxafótr in *Flateyjarbók* I.[11] Thus, while the *draugar* have no specific counterparts in the South Germanic tradition of the **Nibelungenlied,** they illustrate graphically the terror and danger a "hollow hill," filled with the treasure of a (possibly un)dead inhabitant, can possess.

Of course Germanic burial mounds can also be inhabited by dragons, whose nature it is to lie on piles of treasure left in the earth. The most famous mound-dwelling dragon is probably the one Beowulf fights, and there is an Old English gnomic verse which states that barrows full of gold are the proper places for dragons in general: . . . ("The dragon should be on the grave-mound, old and wise, proud of the treasure").[12] Sometimes a man or giant enters a barrow alive and transforms himself into a dragon to guard his gold, but even those dragons that do not inhabit grave mounds *per se* are almost always found dwelling in mountain caverns or on mountainous cliffs high above the sea.[13] Because a dragon is commonly regarded as the most formidable adversary a warrior can encounter, in general only the greatest heroes of Germanic legend become dragon slayers. The rewards are as great as the dangers: in addition to giving up its treasure, a dragon may disclose

secret or esoteric knowledge to a victorious hero, as Fáfnir does in the Eddic poem *Fáfnismál,* and wisdom, as well as the ability to understand the language of birds, can be gained by eating the dragon's heart. Finally, as has already been seen, the touch of a dragon's blood makes a person's skin turn hard as horn.[14]

It is also worth noting that although they are not often linked explicitly to the world of the dead, in both the Scandinavian and German traditions dwarfs are reputed to live under mountains or inside rocks, where they hoard the gold and silver they mine and use their extraordinary skill as smiths to make wonderful swords and other valuable, often magical items. Norse myth credits the dwarfs with making most of the marvelous possessions of the gods, including Odin's Gungni, Thor's hammer Mjollnir, and Freyr's marvelous ship Skíðblaðnir, which is said to be large enough for all the gods to sail in, but can be folded up like a piece of paper and carried in a pocket. However, the specific nature and provenance of the dwarfs is uncertain. In *Gylfaginning,* Snorri Sturluson describes the . . . ("dark elves") as if they were dwarfs, hinting that the two may be related; he says that (like dwarfs) the dark elves live . . . ("down in the earth").[15] In fact, many dwarf-names—such as "Alberich," which translates as "elven-power"—incorporate a form of the word "elf" . . . as one of their components. Snorri gives his characterization of the dwarfs a more ominous note when he asserts in the same work that they . . . ("quickened in the soil and down in the earth like maggots in flesh")[16]—a simile that is literalized when Snorri goes on to say in the next sentence that in reality the dwarfs actually *were* maggots in the flesh of the giant Ymir, from whose body the world was made. They were transformed into dwarfs when the gods gave them human shape and reason, but because of their origin they still prefer to live . . . ("in the earth and in rocks"). Of particular interest is the fact that Snorri names some dwarfs as having come from a grave mound in Joruvellir,[17] a detail that links them with other mound-dwellers and by implication once again with the realm of the dead.[18] It is sometimes assumed that because the dwarfs were created from rocks, they can be turned into rocks again: in the Eddic poem *Alvíssmál,* the purportedly "all-wise" dwarf Alvíss turns into stone when he is tricked by Þórr into remaining outside when the sun rises.

Most German sources agree, however, that if one is clever enough to capture a dwarf by lying in wait outside his cavern, the dwarf will bargain for his release by promising his captor items from his own treasure or even the treasure of another. An example occurs in the twelfth-century *Ruotlieb,* in which the hero surprises a dwarf and thus manages to seize him unawares: the dwarf negotiates for his freedom by promising to reveal the whereabouts of a vast treasure. Like the Nibelung hoard with its two princes, this treasure is guarded by two kings, Immunch and Hartunch, who must be fought before the hoard is won. The episode is plainly an analogue of the hoard-winning scene in the **Nibelungenlied,** and although the two poets were most likely simply working from the same tradition in different centuries, it is tempting to speculate that *Ruotlieb* could be a source of the later poem.[19]

The final Otherworld beings associated with Siegfried's youthful adventures are the giants. As noted above, one Old Norse creation myth describes the earth as having been made from the body of a giant, Ymir, and giants generally play a more important role throughout Norse mythology than do dwarfs or dragons. In the medieval German tradition, however, giants have diminished in both prominence and intelligence. They are considered to be at once dangerous and stupid, not to be matched in size and strength by most men, but relatively easy to outsmart.[20] Certainly neither the giants guarding the Nibelung hoard in the **Nibelungenlied** (Âventiure 3), nor the giant Siegfried fights in *Âvetiure* 8, are a match in intellect or strength for the hero.

It is a hero's job, of course, to acquire a treasure by overcoming its supernatural guardian—whether *draugr* or dwarf, giant or dragon—through cunning and martial prowess. The defeat of the monstrous hoard-guardian traditionally represents an almost ritualized initiation into a new stage in the hero's life, symbolized by his appropriation of the treasure and often of an instrument of power, such as a sword or magical talisman, as well. This kind of fictional initiation sequence can be profitably compared to real-life initiation rituals, such as those studied by anthropologist Arnold van Gennep, who states that although the details may vary according to the society, a typical initiation ritual comprises three distinct parts: (1) temporary expulsion from ordinary society into a so-called "liminal" or "threshold" state, where (2) the initiand undergoes certain prescribed tests to prove his or her worthiness in order to (3) re-enter the social world at a new, higher level of societal and ontological existence.[21] The tests may include a confrontation with a monstrous adversary like a dragon, and often the initiand is forced to undergo a mock death and symbolic rebirth as a sign that the initiation, in Mircea Eliade's words, "is equivalent to a basic change in existential condition."[22] Obviously Siegfried's solitary visit to a liminal place outside of the world and society of Xanten, his victory over the dragon, his acquisition of sword, *tarnkappe*, and hoard from the denizens of a "hollow hill" that is also a grave mound, and finally his successful return to Xanten, provide a good example of the initiation process transformed into heroic narrative. Siegfried's youthful adventures in the Otherworld may thus be seen as a rite of passage, corresponding in narrative function to his *Schwertleite* in the historical world, but altering his ontological condition in a deeper and more decisive fashion than his knighting, which is a promotion in social status alone, could do. Siegfried's experiences serve to set him apart from those characters in the **Nibelungenlied** who have been initiated into knight-hood in the courtly world alone, without having undergone the tests of worthiness an Otherworld initiation entails, and whose merits may therefore be only skin-deep. The contrast between the rites of passage in the two worlds provides a clear rationale for Siegfried's superiority over the Burgundians, a superiority

symbolized by his possession of the sword Balmung, the treasure, and the *tarnkappe.* Hagen's report of Siegfried's adventurous past should therefore not be dismissed as mere fairy-tale ornamentation or the slightly embarrassing traces of an outmoded tradition in an otherwise historical and political epic; the hero's Otherworld initiation is clearly more potent and more significant than any *Schwertleite,* no matter how lavish, and its effects carry over into the courtly world with disastrous results.

The substantive acquisitions that provide evidence for Siegfried's Otherworld initiation—the sword, the *tarnkappe,* the hoard, and the services of the dwarf Alberich as vassal and hoard-guardian—repay closer examination. The idea of a hero's having a special and sometimes magical sword is close to universal in heroic literature, not only in the Germanic tradition but throughout the corpus of Indo-European myth and legend: notable analogues to Balmung include Beowulf's sword Nægling in the Old English poem, þiðrekr's sword Nagelring and Viðga's sword Mímung in the early Norwegian *þiðreks saga af Bern,* and Sigurd's sword Gram in *Volsunga saga.* The *tarnkappe* is less common and therefore more interesting. It appears in connection with dwarfs and dwarf-treasures frequently in the German poetic tradition: an example occurs in the thirteenth-century *Laurin und der kleine Rosengarten,* in which the eponymous hero is a dwarf-king who wears a *tarnkappe* (along with armor dipped in dragon's blood and a magic belt) to fight off intruders into his realm, in this case Dietrich von Bern and his companion Witege.[23] Moreover, certain strophes from the seventh *Âventiure* of the **Nibelungenlied,** normally considered to be later interpolations and thus omitted in modern editions of the poem, state:

> von wilden getwergen   hân ich gehœret sagen,
> einz, heizet tarnkappen,   von wunderliche art:
> swerz hât an sîme lîbe,   der sol vil gar wol sîn bewart.
> Vor slegen unt vor stichen;   in müge ouch niemen sehens
>
> wenn er sî dar inne.   beide hœren unde spehen
> mag er nâch sînem willen,   daz in doch niemen siht;
> er sî ouch vrre sterker,   als uns diu âventiure . . .[24]

One North Germanic counterpart to the *tarnkappe* would seem to be the . . . ("concealing helmets") mentioned in a number of Old Norse sagas.[25] These "helms" are not associated with dwarfs, and sometimes not even with actual helmets, for by the time the sagas were written down in the twelfth and thirteenth centuries, the term . . . was apparently used for any magical means of producing invisibility. At one time, however, the word must have denoted some sort of hat or helmet that was used, like its German counterpart the *tarnkappe,* to make its wearer disappear.[26] A second, more specific analogue to Siegfried's *tarnkappe* in the **Nibelungenlied** is the . . . ("helm of terror")[27] which Sigurd wins by killing the dragon Fˊfnir in the Old Norse versions of the Siegfried story. Judging from the name alone, this is an actual helmet used to terrify the opponents of its wearer. The precise nature of the power of the *œgishjálmr,* however, remains a matter of conjecture, since although Siegfried does not hesitate to wear the *tarnkappe* in his adventures, Sigurd is never explicitly reported to use the *œgishjálmr* at all.

Nor does either hero make use of the hoard in any significant way. Siegfried, of course, officially gives it to Kriemhild as her *Morgengabe* (1116), but the treasure apparently remains untouched in its hollow mountain in Nibelungenland until Kriemhild is coerced by Hagen into bringing it to Worms. It is at this point in the narrative, as the hoard is about to make its final passage from the Otherworld into the historical world, that its contents are described for the first time: the hoard of the Nibelungs is made up entirely of gemstones and gold, and is so large that twelve fully loaded wagons have to make three trips a day for four days in order to remove it from the mountain (1122). More astounding than the hoard's size is its ostensible inexhaustibility, for we are told that "unt ob man al die werlde het dâ von versolt, / sîn newære niht minner einer marke wert" (1123,2-3). This quality may provide the reason why Schilbung and Nibelung, even with Siegfried's help, are unable to divide the hoard satisfactorily, for a hoard that cannot be diminished in value most likely cannot be divided either. The idea of the hoard's indivisible nature is further strengthened by the poet's final revelation concerning the treasure's contents: unnoticed by any of the characters in the poem, the hoard contains a tiny golden rod ("ein rüetelîn," 1124,1b) that, were it to be found and recognized, would give its owner power over the entire world (1124,2-3). The "rüetelîn" is doubtless the Otherworldly embodiment of the political power that possession of the hoard bestows on its owner in the historical world, and such absolute power can be wielded by only one person at a time. If Siegfried is aware of the "rüetelîn," however, he is entirely uninterested in its use, for his political aspirations throughout the poem are focused solely on gaining the love of Kriemhild, not on power for its own sake. Kriemhild's interest in the hoard is as a reminder of Siegfried, not as a means to gain absolute power, and its loss simply provides an additional reason for revenge against her brothers. Hagen and Gunther are another matter, for they are indeed interested in political power *qua* power— that is why they believe they must steal the hoard from Kriemhild, to prevent her from using it to gain a political power base in Worms. Nevertheless, without the "rüetelîn" the Burgundians are as incapable of utilizing the power of the hoard as Schilbung and Nibelung, and they are finally reduced to sinking it in the Rhine to avoid trouble. Still, Hagen plans to return alone and make use of the hoard— and its power—if he can (1137).

If anyone in the poem is both cognizant of the hoard's attributes and able to use them, it is most likely the dwarf Alberich, but like Siegfried, Alberich seems to have no interest in ruling the world. His function is to guard the treasure in the Otherworld for its rightful owner, whoever that owner might be. He makes the transition from serving Ni-

belung and Schilbung to serving Siegfried fairly easily, convinced that the hero's superior strength entitles him to appropriate the treasure. After Siegfried's murder, he serves Kriemhild as he had her husband. When she orders the hoard removed to Burgundy, Alberich obeys her wishes, remarking that he "dare not" . . . 1118,3) withhold the treasure from Kriemhild since as Siegfried's gift it is legitimately hers. Nonetheless, the dwarf hints that he might not have been so acquiescent about moving the hoard to Worms if he had not lost the *tarnkappe,,* his "guoten tarnhût," to Siegfried and could still take advantage of both invisibility and supernatural strength (1119).[28] Certainly he makes no effort to accompany the hoard and its owner to the historical world; Alberich's place is in the Otherworld, and once the hoard has been removed he disappears from the poem.

Alberich reappears, however, in other works relevant to the *Nibelungenlied,* most often in connection with the Dietrich story.[29] As "Álfrekr" in *þiðreks saga af Bern* he is characterized as . . . ("a great thief and the most skillful of all the dwarves," ch. 16),[30] but surprisingly he has no connection either to Sigurd or to the Nibelung hoard in the saga, nor does he own a *tarnkappe* or enjoy extraordinary strength. Instead, in a scene analogous to both *Ruotlieb* and the hoard-winning episode in the *Nibelungenlied,* the dwarf is captured by Dietrich (i.e., þiðrekr) and Hildebrand; he promises them the sword Nagelring along with information about where they can find a treasure in return for his release. As might be expected, to win the treasure the heroes must fight its two guardians in yet another hollow hill, here called a . . . ("earthhouse"). The guardians are Grímr, a man with the strength of twelve, and his even stronger and more formidable troll-wife Hildr. It is a difficult contest; nevertheless, the two heroes eventually prevail, winning the hoard itself and a helm, called "Hildegrímr" after its ill-fated owners. This helm has no special powers like its counterparts the *œgishjálmr* and *tarnkappe,* but it is said to be a valuable treasure in itself, and Dietrich is reported to wear in it battle for a long time afterward.

Alberich plays a more extensive role in the thirteenth-century poem *Ortnit.*[31] Here he is a king of the dwarfs and clearly a more supernatural figure than in either the *Nibelungenlied* or *þiðreks saga af Bern.* He has no need of a *tarnkappe,* since he is invisible by nature and has strength far beyond his physical size; moreover, he is preternaturally wise and at times can predict the future. Only Ortnit, who is wearing a magical ring given to him by his mother, is able to see the dwarf-king. At their first meeting the two fight furiously but are later reconciled, as is also true with Siegfried and Alberich in the *Nibelungenlied.* In fact, it turns out that Alberich is Ortnit's father, and just as the dwarf and his *tarnkappe* help Siegfried during and after Gunther's wooing of Brünhild, Alberich here helps Ortnit in his own bridal-quest, in part by using his skill as a master smith to forge a marvelous sword and impregnable armor for his son.

The most curious element of Alberich's role in the *Nibelungenlied*, however, has no obvious parallels in the analogues to Alberich's story or in other versions of the Siegfried legend: in our poem the dwarf and the hero fight *twice*, once in Âventiure 3 when Siegfried first wins the hoard, and again in Âventiure 8 when Siegfried returns to Nibelungenland to fetch a thousand warriors for Gunther. In each episode Siegfried arrives on the scene in the guise of a stranger, literally so in Âventiure 3 and invisibly with a disguised voice in Âventiure 8; in each he fights both a giant or giants and Alberich—almost to the death—before obtaining a reconciliation and an acknowledgment that he is the dwarf's master and the owner of the hoard. While it has often been recognized that the events of Âventiure 8 are simply another version of Siegfried's experiences in Âventiure 3,[32] precisely why the poet would choose to double the episode in this way has puzzled many readers of the *Nibelungenlied*. Joachim Bumke suggests that the solution lies in the fact that the events of *þiðreks saga af Bern,* ch. 168, are more closely related to Siegfried's Otherworld journey in Âventiure 8 than his hoard-winning in Âventiure 3 seems to be.[33] In *þiðreks saga,* Sigurd arrives at Brünhild's door as a stranger and immediately fights with her door warden, literally breaking down the locked doors of her stronghold, before Brünhild, who apparently does know who he is, intervenes and invites him in. In context, this fight before Brünhild's gate seems just as gratuitous as Siegfried's fight with his own door-wardens. However, if the source of the *Nibelungenlied,* like *þiðreks saga af Bern,* included a truncated version of the traditional fight with a hoard-guardian within its narration of Siegfried's first visit to Brünhild, the *Nibelungenlied* poet may in turn have regarded such a battle as an integral part of the episode, and so have created Siegfried's battle with Alberich and the giant in Nibelungenland directly after his visit to Brünhild on that basis.[34] It may be useful, therefore, to discuss the events of Âventiure 8 in combination with Gunther's bridal-quest to win Brünhild.

Brünhild is the only character besides Siegfried to make a transition from the Otherworld to the historical world. Unfortunately, like Siegfried she finds that her Otherworldly characteristics spell disaster in her new environment. Like many inhabitants of the Otherworld, Brünhild is preternaturally strong, and she has therefore devised tests for her potential suitors based on physical strength rather than on the mannered and artificial rituals of *Minnedienst* currently in fashion in the courtly world at Worms. As long as she is secure in her position as queen of her Otherworld island, Brünhild cares little about the real-world social standing or political power of her suitors; even the vassalage deception becomes important only in the historical world of the Burgundians. In her world Brünhild simply demands a husband whose personal physical prowess can match her own . . . ("giant-strong")[35] abilities. Of course only Siegfried can hope to do so, and Brünhild is even stronger than he is: Siegfried barely overcomes her despite having the help of the *tarnkappe,* which adds the might of twelve men (. . . 337,3a) to his own already formidable strength. It would seem that in the symbolic realm of the Other-

world, personal strength is—or should be—an external manifestation of inner virtue: the man who is strong in the Otherworld will be superior in the historical world as well. The deceptive strategy employed by Siegfried to make Gunther *appear* strong despite his underlying weaknesses has no legitimate place in Brünhild's world; it is a practice imported from the historical world of half-truths and political intrigue.

Siegfried knows and understands the rules of Brünhild's realm, and he knows that Gunther has no chance of winning her on his own. Because of his "real-world" desire to obtain Kriemhild, however, Siegfried uses his knowledge against the queen. He advises Gunther to leave at home his warriors and courtly retainers, symbols of the king's purely political strength, for he knows that in Isenstein only personal strength will matter. Instead of trying to impress Brünhild with an army, therefore, Gunther sets out to sea in a small boat, accompanied only by Hagen, Dancwart, Siegfried (who alone knows the way to Brünhild's land), and twelve sets of magnificent clothing (341-344). Apparently, even though Brünhild's court exists in the Otherworld, it is still a court, and the courtly virtue of magnificence, unlike military might, retains its influence.[36]

Most modern readers of the poem are aware of the fact that in the Old Norse analogues, Siegfried and Brünhild have declared their love and vowed to marry each other before Siegfried's memory of her is destroyed by a magical potion and Brünhild is deceived into marrying Gunther. The fact that in the *Nibelungenlied* Brünhild recognizes Siegfried at first sight and greets him by name, plainly assuming that he is her suitor and with no knowledge of who the Burgundians are, would seem to indicate that the *Nibelungenlied* poet—and thus possibly his medieval audience as well—also knew of the love relationship in other versions of the tale and may even have been hinting at its existence here. The poet makes no explicit reference to a prior relationship between the two; there is simply another layer of irony added to the description of Gunther's bridal quest for anyone aware of the tradition. Less critical attention has been given to the fact that in the same analogues Brünhild is a valkyrie, and anyone aware of the prior love relationship would also be aware of this aspect of her character.[37] Once again Germanic tradition provides a tacit correlation between the Otherworld of the *Nibelungenlied* and the world of the dead, for the valkyries (literally "choosers of the slain") are servants of Odin, the Norse god of battle and death, and their function is first to decide which fighters will die in battle and then to escort the fallen warriors to the god's Otherworld paradise, Valhalla. The valkyries are said to choose only the best and strongest warriors for an afterlife in Valhalla, and the fact that Brünhild uses the same criteria in her choice of a suitor may indicate that the *Nibelungenlied* poet knew of the valkyrie tradition and modified it for his own, very different, uses.

The modification includes a drastic revision in tone, however, for Brünhild's contests with Gunther (and, unbeknownst to her, with Siegfried in the *tarnkappe*) play out as pure farce. The scene looks backward to Siegfried's own earlier tests of worthiness in the Otherworld, which certainly gain in stature by the comparison, as well as forward to his second use of the *tarnkappe* in his almost equally farcical battle with the giant and Alberich in the next *âventiure*. Nonetheless, there is a bitter edge to the comedy, and it lies in the unfeeling attitude which the other characters, and most likely the poet himself, have towards Brünhild. All are clearly unsettled by her prodigious strength; the poet's decision to make the bridal tests comedic reflects his unease. The male characters express their dismay openly: upon seeing Brünhild's initial prowess in the tests, Hagen exclaims, "waz hât der künic ze trût! / jâ sol si in der helle sîn des übeln tiuvels brût" (450,3b-4). Siegfried is simply rude when he tells her at the end of the contests, "Sô wol mich dirre mære . . . daz iuwer hôhverte ist alsô hie gelegen, / daz iemen lebet, der iuwer meister müge sîn" (474,1-3). Even Gunther will declare that Brünhild is an "übeln tiuvel" when, alone with his bride on his wedding night, he is confronted by her Otherworldly strength (649,2a).

In the events following the wedding night, the insensitivity on the part of both poet and characters turns vicious. The poet amplifies the farcical tone of the bedroom scenes in his depiction of the hapless Gunther hanging from a nail on the wall, but he describes, and with evident satisfaction (cp. 675-76), what is in fact a violent marital rape. McConnell has suggested that Siegfried's attitude toward Brünhild is based in the hero's stated belief in male dominance, pointing out that as he wrestles furiously with Brünhild in Gunther's bed, Siegfried is explicitly said to think that by forcing her to submit he is somehow preventing other women from following the queen's example and therefore advancing the cause of men in general (673). McConnell adds that "it is quite possible that Siegfried considers Brünhild to be a threat to society in her 'Amazon-like' state."[38] But a belief in male dominance is not simply part of Siegfried's characterization; the poet clearly shares the hero's views, and we may assume that at least half of his audience did as well.

Brünhild's Otherworldly strength disappears with her loss of virginity in yet another folktale motif that acquires symbolic importance in the **Nibelungenlied**. Not only must the former queen of an Otherworld realm accommodate her behavior to the rules of a male-dominated, courtly society, but she discovers in addition that if she is to have any influence—or pose any threats—within that society she must learn to play the games of duplicity and political machination that prevail in the historical world. She therefore competes for precedence with her rival Kriemhild, conceals her motives for persuading Gunther to invite Siegfried and Kriemhild back to Worms, and possibly even conspires with Hagen in Siegfried's murder. Kriemhild at any rate assumes collusion between the two when she hears of Siegfried's death and cries out, "ez hât gerâten Prünhilt, daz ez hât Hagene getân" (1010,4). Once she is forced by her loss of virginity to become an active partici-

pant in Burgundian power politics, Brünhild's outward appearance no longer matches her inner reality, and it is this more than anything else that is symbolized by her forfeiture of her Otherworldly strength.

It is therefore fitting that Brünhild's initial defeat in Isenstein is followed in the next *âventiure* by a display of Siegfried's strength in the Otherworld in a graphic demonstration of what Gunther never had and what the queen will lose by her marriage. Parallels to the earlier episode include the fact that in each *âventiure* Siegfried acts while invisible in the *tarnkappe,* and in each he defeats an opponent whose strength is equivalent to (or even greater than) his own. The element of farce continues into *Âventiure* 8 as well, since Siegfried's disguise in Nibelungenland seems prompted by high spirits rather than a serious attempt at deception, and the image of Alberich having his beard tugged by an invisible opponent (497) parallels that of Brünhild's defeat: it is simultaneously comic and humiliating. But although Bumke is no doubt correct in suggesting that the scene seems to have been modeled on an analogue to Siegfried's first visit to Brünhild and is best considered as part of the bridal quest, its full function is more complicated. In addition to incorporating parallels with the earlier *âventiure,* the **Nibelungenlied** poet structures *Âventiure* 8 as the counterpart of a later scene as well, namely, Hagen's fight with the ferryman before crossing the Danube into Etzel's land in *Âventiure* 25.

Like Siegfried and Brünhild, Hagen, too, has ties to the Otherworld. Those ties are implied in the **Nibelungenlied** by the fact that Hagen not only knows who Siegfried is at first sight (86), but also knows enough about him to tell the Burgundians the story of his youthful adventures in the Otherworld (87-100). By way of contrast, in *þiðreks saga af Bern* Hagen's relationship to the Otherworld is made explicit: there he is the son of an elf who found the Burgundian queen asleep in her garden and fathered a child on her, thus making Hagen half-brother to the Burgundian princes. Still, in both the saga and the poem, Hagen's most significant encounter with the forces of the Otherworld takes place as he is leading the Burgundian forces into Etzel's Hungary, and it is in this episode that the parallels to *Âventiure* 8 are to be found.

In *Âventiure* 8, Siegfried travels alone to Nibelungenland in a small boat to retrieve a thousand of his Nibelung warriors; to do so, he must cross a boundary or "threshold" separating the historical world from the Otherworld. As we have seen, the literal threshold of Siegfried's stronghold in that world is guarded by a giant doorkeeper and the dwarf Alberich. Both are Siegfried's servants and would be expected to recognize him, so Siegfried disguises himself as a stranger in order to indulge in a playful, but still quite dangerous and apparently unnecessary battle with them. He then ferries the thousand warriors back to Isenstein to accompany Gunther and Brünhild to Worms. In *Âventiure* 25 Hagen is similarly trying to take a thousand "Nibelung" warriors (as the Burgundians are now called) to Etzel's land, but he finds himself faced with the physical boundary of the Danube, which functions here as a symbolic threshold between the familiar world of Worms and the more remote and exotic world of Etzel's realm. Like Siegfried, Hagen battles a recalcitrant and violent threshold guardian in the person of the ferryman, and he also resorts to a disguise, albeit in precisely the opposite manner in which it is used by Siegfried: rather than impersonating a stranger in order to avoid recognition as a returning friend, Hagen impersonates a returning friend in order to avoid recognition as a stranger. The resulting violence is serious rather than slapstick, and the scene ends in Hagen's murder of the ferryman, which forces him to ferry all one thousand warriors across the river himself in an astounding display of almost Otherworldly strength. It is worth pointing out that in describing the folktale qualities of Âventiure 8, Bumke asks wryly if we are really to believe the preposterous idea that all one thousand Nibelung warriors made the trip back to Isenstein in the same boat that Siegfried had arrived in.[39] When Siegfried's actions are compared to Hagen's behavior in Âventiure 25, however, the absurdity of the idea is lessened by the force of the parallel.

It is in Âventiure 25 as well that Hagen encounters the last inhabitants of the Otherworld to appear in the poem, in the form of two beautiful women, the "merwîp," whom he discovers bathing in a clear spring. These figures do not arise from a clearly discernible or widespread tradition in Germanic legend, and scholars are often uncertain of precisely how to translate the word "merwîp" into English: a quick survey reveals "water sprites," "water-fairies," "nixies," and "mermaids."[40] Their counterparts in piðreks saga af Bern are designated by the simple Old Norse equivalent to the Middle High German word, . . . ("sea-women"). Nonetheless, the function of the merwîp in the poem—to prophesy the outcome of the Burgundian expedition— is one that is widely attributed to female figures in general within the Germanic tradition, from Tacitus through the Middle Ages.[41] The prophetic knowledge of the two merwîp is both surprising and specific: they know Hagen by name and ancestry, calling him Aldrian's son (. . . 1539,2b), they give him specific directions as to how to find and handle the ferryman (which Hagen only partly follows), and most importantly, they tell him that none of the Burgundians will return from their journey alive, excepting only the chaplain. Hagen immediately tests the prophecy as best he can by attempting to drown the priest. When he nevertheless survives and swims safely back to the Burgundian side of the river, Hagen becomes certain that the merwîp are telling the truth, and in a final grand gesture he sinks the ferryboat, thereby destroying the possibility of anyone else turning back to Worms.

Clearly the two episodes are meant in part to provide a comparison of Siegfried's and Hagen's dealings with the Otherworld and its inhabitants; such a comparison serves to emphasize the distinction between what Edward R. Haymes has called the "bright" hero Siegfried and the "dark" hero Hagen in both character and behavior.[42] As a "bright" hero, Siegfried typifies the traditional Indo-European conception of heroism: he slays the evil dragon, wins the beautiful princess, lives his life in accordance with societal standards, and dies nobly but tragically at a young age; he can be identified not only with Sigurd and Beowulf, but also with the god Baldr. By way of contrast, "dark" heroes like Hagen work evil as easily as good; Haymes remarks that although the hero's "participation in the dark side of life makes him a questionable model for behavior . . . it does not disqualify him from being both the structural hero of a narrative and an object of awe and admiration."[43] Thus Hagen, like Siegfried, participates in the archetypal "monomyth" of the hero, first articulated by Joseph Campbell and most often used to interpret stories of "bright" rather than "dark" heroes. McConnell likewise sees Hagen as a heroic counterpart to Siegfried, asserting that in his encounter with the Otherworldly figures of the merwîp and the events that follow, Hagen has "undergone a kind of initiation" that may be compared to Siegfried's earlier experiences in the Otherworld and that serves to designate Hagen as the true hero of the rest of the poem.[44]

In fact, Hagen's experiences with the merwîp and the ferryman as threshold guardians, his crossing of the Danube with all his companions, and his final sinking of the boat behind them, would seem to symbolize the Nibelung warriors' passage into the Otherworld as surely as do the trip to Isenstein or Siegfried's voyage to Nibelungenland. The difference, and it may not be as great a difference as it initially appears, is that the earlier crossings are seemingly into a daylight world of magic and marvels, while the passage over the Danube leads only to darkness and death.

It is easy to see Âventiure 25 as representing, if not a literal journey into the Otherworld, at least an incursion of Otherworldly motifs into the historical world. Gottfried Weber has described the episode as "von der Dunkelheit und Wildheit übernatürlicher Kräfte durchzogen,"[45] and it is in fact the last truly supernatural episode of the poem. It is less easy to see the events which follow in Etzelnburg as transpiring in a world significantly different from that of Worms or Xanten. Perhaps the poem's original audience found the differences easier to perceive: Hatto points out that while much of the geography of the Burgundians' journey would have been "intimately known" to a contemporary audience, as they approach Etzel's Hungary the Burgundians would have seemed to "draw away into a distant past . . . in a place grown shadowy and remote."[46] The major transition, however, and one discernible by medieval and modern audiences alike, is in atmosphere. Once both Hagen and the audience realize fully that the annihilation will be absolute, that *no one* will survive the journey, nothing looks the same. Any vestige of ordinary life in the historical world—such as the marriage of Rüdiger's daughter to Giselher in Âventiure 27—becomes acutely ironic, while the progress of events leading to the final destruction takes on an almost mythic air of inevitability. The Burgundians have here entered an Otherworld in which they are not dead, yet are no longer alive in any meaningful way.

Some of this has been suggested before, most notably by Stephen L. Wailes, who states baldly that "in the fall of the Burgundians we are dealing with the Journey to the Other World," and then proceeds to formulate a mythological allegory equating Etzel to "the giant, ogre, or fiend who rules that world" and the Burgundians to "the god who makes the journey."[47] But although the *Nibelungenlied* poet certainly draws on myth in both his plot and his descriptions of the Otherworld, there is no consistent mythological allegory in the poem. Rather, the mythic elements serve to intensify the darkly sinister atmosphere which infuses the last few *âventiuren*, and to underscore the idea that the events that transpire there take place in a symbolic "realm of death"[48] that will become literal by the final strophes.

Thus, although at first glance Etzel's Hungary may seem to have more in common with the historical world of Burgundy and Xanten than with the Otherworld of Isenstein or Nibelungenland, its poetic representation as a literal kingdom of the dead places it firmly in the realm of the Otherworldly. As has been seen, both Nibelungenland and Isenstein have their own connections to the world of the dead in the motif of the hollow hill and in Brünhild's status as a valkyrie, and certainly the *merwîp* on the borders of Etzel's land would not be out of place in either location. Perhaps the relationship between the "bright" Otherworld of Nibelungenland and Isenstein and the "dark" Otherworld of Etzelnburg is best seen as analogous to the relationship between the poem's "bright" and "dark" heroes: each is the equivalent and yet mirror image of the other. Each version of the Otherworld provides a symbolic embodiment of the essence of one character's disposition and experiences, and they are thus structurally equivalent despite differences in specific characteristics. Finally, to paraphrase Ehrismann's comment once again, the poem's representations of the Otherworld also serve to provide the *Nibelungenlied* with enough of the "alten Zauber" of myth and *Märchen* to create a symbolic structure on which the poet's courtly epic, traditionally based yet newly conceived, can be built.

Notes

1. Although the term "Otherworld" is a general one, in this context I am borrowing it from Winder McConnell, *The Nibelungenlied,* Twayne's World Authors Series 712 (Boston: Twayne, 1984) 28ff.

2. Walter Johannes Schröder, *Das Nibelungenlied: Versuch einer Deutung* (Halle: Niemeyer, 1954) 22. See also McConnell 28-45, and Edward R. Haymes's essay in this volume.

3. Jan de Vries, *Heroic Song and Heroic Legend,* trans. B. J. Timmer (London: Oxford University Press, 1963) 64.

4. Walter Falk, *Das Nibelungenlied in seiner Epoche: Revision eines romantischen Mythos.* (Heidelberg: Winter, 1974) 120.

5. Otfrid Ehrismann, *Nibelungenlied. Epoche—Werk—Wirkung* (Munich: Beck, 1987) 126.

6. In Ehrismann's view, Siegfried is "der personifizierte Schwebezustand zwischen Gegenwart und Vorziet" (113).

7. Quotations from *Das Nibelungenlied* are from the Karl Bartsch/Helmut de Boor edition, 21st edition by Roswitha Wisniewski, Deutsche Klassiker des Mittelalters (Wiesbaden: Brockhaus, 1979) and are identified within the text by strophe and verse number.

8. Rudolf Simek, ed., *Dictionary of Northern Mythology,* trans. Angela Hall (Cambridge: Brewer, 1993) 347.

9. Magnus Magnusson and Hermann Pálsson, eds. and trans., *Njal's Saga* (Harmondsworth: Penguin, 1960) ch. 14. Other notable examples occur in *Gisla saga, Eyrbyggja saga,* and *Landnamabók.*

10. Simek 50.

11. The best study of the *draugar* remains Nora K. Chadwick, "Norse Ghosts: A Study in the *Draugar* and the *Haugbúi,*" *Folk-Lore* 57 (1948): 50-65, 106-127. Other sagas featuring troublesome *draugar* include *Eyrbyggja saga, Flóamanna saga, Hávarðar saga Ísfirðings, Laxdola saga,* and *Svarfdola saga.*

12. "Maxims II," in Elliott Van Kirk Dobbie, ed., *The Anglo-Saxon Minor Poems* (New York: Columbia University Press, 1942) 26a-27b.

13. For two examples of Norse grave mound battles that feature dragons rather than *draugar,* see *Játmundar saga ljúfa* and *Gull-Póris saga.*

14. For a more extensive account of the *Nibelungenlied* dragon and its analogues, see John L. Flood's essay in this volume, as well as Joyce Tally Lionarons, *The Medieval Dragon: The Nature of the Beast in Germanic Tradition* (Enfield Lock, Middlesex: Hisarlik, 1997).

15. Anthony Faulkes, ed., *Edda: Prologue and Gylfaginning* (Oxford: Clarendon, 1982) 19.

16. Faulkes 15.

17. Faulkes 15-16.

18. Simek (68) says that the concept "dwarf" may have arisen either from the idea of nature spirits or that of "demons of death."

19. For this suggestion as well as for information on *Ruotlieb* as an analogue, I am indebted to an unpublished paper presented by Paul Battles at the 32nd International Congress on Medieval Studies, held in May, 1997 at Kalamazoo, Michigan.

20. Simek 107.

21. Arnold van Gennep, *The Rites of Passage,* trans. Monika B. Vizedom & Gabrielle L. Caffee (London: Routledge & Kegan Paul, 1909); see also Victor Turner, *The Ritual Process: Structure and Anti-Structure* (Ithaca: Cornell University Press, 1969).

22. Mircea Eliade, *Rites and Symbols of Initiation: The Mysteries of Birth and Rebirth,* trans. Willard R. Trask (New York: Harper, 1958) x.

23. Karl Müllenhoff, ed., *Laurin und Walberan, Deutsches Heldenbuch,* 5 vols. (1866; rpt. Berlin: Weidmann, 1963) 1: 201-257.

24. Karl Bartsch, ed., *Das Nibelunge Nôt* (Leipzig: Brockhaus, 1870) 53n.

25. Hilda Ellis Davidson, "The Hoard of the Nibelungs," *Modern Language Review* 37 (1942): 477. Davidson cites examples of *hulipshálmir* occurring in *Ólafs saga Tryggvasonar, Fóstbrœðra saga, Þorskfirðinga saga,* and *Bósa saga.*

26. Jacqueline Simpson, "Olaf Tryggvason versus the Powers of Darkness," in Venetia Newell, ed., *The Witch Figure* (London and Boston: Routledge and Kegan Paul, 1973) 169.

27. Interestingly enough, the *œgishjálmr* may ultimately have classical roots: Simek points out that the function of the Greek *aigis,* like the *œgishjálmr,* is to terrify, and Greek *aigis* might easily have become attached to Fáfnir's "helm of terror" by a phonetic conflation with Old Norse *œgr,* "terrible" (2).

28. Alberich remarks that if he had the *tarnkappe,* this would never have happened ("[d]och wurdez nimmer . . . getân" 1119.1). The *tarnkappe* does not reappear in the poem after Siegfried subdues Brünhild in the famous bedroom scene, and is never mentioned again after strophe 1119.

29. Once again I am indebted throughout this account of Alberich's history to Paul Battle's 1997 presentation at Kalamazoo.

30. See Guðni Jónsson, ed., *Þiðreks saga af Bern,* 2 vols. (Reykjavík: Íslendingasagnaútgafan, 1954). A modern English translation is available by Edward R. Haymes, *The Saga of Thidrek of Bern* (New York & London: Garland, 1988).

31. J. W. Thomas, trans. and ed., *Ortnit and Wolfdietrich: Two Medieval Romances* (Columbia, SC: Camden House, 1986).

32. Joachim Bumke credits the initial insight to a 1909 article by Karl Droege; see Bumke, "Sigfrieds Fahrt ins Nibelungenland," *PBB* 80 (1958): 255.

33. Bumke 258. Cf. Helmut de Boor, "Kapitel 168 der Thidrekssaga," in Hermann Schneider, ed., *Edda—Skalden—Saga* (Heidelberg: Winter, 1952) 157-172.

34. Bumke 261.

35. Neumann 76.

36. Cp. Ehrismann 126: "Archaisches Ambiente heißt niemals eo ipso *unhöfisches Ambiente.*"

37. For a discussion of Brünhild's history in Germanic legend and literature, see Theodore M. Andersson, *The Legend of Brynhild* (Ithaca and London: Cornell University Press, 1980).

38. McConnell 30.

39. Bumke 254.

40. The translations are from McConnell 32, Hatto 193 and 194, and Edward R. Haymes, *The Nibelungenlied: History and Interpretation* (Urbana and Chicago: University of Illinois Press, 1986) 76 respectively.

41. See Jacob Grimm, *Deutsche Mythologie,* vol. 1 (Göttingen: Dieterich, 1835) under the heading *Weise Frauen,* 328-407. For seeresses in the Norse tradition, see Simek 279.

42. Haymes, *Nibelungenlied* 80, 87.

43. Haymes, *Nibelungenlied* 87.

44. Haymes 74-77; McConnell 37. For Campbell, see *The Hero with a Thousand Faces* (1949; rpt. Princeton: Princeton University Press, 1968).

45. Gottfried Weber, *Das Nibelungenlied: Problem und Idee* (Stuttgart: Metzler, 1963) 136.

46. Hatto 399.

47. Stephen L. Wailes, "The *Nibelungenlied* as Heroic Epic," in Felix J. Oinas, ed., *Heroic Epic and Saga* (Bloomington: Indiana University Press, 1978) 138.

48. Haymes 77.

Winder McConnell (essay date 1998)

SOURCE: "The *Nibelungenlied*: A Psychological Approach" in *A Companion to the "Nibelungenlied"*, edited by Winder McConnell, Camden House, 1998, pp. 172-205.

[*In the following essay, McConnell applies analytical psychology to an exploration of the motivations and dreams of the* Nibelungenlied's *main characters and their relationships, finding much evidence of repression.*]

Science, particularly as evinced in the work of the British biologist, Rupert Sheldrake, as well as in the research of the Swiss physician and psychoanalyst, Willy Obrist, has produced yet further evidence of the validity of core ideas postulated almost a century ago by Carl Gustav Jung, foremost among them the concept of the archetypes of the collective unconscious.[1] It seems reasonable to assume that, as a consequence, greater links, if not cohesion, might have arisen between such (apparently) diverse areas as comparative mythology and religion, literature, biology, and psychology. Yet, despite the far-reaching ramifications of such studies, the disciplines, especially the Humanities and Social Sciences and the Natural Sciences, seem further apart today than ever before. Scientists are often enough skeptical of the forays of their humanist colleagues into physics, chemistry, biology, and psychology. Regrettably, with good reason. Rarely do the latter have any formal training in these areas and the modesty incumbent upon anyone approaching such disciplines as a non-initiate is often precluded by a zeal to promote socio-political agendas which ultimately hampers any real effort at understanding where actual points of intersecting among the disciplines can and do occur.[2] What is touted so often these days as interdisciplinary study is little more than a euphemism for watered-down, baseless curricula fashioned to serve some vague political purpose at the expense of students too young and gullible to recognize the dilettantism and political agendas of their "mentors" and lacking the power to undertake measures to counter it should they recognize the deception. There is certainly a real danger to true interdisciplinary study in such an atmosphere. The latter deserves a better forum and should be encouraged, albeit with the caveat that literary scholars with secondary (or even tertiary) interests in subjects often far afield of their major area of specialization should take care to defer to the recommendations and emendations of experts in those respective fields.

The application of analytical psychology and psychoanalysis in literary exegesis dates back a century. It is not a new methodology, but it has rarely been a popular one.[3] It is impossible to determine precisely why this has been the case, why psychological interpretations of literary works have not enjoyed, for example, the same support as New Criticism or Structuralism. Part of the reason may lie in the danger of reductionism, which, whether the approach be psychological or deconstructionist, invariably culminates in an intellectual cul-de-sac.[4] There is also the question of whether the application of such criteria is unjustifiably anachronistic. Psychological interpretations of literary works in the Freudian and post-Freudian era must necessarily take into account that the creators of such works were aware of the existence of the subconscious and that the primary text itself may revolve around a plot in which clear distinctions are made between the conscious and subconscious. Such was not the case—or so it would seem—in the Middle Ages.

The differentiation between "outer" and "inner" is relatively new. What is obvious, exposed, in short the *persona*, is, in the year 1200, for all intents and purposes, in conformity with *inner* reality. When Hartmann von Aue's protagonist in *Der arme Heinrich* is afflicted with leprosy, he can assume that those who observe him in this state are not merely fearful of becoming infected, or simply repulsed by his appearance, but that they also will have concluded that he has offended against God, that the external affliction is simultaneously a reflection of internal decay or disorder. Beautiful women of the court and handsome knights mirror the inward purity of individuals and the inherent goodness of the court itself.

If one comes to the **Nibelungenlied** from the perspective of analytical psychology, it is thus wise to approach the work with the conscious realization that the terms one will use to describe its characters, action, motivations, motifs, are derived from a terminology unknown to the western world—in the way it is commonly used today—until the last decades of the nineteenth century.[5] Anyone who might have suggested to a thirteenth-century courtier that the Burgundians/Nibelungs were given to "repressing," per-

haps even "denying," their irrevocable fate after they had crossed the Danube on the way to Hungary, that an *animus* had taken hold of Kriemhild who was truly no longer *herself,* would undoubtedly have been met with a vacuous stare. Yet it is quite conceivable that one might have turned to a contemporary as a minstrel-performer held forth on the betrothal of Gotelind and Rüdiger's daughter to Giselher and queried aloud whether the Burgundians, who had wept over the message of doom imparted to them by Hagen just hours previously, had forgotten in the interim that they have no future to which to look forward. The contemporary might even have offered an explanation: "daz wollen si jâ niht hœren!" Moreover, the narrator of ms. B of the **Nibelungenlied** clearly attributes the workings of the devil to Kriemhild's act (see 1394,1), a prepsychological explanation of the psychological phenomenon of giving in to the shadow. My point is that, while objective psychology—and psychologizing—as we understand them today, were foreign to the Middle Ages, the psychological phenomena themselves were present and may well have occasioned more than just passive acceptance on the part of the more astute observers of the time. This is, of course, to attribute to the poet of the **Nibelungenlied** himself a talent for depicting aspects of the human psyche in a way that could well be considered unparalleled in his time. Such a suggestion is not new; it was expressed, in other words (and, in fairness to the author, perhaps with more caution than I might be apt to exercise), in an article written by Walter Haug over ten years ago and which represents, in my view, one of the most insightful contributions to **Nibelungenlied** scholarship that has appeared in the past half century.[6] It also provides an excellent starting point for an analysis of probably the most complex figure within the work: Kriemhild, Princess of Burgundy, Queen of the Netherlands and Nibelungenland, and Queen of the Hungarian Empire.[7]

The present essay is intended as a *prolegomenon* to a larger study planned on German heroic epic and the **Nibelungenlied,** in particular, which will examine these works from the perspective of analytical psychology. I am principally concerned here with the motivations of main characters and the dynamics of their relationships. The terminology employed is largely that developed by Carl Gustav Jung, although it is not exclusively confined to the latter. I believe it is also possible to view the work as a whole from such a vantage point, particularly with respect to the obvious contrast it presents with the vast amount of literature otherwise predominant at that time. Finally, there are some intriguing psychological aspects to be noted regarding the manner in which the **Nibelungenlied** has been received in the twentieth century; in fact, one might suggest that certain manifestations of its *Rezeptionsgeschichte,* particularly over the past nine decades, offer considerable insight into the psyche of twentieth-century man (on this point see Werner Hoffmann's contribution to this volume and pertinent comments in the Introduction).

. . . . .

Die Staubwolken der Reiter, Zeichen des freudigen Aufbruchs, Zeichen der Hoffnung, daß ein riesiges Reich sich aus seiner Trauer erheben wird, Zeichen des Glücks, das man sich von der neuen Königin erwartet, sie werden im Vergleich durchsichtig auf das, was diese Königin tatsächlich bringen sollte: den Feuerbrand, der alles vernichten wird. . . . Was damit geschehen ist, erfaßt man in seiner literaturhistorischen Bedeutung nur völlig, wenn man bedenkt, daß es zuvor in der mittelalterlichen Literatur eine Trennung von Innen und Außen nicht gegeben hat. Das Äußere ist gewissermaßen das Innere.[8]

Walter Haug's description of the Hunnish welcome prepared for Kriemhild reads, in its first part, almost like a film script, and is, in fact, somewhat reminiscent of the activity of the Hunnish scouts in Fritz Lang's 1924 production of *Kriemhilds Rache* when they become aware of Kriemhild's approach. The dichotomy between unrestrained optimism on the part of Etzel and his horde and the "reality" that lies behind the motivation for the queen's removal to Gran and the camp of Etzel is simultaneously unique and devastating. Virtually everything relating to the essence of courtly society that would have meant something to Kriemhild at Worms prior to her marriage to Siegfried and at Xanten prior to her fateful return to Worms, has lost its significance by the time she arrives in the land of the Huns. In his depiction of Kriemhild, the poet of the **Nibelungenlied** has sprung the bounds of medieval expectations; his character is modern, driven by emotions that defy the standard ideal of the time, the pursuit of *mâze*.

I have examined the figure of Kriemhild elsewhere from the viewpoint of animus possession and the significance of the *Klage*-poet's defense of the queen.[9] My contention in that earlier study was to suggest that Kriemhild's isolation and self-isolation within the work, combined with her tendency to repress or deny her shadow while simultaneously turning her back on both motherhood and her obligations as queen, led, in the absence of any real leadership on the part of the men in her life, to an inversion of the *ordo* of things and with Kriemhild completely dominated by the animus. The issue is less one of morality than psychology.[10] Here, too, one can consider the poet of the **Nibelungenlied** to have been unique. The issues raised in the work, along with the motivations of characters, do not tend to be treated solely from the binary perspective of good and bad. To be sure, there is moralizing—consider the manner in which Hagen's killing of Siegfried is recorded by the narrator: "Hagen sîne triuwe vil sêre an Sîfriden brach" (971,4) or "sus grôzer untriuwe solde nimmer man gepflegen" (915,4), as well as the way in which Gunther's role in the whole business is depicted: "swie harte sô in durste, der helt doch niene tranc, / ê daz der künic getrunke; des sagt er im vil bœsen danc" (978,3-4).[11] Yet it is also quite clear that such moralizing with respect to the court at Worms is of limited duration, and that, by the time of the arrival of the Burgundians at the court of Etzel in Gran, the narrator could just as easily have been among the Huns eager to catch a glimpse of the man who had slain Siegfried. Any revulsion that may have previously existed over the manner that the hero of the Netherlands met his death has given way to wonder over his victor:

> . . . dô wunderte dâ zen Hiunen   vil manegen
> küenen man
> umbe Hagen von Tronege,   wie der wære getân.
>
> Durch daz man sagete mære   (des was im genuoc),
> daz er von Niderlande   Sîfriden sluoc,
> sterkest aller recken,   den Kriemhilde man.
> des wart michel vrâge   ze hove nâch Hagene
> getân.

(1732,3-4; 1733)

Morality, when it comes to the murder of Siegfried, is relative. By the twenty-eighth *Âventiure,* no one, including the narrator, is holding Hagen morally responsible for Siegfried's death, other than Kriemhild, of course.[12] It is telling that Kriemhild garners such great praise from the *Klage*-poet for the unrelenting loyalty she demonstrates towards her murdered husband:

> swer ditze mære merken kan,
> der sagt unschuldic gar ir lîp,
> wan daz daz vil edel werde wîp,
> tæte nâch ir triuwe
> ir râche in grôzer riuwe.

(154-158)

Quite clearly, this first commentator on the **Nibelungenlied,** who assumes a position towards Kriemhild that is much closer to what we find in the * C-version than in the manuscripts of the * AB-tradition, chose to focus on *triuwe* as a gender-unbounded concept, in contrast to many of his contemporaries. The latter tended to adhere to the idea of *Männertreue,* most likely harking back to a pre-Christian Germanic ethos, but also combined this with an aversion to any defiance of the courtly ideal of *mâze,* and appear to have reflected a deeply-held belief that women and revenge do not mix, at least with respect to the former becoming instruments of the latter.

There is one thing that can hardly be doubted about Kriemhild—her love for Siegfried.[13] It is not, however, a love in any way comparable to that of, for example, Isolde for Tristan. Neither Siegfried nor Kriemhild is overtaken by the archetype of romantic love, as much as they may appear to pine for each other prior to the marriage. After all, this is a socially acceptable love, legal prior to and certainly *within* marriage, not opposed to the institution, not forbidden, and, for both medieval and modern sentiments, scarcely a romantic love at all. Although a convincing argument could be made that Siegfried and Kriemhild are incompatible partners, particularly with Brünhild in the wings, there is nothing about the union from a sociopolitical standpoint which might be considered inappropriate, other than the circumstances—the deception of Brünhild—which made it possible. Kriemhild's relationship to Siegfried is, nonetheless, not without its problematical side.

Most important, there is Kriemhild's dream, which occupies the last seven strophes of the first *Âventiure,* thus underscoring its pivotal significance for the subsequent unfolding of the plot. No other motif is accorded similar weight in the *Âventiure*. We need not spend an inordinate time on its interpretation, which is delivered in a fairly straightforward, if incomplete, manner by Ute, Kriemhild's mother.[14] The falcon of which she dreams and which she "raises," is a nobleman, who will surely be lost to her (as the falcon is torn apart by two eagles) if God does not protect him. It is, of course, on one level a prediction of things to come with regard to Siegfried and his disastrous relationship to the Burgundian royal family. What is particularly striking about the dream on another level, however, is a) Kriemhild's radical reaction to her mother's interpretation of it and b) the total lack of any further reference to it on her part throughout the rest of the epic. It should also be noted that Kriemhild's first impulse is to protect *herself* from the suffering she now also associates with the "message" of the dream. In apparent contrast to Hagen's dismissal of Ute's dream of the dead birds prior to the departure of the Burgundians for the land of the Huns, Kriemhild takes her dream and her mother's explanation of it very seriously.[15] She believes in its auguring power. Yet, that belief is suspended, or, psychologically speaking, repressed, when Siegfried comes into her life and the possibility looms large for a union between the two of them. It is hard to believe that the dream is simply "forgotten." It served, after all, as the basis for a prolonged period of isolation on Kriemhild's part with respect to the "wooing circuit." Kriemhild's belief in the efficacy of the dream is, perhaps, outmatched by her belief in her husband-to-be's (near) invulnerability. Like Siegfried, she succumbs to *übermüete* which, from a Christian perspective, may be equated with *superbia,* overweening pride, or in terms of analytical psychology—inflation. Kriemhild is by no means the only figure in the *Nibelungenlied* who reads astutely ominous signs provided by various means and who may initially react instinctually—and correctly—to such signs, but who subsequently demonstrates remarkable inconsistency in acting in accordance with this previous knowledge. A similar situation prevails in the second half of the epic with respect to the behavior of the Burgundians following their arrival on the eastern shore of the Danube and the revelations provided to them by Hagen of their inevitable fate.

Kriemhild is not given to complete repression, however, as her anxiety prior to Siegfried's departure to combat the alleged insurrection of Liudeger and Liudegast in the sixteenth *Âventiure* would indicate. This is one of the most complex sections of the *Nibelungenlied* when considered from the perspective of motivation. It seems that there are two views that can be taken of Kriemhild's actions at this point: she is patently naive, or she is remarkably capable of repressing the extent to which she has contributed to besmirching the collective image of Worms and demonstrating, in an almost treacherous manner, her total disregard for its welfare. When she elects to inform Hagen of Siegfried's vulnerable spot, she reverts to the role of the devoted family member, reduces the quarrel between herself and Brünhild to little more than a somewhat nasty familial squabble, and appears to reflect once again the unity between the outer and the inner. It is difficult to conceive

of Kriemhild as being naive, but she has already, through the reversal of her initial reaction to the falcon dream, displayed a tendency to reject certain signs. In this particular instance, it would appear that the two dreams she has of Siegfried's demise, no longer in the metaphor of a falcon, but *as Siegfried,* are fatally *misinterpreted* by her. While Kriemhild envisions the (strong) possibility of Siegfried's death, she imagines it at the hands of the invading Saxons and Danes, and does not appear to consider for a moment that her brother Gunther and *oheim* Hagen, the two eagles of her first dream, have more than enough reason to want the hero of Xanten dead.

It might be contended, however, that Kriemhild is, in fact, quite naive, that she fails to recognize the seriousness of her altercation with Brünhild before the minster and its consequences for the Burgundian court, that she could not conceive of the sanctity of hospitality towards guests being defiled, particularly not in the case of her husband, a loyal military ally of Worms. Does she not, after all, approach Hagen as "family"? Quite true, but then why the doubts expressed later in 920ff., on the heels of her two dreams (in the first, Siegfried is hunted down by two wild boars; in the second, he is crushed by the collapse of two mountains), dreamt *after* her conversation with Hagen? A *Vorahnung* of what is brewing clearly has her in the direst straits, and the reader can well imagine what she is actually thinking when the narrator comments: "Do gedâhtes' an diu mære (sine torst' ir niht gesagen), / diu si dâ Hagenen sagete" (920,1-2a), and this is more starkly underscored two stanzas later: "ich fürhte harte sêre etelîchen rât, / ob man der deheinem missedienet hât, / die uns gefüegen kunnen vîentlîchen haz" (922,1-3). There is an interesting sequence of events here, beginning with the so-called "treachery" of the Saxon and Danish kings, Hagen's seeking out Kriemhild and her betrayal of his vulnerable spot, Kriemhild's dreams on that same night (i.e., *prior* to her hearing about the change in plans), the transformation of the military campaign into a hunt, Siegfried's seeking out Kriemhild to say his good-byes, and finally, Kriemhild's relating to her husband of her two dreams and her fruitless effort to dissuade him from participating in the hunt—stopping short, of course, of actually admitting to him the very sound reasons for her anxiety. Up until the point that Kriemhild herself learns that there is not to be a renewal of the war against the Saxons and the Danes, she could justifiably have identified the two boars and the two mountains with Liudeger and Liudegast. Once she realizes that a hunt has taken the place of the campaign, it is clear that she senses the potential for disaster emanating from much closer to home; her words in stanzas 920 and 922 allude to members of her own family. This is certainly how (a truly naive) Siegfried interprets them: "ine weiz hie niht der liute, die mir iht hazzes tragen. / alle dîne mâge sint mir gemeine holt" (923,2-3).

If Kriemhild had initially reacted only out of selfish interests to the first dream, and then, after having met Siegfried, repressed the "message" of that dream, and if she had, in fact, shown herself to be rather naive in her dealings with Hagen, at this juncture there is clearly no doubt as to the basis of her fears and anxiety. But this raises the highly poignant question: why, as a loving and devoted spouse, does she not make it clear to Siegfried prior to his departure that she has betrayed the one secret that can keep him alive and that he is now *very* vulnerable? The text supplies an answer, although few will be particularly satisfied with it: "(sine torst' ir niht gesagen)" (920,1b). Is it truly *fear* that prevents Kriemhild from taking the one step that might have saved Siegfried's life? She had, in fact, sustained a rather severe beating from Siegfried for the fiasco she had helped to perpetrate before the minster. Is it, then, the fear of a second beating that precludes her divulging her betrayal of her husband? This would appear, in fact, to be the case. The narrator's explanation for Kriemhild's reluctance to say anything to Siegfried can be accepted verbatim: she simply did not dare to tell him. It would seem that Kriemhild has broken a sacred trust between herself and her spouse by having imparted his "ultimate" secret to Hagen, and potentially to many others, a secret brought back from the Otherworld to which only she in the courtly world, as far as we know, was privy. The betrayal of Siegfried begins with Kriemhild,[16] who allows fear to conquer love, although her original intention in telling Hagen of Siegfried's weakness was entirely honorable and focused on preserving her spouse's life.[17]

In a psychological sense, the second half of the *Nibelungenlied* is of less interest than the first, at least insofar as Kriemhild's motivations are concerned. Her course has been plotted from the moment that Siegfried is killed and it is simply re-confirmed with the theft of the *hort*. The narrator, reader/listener, Hagen, Dietrich, the Burgundian kings, Etzel, and Rüdiger—in this approximate order—eventually realize the true/only reason for Kriemhild's marriage to Etzel. Political marriages in the Middle Ages were a matter of course, and, more often than not, involved the creation of alliances, but Kriemhild's union with the Hunnish ruler has only one purpose and that is to secure a power base from which she may eventually be able to avenge the killing of Siegfried as well as the other outrages she has suffered at the hands of her brothers and Hagen. Before turning our attention to other members of the "cast," however, several points warrant comment.

Kriemhild's designation as a "vâlandinne" in the second part of the epic can certainly be justified *from a medieval point of view.* To be sure, injustices have been committed against her, no "champion" has stepped forward to take up her case, she is isolated, but at the same time, she has never comprehended the extent to which her murdered husband, with his "ganz unkontrollierte Naturkraft"[18] constituted a perpetual problem for courtly society as a whole.

It is less Kriemhild's understandable desire for revenge that is striking or alarming than the manner in which this is allowed to consume her as an individual over more than two decades and the extent to which the absolutization of her resolve results in catastrophe for entire nations. Kriemhild's plan could never have been realized, however, with-

out the complicity of various males and the naive or inept leadership of specific rulers who are given more to repression of the obvious, and dangerous than to assuming an active role in preserving their peoples from a cataclysm. What had been characteristic of Kriemhild subsequent to her marriage to Siegfried—an imprudent turning away from her intuition, and then not acting upon it at *the* decisive moment (prior to her husband's final departure)—now holds true for all of the major male players in the work, with the exception of Hagen.

Given the reception of the *Nibelungenlied* in the twentieth century, it may seem almost blasphemous to suggest that, *from a psychological perspective,* Siegfried initially appears to be one of the least interesting characters in the *Nibelungenlied.* He is the archetypal hero: strong, to the point of near invincibility, the "perpetual" friend, or at least aspiring friend (note stanza 155) who manages, however, to create chaos rather than to instill order and stability within society. Siegfried was certainly a hero to the majority of those who heard his praises sung in the Middle Ages. While that is the image that has also tended to prevail through the first half of the twentieth century, it is noteworthy that late medieval depictions of Siegfried—as an irritating apprentice and eventually, in Hans Sachs's *Lied vom Hürnen Seyfrid* (1557), as a poor second to Dietrich in terms of prowess in combat, who even has to seek protection from the latter's wrath in the lap of Crimhilt!—were scarcely as flattering. One should not forget as well the remark made by the anonymous author of the *Klage,* already quoted above: "unt daz er selbe den tôt / gewan von sîner übermuot." This thirteenth-century commentator on the *Nibelungenlied* had relatively little to say about the hero of Xanten and astutely attributed his death in large part to his own failing.

Siegfried may have his vassals and fellow-knights, whether they hail from Xanten or the Otherworld of Nibelungenland, but he is, in the final analysis, *confidant* to no one and, with the possible exception of Kriemhild, has no one to be his *confidant(e).* The hero's solitariness is striking, particularly when we consider the relationship that exists between Hagen and Volker later in the epic, or that between Roland and Oliver in the *Rolandslied.* In marked contrast to the youthful Parzival, who has both male and female mentors to help him in a process of maturation and individuation/transformation which eventually culminates in his ascension to the Grail throne, Siegfried neither encounters, nor does he seek out, older, wiser figures of either sex. He is rather a "loner," although he is given to self-deception when it comes to the matter of friendship. There are indications, however, that Siegfried is not entirely in a psychological vacuum when it comes to knowledge regarding his actual relationship to the Burgundians, specifically Gunther. Prior to informing Siegfried of the attack by Liudeger and Liudegast, Gunther declares:

> "Jane mag ich allen liuten   die swære niht gesagen,
> die ich muoz tougenlîche   in mîme herzen tragen.

man sol stæten vriwenden   klagen herzen nôt."
diu Sîvrides varwe   wart dô bleich unde rôt.

(155)

Siegfried's reaction to Gunther's declaration is to blanch and then to blush. It is clearly a sensitive response to the implication that Gunther does not necessarily consider him among the "stæten vriwenden" but rather that he is counted more among "allen liuten." The very fact that Gunther did not see fit to approach Siegfried immediately with his concerns over the impending Danish-Saxon war should be a sign to the hero of Xanten that he does not belong to the "inner circle." There is much meaning in Siegfried's blanching and blushing, an indication of his "inner" knowledge that he is an outsider. This knowledge is, nonetheless, continually repressed by Siegfried and even denied when he lies dying after being struck down by Hagen. For all of his desire to become a good friend to the Burgundians, and to Gunther, in particular, Siegfried's "otherness," and, in particular, his incapacity to recognize and deal with the darker side of his personality, preclude any "normal" male bonding between himself and, as it appears, anyone else.

The dynamics between Siegfried and Hagen are, in some respects, more subtle than those between Hagen and Kriemhild, but they have led, in at least one instance, to a remarkable bit of scholarly speculation. Prior to examining the latter, however, let us consider the following. Upon arriving at Worms, Siegfried demonstrates no concern whatsoever for the honor of the Burgundians and must certainly offend Hagen (whom he addresses directly), in particular, with his overt declaration of intended conquest. Hagen nonetheless attempts to derive whatever assistance possible from Siegfried in his efforts to enhance the status of Worms, whether that is putting the thought into Gunther's head that he should inform Siegfried about the Danish-Saxon crisis (the clear intention being to engage his help in the forthcoming battle), or "conscripting" him for the wooing mission to Island to procure Brünhild (whereby Hagen fully realizes that Gunther, by himself, is not up to the task). It is his manipulation, after the mission has been successfully completed, that sees Siegfried sent on ahead to Worms to announce, messenger-style, the arrival of the victorious party from Island. Hagen may not have been able to, or even interested in, establishing close, personal ties to Siegfried, but he is fully aware of how valuable the hero could be for Worms if Kriemhild is held out as the ultimate prize. In sum, the relationship, at least from Hagen's standpoint, is one of pragmatism (in contrast, for example, to the affinity developed between Hagen and Volker in the second half of the epic). Even if, as in the case of the wooing of Brünhild, the goal is ill-advised, Hagen's intentions are consistently aimed at the enhancement of Burgundian power and prestige. If the latter is compromised, he will do whatever is necessary to rectify the situation. Hagen's motivation for killing Siegfried is undoubtedly multifaceted in nature, but the major reason is certainly the damage done to Worms, its royal family, their reputation and honor, through the indiscretions of the hero of Xanten and his spouse. It is thus possible to concur to some degree with D. G. Mowatt and Hugh Sacker when they suggest that the murder came about as "Sifrid's punishment for not caring about Worms."[19] Less easy to accept, however, is the Freudian interpretation they accord to the hunt which provides the backdrop for the murder and to the symbolism accorded the act itself: "Is perhaps the whole hunt scene a homosexual hunt, with Hagen and Sifrid the two wild boars of Kriemhilde's dream (921,2), and fatal penetration from the rear Sifrid's punishment for not caring about Worms?"[20]

The matter of Siegfried's sexuality is by no means without interest. He is undoubtedly aware of the attention he receives from the opposite sex in general (note 131,1-3 where the women are always delighted to see Siegfried among the sporting knights, or 135,3-4, in which his looks cause "manec frouwe" to adore him), and, despite his initial qualms about wooing Kriemhild, he is from all indications a successful sexual partner. When sex is alluded to in conjunction with Siegfried, scholars are most likely to concentrate on the bedroom scene in which Siegfried "tames" Brünhild for a hapless Gunther. Mowatt and Sacker maintain that "he is essentially responsible for her loss of maidenhood," but that "he left her to Gunther to deflower."[21] Siegfried is no Tristan, however, as the reservations he expresses in stanza 136 regarding the possibility of even seeing Kriemhild indicate. The Burgundian princess is Siegfried's *anima,* just as he, in many ways, represents her *animus.* As the epitome of courtly existence, Kriemhild in essence becomes the focus of Siegfried's effort to reintegrate himself into society, undertaken subconsciously after his youthful adventures in the otherworldly sphere. Paradoxically, he will adapt less easily to the court than Kriemhild does to his more aggressive sphere. Even the vocabulary used to describe the contemplated sex act (in the case of both Siegfried and Gunther) is not devoid of some bellicose vocabulary: "Die herren kômen beide, dâ si solden ligen. / do gedâht' ir ietslîcher mit minnen an gesigen/den minneclîchen vrouwen" (628,1-3a). The perspective provided by the narrator is solely that of Siegfried's satisfaction, however: "Sîfrides kurzewîle diu wart vil grœzlîche guot" (628,4) and we learn nothing of how Kriemhild fared, although there is no reason to doubt that the pleasure enjoyed was mutual. The desirability of Kriemhild as a lover is not lost on others. The obvious attraction that she and Siegfried have for each other once Kriemhild has appeared physically before him, the image painted of their coming together, prompts many an observing knight to contemplate the pleasures of "being" together with Kriemhild, of making love to her (296,1-3). Siegfried has a sexual persona, and his superiority also in this arena is not to be underestimated when it comes to understanding the relationship between himself and Gunther and hence, through association, to Hagen. It is a persona, however, which is decidedly heterosexual and, from every indication, monogamist: "er næme für si eine niht tûsent anderiu wîp" (629,4; see also 656,2b-3).

There are, of course, obvious sexual overtones to Siegfried's "taming" of Brünhild for Gunther and one can certainly concur with Mowatt and Sacker that Siegfried's bears responsibility for the Icelandic queen's loss of her virginity. Siegfried seems to have anticipated that his help would be needed, as we read in 648,1-2: "Im [= Gunther] unt Sîfride ungelîch stuont der muot./wol wesse, waz im wære, der edel ritter guot." Psychologically, this must be an almost unbearable situation for the Burgundian king. Politically, it could become disastrous, should the antics of the preceding night become widely known. Gunther's sexually inferior status when compared to Siegfried is painfully "rubbed in" through a remark by the latter which may seem to be relatively harmless on the surface: "ich wæne uns ungelîche hînat sî gewesen" (652,2). Gunther is fully aware of Siegfried's sexual prowess and the potential, after the latter's offer of assistance to subdue Brünhild, for a violation of his royal prerogative, hence his rather pathetic statement: "Âne daz du iht triutest" (655,1a). Once assured that, for Siegfried, there is no other woman but Kriemhild, Gunther is quite relieved, although terribly anxious for the day to pass. When it does, however, the poet provides his audience with some excellent insight into the mental state of the Burgundian monarch: "daz was dem künige Gunther beidiu liep unde liet" (665,4). Gunther realizes that there is no other way to "win" Brünhild, but it is a torturous fact that his wife must be "tamed" by another man and there is certainly more than a little ambiguity in his thought: "Den künic ez dûhte lange, ê er si betwanc" (675,1). Gunther remains throughout fully cognizant of the fact that Siegfried held true to his oath not to "violate" Brünhild sexually.[22] He is, however, a medieval sovereign who cannot completely repress the symbolic significance of the later public display of his spouse's ring and belt by his sister after she has declared (lied?) to all and sundry, and more with a sense of pride than of shame, that it was her husband, Siegfried, who first bedded Brünhild.

Previous scholarship has occasionally seen the *Nibelungenhort*—as well as the sword Balmung—as symbolic of Siegfried, hence the added significance of Kriemhild's demand that the hoard be returned to her when she confronts Hagen in the final scenes of the epic and her decapitation of the latter using Siegfried's sword. If this is a correct interpretation, then it is worth noting that the one item in the treasure that is singled out as having particular significance is the magic wand, the *Wünschelrute:* "Der wunsch der lac darunder, von golde ein rüetelîn. / der daz het erkunnet, der möhte meister sîn/wol in aller werlde über ietslîchen man" (1124,1-3). While this can certainly be taken verbatim as the equivalent of the wizard's magic wand, used principally to preclude any diminishing of the treasure, it is intriguing to note that the term *wünschelruote* or *wünschelstap* was also used in the Middle Ages as a euphemism for the male member.[23] The *hort* represents vitality, including sexual vitality,[24] and it is thus possible to view Siegfried himself as the epitome of such vitality, a man who has not only the potential to become "meister" over all men, but also all women, in the world.

We must be cautious, however, about extending this imagery too far. Suffice it to say that Siegfried outdoes Gunther

not only in battle—note their respective roles in the Saxon-Danish war, and also the struggles against Brünhild—but also in the bedroom, irrespective of the fact that both produce sons. It should be underscored once again that Siegfried is not Tristan, he is no Don Juan, although there are certainly aspects of the archetypal *puer aeternus* about him, in the sense that he "remains too long in adolescent psychology."[25] At no time is there any indication that Siegfried himself understands the delicate psychological position in which Gunther must find himself through the very presence of the hero of Xanten and Nibelungenland. Siegfried is simply in every way but one (the ability to form a deep and reliable relationship to his peers) "the better man," and, because it is impossible for him to become any one else's true friend (irrespective of how he may regard himself in the eyes of others), his success in the sexual sphere will inevitably impede a closer relationship to the Burgundian king.

Siegfried is desired by women (possibly including Brünhild), loved by Kriemhild, and himself indicates unequivocally on a number of cases that the princess of Worms is the only woman in his life. At no time is there a hint of homosexuality in his behavior or demeanor. While Mowatt and Sacker have any number of valuable points to make in their commentary, this is one that leads nowhere. What has been said of Siegfried applies as well to Hagen. There is no homosexuality in the *Nibelungenlied,* either symbolically, or otherwise. There is sexual tension between Siegfried and Gunther, Kriemhild and Brünhild, possibly also between Siegfried and Brünhild, and there is sexual (although not necessarily psychological) compatibility between Siegfried and Kriemhild. Sex is used by Kriemhild to sway Etzel, as is fatherhood, it may be used by the Hunnish queen to entice Blœdel to commit treacherous acts against the Burgundians (by offering him the widow of the highly acclaimed hero Nuodung [see also *Alpharts Tod,* 78-79]), but it is, at best, one of several motivating factors within the dynamics of relationships between the various main characters in the *Nibelungenlied,* and it is never anything other than heterosexual in nature.[26]

A number of years ago, Theodore M. Andersson posed the complex and provocative question, "Why does Siegfried die?"[27] He concluded that there was no good reason provided in the *Nibelungenlied;* the Old Norse versions of the tale, on the other hand, offered convincing motivation for the act. Yet we do have the statement made by the *Klage*-poet that the hero of Xanten was killed as a consequence of his *übermuot*. Siegfried's murder—and it will always remain that, regardless of whether one finds it justified or condemnable—can, however, be explained psychologically from the text itself, without recourse to analogues (although this is by no means intended to dispute the possibility that the latter were known to the *Nibelungenlied*-poet and that he, too, like some modern interpreters, saw the potential for an ambiguous interpretation of Brünhild's tears at the sight of Kriemhild sitting next to Siegfried). One might even go so far as to say that the killing was inevitable, given the static nature of an adult child[28] who remains stubbornly oblivious to the serious (negative) ramifications of both his words and deeds on the society around him. Siegfried is not simply Burgundy's "problem." He poses a threat to the stability of the rest of the "epic" world, specifically because of his incapacity to adhere to the norms of the latter, his spontaneity, and his apparent ignoring of the "rules" according to which that world functions. Even in his last moments, Siegfried never demonstrates the capacity to confront his shadow. When he proclaims to Gunther and Hagen: "ich was iu ie getriuwe" (989,3a), he is technically quite correct. He had, from his perspective, and perhaps even from the audience's, always been loyal towards the Burgundians, because he had never *intentionally* or, more accurately, *consciously,* undertaken anything to their disadvantage. Siegfried can look back on his participation in the Danish-Saxon war, his indispensable role in procuring Brünhild, the "service" performed for Gunther in "taming" her, as acts performed on behalf of Gunther and the Burgundians and yet none of these are events that can be designated so simply. Prior to leaving on the Danish-Saxon campaign, Siegfried encourages Gunther ". . . sît hie heime . . . belîbet bî den frouwen" (174,1a; 3a). Siegfried's assurances to Gunther that he will protect "beidiu êre unde guot" (174,4b) are sincere, and there is no reason to believe that he *intends* a slight against the monarch with his recommendation that he remain home with the women. One might contend that it is fitting for Gunther to let his liegemen and allies deal with this problem and remain removed from the actual battlefield, but Gunther is not Arthur, sending out knights on *âventiuren.* The specific reference to "staying home with the women" is remarkable. Liudegast is king of Denmark and an active participant in the campaign against Burgundy. It is inconceivable that Etzel would remain "at home with the women" once his hordes have begun to march. Nor do we find Hagen in *Kudrun,* written within three or four decades after the *Nibelungenlied,* or King Hetel, or his adversary King Ludwig, entrusting either their offensive or defensive wars to vassals while they enjoy the relative security of remaining "at home with the women." Yet it is a recommendation to which Gunther accedes and not a word of his reaction is recorded in the text. The reader/listener is left to decide for himself what Gunther must be feeling in this moment. It is not indicated whether or not Siegfried's statement is made before several of the king's liegemen, but even if said to him privately, it casts a rather hapless Gunther into an even more unenviable psychological position as he is forced to realize who is, at this point, the *de facto* power in Burgundy.

When Siegfried accompanies Gunther, together with Hagen and Dancwart, to Island to woo Brünhild—although he originally advised Gunther against it, while Hagen urged the mission with Siegfried's assistance—he is most certainly providing an invaluable service (albeit with the direst consequences) to Worms and its sovereign. Yet, here again, the situation is psychologically volatile. From the outset, it is clear to all and sundry that the entire mission could not be seriously contemplated without the help of

the "initiate" Siegfried, and this becomes patently obvious when the Burgundians eventually confront the "devilish" Brünhild. Moreover Siegfried, who has wished so much to demonstrate his "friendship" towards Gunther and the others (note 156), allows himself a throughly unnecessary remark which can hardly fail to offend the king and his men: "Jane lob' ichz niht sô verre durch die liebe dîn / sô durch dîne swester" (388,1-2a). Once again, there is no response from Gunther and what could he have possibly replied? In short, any potential for real friendship or comradeship is precluded by the unnerving proclivity of Siegfried to say precisely the wrong thing at the wrong time. Let us recall again Siegfried's query of Gunther following the wedding night, one that is made in *full awareness* of what has undoubtedly happened (648,2). The terrible dichotomy is time and time again apparent: Gunther and the Burgundians need Siegfried, he is more than willing to help, but that help is invariably provided in ways as to remind them consistently of the extent to which they are, individually and collectively, inferior to him. In this respect, he provides a striking contrast to a figure such as Beowulf, on whom Hrothgar and the Danes depend, but who never creates the impression that he is a threat to the latter, a hero who is sensitive to the Danish king's position, and also willing to learn from the latter's wisdom and experience, and who leaves for his own homeland before the suspicion of any usurpation of Danish power could be contemplated. In the case of Siegfried, however, there is the ever-present, gloomy realization that Gunther and his men are not up to accomplishing any of these goals themselves and that, from the moment that Siegfried arrived at Worms, they have become "obliged" to him and aware that they are entirely at his mercy.

Why, in fact, does Siegfried die, if one is not prepared to accept the perfectly good explanation to be derived from the text, namely, that one cannot let rest his responsibility for the public humiliation of the Burgundian court? One might cite Jung's explanation as provided in his *Symbols of Transformation*—here referring to Wagner's opera but it can just as easily be applied to the situation in the *Nibelungenlied:* "The subsequent fate of Siegfried is the fate of every archetypal hero: the spear of the one-eyed Hagen, the Dark One, strikes his vulnerable spot."[29] The poet is thus following an established pattern (not just tradition passed on from the oralformulaic forebears of the epic or its immediate written source) that transcends epic aesthetics and expectations and which finds its origins in mythology. Another explanation might be proposed, one that may be feasible from the perspective of medieval thinking (or psychology). In contradistinction to the expectation of conformity prevalent at the time, Siegfried's archetypal features are not confined to heroic acts which are intended to benefit society, but also include a remarkable measure of *individuality* that confronts and defies the interests of the collective. Furthermore, it is into this realm of individual achievement and self-assertion that Kriemhild is inextricably drawn when she weds Siegfried and which causes her to move further and further away from the clan and the interests and welfare of her family. Quite in keeping with this emergence of the individual is the overweening pride, the *übermuot* which exacerbates Siegfried's independent, *spontaneous* tendency towards unreflected action.[30] The reasons for Siegfried's death may well be seen as multifaceted, but the inflationary, unpredictable nature of this transgressor against the prevailing *ordo* of the world constitutes, at the very least, a major subconscious impetus to his removal. His transgressions have in large part to do with the affinity he displays to the Otherworld and the power he has acquired through his successes in that realm. We are reminded here of a *Spruch* by Nietzsche: "Wer mit Ungeheuern kämpft, mag zusehen, daß er nicht dabei zum Ungeheuer wird. Und wenn du lange in einen Abgrund blickst, blickt der Abgrund auch in dich hinein."[31] Siegfried defeats the dragon, but acquires in the process some of what it symbolizes, particularly the capacity for unleashing chaos. If the Otherworld is viewed as a metaphor for the unconscious, it should be recalled that the latter is also the repository for some things best left "below the surface." Siegfried's inability to discern between what should be allowed to emerge from the depths, what might benefit him and society as a whole, and what should justifiably—and wisely—be repressed, can be regarded as a major factor in the unfolding of his own personal tragedy.

Siegfried's nemesis, Hagen, is a highly complex figure who may, however, on the surface at least, create the impression of being relatively onedimensional in terms of his motivation. He, as well as his clan, appear to have one purpose in life, namely, to serve the Burgundian royal household. All of Hagen's actions take Worms and the welfare of Burgundy as represented by its kings as their point of departure. He will later be designated by the narrator as "cin helflîcher trôst" (1526,2b) and also by Dietrich as the "trôst der Nibelunge" (1726,4a), an allusion that should be understood in both a physical and spiritual sense. It is worth noting from the outset that Hagen is not accorded overtly *personal* ambitions by the poet. For all intents and purposes, any hopes, dreams, wishes, that he may have are identical to what he would consider to be the best course of action for Burgundy, which is not to suggest, however, that Hagen does not jealously guard his own particular position within the hierarchy of the court, one that he has clearly assumed in accordance with a venerable tradition. He is the quintessential "company man," who sees his purpose in enhancing and upholding the stature of Worms. Hagen subscribes to, and upholds, the traditional code of honor and loyalty, albeit defined within the context of the clan. As such, he is the avowed enemy of anyone or anything which might compromise the physical or "metaphysical" welfare of the Burgundians.

Hagen enjoys a unique position at the Burgundian court among other things because of his wide knowledge of the world outside its immediate confines: "Dem sint kunt diu rîche und ouch diu vremden lant" (82,1). As his later encounter with the water sprites on the way to Etzel's camp illustrates, this knowledge extends to the Otherworld, not surprising given the connection Hagen has in Norse ana-

logues to the world of lower mythology, his father having been an elf. He knows of Siegfried, and correctly surmises that the magnificent "recke" who appears in Worms in *Âventiure* 3 is none other than the legendary hero. For all of his "otherness," however, and his somewhat solitary nature—we have no reason to believe that Hagen enjoys any sort of "personal" life outside his relationship to the royal household; a wife and family are never mentioned in connection with him. Hagen is well integrated into Burgundian society and is fully aware and, for the most part, respectful of, the rules that govern the often delicate relationship to peers and superiors. Siegfried's arrival in Worms is not the occasion for unreserved rejoicing. Hagen recommends that he be accorded the appropriate reception, but the motivation behind his advice to Gunther in this respect may well betray more than understandable caution and prudence, namely, fear:

> "Wir suln den herren enpfâhen deste baz,
> daz wir iht verdienen des jungen recken haz.
> sîn lîp der ist sô küene, man sol in holden hân.
> er hât mit sîner krefte sô menegiu wunder getân."
>
> (101)

From the outset, that fear precludes any real possibility that Siegfried and Hagen might eventually develop a warriors' friendship. There is anxiety in Hagen's voice when he continues: "er stêt in der gebære, mich dunket, wizze Krist, / ez ensîn niht kleiniu mære, dar umb' er her geriten ist" (103,3-4). In four brief stanzas, Siegfried essentially justifies the anxiety that Hagen has hinted at, as he moves from recognition of the great "recken" associated with Worms, to its kings, his own status within society, and his intention to earn a name for himself by seizing Burgundian vassals and property. This confrontation, initiated by the intended "guest," sets the essential tone for the relationship which will evolve between Siegfried and the Burgundians. Although Hagen (along with Gernot) is reported as having countered Siegfried's claims in 114,4, it is not until stanza 121 that his words are actually recorded:

> Dô sprach der starke Hagene: "uns mac wol wesen leit,
> allen dînen degenen, daz er ie gereit
> durch strîten her ze Rîne; er soltez haben lân.
> im heten mîne herren sölher leide niht getân."

The reader notes that Hagen's words do not constitute a threat against Siegfried, that they are not indicative of an angry, indignant outburst, but are rather more a reflection of the anxiety he had earlier demonstrated when commenting on Siegfried's stature and reputation. Gunther had been somewhat dismayed over the relative silence demonstrated by his liegeman in the face of Siegfried's challenge (119,3: "daz der sô lange dagete, daz was dem künege leit"). Why had, in fact, Hagen not stepped forward? Why is it left to Ortwin, his nephew, to take up the gauntlet? This is not lost on Siegfried, who provokingly remarks: "War umbe bîtet Hagene und ouch Ortwîn, / daz er niht gâhet strîten mit den friwenden sîn" (125,1-2). Gernot apparently makes it clear to Hagen and Ortwin that they are not to respond to Siegfried's obvious provocation and it is he who extends, despite the latter's arrogance, a warm welcome to the hero. One wonders, however, precisely how Hagen would or could have responded, had Gernot not intervened. He is fully aware of Siegfried's near-invulnerability, and a clash of arms at this juncture could well leave not only himself and his nephew slain, but also the entire Burgundian royal family decimated. Consider Hagen's position; it has already been pointed out that Gunther is somewhat disappointed with his lack of action, he is openly challenged by Siegfried, but dare he move against him, even if not restrained by Gernot? Inasmuch as Hagen's *raison d'être* centers around his ability to protect and enhance the Burgundian monarchy, he cannot undertake a thing at this moment without the possibility that the devastating consequences alluded to above will become fact. That means, however, that he must suffer the indignity of leaving Siegfried's challenge unanswered, at least for now.

From the outset, Hagen is cast into an adversarial relationship with Siegfried that is not of his making, and forced to endure an outrage that cannot help but compromise both his individual sense of honor as well as the collective image of the court. Yet Siegfried possesses a remarkable talent for dissipating—on the surface—the understandable resentment he has undoubtedly evoked among the Burgundians present at this arrival scene, for the narrator comments in 129,4: "in sach vil lützel iemen, der im wære gehaz." To what extent we may take the litotes "vil lützel" to apply to everyone is, however, debatable. Hagen may slip temporarily into the background as Siegfried whiles away his time for a year at the Burgundian court hoping to catch a glimpse of Kriemhild, but this does not mean that he will have necessarily forgotten (or trivialized) the significance of Siegfried's initial appearance at Worms. Given the circumstances that prevail subsequent to Kriemhild's move to the land of the Huns, it is most likely that her brothers, at this point, adapt to Siegfried's presence at court to such an extent that they are able to repress the unpleasantries of the initial encounter. Hagen will not forget; when he asks Gunther, following the announcement of the approaching war with the Saxons and the Danes, "wan muget irz Sîvride sagen" (151,4b), it is completely in accord with the role of the competent royal advisor. On another level, however, it is just as feasible to see Hagen's "advice" as calculated to place Siegfried, at least on the surface, into the role of someone serving Worms, in compensation for the manner in which the Burgundians have been relegated into second-power status by his overbearing, if youthful, "naturalness." Stanza 331 (Hagen's suggestion that Siegfried be engaged for the wooing mission to Iceland) and 532 (Hagen's urging of Gunther to have Siegfried take the message to Worms that they are returning with Brünhild) provide further evidence of a manipulative, perhaps compensatory, effort by Hagen to have Siegfried not only serve Worms but also be controlled by what he, Hagen, has recommended. Once again, we are dealing with different levels of motivation and purpose.

Hagen has not actively contemplated the death of Siegfried from the moment it became clear that he would always remain a potential threat to Burgundian power and prestige. It appears that as long as he can be contained or controlled, as in the above instances, Hagen, something of a medieval *Realpolitiker,* is content to let matters stand. The quarrel of the queens before the minster, however, precludes a continuation of such a policy. Containment is no longer an option. Nothing, up to that point, had approximated the damage done to Burgundian image, including Siegfried's arrogant behavior upon his arrival. The public suggestion that Gunther had been cuckolded by the upstart from Xanten is not something that can be repressed or for which some sort of compensation can be found. Yet, it provides—at Brünhild's urging—only the immediate impetus for the murder.

Highly revealing is Hagen's statement to the despairing Burgundian kings after the deed has been done:

> Dô sprach der grimme Hagene: "Jane weiz ich,
>   waz ir kleit.
> ez hât nu allez ende   uncer sorge unt unser leit.
> wir vinden ir vil wênic,   die getürren uns bestân.
> wol mich, deich sîner hêrschaft   hân ze râte getân."
>
>   (993)

Several things can be established from this statement: 1) Hagen feels no remorse about having killed Siegfried and is somewhat chagrined over the fact that the kings do; 2) he appears to believe, paradoxically, that all of the worries and cares of the Burgundians are at an end—precisely what these are will need further elucidation; 3) the act of killing Siegfried brings with it enhanced political and military stature for the Burgundians for no one will dare challenge them now; 4) Hagen takes a considerable degree of personal satisfaction for having been the one to have put an end to Siegfried's *hêrschaft.* Precisely what Hagen means by "unser sorge unt unser leid" is not explained in any detail, although the obvious immediate reference would be to the sense of helplessness perceived by the Burgundians in the face of the dishonor done their court by Kriemhild's indiscretion in front of the minster. It is quite possible, likely, in fact, that the significance of the comment is much more far-reaching. There is a sense of relief that is conveyed by 993,2 and underscored by the presence of "allez." From Hagen's perspective, the Burgundians have long suffered under Siegfried's *hêrschaft,* his overbearing demeanor, unpredictability, his thoughtlessness, recklessness, his *übermuot.* But Hagen uses the first person plural in his comment and the reader/listener can be sure that while his murder, in Hagen's view, ought to remove the collective anxiety created by his very presence, Hagen himself is relieved to be rid of the man who, on numerous occasions, has cast him into the shadows and relegated him (and his king, in fact, if not in theory) to secondary status. It is thus quite understandable that Hagen immediately follows this comment with an assertion of new-found (or restored?) Burgundian (military/political) power. Particularly revealing is the emphasis he places on the fact that it was *he* who has put an end to the hero's *hêrschaft,* a term which has a range of meaning extending from "dominion, control, power" to "pride, arrogance."[32] It is one of the few instances in the *Nibelungenlied* when we are afforded some insight into Hagen's innermost feelings.

While the argument can be made that Hagen's killing of Siegfried was ultimately a necessity for society as a whole, the immediate consequence of his death is a sense of re-established *individual* and *collective* power, but this is viewed almost exclusively from Hagen's vantage point. His words in stanza 993 are, of course, remarkably ironic: the real troubles of the Burgundians are only about to begin. While it is questionable whether a true reconciliation with Kriemhild could ever have been effected without some action being taken against Hagen, the unchecked inflationary stance of the latter following Siegfried's death, together with the fact that no one of stature steps forward to champion her cause, contributes directly to the queen's increased isolation from her family (irrespective of her decision to remain in Worms rather than journey back to Xanten to raise her son) and distance from courtly norms. Hagen makes it quite clear from the outset that he is unconcerned about Kriemhild's reaction: "ez ahtet mich vil ringe, swaz si weinens getuot" (1001,4), but he goes further and takes deliberate steps to intensify her suffering. The narrator states succinctly the motivation for Hagen's provocation of Siegfried's widow: "Von grôzer übermüete muget ir hœeren sagen, / und von eislîcher râche" (1003,1-2a). Kriemhild is targeted by Hagen not only for the manner in which she compromised Burgundian honor in her confrontation with Brünhild. Hagen has clearly not forgotten the (as he must view it, reckless and provocative) way in which, in total disregard for a long-standing and virtually sacrosanct tradition, Kriemhild expressed her wish that he, along with Ortwin and various other knights from Worms, return with her to Siegfried's homeland (note 697-699). Once again, we have a "transgression" on two levels, the individual and the collective. From the moment she had become Siegfried's spouse, Kriemhild had turned her back on the interests of Worms and demonstrated abject callousness towards Hagen's pivotal role as chief counselor to the Burgundians. Where wisdom is called for, Hagen now allows a psychological need for revenge to prevail. Nor is the act done openly, but rather: "Er hiez in tougenlîchen legen an die tür" (1004,1), although one wonders why he bothers, for it is certainly clear to Kriemhild who has been behind the act: "ez hât gerâten Prünhilt, daz ez hât Hagene getân" (1010,4).

It is, of course, the Hagen-Kriemhild dichotomy/ antagonism which has particularly fascinated generations of scholars. From the moment of Siegfried's murder, the epic appears to revolve around the two of them, even if they themselves are frequently relegated to the background. From a psychological point of view, it can be asserted that Hagen remains relatively consistent, static, throughout the plot; we at no time can discern a change in personality or in motivation, irrespective of the lack of wisdom we may ascribe to some of his actions or advice given the Burgun-

dians. He is, as ever, committed to the physical and spiritual welfare of Worms. On occasion, he may also demonstrate an (understandable) degree of self-interest, as in his initial, negative reaction to the invitation from Etzel and Kriemhild to the Burgundians to visit the Hunnish court, but there can never be any doubt that his top priority remains his resolve to serve Worms, even to the point of insuring that they die with honor.

In this highly personal feud, Kriemhild may also be seen as adhering consistently to her principles (regardless of whether or not they fly in the face of the accepted norms of a basically warrior-oriented society), certainly as much as is the case with Hagen. If the latter is concerned with preservation (of Burgundian power, prestige, but above all, honor), Kriemhild's focus is on restoration of those things of which she has been deprived: honor, power, the *hort* (which has frequently been seen as symbolic of Siegfried himself). In both instances, the respective goals are to be achieved at any price. Hagen leads the entire Burgundian warrior class along with his kings into a foretold death, and he certainly knows that this is their fate once the chaplain has survived his attempt to drown him. Kriemhild is just as prepared to sacrifice any and all, including her son Ortlieb, to the realization of her aim. If we adhere to ms. B in our interpretation of the work, it seems that the poet/narrator's sentiments towards the conclusion of the tale lie squarely with Hagen and the Burgundians, even if he includes references to their "übermuot" in refusing to let Etzel know the true state of affairs. Yet his voice is not the only one that must be noted in this regard. The scribe of ms. C was most certainly at pains to avoid any "demonization" of Kriemhild such as we experience in B, while the author of the *Nibelungenklage* went so far as to insist that Kriemhild's place in heaven is assured, given the loyalth she has demonstrated towards Siegfried: "sît si durch triuwe tôt gelac, / in gotes hulden manegen tac / sol si ze himele noch geleben."[33] Opinions on Kriemhild's behavior were undoubtedly quite diverse in the early thirteenth century, with some contemporaries basing their judgment on the queen's association with the devil (note 1394,1-2: "Ich wæne der übel vâlant Kriemhilde daz geriet, / daz sie sich mit friuntschefte von *Gunthere* schiet"), and, from their perspective, her own "transformation" into a "vâlandinne" (as proclaimed by both Dietrich [1748,4a] and Hagen [2371,4a]), in complete conformity with a traditional patriarchal stance towards the appropriate role of the female in feudal society. Others, however (and they were most likely males), laid the blame for the cataclysm squarely at Hagen's door (and to a lesser degree at Gunther's) and, while not repressing the extent to which Kriemhild was clearly ready to achieve her aim, demonstrated sympathy with the situation in which she found herself, condemned the injustices done her—the murder of Siegfried and the *hort*—and were even prepared to express admiration for her absolute adherence to the principle of loyalty.

There is a noteworthy difference between Hagen and Kriemhild with respect to their psychological states as manifested in the second half of the *Nibelungenlied* and it is here that we return to the thesis propounded by Walter Haug. Whereas Hagen is decidedly overt in his actions from the time that he steals the *hort* on, Kriemhild's are patently covert. Her machinations, as Haug as pointed out, do not simply constitute the often laudable trait of *list,* but rather serve to underscore a basic transformation of her personality. While the medieval narrator has ascribed the latter in pre-psychological terms to the workings of the devil, the post-Freudian, Jungian literary critic might suggest that Kriemhild has succumbed to the *animus* or the *shadow.* As autonomous archetypes, both have, in fact, something in common with the earlier concept of Satan. Kriemhild's re-ascent to a position of power as the spouse of Etzel does not function as a compensatory balance for the inner turmoil and fury she has nurtured since the murder of Siegfried and which she is not always successful in concealing, as Dietrich's comments to the Burgundians upon their arrival in the land of the Huns would indicate: "Kriemhilt noch sêre weinet den helt von Nibelunge lant" (1724,4); "ich hœre alle morgen weinen unde klagen / mit jâmerlîchen sinnen daz Etzelen wîp" (1730,2-3).[34] Rather, it serves solely to allow the shadow greater control over her psyche. Thus, while Kriemhild may still symbolize a new beginning for Etzel and the Huns, in reality her nurturing, mothering, "feminine" side has been completely subsumed beneath the aggressive aims of the *animus/ shadow.* Nowhere is this more in evidence than in her apparently complete lack of grief over Hagen's decapitation of her son Ortlieb (the second offspring on whom she has turned her back), whose head lands in her lap (1961,3). External and internal features no longer correspond, whereas with Hagen they could not be in greater accord as the epic moves inexorably towards the final debacle.

The scenes of confrontation between Hagen and Kriemhild following the arrival of the Burgundians at Gran are masterpieces of dramatic technique. While Kriemhild may greet (only) Giselher with a kiss, the welcome is done "mit valschem muote" (1737,2b). There is nothing "false," however, about Hagen's retort to Kriemhild's query regarding the status of the *hort:* "Jâ bringe ich iu den tiuvel" (1744,1a) which is followed up by a specific reference to his sword, none other than Siegfried's Balmung: "daz swert an mîner hende des enbringe ich iu nieht" (1744,4). Kriemhild's request that all weapons be handed over to her is also rejected outright—by Hagen, not by Gunther or any of the other kings. They have yet to speak. What is most intriguing about this scene is one comment by the narrator that would indicate Kriemhild's conscious awareness that her plans for revenge are not within the parameters of acceptable behavior towards guests. When Dietrich publicly refers to her as a "vâlandinne" (1749,4a), she feels such shame that, speechless, she has no recourse but to retreat: "Des schamte sich vil sêre daz Etzelen wîp" (1749,1). Kriemhild still retains awareness of what is right and what is no longer within the framework of accepted, courtly behavior, but the sparring between herself and Hagen creates its own dynamic which will eventually occasion the deaths of tens of thousands. The poet proceeds

quite rapidly to the next encounter, the scene before Kriemhild's palace, to which only Hagen and Volker advance ("Noch liezen si die herren ûf dem hove stân," 1760,1) and where they sit down on a bench in full view of Kriemhild's window. This is deliberate provocation on Hagen's part, which is further intensified by his refusal to stand up in her presence, electing instead to remain seated with Siegfried's sword placed across his lap. The narrator himself suggests that this was done precisely by Hagen to cause her distress: ". . . weinen si began/ich wæne, ez hete dar umbe der küene Hagene getân," 1784,3b-4). While this may be attributed to "übermüete" (note 1783,1a), it can simultaneously be regarded as testimony to Hagen's "inner" sovereignty, for we should not forget that he *knows* full well that neither he nor the others will ever leave here alive. He openly admits that he killed Siegfried and associates this directly with Kriemhild's insulting of Brünhild (1790,3-4). All of this transpires before some assembled Huns, who quickly recognize that it is suicidal to attack Hagen and Volker and whose withdrawal causes Kriemhild even greater grief (1799,2).

What we witness here is Hagen in relative control, not only of the Burgundians, whom he has served as *de facto* leader on the journey to the land of the Huns, but also, if temporarily, of the situation in Gran, Kriemhild's "home ground," so to speak. It is not correct to suggest that Hagen no longer has anything to lose. His honor and his sense of (inner) sovereignty are to him paramount and in the current situation—he realizes he has absolutely no control over its (external, physical) outcome—both can only be maintained by refusing to concede to Kriemhild on a single point. Once again, power is at the heart of it all, albeit for Hagen now internalized, as the Burgundians do not have a chance of emerging victorious in a conflict against the Huns. In this respect, one might well maintain that he ultimately proves victorious over Kriemhild at the conclusion of the epic, yet the reaction of Etzel to his death would indicate that externally, at least, from the perspective of the male survivors of the catastrophe, his demise was less than "honorable":

> "Wâfen", sprach der fürste, "wie ist nu tôt gelegen
> von eines wîbes handen der aller beste degen,
> der ie kom ze sturme oder ie schilt getruoc!
> swie vîent ich im wære, ez ist mir leide genuoc."
>
> (2374)

Walter Haug has declared that the *Nibelungenlied* is one of the most "modern" works of its time. It transcends contemporary expectations, dissolves the assumed uniformity between inner and outer (particularly in the person of Kriemhild, but also with regard to the epic as a whole), depicts a world in which forces that fester below the surface are decisive and it is the latter which ultimately determine man's fate. In this respect, the dreams of the *Nibelungenlied* should be accorded the highest significance, not for the transformative influence they have on individuals—too often their meaning(s) are repressed by the recipients of the dream-material—but for the manner in which they herald a rather black future involving the demise of both individuals and societies. Understood and acted upon, the dream can effect a positive transformation on various levels. Repressed or ignored, it may remain simply the harbinger of catastrophe.

. . . . .

The transformative power of the dream, in this instance, a dream based on the Nibelungen theme, can be demonstrated for the father of analytical psychology himself, Carl Gustav Jung. On December 18, 1913, less than a year prior to the outbreak of World War I, Jung had a dream, subsequently recorded, in which, together with the assistance of a "brown-skinned man, a savage," he killed the approaching hero, Siegfried.[35] Jung, convinced that the latter must die, shoots Siegfried with a rifle as the latter rushes down the side of a mountain in a chariot that has been fashioned from the bones of the dead. Given Siegfried's standing (at the time) as a relatively unproblematic hero in the German-speaking regions of Europe, Jung's killing of him understandably appalled him in his dream and caused him concern over the possibility of discovery. This was alleviated somewhat by a heavy downpour which Jung believed would eradicate any traces of the "crime" he had committed. His guilt, however, was not purged. Jung provided his own interpretation of the dream, which is worth noting:

> When I awoke from the dream, I turned it over in my mind, but was unable to understand it. I tried therefore to fall asleep again, but a voice within me said: "You *must* understand the dream, and must do so at once!" The inner urgency mounted until the terrible moment came when the voice said, "If you do not understand the dream, you must shoot yourself!" In the drawer of my night table lay a loaded revolver, and I became frightened. Then I began pondering once again, and suddenly the meaning of the dream dawned on me. "Why, that is the problem that is being played out in the world." Siegfried, I thought, represents what the Germans want to achieve, heroically to impose their will, have their own way. . . . I had wanted to do the same. But now that was no longer possible. The dream showed that the attitude embodied by Siegfried, the hero, no longer suited me. Therefore it had to be killed.[36]

Jung's interpretation of his Siegfried dream as recorded in this biography requires, however, some augmentation. The year 1913 was one of crisis for Jung. It was the year in which he broke with Freud, gave up his professorship at the University of Zurich, and toyed with the idea of suicide. David Rosen provides some of the "missing pieces":

> [O]n December 18, 1913, Jung went through a suicidal crisis and underwent what I would call "egocide." . . . Jung dreamed that he teamed up with a dark-skinned savage and they shot and killed Siegfried. . . . Jung tells that he was frightened because in the drawer of his night table lay a loaded revolver. Fortunately for him, and us, Jung committed egocide, not suicide. . . . Jung and his "primitive shadow" psychically murdered this negative side of Jung's ego-image and identity. Of course, Siegfried also sounds like Sigmund, which af-

firms that this is a killing of the heretofore dominant Freudian egoimage or Jung's *false self*.[37]

The interpretations offered by both Rosen and Stevens are convincing, but Jung's dream is also significant in another way. Siegfried had to be killed, yet the killing evoked a sense of revulsion in the killer. In the *Nibelungenlied* there can be little doubt that, apart from the relief, perhaps even enthusiasm shown by Hagen after committing the murder, there is, to be sure, little joy among anyone else over what has transpired (note, in particular, 991-992). Yet there is the unstated "understanding" on the part of the Burgundian royal family (and perhaps, in the wake of the killing, by figures such as Dietrich and Rüdiger) that it had to be done. Jung could no longer accept Freud's dogma, particularly with respect to the sexual complex, and his rejection of the idea of the collective unconscious. Worms, and the rest of the courtly world, would likewise have been hard pressed to tolerate further the unpredictability and (albeit naive) arrogance of Siegfried.

. . . . .

The contemporary literary scholar is hardly in a position to approach the *Nibelungenlied* and its major protagonists from a black-white viewpoint. Kriemhild will continue to have her detractors, but they will also concede that, even if transformed into a she-devil, she is not entirely to blame for the metamorphosis. Her defenders can hardly ignore the manner in which absolute adherence to her goal of revenge allows events to hurtle out of control. Siegfried will scarcely be seen at the turn of the third millennium as the apotheosis of a sun-god, a reflection of Baldr, or simply a decent, if naive, hero who makes some fatal errors of judgment. He has partaken of the Otherworld and the dragon's blood, and his inability to re-integrate himself fully into the mores and expectations of courtly society augurs ill for his own future as well as that of everyone else, particularly if his unpredictability and spontaneity are not kept in check.[38] He carries the seeds of chaos within him. He can be malicious, as when he unnecessarily chides Brünhild for having lost in Island, consciously or subconsciously demonstrating at the same time the pride he takes in having been the one to defeat her at her own game. His lack of foresight and his arrogance in retiring from Gunther's bedchamber with his "booty" prove the catalyst for his ultimate demise. Hagen will most assuredly avoid nowadays the unequivocal condemnation he suffered at the hands of the poet of the *Klage*. In the earlier part of this century he served in Germany either as a symbol of treachery—after World War I—while he was later depicted, during World War II, as the quintessence of bravery, loyalty, and honor. Gunther may continue to experience a "bad press" as a weak king in the medieval tradition, but he will also have his advocates who can point to his laudable (if fruitless) efforts to maintain stability in a highly precarious and finely-balanced world and who, when combat became inevitable, certainly gave an excellent account of himself from the perspective of the warrior ethics prevalent at the time. Much the same thing could be said of Etzel, as it could of Rüdiger, Dietrich, Gernot, and Giselher.

In short, they are all—whether prominently profiled or of a more secondary nature—figures which defy a black-white categorization.

If one were to select a key term from the vocabulary of analytical psychology which pertains to characters, actions, motifs, and even the major theme of the *Nibelungenlied,* then this could certainly be repression, on the part of Siegfried with respect to his "otherness," which so often results in arrogant, reckless behavior; on the part of Kriemhild, who refuses to recognize the true significance of her public quarrel with Brünhild before the minster and later "buries" the fact that without her (albeit inadvertent) assistance, Siegfried would hardly have met his death. It also applies to the reception of dreams in the *Nibelungenlied.* Kriemhild "forgets" her initial dream and acts against what she realized (in 17,4) to be in her own best interests; Siegfried pays no attention whatsoever to the two dreams Kriemhild has had on the night before the hunt. The Burgundians, including (initially) Hagen, repress Ute's dream in which all the birds of the land were dead. Having crossed the Danube, the vast majority of the Burgundian force appears to put behind it rather quickly the confirmation from Hagen that they will not return alive from the land of the Huns; other than Hagen and Volker, none of them show any visible reaction to the information passed on by Dietrich upon their arrival that Kriemhild continues to mourn for her murdered Siegfried. Etzel never appears to acknowledge the unrelenting grief expressed by Kriemhild for her first husband.[39] Both Etzel and Kriemhild—although the former is visibly shaken—remain inactive following Hagen's prophecy that their son Ortlieb does not appear long for this world (1918, 3-4). These are only some of the more poignant instances of repression within the work. But it is *not* apparent in the narrator/author of the epic, an individual who never falls into the trap of assuming a correlation between the "inner" and the "outer," but who is rather constantly aware, and reminds his audience of the fact, that "Sein" and "Schein" are not in accord with one another.

But what of the epic *Nibelungenlied* as a whole? In his own right the poet was—in thirteenth-century terms—a highly astute *Menschenkenner,* whose characters may well have mirrored actual historical personalities, but who certainly, in several instances, transcended the image of typical, fictionalized kings, queens, margraves, and vassals to become individualized personalities designed to impart the entire range of human emotions. Yet the *Nibelungenlied* does not give up conclusively any of its secrets with regard to authorial intentionality. It is left to the reader to decide. Certainly it may be contended that the "message" of 2378,4: "als ie diu liebe leide z'aller jungeste gît" (which harks back to Kriemhild's words in 17,3: "wie liebe mit leide ze jungest lônen kan," albeit in this earlier reference pertaining specifically to the relationship of women to men) constitutes the major thrust of the epic, a philosophical (and psychological) countering of the cyclical structures of courtly romances with their happy endings and emphasis on continuity. Perhaps it was intended

as a lesson for rulers, in specific or in general, that the reins of power must be grasped tightly, that kings must be kings in fact as well as in name. The antagonistic relationship between the feminine and the masculine is amply attested to throughout the work, whether in the wooing of Brünhild in Island (note Siegfried's biting remark to Brünhild in 474,la, 3: "Sô wol mich dirre mære . . . daz iemen lebet, der iuwer meister müge sîn"), the unacceptable idea that occurs to Siegfried during his wrestling match with Brünhild, that, should he lose, all women ("elliu wîp) would become arrogant ("tragen gelpfen muot") towards their spouses (673), or in the drastic reaction of both Etzel and Hildebrand (as well, we may assume, as Dietrich and any other warriors of stature who have not been killed in the preceding slaughter) to the death of a defenseless Hagen by the hand of a woman (2373ff.). Yet it does not culminate in any programmatic declaration of the "proper" place of the sexes within society. As we have witnessed from both the manuscript tradition as well as the appended *Klage,* Kriemhild was most assuredly not without her sympathizers in the thirteenth century.

Finally, we may also have in this anonymous author a cynic, even a nihilist, who was highly influenced by the tragic lays of the past and who (in contrast to the authors of the romances of the period) felt no need to temper the "message" of irrevocable fate through a vision of a better world to come. Even if we can believe that his audience of eight hundred years ago was intended to recognize the "model" comportment and virtuous bearing of those facing their doom—something which more modern audiences have, in fact, also done throughout the past two hundred years—this poet ultimately concentrated squarely on one particular archetype: the "shadow" side of man and his proclivity to destruction.

Notes

1. See, in particular, Rupert Sheldrake, *A New Science of Life. The Hypothesis of Formative Causation* (Los Angeles: Tarcher, 1981); The *Presence of the Past. Morphic Resonance and the Habits of Nature* (New York: Vintage, 1989); Willy Obrist, *Archetypen. Naturund Kulturwissenschaften bestätigen C. G. Jung* (Olten and Freiburg im Breisgau: Walter, 1990).

2. Note Paul R. Gross and Norman Levitt, *Higher Superstition* (Baltimore: The Johns Hopkins Press, 1994). I am grateful to my (scientist) colleague, Richard Falk, a humanist in his own right, for first having made me aware of this work and for the opportunity to discuss with him on numerous occasions the potential for true interdisciplinary work between the Sciences and the Humanities.

3. Nonetheless, the frequency with which the word "psychology" (or one of its cognates), as well as specific terms grained from that discipline are used in literary interpretations of medieval works is remarkable. As one example I cite the recent German translation of John Evert Härd's book, *Das Nibelungenlied. Wertung und Wirkung von der Romantik bis zur*

Gegenwart, trans. from the Swedish by Christine Palm (Tübingen and Basel: Francke, 1996): "Die archetypische Struktur der Sage von *Tristan und Isolde* . . ." (22); "Im *Nibelungenlied* ist die Intrige psychologischer Art . . ." (30); ". . . die schöne höfische Welt wird zerschlagen, indem die elementaren, destruktiven Triebe des Menschen losgelassen werden, das ist das Grundthema des *Nibelungenlieds* . . ." (35); "In der Schilderung von Kriemhilds Verhalten während dieser Begegnung [between her and Hagen prior to the fatal hunt] . . . liegt eine eigenartige Zweideutigkeit, eine psychologische Unwahrscheinlichkeit . . ." (43); ". . . ein psychologisch motiviertes Intrigenspiel" (83); "Es sind die psychologischen Bindungen zwischen den Menschen, die sich überschneidenden Loyalitäten, die nach Dilthey dem Werk seine Spannungstruktur geben . . ." (117); ". . . er ersetzt übernatürliche Erklärungen durch psychologische . . ." (119). Such examples could be augmented at will.

4. See John M. Ellis, *Against Deconstruction* (Princeton: Princeton University Press, 1989).

5. A noteworthy psychological contribution to the field of Nibelungen reception is to be found in Jean Shinoda Bolen's *Ring of Power. The Abandoned Child, The Authoritarian Father, and the Disempowered Feminine. A Jungian Understanding of Wagner's Ring Cycle* (San Francisco: Harper, 1993).

6. Walter Haug, "Montage und Individualität im *Nibelungenlied,*" in Fritz Peter Knapp, ed., *Nibelungenlied und Klage. Sage und Geschichte, Struktur und Gattung. Passauer Nibelungengespräche 1985* (Heidelberg: Winter, 1987) 279-293.

7. Although the movement away from an automatic assumption of a correspondence between the outer and the inner is incidental to her argument, Joyce Tally Lionarons has also intimated that such a split has occurred with respect to the figure of Brünhild in the *Nibelungenlied.* Note p. 167 above.

8. Haug 277, 281.

9. Winder McConnell, "Animus Possession in Kriemhild: A Medieval Insanity Plea?" *Journal of Evolutionary Psychology* 11.1-2 (1990): 22-33.

10. In this respect, I cannot concur with Jerold Frakes, whose 1994 work, *Brides and Doom,* a marxist-feminist approach to the *Nibelungenlied, Klage,* and *Kudrun,* completely avoids the possibility of any explanation for Kriemhild's behavior which is not rooted in the socio-political sphere. I do think that his criticism of the moral(istic) approach that has been taken by scholars (and, perhaps, the poets themselves) towards Kriemhild and other prominent females in the epics of the period is justified—albeit without the ad hominems which lead Frakes into the paradox of moralizing on moralizing— insofar as it points to a rather one-sided limiting of possibilities for interpretation of the figure's actions. However,

where scholars, attempting to view the plots from the perspective of thirteenth-century audiences, have agreed with the poets, narrators, and figures within the epics themselves who have labeled Kriemhild and Gerlind (in *Kudrun*) as *vâlandinnen,* they have not been incorrect (although Kriemhild most certainly had her admirers as well as detractors, as the *Klage,* and undoubtedly the scribe of ms. C, have so aptly demonstrated). They may simply have not gone far enough, namely, to have also considered the male protagonists as being just as responsible for the onset of chaos (once again with the obvious exception of the *Klage* poet). See Jerold C. Frakes, *Brides and Doom. Gender, Property, and Power in Medieval German Women's Epic* (Philadelphia: University of Pennsylvania Press, 1994).

11. Quotations from the *Nibelungenlied* are based on the edition by Karl Bartsch and Helmut de Boor, 21st revised ed. by Roswitha Wisniewski, Deutsche Klassiker des Mittelalters (Wiesbaden: Brockhaus, 1979).

12. Even the author of the *Klage,* who is otherwise ill-disposed towards Hagen and basically views him as responsible for the catastrophic events in which the *Nibelungenlied* culminates, attributes Siegfried's death to his arrogance. See *Diu Klage. Mit den Lesarten sämtlicher Handschriften,* ed. Karl Bartsch (1875; rpt. Darmstadt: Wissenschaftliche Buchgesellschaft, 1964), vv. 38-39: "unt daz er selbe den tôt / gewan von sîner übermuot."

13. Noteworthy here are Gottfried Weber's comments: "Dass Kriemhildens, der ursprünglichen und ungewandelten, Wesen Liebe ist, daß sich ihre weibliche Art ganz und gar erfüllen wird in dem *undertân*-Sein gegenüber dem Geliebten . . . was es überhaupt mit der Kriemhilden-Minne auf sich hat, erzählt der im Seelischen verhaltene und karge Dichter nirgends unmittelbar; das wenige, was er überhaupt sagt, gestattet vorerst kaum einen Einblick in die unbegrenzten Tiefen von Kriemhildens Liebesmöglichkeiten. . . . Worauf der Dichter hinzielt, ist gleichwohl überaus deutlich: es soll offenkundig werden, daß sich Kriemhilt nicht in sich, sondern nur in dem Manne ihrer Liebe erfüllt—in dem grenzenlosen Hingegebensein ihrer Seele an Sîvrit." See Gottfried Weber, *Das Nibelungenlied. Problem und Idee* (Stuttgart: Metzler, 1963) 5.

14. See the comments by Theodor Reik in his short article, "Kriemhilds Traum," *Zentralblatt für Psychoanalyse. Medizinische Monatsschrift für Seelenkunde* 2 (1912): 416-417: "Der Vogel als Penissymbol wird hier von der kundigen Ute bestätigt. . . . Es ist wahrscheinlich, dass sich in der reifen Jungfrau die Libido regt und verdrängt wird. . . . Der ungestillte Trieb schlägt in sadistische Tendenzen um. . . . [D]as Zerfleischen des Vogels zeigt sadistische Tendenzen und ist zugleich der Wunsch nach der höchsten Lust. Der Angstaffekt ist aus dem Bewusstsein, das die verbotenen Wünsche kontrolliert, leicht zu verstehen.

. . . Und am Schlusse bricht die angeborene und durch ungenügende Sexualbefriedigung verstärkte sadistische Komponente sich elementar Bahn." It might be noted at this point that the editor of the *Zentralblatt für Psychoanalyse* was Sigmund Freud and that one of the individuals listed under "Unter Mitwirkung von" was C. G. Jung.

15. Hagen appears to be disinclined to pay any attention to the dream that Ute has prior to the Burgundians' departure for the land of the Huns, but his "rejection" is possibly posturing for the benefit of the kings and may not necessarily reflect his true attitude towards what is, after all, one of the most common forms of prophecy in his time. He will certainly take very seriously the next prophecy, that offered by the water sprite prior to crossing the Danube.

16. Unless we wish to contend that Siegfried had already betrayed himself through having helped Gunther to procure Brünhild, instead of recognizing that he was the one destined to defeat her in the trials in Iceland and thus, in keeping with the rules of the game, should have been the one to wed her. The question may certainly be posed: would not Siegfried and Brünhild have constituted a much more suitable pair than Siegfried and Kriemhild? Even were we to ignore the Norse analogues (which may well have been known to the German scribe), a union between Brünhild and Siegfried would scarcely have led to the compromising situation in which the hero finds himself in the sixteenth *Âventiure*. Brünhild and Siegfried would have complemented each other in a way that could never be possible for Siegfried and Kriemhild.

17. One occasionally encounters the suggestion that Kriemhild subconsciously wished to "remove" Siegfried, assume his power and possession of his *hort*. Such an interpretation would be predicated upon an *a priori* desire on the part of the queen for absolute power, as well as possible resentment over Siegfried's rejection of the lands to which she was entitled upon marrying and the beating he gave her after her indiscretion before the minster. The text, however, offers no support for any interpretation that Kriemhild *consciously* contemplated such a move. Siegfried may even fit the pattern of the average medieval knight when it comes to wife-beating, but this arouses, at the most, fear within Kriemhild, not fury. Siegfried, whether as a symbol or as a person, is an integral part of Kriemhild's life. On a subconscious level, it might be contended that, in the wake of Siegfried's murder, she may attempt to find some sort of compensation in the *Nibelungenhort* with its *Wünschelrute* (note below), and the power it endows which, as Hagen fully realizes, could prove dangerous for Worms. Her daily lamenting in the land of the Huns would lead one to believe that the love she still held for Siegfried was as sincere as the remorse felt over his death and the fury directed at the perpetrators of the deed, undoubtedly intensified all the

more through the ever-present realization of her own part in the affair. Note, however, Härd's brief and intriguing allusion to possible ulterior motives on the part of Kriemhild: "Streng genommen wird Siegfried von ihr verraten, und geschieht das wirklich völlig unabsichtlich und ahnungslos?" (43).

18. Weber 24.

19. D. G. Mowatt and Hugh Sacker, *The Nibelungenlied. An Interpretative Commentary* (Toronto: University of Toronto Press, 1967) 92.

20. Mowatt/Sacker 92.

21. Mowatt/Sacker 71.

22. Scholars have always assumed that Brünhild was a virgin until bedded by Gunther following the wrestling match with Siegfried. The assumption makes perfectly good sense, as one would otherwise expect an earlier "deflowering" to have occurred (in Isenstein) only had a worthy suitor appeared before Siegfried/Gunther, in which case Brünhild would have already been married. Provided, then, that we may assume that Brünhild remained chaste while a sovereign in Island (i.e., that she was not given to using men for her own sexual gratification), Gunther would have had physical proof on the second wedding night of his wife's "purity" (and thus his "friend's integrity"). He would objectively *know* that Siegfried had not overstepped his bounds, at least in the sexual arena. That knowledge, however, will not necessarily compensate for the psychological realization (and frustration) that, were it not for Siegfried, he would conceivably never have been able to consummate his marriage to Brünhild. Unlike Gunther, Brünhild can never enjoy complete assurance that it was not, in fact, Siegfried who "deflowered" her, following a brief interlude subsequent to the taming episode, and the *timing* of his removal of her ring and belt, namely, *prior* to intercourse, could provide her (as it must later those in attendance during the quarrel before the minster) with symbolic evidence that it could only have been Siegfried, in the guise of Gunther, who bedded her. Siegfried, in his arrogance, may have deprived Brünhild of both objects as though they were "war booty," but for Brünhild (and everyone else, including Kriemhild) they are sexual trophies. In this sense, the *Nibelungenlied* differs radically from the *Volsunga saga*, in the thirty-second chapter of which Brynhild urges the death of Sigurd and his son in full cognizance of the fact that the hero had kept his vows and not violated her (having placed his sword between them in bed). From Brünhild's perspective, the realization that Siegfried was with her at all on her second wedding night, with all of the ramifications it holds for prior events in Island, can only have shattered forever any illusions she may have entertained of a correspondence between inner and outer reality.

23. Note Konrad von Megenberg, *Das Buch der Natur. Die erste Naturgeschichte in deutscher Sprache,* ed.

Franz Pfeiffer (1861; rpt. Hildesheim: Olms, 1962) 38 "Von den Zaichen ob ain fraw swanger sei oder niht": "daz ander zaichen ist, daz diu wünschelruot oben trucken ist an dem haupt und daz si die muoter vast seugt," and 399 "Von dem weizen Senif": "aber daz wilde [Kraut] pringt daz harmwazzer und erweckt die unkäusch, wan es sterkt den wünschelstab und daz würkt allermaist des krautes sâm."

24. C. G. Jung, in a reference to Kluge's *Etymologisches Wörterbuch,* has suggested that the original Indo-European root of the word *hort, *kuth,* is "possibly related to . . . 'cavity, female genitals'" (*Symbols of Transformation,* 2nd ed., Bollingen Series XX [Princeton: Princeton University Press, 1976] 364).

25. Marie-Louise von Franz, *Puer Aeternus. A Psychological Study of the Adult Struggle with the Paradise of Childhood,* 2nd ed. (Boston: Sigo, 1981) 1.

26. Note, in this regard, the article by C. Stephen Jaeger, "Mark and Tristan: The Love of Medieval Kings and their Courts," in Winder McConnell, ed., *in hôhem prîse. A Festschrift in Honor of Ernst S. Dick,* GAG 480 (Göppingen: Kümmerle, 1989) 183-197.

27. Theodore M. Andersson, "Why does Siegfried die?", in Stephen J. Kaplowitt, ed. *Germanic Studies in Honor of Otto Springer* (Pittsburgh: K & S Enterprises, 1978) 29-39.

28. See my article, "Inflation and the Gifted Child: The Case of Siegfried," *Journal of Evolutionary Psychology* 9 (1988; nos. 1/2): 127-140.

29. Jung, *Symbols of Transformation* 389.

30. Inflationary tendencies are, of course, by no means limited to the individual, as is demonstrated by the later allusion to the collective *übermuot* (1865,4a) of the Burgundians by declining to inform Etzel of the true state of affairs.

31. Ivo Frenzel, ed., *Friedrich Nietzsche. Werke in zwei Bänden,* based on the three-volume Hanser edition by Karl Schlechta (Munich: Hanser, 1967) 2: 70.

32. See Matthias Lexer, *Mittelhochdeutsches Handwörterbuch,* 3 vols. (1872; rpt. Stuttgart: Hirzel, 1974) 1: cols. 1261-1262. Hagen's remark in 993,4 is reminiscent of the biting comment made by Siegfried to Brünhild in 474,1-3 following his victory over her in Island.

33. Karl Bartsch, ed., *Diu Klage mit den Lesarten sämtlicher Handschriften* (1875; rpt. Darmstadt: Wissenschaftliche Buchgesellschaft, 1964) vv. 571-573.

34. The pattern-like quality of this lamenting underscored by Dietrich's reference to "alle morgen" makes it virtually inconceivable to believe that Etzel is not aware of his wife's state of mind. One has the impression, however, that Etzel is given to repressing the obvious, whether it is the state of Kriemhild's psyche, the significance of Volker's slaying of the garish Hun, the appearance of the Burgundians at his court in full armor, or even the biting comment by Hagen concerning Ortlieb's (lack of a) future. He is not alone in this respect. The Burgundians themselves, with the notable exception of Hagen, fail to read—or simply deny—any of the signs of their impending doom, demonstrate remarkable lack of intuition with regard to the motivations of their sister, and, even when informed by Hagen that they will not return from the land of the Huns, appear to repress this information as they continue on to Bechelaren and Gran. How else can one explain their obvious joy over the betrothal of Rüdiger's daughter to Giselher?

35. Carl Gustav Jung, *Memories, Dreams, Reflections,* recorded and edited by Aniela Jaffé, rev. ed., trans. Richard and Clara Winston (New York: Vintage Books, 1965) 180.

36. Jung 180.

37. David Rosen, *The Tao of Jung. The Way of Integrity* (Arkana: Penguin, 1997) 65-66. See also 4-5. Note as well Anthony Stevens, *Private Myths. Dreams and Dreaming* (Cambridge, MA: Harvard University Press, 1995) 124: ". . . Jung omits to say that it also represented what Freud wanted to achieve—heroically to impose *his* will, have *his* own way. And now *that* was no longer possible. In this dream, Jung is finally sacrificing Freud as his heroic role model and replacing him by a willingness to undertake his own descent into the underworld. . . . Siegfried was thus a complex figure in which were condensed (1) the heroic mentor, Freud; (2) the young sun-god, the aged sun-god's 'Son and Heir' and 'Crown Prince'; and (3) a transcendent symbol capable of reconciling the differences between the two men. His death meant that Jung had finally put all that behind him and committed himself to his *own* process, the discovery of his own psychological truth."

38. Something Gunther may well recognize and hence his hesitation to accede to Brünhild's request that her sister-in-law and her husband be invited to Worms, to which Gunther can offer only the lame reservation that Kriemhild and Siegfried live far away! Intriguingly, Siegfried offers the same excuse to Kriemhild, who is eager to take advantage of the invitation. Both men appear to "know" intuitively that it is best if these particular constellations are kept apart!

39. This was not lost, however, on Fritz Lang, whose portrayal of Etzel in his film, *Kriemhilds Rache,* was that of a ruler fully aware of the inability of his spouse to put the past behind her and to turn to the future.

FURTHER READING

Criticism

Bäuml, Franz H. "Transformations of the Heroine: From Epic Heard to Epic Read." *The Role of Woman in the*

Middle Ages, edited by Rosmarie Thee Morewedge, pp. 23-40. Albany: State University of New York Press, 1975.

Historical study that considers three different types of transmission for the *Nibelungenlied.*

————, and Eva-Marie Fallone. *A Concordance to the "Nibelungenlied" (Bartsch-De Borr Text).* Leeds: W. S. Maney and Son Ltd, 1976, 901p.

Includes index to structural patterns, a frequency ranking list, and a reverse index.

Bostock, J. K. "The Message of the *Nibelungenlied.*" *Modern Language Review* LV, No. 2 (April 1960): 200-12.

Proposal for what the contemporary audience may have understood as the author's purpose in writing the *Nibelungenlied.*

Capek, Michael J. "A Note on Oral Formulism in the *Nibelungenlied.*" *Modern Language Notes* 80, No. 4 (October 1965): 487-89.

Lines from the *Nibelungenlied* that suggest an oral tradition in its composition.

Ellis, Hilda R. "The Hoard of the Nibelungs." *Modern Language Review* XXXVII, No. 4 (October 1942): 466-79.

Discusses form in the traditional tale of the dragon and the treasure.

Fenik, Bernard. *Homer and the "Nibelungenlied:" Comparative Studies in Epic Style.* Cambridge, Mass.: Harvard University Press, 1986, 211p.

Study of the *Nibelungenlied*'s use of symmetry and parallelism.

Gillespie, G. T. "*Die Klage* as a Commentary on *Das Nibelungenlied.*" *Probleme Mittelhochdeutscher Erzählformen: Marburger Colloquium 1969,* pp. 153-177. Berlin: Erich Schmidt Verlag, 1972.

Examination of how the sequel to the *Nibelungenlied* interprets the tale in a Christian vein.

Haymes, Edward R. "Hagen the Hero." *Southern Folklore Quarterly* 43, No. 1-2 (1979): 149-55.

Analysis of how Hagen's heroism in the second half of the *Nibelungenlied* supports the idea that the story was in the process of development.

King, K. C. "The Message of the *Nibelungenlied*—A Reply." *Modern Language Review* LVII, No. 4 (October 1962): 541-50.

Poses objections to Bostock's article (see above.)

McConnell, Winder. "Marriage in the *Nibelungenlied* and *Kudrun.*" *Spectrum Medii Aevi: Essays in Early German Literature in Honor of George Fenwick Jones,* edited by William C. McDonald, pp. 299-320. Göppingen: Kümmerle Verlag, 1983.

Contrasts the weddings depicted in the *Nibelungenlied* and the *Kudrun.*

Mowatt, D. G. and Hugh Sacker. *The "Nibelungenlied:" An Interpretive Commentary.* Toronto: University of Toronto Press, 1967, 144p.

Study intended to advance understanding and stimulate discussion about the *Nibelungenlied.*

Renoir, Alain. "Levels of Meaning in the *Nibelungenlied*: Sifrit's Courtship." *Neuphilologische Mitteilungen* LXI, No. 4 (1960): 353-61.

Describes two distinct levels of interpretation of Sifrit and Kriemhilt's love relationship.

Sacker, Hugh. "The Message of the *Nibelungenlied,* and the Business of the Literary Critic." *Modern Language Review* LVIII, No. 2 (April (1963): 225-27.

Responds to Bostock and King (see above) and defends a textual analysis approach.

Salmon, P. B. "Why Does Hagen Die?" *German Life & Letters* XVII, No. 1 (October 1963): 3-13.

Analyzes the events that lead to the final scenes of the *Nibelungenlied.*

————. "The German-ness of the *Nibelungenlied.*" *New German Studies* 4, No. 1 (Spring 1976): 1-26.

Argues that the C-Text is the most refined text of the *Nibelungenlied.*

Thorp, Mary. *The Study of the "Nibelungenlied:" Being the History of the Study of the Epic and Legend from 1755 to 1937.* Oxford: Clarendon Press, 1940, 196p.

Study of the change in public and critical opinion of the *Nibelungenlied* since the thirteenth century.

Wailes, Stephen L. "Bedroom Comedy in the *Nibelungenlied.*" *Modern Language Quarterly* 32, No. 4 (December 1971): p. 365-76.

Analyzes the *Nibelungenlied*'s bedroom scenes and contends that the poet intended them to be comical.

Wakefield, Ray M. *Nibelungen Prosody.* The Hague: Mouton, 1976, 116p.

Study of different readings of the *Nibelungenlied,* focusing on rhythm patterns.

Additional coverage of the *Nibelungenlied* is contained in the following source published by the Gale Group: *Epics for Students.*

Lamentations
c. 587 B.C.-86 B.C.

(Also known as *How* and *Dirges*) Hebrew poems.

INTRODUCTION

Traditionally attributed to Jeremiah, *Lamentations* is a short book in the Old Testament section of the *Bible* consisting of five poems. Each poem comprises a chapter describing the common sorrow and suffering of the survivors of the devastation of Jerusalem after the Babylonian siege of 587 B.C. The Hebrew title of *Lamentations* translates as *How* and comes from the first word of the book—a groan. With its first four poems written in the form of alphabetic acrostics, *Lamentations*'s structure is elaborate and the exact significance of its pattern somewhat controversial. It is the first widely accepted work exhibiting the definite dirge meter. While placed with Writings rather than among the Prophets in the Jewish canon, in the Greek Septuagint and in most English translations of the *Bible* it is found immediately after the *Book of Jeremiah*. The three major sources for the text of *Lamentations* are the Hebrew text, the Septuagint, and the Peshitta. The Hebrew text is remarkably well-preserved and thus of great use to scholars for study of Hebrew meter. *Lamentations* is a classic work—some say a peerless example—in the expression of communal grief and its power and depth have been admired for many centuries.

PLOT AND MAJOR CHARACTERS

Lamentations changes over the course of its five poems. Initially it chronicles the aftermath of the fall of Jerusalem. The poet describes the once-great city that is now desolate. It is compared to a queen who has become a slave, crying bitter tears, feeling inconsolable grief, humiliated before her enemies. The second poem describes the human suffering and horrible living conditions closer to the time of the actual fall of the city—conditions that the poet asserts have never been endured by anyone before. Starving mothers eat their children and even walls lament. The pain goes as deep as the sea. Young and old alike have been slaughtered by the Lord, who is likened to an enemy. God has laid waste the land and pitilessly rejected all whom He once embraced. Blame is also allocated to prophets and oracles who did not perform their duties. The central poem is traditionally accepted as the most important, according to many experts, and it introduces some measure of hope. Although it continues to relate horrors, they are more general in nature. The poet finds reason for hope in the notion that God will not stay

angry at his chosen people forever. They admit their sins—an essential step to forgiveness. The fourth poem is similar to the second. It says that it would have been better to have died from the sword than to starve to death or resort to cannibalism of one's own children. Sin is declared the cause of Jerusalem's fall, particularly the sins of the priests and the prophets. The final poem lays out to God all the suffering His people have endured and implores Him to restore the nation of His anointed ones. The form of *Lamentations* is mixed and the speaking voice of the book changes in the course of the poems. Jerusalem addresses the Lord in the first chapter. In the second the poet himself speaks, but again Jerusalem delivers the words near the end of the poem. The course of the third poem shifts from "I" to "we," but the identity of the "I" has been interpreted variously by different scholars. William F. Lanahan contends that it is in the voice of the defeated soldier, and that chapter four reflects the voice of the bourgeoisie. The final poem is communa—the survivors of Jerusalem's ruin praying to God for relief from their torments.

MAJOR THEMES

The major theme of *Lamentations* is the suffering and starvation following the capture of Jerusalem and the principal question this raises, Why has this happened? Were the Babylonians used as an instrument of the Lord? Did God's destruction of the city break his covenant with the Jewish people? Was God punishing them for their sins, with the purpose of their eventual rehabilitation? Or has He forsaken them utterly? Should they no longer have faith in the Lord? Nothing so severe had ever happened to Israel before and survivors desperately try to make sense of their situation. The poet answers that sin was the cause of the decimation. The particular sins are not adequately enumerated, but they clearly must have been serious, for Zion admits that it deserves what it has received.

CRITICAL RECEPTION

As with all books comprising the *Bible,* a prodigious amount of scholarship has been devoted to all aspects of *Lamentations.* Contentious disagreements among scholars are common in all areas of research concerning these poems. One avenue of study concerns its theological message. Some scholars argue there is one and only one, others argue that there are many interpretations that work on different levels, while yet others say there is no theological message at all. Another area of interest is the importance of the book's alphabetical composition; many scholars believe that far from being just a display of poetic virtuosity, the acrostics emphasize the completeness of the treatment rendered in the poems. Among other major interests of biblical scholars studying *Lamentations* are its authorship, its date of creation, and its structure. There is extreme disagreement regarding the unity of *Lamentations,* not only whether Jeremiah was the author but whether only one person was responsible for the poems. Theodore H. Robinson, for example, states that "internal evidence makes it practically certain that they are not all the work of a single author." Some scholars assert that *Lamentations* is in Jeremiah's style and William Walter Cannon has furnished dozens of parallel phrases and concerns in *Jeremiah.* Other scholars insist that these parallels are insignificant, that the differences are more important, and that "Jeremiah is out of the question as author of the songs," as Georg Fohrer puts it. Many different compositional arrangements have been proposed, with some scholars assigning certain chapters to one author, other chapters to someone else. The majority view of scholars is that the book—or at least the first four chapters—was absolutely written almost contemporaneously with the fall of Jerusalem by an eyewitness or eyewitnesses; the minority vociferously insist that the book was composed over a period spanning up to some four hundred years. Samuel Tobias Lachs, to use the most extreme example, lays out a case that the fifth poem is from the second century B.C. While many scholars view the final chapter as clearly different from the preceding four, others, notably William H. Shea, maintain that the fifth poem is vital to the overall structure of *Lamentations.* Such controversies continue to be argued both seriously and passionately.*Lamentations* is highly praised for its literary and poetic merits. Lanahan, for example, credits the poet's "manifold creative insight" in using multiple personae in the speaking voice. The most common criticism of the work is that its creator may have occasionally subsumed his message in order to fit it into the acrostic structure; this criticism is vigorously challenged by many other critics. Scholars have made advances in grammatical analysis in modern times concerning the text itself, yielding more accurate readings of certain passages: Marvin H. Pope has rendered a highly praised version of the last three verses of the fifth chapter of *Lamentations,* and Mitchell Dahood has made remarkable improvements to specific lines that he believes were compromised by spelling mistakes in source texts.

PRINCIPAL WORKS

Principal English Translations

"Song of Songs" and "Lamentations": A Commentary and Translation (translated by Robert Gordis) (poems) 1974

Lamentations (translated by Iain W. Provan) (poems) 1991

Lamentations: A New Translation with Introduction and Commentary (translated by Delbert R. Hillers) (poems) 1992

"Jonah" & "Lamentations" (translated by Robert B. Salters) (poems) 1994

The Book of Lamentations (translated by Rosario Castellanos and Esther Allen) (poems) 1998

"Eichah"/"Lamentations": A New Translation with a Commentary Anthologized from Talmudic, Midrashic, and Rabbinic Sources (translated by Meir Zlotowitz) (poems) 1999

CRITICISM

Theodore H. Robinson (essay date 1947)

SOURCE: *"Lamentations,"* in *The Poetry of the Old Testament,* Duckworth, 1947, pp. 205-16.

[*In the following excerpt, Robinson discusses the general characteristics of the verses in* Lamentations, *their varying levels of emotional intensity, and their probable order of composition.*]

We have already seen something of what a "dirge" meant in the ancient world. Originally, no doubt, a funeral spell intended to keep the dead in his place and prevent him from annoying the living, it gradually developed into a genuine expression of the grief felt by survivors at the loss of one whom they loved. We may suppose that there were traditional and conventional formulae which would serve both purposes, and we gather from such a passage as Jer. 9:17 ff. that there was a recognized profession, composed of women, who went through a regular course of training in their work. They had to know the right words which would both allay the spirit of the dead and excite the tears of the living. Authorship of these dirges, however, was not necessarily confined to the professional women, and in II Chron. 35:25 we have a statement to the effect that Jeremiah composed a dirge over Josiah, together with a reference to a book of dirges.

It is, perhaps, this note which has given rise to the tradition that Jeremiah was the actual author of our present **Book of Lamentations** or "Dirges." It is beyond dispute that they, or some of them, are worthy of his poetic genius, and the book which bears his name attests the fact that he could and did compose works of this kind, cf. Jer. 9:19, 21. These, however, are very brief, comparable to the dirge of Amos over the fallen virgin of Israel (Am. 5:2), and are very different from the long and rather elaborate poems preserved in **Lamentations.** Occasionally, too, we have suggestions of a point of view which we can hardly associate with Jeremiah. When, for example, the poet in Lam. 5:7 lays the blame for Judah's disasters on an earlier generation, he is directly contradicting the principle which Jeremiah laid down in Jer. 31:29-30, where the prophet insists that the sinner alone must suffer for his wrongdoing—a doctrine to be more fully developed by Ezekiel. Again, Lam. 4:20 clearly refers to the ruined and captured king, and we can hardly imagine Jeremiah speaking of Zedekiah thus:

> "The breath of our nostrils, the anointed of the Lord,
>   Was taken in their pits,
>   Of whom we said, under his shadow
>   We shall live among the nations."

But while we may find it impossible to accept the tradidition which ascribes the book to Jeremiah, there is abundant reason for assigning it, or part of it, to the age in which he lived, and to use it as a historical document illustrating the calamity which he had foreseen for forty years before it fell.

For the book is not a unity; it does not pretend to be. It is a collection of five poems, four of them dirges in the strict sense, and the fifth a Psalm such as Israel's poets often uttered in times of distress. Each has its own literary characteristics, and internal evidence makes it practically certain that they are not all the work of a single author. They are not of equal literary merit, and they vary a good deal in the intensity of their feeling. While the first four, at any rate, may reasonably be referred to the siege of Jerusalem by Nebuchadrezzar, to the fall of the city and to its consequent desolation, we get the impression that some are nearer than others to actual disasters which they describe.

Chs. 1-4 are acrostic poems, though no two of them are exactly alike in their construction. In chs. 1, 2 and 4, the poet has assigned a stanza to each letter, but it occurs only at the head of the first line in the stanza. In ch. 3, as in Ps. 119, the poem falls into groups of three lines each, one group to every letter, and each line of the group begins with the proper letter. At the same time, the groups are not stanzas in the same sense as they are in 1, 2 and 4, since it is possible for the sense to be continued from one group to another, and the first line of a letter-group may be more closely associated with what precedes than with what follows. The verse-division in the English versions reflects this difference, for in chs. 1, 2 and 4 each letter-group is counted as a single verse, while in ch. 3 every line stands by itself. Thus chs. 1, 2 and 3 have the same number of lines, though the first two have only 22 verses while the third has 66.

Looking at these external characteristics we note that the four poems take the following forms:

Ch. 1 is an acrostic poem in which a stanza of three lines begins with its appropriate letter. The order of the alphabet is that which is now universally adopted, and goes back to ancient times.

Ch. 2 is also an acrostic poem in which a stanza of three lines begins with its appropriate letter, but the order of the alphabet differs slightly from the normal, since the letter . . . Pe, usually the seventeenth, comes before . . . Ayin, usually the sixteenth (the common arrangement may be seen in those Bibles which print the Hebrew letters at the head of each stanza in Ps. 119).

Ch. 3 is an acrostic in which three lines all begin with the same letter. Here, as in ch. 2, the usual order of . . .[Ayin, Pe] is reversed.

Ch. 4 is an acrostic in which a stanza of two lines is assigned to each letter. Otherwise it resembles ch. 2.

The metre in all these is that which seems most appropriate to the dirge, i.e., 3 : 2 varied occasionally with 2 : 2. It was, in fact, in this book that a definite metre, of the kind now generally admitted first attained wide acceptance, and though earlier students recognized only the 3 : 2 (a theory which led to some curious results), it received the name of Qinah, or "dirge," metre. It was not till long afterwards that it was noticed in other poems which could not possibly be classed as "dirges," e.g., in Ps. 23.

The first poem gives us a picture of the desolation of Jerusalem and of her people. It opens with the characteristic Hebrew groan—How! It is not a question, it is an exclamation of suffering, and stands outside the metrical scheme of the verse. This "anacrusis" is not infrequently used by the Hebrew poets to give emotional emphasis to what follows. The first line gives the key to the whole poem; the city that was once so great and beautiful, the place that once stood so high in the esteem of the peoples, has now fallen to the depths. Once populous, now she is lonely, for her inhabitants are gone. She had been powerful, now she is no more than a widow. She had been the mistress of others, and now she herself has to submit to forced labour, like any subject tribe. As we read we see more and more of the desolation. The land about her is deserted, for its people have been carried away captive, and her own inhabitants too have gone with them. She can find neither comfort nor sympathy from those about her; they mock at her and glory in her fall. The poet owns that her troubles are a just punishment for her sins, and in them he sees the hand of Yahweh at work. He cannot imagine that Yahweh is helpless, but He has not even protected His own sanctuary. Priests and elders, the chiefs in Church and State, are alike helpless, and perish of starvation. Yahweh, whom she has offended, is her only hope, and to Him she appeals for aid and restoration.

As we read this deeply moving expression of sorrow, we are struck by the fact that there is little or no reference to the actual horrors of siege and sack. It is the result of the fall of the city, not the terrible event itself, which fills the poet's mind. We shall realize this more fully when we come to glance at some of the other poems, and it has an important bearing on the date of the poem. It goes without saying that it must be placed earlier than any attempt to restore Jerusalem, and comes, therefore, from the time of the exile. But it is not to be placed near the beginning of that period. The first keen anguish has died away, and left a dull aching sorrow. Though there may never have been elsewhere pain like the pain of Jerusalem, it is no new thing; the wound is far from freshly inflicted. We might almost say that she was growing accustomed to her desolation, and it is a condition rather than a disastrous event which gives rise to the poet's utterance. In spite of the somewhat artificial flavour which an acrostic inevitably produces, the language has a solemn beauty, and whether we will or no we are carried back into the actual circumstances which called the dirge forth. The poem stands high among the world's lyrics of sorrow.

Ch. 2 may well be thought to stand even higher. In form, as we have seen, it closely resembles ch. 1, differing only in the places taken by two letters of the alphabet. Like the first poem, the second is a cry of woe and desolation, but it is much nearer to the actual disaster. The poet still remembers keenly incidents of the siege, the famine which destroyed more people than the weapons of the enemy, the corpses lying about the streets, the slaughter even of sacred persons, the cannibalism of mothers driven mad by hunger. It is not so much the desolation which followed on the sack of Jerusalem as the fearful details of the siege and capture which have impressed themselves upon him. In other ways the general atmosphere is much the same as in ch. 1; we observe here also the heart-rending contrast between the glorious past and the ghastly present, the exultant mockery of jealous and hostile neighbours. An interesting feature of the poet's thought is the way in which he sees the hand of Yahweh in all that has happened. Take v. 17 for example:

"Yahweh hath done that which he had devised;
   He hath fulfilled his word;
As he had commanded in days of old,
   He hath cast down, pitiless;
And he hath caused the enemy to rejoice over
                                                    thee,
   He hath set up the horn of thine adversaries."

Or again in v. 21, where Yahweh is directly addressed:

"They lie on the ground in the streets—
   Young and old;
My virgins and my young men
   Are fallen by the sword;
Thou hast slain in the day of thine anger,
   Thou hast slaughtered, hast not pitied."

Even Yahweh's sanctuary has not been spared:

"And he hath done violence to his tabernacle as it were a
         garden,
      He hath destroyed his place of assembly;
Yahweh hath caused to be forgotten in Zion
      Solemn assembly and sabbath,
And hath despised in the indignation of his anger
         King and priest."
                                          (v. 6).

Truly "Yahweh has become as an enemy" (v. 5). It is rather striking that, in these circumstances, there is little or no reference to the sins, either of the fathers or of the generation which actually suffered the horrors which the poet

had seen. There can be no doubt that he had seen them; his feeling is too keen to let us think that he was relying on tradition or on hearsay. What is more, they were comparatively fresh in his memory. There is a great difference between the emotional tone of this chapter and that of ch. 1. Both are steeped in pain, but here the poignant agony of grief has not yet settled down into the ache of sorrow. We must place this poem very near the beginning of the exilic period.

When we reach ch. 3 we are conscious at once of being in an entirely different atmosphere. The metre is still that of the Qinah, but this by no means compels us to regard the poem as a dirge. The use of the acrostic letter at the beginning of each of the three lines assigned to it gives an artificial air to the whole. The gloom is far from being so intense as it was in the first two chapters. Vv. 25-27, for example, all begin with the word "good." This may be due in part to the demands of the acrostic, for comparatively few Hebrew words start with . . .[that] letter, and acrostic writers often have to fall back on ". . .the common Hebrew word for "good." But we have other signs of a more hopeful attitude than appears in other chapters. It seems clear that the poet either has found, or expects to find in the near future, release from his troubles and vengeance on his enemies. There is, too, a certain lack of detail, a vagueness in speaking of the distress into which the poet has fallen, which contrasts very strongly with the wealth of detail offered us by other poems in the book. Occasionally we get hints of quotation from other writings; the opening words of v. 28 suggest an acquaintance with 1:1. It is surely not too fanciful to see in v. 30 a reminiscence of Is. 50:6. We naturally recall Jer. 9:1 on reading v. 48, and with vv. 12-13 we may compare Job 6:4, 16:12. The fact is that this poem is not a "dirge" at all, even in the somewhat wide sense which allows the term to include laments over cities and communities as well as over individuals. It belongs to the same class as a number of the Psalms, especially to those which cry out for deliverance from the threats of an enemy. There is confession of sin in v. 42, though the precise type of offence is not specified. The whole would be very suitable for use on some fast day, proclaimed as a result of national disaster in order to recover the favour of Yahweh and so win deliverance and triumph.

The date of this poem is not easy to determine. The passages which remind us of other writings are never direct quotations, though their language gives us good ground for supposing that this poet was acquainted with them. It is difficult to associate the piece with the fall of Jerusalem at all, and, as we have seen, we have to admit the possibility that it is even later than the book of Job. That would probably carry it down to a point rather late in the fourth century B.C. At the same time the parallels may be accidental, however unlikely this may seem at first sight, and in that case the poem may be earlier.

With ch. 4 we are back once more in the atmosphere of 586 B.C. The poem differs from ch. 2 mainly in having a two-line instead of a three-line stanza, but in other respects the two are closely similar and may be the work of the same poet. There is, perhaps, a tendency to dwell rather more on the horrors of the siege, and especially on the reaction of the women and children. The pitiful condition of these little ones appealed to the poet strongly. He has seen them suffering the agonies of thirst, perishing of hunger, and calling for the food which none can give. Little babies cry out at their mothers' dry breasts, and older children appeal in vain to their fathers for bread. Still more horrible is the cannibalism to which the starving women were reduced, slaughtering, cooking and eating even their own offspring. Incidentally it may be noted that Josephus records similar occurrences during the final siege of Jerusalem in A.D. 70. The poet feels strongly, too, the contrast between what was and what is. In former times the city had been rich in many ways, some had lived in real luxury, and, still more, her people had been beautiful and strong. Now all was changed:

> "They that did feed delicately
>   Are desolate in the streets:
> They that were brought up in scarlet
>   Embrace dunghills."
>
>   (v. 5.)

> "Their visage is blacker than coal;
>   They are not known" (i.e. not recognisable)
> "in the streets:
>   Their skin cleaveth to their bone;
>   It is withered, it is become as a stick."
>
>   (v. 8.)

In vv. 18-20 we live again through the actual fall of the city. The enemy is already through the walls, and, sword in hand, hunts down the wretched inhabitants, chasing them through the streets. The king, as we hear elsewhere, made his way out of the city and fled towards Jordan. The language of the poet suggests that he was among the small group who got away with Zedekiah, for he speaks as if the pursuit had been swift behind himself. He seems, too, to have been a faithful attendant on his royal master, for the climax of the disaster is reached when the enemy overtakes and captures the "breath of our nostrils, the anointed of Yahweh."

While the leading *motif* is the actual suffering, there is room for some reflection, and the poet realises that the punishment now fallen on Jerusalem is due to sin. But it is especially the sin of those who should have led the people to righteousness, the prophets and the priests (v. 13), which is responsible, for they "have shed the blood of the just in the midst of her." A study of the utterances delivered by Jeremiah will bear out this point of view, and will help to reinforce the strong impression, which we get from all sides of the matter, that this poem is the work of one who had lived through the great catastrophe and was writing while its details were still fresh in his mind.

Ch. 5 stands apart from the other four in several ways. Its metre is 3 : 3, not that of the Qinah, and it is not an acros-tic poem. It does, however, contain 22 verses, the right number for an acrostic. Perhaps a writer of such pieces wrote his poem first as it came into his mind, and then went over it again, substituting for the first word in each verse one which began with the appropriate letter. The chapter may, then, have been written for acrostic treatment and been left incomplete, i.e., without the final process.

In general character it is nearer to ch. 3 than to any of the others. It is a picture of desolation and distress, of a people worn by famine and groaning under the yoke. Once only is there reference to the plight of the city itself, and that is couched in quite general terms—Zion is desolate and wild animals wander over the ruined site. But we hear nothing of the process by which this came about, no word of siege or slaughter at the hands of an enemy. The nearest thing is the treatment of the women described in v. 11. There is nothing which speaks directly of exile, though some of the language might well have been used by Jewish captives in Mesopotamia. The old social and political order has broken up, and those who once had been the most prominent among the people have either disappeared or been reduced to degrading labour. There is constant danger from violence, but it does not seem to be the more or less organized persecution of a tyrannous conqueror, but rather that which arises from the presence of marauding and thievish bands.

In a word, the conditions are those which we know to have prevailed in the later period of the exile, and, to some extent, after the first return to Palestine. There may have been other ages in the post-exilic history to which the poem might be referred, but, in so far as we have details, there is none that fits it better than the latter part of the sixth century.

We may sum up. *Lamentations* consists of five poems, of varying authorship and of different dates. The only thing they have in common is that they are poems written in deep distress, though this is far more intense in some cases than in others. All may, and some must, be assigned to the period of the exile, and all appear to have been written in Palestine. Two of them, chs. 2 and 4, are very early in the period, and come from a time immediately after the fatal siege of Jerusalem. They may even be the work of the same writer, for both shew a superlative degree of poetic excellence. A little behind these two, both in time and in quality, comes ch. 1, whose date may be roughly between 570 and 560. B.C. Finally, not earlier than the end of the exilic period, we have ch. 5, and, possibly, ch. 3, though this, if any, is likely to be later than the return from the exile. It is noticeable, too, that these two poems fall some way below the high artistic standard reached by the rest—again we feel that ch. 3 stands even after ch. 5. This does not mean that these two pieces are on a low level as compared with work of similar tone, either in Hebrew or in other literature. They are well up to the average, and the book, small as it is, remains the classic example of literary beauty rising out of the deepest suffering.

Norman K. Gottwald (essay date 1962)

SOURCE: "The Theology of Doom" and "The Theology of Hope," in *Studies in the "Book of Lamentations,"* SCM Press Ltd, 1962, pp. 63-111.

[*In the following excerpt, Gottwald argues that* Lamentations *stresses the unique nature of the fall of Jerusalem and Israel's sins in order to convince its audience that the destruction must have been the will of God and that, in the face of discouraging external conditions, hope of renewal can nevertheless be found.*]

The fall of Jerusalem was a clarion call to the entire rethinking of Hebrew religion. In the truest sense this historic crisis was unparalleled in all Israel's history. At no time in the four hundred years of the monarchy, with the exception of the campaign of Shishak (*c.* 935), had the sacred city of Jerusalem been captured, much less destroyed, nor had the theocracy been interrupted. Now the sombre announcements of the prophets had come to pass. To the exile of king and leaders and the destruction of the city were added famine and slaughter. To an historical faith this catastrophe could well have been fatal. A survey of exilic literature, wherein is embodied the responses of Israel to the crucible of national calamity, makes it abundantly clear that Lamentations is far from being a case of literary exaggeration or warped hypochondria.[1]

One of the first to observe the grand scale of the tragedy lamented in our book was Bishop Lowth who said:

> Grief is generally abject and humble, less apt to assimilate with the sublime; but when it becomes excessive, and predominates in the mind, it rises to a bolder tone, and becomes heated to fury and madness. We have a fine example of this from the hand of Jeremiah when he exaggerates the miseries of Zion.[2]

Wiesmann, noting the same fact, remarked: 'The sensual nature comes into its own, indeed appears in its complete weakness: the travails of suffering find full expression, according to Oriental manner, with a certain extravagance.'[3] This 'fury and madness', this 'extravagance' of emotion is noticeable to any alert reader. It need not be contested that this is the customary temper of the Semite, but the grief of *Lamentations* had the deeper significance that from the Hebrew point of view it laments a supreme historical and, therefore, religious catastrophe.

Nearly every strophe of the ***Book of Lamentations*** could be cited in proof of the magnitude and severity of the misfortune. In particular the cumulative effect of the strophes in which Yahweh is pictured as chastening his people is overwhelming (1.13-15; 2.1-8; 3.1-19). The purpose of this unrelenting heaping up of misery is to stress the unique nature of the catastrophe, the worst feature being Israel's apparent alienation from God (2.1, 6-7; 3.17, 18, 31, 33, 49, 50; 5.20, 22).

In several passages the uniqueness of the suffering inflicted is actually stated and underlined. To the passers-by the daughter of Zion importunately appeals:

> Is it nothing to you, all you who pass by? Behold and consider
> If there is any pain like my pain, which was dealt to me,
> Which Yahweh inflicted in the day of his fierce anger.

(1.12)

This outcry is intended as more than dramatics, although its rhetorical form cannot be denied. Here is a plea for the casual traveller to pause and consider if he has ever beheld such suffering. Perhaps on the grounds of dispassionate reflection alone, forgetting for the moment that it is the despised Zion that suffers, he may have mercy. It is easy to see why Christians have applied this awesome exclamation to the crucifixion of Jesus, for it has a solitariness and anguish akin to that devastating question, 'My God, my God, why hast thou forsaken me?' There is the same piercing quality of irremediable desolation expressed in it.

In the second poem the pivotal strophe is that which follows the withering catalogue of Yahweh's destructive acts:

> How shall I uphold you, with what shall I compare you, O
>   daughter of Jerusalem?
> To what shall I liken you, and how comfort you, virgin
>   daughter of Zion?
> For great as the sea is your ruin; who can heal you?

(2.13)

Here the setting has become almost cosmic. Neither heaven nor earth can adduce an analogy to the magnitude of Zion's ruin. It is plainly incalculable. Only the vast, mysterious, and chaotic depths of the sea offer any point of comparison with the extent of Jerusalem's destruction. In the wake of this sweeping pronouncement we are appropriately introduced to the various groups who are inadequate for the comfort and healing of Judah. Neither prophets (2.14), nor the passers-by (2.15), nor the enemy (2.16) are capable of assuaging her wounds. As a matter of fact, like salt rubbed in an open sore, they only intensify the suffering. Failing all human help, the poet urgently summons Zion:

> Cry aloud to the Lord! . . .
> Arise, cry out in the night! . . .
> Lift up your hands to him! . . .

(2.18*a*, 19*ae*)

The nadir of Jerusalem's despair has been reached, and the sun of faith begins its circle toward the zenith. Disabused of all illusions, Zion knows that all her trust in earthly deliverance, whether in prophet or king or foreign aid, is ineffectual. The picture of inconsolability in 2.13 is indeed one of the most moving expressions of grief and ruin in all literature and yet it only serves to intensify the need for turning to the Lord. Precisely as in Job, Lamentations gives not the slightest trace of a leaning toward atheism or agnosticism.

Our final example leads logically to the theme of sin but deserves to be discussed in the present context because it boldly links unparalleled suffering with unparalleled sin.

> The iniquity of the daughter of my people is greater than the
> sin of Sodom;
> She was overthrown in a moment and no hands were laid upon
> her.
>
>   (4.6)

The shock of this sort of comparison is apparent. Our poet says in effect: 'Yes, there was one cataclysm which can be compared to Jerusalem's ruin, but, terrible as it was, the fall of Sodom and Gomorrah pales beside the present disaster!'

From the eighth-century prophets onwards, the celebrated Cities of the Plain, Sodom and Gomorrah (cf. Admah and Zeboiim, Gen. 10.19; 14.28), made famous by the vivid J story of Gen. 19, became proverbial for the divine judgment, particularly with respect to its suddenness, its violence and its finality.[4] It is noteworthy that in all the pre-exilic passages Sodom and its sister cities are the stock terms for divine judgment on sin. They serve as the norm for punishment, inasmuch as these cities suffered the most terrible punishment ever meted out. In each of the above references the sins of Israel (or the foreign lands) are considered to be perilously like the sins of the wicked cities of antiquity. But in all these cases Sodom and Gomorrah remain the standard which the other judgments approximate or equal. Only in exilic times do we find the sin of the nation *exceeding* that of the legendary cities! The only analogy to the Lamentations passage is in the address to the harlot Jerusalem by Ezekiel, who writes at precisely the same historical juncture:

> And your elder sister in Samaria, who lived with her daughters to the north of you; and your younger sister, who lived to the south of you, is Sodom with her daughters. Yet you were not content to walk in their ways, or do according to their abominations; within a very little time you were more corrupt than they in all your ways. As I live, says the Lord God, your sister Sodom and her daughters have not done as you and your daughters have done. (16.46-48)

The special import of the **Lamentations** reference is that it reasons from the punishment to the sin in keeping with the most unerring Deuteronomic faith. In what respect was Zion's punishment greater than Sodom's? The latter fell by a divine holocaust from heaven which was presumably instantaneous and relatively painless for the inhabitants. 'No hands were laid upon her', but hands *have* been laid upon Jerusalem—the coarse, plundering, destructive hands of the enemy (cf. 1.7, 10, 14; 2.7; 5.8). So the fitness of the ancient Cities of the Plain as an analogy to the Fall of Jerusalem is rejected as inadequate. The earlier statements of unparalleled suffering (1.12; 2.13) are emphatically confirmed. A symbol long honoured as the epitome of divinely inflicted punishment is shattered and cast aside. The ruin of Jerusalem, **Lamentations** insists, defies all categorizing and comparison; it is *sui generis*.[5]

What has brought on the doom? The confession of sin, not once or twice but repeatedly, not perfunctorily or incidentally but earnestly and fundamentally, suggests the reason for the calamity. All five of the poems which comprise the **Book of Lamentations** witness to the prophetic concept of sin and thus form one link in the long chain of evidence bearing out the importance of **Lamentations** as a justification and preservation of the teaching of the prophets. Even chapter two, conspicuous in its accusations of the deity, has an awareness of sin. The prophets are at fault because they did not expose the national guilt in order to prevent captivity (2.14). All the frightful judgments might have been averted had the trusted leaders been faithful to their calling and had the sinful people heeded their warning.

The statements of guilt and responsibility for sin are presented in different ways. Sometimes they are found in the poet's description of the city (1.5d, 8a, 9a; 4.6, 13ab), sometimes in direct address to the city (2.4ad; 4.22ab), and then again they appear as confessions on the lips of the city or nation (1.14, 18ab, 22cd; 3.42; 5.7, 16). The admission of sin by the offender is an absolute necessity if forgiveness is desired. Prov. 28.13, 'He who hides his sins shall not prosper, but he who confesses and forsakes them, shall have mercy,' is a good summary of the Biblical ethos concerning the effectiveness of confessional prayer. In the next chapter we shall explore the character of the repentance which is implied in the very act of acknowledging sin.

With one possible exception the sin is manfully shouldered by the contemporary generation. In 5.7 we read: 'Our fathers sinned and are not; we bear their guilt.' It may be that the 'fathers' are not those of the preceding generations but rather the leaders or eminent among the Jews. In other words, it may be said of the former leaders who are now in captivity that they 'are not', i.e. so far as the Jerusalem community is concerned they have ceased to exist. There is evidence for the usage of . . . '*ābh*, 'father', with respect to rulers, priests, prophets, noblemen (cf. Gen. 45.8; Judg. 17.10; 18.19; I Sam. 24.11; II Kings 2.12; 3.13; 6.21; 13.14; II Chron. 2.12). But even if it is to be referred more naturally to the ancestors, it is not a categorical shifting of responsibility because in the same poem the people aver: 'The crown has fallen from our head; woe to us, for we have sinned!' (5.16). From the Hebrew point of view there is no incompatibility in the entertaining of these two ideas, as indeed the case of Jeremiah so clearly confirms (cf. Jer. 14.20 and 16.10-13). In fact it was the attempted reconciliation of these two elements of Hebrew experience that was to beome one of the major endeavours of Judaism.[6]

First we note that the sin is the equal of the suffering. The sin which has invoked Jerusalem's downfall is more heinous than the coarse sensuality of Sodom and Gomorrah

(4.6). Twice the infinitive absolute is used to reinforce the seriousness of the sin (1.8a, 20d). Her sin has been so blatant that the nations mock and desert her (1.5, 8). Her sharp reversal of fortune was solely because of her sin (1.9). The burden of iniquity was so great when placed on the back of the daughter of Zion that she was crushed to the ground (1.14). Her rebellion was so flagrant that Yahweh was unable to forgive (3.42). The evil of Zion and her people was as foul as leprosy (4.13-15). There can be no mistake about the sincerity of the closing summation:

> The crown has fallen from our head; woe to us, for we have
> sinned!
> Because of this our heart is faint, because of these our eyes are
> darkened.
>
> (5.16,17)

As to the specific sins which constitute the great iniquity of Judah, we are surprised that more detail is not given. It may be that the incisive teaching of the prophets, contained in the denunciatory oracles of Amos, Hosea, Isaiah, and Jeremiah, is here presupposed as the content of the disobedience. Or this may be a deliberate omission expressive of the poet's conviction that the sin of Judah was much more serious and deep-rooted than the combination of many overt acts. This would continue the interpretation of Jeremiah, who internalized and radicalized sin to the extent that it could no longer be thought of as simply the violation of commandments imposed from without (cf. esp. 4.14; 13.23; 17.9, 10; 31.33-35). Also, it is not typical for the lament genre to confess sin. Laments in the Psalter that are true confessions are rare (e.g., 51; 130).

The one sin that is specified in **Lamentations** is the irresponsible leadership of the priests and prophets who were remiss in two respects. On the one hand, they were guilty of dereliction of duty in that they delighted in frothy visions of peace and prosperity and failed to warn Judah of her sin and the coming judgment (2.14). On the other hand, they actually participated in the oppression of the righteous, even shedding their blood (4.13). Beyond this the detailed features of the national sin are not sketched. But one thing is sure: the sin is not laid solely at the door of the religious leadership, but is shared equally by the populace. This can be seen in the distinction that is made between the prophet's falsity and 'thy guilt' (2.14). The same is implied, furthermore, in the earnestness of the national confession of guilt and by the fact that, even when priests and prophets have been slain, banished, or carried into exile, the heavy hand of Yahweh's judgment is still upon the community. In fact the gravity of the defection of the religious leaders is only significant in terms of the national destiny and the national default.[7]

The scope and seriousness of the sin is indicated by the several terms employed to describe it[8]: . . . *pešaʻ*, basically 'transgression, rebellion or infringement', stresses activity (1.5, 14, 22; 3.42); . . . *hēṭ'*, primarily 'failure or falling short', is sin from the standpoint of a norm or formal standard (1.8; 3.39; 4.6, 13, 22; 5.7, 16); . . . *'āwōn*, 'crookedness or straying', is sin from the standpoint of content (2.14; 4.6, 13, 22; 5.7); . . . *mārāh*, 'obstinacy, refractoriness or rebellion' (1.18, 20; 3.42); and . . . *tumeʻāh*, 'uncleanness' (1.9; 4.15). In this connection it may be significant that . . . *šeghāghāh*, 'sin out of ignorance and inadvertence', which does not appear in the prophets, is also avoided in **Lamentations,** inasmuch as the sin of Judah had long been heralded by the prophets and was therefore inexcusable. It is evident that the several words were used to impress the sin upon the hearer and to enable the Judeans to confess wholeheartedly their iniquity before Yahweh.

The confession of sin with such radical vehemence is one of the ways in which our book shows its superiority over all extra-Biblical, and one may also add, over all Biblical laments. Apart from the unusual addendum to the Sumerian Lamentation over Ur,[9] the laments of the ancient Near East known to this writer do not take seriously the connection between national sin and national judgment. This fact testifies eloquently to that deep and sensitive awareness of sin which was the fruition of the prophetic faith of Israel. It demonstrates that sin, both as disobedience and disruption, was understood in exilic Israel. Judaism, with all its defensiveness and exclusivism, developed a deep and interior sense of sin (cf. Ezra 9; Neh. 9; Dan. 9; Sir. 21.1; 39.5; Prayer of Manasseh).[10]

While any such distinction in **Lamentations** is not articulate (as it is nowhere articulate in the Bible), one senses, both in the transcendent imperious will of the deity and in the tragic brokenness of the social organism, a wedding of faith and social morality that was to be one of the great gifts of Judaism to the world. The poet in **Lamentations** shows us that the collective defiance of the word of the Lord (1.18) has resulted in the deepest ruptures of the community life (2.9, 14; 5.1-17). Often in the course of subsequent history there has been a tendency to turn on the one side into an arbitrary tyranny of the divine and on the other into a self-contained ethics. The latter would have been unthinkable for the Hebrews, who knew nothing of autonomous arts, autonomous politics or autonomous culture of any sort. But, the Hebrews, with the possible exception of certain apocalyptists, were not constrained to make of God an arbitrary despot. Unlike the Greek pantheon, Yahweh had the ultimate welfare of his world ever in mind. While for **Lamentations,** as for all Hebrew thought, there is a definite qualitative chasm between God and man, it nevertheless is true that at the same time man is the child of God and fulfills God's purposes in his historical life. This puts all the 'commands' of God in a new perspective and opens up the possibility of talking about natural law, even though the questions of natural law and autonomous ethics do not appear in the Old Testament itself. Nevertheless, the conditions are all there except the humanistic assumption. There is even in the naive faith of the Deuteronomist an expression of the Hebrew conviction that the good of God and good of man are One Good. In this sense Hebrew faith already presupposes and contains, though embryonically, the tensions of later theology. It is not untrue to Biblical faith to raise such rational questions as: Is God or the Good prior? Is an autonomous ethics possible? At least it is not untrue to Biblical faith if it be allowed that the modern religious man may ask religious questions in forms not precisely equivalent to those of the Bible.

The conviction that the nation which lives righteously and trusts God shall be blessed arises out of the fundamental conviction that there are not several goods at conflict with one another but One Good which is the will of Yahweh. Conversely there are not several sins but One Sin which is rebellion against the will of Yahweh. Social ethics, which lay all men under a common obligation, must, therefore, stem from monotheism. It is the given order, created by the One God Yahweh, which rescues the activities of men from sheer arbitrariness and lends them structure. This is why Hebrew religion and Hebrew ethics can never be unravelled to anyone's satisfaction. All rebellion against God is thus not simply rebellion against an 'other' but also against the self and the whole created order, so intimately is the welfare of all created things bound up with adherence to the ways of the creator.[11] One of the great contributions of the Wisdom literature was to make this point articulate. **Lam.** 3.34-39 is cast against the background of the Creator God, whose ways may be mysterious, but whose purposes are always for the good of his creation. There is, then, one may venture to say, already observable in Lamentations the foundation for the insight that evil and the disintegration of human society are inextricably bound together. There is, in terms of Tillich's philosophical theology, both an autonomy and a heteronomy within theonomy.[12] The terrible poignancy of the confession of sin in Lamentations is that Zion, by her rebellion, has destroyed herself.

But to attempt to rationalize sin in terms of its social consequences is not to equate the punishment thereof with a troubled conscience, or with the slow working out of requital through the process of moral 'sowing and reaping'. The interventionist ethos of Hebraism is more vivid and direct than that. The **Book of Lamentations** is distinguished by the repeated emphasis upon the wrath of Yahweh which acts directly in dealing out retribution.[13] Commensurable with the suffering and sin is the anger of Yahweh. The most common term for wrath is . . . *'aph,* also 'nostril', a derivative of . . . *'ānaph,* 'breathe or snort' (1.12; 2.1, 3, 21, 22; 3.43, 66; 4.11). Other terms are . . . *hārōn,* from . . . *hārāhn,* which has the basic notion of 'burning or kindling' (never alone in Lamentations but three times with . . . *'appō,* 1.12; 2.3; 4.11); . . . *hēmāh,* from . . . *yāam,* with the idea of heat (cf. Aramaic . . . *yᵉham,* usually for sexual impulse of animals, 2.4; 4.11); *'ebhrāh,* from . . . *'ābhar,* which suggests 'overflow, excess, outburst' (2.2; 3.1); and . . . *za'am,* or 'indignation' (2.6). The verb . . . *qāçaph,* 'to be wrathful' (5.22) completes the vocabulary. Yahweh's wrath is represented as being 'poured out' . . . *šāphakh,* 2.4; 4.11) and as 'ac-

complished or spent' (. . . *kālāh,* 4.11). Elsewhere he is pictured as 'wrapping himself in anger' (. . . *sākhakh,* 3.43), which like a cloud is impenetrable to prayer (3.44).

The real dynamic of the motif of Yahweh's wrath, however, is lost unless one studies it in close connection with the contexts where it occurs. Only by detailed analysis of the text of Lamentations can the interpreter grasp the fierceness and violence of the divine punishment. Central to the whole matter of the inter-relation of suffering, sin, and wrath is the direct activity of Yahweh in the city's destruction. Sin against God has aroused the divine wrath and that wrath has inflicted punishment without measure or mercy. Lest the reader overlook the true nature of the disaster, the poet ceaselessly reiterates the theme of Yahweh as the relentless, destroying God. Only in the last poem is explicit reference lacking to this motif, but the framework of the chapter, beginning and ending with an appeal for Yahweh to consider and restore the city, as well as the uneasy question of the conclusion, presupposes the earlier belief in the dreadful reprisal of the Lord.

In his monograph on Yahweh as a warrior or military commander, Henning Fredriksson calls attention to the frequent idea of God as the general of foreign armies (cf. e.g. Jer. 50.9; Isa. 41.2, 25; 43.17; Ezek. 26.7; 28.7).[14] Perhaps the most famous expression is that of Assyria as the rod of the divine wrath described by Isaiah of Jerusalem (10.5 ff). From this notion arose the more shocking image of Yahweh himself as the destroyer. In Amos (1.3-2.5) he sends the fire of judgment, not eschatological but simply military (cf. use of the idiom . . . 'to send or kindle fire', in Josh. 8.8, 19; Jud. 1.8; 9.49; 20.48; II Sam. 14.30 f).[15] Yahweh is the one who 'smashes the bars', presumably of the city gates (Amos 1.4 f; Isa. 45.2; Ps. 107.16). But, as Fredriksson observes, the direct destructive work of Yahweh is exemplified in Lamentations far more baldly than in any other Old Testament book.[16] More ruthless and detailed than even the judgments and punitive messages of the prophets is the inexorable coming of Yahweh as he methodically reduces Zion to ruins. The role of the Divine Punisher is most prominent in four series of strophes; in these passages is concentrated the full impact of the judgment (1.13-15; 2.1-8; 3.1-18, 43-45). The passages may, in turn, be divided into those that represent Yahweh's unmediated action against the nation and those that picture the nation in personified lament.

The second category draws into play the terminology of the individual lament which appears to have been fairly well stylized and rather widely circulated, at least in post-exilic times. Our poet has transferred this imagery of terrible affliction to the nation conceived first, in the form of the daughter of Zion and later, in the person of the prophet Jeremiah. By looking at the verbs descriptive of Yahweh's judgment we get some appreciation of the ferocity and savagery, indeed the vicious glee, with which he carried out his plan. The general term for the punishment inflicted is *hōghāh,* 'to afflict' (1.5, 12) but it is embellished by imagery declaring that Yahweh cast fire into her bones, stretched a net to entangle her feet (1.13), impressed a yoke of sin upon her (1.14), spurned her warriors, summoned a festival of slaughter and trod the bloody 'winepress' (1.15).

Yet the first chapter is only a foretaste of what appears in the third poem where the severity of the divine punishment mounts almost to the breaking point. The suffering man depicted is the prophet Jeremiah as a type or representative of the suffering nation; his chastisements are administered by the rod of Yahweh's wrath. . . . But the initial announcement of the lamenting figure is an understatement of the fury to come. In rapid succession Yahweh drives him into darkness (3.2), turns a continually hostile hand against him (3.3), wears away his bodily strength and substance (3.4), besieges him (3.5), makes him dwell in the darkness of death (3.6), walls off his path with stones (3.7, 9), burdens him with chains (3.7), ignores his prayer (3.8), ambushes and tears him like a wild beast (3.10, 11), pierces him with arrows (3.12, 13), sates him with poisonous food and drink (3.15), breaks his teeth (3.16) and forces him to cower in ashes (3.16). It is no wonder that the man cries out in despair:

> Thou hast rejected me from peace; I have forgotten good,
> So I say, 'Gone is my endurance, my hope from Yahweh.'
>
> (3.17, 18)

When we remember the historic circumstances which underlie the extravagance of the third chapter, the imagery does not appear unreasonable. Jeremiah's rejection by his countrymen was, to all appearances, the most complete which any prophet ever experienced, at least that rejection is most sensitively preserved in his writings. As to the destruction of Judah, we have already noted that never had the city of Jerusalem and the kingdom at large known such a total and humiliating defeat. While the descriptions are excessive to our Western canons of taste, they are not disproportionate to the suffering as the people of Judah, the prophet Jeremiah, and the poet had experienced it. It is important to remember that to the Israelite what we speak of as 'the fall of Jerusalem' was not a single instantaneous stroke but an agonizing succession of blows, a tragedy compounded of many tragedies, a lingering and excruciating pain persisting in the form of shame and reproach long after the first distresses of the siege and destruction had subsided.

For the more explicit development of the destructive fury of Yahweh, we must turn to the remaining group of passages where the divine initiative is so to the fore that the instrumentality of the judgment, namely, the Neo-Babylonians, vanishes from sight and the grim demolition of Jerusalem is carried out by God himself. This is definitely more than a poetic device; indeed, mere aesthetics would recoil from such a perverse image. It can only be understood as a calculated attempt to attribute each and every one of Zion's tragic misfortunes to the will of Yah-

weh. Thus the secondary cause recedes and the will which originated the destruction is pictured as executing it. *He* (Yahweh) has beclouded the daughter of Zion, cast her glory from heaven to earth, disregarded his footstool (2.1), destroyed the dwellings of Jacob, thrown down the fortifications, hurled king and princes to the ground (2.2), cut off Israel's strength, turned back Israel's hand before the enemy, burned in Jacob as a flaming fire (2.3), bent his bow, set his hand and slain her sons (2.4), become as an enemy, destroyed her palace and fortifications, multiplied mourning and moaning (2.5), pulled down his booth and assembly place, caused festival and Sabbath to be forgotten, spurned king and priest (2.6), rejected altar and sanctuary, measured off the walls for destruction (2.7), and caused wall and rampart to mourn (2.8).

Later in the same poem Zion addresses Yahweh on behalf of her slaughtered inhabitants:

> Thou hast slain in the day of thine anger; thou hast slaughtered
>   without mercy.
> Thou hast called as a day of festival sojourners from round
>   about,
> And in the day of Yahweh's anger there is neither refugee nor
>   survivor.
>
> (2.21*e*-22*d*)

There is also a relevant passage in the third poem where the nation, in a mixture of amazement and self-reprehension, directs a prayer of protest to the Lord:

> Thou hast clothed thyself with anger and pursued, thou hast
>   slain and had no mercy;
> Thou hast clothed thyself in a cloud, prayer is unable to pass
>   through.
> Offscouring and refuse thou hast made us in the midst of the
>   peoples.
>
> (3.43-54)

Elsewhere the mocking enmity of surrounding peoples is openly attributed to Yahweh's decree (1.17). He caused the enemy to rejoice and actually exalted the strength of the foe (2.17), and he has scattered the faithless prophets and priests with his fierce countenance (4.16).

Nowhere in the five poems do we discover any mitigation of the inexorable and pitiless performance of God in the city's overthrow. To be sure other very important and hope-producing aspects of the deity are presented, but the calamity proper is consistently pictured as *planned* and *executed* by Yahweh. Even when the ruthless enemy is the centre of attention it is taken for granted that he is the momentary instrument of God, for 'He (Yahweh) has delivered into the hands of the enemy the walls of her palaces' (2.7) and 'The Lord gave me into the hands of those whom

I cannot withstand' (1.14). One suspects that the repeated insistence upon this point is the poet's way of impressing his conviction on the wavering and doubtful in Judah. How widely the proposition was shared among the Jews remaining in Palestine is difficult to estimate, but in Lamentations it is clearly axiomatic. No accident, no demon, no foreign god was responsible for the plight of Israel, but Yahweh alone. In fact this becomes the basis of the enemy's cruellest scorn: the god who, by your own definition, should have protected you, has destroyed you!

> Listen when I groan! There is none to comfort me;
> All my enemies rejoice over my fate that thou hast done it!
>
> (1.21)

And still more emphatic is the announcement that

> Yahweh has done what he purposed; he has accomplished his
>   threat
> Which he decreed from days of old; he has pulled down
>   without mercy,
> And caused the enemy to rejoice over you; he has exalted the
>   strength of your enemies.
>
> (2.17)

Next to the loss of community with Yahweh and his purposes, the bitterest aspect of doom is the shame and reproach of defeat. The shame of Jerusalem consists primarily in her weakness so that she is unable to stand against the onslaughts of the foe (1.7-10; 2.16). She utterly failed to live up to her self-styled image as the city honoured (1.1e, 8c). As a consequence of the devastating blow which befell her, the nation is overcome with shame. Her disgrace is seen in two directions. In the first place she is swept by revulsion because of her sins (1.8). The daughter of Zion appears in the shocking image of a brazen harlot whose filthiness is publicly known. The force of the word 'filthy' . . . *niddah;* in Lam. *nīdhah*) can be seen in its technical usage for a mestruating woman (Ezek. 18.6; 22.10; 36.17; Lev. 12.2; 15.19, 20; 24-26; 18.19). By her callous persistence in sin, the daughter of Zion has so defiled herself that she is a thing of utter abhorrence to herself and others and in her revulsion she 'turns away' from the gaze of her former lovers (1.8, 9, 17).

In a similar manner the figure of leprosy is used to communicate the horrible aversion felt toward the faithless persons who held positions of religious leadership. The garments of priests and prophets are polluted and the community expels them from its midst with the warning cry of the leper: 'Unclean! Unclean!' (4.13-15). Jerusalem's sin, then, is like a foul and infectious disease that continually contaminates the daughter of Zion, exposing her to the open contempt and ostracism of the larger Near Eastern Community. But in a more limited sense, those especially guilty within the nation, the priests and prophets, are doubly infected and bear a particular scorn and ignominy.

The cruellest shame borne by Zion is the reproach of the enemy and neighbour who delight in mockery and revel in the punishment of Israel. The sharpest sting of Judah's sinfulness is the fact that it has been uncovered to the curious and hateful view of former friends. 'All her admirers despise her, for they have seen her nakedness' . . . '*er-wāthāh*, 1.8, is another word of offence, actually a euphemism for the pudenda, cf. Gen. 9.22, 23; Ezek. 16.37; 23.10, 29; Isa. 20.4; 47.3). And it is evident from 4.21, 22 that the identical shameful exposure of Edom is anticipated, when her sins will be bared to the castigating derision of all the nations, for 'you shall become drunk and strip yourself bare . . . he [Yahweh] will uncover your sins.'

It was observed in the previous chapter that there is a frequent contrast in the ***Book of Lamentations*** between Judah's fall and the enemy's rise. This reversal of fortune is inextricably bound up with a sense of bitter reproach:

> Her enemies have gained the ascendancy, her foes have
>   triumphed.
>
> (1.5 *ab*)

> The enemies see her; they laugh at her annihilation.
>
> (1.7*gh*)

> So that her fall is awesome, with none to comfort her.
> Behold, O Yahweh, my affliction, for the enemy magnifies
>   himself!
>
> (1.9*c-f*)

> Behold, O Yahweh, and consider, for I am despised! (1.11*ef*)
> All my enemies rejoice over my evil that thou hast done it.
>
> (1.21*cd*)

So odious has Judah become that in one passage she declares that Yahweh has made her like garbage or manure (. . .'what has been rejected'; . . .'what has been scraped off or cleared away', cf. Ezek. 26.4 and the Talmudic 'refuse' and the Targumic. . . 'dirt, dung').

Other verses tell of the nations directing taunt songs against the desolated city:

> He has made me a laughing-stock to all my people, their song
>   of derision all the day.
>
> (3.14)

> All our enemies open their mouth at us.
>
> (3.46)

> Thou hast heard their taunts, O Yahweh, all their plans
>   against me,
> The lips of my assailants and their thoughts against

me all the
> day;
Behold their sitting and their rising! For I am their
song of
> derision!

(3.61-63)

The taunt or mocking song must have been a firmly established Semitic genre. One of the earliest fragments of Hebrew poetry preserves just such a derisive song against Heshbon (Num. 21.27-29). Two later taunt songs, though polished by literary finesse and reshaped by prophetic ideas, are instructive for our understanding of the type (Isa. 14, 47). But we are still more fortunate in having retained in the text of Lamentations what appear to be some of the phrases and refrains from the typical exilic taunt song. We cannot know whether they record the actual words that were hurled at Judah by certain of the enemy but it is enough if they retain the spirit. Accompanied as they are by gestures, malicious joy and hateful malignancy, the sharp whiplash of their scorn is not lost to the modern interpreter:

> All who pass by clap their hands at you;
> They hiss and shake their heads at the daughter of
> Jerusalem;
> "Is this the city of which they said 'perfect in beauty,
> the joy of
>> all the earth'?"
> All your enemies open their mouth at you;
> They hiss and gnash their teeth, they say, 'We have
> destroyed
>> her!'
> 'Surely this is the day for which we waited. It is ours!
> We see
>> it!'

(2.15, 16)

It is interesting that in Isa. 14 and 23 we have the same ironic type of question as in 2.15, questions calculated to stress the great chasm between former pretension and present weakness and humiliation. The former accomplish by means of dramatic contrast very nearly the same effect as Shelley achieved in his sonnet 'Ozymandias'.

> Those who see you will stare at you,
>> and ponder over you:
> 'Is this the man who made the earth tremble,
>> who shook kingdoms,
> Who made the world like a desert
>> and overthrew its cities,
> who did not let the prisoners go home?'

(Isa. 14.16, 17)

> 'Is this your exultant city
>> whose origin is from days of old,
> whose feet carried her
>> to settle afar?'

(Isa. 23.7)

The very fact that the greatest shame revealed in the poems is not the personal shame of sin but the public shame of reproach poses the crucial theological issue of a universal God confining himself to a particular people. The light that has fallen on Israel has been gravely refracted, for Israel has all too often understood her Lord as the protector of her national interests and, conversely, she has tended to define God's enemies in terms of her own enemies. From the standpoint of Christianity, and also in the opinion of many adherents of Judaism, a shattering of the theocracy was necessary in order to release the word of God from its too narrow and too selfish confines.

But even in its post-exilic form, Judaism did not become a world religion in actuality. This must be insisted upon in spite of widespread geographical dispersion and, for a period at least, a thriving proselyte movement.[17] The loftiest sentiments of universalism did not set aside the plain fact that to share the religion of the One God Yahweh meant that one must become a Jew culturally. There can be little doubt that the rise of Christianity shut the door on whatever hope there might have been for a truly universal Judaism, or perhaps one ought to say that the universalistic tendencies in Judaism found their expression in the daughter religion of Christianity. At any rate, it appears that only the one 'branch' of Hebrew-Jewish faith, namely Christianity, succeeded in overcoming the connection between faith and nationality. In the very process of doing so it became heretical to the parent faith. It is true that Christianity retained an offence, but in place of the offence of nationality, it placed the offence of the cross (and the related offence of the incarnation).[18] While both were scandals of particularity, the Christian offence was able to cut radically across all levels of society, culture and race—something which Judaism has never quite succeeded in doing. Christ was and is a scandal to the proud man *as man;* Judaism was and is a scandal to the gentile *as gentile.* Christianity therefore realizes all that is best in the historical faith of Hebraism and Judaism but, in addition, lifts this faith to a level where it is accessible to men everywhere, without demanding of them extraneous cultural and ritual submission. This is typified in the fact that Jesus utterly transformed a Jewish title of limited national meaning into a term of universal significance. If it is true that Hebrew faith gives us the necessary understanding of the term *Christ,* it is also true that Jesus invested the title with its decisive content—a content that could never have been predicted or inferred from its Old Testament antecedents.[19] When the Church calls itself 'the New Israel' this simply means that Christians believe themselves to be participating in the promises of God which were not alone *to* Israel but *through* Israel to all the world.

In this criticism of Jewish pride, we do not mean that an insensitivity to the reproach of the enemy and the onlooker would have been the ideal attitude for the poet of **Lamentations.** Without this sting the lament would have been plainly insipid! Furthermore, this sensitivity shows a recognition that all the brutality and cruelty of the foe could not be equated solely with Yahweh's will. Although an instrument in Yahweh's hand, the enemy was not passive. Its wilfulness became apparent in delight over the havoc which it wrought. Nevertheless the fact persists that the great indulgence of Lamentations in the reproach of the enemy is a blemish of national pride not suited to the mission of Israel. Wiesmann argues that by virtue of Israel's uniqueness as the people of revelation, she was 'marked' as the special target of scorn by the surrounding nations. Because of her privileges and peculiarities, Israel was easily incited to pride and nothing would be more rancorous in the breast of surrounding peoples than such superiority.[20] The destruction of Jerusalem should have taught the Jew not only humility toward Yahweh but a greater charity toward the non-Jew. While the distinction has been very hard for men to make, especially religious men, there is a difference between suffering for the sake of one's faith and suffering because of recalcitrance and stubborn pride. It is hard to avoid the conclusion that in the very superbness of Hebraism with its privileges and excellencies there was a perverseness of pride which God had to judge—a perverseness which is not absent from the Christian Church or indeed from any organization or nation that has some basis for self-satisfaction.

Precisely as in the prophets, *Lamentations* does not totally renounce the election doctrine of Israel. In spite of that, by means of the enormity of her sin and the exhortation to patience and a wider trust in the overarching and mysterious ways of God, a number of reservations are introduced into the optimistic formulations of the election faith. Not only is responsibility primary, but there is some indication that Yahweh's purposes are too grand and unpredictable to be limited to one people. From the following in *Lamentations* it is only a short step to the great statements of universalism in Second Isaiah:

> Who is this who speaks and it is so, unless the Lord commands?
> From the mouth of the Most High has there not gone forth
>
> > evil and good?
> Why should a living man murmur, a man because of his sins?
>
> (3.37-39)

In our consideration of the theology of doom in *Lamentations,* we turn finally to the motif of the Day of Yahweh[21] . . . (*yām yhwh*) which forms another link between our book and the prophets. All discussion of the Day of Yahweh begins with Amos who clearly shows that the concept as popularly held in his day was a creation of quasi-religious patriotism (5.18). His comprehension was quite otherwise, for he envisioned stern judgment on gentile and Israelite alike. It is this view of a radical 'root and branch' destruction of evil, regardless of national boundaries, that is perpetuated and restated by a long succession of prophets (Isa. 2.12; Zeph. 1.10-12; Ezek. 7.10; Joel 1.14; Mal. 4.1).[22]

When we examine *Lamentations* we are impressed with the extent to which it bears out this prophetic conviction. In no sense is its conception of the Day of Yahweh related to the popular idea reflected in Amos. There are several references to the Day of Yahweh, although in only one does the usual name appear and this may be a gloss (2.22). But the features of that day accord with the prophetic teaching:

> Is it nothing to you, all you who pass by? Behold and consider
> If there is any pain like my pain which was dealt to me,
> Which Yahweh inflicted *in the day of his fierce anger.*
>
> (1.12, . . . *bᵉyōm hᵃrōn ' appō*)

> O how the Lord has eclipsed in his anger the daughter of Zion!
> Has cast from heaven to earth the glory of Israel!
> And has taken no thought of his footstool *in the day of his anger!*
>
> (2.1, . . . *bᵉyōm 'appō*)

> Young and old lie prostrate in the streets;
> My maidens and young men fall by the sword;
> Thou hast slain *in the day of thine anger; thou hast slaughtered*
> > without mercy.
>
> (2.21, . . . *bᵉyōm 'appekhā*)

> Thou hast called as a day of festival sojourners from round
> > about,
> And *in the day of Yahweh's anger* there is neither refuge nor survivor;
> Those whom I fondled and reared my enemy consumed.
>
> (2.22, . . . *bᵉyōm 'aph-yhwh*)

Of immediate interest in these passages is the identification of the Day of Yahweh with the fall of Jerusalem in confirmation of the prophets' firm faith that it was to be a day of doom for Israel. As Černý observes, the designation of the Day of Yahweh as *past* is absolutely unique to the *Book of Lamentations.*[23] The significance of this fact must not be overlooked. First, it shows the decisive and epochal nature of the fall of the city. If was of such world-shaking import for Israel that it could be described as the Day of Yahweh. This confirms the many other indications of the *sui generis* nature of the catastrophe. Secondly, it should be abundantly clear that Day of Yahweh in our period, at least for the poet of Lamentations, could scarcely have been regarded as the culmination of history, i.e. the point at which history ends in one great act of God. If it had been so regarded, it would have been impossible to equate the fall of the city, however calamitous, with that Day, for it was obvious that history was still in process. Finally, it clarifies for the exegete the basic connotation of the Day of Yahweh. We shall see momentarily that Lamentations not only regards the Day of Yahweh as past but also conceives of it as future (1.21). Were the Day a given period of time consisting of twenty-four hours, or even a single event, such a bifurcation would be ridiculous. But the Day of Yahweh is not any stated period of time.[24] Temporality

The Prophet Jeremiah (c. 650 B.C.-570 B.C.).

is involved only in the sense that Yahweh will act openly in history. Thus it is Yahweh's 'Day' because it is *the time when God acts.* 'Day' is simply that portion of history in which God moves decisively to judge men and to fulfill his purposes. *Lamentations* is thereby able to represent two or more times as the Day of Yahweh, corresponding to the twofold character of his judgment: once upon Israel in the past and again upon the enemy nations in the future. Both of these are Yahweh's Day without any sense of inconsistency. *Lamentations* is unique in this double reference for the Day of Yahweh. It can only be explained in the light of the enormity of the impression made by the fall of the city.

If the Day of Yahweh is essentially the period of time in which Yahweh acts (cf. Mal. 3.17), what is the character of his action? Our book is uniform in its witness that the action of God is the expression of his wrath (cf. Isa. 13.6, 9; Zeph. 1.18; 2.2 f; 3.9 f; Ezek. 7.19). In fact the accepted expression in Lamentations is 'the Day of his anger'. We have already seen how the intense wrath of Yahweh is pictured as afflicting, annihilating, and profaning the city of Jerusalem, its citizens and holy places.

Among the imagery in which the Day of Yahweh is decked out, the most prominent is the *battle-motif.* Yahweh appears as a slaying warrior (2.4, 5, 21; 3.43), drenched in the 'vintage' blood of his victims (1.15), burning (1.13; 2.3-4; 4.11) and demolishing (2.2, 5-6) the city. Some of this imagery has a demonic coloration, attributing to Yahweh functions once cared for by the lesser divinities who intervened capriciously in the affairs of men (cf. Gen. 32.22 ff). Fredriksson singles out for consideration the blazing face of Yahweh which destroys and scatters, a tradition going back to the numinous Sinai experience when it was said that no man could look upon Yahweh's face and live (Ex. 34.29 ff).[25] It is the hostile face of Yahweh that dissipates the faithless leaders (4.16). Yahweh as an archer whose arrows cause sickness and misfortune takes over that function from demonology (3.2 f cf. Job 6.4; 16.12 f; Deut. 32.22; Ps. 38.3; 64.8).[26] We have noted the starkness of the imagery of God's punishment and also the extent to which the secondary cause (the enemy) is overlooked and the primary cause (Yahweh) is emphasized. S. R. Driver remarks that this habit is typical of the Day of Yahweh theme: 'The conception places out of sight the human agents, by whom actually the judgment, as a rule, is effected, and regards the decisive movements of history as the exclusive manifestation of Jehovah's purpose and power.'[27]

The *darkness-motif* of Amos (cf. Isa. 13.9 f; Joel 2.2, 10 f; Ezek. 30.3) is not so explicit in *Lamentations.* The image of Zion as a star eclipsed by the wrath of Yahweh may be an instance (2.1). But unrecognized by most commentators is the *sacrifice-motif* in the reference 'as to a day of appointed festival' (2.22). This ironic word makes explicit and understandable one feature of the Day of Yahweh that appears for the first time in Zephaniah:

> Be silent before the Lord God!
>   For the day of the Lord is at hand;
> the Lord has prepared a sacrifice
>   and consecrated his guests.
> And on the day of the Lord's sacrifice—
>   'I will punish the official and the king's sons
>   and all who array themselves in foreign attire.'

(1.7 f)

It is also found prior to Lamentations in Jer. 46.10:[28]

> That day is the day of the Lord God of hosts,
>   a day of vengeance,
>   to avenge himself on his foes.
> The sword shall devour and be sated,
>   and drink its fill of their blood.
> For the Lord God of hosts holds a sacrifice
>   in the north country by the river Euphrates.

In exilic times and thereafter the sacrifice was developed into the great eschatological feast (cf. Isa. 34.5-7; Ezek. 39.4, 17-20; Pseudo-Isaiah 25.6-8; I Enoch 62.14; II Esdras 6.52; II Baruch 29.4; Luke 14.15-24; Matt. 7.11; 22.2-14).[29] The figure originated perhaps in the popular patriotic idea that the Day of Yahweh was to be a day of joyful deliverance, a truly festal occasion.[30] If the anticipated day was an outgrowth of the cult then the idea of the festival of Yahweh would be all the more understandable.[31] The difficulty is, of course, that each of the facets of the Day of Yahweh permits of the same kind of provincial interpretation. The battle imagery suggests a military origin.[32] The nature imagery suggests a cosmic setting supplied by myth or eschatology.[33] The truth may be that military, cosmic, and cultic imagery was employed to give colour to a conception that was derived from none of these supposed 'sources'.

The ironic twist that the prophets gave to the *sacrifice-motif* was strictly for the purpose of lending force to their persuasion that judgment would begin with God's people. 'Yes,' agrees the grieving poet, 'we came as those who are summoned to a festival. We crowded Jerusalem in anticipation of victory over the Babylonians but on Yahweh's Day none of us escaped. The sword was turned against us and instead of feasting we were feasted upon!' The mention of cannibalism in the context carries overtones of sadism and brutality that underline the demonic spectacle.[34] It is also possible that in the third poem the statements 'he has driven me into darkness and not light' (3.2 cf. Amos 5.18c, 20) and 'like a bear he ambushed me, like a lion in hiding' (3.10 cf. Amos 5.19ab) are employed with the thought that the appalling suffering here inflicted is the Day of Yahweh now realized as Amos predicted it.

Ordinarily commentators discuss the last two strophes of the second poem simply as an instance of unbridled vengefulness. Vengeance is not to be excluded, but, in addition, we find here a crucial reference to the Day of Yahweh as a day of visitation on the nations:

> Listen when I groan! There is none to comfort me;
> All my enemies rejoice over my fate that thou hast done it;
> Bring to pass *the day thou didst proclaim* when they shall be as I!
> Bring all their evil before thee! and do with them
> As thou hast done with me, because of all my sins.
> For great are my groanings and my heart is faint.

> (1.21, 22)

Pedersen remarks that in spite of the protest of Amos, many of the later prophets fostered the view that God would one day smite the foes of Israel and reign over his people as King (cf. Zeph. 3.18, 15; Obad. 15, 21; Isa. 27; 33-35; 52; Ezek. 38.9; Zech. 14; Joel 2.28-3.20).[35] In this spirit the poet of *Lamentations* believed not only that there is a Day of Yahweh for Israel but also a Day of Yahweh for the foe 'when they shall be as I', i.e. when their evils are dealt with. And this is no afterthought in the divine plan but a Day long 'announced' by Yahweh (1.21, . . . *qārā*). Here is something more than mere vengeance; it is the protest of outraged injustice.[36] It is not denied, or in any way excluded, that the fall of the city was a bona fide judgment of Yahweh, but it is felt that the chastisement of Judah did not fully rectify the injustices of history. There is an increment of judgment yet to come. Pun-

ishment of the nations as the logical outgrowth of God's universal rule is similarly accented in the introduction to the foreign oracles of the book of Jeremiah: 'For behold, I begin to do evil at the city which is called by my name, and shall you [the nations] escape unpunished?' (25.29).

That all is not complete with Yahweh's administration of justice is evident in the mockery and glee of the foe. The punishment of Israel did not cure all evil; indeed, it gave opportunity for the lust and vicious traits of the enemy to be indulged (1.21; 2.7, 15, 16; 3.59-63; 4.18, 21; 5.5, 11, 12). Thus we have the germ of the universal judgment when at the Great Assize God will review the evil of all men and reward them as he has prematurely rewarded Israel. Such an outlook is not contradictory to Amos, for the reverse side of the herdsman's teaching about God's universal rule (9.7) was the conviction that the Universal Ruler would hold these nations responsible for their wrongs (1.3-2.3). Given the changed situation of the exile, it was inevitable that this other side of the doctrine would be developed.

The destructive or 'demonic' character of Yahweh was an apprehension of the deity which Hebraism never surrendered. It is crucial, nevertheless, to recognize the way in which pure caprice and arbitrariness were subordinated by the prophets to the righteous purposes of the Most High. In the next chapter we shall have more to say about this 'ethicizing' of the demonic. What is unique in *Lamentations* is the author's fearlessness in boldly asserting the explosive and destructive side of the divine nature. What is of importance is not merely the tremendous power and energy of Yahweh which can destroy the proudest works of man. That which is of enduring significance is the determination and ability of Yahweh to act in history in fulfilment of his announced word. The doom that he has brought upon Judah is not the result of fitful moodiness but is in accordance with the long proclaimed and inevitable requital of disobedience and rebellion. The **Book of Lamentations** was the first to take up the prophets' theme in the wake of the tragedy they announced and to vindicate their claims.

The consequence of this acceptance of the prophetic interpretation of national tragedy was immense. It deserves to be regarded as the greatest single spiritual achievement of the exile. The continuation of Hebrew religion depended upon it, for the survival of Israel's faith was predicated on the existence of at least a nucleus of believers who would be disposed to heed the words of men like Ezekiel and Deutero-Isaiah. **Lamentations,** originating on the home soil of Palestine, addressed to the people and intended for popular consumption, lays bare the heart of the process by which despair was turned to faith and disillusion to hope. In the attributing of the destruction and disorder of the nation to the divine will, strange as it may seem, we may discern the roots of new life. Calamity in itself might profit nothing. Humanly speaking, everything depended on a substantial number of Israelites recognizing the chastening hand of God at work in the unhappy events. Only in this way could history become revelatory with the purposes of God. Following 586 B.C. historical religion wavered perilously between collapse and reaffirmation. What was demanded in a great act of faith was the acceptance of the doom as Yahweh's doing, in large measure attributable to Israel's sins, but even in its incomprehensibility and mystery, still wholly within the designs of God.

. . . . .

Not many years ago the very mention of a message of hope would have been enough to demonstrate beyond the shadow of a doubt that such a message did not originate with the prophets. There was an ironclad 'law' of prophecy which forbade the spokesman of Yahweh ever to hold forth promises or to offer consolation. At least this was the case with the pre-exilic prophets, and, to the degree that certain exilic and post-exilic prophets departed from the word of absolute doom, to that degree they were thought of as forsaking the rigorous prophetic heights and compromising their mission by concessions to the feelings of the people at large.

But all this is changed. It is now widely recognized that the prophet was no mere automaton who had only one thing to say and only one way of saying it, like a record endlessly repeated. A study of the prophets only increases our amazement at their individuality and adaptability in the face of changing circumstances. To cut out all elements of hope from the prophecies of Hosea, Isaiah, and Jeremiah calls for such wholesale surgery on the text and does such violence to the psychology of the prophets themselves, that the pursuit, if not wholly abandoned, is now tempered with much greater caution and reserve.

This is not to say that every passage of hope in the pre-exilic prophets is genuine.[37] Each one must be tested on its own merits and, to a great extent, the negative judgments of previous critics are to be maintained. What must be decried is their doctrinaire presumption which allowed, or even forced, them to reject passages on principle. Even so historically exacting a critic as T. J. Meek has pointed to the likelihood of a prophetic message of hope inasmuch as the combination of threat and promise can be detected in Egyptian writings as early as the Twelfth Dynasty (2000-1800 B.C.).[38]

We have, however, not only the evidence of the writings themselves and the probabilities suggested by Egyptian parallels, but we have the historical survival of prophetic religion. Had the prophets preached destruction only, and held forth no glimmer of hope beyond tragedy, it is difficult to understand how Yahwism could have survived. Again and again students of the Old Testament have observed that Israel affords an amazing exception to the ancient Near Eastern pattern; Hebrew faith did not decline with national adversity but actually was confirmed and deepened. This was in large measure due to the prophetic conviction about chastisement, repentance, conversion, and hope. Martin Noth has given apt expression to the present tendency in prophetic interpretation:

In the midst of the annihilating events of the past one and a half centuries the prophets of the 8th and 7th centuries had not only spoken their warning of the imminent judgment of God, which was already in operation, but at the same time they had occasionally spoken of God's further plans for Israel.[39]

With this in mind, then, it will not seem strange or impossible that **Lamentations,** in its declaration of hope, is taking up a prophetic strain of thought and giving it that development and emphasis which could only have been possible after the predicted calamity had fallen. Specifically, the theology of hope in the **Book of Lamentations** is not a finely wrought description of future glory in the apocalyptic style. It is, rather, the intimation of a bright future which is determined by the nature of Israel's God. This rules out all speculative indulgence about the precise character of the future. On the contrary, this 'theology of hope' concentrates upon the revealed character of the God who determines the future and upon that response which is required of Israel if she is to participate in God's future.

We may begin our tracing of this hope by noting the frequency with which prayer appears in our book. The several imperatives directed to God are of theological importance inasmuch as they show that Yahweh's control of events is still very much alive in Israel's faith. It was true that he appeared utterly intransigent, but it was not thought of as vain to make appeal, for he might have mercy: 'Perhaps there is hope' (3.29b). In addition, Lamentations offers us some knowledge of the exilic ideals of prayer.

The nation begs Yahweh to behold its affliction (1.9ef), its reproach (1.11ef; 5.1), its rebellious exhaustion (1.20), the slaughter of children, youth and religious leaders (2.20). It pleads with the deity to give ear to the entreaty for help (3.56), to judge the cause of the innocent (3.59), and to restore the nation (5.22). The assumption is that Yahweh can do something about these conditions if he so wills. The most natural conclusion, granted the thought world of the ancient Near East, was the one Israel most stoutly resisted. Jerusalem did not fall because of Yahweh's impotence, but because of his strength. Since destruction is never final, affliction may be healed, reproach requited, rebellion forgiven, innocence justified, and the nation revived.

Lamentations makes it plain that appeals to all other quarters are fruitless. The passers-by do not respond with so much as a shred of mercy (1.12) but only add insult to injury by their revilings (2.15). The nations are oblivious to her pain (1.18). They boast in her downfall and make sport of her tragic lot (2.16). Healing from any human source is impossible (2.13). These categorical negations of earthly aid or comfort serve to intensify the urgent summons which the poet addresses to his people to call upon Yahweh (2.18, 19).

One word must be said about the intercessory prayer. 'Lift up your hands to him for your children's lives!' (2.19ef) adjures the poet. Thereupon the daughter of Zion, as the mother of all Israelites, pleads fervently for her children:

the young, the priests and prophets, the aged, the maidens and warriors (2.20-22). One cannot help but think of the poignant picture of the ancestral mother Rachel weeping over her captive young (Jer. 31.15), and the later Jewish figure of the tribal ancestress in deep mourning for her offspring (Baruch 4.8-12; Syr. Bar. 10.16; 4th Esdras 10.7). The same sort of maternal pathos is encountered in the Babylonian mother goddess Ishtar who, after the great deluge, sang the funeral song over annihilated mankind. The fact that she is the goddess and not the nation personified is of course the important difference, but the same passionate intercessory concern is present, although there is no one to whom Ishtar may appeal for she herself has initiated the flood:

> She bewails as one who has given birth:
> 'The generation passed away has become loam
>   because I in the assembly of the gods commanded evil.
>   Yea, I commanded evil in the assembly of the gods,
>   For the destruction of my people I commanded battle.
>   I alone gave birth to my people!
>   And now they fill the sea like spawning fish.'[40]

A second instance of intercessory prayer is 3.49-51 where the poet in his grief vows to weep unceasingly until Yahweh looks down from heaven and beholds. There is the feeling that if he, as the bewailing poet, can be importunate enough he may gain the hearing of Yahweh who will then have mercy upon the whole city.

In his *magnum opus* on prayer, Heiler declares that lamentation is one of the prime ingredients of 'Prophetic' or 'Biblical' prayer and that it is quite in keeping with what he considers that type of prayer's essential content and motive: the unrestricted expression of compelling emotion, an involuntary and spontaneous discharge which the Old Testament figure 'outpouring of the heart' (cf. 2.19*c*) happily depicts.[41] In the Biblical complaint, anxious questions sometimes pass over into bitter reproach (Jer. 4.10; 15.9; 20.7; Hab. 1.2). Heiler cites Lam. 2.20 ff as an example of shockingly blasphemous lament.[42] 'Behold, O Yahweh, to whom thou hast done this!' is the audacious protest. Some construe this as a reference to the election faith of Israel. Overtones of that idea may be present, but a close study of the context would indicate that it applies to the mother and the priest and prophet. In other words, 'Lord, consider what you have done, turning women into cannibals and slaughtering your sacred ones in the holy place!'

We have, then, in *Lamentations* with its insistent appeals for Yahweh to intervene, that peculiar mark of Biblical prayer which naively seems to believe that God does not see atrocity or misfortune unless his special attention is called to it. Moreover there is the belief that importunity will bring results. Was Jesus scoring this attitude when he said 'they shall not be heard for their much speaking' (Matt. 6.7)? Or was he commending it when he urged that

by her very importunity the widow was heard (Luke 18.1-8)? One has the feeling that by the boldest possible statement of the suffering, God will be moved to pity (2.20-22; 3.42-43) and thus the grim aspects of the book, the repetitions of sorrows and horrors are not solely for the catharsis of grief but are also intended to gain God's sympathy and aid. In truth, the chief characteristic of the prayers in *Lamentations* is that they are *motives* calculated to arouse God to action. Indeed this motivation of prayer as a means of *affecting* God survived and took on additional forms in later centuries.

Norman Johnson, in his study of prayer in inter-testamental Judaism, points out that the petitions to God were oftentimes accompanied by fasting, sexual abstinence, donning of sackcloth and ashes, beating of the breast and tearing of garments. These habits, ancient in origin, tended to become conventionalized, but they retained, nevertheless, the coloration of *motives*.[43]

> While many of these practices became a means of cultivating piety in the man himself, there can be little doubt that originally they were projected toward God's mercy and that the original function remained alongside the other.

Lamentations, with all its associated postures and gestures, offers a superb example of Biblical prayer in the starkest and most irreducible form. We see prayer in its naked objective power, passionately directed toward specific purposes. And if it is this aspect of prayer which is most baffling to the modern religious man, who would rather reduce prayer to a psychological act of piety, then it is precisely this aspect which our historical study needs to bring to the attention of Biblical theology as part of the data to which it must do justice even when that data runs counter to the mood of the day.

But what was there in the nature of God which prompted such violent prayer? Again we are thrust back upon the moral categories of sin and righteousness. That Yahweh had been perfectly justified in his harsh treatment of Zion is witnessed by the frequent confessions of sin. In the first and third poems, however, the author expressly enunciates the righteousness of God as a kind of fixed article of faith to which the doubting may cling. The daughter of Zion is made to say, 'Yahweh is righteous for I have rebelled against his word' (1.18*ab*). This is equivalent to saying, 'I have no excuse to offer.' In the middle poem, in what are the climactic verses of the whole composition, there is a magnificent utterance of the Lord's disavowal of all injustice:

> To crush under foot all the prisoners of the earth,
> To turn aside a man's right in the very presence of the Most
>   High,
> To mislead a man in his case, the Lord does not approve.
>
> (3.34-36)

It is because of this assurance that the sorely tried nation is able to entrust its case to Yahweh, for he has contended for Israel's cause in days of old (3.58). He will judge the right of his people in the present crisis (3.59; 4.22). The foundations have been shaken but the divine government of the world is still administered from the steadfast throne of Yahweh. The easy optimism of the old enthronement hymns has vanished but their central affirmation still serves to express the faith of Israel: 'Thou, O Yahweh, dost endure forever, thy throne to generation on generation!' (5.19).

By means of this conviction about the enduring righteousness of Yahweh, his destructive demonic qualities were brought under control. Still, in sketching such a process, we must beware of thinking that for the Israelite this meant subjecting the deity to human definitions of the good.[44] As a matter of fact Yahweh remained self-determined but that self-determination revealed certain fixed points of fidelity and dependability. Because of his mystery and awe, his unassailability as God, there was no criticism of deity such as one finds so openly engaged in by the Greeks, who were able to dethrone the Olympian pantheon, analysing and dismissing them as one might treat any object of sensory perception. If we are speaking from the standpoint of Biblical revelation, the 'moralization of God' was not something which the Hebrews achieved, but something which God himself revealed. No matter what we think of this viewpoint ourselves, a faithful analysis of the mind of exilic Israel requires at this point that we forsake our philosophic and anthropocentric categories. To say this is not to undercut the importance of the historical context in which the righteousness of God was grasped; it is actually to affirm it, for, in Israel's faith, it is only through the medium of the collective historical experience of the covenant people that Yahweh makes himself known.

Rudolph Volz has observed that with the great writing prophets 'the demonic was separated from the holy'.[45] The sheer destructive power of Yahweh was in the service, not of rationally-stated moral norms, but of a righteousness which was holy. It was the great virtue of the category of the Holy that it could take on moral dimensions and still retain the primitive sense of mystery and 'shuddering'.[46] Two outstanding instances of this deepening of the doctrine of God by the interpenetration and fusion of the moral and the 'demonic' so that they become the Holy are found in Hos. 11.9 and Isa. 5.16:

> I will not execute my fierce anger,
>   I will not again destroy Ephraim;
> for I am God and not man,
>   the Holy One in your midst,
>   and I will not come to destroy.

> But the Lord of hosts is exalted in justice,
>   and the Holy One shows himself holy in righteousness.

It is apparent that the *Book of Lamentations* perpetuates this insight, asserting it with all possible vehemence: Yahweh does not crush the captive, brush aside the clamour for justice, nor subvert a man in the rightness of his cause.

We can readily understand how relevant this message was for the dark days of exilic despair. Israel is mistaken if she supposes that Yahweh has acted out of caprice or whimsey. Whatever the enormity and irrationality of the judgment from the human point of view, he has not disregarded the merits of the case. God is chastening Israel because he has her welfare at heart. He is guided by a righteous motive and a righteous goal.

Righteousness thus delineated borders on the covenant love of God.[47] Yahweh's *hesedh* appears triumphant over the miasmal bitterness and despair of the suffering prophet. It is the sufferer's remembrance of that covenant love which renews hope within him:

> O remember my affliction and homelessness, the wormwood
>   and the gall!
> Thou wilt surely remember and bow down to me;
> This I take to heart, therefore I have hope.
> The covenant loyalties . . . of Yahweh that do not
>   fail, his mercies . . . that are not consumed,
> Are new every morning; great is thy faithfulness!
> 'Yahweh is my inheritance!' says my soul, 'therefore I hope
>   in him!'
>
>   (3.19-24)

We are at once reminded of Zeph. 3.5:

> The Lord within her [Jerusalem] is righteous,
>   he does no wrong;
> every morning he shows forth his justice,
>   each dawn he does not fail;
>   but the unjust knows no shame.

Yahweh will not always afflict and reject, but will have mercy according to the abundance of his covenant loyalty. He does not arbitrarily or voluntarily mete out evil.

> For the Lord will not reject forever;
> If he grieves, he will have mercy according to the abundance
>   of his covenant loyalty;
> For he does not afflict from his heart, nor grieve the sons of
>   men.
>
>   (3.31-33)

In contrast to his *hesedh,* Yahweh's affliction and rejection of men is temporary, the necessity in a given circumstance, but never the final word. He brings his anger to an end, but his covenant loyalties are never consumed and his mercies are never exhausted. The expression 'he does not afflict from the heart' is the high watermark in *Lamentations'* understanding of God. As long as such a view of God was held in Israel there was no danger of the extinction of Yahwism. The angry side of his nature, turned so unflinchingly against Jerusalem, is not the determinative factor in the divine purposes. Begrudgingly, regretfully, if there is no other way toward his higher purposes, he may unleash the forces of evil, but 'his heart' is not in it! His deepest and truest intentions are otherwise; they are bent toward *hesedh.* It is easy to see how a view of educational value in suffering could develop from such a faith.

Eichrodt singles out Lam. 3.22 ff as one instance of the strong relationship of the God of love to the sufferer.[48] The most outrageous blows of fortune and the severest chastisement cannot alienate the man who feels this attachment to his God. It is hardly necessary to remind ourselves that this attachment is not a matter of like attracting like, which is the moving spirit in all absorption mysticism and also in the magical religions of the Near East, among whom Israel's faith was an anomaly. The attachment which finds expression in the religion of Israel, beginning as early as Moses, is one which has been established by the prior initiative of God. Israel thus lays no claim upon God, but is claimed by him. This is the primal faith to which the prophets plead for a return. This is the faith of *Lamentations.* In the light of this fatherly connection, the Jews are to perceive God's grace within his judgment or, to state the matter more precisely, to recognize that his judgment was one aspect of his *hesedh,* even though it was not always possible to trace the direct connection between the two.

So intense had been the suffering that it was almost too much to expect that Yahweh would forgive. The poet does not come by his conviction of the divine love easily! Israel's sin had been very great (3.42) and Yahweh's anger pitiless (3.43). Köberle surely misunderstands the passage when he states that the line, 'We have sinned and rebelled; thou hast not forgiven' is proof that the people felt that God was obliged to forgive and therefore they are affronted.[49] But the very opposite is the case. If he does forgive, it will be a marvel of the goodness of God, for 'Why should a living man murmur, a man because of his sins?' (3.39). God, therefore, owes nothing to Israel, but from the ground of the divine mercy it could be hoped and prayed that he might turn his anger and be gracious. Still nothing is guaranteed or automatic, for it is not God's business to forgive, and *Lamentations* closes with the troubled question, 'Or hast thou utterly rejected us? Art thou exceedingly angry with us?' (5.22). Judging by the book as a whole, the poet was thoroughly disabused of Israel's claims upon God. He makes almost nothing of the doctrine of election (2.20*ab?*). Central to his thought, however, was Yahweh's faithfulness to his own nature and purposes which might once again result in favour to the chastised nation. We are left confronting the unfathomable divine love and mercy which can never be calculated but comes only as a gift. This is the sole comfort which the poet has to offer his people but it casts a ray of hope over the otherwise dismal scene.

The great power and incomprehensibility of God were two aspects of the divine nature that post-exilic Judaism seized upon. They were amplified and embellished in the great flood of literature from the sixth century on. Here, after all, was the only security and refuge for a people whose superficial optimism had been crushed by the adversities

of historical life. We meet the omnipotent and veiled God in Ezekiel, Deutero-Isaiah, the P Code, and then again, with renewed emphasis, in Chronicles, Job, Daniel, and extra-canonical literature like Fourth Esdras. Rankin discusses with penetration the importance of the transcendent World-Creator to the post-exilic age and, in particular, notes its significance for the book last-named:[50]

> All that remains is faith in the Creator's will as being wise and good. This line of thought is taken up in Judaism at a much later date in the Fourth Book of Ezra when, after the destruction of Jerusalem by the Romans, the problem of suffering and of providence lay heavy on the heart of the stricken nation.

He fails to realize, however, that this very concern over providence was aroused by a similar historical situation six centuries earlier and that, in *Lamentations,* many of the interests and moods of the Wisdom literature are foreshadowed.

Of course it should not be overlooked that the conditions for the development of these ideas were long latent in the older prophets' stress on God's control of history. For example, Amos' chain of questions is a case in point (3.3-6). They may be understood as more than an effective rhetorical scheme for stating the law of cause and effect. His sense of the overpowering urgency of the divine will is clearly intended and there is more than an inkling of the later magnifying of Yahweh's majesty. But it remained for the exilic and post-exilic eras to exalt the omnipotence and inscrutability and to confess in dust and ashes that his ways were past finding out.

It is very noticeable in Lamentations that the ultimate appeal of the book is not alone to God's love and mercy but also to his unfathomed depths. Precisely as in Job, the very mystery of God is alluded to as at least a partial solution of the thorny problem of suffering:

> Who is this who speaks and it is so, unless the Lord commands?
> From the mouth of the Most High has there not gone forth evil
>   and good?
> Why should a living man murmur, a man because of his sins?

                                            (3.37-39)

The transcendence of God is seen in the appellation for the deity: Most High. . . . It is circular reasoning to date the third poem late because *Elyon* is a supposedly late title.[51] Actually a perusal of the other passages where it appears[52] indicates several which are certainly exilic and some undoubtedly pre-exilic.[53] Furthermore, *Elyon* is a term used in Phoenician and Canaanite literature which in most cases antedates the exile by centuries.[54] Even if the usage of *Elyon* in Lamentations is the first in Hebrew literature, it could not be imagined in a more likely circumstance and context. It is specious to shift the poem to a post-exilic date when all its characteristics authenticate the historical situation of sixth-century Palestine, simply because it uses a word that is not *common* until a later time.

God as the author of evil as well as good was a familiar theme in pre-exilic Israel (e.g. Ex. 4.21; 9.12; I Kings 22.23; Amos 3.6; Zeph. 3.6), but it did not become the subject of critical reflection until Israel had tasted the bitter dregs of that evil. Then the questionings were inevitable. Could this suffering, all of it and in its every grim aspect, be the will of Yahweh? Thus arose the first awareness of complexity within God himself—levels of volition, if you will, which we often designate as permissive and primary will. Some distinction of the sort is presupposed when the same poet could say that 'he does not afflict from the heart' and also that 'from the Most High come forth good and evil.'

With this insight Israel confessed that slowly she was learning the bitterest lesson of the religious life—that there is no simple one to one correspondence between man's hope and God's will. In this sense, *Lamentations* is the true teacher of later Judaism, even more so than the other more prominent exilic books, for its author was the first to acknowledge that his people's sufferings were dealt them by a God whose purposes are not always apparent and, therefore, must forever elude the definitions of even an elected people. *Lamentations* thus goes beyond Deuteronomy and is not far from the chastened spirit of the Talmud: 'It is not in our power', said R. Jannai, 'to explain either the prosperity of the wicked or the afflictions of the righteous.'[55]

It may be assumed that the frequent confession of sin in *Lamentations* presupposes repentance. The recovery of a right relationship with Yahweh involves not only the admission of . . . but repentance, i.e., 'turning'. . . . Israel has turned from Yahweh to sin and her contrition must now express itself in just as definite an act of the will—a turning back to Yahweh. Repentance implies an abrupt break with the offensive conduct or state of mind (cf. Ezek. 14.6; 21.23; Amos 5.14 f; Hosea 14.2; Josh. 24.23; Dan. 4.24).

Following the assurance of God's goodness and love, the nation summons itself, as it were, to return to Yahweh:

> Let us search and examine our ways, and return to Yahweh!
> Let us lift up our hearts not our hands, to God in the heavens!
> We have sinned and rebelled; thou hast not forgiven.
>
> (3.40-42)

Such a 'return' to the Lord is more than a flight to consolation or a petulant play on the divine sympathy. It is accompanied by a searching and re-examination of the national ways (cf. Ps. 32.3, 5). Critical introspection gives way to the lifting of the heart to God and the confession of sin. There is the suggestion here that the poet is aware of the need for a new heart which was a prophetic insight

so superbly stated by Jeremiah (31.31-34). At any rate there is the realization that now the people have done all within their power. They wait penitently and contritely for the divine forgiveness.

Erich Dietrich has called attention to the fact that in the Old Testament, while repentance is often pictured as the work of men, it is also frequently described as the work of God. No contradiction was felt for 'we must herewith emphasize that the Old Testament in general has no systematic doctrine concerning efficient causation'.[56] He singles out the presence of both human and divine operations in certain of the prophets.[57]

It is noteworthy that just this coexistence of the human and divine aspects of repentance is seen in *Lamentations*. The closing exclamation of the book vehemently calls upon the Lord, 'Turn us to thyself, O Yahweh, and we shall be turned!' (5.21). This plea must be interpreted against the backdrop of the utter supineness and exhaustion of God's people so painfully pictured throughout the poem, a lingering abjectness born of wretched servitude and the despairing conditions of life, plus the great burden of sin and guilt that Israel bears. In herself she knows no power to return to Yahweh. But, while the regal vigour of Israel is destroyed (5.16), Yahweh dwells resplendent upon his throne of world government (5.19). The consequence that our poet draws is that if the Jews are to turn to Yahweh then he must initiate the process of returning.

In *Lamentations* 5.21, as in the Jeremiah parallel of 31.18, it is difficult to know whether it should be interpreted politically or spiritually.[58] Certainly it is not a matter of 'pure spirit'. The parallel hemistich, 'renew our days as of old!' sounds suspiciously like a return of the kingship, the temple, and the religious order (cf. 1.7). However there is something additional. In the first place, as Dietrich stresses, this prayer is uttered in Palestine and cannot be explained simply as a return of the exiles.[59] Furthermore if a restoration of political life were primary in the poet's mind, one might have expected the more suitable expression 'restore our fortunes', . . . cf. Deut. 30.3; Jer. 30.3, 18; Ezek. 39.25) instead of 'turn us to thyself.' . . . Here is a clear parallel to 3.41, 'Let us lift up our hearts not our hands *to God.*' But it is this turning to God which Israel, because of the magnitude of her sin and suffering, is unable to accomplish. She has exhausted herself in frenzied prayer and to no effect. Although the modes of his working are not clear, if God were to turn Israel's heart to himself then a true restoration of her fortunes would occur. So there is a definite distinction to be drawn between 'turning to Yahweh' and 'return of fortune'. The one is the precondition of the other, i.e. conversion is required.

This notion becomes increasingly normative for post-exilic Jewish ideas of repentance. The heinousness of sin and the weakness of man were so keenly experienced that the great gulf between God and man had to be bridged by the divine initiative (cf. Zech. 5.5-11; Dan. 12.10). In later Judaism, the cry of *Lam.* 5.21 was incorporated in the Eighteen Benedictions.[60] In Lamentations, therefore, we find repentance not only as the basis of favour and restoration but also repentance as an act made possible by God, namely conversion.

The submissive spirit which the **Book of Lamentations** inculcates is another of the motifs that can best be understood in the wider Near Eastern context. To some extent the stress upon submission is related culturally to the loss of dynamic, the weariness which overcame the Semitic world from the Assyrian era onwards.[61] Albright remarks on several non-Israelite analogies to the submissiveness of the Suffering Servant in Deutero-Isaiah.[62] Valuable as this orientation may be, attention must also be directed to the Hebrew prototypes for the meekness of the Servant. The Prophets Zephaniah (2.3, 10; 3.11 f) and Habakkuk (3.16) contain early examples of the new accent on humility and passivity. But in **Lamentations** we come upon the most outspoken appeals for submission to be found anywhere in the Old Testament:

> Yahweh is good to him who waits for him, to the person who
> >   seeks him;
> It is good that one should silently wait for the salvation of
> >   Yahweh;
> It is good for a man to bear a yoke in his youth.
> He sits alone and is silent since it has been laid upon him;
> He puts his mouth in the dust, perhaps there is hope;
> He gives his cheek to the smiter, he is sated with contempt.

> > > (3.25-30)

Especially striking is the admonition, 'Let him give his cheek to the smiter', for it is in sharp contrast to the reproach and vengeance which elsewhere receive such violent expression. In this passage there is an extinction or suppression of all pride and personal feeling, the stilling of every angry protest. Why this indifference, this almost Stoic forbearance and self-effacement? Because the suffering originates with the Lord and is ultimately an expression of his goodness, the sufferer must wait upon his action (3.25-27). In fact it is good that the yoke of suffering be borne patiently, for even in adversity Yahweh displays his goodness. In the utter dejection of the sufferer, when he lay spent and crushed in the dust, at precisely that moment the possibility of hope was still alive. The grief that Yahweh has dealt out is not wilful nor perpetual but a seasonal chastening and tempering that is bound to give way to his compassion and love (3.31-33).

At first glance this strikes us as quite different from the ordinary prophetic attitude. For example, Jeremiah railed bitterly at his enemies and was restive under their scron. Yet the difference is not so great if it be remembered that submission in **Lamentations** is an admonition, an exemplary standard, and even within the same poem the old cry of vengeance is raised once more (3.66). But to say that submissiveness served as an exhortation is not to rob it of its

meaning, for by means of his faith in Yahweh the poet was able to believe that even the smitings and insults of the foe were embraced in Yahweh's plans, and though only a pervert could delight in the mockery, the present pain could be endured.

The persistence of the submissive spirit as a motif in Hebrew literature is especially evident in Second Isaiah's characterization of the Servant of Yahweh (42.2-4; 49.4; 50.5-7; 53.7). It is easy to believe that this spirit of acquiescence in suffering, in order that God's good purposes might be achieved in his own time and way, was one of Second Isaiah's debts to the **Book of Lamentations.** The fact that the books were written in different lands, **Lamentations** in Palestine and Second Isaiah in Babylon, is no great difficulty. From the prophet Ezekiel it is clear that there was constant communication between the two areas.[63] That the pupil went beyond his mentor is indisputable. For one thing, the goal of exaltation and triumph is much more articulate in the Suffering Servant passages. There is an exuberance and abounding hope which would not have been natural for the dark hours in which our poet wrote. Yet it is conceivable that the patient spirit of Lamentations, plodding though it be, was the necessary prelude to the flights of the Babylonian prophet. It is **Lamentations,** and not Ezekiel or Deutero-Isaiah, which shows how the Jews bore the first dismal doubts and wild griefs and deep despair of their fate and by 'laying the spectres low one by one' were able to preserve their common faith in Yahweh so that at the propitious hour the prophet of a more certain hope might announce the New Creation.

Because in the suffering there was the promise of good, it is clear that the attitude enjoined was not simply passive meekness or a mere compliance with fate. There was some apprehension of the sufferer's participation in the greater good which endures beyond the city's rubble and the nation's fallen pride (3.25-27). It was, to be sure, a punishment for sin and should be accepted without murmur (3.39), but it was also man's part in the divine plan. H. H. Rowley in a comparative study of attitudes concerning submission in suffering as found in Hinduism, Buddhism, Confucianism, Islam, Judaism and Christianity, reports that in the Semitic religions, particularly Judaism and Christianity, the submissiveness is not prostration before an arbitrary destiny but subservience to a greater good which the deity is bringing to pass.[64] Suffering becomes creative and is 'received with an activity of spirit, that seeks to learn its lessons and to appropriate its profit, and not merely with resignation'.[65]

To what extent that spirit has permeated our book is another question. It is not the constant thought which Jerusalem entertains, for she is much more concerned with the bitterness of suffering and the pangs of sin. Yet when there is pause for reflection, some elements of hope and promise insistently emerge. The restive mood of the laments shows that passivity is not the total intent of the poet. His consciousness that the disciplinary suffering is only temporary indicates that the waiting is not fruitless nor without expectation of better things. An intimation of suffering that is purposeful is the central teaching of **Lamentations,** the axis around which all the confessing and lamenting revolves. The resulting submission and resignation became ever more firmly entrenched in the ethos of Judaism (cf. e.g. Sir. 2.1-5; the prose setting of the Book of Job; and in the Talmudic period: *Berakoth 5a,* and *Cant. Rabba* II.16.2).

As a result of our close scrutiny of the religious message of the **Book of Lamentations** we are compelled to assign it to the main stream of Hebrew prophecy. Again and again we have discovered points of essential agreement with the great prophetic teaching. Some critics object that if it were truly in the prophetic tradition the hope offered would be more positive in tone. For example, C. J. Ball contends:[66]

> There is no trace of his [Jeremiah's] confident faith in the restoration of both Israel and Judah (Jer. 3.14-18; 23.3-8; 30-33) nor of his unique doctrine of the New Covenant (Jer. 31.31-34) as a ground of hope and consolation for Zion.

But it should be apparent that Ball, in his anxiety to dismiss Jeremianic authorship, has failed to take into account the several ways of expressing prophetic hope in the future, some quite different than those familiar to Jeremiah. If **Lamentations** deviates in certain respects from Jeremiah, it is no more than the difference between an Amos and a Hosea or an Isaiah and a Micah. Disinclination, or even actual disproof, of Jeremianic authorship must not be confused with the denial of prophetic affinities.

It is equally futile to make the hope innocuous by dating the third chapter after the restoration.[67] All attempts to minimize or deny the optimism of **Lamentations** are in danger of ignoring the peculiar vitality of Hebrew-Jewish faith which is strikingly evidenced, as H. W. Robinson remarks, in the fact that Israel's 'faith in Yahweh increased as her historical position decreased'.[68] It deserves reiteration that the **Book of Lamentations** displays precisely this baffling character: it originates in a period when Israel's historical life is in decline but it bears witness to a quality of faith which has been deepened by the catastrophe and, if anything, is in the ascendancy.

Briefly, how may we formulate the content of the hope which stirred in the mind of the author of **Lamentations?** It is not predicated on the prevailing conditions. There is nothing in the external situation (not even a Cyrus! cf. Isa. 44.28; 45.1-14) to offer the least bit of encouragement. In fact the ruined city and wasted countryside still stagger under the burdens of defeat. Attempts at economic, social, and religious reconstruction have been largely ineffectual (Chap. 5). So it is not surprising that the poet is unable to point to any instrumentality of hope in the contemporary scene. The ground of hope is in the unshakable nature of Yahweh's justice and love. His constancy guarantees that the disappointments and defeats are not ultimate inasmuch as sovereign grace stands behind and beyond them (3.36-

39). As to the particular forms the future restoration would take, we may note the following:

1. There is the hope of universal judgment. The salutary factor in the book's treatment of vengeance, as we have seen, is the recognition that not Israel alone but all mankind must conform to the divine will (1.21-22; 3.34-36, 64; 4.21-22).

2. There is the hope of the satisfaction of guilt. The enormity of Zion's sin has raised the doubt as to whether forgiveness is possible (3.42; 5.22), but the close of the fourth poem states ecstatically that 'thy punishment, O daughter of Zion, is accomplished!' (4.22). And this statement is made in the same poem that so firmly emphasizes the unparalleled magnitude of the sin (4.6)! The fall of Jerusalem, the ruin and bloodshed, a fate worse than Sodom's, was accepted as the just but ample recompense of the guilt of Judah. The tremendous consolation which this oracular word must have brought is conveyed in the enthusiastic praise of the Midrash:[69]

> The Rabbis said: 'Better was the **Book of Lamentations** for Israel than the forty years during which Jeremiah inveighed against them.' Why? Because in it Israel received full settlement for their iniquities on the day of the Temple's destruction. That is what is written, 'the punishment of thine iniquity is accomplished, O daughter of Zion.'

Immediately we recall the comforting words that introduce the prophecies of Second Isaiah (40.1-2). The prophet has taken up the assuring word of Lamentations and added the significant detail of *double* punishment. After years of exile and suffering subsequent to the writing of the fourth chapter, it would be natural to assume that if restitution for past sin had been fully paid at that time, then an excess of atonement had surely accrued to Israel's favour by the time of Cyrus.

3. There is the hope of the end of exile. Those who remained in the land must have felt keenly the loss of Jadah's leadership, especially after the brutal assassination of Gedaliah (Jer. 41). With several thousand of the choice citizens deported to Babylon, the Israel of God was actually a divided Israel until such a time as the exiles might return. In 4.22 the promise of their release is distinctly sounded with the words: . . . *lō' yōsīph l^e haghlōthēkh,* which may be translated either 'he will never again carry you into exile' or 'he will keep you in exile no longer'. The sentiment is the same: the deep longing for a united Israel.

4. There is the hope of political and religious restoration. The content of the plea to 'renew our days as of old' (5.21) implies at the very least a return of national freedom under king and priesthood with independence of movement, re-establishment of civil order and the exercise of worship and festivity.[70] All the sacred memories of a theocracy, of the favours and privileges of a select people, formed a halo around the past. It is too crass to call it po-

litical restoration alone, but it is too abstract and vapid to call it a spiritual restoration. Since Hebraism had so long been institutional, it was impossible to think of a bright future without the reconstruction of those ancient and venerated forms through which God made his will and goodness known. Lamentations thus foreshadows that compound of the devoutly spiritual and the rabidly institutional which formed the ethos of the New Israel (cf. e.g. Psalms and the Priestly Code).

Our delineation of the hope has remained rather indefinite at best. The passage which gives the most eloquent expression to that hope, namely 3.19-33, lacks any concrete account of its object, but it communicates to the sympathetic reader, better than a definition or a programme, the indestructible optimism of those who faced history with the secure faith that the future belonged to their God. With great sobriety and with earnest persuasion the **Book of Lamentations** proclaims Israel's incredible faith in a history creating and controlling God—a faith to which two of the solid facts of history still add their testimony: the survival of Judaism in the face of impossible odds and the rise of Christianity through which the boons of Israelite religion have been spread throughout the world.

Notes

1. Cf. esp. James Muilenburg, 'The History of the Religion of Israel', *The Interpreter's Bible,* Vol. I, p. 331. J. C. Todd begins his *Politics and Religion in Ancient Israel* (London, 1904) with this sweeping claim: 'The Old Testament is the epos of the Fall of Jerusalem. From the first verse of Genesis to the last of Malachi there rings through it the note of the Capture, the Sack, and the Destruction of the City by the Babylonian Army in 586 B.C. That terrible event is the key to the book. The circumstances which led up to it, the disaster itself, and the consequences which followed, form the subject of the whole.'

2. Robert Lowth, *Lectures on the Sacred Poetry of the Hebrews* (Boston, 1815), p. 235.

3. H. Wiesmann, 'Das Leid im Buche der Klagelieder' *Zeitschrift für Aszese und Mystik* 4 (1929), p. 109.

4. Richard Kraetzschmar, 'Der Mythus von Sodoms Ende', *ZAW* 17 (1897), pp. 81-92, argues that Gen. 18-19 contain two literary strands, one in which Yahweh alone is present (singular person) and another where he is represented by three angels (plural person). The whole myth was originally a Canaanite elohim saga accounting for the volcanic destruction of the cities (cf. Isa. 34.9). By a long process, including several editings, it has been appropriated to prophetic Yahwism. But Kraetzschmar does not touch upon the theological significance of the basic myth nor allusions to it in subsequent centuries. In fact, among the later passages, he omits Lam. 4.6.

5. The enormity of the catastrophe is often expressed in exilic and post-exilic writings, cf. e.g., in the confessional prayer of Daniel 9.12: 'He has confirmed his words, which he spoke against our rulers who ruled us, by bringing upon us a great calamity, for under the whole heaven there has not been done the like of what has been done against Jerusalem.'

6. Justus Köberle, *Sünde and Gnade im religiösen Leben des Volkes Israel bis auf Christum* (München, 1905), p. 277.

7. Cf. J. Philip Hyatt, *Prophetic Religion* (Nashville, 1947), pp. 57-60.

8. The explanation of the Hebrew terminology is derived from Brown, Driver and Briggs, *A Hebrew and English Lexicon of the Old Testament* (Oxford, 1906) and Walter Eichrodt, *Theologie des Alten Testaments* (Berlin, 1950), Teil III, pp. 81 f; and G. Quell, G. Bertram, G. Stählin, and W. Grundmann, *Sin* (Kittel's Bible Key Words), London, 1951. Cf. also Pederson, *Israel* (London, 1926) I-II, p. 414.

9. James Pritchard, *Ancient Near Eastern Texts Relating to the Old Testament* (Princeton, 1950), pp. 455-463.

10. Cf. Norman B. Johnson, *Prayer in the Apocrypha and Pseudepigrapha. A Study in the Jewish Concept of God* (Journal of Biblical Literature Monograph Series, Philadelphia, 1948), pp. 24 ff.

11. The idea that sin is not simply rebellion against divine fiat but is inimical to human life is implied in much of the prophetic teaching, but it is unusually clear in Hosea's stress upon the knowledge of God as the foundation of social life (cf. 4.1 f, 6, 14; 7.9; 9.7).

12. Paul Tillich, *Systematic Theology* (Chicago, 1951), Vol. 1, pp. 83 ff. As I understand Tillich's discussion of autonomy and heteronomy, the essential point is that ethics is rooted in the created order. On p. 85 he says: 'Autonomy and heteronomy are rooted in theonomy, and each goes astray when their theonomous unity is broken. Theonomy does not mean the acceptance of a divine law imposed on reason by a highest authority; it means autonomous reason united with its own depth. In a theonomous situation reason actualizes itself in obedience to its structural laws and in the power of its own inexhaustible ground. Since God (theos) is the law (nomos) for both the structure and the ground of reason, they are united in him, and their unity is manifest in a theonomous situation.' So far as the Biblical world view was concerned it naturally pictured God as one who commands from without, but it is improper to conceive of his command solely as an arbitrary imposition. This command or Word of God addressed itself to the structural necessity of man. It was directed toward his best interests as when a father issues orders for the good of his son. This is seen at its deepest level in the Old Testament's insistence that the God of Israel and the Creator God are one and the same. Revelation and nature thus have one ultimate source. It seems to me that this drive toward the unification of religious experience would also have a corresponding tendency

toward the relating of faith and ethics. Precisely this happened in the Wisdom literature. Thus the increasing cosmogonic reflection of Israel during the exile was not primarily speculative but religio-ethical (cf. Muilenburg, *The Interpreter's Bible*, Vol. I, p. 331).

13. Otto Procksch, *Theologie des Alten Testaments* (Gütersloh, 1950), pp. 642 f, points out that the anger of Yahweh illustrates the peculiar vitality of the Hebrew view of God. It is in marked contrast to the emphasis of the best Greek minds upon the imperturbable, the 'apathetic' character of God. . . . But in the nature of the Hebrew-Jewish God there was something unresting, dynamic, irrational, passionate—all of which is best summarized in the category of the Holy.

14. Henning Fredriksson, *Jahwe als Krieger. Studien zum alttestamentlicben Gottesbild* (Lund, 1945), pp. 23-27.

15. Henning Fredriksson, *Jahwe als Krieger. Studien zum alttestamentlichen Gottesbild* (Lund, 1945), p. 93.

16. *Loc. cit.*

17. Cf. Bernard Bamberger, *Proselytism in the Talmudic Period* (Cincinnati, 1939) and his article in *The Universal Jewish Encyclopedia*, Vol. 9, pp. 1-3.

18. A superb discussion of the scandal of the cross can be found in Paul Minear, *Eyes of Faith* (Philadelphia, 1946), pp. 270 f.

19. This concentration of originally independent titles and expectations in Jesus of Nazareth so that, in effect, he remakes the categories, is thoroughly depicted in William Manson, *Jesus the Messiah* (Philadelphia, 1946).

20. Wiesmann, *op. cit.*, p. 108.

21. The origin and import of the Day of Yahweh has been the subject of intense and protracted debate. The two classic works are Hugo Gressmann, *Der Ursprung der israelitischen-jüdischen Eschatologie* (Göttingen, 1905), pp. 141-158, and Sigmund Mowinckel, *Psalmenstudien II. Das Thronbesteigungsfest Jahwäs und der Ursprung der Eschatologie* (Kristiana, 1922). The most searching recent criticisms of their theories are well summarized in Stanley Frost, *Old Testament Apocalyptic. Its Origins and Growth* (London, 1952), pp. 39 ff, and H. W. Robinson, *Inspiration and Revelation in the Old Testament* (Oxford, 1946), pp. 139 ff. Perhaps the most satisfactory line of approach is that taken by J. M. P. Smith, 'The Day of Yahweh', *American Journal of Theology* 5 (1901), pp. 505-533, who stresses the uniqueness of Israelite eschatology as the ancillary of the historical faith in Yahweh. He sees the roots of the conception as early as the Yahwist epic. The most exhaustive recent treatment is that of Ladislav Černý, *The Day of Yahweh and Some Relevant Problems* (Prague, 1948) who strongly accents the social and historical factors which shaped the development of

Hebrew eschatology. When pressed to state wherein the uniqueness of the latter may be found he is driven to affirm that 'it is only this idea of the necessity of change in the existing world which makes the conception of the Day of Yahweh unique among the Hebrews' (p. 98).

22. It is worth noting, however, that the Day of Yahweh, or at least the term, does not appear in Hosea, Micah or Habakkuk. The reason for this omission may well have been a desire to avoid any misunderstanding on the part of the people who, hearing mention of the Day of Yahweh, would have misconstrued it in the nationalistic sense (J. M. P. Smith, *op. cit.*, p. 515).

23. Černý, *op. cit.*, p. 20.

24. *Ibid.*, Chap. I.

25. Fredriksson, *op. cit.*, p. 90.

26. *Ibid.*, p. 95.

27. S. R. Driver, *Joel and Amos*. The Cambridge Bible (Cambridge, 1901), p. 185.

28. The oracle in Jeremiah 46 concerning the Battle of Carchemish is attributed to the prophet of Anathoth by nearly all commentators.

29. Excellent discussions of the eschatological feast in its various developments are found in Frost, *op. cit.*, pp. 52, 90, 152 f; Gressmann, *op. cit.*, pp. 136-141; Mowinckel, *op. cit.*, pp. 296 f.

30. Cf. Georg Hoffmann, 'Versuche zu Amos', *ZAW* 3 (1883), p. 112.

31. Mowinckel's forte is in the cultic interpretation.

32. W. R. Smith, *The Prophets of Israel* (London, 1897), pp. 397 f, argues that the Day of Yahweh originated as a Day of Battle.

33. W. Cossmann, *Die Entwicklung des Gerichtsgedankens bei dem alttestamentlichen Propheten*. Beihefte zur Zeitschrift für die alttestamentliche Wissenschaft 29 (1915), pp. 178 ff, maintains that the Day of Yahweh was originally a term for Yahweh's revelation, devoid of any judgment associations, as the nature imagery clearly shows.

34. Although no direct connection is likely, Černý points to an Assyrian text associating cannibalism with the future judgment. It is predicted that in the reign of a certain prince 'the brother will eat his brother' and 'the people will sell their children for money' (p. 64).

35. Pedersen, *op. cit.*, III-IV, p. 546.

36. Paul Heinisch, *Theology of the Old Testament* (Collegeville, Minnesota, 1950), p. 201, defends certain of the Old Testament expressions of hostility as follows: ' . . . every violent word reflects the consciousness of intimate union with God and a living faith in His justice. The hatred of the pious, whose sentiments the Old Testament hands down to us, is directed primarily against sin, and thereby is elevated

above a merely personal or natural spirit of revenge.' H. G. Mitchell, *The Ethics of the Old Testament* (Chicago, 1912), p. 235, emphasizes the same point: 'Insofar as the instruments that Yahweh has chosen have gone beyond his instructions, they are guilty and must in their turn pay the penalty of their presumption.' Commenting on our book he says: 'The moral tone of the book comes out most strongly in Lam. 4.22, where the author announces to Zion the termination of her suffering, and to Edom the approach of a similar visitation, because the former has satisfied the demands of the divine justice while the latter has not yet atoned for her offences.'

37. J. Philip Hyatt, *Prophetic Religion* (Nashville, 1947), pp. 96-108 suggests useful criteria for determining authentic passages of hope.

38. T. J. Meek, *Hebrew Origins* (New York, 1950 rev. ed.), p. 181.

39. Martin Noth, *The History of Israel* (London and New York, 1958), p. 297.

40. Translated from the German rendering in H. Jahnow, *Das hebräische Leichenlied im Rahmen der Völkerdichtung. BZAW* 36 (1923), p. 177.

41. Friedrich Heiler, *Das Gebet* (Munchen, 1921), pp. 348-354.

42. *Ibid.*, p. 360.

43. Norman B. Johnson, *Prayer in the Apocrypha and Pseudepigrapha. A Study in the Jewish Concept of God. JBL* Monograph Series, Vol. 2, 1948, 72 f.

44. This is the mistake that humanism and religious liberalism usually make. Because, in terms of the evolutionary process as a whole, the moral character of God was relatively late in rising to human consciousness, it is assumed that the discovery was simply an inference from the human situation. The fallacious deduction is to make of God a pious fiction or at best a useful ideal. The historical development of religion neither proves nor disproves the unchanging nature and purpose of God. It is altogether possible that religious man in his discovery of the moral nature of deity laid hold of something as objectively real as the natural sciences in their research into the laws of nature. Only the religious realm of discourse is competent to judge the issues involved. A good example of the approach of religious liberalism to the ethical monotheism of the Old Testament is in I. G. Matthews, *The Religious Pilgrimage of Israel* (New York, 1947), p. 126, where it is said regarding the writing prophets: 'That Yahweh was a moral being was one of their far-reaching contributions to religious thought. This was correlative to their interpretation that the leaders were doomed and that the existing institution violated human rights and dignity. Building on what to them was axiomatic, they concluded that Yahweh was as fair-minded and as just as was man himself. In the world of men, where right was paramount, God himself must be the embodiment of right. This was a step forward in the realm of religious ideas.' Whatever measure of truth may exist in this analysis, when Matthews talks exclusively of human rights and dignity, of inference and ideas, he betrays a wilful disregard of the prophetic frame of thought. An appraisal of this sort completely loses sight of the divine initiative and purpose which was the primary datum of the prophetic experience and message. Such interpretations easily reduce God from the rank of creator and controller of history to a phenomenon in the history of ideas. Can Biblical theology, i.e. theology which attempts to formulate the Hebrew-Christian faith, whether for historical or constructive purposes—can such theology deny the fundamental presupposition upon which the whole tradition rests?

45. Rudolph Volz, *Das Dämonische in Jahwe*. Sammlung gemeinverständlicher Vorträge und Schriften aus dem Gebet der Theologie und Religionsgeschichte 110 (1924), p. 38.

46. Cf. Rudolph Otto, *The Idea of the Holy* (London, 1950), esp. Chap. XIII.

47. Norman Snaith, *The Distinctive Ideas of the Old Testament* (London, 1945), p. 102 surveys the Old Testament usages of the term *hesedh* and concludes that, while it has definite associations with slowness to anger and mercy, its basic meaning is steadfastness and constancy

48. Walter Eichrodt, *Theologie des Alten Testaments* (Berlin, 1950), Vol. 1. p. 124. He regards Lam. 3 as an individual lament, but his insight applies just as well to a national interpretation. Attention is called to other examples from prayer literature, e.g. Job 33.16 ff; 36.15; Jonah 4.2; Sir. 4.17-19; Neh. 9.17, 31; II Chron. 30.9.

49. Justus Köberle, *Sünde und Gnade im religiösen Leben des Volkes Israel* (München, 1905), p. 368.

50. O. S. Rankin, *Israel's Wisdom Literature* (Edinburgh, 1936), p. 17.

51. Gustav Westphal, *Jahwes Wohnstätten nach den Anschauungen der alten Hebräer. BZAW* 15 (1908), pp. 258, 262, gives the typical arguments for regarding *El Elyon* as a late exilic development. He treats the significance of the name, especially in the Balaam Oracles, and concludes that it was originally a Baal title, later applied to Yahweh to express his transcendence over all other gods, and became frequent in use when out of reverence the name of God was no longer spoken.

52. Gen. 14.18-22; Num. 24.16; Deut. 32.8; Ps. 9.3; 18.14 cf. II Sam. 22.14; Ps. 21.8; 46.5; 50.14; 73.11; 77.11; 78.17; 83.19; 87.5; 91.1, 9; 92.2; 107.11; Isa. 14.14.

53. A. R. Johnson, 'The Role of the King in the Jerusalem Cultus', *The Labyrinth,* ed. by S. H. Hooke (London, 1935), pp. 81-85), contends that there was a preIsraelite Elyon cult at Jerusalem. If this is true

then Elyon is an ancient title and our post-exilic theories need drastic revision.

54. Cf. citations in Köhler-Baumgartner, *Lexicon in Veteris Testamenti Libros* (Leiden, 1948-1953), p. 708.

55. *Pirke Aboth* iv. 19. Quoted in C. G. Montefiore, *Lectures on the Origin and Growth of Religion* (London, 1893, 2nd ed.), p. 451, who also remarks: 'No feelings rooted themselves more deeply in Judasim than those of absolute faith in God and unconditional resignation to his will.'

56. Erich Kurt Dietrich, *Die Umkehr (Bekehrung und Busse) im Alten Testamnet und im Judentum* (Stuttgart, 1936), p. 125.

57. *Ibid.*, pp. 122-125, 149-152, 161-165. Cf. e.g. Zeph. 2.1-3 and 3.11-13; Jer. 3.12 f, 22; 4.14; 7.3, 5; 18.11; 25.2; 29.13; 35.15 and 15.9; 24.7; 31.18, 31 f; Ezek. 14.6; 18.21; 33.11 and 11.9 f; 36.25 ff; 37.23; and Isa. 46.12; 55.3 and 44.21 f.

58. Erich Klamroth, *Die jüdischen Exulanten in Babylonien.* Beiträge zur Wissenschaft vom Alten Testament 10 (1912), p. 36, finds that the fifth poem was written in Babylon (cf. v. 2) and says that 5.21 is simply a thoughtless imitation of Jer. 31.18 and thus refers to a purely external restoration. It means simply, 'lead us back from exile to your land, to your residence upon Zion, in order that we may again build an independent nation.'

59. Dietrich, *op. cit.*, p. 127.

60. *Ibid.*, pp. 126 f. This is the famous Shemoneh 'Esreh or Amidah, the principal supplicatory prayer of the Jewish liturgy, v. Elbogen, *Universal Jewish Encyclopedia*, Vol. IV, pp. 22-27 and A. Z. Idelsohn, *Jewish Liturgy and its Development* (New York, 1932), pp. 93-109.

61. W. F. Albright, *From the Stone Age to Christianity* (Baltimore, 1946), p. 240 f and William C. Graham, *The Prophets and Israel's Culture* (Chicago, 1934), pp. 58 f.

62. Albright, *op. cit.*, pp. 254 f.

63. Cf. Henry A. Redpath, *The Book of the Prophet Ezekiel* (London, 1907), p. xxxix, and Volkmar Herntrich, *Ezechielprobleme BZ AW* 51 (1932), p. 129. Herntrich theorizes that, like Ezekiel, Lamentations was a Palestinian product which underwent later Babylonian revision.

64. H. H. Rowley, *Submission in Suffering* (Cardiff, 1951).

65. *Ibid.*, p. 62.

66. C. J. Ball, 'Lamentations', *Encyclopaedia Britannica*, 11th Ed., Vol. 15, p. 128.

67. Alex. R. Gordon, *The Poets of the Old Testament* (London, 1912), p. 77.

68. H. Wheeler Robinson, *Inspiration and Revelation in the Old Testament* (Oxford, 1946), p. 142.

69. A. Cohen, tr., *Midrash Rabbah. Lamentations* (London, 1939), pp. 234 f.

70. J. Pedersen, *Israel*, I-II, p. 488, shows that such a plea does not mean to turn back the progress of time but to bring again the substance of those days for 'the events with their character and substance make time alive'.

Georg Fohrer (essay date 1965)

SOURCE: "Lamentations," in *Introduction to the Old Testament*, Abingdon Press, 1968, pp. 295-99.

[*In the following excerpt from an essay originally written in German in 1965, Fohrer concisely describes the literary type and style of* Lamentations *and discusses what can be deduced of its origin and authorship.*]

. . . 1. *Terminology.* Hebrew manuscripts and printed editions call the book of Lamentations by the first word of chapters 1, 2, and 4, 'êkâ, "Alas, how. . . . " This title, which usually introduces a dirge, is appropriate to the content of the songs. The earlier name, according to Talmud Bab. Baba bathra 15a, was qîlnôt, "dirges," corresponding to the name given in the translations: Greek *threnoi,* Latin *lamentationes,* German *Klagelieder.* In most of the translations the title also ascribes the book to Jeremiah, after whose book it is placed. This view is probably based on II Chron. 35:25, although the laments for Josiah mentioned in this passage, one of which Jeremiah is said to have composed, cannot be identified with the book of Lamentations despite Lam. 4:20. The book serves as the festival scroll of the Ninth of Ab, the date of the destruction of Jerusalem.

2. *Literary type and style.* The book of **Lamentations** comprises five separate songs coterminous with the chapters. It is impossible to assign them to a specific literary type because in many instances we have a mixture of types. The poet's purpose was not to produce an exemplary poetic form but to embody certain specific ideas, to which the form had to accommodate itself.

Chapters 1, 2, and 4, as their initial word suggests, are dirges, more precisely collective dirges mourning perished Jerusalem. Nevertheless, the poet modulates into other literary types. In 1, in contrast to a dirge, Jerusalem herself addresses Yahweh in prayer, confessing her sins; vss. 12-16, 18-22 are composed in the style of an individual lament. In 2, also, the author departs from the dirge form: the poem focuses on Yahweh; after the lament over Jerusalem, the author speaks in his own person, and finally places a prayer in the mouth of the city. Chapter 4 begins as a dirge, but in vss. 17-20 a group speaks in the style of a community lament, and in vss. 21-22 the poet addresses Edom and Zion.

Chapter 3 is for the most part an individual lament, which passes into the style of a community lament in vss. 40-47 and then returns to the earlier form. In vss. 25-39 we find a meditation on the meaning of suffering. The conclusion contains a narrative of deliverance appropriate to a thanksgiving (vss. 55-62) and a prayer that God will curse the enemies; here we have the element of confidence that God will hear the lament and respond to it favorably. The "I" of the song, which alternates with a "we," has been interpreted as a personification of Jerusalem speaking as a sufferer (Eissfeldt*, Gottwald), as a representative speaking in the name of the whole community (Keil, Ewald, Ricciotti, Rinaldi), and as an individual who is merely describing his personal fate and not that of the community as a whole (Budde). It is probably more accurate to follow Rudolph in thinking in terms of an individual who feels himself singled out by God's wrath and presents himself as an example to his people. It is not necessary to draw the conclusion that the poet intends to place these words in the mouth of Jeremiah; he may quite well be speaking on the basis of his own experience.

Chapter 5 is a pure community lament, beginning with an invocation of Yahweh, continuing with a detailed lament over the present misery, and ending with a brief prayer for aid.

This analysis of literary types is followed by most scholars. Kraus, however, pointing to Mesopotamian laments over destroyed temples, particularly the Sumerian temple of Ur, postulates a new literary type, the "lament for the destroyed sanctuary," with a cultic lamentation ceremony as its *Sitz im Leben*. In Mesopotamia, though, such laments do not constitute an independent literary type (which would be quite peculiar as a sort of liturgical composite); they form a sub-category of the general class of laments. The analogous situation in Jerusalem is sufficient explanation for their similarity to the book of Lamentations; furthermore, the considerable differences should not be overlooked. Finally, the extreme mixture of literary types found in the OT songs and the peculiarity of their stylistic form (which will be discussed below) speak against the assumption made by Kraus.

Stylistically, the first four songs are structured as alphabetic songs. In 1 and 2, the first verse of each three-verse strophe begins with the letters of the alphabet in sequence. In 3, each verse of each strophe begins in this way, and in 4, the first verse of each two-verse strophe. In 2, 3, and 4, *pê* precedes *'ayin*, which probably means that the order of the alphabet was not fixed at the time of composition. Chapter 5 is an alphabetizing song; it has as many verses as there are letters in the alphabet. As a consequence of the stylistic form, the intellectual structure of the songs is loose and the presentation somewhat disconnected.

3. *Occasion and content.* The songs depict and were occasioned by the misery and destruction of Jerusalem after its capture by the Babylonians. They were composed on the basis of meditation upon the reasons for this terrible catastrophe. We are dealing here primarily with expressions of personal feeling, albeit clearly intended to have a pastoral ministry toward the others whom disaster had befallen. It is most unlikely, however, that they were intended from the outset for recitation at cultic lamentation ceremonies; such ceremonies are first mentioned in Zech. 7:1-7; 8:18-19, and were probably not introduced until years or decades after the events.[1] Above all, the alphabetic form argues against the assumption of an original cultic purpose; it characterizes the songs as elegies composed by a cultured man, meant primarily for reading and not for recitation.[2]

4. *Origin.* The date of the songs follows from their occasion and content: they presuppose the capture of Jerusalem. Rudolph prefers to date the first song in the time of the first occupation and deportation (597) and the others in the years following the final catastrophe (587). But even if the first song does not explicitly mention the destruction of the city and the temple, vss. 10, 17, 19-20 suggest the same situation as chapters 2-5. All the songs, therefore, probably were composed after the year 587, though we cannot fix a precise date for each of them. Chapters 2, 4, and (in part) 5 exhibit concrete details, while 1 and 3 are written in more general terms; but this is more likely due to the poet's intentions than to greater or lesser temporal proximity to the events. This alone can be safely stated: They were written by an eyewitness and before the situation was changed by Cyrus' emancipation edict in the year 538. To date 1 and 3-5 in the period 170-166 B.C. (Treves) is out of the question.

The place of origin cannot be determined with assurance. Gottwald thinks in terms of composition in Babylonia during the Exile; Sellin* places at least 1, 2, and 4 in Babylonia, while suggesting Jerusalem or Palestine for 3 and 5; Rudolph and Weiser* consider Palestine the place of origin for all the songs. There is no definite evidence for any of these assumptions, however. Since Palestine undoubtedly learned very quickly of Ezekiel's preaching, chapters 2 and 4 could quite easily have come under its influence there. On the other hand, one of the exiles could easily give the impression of having experienced the catastrophe of Jerusalem at firsthand. Therefore the question of where these songs originated must remain undecided.

The songs were probably brought together after the end of the Exile at Jerusalem, in the fifth century at the latest. They were collected for the practical purpose of assembling in one document the songs used for ceremonial commemoration of the destruction of Jerusalem.

5. *Authorship.* Jeremiah is out of the question as author of the songs, although recently Wiesmann has vigorously supported this position. After the catastrophe the prophet did not lament, but admonished the people to acknowledge the fate decreed by God and to obey the Babylonians; he may also have promised salvation to come, a promise contradicted by several verses of Lamentations (cf. 1:10; 4:17, 20b). Neither should the author or authors be sought among the official cult prophets (Kraus), whose guilt is recounted in 2:14 and 4:13 by someone not of their number.

Wiesmann and Rudolph, however, have shown the probability that all the songs were composed by a single author (*pace*, for example, Eissfeldt*). The evidence, despite the fact that 'ayin and *pê* have a different order in 1 than in 2-4, includes similarities of language and content, stylistic form, and the pastoral purpose and basic theological approach of the songs, all of which hold them together as a unity. If 4:17-20 reflects the personal experience and thoughts of the poet, he was among those that hoped for Jerusalem's deliverance to the very last, and appears to have fled Jerusalem with King Zedekiah. The stylistic form, too, suggests that he belonged to the cultured upper class. It does not necessarily follow that he was deported after the catastrophe; he might have been assigned to the circle around Gedaliah.

6. *Significance.* At any rate, the destruction of the state and its capital opened his eyes to the deeper significance of the events and led him to a profound appreciation of what had taken place, a receptiveness to the message of the prophets, and an attempt to help his fellow sufferers, caught in a crisis of faith (Weiser*). He sees God's wrath as the immediate cause of the disaster and attributes God's wrath to the sins of the people, with the priests and cult prophets foremost among the guilty. The only deliverance from misery and despair he sees to be prayer to God, who will be gracious and merciful to a repentant people.

Notes

1. The pilgrimage to Jerusalem described in Jer. 41:5 does not bear witness to such observances, but rather to the continued existence of opportunity for cultic worship at Jerusalem; furthermore, it takes place before the Feast of Booths.

2. Cf. Jahnow, p. 169.

Works Cited

ATD: A. WEISER, 2nd ed., 1962. BK: H.-J. KRAUS, 2nd ed., 1960. BOT: B. N. WAMBACQ, 1957. HAT: M. HALLER, 1940. HK: M. LÖHR, 2nd ed., 1906. HS: T. PAFFRATH, 1932. IB: T. J. MEEK, 1956. KAT/KAT²: W. RUDOLPH, 1939, 1962. KeH: O. THENIUS, 1855. KHC: K. BUDDE, 1898. SAT: H. SCHMIDT, 2nd ed., 1923; W. STAERK, 2nd ed., 1920. SZ: S. OETTLI, 1889. Individual commentaries: H. G. A. EWALD, *Die Dichter des Alten Bundes*, I, 3rd ed., 1866; C. F. KEIL, 1872 (Biblischer Commentar) (Eng. 1880); G. RICCIOTTI, 1924; G. M. RINALDI, 1953; H. WIESMANN, 1954.

B. ALBREKTSON, *Studies in the Text and Theology of the Book of Lamentations*, 1963; J. BÖHMER, "Ein alphabetisch-akrostisches Rätsel und ein Versuch, es zu lösen," *ZAW*, XXVIII (1908), 53-57; C. FLÖCKNER, "Über den Verfasser der Klagelieder," *ThQ*, LIX (1877), 187-280; N. K. GOTTWALD, *Studies in the Book of Lamentations*, 1954; M. LÖHER, "Der Sprachgebrauch des Buches der Klagelieder," *ZAW*, XIV (1894), 31-50; *idem*, "Sind Thr IV und V makkabäisch?" *ibid.*, pp. 51-59; *idem*, "Threni III und die jeremianische

Autorschaft des Buches der Klagelieder," *ibid.*, XXIV (1904), 1-16; H. MERKEL, *Über das alttestamentliche Buch der Klagelieder*, Dissertation, Halle, 1889; C. VAN DER STRAETEN, "La métrique des Lamentations," in *Mélanges de philologie Orientale*, 1932, pp. 193-301; M. TREVES, "Conjectures sur les dates et les sujets des Lamentations," *Bulletin Renan* XCV (1963), 1-3; H. WIESMANN, "Die literarische Art der Klagelieder des Jeremias," *ThQ*, CX (1929), 381-428; *idem*, "Der geschichtliche Hintergrund des Büchleins der Klagelieder," *BZ*, XXIII (1935/36), 20-43; *idem*, "Der Verfasser der Klagelieder ein Augenzeuge?" *Bibl*, X (1936), 71-84; J. K. ZENNER, *Beiträge zur Erklärung der Klagelieder*, 1905.

Commentaries

Commentaries Cited in the Text

ATD: Das Alte Testament Deutsch, Göttingen.

BK: Biblischer Kommentar, Neukirchen.

BOT: De Boeken van het Oude Testament, Roermond en Maaseik.

COT: Commentar op het Oude Testament, Kampen.

EH: Exegetisches Handbuch zum Alten Testament, Münster.

HAT: Handbuch zum Alten Testament, Tübingen.

HK: Handkommentar zum Alten Testament, Göttingen.

HS: Die Heilige Schrift des Alten Testaments, Bonn.

IB: The Interpreter's Bible, Nashville.

ICC: The International Critical Commentary, Edinburgh.

KAT: Kommentar zum Alten Testament, Leipzig.

KAT²: Kommentar zum Alten Testament, Gütersloh.

KeH: Kurzgefasstes exegetisches Handbuch zum Alten Testament, Leipzig.

KHC: Kurzer Hand-Commentar zum Alten Testament (Freiburg i. Br., Leipzig), Tübingen.

SAT: Die Schriften des Alten Testaments, Göttingen.

SZ: Kurzgefasster Kommentar zu den Heiligen Schriften Alten und Neuen Testamentes (ed. Strack-Zöckler), (Nördlingen) München.

Periodicals and Series

A. Alt.: Kleine Schriften A. Alt, Kleine Schriften zur Geschichte des Volkes Israel.

AASOR: Annual of the American Schools of Oriental Research.

ABR: Australian Biblical Review.

AcOr: Acta Orientalia.

AfK: Archiv für Kulturgeschichte.

AfO: Archiv für Orientforschung.

AIPhHOS: Annuaire de l'Institut de Philologie et d'Histoire Orientales et Slaves.

AJSL: American Journal of Semitic Languages and Literatures.

ANET: J. B. Pritchard (ed.), Ancient Near Eastern Texts Relating to the Old Testament, 2nd ed., 1955.

AnSt: Anatolian Studies.

AOT: H. Gressmann (ed.), Altorientalische Texte zum AT, 2nd ed., 1926.

ArOr: Archiv Orientální.

ARM: A. Parrot and G. Dossin (ed.), Archives Royales de Mari.

ARW: Archiv für Religionswissenschaft.

ASTI: Annual of the Swedish Theological Institute in Jerusalem.

AThR: Anglican Theological Review.

BA: The Biblical Archaeologist.

BASOR: Bulletin of the American Schools of Oriental Research.

BEThL: Bibliotheca Ephemeridum Theologicarum Lovaniensium.

BHET: Bulletin d'Histoire et d'Exégèse de l'Ancien Testament.

Bibl: Biblica.

BiOr: Bibliotheca Orientalis.

BJRL: Bulletin of the John Rylands Library.

BMB: Bulletin du Musée de Beyrouth.

BS: Bibliotheca Sacra.

BSOAS: Bulletin of the School of Oriental and African Studies

BWAT: Beiträge zur Wissenschaft vom Alten (und Neuen Testament.

BZ: Biblische Zeitschrift.

BZAW: Beihefte zur Zeitschrift für die Alttestamentliche Wisenschaft.

Canadian JTh: Canadian Journal of Theology.

CBQ: Catholic Biblical Quarterly.

ChQR: Church Quarterly Review.

ColBG: Collationes Brugenses et Gandavenses.

CRAI: Comptes Rendus de l'Académie des Inscriptions et Belle Lettres.

CuW: Christentum und Wissenschaft.

CV: Communio Viatorum.

DTT Dansk Teologisk Tidsskrift.

EstBibl: Estudios Biblicos.

ET: The Expository Times.

EThL: Ephemerides Theologicae Lovanienses.

EThR: Études Théologiques et Religieuses.

EvTh: Evangelische Theologie.

FF: Forschungen und Fortschritte.

GThT: Gereformeerd Theologisch Tijdschrift.

HThR: Harvard Theological Review.

HTSt: Hervormde Teologiese Studies.

HUCA: Hebrew Union College Annual.

HZ: Historische Zeitschrift.

IEJ: Israel Exploration Journal.

Interpr: Interpretation.

Irish ThQ: Irish Theological Quarterly.

JAOS: Journal of the American Oriental Society.

JBL: Journal of Biblical Literature.

JBR: Journal of Bible and Religion.

JCSt: Journal of Cuneiform Studies.

JDTh: Jahrbücher für Deutsche Theologie.

JEA: Journal of Egyptian Archaeology.

JEOL: Jaarbericht van het Vooraziatisch-Egyptisch Gezelschap (Genootschap) Ex Oriente Lux.

JJS: Journal of Jewish Studies.

JNES: Journal of Near Eastern Studies.

JPOS: Journal of the Palestine Oriental Society.

JQR: Jewish Quarterly Review.

JR: Journal of Religion.

JRAS: Journal of the Royal Asiatic Society of Great Britain and Ireland.

JSOR: Journal of the Society of Oriental Research.

JSS: Journal of Semitic Studies.

JThSt: Journal of Theological Studies.

MAA: Mededeelingen der Koninklijke Akademie van Wetenschappen te Amsterdam.

MDAI: Mitteilungen des Deutschen Archäologischen Instituts, Abt. Kairo.

MGWJ: Monatsschrift für Geschichte und Wissenschaft des Judentums.

MIOF: Mitteilungen des Instituts für Orientforschung.

Münchner ThZ: Münchner Theologische Zeitschrift.

MV(Ä)G: Mitteilungen der Vorderasiatisch (-Ägyptisch) en Gesellschaft.

NC: La Nouvelle Clio.

NedThT: Nederlands Theologisch Tijdschrift.

NkZ: Neue Kirchliche Zeitschrift.

NRTh: Nouvelle Revue Théologique.

NThSt: Nieuw Theologisch Tijdschrift.

NTT: Norsk Teologisk Tidsskrift.

NZSTh: Neue Zeitschrift für Systematische Theologie.

OLZ: Orientalistische Literaturzeitung.

Or: Orientalia.

OrBiblLov: Orientalia et Biblica Lovaniensia.

OrChr: Oriens Christianus.

OTS: Oudtestamentische Studiën.

OuTWP: Die Ou Testamentiese Werkgemeenskap in Suid-Afrika.

PAAJR: Proceedings of the American Academy for Jewish Research.

PBA: Proceedings of the British Academy.

PEFQSt: Palestine Oriental Fund, Quarterly Statement.

PEQ: Palestine Exploration Quarterly.

PJ: Preussishce Jahrbücher.

PJB: Palästinajahrbuch.

PRU: Le Palais Royal d'Ugarit.

PSBA: Proceedings of the Society of Biblical Archaeology.

RA: Revue d'Assyriologie et d'Archéologie Orientale.

RB: Revue Biblique.

RdQ: Revue de Qumran.

REJ: Revue des Études Juives.

RES: Revue des Études Sémitiques.

RevBibl: Revista Biblica.

RGG: Die Religion in Geschichte und Gegenwart.

RHA: Revue Hittite et Asianique.

RHPhR: Revue d'Histoire et de Philosophie Religieuses.

RHR: Revue de l'Histoire des Religions.

RIDA: Revue Internationale des Droits de l'Antiquité.

RivBibl: Rivista Biblica.

RThPh: Revue de Théologie et de Philosophie.

SEÅ: Svensk Exegetisk Årsbok.

SJTh: Scottish Journal of Theology.

StC: Studia Catholica.

STKv : Svensk Teologisk Kvartalskrift.

StTh: Studia Theologica cura ordinum theologorum Scandinavicorum edita.

ThBl: Theologische Blätter.

ThGl: Theologie und Glaube.

ThLBL: Theologisches Literaturblatt.

ThLZ: Theologische Literaturzeitung.

ThQ: Theologische Quartalschrift.

ThR: Theologische Rundschau.

ThRev: Theologische Revue.

ThSt: Theological Studies.

ThStKr: Theologische Studien und Kritiken.

ThT: Theologisch Tijdschrift.

ThW: Theologisches Wörterbuch zum Neuen Testament.

ThZ: Theologische Zeitschrift.

Trierer ThZ: Trierer Theologische Zeitschrift.

TTKi: Tidsskrift for Teologi og Kirke.

VD: Verbum Domini.

VT: Vetus Testamentum.

VTSuppl: Supplements to Vetus Testamentum

WdO: Die Welt des Orients.

WuD: Wort und Dienst, Jahrbuch der Theologischen Hochchule Bethel.

WZ: Wissenschaftliche Zeitschrift.

WZKM: Wiener Zeitschrift für die Kunde des Morgenlandes.

ZA: Zeitschrift für Assyriologie.

ZÄS: Zeitschrift für Ägyptische Sprache und Altertumskunde.

ZAW: Zeitschrift für die Alttestamentliche Wissenschaft.

ZDMG: Zeitschrift der Deutschen Morgenländischen Gesellschaft.

ZDPV: Zeitschrift des Deutschen Palästina-Vereins.

ZKTh: Zeitschrift für Katholische Theologie.

ZKWL: Zeitschrift für Kirchliche Wissenschaft und Kirchliches Leben.

ZLThK: Zeitschrift für die gesamte Lutherische Theologie und Kirche.

ZMR: Zeitschrift für Missionskunde und Religionswissenschaft.

ZNW: Zeitschrift für die neutestamentliche Wissenschaft.

ZRGG: Zeitschrift für Religions- und Geistesgeschichte.

ZS: Zeitschrift für Semitistik und verwandte Gebiete.

ZSTh: Zeitschrift für Systematische Theologie.

ZThK: Zeitschrift für Theologie und Kirche.

ZWTh: Zeitschrift für Wissenschaftliche Theologie.

Samuel Tobias Lachs (essay date 1966)

SOURCE: "The Date of Lamentations V," in *The Jewish Quarterly Review*, Vol. LVII, No. 1, July, 1966, pp. 46-56.

[*In the following essay, Lachs contends that the fifth chapter of* Lamentations *was written around 168-65 B.C.E., justifying the conclusion with his interpretations of its verses.*]

Ancient tradition ascribes the authorship of the book of *Lamentations* to the prophet Jeremiah and interprets its content as referring to the destruction of the First Temple by the Babylonians in 586 B.C.E.[1] Down to modern times few have questioned this assumed authorship or the event described. One notable exception in this regard was R. Abraham Ibn Ezra who, in his introduction to Lamentations, made the following observation: ". . . and this is not the scroll burned by Jehoiakim for we do not find [in *Lamentations*] two statements of God which are contained in the book of Jeremiah. One verse reads (Jer. 36.2) 'Take thee a roll of a book and write therein all the words that I have spoken unto thee against Israel, and against Judah, and against all the nations.' The other verse is (*ibid.* 36.29) 'Why hast thou written therein saying: The king of Babylon shall certainly come and destroy this land?' In the scroll of *Lamentations* there is no mention of Babylon or of its king." He raises doubts not only as to Jeremiah's authorship but as to the historical context as well. His commentary to the body of the book is exclusively grammatical and etymological in character and in it he avoids historical treatment of the material. At the beginning of chapter three he cites the rabbinic tradition of Jeremiah's authorship but also offers an alternative explanation to the passage without indicating his own preference.[2]

With the emergence of scientific biblical criticism, most scholars have rejected Jeremiah's authorship of *Lamentations*; few, however, have departed from the position that the background of the five chapters is the period of the destruction of the Temple in 586 B.C.E. They maintain that these chapters were all written not too many years after this event. Biblical scholars, in the main, have concentrated their energies on the question of the unity of the book— i.e. single or multiple authorship. Numerically the consensus favors the latter; the outstanding proponent,

however, of the single authorship theory, in recent years, was the late Prof. Y. Kaufmann whose proof of this thesis is far from convincing.

At the end of the last century, S.A. Fries advanced the theory advocating the Maccabean period for chapters four and five of *Lamentations*.[3] Unfortunately his work was poorly presented and poorly documented, as a result it was attacked and rejected.[4] We feel that there is indeed sufficient evidence to make a case for Maccabean dating of chapter five of the book. Although each element in our line of argument does not constitute positive proof, taken collectively they do produce a plausible hypothesis.

It is obvious to the reader, even upon a cursory examination of chapter five of Lamentations, that it differs radically from the four preceding chapters. Structurally chapters 1-4 are alphabetic acrostics while the fifth, although apparently in imitation of them i.e. it contains twenty-two verses corresponding to the number of the letters of the Hebrew alphabet, lacks the acrostic form. Chapters 1-4 are, in content, elegistic while chapter five is a prayer. The meter of chapters 1-4 is the *qinah* meter i.e. two parts of unequal length, the first has four accents, the second three. The verses in chapter five have four stress accents.

Aside from the structural differences there remains the question of content and frame of reference. Admittedly a prayer of this kind could fit a variety of historical events involving the Temple and the city of Jerusalem. It is our contention that neither the destruction of the Temple in 586 nor the sacking of the Temple by Ptolomy in 320[5] fits the material. The chapter seems to be set against the background of the attack on Jerusalem in 168 B.C.E. by Antiochus IV and the events following.

In the year 171-170 the Egyptians under Eulaeus and Lenaeus, who acted on behalf of the young king Ptolomy VI Philometer made war on Antiochus IV. Antiochus defeated the Egyptians before they had even crossed the desert. On his return in the summer of 170 he invaded Jerusalem, entered the Temple, confiscated much of the gold and valuables and slaughtered many of the Judaeans.[6]

Again in 169-168 Antiochus met the Egyptians and again was victorious. This victory was short lived because Rome intervened and Antiochus had to withdraw from Egypt. On his return he entered Jerusalem, once again slaughtered many thousands and even more he took into captivity and slavery. He sacked the Temple and stripped it of gold and silver as before.[7] After this sacking of Jerusalem Antiochus left a garrison of Macedonians under the leadership of Appolonius and built the fortress *Acra* near the Temple. This was followed by a number of oppressive and degrading edicts among them: A restriction on the observance of the Sabbath and on performing the rite of circumcision under penalty of death.[8] Daily sacrifices in the Temple were abolished—most likely in the summer of 168.[9] About five months later, on the 25th of Kislev, a heathen altar,,the Altar of Desolation" was erected on the site of the old altar and a swine sacrificed on it. The Temple became a shrine to Zeus Olympus.[10]

The sources for this period are *First* and *Second Maccabees* and the *Antiquities* of Josephus. In these works the language, events described and mood relected offer striking parallels to chapter five of *Lamentations*. We suggest, therefore, that this chapter was written against the background of these events sometime between 168-165 B.C.E. before the victory of Judah Maccabee and that it was subsequently appended to the other four chapters. We shall illustrate this thesis by an examination of the verses *seriatim*.

CHAPTER FIVE

V. I. . . .

This is the invocation of the prayer. The author contrasts the former state of the people with the present condition of degradation.[11] The tragedy is more than a defeat at the hands of an enemy; the hallowed mode of worship had been supplanted by the religious rite of the victor, hence the emphasis on "shame." . . . This mood is paralleled in I Macc.: "And great was sadness in Israel, everywhere; both rulers and elders groaned. Maidens and young men languished, the beauty of the women was altered. Every bridegroom took up lamentation and she that sat in a bridal chamber mourned. Shaken was the earth over those who dwell therein and the whole house of Jacob was clothed in shame."[12]

V. 2. . . .

The reference here seems to be the Temple overrun by the foreigner, i.e. the Syrian. . . . The importance of this verse is that it indicates that Jerusalem is inhabited by the foreigner. This agrees with the policy of Antiochus who built the *Acra* and stationed a garrison in Jerusalem; it does not fit the period of Nebuchadnezzar's victory, for he wanted the city destroyed, not inhabited.[13]

V. 3. . . .

The great slaughter and captivity brought about by Antiochus left thousands orphaned and widowed. Because of the confusion which followed it was not known if a man had been killed in the sacking, alive in hiding or had died in captivity hence "like widows" . . . rather than "widows." . . .[14]

V. 4. . . .

The author choses two illustrations to show the present plight of the Judaean—they were reduced to purchasing their water and paying for their wood. The latter is paralleled by the practise of the Seleucid kings of levying a tax on wood. Antiochus III, for example, who was favorably disposed towards the Judaeans removed this tax from them.[15] It may reasonably be assumed that Antiochus IV reinstituted it. The first phrase i.e. the purchase of water is not as clear. Perhaps there was a tax on the water as well.[16]

V. 5. . . .

This verse contains a linguistic problem[17] and a difficulty as to reference. It is perhaps a description of the insurgents under Judah Maccabee who roamed the wilderness and were constantly harassed by the Syrian troops. We suggest that it be read before v. 9 which appears to be a continuation of the description of their hardships.

V. 6. . . .

This is one of the key verses for Maccabean dating. Were one to explain this verse as referring to the period of the destruction of the First Temple there are basic difficulties involved. When did the Judaeans appeal to the Egyptians for food? What is the meaning of Asshur? At that time Asshur was no longer a power. Were one to argue that Asshur is Babylon[18] the passage is still difficult; how could the Judaean appeal to Babylon for assistance when Babylon was the menacing enemy?

Since we suggest a late date for this chapter a citation from a late source is legitimate. In rabbinic literature Asshur is employed as a term for Syria.[19] Applying this meaning to Asshur in this verse we then find a perfect couplet—Egypt and Syria (Asshur) representing the Ptolomies and the Seleucids. The author is bemoaning the fact that the Judaeans, through their leadership, shifted allegiance between Egypt and Syria. The best example of this was the power struggle between the Tobiades and the house of Onias, one siding with Syria, the other with Egypt. . . . Each side of the Judaean leadership wanted certain economic advantages which would accure were Jereusalem made a *polis,* and they appealed either to Egypt or to Syria for this very purpose.[20]

V.7. . . .

This approach i.e. suffering for the sins of the fathers is contrary to the view held both by Jeremiah and Ezekiel[21] who both maintained individual responsibility for actions and a denial of inherited guilt. This is a strong point ruling out not only authorship of Jeremiah but it reflects the thinking of another age. Here the consequence of the acts of others must be borne. The author laments the acts of former generations in that they forsook their God and adopted the Greek way of life. He sees in this the cause of the recent misfortunes which had befallen the people. Had the Judaean remained faithful to his own culture and religion the calamity would have been averted. This verse can be compared with the following: "At that time there came forth from Israel certain lawless men who persuaded many saying, 'Let us go and make a treaty with the heathen around us because ever since we separated from them many evils have come upon us.'"[22] These "evils" may well refer to the economic problems of the Judaeans because they were not able to compete with the Hellenistic communities.[23]

V.8. . . .

The servants are the mercinaries left as a garrison in Jerusalem under Appolonius, a servant of Antiochus IV and the power of this force was represented by the *Acra* which the writer portrays as being unconquerable. This phrase . . . is one indication that this chapter was composed before any victory by the insurgents had taken place.

V.9. . . .

The lives of those fighting the Syrians were in danger because the enemy patroled the edges of the wilderness and also held the towns which were the source of food.[24]

V.10. . . .

One of two interpretations can be given for this verse. It is either a description of the suffering experienced by the troops in the wilderness or by the victims of crucifixion[25] (see below v. 12). If the latter meaning is taken then it should be read after v. 13.

V.11. . . .

Part of every invasion or attack involved plunder and the rape of the female population. . . .

V. 12. . . .

The death penalty spared no one, prince or elder who violated the edicts of the Emperor.[26]

V. 13. . . .

This is a continuation of the description of the crucifixion scene. The second stich deals with the victims "stumbling while carrying the stake." The first part of the verse, however, is difficult.

V. 14. . . .

Because of the persecutions and the sadness of the mood of the people social and communal gatherings naturally ceased.[27]

VV. 15-18. . . .

These four verses all refer to Jerusalem and the Temple after the latter had been converted into a heathen shrine. Verse 15 records the terms . . . indicating that the Temple was the place of joy and happiness[28] but now all this had changed. . . . It is interesting to note the expression "altar of desolation in Maccabees[29] and similar pharases in the book of Daniel.[30] Although it is almost commonplace to connect foxes with a place of desolation[31] the word might well be used here figuratively in the sense of despoilers as in the phrase . . .[32] referring to the Syrians and the Hellenists who defiled the Temple. There may be another reason for the choice of this term—an allusion to the Greeks who cavorted as foxes in the worship of Dionysis; for the celebration of the Dionysia is mentioned in Maccabees.[33]

VV. 19-22. . . .

These four verses constitute the epilogue of the prayer. The author expresses confidence that the Temple will be restored as the permanent dwelling of God (v. 19). He appeals to God to turn His anger from the people for His rejection of them has been too long and difficult to bear (vv. 20, 22). In v. 22 he invokes God's assistance to cause the people to turn in repentance and to renew their way of life as of old i.e. before they had strayed into foreign practises.

Notes

1. Cf. Targ. Lam 1.1. . . . The Bible speaks of Jeremiah composing lamentations on the death of Josiah (II Chr. 35.25) which Josephus claimed were extant in his day (*Antt.* X, 5, 1).

2. Ibn Ezra to Lam. 3. 1. . . .

3. S. A. Fries, "Parallele zwischen den Klageliedern Cap. IV, V undder Maccabäerzeit" in *Zeitschrift für die Alttestamentlische Wissenschaft* (ZfAW) XIII (1893) pp. 110-124.

4. See M. Löhr, "Sind Thr. IV und V Makkabäische?" in *ZfAW*, XIV (1894) pp. 51-60.

5. Cf. Josephus, *Antt.* XII, I.

6. This historical summary is taken from S. Zeitlin, *The Rise and Fall of the Judaean State* (Phila., 1962) pp. 85-89. Cf. I Macc. 1. 16 ff; Josephus, *Antt.* XII, 5.

7. I Macc. 1. 29 ff; II Macc. 5. 1; Josephus, *Antt. loc. cit.*

8. I Macc. 1. 45, 48; II Macc. 6. 6, 10. See also Josephus, *loc. cit.*

9. Cf. I Macc. 1. 45, 54. Zeitlin *op. cit.* p. 89.

10. I Macc. 1. 21; II Macc. 6. 1-2; *Antt. loc. cit.* Cf. Dan. 11.

11. Translating not "Remember O Lord what is come upon us" but "Remember O Lord how it was with us."

12. I Macc. 1. 25-28. Text and translation here and elsewhere in this article are from the Books of Maccabees of *Jewish Apocryphal Literature* of the Dropsie College. . . .

13. II Kings 25. 8 ff; Ps. 79. 1; Is. 64. 9-10 *et al.*

14. On the slaughter and the captivity see: I Macc. 1. 30 ff; Josephus, *Antt.* XII, 5. The fullest description is in II Macc. 5. II ff. In this last citation v. 14 we read, "Within three days eighty thousand were destroyed, forty thousand in hand to hand fighting, an equal number to those slaughtered were sold into slavery."

15. Cf. Josephus, *Antt.* XII, 3.

16. Cf. King Demetrius' letter to the Jews (I Macc. 10. 25 ff) ". . . . Continue to be faithful to us, and we will requite you well for what you are doing in our behalf. We will grant you many exemptions, and give you gifts. For the present, I free you and release

all Jews from the poll taxes, from the customs on salt and from the crown tax." (ll. 27-29) Perhaps a water tax was one not yet remitted.

17. . . . See other suggestions in Kahana *ad hoc.*

18. Eg. Jer. 2. 18 *et al.*

19. Cf. Ket. 10b. . . . See also Yoma 10a. . . .

20. See Zeitlin, *op. cit.* p. 81.

21. Jer. 31. 29; Ezek. 18. 2 *et passim.*

22. I Macc. 1. 11.

23. See Zeitlin's note to I Macc. *ad loc.*

24. . . . On the hunger of the Judaean troops cf. I Macc. 3.17 ". . . then, too, we are faint, for we have had nothing to eat today." In *Antt.* XII, 7 where Josephus follows I Macc. most closely we find, " . . . he saw that his soldiers were backward to fight because their number was small and because they wanted food, *for they were fasting.*" The last phrase is probably Josephus' interpretation rather than fact.

25. On the hunger of the victims of crucifixion and fever frequently accompanying their agonies, see for example: Eusebius, *Eccl. Hist.* III, 8 where he describes the sufferings of the martyrs in Egypt who were crucified and died of hunger.

26. Cf. I Macc. 1.26, cited above, where prince and elder are taken as a couplet. . . .

27. Compare the mood in I Macc. 1. 39 "Her feasts were turned into sadness, her Sabbaths into a reproach, and again (ibid. 1. 26) "both rulers and elders groaned; maidens and young men languished."

28. Cf. Ps. 48.3; Is. 60. 15; 65. 18; Hos. 2. 13; Ps. 149. 3; 150. 4; Jer. 31. 12.

29. I Macc. 1. 54. . . .

30. Dan. 9. 27. . . . Cf. also Dan. 11. 31.

31. Cf. Ezek. 13. 4. . . .

32. Cant. 2. 15.

33. II Macc. 6. 7 ". . . and when the festival of the Dionysia took place, they were compelled to march in the procession for Dionysis, garlanded with ivy wreaths." One of the practices connected with this celebration was that the participants dressed up as animals, more often as fawns and goats but at times as foxes. All of these animals had meaning in the worship of Dionysis. The fox is singled out here either because of the allusion to the fox as a despoiler or its connection with abandoned places.

Thomas F. McDaniel (essay date 1968)

SOURCE: "The Alleged Sumerian Influence upon *Lamentations,*," in *Vetus Testamentum*, Vol. XVIII, No. 2, April, 1968, pp. 198-209.

[*In the following essay, McDaniel examines and rejects the supposed relationship of Sumerian literature to* Lamentations, *basing his conclusion in part on the fact that the parallels that exist are general and that no convincing means of transmission has been found.*]

Sumerian literary catalogues from the early second millenium contain the titles of numerous lamentations over the destruction of Sumerian city-states, including Akkad (Agade), Eridu, Lagash, Nippur, and Ur, and over the whole land of Sumer[1]). Portions of most of these lamentations have been recovered, and parts of several of them have been published in translation, including the "Lamentation Over the Destruction of Ur"[2]), "The Second Lamentation for Ur"[3]), the "Lamentation Over the Destruction of Nippur"[4]), and the "Lamentation Over the Destruction of Akkad"[5]).

Within the past decade statements have been made by several scholars concerning the relationship of these Sumerian lamentations to the biblical **Lamentations,** claiming that the Hebrew book was influenced by and dependent upon the earlier Sumerian works. S. N. Kramer has stated, without going into detail, "there is little doubt that it was the Sumerian poets who originated and developed the 'lamentation' genre . . . and that the Biblical Book of **Lamentations** as well as the 'burden' laments of the prophets, represented a profoundly moving transformation of the more formal and conventional prototypes"[6]). Similarly C. J. Gadd, without detailed discussion, has stated that the biblical **Lamentations** is "manifestly under the influence" of these Sumerian lamentations. He criticizes Norman Gottwald for not giving, in his *Studies in the Book of Lamentations,* sufficient recognition to the alien influence upon the origin, themes and theology of the Hebrew lamentation motif. He states, "certainly not all the harps were left hanging by the waters of Babylon, and some were attuned to sing at home the songs of a strange land'"[7]). Speaking somewhat more emphatically, H.-J. Kraus has stated, "die Klage um das zerstörte Heiligtum von Ur z.B. bietet eine erstaunliche Paralelle zu den Threni . . . Vergleicht man einmal sorgfältig das Klagelied über die Zerstörung von Ur (man könnte auch noch die Klage um die Zerstörung von Akkade hinzunehmen) und die alttestamentlichen Threni, so zeigen sich sowohl im formalen Ansatz wie auch in den Motiven überraschende Parallelen"[8]). Kraus follows these statements by briefly citing (usually with text references only) examples of these parallels.

However, not all biblical scholars are in agreement with these views of Sumerian influence upon the Hebrew **Lamentations.** W. Rudolph, without any discussion, simply states that the parallels are not too close and are due simply to a similar experience and situation[9]). Similarly, Otto Eissfeldt opposes any historical connection between the Sumerian lamentations and the biblical **Lamentations**[10]).

In view of these assertions and reservations on the question of Sumerian influence upon the Hebrew **Lamentations,** a fuller examination of both the evidence and the problems involved merits consideration. In this study the attempt will be made to present and evaluate the parallel motifs appearing in both the Hebrew and Sumerian works, including not only the more probable ones cited by Kraus but other motifs which could possibly suggest literary influence or dependence. A discussion of the problems involved in relating second millenium Sumerian works to sixth century Hebrew poetry, along with some general conclusions, will be given in conclusion. The writer is not a Sumerologist and has had to depend on available translations. He is aware of the limitations that this imposes, especially when it comes to a Sumerian passage where the translators treat the text differently. In such cases, the writer will cite the different translations. The procedure will be to follow the textual sequence of the biblical passages, listing first the relevant lines from the Hebrew *Lamentations,* followed by the Sumerian parallels. Comments and evaluation of the alleged parallels will be given after each parallel cited.

First it is important to note that certain parallels in the Sumerian and Hebrew texts should not be given undue significance in a study of possible literary influence. The experience of most cities in the ancient Near East under siege, and their fate upon subsequent defeat, were usually the same. Poets writing on the general theme of war and defeat, though at different times and at different places, would likely refer to the hunger, famine, pestilence, the social disintegration during the siege, the destruction of the city, the spoils taken by the victor, and the captivity of the conquered following defeat. Therefore, contrary to Kraus, the parallel references in the Hebrew and Sumerian lamentations to hunger and famine, the destruction of the city walls and temple, the burning of the city, the loss of valuables, and the captivity of the inhabitants speak not so much of parallel literary motifs but of the common experience of the vanquished at the hands of the victor[11]). One would normally expect to find in any kind of lamentation numerous references to weeping, crying and mourning. Thus the recurring parallels in *Lam.* i 2 a, 16 a; ii 18-19 *et passim* and IUr 96, 100 *et passim* could hardly be called upon as evidence of literary dependence. It is in these passages which deal with crying that one notes a significant difference between the Hebrew and Sumerian lamentations. In the former it is the personified city, Jerusalem, which weeps and mourns, but in the latter, Ur is never personified and the one who weeps and mourns is the goddess Ningal. Since the metaphor of bitterness which appears in *Lam.* i 4 c and IUr 315-316 is of such a general nature, it should be included among those parallel motifs that cannot reflect any kind of influence.

(a) Hebrew *'êkāh* 'how!' and the Sumerian word translated "alas" (Lam. i 1, ii 1, iv 1, 2 and IUr 41, 81 *et passim*) have been cited by Kraus as a characteristic element of the literary genre which he calls "Klage um das zerstörte Heiligtum"[12]). But the expostulatory particle *'êkāh* is frequently found in other elegiac and non-elegiac passages of the Bible[13]). It is attested in an elegiac passage in Ugaritic, *ikm. yrgm. bn il 'krt,* "how (mournfully) it shall be said

(that) Keret was the son of El" (*UT* 125:20-21)[14]). It seems much more probable that the Hebrew poet had in mind this Hebrew and Northwest Semitic particle than some more remote Sumerian prototype.

(b) "She dwells among the nations, she finds no resting place . . . We are wearied (but) we are given no rest" (i 3 b; v 5); and "I am one who has been exiled from the city, I am one who has found no rest . . . I am one who has been exiled from the house, I am one who has found no dwelling place" (IUr 306-308). Here the point of similarity is the reference to exile followed by an allusion to the lack of rest or a resting (dwelling) place. In the biblical text the reference is to Judah, but in the Ur lamentation the reference is to the goddess. The combination of "exile" and "no rest" into a single motif is not limited to these lamentations. One should compare the similar motif appearing in the covenant warning to Israel, "the Lord will scatter you among all peoples . . . among these nations you shall find no ease, and there shall be no rest for the sole of your foot" (Deut. xxviii 64-65). It seems more reasonable to assume that the poet had in mind these words, rather than knowledge of the words about Ningal which he then transformed into suitable words for the personified Jerusalem.

(c) "The roads of Zion mourn, for none come to the appointed feasts, all her gates are desolate" (i 4 a-b); and "In its lofty gates, where they were wont to promenade, dead bodies were lying about; In its boulevards, where the feasts were celebrated, . . . In all its streets, . . . In its places, where the festivities of the land took place, the people lay in heaps" (IUr 215-217). The parallel references in these lines to "roads" and "gates" are quite dissimilar. In the Hebrew text they are personified, like the city walls in ii 8, but in the Sumerian lamentation there is no parallel personification. The Sumerian poet calls attention to the gates and streets so as to contrast what used to happen in those places with what had happened in defeat and destruction. The mere mention of "gates" and "roads" together in different lamentations over destroyed cities is not suggestive of literary influence.

(d) "From on high he sent fire" (i 13 a); and "upon him who comes from below verily he hurled fire . . . Enlil upon him who comes from above verily hurled the flame" (IUr 259-260). Although both passages make reference to the divine use of fire, the motifs are only superficially related. Fire as a divine instrument is a recurring motif in biblical literature and Canaanite mythology[15]). The burning of conquered cities and the theme of divine use of fire are so sufficiently attested in Syria-Palestine that there is no need to go all the way to Sumer to find a literary parallel or prototype.

(e) "He spread a net for my feet" (i 13 b); and "über Sumer ist das Fangnetz gefallen" (IUr-F 200:30). Kraus includes these lines in his list of parallel motifs. Kramer is less certain of the meaning of this line in the Ur lamentation and translates, "Sumer *is broken up by the gišburru*" (IUr 195). But within the Hebrew literary and prophetic tradition the picture of Yahweh spreading a net was an established motif. Both Hosea and Ezekiel employ the motif, e.g., "I will spread my net over him, and he shall be taken away in my snare; and I will bring him to Babylon . . ." (Ez. xii 13; see also xvii 20; Ho. vii 12).

(f) "How the Lord in his anger . . ." (ii 1a); and "because of the wrath of Enlil" (Akkad 1). A frequently recurring theme in Lam. ii is the anger of Yahweh, and although not mentioned in the IUr lamentation, there are numerous references in the Sumerian lamentations to the wrath of Anu and Enlil[16]). Although Sumerian references to divine wrath appear in lamentations (including for the purpose of this study "The Curse of Agade")[17]) Hebrew references to the wrath of Yahweh are not restricted to this particular genre. A cursory look at any biblical concordance will be sufficient to indicate how widespread the concept of divine wrath was among the ancient Israelites. The Sumerian and Hebrew emphasis upon divine wrath in the interpretation of tragic national events is more likely to reflect an older and more general common religious tradition among the two peoples than literary dependence of the Hebrew poet upon the Sumerian lamentations.

(g) "He has bent his bow like an enemy . . . like an enemy he has slain . . . the Lord has become like an enemy" (ii 4a, 5); and "Mother Ningal in her city like an enemy stood aside. . . . How long, pray, wilt thou stand aside in the city like an enemy? O Mother Ningal, (how long) wilt thou hurl challenges in the city like an enemy?" (IUr 253, 374-375). The simile "like an enemy" as applied to Yahweh does not appear elsewhere in the Bible, although there are other references to Yahweh's being an "enemy". In Ex. xxiii 22, the motif appears as follows, . . ."I will be an enemy to your enemies and an adversary to your adversaries". In Is. lxiii 10, a similar phrase occurs, . . ."he became their enemy". Accordingly, although there is no biblical parallel as close as the same simile in IUr, the idea itself is found in Israel's religious tradition, and the Hebrew poet could well have coined this simile without recourse to a Sumerian prototype.

(h) "The Lord has rejected his altar, he has abandoned[18]) his sanctuary" (ii 7 a); and "Enlil has abandoned . . . Nippur . . . Ninlil has abandoned their house . . ." (IUr 4, 6, *et passim*). The first thirtyseven lines of IUr are a list of the various temples and shrines which the different Sumerian deities had abandoned. By contrast, in the Hebrew **Lamentations** the motif appears only once, assuming that the above translation of MT *ni'ēr* as "abandon" is correct. At best, the parallel is in the word and not in the meaning behind the word. Whereas in the Hebrew text Yahweh has rejected his holy city because of her sin and rebellion, Ningal and Nanna, the deities at Ur, plead for the safety of Ur and affirm her innocence. Only because the gods had not decreed eternal kingship for Ur must they bear with the calamity[19]). The idea of deliberate rejection is not a part of the Sumerian parallel, but it is basic in Yahweh's abandonment of Jerusalem.

(i) "Yahweh has determined to lay in ruins the wall of the daughter Zion. . . . Yahweh has done what he purposed, he has fulfilled his words which he commanded long ago; he has demolished without pity. . . . Who has given this (order) that it should come to pass? Yahweh verily[20]) has given the order" (ii 8 a, 17 a-b; iii 37); and "after they had *pronounced* the utter destruction of my city; after they had *pronounced* the utter destruction of Ur, after they had directed that its people be killed. . . . Anu changed not his command; Enlil altered not the command which he had issued" (IUr 140-142, 168-169). The same theme appears in the second lamentation, "the destruction of my city they verily gave in commission; the destruction of Ur they verily gave in commission; that its people be killed, as its fate they verily commanded" (IIUr-J). These parallel motifs of divine command and purpose are seemingly quite similar. But a closer study of the thought behind these motifs indicates that the similarity is only of words, not of meaning. According to Israelite religious traditions, the destruction of Jerusalem had not been inexorably decreed by Yahweh. What was commanded and purposed by Yahweh was a *covenant relationship* which could not be changed. Obedience would bring blessing; disobedience would bring destruction (see Deut. xxviii and Lev. xvi). Israel's acknowledged rebellion demanded Yahweh's just fulfillment of his word (i 8 a, 18 a). Thus, in the context of Israel's faith, things could have been different if Jerusalem had been either faithful or repentant.

An entirely different understanding lies behind the Sumerian motifs of divine commission. In the myth of "Inanna and Enki: The Transfer of the Arts of Civilization from Eridu to Erech", the poet lists over one hundred "cultural traits and complexes" for which there is a *me*, i.e., "a set of rules and regulation assigned to each cosmic entity and cultural phenomenon for the purpose of keeping it operating forever in accordance with the plans laid down by the deity creating it"[21]). The thirty-eighth *me* cited by the Sumerian poet, in his list of over one hundred, is the *me* of the "destruction of cities"[22]). Apparently Ur's fate was inexorably fixed by this *me*, so that, innocent or not, even the gods' intercession could not change the *me* which Anu and Enlil had established.

There is no need to assume here that the Hebrew poet of **Lamentations** drew from outside his own covenant traditions when he wrote of divine purpose. The parallels with the Sumerian lamentations are only superficial.

(j) "He caused the rampart and wall to lament; they languish together (ii 8); and "O thou brickwork of Ur, a bitter lament set up as thy lament" (IUr 48, 53 *et passim*). The personification of inanimate objects is frequently encountered in funeral songs[23]). What is noteworthy here is the fact that although the verb *'ābal* is used with numerous other inanimate subjects or objects (including gates, land, pastures and the deep), this is the only occurrence where it is used with *bēl wehōmāh*, somewhat like the Sumerian "brickwork". But there is no reasonable basis to assume that though the Hebrew poets independently composed metaphors like "her gates shall lament and mourn" (Is. iii

26) and "her land mourns" (Ho. iv 3), they were influenced by a Sumerian prototype for the motif "rampart and wall lament".

(k)". . . infants and babes faint in the streets of the city. Cry out in the night . . . for the lives of your children who faint with hunger at the head of every street" (ii 11 c, 19); and "the father turned away from his son . . . the child was abandoned . . . Ur like the child of a street which has been destroyed *seeks a place* before thee" (IUr 235-236, 370). The most that can be said of these parallel motifs is that they both refer to children. There is no reference in the Sumerian lamentations to the starvation of the children, nor to the cannibalism mentioned in Lam. ii 10 and iv 20. Falkenstein translates IUr 370 as, "Ur sucht dich wie ein Kind, das sich in den Strassen verloren hat" (IUr-F 210:15), and this fits the parallelism which follows, "thy house, like a man who has lost *everything stretches out* the hands to thee". There are no parallels to these similes in the Hebrew Lamentations.

(1) "My enemies have hunted me like a bird without cause" (iii 52); and "O my (city) attacked and destroyed, my (city) attacked without cause" (IUr 324-325). In the biblical lamentation there is no real assumption of the city's innocence or plea of ignorance, such as appears in IIUr 45-46: "what has my city done to thee, why hast thou turned from it? Enlil, what has my Ur done to thee. . . ." The poet, who combines the motifs of individual and collective Hebrew laments, introduces here the theme of personal innocence, a typical motif of individual laments as found in Ps. xxxv 7, "for without cause they hid their net for me".

(m) "The young men (have quit) their music. The joy of our hearts has ceased; our dancing has turned to mourning" (v 14-15); and "On the *uppu* and *alû* they play not for thee that which brings joy to the heart. . . . Thy song has been turned into weeping. . . . The . . . -music has been turned into lamentation" (IUr 356). This motif of joy being turned into mourning is a recurring one, appearing in numerous Akkadian texts, the eighth century Aramaic Sefire treaty, and prophetic passages (Ez. xxvi 13; Jer. vii 34 *et passim*)[24]. Although the original motif could possibly go back to some Sumerian source, there is no reason to assume that the motif's appearance in v 14-15 is directly related to the Sumerian lamentations.

(n) "Restore us to thyself, O Yahweh, that we may return; renew our days as of old" (v 21); and "O father, my begetter, return my city in its unity to thy side again. O Enlil, return my Ur in its unity to thy side again" (IIUr 55-56). Gadd has called attention to the similarity of these passages[25], but though they are similar it is not necessary to assume literary influence. The plea for renewal is as natural in this context as plea for renewed health in a lamentation due to sickness, e.g. Ps. vi 5, "return O Lord, and rescue my life, save me . . . ' If there is a literary parallel, the poet may well be echoing words from Jeremiah, "restore me that I may return, for thou art the Lord my God" (xxxi 18).

Other more remote parallels could possibly be added to this list, but they would add little evidence either for or against the influence of Sumerian lamentations upon the Hebrew *Lamentations*. These fourteen examples that have been quoted are the closest parallels and include those motifs which are basic to any assumption of literary dependency. Certain preliminary conclusions can be drawn on the basis of this evidence. First, the parallel motifs do not seem to be as "amazing" as Kraus suggests in his commentary. All of the motifs cited from Lamentations are either attested otherwise in biblical literature or have a prototype in the literary motifs current in Syria-Palestine. Second, certain dominant themes of the Sumerian lamentations find no parallel at all in this Hebrew lament. For example, one would expect to find the motif of the "evil storm" (which makes up all of the fifth song and part of the sixth song of IUr, and occurs in IIUr 10) somewhere in the biblical lamentation if there were any real literary dependency.

Any attempt to postulate Sumerian influence upon the Hebrew poets must deal with the problem of how the Hebrew poets of the mid-sixth century had knowledge of this particular Sumerian literary genre of the early second millenium. There is clear evidence that a part of the scribal and learned tradition in the post Sumerian period in Mesopotamia included knowing the Sumerian language and literary works; and even in the West, a part of the (syllabic) cuneiform scribe's learned tradition involved some elementary knowledge of Sumerian[26]. Furthermore, Akkadian versions of Sumerian literary works were known in the West. A large quantity of Babylonian literary fragments, including fragments of the Gilgamesh epic, were found at the Hittite capital of Boghazkhoy; and fragments of Sumero-Babylonian epics have been found at Ras Shamra[27]. Moreover, several fragments of Babylonian literary texts have turned up at Megiddo and Amarna[28]. According to W. G. Lambert, these literary works and traditions moved westward during the Amarna period (14th century) when Babylonian cuneiform was the international language from Egypt to the Persian Gulf[29]. But there is no evidence that these literary works survived in Syria-Palestine. One has to assume with Kramer that, "Sumerian influence penetrated the Bible through Canaanite, Hurrian, Hittite, and Akkadian literature", and with Lambert (who writes with particular reference to the Genesis parallels) that the traditions "reached the Hebrews in oral form"[30].

To date there is no evidence of a literary genre of "lamentations over destroyed cities" in any of the above literatures, though according to A. Leo Oppenheim this genre of the Sumerian literary tradition is reflected in the fourth tablet of the Era Epic which includes a long lament over the destruction of Babylon[31]. Nor is there any evidence that this particular literary tradition moved westward, which is not surprising since there is no special reason to assume that a lamentation over the destruction of a city would have wide popular appeal. Thus without any evidence that the Sumerian literary works survived in Syria-Palestine, or that this particular lamentation genre was known in the West, it is highly improbable that one can reconstruct a reasonable chain of literary transmission. Even if this lamentation genre had been known during the Amarna period, there is no reason to assume that the tradition was kept alive. Residents of Syria-Palestine were more apt to rejoice than lament over the destruction of Mesopotamian cities. If the Hebrew poets of the sixth century had knowledge of this Sumerian lamentation tradition, it is difficult to see how they could have learned of it in Palestine.

On the other hand it is difficult to agree with Gadd that the Hebrews learned and adopted this literary genre during the exile[32]), since there is no evidence that the Israelites were in a mood, so shortly after the fall of Jerusalem, to adopt a foreign form to express the loss of national treasures in lieu of their own rich local literary traditions[33]).

Since the suggested parallel motifs discussed above have at best only general—and quite natural—similarities, and in light of the difficulties encountered in accounting for the transmission of this literary genre down to mid-sixth century Palestine, it seems best to abandon any claim of literary dependence or influence of the Sumerian lamentations on the biblical **Lamentations**. At most the indebtedness would be the *idea* of a lamentation over a beloved city. But since there is such a natural corollary to individual and collective lamentations or funeral laments, indebtedness may properly be discarded.

Notes

1. See S. N. Kramer, "The Oldest Literary Catalogue: A Sumerian List of Literary Compositions Compiled about 2000 B. C.," *BASOR* 88 (Dec., 1942), 10-19; *idem,* "New Literary Catalogue from Ur", *RA* LV (1961), 169-176. For a listing of the lamentations with full bibliographical notations, see Kramer, *Sumerian Literary Texts From Nippur in the Museum of the Ancient Orient at Istanbul, AASOR* XXIII (1944), 33-36; and Maurice Lambert, "La littérature Sumérienne à propos d'ouvrages recents", *RA* LV (1961), 190-191. The term "Sumerian lamentations" in this study refers only to those lamentations which mourn the destruction of Sumerian cities and city-states. It does not include those lamentations concerned with the death of Dumuzi or one of his counterparts.

2. Kramer, *Lamentation Over the Destruction of Ur, OIP* XII (Chicago, 1940); *idem,* "Lamentation Over the Destruction of Ur", in *Ancient Near Eastern Texts Relating to the Old Testament,* ed. James B. Pritchard, 2nd ed. (Princeton, 1955), pp. 455-463 (cited below as I Ur); Maurus Witzel, "Die Klage über Ur", *Or* XIV (1945), 185-235; XV (1946), 46-63; A. Falkenstein, "Klage um die Zerstörung von Ur", in A. Falkenstein and W. von Soden, *Sumerische und akkadische Hymnen und Gebet* (Zürich and Stuttgart, 1953), pp. 192-213 (cited as IUr-F and *SAHG,* respectively).

3. C. J. Gadd, "The Second Lamentation for Ur", in *Hebrew and Semitic Studies Presented to Godfrey*

Rolles Driver, edd. D. W. Thomas and W. D. McHardy (London, 1963), pp. 59-71 (cited below as IIUR); Thorkild Jacobsen, "Primitive Democracy in Ancient Mesopotamia", *JNES* II (1943), 172 (cited below as IIUr-J); A. Falkenstein, "Ibbisin Klage", in *SAHG,* pp. 189-192 (cited IIUr-F).

4. See Kramer, *AASOR* XXIII (1944), 3; M. Lambert, *op. cit.;* and Wilhelm Rudolph, *Das Buch Ruth. Das Hohe Leid. Die Klagelieder (Kommentar zum Alten Testament),* 2nd ed. (Gütersloh, 1962), p. 213, where he cites a passage from Maurus Witzel, *Perlen sumerischer Poesie,* a book which this writer has not seen.

5. This lamentation over Akkad is part of "The Curse of Agade", a historiographic text, and not from the "lamentation" genre like the others cited above. But since it is cited by Hans-Joachim Kraus, *Klagelieder (Threni) (Biblischer Kommentar Altes Testament),* 2nd ed. (Neukirchen, 1960), p. 10, as a parallel lamentation and is included among the "lamentations" translated by Falkenstein (*SAHG,* pp. 187-189), it is included here in this list. See Kramer, *History Begins at Sumer,* Anchor Book ed. (New York, 1959), pp. 228-232; *idem,* "Sumerian Literature", *Analecta Biblica* XII (Rome, 1959), 196-197; *idem,* Sumerian Literature, A General Survey", *The Bible and the Ancient Near East,* ed. G. Ernest Wright (New York, 1961). p. 257; I. J. Gelb, *Old Akkadian Writing and Grammar,* Materials for the Assyrian Dictionary, 2nd ed. (Chicago, 1961), p. 201; Falkenstein, *SAHG,* p. 376.

6. "Sumerian Literature and the Bible", 201.

7. *Op. cit.,* p. 61.

8. *Op. cit.,* pp. 9-10.

9. *Op. cit.,* p. 9.

10. *Einleitung in Das Alte Testament* (Tübingen, 1964), p. 683.

11. Compare Kraus, *op. cit.,* pp. 9-10.

12. *Ibid.* This title seems a little misleading. The whole city-state was destroyed. The Sumerian poets did not restrict themselves to lamenting only the destruction of the temples and shrines. The Sumerians thought in terms of the "destruction of cities" as reflected in a *me* which deals specifically with the destruction of cities (see below, p. 205).

13. On the occurrence in non-elegiac passages see G. S. Glanzman, "Two Notes: Amos 3, 15 and Os. 11, 8-9" *CBQ* XXIII (1961), 230-232.

14. The particle is usually understood as the interrogative particle "how?" with enclitic *mem* (see Cyrus H. Gordon, *Ugaritic Textbook* [*Analecta Orientalia,* 38] [Rome, 1965], 19.147), but in this elegiac context it is more likely to be the expostulatory particle. On the necessity of adding an adverb in the English translation, see Glanzman, *op. cit.,* p. 231.

15. See Delbert R. Hillers, "Amos 7, 4 and Ancient Parallels", *CBQ* XXVI (1964), 221-225; and Patrick D.

Miller, "Fire in the Mythology of Canaan and Israel", *CBQ* XXVII (1965), 256-261, for studies on the use of fire as a divine instrument in Northwest Semitic literature.

16. The title of the lamentation over Akkad in the Old Babylonian literary catalogue is listed as, "Because of the Wrath of Enlil". See Kramer, *BASOR* 88 (1942), 15.

17. See p. 198, note 5.

18. See L. Koehler and W. Baumgartner, *Lexicon in Veteris Testamenti Libros* (Leiden, 1953), *sub voce ni'ēr.*

19. See Gadd, *op. cit.,* p. 61.

20. Reading here the asseverative particle *lu'* for MT *lō'*. For a full discussion with bibliographic notes, see the writer's "Philological Studies in Lamentations", *Biblica* XLIX (1968).

21. S. N. Kramer, *The Sumerians: Their History, Culture, and Character* (Chicago, 1963), p. 115.

22. *Ibid.,* p. 116.

23. See H. Jahnow, *Das hebräische Leichenlied im Rahmen der Völkerdichtung (ZAW* Beiheft 36) (Giessen, 1923), pp. 102-103.

24. See Delbert R. Hillers, *Treaty-Curses and the Old Testament Prophets. (Biblica et Orientalia,* 16) (Rome, 1964,) pp. 57-58.

25. *Op. cit.,* p. 70. Gadd cites (p. 66) one other parallel, namely Lam. ii 6 and IIUr 5, but does not elaborate, and this writer fails to see any similarity between, "Ur like a single reed makes no resistance (?)", and ii 6, "he has broken down his booth like that of a garden . . ." (RSV).

26. See Kramer, "Sumerian Literature", p. 253; *idem,* "Sumerian Literature, A General Survey", 186; and D. J. Wiseman, "Some Aspects of Babylonian Influence at Alalah", *Syria* XXXIX (1962), 180-187.

27. See Hans G. Güterbock, "Hittite Mythology", in *Mythologies of the Ancient World,* ed. S. N. Kramer (New York, 1961), pp. 154-155, 178; and for a recent discussion on Mesopotamian literary works in Syria-Palestine, with references, see W. G. Lambert, "A New Look at the Babylonian Background of Genesis", *JTS* NS XVI (1965), 287-300. See also M. Jean Nougayrol, "L'influence babylonienne à Ugarit, d'après les Textes en cunéiformes classique", *Syria* XXXIX (1962), 28-35.

28. See W. G. Lambert, *op. cit.,* 299.

29. *Op. cit.,* 299-300.

30. Kramer, "Sumerian Literature, a General Survey", 190; and W. G. Lambert, *op. cit.,* 300.

31. *Ancient Mesopotamia* (Chicago, 1964), p. 267. For the Era Epic itself, see F. Gössman, *Das Era-Epos* (Würtzburg, 1956), and reviews of this work by W. G. Lambert in *Afo* XVIII (1958), 395-401; and B. Kienast in *ZA* LIV (1961), 244-249. Lambert suggests that the historical background of this epic is in the Sutü raids and civil war during the reign of Adad-apal-idinna (1067-1046) and that it was composed at the order of Nabû-apal-iddina (c. 880-850) to chronicle the fall and rise of Akkad. See also Erica Reiner, "Plague Amulets and House Blessings", *JNES* XIX (1960), 148-155, for a discussion on the use of parts of the Era Epic on amulets to preserve one from the plague. For an English translation of portions of the text, see Kramer in *Mythologies of the Ancient World,* ed. S. N. Kramer (New York, 1961), pp. 127-135. In terms of literary form, style and motifs, there is little, if any, resemblance between Tablet IV of the Era Epic and the Sumerian lamentations; there is no resemblance to the Hebrew Lamentations. The only apparent parallel is that the three works are concerned with the destruction of a city and references are made to wailing and crying.

32. "The Second Lamentation for Ur", p. 61.

33. For a full discussion of Northwest Semitic lexical and syntactical elements in Lamentations, see the writer's "Philological Studies in Lamentations", *Biblica* XLIX (1968).

Dilbert R. Hillers (essay date 1972)

SOURCE: An introduction to *The Anchor Bible: "Lamentations,"* Doubleday & Company, Inc., 1972, pp. xv-xli.

[*In the following essay, Hillers provides an overview of* Lamentations *and explores a number of topics including its place in the biblical canon; its alphabetic acrostics; its meter, parallelism, syntax, and strophic structure; and its liturgical use.*]

THE MEANING AND PURPOSE OF *LAMENTATIONS*

"In the fifth month, on the seventh day of the month, in the nineteenth year of King Nebuchadnezzar, king of Babylon, Nebuzaradan, captain of the guard, an official of the king of Babylon, entered Jerusalem. He burned down the house of Yahweh, and the king's house; and all the houses in Jerusalem, including every great man's house, he set on fire and burned. The whole army of the Chaldaeans tore down the walls of Jerusalem, all around. . . . The rest of the people who were left in the city, and those who had deserted to the king of Babylon, and the rest of the populace, Nebuzaradan, captain of the guard, took to Babylon as prisoners. The captain of the guard left only some of the poorest in the country to tend the vines and farm the land" (II Kings 25:8-12).

Thus the book of Kings states the facts about the fall of Jerusalem in 587 B.C. *Lamentations* supplies the meaning of the facts. It is first of all a recital of the horrors and atrocities that came during the long siege and its aftermath, but beyond the tale of physical sufferings it tells of the spiritual significance of the fall of the city. For the ancient people chosen by Yahweh it meant the destruction of every cherished symbol of their election by God. In line after line the poet recalls all the precious, sacred things which had been lost or shattered: the city itself, once "the perfection of beauty, the joy of the whole earth"; the city walls and towers, once the outward sign that "God is in the midst of her"; the king, "the anointed of Yahweh, the breath of our nostrils"; the priests, and with them all festive and solemn worship; the prophets, and with them all visions and the living word of God; the land itself, Israel's "inheritance" from Yahweh, now turned over to strangers; the people—dead, exiled, or slaves in their own land. Every sign that had once provided assurance and confidence in God was gone.

Thus *Lamentations* served the survivors of the catastrophe in the first place as an expression of the almost inexpressible horror and grief they felt. Men live on best after calamity, not by utterly repressing their grief and shock, but by facing it, by measuring its dimensions, by finding some form of words to order and articulate their experience. *Lamentations* is so complete and honest and eloquent an expression of grief that even centuries after the events which inspired it, it is still able to provide those in mute despair with words to speak.

The book is not only an expression of grief, however, but a confession. It is not a perplexed search for the meaning of the catastrophe, still less an attempt to evade responsibility for it. Israel's prophets had foretold with unmistakable clarity the destruction of the nation, and divine punishment for the iniquity of the fathers was the well-known, inescapable darker side of the covenant with God. *Lamentations* says "Amen" to the prophetic judgment on the sin of the people, and calls it greater than that of Sodom and Gomorrah. Worst of all had been the iniquity of the spiritual leaders. Hence it was Yahweh himself who had consumed Israel. What had come on them was nothing less than the day of the Lord, the day of his wrath.

Central to the book, however, is an expression of hope. It is the merit of *Lamentations* that it does not quickly or easily promise away the present agony. It does not encourage the remnant of Israel to take comfort in the fathers, or in the exodus, or in the land, or Zion, or the line of David, or any of the old symbols of her status with God. The series of "mighty acts of God" toward Israel had ended with an unmistakable act of judgment, so that the nation's history could be no source of hope. Nor does it at any point forecast a speedy turn in the fortunes of Israel. Instead the book offers, in its central chapter, the example of an unnamed man who has suffered under the hand of God. *To sketch this typical sufferer, this "Everyman," the language and ideas of the psalms of individual lament, a tradition quite separate from the national history, are drawn on.* From near despair, this man wins through to confidence that God's mercy is not at an end, and that his final, inmost will for man is not suffering. From this beginning of hope the individual turns to call the nation to penitent waiting for God's mercy.

The medium through which these various meanings are expressed is a series of poems composed with deliberate artistry. *As is the case with any work of poetic art, so with* **Lamentations,** *the meaning is not fully statable apart from the form in which the author clothed it.* It cannot be reduced to a set of propositions without serious loss. The present writer offers the above merely as a rough restatement of some major themes in the poems, and prefers to take up more detailed discussion of the meaning of the book only in the COMMENTS which accompany the poems.

THE NAME OF THE BOOK

In the Hebrew Bible *Lamentations* has the title 'ēkāh, "How," the initial word of the book. In the Babylonian Talmud, however (Baba Bathra 14b), and in other early Jewish writings, the book is called qīnōt, that is, *Lamentations.* The title in the Greek Bible, *threnoi,* and in the Vulgate, *threni,* is a translation of this Hebrew name. Quite frequently manuscripts and printed editions of the versions will add: "of Jeremiah," or "of Jeremiah the prophet."

PLACE IN THE CANON

The canonicity of *Lamentations* has never been a matter of dispute. The position of *Lamentations* in the canon of the Hebrew scriptures, however, is of some importance for the question of authorship. It is never placed among the Prophets, where the book of Jeremiah stands, but is always somewhere in the third division of the Hebrew canon, the Writings (*Ketubim*). Its exact position among the Writings has varied in different ages and in different communities. The Babylonian Talmud (Baba Bathra 14b) records a very old tradition which lists the Writings "chronologically," that is, according to their traditional date; the five Scrolls (*Megillot*) are not grouped together, and *Lamentations,* which refers to the Babylonian captivity, comes near the end of the list, just before Daniel and Esther. Hebrew bibles, however, reflect liturgical practice in that within the Writings they group the five short books (the "Scrolls," Hebrew *Megillot*) which had come to be read in public worship on five important festivals. The edition commonly used in scholarly study today, Kittel's *Biblia hebraica* (BH³), is based on a manuscript of A.D. 1008 (Codex Leningradensis) which lists the Scrolls in "chronological" order: Ruth, Song of Songs (from when Solomon was young!), Ecclesiastes (from his old age), *Lamentations,* and Esther. In many manuscripts and printed bibles, however, especially those used by Ashkenazic Jews, the order is that in which the festivals come in the calendar: Song of Songs (Passover); Ruth (Weeks, *Shabuot,* Pentecost), *Lamentations* (the Ninth of Ab), Ecclesiastes (Tabernacles, Succoth), and Esther (Purim). The second major tradition puts *Lamentations* just after Jeremiah (Baruch comes between them in some cases). This is the order followed, for example, in the Septuagint (LXX), the ancient Greek translation of the Bible, in the Vulgate, Jerome's Latin translation, and in English Bibles commonly used among Christians. This order was anciently known to Josephus, as may be inferred from his account of the Hebrew canon (*Contra Apionem* I 8), and is also followed by Melito of Sardis (d.

190; see Eusebius *Historia ecclesiastica* IV xxvi 14) and by Origen (Eusebius VI xxv 2). As Jerome explains, this listing fits with an enumeration of the Old Testament books which makes their number agree with the letters of the Hebrew alphabet; "Jeremias cum Cinoth" counts as one book. Jerome, however, does mention the existence of a varying tradition which put **Lamentations** and Ruth with the Writings ("Prologus Galeatus," *Patrologia Latina* 28, cols. 593-604).

THE DATE OF *LAMENTATIONS*

The view commonly held by modern scholars agrees closely with the traditional view, that is, that the book of Lamentations was written not long after the fall of Jerusalem in 587 B.C. The memory of the horrors of that event seems to be still fresh in the mind of the author or authors. Moreover, the book at no point testifies to a belief that things would soon change for the better; the kind of hope that appeared in later exilic times had not yet arisen.

Considerable scholarly effort has been expended on determining the order in which the five separate poems were written, but no consensus exists. Wilhelm Rudolph has argued that chapter 1 must date from the first capture of Jerusalem by the Babylonians, that is, from shortly after 597, not from after 587 B.C. His main reason for this view, which has won some adherents, is that chapter 1 does not speak of the *destruction* of the city and temple as do the other chapters, but only of its capture.[1] This is essentially an argument from silence, and is not a secure basis for separating the chapter from the others chronologically. Before Rudolph, other scholars argued for putting chapter 1 somewhat later than 2 and 4. Furthermore, the evidence of the new Babylonian Chronicle shows that the first siege must have been quite short,[2] which does not fit with the references in the chapter to severe famine (1:11, 19; see commentary on 11). Others have wanted to put chapter 3 later than the others because it has a less vivid description of events in the siege than 2 and 4. The truth is that there is insufficient evidence for a precise chronological ordering of the separate laments.[3]

THE AUTHORSHIP OF *LAMENTATIONS*

That the prophet Jeremiah wrote **Lamentations** is so firmly rooted in traditions about the Bible, in western literature, and even in art, that even after the ascription to Jeremiah was challenged (first in 1712, by H. von der Hardt[4]), discussion of the book's authorship has tended to take the form of listing reasons why Jeremiah could not have written the book, or why he must have, as though the tradition was unanimous. Ancient tradition on this point is not in fact unanimous, however, and it may clarify the question best if the separate traditions are first listed. Then, as though it were a problem of deciding between textual variants, we may ask: which tradition can best account for the origin of the other?

The first tradition does not name any author for the book, and implies that it was not Jeremiah. This is the tradition represented by the Masoretic Text (MT), which says nothing whatever about the authorship of the book, and in which **Lamentations** is separated from Jeremiah and put among the Writings (*Ketubim*); for details see "Place in the Canon," above.

The second tradition is that Jeremiah wrote the book. The Septuagint prefixes these words to the first chapter: "And it came to pass after Israel had gone into captivity, and Jerusalem was laid waste, that Jeremiah sat weeping and composed this lament over Jerusalem and said—." This heading found in the Greek translation may possibly go back to a Hebrew original, for it is Semitic rather than Greek in style. In the Septuagint **Lamentations** is placed with other works by Jeremiah. The Vulgate follows the Greek closely, both in the ordering of the book, and in the heading. The Targum (Aramaic translation) ascribes the book to Jeremiah, but in different words and more briefly. It is in accord with other Jewish tradition as recorded, for example, in the Babylonian Talmud (Baba Bathra 15a). In rabbinic writings passages from **Lamentations** are often introduced by "Jeremiah said." The heading in the Syriac version (Peshitta) titles the work: "The book of **Lamentations** of Jeremiah the prophet." The oldest of these ancient authorities is the Septuagint.

In spite of the great antiquity of this tradition, it is relatively easy to account for it as secondary to the other. In the first place, there was a very natural desire in the early days of biblical interpretation to determine the authorship of anonymous biblical books. As the one major prophetic figure active in Judah just before and after the fall of Jerusalem, Jeremiah was a candidate sufficiently qualified to meet the demands of a none-too-critical age, especially since certain of his words seemed to fit the theme of **Lamentations**: "O that my head were waters, and my eyes a fount of tears, that I might weep day and night for the slain of my people" (9:1[8:23H]). Secondly, there was an explicit statement in the Bible that Jeremiah wrote laments, II Chron 35:25, which is translated here as literally as possible so that some of the difficulties of the verse may stand out: "And Jeremiah sang a lament [or laments] over Josiah. And all the male and female singers spoke of Josiah in their laments, unto this day. And they made them a fixed observance for Israel. And behold they are written in the [book of] Laments." Actually nothing in the extant book of **Lamentations** can be taken as referring to the death of Josiah in 609 B.C. The reference to the king in 4:20 must be to Zedekiah, who was king at the fall of Jerusalem. It is difficult to suppose that the Chronicler is simply mistaken, that he actually intended to ascribe authorship of the canonical book to Jeremiah. It is easier to suppose that he gives correct information: Jeremiah, and others as well, composed laments over Josiah, and these were gathered in a book called **Lamentations,** but this has nothing to do with the extant biblical book. Nevertheless, the Chronicler's statement that Jeremiah wrote Laments would have encouraged the idea that he was the author of **Lamentations,** especially since very early on some passages in the biblical book were taken to refer to Josiah (see the Targum on 1:18; 4:20).[5] To sum up, given the anonymous book of *Lamentations,* it is possible to give a plausible account of how it could have come to be ascribed to Jeremiah, and eventually to be placed after the book of Jeremiah.

If one assumes the opposite, that the book was understood as Jeremiah's from the beginning, it is difficult to suggest any good reason why it was ever separated from his other writings, or circulated without his name. Wiesmann's argument that this was done for liturgical reasons, in order to group Lamentations with the other Scrolls (*Megillot*), is without force, for the oldest listing of the Writings does not group the Scrolls together, and yet includes *Lamentations* (see above, on "Place in the Canon").

In addition, there is evidence within the book which makes it difficult to suppose that Jeremiah wrote it. Certain statements would be, if not impossible, then at least out of character in the mouth of Jeremiah. For example, 4:17, with its pathetic description of how "we" looked in vain for help from "a nation that does not save," is at variance with Jeremiah's outspoken hostility to reliance on help from other nations (Jer 2:18), and the fact that he did not expect help from Egypt (37:5-10). Would Jeremiah, who prophesied the destruction of the temple, have written 1:10? The high hopes set on Zedekiah in 4:20 ("the breath of our nostrils . . . of whom we said, 'In his shadow we will live among the nations'") are not easy to square with Jeremiah's blunt words to the same king: "You will be given into the hand of the king of Babylon" (37:17). "Her prophets find no vision from Yahweh" (2:9) is in the last analysis a rather odd statement from one who prophesied before, during, and after the catastrophe. If 4:19 refers to the flight of Zedekiah (see II Kings 25:4-5) and implies that the author took part, as many suppose (see COMMENT on the passage), then the author was not Jeremiah, who was in prison at the time (Jer 38:28). It may be granted that any of the above-mentioned details has seemed to some scholars compatible with authorship by Jeremiah, and that those who oppose it do not fully agree on which set of arguments proves the case! Even so, these and other details in the book suggest an author or authors more closely identified with the common hopes and fears of the people than it was possible for Jeremiah to be.

Arguments from the language of the book, especially from the vocabulary employed,[6] and from the acrostic form have been used to argue against Jeremianic authorship. These seem indecisive. The lexical evidence seems to suggest that the book has ties with Ezekiel, Second Isaiah, the Psalms, and Jeremiah—that is, its vocabulary not surprisingly resembles that of roughly contemporary writers in some respects.

There is no conclusive evidence as to whether the book is the work of one author, or of several, and both views have been defended in modern times. The unity of form, that is, the fact that all the poems are alphabetic in one way or another, and that the first four have metrical features in common, does suggest that all are the work of one author. One may also point to the fundamental unity in point of view through the whole book, and to resemblances in linguistic detail between one chapter and another. It is possible to read the sequence of chapters as meaningful, which suggests unified authorship or at least intelligent editing. Other scholars, however, find differences in point of view from chapter to chapter (thus 2 and 4 are said to have more of an "eye-witness" character than 1 and 3). The present writer has attempted to interpret the poems as an intelligible unity, whether or not this unity results from one author or from an editor who ordered originally separate works. So as not always to be saying "author or authors," the singular form is regularly used in the NOTES and COMMENTS.

Some modern commentators, notably Gottwald, Albrektson, and Kraus, have devoted much effort to delineating the theological traditions on which the author drew, and on this basis have offered conjectures as to the circles from which the book must have come. In Kraus's opinion the author was apparently from among the cult-prophets or the priesthood of Jerusalem, while according to Gottwald he unites the spirit of both priest and prophet, so that the book may offer evidence that there were indeed cult-prophets in ancient Israel.[7] In spite of the value of these minute examinations of the book's theological content, they come close to overemphasizing the individuality of the writer's theology. In actuality the book betrays little one-sidedness, and if it contains themes from various earlier traditions, it seems possible that the author was a layman, and perhaps, as has often been supposed on the basis of 4:19-20, someone connected with the royal court.

PLACE OF COMPOSITION

The events and conditions with which the book of *Lamentations* deals are without exception located in Judah. Conversely, the book evinces no acquaintance with or special interest in the plight of exiles in Babylon or Egypt. In the absence of any strong evidence to the contrary, then, it seems best to suppose that the book was written in Palestine. Scholars have proposed that the whole book, or parts of it, were composed elsewhere, and it must be conceded that Jews in exile—Ezekiel is a notable example—could be very well informed about conditions back home, but nothing in the book furnishes positive evidence that it was written by an exile.

ALPHABETIC ACROSTICS

All five poems in *Lamentations* are in one way or another shaped according to the Hebrew alphabet. This is most noticeable in the first four poems, which are alphabetic acrostics. *Chapters 1 and 2 are of a relatively simple type,* in which each stanza has three lines, and only the first word of the first line of each is made to conform to the alphabet, so that stanza one begins with *aleph,* stanza two with *beth,* and so on through the twenty-two letters of the Hebrew alphabet. Chapter 4 is of the same type, but here each stanza has only two lines. Chapter 3 is more elaborate: each stanza has three lines, and all three lines are made to begin with the proper letter, so that there are three lines starting with *aleph,* three with *beth,* and so on. No attempt has been made to reproduce this acrostic feature in the translation given below, for obvious reasons, though the Hebrew letters listed beside the stanzas are intended to call the reader's attention to this phenomenon in the original. Monsignor Ronald Knox did carry through the *tour de force* of reproducing the acrostic in his translation of the Bible, and a sample is quoted here (Lam 3:1-7) to give readers an idea of its effect, though it must be said that Knox strains the English language more than the author of Lamentations did the Hebrew.[8]

> Ah, what straits have I not known, under the
>   avenging rod!
> Asked I for light, into deeper shadow the Lord's
>   guidance led me;
> Always upon me, none other, falls endlessly the
>   blow.
> Broken this frame, under the wrinkled skin, the
>   sunk flesh.
> Bitterness of despair fills my prospect,
>   walled in on every side;
> Buried in darkness, and, like the dead,
>   interminably.
> Closely he fences me in, etc.

Chapter 5 is not an acrostic, but has exactly twenty-two lines and thus conforms to the alphabet to a lesser degree. Other biblical poems with twenty-two lines exist—Pss 33, 38, 103—and it is reasonable to suppose that in all these cases the number of lines is chosen intentionally, though none are acrostics.

There are many acrostic poems in the Bible and in other literature, and this commentary is not the place for a full discussion of the form, about which a good deal has been written.[9] Yet it is so prominent a characteristic of *Lamentations* that some explanation of its purpose and effect must be given. There are really two separate questions involved: the history and purpose of the acrostic form as a whole, and the purpose of the author of Lamentations in using it.

Acrostic compositions were written in both ancient Egypt[10] and ancient Mesopotamia.[11] As is well known, the writing systems of these civilizations were not alphabetic, and therefore their acrostics are not alphabetic either. The most elaborate Mesopotamian acrostic is syllabic. The poem has twenty-seven stanzas of eleven lines each. Each line within an individual stanza begins with the same syllable, and taken together the initial syllables of the stanzas spell out a pious sentence: "I, Saggil-kinam-ubbib, the incantation priest, am adorant of the god and the king."[12] The date of this composition is uncertain, but is probably about 1000 B.C., earlier by far than any datable biblical acrostic. It has been common for scholars to minimize the possibility of a connection between biblical use of acrostics and these extra-biblical works, on the ground that these are syllable or word acrostics as opposed to the alphabetic acrostics in-

side the Bible, and that they are meaningfully connected with the sense of the poem, as opposed to the meaningless sequence of the letters in the alphabetic type. In spite of these differences, it seems likely that the basic idea of an acrostic, the idea of weaving a pattern of syllables or letters separate from its content into a composition at the beginning or end of the lines, came into Hebrew literature from outside. The major implication is that in discussing biblical acrostics we are apt to be dealing with a phenomenon that is quite ancient and far from its source.

Many explanations for the purpose of acrostics have been suggested, and it is likely that more than one motive was involved. Especially in later times, in medieval magical and speculative works, ideas about the mystical power of the letters of the alphabet seem to have occasioned use of the acrostic form. A more prosaic purpose of acrostics was to aid the memory. Verse is easier to get by heart than prose, and still easier when the sequence of lines follows a set pattern. Finally, acrostics were written for what may be called artistic purposes, to display the author's skill and to make his work a more skillfully wrought offering to his god and to contribute to the structure of the poem. Several writers have proposed that alphabetic acrostics convey the idea of completeness, that is, that "everything from A to Z" has been expressed.[13]

Against this background we may inquire what led the author of *Lamentations* to use the acrostic form. There is no reason to believe that he or his contemporaries associated magical powers with the alphabet, as was done later. On the other hand, though it is true that acrostic form makes the poems easier to memorize, we have no way of knowing whether this was the author's conscious purpose, or simply an incidental effect. The suggestion that the book was deliberately written as a school exercise (so Munch) is extremely improbable. If the author had any dominating conscious purpose in mind in choosing the acrostic form, it was perhaps to contribute to the artistry of his poems; he thought it made his poems more beautiful. In addition, the acrostic has the effect of controlling and giving form to the poems. It limits and shapes material which is somewhat monotonous and at some points lacking any clear progression of action or thought. Again, it is impossible to be sure that the author consciously intended such an effect.

Those who have expressed an opinion on the artistic worth of these and other acrostic poems in the Bible have generally rated them rather low. Gunkel, for instance, speaks of their composition as "the pious practice of a modest art."[14] Skehan probably speaks for many in confessing to "being immensely and overwhelmingly bored by Ps. 119,"[15] and others may feel similar ennui at *Lamentations.* Certainly there is no great intrinsic merit in being able to compose acrostics; as a technical task it cannot have been very difficult. But not all acrostics are of the same merit. In Ps 119 one has the impression that the writer has chosen a large and difficult form which he labors mightily to fill up, like a tax-blank. In *Lamentations,* the impression is rather of a boundless grief, an overflowing emotion, whose expression benefits from the limits imposed by a confining acrostic form, as from the rather tightly fixed metrical pattern.

A minor peculiarity of the acrostics in chapters 2, 3, and 4 is that two of the letters of the Hebrew alphabet stand in the reverse of their normal order. Usually it is *ayin* before *pe,* and this is the order in chapter 1, but in the other acrostics the sequence is first *pe,* then *ayin.* This peculiarity is found also in the Greek version of Prov 31, and in the opinion of many scholars should be restored in Ps 34, where the conventional order of the alphabet seems to violate the sense. A common explanation, going back to Grotius, is that the order of these letters of the alphabet was not yet fixed at this time. This is sheerly hypothetical, and rather improbable in view of the consistent sequence *ayin-pe* in Ugaritic abecedaries almost a millennium older than **Lamentations,** and in view of the order of the Greek alphabet, but no more reasonable hypothesis has been advanced. In any case, this variation need not point to different authors for chapter 1 and chapters 2-4.

LITERARY TYPES

Hermann Gunkel carried out an analysis of the five poems in **Lamentations** which has been very widely followed since. Chapter 5, he wrote, is a communal lament. Chapter 3 is an individual lament in the main, and chapters 1, 2, and 4 are funeral songs—not for individuals, of course, but political or national funeral songs.[16] As Gunkel himself stated, however, all but chapter 5 are mixed, impure specimens of the categories to which they belong: the individual lament in 3 is interrupted by a communal lament (vss. 40-51). The funeral songs contain elements which do not properly belong there, such as the short prayers for help and the invocation of the name of Yahweh. In Gunkel's view, this admixture of alien elements is due to the relatively late date of **Lamentations;** the book comes from a time when the literary types are no longer kept separate, but are intermingled so thoroughly that even the dominant motif of a particular type may be lost.

Whether this generalization concerning the course of Israel's literary history is valid or not lies outside the scope of this commentary, but it is important to note that we derive relatively little help from from-criticism of the book. If one agrees, for example, that 1, 2, and 4 are funeral songs, one must immediately go on to note the fundamental differences from what is assumed to have been the classic form. Who is supposed to be dead?—the question makes the difficulty evident at once, for the basic situation to which every genuine funeral song is directed is not dominant in these poems. Similarly, in its earlier portion especially chapter 3 may be linked to the psalms of individual lament, but the poem as a whole bursts the confines of this form. Only chapter 5 stays relatively close to the pattern of a traditional literary type. Otherwise, it seems that the writer had no liturgical or literary models which he followed slavishly. On the other hand, in language and imagery he follows tradition rather closely.

SUMERIAN INFLUENCE

The question of Sumerian influence on **Lamentations** is a separate one. S. N. Kramer, who has edited and translated the principal Sumerian laments over ruined cities, has repeatedly stated that the biblical book of **Lamentations** is under the direct influence of Sumerian laments. The latest statement of his opinion is as follows: "Just how deeply this mournful literary genre affected the neighboring lands is unknown, no lamentations have as yet been recovered from Hittite, Canaanite and Hurrian sources. But there is little doubt that the biblical **Book of Lamentations** owes no little of its form and content to its Mesopotamian forerunners, and, that the modern orthodox Jew who utters his mournful lament at the 'western wall' of 'Solomon's' long-destroyed Temple, is carrying on a tradition begun in Sumer some 4,000 years ago. . . ."[17] The Assyriologist Gadd is of the same opinion[18] and such a view has won the adherence of a distinguished commentator on Lamentations, H.-J. Kraus, who writes that the parallels are astounding.[19]

On the opposite side of the question is T. F. McDaniel. Having examined and compared the Sumerian and Akkadian lamentations translated so far, McDaniel concludes that the parallels are not such as to compel one to assume that there was any connection.[20] Such resemblances as do exist can be explained as the result of a common subject matter. Weiser also in his commentary, finds the resemblances to Sumerian laments very general and unconvincing, and the differences in thought and style much more impressive. He rejects emphatically Kraus's idea that before the fall of Jerusalem there was in Israel a liturgical "Lament over the Ruined Sanctuary."

In the opinion of the present writer, it is difficult to see how the Sumerian texts can have had *direct* influence on the biblical **Lamentations.** How could an Israelite writer or writers in the sixth century B.C. have had firsthand acquaintance with these Mesopotamian compositions? One must agree that there are genuine, and occasionally close parallels in wording but these are to be explained in a wider context. In some cases at least, the literary motifs in the Sumerian laments are paralleled elsewhere in Mesopotamian literature, and where there is a parallel in Lamentations there are parallels elsewhere in the Bible. When we find resemblance between these laments from the early second millennium B.C. and **Lamentations,** it is most likely evidence of the general truth that in many respects Israel's literature is dependent on an older tradition, and that Mesopotamian literature made a rich contribution to the tradition.

To illustrate the point made above, note the following examples; the Sumerian texts are quoted in Kramer's translation:[21] "Ur . . . inside it we die of famine // Outside we are killed by the weapons of the Elamites."[22] This is a genuine parallel to Lam 1:20c and the resemblance is rather striking: "Outside the sword killed my children; inside, it was *famine*" (on the last word, see NOTE). But it is also parallel to Ezek 7:15: "The sword outside, and pestilence and famine inside," and also to Jer 14:18 and Deut 32:25. From a Sumerian text related to the lament genre, the "Curse of Agade" comes a close parallel: "Over your *usga*-place,[23] established for lustrations, // May the 'fox of the ruined mounds,' glide his tail."[24] Compare Lam 5:18 "On mount Zion, which lies desolate, foxes prowl about." But the idea that a ruined city should be the haunt of wild animals is found also in Assyrian royal inscriptions, in an Aramaic treaty (Sefîre I A 32-33) and repeatedly in the Bible. Hence the true situation is that we have to do with a literary convention common to Mesopotamian and biblical literature, and not restricted to the lament genre. A few other Sumerian parallels are quoted in the NOTES below; they are meant to illustrate the persistence of ancient literary motifs into late biblical literature, and not to prove a specific connection of *Lamentations* to Sumerian laments.

METER, PARALLEISM, SYNTAX, AND STROPHIC STRUCTURE

The acrostic form of the first four chapters permits us in most cases to divide the poems into lines as the author intended. It is partly due to this fortunate circumstance that *Lamentations* has occupied so prominent a place in the study of Hebrew meter. A more important factor, however, has been the recognition that these lines follow a rhythmic pattern that seems relatively easy to detect and distinguish from other varieties of Hebrew verse. The classic essay on the meter of *Lamentations* is Karl Budde's "Das hebräische Klagelied" (The Hebrew Song of Lament), which appeared in 1882 (ZAW 2, pp. 1-52). Although Budde's views still merit restatement, subsequent studies have made important modifications necessary, and in general the unsatisfactory state of our knowledge of Hebrew metrics, a field in which no theory can claim general acceptance, makes it necessary at present to be very cautious in describing the meter of *Lamentations.*

A brief survey of some competing views may make clear the nature of the difficulty. One major school of thought, the chief representatives being Hölscher,[25] Mowinckel,[26] Horst,[27] and Segert,[28] holds that the decisive characteristic of Hebrew meter (at least in the period we are concerned with) is alternation of stressed and unstressed syllables of the same length, much as in Syriac meter. A more widely followed system has been that of Ley[29] as modified by Sievers[30] and subsequent students. In this system, the basis of Hebrew meter is not syllables, but accents. The various types of lines are distinguished by various numbers and patterns of accents. It is characteristic of followers of this school that rhythmic patterns are symbolized by numbers, thus a line made up of two parts (bicolon), each containing three accents, will be described as 3+3.[31] In recent years a different view has been advocated by David Noel Freedman who describes lines of Hebrew verse according to the number of *syllables* per colon (part of a line) or bicolon, and the rhythmic pattern of syllables within the line, or the number of accents, are not treated as relevant.[32] No full statement of this last theory is yet available, yet it

is bound to attract notice if only because older theories encounter great difficulties and have failed to win general acceptance.

With this present uncertainty over the most basic questions in mind, we may turn back to Budde's views about *Lamentations.* According to Budde, the formal unit in *Lamentations* is a line divided into two parts by a break in sense. The first part of each line is a normal half-line (colon) of Hebrew poetry, while the second part is shorter than the normal colon. This second half-line cannot be only a single word, however, but must be a group of two or more words. Since the first half-line must be at least one word longer, the lines are of the pattern 3+2, 4+3, 4+2, and so on.

Budde found this meter most readily evident in chapter 3, where apparent exceptions are, in his opinion, either indications of textual corruption, or examples of some permissible variants to the normal pattern. For example, occasionally the first colon is shorter than the second, producing a 2+3 line; in such cases one must assume a tension between the artificial poetic rhythm and the actual, natural sentence rhythm. At the cost of somewhat greater effort he goes on to discover the same sort of unbalanced verse in all the lines of chapters 4, 1, and 2, without exception.

Budde went on to assert that this type of verse is found elsewhere in the Bible also, and the evidence suggested that it was the specific meter traditionally used for singing laments over the dead. He therefore titled it *"Qinah"* meter from the Hebrew word for a lament. The potential significance of this theory for the interpretation of *Lamentations* is obvious, for if it is correct the student of the book is given a very useful tool for reconstructing the text of difficult passages, and also possesses clear evidence connecting *Lamentations* to the tradition of funeral songs. (There is very general agreement that chapter 5 is in a different rhythm, being divided into cola of equal length, a pattern extremely common in the Old Testament.)

Since Budde wrote, Sievers especially has shown that in *Lamentations* a sizable proportion of the lines are not in Budde's unbalanced *"Qinah"* meter, but consist of evenly balanced cola.[33] Though scholars would disagree with details of Sievers' own analysis, as he himself anticipated, many would now agree that Budde overstated his case. Some lines are better described as 2+2 (e.g., 4:13a, b) and some are probably 3+3, though there is greater reluctance to recognize the latter type as legitimate, many scholars preferring to emend lines of this sort. Possible examples of 3+3 are 1:1a, 8a, 16a, 21b; 2:9a, 17c, 20a; 3:64, 66; 4:1a, 8b. Thus Budde's view must be modified by saying that the *"Qinah"* line is at best the dominant line in *Lamentations;* other metric patterns occur more or less at random throughout the first four chapters. Atypical verses are especially common in chapter 1, and less so in chapter 3. The result of this mixture is that the meter is not nearly as useful in text-criticism as it might be.

A second major modification of Budde's theory is equally important: the dominant verse-type cannot properly be called *"Qinah"* (Lament) meter, because it is used in various classes of Hebrew poems having nothing to do with laments for the dead. Sievers, one of the first to raise this objection, cites as other passages in this meter Isa 1:10-12 (a prophetic oracle of judgment); Isa 40:9 ff. (an oracle of hope); Jonah 2:2-9[3-10H] (psalm of lament by an individual); Song of Songs 1:9-11 (part of a love song), as well as others.[34] Moreover, certain funeral songs are not in *"Qinah"* meter, notably David's lament over Saul and Jonathan (II Sam 1: 17-27). Though scholars have been willing to concede that this "rhythm that always dies away," as Budde called it, seems very appropriate for poetry of a somber character, we cannot use the meter of **Lamentations** to connect it to a tradition of funeral songs. On the other hand, it is convenient to keep the name *"Qinah"* meter as a handy way of referring to the type.

No attempt has been made in the present translation to reproduce or imitate the meter of the original.[35] Occasionally a line, literally translated, falls into something like the typical *"Qinah"* verse, for example, 3:4:

> He wore out my flesh and skin;
> he broke my bones.

Characterization of the poetic style of **Lamentations** is not complete without some account of the parallelism found in the poems, and as it turns out this raises further questions concerning the meter. Poetic parallelism may be illustrated by almost any verse from chapter 5 of **Lamentations**, for example, 5:2:

> Our land is turned over to strangers;
> Our houses, to foreigners.

The second colon corresponds to and resembles the first, that is, there is a semantic association between "land" and "houses" and between "strangers" and "foreigners," and in this case the verb of the first colon is to be understood also with the second though it is not repeated. Such resemblance between poetic units is, as is well known, a pervasive feature of Hebrew poetry, and is found to some extent throughout **Lamentations.** But parallelism is not present in *all* the lines of Lamentations. (By line I mean a line of Hebrew text as printed in Kittel's *Biblia hebraica*,[36] which is a satisfactory working definition.) Disregarding what has traditionally been called "synthetic" parallelism, that is, cases where a line may be separated into two parts but where there is no clear semantic or grammatical resemblance between the two.[37] 104 out of the 266 lines in the book do not exhibit parallelism (39 per cent). More significant is the contrast between chapter 5 and the first four chapters. There is a much higher proportion of parallelism in 5, where only three lines out of twenty-two (14 per cent) do not have parallelism. One may note that two of these lines, 5:9 and 10, while without internal parallelism, might be regarded as parallel to each other (external parallelism). By contrast, in the first four chapters 101 of 244 lines (41 per cent) do not contain parallelism. This contrast amplifies our notion of the different poetic style employed in chapters 1-4 as over against 5, which is not solely a metrical difference.

Even though others would undoubtedly disagree with the present writer concerning the presence or absence of parallelism in individual verses, the general pattern sketched above may probably be regarded as correct. If so, our description of the meter is affected. We have described it above as consisting of *"Qinah"* verse for the most part, that is lines having a longer first colon, followed by a shorter second colon. Interspersed, it was said, are lines consisting of equal parts. When parallelism is obviously present, there is no difficulty with this description; for example, in 2:7: "Yahweh rejected his own altar; he spurned his sanctuary," there is no problem in deciding what are the cola, and where the division between them lies. But when parallelism is not present, the question of where to divide the verse becomes acute. Or is it correct to assume that the verse is divided at all? Budde, and others after him, speak of a division produced by a "break in sense," but this is vague, and in practice it seems that Budde and others have followed a kind of intuition as to where the caesura comes, rather than any rigorously defined principle. Lines without parallelism consist for the most part of a single sentence, thus, for example, 1:2b: *'ēn lāh mᵉnahām mikkol 'ōhᵃbehā* (word for word: "There-is-not to-her a-comforter out-of-all her-lovers"). To make two parts out of these lines with only one sentence, it is necessary to divide at a great variety of places with respect to syntax: between nominal subject and verb in 1:1c; between a prepositional phrase modifying a verb and a following nominal subject, in 1:1b; between a nominal subject and a prepositional phrase modifying it, in 1:2b; between verb and prepositional phrase modifying it, in 1:3c—and so on through almost every combination of sentence elements. To put it in another way, it seems impossible to define syntactically where the division between cola (caesura) is to be made in these lines. At least no one has yet offered a satisfactory definition.[38] If one is to continue to describe these lines as made up of two cola, then probably it will be necessary to argue that the dominant pattern set up by the lines with parallelism shapes our reading of these lines. Otherwise one may prefer to describe the lines without parallelism as undivided.

Several further observations concerning the poetic style of **Lamentations** arise from studying the syntax of the verbal sentences in the book. In a study so far published only in part,[39] Francis I. Andersen has analyzed all the verbal sentences in Genesis which have more than one modifier following the verb. By modifier is meant any element such as direct object, indirect object, adverb, prepositional phrase functioning as an adverb, etc. The subject of the verb is also classified as a modifier, and studied in relation to the other post-verbal elements. On the basis of over a thousand sentences of this sort, Andersen is able to present an abstract theoretical model of the verbal sentence, showing the relative order of the modifiers with respect to each other. As it turns out, there is a great regularity in this respect, and only about 4 per cent of the examples diverge from the normal order. This study of prose usage provides an extremely useful basis for comparison with **Lamentations.** The results obtained by applying the same methods of analysis to the verbal sentences in **Lamentations** show that a much higher proportion of sentences with two post-verbal modifiers display abnormal order, about 26 per cent (32 of 122 sentences). Most of the abnormal examples in **Lamentations** involve the position of a nominal subject or a nominal direct object with respect to a prepositional phrase. In this sort of sentence the "abnormal" order is nearly as common as the "normal." In sentences with three post-verbal modifiers the contrast is still more marked. According to Andersen's study 64, or about 15 per cent of the 409 examples in Genesis, were aberrant, differing from the normal pattern. Of twenty-seven such sentences in **Lamentations,** nineteen, or 70 per cent, do not follow the pattern most common in Genesis.

It is reasonable to propose as a hypothesis that metrical or rhythmic considerations have dictated this divergence from normal prose order where it takes place. Somewhat surprisingly, this is not obviously true, at least not from the point of view of an accentual system of meter, or as far as "Qinah" meter is concerned. In 2:20c, for example, 'im yē-hārēg bᵉmiqdaš 'ᵃdōnāy kōhēn wᵉnābī' (word-for-word: Are-slain in-the-sanctuary of-the-Lord priest and-prophet?), the order is prepositional phrase=subject, abnormal as compared to what is most common in Genesis. Yet the opposite order would seem to be possible here from the point of view of meter. Variant orders appear within the space of a single colon; compare 1:20b nehpak libbī bᵉqirbī (word-for-word: Is-turned-over my-heart inside-me) to 2:9a tabᵉ'ū bā'āre—šᵉ'āreh^ ("have-sunk into-the-earth her-gates"). Until further refinement of our metrical conceptions or of our knowledge of Hebrew syntax is achieved, the proper conclusion seems to be that in the ordering of these sentence-elements the poet of **Lamentations** was freer than the writers of Genesis, and his choice of a particular order was dictated by what may vaguely be called "stylistic" considerations, rather than meter. Whether this is a characteristic of other Hebrew poetry is as yet undetermined.

One rhythmic consideration does seem to have played a part, however. In sentences with three post-verbal modifiers, the poet shows a marked tendency to put the *longest* element last, regardless of its normal relative order. For example, in 2:6b it is syntactically unusual for the prepositional phrase to precede the nominal direct object:
. . .

> ("has-made-forgotten Yahweh in-Zion festival and-sabbath").

But the compound direct object is very long as compared to the other modifiers in the sentence. Andersen noticed a similar tendency in sentences in Genesis where word order was unusual, so that this may be a rather widespread characteristic of Hebrew sentence rhythm. On the other hand, it is present in such a high proportion of sentences in Lamentations that it may deserve notice as a feature of poetic style.

The acrostic pattern in chapters 1-4 quite obviously divides these poems into units which may for convenience be called strophes, or stanzas. In some cases these strophes correspond to units of thought. Thus, for example, 1:2 presents a unified picture—Zion weeps by night, forsaken by all her friends—quite clearly separated from what goes before and follows after. In other cases, however, the pattern marked off by the acrostic does not coincide with the pattern of thought. Ideas and images may be run-on from one acrostic unit to the next. The last line of the *Daleth* strophe is 3:12, but the image of God as an archer is continued into the first line of the *He* strophe, 3:13. This syncopation seems particularly common in chapter 3; see COMMENT there.

NOTE ON A FEATURE OF POETIC DICTION

Phrases of the pattern "daughter (Heb. *bat*) X," or "virgin daughter (*bᵉtūlat bat*) X" occur twenty times in **Lamentations,** a remarkable number in so short a book, since such phrases occur only about forty-five times in all the rest of the Old Testament. Jeremiah has sixteen of these other occurrences, including eight occurrences of *bat 'ammī* (lit., "daughter of my people"), practically the only occurrence of the term outside **Lamentations** (the exception is Isa 22:4). It is reasonable to conclude that this poetic device was especially popular in the seventh and sixth centuries B.C., although it was no doubt very ancient, since Micah and Isaiah use it.

Lamentations uses *bat Siyyōn*, "Zion," seven times; *bᵉtūlat bat Siyyōn*, once; *bat 'ammī*, "my people," five times; *bat yᵉhūdāh*, "Judah," twice; *bᵉtūlat bat yᵉhūdāh*, once (these last two are not used elsewhere in the Bible); *bat yᵉrūš-ālaim*, "Jerusalem," twice, and *bat 'ᵉdōm,* "Edom," once.

These phrases serve a poetic purpose in two ways. First, they help make explicit the personification of the people or city as a woman. Secondly, they seem to serve metrical purposes. The longer forms, the ones with three elements such as "virgin daughter Zion" are used to stretch out a name so as to make a whole poetic unit (colon) out of it. The shorter, two-part, phrases such as "daughter Zion" seem also to serve metrical purposes, though these are not clearly definable given the present state of understanding of Hebrew metrics. The most easily observable pattern is that phrases of the type "daughter X" tend to stand last in the unit of parallelism (colon). This is true of all occurrences in the Bible with a few exceptions (Jer 4:31; 6:26; 8:21; 51:33; Ps 137:8). There are practically no exceptions to this rule in **Lamentations,** the only possible case (4:3) being open to question textually (see NOTE).

As has been observed by others, the renderings familiar from older English translations, and the Revised Standard Version (RSV), "Daughter *of* Zion," "virgin daughter *of* Zion," etc., are potentially misleading, since the Hebrew phrases refer to the people or city as a whole, and not to a part of it. To put it another way, the relation between the two nouns in such a phrase is one of apposition; the second is not the possessor of the first. Since the main purpose of "daughter" and "virgin daughter" seems to be metrical, they have in most cases been omitted in the present translation. Where this has been done it is mentioned in the NOTES. This omission seemed advisable especially since no thoroughly idiomatic English is available. The new Jewish Publication Society (JPS) version uses "Fair Zion," "Fair Maiden Judah," "my poor people," and the like, which seem fairly close to the effect of the Hebrew.

THE TEXT

The Hebrew text of **Lamentations** is in a relatively good state of preservation, compared to the text of some other biblical books. This advantage in the commentator's favor is to some extent balanced by a corresponding disadvantage: the ancient translations offer relatively little help at those places where the Masoretic text, that is, the received Hebrew text, may be suspected of being corrupt. At the end of a recent thorough study of the text, Bertil Albrektson concludes that the Septuagint, the ancient Greek translation, was based on a text in all essentials identical with the Masoretic text, and the same verdict is offered for the Syriac version.[40] It is now believed that the Greek text of **Lamentations** belongs to the recently identified *kaige* recension,[41] that is to say, the Greek text in our possession is the outcome of a deliberate attempt to accommodate the original Greek translation as closely as possible to a near forerunner of the Masoretic text. Thus the Greek also gives us for the most part a text that already contained the errors and difficulties that are in the standard Hebrew text. Under these circumstances, commentators are compelled to rely to a greater degree on conjectural emendation of corrupt passages than might otherwise be necessary.

Among the Dead Sea scrolls published so far, in addition to small portions of the canonical book **Lamentations,** are several fragments of a poetical composition which incorporates many quotations from **Lamentations,** often in paraphrased form (4Q179).[42] This composition is occasionally cited in the NOTES as an early interpretation of the sense of the text.

LITURGICAL USE

The poems in **Lamentations** may have been used in public mourning over the destruction of Jerusalem immediately after they were written, though the evidence is inconclusive. Nothing in the poems precludes such a use. Formal characteristics, such as the use of "I" in many passages, do not rule out the use in corporate worship, nor does the use of acrostic form compel us to think that chapters 1-4 were intended only for private study and devotion (so Segert). On the other hand, the alternation among various speakers in some of the poems does not justify the conclusion that they were acted out publicly as a ritual drama. Nor is there evidence for the existence of a fixed liturgical practice of "Lament over the Ruined Sanctuary" already in pre-exilic times (against Kraus; see above under LITERARY TYPES). Direct evidence for liturgical use of Lamentations is not available until the Christian era.

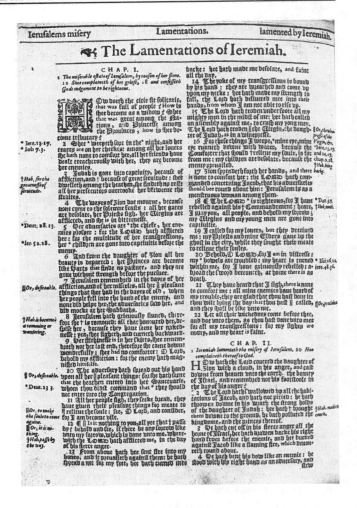

A page from Lamentations, *from a 1630 edition of the* King James Bible.

Public mourning over the destroyed city was carried on from earliest times. Jer 41:5, narrating an event just after the death of Gedaliah, the governor installed over Judah by the Chaldaeans, tells of "eighty men from Shechem, Shiloh, and Samaria who had shaved off their beards, torn their garments, and lacerated their skin," coming to make offering at the house of Yahweh in Jerusalem. Zech 7:3-5, dated to 518 B.C., hence shortly after the return from exile, makes it clear that mourning and fasting in the fifth month (*Ab*) had been going on ever since the city fell. Zech 8:19 also refers to a fast in the fifth month. It is, therefore, reasonable to suppose that the Lamentations were used in connection with this regular public mourning already in the exilic period.

Presumably continuing this ancient practice, later Jewish usage assigns **Lamentations** a place in the public mourning on the 9th of *Ab,* the fifth month, which falls in July or August according to the modern calendar. The 9th is chosen in preference to strict adherence to either of the two biblical dates (II Kings 25:8-9 gives the 7th of *Ab;* Jer 52:12 gives the 10th) because of the tradition that the *sec-*

ond temple fell to Titus on the 9th of *Ab,* and that Bar Kokhba's fortress Betar fell on that date in A.D. 135.

In various Christian liturgies portions of **Lamentations** are used in services on Maundy Thursday, Good Friday, and Holy Saturday, a custom which has resulted in the composition of eloquent musical settings of the text.

In modern times, Leonard Bernstein has used texts from **Lamentations** in his "Jeremiah" Symphony (1942), for mezzo-soprano and orchestra, as did Igor Stravinsky, in his "Threni" (1958), for solo voices, chorus, and orchestra.

Notes

1. See Rudolph's commentary on chapter 1 for details.

2. See Abraham Malamat, "The Last Kings of Judah and the Fall of Jerusalem," *Israel Exploration Journal* 18 (1968), 144-45, for a discussion of the chronology of the events.

3. The idea that one or more chapters of Lamentations come from the Maccabean period was advanced by S. A. Fries, "Parallele zwischen den Klageliedern Cap. IV, V und der Maccabäerzeit," ZAW 13 (1893), 110-24, but found few adherents. S. T. Lachs, "The Date of Lamentations V," JQR, N.S. 57 (1966-67), 46-56, has revived the idea, but his arguments are equally unconvincing.

4. Hardt proposed that the five chapters were written respectively by Daniel, Shadrach, Meshach, Abednego, and King Jehoiachin! See Giuseppe Ricciotti, *Le lamentazione di Geremia* (Turin, Rome, 1924), p. 35. To say that modern critical opinion in this matter was anticipated by Ibn Ezra, as does Lachs, JQR, N.S. 57 (1966-67), 46-47, is erroneous. Ibn Ezra rejects only the rabbinic tradition that Lamentations was the scroll burned by Jeremiah, but not Jeremiah's authorship of the book.

5. The idea that Jopsiah is spoken of in 4:20 was picked up by Saint Jerome and from him by the *Glossa interlinearis,* and thence by later medieval commentators; see Ricciotti, pp. 32-34.

6. The lexical evidence is exhaustively presented in Max Löhr, "Der Sprachgebrauch des Buches der Klagelieder," ZAW 14 (1894), 31-50; cf. "Threni III. und die jeremianische Autorschaft des Buches der Klagelieder," ZAW 24 (1904), 1-16, and "Alphabetische und alphabetisierende Lieder im Alten Testament," ZAW 25 (1905), 173-98, also by Löhr.

7. Gilbert Brunet, in his *Les lamentations contre Jérémie* (Paris, 1968) has recently argued at length that the first four Lamentations were written by a (half-repentant) representative of the nationalist party, probably the high-priest Seraiah, *against* the unpatriotic prophetic party of Jeremiah. The conclusions reached do not agree well with the relatively untendentious character of the book, and are achieved only by a very strained exegesis, a main prop of the argument being that one must distinguish sharply between "enemy," and . . . "foe," throughout the book. Giorgio Buccellati, "Gli Israeliti di Palestina al tempo dell'esilio," *Bibbia e Oriente* 2 (1960), 199-209, argues from passages in Lamentations that the book comes from a party hostile to Gedaliah: a group of Jerusalemites who opposed his governing from Mizpah, of patriots who hated collaborators. The evidence cited is insufficient to render any of these conclusions probable.

8. *The Holy Bible,* trans. Ronald Knox, London, 1955.

9. Extensive discussions, with bibliography, are offered by P. A. Munch, "Die alphabetische Akrostichie in der jüdischen Psalmendichtung," *Zeitschrift der Deutschen Morgenländischen Gesellschaft* 90 (1936), 703-10; Ralph Marcus, "Alphabetic Acrostics in the Hellenistic and Roman Periods," JNES 6 (1947), 109-15; Norman K. Gottwald, Studies in the Book of Lamentations, Studies in Biblical Theology, 14 (London, 1962), pp. 23-32.

10. Adolf Erman, *The Ancient Egyptians,* trans. A. M. Blackman (New York, 1943), pp. lviii-lix, describes several compositions which, while not acrostic in the strictest sense, have the peculiarity that all the stanzas have the same opening word.

11. W. G. Lambert, *Babylonian Wisdom Literature* (Oxford, 1960), p. 67.

12. Lambert, pp. 63-68.

13. Enno Janssen, *Juda in der Exilszeit.* Forschungen zur Religion und Literatur des Alten und Neuen Testaments 69 (Göttingen, 1956), p. 97; Gottwald, loc. cit.

14. Hermann Gunkel, *Die Psalmen,* Handkommentar zum Alten Testament, Göttingen, 1926, on Ps 111.

15. Patrick Skehan, "Wisdom's House," CBQ 29 (1967), 468, note.

16. "Klagelieder Jeremiae," in *Die Religion in Geschichte und Gegenwart,* 2d ed. (Tübingen, 1929), III, cols. 1049-52. In his discussion of the funeral song, Gunkel draws on the study by Hedwig Jahnow, *Das hebräische Leichenlied im Rahmen der Völkerdichtung,* BZAW 36, Giessen, 1923.

17. S. N. Kramer, "Lamentation over the Destruction of Nippur," *Eretz-Israel* 9 (W. F. Albright Volume, Jerusalem, 1969), 89. Cf. his "Sumerian Literature and the Bible," in *Studia Biblica et Orientalia,* III: *Oriens Antiquus,* Analecta Biblica, 12 (Rome, 1959), p. 201.

18. C. J. Gadd, "The Second Lamentation for Ur," in *Hebrew and Semitic Studies presented to G. R. Driver* (Oxford, 1963), p. 61.

19. In the introduction to his commentary, pp. 9-11.

20. T. F. McDaniel, "The Alleged Sumerian Influence upon Lamentations," VT 18 (1968), 198-209.

21. The principal extant Sumerian laments over destroyed cities may be conveniently read in ANET: "The Lamentation over the Destruction of Ur," pp.

455-63; "Lamentation over the Destruction of Sumer and Ur," pp. 611-19; the related "The Curse of Agade," pp. 646-51.

22. ANET, p. 618, lines 403-4.

23. The word *usga,* whose proper translation is uncertain, refers to a part of the temple used for lustrations, according to Kramer, ANET, p. 651, n. 70.

24. ANET, p. 651, lines 254-55.

25. Gustav Hölscher, "Elemente arabischer, syrischer und hebräischer Metrik," BZAW 34 (1920), 93-101.

26. Sigmund Mowinckel, "Zum Problem der hebräischen Metrik," in *Festschrift für Alfred Bertholet* (Tübingen, 1950), pp. 379-94.

27. Friedrich Horst, "Die Kennzeichen der hebräischen Poesie," ThR 21 (1953), 97-121.

28. Stanislav Segert, "Versbau und Sprachbau in der althebräischen Poesie," *Mitteilungen des Instituts für Orientforschung* 15 (1969), 312-21, with references (n. 7) to his earlier studies.

29. Julius Ley, *Grundzüge des Rhythmus, des Vers- und Strophenbaues in der hebräischen Poesie,* Halle, 1887.

30. Eduard Sievers, *Metrische Studien,* I-III, Leipzig, 1901, 1904-5, 1907.

31. Occasionally the same practice is followed in the NOTES and COMMENTS below, without the intention of indicating adherence to the accentual theory.

32. Archaic Forms in Early Hebrew Poetry," ZAW 72 (1960), 101-7; "The Structure of Job 3," *Biblica* 49 (1968), 503-8.

33. *Metrische Studien,* I, Erster Teil, 120-23; Zweiter Teil, 550-63.

34. *Metrische Studien,* I, Erster Teil, 116.

35. Such an undertaking lies beyond my powers; when I attempt metrical translation I achieve something like the following by Vavasour Powell, *Sippor Ba-Pach,* or *The Bird in the Cage* (London, 1662), p. 143:

> How doth the city sit alone
>   that full of people was?
> How is she become a widow?
>   she that was great alas!

Quoted in Rolf P. Lessenich, *Dichtungsgeschmack und althebräische Bibelpoesie im 18. Jahrhundert,* Anglistische Studien, 4 (Cologne, Graz, 1967), p. 11.

36. Otto Procksch, *Theologie des Alten Testaments* (Gütersloh, 1950), pp. 642 f, points out that the anger of Yahweh illustrates the peculiar vitality of the Hebrew view of God. It is in marked contrast to the emphasis of the best Greek minds upon the imperturbable, the 'apathetic' character of God. . . . But in the nature of the Hebrew-Jewish God there was something unresting, dynamic, irrational, passionate—all of which is best summarized in the category of the Holy.

37. If it were desired, one could restate the results in terms of the proportion of synonymous to synthetic parallelism, without change.

38. J. Begrich asserts that the caesura cannot interrupt a construct chain, or fall between the two accented syllables in a word with two accents; obviously these restrictions still leave a great deal of room open. See his "Der Satzstil im Fünfer," ZS 9 (1933-34), 173.

39. The writer regrets the necessity of referring to the conclusions of a work not easily available to readers, and which Professor Andersen would doubtless revise and amplify in some respects before publication. There is, however, no similar work available for comparison. I have taken the liberty of altering Andersen's technical terminology in some respects in favor of terms which, while less precise, are more traditional and hence apt to be more readily intelligible without lengthy explanation. For verbless clauses, the reader is referred to Andersen's monograph *The Hebrew Verbless Clause in the Pentateuch,* New York, Nashville, 1970. For a fuller discussion, see the writer's contribution to the forthcoming Festschrift for J. M. Myers.

40. Bertil Albrektson, *Studies in the Text and Theology of the Book of Lamentations,* Studia Theologica Lundensia, 21 (Lund, 1963), pp. 208-13. The other most important recent treatment of the text is Wilhelm Rudolph, "Der Text der Klagelieder," ZAW 56 (1938), 101-22.

41. Jean-Dominique Barthélemy, *Les devanciers d'Aquila,* Vetus Testamentum Supplements 10 (Leiden, 1963), pp. 33, 138-60, is quite positive about the identification of the Greek text of Ruth, the Song of Songs, and Lamentations as belonging to the *kaige* group, and bases a theory about the beginning of liturgical use of these books on the identification. Frank M. Cross, Jr., "The History of the Biblical Text in the Light of Discoveries in the Judaean Desert," *Harvard Theological Review* 57 (1964), 283, is somewhat more reserved: "Ruth and Lamentations are good candidates" (to be representatives of the recension). See also J. M. Grindel, "Another Characteristic of the Kaige Recension: *nsh/nikos,*" CBQ 31 (1969), 499-513; note that LXX has *nikos* for *nsh* at Lam 3:18 and 5:20.

42. J. M. Allegro, with Arnold A. Anderson, *Qumrân Cave 4,* Discoveries in the Judaean Desert of Jordan, V (Oxford, 1968), pp. 75-77; cf. J. Strugnell, "Notes en marge du volume V des 'Discoveries in the Judaean Desert of Jordan,'" *Revue de Qumrân* 7, No. 26 (1970), 250-52.

Abbreviations

ANET: *Ancient Near Eastern Texts Relating to the Old Testament,* ed. J. B. Pritchard, 3d ed., Princeton, 1969

BDB: F. Brown, S. R. Driver, C.A. Briggs, eds. of Wilhelm Gesenius' *Hebrew and English Lexicon of the Old Testament,* 2d ed., Oxford, 1952

BH[3]: *Biblia hebreica,* ed. Rudolf Kittel, 3d ed., Stuttgart, 1937

BZAW: Beihefte zur Zeitschrift für die alttestamentliche Wissenschaft

CAD: Chicago Assyrian Dictionary

CBQ: Catholic Biblical Quarterly

CTA: *Corpus des tablettes et cunéiformes alphabétiques,* by Andrée Herdner, Paris , 1963

GKC: *Gesenius' Hebrew Grammar,* ed. E. Kautzsch, revised by A. E. Cowley, 2d Eng. ed., Oxford, 1910

JNES: Journal of Near Eastern Studies

JQR: Jewish Quarterly Review

KB[3]: Ludwig Koehler and Walter Baumgartner, *Lexikon in Veteris Testamenti Libros,* 3d ed., Leiden, 1967

ThR: Theologische Rundschau

UT: *Ugaritic Textbook,* by Cyrus H. Gordon, Rome, 1965

VT: Vetus Testamentum

ZAW: Zeitschrift für die alttestamentliche Wissenschaft

ZS: Zeitschrift für Semitistik und verwandte Gebiete

William F. Lanahan (essay date 1974)

SOURCE: "The Speaking Voice in the *Book of Lamentations,*" in *Journal of Biblical Literature,* Vol. 93, No. 1 March 1974, pp. 41-49.

[*In the following essay, Lanahan offers a detailed examination of five distinctive narrative personae in* Lamentations *and explains how their use benefits the work.*]

This examination of the speaking voice in the ***Book of Lamentations*** will not discuss the authorship of the book. The attribution of the work to the prophet Jeremiah is fundamentally a question of historical judgment. The attempt to identify the speaking voice, the subject of our concentration at the moment, is a stylistic concern. In this context, literary criticism sometimes uses the term *persona,* i.e., the mask or characterization assumed by the poet as the medium through which he perceives and gives expression to his world.

The *persona* is not to be thought of as a fiction. It is a creative procedure in the displacement of the poet's imagination beyond the limitations of his single viewpoint so that he may gain a manifold insight into the human experience. The poet's manifold creative insight then becomes the ground by which the reader achieves a more powerful perception of the creative situation. If the use of one *persona* by the poet enriches his intuition, the use of the five *personae* discernible in ***Lamentations*** should of itself deepen and broaden the reader's grasp of the dynamics of the

spiritual experience embodied by the book. Another man's consciousness of the world is available to us only through his statements, and only imperfectly at that; the richer his statement, the more rewarding our entrance into his experience.

The most obvious example of the existence of a *persona* in the ***Book of Lamentations*** appears in the first two chapters, in those verses (1:9c, 11c-22; 2:20-22) during which Jerusalem speaks in her own voice. Obviously, the city of Jerusalem cannot speak except in some figurative sense, but it is precisely this personification of the city which expresses the anguish of these verses. However, this Jerusalem does not merely register a community complaint as a political abstraction; it characterizes itself as a particular woman whose specific feelings are embodied in a certain texture of imagery.

The very existence of the easily identified *persona* of Jerusalem provokes in the reader a reflex awareness of the second voice to be heard in these chapters (1:1-11b, 15a, 17; 2:1-19): a more objective reporter whose cooler descriptive statements contrast with the passionate outbursts of Jerusalem. It is this reporter's voice which may strike the reader as the poet's authentic voice, but such an assessment appears manifestly inadequate and even simplistic after reading the entire book. Distinct voices are discernible in each of the subsequent three chapters. Are we then to stipulate that only one of the five voices speaking in ***Lamentations*** is the "sincere mode" of expression used by the poet? To equate impersonation with hypocrisy in this way would be to confuse an aesthetic category with a moral judgment. When the poet chooses to write certain passages without adopting an alien characterization as his focus of perception, he is making just as explicit and deliberate a decision as he does in adopting a *persona.* Furthermore, to presume that the least radical departure from the comfortably objective viewpoint must be the most authentic speaking voice would be to equate sincerity with the most banal level of imagination and deny vitality to those levels of the poet's consciousness on which he is attempting to grasp a world which is dissolving before his eyes.

On the other hand, if this examination of ***Lamentations*** should succeed in distinguishing five separable *personae* in the course of the book, would it not succeed in destroying the unity of the book, dissecting a totality into a series of discrete statements? Would such a success imply multiple authorship?

On the contrary, the variety of voices sketches the topography of a unique spiritual consciousness which can realize itself only by projecting its grief in its constituent phases by adopting different *personae.* This ultimate unity should emerge as a single controlling awareness from the detailed examination of the five *personae* to which we shall now proceed.

The first voice to be overheard in ***Lamentations*** is that of someone who approaches the city of Jerusalem only to find it deserted and forsaken, abandoned by its inhabitants and oppressed by its enemies, resembling a widow forced to work like a serf (1:1). The roads to Zion and the city gates no longer bustle with traffic; the speaker is particularly aware of the absence of crowds he had seen on some earlier visit to Jerusalem. The precise event which has turned the city into a ghost town is not identified here; only the vacuum is described, the picture of the city's desolation and its emptiness under the punitive will of God (vs. 5). The speaker is preoccupied with the dialectic of past glory and present misery; he perceives the misery only within the memory of the glory. He provides neither continuity nor crisis between past and present; he depicts an image of the suddenly empty city against his recollection of its former activity by a verbal diptych.

He sees that Jerusalem has abruptly become the mere object of the scornful gaze of the passers-by who had once respected her. Now they see her naked, whining, fallen to the ground, her skirts fouled with pollution (vss. 8-9), ravished (vs. 10), her people so hungry that they have sold their own children in order to buy food for themselves (vs. 11). The reporter does not maintain a stringent distinction between Jerusalem-as-city and Jerusalem-as-woman through to the end of this sequence of verses. In either capacity, however, Jerusalem is an object bereft of all dignity, reduced to the level of a thing to be gawked at. The personification functions at this point merely as a rhetorical device by which the city's degradation is intensified. Converting the city into a woman makes her fall all the more shameful. The speaker sees the disgrace of the city as the other passers-by see the disgrace, but he sees it with a certain rudimentary pity when he sees a despondent woman in the ruins of Jerusalem.

When this first voice resumes speaking at the beginning of ch. 2, the emphasis on visual imagery which distinguishes the reporter from the voice of Jerusalem returns as well. He now describes the Lord in the act of destroying Israel. Like an angry warrior the Lord has torn down the fortresses of Judah (vs. 2), he has caused the defeat of the armies (vs. 3), he has turned his own bow and sword against his people and destroyed them with the fire of his wrath (vss. 4-5). Not only did God spurn his own sanctuary, he carefully planned the tearing down of Jerusalem's walls (vss. 7-8). The princes are captives, the prophets without visions, the people without hope (vss. 9-10). At this point, however, a significant shift in tone modifies the reporter's description.

Up to this point the speaker has depicted God as the sacker of the city: epic in his stature, gigantic in his anger, relentless in the totality of his destructiveness. The emptiness of the city noted in ch. 1 can be explained: God has devastated his own city. The reporter is following the sequence of his own perceptions rather than the chronological sequence of events; he has seen the devastation before depicting its infliction, he has discovered the effect before fully identifying the cause for the reader. The imagery of the opening verse of ch. 2 is energetically pictorial, fully

presenting God in terms of physical activity. If the descriptive passages at the beginning of ch. 1 may be classified as static tableaux, this anthropomorphic portrait of God is cinematic. And yet with vs. 9 there is a sudden abatement from the violent activity, a crash of silence.

No one preaches in Jerusalem; everyone now sits mute in the dust. The reporter becomes noticeably sympathetic, for his heart is moved by the starving children, whimpering, fainting, dying (vss. 11-12). He is left without poetic resources, for he feels the grief deeply; and grief like all other pain defies any adequate expression beyond screams and tears. The only simile he can find for the ruination of the city is the wide sea—chaotic, elemental, unbridgeable. Jerusalem fell because her prophets had failed her. Their words were whitewash and frauds (vs. 14), and now the city lies in rubble and silence.

Now there reappear in vss. 15-16 those passers-by who mock the nakedness of Jerusalem in ch. 1 (vs. 8) and to whom Jerusalem has addressed the opening phrases of her soliloquy (v. 12). The reporter has also seen the city but has not mocked; his sympathy for her has so far transcended mere observation that he experiences the same churning of the bowels (2:11) that Jerusalem has also experienced (1:20). The only appropriate procedure now is to lament the misery of the city, but since that is Jerusalem's personified role in the earlier chapter, the reporter now invites her to resume her outcry (vss. 18-19).

The reporter might have seen no more than the jeering passers-by saw except for the entropic spasm sparked by the sight of the starving children. In that one moment of commiseration with its kinesthetic reflex the description loses its purely analytic, pictorial texture. Now the voice of Jerusalem is not merely inserted between two reportorial statements; it responds to the reporter's invitation to speak, as if the surrender of the aloofness of the spectator prompted a dialogue.

The second voice of *Lamentations* is that of Jerusalem herself, i.e., the hypostatized anguish of the fallen city. She begins by appealing to God to consider her humiliation (1:11c) and to the passers-by to consider her pain (vs. 12). The cry is not for further looking at her misery but for pitiful looking; no longer can Jerusalem allow herself to be a mere object to be observed, but rather she requires humane attentiveness, a look accompanied by compassion. True, she has been demeaned by God in his anger, burnt, trapped in the net, yoked by the neck (vss. 13-14), but she is also the mother of the dead young soldiers, weeping for the misery of her children (vss. 15-16). Jerusalem willingly admits the folly of her past behavior towards God in her making of futile alliances with the gentiles (vss. 18-19), but her poor people are now suffering captivity (vs. 18), famine (vs. 19), and violent death (vs. 20), while her oppressors rejoice (vs. 21). Jerusalem is totally powerless and abandoned, inconsolable and despondent; her only prayer is not for delivery, but for the equal affliction of her oppressors by God's anger (vs. 22).

The imagery employed by Jerusalem in her lament is in striking contrast to the visual imagery employed by the reporter. Through these verses she speaks of herself as trapped in a net, given over to her enemies; in her midst lies a heap of her dead warriors who have been crushed out in the winepress; her eyes run with tears; she is filled with pain; her bowels are churning and her heart is turning over; she is groaning and heartsick. Not only do such statements convey her deepest feelings, but they also associate her passions with a sense of kinesthetic oppression. The subjective awareness insisted upon in these verses is that internal experience one has of one's own vital organs, one's posture, one's musculature, one's freedom to move within one's personal sphere of space.

The kinesthetic sense is the most personally experienced, the most interiorly focused, the most difficult to communicate in words of the human sensorium. Of all the senses it is the most unlike seeing; it allows no distancing, no perspective, no proportion, no analytical judgment. From the vague discomfort of subliminal indigestion to the blinding pain of insupportable anguish, it cannot be blinked away by the conscious mind. One blurs one's awareness with analgesics or one falls into unconsciousness, but one cannot think oneself free. Even her admission of guilty responsibility cannot alleviate Jerusalem's suffering. Self-reproach does not soften the pain.

The judgmental attitude belongs rather to the passers-by, and it is only the reporter's rush of compassion for the children which stands between him and the "Jerusalem is simply getting just what she deserves" sneers of those other, disengaged observers of her misery. It is through entropy, the physiological accompaniment to his sympathy, that the reporter enters into the sorrow of Jerusalem. When towards the end of ch. 2 (vss. 18-19) he invites the city to cry out once again, he phrases his cue to Jerusalem in the kinesthetic range of imagery: cry from the heart, weep like a perpetual flood, and pour out your heart; arise and do not rest, lift up your hands.

The voice of Jerusalem offers a final prayer lacking in any petition for specific help. She simply calls upon God to look upon the effects of his angry handiwork with pity (2:20-22). Her prayer evokes the imagery of falling and lying still, of failing to run away and of being wiped out, the awareness of stasis, of nightmare paralysis. But if God will but look at this ruin, Jerusalem need ask nothing more.

The voices in chs. 3 and 4 seem to express individual perceptions in concrete situations. If the reader wishes to interpret certain aspects of the statements in these chapters as metaphor and convention because of parallel usages elsewhere in the Scriptures, he simply shifts the level of characterization from the individual speaker to the typical or even the allegorical speaker. In doing this, however, the reader who would detach the metaphor from its concrete basis in an individual *persona* runs the risk of accusing the poet of weaving a fabric of clichés without cohesive reference to a successfully rounded characterization. Thus, in ch. 3, the poet has assumed the *persona* of a defeated soldier; for a soul beleaguered by the world to assume the guise of a crusader is familiar enough in the mystical tradition since Paul, but to regard this as an outworn convention in our time is to ignore the original power of the *persona*. The speaker in ch. 3 may or may not have been a veteran of the siege of Jerusalem; the fact is that the poet perceives his spiritual downfall through the eyes of a defeated soldier.

That the speakers of chs. 3 and 4 enjoy the right to be distinguished from each other as well as from the reporter and Jerusalem receives some support from a consideration of formal patterns of composition in the first four chapters of *Lamentations*. These four chapters practise that deliberate manipulation of words common enough in Hebrew poetry, the acrostic structure. Chs. 1, 2, and 4 begin each of their strophes with the letters of the Hebrew alphabet in sequential order; ch. 3 is even more insistent on the structure by beginning each line within its three-line strophes with the same initial letter, changing from strophe to strophe in sequence. Ch. 4, on the other hand, provides only two lines to a strophe, while the earlier chapters have three lines to the strophe. Poetic form, therefore, unites chs. 1 and 2 into a unit while it sets off chs. 3 and 4. And yet the poetic form in each chapter is still a variation on the same fundamental structure of the alphabetical sequence. Such a structure offers the lamentations a movement of irreversible progression towards inevitable completion with the last letter of the alphabet. There is an inexorable certitude about the total fulfillment of God's punitive will. No chapter reaches a climax; there is merely the sense of denouement, the realization that the experiences march on and on towards exhaustive recitation.

The voice in ch. 3 is the *persona* of a soldier, a veteran who has endured hard use in the war. He protests that he was led into defeat by an officer who wished him to be defeated; we have already been told that it was God who led the army to defeat (1:15; 2:3-5, 22). The speaker has suffered fatigue and hunger (vs. 2), was held prisoner, and then wandered about amidst obstacles (vs. 3), fearfully and warily expected ambush at every turn (vs. 4), has been wounded in his vitals (vs. 5). His final bitterness is that he has become the butt of everyone's contempt (vs. 5). God has trampled him in the dirt so that he feels only despair (vs. 6). Despite his pain and dishonor, however, the young man (vs. 8) is still flexible enough to hope for an ultimate exoneration (vss. 7c-13), because God will not deny justice to anyone forever. A battle has been lost, but perhaps not the war.

The distinction between past and present in the chapter thus far is the veteran's shift from recollection to evaluation. The speaker is now pausing in the memories of his pains to reflect on God's nature and to discover some measure of vague hope. The future can be envisioned only as that time beyond the present moment when God will no longer continue to punish his people. The only real time for the veteran is the present moment of reflective pause; the veteran can now dismiss his former sufferings since they were deserved by his past sins, and he can at least find some comfort in his boast that he has managed to survive into this present moment (vs. 13), an authentic axiom in the mouth of a regular soldier.

The veteran now turns to exhort some unidentified comrades (vs. 14), rallying them, urging them to admit their own guilt and to seek God in prayer as he has done. He leads them in prayer, but his self-confident intention fails him, and he erupts in an outburst of grief over God's withdrawal from his people (vss. 14c-15), the mockery of the victorious enemy (vs. 16), his blinding tears of defeat (vs. 17), and his entrapment in a pit filling up with water (vs. 18). At vs. 16c, the veteran reverts to the first person singular, giving up his group role in order to express his individual grief. He beseeches God to look with pity on his plight, for he is the victim of plots and jeers, and he invokes God to punish his enemies in the measure they deserve (vs. 22).

The veteran has passed through several phases of guilt, which he expresses in terminology most appropriate to a defeated soldier. At first he gratifies his desire to rationalize his own guilt by blaming his dishonor on God or on circumstances beyond his own control: his officer betrayed him into defeat, he was poorly supplied, he was captured, he was wounded. But he must still sustain the contempt of his countrymen, who find in him a scapegoat for their ruin, and of his enemies, who despise him as a loser. Another opportunity to evade his own guilt now presents itself: since God will someday provide another chance for him, he may simply disown his own share in the recent catastrophe. But this ready decision to confess and forget his own responsibility through a gesture of quick dismissal leads him not to the consolation of prayer and comradeship but to another outburst of self-pity.

The dominant image throughout the chapter has been that of encirclement: the speaker has been imprisoned, trapped in the drowning-pit, surrounded by his enemies, the guilt-ridden veteran can really escape neither by prayer nor by the subterfuge of self-exoneration. No delusion can release him from the inescapable trap, his own memory. If a man's memory constitutes his identity, the pit from which the veteran cannot rescue himself is himself.

In a final outburst of defiance against his enemies, he in fact admits his own impotency to strike out on his own behalf. His is no more than a partial vision of the meaning of his own condition: while acknowledging his own guilt and the justice of God's punishment, he cannot surrender to the whole truth of his own share in the responsibility for the catastrophe.

If the voice of the veteran seems to echo the voice of Jerusalem, the voice of ch. 4 corresponds to the reporter's. The veteran feels himself trapped, the victim of the mocker's jeers; the city feels herself fallen, the object of the scorn of the passers-by. Their outcries are passionate, subjective, self-expressive, concerned with pity. The reporter is, in the main, detached, objective, descriptive, analytical; his compassion is evoked, a mirror, a reaction rather than a statement. The bourgeois who is the voice of ch. 4 recapitulates these attitudes in several ways.

The bourgeois is surprised by the economic and social upheaval within the fallen city. That gold and jewels are now treated with scorn is not only an exclamation leading to a simile comparing the maltreated citizens of Jerusalem, formerly of high regard, to discarded potsherds in their present condition (4:1-2) but also a transcendent statement about the devalued standards of life in the city. In this thoroughly disrupted society, gold is despised because it can no longer buy anything. There is nothing to buy: the starving children are worse off than the jackals' cubs, the rich are eating garbage (vss. 3-5). The aristocrats, once so fair to behold, are now reduced to skeletons; mothers cook and eat their own children (vss. 7-8, 10). God in his anger destroyed Jerusalem to the surprise of the world (vss. 11-12) because of the corruption of the prophets and priests (vss. 13-16). The harshness of this description of the aftermath of Jerusalem's fall and the analysis of its causes are hardly relieved by the cynicism: Jerusalem must have been worse than Sodom, which was destroyed in an instant and without all this agony (vs. 6); similarly, those who were killed violently in the fighting were luckier than those who survived only to starve to death in the city. The awareness of the difference between past and present, the note of mockery, and the pictorial presentation not only echo the reporter, but also introduce a comparison between this voice and the mocking passer-by who has appeared as a shadowy observer in all three of the earlier chapters of *Lamentations.*

The speaker is describing the total collapse of the state as a nation, as a people, and as a culture. His mind has operated on the level of social regalia, and he is both horrified and fascinated by the disjointing of the hierarchical structure of his world. In his old world, there were aristocrats above and beggars below. Now the aristocrats have lost the emblems of their prestige. Those who had built their identities on wealth and status now reveal in their downfall the destruction of that social structure which had once afforded them the deference due to their position. They have come to disregard the gold and jewelry, clothes and grooming which were the props of their former glory. Ironically, it was the failure of leadership that incurred God's wrath; since the leaders refused to fulfill their function, they have been deprived of its forms. The utter devaluation of what was once considered the measure of achievement and dignity is itself God's judgment on Jerusalem: the emptiness of the aristocratic class has been revealed as both the cause and the symbol of the ruination. The speaker does not seem to grasp this clearly. He is the average citizen who is both amazed and somewhat gratified at the reversal which has reduced his leaders to beggary and which has inverted society so thoroughly that the first have indeed been made last, the exalted have indeed been humbled.

But the bourgeois has some sense of identity with his fellow-citizens. He shifts to the first person plural in order to describe the widespread foreboding of danger experienced either while staying in the besieged city (vss. 17-18) or while attempting to flee to the mountains or into the desert (vss. 19-20). He is a man who had accepted the social structure of his world at face value, and his feelings have seemed less intense than any of the other three voices heard in the book. His has been but a kind of dismay at the dissolution of familiar social distinctions by which he had once oriented his life. Now the reader discovers the great shock to the bourgeois, the peril he feels in the once familiar streets of his own city. There is neither security within the city nor freedom from fear outside it. His sense of comfortable space, as well as his sense of hierarchy, has been destroyed. The formlessness of his society consequent to the unmasking of the instability of its values has found a spatial correlative. His present world is, therefore, a wreck of shattered perspectives. His categories of orderliness and precedence have been totally ruptured. His complacency in a world filled with landmarks is now replaced by the vertigo of nothing; the vacuum resides in his absolute surprise before the hollowness of everything he had previously assumed to be successful and safe.

Yet the bourgeois is incapable of understanding the bitter irony of all this. All that is left to him is the spiteful wish that his own sense of chaos may now be transferred elsewhere so that the distant enemy will also suffer this same shock of dislocation. His final word, his curse on Edom and Uz (vss. 21-22), implies that willful indulgence in moral anarchy functions as the universal cause of inevitable material ruin in any society. His ultimate resolution thus comprises neither insight nor resignation, but merely an ineffectual tantrum of vindictiveness. He thus falls short of the reporter's final empathy and compassion. After he has observed the chaos and experienced the confusion, his reaction is the wish that the evil be spread out even further.

The voice of ch. 5 of *Lamentations* is a choral voice. It is made up of the people of Jerusalem as a community, out of a shared misery and a common purposive atttitude towards God. The chorus is not simply the reporter, the city, the veteran, and the bourgeois speaking together; the chorus has its own character, subsuming each individual *persons* in an act of prayer which transcends the viewpoints and the inadequacies which the poet perceived and expressed through the first four chapters.

The first four chapters enjoy a certain unity in that they share significant underlying perspectives, a unique spiritual orientation towards the experiences they convey. They share a narrative constant in the passers-by who jeer at Jerusalem, who resemble the reporter without achieving his compassion, who mock the veteran as scapegoat and victim, who may include the bourgeois whose wonderment at the downfall of the city does not preclude an element of cynical satisfaction. The heckling laughter of those who walk by without emotional involvement echoes through the chapters as a counterpoint to the appeals for pity, the prayers, the curses of the suffering. The passers-by act as a pivot of recognition on which the reader can swing from the passionate outcries to the detached observations as on a fixed moment in time. The reader can recognize that the subjective examination of one *persona* has been simultaneous with the objective description by another by the sound of mockery from the passers-by.

The first chapters also share the thematic constant of the hungry children. Jerusalem as the desolate woman represents the continuum of past guilt into present degradation, but the destruction of the children testifies to the impossibility of a future. In the present misery, the children are not only starving, they are even being sold so that their parents may buy food and ultimately they are being consumed by their own mothers. The poet sees that the cannibalism is wiping out the final vestige of instinctive human love as the nation consumes the vehicles and creators of its future. The present moment of anguish is thus the absolute pause between a corrupt and irrecoverable past and an unimaginable future.

The first chapters, as already noted, share an acrostic structuring in their poetic formulation. The final chapter, however, has no such acrostic pattern. The inevitable conclusion intended by the alphabetical sequence is inconceivable in the final moment of the book. No new sequence of events or emotions has been initiated. There has been, after all, no real progression in the course of the book: shock, fatigue, despair, disorientation have reached in the fifth chapter a declaration of the communal awareness of Jerusalem's total destruction.

The chorus addresses its prayer to God to express its need for relief, not to express any firm hope in prompt deliverance. The fund of torments has simply been exhausted; there remains no possible suffering which has not already been inflicted and endured. Now the people have seen the nothingness underlying the life which had separated them from God. They grope their way towards him as towards the only plausible explanation of their human finitude and the only possible source of relief from their anguish.

The chorus voices its sense of imprisonment within the present bankruptcy of the people whom God has abandoned. The community is left in a vacuum, with nothing as strong as hope or confidence or trust. It retains only conviction, the conviction that God will finally lift his punishing hand from his people. Quantity rather than quality is now the issue. No longer need anyone ask, "Should Jerusalem suffer?" Admittedly she must, and does. The question is, "How long shall Jerusalem continue to suffer?" The chorus ends its prayer, suspended without a definite answer.

The only answer to the mystery of God's relationship to his people is provided, not by a sixth *persona* speaking for the Name, but in the community's conviction that accompanies and supports the implicit litotes: our God is not unrelenting.

Robert Gordis (essay date 1974)

SOURCE: "The Conclusion of the *Book of Lamentations* (5:22)," in *Journal of Biblical Literature*, Vol. 93, No. 2, June, 1974, pp. 289-93.

[*In the following essay, Gordis considers and rejects assorted approaches to the problematic closing verse in* Lamentations *and offers his own interpretation based on a different reading of the syntactic structure employed.*]

The closing verse in *Lamentations* is crucial for the meaning and spirit of the entire poem.[1] In spite of the simplicity of its style and the familiarity of its vocabulary, it has long been a crux. After the plea in vs. 21, "Turn us to yourself and we will return, renew our days as of old," vs. 22 . . . seems hardly appropriate, particularly as the conclusion of the prayer.

(1) The extent of the difficulties posed by the verse may perhaps be gauged by the desperate expedient adopted, e.g., in the (1917) JPSV, of virtually inserting a negative into the text, thus diametrically reversing its meaning: "Thou canst not have utterly rejected us, and be exceeding wroth against us."

A variety of other interpretations have been proposed, all of which suffer from grave drawbacks:

(2) To treat the verse as an interrogative: "Or have you rejected us, are you exceedingly angry with us?"[2] There is, however, no evidence for rendering *kî' im* as "or," whether interrogatively or otherwise, and this interpretation has found few modern defenders.

(3) To delete *'im* on the grounds that it is not expressed by the LXX or the Peš and is missing in six medieval Hebrew MSS. The verse is then rendered: "For you have indeed rejected us, etc." It is probable that the ancient versions, endeavoring to make sense of a difficult phrase, rendered it *ad sensum.* As Hillers notes, the MT is to be preferred as the *lectio difficilior.* Moreover, the idea remains inappropriate at the end of a penitential prayer for forgiveness and restoration.

(4) A better approach is to treat the verse as a conditional sentence: "If you should reject us, you would be too angry against us,"[3] or "If thou hast utterly rejected us, then great has been thy anger against us."[4] Actually, there is no true conditional sentence here, stich *b* being completely parallel to stich *a,* and adding nothing new to the thought.[5] In addition, the difficulty mentioned above inheres in this view as well—it offers a very unsatisfactory conclusion to a penitential poem.

(5) To understand the *ki' im* as "unless," on the basis of such passages as Gen 32:27, . . . "I shall not let you go unless you bless me," and to render this passage, "Turn us to yourself . . . unless you have despised us," i.e., completely rejected us.[6] But as Albrektson points out, in all such instances *ki' im* is used only after a clause containing or implying a negative. The syntactic difficulty aside, the problem of meaning remains: a plea for divine favor is logically and psychologically incompatible with the idea of a possible total rejection by God. A despairing Job may contemplate the possibility of complete alienation from God; a psalmist, however harried and embittered by misfortune, has not surrendered the hope of succor and restoration.

(6) Having rejected all other interpretations, Hillers finds "one remaining possibility—to render the verse adversatively, "But instead you have utterly rejected us, you have been very angry with us."[7] He seeks to buttress this view by three lines of argument:

(a) This interpretation is supported by Jewish liturgical practice, which ordains that in the synagogue reading of the closing sections of Isaiah, Malachi, Ecclesiastes, and *Lamentations* the last verse of the text is not to be the conclusion, by having the penultimate sentence repeated, so as not to end with "a somber verse."[8]

But even if the synagogue usage be allowed as evidence, it offers no proof for this interpretation. In each of these instances, the reason for not concluding with the final verse is not "the somber verse," but the negative character of the *closing phrase.* In Isa 66:24, the prophet describes the utter destruction and degradation of the wicked. Malachi 3:24 foretells the restoration of unity between parents and children. Eccl 12:12 declares that God will judge all men's actions. None of these ideas are felt to be negative either in biblical or post-biblical thought. They all deal with manifestations of God's power and justice. What the ancient reader found unpalatable and, therefore, sought to avoid ending with was an unpleasant phrase, "a stench to all flesh," "I shall smite the land in total destruction," "upon every deed, good or evil." Similarly in this passage, the closing phrase, "you have been very angry with us," is the reason for the synagogue practice. Hence nothing can be inferred with regard to the specific meaning assigned to the verse as a whole or to the conjunction and to stich *a* in particular.

(b) In further justification of this rendering, Hillers declares that "other laments similarly end on a low key, e.g., Jer 14:9; Ps 88, 89." However, the description of the passage as being "in a low key," would seem to be an understatement. If it is, as Hillers avers, a statement of present realities, it is strongly negative.

Nor can these other passages cited be adduced in favor of this view. Jer 14:9, far from ending on a low key, has a highly appropriate conclusion, paralleling vs. 21 in this chapter. It is a passionate plea for God's help: "Your name is called upon us, do not forsake us!"

In Psalm 89, the plea is expressed in vs. 51a, while vs. 52 is a subordinate clause, giving the grounds for the urgency of the appeal:

> Remember, O Lord, how thy servant is scorned
>> How I bear in my bosom the insults of the

people
    with which thine enemies taunt, O Lord,
        with which they mock the footsteps of thy
anointed.[9]

Of the three passages adduced, Psalm 88 does, indeed, end upon a negative note. It seems clear, however, that the surviving text is incomplete and that we have only part of a description of the poet's estrangement and isolation from his fellows. The theme is very similar to that of Job 19:13-19. The conclusion to Psalm 88 can scarcely be described as a satisfactory close to the poem on any count.[10]

(c) Hillers explains that the verse "merely restates the present fact: Israel does stand under God's severe judgment." However, the alleged matter-of-fact statement contradicts the cry of vs. 20: "Why have you forsaken us so long?" and is totally incompatible with the plea of vs. 22, "Turn us back to you, etc."[11]

In sum, this interpretation, like those cited above, offers what must be described as an inappropriate conclusion to the poem.

I would venture to propose another approach. As we have noted above, Psalm 89 ends with a plea extending over two verses, the petition being expressed by a main clause containing the petition (vs. 51), while the supporting grounds or circumstances are presented in a following subordinate clause (vs. 52). The passage in *Lamentations* exhibits the same syntactic structure, the plea being expressed by the main clause (vs. 21), and the circumstances surrounding the petition being contained in a subordinate clause (vs. 22).

The problem here has been the precise meaning of the conjunction. I believe that in this passage *ki' im* is to be rendered "even if, although." This dual conjunction is used widely and rather loosely in biblical Hebrew in a variety of meanings listed in the lexicons. However, in several instances, the conjunction is best rendered "even if, although."[12] That this meaning has not been clearly recognized is due to the difficult passages in which it occurs:

Jer 51:14: . . . "though I have filled you with men like the locust (i.e., increased your population), yet they (i.e., your assailants) lift up their shout against you."[13]

Isa 10:22: . . . "even if your people, O Israel, will be like the sand of the sea, only a remnant will return."[14]

Amos 5:22: . . . "even if you offer up to me your holocausts and gift offerings, I will not accept them."[15]

This meaning is highly appropriate in Lam 3:32 as well: . . ."though he has afflicted, he will have pity according to his great mercies."

The meaning "although, even though" which we have postulated for the double conjunction may be the result of a transposition, *kî' im = 'im kî*. We may cite as an analogy

the use of *kî gam* which has the meaning "although" in Eccl 4:14; 8:12, 16. This usage, characteristic of Qoheleth, is equivalent to *gam kî*, "even if, although" (Isa 1:15; Hos 8:10; 9:16; Ps 23:4), and likewise introduces a subordinate clause.[16]

A syntactic change in the use of the conjunction "although" appears to have developed in the post-exilic period. In the pre-exilic usage, the subordinate clause introduced by the conjunction *precedes* the main clause (*kî' im*, Amos 5:22; Isa 10:22; Jer 51:14; *gam kî*, Hos 8:10; 9:16; so also Ps 23:4; Prov 22:6). Though post-exilic writers continue this sequence (Lam 3:8, 32), they nevertheless feel free to vary it by having the main clause *precede* the subordinate clause (*kî' im* in this passage; *kî gam* in Eccl 4:14; 8:12, 16). Obviously, from the standpoint of logic, either sequence of clauses is entirely proper.[17]

It remains to add that the verbs in this passage are to be understood as pluperfects.[18] We now have a vigorous, clear, and appropriate conclusion to the penitential prayer in the last three verses of *Lamentations*:

> Why do you neglect us eternally,
>   forsake us for so long?
> Turn us to yourself, O Lord, and we shall return;
>   renew our days as of old,
> even though you had despised us greatly
>   and were very angry with us.

Notes

1. As recognized by D. R. Hillers, *Lamentations* (AB 7A; Garden City: Doubleday, 1973) 100.

2. So RSV: "Why dost thou forget us for ever, why dost thou so long forsake us?"

3. So Ehrlich, *Randglossen zür hebräischen Bibel* (Leipzing: Hinrichs, 1914), 7. 854; T. Meek, *IB* (Nashville: Abingdon, 1956), 6. 38.

4. So NEB.

5. The verbs in both stichs are virtually synonymous, and the infinitive absolute construction in stich *a* parallels '*ad m^{e}ōd*' in stich *b*.

6. So W. Rudolph, "Der Text der Klagelieder," *ZAW* 51 (1933) 120.

7. AB, following the Vulgate, Luther, AV and P. Volz (*TLZ* 22 [1940] 82-83).

8. AB, 101.

9. So RSV.

10. It is, of course, possible to assume that this poem is also incomplete, but this approach is a procedure to be adopted only when no other is available, and Hillers properly does not include this view among the possible options. In addition, virtually all scholars are agreed that the existence of 22 verses in the chapter, identical with the number of letters in the alphabet, is not accidental; it represents a variant of the acrostic pattern characteristic of chs. 1-4.

11. As Rudolph correctly points out.

12. Cf. BDB, *s.v.,* 474-75; KB, 431.

13. See BDB, 475a, who cite Ewald, Keil, Cheyne; so also W. Rudolph, *Jeremia* (HAT; Tübingen: Mohr, 1947), 266. Other commentators render the clause, "I will surely fill them with assailants" (Hitzig, RSV), but this requires construing *millē'tik* as a perfect of certitude, which appears awakward in this context. Hence NEB follows the view we have adopted, rendering freely, "Once I filled you with men, countless as locusts, yet a song of triumph shall be chanted over you."

14. The rendering *kî* as "for" disguises, but does not obviate, the difficulty involved in treating vs. 22 as the reason for vs. 21. Actually, the second verse offers no reason for the first; it expresses the same idea as the first, but with greater emphasis.

15. Here, too, *kî* does not introduce the reasons for vs. 21.

16. For a discussion of these passages in Ecclesiastes, see R. Gordis, *Koheleth—The Man and His World* (3rd ed.; New York: Schocken, 1968), 244, 297-98. There is virtually complete agreement on the meaning of *kî gam* in 4:14; on 8:12, see BDB, 169, *s.v.* § 6. We believe this meaning for the double conjunction most appropriate in all three passages.

17. It may be added that in medieval Hebrew, *we'im* is frequently used in the sense, "although, even if." Thus in *Bᵉrah Dōdî,* the *Gᵉ'ûlāh piyyût* recited on the Second Day (as well as the other days) of Passover, the usage occurs no less than nine times in the meaning "though," e.g., *bᵉrah dôdî el mâkôn lᵉšibtāk wᵉim 'ābarnû 'et bᵉrîtāk, 'ānā zᵉkōr,* "Fly, my beloved, to your established dwelling and though we have transgressed your convenant, remember, pray, etc." (*Sabbath & Festival Prayer Book* [New York: Rabbinical Assembly and United Synagogue, 1946], 182-83).

18. Cf. S. R. Driver, *Hebrew Tenses* (Oxford: Clarendon, 1892), 22: "The perfect is used where we should employ by preference the pluperfect, i.e., in cases where it is desired to bring two actions in the past into a special relation with each other, and to indicate that the action described by the pluperfect was completed before the other took place. The function of the pluperfect is thus to throw two events into their proper perspective as regards each other; but the tense is to some extent a superfluous one—it is an elegance for which Hebrew possesses no distinct form, and which even in Greek, as is well known, both classical and Hellenistic is constantly replaced by the simple aorist."

Michael S. Moore (essay date 1983)

SOURCE: "Human Suffering in *Lamentations*," in *Revue Biblique,* Vol. 90, No. 4, October, 1983, pp. 534-55.

[*In the following essay, Moore critiques attempts at finding unity in* **Lamentations** *and contends that its theme and structure work together to express grief and promote hope.*]

Among most recent studies of the theological import of *Lamentations,* the approaches of Norman Gottwald[1] and Bertil Albrektson[2] have dominated discussion. It is Gottwald's view, first of all, that a single "key" to the theology of **Lamentations** can be found—a position which is problematic from the very outset.[3] Secondly, Gottwald believes that this "key" to the theology of the book is to be found in the tension between deuteronomic faith and the tragic facts of history underlying the book. During the Josianic reform the older, more conservative beliefs were reasserted in certain Israelite circles with regard to the perpetual problem of evil. The deuteronomic solution, according to Gottwald, consisted of the simplistic view that sin *always* brings punishment while faith *always* brings forth vindication of the faithful elect.

To this neat and tidy solution, however, history quickly raised several unexplainable tragedies. Josiah, the righteous reformer, dies in battle (608). Jehoiachin and several thousand citizens are deported to Mesopotamia after an abortive rebellion attempt (597). Even Jerusalem suffers the ignobilies of besiegement, starvation, defeat, and slavery (586). To Gottwald, therefore, **Lamentations** is a serious theological document struggling with this perennial dilemma: Why do the righteous suffer? It is the first time in Israel's turbulent history that a sensitive writer has to face this problem, stripped of all the old symbols of Yahweh's favor the city, the temple, the people, the torah. The "daughter of Jerusalem" must now deal directly with the "divine warrior," Yahweh of Hosts. The prophetic warnings have now been fulfilled, but in such a terrible way that the simplistic approach of the deuteronomists is found wanting.

Albrektson challenged this interpretation by going directly to the heart of Gottwald's thesis and asking whether there had ever existed, in fact, any such "tension" between *deuteronomic* faith and history. Accepting Gottwald's basic premise that **Lamentations** was written to explain the hideous circumstances attending the events of 586 within an overall framework of tension between Israelitic faith and the tragic events of history, he nevertheless rejected outright the view that such a pristine "deuteronomic" faith had ever commanded the full attention of the populace.[4] More probably, Albrektson submits, the people living in and around Jerusalem had allowed themselves to be lulled to sleep via the hundreds of sermons and liturgies they had repeatedly heard extolling *ad absurdum* the beauty, sanctity, and even impregnable inviolability of Zion, God's "footstool." Thus, when Zion fell, so did their faith. Albrektson sees **Lamentations,** therefore, as a document designed to lead Israel back to faith in a *person* rather than a *place.* In fact, Albrektson submits, Gottwald's thesis holds only if one can prove that such a deuteronomic faith was universally (or at least quasi-universally) held in Israel—that Israel could ever have been, *in toto,* truly "righteous."

In other words, Albrektson is simply not willing to build a theology of *Lamentations* on such an attractive, yet unproven assumption, though he is not then trying to dismiss Gottwald's work as completely misguided. In the latter pages of his approach he seems to be trying, in fact, to offer a synthesis of the two theses,[5] a process which is later picked up by P. Ackroyd within his broader attempt to articulate a "theology of the Exile."[6]

The problem with both of these hypotheses is that both put forward the conviction, *a priori*, that *a* single theological focal point can not only be found in this mini-collection of laments over Jerusalem, but also that such a postulated focal point might then serve as *the* major theological trust of the book; all else is secondary. This kind of a methodological approach is often suspect in works wherein authorship, time, and place of composition are generally recognized and accepted; it is highly suspect in a diffuse collection of poetic compositions like the "books" of Psalms and *Lamentations*. Accordingly, there will probably always be critical minds who justifiably question this kind of biblical theological approach, based as it is on so many unproven (and unproveable) assumptions, correlations, and questionable conclusions. It seems to me that one might safely go as far as to say that deuteronomic and Zion traditions serve as contributing traditional sources for the development of the theology articulated in Lamentations, but to focus either upon one of these or even upon some sort of synthesis between the two eventually proves to be inadequate for the following reasons:

(1) To posit a single theological focus one most likely will have to base such a focus upon some kind of theory of unity between the individual chapters. As will be shown below, neither Gottwald nor Albrektson are the first to try this (theological focus+unity of form/material), even though neither of them explicitly link the two together in their respective analyses.

(2) To posit a single theological focus would most likely imply that the poet(s) responsible for this collection of laments was calculatedly conscious of "doing theology" in the modern sense of the expression: i.e., that there was a deliberate attempt here to go *beyond* the crying need to begin Israel's "grief work"[7] *on to* the development of a theological treatise. Is *Lamentations* really an objectively thought-out theological treatise? Is this document anything more than what it claims to be, viz. a lament over Jerusalem? Doubtless the author(s) stood within a particular traditional framework (deuteronomistic? zionistic?), but was he *consciously* and *methodically* employing all the stock symbols, phrases, and poetic word-pairs[8] of this alleged historico/theological tradition in order to facilitate a communal lament? In other words, was he *intentionally* attempting to construct a theology?[9] I am more inclined to believe that the hard theologizing about these events came later.[10] There had to be some time to think it all through first. Such tragedies have to be absorbed into one's consciousness before one can then begin to "explain" them in any coherent way. How many soundly-reasoned books on

the holocaust in Nazi Germany were written (by Jews) within the first decade or two after the liberations of Dachau, Buchenwald, or Auschwitz?[11] How many carefully-reasoned historical analyses about the Vietnam war have yet been written (by Americans) since the fall of Saigon?[12] In addition, the persistent uncertainty among so many scholars as to the very existence of a theological focal point within this collection of poems makes it seem much more likely that *Lamentations,* composed and collected as it was so close to the events depicted within it,[13] was primarily designed only to lament the nation's destruction, to put forward a first step toward picking up the emotional pieces, to articulate the anger, guilt, despair, and stubborn hopes of a nation too shell-shocked to begin this necessary "grief work" without help.[14] This is not to deny that significant theological themes surface and resurface here and there throughout the book, but it is to affirm that the historical context within which it was composed precluded the kind of theological questions and answers one finds more carefully articulated in full-fledged works like Deutero-Isaiah and Ezekiel.

(3) To posit a single theological focus tends, in the final analysis, to reduce and constrict the variegated impact of *Lamentations*' broad theological thrust. It tends to force the "secondary" themes out of the picture. One could well reissue here the question that H. H. Schmid has raised to pentateuchal research and apply it to the present state of research into *Lamentations*' theology:

> Has the text more often been adjusted to our hypotheses than our hypotheses to the text?[15]

This paper is an attempt to shed more light on one of these "secondary" themes, to try to place it in some kind of a proper perspective within the overall message of the book without distorting the theological impact of the whole. I am suggesting here that *one* of the primary messages of *Lamentations* is the theme of human suffering.[16] This seems to be such an obvious conclusion from even a cursory reading of the book, yet few (if any) of the treatments I have read have assigned this theme more than a peripheral place. This is unfortunate, because a careful study of the metaphorical as well as historical passages which deal with human suffering—from the starving of infants to the sorrow of the aged—not only points the way toward the illumination of a major theme in a biblical document, but also opens the door a bit wider to the kind of biblical interpretation which can speak more directly to the present needs of a war-torn world. What is God saying here about his relationship to suffering humanity? What was the poet(s) trying to accomplish here? What were his priorities? What theological (and even psychological) value might Lamentations have today were the light of interpretation focused squarely on this neglected theme?

I. The problem of unity within the book of *Lamentations* has long intrigued scholars. Many expressed profound doubt at the end of the previous century that *Lamentations* might ever be characterized a unified document in any sense of the term—neither formally nor in terms of its theological content.[17] Others had allegedly uncovered what they believed to have been the author's (in most cases, Jeremianic authorship was assumed) conscious attempt to structure the book. Some sought a middle solution—that the poems were individually composed, and that a later redactor deliberately arranged and modified them according to *his* pre-thought-out plan. Some of these theses are worth re-examining here.[18]

Hermann Wiesmann has been quoted often by modern scholars as one who championed the theological unity of the book, yet even though his work laid the foundation for later serious theological inquiry,[19] both Gottwald and Albrektson (to take two prominent examples) hastily dismiss the implications of his approach, linking it to primitive Roman Catholic theology.[20] Perhaps his later work (particularly his *Die Klagelieder* commentary)[21] has gone far enough to earn this opprobrium, but his earlier work, particularly his article "Der planmässige Aufbau der Klagelieder des Jeremias," cannot fairly be so criticized.[22] In it, Wiesmann stakes out a carefully balanced position, meticulously distinguishing his views from some of the more radical "unity" theories then in circulation, particularly among German scholars. Though descriptive in approach (i.e., not tied exclusively to form-, literary-, or traditio-critical foundations), I found none of the theological excesses in it of the sort Rudolph describes (though not in a description of Wiesmann *per se*).[23] Instead, I found what can only properly be described as the beginning point for the modern theological discussion.[24]

Though several scholars in Wiesmann's day rejected outright the unity of the book, a few older, conservative scholars tried hard to construct strong "unity" hypotheses, often linking them to attempts to salvage Jeremianic authorship from critical attack. W. M. L. de Wette proposed that the destruction of the city seemed to be set out in clearly recognizable stages from poem to poem, thus leading one to the conclusion that such linkages had been deliberately arranged from a pre-set structural outline.[25] Wiesmann rejected this "gradational" approach because the text presents no evidence for it. Each poem assumes, either implicitly or explicitly, that Jerusalem has been utterly destroyed (even chapter 1, *contra* Rudolph). H. Ewald held that the author took five pre-written, scattered laments and re-worked them into a unified whole.[26] C. F. Keil accepted this theory with the *proviso* that the author/collector did *not* work around a definite theological focal point (such as the theology of hope embedded in 3.22-33), yet still must have operated from some sort of "well thought-out plan."[27] Wiesmann saw through this inconsistency right away by noting wryly that Keil failed to spell out what exactly that "well-thought-out plan" might have been.[28] He saved his strongest criticism, however, for the "unity" thesis put forward by Eduard Naegelsbach.

Naegelsbach took this developing line of approach (i.e., the attempts of de Wette, Ewald, Keil, and others to build a portrait of the book's unity primarily upon *external*

characteristics) to its logical extreme. For Naegelsbach, the expression of hope in 3.22-42 is the "culmination-point of the whole book."[29] Like the peak of a mountain, everything in the preceding verses leads up to it, while everything in the succeeding verses leads back downward. Chapters 1 and 2, 4 and 5 represent the night of misery after the fall of the nation. For Naegelsbach, however, these chapters served merely to bracket what for him was the dominant thrust of the poet's message. Chapters 1 and 2 were constructed like a crescendo leading to this volcanic peak; chapter 4 and 5 served as decrescendo. Chapter 3 itself was separated into three parts: (1) 3.1-21 was supposed to represent the night of doubt (3.1-18), followed by the dawn of hope (3.19-21); (2) this hope then bursts forth like the rays of the sun (3.22-40)—heavenly trust is rekindled, God's love is reaffirmed; (3) this paroxysm then subsides back into the twilight (i.e., historical reality begins to sink back in—3.40-42), followed by ultimate return to a night of anguish (3.43-66). Naegelsbach also found it important to stress, in support of his thesis, that the poetic intensity of the first two chapters built to a high point in chapter 3, whereas chapters 4 and 5 were not to be considered artistically comparable to chapters 1 and 2. The 3-line acrostic of chapters 1 and 2 intensifies in chapter 3 where every line has to be chosen with care, while chapter 4 suddenly abandons this style for a 2-line structure. Chapter 5 then abandons the acrostic altogether.

Without even pausing to salute the ingenuity of Naegelsbach's thesis, Wiesmann promptly rejected it[30] because (1) if the poet truly wanted to structure his work thus around a message of hope, why lead the people to the light of day only to lead them back down into the gloom of night? This makes no sense. Further, it might even be characterized as a cruel, teasing joke to so play with their emotions like that. What might he have been trying to accomplish with such a message? (2) Though the poet indeed struggles through from "night" to "day" in a literary sense in the third chapter, the *theological* message could not have been that suffering is only a proof from God that he still cares; i.e., the more one suffers under God's punishing hand, the more one might be convicted of God's chastening concern. Rather, the point of chapter 3 is that one who stands in the midst of suffering should never give up hope in God's love and grace, even when it is most difficult to perceive these positive qualities in the Deity.[31] In fact, Wiesmann would argue here against Budde[32] that the misery of the people is introduced in an individual lament in chapter 3 *not* merely to provide a literary focal point for the whole book, but to give suffering people a tangible model of dignified behavior in the midst of famine, war, and cannibalism. (3) Finally, Wiesmann crisply rejects the notion that chapters 4 and 5 are in any way inferior to the rest of the book.[33]

What kind of unity, therefore, did Wiesmann ascribe to the book? Wiesmann was the first to reject the placement of any artificially-constructed *external* schema over the book while at the same time insisting that the book's *internal* characteristics coherently set forth a substantive unity upon which one might then go on to build a relevant theology.[34] He summarizes his position in a cogent résumé:

> Our five songs do picture a unity, and indeed, not merely from external considerations (because they are unified in a collection like some of Psalms), but also on inner grounds. Therefore, *(a)* they are first of all composed around a similar situation: all set forth the destruction of Jerusalem and the misfortune which thereby came over the people. Further, *(b)* they collectively draw these mournful events into the realm of their concern and place them opposite similar situations: there resounds within all of them a lament over the terrible fall of the kingdom (as well as) the voices of profoundest pity for its unfortunate inhabitants. *(c)* The same basic views are then drawn through all the fragments: concerning the reasons for this fate, the results of the affliction, the instruments of punishment, etc. *(d)* All follow, further, the same goal: the consolation of the people and their return to the Lord.[35]

The advantages of Wiesmann's thesis of *internal* unity are several:

(1) His thesis rests on the text itself, not on a superimposed literary schema (Naegelsbach), a hypothetical explanation for the historico/theological background of the book (Gottwald, Albrektson),[36] a cultic hypothesis which lays too much stress on the unproved assumption that these laments (particularly the mixture of individual and communal laments in chapter 3) were originally composed to be sung by an individual+a chorus (Kraus),[37] nor a complex theory of compositional stages (several years, same author—Rudolph;[38] chapters, in order of composition: 4, 1, 2, 3 over a 27-day period—Brunet).[39] Whatever else one might say in criticism of Wiesmann's thesis, it is hard to find fault with him here. Granted, he sometimes gets carried away' as, for example, when he asserts that all five chapters have a description of Yahweh's righteousness[40] (neither chapter 4 nor chapter 5 explicitly ascribe righteousness to Yahweh), or when he overreacts to the theses of Budde and Naegelsbach on chapter 3 and neglects to point out the genuine lexical and historical points-of-contact between chapter 3 and the rest of the book,[41] but his basic desire to let the text interpret itself is quite refreshing.

(2) Wiesmann's emphasis on *internal* unity may be unpalatable to form critics interested in artistic purity (Jahnow),[42] or to source critics interested in multiple-authorship hypotheses (Löhr),[43] but it has already proved acceptable (and should so continue) to many scholars, probably because it is so adaptable.[44] One can accept it and still remain consistent to positions either for or against Jeremianic authorship, Babylonian vs. Palestinian *Sitze im Leben*, deuteronomistic vs. Zionistic background, oral vs. written original composition, multiple vs. single authorship, or any number of still-unsolved *external* problems related to the book. This needs to be underscored, especially to anyone truly interested in uncovering the theological message concealed here (cf. 3.44!). The alternative is to posit that neither the poet (if individual authorship is assumed) nor

poet(s)/redactor(s) were at all interested in conveying an intelligible theological message to Israel at a time when she most needed a word from God.

(3) Lastly, Wiesmann's approach, via emphasizing the *internal* unity of *Lamentations,* effectually opens the way for further theological investigation into the several themes articulated in the book as well as the way in which these themes are interwoven and interlocked. Moreover, it helps to open up clearer avenues for contemporary exposition, interpretation, and application.[45] Application of a process hermeneutic, for example, to the themes of human suffering or divine consolation might yield fruitful results, if responsibly administered.[46] The same could be said for either a structuralist or a non-structuralist literary analysis.[47] The following discussion, in fact, will seek to focus on the theme of human suffering in *Lamentations* from such a predominantly nonstructuralist literary approach, operating within these minimal formal guidelines:

(a) The intention here will be to set aside, for a moment, the historical problems associated with the book and focus instead on its literary structure. The risk inherent in this kind of approach, of course, is that the meaning of the text will be distorted into something it was never intended to be. This risk will be placed here under a watchful eye. I have no desire to follow in the foot-steps of Naegelsbach or de Wette. Further, the objection could be raised that this kind of approach is applicable only to material that was self-consciously written as literature.[48] In *Lamentations'* case the manifest employment of the acrostic literary form ought to quell objections from this quarter.[49]

(*b*) Secondly, the intention here is to focus on deep structures underneath the surface of the text, rather than surface structures like words, metaphors, or genres. This should prove particularly fruitful in a work like *Lamentations,* since it is a document of such deep human emotion. One will need to deal with words and metaphors in order to begin this process, but the *intention* here, so long as it can be objectively justified, is to try to dig deeper into the mind and heart of the poet(s) who composed this series of laments over Zion. I am consciously attempting to construct a theological statement about the book in the tradition begun by Wiesmann. The only major difference here is that I will be making use of some contemporary hermeneutical tools which Wiesmann either could not or chose not to employ in his own distinctive approach. Moreover, since it is highly doubtful that the poet(s) was consciously trying to construct a theology in the modern sense,[50] it seems to me that one eventually *has* to adopt some sort of internalistic approach in order to get at the full meaning of the text. I am under no illusions that the approach offered here will enable us to "map the mind"[51] of the author(s) of *Lamentations*—the sour impression which is sometimes left by practitioners of this methodological approach. The goal here will be simply to focus attention upon one (and only one) of the major themes of the book, *not* offer a composite, complete theology.

II. Delbert Hillers,[52] in the introduction to his Anchor Bible commentary on *Lamentations,* notes the unusually large number of metaphorical epithets for the Israelite people found in the book. The phrase *bath—X* or *b^ethūlath bath—X* occurs 20 times here whereas it occurs only about 45 times in the entire OT. In addition, the majority of the other occurrences are to be found in Jeremiah. Hillers then goes on to make some valuable comments which seek to explain this exceptionally prevalent usage in Lamentations; viz., (1) that it appears to offer the poet a flexible metrical unit which can be expanded or contracted according to need,[53] and (2) "they help make explicit the personification of the people or city as a woman."[54] This second explanation deserves further development. Why did the poet seek to personify the misery of the people via such epithets? What was he trying to make explicit; i.e., what are the historical referents behind these epithetical symbols?

A careful concordial analysis of the text of all five of these poems reveals that behind these metaphorical epithets stands an astonishingly complete spectrum of non-metaphorical terms for nearly every age, sex, and class of humanity. Babes, sucklings, children, boys, young men, young women, mothers, fathers, and old men are portrayed in the book suffering differing degrees of trauma. Slaves, priests, prophets, widows, orphans, princes, and kings are all there as well. . . .

In addition to this mass of data, some rather striking structural characteristics come immediately to light when one begins to note the fashion by which this theme of human suffering is presented. I agree with Gottwald that the writer(s) of Lamentations was much more interested in conveying his message than in maintaining artistic purity. In particular, Gottwald's response to Jahnow's assertion (that the free mixture of types and images in the first four poems was due to a lack of ". . . the powerful originality of a unitary artistic conception")[55] lands right on target: (1) Had the poet focused only upon the figure of the mother of Zion, the poem would have lacked concreteness; (2) had he focused only upon the actual scenes of the dead, the work would have lacked the communal appeal which he sought to effect. The author "would not sacrifice a realistic lament in order to achieve artistry."[56]

The debate over literary types, however, offers little help to the expositor interested in probing underneath the surface to the deeper meaning of these epithets and historical word-symbols. Agreement with the contention that theological intention overrides artistic design does not necessarily mean that this book is therefore a-structural. The question is, what *kind* of structure? Deep structure or surface structure? Debates over acrostic forms and types of lament-forms are predominantly interested in analyzing the surface structures of this material. A closer reading into the deeper structures reveals a very interesting pattern—a pattern which explicitly has to do with the way in which the theme of human suffering is interwoven throughout the book. Perhaps the most convenient way to present this pattern would be to trace its contours within each chapter:

Chapter 1—Four times in this chapter there is a sudden shift from 3rd to 1st person. In three of the instances[57] the poet turns to the 1st-person prayer (1.11), lament (1.16),[58] and admonition to the nations (1.18) in particularly noteworthy contexts. In 1.11 he employs a metaphorical term for children (*mah^amaddēhem*—Qere) which could have been designed as a word play with *mah^amaddēhā* in 1.10: i.e., it is one thing for the enemy to invade the sanctuary compound and steal what is precious to him, but the thought of little children having to be sold for food wrenches out of the poet a sudden 1st-person prayer to Yahweh: "Look, O Lord, and behold!" Similarly, in v. 16 the shift comes not after a complaint about the activities of the enemy (v. 14), but after pointing out the outcome of the human tragedy (cf. *bahūray, b^ethūlath bath y^ehādāh* in v. 15; *bhānay* in v. 16). The 1st-person admonition which concludes the chapter (beginning in v. 18) commences the delineating description of "my pain" *(mak'ōbhī)* with a mourning over the captivity of *b^ethūlōthay ūbhahūray* before any other kind of pain. This is complemented by another prayer for Yahweh to behold the poet's distress (vss. 20-22).

Chapter 2—The first ten verses of chapter 2 read like a 3rd-person laundry-list of images and metaphors which all attempt to describe the depth and breadth of Yahweh's destructive power. Significantly, however, it is not until the visual images of the *ziqnā bath siyyōn* and the *b^ethūlōth y^erūšālāim* flash across the poet's mind that we find the first shift to the 1st person in v. 11. In that verse the poet elaborates the reasons for his lament by narrating what he had seen which could have so moved him to tears: the sight of *'ōlēl* and *yōnēq* starving to death in their mothers' laps. Note that here the metaphorical epithet *(bath 'ammī)* is placed in parallel with the historical term(s) *('ōlēl w^eyōnēq),* a device which is often repeated throughout the book (1.6, *bath siyyōn & śārehā*; 1.15, *b^ethūlath bath y^e- hūdāh & bahūray/' abbīray*: 2.5, *bath y^ehūday & yisrā'el*; 2.15, *bath y^erūšālaim & hā'īr*; 3.48, *bath 'ammī & 3.51, b^enōth 'īrī*;[59] 4.3, *bath 'ammī & y^e'ēnīm* (Qere); 4.6, *bath 'ammī & s^edōm*). This heartbreaking memory promptly leads to a short series of rhetorical questions which underline the helpless agony he was trying to put into words (v. 13). The intervening 2nd-person material is finally disrupted again by a series of imperative verbs which begins in v. 18 and extends through v. 20 (*sa^'aqī,[60] horīdhī, 'al titt^enī, qūmī, rōnnī, šiphkī, ś^e'ī*). As the last of these everlouder hammer-blows strikes the page, the poet . . . s thoughts stubbornly return to his now-frantic concern for the "lives of your childre." This recurrent theme finally drags out of him a concluding prayer, wherein he begs Yahweh to watch: the starvation of women compelling them to eat their own children; the choice young men and maidens dying violently by the sword; the enemy utterly destroying "those whom I fondled and nurtured."

Chapter 3—Saturated as this chapter is with the 1st-person format of the individual lament,[61] no dramatic 3rd to 1st person shifts occur here. This is not surprising. Moreover, the overt personalization of the poet's agony (which is more communally expressed in the other four laments) consequently inhibits his concern here for the suffering of the various social groupings within his community. His interests are dominantly personal, not public. Accordingly, there are no terms for suffering humanity here and only two brief epithetical symbols in vss. 48 and 51 (*bath 'ammī* in v. 48; *b^{e}nōth 'īrī* in v. 51). The first person plural contexts within which these two epithets are found switch smoothly to the first person singular in the verse which concludes with *bath 'ammī* and continues through its parallel in v. 51, but the frenzied statements thereafter which lead up to the vocative prayer-plea in v. 55 make it clear that the poet's concern in this third chapter has been deliberately focused more upon personal suffering than upon collective suffering.

Chapter 4—In chapter 4 the first ten verses are structured around three comparisons. Each of these comparisons is itself structured around the repeated phrase, *bath 'ammī*. In verse 3 the jackals are portrayed as creatures which remember, even under stress, to feed their young, but *bath 'ammī* has become cruel. The second contrast follows up on this ominous beginning, sketching a pathetic picture of starving children (who once had so much to eat, such nice clothes to wear) and comparing the present destruction of *bath 'ammī* with the well-known judgment over Sodom (v. 6): the poet asserts that Jerusalem's chastisement is greater. Verse 10 is one of the most poignant passages in the book. Compassionate women, no longer able to stand the sight of their little ones in such unbearable agony, and realizing that even death by the sword was preferable to the slow, lingering pain of starvation (cf. Josephus, *Wars* VII, 8, 6), mercifully kill and cook their children for food. All three comparisons move relentlessly deeper into the poet's horror-numbed mind as the scenes of these atrocities are poured out on the page.[62] The second half of the poem begins yet another 3rd-person laundry-list of the afflicted (3.12-16). Standard word-pairs[63] are employed via well-worn formulae: *nābhī'/kōhēn* (4.13; cf. 2.20; Isa. 28.7; Jer. 2.8, 26; 4.9; 5.31; etc.); and *kōhēn/zāqēn* (4.16; cf. 1.19; Ezek. 7.26; Jer. 19.1; 29.1). *Zāqēn*, however, has a double meaning in Lamentations. Of the 6 times it is employed, 4 occurrences are in rather standard word-pairs. Twice, however (2.10; 5.14), the word broadly refers to the aged men of the city, not necessarily the political/business leadership. At any rate, the shift from 3rd to 1st person occurs right here in v. 17 after the word *z^{e}qēnīm*. It is difficult to say how deliberate this shift may have been, or whether the term's other connotation might have been at all the poet's mind when he decided to make this shift.

Chapter 5—This final chapter, which so many have relegated to a later date[64] (and sometimes separate place)[65] of composition, nevertheless admirably serves as a strong recapitulation of the "suffering humanity" theme we have already traced through the first four poems. This 1st-person plural communal lament, a prayer from start to finish, is carefully stocked with references to a large segment of the human groupings heretofore discovered underneath the surface of this material:

(a) orphans (5.3)

(b) mothers (5.3)

(c) fathers (5.7)

(d) women (5.11)

(e) virgins (5.11)

(f) princes (5.12)

(g) elders (5.12)

(h) young men (5.13)

(i) young boys (5.13)

(j) old men (5.14)

(k) young men (5.14)

Some are placed in standard word-pairs, though not all; some are repeated with different connotational nuances; some are mentioned here for the first time in the book. The semantic weight, however, in this last chapter appears to be laid more upon what these people used to *do* (but have now ceased doing) than upon who they *are* and how much they have suffered. So many distinctively *human* activities have now been silenced. So many distinctively *human* institutions have been battered and bludgeoned. So many distinctively *human* freedoms have been violently and callously taken away. The aftermath of human carnage is here grimly charcoaled for us in chiaroscuro shades of greys and browns. Life now limps along without direction or zest. The sparkling colors which could have brought animation to this scene no longer radiate from the poet's palette. The canvas is grey and vacant. Yahweh's wrath has burned them away.

III. Patrick D. Miller's remarks in a recently-published article have particular relevance here at the conclusion of this paper:

> The interpretative task is not tied to the search for a single explanation for a particular lament, but can center in opening up through different stories and moments examples of the human plight that may be articulated through the richly figurative but stereotypical language of the laments.[66]

(1) Although Miller is responding *(a)* to rather slavish attempts to locate precisely who the "enemies" in a particular lament might have been,[67] and *(b)* to the debate over the exact historical sequencing of Jeremiah's laments and the Psalms of lament by *(c)* attempting to relocate the laments more closely to their narrative and historical contexts, the implications of his statement go much farther than this. I heartily agree with him that there needs to be more flexibility with regard to contemporary analyses of lament-forms. In fact, a review of *Lamentations*' history of theological interpretation, as it has been briefly sketched above, confirms his concern that this kind of flexibility is acutely needed. It is particularly applicable here because so many interpretations assume *(a)* that a single "key" to the theology of this corpus might be produced, and *(b)*

that such a theological "key" might then lead the way to full exposition of the biblical message, almost as if the poet consciously intended that such a theological "key" be found. Furthermore, *(c)* such a methodological approach overly reduces and constricts the message of the book, because all other themes must now be labelled "secondary." This usually means that they do not receive adequate attention and are therefore simply allowed to lie dormant in the text.

(2) Wiesmann intuitively understood this when he pleaded for a theological interpretation which focused more on *internal* than *external* characteristics. Not surprisingly, this approach has not endeared him to critics, even though so many of his original theological insights, following his own careful approach, have been recognized, elaborated, and synthesized in several of their own theologies of Lamentations. Because there is still so much uncertainty over so many external characteristics related to this document, Wiesmann's approach is very attractive as a way out of the impasse, even though it, too, has to be treated critically. His stubborn insistence that God's judgment as well as his compassion are held in tension throughout all five chapters points the way toward a balanced methodological blueprint for further investigation. "Dissective" approaches are no more of an attractive alternative than are "single key" approaches. Wiesmann managed to avoid both extremes, at least in his earlier work. Therefore, a critically-adapted version of his methodological approach to these texts ought now to make it possible for one to fashion a relevant, balanced theology on any one of these long-dormant "secondary" themes, as long as one steadfastly guards against the temptation to make such analyses new "keys" to the Theology of **Lamentations.**

(3) With the aid of some newer hermeneutical tools, the deeper structures of the book might now be made a bit more accessible to the expositor's eye. The analysis offered here has shown that a preeminent concern of the poet was to portray the horrifying scope of human suffering which he had witnessed with his own eyes when Jerusalem fell (could a redactor really have captured this?). Subtle shifts of viewpoint as well as macabre word-plays[68] lying under the surface of these laments most often occur in explicit contexts of human suffering as the poet(s) pours out the condensed pain stored up in the depths of his heart. Though his *thoughts* often turn to God, his *feelings* just as often turn to his beloved *'ammī*. Like a survivor from a concentration camp, he had had to suppress some grisly, nauseating memories. Wisely, he decided not to repress these powerful emotions, but tried instead to give artistic expression to them. **Lamentations,** the result of this "grief work," itself becomes the focal-point for the grief work of an entire nation. Its psychological insights profoundly stimulated the survivors of the holocaust to grieve the loss of their loved ones. Its theological underpinnings, however, insured forever that this grieving process would remain a therapeutic one. Thus, **Lamentations** provided (and still provides) the essential, fundamental element which every survivor needs to carry on—hope.

Notes

1. *Studies in the Book of Lamentations,* Studies in Biblical Theology 14 (London: SCM, 1954), esp. pp. 47ff.

2. *Studies in the Text and Theology of the Book of Lamentations,* Studia Theologica Lundensia 21 (Lund: CWK Gleerup, 1963), esp. pp. 214ff.

3. Curiously, none of the primary reviews of Gottwald's book noted this deficiency. Cf. J. F. McDonnell, *CBQ* 17 (1955): 517-18; J. Mauchline, *ET* 66 (1954-55): 230; J. H. Gailey, Jr., *Inter* 9 (1955): 471-72; D. W. Thomas, *JTS* 6 (1955): 262-65; W. A. Dowd, *TS* 16 (1955): 282. Cf. Albrektson, *Lamentations,* p. 238: "It (is) . . . debatable whether one can speak at all of 'the key' in the singular."

4. Albrektson, *Lamentations,* p. 218.

5. *Ibid.,* p. 219, 231ff.

6. Ackroyd, *Exile and Restoration, OTL* (Philadelphia: Westminster, 1968), s.v. "Gottwald" and "Alkrektson" in the author's index.

7. "Grief work" is a phrase which will be used repeatedly in this paper. An excellent introduction to this psychological process can be found in Elisabeth Kubler-Ross, *On Death and Dying* (New York: MacMillan, 1969). In this landmark study, Kübler-Ross sets out her now-famous "five stages" of this process: (1) denial and isolation, (2) anger, (3) bargaining, (4) depression, and (5) acceptance. Traces of all of these stages might quite readily be noted in Lamentations. Kübler-Ross would be the first to caution, however, that these five stages should not be set into an overly-rigid, staircase-type continuum (cf. p. 138).

8. Cf. W. R. Watters, *Formula Criticism and the Poetry of the Old Testament, BZAW* 138 (Berlin/New York: de Gruyter, 1976), esp. pp. 132f, 210-215. His conclusions appear most succinctly on pp. 146-47: "While formula criticism is not the final solution to all the questions about Hebrew poetry, it nevertheless will go a long way toward helping us repair and relate texts. And it alone just might be the key to a better understanding of the meter." While not uncritically accepting this thesis *in toto,* J. Scharbert *BZ* 22, 2 (1978): 289, nevertheless feels that his discussion of the important function played by word-pairs in OT poetry is much more digestible than his broader discussion about "formulas."

9. *Contra* Albrektson, *Lamentations,* pp. 215f, 238f, though Albrektson does concede that "elements from different traditions can be found in the same author or in the same work, but this does not in itself mean that any real synthesis has been established."

10. For example, simple confessions of sin (*Lam.* 5.7) are _ater spelled out in more categorical detail (*Ezek.* 18), as theologians are forced to deal with the questions raised by the great catastrophe: individual vs. collective sin; justice vs. injustice, particularly of

Yahweh's actions; the need for a new spirit, not just a chastened heart, etc. Lamentations is a theological document, but one which "presupposes and contains, though embryonically, the tensions of later theology," Gottwald, *Lamentations,* p. 71. Cf. also W. Rudolph, *Die Klagelieder, KAT* XVII-3 (Gütersloh: Gerd Mohn, 1963), p. 194.

11. One of the survivors in Dorothy Rabinowitz's *New Lives: Survivors of the Holocaust Living in America* (New York: Knopf, 1976), p. 222, is described in a precise prose which relates how one had to learn to think in order to survive the holocaust of the 1940's: "A person had to summon all his wits, and to focus entirely on the present. One had to learn the rules and search for the signals that told how things were done in the new situation, to find out what the dangers were, whom to trust, what resources to count on. In a new situation there was no place for yesterday's problems. It was only when he was much older that he took to brooding. And he did take to it: he had the brooder's memory, the passion for details, the tireless capacity for rage. But that was in the future, when life was easier."

12. Donald Zagoria, *Vietnam Triangle: Moscow, Peking, Hanoi* (New York: Pegasus, 1967), writing at the height of U.S. involvement in the war, stated: "Our action has resembled that of a bull in a china shop more than that of a surgeon performing a delicate operation on the body politic of a distant and strange nation. One can only hope that the lesson of this tragic experience is being learned. But the signs are not hopeful. We continue with what must be a vain effort to rescue political failure by crude military pressure." Apparently, the hard thinking that was lacking in 1967 is still lacking in 1983, if the developing chaos in Central American/U.S. relations is any indication of the "lessons learned" in Vietnam.

13. On this point I am in basic agreement with W. W. Cannon, *The Authorship of Lamentations, BS* 81 (1924): 43ff, and W. Rudolph, *Die Klagelieder,* p. 193, against H. Wiesmann, *Der Verfasser der Klagelieder ein Augenzeuge?, Bib* 17 (1936): 84, viz. that Lamentations contains all the qualities of an eyewitness account.

14. H.-J. Kraus' argument, *Klagelieder (Threni),*[2] *BK* 20 (Neukirchen: Neukirchener Verlag, 1960), pp. 13-14, that all five songs stand in close relationship to the events depicted in 587, seems to me to be the safest explanation for the phenomena contained in the text. Rudolph at least agrees (*Klagelieder,* p. 193) that there probably was not a "Babylonian reworking" of this material; I hold a similar view, though for different reasons (cf. below).

15. *Der sogenannte Jahwist* (Zurich: Theologischer Verlag, 1976), p. 12.

16. Gottwald's criticism (*Lamentations,* p. 52) of Wiesmann's overdevelopment of the "suffering" theme, as an abstract notion cut off from its historical roots, is well taken.

17. Cf. the views of F. Montet, *Étude sur le livre des Lamentations* (Genève, 1875), p. 27, who believed that the "livre" was little more than a loose ensemble of poems thrown together "sans ordre." E. Reuss, *Das alte Testament* (Braunschweig, 1892), V, p. 295, was of the opinion that neither a logical development of thought nor an ordered series of pictures was traceable in the book. T. Nöldeke accused the exegetes of his day, at least those who had claimed to have found such logical developments of thought from chapter to chapter, of gross eisegesis, of "reading back conceptions which cannot be found therein from an unprejudiced reading" *Die alttestamentliche Literatur* (Leipzig, 1868), p. 145.

18. Some delimitations before reviewing these opinions: *(a)* nothing prior to the 19th century will be consulted; *(b)* there will be no attempt here to deal directly with the issues of date, authorship, or place of composition, though my own views will inevitably be intimated as the discussion unfolds; *(c)* the focal point of the following section will be the arguments both for and against the unity of the book. Since so few modern discussions have dealt with this problem, the opinions of older scholars had to be consulted to lay the foundation for the analysis here. For lack of time and space, only a representative sampling can be presented.

19. Gottwald's praise is magnanimous—"Wiesmann (is) the only scholar known to the present writer who has made a close scrutiny of the theology" (*Lamentations,* p. 52)—even if strongly tempered. Similarly, Rudolph, after criticizing him for his opinions on the book's date, 1 efers the reader to Wiesmann's commentary for detailed exposition of the factors which bring internal harmony to the biblical material (*Klagelieder,* p. 193).

20. Gottwald, *Lamentations,* p. 52; Albrektson, *Lamentations,* p. 215.

21. H. Wiesmann, *Die Klagelieder übersetzt und erklärt* (Frankfurt, 1954).

22. *Biblica,* 7 (1926): 146-61.

23. Rudolph, *Klagelieder,* p. 195.

24. Most of the following citations were taken directly from H. Wiesmann's article, *Der planmässige,* I have not checked all these sources.

25. *Lehrbuch der hist.-krit. Einleitung in die kanon. und apokryph. Bücher des AT,*[6] (Berlin, 1845), para. 273.

26. *Die Dichter des alten Bundes*[2] (Göttingen, 1866), 1/2, p. 323.

27. *Die Klagelieder Jeremia's* (Leipzig, 1872), p. 546.

28. *Der planmässige,* pp. 155-56.

29. *Die Klagelieder,* (Leipzig, 1868), p. VIIf.

30. *Der planmässige,* pp. 156-57.

31. From Wiesmann's own review of Naegelsbach's thesis, I wonder if he is fairly representing him at this point.

32. *Das hebräische Klagelied, ZAW* (1882): 1ff.

33. *Der planmässige,* p. 157.

34. Ironically, Rudolph has fundamentally misunderstood what Wiesmann was trying to say when he lumps him into the same category as Ewald, Keil, and Naegelsbach (*Klagelieder,* p. 196).

35. *Der planmässige,* pp. 155-56.

36. This statement should be interpreted only as a tempering criticism, *not* a complete rejection.

37. Kraus, *Klagelieder,* pp. 12, 15. Kraus' postulation of a new literary type, the "lament for the destroyed sanctuary," as well as its alleged *Sitz im Leben* among the cult prophets has come under strong criticism. Cf. *Lam.* 2.14; 4.13, and G. Fohrer, *Einleitung in das alte Testament* (Heidelberg: Quelle and Meyer, 1965)—ET by D. Green (Nashville: Abingdon, 1968), pp. 297-98; T. F. McDaniel, *The Alleged Sumerian Influence upon Lamentations, VT,* 18 (1968): 198-209; B. S. Childs, *Introduction to the Old Testament as Scripture* (Philadelphia: Westminster, 1979), p. 592.

38. *Der Klagelieder,* p. 193. I fail to see Rudolph's evidence for identical authorship of chapters 4 and 5 from the passages he cites on p. 194: *Lam.* 4.1f & 5.16a; 4.16b & 5.12; 4.17 & 5.6.

39. G. Brunet, *Les Lamentationes contre Jérémie* (Paris: Presses Universitaires de France, 1968). Eissfeldt rejected his thesis entirely (as have many others) as strained and artificial, but applauded his attempt to draw parallels between modern history and Jerusalem's situation in 587 B.C.E. as "a deepening of the understanding of Lamentations," *ThLZ* 94 (1969): 819.

40. *Der planmässige,* pp. 150-51.

41. *Ibid.,* p. 156. N. B. Rudolph's critique, *Der Klagelieder,* pp. 193-94.

42. H. Jahnow, *Das Hebräische Leichenlied, BZAW* 36 (Berlin, 1923).

43. *Threni III und die jeremianische Autorschaft des Buches der Klagelieder, ZAW* 24 (1904): 1-16.

44. Cf. nt. 19 above.

45. I fail to understand either why *(a)* Wiesmann chose only to emphasize the themes of *punishment* and *lament* in his concluding remarks, or *(b)* why he felt compelled to return to a quasi-external structure by submitting a rise-and-fall developmental pattern for these two themes, since he so carefully avoids it, even criticizes it in the preceding pages ("Der planmässige," pp. 160-61).

46. See the thorough analysis and critique of process theology by N. L. Geisler, *Process Theology,* in S. N. Gundry and A. F. Johnson., eds, *Tensions in Contemporary Theology* (Chicago: Moody, 1976), pp. 237-84. For an interesting application of such a process hermeneutic to a biblical text, cf. G. W. Coats, *The Way of Obedience: Traditiohistorical and Hermeneutical Reflections on the Balaam Story, Semeia,* 24 (1982): 53-79.

47. Cf. J. Barr, *Reading the Bible as Literature, BJRL,* 56 (1973): 10-33; J. D. Crossan *A Basic Bibliography for Parables Research, Semeia,* 1 (1974): 236-73.

48. Cf. D. Robertson, *Literature, the Bible as, IDBSupp* (Nashville: Abingdon, 1976), p. 549.

49. Even W. R. Watters, in a study which is primarily concerned with the characteristics of oral poetry, candidly admits that Lamentations "was written poetry from the beginning" (*Formula Criticism,* p. 133).

50. Cf. above.

51. Cf. Roberston, *Literature,* p. 549.

52. *Lamentations,* AB (Garden City, New York: Doubleday, 1972).

53. Cf. F. M. Cross, *Canaanite Myth and Hebrew Epic* (Cambridge: Harvard Univ. Press, 1973), p. 52, on the flexibility of even the most ancient near eastern epithets. Cf. also chapter 4, *Word Pairs and the Creativity of the Hebrew Poet,* in Watters, *Formula Criticism,* pp. 81ff.

54. *Lamentations,* p. xxxviii. . . .

55. Jahnow, *Leichenlied,* p. 172.

56. Gottwald, *Lamentations,* p. 36.

57. The shift in 1.9c seems premature. N.B. *(a)* only 3 f s suffixes elsewhere in the verse; *b* return of 3 f s suffix in vss. 10-11b; *c* Bohairic and Ambrose read ʻonyāh for ʻonyī in 1.9c.

58. Granted, the shift here is not from 3rd to 1st person. An analysis of the usage of the first person singular pronoun ʼ^{a}nī, however, reveals that this is one of only 4 verses in the book wherein ʼ^{a}nī occurs—and here in conjunction with *mimmennī* (cf. 1.21; 3.1, 63).

59. *bath ʻammī* and *b^{e}nôth ʻīrī* (3.51) could also be taken as parallel metaphorical epithets. There seems to be no convincing reason to drop the suffix (cf. Albrektson *Lamentations,* p. 161f).

60. Reading *sa^{ca}qī* with Budde, *Die Dichter,* p. 335, in view of *horīdhī* and *ʼal titt^{e}nī* in v. 18b and c.

61. Previous debate has centered on genre: individual vs. communal lament-forms in chapter 3. Cf. Löhr's review of the arguments both for and against each position ("Threni III"). Gottwald thinks that the poet, steeped in the milieu of "corporate personality," never had a real problem with genre and cautions moderns not to become chained to "ironclad rules" and "sheer arbitrariness" (*Lamentations,* p. 41). W. Whallon attacks Gunkel's programmatic categorization of *Gattungen* in Gunkel's *Einleitung in die Psalmen* (Göttingen, 1933), noting these fundamental weaknesses: *(a)* assumption of a uniform culture; *(b)*

primitive association of the literature we possess with the religious life of the ancient community; (c) overemphasis on the Psalms as liturgical from the very first, and the source of all *Gattungen* in the OT (cf. *Formula, Character, and Context,* p. 162, cited in Watters, *Formula Criticism,* p. 34).

62. Cf. Josephus, *Wars,* V, 10, 2-3, for a grisly description of what famine can do to a family under wartime conditions. J. J. M. Roberts (private correspondence) offers another reason for this maternal cannibalism: "The point is not that they *mercifully* kill, but that hunger drives these women to lose their compassionate character and to eat their children to still their own tormenting hunger!".

63. Watters, *Formula Criticism,* pp. 212-213.

64. All of the commentaries already cited plus the standard Introductions of Fohrer, Eissfeldt (*The OT: An Introduction,* 1965), Childs, and Harrison (*Introduction to the OT,* 1969) deal extensively with the opinions found in the literature.

65. *Ibid.*

66. *Trouble and Woe: Interpreting the Biblical Laments, Inter,* 37, 1 (Jan. 1983): 45.

67. Building on C. Wastermann's categories of "God," "mourner," and "enemies" in *Struktur und Geschichte der Klage im AT, ZAW,* 66 (1954): 44-80.

68. R. Gordis, *The Song of Songs and Lamentations*[2] (New York: KTAV, 1974), frequently notes the existence of word-plays scattered throughout the text; e.g., *ad loc.* on 1.8, where he suggests that *niddāh* was deliberately chosen because it might mean either "unclean" or "object of scorn." Cf. also *zōlēlāh* in 1.11: older meaning, "gluttonous," secondary meaning, "despised, worthless." The sinister word-play on *mah^a maddē* (1.10; 1.11) has already been noted above (). Perhaps the most menacing example is found in the way the poet plays with the root *'ll.* Cf. the way in which the noun *'ōlēl* and the verb *'ālal* dance together in 2.20; 1.22; 1.12 (N.B. *mah^{a}maddē-hem* in 1.11); 3.51.

Delbert R. Hillers (essay date 1983)

SOURCE: "History and Poetry in *Lamentations,*" in *Currents in Theology and Mission,* Vol. 10, 1983, pp. 155-61.

[*In the following essay, Hillers explores the reasons behind the lack of historical material in* Lamentations *and explains that what little of it can be found owes more to literary and religious traditions than to history.*]

While in Jerusalem several years ago I remarked to a friend, an historian at the Hebrew University, that I was working on a commentary on *Lamentations.* He expressed great interest, attracted by the possibility of extracting from the series of poems some historical data to flesh out the bare picture of the fall of Jerusalem given in Kings. Encouraged by his suggestion, I dived into the book again and came up almost completely empty. For though Lamentations was written soon after an overpowering historical event, it provides almost no historical information and is related to "history" in an indirect, mediated fashion.

These conclusions will be elaborated in more detail below, but are stated thus baldly here because they raise the question of how central "history" is in Old Testament religion. That "history" is the particular arena of divine action and divine revelation has been a prominent assertion of many recent theologians. "The Old Testament is a history book" (von Rad). "God reveals himself in historical events, and not in ageless myths or in a system of propositions" (Noth). "Israel is distinguished by the fact that it experienced the reality of God not in the shadows of a mythical primitive history but more and more decisively in historical change itself" (Pannenberg). Thus in these and many other thinkers about the Old Testament—also in America—history is considered significant and vital as contingent, concrete event, free and unexpected, as opposed to any timeless scheme, either the myths of the ancient world or the rigid dogmatics of the present time.

Such stress on history as a religious category is probably somewhat less popular now, but is perhaps still sufficiently alive that an examination of a biblical book in this connection may not be completely out-of-date. This critical review of history as a religious category is deliberately exegetical rather than philosophical, and is deliberately limited to **Lamentations** and some related compositions, with no claim to be more universal in scope.

One is struck, in reading **Lamentations,** by the dearth of specific dates and such details as personal names and placenames. The Kings account of the Fall of Jerusalem is rich in these respects: the conquerer is Nebuzaradan, and his specific title . . . , "Captain of the Guard," is added; he enters the city in the fifth month, on the seventh day of the month, which was the 19th year of King Nebuchadnezzar. **Lamentations** does not even inform us that the conquerers were from Babylon, and far from telling us the name of Babylon's king or the name of the general, does not even supply us the name of Israel's king. Of foreign nations only Edom is mentioned, in a curse on her for her part in the spoiling of Israel. And there is a great reduction in contrast to the prose account. The cast of actors is reduced to two: Yahweh and Israel, and the latter is so passive that one can almost speak of Yahweh as the only actor. Of course one may observe that if, as is likely, **Lamentations** was written soon after the event, then the congregation of worshippers knew the details; they knew the dates, they knew the names, and did not need to be reminded. But this objection to the point made here seems rather irrelevant to me. The related passage in Kings was evidently also written soon after the events, and the author *did* think it important to give the details. We have to do with a question of the writer's intention, and his conception of what was important, and the poet, however much his hearers may have known or forgotten, did not think it important to give historical details in the same way that the prose writer did.

Some of what *Lamentations* does seem to tell us turns out to be shaped by the literary and religious tradition, not by observation. There is much material in the book that cannot conceivably be called historical information, long passages where the language is obviously metaphorical, or where Yahweh is presented as the destroyer of Israel in a series of poetic images. This does not at the moment concern us. But there are some passages where one might suppose historical evidence is being communicated, even if that was not the author's main purpose. On examination, however, these prove to reflect literary and religious tradition more than fact. Chapter 5:18 provides a simple, almost trivial example. "On Mount Zion, which lies desolate, foxes prowl about." The historian Enno Janssen, writing of Judah in the Period of the Exile (*Juda in der Exilszeit*), quite understandably turns to *Lamentations* to support the meager amount that we know about this period, and he lights on this verse. The question concerning him is a typical historian's question: how many people were left in Jerusalem, if any? Evidently there were some, he answers, yet the city is badly enough ruined that wild animals live there, even right on the site of the temple: see *Lam.* 5:18. Beginning with Mesopotamian texts from the end of the 3rd Millennium B.C., we have many examples from outside the Bible of a rather stereotyped description of a ruined city, often including the idea that wild animals now roam in the streets of the ruin.

This turns up in the Bible also, in Isa. 34 and 13, and in Zeph. 3. Thus for example Isa. 34:11f speaks of Edom: "The hawk and the porcupine shall inherit it, and the owl and the raven shall dwell in it. It shall become a dwelling of jackals, an abode for ostriches; and desert animals shall meet with jackals, the satyr shall meet with his fellow." This is not only literary convention, but reflects a religious conviction as well. One of the curses attached to the first Sefire treaty (Sef I A 32-33) says: "And may Arpad become a mound to (house the desert animal) and the gazelle and the fox and the hare and the wildcat and the owl and the (?) and the magpie." Israel conceived of her relation to Yahweh under the form of a treaty, from very early times, I believe, but certainly by the time of Jeremiah, and part of this treaty with God was the conception that if Israel broke it, the curses of the covenant would come upon her. The author of *Lamentations* is at this point making a religious point, that Jerusalem has suffered the typical fate of a rebellious city, and he is following a literary commonplace—Jerusalem is described the way ruined cities have been described for a very long time.

As a further example of how the literary tradition shapes a poet's description of historical events, we take a more problematic case: the description of famine and specifically of cannibalism found in *Lamentations*. There is no doubt that the people of Jerusalem suffered famine. According to Kings "On the ninth day of the fourth month

the famine was so severe in the city that there was no food for the people of the land." As a result the king and a party of others fled. This episode came after the city had been under siege for a year and a half; even though the siege was lifted at one point when the Egyptians diverted the Babylonian army, which probably happened in summer of 588, we still must reckon that the people had lived for a solid year on what was stored within the town.

Thus it is not problematic that *Lamentations* makes repeated reference to hunger. "As the children and babies fainted in the streets of the city they said to their mothers. 'Where is there grain and wine?'" (2:11-12) Commentators have wondered whether the little children would have called out for wine along with their bread, but that is probably being hyper-critical. There is no difficulty with the main point: "My priests and elders expired in the city while seeking food to keep alive." The problem is with the references to cannibalism: "Look, Yahweh, and consider who it was you treated so—Should women eat what they bore, the children they have raised?" (2:20) "The very women, the kindly women, cooked their own children. That was the food they had when my people was ruined." (4:10) There is no mention of this in the prose accounts of the fall of Jerusalem. Does *Lamentations* thus provide us with a grisly detail to add to our histories?

One can raise this question if only because cannibalism as a result of prolonged starvation is an extreme of human behavior which is not so terribly common. People can starve to death without sinking to this. Yet these passages in *Lamentations* are not completely isolated in the Bible. In a well-known passage from the cycle of Elisha stories set in the time of the siege of Samaria (2 Kings 6:28-30), a woman complains to the king: "This woman said to me, 'Give your son, that we may eat him today, and we will eat my son tomorrow.' So we boiled my son and ate him." The other woman does not keep her part of the bargain, as it turns out. One would be more certain about this reference to cannibalism if it were in a source with higher historical reliability; the Elisha stories, as is well-known, contain many touches of legend and folk-lore. Josephus does tell of cannibalism on the occasion of the great siege of Jerusalem by the Romans in 70 A.D. (Jewish War VI 3, 4.) His account is highly circumstantial, with the name of the guilty woman and many details, and so is perhaps not to be questioned, though it also contains calculated literacy devices, such as dramatic speeches which Josephus made up. Oppenheim has gathered references to cannibalism in Akkadian literature. In historical writing we have such references to two version of Ashurbanipal's campaign against the Arabs who were on the side of Shamashshumukin: "The remainders (of the Arab troops) who succeeded to enter Babylon ate (there) each other's flesh in their ravenous hunger." In another version: "Irra, the Warrior (i.e., pestilence) struck down Uate', as well as his army, who had not kept the oaths sworn to me and had fled before the onslaught of Ashur, my lord—had run away from them Famine broke out among them and they ate the flesh of their children against their hunger." Provisionally we may say that cannibalism is mentioned in Assyrian historical records, but we will later want to reexamine these passages.

Cannibalism is also a feature of the literary tradition, and this is where the doubt arises. In Mesopotamia, we have mention of it in the Atrahasis epic, an Old Babylonian composition of greatest interest to Bible students because of its flood account, which supplements that in the Gilgamesh epic and is in some respects closer to the Noah story. According to this epic, before Enlil hit on the idea of using the flood against the bothersome race of mankind, he tried to wipe them out by hunger. (Assyrian recension "S" rev. vi 1-15) "When the second year arrived they suffered the itch. When the third year arrived the people's features were distorted by hunger. When the fourth year arrived their long legs became short, their broad shoulders became narrow, they walked hunched in the street. When the fifth year arrived daughter watched the mother's going in, But the mother would not open her door to the daughter. The daughter watched the scales at the sale of the mother, The mother watched the scales at the sale of the daughter. When the sixth year arrived they served up the daughter for dinner, they served up the son for food . . . One house consumed another. Their faces were overlaid like dead malt. The people were living on the edge of death." This is the end of the description. Note that cannibalism is the limit, the extreme stage. The earliest reference to cannibalism known to me is in the Curse of Agade, a text I mentioned above, from about 2000 B.C. "May the oxen-slaughterer, slaughter (his) wife (instead), May your sheep-butcher butcher his child (instead)."

The curses attached to Mesopotamian treaties from the eighth and seventh centuries B.C. repeatedly threaten treatybreakers with cannibalism, and this is done in terms at times very close to the literary tradition. To quote just one specimen, note Esarhaddon's treaty: "A mother [will close her door] against her own daughter. In your hunger eat the flesh of your sons. Let one eat the flesh of another." Here two stages are cited in the same order as in the Epic: first the mother refuses her daughter access to food by barring the door in her face; then the climactic stage, namely cannibalism. It is this very frequent occurrence of cannibalism among the treaty-curses which leads me to question the historical value of such references in Ashurbanipal's annals. Let me cite again the passage on the sufferings of the Arabians for an example of how it is possible that the treaty pattern, or covenant theology if you prefer, may have shaped Assyrian "history": "Famine broke out among them and they ate the flesh of their children against their hunger. (The gods) inflicted quickly upon them (all) the curses written down in their sworn agreements." The writer goes on to quote almost verbatim another curse attested in the treaties.

Israelite covenants also had such a curse—one mentioning cannibalism—attached, to judge from the conclusion to covenant legislation in Deuteronomy and Leviticus. Thus Lev. 26:29 "You shall eat the flesh of your sons, and you shall eat the flesh of your daughters." The version in Deuteronomy is much expanded, and is too gruesome to quote. I will mention only that the author of Deuteronomy heightens the effect of his curse by saying this will be done by "the most tender and delicately bred" man or woman. As you may recall, Lam. 4:10 makes the same point: The women themselves, "the kindly women" committed the awful crime. Jeremiah threatens Israel with doom in similar words: "And I will make them eat the flesh of their sons and the flesh of their daughters. Each shall eat another's flesh." Isaiah (9:19-20) and Ezekiel (5:10) say much the same thing.

This may suffice to make clear the problem with history as depicted in the poetry of *Lamentations.* The events are not given to us direct, but as refracted through an age-old tradition, a tradition both literary and religious. In literature this was how one stated that the utmost starvation had taken place. This we may propose is one of the traditional limits in Israelite literary style. The sky is the traditional limit for height, the earth for depths, stars and locusts for great number, the sea for breadth, Sodom and Gomorrah for wickedness, and cannibalism for the limit, the extreme of famine. If the author of *Lamentations* says "For your ruin is as vast as the sea" using a simile as old as Ugaritic literature, or can say that the iniquity of his people was greater than that of Sodom and Gomorrah, then we may suppose him capable of saying that the people turned cannibals, as a traditional and expressive way of depicting the severity of the suffering. From the religious side, this was a way of asserting that Yahweh had done what he threatened. The author of *Lamentations* quotes one curse from (or at any rate a traditional curse) Deuteronomy at 1:5 when he says "Her enemies have become the head." Compare Deut. 28:44 "He shall be the head, and you will be the tail." So it is not inconceivable that also in referring to cannibalism his main interest was in asserting that covenantbreach had brought its inevitable consequences. One of the apocrypha, Baruch, makes this connection explicit: (2:1-2) "Nowhere under heaven have such deeds been done as were done in Jerusalem, thus fulfilling what was foretold in the law of Moses, that we should eat the flesh of our children . . . ."

Thus such "history" as we have in *Lamentations* is not told with an eye to the unique, particular unrepeatable, contingent circumstances; it is experienced and narrated in conformity to certain pre-existing literary and religious patterns.

Turning to the more strictly theological question with which we began, is God represented in *Lamentations* as revealing himself in history? In one sense, the answer is obviously in the affirmative. Long passages in the book speak of what happened to Judah in 587 B.C. as the action of Yahweh. "You who pass by on the road, consider and see: Is there any pain like my pain—that which he caused me, Which Yahweh inflicted on me the day of his burning anger? From on high he sent fire and sank it into my bones. He stretched a net for my feet; he turned me back. . . .

The Lord heaped up in my midst all my strong men, then summoned an assembly against me to crush my young warriors." There is no question that Yahweh is active in human history; he so dominates the book as to make it more appropriate to question whether Babylon had anything to do with the fall of Jerusalem! Yahweh's sphere is obviously not a remote divine world, where he confronts other gods in myth, but the world of human beings, and conversely, the world of mankind is not sealed off from divine action, but open to it at every point.

But in another sense the book provides a basis for questioning the point of view of the theologians cited above. Historical events are not presented as though by themselves they are revelatory. Instead there always seems to be present the idea that an event must be expected or predicted in some way to be meaningful. It must conform to an existing conception of what divine action is. "Yahweh has done what he planned; he has carried out what he said he would, What he commanded from olden times." To say, as Pannenberg does, that he is revealed "in historical change itself" does not seem to apply to this book. I wonder if it applies even to the prose narrative in Kings? One can raise a similar objection to the rather more extreme statements by Hans Walter Wolff, who asserts that the Old Testament person was interested neither in the thought forms of myth, with its idea of return and recurrence, nor in a world-order of action and consequences—"Rather now it is the unforeseen fact which attracts interest, the change in history, the new in the irreversible progress of events." The fall of Jerusalem was scarcely an unforeseen fact, yet it is the only one our author is really interested in. He presents it in a style which emphasizes, not the new and particular in the situation, but its conformity to old pattern; he presents the catastrophe as the fulfillment and confirmation of a preexisting religious conception. If so, this reduces the contrast between "history" and myth or propositional theology.

Was an Israelite's self-understanding, his hope, grounded in a set of events in history as some theologians have affirmed?

When we turn to *Lamentations,* it is to discover that Israel's history plays practically no role in this book, intended to help a despairing community, whatever. The only meager references to anything in the national past other than the recent destruction of the city are the statement "Our fathers have sinned," the allusions to the sin of prophets and priests, and to the sinful policy of foreign alliances. But there is no reference to the mighty acts of God, for very good and obvious reasons! The last mighty act of God had been an act of judgment. Yahweh had brought about his "day"—judgment day, we might say, and our author is sufficiently imbued with the spirit of the prophets to know that there can be no appeal now to the ancient acts by which God had given Israel assurance of her election.

Instead of turning to history, he turns to another area of religious experience to be able to interpret the catastrophe.

That is the area of individual experience, what the individual faithful Israelite had found to be true of God in his private life, not in the national life. The individual is not here called on to interpret his destiny in light of the national history, but the nation is called on to learn from individual experience. At a time when it was pointless for them to say, "We have Abraham as our father," they are directed to a separate resource of assurance: the typical experiences of the hard-pressed believer (e.g., *Lam.* 3:22-36). *Lamentations* is demonstrably not unique in this respect. The Psalms of complaint by the individual are the most common type in the psalter, and in all of them there is not one reference to the national history. I am not suggesting that history, the particular events which Israel identified as acts of God, did not ever provide assurance and self-understanding to the Israelite. But *Lamentations* and the psalms of Lament (not to mention the wisdom literature) suggest that Israel's religion was complex enough to encompass a wider range of ideas.

W. C. Gwaltney, Jr. (essay date 1983)

SOURCE: "The Biblical *Book of Lamentations* in the Context of Near Eastern Lament Literature" in *Scripture in Context II: More Essays on the Comparative Method,* edited by William W. Hallo *et al.*, Eisenbrauns, 1983, pp. 191-211.

[*In the following essay, Gwaltney summarizes the history of Mesopotamian laments, analyzes their forms, and argues that the gaps in the record that caused Thomas F. McDaniel (see excerpt above) to reject the notion of Sumerian influence on* Lamentations *have now been bridged.*]

1. INTRODUCTION

The biblical book of *Lamentations* has enjoyed a surprising renewal of interest in recent years. In extensive studies over the past twenty years the text, philology, and theology of *Lamentations* have received the lion's share of attention.[1] Other questions remain unanswered, however. What are we to make of the five compositions comprising *Lamentations* in terms of poetic analysis? May we reconstruct these compositions in a metrical pattern as *Biblica Hebraica* did? Is Freedman's syllable-count method[2] to be preferred to the older system of counting stresses? May we even use the concept of meter in regard to Hebrew and Near Eastern poetry? What are the characteristics of Near Eastern poetry anyway? The question of poetry, metrics, and the use of acrostics is far from settled.

Another matter of serious note has been treated in the commentaries in a somewhat cavalier manner. What are the Near Eastern antecedents of the kind of literature we find in the biblical book of *Lamentations*? To date only one serious attempt (that of McDaniel[3]) has appeared in print to explore the claim of Kramer:

There is little doubt that it was the Sumerian poets who originated and developed the "lamentation" genre—

there are Sumerian examples dating possibly from as early as the Third Dynasty of Ur . . . and as late as the Parthian period . . . and that the Biblical *Book of Lamentations,* as well as the "burden" laments of the prophets, represent a profoundly moving transformation of the more formal and conventional Mesopotamian prototypes.[4]

Ten years later Kramer wrote:

> But there is little doubt that the biblical *Book of Lamentations* owes no little of its form and content to its Mesopotamian forerunners, and that the modern orthodox Jew who utters his mournful lament at the "western wall" of "Solomon's" long-destroyed Temple, is carrying on a tradition begun in Sumer some 4,000 years ago, where "By its (Ur's) walls as far as they extended in circumference, laments were uttered."[5]

Because of advances in the realm of Sumerian and Akkadian literary analysis during the 1970s, a reappraisal of Thomas F. McDaniel's pioneer critique is imperative to investigate this question of possible Sumerian antecedents. This paper will argue that McDaniel's conclusions can no longer be maintained and that Kramer's views are more defensible now than when he made them in 1959 and 1969.

McDaniel begins by pitting Kramer,[6] Gadd,[7] and Kraus[8] against Rudolph[9] and Eissfeldt[10] to demonstrate that scholarly opinion is divided on the question of Sumerian influence on the biblical *Lamentations* (pp. 199f.). He then proceeds to "present and evaluate the parallel motifs appearing in both the Hebrew and Sumerian works . . ." (p. 200). These "parallel motifs" number fourteen and represent terms, concepts, and choices in wording. McDaniel then judges, "All of the motifs cited from *Lamentations* are either attested otherwise in biblical literature or have a prototype in the literary motifs current in Syria-Palestine."[11] Furthermore McDaniel affirms that

> certain dominant themes of the Sumerian lamentations find no parallel at all in this Hebrew lament. For example, one would expect to find the motif of the "evil storm" . . . somewhere in the biblical lamentation if there were any real literary dependency.[12]

Next McDaniel questions how a second millennium Mesopotamian genre could have influenced a first millennium Palestinian work. He argues that evidence is lacking to demonstrate the survival of an eastern cuneiform tradition in Iron-age Syro-Palestine. The only possible means he sees to bridge this spatial and temporal chasm is the intervening Canaanite, Hurrian, and Hittite literature whose remains have failed to provide us with exemplars of the lament genre. He also disagrees with Gadd's contention that exiled Judeans adopted this genre in Babylon. He reasons that exiled Israelites would not have been in any mood to adopt a literary form of their captors, especially since they had "their own rich local literary traditions" (p. 209). "At most the indebtedness would be the *idea* of a lamentation over a beloved city."[13] Of his arguments, the most crippling to Kramer's, Gadd's, and Kraus's position

is the spatial and temporal gap separating *Lamentations* from the Sumerian city-laments. This paper will summarize the history of the Mesopotamian lament genre, give a brief analysis of the later evolved lament form, and show that there no longer exists a significant spatial and temporal gap between the Mesopotamian congregational lament form and the biblical book.

II. Mesopotamian Laments

Early Mesopotamian Lamentations

Following the pioneering publications of Kramer[14] and Jacobsen[15] in the 1940s and 1950s a younger group of scholars (W. W. Hallo,[16] Mark E. Cohen,[17] Raphael Kutscher,[18] Joachim Krecher,[19] and Margaret Green[20]) has delineated and analyzed the Sumero-Akkadian genre of laments in dissertations, articles, and monographs. Although it is still premature to attempt a definitive treatment of the genre, the broad outline of the development of laments in Mesopotamian culture can be shown to span nearly two millennia.

Kramer remarked as early as 1969 that the "incipient germ [of the lament genre] may be traced as far back as the days of Urukagina, in the 24th century B.C."[21] He cited a list of temples and shrines of Lagash which had been burned, looted, or otherwise defiled by Lugalzagessi as being the first step in the creation of the lament genre. No laments are extant for the Akkadian, Gutian, or Ur III eras. Laments were invented as a literary response to the calamity suffered throughout Sumer about 2000 B.C.E. immediately after the sack of Ur in the days of Ibbi-Sin, the last of the Third Dynasty rulers of Ur.

At present five Old Babylonian Sumerian city-laments form the earliest stage of the lament genre. They are the "Lamentation over the Destruction of Ur"[22] which has received the greatest amount of attention, the "Lamentation over the Destruction of Sumer and Ur,[23]" the "Nippur Lament" to be published by Å. Sjöberg,[24] the "Uruk Lament," edition in preparation by M. Civil and M. W. Green,[25] and the "Eridu Lament," critical edition by M. W. Green.[26] The so-called "Second Lamentation for Ur," the "Ibbi-Sin Lamentation," and the "Lamentation over the Destruction of Sumer and Akkad" have all turned out to be parts of the "Lamentation over the Destruction of Sumer and Ur."[27] Nor are we including here the so-called "Curse of Agade" even though it employs lament or complaint language.[28] The usually accepted *terminus ante quem* for the five major city-laments is 1925 B.C.E.[29]

The city-laments describe one event,[30] were written largely in the Emesal dialect of Sumerian[31] by *gala*-priests, and were composed to be recited in ceremonies for razing Ur and Nippur sanctuaries in preparation for proper restoration.[32] They were not reused in later rituals and did not become a part of the priests' ritual stock of available religious poetry for liturgical use. In the Old Babylonian scribal schools they became a part of the scribal curriculum but ceased to be copied during the First Millennium.

Kutscher, remarking about the literary merit of these city-laments, writes, "From a literary point of view these laments display a masterful use of the classical Sumerian language, freshness of style and a sincere creative effort.'[33]

THE OLD BABYLONIAN ERSEMMA

The second stage in the history of the Mesopotamian lament genre occurred in the Old Babylonian era with the nearly simultaneous creation of the *eršemma*-composition and the *balag*-lament. Cohen suspects that the *eršemma*, a liturgical composition of the *gala*-priests in Emesal dialect, may have preceded the *balag* slightly on the grounds that the *eršemma* had a more compact form while the *balag* appears to have had a more composite nature.[34] Unfortunately, clear textual evidence is lacking for us to fix priority within the Old Babylonian period.

Although the term *eršemma* means "wail of the *šèm*-([Akkadian] 'hal 'allatu-) drum," not all *eršemmas* are completely mournful since at points the subject matter served to praise a god.[35] However, a large percentage of *eršemma*-subject matter centered on catastrophes or the dying-rising myth of Inanna, Dumuzi, or Geshtinanna.[36] Kramer as recently as 1975 published two Old Babylonian *eršemma*-incipit catalogs from the British Museum from which he isolated no less than 109 *eršemmas*.[37] Of these, about 100 are unknown to us at this time. Cohen has demonstrated that in general the Old Babylonian *eršemmas* are characterized as being a single, compact unit addressed to a single deity.[38] Cohen has also contended that the *gala*-priests, when called upon repeatedly to provide more liturgical compositions to be chanted on the occasion of rebuilding cities and temples, borrowed *eršemma* material to create new *eršemmas* and appropriated hymnic Emegir material for insertion into new *eršemmas*.[39] Also Old Babylonian *eršemmas* and *balags* occasionally shared lines of text.[40] Cohen was not able to determine the direction of this borrowing.[41] The exact Old Babylonian cultic use of the *eršemma* remains a mystery, although we may speculate that they were intoned in a liturgical context similar to that of the *balag*-laments.[42]

THE OLD BABYLONIAN BALAG

The *balag* was created as a lamentation form about 1900 B.C.E. as a literary outgrowth of the older city-lament. In support of this thesis Cohen has established a "high probability of direct relationship between the city-laments and the *balag*-lamentations"[43] by examining four factors: 1) the structure and form of city-laments and Old Babylonian *balags*,[44] 2) their content,[45] 3) their ritual use,[46] and 4) whether there was sufficient opportunity for development to occur.[47] Even though we may conclude there was a close association between the *balag*-lament and its older city-lament predecessor, we must note several differences between the two. City-laments were composed for one specific "performance" to be retired afterwards to the scribal academy as a classical work;[48] *balags* were adopted for further liturgical use and were copied over and over down into the Seleucid era. City-lament subject matter

concentrated on one specific disaster in detailed description; *balags* were more general in their description of disaster and could be borrowed from city to city. City-laments were used in a narrow setting of temple demolition and reconstruction; *balags* were recited in broader contexts apparently as "congregational laments."

Although most compositions of this genre were not called by the title *"balag"* in the Old Babylonian era, five examples in which such was the case have been recovered.[49] One of these five, a *balag* to Dumuzi (CT 42, 15), was composed in the Larsa period about 1870 B.C.E.[50] Kutscher has explained this low number of labeled examples as arising from the fact that the term *"balag"* in Babylonian times designated function, not generic title. The composition was to be intoned to the accompaniment of the *balag*-instrument,[51] in all likelihood a drum.[52] Cohen observed that the unusual length of the *balags* caused them to be written on large tablets or in series of smaller tablets so that the final lines with their colophons were lost in many cases with the result that the designation *"balag"* is missing.[53] The form of the general all-purpose lament had already emerged in the Old Babylonian era even though the label *"balag"* was not always attached to the extant Old Babylonian recensions.

Kutscher's publication of YBC 4659[54] which preserves stanzas IV-XIII of the *balag, a-ab-ba u-lu-a* (Oh Angry Sea), makes clear that even in its Old Babylonian form this particular *balag* may be roughly divided in half.[55] The first half was devoted to lamentation presumably to be chanted during ceremonies at the demolition of an old temple. The second half (a hymn and prayer to Enlil) was probably "recited during the ceremonies marking the laying of the foundation to the new temple."[56] Cohen points to the concluding line in some Old Babylonian *balags*, "This supplication . . . return the 'x-temple' to place," as indicating the use of the *balag* in temple-restoration ceremonies.[57] The Old Babylonian *balags* also appear to have been included in liturgies for various festivals and for certain days of the month.[58]

THE FIRST MILLENNIUM BALAG AND ERSEMMA

The Middle Babylonian period marked an advance in the lament genre although documentary evidence for it is meager. In fact, none of the main Emesal hymnic types of the first millennium—the *balag*, the *eršemma*, the *šuilla*, and the *eršahunga*—are attested in Middle Babylonian times.[59] Several *eršemmas* were possibly composed during Kassite times, however. Cohen somewhat tentatively suggests that the joining of *balag*-laments with *eršemma*-compositions to form a new composite genre occurred at some point during the Kassite era (ca. 1600-1160 B.C.E.).

> During the Middle Babylonian period the two genres [*balag* and *eršemma*] had apparently been so closely identified with each other, presumably on the basis of ritual function, that each *balag* was assigned one *eršemma* as its new conclusion. The *eršemma* was then reworked, adopting a second concluding unit which

contained the plea to the heart of the god and the con-commitant [sic] list of deities, although this list was drastically reduced in size from the final *kirugu* of the Old Babylonian lamentation.[60]

Interestingly, Kutscher was able to amass exemplars of the Old Babylonian *balag* titled *a-ab-ba hu-luh-ha* (Oh Angry Sea) for the Old Babylonian, Neo-Assyrian, Neo-Babylonian, and Seleucid periods but could not locate even a one-line scrap of Kassite origin.[61] Even the Middle Assyrian era provided two scraps consisting of eight lines of text.[62] A Middle Babylonian catalog may, however, list Kutscher's *balag* under the title *a-ab-ba hu-luh-ha ᵈen-líl-lá*.[63]

Precisely how the text of earlier *balag*s and *eršemma*s passed into the first millennium from their Old Babylonian point of origin is not totally clear. We may postulate, however, that these compositions had become essential ingredients in liturgies and were, therefore, preserved by the clergy. At any rate, from the Neo-Assyrian period through the Seleucid, *balag-eršemma* laments are excep-tionally well documented from three major sources: 1) in-cipit catalogs, 2) ritual calendar tablets, and 3) copies of the laments themselves together with their colophons indicating *inter alia* the nature of the genre.

During the first millennium older lament material from both *balag*s and *eršemma*s became somewhat interchange-able. Cohen was able to produce two *eršemma*s of this era which had been created from earlier *balag* material with some modification.[64] The more general term *ér* = "lament," came to be used for the wide range of lamentations in keeping with the broadening of both the form and its func-tion.

The ritual use of the *balag-eršemma* in the first millen-nium was even broader than in the Old Babylonian era. Numerous texts detailing the cultic performance of *gala*- (Akkadian *kalû*-) priests reveal how the *balag-eršemma* la-ments were integrated into complex rituals for a variety of situations.[65] Furthermore, the *balag-eršemma*s provided the ritual wording for ceremonies conducted on certain days of the month as noted in numerous calendar texts.[66] Often on such occasions a lament was recited while offerings and libations were being presented to a deity. The *balag-eršemma* continued to be sung on the occasion of razing an old building.[67] Caplice has given us a case of a lament's being chanted as a part of a *namburbi*-ritual for warding off a portended evil.[68] Cohen has also presented other examples when an evil portent prompted a *namburbi*-ritual which included a god-appeasing lament.[69] Thus the lament served the purpose of tranquilizing the potentially destruc-tive god so that catastrophe could be prevented. The ritual for covering the sacred kettledrum involved the singing of a balag with its *eršemma* accompanied by the newly covered kettledrum later on in the rite.[70] Libations and of-ferings were not presented on this occasion. Cohen interpreted the occasion as a formal testing of the drum.

III. Analysis of Lamentation Form

City-Laments

On its most superficial level of organization the city-laments were divided into "songs" called *kirugu*, usually equated with Akkadian *šēru* = Hebrew *šîr*.[71] The number and length of these stanzas were seemingly at the compos-ers' discretion. Each stanza, except the last, was followed by a one or two line unit called *gišgigal*, usually interpreted as "antiphon."[72] The *gišgigal* summarized the content of its *kirugu* or repeated a key line or two from the *kirugu*. Beyond these divisions the city-laments seem not to have had further formal external structure.[73]

Margaret Green in an unpublished Chicago dissertation[74] has discussed the poetic devices used in the city-laments.[75] Significant among these devices are: 1) the use of couplets, triplets, and even longer units of lines in which only one element is changed from line to line, 2) parallelism, 3) repeating units of a part of a line or a whole line or several lines, 4) complex interweaving of two or more refrains, and 5) use of lists. All these devices appear in Sumerian poetry of various genres and are not restricted to laments. Beyond these structural techniques two other characteristics appear to a greater or lesser extent in all five citylaments. For one thing, the composition alternates between first, second, and third persons. Such change in speaker pos-sibly reflects the dramatic function of the city-laments. Furthermore, the dialect alternates between Emesal and standard Emegir Sumerian. This alternation has provoked a minor debate over whether the city-laments were "Eme-sal compositions" or "Emegir compositions."[76] Without entering the technicalities of this question, we may observe that whenever a goddess speaks the Emesal dialect is used. In spite of Green's argument, however,[77] we are not yet entitled to judge that every occurrence of Emesal implies a female speaker. *Gala*-priests intoned a wide range of litur-gies in the Emesal dialect even when a female speaker is not implied.[78]

Although the five preserved city-laments are quite individualized in theme and theme development as well as in style and structure, they have certain underlying themes in common.[79] The most prominent theme is destruction of the total city: walls, gates, temples, citizens, royalty, nobil-ity, army, clergy, commoners, food, crops, herds, flocks, villages, canals, roads, customs, and rites. Life has ceased. A second common theme lies in the concept that the end has come upon Sumer by virtue of a conscious decision of the gods in assembly. The invading hordes, whether Sub-arians, Elamites, Amorites, or Gutians, "storm" the land by the "word" of the gods. A third theme centers around the necessary abandonment of the city by the suzerain-god, his consort, and their entourage. The lament may scold the god for his callous abandonment. The goddess in longer or shorter monologues pleads with either her divine spouse or Enlil or the council of gods to show mercy and relent. In the fourth place, the city-laments either specifi-cally mention, or at least presume, restoration of the city or sanctuary. As a fifth common element, the chief god eventually returns to his city with his entire company. The five laments do not all handle this theme in identical fashion, but in every case the gods' return is indispensable to the plot. The final common thematic element is a concluding prayer to the concerned god involving either praise, plea, imprecation against the enemy, self-abasement, or a combination of these elements.

The exact cultic circumstances for the recitation of the city-laments is not totally agreed upon. Jacobsen proposed that their "Sitz im Kultus" was the demolition of the ruins of a temple and its rebuilding.[80] Hallo[81] and Cohen[82] have followed this line of thinking. Green, however, offers the alternative that the lament was performed by the king in his priestly function at the installation ceremony when the god's statue returned to its refurbished shrine.[83] The god's leaving may not always have been caused by foreign devastation but may have been forced by needed renovations of the temple in peacetime.[84] That the five major city-laments arose from something more serious than a renovation in peacetime appears evident from the extreme violence they depict. Perhaps Green's suggestion has merit in explaining the function of Old Babylonian *balag*s and *eršemma*s. As for the king's reciting the lament before the cult image, we may question the king's acumen and literacy to read and recite both Emesal and Emegir dialects in complex poetry.

FIRST MILLENNIUM BALAG-ERSEMMAS

The first millennium composite lament form, the *balag-eršemma,* has been clarified by Kutscher in his study of the history of the long-lived *balag* called *a-ab-ba hu-luh-ha* (Oh Angry Sea). He shows that this *balag* originated in Old Babylonian times but was expanded for public ritual use during Neo-Assyrian, Neo-Babylonian, and Seleucid times in at least nine recensions.[85]

In terms of poetic devices this *balag* in Emesal makes use of the usual techniques: repetition, refrain, parallelism, listing, division into stanzas (unlabeled in some recensions), use of divine epithets, and apparent antiphonal performance. The *gišgigal*-unit (antiphon) is absent.

The later form of this lament may be outlined as follows:[86]

A. "Prayerful Lament," lines 1-152 (stanzas II-X)

1. Enlil's epithets, lines 1-12 (stanza II)

2. Nippur's and Babylon's ruin, lines 13-27 (stanza II)

3. "How long?" plea to Enlil, lines 28-40 (stanza III)

4. Wailing and mourning, lines 41-48 (stanza IV)

5. Enlil's power, lines 49-72 (stanza V)

6. Enlil's dignity, lines 73-98 (stanzas VI-VII)

7. "How long?" plea with "return to the land!", lines 99-118 (stanza VIII)

8. Enlil's dignity, lines 119-25 (stanza IX)

9. Plea to Enlil to "restore (your) heart," lines 126-52 (stanza X)

B. Hymn to Enlil, lines 153–236 (stnzas XI-XVII)

1. Enlil sleeps, lines 153-59 (stanza XI)

2. List of devastated areas of the city, lines 160-71 (stanza XI)

3. Let Enlil arise!, lines 172-84 (stanza XII)

4. Enlil sees the devastation, lines 185-91 (stanza XIII)

5. Enlil caused the destruction, lines 192-212 (stanzas XIV-XV)

6. The exalted Enlil, lines 213-24 (stanza XVI)

7. Lines 225-36 (stanza XVII) broken

C. *Eršemma,* lines 237–96

1. Plea for Enlil to "turn around and look at your city!", lines 237-53

2. Plea for Enlil to "turn around and look at your city!" from various locations, lines 254-72

3. The flooded cities in couplets, lines 273-80

4. The gluttonous man starves, lines 281-82

5. The fractured family, lines 283-87

6. The population rages, lines 288-91

7. Death in the city streets, lines 292-96

We may observe that section A (stanzas II-X) calls attention to Enlil's destructive power as evidenced by the devastation. Section B (stanzas XI-XVII) concentrates on awakening Enlil in hopes of encouraging his return so that the city may regain its lost glory. The *eršemma* seeks to inspire some spark of pity within Enlil.

Cohen demonstrates that the *balag* exhibited a certain development within its history.[87] In its Old Babylonian form the *balag* like the city-lament had a rather formal external structure of *kirugu*-divisions in which each stanza was followed by "first, second, etc. *kirugu.*"[88] In some cases there followed a one-line *gišgigal* (antiphon) as in the city-lament. Many scribes set the *kirugu* and *gišgigal* off by horizontal lines across the text both above and below these labels. As time passed, the labels tended to drop out leaving only the horizontal lines to mark stanzas. Another Old Babylonian convention of *balag* construction was the "heart pacification-unit" in the concluding stanza of older Enlil-*balags*.[89] *Balags* to other divinities omit this plea that the wrathful god's heart and liver might be pacified. Following this unit comes the formula expressing the wish that x-temple should return to its place, then the rubric *kiš-ubim* which means something like "coda."

Modification in *balag* structural organization became necessary, however, following the later joining of *balag* and *eršemma*. Each first millennium *balag*-lament had an *eršemma* attached to its end. In its new function as last stanza the *eršemma* had to be redesigned.[90] For one thing, even though their first millenium counterparts always were one-unit compositions, the first millennium *eršemmas* often consist of two or three units each.[91] In these cases the last unit either begins with or contains a "heart pacification-unit" which seems to have originated in Old Babylonian Enlil *balags*. The "heart pacification" is followed by a list of gods who were to add their pleas to those of the priests and worshipers. In this composite form the *balag-eršemma* continued to serve as liturgical material during hundreds of years through the Seleucid era.

When comparing these later laments with their ancient ancestors, the city-laments, the modern literary critic may think of them as grossly inferior. Kutscher,[92] for example, uses such descriptions as "repetitive," "unimaginative," "composed to a large extent of clichés, and devoid of poetic rhythm," "stereotyped," and we may add boring. Their longevity and broad range of use suggest to us, however, that the ancients found great merit in them.

IV. THE FIRST MILLENNIUM MESOPOTAMIAN LAMENT AND BIBLICAL *LAMENTATION*

In order to draw meaningful comparisons between the book of **Lamentations** and Mesopotamian laments we will create a typology in summary form for the first millennium Mesopotamian lament genre under four major headings: Ritual Occasions, Form/Structure, Poetic Techniques, and Theology. Then we will compare the book of Lamentations with this typology to formulate a hypothesis regarding the relationship of the two.

In the present state of cuneiform scholarship[93] we find four categories of religious circumstances when lamentations were employed in the cults of Mesopotamia. They are: 1) before, during, or after daily sacrifices and libations to a wide range of deities, 2) special services, feasts, or rituals like the Akitu festival or the ritual for covering the sacral kettledrum, 3) *namburbi* incantation rites to forestall impending doom, and 4) especially those circumstances of pulling down sacred buildings to prepare the site for rebuilding.

The structure of first millennium laments was flexible but usually followed a broad pattern as follows:

1) praise to the god of destruction, usually Enlil

2) description of the destruction

3) lamenting the destruction ("How long?")

4) plea to the destructive god to be pacified

5) plea to the god to gaze upon the destruction

6) plea to other deities (often a goddess) to intercede

7) further description of the ruin.

Those poetic techniques employed by lament composers may be outlined under the following captions:

1) interchange of speaker (third, second, first person) involving description (third person), direct address (second person), monologue (first person), dialogue (first, second, and third persons)

2) use of woe-cries and various interjections

3) use of Emesal dialect apparently to simulate high-pitched cries of distress and pleading

4) heavy use of couplets, repeating lines with one word changed from line to line, and other devices of parallelism

5) antiphonal responses

6) tendency to list or catalog (gods, cities, temples, epithets, victims, etc.)

7) use of theme word or phrase which serves as a cord to tie lines together, or whole stanzas.

We may outline the underlying ideas under three major captions: divinity, humanity, and causality.

A. Divinity

1) The god of wrathful destruction, usually Enlil, abandons the city, a signal for devastation, often called a "storm," to begin.

2) This chief god may bring the havoc himself or may order another deity to attack the city or sanctuary.

3) In any case, Enlil's will is irresistible; he has the backing of the council of gods.

4) Enlil is described and addressed in anthropomorphic terms:

a) a warrior

b) the shepherd of the people

c) his word destroys

d) his "heart" and "liver" must be soothed

e) he must be roused from sleep

f) he must inspect the ruins to see what has occurred

g) he must be cajoled to change his mind.

5) Yet there is an unknowable quality to Enlil; he is unreachable.

6) Lesser deities must intercede with the chief god to bring an end to the ruin.

B. Humanity

Surprisingly, humans are of little significance in the laments. The gods occupy the limelight. The following ideas about the place of human beings do emerge, however:

1) Human tragedy is described in terms of

a) death

b) exile

c) madness

d) disruption of families

e) demolishing the buildings associated with the general population.

2) Mesopotamian society placed great emphasis on job definition; it is a tragedy when people cannot fulfill their jobs.

3) The citizens were seen as Enlil's flock but were "trampled" by Enlil.

4) The only response the population can make to the disaster is to mourn and offer sacrifices and libations. There seems to be a pervading sense of helplessness before the gods' power.

5) A gap separates the citizens and the gods. People must keep their distance. A sign of the tragedy is that the temple is demolished and people can see into the holy sanctuary.

C. Causality

In Mesopotamian experience ultimate causation lies in the largely unseen world of the gods. Storms of barbarians may crash upon the city, but they were called upon the scene by a decision of Enlil in consultation with the council of the gods. The emphasis of the laments is upon the power of the divine, not upon the rightness of the decision. There appears no resort to the justness of the gods. The humans have committed no particular crime or sin which moves the gods to their decision. The devastation is not judgment on evil humans. In fact the Eridu lament says, "The storm, which possesses neither kindness nor malice, does not distinguish between good and evil."[94]

There does appear to be a primitive magical use made of the laments, however. To recount the havoc and recite the appeasement of the god is the same as experiencing the disaster physically. The lament becomes a means of avoidance of ruin, in other words, a means of controlling the causality which resides with the gods.

When we look at the biblical *Lamentations* in the light of this typology, we are impressed with both similarities and differences. In order to move from the clearest to the least clear category, we begin with some observations relative to the theology of *Lamentations*. Those points of similarity and difference are:

1) God's majesty and irresistible power, 5:19 (but *Lamentations* goes beyond Mesopotamian laments by insisting on God's righteousness in 1:18, 3:22, 26, 32)

2) God was the cause of the city's fall, 1:5, 12-15, 17; 2:1-8, 17; 3:1-16 (God brings misery on the "man"), 32-38, 43-45; 4:11, 16; 5:22

3) God abandoned his city, 2:1 (refused to remember), 6 (spurned), 7 (spurned and rejected), 8 (thought to destroy); 5:20-22

4) God as a mighty warrior, 2:2-8, 20-22; 3:4-13, 16, 34; 4:11

5) God's wrath, 2:1-4, 6, 21, 22; 3:1, 43, 65-66; 4:11

6) God caused the destruction by his word, 2:17; 3:37, 38

7) God called upon to look at the havoc, 1:9, 11; 2:20; 3:61 (God is to hear the enemy's plots), 63; 4:16 (God refuses to look); 5:1 (God is to remember)

8) a goddess wanders about the destroyed city and bemoans its sad plight (Of course, Israelite theology could not tolerate such an idea, but the city Jerusalem fulfills this role especially in 1:12-17)

9) God to be aroused from sleep is totally lacking in biblical Lamentations

10) God's heart to be soothed and his liver pacified is likewise missing

11) God called upon to return to his abandoned city is missing

12) The theme of lesser gods called upon to intercede with the destroyer god is obviously lacking.

More space is devoted to humans and their plight in biblical *Lamentations* than in Mesopotamian laments. In both, the personified city occupies much of the description. Social grouping appears in rather general terms: king, princes, and elders; priests, prophets, and Nazirites; army men, pilgrims, and citizens; old men, mothers, young men, virgins, children, and infants; orphans and widows. Skilled craftsmen are not enumerated. The description of the horrors of war suffered by the population is in some ways a bit more gruesome in the biblical *Lamentations*. For example, young and old dying in the streets of thirst and hunger, the lethargic march of the priests, mothers eating their children, cruel enslavement of one-time nobles, the shame of ridicule and exposure—all are expressed in poignant detail.

As in the Mesopotamian laments the biblical *Lamentations* clearly placed ultimate causation with God, but God is justified in the decision since the citizenry of Jerusalem was guilty of numerous crimes (1:5, 8, 18, 20; 4:6). The prophets (2:14; 4:13), priests (4:13), and fathers (5:7) must bear a large portion of the guilt for their failure to correct the evils which prompted God to take his angry action. God's extreme action in warring against Jerusalem has produced repentance on the part of the survivors, however. Now the mercy and love of God are being sought to change the fortunes of the people and, especially, the city.

In comparing poetic techniques, we find the interchange of speaker involving first, second, and third persons with accompanying change in perspective reminiscent of dramatic or liturgical performance. Likewise woe-cries and interjections occur to intensify dramatic effect. Parallelism of various orders runs throughout the five *Lamentations* poems. Only the Mesopotamian predilection for cataloging is lacking in biblical *Lamentations*.

In addition, other strategies utilized by Mesopotamian laments appear in biblical *Lamentations* either directly or with modification. Among these devices are: the poet addresses God (1:10 and the whole of chapter 5), but God never answers; the poet addresses or questions Jerusalem who seems to function in *Lamentations* much as the goddess functions in Mesopotamian laments (2:13-16, 18-19; 4:21, 22); invective against the enemy (1:21, 22; 3:55-66; 4:21, 22), the city which weeps or speaks (1:1-3, 8, 9, 11-15, 16, 18-20, 22; 2:11, 20-22; 3:48-51, 55-66; 5:17), the city ridiculed or embarrassed (1:7, 8, 17, 19, 21; 2:15-17; 3:14 (the *"man"*), 30 (the "man"), 45 (the citizens), 46, 63; 4:12, 15), detailed description of the carnage (1:4, 5, 18-20; 2:2, 5-12, 20-22; 3:4-16 [the "man" is a prisoner]; 4:1-10, 14-15, 17-19; 5:1-18). The stock-in-trade woe-cry "How long?" does not occur in biblical *Lamentations*. Neither is restoration stated though we may infer that the total work envisions Jerusalem's rebuilding as do several statements which recall God's mercy (3:22-27, 31-33; 4:21, 22; 5:20-22).[95]

When we come to a comparison of structure and organization, we find a decided lack of similarity. God is not honored by reciting a long list of epithets. The simple order of movement perceivable in Mesopotamian laments does not occur (abandonment, invasion by the "storm," plea to the god to awake, rouse himself, and gaze upon the ruins, lesser gods involved to add weight to the pleas, further recalling the ruination). Each of the five poems does show "poetic development" especially discernable in change of speaker, but not a plot type of movement.

We come finally to the question of cultic context. On this question we are without documentation to inform us. Of the four cultic occasions when first millennium Mesopotamian laments were recited, the most likely candidate for the biblical is that of temple restoration.

Jer 41:5 informs us that some 80 mourners of Shechem, Shiloh, and Samaria brought offerings and incense to the "House of Yahweh" during the Gedaliah days following the temple's destruction at the hands of the Babylonians. The signs of their mourning were shaved off beards, ripped clothing, and gashed skin. Zech 7:3-5 refers to mournful fasts at Jerusalem in the fifth and seventh months which have been observed "these 70 years." Apparently a commemoration of the sack of Jerusalem and the burning of the Temple occurred in the fifth month and a memorial to the slain Gedaliah in the seventh month. Zech 8:19 adds to the fifth and seventh month fasts by citing fasts in the fourth month (the breaching of the walls) and in the tenth month (the onset of Nebuchadnezzar's final siege). We may assume from the statement in Jer 41:5 that some form of religious practice continued on the site of the largely demolished Temple. The other fasts likewise focused on the ruined city, walls, and Temple. Finally the time came for rebuilding the Temple immediately following the Persian conquest of Babylon and Cyrus's edict of toleration in 539. Exiles, including priests from Babylonia familiar with long practiced Mesopotamian liturgies for rebuilding demolished shrines, joined with their brothers who had been left behind "these 70 years" to live within sight of the ruins and to fast and mourn among the Temple's ruins. Together they bewailed the fallen sanctuary as clearing the site began in preparation for reconstruction. Such an occasion would provide a fit setting for the recitation of *Lamentations* and could have provided the impetus for writing or editing these five lament-poems for the performance.

V. Conclusion

McDaniel rejected direct Sumerian influence on the biblical *Lamentations* on the grounds that there was too great a gap between them in terms of both time and space.[96] Furthermore he argued that there were no distinctively Mesopotamian elements in the biblical book.[97] On the basis of the discoveries of the 1970s we can now fill the gap in time between the city-laments and biblical *Lamentations* with the lineal liturgical descendants of the city-laments, the *balag-eršemmas*. Gadd's suggestion[98] that the Babylonian Exile provided the opportunity for the Jewish clergy to encounter the laments has proved correct. We may add that the exiles of the Northern Kingdom also had similar opportunities in the cities of Assyria to observe or participate in these rituals. Thus the spatial gap has been closed also. Beyond these considerations, we have demonstrated strong analogies between the Mesopotamian lament typology and that of the biblical book of *Lamentations* though there were dissimilarities also. Because of the polytheistic theology underlying the Mesopotamian laments and their ritual observance, they could not be taken over without thorough modification in theology and language.

Still the biblical book of **Lamentations** was more closely associated with the Near Eastern lament genre than simply borrowing the "idea" of a lament over the destruction of a city as McDaniel conceded.

[Addendum:

Mark E. Cohen's significant study, *Sumerian Hymnology: The Eršemma* (HUCA Supplement 2 [Cincinnati: Hebrew Union College-Jewish Institute of Religion, 1981]), appeared while this study was in press, and consequently, could not be incorporated into the body of this essay. Although most of Cohen's later conclusions were anticipated in the earlier form of his dissertation, one major refinement requires a modification in the discussion of the first millennium *eršemma* offered above.

On pages 27, 41, and 42 Cohen calls attention to *eršemmas* labeled *kidudû* which appear in incipit lists unrelated to any *balag*. These independent *eršemmas* were recited in various ceremonies such as those relating to the covering of the sacred building. Thus the *eršemma* enjoyed two forms of usage in the first millennium, that is, as a separate work and as the last section of the composite *balag-eršemma*, The recognition of this independent status of the *eršemma* does not alter the conclusions drawn concerning the composite *balag-eršemma*, however.]

Notes

1. Several studies must be highlighted as bringing scholarly criticism up to date on Lamentations. Delbert Hiller's volume, *Lamentations,* in the Anchor Bible series (Garden City: Doubleday, 1972) is a good starting point because of its clear statement of the critical problems relating to Lamentations, its selective bibliography, and its informative and balanced notes. Hillers made good use of several noteworthy studies from the 1960s which applied the best of available scholarship to questions of text, philology, higher criticism, theology, and form analysis. Those leading commentaries were A. Weiser's *Klagelieder* (ATD 16; G¨ttingen: Vandenhoeck and Ruprecht, 1962) pp. 297-370, W. Rudolph's *Das Buch Ruth—Das Hohe Lied—Die Klagelieder* (KAT 17/1-3; Gütersloh: Gütersloher Verlagshaus Gerd Mohn, 1962), and Hans-Joachim Kraus's *Klagelieder* (BKAT 20; 3d ed.; Neukirchen-Vluyn: Neukirchener Verlag, 1968). These three German commentaries provide exhaustive bibliographies as well. Norman Gottwald's chief contribution, *Studies in the Book of Lamentations* (SBT 1/14, 2d ed.; London: SCM, 1962), lies in his perceptive treatment of Lamentations' theology. Specific texts within Lamentations have been elucidated by numerous detailed studies. Bertil Albrektson (*Studies in the Text and Theology of the Book of Lamentations* [Lund: CWK Gleerup, 1963]) has communicated an extremely valuable tool, a critical Syriac text of Lamentations, and has made a detailed study of the MT in the light of LXX, Peshitta, and Latin versions. Gottlieb's shorter study

(*A Study on the Text of Lamentations* [Århus: Det Laerde Selskab, 1978] = Acta Jutlandica 48, Theolgy Series 12) discusses textual matters either not treated by Albrektson or those where Gottlieb wishes to take issue with Albrektson or others. The essay of Lanahan, ("Speaking Voice in the Book of Lamentations, *JBL* 93 [1974] 41-49) draws attention to the literary and dramatic effect of the change of speaker in Lamentations.

2. D. N. Freedman, "Acrostics and Metrics in Hebrew Poetry," *HTR* 65 (1972) 367-92.

3. Thomas F. McDaniel, "The Alleged Sumerian Influence upon Lamentations," *VT* 18 (1968) 198-209.

4. S. N. Kramer, "Sumerian Literature and the Bible," AnBib 12 (Studia Biblica et Orientalia 3 [1959]) 201, n. 1.

5. S. N. Kramer, "Lamentation over the Destruction of Nippur: A Preliminary Report," *Eretz Israel* 9 (1969) 90.

6. McDaniel draws from Kramer's published work as of 1968 including "The Oldest Literary Catalogue: A Sumerian List of Literary Compositions Compiled about 2000 B.C.," *BASOR* 88 (1942) 10-19; "New Literary Catalogue from Ur," *RA* 55 (1961) 169-76; *Sumerian Literary Texts from Nippur in the Museum of the Ancient Orient at Istanbul* (AASOR 23; New Haven: American Schools of Oriental Research, 1943-44) 32-35; *Lamentation over the Destruction of Ur* (Assyriological Studies 12; Chicago: University of Chicago, 1940); "Lamentation over the Destruction of Ur," *ANET*[2] 455-63; "Sumerian Literature, A General Survey," *The Bible and the Ancient Near East* (Albright Anniversary Volume; Garden City: Doubleday, 1961) 249-66.

7. McDaniel cites C. J. Gadd, "The Second Lamentation for Ur," *Hebrew and Semitic Studies Presented to Godfrey Rolles Driver* (ed. D. W. Thomas and W. D. McHardy; Oxford: Oxford University, 1963) 59-71.

8. McDaniel cites Hans-Joachim Kraus, *Klagelieder (Threni)* (BKAT 20; 2d ed.; Neukirchen-Vluyn: Neukirchener Verlag, 1960) 10.

9. McDaniel cites Wilhelm Rudolph, *Das Buch Ruth—Das Hohe Lied—Die Klagelieder,* p. 9.

10. McDaniel cites Otto Eissfeldt, *Einleitung in das Alte Testament* (3d ed.; Tübingen: Mohr, 1964) 683.

11. McDaniel, "Sumerian Influence," 207.

12. Ibid.

13. McDaniel, "Sumerian Influence," 209.

14. See above, n. 6. Add to the Kramer bibliography: "Literary Texts from Ur VI, Part II," *Iraq* 25 (1963) 171-76; "Lamentation over the Destruction of Sumer and Ur," *ANET*[3] 611-19; and "Two British Museum iršemma 'Catalogues,'" StudOr 46 (1975) 141-66.

15. See T. Jacobsen in his review of Kramer, *Lamentation over the Destruction of Ur* in *AJSL* 58 (1941)

219-24; *Proceedings of the American Philosophical Society* 107 (1963) 479-82.

16. See especially W. W. Hallo, "Individual Prayer in Sumerian: The Continuity of a Tradition," *JAOS* 88 (Speiser Anniversary Volume, 1968) 71-89, where he traced the development of the individual lament from the older letter-prayer genre. Other articles of W. W. Hallo relating to Sumerian literary genre history include: "The Coronation of Ur-Nammu," *JCS* 20 (1966) 133-41; "The Cultic Setting of Sumerian Poetry," *Actes de la XVIIᵉ Rencontre assyriologique internationale* (Ham-sur-Heure: Universite Libre de Bruxelles, 1970) 116-34; "Another Sumerian Literary Catalogue?" StudOr 46 (1975) 77-80 with additions in StudOr 48:3; and "Toward a History of Sumerian Literature," *Sumerological Studies in Honor of Thorkild Jacobsen on His Seventieth Birthday* (Assyriological Studies 20; Chicago: University of Chicago, 1975) 181-203.

17. Mark E. Cohen, *Balag-compositions: Sumerian Lamentation Liturgies of the Second and First Millennium B.C.* (Sources from the Ancient Near East, vol. 1, fasc. 2; Malibu: Undena, 1974) and *The eršemma in the Second and First Millennia B.C.* (Unpublished doctoral dissertation at the University of Pennsylvania, n.d.). [See Addendum.]

18. Raphael Kutscher, *Oh Angry Sea (a-ab-ba hu-luḫ-ḫa): The History of a Sumerian Congregational Lament* (Yale Near Eastern Researches 6; New Haven: Yale University, 1975).

19. Joachim Krecher, *Sumerische Kultlyrik* (Wiesbaden: Otto Harrassowitz, 1966).

20. Margaret W. Green, *Eridu in Sumerian Literature* (Unpublished doctoral dissertation at the University of Chicago, 1975), chap. 9: "Sumerian Lamentations" and chap. 10: "The Eridu Lament." See also M. W. Green, "The Eridu Lament," *JCS* 30 (1978) 127-67.

21. Kramer, *Eretz Israel* 9 (1969) 89.

22. See Kramer's treatments cited in n. 4.

23. See Kramer, "Lamentation over the Destruction of Sumer and Ur," *ANET*³ 611-19.

24. Green, *Eridu*, 279. See also D. O. Edzard, *Die "Zweite Zwischenzeit" Babyloniens* (Wiesbaden: Otto Harrasowitz, 1957) 86-90.

25. Ibid.

26. Green, *Eridu*, chap. 10, 326-74 and Green, "Eridu Lament," 127-67.

27. See Kramer, *ANET*³ 612 and n. 9 as well as C. J. Gadd and S. N. Kramer, *Literary and Religious Texts, Ur Excavation Texts, 6, Part 2* (London: British Museum, 1966) 1 for the joins of tablets to show the unity of these fragments.

28. See Kramer's comments in "The Curse of Agade: The Ekur Avenged," *ANET*³ 646f. See also M. W. Green's remarks in Green, *Eridu*, 279f. and Kutscher's in *Oh Angry Sea*, 1.

29. Cohen, *balag*, 9. M. W. Green ("Eridu Lament," 129f.) raises the possibility of finding the origin of the Eridu lament in the reign of Nur-Adad of Larsa (1865-50 B.C.E.) but prefers an earlier date in the reign of Išme-Dagan of Isin (1953-35).

30. Cohen, *balag*, 11.

31. Kutscher (*Oh Angry Sea*, 3) claims that city-laments were written in the standard Emegir dialect, while Cohen (*balag*, 11 and 32) claims they were Emesal compositions.

32. See Cohen, *balag*, 11.

33. Kutscher, *Oh Angry Sea*, 3.

34. Cohen, *eršemma*, 24.

35. Cohen, *eršemma*, 9.

36. Ibid.

37. Kramer, "Two British Museum iršemma 'Catalogues,'" StudOr 46 (1975) 141-66.

38. Cohen, *eršemma*, 9f., 12.

39. Cohen, *eršemma*, 22-24.

40. Cohen, *eršemma*, 24.

41. Ibid.

42. Cohen, *eršemma*, 27f.

43. Cohen, *balag*, 11.

44. Cohen, *balag*, 9f.

45. Cohen, *balag*, 10f.

46. Cohen, *balag*, 11.

47. Ibid.

48. Ibid.

49. Cohen, *balag*, 6.

50. Cohen, *balag*, 12.

51. Kutscher, *Oh Angry Sea*, 3.

52. Cohen, *balag*, 31 (Excursus on the *balag*-instrument).

53. Cohen, *balag*, 6.

54. Kutscher, *Oh Angry Sea*, 25-27 (history of YBC 4659), 52-54 (transliteration of YBC 4659), 143-53 (translation of the composite text), plates 6 and 7 (copies of YBC 4659 [*sic!* Captions inadvertently interchanged with those of Plates 1 and 2. Ed.]).

55. See Kutscher, *Oh Angry Sea*, 6f., for this interpretation.

56. Kutscher, *Oh Angry Sea*, 7.

57. Cohen, *balag*, 11.

58. Cohen, *balag*, 13, 15.

59. See E. Sollberger's remarks in his review of J. Krecher, *Kultlyrik*, which was published in *BO* 25 (1968) 47a.

This hiatus in documentation is probably caused by the fact that following the fall of Babylon about 1600

B.C.E. the scribal schools of Nippur and Babylon closed, and their scholars, taking their texts with them, fled southward to the Sealand. Under the Kassites, however, new scribal schools were established to perpetuate the classical literary tradition. In this corpus, which Hallo calls "Post-Sumerian" and "Bilingual," cultic texts and especially laments dominated. In fact, this bilingual collection survived as the canon for the remainder of the history of classical Mesopotamian literature through the Seleucid era into the Arsacid period. See W. W. Hallo, "Problems in Sumerian Hermeneutics," *Perspectives in Jewish Learning* 5 (1973) 6f. and "Toward a History of Sumerian Literature," 189-91, 198, 201, on bilinguals in the history of the canons.

60. Cohen, *balag*, 9.

61. See Kutscher, *Oh Angry Sea*, 9f., for a chart of the texts he was able to combine to reconstruct this *balag*.

62. Kutscher, *Oh Angry Sea*, 11. Kutscher's Ca (=VAT 8243, 11. 32-37) and Db (=VAT 8243, 11. 142 and 143).

63. Kutscher, *Oh Angry Sea*, 17 (TMHnF 53:21).

64. Cohen, *eršemma*, 25f.

65. See, for example, Kutscher, *Oh Angry Sea*, 5; Cohen, *balag*, 13-15.

66. Cohen, *balag*, 13-15.

67. Cohen, *balag*, 13.

68. Caplice, "Namburbi Texts in the British Museum, IV," *Or* 39 (1970) 118f.

69. Cohen, *balag*, 14f.

70. Ibid.

71. On *kirugu* see A. Falkenstein, "Sumerische religiöse Texte," *ZA* 49 (1950) 104f. where he interpreted the term as meaning "to bow to the ground." *Šēru* is probably related to Sumerian *šîr*, a generic title for poetry and/or song; see *AHW* 1219a. See also Green, *Eridu*, 283-85.

72. On *gišgigal* see A. Falkenstein, "Sumerische religiöse Texte," 92, 93, 97f., 101. Falkenstein interpreted the term simply as "antiphon." See also Green, *Eridu*, 285f. See *AHW* 641a, sub *me/ihru*, 3) where *giš-gál* = *mi-hir za-ma-ri* = antiphonal song and *giš-gi⁴-gál* = *me-eh-ru/rù*.

73. See Cohen, *balag*, 8 and Green, *Eridu*, 283-86 on structural matters.

74. See n. 20 above.

75. See Green, *Eridu*, 286-89. For a fuller analysis of Sumerian poetic form, see C. Wilcke, "Formale Gesichtspunkte in der sumerischen Literatur," *Assyriological Studies* 20 (Chicago: University of Chicago, 1975) 205-316.

76. See n. 31 above.

77. Green, *Eridu*, 288f.

78. Kutscher (*Oh Angry Sea*, 5) takes the position that *gala*-priests "specialized in Emesal" and that when they composed or recited compositions in worship settings, they employed the Emesal dialect. Krecher (*Kultlyrik*, 27f.), however, maintains that other cult personnel, namely the *nārū*-singer, also sang the Emesal compositions. Krecher, however, admits that the Emesal songs were almost exclusively sung by the *kalû*-(=*gala*)priests. Cohen (*balag*, 11) attributes the composition of the city-laments, as well as *balag*s and *eršemma*s, to the *kalû*-priests. See also Cohen, *balag*, 13, 15, and 32 as well as Cohen, *eršemma*, 9, 11, 17, and 24. Hallo ("Individual Prayer in Sumerian: The Continuity of a Tradition," *JAOS* 88 [1968] 81b) shows that "the later penitent commissioned the gala-singer to recite his prayer orally." Such *erša hunga*-prayers were also composed in Emesal (see Krecher, *Kultlyrik*, 25 and Hallo, "Individual Prayer," 80-82) and were recited, at least on occasions, to the accompaniment of the *halhallatu*-drum (Cohen, *eršemma*, 27). For a discussion of the *gala*-priests as Old Babylonian cult personnel, see J. Renger, "Untersuchungen zum Priestertum der altbabylonischen Zeit," *ZA* 59 (1969) 189-95.

79. In outlining these six common themes I am following Green, *Eridu*, 295-310.

80. Jacobsen, *AJSL* 58 (1941) 219-24.

81. Hallo, "Cultic Setting," 119.

82. Cohen, *balag*, 11.

83. Green, *Eridu*, 309f.

84. Green, *Eridu*, 311f.

85. Kutscher, *Oh Angry Sea*, 21.

86. Translation in Kutscher, *Oh Angry Sea*, 143-53.

87. Cohen, *balag*, 8, 11f.

88. Cohen, *balag*, 8.

89. Cohen, *eršemma*, 17.

90. Cohen, *eršemma*, 28.

91. Cohen, *eršemma*, 12.

92. Kutscher, *Oh Angry Sea*, 4.

93. Cohen, *eršemma*, 9f., 27f.; Cohen, *balag*, 11, 13-15; Kutscher, *Oh Angry Sea*, 6f.; Krecher, *Kultlyrik*, 18-25, 34.

94. Green, *Eridu*, 342, 1. 1:20.

95. See Gottwald's discussion of the interplay of doom and hope in Lamentations in his chap. 3 ("The Key to the Theology of Lamentations"), chap. 4 ("The Theology of Doom") and chap. 5 ("The Theology of Hope") in *Studies in the Book of Lamentations*.

96. McDaniel, "Sumerian Influence," 207f.

97. McDaniel, "Sumerian Influence," 207.

98. Gadd, "Second Lamentation," 61, cited in McDaniel, "Sumerian Influence," 209.

99. McDaniel, "Sumerian Influence," 209.

ABBREVIATIONS

AASOR: Annual of the American Schools of Oriental Research

AB: Anchor Bible

AfO Archiv für Orientforschung:

AHR American Historical Review:

AHW: W. von Soden, *Akkadisches Handwörterbuch*

AJSL: American Journal of Semitic Languages and Literatures

ANEH: W. W. Hallo and W. K. Simpson, *The Ancient Near East: A History*

ANEP: James B. Pritchard (ed.), *The Ancient Near East in Pictures*

ANET: J. B. Pritchard (ed.), *Ancient Near Eastern Texts*

AOAT: Alter Orient und Altes Testament

AOS: American Oriental Series

ARW: Archiv für Religionswissenschaft

AS: Assyriological Studies

ASOR: American Schools of Oriental Research

ASTI: Annual of the Swedish Theological Institute

ATD: Das Alte Testament Deutsch

ATR: Anglican Theological Review

BAR: Biblical Archaeologist Reader

BARev: Biblical Archaeology Review

BASOR: Bulletin of the American Schools of Oriental Research

BHT: Beiträge zur historischen Theologie

Bib: Biblica

BiOr: Bibliotheca Orientalis

BJRL: Bulletin of the John Rylands University Library of Manchester

BKAT: Biblischer Kommentar: Altes Testament

BO: Bibliotheca Orientalis

BR: Biblical Research

BTB: Biblical Theology Bulletin

BZAW: Beihefte zur *ZAW*

CAD: The Assyrian Dictionary of the Oriental Institute of the University of Chicago

CAH: Cambridge Ancient History

CBQ: Catholic Biblical Quarterly

CQR: Church Quarterly Review

Enc Jud: Encyclopaedia Judaica

Exp Tim: Expository Times

HSS: Harvard Semitic Series

HTR: Harvard Theological Review

HUCA: Hebrew Union College Annual

ICC: International Critical Commentary

IEJ: Israel Exploration Journal

JANESCU: Journal of the Ancient Near Eastern Society of Columbia University

JAOS: Journal of the American Oriental Society

JBL: Journal of Biblical Literature

JCS: Journal of Cuneiform Studies

JEA: Journal of Egyptian Archaeology

JNES: Journal of Near Eastern Studies

JQR: Jewish Quarterly Review

JSOT: Sup Journal for the Study of the Old Testament, Supplements

JSS: Journal of Semitic Studies

JTS: Journal of Theological Studies

KAT: E. Sellin (ed.), Kommentar zum A.T.

MSL: Materilien zum Sumerischen Lexikon

MVAG: Mitteilungen der vorderasiatisch-ägyptischen Gesellschaft

NICOT: New International Commentary on the Old Testament

OIP: Oriental Institute Publications

Or: Orientalia (Rome)

OrAnt: Oriens antiquus

OTL: Old Testament Library

OTS: Oudtestamentische Studiën

RA: Revue d'assyriologie et d'archéologie orientale

RB: Revue Biblique

REg: Revue d'égyptologie

RLA: Reallexikon der Assyriologie

RSR: Recherches de science religieuse

SACT: S. T. Kang, *Sumerian and Akkadian Cuneiform Texts*

SANE: Sources from the Ancient Near East

SBLMS: Society of Biblical Literature Monograph Series

SBS: Stuttgarter Bibelstudien

SBT: Studies in Biblical Theology

Sem: Semitica

StudOr: Studia Orientalia

TDOT: Theological Dictionary of the Old Testament

TLZ: Theologische Literaturzeitung

TynBul: Tyndale Bulletin

UF: Ugarit-Forschungen

VT: Vetus Testamentum

VTSup: Vetus Testamentum, Supplements

WMANT: Wissenschaftliche Monographien zum Alten und Neuen Testament

WO Die Welt des Orients

YNER Yale Near Eastern Researches

ZA Zeitschrift für Assyriologie

ZÄS Zeitschrift für Ägyptische Sprache und Altertumskunde

ZAW Zeitschrift für die alttestamentliche Wissenschaft

ZDPV Zeitschrift des deutschen Palästina-Vereins

FURTHER READING

Criticism

Albrektson, Bertil. *Studies in the Text and Theology of the "Book of Lamentations."* Lund, Sweden: CWK Gleerup, 1963, 258p.

> Critical edition of the Peshitta text that includes divergences from the Hebrew text and the Septuagint.

Alexander, Philip S. "The Textual Traditions of Targum *Lamentations*." *Abr-Nahrain* XXIV (1986): 1-26.

> Study of Targum *Lamentations* offered as a general approach that can be pursued in editing any biblical text.

Cannon, William Walter. "The Authorship of *Lamentations*." *Bibliotheca Sacra* 81 (1924): 42-58.

> Critique of arguments that Jeremiah was not the sole author of *Lamentations*.

Cross, Frank Moore. "Studies in the Structure of Hebrew Verse: The Prosody of *Lamentations* 1:1-22." *The Word of the Lord Shall Go Forth,* pp. 129–55. .Winona Lake, Ind.: Eisenbrauns, 1983.

> Study of the Qinah meter in *Lamentations*.

Dahood, Mitchell. "New Readings in *Lamentations*." *Biblica* 59, No. 2 (1978): 174-97.

> Examination of specific verses of *Lamentations* that may be improved by correcting probable defective spellings in source texts.

Gadd, C. J. "The Second Lamentation for Ur." *Hebrew and Semitic Studies,* edited by D. Winton Thomas and W. D. McHardy, pp. 59–71. Oxford: Clarendon Press, 1963.

> Translation of and notes for an early lamentation that may have influenced *Lamentations*.

Gordis, Robert. "Commentary on the Text of *Lamentations* (Part Two)." *The Jewish Quarterly Review* LVIII, No. 1 (July 1967): 14-33.

> Explanation for difficulties in understanding the third chapter of *Lamentations*. Gordis discusses "fluid personality" and adopting a psychological rather than a logical reading.

Gray, George Buchanan. "Parallelism and Rhythm in the *Book of Lamentations*." In *The Forms of Hebrew Poetry,* pp. 87–120. 1915. Reprint. New York: KTAV Publishing House, 1972.

> Analysis of the differences in the use of parallelism in the first four chapters of *Lamentations*.

Johnson, Bo. "Form and Message in *Lamentations*." *Zietschrift für die Alttestamentliche Wissenschaft* 97, No. 1 (1985): 58–73.

> Examines the structure of *Lamentations* and contends that its careful design and alphabetic composition points to and emphasizes its intended message.

Shea, William H. "The *qinah* Structure of the *Book of Lamentations*." *Biblica* 60, No. 1 (1979): 103-07.

> Analysis of pattern and structure of *Lamentations* that emphasizes linking together its five books.

Sir Orfeo
c. 13th century

Middle English poem.

INTRODUCTION

Sir Orfeo, a romance composed by an unknown Celtic author, was loosely adapted from the classic Greek story of Orpheus and Eurydice. The earliest Middle English version is found among other tales in the Auchinleck manuscript, which dates from about 1330-1340 and may have been owned by Geoffrey Chaucer. On the basis of linguistic studies, *Sir Orfeo* appears to have been written sometime during the second half of the 13th century. The tale, its chief version consisting of 602 short lines of rhyming couplets, tells the tale of King Orfeo, a harp player without equal. His wife, Heurodis, is abducted by the fairy King but Orfeo, through his harp playing, manages to bring her back to the land of mortals. Among the many notable differences between the Celtic and the Greek renditions are the setting and the ending: in *Sir Orfeo* the main resolution occurs in Fairyland instead of Hades, and the ending is a happy one. *Sir Orfeo* is regarded by critics as one of the finest examples of the Breton lay.

PLOT AND MAJOR CHARACTERS

At the beginning of May, King Orfeo's wife falls into a deep sleep under an imp, or grafted, tree and dreams she is abducted by the King of the fairies, shown his fantastic kingdom, and told that, come tomorrow, she will be kept there forever. She awakes distraught, tears her robes to shreds and claws at her face, making it bleed profusely. To thwart the realization of the dream, Orfeo has hundreds of knights guard Heurodis, but they prove ineffective as the fairy King uses enchantment to take her away effortlessly. Orfeo is beyond consoling and abandons his kingdom to the charge of his steward. Having lost the fairest lady who ever lived, Orfeo swears he will never look upon another woman and takes to the woods barefoot, totally without material possessions except for his cloak and his harp. Living off nuts, roots, and bark for more than ten years, Orfeo wanders aimlessly. His only respite from grief comes from playing his harp, which soothes him and enchants both bird and beast. One day, he chances upon his wife among a group of ladies from the fairy kingdom. Although Orfeo's appearance shows the effect of a decade in the wilderness, and his hair is rough and hangs to his waist, Heurodis recognizes him instantly. Overcome with emotion, neither can speak to the other. Orfeo follows her through a rock and below ground to the fairy kingdom. He gains permission from the porter to enter the castle made of gold and dazzling jewels, by virtue of being a minstrel. Inside the castle Orfeo plays his harp for the fairy King, who is so impressed that he offers Orfeo whatever he cares to request. Orfeo demands Heurodis and, although the fairy King hesitates to give her to him because the couple seem so mismatched, he honors his word and relinquishes her. Orfeo returns to his kingdom but does not reveal his identity until he tests his steward's loyalty. The steward passes the test, Orfeo makes his true identity known, and Orfeo and Heurodis are newly crowned. They live and rule in peace until their deaths, upon which, the steward becomes king.

MAJOR THEMES

Ultimately, *Sir Orfeo* is a tale of loyalty and devotion. Set in a scene rich with Celtic folklore, the poem involves magic and enchantment, a King who loses everything only to regain it after years of suffering, fidelity to spouse and to lord, love, and music. The music of the harp was considered sacred by the Celts and represents harmony; its power is such that it can restore order, even overcoming the fairy King. Notable is the fact that Orfeo does not have to search for his wife, as is the case in similar tales; scholar K. R. R. Gros Louis interprets Orfeo's suffering as representing Christian penance and the return of Heurodis through the grace of God.

CRITICAL RECEPTION

Sir Orfeo is unanimously and highly praised by critics. Laura A. Hibbard calls its grace and beauty exceptional and states, "Brief, yet vivid, the little tale is inimitably fresh in style and content." Dorena Allen calls its author a genius at adaptation. Other critics echo these statements. Much effort has been made to trace the roots of *Sir Orfeo;* most scholars presume that the Middle English version comes from an adaptation of a now-lost Old French version. Several texts have been demonstrated to contain similarities but no proposal of a single source for all the non-Classical elements has been satisfactory; Allen argues that such a search must be fruitless because it is a hunt for something that probably never existed. Critics have pointed out that *Sir Orfeo*'s Greek, Christian, Celtic, and French elements are divergences from the typical poetry of its time. To cite one example, this tale is the only one known in which the action of mortals in Fairyland takes place in the land of the living and not of the dead. Some scholars are fascinated by the nature of Heurodis's state, which has similarities with mythical death but is distinctly different.

Critics continue to disagree about interpretations of *Sir Orfeo,* many asserting that the poem contains multiple levels of allegory. In addition, scholars have devoted themselves to the study of manuscript variations, errors, and omissions. A. J. Bliss has gone so far as to reconstruct the missing beginning of the Auchinleck manuscript in a faithful style. The timeless themes of *Sir Orfeo* and its ability to accomodate new interpretations continue to attract readers and scholars alike.

PRINCIPAL WORKS

Principal English Editions

"Havelok" and *"Sir Orfeo"* (translated by Robert Montagu) (poetry) 1954
Sir Orfeo (edited by A. J. Bliss) (poetry) 1966
"Sir Gawain and the Green Knight," *"Pearl,"* and *"Sir Orfeo"* (translated by J. R. R. Tolkien) (poetry) 1975

CRITICISM

George Lyman Kittredge (essay date 1886)

SOURCE: "Sir Orfeo," *American Journal of Philology*, Vol. VII, No. 25, 1886, pp. 176-202.

[*In the following essay, Kittredge examines several Breton lays and explains how French, Celtic, and Irish influences made* Sir Orfeo *different from the others.*]

Dating from the end of the thirteenth century, when imitation, not originality, was the rule in English writing, the Romance or Lay of *Sir Orfeo* is not more remarkable for its grace and beauty than for the freedom with which it handles the classic mythology. The ultimate source of the poem is evidently the story of Orpheus and Eurydice as told by Virgil and Ovid, but so different is the romance from any known version of this story that, if the English minstrel had not called his hero and heroine Orfeo and Heurodys, his indebtedness to the ancients would be hard to prove. The present discussion aims to show the direct antecedents of the *Orfeo,* and to throw some light on the causes that have led the story so far away from its original shape.[1]

In the first place, the poem professes to be a Breton lay. This claim is made not only in the opening lines—which, as almost identical with the beginning of the English Lay le Fresne, and possibly borrowed from that poem, may be left out of account[2]—but also very distinctly in the closing verses:

> Harpours in Bretaine afterþan
> Herd hou þis mervaile bigan,
> And made herof a lay of gode likeing
> And nempned it after the king:
> Þat lay Orfeo is yhote,
> Gode is þe lay, swete is þe note.
> Þus com Sir Orfeo out of his care.
> God graunt ous alle wele to fare.

> (vv. 595 ff. Zielke.)

If these lines are to be taken seriously, and not as a literary artifice, they prove that the *Orfeo* is translated from some French poem[3] purporting—like any one of Marie's collection—to give the substance of a Breton lay. Only through the French could a Breton lay get into English; from none but a French poem could verses like these be derived. If, however, the lines are a mere flourish on the part of the English minstrel, intended to gain respect for his piece, of course they prove nothing.[4] Comparison may help decide the question.

Besides the *Orfeo* there are six Middle English poems that profess to be Breton lays. These are: (1) Lay le Fresne, (2) Sir Launfal, (3) Sir Gowther, (4) Emare, (5) Chaucer's Franklin's Tale, and (6) the Erl of Tolous. Of these the Fresne and Launfal are free translations from Marie de France. The others are more doubtful.[5]

Sir Gowther has long been recognized as an offshoot of the story of Robert the Devil. The anonymous author twice declares it to be a lay of Britain:

> A lai of Breyten long y soght
> And owt þerof a tale have broght,
>   þat lufly is to tell.

> (vv. 28-30, p. 6, ed. Breul.)[6]

> þis is wreton in parchemyn,
> A story hoþe gud and fyn,
>   Owt off a lai of Breyteyn.

> (vv. 751-3, p. 38.)

The French original of Sir Gowther is unknown, but was doubtless a free translation of some Breton lay. Normandy and Brittany were closely associated. It is chiefly through the Normans that the lays of Brittany have come down to us.[7] The Breton Lay of the Two Lovers, preserved in Marie's version, is founded on a Norman popular tale.[8] Robert the Devil, then, being a Norman story, was within easy reach of any Armorican harper. When the Gowther varies from the Robert, it often approaches Celtic tradition. Robert is devoted to the devil before his birth,[9] but Gowther is actually the son of a demon who has deceived the Duchess of Estryke as Uther cheated Igerne,[10] by putting on the semblance of her husband. The scene in the orchard and the joy of the duke when he finds himself likely to become a father, may be compared with the Lay de Tydorel.[11] There is nothing like them in any version of Robert. Robert repents when he finds himself dreaded and avoided by all. This is after he has murdered the nuns (or hermits). Gowther is brought to his senses rather differently—by a taunt from an old monk, who declares that so wicked a man cannot be of human origin. In like manner Tydorel, the son of a queen and a fairy knight, is set thinking by a young man who has been impressed to tell him stories at night. Tydorel never sleeps, and the young man flings at him the proverb, "Qui ne dort n'est pas d'ome" (vv. 329-30). In all three poems, Gowther, Tydorel, and the romance of Robert,[12] the son, when once his suspicions are excited, rushes into his mother's chamber with drawn sword and forces her to confess. These considerations perhaps justify us in regarding Sir Gowther as really founded on a Breton lay.[13]

Emare ends with the usual prayer, before which come these lines:

> Thys ys on of Brytayne layes,
> That was used by olde dayes,
> Men callys playn the garye.

(vv. 1030-2.)[14]

The story of Emare is very much like the Tale of the Man of Lawe, from which it differs chiefly in having a disagreeable beginning. Chaucer's tale comes directly from Trivet's Life of Constance,[15] but other versions were current in the Middle Ages,[16] and one of them may easily have come to the ears of a Breton harper. The title of the lay is perhaps preserved in a French form in the verse "Men callys playn the garye," which I take to mean that the lay is called "La Garie"—"the saved or preserved one"—an appropriate name.[17] The direct original of the English poem was doubtless a French version of this lay.

The Franklin's Tale, if we may take the franklin's word for it, is founded on one of the "layes" which "these olde, gentil Britons" made "of diverse aventures" (C. T. 11,021 ff.). No such lay, however, is extant, and it is not impossible that Chaucer simply took the story from Boccaccio,[18] changed the setting, and referred the adventure to "Armorik, that called is Britayne." For Chaucer handled his material with conscious literary art, and is much more likely to have treated a tale in this fashion than the obscure translator who has left us Emare. Against this it may be urged that the Franklin's Tale has some Breton proper names, and that, in general, the plot would have been attractive to the Armorican minstrels. The story came from the East, and may have reached Chaucer through a lay of Brittany.[19]

The Erl of Tolous speaks for itself thus:

> Yn Rome thys gest cronyculyd ys,
> A lay of Bretayn callyd ywys
> And evyr more schall be.

(vv. 1219-21, p. 279 Lüdtke.)

Gustav Lüdtke, who has studied this story with wonderful industry and acuteness, has no misgivings in referring the English poem to a lost French Comte de Toulouse, and that, in turn, back to a Breton lay. These English and French versions, he thinks, followed their respective originals with fidelity.[20]

For all six of the poems we have examined, a Breton source may reasonably be claimed. It appears, then, that Middle English authors, however recklessly they appealed to "the book," or "the history," or "the romance," did not call their poems Breton lays unless they meant what they said. In the absence of evidence to the contrary, we may infer that the author of Sir Orfeo was equally in earnest—that is, that the French piece from which he translated, professed to be a rendering of a Breton lay.

That such a lay once existed is shown by two well-known passages. The first is from the Lai de l'Espine, mistakenly ascribed by De la Rue to Guillaume le Normand[21] and by Roquefort to Marie de France.[22] The king of "Bretaigne" and his knights listen to music after hunting:

> Le Lais escoutent d'Aielis,
> Que uns irons sone en sa rote;
> Mout doucement le chante et note.
> Apriès celi d'autre commenche,
> Nus d'iaus ni noise ne ni tenche;
> Le Lai lor sonne d'Orphéy.

(vv. 180-5.)[23]

The second is from the first version of Floire et Blanceflor. Among the wonders shown by the magician to entertain Floire is an image of gold:

> . . . grant com un vilains:
> Une harpe tint en ses mains,
> Et harpe le lai d'Orphéy:
> Onques nus hom plus n'en oï
> Et le montée et l'avalée.

(Ed. Du Méril, p. 231.)[24]

These two passages show that the Lai d'Orphéy was well known and popular. They show also that it was a genuine lay of Brittany, and not a French poem merely pretending to give the story of a lay which, after all, did not exist; for the French versions—genuine or counterfeit—of Breton lays were probably not sung or accompanied by the harp or rote.[25] They simply gave the plot of the real or pretended lay in rhymed couplets, with no attempt to preserve its rhythmical structure, and, if it were possible to sing them at all, could have been set only to a monotonous strain[26] quite different from the tune here indicated.

It is impossible not to identify this Breton lay with the original of our *Sir Orfeo*. The existence of a French intermediary cannot be directly proved[27]—for the three or four other places in which the story of Orpheus is mentioned in Old French literature have no necessary connection with the lay[28]—but must certainly be inferred as our only means of connecting the English poem with the lay of Brittany.

At this point it may reasonably be asked: Have we any other examples of Breton lays composed on classical themes? This question must be answered in the negative;

for the various poems that have been at one time or another cited as such examples—Aristotle,[29] Pyramus and Thisbe,[30] Narcissus,[31] etc.—have nothing to do with Brittany. This, however, should not damage the credit of *Sir Orfeo*. The Aristotle, etc., do not profess to be anything but *contes* or *ditiés*. The word *lay* does not occur in any of them. They tell neither for nor against the alleged source of the English poem. The question must be decided without their aid.

The Breton lays, now generally agreed to be of Armorican origin, attained their greatest popularity in the eleventh and twelfth centuries. Most of them naturally were on Celtic subjects, and laid their scenes in Celtic countries—Great and Little Britain, Ireland and Scotland. But the Armorican minstrels did not confine themselves Celtic to themes. Their music was famous throughout France. "Le Moyen-Age," says Joly, "est un grand enfant qui, comme tous les enfants, demande sans cesse qu'on lui conte des nouvelles histoires. Ses fournisseurs habituels vont puiser á toutes les sources."[32] Among these purveyors were the Bretons:

> Mult unt esté noble barun
> cil de Bretaigne, li Bretun.
> Jadis suleient par pruësce,
> par curteisie e par noblesce
> des aventures que oeient,
> ki a plusurs genz aveneient,
> faire les lais pur remembrance,
> qu'um nes meïst en ubliance.
>
> (Lai d'Equitan, vv. 1-8.)[33]

So in *Sir Orfeo:*

> When þey (*sc.* Brytouns) myght owher heryn
> Of aventures þat þer weryn,
> þey toke her harpys wiþ game,
> Maden layes and af it name.
>
> (vv. 17-20 Zielke.)[34]

We have already seen Breton jongleurs appropriating the Norman stories of Robert the Devil and the Two Lovers, as well as the Aquitanian tradition of the Earl of Toulouse. In the Lai d'Havelok, an Anglo-Danish local legend is in like manner made the subject of a Breton lay.[35] In a word, the Armorican minstrels picked up good stories wherever they could find them,[36] and nothing is more likely than that, in their wanderings, they heard somebody tell the tale of Orpheus and Eurydice.

This might have happened either in England or in the South of France, where Ovid and Virgil were well known,[37] and where the Breton harpers were also no strangers.[38] However it came about, there is nothing remarkable in their hearing the story. It was a subject for popular poetry—or, at least, for the lightest style of monkish verse—as early as the tenth century, when the monk Froumont wrote to the Abbot of Tegernsee:

> Si . . . Dulcifer aut fabulas possem componere mendas,
>
> Orpheus ut canfans Eurydicen revocat,[39]

and it may have reached Breton ears in some cantilena similar to that De Narcisso mentioned by Peter Cantor in the twelfth century as performed by a strolling musician.[40]

Our Breton harper, however, probably got the story by word of mouth and in no very accurate shape; and, in making it over into a lay, he must inevitably have changed the story still further to make it square with his own beliefs and traditions and those of his auditors. In this process, such parts of the classic myth as were within his circle of ideas were retained with least alteration; such things as he could not understand, were cast aside or forgotten; many points were misunderstood and unwittingly misrepresented. In short, the Ovidian story became a Breton lay in every sense—short, romantic, Celtic. This the French translator must have rendered without much change, his aim being to tell the tale of a favorite lay, not to restore an antique. And from this French version came our English *Orfeo,* freely handled, no doubt, but with no essential variation.

The French element in the *Orfeo* is rather pervasive than striking. The English element is seen in the parliament which is to appoint a new king if Orfeo does not come back (vv. 214-16), and perhaps in the steward, though that personage reminds one of the seneschal so often met with in old French poems. The Celtic element has never been discussed, and, if it can be shown to exist in any considerable degree, will serve not merely to clinch what has so far been said as to the origin and transmission of our poem, but also as independent and sufficient proof that the *Orfeo* is what it professes to be—a Breton lay. If our genesis is correct, we shall find the *Orfeo* preserving or rejecting the incidents of the classic story according as they agree or disagree with Celtic ideas and traditions.

On this principle, we should expect the harping of Orpheus to be made much of in *Sir Orfeo.* The respect felt by all Celtic nations for their harpers is famous. Every baron should have three things, said the Welsh laws—his harp, his cloak, and his chessboard.[41] In the time of Richard II the Irish kings still treated their minstrels with a consideration that shocked the English ambassador.[42] In this respect the *Orfeo* meets our expectation. Orfeo is not only the best of harpers, he is a king. The Celts were fond of putting the harp into the hands of kings and princes. Every one will think of Tristram and Yseut and Mark.[43] Glasgerion was a king's son and a Briton.[44] No less than three of the Welsh bards were royal.[45] Above all, the British king Blegabres[46] must not be forgotten. He knew "de tos estrumens maistrie, et de diverse canterie; et mult sot de lais et de note . . .

> Porce qu'il ert de si bon sens
> Disoient li gent, à son tens,
> Que il ert Dex des jogléors,
> Et Dex de tos les chantéors."
>
> (Roman de Brut., vv. 3763-5, 3773-6; Le Roux de Lincy, I 178-9.)

With this royal patron and god of music may be compared the crowned figure seated on a throne and playing on that eminently Celtic instrument, the crwt, found in a manu-script in the French National Library.[47]

The power exercised by the harp of Orpheus over the beasts of the wood is carefully preserved in the lay; for, though this trait occurs oftener in Norse than in Celtic, it cannot be claimed as the exclusive property of any people, and would doubtless have been retained by any mediaeval minstrel who had undertaken to work over the classic tale.[48] The Celts were no strangers to marvellous feats of minstrelsy. The Irish had a wild tale of the three sons of Uaithne, who harped at the court of Ailill one day till twelve men died of weeping;[49] and another of the three tunes played on a magic harp by Dagde in the hall of his foes: "He played them the Goltraighe until their women cried tears. He played them the Gentraighe until their women and youths burst into laughter. He played them the Suantraighe until the entire host fell asleep."[50] Nearer the *Orfeo* is the harping of Glasgerion, who, if not Glas Keraint, is a Briton at least.[51] And curiously parallel is the power with which Tyolet, the hero of a Breton lay, had been endowed by a fairy—the power of attracting wild beasts, when he wished, by whistling.[52]

In the lay, as in the myth, Orpheus wins back his wife by his music; and this is a trait that we should have expected a Breton to preserve. At the same time, almost every feature of the picture has been retouched. In Ovid, Orpheus frankly avows his errand, and his song is an appeal to Pluto and Proserpine to restore Eurydice. In the lay he appears as a wandering minstrel, charms the court of the fairy king with his playing, and, on being promised whatever boon he may ask, demands the lady asleep under the tree yonder. In these changes a strong resemblance may be noticed to the peculiarly Celtic romance of Tristram. An Irish harper presents himself at the court of King Mark, but refuses to play till he is promised a gift. Mark assures him he shall have whatever he may choose; whereupon the minstrel, after a tune or two, claims the queen. Mark is in despair, but must keep his word or give up all title to royalty, for no liar can be king.[53] The parallel is very close. In both cases we have the same reluctance to keep faith, and the same warning that it is a foul thing to hear a lie from a king's mouth.

Another point in which the *Orfeo* is reasonably close to Ovid is the despair of the bard and his solitary life in the woods.[54] In this the lay, which is much more circumstantial than the Latin, may be compared with the romance of Iwain and with the story of Merlin Silvestris.[55]

The great difference between our poem and its original—the central variation which in a manner conditions all the rest—consists in the change of scene from Hades to fairyland, and the substitution of the King of Fairies for Pluto. If this change is not in the direction of Celtic tradition, nothing can establish the claim of the *Orfeo* to be a Breton production. Fortunately, the question admits of no doubt. The fairies in the English poem have nothing Teutonic about them. They are not gnomes, or trolls, or kobo-lds, or brownies, or nixies. They are not the mischievous diminutive creatures that abound in German popular tales. They are precisely those mysterious, reverend beings, of human size and more than mortal power and beauty, in which Celtic imagination delighted. Two or three minor points in which the fairies of the *Orfeo* resemble Celtic tradition may be mentioned before we come to the main question.

In the woods Orfeo often saw hosts of fairy knights with flying banners and gleaming arms, "ac never he nist whider þai wold" (vv. 287-94). Similar apparitions were common in Little Britain in the twelfth century and earlier. "In Britannia minore visae sunt praedae nocturnae militesque ducentes eas cum silentio semper transeuntes."[56] The Irish fairy chiefs had always soldiers under their command and engaged in murderous combats with each other.[57] The knights and ladies, a hundred each, on snow-white steeds, that accompany the fairy king in *Sir Orfeo,* may be compared with the fourscore damsels, each with her *ami,* that Lorosis (in the Lai du Trot[58]) saw, in a sort of fairy vision, riding out of the wood. Too much stress must not, however, be laid on these minor matters.

The scene in which *Sir Orfeo* departs farthest from its classic source is that of the carrying off of Eurydice. The queen had gone to sleep in her orchard under an ympe-tree. Her sleep was long and heavy, but her maidens dared not wake her. When it passed, she was out of her wits, and tore her hair and scratched her cheeks. She was conveyed to her chamber, where the king immediately visited her. To him she revealed that while she was under the tree a gentle knight had summoned her to come and speak with his king; that on her refusal he had called his lord, who came with a score of knights and ladies and put her on a steed by his side; that this king had then carried her to a fair palace, the magnificence of which he showed her, and had at last brought her back to the ympe-tree, where he left her with the words:

> Loke, dame, to morwe þatow be
> Rit here under þis ympetre,
> And þan þou schalt wiþ ous go
> And live wiþ ous ever mo.
> And if þou makest ous ylet,
> Whàr þou be, þou worst yfet,
> And totore þine limes al
> þat noþing help þe no schal;
> And þei þou best so totorn,
> ete þou worst wiþ ous yborn.
>
> (vv. 163-72 Zielke.)

On the morrow the king and queen took their place under the tree, surrounded by two (ten) hundred knights, who swore that they would live and die before the queen should be taken from them.

> Ac ete amiddes hem ful rit
> þe quen was oway ytvit,
> Wiþ fairi forþ ynome,
> Men wist never wher sche was bicome.
>
> (vv. 189-92.)

The fairy marauders in this adventure seem to have been visible to the queen alone.

Apparently it is her sleeping under an ympe (or grafted) tree that gives the fairies power over Heurodys. This comes out later in the poem, when Orfeo sees in fairyland very many mortals who had been stolen away as they slept their "undertides" (vv. 339-440; cf. the reading of MS O). "Thomas of Erceldoune (in the Romance) is lying under a semely (derne, cumly) tree, when he sees the fairy queen. The derivation of that poem from Ogier le Danois shows that this must have been an apple-tree."[59] That Tam Lane was taken by the fairies while sleeping under an apple-tree[60] certainly seems to be, in like manner, a Celtic survival. In Sir Gowther the devil beguiles the duchess in her orchard. The Breton Lay de Tydorel[61] furnishes a curious parallel. The queen, who is disporting herself in her orchard with her maidens, falls, like Heurodys, into a heavy and unnatural sleep[62] under an "ente qu'ele choisi" (v. 30). On waking, she sees nothing of her attendants, but is approached by a knightly stranger, who asks her love. "If you refuse me," he threatens, "je m'rai, vos remaindrez: Sachiez ja mes joie n'avrez" (vv. 67-8). This knight is altogether supernatural, and his influence over the queen mysterious.[63] His home is under the waters of a neighboring lake.

I wish especially to call attention, however, to the correspondence between this scene in *Sir Orfeo* and a similar scene in the Irish epic tale of the Wooing of Etain (Tochmarc Etaine).

Etain was the wife of Eochaid Airem, supreme king of Ireland, and Midir, a fairy chief, was deeply in love with her. One fine day in summer Eochaid saw approaching his palace a bright-eyed, yellow-haired warrior, clad in purple and armed with a five-pointed lance and a buckler adorned with gold. The stranger gave his name as Midir, and proposed a game of chess. The king, secure in his reputation as the best chess-player in Ireland, promised Midir whatever he wished if he could win the game. Midir was successful and demanded Etain, but was, with difficulty, put off for a year, and, at the year's end, for a month. At the close of this month the king held high court at Tara. As night came on, he shut himself up in his palace with his queen. The doors were barred; the courtyard was manned by a line of vigilant guards, with strict orders to let no one pass; in the great hall of audience sat the king and queen, surrounded by the chief lords and choice warriors of the realm, each resolved to prevent the fairy chief from taking away his prize by force. The hour of midnight approached. Suddenly Eochaid was horrified to see Midir in the midst of the hall. No one had seen him enter, nor had the doors been unfastened. The unwelcome visitant advanced to the queen, whom he addressed in a song of invitation: "O, fair woman, will you come with me to my beautiful country, where all are beautiful, where none is sad or silent, where teeth are white and eyebrows black, where the hue of the foxglove is on every cheek? Beautiful are the plains of Inisfail, but they are as nothing to our great plains. Intoxicat-

ing is the beer of Inisfail, more intoxicating is the beer of the Great Country. There rivers run with wine. There old age is unknown. There love is unforbidden. O, fair woman, will you come with me?"[64] Etain refused to go without her husband's consent. Midir demanded permission to put his arm around the queen's waist. To this demand the king was obliged to accede. Immediately the fairy chieftain shifted his spear to his left hand, and, encircling Etain with his right arm, rose aloft and disappeared with her through the smoke-hole in the roof. Nobody could touch him or hinder his flight. Rushing out of the palace, the warriors saw two swans floating in the air, their long white tails united by a golden yoke. The birds were too far off to be followed, and soon disappeared altogether.[65] According to O'Curry's synopsis of the story, Midir was visible only to the king and queen, and the former was "so overcome by some supernatural influence that he was not only powerless to oppose him, but even unable to apprise the company of what was going on."[66]

The resemblances of this scene to *Sir Orfeo* need no emphasizing. The beautiful fairy warrior Midir corresponds to the fairy king; the song describing the delights of the Great Country to the tempting sight of fairyland granted Heurodys in her vision. Both Eochaid and Orfeo surround themselves with guards on the fatal day. In both lay and story the ravisher comes suddenly and mysteriously; in both, the warriors, if they see the fairy prince, have no power to resist his occult influence; in both the queen is carried off, nobody knows whither. In all the particulars, then, of the loss of Eurydice, *Sir Orfeo* is utterly at variance with Ovid and strikingly similar to a famous Celtic tale.

Heurodys is not taken to Hades, but to fairyland. We left the lay at the same point at which we now leave the Irish story. The queen had been stolen away "with fairy." Her husband and his court were at their wit's end. Orfeo immediately abandoned his realm, leaving his steward in charge, and plunged into the woods, harp in hand. After ten years of wild life (already noticed) he recognized his wife one day among a troop of ladies in the wood. Though the recognition was mutual, neither spoke,[67] and Heurodys was soon hurried off by her companions, resolutely pursued by Orfeo. The ladies rode "in at a rock," which was the entrance to fairyland. Three miles the king followed them into the hillside, when he came to "a fair country, as bright as sun on summer's day, smooth and plain and all green." In the midst was a splendid castle, the walls of which shone like crystal. Within were spacious dwellings of precious stones; the worst pillar was of gold. The land was never dark, for the rich stones gave light in the nighttime. In the castle, under a "pavilion," sat a king and queen whose raiment shone so brightly that Orfeo could not look upon it. A hundred knights waited on the king. Among other stolen mortals, Orfeo saw his wife, asleep under an imp-tree.[68] He gained her freedom,[69] as we have already seen, and returned with her in safety to his kingdom, where, concealing his identity, he tested the fidelity of the steward. The steward was faithful, and the king revealed himself. A new coronation followed, and Orfeo and Heurodys lived happily till the end of their days.

Zielke oddly remarks that a subterranean situation for fairyland is peculiar to the **Orfeo**—"diese Oertlichkeit des Feenlandes ist unserm Gedichte eigenthümlich, da wir dasselbe sonst auf eine Insel im Ocean oder in dichte Wildnisse verlegt finden" (p. 135). He is thinking evidently of the Isle of Avalon[70] and the Forest of Breceliant.[71] But we do find fairyland underground often enough, and under Celtic ground, too. Thus, not long before the time of Giraldus Cambrensis, a Welsh youngster, one Elidurus, who was playing truant and hiding "in concava fluvii cujusdam ripa," was led through subterranean passages "usque in terram pulcherrimam, fluviis et pratis, silvis et planis distinctissimam" which was ruled over by a king.[72] This is no doubt the same realm in which Herla, a king, "antiquissimorum Britonum," passed three centuries as three days. To reach it Herla had to enter "cavernam altissimae rupis" and travel some distance,[73] precisely as in **Orfeo**. So in Shropshire a cavern called the Ogo Hole is still pointed out as the entrance to fairyland,[74] and a cave in North Wales has a like uncanny reputation.[75] To these may be added the Peak Cavern in Derbyshire, at the bottom of which a swineherd, who had descended in search of a lost sow, found a land where men were reaping, though it was cold weather in the world above.[76] His sow was restored to him by the "praepositus" of that land. Add the Wolf Pits in Suffolk, out of which ascended the famous green children, who inhabited (so one of them said) a beautiful country sacred to St. Martin.[77] And Eldon Hill, in the Romance of Thomas of Erceldoune into which the queen of fairy led True Thomas,

> Vndir-nethe a derne lee
>   Whare it was dirke als mydnyght myrke,
> And euer þe water till his knee
>   The montenans of dayes three,

before they came in sight of the fairy castle.[78] Similarly the young Tam Lin was caught away by the fairies "in you green hill to dwell."[79]

I am aware that most of the cases so far cited may be challenged as either not pure Celtic or not quite to the point. But in carrying out our comparison between **Sir Orfeo** and the Wooing of Etain, we shall find an underground fairyland in virgin Celtic soil.

We left Midir flying through the air with his prize. As soon as King Eochair came to himself, he sent out his chief Druid, Dalân, with orders not to return without Etain. After a year of fruitless toil, Dalân discovered, "through his keys of science and his ogam," that the queen was concealed in Midir's palace in the hill of Bri Leith. The king mustered an army and proceeded to dig into the hill. As the miners approached the precincts of the fairy palace, the wily Midir displayed upon the hillside fifty beautiful women all exactly like Etain in dress and person, so that Eochaid could not distinguish his wife among them till she made herself known. Then he carried her back to Tara

with him in safety. He had recovered his wife from the underground fairy mansion no less effectually than Orfeo, though in a different way.

I have called Midir a fairy chief, but he deserves a more careful definition. By the year 1100 two or three lines of heathen belief and tradition had become almost inextricably tangled in the superstition and the literature of Ireland. In common with all Celtic peoples, the ancient Irish believed in a beautiful country beyond the sea, inhabited by gods and sometimes visited by heroes. This Elysium, related to the Avalon of Arthurian romance and the Terra Repromissionis Sanctorum of the legends, was called the Land of Promise (Tír Tairngire), the Land of the Land of the Living (Tír na mBeo), the Land of the Youthful (Tír na nOg), the Pleasant Plain (Mag Mell), etc.[80] The Irish also believed in certain divinities who lived underground and were called Aes Sídhe, and in other divinities, called Tuatha Dê Danann, who, if not originally identical with the Aes Sídhe, were in time confounded with them.[81] Properly the blissful land beyond the sea had nothing to do with the Aes Sídhe; but, by the beginning of the twelfth century, the Irish had long been Christians, their deities had been either euhemerized into mortals or degraded into demons and fairy chiefs, and they found it no easier to carry two sets of fairies and two fairylands in the mind without confusion, than the Greeks found it to keep their Chthonian and their Uranian gods always sharply distinguished. Hence they located the Aes Sídhe sometimes in the interior of pleasant green hills, sometimes in Tír Tairngire;[82] and Tír Tairngire—now fairyland—was sometimes regarded as underground, or as having a fairy-hill for its vestibule, or, perhaps, as dotted with green hills, in which its people dwelt. Thus, in the Adventures of Condla the Fair, the fêe (Windisch's word) invites Condla to the Land of the Living and the Pleasant Plain, but adds that the inhabitants are called Aes Sídhe, "for they have their dwellings in large, pleasant green hills." Condla finally departs with her in a crystal canoe.[83]

We can now understand Midir better. Originally a good, one of the Aes Sídhe, he is thought of in the Wooing of Etain as a fairy in the Celtic sense—a being of human stature, wonderful beauty, and extraordinary powers. He resides in a sídh or fairy-hill, whence he can come forth among men, visibly or invisibly, as he may perfer.[84] He describes his abode in a song intended originally, no doubt, as a description of the Land of the Living, but in this the twelfth century saw no contradiction. As soon as the Irish imagination entered the hill of Bri Leith, it lost itself and saw there all the wonders that former times had appropriated to the country beyond the sea. We may compare other Irish descriptions of fairyland. In the Sickness of Cuchlainn, also in the Book of the Dun Cow, the abode of the goddess Fand is called Hill of the Fairies (Dintsid), Powerful Plain of Trogaigi, and Mag Mell.[85] It is a country "bright and noble, in which is not spoken falsehood or guile"; it is a flowery plain; there are champions with gleaming arms and shining raiment; there are lovely women feasting. There sits King Labraid in his palace, surrounded by thousands of warriors. His hair is yellow as gold and fastened with a golden apple.[86] We see plainly the fusion of different elements into a more or less harmonious whole. This fusion had been fully accomplished by the year 1100—and we are here concerned with no earlier state of these stories.

Enough has probably been said to show that it is reasonable to regard the *Orfeo* in the light in which it puts itself—that is, as a Breton lay. Coincidences with Celtic story are too many to admit of any other conclusion. The conspicuous place which Irish literature has occupied in our investigation prompts a further question: Did the Breton *Orfeo* come into direct contact with Irish tradition? That is, are the striking resemblances we have noticed due (1) to the fact that the story of Midir represents views common to all Celts—the property as well of a Breton harper as of an Irish bard[87]—or (2) to the fact that the Breton author of our lay had heard from some Irishman the story of Midir or the like, and had consciously or unconsciously mixed it with the classic myth? Since either of these hypotheses accounts for the phenomena, neither can with certainty be proved. Still many features of *Sir Orfeo* agree more closely with Irish tradition than with anything demonstrably Breton or common Celtic, and it is easy to show that a Breton harper may have heard the Wooing of Etain much as we have it.

There is no difficulty about dates. The Leabhar na hUidhre, which contains the Irish story, is a MS written before 1106. If it were necessary (as it is not) to suppose any earlier date than this for the Breton *Orfeo,* there would still be no difficulty, for the contents of the Leabhar are of unknown antiquity, and, even in their present form, must antedate the MS considerably.

Nor need there be any hesitation as to means of transmission. Intercourse between Ireland and Wales on the one hand, and Wales and Brittany on the other, was brisk and not unfruitful in a literary way.[88] Several of the Mabinogion are thought to betray an Irish source.[89] When Lord Rhys held, in 1177, a great feast in South Wales, "he instituted two species of contests—one between the bards and poets, and another between the harpers, pipers, and those who played upon the crwth . . . , and this feast was announced a full year before it took place, in Wales, England, Scotland, and Ireland, and many other countries."[90] Gruffydd ab Kynan, who had taken refuge in Ireland, brought back with him on his return divers cunning musicians, who are said to have reformed the music of Wales.[91] Similarly it was no uncommon thing for a Welsh prince to spend some time in Armorica. A famous example is Rhys ab Tewdwr, who, on his return from Brittany to take the crown of South Wales in 1077, "brought with him," it is said, "the system of the Round Table, which at home had become quite forgotten, and restored it as it was with regard to minstrels and bards."[92] Thus closely associated with both countries, Wales might well have served as an intermediary in the transmission of Irish stories to Brittany.[93]

But we are not driven to this expedient. The fame of the Irish harpers was not confined to their native island. Early celebrated in Great Britain,[94] their renown was at its height there in the twelfth century, from which dates the enthusiastic testimony of Giraldus;[95] and there is evidence that, by his time, they had visited the Continent in considerable numbers. From the eighth to the fourteenth century they "appear to have wandered about the north of Europe,"[96] and it is even thought they got as far south as Italy. Vincentio Galilei declares without hesitation that the harp was introduced—or reintroduced—into that country from Ireland[97]—an opinion which has won some assent.[98] Of course these harpers carried their national stories with them, and nothing is more likely than that they imparted some of them to their Celtic brethren in Brittany, with whom they would naturally affiliate. To such intercourse, perhaps, more than to Welsh agency, we owe what seem to be Irish elements in the beautiful Breton Lay de Guigamor.[99] There is even said to have been a lay on an out-and-out Irish subject—which had, however, become cosmopolitan through the Latin version—the Voyage of St. Brandan.[100] In the Roman de Renart, the fox, masquerading as an Anglo-Norman jongleur, declares:

> Ge fot savoir bon lai Breton
> Et de Merlin et de Noton,
> Del roi Artu et de Tristan,
> Del chevrefoil, de saint Brandan.

> (i 2389-92, I 67 Martin; 12,149-52, II 95-6 Méon.)

More than all this, we have, in an undoubted Breton lay, clear proof that Irish harpers not only played their national melodies, but that they excelled in the performance of genuine lays of Brittany. Curiously enough, the passage that shows this gives the Lai d'Orphéy as one of the pieces thus performed. The quotation has already been made for another purpose:

> Le lais escoutent d'Aielis,
> Que uns irois sone en sa rote;
> Mout doucement le chante et note.
> Apriès celi d'autre commenche,
> Nus d'ïaus ni noise ne ni tenche;
> Le Lai lor sone d'Orphéy.

> (Lai de l'Espine, vv. 180 ff.)

Here an Irish harper plays two lays before the King of Bretaigne. M. Gaston Paris draws this inference: "La conclusion à tirer . . . semble être que les lais étaient connus en Irlande et executés parfois par des Irlandais." With the first of these propositions we need not concern ourselves; the second is certainly borne out by the evidence. That these wandering minstrels knew the story of Etain goes without saying. It was their business to know stories and to tell them. In this way, then, the tale of Midir and Etain may have reached Breton ears.

The results of our investigation appear then to be: (1) that *Sir Orfeo* is translated from a French version of a Breton lay; (2) that this lay varied from the classical story in the direction of Celtic tradition, and that these variations are in general preserved in the English poem. Further, that these variations, since they coincide in part with Irish tales, and since Irish harpers were known in Brittany, may probably have been made under the influence of stories picked up by some Armorican jongleur from an Irish brother. And, finally, that it is not absurd to conjecture that in the Wooing of Etain we have the very tale which, mixed with the imperfectly understood myth of Orpheus, produced the Breton lay of which the English poem is the sole surviving version.

Notes

1. I have used the excellent edition of Dr. Oscar Zielke: *Sir Orfeo,* ein englisches Feenmärchen aus dem Mittelalter. Breslau, 1880. Dr. Zielke was obliged to print his book with a less detailed account of the literary history of the poem than he had intended to give. His untimely death has probably robbed us of all chance of seeing his ideas in any fuller form. If he left any notes behind him, it is to be hoped they will soon be published.

2. These lines are found in the Harleian MS and the Bodleian MS. The Auchinleck MS lacks them, but the omission is satisfactorily explained by the mutilated condition of that famous quarto. There is no *a priori* reason why the verses should be regarded as borrowed by the *Orfeo* rather than by Le Fresne. They fit the former quite as well as the latter, and there is nothing in the French original of the Lay le Fresne from which they can be derived. The English Lay le Fresne is preserved only in the Auchinleck MS, which also contains the oldest copy of *Sir Orfeo.*

3. F. Lindner (Englische Studien, V 166 ff.) argues vigorously against a French, and for an Italian origin for *Sir Orfeo.* Most of his reasoning seems to me to have very little in it. He certainly does not prove that it is even possible that the *Orfeo* had other than an immediate French source. His only real argument for an Italian derivation is based on the form *Orfeo.* It is doubly unnecessary to discuss Lindner's article at length, as it has been already satisfactorily answered by Einenkel (Anglia, Anzeiger, V 13 ff.). Einenkel refers *Sir Orfeo* to a "verlorengegangenes franz. lay, dessen inhalt dem ersten englischen Erzähler oder Abfasser der Dichtung nur noch schwach erinnerlich war" (p. 17). Zielke (p. 136) refuses to decide whether the interweaving of the classical mythòlogy with the fairy belief "das werk unsers Dichters resp. seines französischen Gewährsmannes gewesen ist, oder bereits zuvor bestanden hat."

4. The verses are found in two MSS, the Bodleian and the Auchinleck; they are wanting in the Harleian. According to Zielke's genealogy of the MSS (p. 25), anything found in the Auchinleck, and at the same time in either of the other two MSS, must belong to the poem in its oldest English state.

5. Wolf, Ueber die Lais, p. 216, says that the Cokwold's Daunce is "nachweisbar auf ein bretonisches Lai gegründet." He seems to regard it as a parody on the Lai du Corn (p. 177). Wright's text of this piece, which calls itself not a lay, but a bourd, may be found in Karadjan's Frühlingsgabe.

6. I have used Breul's text (1883), but have not seen his prolegomena.

7. Cf. Aubertin, Hist. de la Langue et Litt. franç. 1203-4. At the beginning of the eleventh century, the Norman historian Dudon de Saint-Quentin, "pour que la gloire du duc Richard Ier se répandît dans le monde, conjurait les harpeurs armoricains de venir en aide aux clercs de Normandie."—P. Paris, Les Romans de la Table Ronde, I 7.

8. See R. Köhler's n. in Warnke's ed. of the Lais, pp. lxxxv-viii. G. Paris (Rom. VIII 34) says that the story is not yet forgotten in Normandy.

9. Romans de R. le Diable (thirteenth century), ed. Trebutien, 1837, sig. A ii; Miracle de Nostre Dame de R. le Dyable, ed. Fournier, p. 36; ed. Paris and Robert, Miracles de Nostre Dame, No. 33, VI 27-8; Robert the Deuyll, Thomas, Early Prose Romances, 2d ed., I 7; Roberte the Deuyll (Eng. poem), ed. Herbert, 1798, p. 6.

10. Geoffrey of Monmouth, viii 19, p. 117 Schulz; Eng. prose Merlin, Ch. iv, pp. 76-7, ed. Wheatley; Girald. Cambr., Itin. Kamb. I 12, Opera, ed. Dimock, VI 96; Eulogium Historiarum, ed. Haydon, II 305.

11. An undoubted Armorican lay, first printed by G. Paris, Rom. VIII 67-72.

12. Ed. Trebutien, sig. A iiii; Tydorel, 339 ff. In the Miracle (ed. Paris and Robert, pp. 24-5), the Eng. poem (pp. 22-3), and the Eng. prose version (Thoms, I 20), Robert does not threaten, but beseech, and there are other differences.

13. Cf. F. Wolf, Ueber die Lais, p. 219.

14. Ritson, Anc. Eng. Metr. Romancëes, II 247; cited by De la Rue, Recherches sur les ouvrages des bardes de la Bretagne armoricaine, 1815, p. 9, who remarks that the original Breton and the French appear to be lost. De la Rue also cites the Franklin's Tale.

15. Edited by Brock for Chaucer Society, Originals and Analogues.

16. Merelaus the Emperor, in the Eng. Gesta Romanorum, Herrtage, p. 311; Matthew Paris, Vita Offae Primi, ed. Wats, 1684, pp. 965-8, etc. Cf. Skeat's Introduction to the Man of Law's Tale, and Van der Hagen, Gesammtabenteuer, I c-civ, 135 ff.

17. Ritson quite misunderstands the passage. His explanation of it is even absurd (III 333). I know of no attempt made to interpret it since his day. Cf. with the title "Lai la Garie," the "Lai del Désiré" (Michel, Lais inédits, 1836, p. 1).

18. Decam. x 5; Filocopo, lib. v, qu. 4.

19. See Landau, Die Quellen des Decamerone, 2d ed., 1884, pp. 94, 95, 100, 248.

20. Erl of Tolous, pp. 131, 163. Lüdtke thinks the Breton lay was founded directly on Aquitanian tradition. Wolf, who derives the story differently, has no doubt that the English romance is from an Armorican lay

(Ueber die Lais, p. 217). On the story and its connections, see Child, Eng. and Scottish Popular Ballads, II 33 ff., who calls attention to a point of similarity between the Erl and the Lai du Corn (p. 43, n. ‡).

21. G. Paris, R'om. VIII 35.

22. Mall, De Aetate Rebusque Mariae Francicae, p. 56.

23. Roquefort, Poèsies de Marie de France, 1556. I have given vv. 181-2 as they stand in the MS of the Bibl. Nat. (nouv. acq., fonds franc. 1104) according to G. Paris, Rom. VIII 36. Roquefort reads "Que uns Yrois doucement note, Mout le sonne ens sa rote."

24. Bekker, vv. 861 ff., in Philol. u. hist. Abhandl. der Akad. der Wiss. zu Berlin, 1844. The whole episode of the magician is relegated to an appendix by Du Mèril as being spurious.

25. G. Paris, Ròm. VIII 33.

26. Fétis, Hist. gènèrale de la Musique, V 46-7.

27. The passages cited from the Lai de l'Espine and Floire and Bl., together with the Sept Sages ("et bien aues oi conter, Com Alpheus ala harper En infier por sa femme traire. Apolins fu si deboinaire K'il li rendi par tel conuent S'ele ne s'aloit regardant. Femme est tous iors plainne d'enuie, Regarda soi par mesproisie," vv. 27-34, p. 2 Keller), are commonly said (as by Zielke, p. 131) to prove the existence of a French poetical Orpheus in the twelfth century. Though I have no doubt of the conclusion, I do not think it follows from the premises. In the Sept Sages the writer seems to refer simply to the classical story, with a mischievous perversion by which the blame of the catastrophe is thrown on Eurydice. In the Espine the minstrel does not sing in French. In Fl. and Bl. the image does not sing at all. The tunes of the Breton lays were known all over France before the words came to be translated (cf. G. Paris, Rom. VII 1). To infer from these two places that a twelfth-century French Lai d'Orphèy existed, is to confuse the Breton original with a French translation.

28. There are two versions of the classical story in Old French, one, a fragment, pub. by Ritter in the Bulletin de la Soc. des Anc. Textes Franc. 1877, pp. 99 ff.; the other, part of the Confort d'ami of Guillaume de Machaut, as contained in the Bern MS, printed in part by Zielke, pp. 132-3. The episode is not contained in the Paris MS from which Tarbé published the Confort. The Bern MS is the same (No. 218) from which Sinner (Extraits de quelques Poësies du XII, XIII et XIV Siécle, 1759, p. 35) cites: "Le Poëte assure d'avoir trés souvent vû la chanson qu'Orphée recita devant Pluton. Cela est positif.

> Jai son lay maintesfois vû
> Et l'ai de chief en chief leu."

The lay of Orpheus here mentioned is simply his song in Hades, reported in full by Ovid, and not to be confounded with anything Armorican. On Guillaume de Machaut see Wolf, pp. 141, 168. He was an industrious writer of *lyrical* lays, and probably here used the word in that sense. These lyrical

poems have nothing to do with the narrative lays. A Descent of Orpheus to Hell is also found in a Geneva MS, and is perhaps identical with Guillaume's. See Wolf, Ueber die Lais, pp. 238-40; Du Méril, Floire et Blanceflor, Introd., p. clxxij, n. I; cf. Zielke, pp. 130-33.

29. Barbazon-Méon, III 96; Montaiglon and Raynaud, Recueil général des fabliaux, V 243. The title given is *Le Lai d'Aristote;* the colophon, *Explicit li lais d'A.,* but the word *lai,* or *Breton,* does not occur in the piece. The story is of Oriental origin; see Von der Hagen, Gesammtabenteuer, I 21-35 (Aristoteles und Fillis), and the Introduction, pp. lxxv ff., and compare Zingerle in Pfeiffer's Germania, XVII 306-9. That the poem has nothing to do with the lays of Brittany was remarked in 1814 by De la Rue, Recherches, p. 26. It occurs, to be sure, among the poems collected, under the general title of "Les lais de Breteigne," in the MS from which Gaston Paris published Lais inédits in Rom. VIII 29 ff., but this shows merely that the compiler of that collection could not distinguish a true lay from a false. The MS is not earlier than the end of the thirteenth century—later by more than a hundred years than the time when Marie began her work of translation. P. Meyer (Rom. I 192) notes that Henri d'Andeli, the author of the poem, calls his work a *ditié* (v. 38), and that the title *Lais* comes from MS 837 (old 7218), whereas the other MSS of the same version have simply *Explicit Aristotes.* Henri was canon of Rouen in 1207.

30. Barbazon-Méon, IV 326-54. Cf. Hist. Litt. XIX 765. The poem is a stupid working over of Ovid, M. v 10 ff. For a comparison, see Bartsch, Ovid im Mittelalter, pp. lx ff. Bartsch, who gives ample evidence of the popularity of the story in the Middle Ages, properly calls this piece a fabliau, but Paulin Paris speaks of the Lai de Pirame et Thisbé as a genuine Breton production in the same breath with Garin, Graelent, Ignaure, etc. (Les Romans de la Table Ronde, I 23). Wolf, p. 54, mentions a "Lai de la courtoise Thisbé."

31. Barbazon-Méon, IV 143-75. Cf. Bartsch, Ovid im Mittelalter, pp. lvii ff. The author has handled his orginal (Ov. M. iii 339-510) rather freely, and has touched on popular superstition (especially vv. 454, 650, 655). "Les Bretons prirent quelquefois leurs sujets dans la Mythologie, comme *le Lai de Narcisse,*" says De la Rue, Recherches, p. 28; but this poem is not a lay, even in its title, which is *De Narcisus.* Wolf conjectures that the piece, as we have it, is an adaptation of the Cantilena de Narcisso mentioned by Peter Cantor, Verbum Abbreviatum, cap. 27, in the first half of the twelfth century (Ueber die Lais, p. 51). Cf. Hist. Litt. XIX 761, where the matter is confused.

32. A. Joly, Benoit de Sainte-More et le Roman de Troie, 17.

33. Warnke, Die Lais der Marie de France, 1885, p. 41. The source of this very lay is by no means evident. R. Köhler (n. to Warnke, p. lxi) can cite only Die dri münche von Kolmære, V. d. Hagen, Gesammtabenteuer, No. 62, III 163, as in some respects parallel.

34. So, almost word for word, in the English Lay le Fresne, vv. 15 ff., as published by Varnhagen, Anglia, III 415.

35. See Wolf, Ueber die Lais, pp. 68, 217; Ten Brink, Gesch. der. engl. Litt., I 227. It will not do to be too positive, however, that the Havelok ever passed through Breton hands. The question is difficult and has never been adequately discussed. Madden, in his elaborate introduction, pp. v-vi, dismisses it with scant notice. Wright merely remarks that the term "Breton lay" had become almost proverbial, and adds that it is not at all likely that Havelok ever existed in a Breton version (Chron. de Geoffrey Gaimar, ed. for Caxton Soc., App., p. 3). As to the English Havelok, it cannot be directly derived from the French, though most scholars seem to think so. Storm, for instance, remarks (Englische Studien, III 533): "The English lay, on the whole, corresponds to the French; only some details and names are different." On the contrary, the two poems differ in almost every particular. The English version is about three times as long as the French, and ought not to be called a lay—as even Skeat has named it—but a *gest,* as it styles itself. Storm's suggestion that the Lay "is come to the Norman poet from the Welsh" deserves examination.

36. On the miscellaneous stock-in-trade of a Breton jongleur, see Paulin Paris, Rom. de la Table Ronde, I 15, though some of the classical traits he finds in the Arthurian romances may more probably be credited to Chrestien and his like than to the Celts. Ovid is mentioned once in Marie's Lais, Guigemer, 239.

37. Cf. Bartsch, Ov. im Mittelalter, pp. i, xi.

38. Wolf, Ueber die Lais, p. 10. G. Paris suggests (Rom. XII 362; cf. VIII 364) that the source of the lost Provencal romance from which were derived the biography of Guilhem de Cabestaing and Boccaccio's novel of Guardastagno (Dec. iv 9) was the Breton Lay of Guiron (Gurun, Gorhon, Goron). Cf. Wolf, pp. 236-8, as to this lay:

39. Wolf, pp. 238-9. Froumont's poem (not seen by me) is in Pezii Thesaur. Anecd. II i, 184. In the Carmina Burana (from a MS of the thirteenth century, and mentioning events from 1175 to 1208) we read of "Narcissus floriger, Orpheusque plectiger, Faunus quoque corniger," p. 117 (cited by Bartsch, p. civ).

40. Cited above, p. 183, n. 4: Hi similes sunt cantantibus fabulas et gesta, qui videntes cantilenam de Landrico non placere auditoribus, statim incipiunt de Narcisso cantare: quod si nec placuerit, cantant de alio (Fauriel, Hist. de la Poësie prov., III 489).

41. Wotton and Williams, Leges Walliae, p. 301; quoted by Fétis.

42. Walker, Irish Bards, I 180.

43. Michel, Tristan, II 106; Gottfried v. Strassburg, 8058-71. (Wolf, p. 53.)

44. Cf. Child, English and Scottish Popular Ballads, II 137.

45. Price, Literary Remains, I 133, 325-6.

46. This was Blegywyrd ab Seisyllt, 56th supreme king of Great Britain, according to E. Jones (Welsh Bards, 3d ed., 1808, I 1), who cites Tyssilio's Welsh Chron., etc.

47. The figure is playing, with a bow held in the left hand, on a three-stringed instrument. A copy is given by Bottée de Toulmon, Mémoires de la Soc. royale des Antiquaires, 2ᵉ Série, VII 154, and by Fétis, Hist. gén. de la Musique, IV 345.

48. For many examples of the power of the harp see Child, II 137. Add Kalevala, Schiefner's transl., Rune 41, pp. 240 ff. Professor Child mentions Orpheus, and notes that in the Scandinavian ballad Harpans Kraft (Grundtvig, II 65-8, etc.), "the harper is a bridegroom seeking (successfully) to recover his bride, who has been carried down to the depths of the water by a merman." It is not impossible that we have here another offshoot of the classic story, developed under Scandinavian, as the *Orfeo* under Celtic influence. The Shetland ballad given by Child (I 217) with the title *King Orfeo* is apparently from the English romance.

49. Tain Bo Fraich (The Cow-Spoil of Fraech), in the Book of Leinster, a MS of the twelfth century; O'Curry, Manners and Customs of the Anc. Irish, III 220; H. d'Arbois de Jubainville, Cours de Litt. celtique, I 58, Essai d'un Catalogue, pp. 217=18.

50. Cath Maige Tured na Fomorach (Battle of Mag Tured against the Fomorians), in O'Curry, Manners and Customs, III 214. Cf. Arbois de Jubainville, Cours, II 191; Essai d'un Catalogue, pp. 80-1.

51. See Child; II 137; cf. Price, Lit. Remains, I 151-2.

52. Lay de Tyolet, vv. 42-8, published by G. Paris, Rom. VIII 67.

53. Michel, Tristan, II 126; Sir Tristrem, ii 63-6 Scott, 165-8, II 50-1 Kölbing; Tristrams Saga og Ìsondar, 49-50, I 61 Kölbing, pp. 105-6 Brynjùlfson; Gottfried v. Strassburg, 13,108 ff., II 99 ff. Bechstein. The details, of course, differ somewhat.

54. Cf. Met. × 72 ff.

55. In the Latin poetical Vita Merlini (formerly ascribed to Geoffrey of Monmouth), vv. 73 ff. Cf. the Welsh poem Avallenau (The Apple Trees), st. 15 (18). Both these are printed by A. Schulz, Die Sagen von Merlin, pp. 275, 75; the latter also by Stephens, Literature of the Kymry, 2d ed., pp. 212-22. Cf. Girald. Cambr., Descriptio Kambriae, ii 8, Opera, ed. Dimock, V 133, cited by Schulz.

56. Ex quibus Britones frequenter excusserunt equos et animalia, et eis usi sunt, quidam sibi ad mortem, quidam indemniter (Walter Mapes, De Nugis Curialium, iv 13, p. 180 Wright). It does not appear that the knights seen by Orfeo had any booty with them; perhaps he did not see them on their return!

57. As in the Serglige Conculainn, A. de Jubainville, Cours, II 354-5; cf. p. 361. Compare the procession of fairy knights in the ballad of Tam Lin (Child, No. 29, A 27, 29, 41; B 25, 27, 39; I 342 ff.).

58. vv. 76 ff., Monmerquè and Michel, Lai d'Ignaurès, etc., p. 74. As to the fondness of fairies for white horses, cf. Child, I 339.

59. Child, I 340, who adds: "Special trees are considered in Greece dangerous to lie under in summer and at noon, as exposing one to be taken by the nereids or fairies . . . Schmidt, Volksleben der Neugriechen, p. 119." Is not this connected with the belief in a δαιμσνισν μεσημβρινσν (LXX Psalm. xci 6), as to which see Rochholz, Deutscher Unsterblichkeits-glaube, pp. 62 ff., 67 ff., and cf. Lobeck, Aglaoph., pp. 1092-3.

60. Child, No. 39, G 26; I 350. In D 14 Tomlin falls asleep by a fairy-hill. In the Percy MS version of Launfal (Sir Lambwell, 55-65, Hales and Furnivall; cf. Malone fragment, vv. 43 ff.) the hero goes to sleep under a tree, and on waking sees two fairy maidens approaching. In Thomas Chestre's Launfal he is sitting under a tree, not asleep (vv. 226-7). In Marie's Lai de Lanval there is neither tree nor nap (vv. 45-55).

61. Pub. by G. Paris, Rom. VIII 67.

62. Molt durement m'apesanti, v. 375.

63. He abandons the queen when their amour is discovered, not for fear of an *éclaircissement*—for the witness dies at once—but in accordance with his fairy nature, which cannot bear that his union with a mortal should be known. Compare the conduct of Lanval's mistress, of Graelent's (in the Lai de Graelent, 503 ff.; Roquefort, Poésies de Marie de France, I 522), of Lionbruno's in the Italian tale (Crane's Ital. Pop. Tales, p. 141).

64. This song is translated (1) by O'Curry, Manners and Customs, II 192-3; (2) more literally, by Sullivan, Id., III 191 n.; (3) by A. de Jubainville, Cours, II 317-18. I have followed O'Curry in inserting it here. De Jubainville is not clear on this point. Apparently he makes Midir sing the song on one of his clandestine visits to Etain. He remarks that the poem does not belong to the story. This is very probably true; but it was part of the story in 1100 (the approximate date of the Book of the Dun Cow) or earlier, and for our present purpose we need not go farther back than that.

65. Swans, whether they properly belong to this story or not, are not unknown in Breton lays. In the Lay de Doon, v. 140 (Rom. VIII 62), the knight is required to ride as fast as a swan can fly. In Marie's Lai de Milun the hero and his love, in South Wales, send letters to and fro by a tame swan for twenty years.

66. In this story I have generally followed the analysis of A. de Jubainville (Cours, II 312-22), which is fuller and probably more trustworthy than that of O'Curry (Manners and Customs, II 192-4). In some cases, however, where O'Curry is evidently following copy closely, I have preferred his version, noting, however, any essential variation from De Jubainville. The Irish text has been edited from the Leabhar na hUidhre by Windisch, Irische Texte, pp. 117-30, but this book has been beyond my reach in more senses than one. See further Ed. Müller, Revue Celtique, III 350 ff.; O'Grady, Hist. of Ireland, I 88-93. The Leabhar na hUidhre version is fragmentary and lacks the account of the recovery of Etain. The chess-scene is translated by O'Donovan, Book of Rights, Introd., pp. lxi-lxii.

67. Zielke (p. 137) thinks this may be a reminiscence of the condition of not looking back imposed on Orpheus in Ov. M. x 51; Virg. Georg. iv 487-91. If there is anything more than meets the view in this passage of the romance, I should rather compare the widespread superstition that it is dangerous to speak to witches, ghosts, and fairies. "They are fairies; he that speaks to them shall die" (Merry Wives, v 5). Cf. Child, I 322, to whose citations may be added Waldron, Isle of Man, Manx Soc. ed., p. 67.

68. The passage describing the stolen mortals seen by Orfeo in fairyland (vv. 385-406) is very remarkable. Zielke (p. 137) sees classic elements in it, and perhaps he is right. All sorts of fairies—Celtic and other—are prone to carry away people.

69. "Bedb was a fairy potentate who, with his daughters, lived under Sidh-ar-Femhin, a hill or fairy mansion on the plain of Cashel. To this subterranean residence a famous old harper named Cliach is said to have obtained access by playing his harp near the spot until the ground opened and admitted him into the fairy realm" (O'Hanlon, Irish Folk-Lore, Gentleman's Magazine, 1865, Pt. II; Gentl. Mag. Library, ed. Gomme, IV (Eng. Tradit. Lore) 22). Orfeo recognizes his wife "by her clothes" (v. 406). The modern Irish "fairy doctress" is said by O'Hanlon (p. 13) to tell some token or peculiarity of dress by which the rescuer may distinguish his lost friend amidst the fairy troop as it sweeps past on Hallowe'en.

70. See R. Köhler's n. in Warnke's ed. of Marie's Lais, p. lxxxiii, n.

71. Cf. Brun de la Montaigne, 562-7, ed. P. Meyer, p. 20, and Préface, p. xii.

72. Girald. Cambr., Itin. Kambriae, i 8, Opera, ed. Dimock, VI 75, cited by Wright, St. Patrick's Purgatory, p. 83. Cf. Peter Roberts, Cambrian Pop. Antiquities, 1815, pp. 195-201.

73. Gault. Mapes, De Nugis Curial. i II, p. 16 Wright. In this case, as in the story of Elidurus, the fairies are called pygmaei.

74. Welsh *ogof*, a cavern, Burne and Jackson, Shropshire Folk-Lore, 1883, p. 57.

75. Wirt Sikes, British Goblins, p. 99.

76. Gerv. Tilb., Otia Imperialia, p. 975 (iii 45, p. 24 Liebrecht, whose n., pp. 117 ff., should be compared), cited by Sir Walter Scott, On the Fairies of Popular Superstition.

77. Guil. Neubrig., Rer. Angl. i 27, ed. Hearne, I 90-93; Radulph. de Coggeshale, Chron. Angl., ed. Stephenson, pp. 118-20. The accounts differ slightly. Ralph does not mention St. Martin. I owe the references to Wright, St. Patrick's Purgatory, p. 84. The date is some time in the reign of Henry II.

78. Sts. 30-31, Murray, p. 10, vv. 169-73.

79. Child, No. 39, A 23, I 342. Cf. Gentleman's Magazine, 1832, Pt. 2, p. 223; Gentleman's Mag. Library, ed. Gomme, IV 52: "In Scotland the fairies dwell under the little green hills."

80. See particularly E. Beauvois, Rev. de l'Hist. des Réligions, VII (1883) 288 ff. Cf. Joyce, Old Celtic Romances, pp. 405, 410; Kuno Meyer, Cath Finntrága, Oxf., 1885, Introd., p. xiii.

81. A. de Jubainville, Cours, II 140 ff.; O'Curry, MS Materials, pp. 504-5; Joyce, pp. 401-2; Kuno Meyer, p. xi.

82. Meyer, pp. xii-xiii.

83. Echtra Condla Chaim in the Leabhar na h Uidhre. Windisch, Rev. Celtique, V 389-90; A. de Jubainville, Cours, II 192-3; Joyce, Old Celtic Romances, pp. 106-11; Beauvois, Revue de l'Hist. des Réligions, VII (1883) 288-90. De Jubainville regards this fairy maiden as the Celtic death-messenger. His brochure, Le Dieu de la Mort, Troyes, 1879, I have not seen. Beauvois (p. 290, n. I) declares that "cette opinion n'est cinfirmée ni par la présente légende ni par les suivantes." Whatever she was originally, to the Irish of the eleventh and twelfth centuries she was merely, as Windisch calls her, a fée.

84. De Jubainville, Revue Archéol., 1878, I 390-91; Cours, II 143-4.

85. Beauvois, Rev. de l'Hist. des Réligions, VII 291.

86. Serglige Conculainn in the Leabhar na hUidhre. Original in Windisch's Irische Texte, pp. 205-27. I have used the translation given by Gilbert, Facsimiles of the National MSS of Ireland, Pt. II (1878), Appendix IV F. Two parallels may be noted—first, the bright raiment, cf. *Sir Orfeo*, vv. 413-14; second, the means of light, cf. with *Sir Orfeo*. vv. 367-70, the words of the Irish piece: "The noble candle which is there is the brilliant precious stone." Not much emphasis can be laid on this, however. Carbuncles are a commonplace in mediaeval literature. See Bartsch, Herzog Ernst, pp. clxi ff.

87. In favor of this might be cited the Welsh fairyland, Annwn, with its king Arawn, the description of whose castle, and wife, and courtiers, in the tale of Pwyll, Prince of Dyved (Mabinogion, tr. by Lady Charlotte Guest, Pt. V, pp. 41-2), is not unlike the similar place in *Orfeo*. Gwyn ap Nudd is also called lord of Annwn and of the Tylwyth Teg, who are fairies of human size, as well as of the elves. See the tale of Kilhwch and Olwen (Mabinogion, IV 259, 305, and cf. Lady Guest's n., pp. 323-6). But both these Mabinogion are thought to be full of Irish elements (Sullivan, Celtic Lit., Encycl. Brit., 9th ed., V 321-2). Cf., as to Gwyn and his subjects, Keightley, Fairy Mythol., II 196 ff., Price, Lit. Remains, I 146-7, 285-7; Stephens, Lit. of the Kymry, pp. 183 ff. It should be noted that Gwyn is said to have stolen Creiddylad (Cordelia), the daughter of Lludd Llaw Ereint (Lear), from her betrothed husband Gwythyr; but Arthur restored the maiden to her father, stipulat-

ing that the two suitors "should fight for her every first of May, from thenceforth until the day of doom" (Mabinog. IV 305). Here may be mentioned the romance or ballad of Burd Ellen, an outline of which Jamieson (Illustrations of Northern Antiquities, pp. 398-403) gives from his recollection of the shape in which it was told him in his youth by a country tailor. The story has several correspondences with *Sir Orfeo*. Warluck Merlin appears in it as advising Child Rowland.

88. Note the importance of Ireland in Arthurian romance. Compare, too, the Lai de Melion (Monmerqué and Michel, Lai d'Ignaurés, etc., pp. 43-67), in which the scene is partly laid in Ireland, though Marie's Bisclavret, of which Melion is a variant, is intensely Breton. The werewolf superstition is still alive in Brittany. See Baring-Gould, Book of Werewolves, Ch. I.

89. Sullivan, Celtic Literature, Encycl. Britannica, 9th ed., V 321-2.

90. Caradoc's Chron., in the Myvyrian Archaiology, II 574, as quoted by Stephens, Lit. of the Kymry, pp. 324-5.

91. Powell (Hist. of Cambria, ed. 1584, p. 191, not seen by me) says they "devised in a manner all the instrumental music that is now there used" (Walker, Irish Bards, 2d ed., I 143); but Thomas Stephens, who discusses the subject at some length (Lit. of the Kymry, 2d ed., pp. 56-65), is inclined to think that the chief innovation was the use of the bagpipes.

92. Stephens, Lit. of the Kymry, p. 322, quoting Iolo MSS, p. 630.

93. Cornubia vero, et Armorica Britannia lingua utuntur fere persimili, Kambris tamen, propter originalem conventiam, in multis adhuc et fere cunctis intelligibili (Girald. Cambr., Itin. Kambriae, i 6, Dimock, VI 177). It is often asserted now-a-days that a Welshman can make himself understood in Brittany, but this Price denies (Literary Remains, I 35, 108).

94. An Irish king in the sixth century is said to have sent a joculator to the Welsh court for political purposes. The minstrel delighted the king and nobles by his harping and singing (D'Alton, Social and Polit. State of People of Ireland, Trans. R. I. A. XVI (1830) 225). Ethodius of Scotland, cum, de more procerum Scotorum, fidicinem ex Hibernia in cubiculo suo pernoctantem haberet, ab eo noctu occisus fuit (Buchanan, Rer. Scotic. Hist. IV 25, cited by Walker, I 98). The passage may be found in Ruddiman's ed., 1725, I 118. On the popularity of these harpers in later times, see D'Alton, pp. 162, 225, 226, 338-9; Walker, I 177.

95. Top. Hib. iii 11, Dimock, V 153. Cited by Sir James Ware, Antiq. of Ireland, p. 184 (in Vol. I of his Whole Works Concerning Ireland, translated by Walter Harris, Dublin, 1764).

96. Sullivan, Introd. to O'Curry, Manners and Customs, I dxix.

97. As this passage has been oftener cited than seen, I may be pardoned for giving it at some length: "Fra

gli strumenti adunque di corde che sono hoggi in vso in Italia, ci è primamente l'Harpa, la quale non è altro che vn' antica Cithara di molte corde; se bene di forma in alcuna cosa differente . . . Fu portata d'Irlanda à noi questo antichissimo strumento (commemorato da Dante) doue si lauorano in excellenza & copiosamēte: gli habitatori della quale isola si esercitano molti & molti secoli sono in esse, oltre all' essere impresa particolare del regno; la quale dispingano & sculpiscono negli edifizij pubblici & nelle monete loro" (Dialogo di Vincentio Galilei Nobile Fiorentino della Musica Antica, et della Moderna. In Fiorenza, MDLXXXI, p. 143). The author then describes the Irish harp. In spite of the plain meaning of Vincentio, both D'Alton (Social and Polit. State of People of Ireland, Royal Irish Acad. Trans. XVI (1830) 339), and Sullivan (Introd. to O'Curry's Manners and Customs, I dxix) quote him as authority for the statement that Dante says the harp was introduced into Italy from Ireland. The mistranslation appears to be due to E. Jones (Mus. and Poet. Relicks of the Welsh Bards, 3d ed., 1808, I 95). Of course the passage means simply that Dante has mentioned the harp (Paradiso xiv 118).

98. Sullivan, p. dxx, who cites "Doni, Lyra barberina, etc., Flor., 1763, I 20," which I have not seen.

99. Published by G. Paris, Rom. VIII 51 ff. Compare with this lay, besides the citations of the editor, the ancient Irish tale of Loegaire (A. de Jubainville, Cours, II 356 ff.); the seventeenth-century Oisín in Tirnanoge (Joyce, Old Celtic Romances, pp. 395-9; Windisch, Verhandlungen der 33sten. Versammlg. deutscher Philologen, p. 26), and the story of the ancient British king Herla (Mapes, De Nugis Curial. i II, pp. 14-17 Wright). The resemblance consists in the disastrous effect of eating earthly food or touching the ground on returning to this earth from fairyland. De Jubainville (II 363) compares the fate of Crimthann, but the similarity is doubtful.

100. The Latin Life of St. Brandan is perhaps as old as the ninth century. See, on the whole matter, A. Graf, La Leggenda del Paradiso Terrestre, pp. 33-6, 90 ff.; E. Beauvois, L'Éden occidental, Revue de l'Hist. des Réligions, VII (1883) 693, n. 4. As to the alleged Breton lay, the evidence of Reynard is not altogether conclusive, though it is accepted by Wolf, p. 59, and by Schröder, Sanct Brandan, Introd., p. vi. Basse-Bretagne had its own adventurous voyagers, the monks of Saint-Mathieu (Beauvois, pp. 680-84).

Lucian Foulet (essay date 1906)

SOURCE: "The Prologue of *Sir Orfeo*," *Modern Language Notes*, Vol. XXI, No. 2, February, 1906, pp. 46-50.

[*In the following essay, Foulet examines the prologue to* Sir Orfeo, *suggests its probable origin, and attempts to explain inconsistencies in the use of the word "lay" and "adventure."*]

Sir Orfeo,[1] one of the most charming among the middle English romances, has received a good deal of attention at the hands of scholars: it has been conclusively shown that it is a translation from a now lost French original, and its points of contact with varied Celtic legends have been made the subject of careful study.[2] Its opening lines, however, which do not constitute a part of the tale itself, have been generally left out of account, except in so far as their probable source has been—with every reason—sought in the lais of Marie de France.[3] Their purpose is to give us an account of the origin of the so-called Breton lays. It may repay us to examine them a little more closely.

In the first place, are we right in ascribing them to *Sir Orfeo*? As far as I know, this point is still undecided. These lines are found in only two out of three manuscripts, in which *Sir Orfeo* has come down to us, and, on the other hand, they are almost identical with the beginning of the *Lay le Freine*[4] (which is, as is well known, a translation of one of Marie's Lais). To which of the two poems did they originally belong? The evidence of the manuscripts is quite inconclusive, as the Auchinleck manuscript in which these lines are wanting, is by no means in a perfect state of preservation.[5] The question must be settled otherwise. An examination of the contents of these opening verses soon points to the fact that *Sir Orfeo* is the poem where they belong by right. Let us suppose, for argument's sake, that they were written by the author of the *Lay le Freine*. How did he happen upon them? Clearly he could not have taken them from his original, where the tale is preceded only by two verses of rather vague import.[6] On the other hand, the information they give us was borrowed—as was long ago shown by Zupitza—from the prologues or conclusions of several of Marie's lays. How are we to understand this? Did Zupitza mean that the English poet got his hints himself out of Marie? In that case, we should picture him to ourselves as a presumably faithful translator in the tale proper but as a somewhat laborious compiler in the introduction to the tale. The supposition is of course possible, but not very probable. Or are we not rather to admit that the work of compilation, such as it was, was done by a French poet and that the author of *Sir Orfeo* translated his preface as well as his tale? We must take into account that the prologue of *Sir Orfeo*—by the nature and the extent of the information it gives—stands alone[7] in middle English literature. But French literature of the thirteenth century provides us with quite a number of parallels. It is enough here to mention the prologues of *Doon, Tydorel,* and the whole *lai du Lecheor*. It is therefore most likely that their English counterpart at the beginning of *Sir Orfeo* was itself a pretty literal translation from the French; as Marie's *Le Fraisne* contains nothing of the sort, it must have opened the French *lai d' Orphée*. It must be noted that the closing lines of *Sir Orfeo*—presumably translated from the French like the rest—are quite in keeping with the prologue.[8]

Provided with that introduction which we are thus led to assign to it, the French *lai d' Orphée* appears in a rather new light. It reveals itself to us at once as one of the younger lais, belonging to the second or the third generation.[9] It was of course only after Marie's work was done

IV.

Romance of King Orfeo.

———o———

THIS beautiful fairy romance-poem is founded on the classical tale of Orpheus and Eurydice, but metamorphosed in a manner that would lead us to believe that the compiler had either a very imperfect knowledge of his original, or that the variations were intentional. In the latter case, it is clear that much ingenuity and taste have been displayed; and even if the other supposition be correct, the metamorphosis of hell into fairyland cannot but be an inprovement. Three copies of this romance, which has been conjectured with much probability to be a translation from the French, are known to exist; one in MS. Harl. 3810, printed by Ritson, another in the Auchinleck MS., printed by Mr Laing, and a third in MS. Ashmole 61, lf. 151, the text we have here selected. According to the Auchinleck and Harleian MSS., Orpheo's father " was comen of King Pluto," and Chaucer speaks of Pluto and Proserpina as the king and queen of Faëry. The Edinburgh MS. reads Juno for Proserpina, but the variation is immaterial. The circumstance, however, seems to add one more proof to those adduced by Mr Wright, of the interchange between legends and popular fictions. The " Traitie of Orpheus kyng," by Robert Henryson, printed at Edinburgh in 1508, and re-

ROMANCE OF KING ORFEO. 83

printed in 1827, merely relates to the classical story, and it will be enough for us to refer to the extracts given by Mr Laing in his " Select Remains of the Ancient Popular Poetry of Scotland," 4to. Edinb. 1822. The Ashmolean MS. is a far better version than that printed by Ritson, and, although it agrees rather closely with the copy in the Auchinleck MS., it is more complete at the commencement, and in many respects superior to it, the MS. itself, however, being not more ancient than the time of Henry VI.

KING ORFEW,

MERY tyme is in Aperelle,[1]
That mekyll schewys of manys wylle;
In feldys and medewys flow[r]ys spryng,
In grovys and wodes foules syng:
Than wex ʒong men jolyffe,
And than prevyth man and wyffe.
The Brytans, as the boke seys,
Off diverse thinges thei made ther leys;
Som thei made of herpynges,
And some of other diverse thinges;
Some of werre and some off wo,
Some of myrthys and joy also
Some of trechery and some off gyle,
Some of happys that felle some whyle,
And some be of rybawdry,
And many ther bene off fary:
Off all the venturys men here ore se,
Most off luffe fore-soth thei be,
That in the leys ben i-wrouʒht.
Fyrst fond and forth brouʒht.

[1] The introductory portion is not found in the Auchinleck MS., but it is given in Ritson's version, with some variation.

A page from Sir Orfeo, *from Joseph Ritson's* Fairy Tales, Legends, and Romances Illustrating Shakespeare, *1875.*

that later poets could turn to her for information; and we shall see a little further on that it was not even till the collection of the French lays, such as we know it, was nearly complete that the prologue of *Orphée* could have been written. It was then composed at a time when there was a good deal of talk about, but very little knowledge of, the old Bretons; most of the writers of lais confined themselves to rehandling themes already treated by Marie.[10] Between an introduction and a conclusion closely modeled on her prologues and epilogues, clever but unimaginative *jongleurs* would insert a story that sometimes was also taken from Marie, sometimes borrowed from quite a different source. So in *Doon* a tale of Eastern origin was fused with a legend which on examination proves to be nothing else but that of *Milun;* the result of that most artificial fusion was called by its proud author a lai. The author of *Havelock* took bodily out of Gaimar's chronicle a rather lengthy passage narrating a fine old legend; he slightly modified it, and, adorning it with a prologue and a conclusion in the style and at times the phraseology of Marie, he forthwith launched into the world, at the beginning of the thirteenth century, a new Breton lai, as genuine as many others of the same time. Just in the same manner, we may suppose,

the author of *Orphée* rehandled a Classic myth and worked it over into a lai. But for ingenuity and knowledge of the technique of his trade, he was certainly far above the usual run of the thirteenth century lay-writers; his adaptation is so clever that, had he not retained the Classical names, it might have been difficult to prove his acquaintance with the Classic tale.[11] There is little doubt that the adaptation was his own work; he wrote at too late a day for us to be able to assume that he drew on a Breton original. Was he nevertheless influenced, in his work of rehandling, by Celtic legends more or less similar to the Classic myth, which were known to him in a French form now lost?[12] Or did he simply turn for the colouring and the new matter he wanted to the Arthurian romances or the *romans d'aventure* of his own time, and thus apply to the tale itself very much the same method as to the introduction?[13] I feel rather inclined to adopt the second solution, but in the absence of quite conclusive evidence one way or the other, it is perhaps wiser to leave the question undecided.

In returning to the Prologue, we tread upon safer ground, for in this case we have both the copy (in its English translation) and the original (Marie). Let us not look here for genuine and accurate information on the Breton Lais; in the thirteenth century the Bretons had for a long time ceased to be very distinct figures, and the memory of them grew every day dimmer. In so far as they were represented as makers of Lays, that memory was mainly kept up by a literary tradition which went back to Marie; the chief interest of the introductions to the thirteenth century Lays lies in that they allow us to form an idea as to how that tradition developed or in other terms how readers of that time understood Marie and the somewhat obscure indications of her prologues. The text of our prologue is rather uncertain; the three manuscripts, H, O and F[14] have different readings for almost every line, and although the variations are mostly very slight they are not always so. For ll. 1-4 it is obvious that H and F present the best reading; O modified rather clumsily the original text, without, it is true, greatly altering the meaning. Ll. 5-12: here the three manuscripts are in almost complete agreement. In the following lines, variations are more significant; let us, for instance, compare H and F:

	H.		*F.*
13	In Brytain þis layes arne ywryte,	13	In Breteyne bi hold time
	Furst yfounde and forþe ygete,		This layes were wrought, so seith this rime.
	Of aventures þat fillen by dayes		When kinges might our yhere
	Wherof Brytouns made her layes,		Of ani mervailes that ther were,
17	When þey myght owher heryn	17	Thai token an harp in gle and game,
	Of aventures þet þer weryn,		And maked a lay and gaf it name.
	Þey toke her harpys wiþ game,		
	Maden layes and af it name.		

Which of the two gives the best reading? To be sure, one might contend that although the two texts are somewhat different the meaning is substantially the same. It is possible that by the lays which are 'written' in Brittany, H simply means the songs that were composed on the occasion of the 'adventures' and to which another reference is made and—awkwardly enough—a third one in lines 19 and 20. In that case then, there would seem to be almost a contradiction between lines 13-14 and lines 19-20. The process of composition denoted by lines 19-20 hardly implies a writing down of the songs, in fact, seems to exclude the idea of it. But it is far more likely that the scribe of H got here a little confused; having in his mind the tale of Orfeo which he was making ready to copy he imagined—in a probably obscure and rather unconscious manner—the Breton lays to be at once and at the same time, songs sung to the harp and narrative poems written for the enjoyment of a reading public. But was this the idea of the English author of our prologue? That does not seem probable in this passage at least. He does not say that he is go-

ing to tell us a lay, but only to relate one of those 'adventures' in memory of which the Bretons used to make lays.

> Of aventures, þat han befalle,
> Y can sum telle, but nought all.
> Herken, lordyngs, þat ben trewe,
> And y wol ou telle of Sir Orphewe.

Cf. F:

> Now of this aventours that weren yfalle
> Y can tel sum, ac nought alle.
>
> (11. 18-20).[15]

In the same manner, while in the closing verses of the romance, he mentions a lay, he by no means says that that Breton lai—a musical piece made to be sung to a tune—is identical with the story he has just told us; in fact, his words imply the reverse.

> Harpours in Bretaine afterþan
> Herd, hou þis mervaile bigan,
> And made herof a lay of gode likeing
> And nempned it after þe king:
> Þat lay Orfeo is yhote,
> Gode is þe lay, swete is þe note.[16]

The author of **Sir Orfeo** makes here the same careful distinction between the tale ('conte' or 'aventure') and the Breton lai that Marie had made in *Guigemar*[17] and others of her lays (although not in all of them). For the passage under discussion the text of F seems therefore to give the best reading.[18]

We are now in a better position to notice and discuss another confusion for which this time the scribes are not responsible, for it must have taken place already in the French original.[19] The author of *Orphée* had certainly distinguished between the 'adventure' and the 'lai': this distinction, together with sundry information on the old Bretons, he had of course borrowed from Marie. The consequence is that, wherever in his prologue we catch, as it were, an echo of Marie, we notice that 'lay' means *song* and nothing else (II. 1-4: H, O, F; II. 13-20 F, cf. II. 15-24 H).[20] But in II. 5-12 (substantially the same in the three manuscripts), which do not come from the *Lais*, we meet with a rather different conception. Here the author wanted to give his readers an idea of the subjects which the harpers of old sang in their lays; no easy task, we may believe, for a man of the thirteenth century; one had scarcely then an opportunity to listen to a genuine Breton lay. The best way out of the difficulty was perhaps to turn for information to the rather numerous so-called (French) lays which claimed to tell, with more or less fidelity, the adventures out of which the Bretons had made their lays. And there can be little doubt that in lines 5-12 our author refers us, not to the original Breton lays, but to the works of Marie, Renaut and to the anonymous lays:

> Sum ben of wele und sum of wo,
> And sum of joy and merþe also,

Sum of trechery and sum of gyle,
And sum of happes, þat fallen by whyle,
Sum of bourdys and sum of rybaudry,
And sum þer ben of þe feyre.
Off alle þing þat men may se,
Moost o lowe forsoþe þey be.

To be sure, one cannot sum up in more felicitous terms the contents of the *French* lays.[21] But it is obvious that we are getting rather far from the Bretons; nobody at the time of Marie would have dreamed of ascribing to them songs of 'bourdys' and 'rybaudry'; surely the poetess would have denied the charge most indignantly. We must wait many years before we can find in the authors of *Ignaure, Lecheor* and *Nabaret* men ready to agree on this point with our ingenious *trouvère*. Of course, by thus going for his examples of Breton lays to collections of French tales, he ran the risk of mixing up quite different things; he was almost inevitably led to assign to the latter a name which by right belonged only to the former:

Þe layes þat ben of harpyng
Ben yfounde of frely thing.
Sum ben of wele and sum of wo . . .
Sum of bourdys and sum of rybaudry.

It must be said at once, that this confusion is not peculiar to our author; it was made in his own time by more than one lay-writer. As a matter of fact, it can be traced back to Marie herself. While in the oldest of her tales, *Guigemar,* and in some others, she kept carefully apart the two notions of 'tale' written for readers and 'lai' sung to a tune, there is no doubt but that in several others she inclined to call her own tale a *lai* as well as the real or pretended original Breton song. Contradictions and hesitations such as these rather puzzled her imitators in the following age. Some consistently maintained the distinction between 'tale' and 'lay' to the end; others, more or less consciously or willingly, failed to perceive or keep up that distinction, and thereby contributed to assign to the word 'lai,' the only sense of which, up to Marie's time, had been song, a new meaning, that of short narrative poem on a subject connected with the 'matière de Bretagne.'[22] The lost *lai d' Orphée,* we may now conclude, had certainly its share in that most curious development, and in any study of the evolution of the lai (the word and the thing) must be mentioned and discussed by the side of *Doon, Lecheor* and *Tyolet.* English literature, too, as we know, welcomed, for a time, that novel use of an old word, and it is not absurd to suppose that the English translation of *Orphée,* our **Sir Orfeo,** had a good deal to do with that departure from tradition.

Notes

1. *Sir Orfeo,* ein englisches Feenmärchen aus dem Mittelalter, hgg. von Dr. Oscar Zielke, Breslau, 1880.

2. See especially Kittredge, *Am. Journ. of Philology,* VII, 176 ff.

3. Zupitza, *Engl. Stud.,* X, p. 42.

4. Published by Varnhagen, *Anglia,* III, 415 ff.

5. Cf. Kittredge, p. 176, n. 2, and Zielke, p. 22.

6. Le lai del Fraisne vus dirai | sulune le cunte que jeo sai.

7. With the exception of the *Franklin's Tale.* But it is not absurd to suppose that Chaucer had the opening lines of *Sir Orfeo* in mind when he wrote his own prologue to the *Franklin's Tale.* I hope to come back to this point in a subsequent paper.

8. Ll. 595-600: "Harpours in Bretaine afterþan | Herd, hou þis mervaile bigan, | And made herof a lay of gode likeing | And nempned it after þe king: þat lay Orfeo is yhote, | Gode is þe lay, swete is þe note." Cf. *Guigemar,* 883-886; *Graelent,* 3-4. Cf. G. Paris, *Hist. Litt. de la France,* XXIX, 500-501.

9. I agree with Prof. Kittredge (see pp. 180-182) that the passages often cited from the *Lai de l' Espine* (ll. 180-185) and *Floire et Blanceflor* (ed. Du Méril, p. 231), have nothing to do with the French original of *Sir Orfeo,* although I cannot think that they refer us to a genuine Breton lay.

10. For all that concerns the so-called anonymous Lais and their attitude towards Marie, see *Zts. f. rom. Phil.,* XXIX, 19 ff.

11. Cp. Zielke, p. 4.

12. Prof. Kittredge admits the existence of a Breton lay which the French translator probably rendered without much change. But his main thesis—namely, that we have to do here with an adaptation of the Ovidian story to Celtic beliefs and traditions—is not absolutely bound up, it seems to me, with the assertion that there ever existed such a lay. Even Marie, in my opinion, can hardly be shown to have had access to 'Breton lays.' And yet some of her stories which she got from French written sources or by word of mouth from French *jongleurs,* undoubtedly go back to Celtic traditions. The case might be the same with the author of *Orphée.*

13. Cf. Zielke, *Sir Orfeo,* p. 137: Vieles von dem beiwerke, mit dem der dichter seine romanze geschmückt hat, kehrt in der weltliteratur jener zeit wieder. So erinnert uns die scene der thronentsagung an Guillaume d' Angleterre: das traurige Leben, welches Orfeo im walde führt, an Iwein und Parthenopeus; die ausstattung des feenschlosses an Beves und Flandrijs; die aufforderung des feenkönigs an Orfeo, sich den lohn für seine kunst selbst zu bestimmen, an Tristan, [Cf. Kittredge, p. 188]; das wechseln der kleider an Horn, William of Palerne und Beves.

14. H (Harleian MS.), O (Bodleian MS.), F (Lay le Freine preserved only in the Auchinleck MS.). The Auchinleck MS. of *Sir Orfeo* lacks the introduction. Cf. Zielke, 22 ff., and Varnhagen, *Anglia,* III, 415.

15. The next two lines in F: "Ac herkneth lordinges sothe to sain | Ichil you telle Lay le Frain" are obviously a translation of the opening lines of Marie's lai: "Le lai del Fraisne vus dirai | sulunc le cunte que jeo sai."

16. These lines are lacking in H, but are found both in A and O. Cf. Kittredge, p. 177, n. 2.

17. *Guigemar,* ll. 19-21: Les *contes* que jo sai verais, | dunt li Bretun unt fait les *lais,* | vos conterai assez briefment. Cf. ll. 883-884: De cest *cunte* qu'oï avez | fu Guigemar li *lais* trovez.

18. An examination of the first lines of O for this passage confirms our interpretation. But towards the end of it the scribe falls into the same blunder as the copyist of H: þat in þe leys ben *iwrouht* | Fyrst fond and forþe *brouht* | of aventours þer fell some deys | þe Bretonys þerof made þer leys | Off kynges þat before us were, | When þey myt any woundres here | þey lete þem *wryte* as it were do, | And þer among is sir Orfewo (ll. 13-20). The end is obviously shortened.

19. At the same time it sufficiently accounts for the blunder of the scribe of H.

20. See the passages of Marie made use of by the author of *Orphée* in the article of Zupitza already quoted.

21. It is, therefore, quite fitting that W. Hertz should have opened his collection of lays in his *Spielmanns Buch* by a rendering of *Sir Orfeo.* But whether our prologue was actually meant by its author to be the introduction to a large collection of lays, as Mr. Brugger suggests in *Zts. f. fr. Spr. u. Litt.,* XX, 154, n. 103, is doubtful.

22. On this point, see *Zts. f. rom. Phil.,* XXIX, 299 ff.

Gabrielle Guillaume (essay date 1921)

SOURCE: "The Prologues of the *Lay le Freine* and *Sir Orfeo,*" *Modern Language Notes,* Vol. XXXVI, No. 8, December, 1921, pp. 458-64.

[*In the following essay, Guillaume explains why she doubts Lucien Foulet's assertions (see excerpt above) concerning the prologue to* Sir Orfeo, *and advances her own: the prologue was written not by a French, but by an English author; the prologue's author also wrote the* Lay le Freine; *and the prologue was borrowed by* Sir Orfeo's *author.*]

The only known copy of the Middle-English Breton *Lay le Freine,* preserved in the famous Auchinleck Manuscript, has a prologue which differs but slightly from the prologue prefixed to two of the three extant copies of the Middle-English Breton Lay, *Sir Orfeo.*[1] It is still an open question whether the Prologue originally belonged to the *Lay le Freine* or to *Sir Orfeo.* Lucien Foulet,[2] the only scholar who has examined the question in detail, held that the verses belonged to the French original of *Sir Orfeo,* and were borrowed for the *Lay le Freine.* His argument can be summed up as follows. A portion of the Prologue (vv. 13-18), as Zupitza[3] showed, is made up of phrases taken here and there from the epilogues and prologues of Marie de France's different lays. The *Lay le Freine,* on the other hand, is a "presumably faithful" translation of Marie's *Lai del Fraisne.* One can hardly suppose that the same author was at once a faithful translator and a compiler. M. Foulet granted that it was "possible," but not

"very probable." He also pointed out that this Prologue stands alone in Middle-English literature, but that French literature of the thirteenth century provides us with a number of parallels (the prologues of *Doon, Tydorel,* the *Lai du Lecheor* and *Tyolet*[4]). M. Foulet believed that it was simply in imitation of these that the contemporary French author of *Orfeo* complied his prologue. He recognized that the form of the Prologue in the *Orfeo* texts is inferior to that in *le Freine,* but this he ascribed to scribal carelessness.

M. Foulet's two main points rest on assertions which seem to me doubtful. The evidence at best is scant, but such as it is, I think it suggests quite different results. I believe (a) that the Prologue was not written by a French author, (b) that the English author of the Prologue was also the author of the *Lay le Freine,* (c) that this Prologue was borrowed by the author of *Sir Orfeo.*

A. THE PROLOGUE WAS NOT WRITTEN BY A FRENCH AUTHOR.

The prologue of the *Lay le Freine* is not similar to those of the extant thirteenth century French lays. By its form and the nature of its information, it stands as much alone among French lays as among English. It is a serious and well-composed introduction which was intended, perhaps, as Brugger[5] suggested, not only for the *Lay le Freine,* but for a collection of lays. It may be divided into three parts. In the first part (vv. 1-12), written in the present tense, we have the writer's own commentary on a number of lays which he seems to have just read. It is a brief, just and faithful summary of the contents of the Breton lays. All the varieties of theme which he indicates are to be found in Marie de France's lays, except for the "bourdes and ribaudy" (v. 9). This fact leads M. Foulet[6] to remark that the author had probably in mind the short French "fabliaux" which exactly answer to this description. In the second part (vv. 13-18) written in the past tense, the writer reports what he has read about the origin of these lays; "so seið ðis rime" (v. 14), in the present tense, refers very likely to Marie's different prologues and epilogues. This, by the way, is the only part which M. Foulet took into consideration. In the third part (vv. 19-28), after a general explanation to his audience of the lays of Britain, the poet comes to the particular one which he is going to retell, the *Lay le Freine,* and asserts that it is "on ensaumple fair with alle"[7] (v. 27).

In comparison with this Prologue, those of the other lays offer notable differences. The prologues of *Tydorel* and *Doon* are very short (not over 6 lines) and of vague import. In the prologue of the *Lai du Lecheor* the author develops only the theme of the second part of the prologue of the *Lay le Freine;* in the prologue of *Tyolet,* only that of the second and the third parts. We can say, therefore, that the first part of the *Freine* prologue is an original piece of work. The French authors' treatment, moreover, of the second part, that is to say, of the information they found in Marie's prologues and epilogues as to her sources, is widely different from that of the English author. The latter seems to have chosen carefully and to have translated faithfully the most important and distinctive phrases of Marie about the origin of her lays. This close dependence on Marie's prologues argues familiarity with her lays and not with the later ones. The French lay-writers, on the contrary, let their fancy wander and amplified freely Marie's information, as for instance the author of *Tyolet*, who tells us that the adventures:

> mises estaient en latin
> et en escrit em parchemin[8]

(vv. 29-30)

or the author of the *Lai du Lecheor* who imagined a fair gathering of ladies and knights and introduced ladies as lay-tellers. Theirs was the tone of the conventional, artificial, sophisticated, half-amused and sceptical French writers, or that of the courtly Chaucer in the prologue to his "Breton lay," *The Franklin's Tale*. The tone of the author of the prologue of the *Lay le Freine* is that of a simple-minded and credulous writer as most of the English writers of romance of that time seem to have been.

B. THE AUTHOR OF THE PROLOGUE WAS THE AUTHOR OF THE LAY LE FREINE.

The belief that the author of the Prologue was English clears the way for the further ascription to him of the *Lay le Freine*. M. Foulet rejected this chiefly because he felt it unlikely that the "presumably faithful translator" of the lay was also the "laborious compiler" of the Prologue. The argument might be of weight if the author of the lay were no more than M. Foulet suggested. But a close comparison of Marie's *Lai del Fraisne* and the English *Lay le Freine* reveals distinctive traits of style and thought on the part of the English poet, which mark in his work an unexpected freedom and originality and prove him to be much more than a mere translator. He modified Marie's style and bettered the story by avoiding her unnecessary repetitions,[9] suppressing irrelevant comments,[10] shifting certain details of place and character from the place they occupied in her poem to one that seemed to him more appropriate.[11] He made a greater use of direct discourse, thus adding directness, power, swiftness, realism to the story.[12] He succeeded in setting out the most important points of the story and in combining the various elements in the plot, as, for instance, in the introductory scene which he most skillfully modified. He introduced a lively dialogue between the lord's messenger and his neighbour and delayed intentionally the telling of the essential fact: the birth of the twins. He kept the fact of the double birth until it might be given as the messenger's news (v. 54) to the neighbour's wife and so be followed by her fatal utterance. Thus the English writer managed a surprise not only for the neighbour but also for the reader, and brought emphasis on the fact that the lady had two children and on the subsequent remark of her neighbour, both important facts for in them lies the knot of the story. He popularized the aristocratic little story and he gave it not only the realism of an actual

world in his treatment of nature, and of manners and customs, but he filled it with the very air of his own fourteenth century England.[13] In brief, his lay can not so much be called a "translation" as a "transformation" of Marie's. But though he dealt freely with his material, he did not deal at all extravagantly with it, he did not allow himself to do more than draw out of his French original what it held in suggestion.

It has already been pointed out that the Prologue is in part a mosaic, a clever combination of phrases borrowed from Marie. Yet the Prologue has also a distinctive character, a real independence of its own. In these qualities of likeness and unlikeness, it corresponds exactly with those which distinguish the English lay from its source. Since the Prologue is used to introduce the lay, since they both evince the same treatment of source material, it seems only reasonable to ascribe them both to the same author. As a final bit of evidence we may note that v. 22:

> Ichil ou telle Lay le Frayn,

is the literal translation of the first line of *Marie's Lai del Fraisne*:

> Le lai del Fraisne vus dirai;

thus proving unquestionably the relationship between the Prologue and the poem.

C. THE PROLOGUE WAS BORROWED BY THE AUTHOR OF SIR ORFEO.

The evidence from **Orfeo** goes far to support this view. The author of the Prologue was evidently familiar with Marie's works; the author of **Sir Orfeo** shows no sign of direct borrowing. Yet demonstrably he was familiar with the Middle-English version of *le Freine*. For instance, lines 35-36 of **Sir Orfeo** in which the king is said to go:

> Þurch wode and over heþ
> Into þe wildernes he geþ,

are clearly reminiscent of lines 147-8 of *Freine*:

> And passed over a wild heþ
> Þurch feld and þurch wode hye geþ.

A phrase about "lovesum eien" is used for the queen in **Sir Orfeo** (v. 109) and the heroine of the *Lay le Freine* (v. 269), but this is not a striking resemblance as it was so common an expression in the world of romance. The mention in the two lays of a "holow tree," is however, worthy of note. It is said of Sir Orfeo that:

> His harp
> He hidde in a holwe tree

(v. 265-66)

whereas it is said in the *Lay le Freine* that the maiden placed the child in an ash-tree whose:

> bodi was holow as mani on is

(v. 176)

This detail was the *Freine* poet's own invention and belonged naturally enough to the story. In **Orfeo** its more casual use suggests borrowing. Had we the French text of **Orfeo** and could we show that the Middle-English translator had freshened it with his humor, simplicity and literalness as did the author of the *Freine,* we might rely more largely on the parallelism in style and spirit between the two poems. **Orfeo** has perhaps, the maturer touch, which would be natural, if it were, as I believe, a later poem by the same author as *le Freine,* but in any case the *heð* and *geð* rhyme establishes the dependence of **Orfeo** upon the Middle-English *Freine.*[14]

If this relationship is true for the two poems, it must also be true for the prologues. M. Foulet admitted the inferiority of the *Prologue* in the two late texts of **Orfeo** in which it is found. His own theory of scribal carelessness could explain the situation much better if the prologue were indeed simply an addition foisted from *le Freine* to **Orfeo,** and did not belong to the author's original version. It should also be noted that the transformation in **Orfeo** of line 3 of the *Freine* prologue:

> Layes þat ben *in* harping

to:

> Þe layes þat ben *of* harping

is a most suggestive change. There is no doubt that the preposition was originally *in* and that the line meant "lays that are sung with the harp." It has been changed to *of* in **Sir Orfeo** in order that the line might apply especially to **Sir Orfeo** and mean "lays which tell about harping." It is awkward and out of place in lines which were intended to give a characterization of Breton lays in general.

Notes

1. The *Auchinleck MS. W.* 4, I, Advocates' Library, Edinburgh, early 14th cent. *Orfeo* without the Prologue is written on ff. 300-303 by the scribe who wrote the *Lay le Freine* on ff. 261ª-262ª. The text of *Orfeo* in *Harleian MS.* no. 3810, British Museum, early 15th cent. and in *Ashmolean MS.* no. 61, Oxford, later 15th cent. are evidently derived from the same source. Cf. Zielke's edition, Breslau, 1889.

2. L. Foulet, The Prologue of *Sir Orfeo, Modern Language Notes,* vol. XXI, no. 2, February 1906, pp. 46-50.

3. J. Zupitza, *Englische Studien,* vol. 10 (1886), p. 42.

4. L. Foulet, Marie de France et les lais bretons, *Zeitschrift für Roman. Philologie,* 29 (1905), pp. 19-56: the prologue of the *Lay le Freine* "est l'equivalent anglais du prologue de *Tyolet.*" *Tyolet* and the other three lays have been published by Gaston Paris, *Romania,* VIII, p. 29 ff.

5. Brugger, *Zts. f. fr. Spr. u. Litt.,* xx, p. 154, n. 103.

6. L. Foulet, "The Prologue of *Sir Orfeo,*" *Modern Language Notes,* vol. XXI, p. 50.

7. 23-28 are not to be found in the prologue prefixed to *Sir Orfeo.*

8. See L. Foulet's comment on those two lines, *Zts. f. Roman. Philologie,* 29, 1905, pp. 19-56.

9. Concerning the birth of the twins, Marie said 8 times, in 85 lines (vv. 11, 15, 35, 41, 67, 70, 83, 85) that the ladies had "dous enfanz," "dous fiz" or "filles." The English writer mentioned the fact only 3 times (vv. 54, 69, 87) and in this reticence and the reshaping of the whole passage gave the fact more importance.

   The porter of the abbey in the French poem, orders his daughter to take care of the baby and tells her in detail what she must do (vv. 198, 201-2), and in the following lines (vv. 203-6) what she did is repeated at length. The English writer summed up in one line the porter's orders (v. 201). He likewise summed up in one line (v. 247) Marie's unnecessary passage (vv. 308-12).

10. The English writer omitted vv. 59-64 in which we are told what happened to the lady who had been falsely accused. She is not mentioned again in either version. Note also omission of vv. 178-180.

11. Concerning the abbess's disclosure to Freine of how the girl was found in the ash-tree and the delivery to her of "the pel and the ring," Marie gave these details to her readers casually (vv. 305-12); the English writer gave motives for this disclosure and delivery, which he shifts from the second part to the first (vv. 241-50). This change made it more closely connected with the rest of the story as it allowed him to suggest Freine's personality and to bring emphasis on the special problem of the second part of the story, i. e., Freine's unknown birth.

   He shifted the scene between the porter and his daughter (F. vv. 197-202) to a similar scene between the porter and the abbess (E. vv. 211-24) who is to play, from now on, an important role.

12. In 6 cases he used direct instead of indirect discourse:

E. vv. 39-42	correspond to	F. vv. 15-18
E. vv. 116-18	correspond to	F. vv. 95
E. vv. 273-76	correspond to	F. vv. 268-70
E. vv. 49-54	correspond to	F. vv. 22
E. vv. 220-24	correspond to	F. vv. 216-18
E. vv. 279-84	correspond to	F. vv. 271-78

    (E. stands for English and F. for French).

13. See E.'s telling of the maiden's adventures through the winter long moonlit night (E. vv. 145-60, compare with F. vv. 135-52); his characterization of the morning (E. vv. 180-82).

14. Compare also v. 267 *Orfeo* with v. 150 *Freine;* v. 135 *Orfeo* with v. 220 *Freine,* about the weather. Winter time, birds "on bou," "foules" are mentioned in the two lays.

Laura A. Hibbard (essay date 1924)

SOURCE: *"Sir Orfeo"* in *Mediaeval Romance in England: A Study of the Sources and Analogues of the Non-Cyclic Metrical Romances*, Oxford University Press, 1924, pp. 195-99.

[*In the following essay, Hibbard briefly describes the known versions of* Sir Orfeo *and traces the work's sources and development through the centuries.*]

VERSIONS. The earliest extant version in Middle English of the **Lay of Sir Orfeo** is found in the early fourteenth-century Auchinleck manuscript. The poem contains 602 lines in short riming couplets and is to be ascribed to the South-Midland district (Zielke, p. 55). The two fifteenth-century manuscripts, Harleian 3810 and Ashmole 61, seem to be minstrel variants of a second version (y) derived from the same source as the Auchinleck text (Zielke, p. 25). The original poem was probably composed about the end of the thirteenth century.

Coming at a time when "imitation and not originality was the rule in English writing," the grace and beauty of **Orfeo** are the more exceptional. Brief yet vivid, the little tale is inimitably fresh in style and content. So artless it seems, that a ballad-like quality has been claimed for it (*Cambridge Hist.*, 1, 328). Ballad-like it is in the simplicity of its theme,—a king's rescue of his queen out of fairy land, in the bright distinctness of its few characters, Orfeo himself, his queen, Heurodis, a fairy king, a porter and a faithful steward, and in an occasional humorously laconic phrase. But the poem is not without indications of conscious artistry. Such descriptions as that of the hundred-towered, crystal-shining castle of the fairy king (v. 387 ff.), or of the fairy company riding on snow-white steeds (v. 109 ff.), show deliberate pictorial sense, and in the passage (v. 245) which contrasts Orfeo's life in his royal hall with his misery on the desolate, freezing moor, there is conscious pathos. If **Orfeo** is minstrel verse,[1] it is of very high order and far removed from such a true offspring of popular verse as the ballad into which it was ultimately fashioned.

The ballad of **King Orfeo** (Child, *Ballads*, No. 19) was not written down until late in the nineteenth century, in Unst, Shetland; but in its choral and dramatic form it is, as Gummere (p. 224) pointed out, of ancient structural type, its story evidently an oral, traditional version of the lay. The ballad contains seventeen two-line stanzas with an unintelligible refrain that may originally have been composed of Danish words. Of these stanzas two, twice repeated, tell of Orfeo's playing:

> And first he played da notes o noy,
> An dan he played da notes o joy.

> An dan he played da göd gabber reel,
> Dat meicht ha made a sick hert hale.

In other words the ballad is almost exclusively interested in Orfeo, the music-maker, and presents the episode in which his skill recovers for him Lady Isabel, in the most abbreviated narrative form.

ORIGIN. A few specifically English touches such as that which turns Thrace into Winchester, "a cite of noble defens," or that which makes Orfeo summon his people to a "parlement" to appoint a new king when he shall be dead, are but slight modifications of a story recognizably classical in origin. Through Ovid (*Metamorphoses*, X), Virgil (*Georgics,* IV, 454 ff.), and Boethius (*Philosophiae Consolationis*, III, metre XII), the favorite classic authors of the Middle Ages, the tragic Greek legend of Orpheus and Eurydice was widely known. In England[2] as early as the ninth century King Alfred had translated it from Boethius, and in France we have it alluded to in the tenth century by the monk, Froudmont of Tegernsee (Zielke, p. 130). By the twelfth century it had been turned from Latin into French verse and there are extant two Old French fragments of the classical story (Kittredge, p. 182, p. I). But obviously no version that kept to the classical form could adequately account for the Middle English version nor for the Breton lay from which it claims descent.[3]

The English poem shows that the Greek legend has been transformed under the influence of a different racial culture and belief. The dim Hades of Greek myth has become a glowing enchanting Otherworld;[4] the sad Greek gods of the dead have turned to beautiful, passionate, and mysterious fairy beings. Folk superstition has intruded itself in the scene in which the Otherworld king gains power over Heurodis, the mediaeval Eurydice, not because she dies, but because she falls asleep under a "fairy tree."[5] In his study of **Orfeo** Kittredge indicated not only the general influence of what seems to be primarily Celtic folk-lore, but the specific modification besides of the classic legend under the probable influence of one of the most famous tales known to Irish minstrels, the Wooing of Etain (*Tochmarc Etain*),[6] written down in at least one extant manuscript before 1106. In this, as in **Orfeo,** Etain, the happy wife of Eochaid, high king of Ireland, is stolen away by Midir, a fairy king, to whom in a former life she has been wedded.[7] Like the fairy king in **Orfeo,** Midir sings to her of his marvellous Otherworld realm; like Heurodis, Etain, though guarded by her mortal husband's warriors, is spirited away through the air, and is recovered at last from a fairy hill. The recovery itself, accomplished in the *Etain* story by a siege of the fairy hill, is not paralleled in the later romance. **Orfeo** draws for this part of the story, it would seem, on an earlier episode in the Irish legend. At his first coming to Eochaid's court, Midir, disguised, lures the king into the rash promise to give Midir whatsoever he should desire if Midir wins a game of chess. Eochaid admits the sanctity of the promise even when Midir asks for Etain. So also in the **Lay,** Orfeo, disguised as a minstrel, wins the rash promise of high reward from the fairy king. Like the mortal Eochaid, the fairy king keeps his promise even though Orfeo promptly demands the stolen lady. "Stories of a woman thus won and lost by a ruse between mortals and immortals seem to have been a favorite type among the Celts" (Schoepperle, *Tristan*, II, 428). The same these is found in numerous Celtic tales of which the most famous, perhaps, are the Irish Diarmid and Grainne story, the Welsh tale of the wedding of Pwyll in the *Mabinogion,* and the French and Norse versions of *Tristan.* In **Orfeo** the abduction episode and its happy sequel, for which there is no parallel in the classic legend, seem to represent characteristic Celtic adaptations.[8]

The evidence of Celtic influence makes more credible the reference in **Orfeo** to an original "Breton" lay as its source, especially as this is supported by a reference in the *Lai de l'Espine* (ed. R. Zenker, *Zts. f. rom Phil.* XVII, 233) to a musical *Lai d'Orphey* sung by an Irish harper (Kittredge, p. 201). It is conceivable that the bilingual Breton minstrels may have turned the Orpheus story into the form of a lay which the Irish minstrel learned and sang, or that the latter himself, knowing the form and assured popularity of the "Breton lays," may have worked the transformation of the original story. In Bretonizing the original legend it was *infused with Celtic "magic"* and turned, as were all the extant lays, into *swift-flowing French couplets.* From this form the story then passed into Middle English. It is probable that the English version owes to its French original those special qualities which make it "nearly perfect as an English representative of a Breton lay—its *brevity and romantic charm*" (Ker, *English Literature, Mediaeval,* p. 127).

Notes

1. Ker's illustrative reference (*Eng. Lit. Mediaeval,* p. 127) to the lines in *Orfeo* on the wandering minstrels who must proffer their glee, however inhospitable their reception, is far from proving that the author of *Orfeo* was a minstrel. Necessarily the poem says much of minstrelsy, but so, also, and in a very different tone, does *Sir Cleges,* a typical minstrel tale. The quality and effect of *Orfeo* is far less popular than *Cleges.*

2. For the history of the *Orpheus* legend in English literature see Wirl's dissertation. He discussed the Alfredian and Chaucerian versions of Boethius, the *Lay of Sir Orfeo,* the *Orpheus* fable of Robert Henryson (Scottish Text Soc., vol. LVIII, 1908), which was entirely uninfluenced by the *Lay,* and various allusions to the legend by writers of the fifteenth, sixteenth, and seventeenth centuries.

3. Cf. V. 1-24 and V. 595. The opening lines, which generalize on the usual contents of Breton lays, are practically identical with those which make up the Prologue of the *Lay le Fresne.* Foulet, p. 46 ff., believed they belonged to the French original of *Sir Orfeo* and were borrowed from *Fresne.* Miss Guillaume, p. 463, noted that as the Prologue occurs only in the two fifteenth-century texts of *Orfeo,* as it is inferior to the text given in *Fresne,* and as the text of *Orfeo* shows direct borrowing from *Fresne,* it is more reasonable to suppose that the Prologue itself in *Orfeo* was borrowed from the other poem.

4. The pagan Irish Otherworld was a fairy realm which lay beneath or beyond the sea, or was hidden in a mound. For details concerning its pleasant landscape and the Perilous Passage which commonly led to it, see A. C. L. Brown, "Iwain," *Harvard Studies in Phil. and Lit.* VIII (1903); L. Paton, *Studies in the Fairy Mythology of Arthurian Romance,* p. 83 ff., Boston, 1903; T. B. Cross, "The Celtic Origin of the Lay of Yonec," *Revue Celt.* XXXI, 461, n. 3; Hibbard, "The Sword Bridge of Chrétien de Troyes and Its Celtic Original," *Rom. Rev.* IV, 178 ff. (1913). Even H. R. Patch, who discredited in his study of "Mediaeval Descriptions of the Otherworld," *PMLA.* XXXIII (1918) the idea of Celtic influence on these descriptions, admitted (p. 612) that the idea of a fairy hill was peculiarly Celtic, and noted that in the *Lay,* Orfeo followed the fairy throng "in at the roche" as the only means of penetrating the fairy hill. There is, however, a genuine reminiscence of the classic legend in *Orfeo* in the description of the fairyland as a place of the dead and of the court held by the fairy king.

5. Kittredge, p. 189, thought this "a Celtic survival," although he admitted that the idea of danger of sleeping under special trees, because it exposed one to the power of the fairies, was not an exclusively Celtic idea. For arguments against considering this "orchard scene" in any way Celtic see Ogle's arguments (*Sir Gowther* bibliography).

6. See *Bibliography of Irish Philology and Printed Literature,* ed. R. I. Best, Dublin, 1913; Schoepperle, *Tristan,* II, 422, n. 3.

7. There is no suggestion in *Orfeo* of any former relationship between Heurodis and the fairy king. But this detail from the Old Irish stories survives in some versions of the Rape of Guinevere in connection with the lover who appears as Meliagrance in Malory, *Morte Darthur,* XIX, ch. 2. In the older versions of this episode she is stolen by a supernaturally splendid person who as lover or husband has a claim to her prior to Arthur's. (Webster, "Arthur and Charlemagne," *Eng. Stud.* 1906, XXXVI, 348 ff.; Schoepperle, II, 528-31).

8. Cf. Schoepperle *Tristan,* II, 541-4; for a detailed comparison of the abduction episode in *Orfeo* with that in the stories of Tristan and Guinevere.

Bibliography

TEXTS:

(1) Auchinleck MS. ed. Laing, *Select Remains of Ancient Popular Poetry of Scotland,* Edin. 1822, 1884; O. Zielke, Breslau, 1880 (a critical edition); M. Shackford, *Legends and Satires,* p. 141 ff., Boston, 1913; A. Cook, *A Literary Middle English Reader,* Boston, 1915; (2) Ashmole 61, Bodleian, ed. Halliwell, *Illustrations of the Fairy Mythology of A Midsummer Night's Dream,* Lond., 1895; (3) Harleian 3910, Brit. Mus., Ritson, II, 248 ff., 1884. Trans. E. E. Hunt, Cambridge, Mass., 1909; E. Rickert, *Romances of Love,* p. 32 ff.; Weston, *Chief ME. Poets,* p. 133.

STUDIES AND ANALOGUES:

Körting, _Grundriss,_ p. 160; Wells, _Manual,_ p. 783.

Foulet, L. "The Prologue of _Sir Orfeo,_" _MLN._ XXI, 46-50 (1906). Guillaume, G. "The Prologues of the _Lay le Freine_ and _Sir Orfeo,_" _MLN._ XXXVI, 458-64 (1921).

Gummere, F. B. _The Popular Ballad,_ Boston, 1908.

Ker, W. _English Literature, Mediaeval,_ p. 127-29, N. Y., 1912.

Kittredge, G. L. "Sir Orfeo," _Amer. Jour. Phil._ VII, 176-202 (1886).

Marshall, L. E. "Greek Myths in Modern English Poetry," _Studi di filologia moderne,_ v, 203-32 (1912).

Schofield, W. _English Literature—to Chaucer,_ pp. 184-86. N. Y., 1906.

Wirl, J. "Orpheus in der engl. Literatur," _Wiener Beiträge,_ XL (1913); rev. _Archiv,_ CXXXII, 239.

Roger Sherman Loomis (essay date 1936)

SOURCE: "_Sir Orfeo_ and Walter Map's _De Nugis,_" _Modern Language Notes,_ Vol. LI, No. 1, January, 1936, pp. 28-30.

[_In the following essay, Loomis advances the idea that a story included by Walter Map in his collection of court tales served as one of the elements of the French original of_ Sir Orfeo.]

The Middle English lai of **Sir Orfeo** has been reprinted several times in recent years, the last edition being found in _Middle English Metrical Romances,_ edited by W. H. French and C. B. Hale (N. Y., 1930). Allusions in French literature to a "lai d'Orfey" render certain the existence of a French original, now lost.[1] The authentic Celtic character of the lai has been rendered equally certain by the studies of Professor Kittredge, Professor Schoepperle, and Professor Laura Hibbard Loomis.[2] Professor Patch has also called attention to some Celtic and romance analogs for the supernatural realm under the hill,[3] to which may be added the fifteenth century _Turk and Gawain._[4]

Both Kittredge and Patch have noted the affinity of **Sir Orfeo** and the tale of Herla related by Walter Map in his _De Nugis Curialium._[5] King Herla is represented as entering the side of a cliff and after an interval seeing a brilliantly shining castle, whose lord entertains him; and in this respect Orfeo and Herla have similar adventures. Moreover, the realm which Orfeo and Herla visit is identified with the abode of the dead:[6] In the Middle English poem it is filled with the slain; in Map's story Herla is warned on departing not to set foot to ground, and an attendant who does so, falls into dust,—a conclusion which closely parallels the early Irish _Voyage of Bran._[7] By what seems to be an odd coincidence, Map also describes Herla as

leader of the phantom host,[8] and elsewhere says that it was last seen in Wales about noon in the first year of the reign of Henry II.[9] For this same host is plainly described in **Sir Orfeo:**

> Wele atourned ten hundred knites,
> Ich yarmed to his rites,
> Of cuntenaunce stout and fers,
> Wiþ mani desplaid baners,
> And ich his swerd ydrawe hold,
> Ac neuer he [Orfeo] nist whider þai wold.

(vv. 289-94)

The Irish parallels adduced by Kittredge, the Arthurian parallels adduced by Miss Schoepperle, the Welsh parallels found in Walter Map should leave no doubt of the Celticity of **Sir Orfeo.**

Walter Map in another story, moreover, furnishes a Breton parallel which has been completely overlooked,[10] and which is interesting as confirmation of the prolog of **Sir Orfeo,** which definitely states that the poem is of Breton origin.[11]

> Quia de mortibus quarum iudicia dubia sunt incidit oracio, miles quidam Britannie minoris uxorem suam amissam diuque ploratam a morte sua in magno feminarum cetu de nocte reperit in conualle solitudinis amplissime. Miratur et metuit et cum redivivam videat quam sepelierat, non credit oculis, dubius quid a fatis agatur. Certo proponit animo rapere, ut de rapta vere gaudeat, si vere videt, vel a fantasmate fallatur, ne possit a desistendo timiditatis argui. Rapit eam igitur, et gavisus est ejus per multos annos conjugio, tam iocunde tam celebriter, ut prioribus, et ex ipsa suscepit liberos, quorum hodie progenies magna est, et filii mortue dicuntur.

In **Sir Orfeo** likewise we have a knight who long seeks his wife, finds her in a great company of ladies in a remote region, wins her back, and lives long afterward with her, though she has been among the dead.

It may be suspected that this tale of Map's is an echo of the "lai d'Orfey," since it seems to have been written about 1182[12] and the lai might well have been earlier. Yet the complete absence of any feature from the Mider story, which has so profoundly affected the **Orfeo,** seems to indicate clearly that the story related by Map was not derived from the French lai, but on the contrary is one of the elements which combined with the classic story of Orpheus, the Irish tale of Mider and Etain, Welsh or Breton traditions of the Wild Hunt, the Phantom Host, and the subterranean palace of the dead, to form the French original of the altogether delightful **Sir Orfeo.**

Notes

1. Listed in _American Journal of Philology,_ VII (1886), 181; _Studj Romanzi,_ XIV (1917), 193-95. Add _Vulgate Version of the Arthurian Romances,_ ed. H. O. Sommer (Washington), IV, 290. The reference to Alpheus in the _Roman des Sept Sages_ (ed. Jean Mis-

rahi, Paris, 1933, v. 28) does not concern the lai but the classical story.

2. *Am. Journ. of Phil.,* VII, 176-202. G. Schoepperle, *Tristan and Isolt* (London, Frankfort, 1913), II, 541-44. L. A. Hibbard, *Mediaeval Romance in England* (N. Y., 1924), 195-99.

3. *PMLA.,* XXXIII (1918), 612. Cf. L. C. Wimberly, *Folklore in English and Scottish Ballads* (Chicago, 1928), 130, 332.

4. *Percy Folio MS.,* ed. Furnivall and Hales (London, 1867-9), I, 90-102. Cf. R. S. Loomis, *Celtic Myth and Arthurian Romance* (N. Y., 1927), 100-102.

5. Ed. M. R. James (Oxford, 1914), 13. Trans. M. R. James (Cymmrodorion Record Series, No. 9, London, 1923), 13. Trans. Tupper and Ogle (London, 1924), 15. Cf. E. S. Hartland, *Science of Fairytales,* 178, 234.

6. It is only in comparatively late medieval texts that the Celtic Otherworld is depicted as a land of the dead. In the earlier texts no dead persons are ever encountered there, and human beings often return from it. Originally a blissful land of the gods, visited only by an occasional rare mortal, it came to be confused with the land of the dead and the Christian hell. Cf. *Folklore,* XVIII, 121.

7. M. Joynt, *Golden Legends of the Gael* (Dublin, n. d.), Part I, 55f. Cf. *ibid.,* 48.

8. Also of the Wild Hunt. Cf. *Romanic Rev.,* III (1912), 191; XII (1921), 286.

9. Trans. James, 207. Trans. Tupper and Ogle, 233.

10. Ed. James, 173. Trans. James, 187. Trans. Tupper and Ogle, 218.

11. *Am. Journ. of Phil.,* VII, 183-85. On the lai question cf. Marie de France, *Lais,* ed. Warnke (Halle, 1925), xx-xl, and Brugger's review. *Zts. f. franz. Sprache u. Lit.,* XLIX (1926), 120 ff.

12. Trans. James, p. xii.

A. J. Bliss (essay date 1954)

SOURCE: Introduction to *Sir Orfeo,* Oxford University Press, 1954, pp. ixxlviii.

[*In the following excerpt, Bliss describes the three extant manuscripts of* Sir Orfeo *and briefly analyzes its literary qualities.*]

MANUSCRIPTS

1. **Sir Orfeo** is extant in three manuscripts, the Auchinleck MS. (Advocates' 19. 2. 1), here designated A, MS. Harley 3810, here designated H, and MS. Ashmole 61 (Bodleian 6922*), here designated B.

THE AUCHINLECK MS.

2. The Auchinleck MS.[1] is a stout folio volume containing 332 vellum leaves measuring 19 × 25 cm.; they must once have been larger, since in some places the binder's knife has cropped off marginal annotations. The manuscript has been much mutilated; most of the rather crude illuminations have been excised, and a large number of leaves have been completely cut away. The foliation includes two leaves of which only a narrow strip remains, so that the last leaf is numbered 334. Eight of the missing leaves have been recovered.[2] The present contents of the volume must originally have occupied fifty-two gatherings of eight leaves each; more gatherings must have been lost from the beginning of the manuscript, for the articles are numbered in a contemporary hand, and what is now the first article bears the number *vi;* still more gatherings have been lost between folios 277 and 278, for only four articles remain to fill the gap between *xxxvii* and *li* of the contemporary numbering.

3. The date of the manuscript can be established by internal evidence. Other manuscripts of the *Short Metrical Chronicle* bring the history of England up to the accession of Edward II, and conclude with a short prayer for *our ong king Edward.* In the Auchinleck MS. a passage is inserted between the accession of Edward II and the prayer, briefly relating the troublesome reign and death of the king and the accession of his son; *our ong king Edward* is now clearly Edward III. Since the manuscript contains two other articles concerned with the troubles of the reign of Edward II, it may confidently be dated about 1330, shortly after the accession of Edward III. The manuscript was written by six different scribes and contains a large variety of romances, saints' lives, and moral and political poems: **Sir Orfeo,** written by Scribe I, is now the thirty-eighth article; it was omitted from the contemporary numeration, for the preceding and following articles bear the numbers *li* and *lii* respectively.

4. Nothing is known of the history of the manuscript until it came into the possession of Lord Auchinleck, whose signature stands on the inner fly-leaf: *Alex^r. Boswel / Auchinleck / 1740.* 'Lord Auchinleck gave the manuscript to the Advocates' Library, and recorded the gift at the foot of the first folio: *Bibliothecæ Fac: Iur: Edinb: Hunc librum donat / Alex^r. Boswel / 1744.* Mrs. Loomis has convincingly argued that the manuscript was produced as a commercial venture by a London bookshop, and that it may have belonged to Chaucer.[3] In default of concrete evidence no certainty is possible; but the case for a London origin, at least, is very strong.

5. The Auchinleck version of **Sir Orfeo** has been printed in the following works:

D. Laing, *Selected Remains of Ancient Popular Poetry of Scotland,* 1822 [no pagination or signatures].

W. C. Hazlitt, *Early Popular Poetry of Scotland,* 1895, i. 64-80.

O. Zielke, *Sir Orfeo, ein englisches Feenmärchen aus dem Mittelalter,* 1880.

A. S. Cook, *A Literary Middle English Reader,* 1915, 88-107.

K. Sisam, *Fourteenth Century Verse and Prose,* 1921, 14-31.

G. Sampson, *The Cambridge Book of Prose and Verse,* 1924, 265-74. [Selections.]

W. H. French and C. B. Hale, *Middle English Metrical Romances,* 1930, 321-42.

MS. HARLEY 3810

6. MS. Harley 3810 is a small quarto volume consisting of several unconnected manuscripts bound up together. The first of these contains thirty-four paper folios measuring 14.5×10 cm., each cut out and separately mounted, and is written throughout in an angular hand of the beginning of the fifteenth century. This manuscript contains only six articles, of which *Sir Orfeo* is the first; the remaining articles are moral and religious pieces. The first two folios are badly stained and rubbed, and some passages have been inked over by a later hand. On the verso of the last folio a sixteenth-century hand has written the following inscription: *Hic liber olim fuit liber Will'mi Shaw cler' et Cur¹ de Baddesly Clinton: Eccl'a.* Nothing is known of this William Shaw, but the location of the manuscript in Warwickshire is plausible on linguistic grounds (see § 32).

7. The Harleian version of *Sir Orfeo* has only once been printed:

J. Ritson, *Ancient Engleish Metrical Romanceës,* 1802, ii. 248-69.

Readings from this manuscript were printed by Zielke, and the missing lines at the beginning of the Auchinleck version were supplied from this manuscript by Cook, Sisam, and French and Hale.

MS. ASHMOLE 61

8. MS. Ashmole 61 is a tall narrow folio volume containing 162 paper folios measuring 42×14.5 cm. The paper sheets are now folded along the greater length, but they were evidently supplied folded along the shorter length, since a horizontal crease runs across the middle of each folio. The sheets of the third, fourth, and fifth gatherings are watermarked with a ring surmounted by a crown and an equal-armed cross; this design closely resembles Briquet's No. 694,[4] Palermo, 1479, 30×42 cm. The sixth, seventh, and eighth gatherings are watermarked with two variants of the same design, an outstretched hand surmounted by a six-leaved flower, which closely resembles Briquet's No. 11159, Genoa, 1483, 29×42 cm. The tenth, eleventh, twelfth, thriteenth, and fourteenth gatherings are watermarked with two variants of the same design, a uni-

corn with lowered head, one of which is identical with Briquet's No. 10116, Deville, 1488, 20.5×42 cm. It seems clear that the manuscript was compiled over a period of years; it is written in a clear but coarse hand of the end of the fifteenth century; minor variations in the hand seem to be due to different pens and inks. If the identification of the watermarks is reliable (and the correspondence of the sizes is very striking) *Sir Orfeo,* which begins the thirteenth gathering, must have been written after 1488.

9. The manuscript contains forty-one articles: romances, saints' lives, and various moral and religious pieces. *Sir Orfeo* is the thirty-ninth article. After eighteen of the articles the scribe has written *Amen quod Rate* (once, *Rathe*): Rate was presumably the name of the scribe. Dr. J. T. T. Brown devoted two long articles[5] to the propositions that Rate was the author of the pieces to which he appended his name; that he was the author of *Ratis Raving;* and that he was David Rate, chaplain of King James IV of Scotland. All these propositions were convincingly refuted by Ritchie Girvan.[6] Nothing is known of the provenance of the manuscript, but on linguistic grounds it must be located in the north-east Midlands (see § 33).

10. The Ashmole version of *Sir Orfeo* has been printed in the following works:

J. O. Halliwell[-Phillipps], *Illustrations of the Fairy Mythology of Shakespeare's Midsummer Night's Dream,* 1845, 37-55.

W. C. Hazlitt, *Fairy Tales, Legends and Romances,* 1875, 83-100.

Scottish Antiquary, xvi (1902), 30-38.

Readings from this manuscript were printed by Zielke, and the missing lines at the beginning of the Auchinleck version were supplied from this manuscript by Hazlitt, *Selected Remains. . . .*

. . . . .

LITERARY QUALITIES

51. Critics are unanimous in their praise of *Sir Orfeo;* but its success is usually attributed rather to the potency of the magical atmosphere than to any particular skill on the part of the author. In fact, the poem is an outstanding example of narrative skill, and the author's artistry is such that his technical brilliance may at first sight be mistaken for untutored simplicity.[7]

ANALYSIS OF THE POEM

52. Structurally the poem may be divided into a brief prologue and three sections of approximately equal length. The prologue extends from the beginning to line 56, the first section from line 57 to line 194, the second section from line 195 to line 476, the third section from line 477 to the end. The prologue itself has three divisions: the first tells what kind of story *Sir Orfeo* is; the second, that Or-

feo was an exceptionally skilful harper; the third, that he was a man of high birth and authority, and that his wife was a paragon of all the virtues. In a very few lines the reader is told everything that is vital to his understanding of the story, and nothing that is superfluous. Orfeo's musical accomplishment makes the fairy king's rash promise plausible; his high estate adds poignancy to his destitution in the wilderness; and the beauty and virtue of Heurodis explain his eagerness to recover her at any cost.

53. The first main section of the poem tells of the abduction of Heurodis. It opens with a description of a fine May morning; a description which at first sight appears to be no more than a conventional medieval device. But in fact the peaceful orchard scene serves two useful purposes: it explains how Heurodis came to put herself in the power of the fairies, and it emphasizes by contrast the ghastliness of her mad terror on awaking from her dream. Now for the first time we meet a characteristic device of the author of *Sir Orfeo,* the use of suspense to heighten the vividness of the action. Heurodis falls asleep under a tree, and awakes speechless with distress; her maidens run for help, and she is carried into the palace; Orfeo is fetched and implores her to explain the reason for her dreadful behaviour. All this time the reader remains in ignorance of the cause of her distress: like Orfeo, he has to wait until the queen is sufficiently recovered to talk coherently. Also noteworthy is the author's skilful use of dialogue to convey intimate marital affection between Orfeo and Heurodis. Still a further effective narrative device is to be found in the description of the abduction of the queen. Orfeo's pathetically inadequate precautions, the troops of armed knights ready to fight to the death in the queen's defence, are described at some length; but the actual abduction is over in an instant, as mysteriously for the reader as it must have been for the witnesses:

> Ac ete amiddes hem ful rit
> Þe quen was oway y-tvit.

54. The second section tells of Orfeo's long search for Heurodis, and of his eventual success. At the beginning the magical atmosphere so finely created by the abduction scene is somewhat dissipated by the practical details of Orfeo's disposal of his kingdom, and the first part of the section is devoted to the recapture of the enchantment. First comes an episode appropriately preserved from the classical legend, in which Orfeo charms the wild beasts of the forest with his music. Next follows the fairy hunt, with hounds and huntsmen in full array; but it is all a strange pretence, the sound of the horns, the shouts, the baying of the hounds are heard only faintly, and *no best þai no nome.* Then there is the fairy army, and the dance, and last of all the party of ladies hawking along the river. Here there is a difficulty very neatly surmounted: the enchanted atmosphere so skilfully evoked is now no longer appropriate, for Orfeo is now to meet his wife, and must be in no doubt that she is really alive and not merely an illusion; the reader must somehow be prepared to encounter reality again. It is very simply but effectively done: whereas the first hunt had taken no game, this time *Ich faucoun his*

þray slou. The remainder of the section, which tells how Orfeo entered the land of fairy and recovered his wife, is narrated quite straightforwardly, with an effective use of dialogue.

55. The third section tells of Orfeo's return to his kingdom and his welcome by his faithful steward. At first sight the whole of this section seems superfluous; the poem might well have ended with a brief 'happy ever after'. In fact the addition of the final episode gives the whole story its proper balance by making the scenes of enchantment, already psychologically central, physically central as well; moreover it allows the author to achieve a notable climax, once again by the use of suspense, but in rather a different way. In the first instance the reader himself was kept in suspense; this time he is in the secret from the beginning, and is allowed to surmise the steward's gradual comprehension as Orfeo in his impenetrable disguise puts his hypothetical case:

> 'Steward, herkne now þis þing!
> Ʒif ich were Orfeo þe king,
> & hadde y-suffred ful ore
> In wilderness miche sore, . . .

and so on for eighteen lines of sustained condition.

56. It would be easy to multiply instances of the author's rare tact in constructing his story and framing it in exactly the most effective words. Such consummate skill is scarcely to be found in ME outside the work of Chaucer and the *Gawain* poet, and is certainly not to be expected in what purports to be a 'popular' romance; its rarity is attested by the brutality with which both the later scribes of *Sir Orfeo* have ruined some of its most characteristic effects. One example must suffice: the climax of suspense which I have just discussed is altogether missing from H, and badly mutilated in B. In H Orfeo reveals his identity as soon as he is sure that the steward has remained loyal:

> 'Syr,' he seyde, 'Y am Orpheo þe kyng.'

In B he begins to state his hypothesis, and then ridiculously breaks off:

> 'Syr stuerd, lystyns now þys thing!
> Ʒiff j were Orfeo þe kyng
> —Ther-for, stewerd, lystyns to me:
> Now þou may þe kyng her se.' . . .

Notes

1. For a full description see E. Kölbing, 'Vier Romanz Handschriften', *EngSt* vii (1884), 177-201, supplemented by A. J. Bliss, 'Notes on the Auchinleck Manuscript', *Speculum,* xxvi (1951), 652-8.

2. Four of the leaves are in MS. University of Edinburgh 218, the remaining four are in the library of the University of St. Andrews; see G. V. Smithers, 'Two newly-discovered fragments from the Auchinleck MS.', *M* xviii (1949), 1-11.

3. L. H. Loomis, 'Chaucer and the Auchinleck MS', in *Essays and Studies in Honour of Carleton Brown*, 1940, 111-28; 'Chaucer and the Breton Lays of the Auchinleck MS.', *SP* xxxviii (1941), 14-33; 'The Auchinleck MS. and a possible London bookshop of 1330-1340', *PMLA* lvii (1942), 595-627; 'The Auchinleck *Roland and Vernagu* and the *Short Chronicle*', *MLN* lx (1945), 94-97. See also H. M. Smyser, '*Charlemagne and Roland* and the Auchinleck MS.', *Speculum*, xxi (1946), 275-88.

4. See C. M. Briquet, *Les Filigranes*, 1909.

5. J. T. T. Brown, 'The Poems of David Rate', *Scottish Antiquary*, xi (1897), 145-55; 'The Author of *Ratis Raving*', *Bonner Beiträge zur Anglistik*, v (1900), 144-61.

6. R. Girvan, *Ratis Raving*, STS 1939, xxxiii-xxxvii.

7. For an admirable criticism from a standpoint rather different from mine, see G. Kane, *Middle English Literature*, 1951, 80-84.

Abbreviations

E&GS: English and Germanic Studies

EngSt: Englische Studien

E&S: Essays and Studies by Members of the English Association

M: Medium vum

MLN: Modern Language Notes

MLR: Modern Language Review

PMLA: Publications of the Modern Language Association of America

RES: Review of English Studies

RevCelt: Revue Celtique

RomRev: Romanic Review

SATF: Société des Anciens Textes Français

SP: Studies in Philology

STS: Scottish Text Society

ZfdA: Zeitschrift für deutsches Altertum

ZfrP: Zeitschrift für romanische Philologie

Dorena Allen (essay date 1964)

SOURCE: "Orpheus and Orfeo: The Dead and the *Taken*," *Mediem Aevum*, Vol. XXXIII, No. 2, 1964, pp. 102-11.

[*In the following essay, Allen argues that fairy tradition is central to* Sir Orfeo *and that, because the tale originated from the substitution of fairy elements in place of Greek myths, the search for its "elusive Celtic source" should be abandoned.*]

The genius of the poet of *Sir Orfeo* lies not in creation but in adaptation, in refashioning for his own purposes material which he shares with countless generations of popular story-tellers. In its chivalric splendour and in its concern with love, honour and loyalty, the poem mirrors his tastes and preoccupations and those of his age, but for its rich and curious detail and for its very subject it draws upon beliefs which were to live on almost unchanged for centuries in the more distant parts of the British Isles.[1] All this is, of course, common knowledge. What is less generally realized is that the fairy faith might include more than the opinion that there existed a dreaded but picturesque race of immortal beings. Inseparable from it were ideas about man himself—about the relationship of soul and body, about the nature of death and immortality—which to us are so alien as to be almost incomprehensible; and it is from them, and not from its author, that our poem derives contradictions and absurdities which must have troubled many readers. Heurodis is carried off by the fairy host while to her watching attendants she appears to be peacefully asleep in her own orchard; her going, nevertheless, is presented not as a dream, but as an objective event:

> As ich lay þis vndertide
> And slepe vnder our orchardside
> Þer come to me to fair knites
> Wele y-armed al to rites,
> And bad me comen an heiing
> And speke wiþ her lord þe king:
> And ich answerd at wordes bold,
> Y no durst nout, no y nold.
> Þai pricked oain as þai mit drive.
> Þo com her king, also blive . . .
> Wold ich, nold ich, he me nam,
> And made me wiþ him ride . . .
> And seþþen me brout oain hom
> Into our owhen orchard . . .

(ll. 133-163)

Ought we to see in the supposed inconsistency a deliberate heightening of the vividness of Heurodis' words?[2] So subtle an explanation is, I think, unnecessary. In modern tales of the *sidhe* many of the actors consort with the fairy host while to their families they seem to be safe in their beds—a survival of the wide-spread primitive conception that during life, and especially during sleep or unconsciousness, the 'soul' or 'self' is able to wander from the body on adventures of its own.[3] The poet has been neither careless nor ingenious: he has simply preserved a feature which is as traditional as most of the rest of his material.

But for the study of *Sir Orfeo* the interest of this less familiar side of the fairy creed extends beyond its usefulness in resolving isolated difficulties. Behind one neglected and misunderstood episode there lies a belief which, as I hope to show, suggests a new approach to a more general and more important problem: the origin of the entire poem. It is this episode, and the wider implications of what it contains, that I propose to consider. The scene is in the castle of the fairy king:

> Þan he (Orfeo) gan bihold about al
> And seie liggeand wiþin þe wal
> Of folk þat were þider y-brout
> And þout dede, and nare nout.
> Sum stode wiþouten hade,
> And sum non armes nade,
> And sum þurch þe body hadde wounde
> And sum lay wode, y-bounde,
> And sum armed on hors sete,
> And sum astrangled as þai ete,
> And sum were in water adreynt,
> And sum wiþ fire al forschreynt.
> Wiues þer lay on child-bedde,
> Sum ded and sum awedde,
> And wonder fele þer lay bisides,
> Rit as þai slepe her undertides.
> Eche was þus in þis warld y-nome,
> Wiþ fairi þider y-come.

(ll. 387-404)

Against the glittering magnificence of the background nothing could be more hideously unexpected than this assembly of maimed and suffering figures. Their presence is usually dismissed as a distorted and incongruous reminiscence of the classical Hades,[4] but this temptingly obvious explanation ignores one inconvenient fact: that in ll. 389-90 the poem states explicitly that they are *not* dead:

> of folk þat were þider y-brout
> And þout dede, and nare nout.

How can the decapitated and the asphyxiated, the burnt and the drowned be said still to live? To us these lines may seem at the worst nonsensical, at the best a clumsy attempt to reconcile the irreconcilable mythologies of Hades and fairyland;[5] but less than a hundred years ago an Irish or a Scottish countryman would have recognized in them the echo of his own convictions:

> Very few die at all, most are *taken*.
> When a man dies, he does not die at all, but the *daoine maithe* take him away.
> No-one dies, but the *daoine maithe* take him away, and leave something else in his place.
> Not one in twenty dies a true death, they all pass into another life.[6]

These speakers believed that many, perhaps most, of those who were thought to die were in reality no more dead than Orfeo's stolen Heurodis. In their last agony they too had been carried off, body and soul, by the triumphant *sidhe*, and a lifeless changeling, a cunningly fashioned image of wood or straw, left in the place of each.[7] Inside the hollow hill the 'dead' and the *taken* endured the same captivity, and tale after tale demonstrated that both could be won back in the same ways, and with the same ease.[8] Certainly fairyland was not the home of the dead, the Celtic Hades, as it has been so often and so misleadingly called: with or

without a semblance of dying, its mortal inhabitants had passed unchanged, in earthly flesh and blood, from one world to another.[9]

Inside the fairy castle Heurodis and her companions remain exactly as they were at the moment when they were abducted, stretched in sleep, or frozen in grotesque attitudes of apparent death. The catalogue of ll. 391 ff. is only too likely to have been varied, elaborated and deformed by any reciter or scribe into whose hands it has happened to fall (in the Ashmole manuscript it is among the most mangled portions of the whole text); the greater part of it, nevertheless, is still explicable in terms of fairy superstition. One group of captives lie 'wode, y-bounde' (l. 394): similarly, in the Ireland of the nineteenth century, delirium was still looked upon as an infallible sign that the sick man's spirit (or, more accurately, his *taise*) was already with the *daoine maithe,* who would soon, at his death, claim his body as well.[10] With the rest, a different principle is at work. Their lives have been cut short suddenly, by violence, accident or misadventure; and here we may discern a reflection of the assurance which, for later generations, lightened the peculiar pathos of untimely and unexpected death: that so to die was not to perish, but to join the fairy host.[11] For some parts of the list a more specific justification can also be found. Those who died in child-birth and those who died by drowning were invariably considered to be *taken*,[12] and are placed in fairyland also by our poem (ll. 397 and 399). The mutilated of ll. 391-2 may have suffered the bloody violence with which, earlier in the poem, Heurodis herself is threatened;[13] the wounded of l. 393—and possibly the horsemen of l. 395—may have met the same fate as Thomas Reid, who died in the Battle of Pinkye, but whom Bessie Dunlop saw among the *sidhe*.[14] For the rest of the catalogue (ll. 396 and 398) there are to my knowledge no exact parallels, but since almost any unnatural death was attributed to the *good people*, it is impossible to say whether we owe these remaining lines to a single narrator's whim or to authentic popular tradition.[15]

If my arguments have so far depended almost solely upon modern evidence, my excuse must be that the early material at our disposal is inevitably limited and scattered. Until the nineteenth century a belief which was essentially the property of the illiterate stood little chance of surviving in any written record. Normally it would find expression not in statement but in narrative, in tales of the unmasking of changelings, or of the recovery from the *sid* of those mourned as dead, but until folklore became a respectable study, these unpolished accounts of supposedly everyday events would be preserved only by accident, or through the curiosity or credulity of a few educated men. The proceedings of the witchcraft trials and the *Secret Commonvealth* of Robert Kirk bear witness that many Scots of the sixteenth and seventeenth centuries were persuaded that in fairyland the dead still lived,[16] while earlier, and well before the date of our poem, the same conviction may be traced in a small number of stories which have been handed down to us by Latin writers. In recent times this belief was both distinctively Celtic and distinctively Gaelic, but at one time it was probably current also in Brittany.[17] Of the tales I am about to quote, one is undoubtedly Irish, and another is set in Britain the Less. The first comes from a description of the Wonders of Ireland which, round about the year 1076, Patrick, Bishop of Dublin, composed in halting Latin verse.[18] In it the *sidhe* appear in Latin and Christian guise as *daemones;* otherwise, the passage speaks for itself with admirable clarity:

> Haec res mira solet numeros celebrantibus addi.
> Vir bonus et verax aliquid mirabile vidit.
> Quondam namque die volucres in flumine cernens
> Proitiens lapidem percussit vulnere cignum
> Prendere quam cupiens tunc protinus ille cucurrit.
> Sed properante viro mire est ibi femina visa,
> Quam stupido viso aspiciens haec querit ab illa
> Unde fuit, quid ei accidit, aut quo tempore venit.
> Haec: infirma fuit, inquit ei, et tunc proxima morti
> Atque putata meis sum, quod defuncta videbar,
> Demonibus sed rapta fui cum carne repente.
> Hanc vix crediblem rem tunc audivit ab illa,
> Quam secum ducens saciavit veste ciboque
> Tradidit atque suis credentibus esse sepultam
> Qui quod erat factum vix credere iam potuerunt.

The history of the *miles Britanniæ Minoris* from Walter Map's *De Nugis Curialium* is already well-known to students of *Sir Orfeo,* but for the wrong reasons. Its confusion of the dead and the *fatæ* has won it fame as the ancestor of the mediæval poem, as a 'Celtic tale which had already been contaminated with the classical legend of Orpheus'.[19] A glance at the passage in question will show how ill-founded this theory is. In Dist. II xiii Map gives a brief summary:

> . . . miles quidam uxorem suam sepellisse reuera mortuam, et a chorea redibuisse raptam, et postmodum ex eo filios et nepotes suscepisse, et perdurare sobolem in diem istum, et eos qui traxerunt inde originem in multitudinem factos, qui omnes ideo 'filii mortuae' dicuntur.

In Dist. IV viii the story is told in full:

> Miles quidam Britanniæ Minoris uxorem suam amissam diuque ploratam a morte sua in magno feminarum cetu de nocte reperit in conualle solitudinis amplissime. Miratur et metuit, et cum rediuiuam uideat quam sepelierat, non credit oculis, dubius quid a fatis agatur. Certo proponit animo rapere, ut de rapta uere gaudeat, si uere uidet, uel a fantasmate fallatur, ne possit a desistendo timidiatis argui. Rapit eam igitur, et gauisus est eius per multos annos coniugio, tam ioconde, tam celebriter, ut prioribus . . .

This tale resembles our poem only in the common-place motifs of the fairy dance and the company of women, and for it no more complicated explanation is needed than that which Hartland[20] gave long ago: that Map had, not surprisingly, misunderstood an account of the recovery from the *sidhe* of a woman who, like so many others, was not dead, but *taken.*

Our remaining examples are provided, more unexpectedly, by Petronius Arbiter and Thomas of Chantimpré, and are set, disconcertingly enough, in Italy and in Flanders. In every other respect, however, they might be from the lips of a Gaelic story-teller; and in them we must have tales of Celtic origin with which, in ways too fortuitous to be discovered, Italian and Flemish narrators have become acquainted, and to which they have given a local colouring. In Chap. 63 of the *Cena Trimalchionis* Petronius reproduces a changeling story. In it the *sidhe* (or, in their pagan Latin dress, the *strigæ*) replace the corpse by an image some time *after* the victim's apparent death, just as in modern tales the exchange may be postponed until the wake, or the progress to the church yard:[21]

> Cum adhuc capillatus essem, nam a puero vitam Chiam gessi, ipsimi nostri delicatus decessit, mehercules margaritum, caccitus et omnium numerum. Cum ergo illum mater misella plangeret, et nos tum plures in tristimonio essemus, subito strigae coeperunt; putares canem leporem persequi. Habebamus tunc hominem Cappadocem, longum, valde audaculum et qui valebat: poterat bovem iratum tollere. Hic audacter stricto gladio extra ostium procucurrit, involuta sinistra manu curiose, et mulierem tanquam hoc loco—salvum sit, quod tango—mediam traiecit. Audimus gemitum, et (plane non mentiar) ipsas non vidimus. Baro autem noster introversus se proiecit in lectum, et corpus totum lividum habebat quasi flagellis caesus, quia scilicet illum tetigerat mala manus. Nos cluso ostio redimus iterum ad officium, sed dum mater amplexerat corpus filii sui, tangit et videt manuciolum de stramentis factum. Non cor habebat, non intestina, non quicquam: scilicet iam puerum strigae involaverant, et supposuerant stramenticium vavatonem.

In Chap. LVII of the second book of his *Bonum Universale* Thomas of Chantimpré enumerates the outrages of the *Dusii,* spirits who inhabit mountains and groves; and it is here that he inserts the tales which merit our attention.[22] They have more pretensions to plot than any of the others we have examined: they combine the two ever-popular topics of the changeling and of the winning-back of the dead, and their climax is of a kind particularly favoured by later story-tellers, a dramatic disclosure at the wake. In 'Guerthenae' in Brabant a young girl dies . . .

> . . . iuvenis amator puellæ de villa eadem in crepusculo noctis pergebat ad aliam, et dum per dumeta transiret, audivit vocem quasi feminæ lamentantis, Sollicitus ergo discurrens et quærens, auditam invenit puellam quam mortuam æstimabat, cui et dixit: 'mortuam te plangunt tui, et huic unde venisti?' 'Ecce', ait, 'vir ante me vadit qui deducit me'. Stupefactus ad hoc iuvenis, cum neminem alium nisi solam puellam videret, audacter rapit eam, et in domo extra villam protinus occultavit.

He goes to the girl's father, and asks for her hand in marriage. Amazed, the father consents, if he can bring her back to life and health.

> Mox iuvenis, cum relevasset linteum quo cooperta putabatur, figmentum mirabile, quale a nullo hominum fi-

eri potuit, invenerunt. Dicitur autem ab illis qui figmenta huiusmodi diabolica inspexerunt, ea esse interius putrido ligno similia, levi exterius pellicula superducta. Hinc reducta puella est, et patri reddita, sanaque post dies aliquot dictum iuvenem maritum accept, et usque ad tempora nostra incolumis perduravit.

The next section contains an almost identical story:

Simili prope modo, cum quidam in confinio Flandriæ sororem languidam et mortuam putatam, sub eadem die, antequam sepeliretur figmentum, inter arundineta iuxta maris littora reperisset, reduxit eam ad propria, et ingressus domum ubi ab amicis quasi mortua plangebatur, discoopertum figmentum extracto gladio in frusta conscidit, horrentibus cunctis atque clamantibus, cur in funus sororis tanta crudelitate sæviret. Et mox subridens, 'crudelis' inquit 'videor in sororem, non est illud sororis corpus, sed figmentum et illusio dæmonum'. Et hæc dicens secum cunctos accepit, et duxit ad domum propriam, et eis sororem reductam ostendit. Et hæc usque ad tempora nostra permansit.

The conclusions which emerge from these tales are both unambiguous and reassuring. They are centuries older than the main body of our evidence, yet in them we find the same endlessly repeated events used to clothe the same constant articles of faith: the survival of the dead, the hope of their return, and (since the victims include a woman of child-bearing age, a little boy, and an unmarried girl) the association of abduction and untimely death. There could be no clearer confirmation of much of my interpretation, and no better illustration of the unchangingness of popular tradition and of popular belief.

About the origin of *Sir Orfeo* all that is certain is that in it we have a remote and Celtic descendant of the legend of Orpheus and Eurydice; beyond that, everything is a matter of speculation, particularly the exact nature of the imaginative process by which that legend was remoulded. (From the remoulding of the legend itself must, of course, be distinguished the accretion to it, in its new form, of motifs from fairy superstition, which is not here our concern.) Since Kittredge's time most scholars have followed him in assuming that the events of the classical myth were combined by an Irish or a Breton story-teller with those of an already current native tale; but none known to us, whether the celebrated *Tochmarc Etaine* or any other, is in fact sufficiently like the mediæval poem to be justly regarded as its Celtic parent.[23] How then did the story of Orpheus become the story of Orfeo? To that question I should like to propose an answer which, if it is accepted, will enable us to abandon for ever the search for *Sir Orfeo's* elusive Celtic source. The poem as we know it owes its existence to an act of substitution, the substitution of *taking* for death and of the *sid* for Hades: by that change the myth enters into fairy tradition, and upon it the presence of all *Sir Orfeo's* strange and marvellous detail depends. The reasons for that substitution must by now be quite evident. To a Gaelic or a Breton narrator the fable of Orpheus' quest for his lost wife would seem at once familiar and oddly unfamiliar: the tales to which he was accustomed

described the recovery not of the dead, but of the abducted, of those wrongly imagined to have died. In recounting his newly-acquired material, he would naturally restore to it what was for him its proper condition. Instead of a 'blending' or a 'fusing' (to borrow the terms usually employed) of two independent tales, there would be a reinterpretation of the ancient legend by one who believed, as his countrymen did for centuries, that death might be no more than an illusion and a deceit.

The resulting story may already have had the famous happy ending of *Sir Orfeo,* for both Euripides and Isocrates[24] allow Eurydice to be reunited with her husband for once and for all, and there are indications that this account may have survived into the Middle Ages, alongside the better-loved and more pathetic Vergilian version.[25] It would, however, disagree with the extant poem in one important particular: in it the heroine would appear to die. The eventual loss of this feature can be explained quite simply. In popular tradition tales of the rescue or the return of the 'dead' and of the *taken* were both equally frequent, and the boundary between them was extremely ill-defined. The supposed death of the victim, which alone distinguished the first type of narrative from the second, did not always occupy a prominent position (in one of the tales in Wentz's collection it is added as a mere afterthought),[26] and might be present in some versions of a story and absent in others. J. M. Synge and Hans Hartmann both retell the same tale: every night a woman would come back from the *sidhe* to her home for food, and during these visits she disclosed to her husband that he might win her back by dragging her from her horse as the fairy procession rode past a certain spot. In Synge's version the heroine is believed to be dead and buried, in Hartmann's, there is no word of her 'death'.[27] For those who held the fairy faith, it little mattered whether counterfeit death or undisguised abduction befell a man or woman. Against this background the change which concerns us ceases to be at all surprising. As our story passed from narrator to narrator, the 'death' of the hero's wife might easily come to receive less and less attention. In time it might, with equal ease, disappear altogether, and there would be left the straightforward account of rescue from the *sid* which forms the basis of *Sir Orfeo.*

The often-praised lightness and charm of *Sir Orfeo* are deceptive: the distinctive flavour of the poem comes not from them, but from a unique and haunting combination of fourteenth-century graces and immemorial fears. The world of the poem, for all its outward elegance, is still the primitive world of popular belief, a world in which men are forever surrounded and threatened by cruel and capricious beings:

'Loke, dame, tomorwe þatow be
Rit here vnder þis ympe-tre,
And þan þou schalt wiþ us go
And live wiþ ous euermo.
And if þou makest ys ylet
Whar þou be, þou worst yfet,
And totore þine limes al

Þat noþing help þe no schal,
And þei þou best so totorn
Ʒete þou worst wiþ ous yborn.'

(11. 165-174)

Upon this sense of danger and unease the poem relies for its strength, for in its subject it has none of the grave yet passionate dignity of the antique myth—to win back the dead requires a love strong enough to overcome the laws of nature, to win back the *taken* requires only cunning and resolution. The gulf which separates the two tales is best exemplified in the scenes which are enacted before Pluto and before the fairy king. By his music Orpheus forces the inexorable powers of death to feel pity for human grief and human longing:

Tandem 'vincemur' arbiter
Umbrarum miserans ait
'Donamus comitem viro
Emptam carmine coniugem'.

(Boethius *De Consolatione Philosophiæ* III, xii)

In **Sir Orfeo** resource has taken the place of feeling, and the recovery of Heurodis turns upon a short battle of wits between her captor and her husband. The happy ending of the mediæval poem (if it is indeed an innovation) is only one manifestation of an all-pervasive difference in quality. In spirit the story of Orpheus and the story of Orfeo have very little in common, and between them lies a belief in which death itself loses its bitterness and finality, and is swallowed up in enchantment.

Notes

1. The poem is an early representative of the fairy abduction story which later is particularly characteristic of popular Celtic tradition, and of which a work such as Sean O'Suilleabhain's *Handbook of Irish Folklore* (Dublin 1942) will provide countless examples. The *sidhe* of *Sir Orfeo* are admirably typical of their kind in their love of fine clothes and white horses [ll. 145 ff. compare L. C. Wimberly *Folklore in the English and Scottish Ballads* (Chicago 1928) p. 188; J. G. Campbell *Superstitions of the Highlands and Islands of Scotland* (Glasgow 1900) p. 148; P. Kennedy *Legendary Fictions of the Irish Celts* (London 1860), p. 113], and in their human past times of hunting, dancing and fighting [ll. 282 ff., compare O'Suilleabhain, op. cit. p. 460 ff.; Wimberley, op. cit., p. 194 ff.; J. Crofton Croker *Fairy Legends of the South of Ireland* (London 1870) p. 218]. On the perils of sleeping outside on May Day see O'Suilleabhain, op. cit. p. 473, and Hans Hartmann *Über Krankheit, Tod, und Jenseitsvorstellungen in Irland* (Halle 1942) p. 139 ff.; on the perils of sleeping beneath a tree see F. J. Child *English and Scottish Ballads* (New York 1956) I 340, and II 505, and G. L. Kittredge *American Journal of Philology* VII 190. The hollow hill and the green plain of fairyland are traditional [see H. R. Patch *The Other World* (Harvard 1950) p. 46 ff.] as are the brilliance and splendour of the fairy

castle [see Child, loc. cit.; Kennedy, *op. cit.*, p. 116; Robert Kirk *The Secret Commonwealth* (Edinburgh 1815) p. 5]; but, despite the parallels adduced by A. J. Bliss in his edition of *Sir Orfeo* (Oxford 1954) p. xxxviii, its crystalline wall, pillars of gold, and glowing carbuncles do not necessarily derive from Celtic visions of the Other World, since they may be found in descriptions of any magnificent building, from the heavenly Jerusalem to the palace of Prester John. (See Patch, op. cit. p.149 f. and 203 f.)

2. As is suggested by Constance Davies *MLR* LVI 161.

3. See H. Hartmann op. cit., p. 118 and 147 ff. The Irish term for this wandering soul is *taise,* for which English has no equivalent. The *taise* is not a disembodied spirit: it is both visible and tangible, and is in all respects indistinguishable from the man himself.

4. See G. V. Smithers *Mæ* XXII 85 f., and Constance Davies, loc. cit. 164.

5. As is suggested by Constance Davies *id.*

6. Quoted from material in the possession of the Irish Folklore Commission, Dublin, by kind permission of Professor J. Delargy. These remarks were recorded in this century by collectors working in Gaelic-speaking Ireland.

7. See H. Hartmann op. cit., p. 168.

8. See H. Hartmann op. cit. p. 176.

9. On this point see H. Hartmann op. cit. p. 162 and 176, and Elisabeth Hartmann *Die Trollvorstellungen in dem Sagen und Märchen der Skandinavischen Volker* (Stuttgart-Berlin 1936) p. 86 f. In modern Scotland and Ireland the dead and the inhabitants of fairyland were, admittedly, sometimes confused, but this confusion is directly and explicitly contradicted in the remarks just quoted, and is explained by H. Hartmann (op. cit. p. 160 f.) as a corruption of the belief I have been describing. Some mediæval and renaissance authors identify Pluto and Proserpina with the fairy king and queen (Chaucer *Merchant's Tale* ll. 983 ff., Dunbar *Golden Targe*, ll. 124 f., Henryson *Orpheus and Eurydice* 11. 110 ff., T. Campion, in *Elizabethan Lyrics* ed. N. Ault (London 1949) p. 151): this identification probably depends mainly upon the learned equation of Diana in her multiplicity of aspects with the fairy queen on one hand and with Proserpina in the other. (See Prudentius *Contra Symmachum* I 367; Servius, comm. on *Ecl.* iii 27; Albericus I, *Theogony* II xii ii.) L. H. Loomis has demonstrated that Chaucer probably also had in mind *Sir Orfeo* itself (*Studies in Philology* XXXVIII 14 ff.); and in a later article I hope to show that Henryson too was influenced by our poem.

10. See H. Hartmann op. cit. p. 147.

11. See H. Hartmann loc. cit. and Reidar Th. Christiansen *Folkliv* 1938 p. 330 ff.

12. See H. Hartmann op. cit. p. 125 and 144. For the belief that the drowned are *taken* there is one very

early scrap of evidence. In the Bodleian MS of the Dinnsenchas (Rawlinson B 506, ed. by Whitely Stokes in *Folklore* III 467 ff.) the scribe has added to the story of Tuag, who was drowned as she was being carried away to become Mannanan's bride, the note *no comad e Mannanan fesin nodos-berid* (or perhaps it was M. himself carrying her off). In making this addition, he may have been inspired by the conviction that the drowned had become the captives of the beings who ruled over the water where they had lost their lives.

13. For modern parallels see *Bealoideas* VII p. 85 f., and J. M. Synge *The Aran Islands* (Dublin 1911) p. 60.

14. See the trial of Bessie Dunlop for witchcraft in R. Pitcairn *Ancient Criminal Trials of Scotland.* (Edin. 1833) I 49 ff.

15. Death by fire and death by water conventionally go together: see *Floris and Blancheflour* 1. 383 ff. and *Richard Coeur de Lion* l. 1635 ff. The inclusion in the catalogue of the drowned (which certainly does come from popular superstition) may therefore have suggested to a narrator the addition of the burned to the list.

16. See Pitcairn op. cit. p. 49 ff. and 161 ff., and Kirk op. cit. p. 5 and 12.

17. See H. Hartmann op. cit. p. 161.

18. Ed. by Mommsen in *Monumenta Germanica Historica,* Auctorum Antiquissimorum XIII 218 ff. Patrick was almost certainly translating into Latin a vernacular list of marvels: see A. Gwynn *The Writings of Bishop Patrick* (Dublin 1955) p. 126 ff.

19. Bliss op. cit. p. xxxiii, and Smithers *M* XXII 86 ff.

20. E. S. Hartland *Science of Fairytales* (London 1925) p. 343.

21. For the delay in the exchange compare H. Hartmann op. cit. p. 169 ff. In Chap. 38 of the *Cena Trimalchionis* Petronius refers to another tale of Celtic provenance: that of the leprechaun's cap and the crock of gold. For a discussion of both passages see E. Hartmann *Zeitschrift für Folkskunde, neue Folge,* Band 7 (1937) 308 ff.

22. Thomas of Chantimpré *Bonum Universale de Apibus* II lvii § 20 and 21, p. 552 f. in Douai ed. of 1605. For modern stories with a similar climax see H. Hartmann op. cit. p. 175 ff.

23. Kittredge loc. cit. p. 176-202; Smithers loc. cit. p. 86 ff.; J. Burke Severs *Studies in Medieval Literature in Honour of A. C. Baugh* (Philadelphia 1961) 194 ff. Bliss's rejection of *Tochmarc Etaine* as a source for *Sir Orfeo* (op. cit. p. xxxiii ff.) seems to me to be quite convincing. They resemble each other closely only in that in each the intended victim is warned, and a guard is set to prevent her abduction. A motif of this kind cannot be used to prove anything about the relationship between two tales, since it would appear that it was not proper to any one story. It is found elsewhere, in places as diverse as Map's *De Nugis Curialium* (see Dis. II, cap. xxix, where Map uses it to embroider a narrative taken from *Pseudo-Turpin* chap. 7), and a modern Irish story (see *Bealoideas VII* 85 f.), and was probably a story-teller's device which could be employed in any appropriate situation. The game of chess or cards (which also occurs in the *Tochmarc Etaine*) is a good example of the same kind of 'free' motif in Irish story-telling: see Miles Dillon, *Irish Sagas* (Dublin 1959) p. 19. With the relationship between *Sir Orfeo* and another suggested source, Map's tale of the *miles Britanniae Minoris* (R. S. Loomis, *MLN* LI 28 ff., C. Davies *MLR* XXXI 354 ff.) I have already dealt.

24. Euripides *Alcestis* 357 ff.; Isocrates (ed. F. Blass Leipzig 1898) Oratio xi 7.

25. A twelfth-century sequence speaks unambiguously and without qualification of Orpheus' recovery of his bride: see G. M. Dreves *Analecta Hymnica* VIII (Leipzig 1890) 33. Two manuscript illustrations known to me show Orpheus and Eurydice walking away from the mouth of Hell together: see F. Saxl and H. Meier *Catalogue of Astrological and Mythological MSS of the Latin Middle Ages* III (London 1953) pl. xl, and J. van den Gheyn ed. *Epitre D'Othea,* 100 *miniatures reproduced from the MS of Jean Mielot* (Brussels 1913), pl. 70. P. Dronke discusses the whole problem thoroughly in *Classica et Medievalia* XXIII 198-215.

26. Y. E. Wentz *The Fairy Faith in Celtic Countries* (Rennes 1909) p. 66.

27. Synge op. cit., p. 210, Hartmann op. cit., p. 177. The two accounts differ in their degree of alaboration and in their endings, but are undoubtedly versions of the same story.

Bruce Mitchell (essay date 1964)

SOURCE: "The Faery World of *Sir Orfeo*," *Neophilologus* Vol. 48, 1964, pp. 155-59.

[*In the following excerpt, Mitchell argues that the sinister elements of* Sir Orfeo *constitute an inappropriate addition made to the original work.*]

Writing of **Sir Orfeo,** Kane observes that

> no other romance conveys so strong an impression of contact with another existence older, colder and less happy than our own, sinister in the chill of its beauty. . . . The mortal characters in the romance are made good and loyal while a boundless suggestion of unexplored evil is ascribed to the other world and its inhabitants.[1]

He then traces the growth of 'imminent evil' in the poem until

> the sense of danger . . . is confirmed, and the mask of beauty is stripped from faery when in the courtyard of

the palace Orfeo sees a horror, the figures of the taken mortals in the attitudes of their moments of capture. Now the open conflict between Orfeo and the evil forces begins; he emerges victorious when he rebukes the king for failing to honour his promise. . . . At this moment the power and spell of faery breaks, the evil beauty finally falls away, and thereafter a sense of relief from anxiety and oppressiveness, of *blitheness* in the mediaeval sense of the word develops in the romance until it reaches its climax in the final recognition of Orfeo.[2]

It seems to me that without the scene in the courtyard (Auchinleck MS., lines 391-400, Ashmole MS., lines 382-9), this impression of sinister chill would have no basis at all. The faery world is certainly mysterious. But where is the evidence for Kane's observation that it is an 'evil' land peopled by a 'hostile race'?[3] Certainly the mysterious huntsmen take no beast (lines 281-8)[4] while each of the sixty ladies is successful (lines 303-313). But why does this give a suggestion of 'envy'?[5] It serves rather to emphasize the other-worldliness of the unsuccessful hunters. Indeed, all the evidence from the poem apart from the courtyard scene suggests that the faery world is a pleasant place. It is peopled by fair creatures (lines 135-48). It has a fine palace set in beautiful country (lines 157-60 and 349-68) which is so bright that Orfeo thinks he is in Paradise (lines 369-76). The phantom knights and ladies do no harm (lines 281-302). Dame Heurodis is unharmed (lines 405-8, 455-6, and 460), though we might not expect this after the ghastly catalogue of lines 391-400. The King and Queen are noble and kindly people who treat Orfeo politely (lines 409 ff.). The King has a sense of humour (lines 457-62) and his reluctance to honour his promise is not unknown among even the noblest mortals of Celtic legend.[6] Finally, however, he releases Heurodis and allows Orfeo to lead her out of his realms (lines 469-476). Where is the hostility and sinister chill in all this?

Apart from the courtyard scene, the strongest evidence for its existence is the conduct of Dame Heurodis when she awakes from sleep under the *ympe-tre* (Auchinleck MS., lines 69 ff.). Bliss rightly speaks of 'the ghastliness of her mad terror' and of 'her dreadful behaviour'.[7] But this is not proof that the other world is ghastly. It is one of the achievements of the poet of *Sir Orfeo* that he has made credible the love of Orfeo and Heurodis, and her reaction is the natural one of a loving wife soon to be mysteriously and compulsorily torn from her husband. Lovers about to be separated by war or death have experienced similar emotions, and here the suddenness and strangeness of the incomprehensible summons is enough to account for Heurodis's conduct. Would we expect her to pack her bags calmly and await the arrival of the Faery King?

Whatever impression of sinister chill there may be in the poem—and I have never been able to experience it or believe in it—must have its origin in the courtyard scene. Were these lines an original part of the poem? I take leave to doubt it: without them we have a perfectly smooth progression, as in the Harley MS. (which omits them all), and their absence eliminates certain inconsistencies.

The lines I suspect are, in the Auchinleck MS., lines 391-400:

> Sum stode wiþ-outen hade,
> & sum non armes nade,
> & sum þurth þe bodi hadde wounde,
> & sum lay wode, y-bounde,
> & sum armed on hors sete,
> & sum astrangled as þai ete;
> & sum were in water adreynt,
> & sum wiþ fire al for-schreynt.
> Wiues þer lay on child-bedde,
> Sum ded & sum awedde, . . .

These have no counterpart in the Harley MS. But in the Ashmole MS., lines 382-9 read:

> Som þer stod wyth-outyn hede,
> And some armys non hade,
> And som, þer bodys had wounde,
> And som onne hors þer armys sette,
> And som wer strangyld at þer mete,
> And men þat wer nomen wyth þem ete;
> So he saw þem stonding þer.
> Than saw he men & women in fere: . . .

Only the Auchinleck MS. has the particularly offending couplet (lines 399-400)

> Wiues þer lay on child-bedde,
> Sum ded & sum awedde,

which so blatantly contradicts line 390 of the same MS.

> & þout dede, & nare nout.

It seems incredible to me that this contradiction was really part of the original poem. Such an insensitive artistic blemish cannot be excused (though it may be explained) by any confusion of the classical and Celtic underworlds, and if we accept it we must on this point at any rate take issue with Ker's comment that the poem 'is all in good compass, and coherent; nothing in it is meaningless or ill-placed'.[8]

This particular difficulty and the problem of their general inconsistency with the picture of the faery world we are given elsewhere in the poem would be happily solved by the omission of Auchinleck MS., lines 391-400, and Ashmole MS., lines 382-9, on the ground that their common ancestor was an interpolation by some scribe or minstrel. Since the passage is represented in both the Auchinleck and the Ashmole MSS., the interpolation must have occurred early, either in the Auchinleck MS. itself (or an ancestor of it) if the other two MSS. are descended directly from it, or in the manuscript which lies behind the Auchinleck MS. and the common ancestor of the Ashmole and Harley MSS.[9] The absence of the passage from the Harley MS. is purely coincidental, proving nothing beyond what we already know—that mediaeval scribes and minstrels were not particularly concerned with accurate transmission. That they were just as likely to add passages as to omit them is clear from Bliss's examination of the divergences between these three MSS. of *Sir Orfeo*.[10] Cases particularly relevant are the insertion at the beginning of the Ashmole MS. of six lines borrowed from *Arthour and Merlin* and of nine lines after line 134 in the same manuscript, the first eight of which are nearly identical with the Auchinleck MS., lines 71-8, and the Ashmole MS., lines 59-66. There are, of course, many other additions, omissions, and transpositions, some of them in the offending passages themselves. All of these serve to show that the original of the lines I should like to omit could have been interpolated.

Constance Davies has recently pointed out that some of the elements in *Sir Orfeo* which cannot be explained from Celtic sources or from classical versions of the Orpheus legend may well have their origin in the works of Virgil. She compares the passages with which we are particularly concerned with *Aeneid,* Book VI lines 273-286, and observes:

> What Aeneas saw in the forecourt of Orcus was very similar to that which Orfeo saw in the courtyard of the fairy king's castle; all kinds of horrors had 'made their beds' there, but where Virgil has enumerated abstractions and the customary grisly inhabitants of Tartarus, the author of *Orfeo* has presented a picture of examples, an oddly assorted gathering of people, most of whom would have been found, in the Middle Ages, in Purgatory, because they had died suddenly and unshriven— the burnt, the drowned, women who had died mad in labour, soldiers killed in battle and those who, like Hamlet's father, had been taken, 'grossly, full of bread' and had died choking. None of them has a right to a home in Fairyland, at least, not according to the ancient tradition concerning that place; all who go there are either stolen or lured from earth on account of their beauty or desirability. That Heurodis should be there is intelligible, but the rest seem to belong to the Christian otherworld of punishment, which, in the Middle Ages, owed many of its features to the pagan conception of Tartarus; both were places in which the wicked or the unassoiled found themselves after death and every traveller who had the temerity to visit them, were he an Orpheus, an Aeneas or a Knight Owen had his sight seared with visions of human agony. Orpheus descended into Hades, Orfeo tunnelled into Fairyland; the two stories which are so successfully merged in other parts of *Orfeo* are just here a little divergent, or perhaps it is that the classical element is for the moment uppermost and has, in its detail, been partly overlaid with contemporary notions. In any case, the similarity between the settings is very close.[11]

This may well throw light on the source of the offending passages and may help to show that such a description of the horrors of Purgatory or Hell could have become a rhetorical formula and part of the minstrel stock-in-trade: compare Chaucer's terrible catalogue of those to be seen in the temple of Mars in *The Knightes Tale,* lines 1137 ff. (Group A, lines 1995 ff., in Skeat's seven-volume edition). But it is of particular interest to us, not only because it shows how wildly incongruous these passages are with the

rest of *Sir Orfeo,* but also because it suggests how the very similarity of the settings may have led to the early interpolation of their original.

I would therefore argue that the original of these offending passages was not in the first instance part of the poem. The inept discrepancy between line 390 and line 400 of the Auchinleck MS., the fact that these passages as a whole prepare us for a dead rather than a living Heurodis,[12] and their inconsistency with the faery world as it is described elsewhere in the poem, seem to me good grounds for seeing here another and earlier example of the 'brutality' to which Bliss tellingly objects:

> It would be easy to multiply instances of the author's rare tact in constructing his story and framing it in exactly the most effective words. Such consummate skill is scarcely to be found in ME outside the work of Chaucer and the *Gawain* poet, and is certainly not to be expected in what purports to be a 'popular' romance; its rarity is attested by the brutality with which both the later scribes of *Sir Orfeo* have ruined some of its most characteristic effects.[13]

Notes

1. G. Kane, *Middle English Literature* (Methuen, 1951), p. 81.

2. ibid., p. 83.

3. ibid., p. 82.

4. The line references in the rest of this paragraph are to the Auchinleck MS.

5. ibid., p. 83.

6. See K. Sisam, *Fourteenth Century Verse and Prose* (Oxford, 1946), p. 211.

7. A. J. Bliss, *Sir Orfeo* (Oxford, 1954), p. xlii.

8. W. P. Ker, *Mediaeval English Literature* (Oxford, 1948), p. 94.

9. See Bliss, op. cit., p. xv.

10. ibid., pp. xv-xvii.

11. *Modern Language Review,* lvi (1961), 164-5.

12. See Bliss, op. cit., p. xlii-iii.

13. ibid., p. xliii.

FURTHER READING

Criticism

Bliss, A. J. "*Sir Orfeo*, Lines 1-46." *English and Germanic Studies* V (1952-53): 7-14.

> Offers an examination of *Sir Orfeo* manuscript variations, and a reconstruction of the missing first forty-six lines from the Auchinleck manuscript.

————. "Classical Threads in *Orfeo*." *Modern Language Review* LVI, No. 2 (April 1961): 161-66.

Exploration of the parallels between *Sir Orfeo* and classical legends.

Davies, Constance. "Notes on the Sources of *Sir Orfeo*." *Modern Language Review* XXXI (1936): 354-57.

Assessment of the impact that the legend of the Filii Mortue had on *Sir Orfeo*.

Donovan, Mortimer J. "Herodis in the Auchinleck *Sir Orfeo*." *Medium Aevum* XXVII, No. 3 (1958): 162-65.

Discussion of the importance of variant spellings of the Queen's name in *Sir Orfeo*.

Kane, George. "The Middle English Metrical Romances." *Middle English Literature: A Critical Study of the Romances—the Religious Lyrics,* "Piers Plowman," pp. 80-84, 1951. New York: Barnes & Noble, Inc., 1970.

Appreciative comments on the author's literary abilities.

Marshall, L. E. "Greek Myths in Modern English Poetry: *Orpheus and Eurydice*. I." *Studi di Filologia Moderna* V, No. 1-2 (1912): 203-32.

Summaries of many English variations of the Greek Orpheus tale.

Schofield, William Henry. "Romance: The Breton Lays in English." *English Literature: From the Norman Conquest to Chaucer,* pp. 179-201. London: Macmillan and Co., Limited, 1921.

Examination of eight different Breton lays.

How to Use This Index

The main references

> **Calvino, Italo**
> 1923-1985 .... CLC **5, 8, 11, 22, 33, 39,**
> **73; SSC 3**

list all author entries in the following Gale Literary Criticism series:

BLC = *Black Literature Criticism*
CLC = *Contemporary Literary Criticism*
CLR = *Children's Literature Review*
CMLC = *Classical and Medieval Literature Criticism*
DA = *DISCovering Authors*
DAB = *DISCovering Authors: British*
DAC = *DISCovering Authors: Canadian*
DAM = *DISCovering Authors: Modules*
    DRAM: Dramatists Module; MST: Most-Studied Authors Module;
    MULT: Multicultural Authors Module; NOV: Novelists Module;
    POET: Poets Module; POP: Popular Fiction and Genre Authors Module
DC = *Drama Criticism*
HLC = *Hispanic Literature Criticism*
LC = *Literature Criticism from 1400 to 1800*
NCLC = *Nineteenth-Century Literature Criticism*
NNAL = *Native North American Literature*
PC = *Poetry Criticism*
SSC = *Short Story Criticism*
TCLC = *Twentieth-Century Literary Criticism*
WLC = *World Literature Criticism, 1500 to the Present*

The cross-references

> See also CANR 23; CA 85-88;
> obituary CA116

list all author entries in the following Gale biographical and literary sources:

AAYA = *Authors & Artists for Young Adults*
AITN = *Authors in the News*
BEST = *Bestsellers*
BW = *Black Writers*
CA = *Contemporary Authors*
CAAS = *Contemporary Authors Autobiography Series*
CABS = *Contemporary Authors Bibliographical Series*
CANR = *Contemporary Authors New Revision Series*
CAP = *Contemporary Authors Permanent Series*
CDALB = *Concise Dictionary of American Literary Biography*
CDBLB = *Concise Dictionary of British Literary Biography*
DLB = *Dictionary of Literary Biography*
DLBD = *Dictionary of Literary Biography Documentary Series*
DLBY = *Dictionary of Literary Biography Yearbook*
HW = *Hispanic Writers*
JRDA = *Junior DISCovering Authors*
MAICYA = *Major Authors and Illustrators for Children and Young Adults*
MTCW = *Major 20th-Century Writers*
SAAS = *Something about the Author Autobiography Series*
SATA = *Something about the Author*
YABC = *Yesterday's Authors of Books for Children*

Literary Criticism Series
Cumulative Author Index

Anderson, C. Farley
See Mencken, H(enry) L(ouis); Nathan, George Jean

Anderson, Jessica (Margaret) Queale 1916- .... **CLC 37**
See also CA 9-12R; CANR 4, 62

Anderson, Jon (Victor) 1940- . **CLC 9; DAM POET**
See also CA 25-28R; CANR 20

Anderson, Lindsay (Gordon) 1923-1994 .... **CLC 20**
See also CA 125; 128; 146; CANR 77

Anderson, Maxwell 1888-1959 .... **TCLC 2; DAM DRAM**
See also CA 105; 152; DLB 7, 228; MTCW 2

Anderson, Poul (William) 1926- .... **CLC 15**
See also AAYA 5, 34; CA 1-4R, 181; CAAE 181; CAAS 2; CANR 2, 15, 34, 64; CLR 58; DLB 8; INT CANR-15; MTCW 1, 2; SATA 90; SATA-Brief 39; SATA-Essay 106

Anderson, Robert (Woodruff) 1917- .... **CLC 23; DAM DRAM**
See also AITN 1; CA 21-24R; CANR 32; DLB 7

Anderson, Sherwood 1876-1941 ..... **TCLC 1, 10, 24; DAB; DAC; DAM MST, NOV; SSC 1; WLC**
See also AAYA 30; CA 104; 121; CANR 61; CDALB 1917-1929; DA3; DLB 4, 9, 86; DLBD 1; MTCW 1, 2

Andier, Pierre
See Desnos, Robert

Andouard
See Giraudoux, (Hippolyte) Jean

Andrade, Carlos Drummond de CLC 18
See also Drummond de Andrade, Carlos

Andrade, Mario de 1893-1945 .... **TCLC 43**

Andreae, Johann V(alentin) 1586-1654 .... **LC 32**
See also DLB 164

Andreas-Salome, Lou 1861-1937 ... **TCLC 56**
See also CA 178; DLB 66

Andress, Lesley
See Sanders, Lawrence

Andrewes, Lancelot 1555-1626 .... **LC 5**
See also DLB 151, 172

Andrews, Cicily Fairfield
See West, Rebecca

Andrews, Elton V.
See Pohl, Frederik

Andreyev, Leonid (Nikolaevich) 1871-1919 .... **TCLC 3**
See also CA 104; 185

Andric, Ivo 1892-1975 .... **CLC 8; SSC 36**
See also CA 81-84; 57-60; CANR 43, 60; DLB 147; MTCW 1

Androvar
See Prado (Calvo), Pedro

Angelique, Pierre
See Bataille, Georges

Angell, Roger 1920- .... **CLC 26**
See also CA 57-60; CANR 13, 44, 70; DLB 171, 185

Angelou, Maya 1928- .... **CLC 12, 35, 64, 77; BLC 1; DA; DAB; DAC; DAM MST, MULT, POET, POP; WLCS**
See also AAYA 7, 20; BW 2, 3; CA 65-68; CANR 19, 42, 65; CDALBS; CLR 53; DA3; DLB 38; MTCW 1, 2; SATA 49

Anna Comnena 1083-1153 .... **CMLC 25**

Annensky, Innokenty (Fyodorovich) 1856-1909 .... **TCLC 14**
See also CA 110; 155

Annunzio, Gabriele d'
See D'Annunzio, Gabriele

Anodos
See Coleridge, Mary E(lizabeth)

Anon, Charles Robert
See Pessoa, Fernando (Antonio Nogueira)

Anouilh, Jean (Marie Lucien Pierre) 1910-1987 .... **CLC 1, 3, 8, 13, 40, 50; DAM DRAM; DC 8**
See also CA 17-20R; 123; CANR 32; MTCW 1, 2

Anthony, Florence
See Ai

Anthony, John
See Ciardi, John (Anthony)

Anthony, Peter
See Shaffer, Anthony (Joshua); Shaffer, Peter (Levin)

Anthony, Piers 1934- .... **CLC 35; DAM POP**
See also AAYA 11; CA 21-24R; CANR 28, 56, 73; DLB 8; MTCW 1, 2; SAAS 22; SATA 84

Anthony, Susan B(rownell) 1916-1991 .... **TCLC 84**
See also CA 89-92; 134

Antoine, Marc
See Proust, (Valentin-Louis-George-Eugene-) Marcel

Antoninus, Brother
See Everson, William (Oliver)

Antonioni, Michelangelo 1912- .... **CLC 20**
See also CA 73-76; CANR 45, 77

Antschel, Paul 1920-1970
See Celan, Paul
See also CA 85-88; CANR 33, 61; MTCW 1

Anwar, Chairil 1922-1949 .... **TCLC 22**
See also CA 121

Anzaldua, Gloria 1942-
See also CA 175; DLB 122; HLCS 1

Apess, William 1798-1839(?) .... **NCLC 73; DAM MULT**
See also DLB 175; NNAL

Apollinaire, Guillaume 1880-1918 .. **TCLC 3, 8, 51; DAM POET; PC 7**
See also Kostrowitzki, Wilhelm Apollinaris de
See also CA 152; MTCW 1

Appelfeld, Aharon 1932- .... **CLC 23, 47**
See also CA 112; 133; CANR 86

Apple, Max (Isaac) 1941- .... **CLC 9, 33**
See also CA 81-84; CANR 19, 54; DLB 130

Appleman, Philip (Dean) 1926- .... **CLC 51**
See also CA 13-16R; CAAS 18; CANR 6, 29, 56

Appleton, Lawrence
See Lovecraft, H(oward) P(hillips)

Apteryx
See Eliot, T(homas) S(tearns)

Apuleius, (Lucius Madaurensis) 125(?)-175(?) .... **CMLC 1**
See also DLB 211

Aquin, Hubert 1929-1977 .... **CLC 15**
See also CA 105; DLB 53

Aquinas, Thomas 1224(?)-1274 ..... **CMLC 33**
See also DLB 115

Aragon, Louis 1897-1982 .. **CLC 3, 22; DAM NOV, POET**
See also CA 69-72; 108; CANR 28, 71; DLB 72; MTCW 1, 2

Arany, Janos 1817-1882 .... **NCLC 34**

Aranyos, Kakay
See Mikszath, Kalman

Arbuthnot, John 1667-1735 .... **LC 1**
See also DLB 101

Archer, Herbert Winslow
See Mencken, H(enry) L(ouis)

Archer, Jeffrey (Howard) 1940- ...... **CLC 28; DAM POP**
See also AAYA 16; BEST 89:3; CA 77-80; CANR 22, 52; DA3; INT CANR-22

Archer, Jules 1915- .... **CLC 12**
See also CA 9-12R; CANR 6, 69; SAAS 5; SATA 4, 85

Archer, Lee
See Ellison, Harlan (Jay)

Arden, John 1930- .... **CLC 6, 13, 15; DAM DRAM**
See also CA 13-16R; CAAS 4; CANR 31, 65, 67; DLB 13; MTCW 1

Arenas, Reinaldo 1943-1990 . **CLC 41; DAM MULT; HLC 1**
See also CA 124; 128; 133; CANR 73; DLB 145; HW 1; MTCW 1

Arendt, Hannah 1906-1975 .... **CLC 66, 98**
See also CA 17-20R; 61-64; CANR 26, 60; MTCW 1, 2

Aretino, Pietro 1492-1556 .... **LC 12**

Arghezi, Tudor 1880-1967 .... **CLC 80**
See also Theodorescu, Ion N.
See also CA 167

Arguedas, Jose Maria 1911-1969 .... **CLC 10, 18; HLCS 1**
See also CA 89-92; CANR 73; DLB 113; HW 1

Argueta, Manlio 1936- .... **CLC 31**
See also CA 131; CANR 73; DLB 145; HW 1

Arias, Ron(ald Francis) 1941-
See also CA 131; CANR 81; DAM MULT; DLB 82; HLC 1; HW 1, 2; MTCW 2

Ariosto, Ludovico 1474-1533 .... **LC 6**

Aristides
See Epstein, Joseph

Aristophanes 450B.C.-385B.C. .... **CMLC 4; DA; DAB; DAC; DAM DRAM, MST; DC 2; WLCS**
See also DA3; DLB 176

Aristotle 384B.C.-322B.C. .... **CMLC 31; DA; DAB; DAC; DAM MST; WLCS**
See also DA3; DLB 176

Arlt, Roberto (Godofredo Christophersen) 1900-1942 .... **TCLC 29; DAM MULT; HLC 1**
See also CA 123; 131; CANR 67; HW 1, 2

Armah, Ayi Kwei 1939- . **CLC 5, 33; BLC 1; DAM MULT, POET**
See also BW 1; CA 61-64; CANR 21, 64; DLB 117; MTCW 1

Armatrading, Joan 1950- .... **CLC 17**
See also CA 114; 186

Arnette, Robert
See Silverberg, Robert

Arnim, Achim von (Ludwig Joachim von Arnim) 1781-1831 ..... **NCLC 5; SSC 29**
See also DLB 90

Arnim, Bettina von 1785-1859 .... **NCLC 38**
See also DLB 90

Arnold, Matthew 1822-1888 ..... **NCLC 6, 29, 89; DA; DAB; DAC; DAM MST, POET; PC 5; WLC**
See also CDBLB 1832-1890; DLB 32, 57

Arnold, Thomas 1795-1842 .... **NCLC 18**
See also DLB 55

Arnow, Harriette (Louisa) Simpson 1908-1986 .... **CLC 2, 7, 18**
See also CA 9-12R; 118; CANR 14; DLB 6; MTCW 1, 2; SATA 42; SATA-Obit 47

Arouet, Francois-Marie
See Voltaire

Arp, Hans
See Arp, Jean

Arp, Jean 1887-1966 .... **CLC 5**
See also CA 81-84; 25-28R; CANR 42, 77

Arrabal
See Arrabal, Fernando

Arrabal, Fernando 1932- ... **CLC 2, 9, 18, 58**
See also CA 9-12R; CANR 15

Bakhtin, M.
See Bakhtin, Mikhail Mikhailovich
Bakhtin, M. M.
See Bakhtin, Mikhail Mikhailovich
Bakhtin, Mikhail
See Bakhtin, Mikhail Mikhailovich
Bakhtin, Mikhail Mikhailovich
1895-1975 .... **CLC 83**
See also CA 128; 113
Bakshi, Ralph 1938(?)- .... **CLC 26**
See also CA 112; 138
Bakunin, Mikhail (Alexandrovich)
1814-1876 .... **NCLC 25, 58**
Baldwin, James (Arthur) 1924-1987 . **CLC 1,
2, 3, 4, 5, 8, 13, 15, 17, 42, 50, 67, 90,
127; BLC 1; DA; DAB; DAC; DAM
MST, MULT, NOV, POP; DC 1; SSC
10, 33; WLC**
See also AAYA 4, 34; BW 1; CA 1-4R; 124;
CABS 1; CANR 3, 24; CDALB 1941-
1968; DA3; DLB 2, 7, 33; DLBY 87;
MTCW 1, 2; SATA 9; SATA-Obit 54
Ballard, J(ames) G(raham)
1930-1964 .... **CLC 3, 6, 14, 36; DAM
NOV, POP; SSC 1**
See also AAYA 3; CA 5-8R; CANR 15, 39,
65; DA3; DLB 14, 207; MTCW 1, 2;
SATA 93
Balmont, Konstantin (Dmitriyevich)
1867-1943 .... **TCLC 11**
See also CA 109; 155
Baltausis, Vincas
See Mikszath, Kalman
Balzac, Honore de 1799-1850 ... **NCLC 5, 35,
53; DA; DAB; DAC; DAM MST, NOV;
SSC 5; WLC**
See also DA3; DLB 119
Bambara, Toni Cade 1939-1995 ...... **CLC 19,
88; BLC 1; DA; DAC; DAM MST,
MULT; SSC 35; WLCS**
See also AAYA 5; BW 2, 3; CA 29-32R;
150; CANR 24, 49, 81; CDALBS; DA3;
DLB 38; MTCW 1, 2; SATA 112
Bamdad, A.
See Shamlu, Ahmad
Banat, D. R.
See Bradbury, Ray (Douglas)
Bancroft, Laura
See Baum, L(yman) Frank
Banim, John 1798-1842 .... **NCLC 13**
See also DLB 116, 158, 159
Banim, Michael 1796-1874 .... **NCLC 13**
See also DLB 158, 159
Banjo, The
See Paterson, A(ndrew) B(arton)
Banks, Iain
See Banks, Iain M(enzies)
Banks, Iain M(enzies) 1954- .... **CLC 34**
See also CA 123; 128; CANR 61; DLB 194;
INT 128
Banks, Lynne Reid CLC 23
See also Reid Banks, Lynne
See also AAYA 6
Banks, Russell 1940- .... **CLC 37, 72**
See also CA 65-68; CAAS 15; CANR 19,
52, 73; DLB 130
Banville, John 1945- .... **CLC 46, 118**
See also CA 117; 128; DLB 14; INT 128
Banville, Theodore (Faullain) de
1832-1891 .... **NCLC 9**
Baraka, Amiri 1934- . **CLC 1, 2, 3, 5, 10, 14,
33, 115; BLC 1; DA; DAC; DAM MST,
MULT, POET, POP; DC 6; PC 4;
WLCS**
See also Jones, LeRoi
See also BW 2, 3; CA 21-24R; CABS 3;
CANR 27, 38, 61; CDALB 1941-1968;
DA3; DLB 5, 7, 16, 38; DLBD 8; MTCW
1, 2

Barbauld, Anna Laetitia
1743-1825 .... **NCLC 50**
See also DLB 107, 109, 142, 158
Barbellion, W. N. P. TCLC 24
See also Cummings, Bruce F(rederick)
Barbera, Jack (Vincent) 1945- .... **CLC 44**
See also CA 110; CANR 45
Barbey d'Aurevilly, Jules Amedee
1808-1889 .... **NCLC 1; SSC 17**
See also DLB 119
Barbour, John c. 1316-1395 .... **CMLC 33**
See also DLB 146
Barbusse, Henri 1873-1935 .... **TCLC 5**
See also CA 105; 154; DLB 65
Barclay, Bill
See Moorcock, Michael (John)
Barclay, William Ewert
See Moorcock, Michael (John)
Barea, Arturo 1897-1957 .... **TCLC 14**
See also CA 111
Barfoot, Joan 1946- .... **CLC 18**
See also CA 105
Barham, Richard Harris
1788-1845 .... **NCLC 77**
See also DLB 159
Baring, Maurice 1874-1945 .... **TCLC 8**
See also CA 105; 168; DLB 34
Baring-Gould, Sabine 1834-1924 ... **TCLC 88**
See also DLB 156, 190
Barker, Clive 1952- ...... **CLC 52; DAM POP**
See also AAYA 10; BEST 90:3; CA 121;
129; CANR 71; DA3; INT 129; MTCW
1, 2
Barker, George Granville
1913-1991 .... **CLC 8, 48; DAM POET**
See also CA 9-12R; 135; CANR 7, 38; DLB
20; MTCW 1
Barker, Harley Granville
See Granville-Barker, Harley
See also DLB 10
Barker, Howard 1946- .... **CLC 37**
See also CA 102; DLB 13
Barker, Jane 1652-1732 .... **LC 42**
Barker, Pat(ricia) 1943- .... **CLC 32, 94**
See also CA 117; 122; CANR 50; INT 122
Barlach, Ernst (Heinrich)
1870-1938 .... **TCLC 84**
See also CA 178; DLB 56, 118
Barlow, Joel 1754-1812 .... **NCLC 23**
See also DLB 37
Barnard, Mary (Ethel) 1909- .... **CLC 48**
See also CA 21-22; CAP 2
Barnes, Djuna 1892-1982 .... **CLC 3, 4, 8, 11,
29, 127; SSC 3**
See also CA 9-12R; 107; CANR 16, 55;
DLB 4, 9, 45; MTCW 1, 2
Barnes, Julian (Patrick) 1946- .... **CLC 42;
DAB**
See also CA 102; CANR 19, 54; DLB 194;
DLBY 93; MTCW 1
Barnes, Peter 1931- .... **CLC 5, 56**
See also CA 65-68; CAAS 12; CANR 33,
34, 64; DLB 13; MTCW 1
Barnes, William 1801-1886 .... **NCLC 75**
See also DLB 32
Baroja (y Nessi), Pio 1872-1956 ..... **TCLC 8;
HLC 1**
See also CA 104
Baron, David
See Pinter, Harold
Baron Corvo
See Rolfe, Frederick (William Serafino
Austin Lewis Mary)
Barondess, Sue K(aufman)
1926-1977 .... **CLC 8**
See also Kaufman, Sue
See also CA 1-4R; 69-72; CANR 1

Baron de Teive
See Pessoa, Fernando (Antonio Nogueira)
Baroness Von S.
See Zangwill, Israel
Barres, (Auguste-) Maurice
1862-1923 .... **TCLC 47**
See also CA 164; DLB 123
Barreto, Afonso Henrique de Lima
See Lima Barreto, Afonso Henrique de
Barrett, (Roger) Syd 1946- .... **CLC 35**
Barrett, William (Christopher)
1913-1992 .... **CLC 27**
See also CA 13-16R; 139; CANR 11, 67;
INT CANR-11
Barrie, J(ames) M(atthew)
1860-1937 .... **TCLC 2; DAB; DAM
DRAM**
See also CA 104; 136; CANR 77; CDBLB
1890-1914; CLR 16; DA3; DLB 10, 141,
156; MAICYA; MTCW 1; SATA 100;
YABC 1
Barrington, Michael
See Moorcock, Michael (John)
Barrol, Grady
See Bograd, Larry
Barry, Mike
See Malzberg, Barry N(athaniel)
Barry, Philip 1896-1949 .... **TCLC 11**
See also CA 109; DLB 7, 228
Bart, Andre Schwarz
See Schwarz-Bart, Andre
Barth, John (Simmons) 1930- ... **CLC 1, 2, 3,
5, 7, 9, 10, 14, 27, 51, 89; DAM NOV;
SSC 10**
See also AITN 1, 2; CA 1-4R; CABS 1;
CANR 5, 23, 49, 64; DLB 2, 227; MTCW
1
Barthelme, Donald 1931-1989 ... **CLC 1, 2, 3,
5, 6, 8, 13, 23, 46, 59, 115; DAM NOV;
SSC 2**
See also CA 21-24R; 129; CANR 20, 58;
DA3; DLB 2; DLBY 80, 89; MTCW 1, 2;
SATA 7; SATA-Obit 62
Barthelme, Frederick 1943- ...... **CLC 36, 117**
See also CA 114; 122; CANR 77; DLBY
85; INT 122
Barthes, Roland (Gerard)
1915-1980 .... **CLC 24, 83**
See also CA 130; 97-100; CANR 66;
MTCW 1, 2
Barzun, Jacques (Martin) 1907- ...... **CLC 51**
See also CA 61-64; CANR 22
Bashevis, Isaac
See Singer, Isaac Bashevis
Bashkirtseff, Marie 1859-1884 .... **NCLC 27**
Basho
See Matsuo Basho
Basil of Caesaria c. 330-379 .... **CMLC 35**
Bass, Kingsley B., Jr.
See Bullins, Ed
Bass, Rick 1958- .... **CLC 79**
See also CA 126; CANR 53; DLB 212
Bassani, Giorgio 1916- .... **CLC 9**
See also CA 65-68; CANR 33; DLB 128,
177; MTCW 1
Bastos, Augusto (Antonio) Roa
See Roa Bastos, Augusto (Antonio)
Bataille, Georges 1897-1962 .... **CLC 29**
See also CA 101; 89-92
Bates, H(erbert) E(rnest)
1905-1974 . **CLC 46; DAB; DAM POP;
SSC 10**
See also CA 93-96; 45-48; CANR 34; DA3;
DLB 162, 191; MTCW 1, 2
Bauchart
See Camus, Albert

Benjamin, David
See Slavitt, David R(ytman)
Benjamin, Lois
See Gould, Lois
Benjamin, Walter 1892-1940 .... **TCLC 39**
See also CA 164
Benn, Gottfried 1886-1956 .... **TCLC 3**
See also CA 106; 153; DLB 56
Bennett, Alan 1934- .... **CLC 45, 77; DAB; DAM MST**
See also CA 103; CANR 35, 55; MTCW 1, 2
Bennett, (Enoch) Arnold
1867-1931 .... **TCLC 5, 20**
See also CA 106; 155; CDBLB 1890-1914; DLB 10, 34, 98, 135; MTCW 2
Bennett, Elizabeth
See Mitchell, Margaret (Munnerlyn)
Bennett, George Harold 1930-
See Bennett, Hal
See also BW 1; CA 97-100; CANR 87
Bennett, Hal CLC 5
See also Bennett, George Harold
See also DLB 33
Bennett, Jay 1912- .... **CLC 35**
See also AAYA 10; CA 69-72; CANR 11, 42, 79; JRDA; SAAS 4; SATA 41, 87; SATA-Brief 27
Bennett, Louise (Simone) 1919- ...... **CLC 28; BLC 1; DAM MULT**
See also BW 2, 3; CA 151; DLB 117
Benson, E(dward) F(rederic)
1867-1940 .... **TCLC 27**
See also CA 114; 157; DLB 135, 153
Benson, Jackson J. 1930- .... **CLC 34**
See also CA 25-28R; DLB 111
Benson, Sally 1900-1972 .... **CLC 17**
See also CA 19-20; 37-40R; CAP 1; SATA 1, 35; SATA-Obit 27
Benson, Stella 1892-1933 .... **TCLC 17**
See also CA 117; 155; DLB 36, 162
Bentham, Jeremy 1748-1832 .... **NCLC 38**
See also DLB 107, 158
Bentley, E(dmund) C(lerihew)
1875-1956 .... **TCLC 12**
See also CA 108; DLB 70
Bentley, Eric (Russell) 1916- .... **CLC 24**
See also CA 5-8R; CANR 6, 67; INT CANR-6
Beranger, Pierre Jean de
1780-1857 .... **NCLC 34**
Berdyaev, Nicolas
See Berdyaev, Nikolai (Aleksandrovich)
Berdyaev, Nikolai (Aleksandrovich)
1874-1948 .... **TCLC 67**
See also CA 120; 157
Berdyayev, Nikolai (Aleksandrovich)
See Berdyaev, Nikolai (Aleksandrovich)
Berendt, John (Lawrence) 1939- ...... **CLC 86**
See also CA 146; CANR 75; DA3; MTCW 2
Beresford, J(ohn) D(avys)
1873-1947 .... **TCLC 81**
See also CA 112; 155; DLB 162, 178, 197
Bergelson, David 1884-1952 .... **TCLC 81**
Berger, Colonel
See Malraux, (Georges-)Andre
Berger, John (Peter) 1926- .... **CLC 2, 19**
See also CA 81-84; CANR 51, 78; DLB 14, 207
Berger, Melvin H. 1927- .... **CLC 12**
See also CA 5-8R; CANR 4; CLR 32; SAAS 2; SATA 5, 88
Berger, Thomas (Louis) 1924- .. **CLC 3, 5, 8, 11, 18, 38; DAM NOV**
See also CA 1-4R; CANR 5, 28, 51; DLB 2; DLBY 80; INT CANR-28; MTCW 1, 2

Bergman, (Ernst) Ingmar 1918- ...... **CLC 16, 72**
See also CA 81-84; CANR 33, 70; MTCW 2
Bergson, Henri(-Louis) 1859-1941 . **TCLC 32**
See also CA 164
Bergstein, Eleanor 1938- .... **CLC 4**
See also CA 53-56; CANR 5
Berkoff, Steven 1937- .... **CLC 56**
See also CA 104; CANR 72
Bermant, Chaim (Icyk) 1929- .... **CLC 40**
See also CA 57-60; CANR 6, 31, 57
Bern, Victoria
See Fisher, M(ary) F(rances) K(ennedy)
Bernanos, (Paul Louis) Georges
1888-1948 .... **TCLC 3**
See also CA 104; 130; DLB 72
Bernard, April 1956- .... **CLC 59**
See also CA 131
Berne, Victoria
See Fisher, M(ary) F(rances) K(ennedy)
Bernhard, Thomas 1931-1989 ..... **CLC 3, 32, 61**
See also CA 85-88; 127; CANR 32, 57; DLB 85, 124; MTCW 1
Bernhardt, Sarah (Henriette Rosine)
1844-1923 .... **TCLC 75**
See also CA 157
Berriault, Gina 1926-1999 .... **CLC 54, 109; SSC 30**
See also CA 116; 129; 185; CANR 66; DLB 130
Berrigan, Daniel 1921- .... **CLC 4**
See also CA 33-36R; CAAS 1; CANR 11, 43, 78; DLB 5
Berrigan, Edmund Joseph Michael, Jr.
1934-1983
See Berrigan, Ted
See also CA 61-64; 110; CANR 14
Berrigan, Ted CLC 37
See also Berrigan, Edmund Joseph Michael, Jr.
See also DLB 5, 169
Berry, Charles Edward Anderson 1931-
See Berry, Chuck
See also CA 115
Berry, Chuck CLC 17
See also Berry, Charles Edward Anderson
Berry, Jonas
See Ashbery, John (Lawrence)
Berry, Wendell (Erdman) 1934- .. **CLC 4, 6, 8, 27, 46; DAM POET; PC 28**
See also AITN 1; CA 73-76; CANR 50, 73; DLB 5, 6; MTCW 1
Berryman, John 1914-1972 ... **CLC 1, 2, 3, 4, 6, 8, 10, 13, 25, 62; DAM POET**
See also CA 13-16; 33-36R; CABS 2; CANR 35; CAP 1; CDALB 1941-1968; DLB 48; MTCW 1, 2
Bertolucci, Bernardo 1940- .... **CLC 16**
See also CA 106
Berton, Pierre (Francis Demarigny)
1920- .... **CLC 104**
See also CA 1-4R; CANR 2, 56; DLB 68; SATA 99
Bertrand, Aloysius 1807-1841 .... **NCLC 31**
Bertran de Born c. 1140-1215 .... **CMLC 5**
Besant, Annie (Wood) 1847-1933 ..... **TCLC 9**
See also CA 105; 185
Bessie, Alvah 1904-1985 .... **CLC 23**
See also CA 5-8R; 116; CANR 2, 80; DLB 26
Bethlen, T. D.
See Silverberg, Robert
Beti, Mongo CLC 27; BLC 1; DAM MULT
See also Biyidi, Alexandre
See also CANR 79

Betjeman, John 1906-1984 ...... **CLC 2, 6, 10, 34, 43; DAB; DAM MST, POET**
See also CA 9-12R; 112; CANR 33, 56; CDBLB 1945-1960; DA3; DLB 20; DLBY 84; MTCW 1, 2
Bettelheim, Bruno 1903-1990 .... **CLC 79**
See also CA 81-84; 131; CANR 23, 61; DA3; MTCW 1, 2
Betti, Ugo 1892-1953 .... **TCLC 5**
See also CA 104; 155
Betts, Doris (Waugh) 1932- ...... **CLC 3, 6, 28**
See also CA 13-16R; CANR 9, 66, 77; DLBY 82; INT CANR-9
Bevan, Alistair
See Roberts, Keith (John Kingston)
Bey, Pilaff
See Douglas, (George) Norman
Bialik, Chaim Nachman
1873-1934 .... **TCLC 25**
See also CA 170
Bickerstaff, Isaac
See Swift, Jonathan
Bidart, Frank 1939- .... **CLC 33**
See also CA 140
Bienek, Horst 1930- .... **CLC 7, 11**
See also CA 73-76; DLB 75
Bierce, Ambrose (Gwinett)
1842-1914(?) .... **TCLC 1, 7, 44; DA; DAC; DAM MST, SSC 9; WLC**
See also CA 104; 139; CANR 78; CDALB 1865-1917; DA3; DLB 11, 12, 23, 71, 74, 186
Biggers, Earl Derr 1884-1933 .... **TCLC 65**
See also CA 108; 153
Billings, Josh
See Shaw, Henry Wheeler
Billington, (Lady) Rachel (Mary)
1942- .... **CLC 43**
See also AITN 2; CA 33-36R; CANR 44
Binyon, T(imothy) J(ohn) 1936- .... **CLC 34**
See also CA 111; CANR 28
Bion 335B.C.-245B.C. .... **CMLC 39**
Bioy Casares, Adolfo 1914-1999 ... **CLC 4, 8, 13, 88; DAM MULT; HLC 1; SSC 17**
See also CA 29-32R; 177; CANR 19, 43, 66; DLB 113; HW 1, 2; MTCW 1, 2
Bird, Cordwainer
See Ellison, Harlan (Jay)
Bird, Robert Montgomery
1806-1854 .... **NCLC 1**
See also DLB 202
Birkerts, Sven 1951- .... **CLC 116**
See also CA 128; 133; 176; CAAE 176; CAAS 29; INT 133
Birney, (Alfred) Earle 1904-1995 .. **CLC 1, 4, 6, 11; DAC; DAM MST, POET**
See also CA 1-4R; CANR 5, 20; DLB 88; MTCW 1
Biruni, al 973-1048(?) .... **CMLC 28**
Bishop, Elizabeth 1911-1979 ..... **CLC 1, 4, 9, 13, 15, 32; DA; DAC; DAM MST, POET; PC 3**
See also CA 5-8R; 89-92; CABS 2; CANR 26, 61; CDALB 1968-1988; DA3; DLB 5, 169; MTCW 1, 2; SATA-Obit 24
Bishop, John 1935- .... **CLC 10**
See also CA 105
Bissett, Bill 1939- .... **CLC 18; PC 14**
See also CA 69-72; CAAS 19; CANR 15; DLB 53; MTCW 1
Bissoondath, Neil (Devindra)
1955- .... **CLC 120; DAC**
See also CA 136
Bitov, Andrei (Georgievich) 1937- ... **CLC 57**
See also CA 142
Biyidi, Alexandre 1932-
See Beti, Mongo
See also BW 1, 3; CA 114; 124; CANR 81; DA3; MTCW 1, 2

Bromell, Henry 1947- .... CLC 5
See also CA 53-56; CANR 9

Bromfield, Louis (Brucker)
1896-1956 .... TCLC 11
See also CA 107; 155; DLB 4, 9, 86

Broner, E(sther) M(asserman)
1930- .... CLC 19
See also CA 17-20R; CANR 8, 25, 72; DLB 28

Bronk, William (M.) 1918-1999 .... CLC 10
See also CA 89-92; 177; CANR 23; DLB 165

Bronstein, Lev Davidovich
See Trotsky, Leon

Bronte, Anne 1820-1849 .... NCLC 4, 71
See also DA3; DLB 21, 199

Bronte, Charlotte 1816-1855 ...... NCLC 3, 8, 33, 58; DA; DAB; DAC; DAM MST, NOV; WLC
See also AAYA 17; CDBLB 1832-1890; DA3; DLB 21, 159, 199

Bronte, Emily (Jane) 1818-1848 ... NCLC 16, 35; DA; DAB; DAC; DAM MST, NOV, POET; PC 8; WLC
See also AAYA 17; CDBLB 1832-1890; DA3; DLB 21, 32, 199

Brooke, Frances 1724-1789 .... LC 6, 48
See also DLB 39, 99

Brooke, Henry 1703(?)-1783 .... LC 1
See also DLB 39

Brooke, Rupert (Chawner)
1887-1915 .... TCLC 2, 7; DA; DAB; DAC; DAM MST, POET; PC 24; WLC
See also CA 104; 132; CANR 61; CDBLB 1914-1945; DLB 19; MTCW 1, 2

Brooke-Haven, P.
See Wodehouse, P(elham) G(renville)

Brooke-Rose, Christine 1926(?)- ...... CLC 40
See also CA 13-16R; CANR 58; DLB 14

Brookner, Anita 1928- .... CLC 32, 34, 51; DAB; DAM POP
See also CA 114; 120; CANR 37, 56, 87; DA3; DLB 194; DLBY 87; MTCW 1, 2

Brooks, Cleanth 1906-1994 .. CLC 24, 86, 110
See also CA 17-20R; 145; CANR 33, 35; DLB 63; DLBY 94; INT CANR-35; MTCW 1, 2

Brooks, George
See Baum, L(yman) Frank

Brooks, Gwendolyn 1917- ..... CLC 1, 2, 4, 5, 15, 49, 125; BLC 1; DA; DAC; DAM MST, MULT, POET; PC 7; WLC
See also AAYA 20; AITN 1; BW 2, 3; CA 1-4R; CANR 1, 27, 52, 75; CDALB 1941-1968; CLR 27; DA3; DLB 5, 76, 165; MTCW 1, 2; SATA 6

Brooks, Mel CLC 12
See also Kaminsky, Melvin
See also AAYA 13; DLB 26

Brooks, Peter 1938- .... CLC 34
See also CA 45-48; CANR 1

Brooks, Van Wyck 1886-1963 .... CLC 29
See also CA 1-4R; CANR 6; DLB 45, 63, 103

Brophy, Brigid (Antonia)
1929-1995 .... CLC 6, 11, 29, 105
See also CA 5-8R; 149; CAAS 4; CANR 25, 53; DA3; DLB 14; MTCW 1, 2

Brosman, Catharine Savage 1934- ..... CLC 9
See also CA 61-64; CANR 21, 46

Brossard, Nicole 1943- .... CLC 115
See also CA 122; CAAS 16; DLB 53

Brother Antoninus
See Everson, William (Oliver)

The Brothers Quay
See Quay, Stephen; Quay, Timothy

Broughton, T(homas) Alan 1936- ..... CLC 19
See also CA 45-48; CANR 2, 23, 48

Broumas, Olga 1949- .... CLC 10, 73
See also CA 85-88; CANR 20, 69

Brown, Alan 1950- .... CLC 99
See also CA 156

Brown, Charles Brockden
1771-1810 .... NCLC 22, 74
See also CDALB 1640-1865; DLB 37, 59, 73

Brown, Christy 1932-1981 .... CLC 63
See also CA 105; 104; CANR 72; DLB 14

Brown, Claude 1937- .... CLC 30; BLC 1; DAM MULT
See also AAYA 7; BW 1, 3; CA 73-76; CANR 81

Brown, Dee (Alexander) 1908- . CLC 18, 47; DAM POP
See also AAYA 30; CA 13-16R; CAAS 6; CANR 11, 45, 60; DA3; DLBY 80; MTCW 1, 2; SATA 5, 110

Brown, George
See Wertmueller, Lina

Brown, George Douglas
1869-1902 .... TCLC 28
See also CA 162

Brown, George Mackay 1921-1996 ... CLC 5, 48, 100
See also CA 21-24R; 151; CAAS 6; CANR 12, 37, 67; DLB 14, 27, 139; MTCW 1; SATA 35

Brown, (William) Larry 1951- .... CLC 73
See also CA 130; 134; INT 133

Brown, Moses
See Barrett, William (Christopher)

Brown, Rita Mae 1944- .... CLC 18, 43, 79; DAM NOV, POP
See also CA 45-48; CANR 2, 11, 35, 62; DA3; INT CANR-11; MTCW 1, 2

Brown, Roderick (Langmere) Haig-
See Haig-Brown, Roderick (Langmere)

Brown, Rosellen 1939- .... CLC 32
See also CA 77-80; CAAS 10; CANR 14, 44

Brown, Sterling Allen 1901-1989 ...... CLC 1, 23, 59; BLC 1; DAM MULT, POET
See also BW 1, 3; CA 85-88; 127; CANR 26; DA3; DLB 48, 51, 63; MTCW 1, 2

Brown, Will
See Ainsworth, William Harrison

Brown, William Wells 1813-1884 ... NCLC 2, 89; BLC 1; DAM MULT; DC 1
See also DLB 3, 50

Browne, (Clyde) Jackson 1948(?)- ... CLC 21
See also CA 120

Browning, Elizabeth Barrett
1806-1861 ...... NCLC 1, 16, 61, 66; DA; DAB; DAC; DAM MST, POET; PC 6; WLC
See also CDBLB 1832-1890; DA3; DLB 32, 199

Browning, Robert 1812-1889 . NCLC 19, 79; DA; DAB; DAC; DAM MST, POET; PC 2; WLCS
See also CDBLB 1832-1890; DA3; DLB 32, 163; YABC 1

Browning, Tod 1882-1962 .... CLC 16
See also CA 141; 117

Brownson, Orestes Augustus
1803-1876 .... NCLC 50
See also DLB 1, 59, 73

Bruccoli, Matthew J(oseph) 1931- ... CLC 34
See also CA 9-12R; CANR 7, 87; DLB 103

Bruce, Lenny CLC 21
See also Schneider, Leonard Alfred

Bruin, John
See Brutus, Dennis

Brulard, Henri
See Stendhal

Brulls, Christian
See Simenon, Georges (Jacques Christian)

Brunner, John (Kilian Houston)
1934-1995 .... CLC 8, 10; DAM POP
See also CA 1-4R; 149; CAAS 8; CANR 2, 37; MTCW 1, 2

Bruno, Giordano 1548-1600 .... LC 27

Brutus, Dennis 1924- .... CLC 43; BLC 1; DAM MULT, POET; PC 24
See also BW 2, 3; CA 49-52; CAAS 14; CANR 2, 27, 42, 81; DLB 117, 225

Bryan, C(ourtlandt) D(ixon) B(arnes)
1936- .... CLC 29
See also CA 73-76; CANR 13, 68; DLB 185; INT CANR-13

Bryan, Michael
See Moore, Brian

Bryan, William Jennings
1860-1925 .... TCLC 99

Bryant, William Cullen 1794-1878 . NCLC 6, 46; DA; DAB; DAC; DAM MST, POET; PC 20
See also CDALB 1640-1865; DLB 3, 43, 59, 189

Bryusov, Valery Yakovlevich
1873-1924 .... TCLC 10
See also CA 107; 155

Buchan, John 1875-1940 .... TCLC 41; DAB; DAM POP
See also CA 108; 145; DLB 34, 70, 156; MTCW 1; YABC 2

Buchanan, George 1506-1582 .... LC 4
See also DLB 152

Buchheim, Lothar-Guenther 1918- .... CLC 6
See also CA 85-88

Buchner, (Karl) Georg 1813-1837 . NCLC 26

Buchwald, Art(hur) 1925- .... CLC 33
See also AITN 1; CA 5-8R; CANR 21, 67; MTCW 1, 2; SATA 10

Buck, Pearl S(ydenstricker)
1892-1973 .... CLC 7, 11, 18, 127; DA; DAB; DAC; DAM MST, NOV
See also AITN 1; CA 1-4R; 41-44R; CANR 1, 34; CDALBS; DA3; DLB 9, 102; MTCW 1, 2; SATA 1, 25

Buckler, Ernest 1908-1984 .... CLC 13; DAC; DAM MST
See also CA 11-12; 114; CAP 1; DLB 68; SATA 47

Buckley, Vincent (Thomas)
1925-1988 .... CLC 57
See also CA 101

Buckley, William F(rank), Jr. 1925- . CLC 7, 18, 37; DAM POP
See also AITN 1; CA 1-4R; CANR 1, 24, 53; DA3; DLB 137; DLBY 80; INT CANR-24; MTCW 1, 2

Buechner, (Carl) Frederick 1926- . CLC 2, 4, 6, 9; DAM NOV
See also CA 13-16R; CANR 11, 39, 64; DLBY 80; INT CANR-11; MTCW 1, 2

Buell, John (Edward) 1927- .... CLC 10
See also CA 1-4R; CANR 71; DLB 53

Buero Vallejo, Antonio 1916- ..... CLC 15, 46
See also CA 106; CANR 24, 49, 75; HW 1; MTCW 1, 2

Bufalino, Gesualdo 1920(?)- .... CLC 74
See also DLB 196

Bugayev, Boris Nikolayevich
1880-1934 .... TCLC 7; PC 11
See also Bely, Andrey
See also CA 104; 165; MTCW 1

Bukowski, Charles 1920-1994 ... CLC 2, 5, 9, 41, 82, 108; DAM NOV, POET; PC 18
See also CA 17-20R; 144; CANR 40, 62; DA3; DLB 5, 130, 169; MTCW 1, 2

Bulgakov, Mikhail (Afanas'evich)
1891-1940 . TCLC 2, 16; DAM DRAM, NOV; SSC 18
See also CA 105; 152

Bulgya, Alexander Alexandrovich
1901-1956 .... **TCLC 53**
See also Fadeyev, Alexander
See also CA 117; 181

Bullins, Ed 1935- .... **CLC 1, 5, 7; BLC 1;**
DAM DRAM, MULT; DC 6
See also BW 2, 3; CA 49-52; CAAS 16;
CANR 24, 46, 73; DLB 7, 38; MTCW 1,
2

Bulwer-Lytton, Edward (George Earle
Lytton) 1803-1873 .... **NCLC 1, 45**
See also DLB 21

Bunin, Ivan Alexeyevich
1870-1953 .... **TCLC 6; SSC 5**
See also CA 104

Bunting, Basil 1900-1985 ..... **CLC 10, 39, 47;**
DAM POET
See also CA 53-56; 115; CANR 7; DLB 20

Bunuel, Luis 1900-1983 .. **CLC 16, 80; DAM**
MULT; HLC 1
See also CA 101; 110; CANR 32, 77; HW
1

Bunyan, John 1628-1688 ... **LC 4; DA; DAB;**
DAC; DAM MST; WLC
See also CDBLB 1660-1789; DLB 39

Burckhardt, Jacob (Christoph)
1818-1897 .... **NCLC 49**

Burford, Eleanor
See Hibbert, Eleanor Alice Burford

Burgess, Anthony -1993 .... **CLC 1, 2, 4, 5, 8,**
10, 13, 15, 22, 40, 62, 81, 94; DAB
See also Wilson, John (Anthony) Burgess
See also AAYA 25; AITN 1; CDBLB 1960
to Present; DLB 14, 194; DLBY 98;
MTCW 1

Burke, Edmund 1729(?)-1797 .... **LC 7, 36;**
DA; DAB; DAC; DAM MST; WLC
See also DA3; DLB 104

Burke, Kenneth (Duva) 1897-1993 ... **CLC 2,**
24
See also CA 5-8R; 143; CANR 39, 74; DLB
45, 63; MTCW 1, 2

Burke, Leda
See Garnett, David

Burke, Ralph
See Silverberg, Robert

Burke, Thomas 1886-1945 .... **TCLC 63**
See also CA 113; 155; DLB 197

Burney, Fanny 1752-1840 .. **NCLC 12, 54, 81**
See also DLB 39

Burns, Robert 1759-1796 . **LC 3, 29, 40; DA;**
DAB; DAC; DAM MST, POET; PC 6;
WLC
See also CDBLB 1789-1832; DA3; DLB
109

Burns, Tex
See L'Amour, Louis (Dearborn)

Burnshaw, Stanley 1906- .... **CLC 3, 13, 44**
See also CA 9-12R; DLB 48; DLBY 97

Burr, Anne 1937- .... **CLC 6**
See also CA 25-28R

Burroughs, Edgar Rice 1875-1950 . **TCLC 2,**
32; DAM NOV
See also AAYA 11; CA 104; 132; DA3;
DLB 8; MTCW 1, 2; SATA 41

Burroughs, William S(eward)
1914-1997 .. **CLC 1, 2, 5, 15, 22, 42, 75,**
109; DA; DAB; DAC; DAM MST,
NOV, POP; WLC
See also AITN 2; CA 9-12R; 160; CANR
20, 52; DA3; DLB 2, 8, 16, 152; DLBY
81, 97; MTCW 1, 2

Burton, SirRichard F(rancis)
1821-1890 .... **NCLC 42**
See also DLB 55, 166, 184

Busch, Frederick 1941- .... **CLC 7, 10, 18, 47**
See also CA 33-36R; CAAS 1; CANR 45,
73, 92; DLB 6

Bush, Ronald 1946- .... **CLC 34**
See also CA 136

Bustos, F(rancisco)
See Borges, Jorge Luis

Bustos Domecq, H(onorio)
See Bioy Casares, Adolfo; Borges, Jorge
Luis

Butler, Octavia E(stelle) 1947- .... **CLC 38,**
121; BLCS; DAM MULT, POP
See also AAYA 18; BW 2, 3; CA 73-76;
CANR 12, 24, 38, 73; CLR 65; DA3;
DLB 33; MTCW 1, 2; SATA 84

Butler, Robert Olen (Jr.) 1945- .... **CLC 81;**
DAM POP
See also CA 112; CANR 66; DLB 173; INT
112; MTCW 1

Butler, Samuel 1612-1680 .... **LC 16, 43**
See also DLB 101, 126

Butler, Samuel 1835-1902 . **TCLC 1, 33; DA;**
DAB; DAC; DAM MST, NOV; WLC
See also CA 143; CDBLB 1890-1914; DA3;
DLB 18, 57, 174

Butler, Walter C.
See Faust, Frederick (Schiller)

Butor, Michel (Marie Francois)
1926- .... **CLC 1, 3, 8, 11, 15**
See also CA 9-12R; CANR 33, 66; DLB
83; MTCW 1, 2

Butts, Mary 1892(?)-1937 .... **TCLC 77**
See also CA 148

Buzo, Alexander (John) 1944- .... **CLC 61**
See also CA 97-100; CANR 17, 39, 69

Buzzati, Dino 1906-1972 .... **CLC 36**
See also CA 160; 33-36R; DLB 177

Byars, Betsy (Cromer) 1928- .... **CLC 35**
See also AAYA 19; CA 33-36R, 183; CAAE
183; CANR 18, 36, 57; CLR 1, 16; DLB
52; INT CANR-18; JRDA; MAICYA;
MTCW 1; SAAS 1; SATA 4, 46, 80;
SATA-Essay 108

Byatt, A(ntonia) S(usan Drabble)
1936- ..... **CLC 19, 65; DAM NOV, POP**
See also CA 13-16R; CANR 13, 33, 50, 75;
DA3; DLB 14, 194; MTCW 1, 2

Byrne, David 1952- .... **CLC 26**
See also CA 127

Byrne, John Keyes 1926-
See Leonard, Hugh
See also CA 102; CANR 78; INT 102

Byron, George Gordon (Noel)
1788-1824 .... **NCLC 2, 12; DA; DAB;**
DAC; DAM MST, POET; PC 16; WLC
See also CDBLB 1789-1832; DA3; DLB
96, 110

Byron, Robert 1905-1941 .... **TCLC 67**
See also CA 160; DLB 195

C. 3. 3.
See Wilde, Oscar (Fingal O'Flahertie Wills)

Caballero, Fernan 1796-1877 .... **NCLC 10**

Cabell, Branch
See Cabell, James Branch

Cabell, James Branch 1879-1958 .... **TCLC 6**
See also CA 105; 152; DLB 9, 78; MTCW
1

Cable, George Washington
1844-1925 .... **TCLC 4; SSC 4**
See also CA 104; 155; DLB 12, 74; DLBD
13

Cabral de Melo Neto, Joao 1920- ... **CLC 76;**
DAM MULT
See also CA 151

Cabrera Infante, G(uillermo) 1929- . **CLC 5,**
25, 45, 120; DAM MULT; HLC 1; SSC
39
See also CA 85-88; CANR 29, 65; DA3;
DLB 113; HW 1, 2; MTCW 1, 2

Cade, Toni
See Bambara, Toni Cade

Cadmus and Harmonia
See Buchan, John

Caedmon fl. 658-680 .... **CMLC 7**
See also DLB 146

Caeiro, Alberto
See Pessoa, Fernando (Antonio Nogueira)

Cage, John (Milton, Jr.) 1912-1992 . **CLC 41**
See also CA 13-16R; 169; CANR 9, 78;
DLB 193; INT CANR-9

Cahan, Abraham 1860-1951 .... **TCLC 71**
See also CA 108; 154; DLB 9, 25, 28

Cain, G.
See Cabrera Infante, G(uillermo)

Cain, Guillermo
See Cabrera Infante, G(uillermo)

Cain, James M(allahan) 1892-1977 .. **CLC 3,**
11, 28
See also AITN 1; CA 17-20R; 73-76;
CANR 8, 34, 61; DLB 226; MTCW 1

Caine, Hall 1853-1931 .... **TCLC 97**

Caine, Mark
See Raphael, Frederic (Michael)

Calasso, Roberto 1941- .... **CLC 81**
See also CA 143; CANR 89

Calderon de la Barca, Pedro
1600-1681 .... **LC 23; DC 3; HLCS 1**

Caldwell, Erskine (Preston)
1903-1987 .. **CLC 1, 8, 14, 50, 60; DAM**
NOV; SSC 19
See also AITN 1; CA 1-4R; 121; CAAS 1;
CANR 2, 33; DA3; DLB 9, 86; MTCW
1, 2

Caldwell, (Janet Miriam) Taylor (Holland)
1900-1985 .. **CLC 2, 28, 39; DAM NOV,**
POP
See also CA 5-8R; 116; CANR 5; DA3;
DLBD 17

Calhoun, John Caldwell
1782-1850 .... **NCLC 15**
See also DLB 3

Calisher, Hortense 1911- ..... **CLC 2, 4, 8, 38,**
134; DAM NOV; SSC 15
See also CA 1-4R; CANR 1, 22, 67; DA3;
DLB 2; INT CANR-22; MTCW 1, 2

Callaghan, Morley Edward
1903-1990 ...... **CLC 3, 14, 41, 65; DAC;**
DAM MST
See also CA 9-12R; 132; CANR 33, 73;
DLB 68; MTCW 1, 2

Callimachus c. 305B.C.-c.
240B.C. .... **CMLC 18**
See also DLB 176

Calvin, John 1509-1564 .... **LC 37**

Calvino, Italo 1923-1985 .... **CLC 5, 8, 11, 22,**
33, 39, 73; DAM NOV; SSC 3
See also CA 85-88; 116; CANR 23, 61;
DLB 196; MTCW 1, 2

Cameron, Carey 1952- .... **CLC 59**
See also CA 135

Cameron, Peter 1959- .... **CLC 44**
See also CA 125; CANR 50

Camoens, Luis Vaz de 1524(?)-1580
See also HLCS 1

Camoes, Luis de 1524(?)-1580 .... **PC 31**
See also HLCS 1

Campana, Dino 1885-1932 .... **TCLC 20**
See also CA 117; DLB 114

Campanella, Tommaso 1568-1639 .... **LC 32**

Campbell, John W(ood, Jr.)
1910-1971 .... **CLC 32**
See also CA 21-22; 29-32R; CANR 34;
CAP 2; DLB 8; MTCW 1

Campbell, Joseph 1904-1987 .... **CLC 69**
See also AAYA 3; BEST 89:2; CA 1-4R;
124; CANR 3, 28, 61; DA3; MTCW 1, 2

Campbell, Maria 1940- .... **CLC 85; DAC**
See also CA 102; CANR 54; NNAL

Codrescu, Andrei 1946- .... **CLC 46, 121; DAM POET**
See also CA 33-36R; CAAS 19; CANR 13, 34, 53, 76; DA3; MTCW 2

Coe, Max
See Bourne, Randolph S(illiman)

Coe, Tucker
See Westlake, Donald E(dwin)

Coen, Ethan 1958- .... **CLC 108**
See also CA 126; CANR 85

Coen, Joel 1955- .... **CLC 108**
See also CA 126

The Coen Brothers
See Coen, Ethan; Coen, Joel

Coetzee, J(ohn) M(ichael) 1940- ...... **CLC 23, 33, 66, 117; DAM NOV**
See also CA 77-80; CANR 41, 54, 74; DA3; DLB 225; MTCW 1, 2

Coffey, Brian
See Koontz, Dean R(ay)

Coffin, Robert P(eter) Tristram
1892-1955 .... **TCLC 95**
See also CA 123; 169; DLB 45

Cohan, George M(ichael)
1878-1942 .... **TCLC 60**
See also CA 157

Cohen, Arthur A(llen) 1928-1986 ...... **CLC 7, 31**
See also CA 1-4R; 120; CANR 1, 17, 42; DLB 28

Cohen, Leonard (Norman) 1934- ...... **CLC 3, 38; DAC; DAM MST**
See also CA 21-24R; CANR 14, 69; DLB 53; MTCW 1

Cohen, Matt 1942-1999 .... **CLC 19; DAC**
See also CA 61-64; CAAS 18; CANR 40; DLB 53

Cohen-Solal, Annie 19(?)- .... **CLC 50**

Colegate, Isabel 1931- .... **CLC 36**
See also CA 17-20R; CANR 8, 22, 74; DLB 14; INT CANR-22; MTCW 1

Coleman, Emmett
See Reed, Ishmael

Coleridge, Hartley 1796-1849 .... **NCLC 90**
See also DLB 96

Coleridge, M. E.
See Coleridge, Mary E(lizabeth)

Coleridge, Mary E(lizabeth)
1861-1907 .... **TCLC 73**
See also CA 116; 166; DLB 19, 98

Coleridge, Samuel Taylor
1772-1834 .... **NCLC 9, 54; DA; DAB; DAC; DAM MST, POET; PC 11; WLC**
See also CDBLB 1789-1832; DA3; DLB 93, 107

Coleridge, Sara 1802-1852 .... **NCLC 31**
See also DLB 199

Coles, Don 1928- .... **CLC 46**
See also CA 115; CANR 38

Coles, Robert (Martin) 1929- .... **CLC 108**
See also CA 45-48; CANR 3, 32, 66, 70; INT CANR-32; SATA 23

Colette, (Sidonie-Gabrielle)
1873-1954 . **TCLC 1, 5, 16; DAM NOV; SSC 10**
See also CA 104; 131; DA3; DLB 65; MTCW 1, 2

Collett, (Jacobine) Camilla (Wergeland)
1813-1895 .... **NCLC 22**

Collier, Christopher 1930- .... **CLC 30**
See also AAYA 13; CA 33-36R; CANR 13, 33; JRDA; MAICYA; SATA 16, 70

Collier, James L(incoln) 1928- .... **CLC 30; DAM POP**
See also AAYA 13; CA 9-12R; CANR 4, 33, 60; CLR 3; JRDA; MAICYA; SAAS 21; SATA 8, 70

Collier, Jeremy 1650-1726 .... **LC 6**

Collier, John 1901-1980 .... **SSC 19**
See also CA 65-68; 97-100; CANR 10; DLB 77

Collingwood, R(obin) G(eorge)
1889(?)-1943 .... **TCLC 67**
See also CA 117; 155

Collins, Hunt
See Hunter, Evan

Collins, Linda 1931- .... **CLC 44**
See also CA 125

Collins, (William) Wilkie
1824-1889 .... **NCLC 1, 18**
See also CDBLB 1832-1890; DLB 18, 70, 159

Collins, William 1721-1759 . **LC 4, 40; DAM POET**
See also DLB 109

Collodi, Carlo 1826-1890 .... **NCLC 54**
See also Lorenzini, Carlo
See also CLR 5

Colman, George 1732-1794
See Glassco, John

Colt, Winchester Remington
See Hubbard, L(afayette) Ron(ald)

Colter, Cyrus 1910- .... **CLC 58**
See also BW 1; CA 65-68; CANR 10, 66; DLB 33

Colton, James
See Hansen, Joseph

Colum, Padraic 1881-1972 .... **CLC 28**
See also CA 73-76; 33-36R; CANR 35; CLR 36; MAICYA; MTCW 1; SATA 15

Colvin, James
See Moorcock, Michael (John)

Colwin, Laurie (E.) 1944-1992 .... **CLC 5, 13, 23, 84**
See also CA 89-92; 139; CANR 20, 46; DLBY 80; MTCW 1

Comfort, Alex(ander) 1920- .... **CLC 7; DAM POP**
See also CA 1-4R; CANR 1, 45; MTCW 1

Comfort, Montgomery
See Campbell, (John) Ramsey

Compton-Burnett, I(vy)
1884(?)-1969 .... **CLC 1, 3, 10, 15, 34; DAM NOV**
See also CA 1-4R; 25-28R; CANR 4; DLB 36; MTCW 1

Comstock, Anthony 1844-1915 ...... **TCLC 13**
See also CA 110; 169

Comte, Auguste 1798-1857 .... **NCLC 54**

Conan Doyle, Arthur
See Doyle, Arthur Conan

Conde (Abellan), Carmen 1901-
See also CA 177; DLB 108; HLCS 1; HW 2

Conde, Maryse 1937- .... **CLC 52, 92; BLCS; DAM MULT**
See also BW 2, 3; CA 110; CANR 30, 53, 76; MTCW 1

Condillac, Etienne Bonnot de
1714-1780 .... **LC 26**

Condon, Richard (Thomas)
1915-1996 ...... **CLC 4, 6, 8, 10, 45, 100; DAM NOV**
See also BEST 90:3; CA 1-4R; 151; CAAS 1; CANR 2, 23; INT CANR-23; MTCW 1, 2

Confucius 551B.C.-479B.C. .. **CMLC 19; DA; DAB; DAC; DAM MST; WLCS**
See also DA3

Congreve, William 1670-1729 .... **LC 5, 21; DA; DAB; DAC; DAM DRAM, MST, POET; DC 2; WLC**
See also CDBLB 1660-1789; DLB 39, 84

Connell, Evan S(helby), Jr. 1924- . **CLC 4, 6, 45; DAM NOV**
See also AAYA 7; CA 1-4R; CAAS 2; CANR 2, 39, 76; DLB 2; DLBY 81; MTCW 1, 2

Connelly, Marc(us Cook) 1890-1980 . **CLC 7**
See also CA 85-88; 102; CANR 30; DLB 7; DLBY 80; SATA-Obit 25

Connor, Ralph TCLC 31
See also Gordon, Charles William
See also DLB 92

Conrad, Joseph 1857-1924 .... **TCLC 1, 6, 13, 25, 43, 57; DA; DAB; DAC; DAM MST, NOV; SSC 9; WLC**
See also AAYA 26; CA 104; 131; CANR 60; CDBLB 1890-1914; DA3; DLB 10, 34, 98, 156; MTCW 1, 2; SATA 27

Conrad, Robert Arnold
See Hart, Moss

Conroy, Pat
See Conroy, (Donald) Pat(rick)
See also MTCW 2

Conroy, (Donald) Pat(rick) 1945- ... **CLC 30, 74; DAM NOV, POP**
See also Conroy, Pat
See also AAYA 8; AITN 1; CA 85-88; CANR 24, 53; DA3; DLB 6; MTCW 1

Constant (de Rebecque), (Henri) Benjamin
1767-1830 .... **NCLC 6**
See also DLB 119

Conybeare, Charles Augustus
See Eliot, T(homas) S(tearns)

Cook, Michael 1933- .... **CLC 58**
See also CA 93-96; CANR 68; DLB 53

Cook, Robin 1940- .... **CLC 14; DAM POP**
See also AAYA 32; BEST 90:2; CA 108; 111; CANR 41, 90; DA3; INT 111

Cook, Roy
See Silverberg, Robert

Cooke, Elizabeth 1948- .... **CLC 55**
See also CA 129

Cooke, John Esten 1830-1886 .... **NCLC 5**
See also DLB 3

Cooke, John Estes
See Baum, L(yman) Frank

Cooke, M. E.
See Creasey, John

Cooke, Margaret
See Creasey, John

Cook-Lynn, Elizabeth 1930- . **CLC 93; DAM MULT**
See also CA 133; DLB 175; NNAL

Cooney, Ray CLC 62

Cooper, Douglas 1960- .... **CLC 86**

Cooper, Henry St. John
See Creasey, John

Cooper, J(oan) California (?)- .... **CLC 56; DAM MULT**
See also AAYA 12; BW 1; CA 125; CANR 55; DLB 212

Cooper, James Fenimore
1789-1851 .... **NCLC 1, 27, 54**
See also AAYA 22; CDALB 1640-1865; DA3; DLB 3; SATA 19

Coover, Robert (Lowell) 1932- ...... **CLC 3, 7, 15, 32, 46, 87; DAM NOV; SSC 15**
See also CA 45-48; CANR 3, 37, 58; DLB 2, 227; DLBY 81; MTCW 1, 2

Copeland, Stewart (Armstrong)
1952- .... **CLC 26**

Copernicus, Nicolaus 1473-1543 .... **LC 45**

Coppard, A(lfred) E(dgar)
1878-1957 .... **TCLC 5; SSC 21**
See also CA 114; 167; DLB 162; YABC 1

Coppee, Francois 1842-1908 .... **TCLC 25**
See also CA 170

Coppola, Francis Ford 1939- ... **CLC 16, 126**
See also CA 77-80; CANR 40, 78; DLB 44

Corbiere, Tristan 1845-1875 .... **NCLC 43**

Corcoran, Barbara 1911- .... **CLC 17**
See also AAYA 14; CA 21-24R; CAAS 2;
CANR 11, 28, 48; CLR 50; DLB 52;
JRDA; SAAS 20; SATA 3, 77

Cordelier, Maurice
See Giraudoux, (Hippolyte) Jean

Corelli, Marie 1855-1924 .... **TCLC 51**
See also Mackey, Mary
See also DLB 34, 156

Corman, Cid 1924- .... **CLC 9**
See also Corman, Sidney
See also CAAS 2; DLB 5, 193

Corman, Sidney 1924-
See Corman, Cid
See also CA 85-88; CANR 44; DAM POET

Cormier, Robert (Edmund) 1925- ... **CLC 12,
30; DA; DAB; DAC; DAM MST, NOV**
See also AAYA 3, 19; CA 1-4R; CANR 5,
23, 76; CDALB 1968-1988; CLR 12, 55;
DLB 52; INT CANR-23; JRDA; MAI-
CYA; MTCW 1, 2; SATA 10, 45, 83

Corn, Alfred (DeWitt III) 1943- .... **CLC 33**
See also CA 179; CAAE 179; CAAS 25;
CANR 44; DLB 120; DLBY 80

Corneille, Pierre 1606-1684 ..... **LC 28; DAB;
DAM MST**

Cornwell, David (John Moore)
1931- .... **CLC 9, 15; DAM POP**
See also le Carre, John
See also CA 5-8R; CANR 13, 33, 59; DA3;
MTCW 1, 2

Corso, (Nunzio) Gregory 1930- .... **CLC 1, 11**
See also CA 5-8R; CANR 41, 76; DA3;
DLB 5, 16; MTCW 1, 2

Cortazar, Julio 1914-1984 ... **CLC 2, 3, 5, 10,
13, 15, 33, 34, 92; DAM MULT, NOV;
HLC 1; SSC 7**
See also CA 21-24R; CANR 12, 32, 81;
DA3; DLB 113; HW 1, 2; MTCW 1, 2

Cortes, Hernan 1484-1547 .... **LC 31**

Corvinus, Jakob
See Raabe, Wilhelm (Karl)

Corwin, Cecil
See Kornbluth, C(yril) M.

Cosic, Dobrica 1921- .... **CLC 14**
See also CA 122; 138; DLB 181

Costain, Thomas B(ertram)
1885-1965 .... **CLC 30**
See also CA 5-8R; 25-28R; DLB 9

Costantini, Humberto 1924(?)-1987 . **CLC 49**
See also CA 131; 122; HW 1

Costello, Elvis 1955- .... **CLC 21**

Costenoble, Philostene
See Ghelderode, Michel de

Cotes, Cecil V.
See Duncan, Sara Jeannette

Cotter, Joseph Seamon Sr.
1861-1949 ...... **TCLC 28; BLC 1; DAM
MULT**
See also BW 1; CA 124; DLB 50

Couch, Arthur Thomas Quiller
See Quiller-Couch, SirArthur (Thomas)

Coulton, James
See Hansen, Joseph

Couperus, Louis (Marie Anne)
1863-1923 .... **TCLC 15**
See also CA 115

Coupland, Douglas 1961- .... **CLC 85, 133;
DAC; DAM POP**
See also AAYA 34; CA 142; CANR 57, 90

Court, Wesli
See Turco, Lewis (Putnam)

Courtenay, Bryce 1933- .... **CLC 59**
See also CA 138

Courtney, Robert
See Ellison, Harlan (Jay)

Cousteau, Jacques-Yves 1910-1997 .. **CLC 30**
See also CA 65-68; 159; CANR 15, 67;
MTCW 1; SATA 38, 98

Coventry, Francis 1725-1754 .... **LC 46**

Cowan, Peter (Walkinshaw) 1914- .... **SSC 28**
See also CA 21-24R; CANR 9, 25, 50, 83

Coward, Noel (Peirce) 1899-1973 . **CLC 1, 9,
29, 51; DAM DRAM**
See also AITN 1; CA 17-18; 41-44R;
CANR 35; CAP 2; CDBLB 1914-1945;
DA3; DLB 10; MTCW 1, 2

Cowley, Abraham 1618-1667 .... **LC 43**
See also DLB 131, 151

Cowley, Malcolm 1898-1989 .... **CLC 39**
See also CA 5-8R; 128; CANR 3, 55; DLB
4, 48; DLBY 81, 89; MTCW 1, 2

Cowper, William 1731-1800 . **NCLC 8; DAM
POET**
See also DA3; DLB 104, 109

Cox, William Trevor 1928- ... **CLC 9, 14, 71;
DAM NOV**
See also Trevor, William
See also CA 9-12R; CANR 4, 37, 55, 76;
DLB 14; INT CANR-37; MTCW 1, 2

Coyne, P. J.
See Masters, Hilary

Cozzens, James Gould 1903-1978 . **CLC 1, 4,
11, 92**
See also CA 9-12R; 81-84; CANR 19;
CDALB 1941-1968; DLB 9; DLBD 2;
DLBY 84, 97; MTCW 1, 2

Crabbe, George 1754-1832 .... **NCLC 26**
See also DLB 93

Craddock, Charles Egbert
See Murfree, Mary Noailles

Craig, A. A.
See Anderson, Poul (William)

Craik, Dinah Maria (Mulock)
1826-1887 .... **NCLC 38**
See also DLB 35, 163; MAICYA; SATA 34

Cram, Ralph Adams 1863-1942 ..... **TCLC 45**
See also CA 160

Crane, (Harold) Hart 1899-1932 .... **TCLC 2,
5, 80; DA; DAB; DAC; DAM MST,
POET; PC 3; WLC**
See also CA 104; 127; CDALB 1917-1929;
DA3; DLB 4, 48; MTCW 1, 2

Crane, R(onald) S(almon)
1886-1967 .... **CLC 27**
See also CA 85-88; DLB 63

Crane, Stephen (Townley)
1871-1900 .... **TCLC 11, 17, 32; DA;
DAB; DAC; DAM MST, NOV, POET;
SSC 7; WLC**
See also AAYA 21; CA 109; 140; CANR
84; CDALB 1865-1917; DA3; DLB 12,
54, 78; YABC 2

Cranshaw, Stanley
See Fisher, Dorothy (Frances) Canfield

Crase, Douglas 1944- .... **CLC 58**
See also CA 106

Crashaw, Richard 1612(?)-1649 .... **LC 24**
See also DLB 126

Craven, Margaret 1901-1980 .... **CLC 17;
DAC**
See also CA 103

Crawford, F(rancis) Marion
1854-1909 .... **TCLC 10**
See also CA 107; 168; DLB 71

Crawford, Isabella Valancy
1850-1887 .... **NCLC 12**
See also DLB 92

Crayon, Geoffrey
See Irving, Washington

Creasey, John 1908-1973 .... **CLC 11**
See also CA 5-8R; 41-44R; CANR 8, 59;
DLB 77; MTCW 1

Crebillon, Claude Prosper Jolyot de (fils)
1707-1777 .... **LC 1, 28**

Credo
See Creasey, John

Credo, Alvaro J. de
See Prado (Calvo), Pedro

Creeley, Robert (White) 1926- .. **CLC 1, 2, 4,
8, 11, 15, 36, 78; DAM POET**
See also CA 1-4R; CAAS 10; CANR 23,
43, 89; DA3; DLB 5, 16, 169; DLBD 17;
MTCW 1, 2

Crews, Harry (Eugene) 1935- ..... **CLC 6, 23,
49**
See also AITN 1; CA 25-28R; CANR 20,
57; DA3; DLB 6, 143, 185; MTCW 1, 2

Crichton, (John) Michael 1942- .... **CLC 2, 6,
54, 90; DAM NOV, POP**
See also AAYA 10; AITN 2; CA 25-28R;
CANR 13, 40, 54, 76; DA3; DLBY 81;
INT CANR-13; JRDA; MTCW 1, 2;
SATA 9, 88

Crispin, Edmund **CLC 22**
See also Montgomery, (Robert) Bruce
See also DLB 87

Cristofer, Michael 1945(?)- ... **CLC 28; DAM
DRAM**
See also CA 110; 152; DLB 7

Croce, Benedetto 1866-1952 .... **TCLC 37**
See also CA 120; 155

Crockett, David 1786-1836 .... **NCLC 8**
See also DLB 3, 11

Crockett, Davy
See Crockett, David

Crofts, Freeman Wills 1879-1957 .. **TCLC 55**
See also CA 115; DLB 77

Croker, John Wilson 1780-1857 .... **NCLC 10**
See also DLB 110

Crommelynck, Fernand 1885-1970 .. **CLC 75**
See also CA 89-92

Cromwell, Oliver 1599-1658 .... **LC 43**

Cronin, A(rchibald) J(oseph)
1896-1981 .... **CLC 32**
See also CA 1-4R; 102; CANR 5; DLB 191;
SATA 47; SATA-Obit 25

Cross, Amanda
See Heilbrun, Carolyn G(old)

Crothers, Rachel 1878(?)-1958 .... **TCLC 19**
See also CA 113; DLB 7

Croves, Hal
See Traven, B.

Crow Dog, Mary (Ellen) (?)- .... **CLC 93**
See also Brave Bird, Mary
See also CA 154

Crowfield, Christopher
See Stowe, Harriet (Elizabeth) Beecher

Crowley, Aleister **TCLC 7**
See also Crowley, Edward Alexander

Crowley, Edward Alexander 1875-1947
See Crowley, Aleister
See also CA 104

Crowley, John 1942- .... **CLC 57**
See also CA 61-64; CANR 43; DLBY 82;
SATA 65

Crud
See Crumb, R(obert)

Crumarums
See Crumb, R(obert)

Crumb, R(obert) 1943- .... **CLC 17**
See also CA 106

Crumbum
See Crumb, R(obert)

Crumski
See Crumb, R(obert)

Crum the Bum
See Crumb, R(obert)

Crunk
See Crumb, R(obert)

Crustt
See Crumb, R(obert)

Cruz, Victor Hernandez 1949-
See also BW 2; CA 65-68; CAAS 17; CANR 14, 32, 74; DAM MULT, POET; DLB 41; HLC 1; HW 1, 2; MTCW 1

Cryer, Gretchen (Kiger) 1935- .... **CLC 21**
See also CA 114; 123

Csath, Geza 1887-1919 .... **TCLC 13**
See also CA 111

Cudlip, David R(ockwell) 1933- .... **CLC 34**
See also CA 177

Cullen, Countee 1903-1946 .... **TCLC 4, 37; BLC 1; DA; DAC; DAM MST, MULT, POET; PC 20; WLCS**
See also BW 1; CA 108; 124; CDALB 1917-1929; DA3; DLB 4, 48, 51; MTCW 1, 2; SATA 18

Cum, R.
See Crumb, R(obert)

Cummings, Bruce F(rederick) 1889-1919
See Barbellion, W. N. P.
See also CA 123

Cummings, E(dward) E(stlin) 1894-1962 .... **CLC 1, 3, 8, 12, 15, 68; DA; DAB; DAC; DAM MST, POET; PC 5; WLC**
See also CA 73-76; CANR 31; CDALB 1929-1941; DA3; DLB 4, 48; MTCW 1, 2

Cunha, Euclides (Rodrigues Pimenta) da 1866-1909 .... **TCLC 24**
See also CA 123

Cunningham, E. V.
See Fast, Howard (Melvin)

Cunningham, J(ames) V(incent) 1911-1985 .... **CLC 3, 31**
See also CA 1-4R; 115; CANR 1, 72; DLB 5

Cunningham, Julia (Woolfolk) 1916- .... **CLC 12**
See also CA 9-12R; CANR 4, 19, 36; JRDA; MAICYA; SAAS 2; SATA 1, 26

Cunningham, Michael 1952- .... **CLC 34**
See also CA 136

Cunninghame Graham, R. B.
See Cunninghame Graham, Robert (Gallnigad) Bontine

Cunninghame Graham, Robert (Gallnigad) Bontine 1852-1936 .... **TCLC 19**
See also Graham, R(obert) B(ontine) Cunninghame
See also CA 119; 184; DLB 98

Currie, Ellen 19(?)- .... **CLC 44**

Curtin, Philip
See Lowndes, Marie Adelaide (Belloc)

Curtis, Price
See Ellison, Harlan (Jay)

Cutrate, Joe
See Spiegelman, Art

Cynewulf c. 770-c. 840 .... **CMLC 23**

Czaczkes, Shmuel Yosef
See Agnon, S(hmuel) Y(osef Halevi)

Dabrowska, Maria (Szumska) 1889-1965 .... **CLC 15**
See also CA 106

Dabydeen, David 1955- .... **CLC 34**
See also BW 1; CA 125; CANR 56, 92

Dacey, Philip 1939- .... **CLC 51**
See also CA 37-40R; CAAS 17; CANR 14, 32, 64; DLB 105

Dagerman, Stig (Halvard) 1923-1954 .... **TCLC 17**
See also CA 117; 155

Dahl, Roald 1916-1990 ...... **CLC 1, 6, 18, 79; DAB; DAC; DAM MST, NOV, POP**
See also AAYA 15; CA 1-4R; 133; CANR 6, 32, 37, 62; CLR 1, 7, 41; DA3; DLB

139; JRDA; MAICYA; MTCW 1, 2; SATA 1, 26, 73; SATA-Obit 65

Dahlberg, Edward 1900-1977 .. **CLC 1, 7, 14**
See also CA 9-12R; 69-72; CANR 31, 62; DLB 48; MTCW 1

Daitch, Susan 1954- .... **CLC 103**
See also CA 161

Dale, Colin TCLC 18
See also Lawrence, T(homas) E(dward)

Dale, George E.
See Asimov, Isaac

Dalton, Roque 1935-1975
See also HLCS 1; HW 2

Daly, Elizabeth 1878-1967 .... **CLC 52**
See also CA 23-24; 25-28R; CANR 60; CAP 2

Daly, Maureen 1921-1983 .... **CLC 17**
See also AAYA 5; CANR 37, 83; JRDA; MAICYA; SAAS 1; SATA 2

Damas, Leon-Gontran 1912-1978 .... **CLC 84**
See also BW 1; CA 125; 73-76

Dana, Richard Henry Sr. 1787-1879 .... **NCLC 53**

Daniel, Samuel 1562(?)-1619 .... **LC 24**
See also DLB 62

Daniels, Brett
See Adler, Renata

Dannay, Frederic 1905-1982 . **CLC 11; DAM POP**
See also Queen, Ellery
See also CA 1-4R; 107; CANR 1, 39; DLB 137; MTCW 1

D'Annunzio, Gabriele 1863-1938 ... **TCLC 6, 40**
See also CA 104; 155

Danois, N. le
See Gourmont, Remy (-Marie-Charles) de

Dante 1265-1321 .... **CMLC 3, 18, 39; DA; DAB; DAC; DAM MST, POET; PC 21; WLCS**
See also Alighieri, Dante
See also DA3

d'Antibes, Germain
See Simenon, Georges (Jacques Christian)

Danticat, Edwidge 1969- .... **CLC 94**
See also AAYA 29; CA 152; CANR 73; MTCW 1

Danvers, Dennis 1947- .... **CLC 70**

Danziger, Paula 1944- .... **CLC 21**
See also AAYA 4; CA 112; 115; CANR 37; CLR 20; JRDA; MAICYA; SATA 36, 63, 102; SATA-Brief 30

Da Ponte, Lorenzo 1749-1838 .... **NCLC 50**

Dario, Ruben 1867-1916 .... **TCLC 4; DAM MULT; HLC 1; PC 15**
See also CA 131; CANR 81; HW 1, 2; MTCW 1, 2

Darley, George 1795-1846 .... **NCLC 2**
See also DLB 96

Darrow, Clarence (Seward) 1857-1938 .... **TCLC 81**
See also CA 164

Darwin, Charles 1809-1882 .... **NCLC 57**
See also DLB 57, 166

Daryush, Elizabeth 1887-1977 ...... **CLC 6, 19**
See also CA 49-52; CANR 3, 81; DLB 20

Dasgupta, Surendranath 1887-1952 .... **TCLC 81**
See also CA 157

Dashwood, Edmee Elizabeth Monica de la Pasture 1890-1943
See Delafield, E. M.
See also CA 119; 154

Daudet, (Louis Marie) Alphonse 1840-1897 .... **NCLC 1**
See also DLB 123

Daumal, Rene 1908-1944 .... **TCLC 14**
See also CA 114

Davenant, William 1606-1668 .... **LC 13**
See also DLB 58, 126

Davenport, Guy (Mattison, Jr.) 1927- .... **CLC 6, 14, 38; SSC 16**
See also CA 33-36R; CANR 23, 73; DLB 130

Davidson, Avram (James) 1923-1993
See Queen, Ellery
See also CA 101; 171; CANR 26; DLB 8

Davidson, Donald (Grady) 1893-1968 .... **CLC 2, 13, 19**
See also CA 5-8R; 25-28R; CANR 4, 84; DLB 45

Davidson, Hugh
See Hamilton, Edmond

Davidson, John 1857-1909 .... **TCLC 24**
See also CA 118; DLB 19

Davidson, Sara 1943- .... **CLC 9**
See also CA 81-84; CANR 44, 68; DLB 185

Davie, Donald (Alfred) 1922-1995 .... **CLC 5, 8, 10, 31; PC 29**
See also CA 1-4R; 149; CAAS 3; CANR 1, 44; DLB 27; MTCW 1

Davies, Ray(mond Douglas) 1944- ... **CLC 21**
See also CA 116; 146; CANR 92

Davies, Rhys 1901-1978 .... **CLC 23**
See also CA 9-12R; 81-84; CANR 4; DLB 139, 191

Davies, (William) Robertson 1913-1995 .... **CLC 2, 7, 13, 25, 42, 75, 91; DA; DAB; DAC; DAM MST, NOV, POP; WLC**
See also BEST 89:2; CA 33-36R; 150; CANR 17, 42; DA3; DLB 68; INT CANR-17; MTCW 1, 2

Davies, Walter C.
See Kornbluth, C(yril) M.

Davies, William Henry 1871-1940 ... **TCLC 5**
See also CA 104; 179; DLB 19, 174

Da Vinci, Leonardo 1452-1519 ..... **LC 12, 57, 60**

Davis, Angela (Yvonne) 1944- .... **CLC 77; DAM MULT**
See also BW 2, 3; CA 57-60; CANR 10, 81; DA3

Davis, B. Lynch
See Bioy Casares, Adolfo; Borges, Jorge Luis

Davis, B. Lynch
See Bioy Casares, Adolfo

Davis, H(arold) L(enoir) 1894-1960 . **CLC 49**
See also CA 178; 89-92; DLB 9, 206; SATA 114

Davis, Rebecca (Blaine) Harding 1831-1910 .... **TCLC 6; SSC 38**
See also CA 104; 179; DLB 74

Davis, Richard Harding 1864-1916 .... **TCLC 24**
See also CA 114; 179; DLB 12, 23, 78, 79, 189; DLBD 13

Davison, Frank Dalby 1893-1970 ..... **CLC 15**
See also CA 116

Davison, Lawrence H.
See Lawrence, D(avid) H(erbert Richards)

Davison, Peter (Hubert) 1928- .... **CLC 28**
See also CA 9-12R; CAAS 4; CANR 3, 43, 84; DLB 5

Davys, Mary 1674-1732 .... **LC 1, 46**
See also DLB 39

Dawson, Fielding 1930- .... **CLC 6**
See also CA 85-88; DLB 130

Dawson, Peter
See Faust, Frederick (Schiller)

Day, Clarence (Shepard, Jr.) 1874-1935 .... **TCLC 25**
See also CA 108; DLB 11

Day, Thomas 1748-1789 .... **LC 1**
See also DLB 39; YABC 1

Diaz del Castillo, Bernal 1496-1584 .. **LC 31;**
HLCS 1

di Bassetto, Corno
See Shaw, George Bernard

Dick, Philip K(indred) 1928-1982 ... **CLC 10,**
30, 72; DAM NOV, POP
See also AAYA 24; CA 49-52; 106; CANR
2, 16; DA3; DLB 8; MTCW 1, 2

Dickens, Charles (John Huffam)
1812-1870 .... **NCLC 3, 8, 18, 26, 37, 50,**
86; DA; DAB; DAC; DAM MST, NOV;
SSC 17; WLC
See also AAYA 23; CDBLB 1832-1890;
DA3; DLB 21, 55, 70, 159, 166; JRDA;
MAICYA; SATA 15

Dickey, James (Lafayette)
1923-1997 .... **CLC 1, 2, 4, 7, 10, 15, 47,**
109; DAM NOV, POET, POP
See also AITN 1, 2; CA 9-12R; 156; CABS
2; CANR 10, 48, 61; CDALB 1968-1988;
DA3; DLB 5, 193; DLBD 7; DLBY 82,
93, 96, 97, 98; INT CANR-10; MTCW 1,
2

Dickey, William 1928-1994 .... **CLC 3, 28**
See also CA 9-12R; 145; CANR 24, 79;
DLB 5

Dickinson, Charles 1951- .... **CLC 49**
See also CA 128

Dickinson, Emily (Elizabeth)
1830-1886 ..... **NCLC 21, 77; DA; DAB;**
DAC; DAM MST, POET; PC 1; WLC
See also AAYA 22; CDALB 1865-1917;
DA3; DLB 1; SATA 29

Dickinson, Peter (Malcolm) 1927- .. **CLC 12,**
35
See also AAYA 9; CA 41-44R; CANR 31,
58, 88; CLR 29; DLB 87, 161; JRDA;
MAICYA; SATA 5, 62, 95

Dickson, Carr
See Carr, John Dickson

Dickson, Carter
See Carr, John Dickson

Diderot, Denis 1713-1784 .... **LC 26**

Didion, Joan 1934- .... **CLC 1, 3, 8, 14, 32,**
129; DAM NOV
See also AITN 1; CA 5-8R; CANR 14, 52,
76; CDALB 1968-1988; DA3; DLB 2,
173, 185; DLBY 81, 86; MTCW 1, 2

Dietrich, Robert
See Hunt, E(verette) Howard, (Jr.)

Difusa, Pati
See Almodovar, Pedro

Dillard, Annie 1945- .. **CLC 9, 60, 115; DAM**
NOV
See also AAYA 6; CA 49-52; CANR 3, 43,
62, 90; DA3; DLBY 80; MTCW 1, 2;
SATA 10

Dillard, R(ichard) H(enry) W(ilde)
1937- .... **CLC 5**
See also CA 21-24R; CAAS 7; CANR 10;
DLB 5

Dillon, Eilis 1920-1994 .... **CLC 17**
See also CA 9-12R; 182; 147; CAAE 182;
CAAS 3; CANR 4, 38, 78; CLR 26; MAI-
CYA; SATA 2, 74; SATA-Essay 105;
SATA-Obit 83

Dimont, Penelope
See Mortimer, Penelope (Ruth)

Dinesen, Isak -1962 .. **CLC 10, 29, 95; SSC 7**
See also Blixen, Karen (Christentze
Dinesen)
See also MTCW 1

Ding Ling CLC 68
See also Chiang, Pin-chin

Diphusa, Patty
See Almodovar, Pedro

Disch, Thomas M(ichael) 1940- ... **CLC 7, 36**
See also AAYA 17; CA 21-24R; CAAS 4;
CANR 17, 36, 54, 89; CLR 18; DA3;
DLB 8; MAICYA; MTCW 1, 2; SAAS
15; SATA 92

Disch, Tom
See Disch, Thomas M(ichael)

d'Isly, Georges
See Simenon, Georges (Jacques Christian)

Disraeli, Benjamin 1804-1881 ... **NCLC 2, 39,**
79
See also DLB 21, 55

Ditcum, Steve
See Crumb, R(obert)

Dixon, Paige
See Corcoran, Barbara

Dixon, Stephen 1936- .... **CLC 52; SSC 16**
See also CA 89-92; CANR 17, 40, 54, 91;
DLB 130

Doak, Annie
See Dillard, Annie

Dobell, Sydney Thompson
1824-1874 .... **NCLC 43**
See also DLB 32

Doblin, Alfred TCLC 13
See also Doeblin, Alfred

Dobrolyubov, Nikolai Alexandrovich
1836-1861 .... **NCLC 5**

Dobson, Austin 1840-1921 .... **TCLC 79**
See also DLB 35; 144

Dobyns, Stephen 1941- .... **CLC 37**
See also CA 45-48; CANR 2, 18

Doctorow, E(dgar) L(aurence)
1931- .... **CLC 6, 11, 15, 18, 37, 44, 65,**
113; DAM NOV, POP
See also AAYA 22; AITN 2; BEST 89:3;
CA 45-48; CANR 2, 33, 51, 76; CDALB
1968-1988; DA3; DLB 2, 28, 173; DLBY
80; MTCW 1, 2

Dodgson, Charles Lutwidge 1832-1898
See Carroll, Lewis
See also CLR 2; DA; DAB; DAC; DAM
MST, NOV, POET; DA3; MAICYA;
SATA 100; YABC 2

Dodson, Owen (Vincent)
1914-1983 .... **CLC 79; BLC 1; DAM**
MULT
See also BW 1; CA 65-68; 110; CANR 24;
DLB 76

Doeblin, Alfred 1878-1957 .... **TCLC 13**
See also Doblin, Alfred
See also CA 110; 141; DLB 66

Doerr, Harriet 1910- .... **CLC 34**
See also CA 117; 122; CANR 47; INT 122

Domecq, H(onorio) Bustos)
See Bioy Casares, Adolfo

Domecq, H(onorio) Bustos
See Bioy Casares, Adolfo; Borges, Jorge
Luis

Domini, Rey
See Lorde, Audre (Geraldine)

Dominique
See Proust, (Valentin-Louis-George-
Eugene-) Marcel

Don, A
See Stephen, SirLeslie

Donaldson, Stephen R. 1947- .... **CLC 46;**
DAM POP
See also CA 89-92; CANR 13, 55; INT
CANR-13

Donleavy, J(ames) P(atrick) 1926- .... **CLC 1,**
4, 6, 10, 45
See also AITN 2; CA 9-12R; CANR 24, 49,
62, 80; DLB 6, 173; INT CANR-24;
MTCW 1, 2

Donne, John 1572-1631 .... **LC 10, 24; DA;**
DAB; DAC; DAM MST, POET; PC 1;
WLC
See also CDBLB Before 1660; DLB 121,
151

Donnell, David 1939(?)- .... **CLC 34**

Donoghue, P. S.
See Hunt, E(verette) Howard, (Jr.)

Donoso (Yanez), Jose 1924-1996 ... **CLC 4, 8,**
11, 32, 99; DAM MULT; HLC 1; SSC
34
See also CA 81-84; 155; CANR 32, 73;
DLB 113; HW 1, 2; MTCW 1, 2

Donovan, John 1928-1992 .... **CLC 35**
See also AAYA 20; CA 97-100; 137; CLR
3; MAICYA; SATA 72; SATA-Brief 29

Don Roberto
See Cunninghame Graham, Robert
(Gallnigad) Bontine

Doolittle, Hilda 1886-1961 . **CLC 3, 8, 14, 31,**
34, 73; DA; DAC; DAM MST, POET;
PC 5; WLC
See also H. D.
See also CA 97-100; CANR 35; DLB 4, 45;
MTCW 1, 2

Dorfman, Ariel 1942- ...... **CLC 48, 77; DAM**
MULT; HLC 1
See also CA 124; 130; CANR 67, 70; HW
1, 2; INT 130

Dorn, Edward (Merton)
1929-1999 .... **CLC 10, 18**
See also CA 93-96; CANR 42, 79; DLB 5;
INT 93-96

Dorris, Michael (Anthony)
1945-1997 .... **CLC 109; DAM MULT,**
NOV
See also AAYA 20; BEST 90:1; CA 102;
157; CANR 19, 46, 75; CLR 58; DA3;
DLB 175; MTCW 2; NNAL; SATA 75;
SATA-Obit 94

Dorris, Michael A.
See Dorris, Michael (Anthony)

Dorsan, Luc
See Simenon, Georges (Jacques Christian)

Dorsange, Jean
See Simenon, Georges (Jacques Christian)

Dos Passos, John (Roderigo)
1896-1970 ... **CLC 1, 4, 8, 11, 15, 25, 34,**
82; DA; DAB; DAC; DAM MST, NOV;
WLC
See also CA 1-4R; 29-32R; CANR 3;
CDALB 1929-1941; DA3; DLB 4, 9;
DLBD 1, 15; DLBY 96; MTCW 1, 2

Dossage, Jean
See Simenon, Georges (Jacques Christian)

Dostoevsky, Fedor Mikhailovich
1821-1881 . **NCLC 2, 7, 21, 33, 43; DA;**
DAB; DAC; DAM MST, NOV; SSC 2,
33; WLC
See also DA3

Doughty, Charles M(ontagu)
1843-1926 .... **TCLC 27**
See also CA 115; 178; DLB 19, 57, 174

Douglas, Ellen CLC 73
See also Haxton, Josephine Ayres; William-
son, Ellen Douglas

Douglas, Gavin 1475(?)-1522 .... **LC 20**
See also DLB 132

Douglas, George
See Brown, George Douglas

Douglas, Keith (Castellain)
1920-1944 .... **TCLC 40**
See also CA 160; DLB 27

Douglas, Leonard
See Bradbury, Ray (Douglas)

Douglas, Michael
See Crichton, (John) Michael

Douglas, (George) Norman
1868-1952 .... **TCLC 68**
See also CA 119; 157; DLB 34, 195
Douglas, William
See Brown, George Douglas
Douglass, Frederick 1817(?)-1895 .. **NCLC 7,
55; BLC 1; DA; DAC; DAM MST,
MULT; WLC**
See also CDALB 1640-1865; DA3; DLB 1,
43, 50, 79; SATA 29
Dourado, (Waldomiro Freitas) Autran
1926- .... **CLC 23, 60**
See also CA 25-28R; 179; CANR 34, 81;
DLB 145; HW 2
Dourado, Waldomiro Autran 1926-
See Dourado, (Waldomiro Freitas) Autran
See also CA 179
Dove, Rita (Frances) 1952- .... **CLC 50, 81;
BLCS; DAM MULT, POET; PC 6**
See also BW 2; CA 109; CAAS 19; CANR
27, 42, 68, 76; CDALBS; DA3; DLB 120;
MTCW 1
Doveglion
See Villa, Jose Garcia
Dowell, Coleman 1925-1985 .... **CLC 60**
See also CA 25-28R; 117; CANR 10; DLB
130
Dowson, Ernest (Christopher)
1867-1900 .... **TCLC 4**
See also CA 105; 150; DLB 19, 135
Doyle, A. Conan
See Doyle, Arthur Conan
Doyle, Arthur Conan 1859-1930 .... **TCLC 7;
DA; DAB; DAC; DAM MST, NOV;
SSC 12; WLC**
See also AAYA 14; CA 104; 122; CDBLB
1890-1914; DA3; DLB 18, 70, 156, 178;
MTCW 1, 2; SATA 24
Doyle, Conan
See Doyle, Arthur Conan
Doyle, John
See Graves, Robert (von Ranke)
Doyle, Roddy 1958(?)- .... **CLC 81**
See also AAYA 14; CA 143; CANR 73;
DA3; DLB 194
Doyle, Sir A. Conan
See Doyle, Arthur Conan
Doyle, Sir Arthur Conan
See Doyle, Arthur Conan
Dr. A
See Asimov, Isaac; Silverstein, Alvin
Drabble, Margaret 1939- ...... **CLC 2, 3, 5, 8,
10, 22, 53, 129; DAB; DAC; DAM
MST, NOV, POP**
See also CA 13-16R; CANR 18, 35, 63;
CDBLB 1960 to Present; DA3; DLB 14,
155; MTCW 1, 2; SATA 48
Drapier, M. B.
See Swift, Jonathan
Drayham, James
See Mencken, H(enry) L(ouis)
Drayton, Michael 1563-1631 ..... **LC 8; DAM
POET**
See also DLB 121
Dreadstone, Carl
See Campbell, (John) Ramsey
Dreiser, Theodore (Herman Albert)
1871-1945 .... **TCLC 10, 18, 35, 83; DA;
DAC; DAM MST, NOV; WLC**
See also CA 106; 132; CDALB 1865-1917;
DA3; DLB 9, 12, 102, 137; DLBD 1;
MTCW 1, 2
Drexler, Rosalyn 1926- .... **CLC 2, 6**
See also CA 81-84; CANR 68
Dreyer, Carl Theodor 1889-1968 ...... **CLC 16**
See also CA 116
Drieu la Rochelle, Pierre(-Eugene)
1893-1945 .... **TCLC 21**
See also CA 117; DLB 72

Drinkwater, John 1882-1937 .... **TCLC 57**
See also CA 109; 149; DLB 10, 19, 149
Drop Shot
See Cable, George Washington
Droste-Hulshoff, Annette Freiin von
1797-1848 .... **NCLC 3**
See also DLB 133
Drummond, Walter
See Silverberg, Robert
Drummond, William Henry
1854-1907 .... **TCLC 25**
See also CA 160; DLB 92
Drummond de Andrade, Carlos
1902-1987 .... **CLC 18**
See also Andrade, Carlos Drummond de
See also CA 132; 123
Drury, Allen (Stuart) 1918-1998 .... **CLC 37**
See also CA 57-60; 170; CANR 18, 52; INT
CANR-18
Dryden, John 1631-1700 .... **LC 3, 21; DA;
DAB; DAC; DAM DRAM, MST,
POET; DC 3; PC 25; WLC**
See also CDBLB 1660-1789; DLB 80, 101,
131
Duberman, Martin (Bauml) 1930- ..... **CLC 8**
See also CA 1-4R; CANR 2, 63
Dubie, Norman (Evans) 1945- .... **CLC 36**
See also CA 69-72; CANR 12; DLB 120
Du Bois, W(illiam) E(dward) B(urghardt)
1868-1963 ... **CLC 1, 2, 13, 64, 96; BLC
1; DA; DAC; DAM MST, MULT,
NOV; WLC**
See also BW 1, 3; CA 85-88; CANR 34,
82; CDALB 1865-1917; DA3; DLB 47,
50, 91; MTCW 1, 2; SATA 42
Dubus, Andre 1936-1999 ..... **CLC 13, 36, 97;
SSC 15**
See also CA 21-24R; 177; CANR 17; DLB
130; INT CANR-17
Duca Minimo
See D'Annunzio, Gabriele
Ducharme, Rejean 1941- .... **CLC 74**
See also CA 165; DLB 60
Duclos, Charles Pinot 1704-1772 .... **LC 1**
Dudek, Louis 1918- .... **CLC 11, 19**
See also CA 45-48; CAAS 14; CANR 1;
DLB 88
Duerrenmatt, Friedrich 1921-1990 ... **CLC 1,
4, 8, 11, 15, 43, 102; DAM DRAM**
See also CA 17-20R; CANR 33; DLB 69,
124; MTCW 1, 2
Duffy, Bruce 1953(?)- .... **CLC 50**
See also CA 172
Duffy, Maureen 1933- .... **CLC 37**
See also CA 25-28R; CANR 33, 68; DLB
14; MTCW 1
Dugan, Alan 1923- .... **CLC 2, 6**
See also CA 81-84; DLB 5
du Gard, Roger Martin
See Martin du Gard, Roger
Duhamel, Georges 1884-1966 .... **CLC 8**
See also CA 81-84; 25-28R; CANR 35;
DLB 65; MTCW 1
Dujardin, Edouard (Emile Louis)
1861-1949 .... **TCLC 13**
See also CA 109; DLB 123
Dulles, John Foster 1888-1959 .... **TCLC 72**
See also CA 115; 149
Dumas, Alexandre (pere)
See Dumas, Alexandre (Davy de la
Pailleterie)
Dumas, Alexandre (Davy de la Pailleterie)
1802-1870 ...... **NCLC 11, 71; DA; DAB;
DAC; DAM MST, NOV; WLC**
See also DA3; DLB 119, 192; SATA 18
Dumas, Alexandre (fils)
1824-1895 .... **NCLC 71; DC 1**
See also AAYA 22; DLB 192

Dumas, Claudine
See Malzberg, Barry N(athaniel)
Dumas, Henry L. 1934-1968 .... **CLC 6, 62**
See also BW 1; CA 85-88; DLB 41
du Maurier, Daphne 1907-1989 .. **CLC 6, 11,
59; DAB; DAC; DAM MST, POP; SSC
18**
See also CA 5-8R; 128; CANR 6, 55; DA3;
DLB 191; MTCW 1, 2; SATA 27; SATA-
Obit 60
Du Maurier, George 1834-1896 ..... **NCLC 86**
See also DLB 153, 178
Dunbar, Paul Laurence 1872-1906 . **TCLC 2,
12; BLC 1; DA; DAC; DAM MST,
MULT, POET; PC 5; SSC 8; WLC**
See also BW 1, 3; CA 104; 124; CANR 79;
CDALB 1865-1917; DA3; DLB 50, 54,
78; SATA 34
Dunbar, William 1460(?)-1530(?) .... **LC 20**
See also DLB 132, 146
Duncan, Dora Angela
See Duncan, Isadora
Duncan, Isadora 1877(?)-1927 .... **TCLC 68**
See also CA 118; 149
Duncan, Lois 1934- .... **CLC 26**
See also AAYA 4, 34; CA 1-4R; CANR 2,
23, 36; CLR 29; JRDA; MAICYA; SAAS
2; SATA 1, 36, 75
Duncan, Robert (Edward)
1919-1988 .... **CLC 1, 2, 4, 7, 15, 41, 55;
DAM POET; PC 2**
See also CA 9-12R; 124; CANR 28, 62;
DLB 5, 16, 193; MTCW 1, 2
Duncan, Sara Jeannette
1861-1922 .... **TCLC 60**
See also CA 157; DLB 92
Dunlap, William 1766-1839 .... **NCLC 2**
See also DLB 30, 37, 59
Dunn, Douglas (Eaglesham) 1942- .... **CLC 6,
40**
See also CA 45-48; CANR 2, 33; DLB 40;
MTCW 1
Dunn, Katherine (Karen) 1945- .... **CLC 71**
See also CA 33-36R; CANR 72; MTCW 1
Dunn, Stephen 1939- .... **CLC 36**
See also CA 33-36R; CANR 12, 48, 53;
DLB 105
Dunne, Finley Peter 1867-1936 ...... **TCLC 28**
See also CA 108; 178; DLB 11, 23
Dunne, John Gregory 1932- .... **CLC 28**
See also CA 25-28R; CANR 14, 50; DLBY
80
**Dunsany, Edward John Moreton Drax
Plunkett** 1878-1957
See Dunsany, Lord
See also CA 104; 148; DLB 10; MTCW 1
Dunsany, Lord -1957 .... **TCLC 2, 59**
See also Dunsany, Edward John Moreton
Drax Plunkett
See also DLB 77, 153, 156
du Perry, Jean
See Simenon, Georges (Jacques Christian)
Durang, Christopher (Ferdinand)
1949- .... **CLC 27, 38**
See also CA 105; CANR 50, 76; MTCW 1
Duras, Marguerite 1914-1996 . **CLC 3, 6, 11,
20, 34, 40, 68, 100; SSC 40**
See also CA 25-28R; 151; CANR 50; DLB
83; MTCW 1, 2
Durban, (Rosa) Pam 1947- .... **CLC 39**
See also CA 123
Durcan, Paul 1944- .... **CLC 43, 70; DAM
POET**
See also CA 134

Durkheim, Emile 1858-1917 .... **TCLC 55**

Durrell, Lawrence (George)
1912-1990 .... **CLC 1, 4, 6, 8, 13, 27, 41;**
DAM NOV
See also CA 9-12R; 132; CANR 40, 77;
CDBLB 1945-1960; DLB 15, 27, 204;
DLBY 90; MTCW 1, 2

Durrenmatt, Friedrich
See Duerrenmatt, Friedrich

Dutt, Toru 1856-1877 .... **NCLC 29**

Dwight, Timothy 1752-1817 .... **NCLC 13**
See also DLB 37

Dworkin, Andrea 1946- .... **CLC 43**
See also CA 77-80; CAAS 21; CANR 16,
39, 76; INT CANR-16; MTCW 1, 2

Dwyer, Deanna
See Koontz, Dean R(ay)

Dwyer, K. R.
See Koontz, Dean R(ay)

Dwyer, Thomas A. 1923- .... **CLC 114**
See also CA 115

Dye, Richard
See De Voto, Bernard (Augustine)

Dylan, Bob 1941- .... **CLC 3, 4, 6, 12, 77**
See also CA 41-44R; DLB 16

E. V. L.
See Lucas, E(dward) V(errall)

Eagleton, Terence (Francis) 1943- .. **CLC 63,**
132
See also CA 57-60; CANR 7, 23, 68;
MTCW 1, 2

Eagleton, Terry
See Eagleton, Terence (Francis)

Early, Jack
See Scoppettone, Sandra

East, Michael
See West, Morris L(anglo)

Eastaway, Edward
See Thomas, (Philip) Edward

Eastlake, William (Derry)
1917-1997 .... **CLC 8**
See also CA 5-8R; 158; CAAS 1; CANR 5,
63; DLB 6, 206; INT CANR-5

Eastman, Charles A(lexander)
1858-1939 .... **TCLC 55; DAM MULT**
See also CA 179; CANR 91; DLB 175;
NNAL; YABC 1

Eberhart, Richard (Ghormley)
1904- .. **CLC 3, 11, 19, 56; DAM POET**
See also CA 1-4R; CANR 2; CDALB 1941-
1968; DLB 48; MTCW 1

Eberstadt, Fernanda 1960- .... **CLC 39**
See also CA 136; CANR 69

Echegaray (y Eizaguirre), Jose (Maria
Waldo) 1832-1916 .... **TCLC 4; HLCS 1**
See also CA 104; CANR 32; HW 1; MTCW
1

Echeverria, (Jose) Esteban (Antonino)
1805-1851 .... **NCLC 18**

Echo
See Proust, (Valentin-Louis-George-
Eugene-) Marcel

Eckert, Allan W. 1931- .... **CLC 17**
See also AAYA 18; CA 13-16R; CANR 14,
45; INT CANR-14; SAAS 21; SATA 29,
91; SATA-Brief 27

Eckhart, Meister 1260(?)-1328(?) ... **CMLC 9**
See also DLB 115

Eckmar, F. R.
See de Hartog, Jan

Eco, Umberto 1932- .... **CLC 28, 60; DAM**
NOV, POP
See also BEST 90:1; CA 77-80; CANR 12,
33, 55; DA3; DLB 196; MTCW 1, 2

Eddison, E(ric) R(ucker)
1882-1945 .... **TCLC 15**
See also CA 109; 156

Eddy, Mary (Ann Morse) Baker
1821-1910 .... **TCLC 71**
See also CA 113; 174

Edel, (Joseph) Leon 1907-1997 .. **CLC 29, 34**
See also CA 1-4R; 161; CANR 1, 22; DLB
103; INT CANR-22

Eden, Emily 1797-1869 .... **NCLC 10**

Edgar, David 1948- .. **CLC 42; DAM DRAM**
See also CA 57-60; CANR 12, 61; DLB 13;
MTCW 1

Edgerton, Clyde (Carlyle) 1944- ...... **CLC 39**
See also AAYA 17; CA 118; 134; CANR
64; INT 134

Edgeworth, Maria 1768-1849 .... **NCLC 1, 51**
See also DLB 116, 159, 163; SATA 21

Edmonds, Paul
See Kuttner, Henry

Edmonds, Walter D(umaux)
1903-1998 .... **CLC 35**
See also CA 5-8R; CANR 2; DLB 9; MAI-
CYA; SAAS 4; SATA 1, 27; SATA-Obit
99

Edmondson, Wallace
See Ellison, Harlan (Jay)

Edson, Russell **CLC 13**
See also CA 33-36R

Edwards, Bronwen Elizabeth
See Rose, Wendy

Edwards, G(erald) B(asil)
1899-1976 .... **CLC 25**
See also CA 110

Edwards, Gus 1939- .... **CLC 43**
See also CA 108; INT 108

Edwards, Jonathan 1703-1758 .... **LC 7, 54;**
DA; DAC; DAM MST
See also DLB 24

Efron, Marina Ivanovna Tsvetaeva
See Tsvetaeva (Efron), Marina (Ivanovna)

Ehle, John (Marsden, Jr.) 1925- ...... **CLC 27**
See also CA 9-12R

Ehrenbourg, Ilya (Grigoryevich)
See Ehrenburg, Ilya (Grigoryevich)

Ehrenburg, Ilya (Grigoryevich)
1891-1967 .... **CLC 18, 34, 62**
See also CA 102; 25-28R

Ehrenburg, Ilyo (Grigoryevich)
See Ehrenburg, Ilya (Grigoryevich)

Ehrenreich, Barbara 1941- .... **CLC 110**
See also BEST 90:4; CA 73-76; CANR 16,
37, 62; MTCW 1, 2

Eich, Guenter 1907-1972 .... **CLC 15**
See also CA 111; 93-96; DLB 69, 124

Eichendorff, Joseph Freiherr von
1788-1857 .... **NCLC 8**
See also DLB 90

Eigner, Larry **CLC 9**
See also Eigner, Laurence (Joel)
See also CAAS 23; DLB 5

Eigner, Laurence (Joel) 1927-1996
See Eigner, Larry
See also CA 9-12R; 151; CANR 6, 84; DLB
193

Einstein, Albert 1879-1955 .... **TCLC 65**
See also CA 121; 133; MTCW 1, 2

Eiseley, Loren Corey 1907-1977 .... **CLC 7**
See also AAYA 5; CA 1-4R; 73-76; CANR
6; DLBD 17

Eisenstadt, Jill 1963- .... **CLC 50**
See also CA 140

Eisenstein, Sergei (Mikhailovich)
1898-1948 .... **TCLC 57**
See also CA 114; 149

Eisner, Simon
See Kornbluth, C(yril) M.

Ekeloef, (Bengt) Gunnar
1907-1968 ... **CLC 27; DAM POET; PC**
23
See also CA 123; 25-28R

Ekelof, (Bengt) Gunnar
See Ekeloef, (Bengt) Gunnar

Ekelund, Vilhelm 1880-1949 .... **TCLC 75**

Ekwensi, C. O. D.
See Ekwensi, Cyprian (Odiatu Duaka)

Ekwensi, Cyprian (Odiatu Duaka)
1921- ...... **CLC 4; BLC 1; DAM MULT**
See also BW 2, 3; CA 29-32R; CANR 18,
42, 74; DLB 117; MTCW 1, 2; SATA 66

Elaine **TCLC 18**
See also Leverson, Ada

El Crummo
See Crumb, R(obert)

Elder, Lonne III 1931-1996 .... **DC 8**
See also BLC 1; BW 1, 3; CA 81-84; 152;
CANR 25; DAM MULT; DLB 7, 38, 44

Eleanor of Aquitaine 1122-1204 ... **CMLC 39**

Elia
See Lamb, Charles

Eliade, Mircea 1907-1986 .... **CLC 19**
See also CA 65-68; 119; CANR 30, 62;
DLB 220; MTCW 1

Eliot, A. D.
See Jewett, (Theodora) Sarah Orne

Eliot, Alice
See Jewett, (Theodora) Sarah Orne

Eliot, Dan
See Silverberg, Robert

Eliot, George 1819- . **NCLC 4, 13, 23, 41, 49,**
89; DA; DAB; DAC; DAM MST, NOV;
PC 20; WLC
See also CDBLB 1832-1890; DA3; DLB
21, 35, 55

Eliot, John 1604-1690 .... **LC 5**
See also DLB 24

Eliot, T(homas) S(tearns)
1888-1965 ...... **CLC 1, 2, 3, 6, 9, 10, 13,**
15, 24, 34, 41, 55, 57, 113; DA; DAB;
DAC; DAM DRAM, MST, POET; PC
5, 31; WLC
See also AAYA 28; CA 5-8R; 25-28R;
CANR 41; CDALB 1929-1941; DA3;
DLB 7, 10, 45, 63; DLBY 88; MTCW 1,
2

Elizabeth 1866-1941 .... **TCLC 41**

Elkin, Stanley L(awrence)
1930-1995 .. **CLC 4, 6, 9, 14, 27, 51, 91;**
DAM NOV, POP; SSC 12
See also CA 9-12R; 148; CANR 8, 46; DLB
2, 28; DLBY 80; INT CANR-8; MTCW
1, 2

Elledge, Scott **CLC 34**

Elliot, Don
See Silverberg, Robert

Elliott, Don
See Silverberg, Robert

Elliott, George P(aul) 1918-1980 .... **CLC 2**
See also CA 1-4R; 97-100; CANR 2

Elliott, Janice 1931- .... **CLC 47**
See also CA 13-16R; CANR 8, 29, 84; DLB
14

Elliott, Sumner Locke 1917-1991 ..... **CLC 38**
See also CA 5-8R; 134; CANR 2, 21

Elliott, William
See Bradbury, Ray (Douglas)

Ellis, A. E. **CLC 7**

Ellis, Alice Thomas **CLC 40**
See also Haycraft, Anna (Margaret)
See also DLB 194; MTCW 1

Ellis, Bret Easton 1964- ..... **CLC 39, 71, 117;**
DAM POP
See also AAYA 2; CA 118; 123; CANR 51,
74; DA3; INT 123; MTCW 1

Ellis, (Henry) Havelock
1859-1939 .... **TCLC 14**
See also CA 109; 169; DLB 190

Ellis, Landon
See Ellison, Harlan (Jay)

Farah, Nuruddin 1945- ...... **CLC 53; BLC 2; DAM MULT**
See also BW 2, 3; CA 106; CANR 81; DLB 125

Fargue, Leon-Paul 1876(?)-1947 .... **TCLC 11**
See also CA 109

Farigoule, Louis
See Romains, Jules

Farina, Richard 1936(?)-1966 .... **CLC 9**
See also CA 81-84; 25-28R

Farley, Walter (Lorimer)
1915-1989 .... **CLC 17**
See also CA 17-20R; CANR 8, 29, 84; DLB 22; JRDA; MAICYA; SATA 2, 43

Farmer, Philip Jose 1918- .... **CLC 1, 19**
See also AAYA 28; CA 1-4R; CANR 4, 35; DLB 8; MTCW 1; SATA 93

Farquhar, George 1677-1707 ... **LC 21; DAM DRAM**
See also DLB 84

Farrell, J(ames) G(ordon)
1935-1979 .... **CLC 6**
See also CA 73-76; 89-92; CANR 36; DLB 14; MTCW 1

Farrell, James T(homas) 1904-1979 . **CLC 1, 4, 8, 11, 66; SSC 28**
See also CA 5-8R; 89-92; CANR 9, 61; DLB 4, 9, 86; DLBD 2; MTCW 1, 2

Farren, Richard J.
See Betjeman, John

Farren, Richard M.
See Betjeman, John

Fassbinder, Rainer Werner
1946-1982 .... **CLC 20**
See also CA 93-96; 106; CANR 31

Fast, Howard (Melvin) 1914- .. **CLC 23, 131; DAM NOV**
See also AAYA 16; CA 1-4R, 181; CAAE 181; CAAS 18; CANR 1, 33, 54, 75; DLB 9; INT CANR-33; MTCW 1; SATA 7; SATA-Essay 107

Faulcon, Robert
See Holdstock, Robert P.

Faulkner, William (Cuthbert)
1897-1962 .... **CLC 1, 3, 6, 8, 9, 11, 14, 18, 28, 52, 68; DA; DAB; DAC; DAM MST, NOV; SSC 1, 35; WLC**
See also AAYA 7; CA 81-84; CANR 33; CDALB 1929-1941; DA3; DLB 9, 11, 44, 102; DLBD 2; DLBY 86, 97; MTCW 1, 2

Fauset, Jessie Redmon
1884(?)-1961 .... **CLC 19, 54; BLC 2; DAM MULT**
See also BW 1; CA 109; CANR 83; DLB 51

Faust, Frederick (Schiller)
1892-1944(?) .... **TCLC 49; DAM POP**
See also CA 108; 152

Faust, Irvin 1924- .... **CLC 8**
See also CA 33-36R; CANR 28, 67; DLB 2, 28; DLBY 80

Fawkes, Guy
See Benchley, Robert (Charles)

Fearing, Kenneth (Flexner)
1902-1961 .... **CLC 51**
See also CA 93-96; CANR 59; DLB 9

Fecamps, Elise
See Creasey, John

Federman, Raymond 1928- .... **CLC 6, 47**
See also CA 17-20R; CAAS 8; CANR 10, 43, 83; DLBY 80

Federspiel, J(uerg) F. 1931- .... **CLC 42**
See also CA 146

Feiffer, Jules (Ralph) 1929- ..... **CLC 2, 8, 64; DAM DRAM**
See also AAYA 3; CA 17-20R; CANR 30, 59; DLB 7, 44; INT CANR-30; MTCW 1; SATA 8, 61, 111

Feige, Hermann Albert Otto Maximilian
See Traven, B.

Feinberg, David B. 1956-1994 .... **CLC 59**
See also CA 135; 147

Feinstein, Elaine 1930- .... **CLC 36**
See also CA 69-72; CAAS 1; CANR 31, 68; DLB 14, 40; MTCW 1

Feldman, Irving (Mordecai) 1928- ..... **CLC 7**
See also CA 1-4R; CANR 1; DLB 169

Felix-Tchicaya, Gerald
See Tchicaya, Gerald Felix

Fellini, Federico 1920-1993 .... **CLC 16, 85**
See also CA 65-68; 143; CANR 33

Felsen, Henry Gregor 1916-1995 ..... **CLC 17**
See also CA 1-4R; 180; CANR 1; SAAS 2; SATA 1

Fenno, Jack
See Calisher, Hortense

Fenollosa, Ernest (Francisco)
1853-1908 .... **TCLC 91**

Fenton, James Martin 1949- .... **CLC 32**
See also CA 102; DLB 40

Ferber, Edna 1887-1968 .... **CLC 18, 93**
See also AITN 1; CA 5-8R; 25-28R; CANR 68; DLB 9, 28, 86; MTCW 1, 2; SATA 7

Ferguson, Helen
See Kavan, Anna

Ferguson, Niall 1967- .... **CLC 134**

Ferguson, Samuel 1810-1886 .... **NCLC 33**
See also DLB 32

Fergusson, Robert 1750-1774 .... **LC 29**
See also DLB 109

Ferling, Lawrence
See Ferlinghetti, Lawrence (Monsanto)

Ferlinghetti, Lawrence (Monsanto)
1919(?)- .... **CLC 2, 6, 10, 27, 111; DAM POET; PC 1**
See also CA 5-8R; CANR 3, 41, 73; CDALB 1941-1968; DA3; DLB 5, 16; MTCW 1, 2

Fern, Fanny 1811-1872
See Parton, Sara Payson Willis

Fernandez, Vicente Garcia Huidobro
See Huidobro Fernandez, Vicente Garcia

Ferre, Rosario 1942- .... **SSC 36; HLCS 1**
See also CA 131; CANR 55, 81; DLB 145; HW 1, 2; MTCW 1

Ferrer, Gabriel (Francisco Victor) Miro
See Miro (Ferrer), Gabriel (Francisco Victor)

Ferrier, Susan (Edmonstone)
1782-1854 .... **NCLC 8**
See also DLB 116

Ferrigno, Robert 1948(?)- .... **CLC 65**
See also CA 140

Ferron, Jacques 1921-1985 .... **CLC 94; DAC**
See also CA 117; 129; DLB 60

Feuchtwanger, Lion 1884-1958 .... **TCLC 3**
See also CA 104; DLB 66

Feuillet, Octave 1821-1890 .... **NCLC 45**
See also DLB 192

Feydeau, Georges (Leon Jules Marie)
1862-1921 .... **TCLC 22; DAM DRAM**
See also CA 113; 152; CANR 84; DLB 192

Fichte, Johann Gottlieb
1762-1814 .... **NCLC 62**
See also DLB 90

Ficino, Marsilio 1433-1499 .... **LC 12**

Fiedeler, Hans
See Doeblin, Alfred

Fiedler, Leslie A(aron) 1917- .. **CLC 4, 13, 24**
See also CA 9-12R; CANR 7, 63; DLB 28, 67; MTCW 1, 2

Field, Andrew 1938- .... **CLC 44**
See also CA 97-100; CANR 25

Field, Eugene 1850-1895 .... **NCLC 3**
See also DLB 23, 42, 140; DLBD 13; MAICYA; SATA 16

Field, Gans T.
See Wellman, Manly Wade

Field, Michael 1915-1971 .... **TCLC 43**
See also CA 29-32R

Field, Peter
See Hobson, Laura Z(ametkin)

Fielding, Henry 1707-1754 ..... **LC 1, 46; DA; DAB; DAC; DAM DRAM, MST, NOV; WLC**
See also CDBLB 1660-1789; DA3; DLB 39, 84, 101

Fielding, Sarah 1710-1768 .... **LC 1, 44**
See also DLB 39

Fields, W. C. 1880-1946 .... **TCLC 80**
See also DLB 44

Fierstein, Harvey (Forbes) 1954- .... **CLC 33; DAM DRAM, POP**
See also CA 123; 129; DA3

Figes, Eva 1932- .... **CLC 31**
See also CA 53-56; CANR 4, 44, 83; DLB 14

Finch, Anne 1661-1720 .... **LC 3; PC 21**
See also DLB 95

Finch, Robert (Duer Claydon)
1900- .... **CLC 18**
See also CA 57-60; CANR 9, 24, 49; DLB 88

Findley, Timothy 1930- . **CLC 27, 102; DAC; DAM MST**
See also CA 25-28R; CANR 12, 42, 69; DLB 53

Fink, William
See Mencken, H(enry) L(ouis)

Firbank, Louis 1942-
See Reed, Lou
See also CA 117

Firbank, (Arthur Annesley) Ronald
1886-1926 .... **TCLC 1**
See also CA 104; 177; DLB 36

Fisher, Dorothy (Frances) Canfield
1879-1958 .... **TCLC 87**
See also CA 114; 136; CANR 80; DLB 9, 102; MAICYA; YABC 1

Fisher, M(ary) F(rances) K(ennedy)
1908-1992 .... **CLC 76, 87**
See also CA 77-80; 138; CANR 44; MTCW 1

Fisher, Roy 1930- .... **CLC 25**
See also CA 81-84; CAAS 10; CANR 16; DLB 40

Fisher, Rudolph 1897-1934 .. **TCLC 11; BLC 2; DAM MULT; SSC 25**
See also BW 1, 3; CA 107; 124; CANR 80; DLB 51, 102

Fisher, Vardis (Alvero) 1895-1968 ...... **CLC 7**
See also CA 5-8R; 25-28R; CANR 68; DLB 9, 206

Fiske, Tarleton
See Bloch, Robert (Albert)

Fitch, Clarke
See Sinclair, Upton (Beall)

Fitch, John IV
See Cormier, Robert (Edmund)

Fitzgerald, Captain Hugh
See Baum, L(yman) Frank

FitzGerald, Edward 1809-1883 .... **NCLC 9**
See also DLB 32

Fitzgerald, F(rancis) Scott (Key)
1896-1940 .. **TCLC 1, 6, 14, 28, 55; DA; DAB; DAC; DAM MST, NOV; SSC 6, 31; WLC**
See also AAYA 24; AITN 1; CA 110; 123; CDALB 1917-1929; DA3; DLB 4, 9, 86; DLBD 1, 15, 16; DLBY 81, 96; MTCW 1, 2

Fitzgerald, Penelope 1916- ... **CLC 19, 51, 61**
See also CA 85-88; CAAS 10; CANR 56, 86; DLB 14, 194; MTCW 2

Freeman, Mary E(leanor) Wilkins
1852-1930 .... **TCLC 9; SSC 1**
See also CA 106; 177; DLB 12, 78, 221

Freeman, R(ichard) Austin
1862-1943 .... **TCLC 21**
See also CA 113; CANR 84; DLB 70

French, Albert 1943- .... **CLC 86**
See also BW 3; CA 167

French, Marilyn 1929- .... **CLC 10, 18, 60; DAM DRAM, NOV, POP**
See also CA 69-72; CANR 3, 31; INT CANR-31; MTCW 1, 2

French, Paul
See Asimov, Isaac

Freneau, Philip Morin 1752-1832 ... **NCLC 1**
See also DLB 37, 43

Freud, Sigmund 1856-1939 .... **TCLC 52**
See also CA 115; 133; CANR 69; MTCW 1, 2

Friedan, Betty (Naomi) 1921- .... **CLC 74**
See also CA 65-68; CANR 18, 45, 74; MTCW 1, 2

Friedlander, Saul 1932- .... **CLC 90**
See also CA 117; 130; CANR 72

Friedman, B(ernard) H(arper)
1926- .... **CLC 7**
See also CA 1-4R; CANR 3, 48

Friedman, Bruce Jay 1930- ...... **CLC 3, 5, 56**
See also CA 9-12R; CANR 25, 52; DLB 2, 28; INT CANR-25

Friel, Brian 1929- .... **CLC 5, 42, 59, 115; DC 8**
See also CA 21-24R; CANR 33, 69; DLB 13; MTCW 1

Friis-Baastad, Babbis Ellinor
1921-1970 .... **CLC 12**
See also CA 17-20R; 134; SATA 7

Frisch, Max (Rudolf) 1911-1991 ... **CLC 3, 9, 14, 18, 32, 44; DAM DRAM, NOV**
See also CA 85-88; 134; CANR 32, 74; DLB 69, 124; MTCW 1, 2

Fromentin, Eugene (Samuel Auguste)
1820-1876 .... **NCLC 10**
See also DLB 123

Frost, Frederick
See Faust, Frederick (Schiller)

Frost, Robert (Lee) 1874-1963 .. **CLC 1, 3, 4, 9, 10, 13, 15, 26, 34, 44; DA; DAB; DAC; DAM MST, POET; PC 1; WLC**
See also AAYA 21; CA 89-92; CANR 33; CDALB 1917-1929; DA3; DLB 54; DLBD 7; MTCW 1, 2; SATA 14

Froude, James Anthony
1818-1894 .... **NCLC 43**
See also DLB 18, 57, 144

Froy, Herald
See Waterhouse, Keith (Spencer)

Fry, Christopher 1907- .... **CLC 2, 10, 14; DAM DRAM**
See also CA 17-20R; CAAS 23; CANR 9, 30, 74; DLB 13; MTCW 1, 2; SATA 66

Frye, (Herman) Northrop
1912-1991 .... **CLC 24, 70**
See also CA 5-8R; 133; CANR 8, 37; DLB 67, 68; MTCW 1, 2

Fuchs, Daniel 1909-1993 .... **CLC 8, 22**
See also CA 81-84; 142; CAAS 5; CANR 40; DLB 9, 26, 28; DLBY 93

Fuchs, Daniel 1934- .... **CLC 34**
See also CA 37-40R; CANR 14, 48

Fuentes, Carlos 1928- .. **CLC 3, 8, 10, 13, 22, 41, 60, 113; DA; DAB; DAC; DAM MST, MULT, NOV; HLC 1; SSC 24; WLC**
See also AAYA 4; AITN 2; CA 69-72; CANR 10, 32, 68; DA3; DLB 113; HW 1, 2; MTCW 1, 2

Fuentes, Gregorio Lopez y
See Lopez y Fuentes, Gregorio

Fuertes, Gloria 1918- .... **PC 27**
See also CA 178, 180; DLB 108; HW 2; SATA 115

Fugard, (Harold) Athol 1932- . **CLC 5, 9, 14, 25, 40, 80; DAM DRAM; DC 3**
See also AAYA 17; CA 85-88; CANR 32, 54; DLB 225; MTCW 1

Fugard, Sheila 1932- .... **CLC 48**
See also CA 125

Fukuyama, Francis 1952- .... **CLC 131**
See also CA 140; CANR 72

Fuller, Charles (H., Jr.) 1939- .... **CLC 25; BLC 2; DAM DRAM, MULT; DC 1**
See also BW 2; CA 108; 112; CANR 87; DLB 38; INT 112; MTCW 1

Fuller, John (Leopold) 1937- .... **CLC 62**
See also CA 21-24R; CANR 9, 44; DLB 40

Fuller, Margaret
See Ossoli, Sarah Margaret (Fuller marchesa d')

Fuller, Roy (Broadbent) 1912-1991 ... **CLC 4, 28**
See also CA 5-8R; 135; CAAS 10; CANR 53, 83; DLB 15, 20; SATA 87

Fuller, Sarah Margaret 1810-1850
See Ossoli, Sarah Margaret (Fuller marchesa d')

Fulton, Alice 1952- .... **CLC 52**
See also CA 116; CANR 57, 88; DLB 193

Furphy, Joseph 1843-1912 .... **TCLC 25**
See also CA 163

Fussell, Paul 1924- .... **CLC 74**
See also BEST 90:1; CA 17-20R; CANR 8, 21, 35, 69; INT CANR-21; MTCW 1, 2

Futabatei, Shimei 1864-1909 .... **TCLC 44**
See also CA 162; DLB 180

Futrelle, Jacques 1875-1912 .... **TCLC 19**
See also CA 113; 155

Gaboriau, Emile 1835-1873 .... **NCLC 14**

Gadda, Carlo Emilio 1893-1973 .... **CLC 11**
See also CA 89-92; DLB 177

Gaddis, William 1922-1998 ... **CLC 1, 3, 6, 8, 10, 19, 43, 86**
See also CA 17-20R; 172; CANR 21, 48; DLB 2; MTCW 1, 2

Gage, Walter
See Inge, William (Motter)

Gaines, Ernest J(ames) 1933- ...... **CLC 3, 11, 18, 86; BLC 2; DAM MULT**
See also AAYA 18; AITN 1; BW 2, 3; CA 9-12R; CANR 6, 24, 42, 75; CDALB 1968-1988; CLR 62; DA3; DLB 2, 33, 152; DLBY 80; MTCW 1, 2; SATA 86

Gaitskill, Mary 1954- .... **CLC 69**
See also CA 128; CANR 61

Galdos, Benito Perez
See Perez Galdos, Benito

Gale, Zona 1874-1938 .... **TCLC 7; DAM DRAM**
See also CA 105; 153; CANR 84; DLB 9, 78, 228

Galeano, Eduardo (Hughes) 1940- . **CLC 72; HLCS 1**
See also CA 29-32R; CANR 13, 32; HW 1

Galiano, Juan Valera y Alcala
See Valera y Alcala-Galiano, Juan

Galilei, Galileo 1546-1642 .... **LC 45**

Gallagher, Tess 1943- ...... **CLC 18, 63; DAM POET; PC 9**
See also CA 106; DLB 212

Gallant, Mavis 1922- .. **CLC 7, 18, 38; DAC; DAM MST; SSC 5**
See also CA 69-72; CANR 29, 69; DLB 53; MTCW 1, 2

Gallant, Roy A(rthur) 1924- .... **CLC 17**
See also CA 5-8R; CANR 4, 29, 54; CLR 30; MAICYA; SATA 4, 68, 110

Gallico, Paul (William) 1897-1976 ..... **CLC 2**
See also AITN 1; CA 5-8R; 69-72; CANR 23; DLB 9, 171; MAICYA; SATA 13

Gallo, Max Louis 1932- .... **CLC 95**
See also CA 85-88

Gallois, Lucien
See Desnos, Robert

Gallup, Ralph
See Whitemore, Hugh (John)

Galsworthy, John 1867-1933 .... **TCLC 1, 45; DA; DAB; DAC; DAM DRAM, MST, NOV; SSC 22; WLC**
See also CA 104; 141; CANR 75; CDBLB 1890-1914; DA3; DLB 10, 34, 98, 162; DLBD 16; MTCW 1

Galt, John 1779-1839 .... **NCLC 1**
See also DLB 99, 116, 159

Galvin, James 1951- .... **CLC 38**
See also CA 108; CANR 26

Gamboa, Federico 1864-1939 .... **TCLC 36**
See also CA 167; HW 2

Gandhi, M. K.
See Gandhi, Mohandas Karamchand

Gandhi, Mahatma
See Gandhi, Mohandas Karamchand

Gandhi, Mohandas Karamchand
1869-1948 .... **TCLC 59; DAM MULT**
See also CA 121; 132; DA3; MTCW 1, 2

Gann, Ernest Kellogg 1910-1991 ..... **CLC 23**
See also AITN 1; CA 1-4R; 136; CANR 1, 83

Garber, Eric 1943(?)-
See Holleran, Andrew
See also CANR 89

Garcia, Cristina 1958- .... **CLC 76**
See also CA 141; CANR 73; HW 2

Garcia Lorca, Federico 1898-1936 . **TCLC 1, 7, 49; DA; DAB; DAC; DAM DRAM, MST, MULT, POET; DC 2; HLC 2; PC 3; WLC**
See also Lorca, Federico Garcia
See also CA 104; 131; CANR 81; DA3; DLB 108; HW 1, 2; MTCW 1, 2

Garcia Marquez, Gabriel (Jose)
1928- .... **CLC 2, 3, 8, 10, 15, 27, 47, 55, 68; DA; DAB; DAC; DAM MST, MULT, NOV, POP; HLC 1; SSC 8; WLC**
See also Marquez, Gabriel (Jose) Garcia
See also AAYA 3, 33; BEST 89:1, 90:4; CA 33-36R; CANR 10, 28, 50, 75, 82; DA3; DLB 113; HW 1, 2; MTCW 1, 2

Garcilaso de la Vega, El Inca 1503-1536
See also HLCS 1

Gard, Janice
See Latham, Jean Lee

Gard, Roger Martin du
See Martin du Gard, Roger

Gardam, Jane 1928- .... **CLC 43**
See also CA 49-52; CANR 2, 18, 33, 54; CLR 12; DLB 14, 161; MAICYA; MTCW 1; SAAS 9; SATA 39, 76; SATA-Brief 28

Gardner, Herb(ert) 1934- .... **CLC 44**
See also CA 149

Gardner, John (Champlin), Jr.
1933-1982 ...... **CLC 2, 3, 5, 7, 8, 10, 18, 28, 34; DAM NOV, POP; SSC 7**
See also AITN 1; CA 65-68; 107; CANR 33, 73; CDALBS; DA3; DLB 2; DLBY 82; MTCW 1; SATA 40; SATA-Obit 31

Gardner, John (Edmund) 1926- ...... **CLC 30; DAM POP**
See also CA 103; CANR 15, 69; MTCW 1

Gardner, Miriam
See Bradley, Marion Zimmer

Gardner, Noel
See Kuttner, Henry

Gardons, S. S.
See Snodgrass, W(illiam) D(e Witt)

Garfield, Leon 1921-1996 .... **CLC 12**
   See also AAYA 8; CA 17-20R; 152; CANR
   38, 41, 78; CLR 21; DLB 161; JRDA;
   MAICYA; SATA 1, 32, 76; SATA-Obit 90
Garland, (Hannibal) Hamlin
   1860-1940 .... **TCLC 3; SSC 18**
   See also CA 104; DLB 12, 71, 78, 186
Garneau, (Hector de) Saint-Denys
   1912-1943 .... **TCLC 13**
   See also CA 111; DLB 88
Garner, Alan 1934- ..... **CLC 17; DAB; DAM POP**
   See also AAYA 18; CA 73-76, 178; CAAE
   178; CANR 15, 64; CLR 20; DLB 161;
   MAICYA; MTCW 1, 2; SATA 18, 69;
   SATA-Essay 108
Garner, Hugh 1913-1979 .... **CLC 13**
   See also CA 69-72; CANR 31; DLB 68
Garnett, David 1892-1981 .... **CLC 3**
   See also CA 5-8R; 103; CANR 17, 79; DLB
   34; MTCW 2
Garos, Stephanie
   See Katz, Steve
Garrett, George (Palmer) 1929- .. **CLC 3, 11, 51; SSC 30**
   See also CA 1-4R; CAAS 5; CANR 1, 42,
   67; DLB 2, 5, 130, 152; DLBY 83
Garrick, David 1717-1779 .... **LC 15; DAM DRAM**
   See also DLB 84
Garrigue, Jean 1914-1972 .... **CLC 2, 8**
   See also CA 5-8R; 37-40R; CANR 20
Garrison, Frederick
   See Sinclair, Upton (Beall)
Garro, Elena 1920(?)-1998
   See also CA 131; 169; DLB 145; HLCS 1;
   HW 1
Garth, Will
   See Hamilton, Edmond; Kuttner, Henry
Garvey, Marcus (Moziah, Jr.)
   1887-1940 ...... **TCLC 41; BLC 2; DAM MULT**
   See also BW 1; CA 120; 124; CANR 79
Gary, Romain CLC 25
   See also Kacew, Romain
   See also DLB 83
Gascar, Pierre CLC 11
   See also Fournier, Pierre
Gascoyne, David (Emery) 1916- .... **CLC 45**
   See also CA 65-68; CANR 10, 28, 54; DLB
   20; MTCW 1
Gaskell, Elizabeth Cleghorn
   1810-1865 .... **NCLC 70; DAB; DAM MST; SSC 25**
   See also CDBLB 1832-1890; DLB 21, 144,
   159
Gass, William H(oward) 1924- . **CLC 1, 2, 8, 11, 15, 39, 132; SSC 12**
   See also CA 17-20R; CANR 30, 71; DLB
   2, 227; MTCW 1, 2
Gassendi, Pierre 1592-1655 .... **LC 54**
Gasset, Jose Ortega y
   See Ortega y Gasset, Jose
Gates, Henry Louis, Jr. 1950- .... **CLC 65; BLCS; DAM MULT**
   See also BW 2, 3; CA 109; CANR 25, 53,
   75; DA3; DLB 67; MTCW 1
Gautier, Theophile 1811-1872 .. **NCLC 1, 59; DAM POET; PC 18; SSC 20**
   See also DLB 119
Gawsworth, John
   See Bates, H(erbert) E(rnest)
Gay, John 1685-1732 .. **LC 49; DAM DRAM**
   See also DLB 84, 95
Gay, Oliver
   See Gogarty, Oliver St. John
Gaye, Marvin (Penze) 1939-1984 ..... **CLC 26**
   See also CA 112

Gebler, Carlo (Ernest) 1954- .... **CLC 39**
   See also CA 119; 133
Gee, Maggie (Mary) 1948- .... **CLC 57**
   See also CA 130; DLB 207
Gee, Maurice (Gough) 1931- .... **CLC 29**
   See also CA 97-100; CANR 67; CLR 56;
   SATA 46, 101
Gelbart, Larry (Simon) 1923- .... **CLC 21, 61**
   See also CA 73-76; CANR 45
Gelber, Jack 1932- .... **CLC 1, 6, 14, 79**
   See also CA 1-4R; CANR 2; DLB 7, 228
Gellhorn, Martha (Ellis)
   1908-1998 .... **CLC 14, 60**
   See also CA 77-80; 164; CANR 44; DLBY
   82, 98
Genet, Jean 1910-1986 .. **CLC 1, 2, 5, 10, 14, 44, 46; DAM DRAM**
   See also CA 13-16R; CANR 18; DA3; DLB
   72; DLBY 86; MTCW 1, 2
Gent, Peter 1942- .... **CLC 29**
   See also AITN 1; CA 89-92; DLBY 82
Gentile, Giovanni 1875-1944 .... **TCLC 96**
   See also CA 119
Gentlewoman in New England, A
   See Bradstreet, Anne
Gentlewoman in Those Parts, A
   See Bradstreet, Anne
George, Jean Craighead 1919- .... **CLC 35**
   See also AAYA 8; CA 5-8R; CANR 25;
   CLR 1; DLB 52; JRDA; MAICYA; SATA
   2, 68
George, Stefan (Anton) 1868-1933 . **TCLC 2, 14**
   See also CA 104
Georges, Georges Martin
   See Simenon, Georges (Jacques Christian)
Gerhardi, William Alexander
   See Gerhardie, William Alexander
Gerhardie, William Alexander
   1895-1977 .... **CLC 5**
   See also CA 25-28R; 73-76; CANR 18;
   DLB 36
Gerstler, Amy 1956- .... **CLC 70**
   See also CA 146
Gertler, T. CLC 34
   See also CA 116; 121; INT 121
Ghalib NCLC 39, 78
   See also Ghalib, Hsadullah Khan
Ghalib, Hsadullah Khan 1797-1869
   See Ghalib
   See also DAM POET
Ghelderode, Michel de 1898-1962 ..... **CLC 6, 11; DAM DRAM**
   See also CA 85-88; CANR 40, 77
Ghiselin, Brewster 1903- .... **CLC 23**
   See also CA 13-16R; CAAS 10; CANR 13
Ghose, Aurabinda 1872-1950 .... **TCLC 63**
   See also CA 163
Ghose, Zulfikar 1935- .... **CLC 42**
   See also CA 65-68; CANR 67
Ghosh, Amitav 1956- .... **CLC 44**
   See also CA 147; CANR 80
Giacosa, Giuseppe 1847-1906 .... **TCLC 7**
   See also CA 104
Gibb, Lee
   See Waterhouse, Keith (Spencer)
Gibbon, Lewis Grassic TCLC 4
   See also Mitchell, James Leslie
Gibbons, Kaye 1960- .... **CLC 50, 88; DAM POP**
   See also AAYA 34; CA 151; CANR 75;
   DA3; MTCW 1; SATA 117
Gibran, Kahlil 1883-1931 .... **TCLC 1, 9; DAM POET, POP; PC 9**
   See also CA 104; 150; DA3; MTCW 2
Gibran, Khalil
   See Gibran, Kahlil

Gibson, William 1914- .. **CLC 23; DA; DAB; DAC; DAM DRAM, MST**
   See also CA 9-12R; CANR 9, 42, 75; DLB
   7; MTCW 1; SATA 66
Gibson, William (Ford) 1948- ... **CLC 39, 63; DAM POP**
   See also AAYA 12; CA 126; 133; CANR
   52, 90; DA3; MTCW 1
Gide, Andre (Paul Guillaume)
   1869-1951 . **TCLC 5, 12, 36; DA; DAB; DAC; DAM MST, NOV; SSC 13; WLC**
   See also CA 104; 124; DA3; DLB 65;
   MTCW 1, 2
Gifford, Barry (Colby) 1946- .... **CLC 34**
   See also CA 65-68; CANR 9, 30, 40, 90
Gilbert, Frank
   See De Voto, Bernard (Augustine)
Gilbert, W(illiam) S(chwenck)
   1836-1911 .... **TCLC 3; DAM DRAM, POET**
   See also CA 104; 173; SATA 36
Gilbreth, Frank B., Jr. 1911- .... **CLC 17**
   See also CA 9-12R; SATA 2
Gilchrist, Ellen 1935- ...... **CLC 34, 48; DAM POP; SSC 14**
   See also CA 113; 116; CANR 41, 61; DLB
   130; MTCW 1, 2
Giles, Molly 1942- .... **CLC 39**
   See also CA 126
Gill, Eric 1882-1940 .... **TCLC 85**
Gill, Patrick
   See Creasey, John
Gilliam, Terry (Vance) 1940- .... **CLC 21**
   See also Monty Python
   See also AAYA 19; CA 108; 113; CANR
   35; INT 113
Gillian, Jerry
   See Gilliam, Terry (Vance)
Gilliatt, Penelope (Ann Douglass)
   1932-1993 .... **CLC 2, 10, 13, 53**
   See also AITN 2; CA 13-16R; 141; CANR
   49; DLB 14
Gilman, Charlotte (Anna) Perkins (Stetson)
   1860-1935 .... **TCLC 9, 37; SSC 13**
   See also CA 106; 150; DLB 221; MTCW 1
Gilmour, David 1949- .... **CLC 35**
   See also CA 138, 147
Gilpin, William 1724-1804 .... **NCLC 30**
Gilray, J. D.
   See Mencken, H(enry) L(ouis)
Gilroy, Frank D(aniel) 1925- .... **CLC 2**
   See also CA 81-84; CANR 32, 64, 86; DLB
   7
Gilstrap, John 1957(?)- .... **CLC 99**
   See also CA 160
Ginsberg, Allen 1926-1997 .... **CLC 1, 2, 3, 4, 6, 13, 36, 69, 109; DA; DAB; DAC; DAM MST, POET; PC 4; WLC**
   See also AAYA 33; AITN 1; CA 1-4R; 157;
   CANR 2, 41, 63; CDALB 1941-1968;
   DA3; DLB 5, 16, 169; MTCW 1, 2
Ginzburg, Natalia 1916-1991 .... **CLC 5, 11, 54, 70**
   See also CA 85-88; 135; CANR 33; DLB
   177; MTCW 1, 2
Giono, Jean 1895-1970 .... **CLC 4, 11**
   See also CA 45-48; 29-32R; CANR 2, 35;
   DLB 72; MTCW 1
Giovanni, Nikki 1943- .... **CLC 2, 4, 19, 64, 117; BLC 2; DA; DAB; DAC; DAM MST, MULT, POET; PC 19; WLCS**
   See also AAYA 22; AITN 1; BW 2, 3; CA
   29-32R; CAAS 6; CANR 18, 41, 60, 91;
   CDALBS; CLR 6; DA3; DLB 5, 41; INT
   CANR-18; MAICYA; MTCW 1, 2; SATA
   24, 107
Giovene, Andrea 1904- .... **CLC 7**
   See also CA 85-88

Gippius, Zinaida (Nikolayevna) 1869-1945
See Hippius, Zinaida
See also CA 106

Giraudoux, (Hippolyte) Jean
1882-1944 .... **TCLC 2, 7; DAM DRAM**
See also CA 104; DLB 65

Gironella, Jose Maria 1917- .... **CLC 11**
See also CA 101

Gissing, George (Robert)
1857-1903 .... **TCLC 3, 24, 47; SSC 37**
See also CA 105; 167; DLB 18, 135, 184

Giurlani, Aldo
See Palazzeschi, Aldo

Gladkov, Fyodor (Vasilyevich)
1883-1958 .... **TCLC 27**
See also CA 170

Glanville, Brian (Lester) 1931- .... **CLC 6**
See also CA 5-8R; CAAS 9; CANR 3, 70;
DLB 15, 139; SATA 42

Glasgow, Ellen (Anderson Gholson)
1873-1945 .... **TCLC 2, 7; SSC 34**
See also CA 104; 164; DLB 9, 12; MTCW

Glaspell, Susan 1882(?)-1948 . **TCLC 55; DC
10; SSC 41**
See also CA 110; 154; DLB 7, 9, 78, 228;
YABC 2

Glassco, John 1909-1981 .... **CLC 9**
See also CA 13-16R; 102; CANR 15; DLB
68

Glasscock, Amnesia
See Steinbeck, John (Ernst)

Glasser, Ronald J. 1940(?)- .... **CLC 37**

Glassman, Joyce
See Johnson, Joyce

Glendinning, Victoria 1937- .... **CLC 50**
See also CA 120; 127; CANR 59, 89; DLB
155

Glissant, Edouard 1928- . **CLC 10, 68; DAM
MULT**
See also CA 153

Gloag, Julian 1930- .... **CLC 40**
See also AITN 1; CA 65-68; CANR 10, 70

Glowacki, Aleksander
See Prus, Boleslaw

Gluck, Louise (Elisabeth) 1943- .. **CLC 7, 22,
44, 81; DAM POET; PC 16**
See also CA 33-36R; CANR 40, 69; DA3;
DLB 5; MTCW 2

Glyn, Elinor 1864-1943 .... **TCLC 72**
See also DLB 153

Gobineau, Joseph Arthur (Comte) de
1816-1882 .... **NCLC 17**
See also DLB 123

Godard, Jean-Luc 1930- .... **CLC 20**
See also CA 93-96

Godden, (Margaret) Rumer
1907-1998 .... **CLC 53**
See also AAYA 6; CA 5-8R; 172; CANR 4,
27, 36, 55, 80; CLR 20; DLB 161; MAI-
CYA; SAAS 12; SATA 3, 36; SATA-Obit
109

Godoy Alcayaga, Lucila 1889-1957
See Mistral, Gabriela
See also BW 2; CA 104; 131; CANR 81;
DAM MULT; HW 1, 2; MTCW 1, 2

Godwin, Gail (Kathleen) 1937- ..... **CLC 5, 8,
22, 31, 69, 125; DAM POP**
See also CA 29-32R; CANR 15, 43, 69;
DA3; DLB 6; INT CANR-15; MTCW 1,
2

Godwin, William 1756-1836 .... **NCLC 14**
See also CDBLB 1789-1832; DLB 39, 104,
142, 158, 163

Goebbels, Josef
See Goebbels, (Paul) Joseph

Goebbels, (Paul) Joseph
1897-1945 .... **TCLC 68**
See also CA 115; 148

Goebbels, Joseph Paul
See Goebbels, (Paul) Joseph

Goethe, Johann Wolfgang von
1749-1832 ..... **NCLC 4, 22, 34, 90; DA;
DAB; DAC; DAM DRAM, MST,
POET; PC 5; SSC 38; WLC**
See also DA3; DLB 94

Gogarty, Oliver St. John
1878-1957 .... **TCLC 15**
See also CA 109; 150; DLB 15, 19

Gogol, Nikolai (Vasilyevich)
1809-1852 . **NCLC 5, 15, 31; DA; DAB;
DAC; DAM DRAM, MST; DC 1; SSC
4, 29; WLC**
See also DLB 198

Goines, Donald 1937(?)-1974 . **CLC 80; BLC
2; DAM MULT, POP**
See also AITN 1; BW 1, 3; CA 124; 114;
CANR 82; DA3; DLB 33

Gold, Herbert 1924- .... **CLC 4, 7, 14, 42**
See also CA 9-12R; CANR 17, 45; DLB 2;
DLBY 81

Goldbarth, Albert 1948- .... **CLC 5, 38**
See also CA 53-56; CANR 6, 40; DLB 120

Goldberg, Anatol 1910-1982 .... **CLC 34**
See also CA 131; 117

Goldemberg, Isaac 1945- .... **CLC 52**
See also CA 69-72; CAAS 12; CANR 11,
32; HW 1

Golding, William (Gerald)
1911-1993 ..... **CLC 1, 2, 3, 8, 10, 17, 27,
58, 81; DA; DAB; DAC; DAM MST,
NOV; WLC**
See also AAYA 5; CA 5-8R; 141; CANR
13, 33, 54; CDBLB 1945-1960; DA3;
DLB 15, 100; MTCW 1, 2

Goldman, Emma 1869-1940 .... **TCLC 13**
See also CA 110; 150; DLB 221

Goldman, Francisco 1954- .... **CLC 76**
See also CA 162

Goldman, William (W.) 1931- ...... **CLC 1, 48**
See also CA 9-12R; CANR 29, 69; DLB 44

Goldmann, Lucien 1913-1970 .... **CLC 24**
See also CA 25-28; CAP 2

Goldoni, Carlo 1707-1793 .... **LC 4; DAM
DRAM**

Goldsberry, Steven 1949- .... **CLC 34**
See also CA 131

Goldsmith, Oliver 1728-1774 . **LC 2, 48; DA;
DAB; DAC; DAM DRAM, MST, NOV,
POET; DC 8; WLC**
See also CDBLB 1660-1789; DLB 39, 89,
104, 109, 142; SATA 26

Goldsmith, Peter
See Priestley, J(ohn) B(oynton)

Gombrowicz, Witold 1904-1969 .... **CLC 4, 7,
11, 49; DAM DRAM**
See also CA 19-20; 25-28R; CAP 2

Gomez de la Serna, Ramon
1888-1963 .... **CLC 9**
See also CA 153; 116; CANR 79; HW 1, 2

Goncharov, Ivan Alexandrovich
1812-1891 .... **NCLC 1, 63**

Goncourt, Edmond (Louis Antoine Huot) de
1822-1896 .... **NCLC 7**
See also DLB 123

Goncourt, Jules (Alfred Huot) de
1830-1870 .... **NCLC 7**
See also DLB 123

Gontier, Fernande 19(?)- .... **CLC 50**

Gonzalez Martinez, Enrique
1871-1952 .... **TCLC 72**
See also CA 166; CANR 81; HW 1, 2

Goodman, Paul 1911-1972 .... **CLC 1, 2, 4, 7**
See also CA 19-20; 37-40R; CANR 34;
CAP 2; DLB 130; MTCW 1

Gordimer, Nadine 1923- ...... **CLC 3, 5, 7, 10,
18, 33, 51, 70; DA; DAB; DAC; DAM
MST, NOV; SSC 17; WLCS**
See also CA 5-8R; CANR 3, 28, 56, 88;
DA3; DLB 225; INT CANR-28; MTCW
1, 2

Gordon, Adam Lindsay
1833-1870 .... **NCLC 21**

Gordon, Caroline 1895-1981 . **CLC 6, 13, 29,
83; SSC 15**
See also CA 11-12; 103; CANR 36; CAP 1;
DLB 4, 9, 102; DLBD 17; DLBY 81;
MTCW 1, 2

Gordon, Charles William 1860-1937
See Connor, Ralph
See also CA 109

Gordon, Mary (Catherine) 1949- .... **CLC 13,
22, 128**
See also CA 102; CANR 44, 92; DLB 6;
DLBY 81; INT 102; MTCW 1

Gordon, N. J.
See Bosman, Herman Charles

Gordon, Sol 1923- .... **CLC 26**
See also CA 53-56; CANR 4; SATA 11

Gordone, Charles 1925-1995 .... **CLC 1, 4;
DAM DRAM; DC 8**
See also BW 1, 3; CA 93-96, 180; 150;
CAAE 180; CANR 55; DLB 7; INT 93-
96; MTCW 1

Gore, Catherine 1800-1861 .... **NCLC 65**
See also DLB 116

Gorenko, Anna Andreevna
See Akhmatova, Anna

Gorky, Maxim 1868-1936 ..... **TCLC 8; DAB;
SSC 28; WLC**
See also Peshkov, Alexei Maximovich
See also MTCW 2

Goryan, Sirak
See Saroyan, William

Gosse, Edmund (William)
1849-1928 .... **TCLC 28**
See also CA 117; DLB 57, 144, 184

Gotlieb, Phyllis Fay (Bloom) 1926- .. **CLC 18**
See also CA 13-16R; CANR 7; DLB 88

Gottesman, S. D.
See Kornbluth, C(yril) M.; Pohl, Frederik

Gottfried von Strassburg fl. c.
1210- .... **CMLC 10**
See also DLB 138

Gould, Lois **CLC 4, 10**
See also CA 77-80; CANR 29; MTCW 1

Gourmont, Remy (-Marie-Charles) de
1858-1915 .... **TCLC 17**
See also CA 109; 150; MTCW 2

Govier, Katherine 1948- .... **CLC 51**
See also CA 101; CANR 18, 40

Goyen, (Charles) William
1915-1983 .... **CLC 5, 8, 14, 40**
See also AITN 2; CA 5-8R; 110; CANR 6,
71; DLB 2; DLBY 83; INT CANR-6

Goytisolo, Juan 1931- .... **CLC 5, 10, 23, 133;
DAM MULT; HLC 1**
See also CA 85-88; CANR 32, 61; HW 1,
2; MTCW 1, 2

Gozzano, Guido 1883-1916 .... **PC 10**
See also CA 154; DLB 114

Gozzi, (Conte) Carlo 1720-1806 .... **NCLC 23**

Grabbe, Christian Dietrich
1801-1836 .... **NCLC 2**
See also DLB 133

Grace, Patricia Frances 1937- .... **CLC 56**
See also CA 176

Gracian y Morales, Baltasar
1601-1658 .... **LC 15**

Gracq, Julien **CLC 11, 48**
See also Poirier, Louis
See also DLB 83

Grade, Chaim 1910-1982 .... **CLC 10**
See also CA 93-96; 107

Graduate of Oxford, A
  See Ruskin, John
Grafton, Garth
  See Duncan, Sara Jeannette
Graham, John
  See Phillips, David Graham
Graham, Jorie 1951- .... **CLC 48, 118**
  See also CA 111; CANR 63; DLB 120
Graham, R(obert) B(ontine) Cunninghame
  See Cunninghame Graham, Robert
  (Gallnigad) Bontine
  See also DLB 98, 135, 174
Graham, Robert
  See Haldeman, Joe (William)
Graham, Tom
  See Lewis, (Harry) Sinclair
Graham, W(illiam) S(ydney)
  1918-1986 .... **CLC 29**
  See also CA 73-76; 118; DLB 20
Graham, Winston (Mawdsley)
  1910- .... **CLC 23**
  See also CA 49-52; CANR 2, 22, 45, 66;
  DLB 77
Grahame, Kenneth 1859-1932 ...... **TCLC 64;
  DAB**
  See also CA 108; 136; CANR 80; CLR 5;
  DA3; DLB 34, 141, 178; MAICYA;
  MTCW 2; SATA 100; YABC 1
Granovsky, Timofei Nikolaevich
  1813-1855 .... **NCLC 75**
  See also DLB 198
Grant, Skeeter
  See Spiegelman, Art
Granville-Barker, Harley
  1877-1946 .... **TCLC 2; DAM DRAM**
  See also Barker, Harley Granville
  See also CA 104
Grass, Guenter (Wilhelm) 1927- ... **CLC 1, 2,
  4, 6, 11, 15, 22, 32, 49, 88; DA; DAB;
  DAC; DAM MST, NOV; WLC**
  See also CA 13-16R; CANR 20, 75; DA3;
  DLB 75, 124; MTCW 1, 2
Gratton, Thomas
  See Hulme, T(homas) E(rnest)
Grau, Shirley Ann 1929- . **CLC 4, 9; SSC 15**
  See also CA 89-92; CANR 22, 69; DLB 2;
  INT CANR-22; MTCW 1
Gravel, Fern
  See Hall, James Norman
Graver, Elizabeth 1964- .... **CLC 70**
  See also CA 135; CANR 71
Graves, Richard Perceval 1945- .... **CLC 44**
  See also CA 65-68; CANR 9, 26, 51
Graves, Robert (von Ranke)
  1895-1985 .. **CLC 1, 2, 6, 11, 39, 44, 45;
  DAB; DAC; DAM MST, POET; PC 6**
  See also CA 5-8R; 117; CANR 5, 36; CD-
  BLB 1914-1945; DA3; DLB 20, 100, 191;
  DLBD 18; DLBY 85; MTCW 1, 2; SATA
  45
Graves, Valerie
  See Bradley, Marion Zimmer
Gray, Alasdair (James) 1934- .... **CLC 41**
  See also CA 126; CANR 47, 69; DLB 194;
  INT 126; MTCW 1, 2
Gray, Amlin 1946- .... **CLC 29**
  See also CA 138
Gray, Francine du Plessix 1930- ..... **CLC 22;
  DAM NOV**
  See also BEST 90:3; CA 61-64; CAAS 2;
  CANR 11, 33, 75, 81; INT CANR-11;
  MTCW 1, 2
Gray, John (Henry) 1866-1934 ...... **TCLC 19**
  See also CA 119; 162
Gray, Simon (James Holliday)
  1936- .... **CLC 9, 14, 36**
  See also AITN 1; CA 21-24R; CAAS 3;
  CANR 32, 69; DLB 13; MTCW 1

Gray, Spalding 1941- ..... **CLC 49, 112; DAM
  POP; DC 7**
  See also CA 128; CANR 74; MTCW 2
Gray, Thomas 1716-1771 .... **LC 4, 40; DA;
  DAB; DAC; DAM MST; PC 2; WLC**
  See also CDBLB 1660-1789; DA3; DLB
  109
Grayson, David
  See Baker, Ray Stannard
Grayson, Richard (A.) 1951- .... **CLC 38**
  See also CA 85-88; CANR 14, 31, 57
Greeley, Andrew M(oran) 1928- ..... **CLC 28;
  DAM POP**
  See also CA 5-8R; CAAS 7; CANR 7, 43,
  69; DA3; MTCW 1, 2
Green, Anna Katharine
  1846-1935 .... **TCLC 63**
  See also CA 112; 159; DLB 202, 221
Green, Brian
  See Card, Orson Scott
Green, Hannah
  See Greenberg, Joanne (Goldenberg)
Green, Hannah 1927(?)-1996 .... **CLC 3**
  See also CA 73-76; CANR 59
Green, Henry 1905-1973 .... **CLC 2, 13, 97**
  See also Yorke, Henry Vincent
  See also CA 175; DLB 15
Green, Julian (Hartridge) 1900-1998
  See Green, Julien
  See also CA 21-24R; 169; CANR 33, 87;
  DLB 4, 72; MTCW 1
Green, Julien CLC 3, 11, 77
  See also Green, Julian (Hartridge)
  See also MTCW 2
Green, Paul (Eliot) 1894-1981 .... **CLC 25;
  DAM DRAM**
  See also AITN 1; CA 5-8R; 103; CANR 3;
  DLB 7, 9; DLBY 81
Greenberg, Ivan 1908-1973
  See Rahv, Philip
  See also CA 85-88
Greenberg, Joanne (Goldenberg)
  1932- .... **CLC 7, 30**
  See also AAYA 12; CA 5-8R; CANR 14,
  32, 69; SATA 25
Greenberg, Richard 1959(?)- .... **CLC 57**
  See also CA 138
Greene, Bette 1934- .... **CLC 30**
  See also AAYA 7; CA 53-56; CANR 4; CLR
  2; JRDA; MAICYA; SAAS 16; SATA 8,
  102
Greene, Gael CLC 8
  See also CA 13-16R; CANR 10
Greene, Graham (Henry)
  1904-1991 .... **CLC 1, 3, 6, 9, 14, 18, 27,
  37, 70, 72, 125; DA; DAB; DAC; DAM
  MST, NOV; SSC 29; WLC**
  See also AITN 2; CA 13-16R; 133; CANR
  35, 61; CDBLB 1945-1960; DA3; DLB
  13, 15, 77, 100, 162, 201, 204; DLBY 91;
  MTCW 1, 2; SATA 20
Greene, Robert 1558-1592 .... **LC 41**
  See also DLB 62, 167
Greer, Germaine 1939- .... **CLC 131**
  See also AITN 1; CA 81-84; CANR 33, 70;
  MTCW 1, 2
Greer, Richard
  See Silverberg, Robert
Gregor, Arthur 1923- .... **CLC 9**
  See also CA 25-28R; CAAS 10; CANR 11;
  SATA 36
Gregor, Lee
  See Pohl, Frederik
Gregory, Isabella Augusta (Persse)
  1852-1932 .... **TCLC 1**
  See also CA 104; 184; DLB 10
Gregory, J. Dennis
  See Williams, John A(lfred)

Grendon, Stephen
  See Derleth, August (William)
Grenville, Kate 1950- .... **CLC 61**
  See also CA 118; CANR 53
Grenville, Pelham
  See Wodehouse, P(elham) G(renville)
Greve, Felix Paul (Berthold Friedrich)
  1879-1948
  See Grove, Frederick Philip
  See also CA 104; 141, 175; CANR 79;
  DAC; DAM MST
Grey, Zane 1872-1939 . **TCLC 6; DAM POP**
  See also CA 104; 132; DA3; DLB 212;
  MTCW 1, 2
Grieg, (Johan) Nordahl (Brun)
  1902-1943 .... **TCLC 10**
  See also CA 107
Grieve, C(hristopher) M(urray)
  1892-1978 ..... **CLC 11, 19; DAM POET**
  See also MacDiarmid, Hugh; Pteleon
  See also CA 5-8R; 85-88; CANR 33;
  MTCW 1
Griffin, Gerald 1803-1840 .... **NCLC 7**
  See also DLB 159
Griffin, John Howard 1920-1980 ..... **CLC 68**
  See also AITN 1; CA 1-4R; 101; CANR 2
Griffin, Peter 1942- .... **CLC 39**
  See also CA 136
Griffith, D(avid Lewelyn) W(ark)
  1875(?)-1948 .... **TCLC 68**
  See also CA 119; 150; CANR 80
Griffith, Lawrence
  See Griffith, D(avid Lewelyn) W(ark)
Griffiths, Trevor 1935- .... **CLC 13, 52**
  See also CA 97-100; CANR 45; DLB 13
Griggs, Sutton (Elbert)
  1872-1930 .... **TCLC 77**
  See also CA 123; 186; DLB 50
Grigson, Geoffrey (Edward Harvey)
  1905-1985 .... **CLC 7, 39**
  See also CA 25-28R; 118; CANR 20, 33;
  DLB 27; MTCW 1, 2
Grillparzer, Franz 1791-1872 .... **NCLC 1;
  SSC 37**
  See also DLB 133
Grimble, Reverend Charles James
  See Eliot, T(homas) S(tearns)
Grimke, Charlotte L(ottie) Forten
  1837(?)-1914
  See Forten, Charlotte L.
  See also BW 1; CA 117; 124; DAM MULT,
  POET
Grimm, Jacob Ludwig Karl
  1785-1863 .... **NCLC 3, 77; SSC 36**
  See also DLB 90; MAICYA; SATA 22
Grimm, Wilhelm Karl 1786-1859 .. **NCLC 3,
  77; SSC 36**
  See also DLB 90; MAICYA; SATA 22
**Grimmelshausen, Johann Jakob Christoffel
  von** 1621-1676 .... **LC 6**
  See also DLB 168
Grindel, Eugene 1895-1952
  See Eluard, Paul
  See also CA 104
Grisham, John 1955- .... **CLC 84; DAM POP**
  See also AAYA 14; CA 138; CANR 47, 69;
  DA3; MTCW 2
Grossman, David 1954- .... **CLC 67**
  See also CA 138
Grossman, Vasily (Semenovich)
  1905-1964 .... **CLC 41**
  See also CA 124; 130; MTCW 1
Grove, Frederick Philip TCLC 4
  See also Greve, Felix Paul (Berthold
  Friedrich)
  See also DLB 92
Grubb
  See Crumb, R(obert)

Grumbach, Doris (Isaac) 1918- . **CLC 13, 22, 64**
    See also CA 5-8R; CAAS 2; CANR 9, 42, 70; INT CANR-9; MTCW 2

Grundtvig, Nicolai Frederik Severin
    1783-1872 .... **NCLC 1**

Grunge
    See Crumb, R(obert)

Grunwald, Lisa 1959- .... **CLC 44**
    See also CA 120

Guare, John 1938- .... **CLC 8, 14, 29, 67; DAM DRAM**
    See also CA 73-76; CANR 21, 69; DLB 7; MTCW 1, 2

Gudjonsson, Halldor Kiljan 1902-1998
    See Laxness, Halldor
    See also CA 103; 164

Guenter, Erich
    See Eich, Guenter

Guest, Barbara 1920- .... **CLC 34**
    See also CA 25-28R; CANR 11, 44, 84; DLB 5, 193

Guest, Edgar A(lbert) 1881-1959 ... **TCLC 95**
    See also CA 112; 168

Guest, Judith (Ann) 1936- .... **CLC 8, 30; DAM NOV, POP**
    See also AAYA 7; CA 77-80; CANR 15, 75; DA3; INT CANR-15; MTCW 1, 2

Guevara, Che **CLC 87; HLC 1**
    See also Guevara (Serna), Ernesto

Guevara (Serna), Ernesto
    1928-1967 .... **CLC 87; DAM MULT; HLC 1**
    See also Guevara, Che
    See also CA 127; 111; CANR 56; HW 1

Guicciardini, Francesco 1483-1540 ..... **LC 49**

Guild, Nicholas M. 1944- .... **CLC 33**
    See also CA 93-96

Guillemin, Jacques
    See Sartre, Jean-Paul

Guillen, Jorge 1893-1984 .... **CLC 11; DAM MULT, POET; HLCS 1**
    See also CA 89-92; 112; DLB 108; HW 1

Guillen, Nicolas (Cristobal)
    1902-1989 ... **CLC 48, 79; BLC 2; DAM MST, MULT, POET; HLC 1; PC 23**
    See also BW 2; CA 116; 125; 129; CANR 84; HW 1

Guillevic, (Eugene) 1907- .... **CLC 33**
    See also CA 93-96

Guillois
    See Desnos, Robert

Guillois, Valentin
    See Desnos, Robert

Guimaraes Rosa, Joao 1908-1967
    See also CA 175; HLCS 2

Guiney, Louise Imogen
    1861-1920 .... **TCLC 41**
    See also CA 160; DLB 54

Guiraldes, Ricardo (Guillermo)
    1886-1927 .... **TCLC 39**
    See also CA 131; HW 1; MTCW 1

Gumilev, Nikolai (Stepanovich)
    1886-1921 .... **TCLC 60**
    See also CA 165

Gunesekera, Romesh 1954- .... **CLC 91**
    See also CA 159

Gunn, Bill **CLC 5**
    See also Gunn, William Harrison
    See also DLB 38

Gunn, Thom(son William) 1929- .. **CLC 3, 6, 18, 32, 81; DAM POET; PC 26**
    See also CA 17-20R; CANR 9, 33; CDBLB 1960 to Present; DLB 27; INT CANR-33; MTCW 1

Gunn, William Harrison 1934(?)-1989
    See Gunn, Bill
    See also AITN 1; BW 1, 3; CA 13-16R; 128; CANR 12, 25, 76

Gunnars, Kristjana 1948- .... **CLC 69**
    See also CA 113; DLB 60

Gurdjieff, G(eorgei) I(vanovich)
    1877(?)-1949 .... **TCLC 71**
    See also CA 157

Gurganus, Allan 1947- . **CLC 70; DAM POP**
    See also BEST 90:1; CA 135

Gurney, A(lbert) R(amsdell), Jr.
    1930- ..... **CLC 32, 50, 54; DAM DRAM**
    See also CA 77-80; CANR 32, 64

Gurney, Ivor (Bertie) 1890-1937 ... **TCLC 33**
    See also CA 167

Gurney, Peter
    See Gurney, A(lbert) R(amsdell), Jr.

Guro, Elena 1877-1913 .... **TCLC 56**

Gustafson, James M(oody) 1925- ... **CLC 100**
    See also CA 25-28R; CANR 37

Gustafson, Ralph (Barker) 1909- ..... **CLC 36**
    See also CA 21-24R; CANR 8, 45, 84; DLB 88

Gut, Gom
    See Simenon, Georges (Jacques Christian)

Guterson, David 1956- .... **CLC 91**
    See also CA 132; CANR 73; MTCW 2

Guthrie, A(lfred) B(ertram), Jr.
    1901-1991 .... **CLC 23**
    See also CA 57-60; 134; CANR 24; DLB 212; SATA 62; SATA-Obit 67

Guthrie, Isobel
    See Grieve, C(hristopher) M(urray)

Guthrie, Woodrow Wilson 1912-1967
    See Guthrie, Woody
    See also CA 113; 93-96

Guthrie, Woody **CLC 35**
    See also Guthrie, Woodrow Wilson

Gutierrez Najera, Manuel 1859-1895
    See also HLCS 2

Guy, Rosa (Cuthbert) 1928- .... **CLC 26**
    See also AAYA 4; BW 2; CA 17-20R; CANR 14, 34, 83; CLR 13; DLB 33; JRDA; MAICYA; SATA 14, 62

Gwendolyn
    See Bennett, (Enoch) Arnold

H. D. **CLC 3, 8, 14, 31, 34, 73; PC 5**
    See also Doolittle, Hilda

H. de V.
    See Buchan, John

Haavikko, Paavo Juhani 1931- .. **CLC 18, 34**
    See also CA 106

Habbema, Koos
    See Heijermans, Herman

Habermas, Juergen 1929- .... **CLC 104**
    See also CA 109; CANR 85

Habermas, Jurgen
    See Habermas, Juergen

Hacker, Marilyn 1942- ...... **CLC 5, 9, 23, 72, 91; DAM POET**
    See also CA 77-80; CANR 68; DLB 120

Haeckel, Ernst Heinrich (Philipp August)
    1834-1919 .... **TCLC 83**
    See also CA 157

Hafiz c. 1326-1389(?) .... **CMLC 34**

Hafiz c. 1326-1389 .... **CMLC 34**

Haggard, H(enry) Rider
    1856-1925 .... **TCLC 11**
    See also CA 108; 148; DLB 70, 156, 174, 178; MTCW 2; SATA 16

Hagiosy, L.
    See Larbaud, Valery (Nicolas)

Hagiwara Sakutaro 1886-1942 ..... **TCLC 60; PC 18**

Haig, Fenil
    See Ford, Ford Madox

Haig-Brown, Roderick (Langmere)
    1908-1976 .... **CLC 21**
    See also CA 5-8R; 69-72; CANR 4, 38, 83; CLR 31; DLB 88; MAICYA; SATA 12

Hailey, Arthur 1920- ..... **CLC 5; DAM NOV, POP**
    See also AITN 2; BEST 90:3; CA 1-4R; CANR 2, 36, 75; DLB 88; DLBY 82; MTCW 1, 2

Hailey, Elizabeth Forsythe 1938- ..... **CLC 40**
    See also CA 93-96; CAAS 1; CANR 15, 48; INT CANR-15

Haines, John (Meade) 1924- .... **CLC 58**
    See also CA 17-20R; CANR 13, 34; DLB 212

Hakluyt, Richard 1552-1616 .... **LC 31**

Haldeman, Joe (William) 1943- .... **CLC 61**
    See Graham, Robert
    See also CA 53-56; 179; CAAE 179; CAAS 25; CANR 6, 70, 72; DLB 8; INT CANR-6

Hale, Sarah Josepha (Buell)
    1788-1879 .... **NCLC 75**
    See also DLB 1, 42, 73

Haley, Alex(ander Murray Palmer)
    1921-1992 . **CLC 8, 12, 76; BLC 2; DA; DAB; DAC; DAM MST, MULT, POP**
    See also AAYA 26; BW 2, 3; CA 77-80; 136; CANR 61; CDALBS; DA3; DLB 38; MTCW 1, 2

Haliburton, Thomas Chandler
    1796-1865 .... **NCLC 15**
    See also DLB 11, 99

Hall, Donald (Andrew, Jr.) 1928- ...... **CLC 1, 13, 37, 59; DAM POET**
    See also CA 5-8R; CAAS 7; CANR 2, 44, 64; DLB 5; MTCW 1; SATA 23, 97

Hall, Frederic Sauser
    See Sauser-Hall, Frederic

Hall, James
    See Kuttner, Henry

Hall, James Norman 1887-1951 ..... **TCLC 23**
    See also CA 123; 173; SATA 21

Hall, Radclyffe -1943
    See Hall, (Marguerite) Radclyffe
    See also MTCW 2

Hall, (Marguerite) Radclyffe
    1886-1943 .... **TCLC 12**
    See also CA 110; 150; CANR 83; DLB 191

Hall, Rodney 1935- .... **CLC 51**
    See also CA 109; CANR 69

Halleck, Fitz-Greene 1790-1867 .... **NCLC 47**
    See also DLB 3

Halliday, Michael
    See Creasey, John

Halpern, Daniel 1945- .... **CLC 14**
    See also CA 33-36R

Hamburger, Michael (Peter Leopold)
    1924- .... **CLC 5, 14**
    See also CA 5-8R; CAAS 4; CANR 2, 47; DLB 27

Hamill, Pete 1935- .... **CLC 10**
    See also CA 25-28R; CANR 18, 71

Hamilton, Alexander
    1755(?)-1804 .... **NCLC 49**
    See also DLB 37

Hamilton, Clive
    See Lewis, C(live) S(taples)

Hamilton, Edmond 1904-1977 .... **CLC 1**
    See also CA 1-4R; CANR 3, 84; DLB 8

Hamilton, Eugene (Jacob) Lee
    See Lee-Hamilton, Eugene (Jacob)

Hamilton, Franklin
    See Silverberg, Robert

Hamilton, Gail
    See Corcoran, Barbara

Hamilton, Mollie
    See Kaye, M(ary) M(argaret)

Hamilton, (Anthony Walter) Patrick
    1904-1962 .... **CLC 51**
    See also CA 176; 113; DLB 191

Hayaseca y Eizaguirre, Jorge
See Echegaray (y Eizaguirre), Jose (Maria Waldo)

Hayashi, Fumiko 1904-1951 .... **TCLC 27**
See also CA 161; DLB 180

Haycraft, Anna (Margaret) 1932-
See Ellis, Alice Thomas
See also CA 122; CANR 85, 90; MTCW 2

Hayden, Robert E(arl) 1913-1980 . **CLC 5, 9, 14, 37; BLC 2; DA; DAC; DAM MST, MULT, POET; PC 6**
See also BW 1, 3; CA 69-72; 97-100; CABS 2; CANR 24, 75, 82; CDALB 1941-1968; DLB 5, 76; MTCW 1, 2; SATA 19; SATA-Obit 26

Hayford, J(oseph) E(phraim) Casely
See Casely-Hayford, J(oseph) E(phraim)

Hayman, Ronald 1932- .... **CLC 44**
See also CA 25-28R; CANR 18, 50, 88; DLB 155

Haywood, Eliza (Fowler)
1693(?)-1756 .... **LC 1, 44**
See also DLB 39

Hazlitt, William 1778-1830 ...... **NCLC 29, 82**
See also DLB 110, 158

Hazzard, Shirley 1931- .... **CLC 18**
See also CA 9-12R; CANR 4, 70; DLBY 82; MTCW 1

Head, Bessie 1937-1986 .... **CLC 25, 67; BLC 2; DAM MULT**
See also BW 2, 3; CA 29-32R; 119; CANR 25, 82; DLB 117, 225; MTCW 1, 2

Headon, (Nicky) Topper 1956(?)- ..... **CLC 30**

Heaney, Seamus (Justin) 1939- .. **CLC 5, 7, 14, 25, 37, 74, 91; DAB; DAM POET; PC 18; WLCS**
See also CA 85-88; CANR 25, 48, 75, 91; CDBLB 1960 to Present; DA3; DLB 40; DLBY 95; MTCW 1, 2

Hearn, (Patricio) Lafcadio (Tessima Carlos)
1850-1904 .... **TCLC 9**
See also CA 105; 166; DLB 12, 78, 189

Hearne, Vicki 1946- .... **CLC 56**
See also CA 139

Hearon, Shelby 1931- .... **CLC 63**
See also AITN 2; CA 25-28R; CANR 18, 48

Heat-Moon, William Least CLC 29
See also Trogdon, William (Lewis)
See also AAYA 9

Hebbel, Friedrich 1813-1863 .... **NCLC 43; DAM DRAM**
See also DLB 129

Hebert, Anne 1916-2000 .... **CLC 4, 13, 29; DAC; DAM MST, POET**
See also CA 85-88; CANR 69; DA3; DLB 68; MTCW 1, 2

Hecht, Anthony (Evan) 1923- ...... **CLC 8, 13, 19; DAM POET**
See also CA 9-12R; CANR 6; DLB 5, 169

Hecht, Ben 1894-1964 .... **CLC 8**
See also CA 85-88; DLB 7, 9, 25, 26, 28, 86

Hedayat, Sadeq 1903-1951 .... **TCLC 21**
See also CA 120

Hegel, Georg Wilhelm Friedrich
1770-1831 .... **NCLC 46**
See also DLB 90

Heidegger, Martin 1889-1976 .... **CLC 24**
See also CA 81-84; 65-68; CANR 34; MTCW 1, 2

Heidenstam, (Carl Gustaf) Verner von
1859-1940 .... **TCLC 5**
See also CA 104

Heifner, Jack 1946- .... **CLC 11**
See also CA 105; CANR 47

Heijermans, Herman 1864-1924 .... **TCLC 24**
See also CA 123

Heilbrun, Carolyn G(old) 1926- .... **CLC 25**
See also CA 45-48; CANR 1, 28, 58

Heine, Heinrich 1797-1856 .... **NCLC 4, 54; PC 25**
See also DLB 90

Heinemann, Larry (Curtiss) 1944- .. **CLC 50**
See also CA 110; CAAS 21; CANR 31, 81; DLBD 9; INT CANR-31

Heiney, Donald (William) 1921-1993
See Harris, MacDonald
See also CA 1-4R; 142; CANR 3, 58

Heinlein, Robert A(nson) 1907-1988 . **CLC 1, 3, 8, 14, 26, 55; DAM POP**
See also AAYA 17; CA 1-4R; 125; CANR 1, 20, 53; DA3; DLB 8; JRDA; MAICYA; MTCW 1, 2; SATA 9, 69; SATA-Obit 56

Helforth, John
See Doolittle, Hilda

Hellenhofferu, Vojtech Kapristian z
See Hasek, Jaroslav (Matej Frantisek)

Heller, Joseph 1923-1999 . **CLC 1, 3, 5, 8, 11, 36, 63; DA; DAB; DAC; DAM MST, NOV, POP; WLC**
See also AAYA 24; AITN 1; CA 5-8R; CABS 1; CANR 8, 42, 66; DA3; DLB 2, 28, 227; DLBY 80; INT CANR-8; MTCW 1, 2

Hellman, Lillian (Florence)
1906-1984 .. **CLC 2, 4, 8, 14, 18, 34, 44, 52; DAM DRAM; DC 1**
See also AITN 1, 2; CA 13-16R; 112; CANR 33; DA3; DLB 7, 228; DLBY 84; MTCW 1, 2

Helprin, Mark 1947- .... **CLC 7, 10, 22, 32; DAM NOV, POP**
See also CA 81-84; CANR 47, 64; CDALBS; DA3; DLBY 85; MTCW 1, 2

Helvetius, Claude-Adrien 1715-1771 .. **LC 26**

Helyar, Jane Penelope Josephine 1933-
See Poole, Josephine
See also CA 21-24R; CANR 10, 26; SATA 82

Hemans, Felicia 1793-1835 .... **NCLC 71**
See also DLB 96

Hemingway, Ernest (Miller)
1899-1961 .... **CLC 1, 3, 6, 8, 10, 13, 19, 30, 34, 39, 41, 44, 50, 61, 80; DA; DAB; DAC; DAM MST, NOV; SSC 1, 25, 36, 40; WLC**
See also AAYA 19; CA 77-80; CANR 34; CDALB 1917-1929; DA3; DLB 4, 9, 102, 210; DLBD 1, 15, 16; DLBY 81, 87, 96, 98; MTCW 1, 2

Hempel, Amy 1951- .... **CLC 39**
See also CA 118; 137; CANR 70; DA3; MTCW 2

Henderson, F. C.
See Mencken, H(enry) L(ouis)

Henderson, Sylvia
See Ashton-Warner, Sylvia (Constance)

Henderson, Zenna (Chlarson)
1917-1983 .... **SSC 29**
See also CA 1-4R; 133; CANR 1, 84; DLB 8; SATA 5

Henkin, Joshua CLC 119
See also CA 161

Henley, Beth CLC 23; DC 6
See also Henley, Elizabeth Becker
See also CABS 3; DLBY 86

Henley, Elizabeth Becker 1952-
See Henley, Beth
See also CA 107; CANR 32, 73; DAM DRAM, MST; DA3; MTCW 1, 2

Henley, William Ernest 1849-1903 .. **TCLC 8**
See also CA 105; DLB 19

Hennissart, Martha
See Lathen, Emma
See also CA 85-88; CANR 64

Henry, O. TCLC 1, 19; SSC 5; WLC
See also Porter, William Sydney

Henry, Patrick 1736-1799 .... **LC 25**

Henryson, Robert 1430(?)-1506(?) ...... **LC 20**
See also DLB 146

Henry VIII 1491-1547 .... **LC 10**
See also DLB 132

Henschke, Alfred
See Klabund

Hentoff, Nat(han Irving) 1925- .... **CLC 26**
See also AAYA 4; CA 1-4R; CAAS 6; CANR 5, 25, 77; CLR 1, 52; INT CANR-25; JRDA; MAICYA; SATA 42, 69; SATA-Brief 27

Heppenstall, (John) Rayner
1911-1981 .... **CLC 10**
See also CA 1-4R; 103; CANR 29

Heraclitus c. 540B.C.-c. 450B.C. ... **CMLC 22**
See also DLB 176

Herbert, Frank (Patrick)
1920-1986 .... **CLC 12, 23, 35, 44, 85; DAM POP**
See also AAYA 21; CA 53-56; 118; CANR 5, 43; CDALBS; DLB 8; INT CANR-5; MTCW 1, 2; SATA 9, 37; SATA-Obit 47

Herbert, George 1593-1633 ..... **LC 24; DAB; DAM POET; PC 4**
See also CDBLB Before 1660; DLB 126

Herbert, Zbigniew 1924-1998 ..... **CLC 9, 43; DAM POET**
See also CA 89-92; 169; CANR 36, 74; MTCW 1

Herbst, Josephine (Frey)
1897-1969 .... **CLC 34**
See also CA 5-8R; 25-28R; DLB 9

Heredia, Jose Maria 1803-1839
See also HLCS 2

Hergesheimer, Joseph 1880-1954 ... **TCLC 11**
See also CA 109; DLB 102, 9

Herlihy, James Leo 1927-1993 .... **CLC 6**
See also CA 1-4R; 143; CANR 2

Hermogenes fl. c. 175- .... **CMLC 6**

Hernandez, Jose 1834-1886 .... **NCLC 17**

Herodotus c. 484B.C.-429B.C. .... **CMLC 17**
See also DLB 176

Herrick, Robert 1591-1674 .... **LC 13; DA; DAB; DAC; DAM MST, POP; PC 9**
See also DLB 126

Herring, Guilles
See Somerville, Edith

Herriot, James 1916-1995 ..... **CLC 12; DAM POP**
See also Wight, James Alfred
See also AAYA 1; CA 148; CANR 40; MTCW 2; SATA 86

Herris, Violet
See Hunt, Violet

Herrmann, Dorothy 1941- .... **CLC 44**
See also CA 107

Herrmann, Taffy
See Herrmann, Dorothy

Hersey, John (Richard) 1914-1993 .... **CLC 1, 2, 7, 9, 40, 81, 97; DAM POP**
See also AAYA 29; CA 17-20R; 140; CANR 33; CDALBS; DLB 6, 185; MTCW 1, 2; SATA 25; SATA-Obit 76

Herzen, Aleksandr Ivanovich
1812-1870 .... **NCLC 10, 61**

Herzl, Theodor 1860-1904 .... **TCLC 36**
See also CA 168

Herzog, Werner 1942- .... **CLC 16**
See also CA 89-92

Hesiod c. 8th cent. B.C.- .... **CMLC 5**
See also DLB 176

Hollis, Jim
 See Summers, Hollis (Spurgeon, Jr.)
Holly, Buddy 1936-1959 .... **TCLC 65**
Holmes, Gordon
 See Shiel, M(atthew) P(hipps)
Holmes, John
 See Souster, (Holmes) Raymond
Holmes, John Clellon 1926-1988 ...... **CLC 56**
 See also CA 9-12R; 125; CANR 4; DLB 16
Holmes, Oliver Wendell, Jr.
 1841-1935 .... **TCLC 77**
 See also CA 114; 186
Holmes, Oliver Wendell
 1809-1894 .... **NCLC 14, 81**
 See also CDALB 1640-1865; DLB 1, 189;
 SATA 34
Holmes, Raymond
 See Souster, (Holmes) Raymond
Holt, Victoria
 See Hibbert, Eleanor Alice Burford
Holub, Miroslav 1923-1998 .... **CLC 4**
 See also CA 21-24R; 169; CANR 10
Homer c. 8th cent. B.C.- .. **CMLC 1, 16; DA;**
 DAB; DAC; DAM MST, POET; PC
 23; WLCS
 See also DA3; DLB 176
Hongo, Garrett Kaoru 1951- .... **PC 23**
 See also CA 133; CAAS 22; DLB 120
Honig, Edwin 1919- .... **CLC 33**
 See also CA 5-8R; CAAS 8; CANR 4, 45;
 DLB 5
Hood, Hugh (John Blagdon) 1928- . **CLC 15,**
 28
 See also CA 49-52; CAAS 17; CANR 1,
 33, 87; DLB 53
Hood, Thomas 1799-1845 .... **NCLC 16**
 See also DLB 96
Hooker, (Peter) Jeremy 1941- .... **CLC 43**
 See also CA 77-80; CANR 22; DLB 40
hooks, bell **CLC 94; BLCS**
 See also Watkins, Gloria Jean
 See also MTCW 2
Hope, A(lec) D(erwent) 1907- .... **CLC 3, 51**
 See also CA 21-24R; CANR 33, 74; MTCW
 1, 2
Hope, Anthony 1863-1933 .... **TCLC 83**
 See also CA 157; DLB 153, 156
Hope, Brian
 See Creasey, John
Hope, Christopher (David Tully)
 1944- .... **CLC 52**
 See also CA 106; CANR 47; DLB 225;
 SATA 62
Hopkins, Gerard Manley
 1844-1889 .... **NCLC 17; DA; DAB;**
 DAC; DAM MST, POET; PC 15; WLC
 See also CDBLB 1890-1914; DA3; DLB
 35, 57
Hopkins, John (Richard) 1931-1998 .. **CLC 4**
 See also CA 85-88; 169
Hopkins, Pauline Elizabeth
 1859-1930 ...... **TCLC 28; BLC 2; DAM**
 MULT
 See also BW 2, 3; CA 141; CANR 82; DLB
 50
Hopkinson, Francis 1737-1791 .... **LC 25**
 See also DLB 31
Hopley-Woolrich, Cornell George 1903-1968
 See Woolrich, Cornell
 See also CA 13-14; CANR 58; CAP 1; DLB
 226; MTCW 2
Horace 65B.C.-8B.C. .... **CMLC 39**
 See also DLB 211
Horatio
 See Proust, (Valentin-Louis-George-
 Eugene-) Marcel

Horgan, Paul (George Vincent
 O'Shaughnessy) 1903-1995 . **CLC 9, 53;**
 DAM NOV
 See also CA 13-16R; 147; CANR 9, 35;
 DLB 212; DLBY 85; INT CANR-9;
 MTCW 1, 2; SATA 13; SATA-Obit 84
Horn, Peter
 See Kuttner, Henry
Hornem, Horace Esq.
 See Byron, George Gordon (Noel)
Horney, Karen (Clementine Theodore
 Danielsen) 1885-1952 .... **TCLC 71**
 See also CA 114; 165
Hornung, E(rnest) W(illiam)
 1866-1921 .... **TCLC 59**
 See also CA 108; 160; DLB 70
Horovitz, Israel (Arthur) 1939- ...... **CLC 56;**
 DAM DRAM
 See also CA 33-36R; CANR 46, 59; DLB 7
Horton, George Moses
 1797(?)-1883(?) .... **NCLC 87**
 See also DLB 50
Horvath, Odon von
 See Horvath, Oedoen von
 See also DLB 85, 124
Horvath, Oedoen von 1901-1938 ... **TCLC 45**
 See also Horvath, Odon von; von Horvath,
 Oedoen
 See also CA 118
Horwitz, Julius 1920-1986 .... **CLC 14**
 See also CA 9-12R; 119; CANR 12
Hospital, Janette Turner 1942- .... **CLC 42**
 See also CA 108; CANR 48
Hostos, E. M. de
 See Hostos (y Bonilla), Eugenio Maria de
Hostos, Eugenio M. de
 See Hostos (y Bonilla), Eugenio Maria de
Hostos, Eugenio Maria
 See Hostos (y Bonilla), Eugenio Maria de
Hostos (y Bonilla), Eugenio Maria de
 1839-1903 .... **TCLC 24**
 See also CA 123; 131; HW 1
Houdini
 See Lovecraft, H(oward) P(hillips)
Hougan, Carolyn 1943- .... **CLC 34**
 See also CA 139
Household, Geoffrey (Edward West)
 1900-1988 .... **CLC 11**
 See also CA 77-80; 126; CANR 58; DLB
 87; SATA 14; SATA-Obit 59
Housman, A(lfred) E(dward)
 1859-1936 .... **TCLC 1, 10; DA; DAB;**
 DAC; DAM MST, POET; PC 2;
 WLCS
 See also CA 104; 125; DA3; DLB 19;
 MTCW 1, 2
Housman, Laurence 1865-1959 .... **TCLC 7**
 See also CA 106; 155; DLB 10; SATA 25
Howard, Elizabeth Jane 1923- ..... **CLC 7, 29**
 See also CA 5-8R; CANR 8, 62
Howard, Maureen 1930- .... **CLC 5, 14, 46**
 See also CA 53-56; CANR 31, 75; DLBY
 83; INT CANR-31; MTCW 1, 2
Howard, Richard 1929- .... **CLC 7, 10, 47**
 See also AITN 1; CA 85-88; CANR 25, 80;
 DLB 5; INT CANR-25
Howard, Robert E(rvin)
 1906-1936 .... **TCLC 8**
 See also CA 105; 157
Howard, Warren F.
 See Pohl, Frederik
Howe, Fanny (Quincy) 1940- .... **CLC 47**
 See also CA 117; CAAS 27; CANR 70;
 SATA-Brief 52
Howe, Irving 1920-1993 .... **CLC 85**
 See also CA 9-12R; 141; CANR 21, 50;
 DLB 67; MTCW 1, 2
Howe, Julia Ward 1819-1910 .... **TCLC 21**
 See also CA 117; DLB 1, 189

Howe, Susan 1937- .... **CLC 72**
 See also CA 160; DLB 120
Howe, Tina 1937- .... **CLC 48**
 See also CA 109
Howell, James 1594(?)-1666 .... **LC 13**
 See also DLB 151
Howells, W. D.
 See Howells, William Dean
Howells, William D.
 See Howells, William Dean
Howells, William Dean 1837-1920 .. **TCLC 7,**
 17, 41; SSC 36
 See also CA 104; 134; CDALB 1865-1917;
 DLB 12, 64, 74, 79, 189; MTCW 2
Howes, Barbara 1914-1996 .... **CLC 15**
 See also CA 9-12R; 151; CAAS 3; CANR
 53; SATA 5
Hrabal, Bohumil 1914-1997 .... **CLC 13, 67**
 See also CA 106; 156; CAAS 12; CANR
 57
Hroswitha of Gandersheim c. 935-c.
 1002 .... **CMLC 29**
 See also DLB 148
Hsun, Lu
 See Lu Hsun
Hubbard, L(afayette) Ron(ald)
 1911-1986 .... **CLC 43; DAM POP**
 See also CA 77-80; 118; CANR 52; DA3;
 MTCW 2
Huch, Ricarda (Octavia)
 1864-1947 .... **TCLC 13**
 See also CA 111; DLB 66
Huddle, David 1942- .... **CLC 49**
 See also CA 57-60; CAAS 20; CANR 89;
 DLB 130
Hudson, Jeffrey
 See Crichton, (John) Michael
Hudson, W(illiam) H(enry)
 1841-1922 .... **TCLC 29**
 See also CA 115; DLB 98, 153, 174; SATA
 35
Hueffer, Ford Madox
 See Ford, Ford Madox
Hughart, Barry 1934- .... **CLC 39**
 See also CA 137
Hughes, Colin
 See Creasey, John
Hughes, David (John) 1930- .... **CLC 48**
 See also CA 116; 129; DLB 14
Hughes, Edward James
 See Hughes, Ted
 See also DAM MST, POET; DA3
Hughes, (James) Langston
 1902-1967 .... **CLC 1, 5, 10, 15, 35, 44,**
 108; BLC 2; DA; DAB; DAC; DAM
 DRAM, MST, MULT, POET; DC 3;
 PC 1; SSC 6; WLC
 See also AAYA 12; BW 1, 3; CA 1-4R; 25-
 28R; CANR 1, 34, 82; CDALB 1929-
 1941; CLR 17; DA3; DLB 4, 7, 48, 51,
 86, 228; JRDA; MAICYA; MTCW 1, 2;
 SATA 4, 33
Hughes, Richard (Arthur Warren)
 1900-1976 .... **CLC 1, 11; DAM NOV**
 See also CA 5-8R; 65-68; CANR 4; DLB
 15, 161; MTCW 1; SATA 8; SATA-Obit
 25
Hughes, Ted 1930-1998 . **CLC 2, 4, 9, 14, 37,**
 119; DAB; DAC; PC 7
 See also Hughes, Edward James
 See also CA 1-4R; 171; CANR 1, 33, 66;
 CLR 3; DLB 40, 161; MAICYA; MTCW
 1, 2; SATA 49; SATA-Brief 27; SATA-
 Obit 107
Hugo, Richard F(ranklin)
 1923-1982 .... **CLC 6, 18, 32; DAM**
 POET
 See also CA 49-52; 108; CANR 3; DLB 5,
 206

Jackson, Laura (Riding) 1901-1991
See Riding, Laura
See also CA 65-68; 135; CANR 28, 89;
DLB 48

Jackson, Sam
See Trumbo, Dalton

Jackson, Sara
See Wingrove, David (John)

Jackson, Shirley 1919-1965 . **CLC 11, 60, 87;
DA; DAC; DAM MST; SSC 9, 39;
WLC**
See also AAYA 9; CA 1-4R; 25-28R; CANR
4, 52; CDALB 1941-1968; DA3; DLB 6;
MTCW 2; SATA 2

Jacob, (Cyprien-)Max 1876-1944 .... **TCLC 6**
See also CA 104

Jacobs, Harriet A(nn)
1813(?)-1897 .... **NCLC 67**

Jacobs, Jim 1942- .... **CLC 12**
See also CA 97-100; INT 97-100

Jacobs, W(illiam) W(ymark)
1863-1943 .... **TCLC 22**
See also CA 121; 167; DLB 135

Jacobsen, Jens Peter 1847-1885 .... **NCLC 34**

Jacobsen, Josephine 1908- .... **CLC 48, 102**
See also CA 33-36R; CAAS 18; CANR 23,
48

Jacobson, Dan 1929- .... **CLC 4, 14**
See also CA 1-4R; CANR 2, 25, 66; DLB
14, 207, 225; MTCW 1

Jacqueline
See Carpentier (y Valmont), Alejo

Jagger, Mick 1944- .... **CLC 17**

Jahiz, al- c. 780-c. 869 .... **CMLC 25**

Jakes, John (William) 1932- . **CLC 29; DAM
NOV, POP**
See also AAYA 32; BEST 89:4; CA 57-60;
CANR 10, 43, 66; DA3; DLBY 83; INT
CANR-10; MTCW 1, 2; SATA 62

James, Andrew
See Kirkup, James

James, C(yril) L(ionel) R(obert)
1901-1989 .... **CLC 33; BLCS**
See also BW 2; CA 117; 125; 128; CANR
62; DLB 125; MTCW 1

James, Daniel (Lewis) 1911-1988
See Santiago, Danny
See also CA 174; 125

James, Dynely
See Mayne, William (James Carter)

James, Henry Sr. 1811-1882 .... **NCLC 53**

James, Henry 1843-1916 ..... **TCLC 2, 11, 24,
40, 47, 64; DA; DAB; DAC; DAM
MST, NOV; SSC 8, 32; WLC**
See also CA 104; 132; CDALB 1865-1917;
DA3; DLB 12, 71, 74, 189; DLBD 13;
MTCW 1, 2

James, M. R.
See James, Montague (Rhodes)
See also DLB 156

James, Montague (Rhodes)
1862-1936 .... **TCLC 6; SSC 16**
See also CA 104; DLB 201

James, P. D. 1920- .... **CLC 18, 46, 122**
See also White, Phyllis Dorothy James
See also BEST 90:2; CDBLB 1960 to
Present; DLB 87; DLBD 17

James, Philip
See Moorcock, Michael (John)

James, William 1842-1910 .... **TCLC 15, 32**
See also CA 109

James I 1394-1437 .... **LC 20**

Jameson, Anna 1794-1860 .... **NCLC 43**
See also DLB 99, 166

Jami, Nur al-Din 'Abd al-Rahman
1414-1492 .... **LC 9**

Jammes, Francis 1868-1938 .... **TCLC 75**

Jandl, Ernst 1925- .... **CLC 34**

Janowitz, Tama 1957- .. **CLC 43; DAM POP**
See also CA 106; CANR 52, 89

Japrisot, Sebastien 1931- .... **CLC 90**

Jarrell, Randall 1914-1965 .... **CLC 1, 2, 6, 9,
13, 49; DAM POET**
See also CA 5-8R; 25-28R; CABS 2; CANR
6, 34; CDALB 1941-1968; CLR 6; DLB
48, 52; MAICYA; MTCW 1, 2; SATA 7

Jarry, Alfred 1873-1907 . **TCLC 2, 14; DAM
DRAM; SSC 20**
See also CA 104; 153; DA3; DLB 192

Jawien, Andrzej
See John Paul II, Pope

Jaynes, Roderick
See Coen, Ethan

Jeake, Samuel, Jr.
See Aiken, Conrad (Potter)

Jean Paul 1763-1825 .... **NCLC 7**

Jefferies, (John) Richard
1848-1887 .... **NCLC 47**
See also DLB 98, 141; SATA 16

Jeffers, (John) Robinson 1887-1962 .. **CLC 2,
3, 11, 15, 54; DA; DAC; DAM MST,
POET; PC 17; WLC**
See also CA 85-88; CANR 35; CDALB
1917-1929; DLB 45, 212; MTCW 1, 2

Jefferson, Janet
See Mencken, H(enry) L(ouis)

Jefferson, Thomas 1743-1826 .... **NCLC 11**
See also CDALB 1640-1865; DA3; DLB
31

Jeffrey, Francis 1773-1850 .... **NCLC 33**
See also DLB 107

Jelakowitch, Ivan
See Heijermans, Herman

Jellicoe, (Patricia) Ann 1927- .... **CLC 27**
See also CA 85-88; DLB 13

Jemyma
See Holley, Marietta

Jen, Gish CLC 70
See also Jen, Lillian

Jen, Lillian 1956(?)-
See Jen, Gish
See also CA 135; CANR 89

Jenkins, (John) Robin 1912- .... **CLC 52**
See also CA 1-4R; CANR 1; DLB 14

Jennings, Elizabeth (Joan) 1926- ...... **CLC 5,
14, 131**
See also CA 61-64; CAAS 5; CANR 8, 39,
66; DLB 27; MTCW 1; SATA 66

Jennings, Waylon 1937- .... **CLC 21**

Jensen, Johannes V. 1873-1950 ...... **TCLC 41**
See also CA 170

Jensen, Laura (Linnea) 1948- .... **CLC 37**
See also CA 103

Jerome, Jerome K(lapka)
1859-1927 .... **TCLC 23**
See also CA 119; 177; DLB 10, 34, 135

Jerrold, Douglas William
1803-1857 .... **NCLC 2**
See also DLB 158, 159

Jewett, (Theodora) Sarah Orne
1849-1909 .... **TCLC 1, 22; SSC 6**
See also CA 108; 127; CANR 71; DLB 12,
74, 221; SATA 15

Jewsbury, Geraldine (Endsor)
1812-1880 .... **NCLC 22**
See also DLB 21

Jhabvala, Ruth Prawer 1927- . **CLC 4, 8, 29,
94; DAB; DAM NOV**
See also CA 1-4R; CANR 2, 29, 51, 74, 91;
DLB 139, 194; INT CANR-29; MTCW 1,
2

Jibran, Kahlil
See Gibran, Kahlil

Jibran, Khalil
See Gibran, Kahlil

Jiles, Paulette 1943- .... **CLC 13, 58**
See also CA 101; CANR 70

Jimenez (Mantecon), Juan Ramon
1881-1958 .... **TCLC 4; DAM MULT,
POET; HLC 1; PC 7**
See also CA 104; 131; CANR 74; DLB 134;
HW 1; MTCW 1, 2

Jimenez, Ramon
See Jimenez (Mantecon), Juan Ramon

Jimenez Mantecon, Juan
See Jimenez (Mantecon), Juan Ramon

Jin, Ha
See Jin, Xuefei

Jin, Xuefei 1956- .... **CLC 109**
See also CA 152; CANR 91

Joel, Billy CLC 26
See also Joel, William Martin

Joel, William Martin 1949-
See Joel, Billy
See also CA 108

John, Saint 7th cent. - .... **CMLC 27**

John of the Cross, St. 1542-1591 .... **LC 18**

John Paul II, Pope 1920- .... **CLC 128**
See also CA 106; 133

Johnson, B(ryan) S(tanley William)
1933-1973 .... **CLC 6, 9**
See also CA 9-12R; 53-56; CANR 9; DLB
14, 40

Johnson, Benj. F. of Boo
See Riley, James Whitcomb

Johnson, Benjamin F. of Boo
See Riley, James Whitcomb

Johnson, Charles (Richard) 1948- .... **CLC 7,
51, 65; BLC 2; DAM MULT**
See also BW 2, 3; CA 116; CAAS 18;
CANR 42, 66, 82; DLB 33; MTCW 2

Johnson, Denis 1949- .... **CLC 52**
See also CA 117; 121; CANR 71; DLB 120

Johnson, Diane 1934- .... **CLC 5, 13, 48**
See also CA 41-44R; CANR 17, 40, 62;
DLBY 80; INT CANR-17; MTCW 1

Johnson, Eyvind (Olof Verner)
1900-1976 .... **CLC 14**
See also CA 73-76; 69-72; CANR 34

Johnson, J. R.
See James, C(yril) L(ionel) R(obert)

Johnson, James Weldon
1871-1938 .. **TCLC 3, 19; BLC 2; DAM
MULT, POET; PC 24**
See also BW 1, 3; CA 104; 125; CANR 82;
CDALB 1917-1929; CLR 32; DA3; DLB
51; MTCW 1, 2; SATA 31

Johnson, Joyce 1935- .... **CLC 58**
See also CA 125; 129

Johnson, Judith (Emlyn) 1936- .... **CLC 7, 15**
See also Sherwin, Judith Johnson
See also CA 25-28R, 153; CANR 34

Johnson, Lionel (Pigot)
1867-1902 .... **TCLC 19**
See also CA 117; DLB 19

Johnson, Marguerite (Annie)
See Angelou, Maya

Johnson, Mel
See Malzberg, Barry N(athaniel)

Johnson, Pamela Hansford
1912-1981 .... **CLC 1, 7, 27**
See also CA 1-4R; 104; CANR 2, 28; DLB
15; MTCW 1, 2

Johnson, Robert 1911(?)-1938 .... **TCLC 69**
See also BW 3; CA 174

Johnson, Samuel 1709-1784 . **LC 15, 52; DA;
DAB; DAC; DAM MST; WLC**
See also CDBLB 1660-1789; DLB 39, 95,
104, 142

Johnson, Uwe 1934-1984 .. **CLC 5, 10, 15, 40**
See also CA 1-4R; 112; CANR 1, 39; DLB 75; MTCW 1

Johnston, George (Benson) 1913- .... **CLC 51**
See also CA 1-4R; CANR 5, 20; DLB 88

Johnston, Jennifer (Prudence) 1930- . **CLC 7**
See also CA 85-88; CANR 92; DLB 14

Joinville, Jean de 1224(?)-1317 ..... **CMLC 38**

Jolley, (Monica) Elizabeth 1923- ..... **CLC 46; SSC 19**
See also CA 127; CAAS 13; CANR 59

Jones, Arthur Llewellyn 1863-1947
See Machen, Arthur
See also CA 104; 179

Jones, D(ouglas) G(ordon) 1929- ..... **CLC 10**
See also CA 29-32R; CANR 13, 90; DLB 53

Jones, David (Michael) 1895-1974 .... **CLC 2, 4, 7, 13, 42**
See also CA 9-12R; 53-56; CANR 28; CD-BLB 1945-1960; DLB 20, 100; MTCW 1

Jones, David Robert 1947-
See Bowie, David
See also CA 103

Jones, Diana Wynne 1934- .... **CLC 26**
See also AAYA 12; CA 49-52; CANR 4, 26, 56; CLR 23; DLB 161; JRDA; MAI-CYA; SAAS 7; SATA 9, 70, 108

Jones, Edward P. 1950- .... **CLC 76**
See also BW 2, 3; CA 142; CANR 79

Jones, Gayl 1949- ..... **CLC 6, 9, 131; BLC 2; DAM MULT**
See also BW 2, 3; CA 77-80; CANR 27, 66; DA3; DLB 33; MTCW 1, 2

Jones, James 1921-1977 ...... **CLC 1, 3, 10, 39**
See also AITN 1, 2; CA 1-4R; 69-72; CANR 6; DLB 2, 143; DLBD 17; DLBY 98; MTCW 1

Jones, John J.
See Lovecraft, H(oward) P(hillips)

Jones, LeRoi **CLC 1, 2, 3, 5, 10, 14**
See also Baraka, Amiri
See also MTCW 2

Jones, Louis B. 1953- .... **CLC 65**
See also CA 141; CANR 73

Jones, Madison (Percy, Jr.) 1925- ...... **CLC 4**
See also CA 13-16R; CAAS 11; CANR 7, 54, 83; DLB 152

Jones, Mervyn 1922- .... **CLC 10, 52**
See also CA 45-48; CAAS 5; CANR 1, 91; MTCW 1

Jones, Mick 1956(?)- .... **CLC 30**

Jones, Nettie (Pearl) 1941- .... **CLC 34**
See also BW 2; CA 137; CAAS 20; CANR 88

Jones, Preston 1936-1979 .... **CLC 10**
See also CA 73-76; 89-92; DLB 7

Jones, Robert F(rancis) 1934- .... **CLC 7**
See also CA 49-52; CANR 2, 61

Jones, Rod 1953- .... **CLC 50**
See also CA 128

Jones, Terence Graham Parry 1942- .... **CLC 21**
See also Jones, Terry; Monty Python
See also CA 112; 116; CANR 35; INT 116

Jones, Terry
See Jones, Terence Graham Parry
See also SATA 67; SATA-Brief 51

Jones, Thom (Douglas) 1945(?)- .... **CLC 81**
See also CA 157; CANR 88

Jong, Erica 1942- .... **CLC 4, 6, 8, 18, 83; DAM NOV, POP**
See also AITN 1; BEST 90:2; CA 73-76; CANR 26, 52, 75; DA3; DLB 2, 5, 28, 152; INT CANR-26; MTCW 1, 2

Jonson, Ben(jamin) 1572(?)-1637 .. **LC 6, 33; DA; DAB; DAC; DAM DRAM, MST, POET; DC 4; PC 17; WLC**
See also CDBLB Before 1660; DLB 62, 121

Jordan, June 1936- .... **CLC 5, 11, 23, 114; BLCS; DAM MULT, POET**
See also AAYA 2; BW 2, 3; CA 33-36R; CANR 25, 70; CLR 10; DLB 38; MAI-CYA; MTCW 1; SATA 4

Jordan, Neil (Patrick) 1950- .... **CLC 110**
See also CA 124; 130; CANR 54; INT 130

Jordan, Pat(rick M.) 1941- .... **CLC 37**
See also CA 33-36R

Jorgensen, Ivar
See Ellison, Harlan (Jay)

Jorgenson, Ivar
See Silverberg, Robert

Josephus, Flavius c. 37-100 .... **CMLC 13**

Josiah Allen's Wife
See Holley, Marietta

Josipovici, Gabriel (David) 1940- ...... **CLC 6, 43**
See also CA 37-40R; CAAS 8; CANR 47, 84; DLB 14

Joubert, Joseph 1754-1824 .... **NCLC 9**

Jouve, Pierre Jean 1887-1976 .... **CLC 47**
See also CA 65-68

Jovine, Francesco 1902-1950 .... **TCLC 79**

Joyce, James (Augustine Aloysius) 1882-1941 .. **TCLC 3, 8, 16, 35, 52; DA; DAB; DAC; DAM MST, NOV, POET; PC 22; SSC 3, 26; WLC**
See also CA 104; 126; CDBLB 1914-1945; DA3; DLB 10, 19, 36, 162; MTCW 1, 2

Jozsef, Attila 1905-1937 .... **TCLC 22**
See also CA 116

Juana Ines de la Cruz 1651(?)-1695 .... **LC 5; HLCS 1; PC 24**

Judd, Cyril
See Kornbluth, C(yril) M.; Pohl, Frederik

Juenger, Ernst 1895-1998 .... **CLC 125**
See also CA 101; 167; CANR 21, 47; DLB 56

Julian of Norwich 1342(?)-1416(?) . **LC 6, 52**
See also DLB 146

Junger, Ernst
See Juenger, Ernst

Junger, Sebastian 1962- .... **CLC 109**
See also AAYA 28; CA 165

Juniper, Alex
See Hospital, Janette Turner

Junius
See Luxemburg, Rosa

Just, Ward (Swift) 1935- .... **CLC 4, 27**
See also CA 25-28R; CANR 32, 87; INT CANR-32

Justice, Donald (Rodney) 1925- .. **CLC 6, 19, 102; DAM POET**
See also CA 5-8R; CANR 26, 54, 74; DLBY 83; INT CANR-26; MTCW 2

Juvenal c. 60-c. 13 .... **CMLC 8**
See also Juvenalis, Decimus Junius
See also DLB 211

Juvenalis, Decimus Junius 55(?)-c. 127(?)
See Juvenal

Juvenis
See Bourne, Randolph S(illiman)

Kacew, Romain 1914-1980
See Gary, Romain
See also CA 108; 102

Kadare, Ismail 1936- .... **CLC 52**
See also CA 161

Kadohata, Cynthia **CLC 59, 122**
See also CA 140

Kafka, Franz 1883-1924 . **TCLC 2, 6, 13, 29, 47, 53; DA; DAB; DAC; DAM MST, NOV; SSC 5, 29, 35; WLC**
See also AAYA 31; CA 105; 126; DA3; DLB 81; MTCW 1, 2

Kahanovitsch, Pinkhes
See Der Nister

Kahn, Roger 1927- .... **CLC 30**
See also CA 25-28R; CANR 44, 69; DLB 171; SATA 37

Kain, Saul
See Sassoon, Siegfried (Lorraine)

Kaiser, Georg 1878-1945 .... **TCLC 9**
See also CA 106; DLB 124

Kaletski, Alexander 1946- .... **CLC 39**
See also CA 118; 143

Kalidasa fl. c. 400- .... **CMLC 9; PC 22**

Kallman, Chester (Simon) 1921-1975 .... **CLC 2**
See also CA 45-48; 53-56; CANR 3

Kaminsky, Melvin 1926-
See Brooks, Mel
See also CA 65-68; CANR 16

Kaminsky, Stuart M(elvin) 1934- ..... **CLC 59**
See also CA 73-76; CANR 29, 53, 89

Kandinsky, Wassily 1866-1944 .... **TCLC 92**
See also CA 118; 155

Kane, Francis
See Robbins, Harold

Kane, Paul
See Simon, Paul (Frederick)

Kanin, Garson 1912-1999 .... **CLC 22**
See also AITN 1; CA 5-8R; 177; CANR 7, 78; DLB 7

Kaniuk, Yoram 1930- .... **CLC 19**
See also CA 134

Kant, Immanuel 1724-1804 ..... **NCLC 27, 67**
See also DLB 94

Kantor, MacKinlay 1904-1977 .... **CLC 7**
See also CA 61-64; 73-76; CANR 60, 63; DLB 9, 102; MTCW 1

Kaplan, David Michael 1946- .... **CLC 50**

Kaplan, James 1951- .... **CLC 59**
See also CA 135

Karageorge, Michael
See Anderson, Poul (William)

Karamzin, Nikolai Mikhailovich 1766-1826 .... **NCLC 3**
See also DLB 150

Karapanou, Margarita 1946- .... **CLC 13**
See also CA 101

Karinthy, Frigyes 1887-1938 .... **TCLC 47**
See also CA 170

Karl, Frederick R(obert) 1927- .... **CLC 34**
See also CA 5-8R; CANR 3, 44

Kastel, Warren
See Silverberg, Robert

Kataev, Evgeny Petrovich 1903-1942
See Petrov, Evgeny
See also CA 120

Kataphusin
See Ruskin, John

Katz, Steve 1935- .... **CLC 47**
See also CA 25-28R; CAAS 14, 64; CANR 12; DLBY 83

Kauffman, Janet 1945- .... **CLC 42**
See also CA 117; CANR 43, 84; DLBY 86

Kaufman, Bob (Garnell) 1925-1986 . **CLC 49**
See also BW 1; CA 41-44R; 118; CANR 22; DLB 16, 41

Kaufman, George S. 1889-1961 ...... **CLC 38; DAM DRAM**
See also CA 108; 93-96; DLB 7; INT 108; MTCW 2

Kaufman, Sue **CLC 3, 8**
See Barondess, Sue K(aufman)

Kavafis, Konstantinos Petrou 1863-1933
See Cavafy, C(onstantine) P(eter)
See also CA 104

Kavan, Anna 1901-1968 .... **CLC 5, 13, 82**
See also CA 5-8R; CANR 6, 57; MTCW 1

Kavanagh, Dan
See Barnes, Julian (Patrick)

Kavanagh, Julie 1952- .... **CLC 119**
See also CA 163

Kavanagh, Patrick (Joseph)
1904-1967 .... **CLC 22**
See also CA 123; 25-28R; DLB 15, 20;
MTCW 1

Kawabata, Yasunari 1899-1972 ..... **CLC 2, 5, 9, 18, 107; DAM MULT; SSC 17**
See also CA 93-96; 33-36R; CANR 88;
DLB 180; MTCW 2

Kaye, M(ary) M(argaret) 1909- .... **CLC 28**
See also CA 89-92; CANR 24, 60; MTCW
1, 2; SATA 62

Kaye, Mollie
See Kaye, M(ary) M(argaret)

Kaye-Smith, Sheila 1887-1956 .... **TCLC 20**
See also CA 118; DLB 36

Kaymor, Patrice Maguilene
See Senghor, Leopold Sedar

Kazan, Elia 1909- .... **CLC 6, 16, 63**
See also CA 21-24R; CANR 32, 78

Kazantzakis, Nikos 1883(?)-1957 .... **TCLC 2, 5, 33**
See also CA 105; 132; DA3; MTCW 1, 2

Kazin, Alfred 1915-1998 ..... **CLC 34, 38, 119**
See also CA 1-4R; CAAS 7; CANR 1, 45,
79; DLB 67

Keane, Mary Nesta (Skrine) 1904-1996
See Keane, Molly
See also CA 108; 114; 151

Keane, Molly CLC 31
See Keane, Mary Nesta (Skrine)
See also INT 114

Keates, Jonathan 1946(?)- .... **CLC 34**
See also CA 163

Keaton, Buster 1895-1966 .... **CLC 20**

Keats, John 1795-1821 ...... **NCLC 8, 73; DA; DAB; DAC; DAM MST, POET; PC 1; WLC**
See also CDBLB 1789-1832; DA3; DLB
96, 110

Keble, John 1792-1866 .... **NCLC 87**
See also DLB 32, 55

Keene, Donald 1922- .... **CLC 34**
See also CA 1-4R; CANR 5

Keillor, Garrison CLC 40, 115
See also Keillor, Gary (Edward)
See also AAYA 2; BEST 89:3; DLBY 87;
SATA 58

Keillor, Gary (Edward) 1942-
See Keillor, Garrison
See also CA 111; 117; CANR 36, 59; DAM
POP; DA3; MTCW 1, 2

Keith, Michael
See Hubbard, L(afayette) Ron(ald)

Keller, Gottfried 1819-1890 .... **NCLC 2; SSC 26**
See also DLB 129

Keller, Nora Okja CLC 109

Kellerman, Jonathan 1949- .. **CLC 44; DAM POP**
See also BEST 90:1; CA 106; CANR 29,
51; DA3; INT CANR-29

Kelley, William Melvin 1937- .... **CLC 22**
See also BW 1; CA 77-80; CANR 27, 83;
DLB 33

Kellogg, Marjorie 1922- .... **CLC 2**
See also CA 81-84

Kellow, Kathleen
See Hibbert, Eleanor Alice Burford

Kelly, M(ilton) T(errence) 1947- ...... **CLC 55**
See also CA 97-100; CAAS 22; CANR 19,
43, 84

Kelman, James 1946- .... **CLC 58, 86**
See also CA 148; CANR 85; DLB 194

Kemal, Yashar 1923- .... **CLC 14, 29**
See also CA 89-92; CANR 44

Kemble, Fanny 1809-1893 .... **NCLC 18**
See also DLB 32

Kemelman, Harry 1908-1996 .... **CLC 2**
See also AITN 1; CA 9-12R; 155; CANR 6,
71; DLB 28

Kempe, Margery 1373(?)-1440(?) ... **LC 6, 56**
See also DLB 146

Kempis, Thomas a 1380-1471 .... **LC 11**

Kendall, Henry 1839-1882 .... **NCLC 12**

Keneally, Thomas (Michael) 1935- ... **CLC 5, 8, 10, 14, 19, 27, 43, 117; DAM NOV**
See also CA 85-88; CANR 10, 50, 74; DA3;
MTCW 1, 2

Kennedy, Adrienne (Lita) 1931- ..... **CLC 66; BLC 2; DAM MULT; DC 5**
See also BW 2, 3; CA 103; CAAS 20;
CABS 3; CANR 26, 53, 82; DLB 38

Kennedy, John Pendleton
1795-1870 .... **NCLC 2**
See also DLB 3

Kennedy, Joseph Charles 1929-
See Kennedy, X. J.
See also CA 1-4R; CANR 4, 30, 40; SATA
14, 86

Kennedy, William 1928- .. **CLC 6, 28, 34, 53; DAM NOV**
See also AAYA 1; CA 85-88; CANR 14,
31, 76; DA3; DLB 143; DLBY 85; INT
CANR-31; MTCW 1, 2; SATA 57

Kennedy, X. J. CLC 8, 42
See also Kennedy, Joseph Charles
See also CAAS 9; CLR 27; DLB 5; SAAS
22

Kenny, Maurice (Francis) 1929- ..... **CLC 87; DAM MULT**
See also CA 144; CAAS 22; DLB 175;
NNAL

Kent, Kelvin
See Kuttner, Henry

Kenton, Maxwell
See Southern, Terry

Kenyon, Robert O.
See Kuttner, Henry

Kepler, Johannes 1571-1630 .... **LC 45**

Kerouac, Jack CLC 1, 2, 3, 5, 14, 29, 61
See also Kerouac, Jean-Louis Lebris de
See also AAYA 25; CDALB 1941-1968;
DLB 2, 16; DLBD 3; DLBY 95; MTCW
2

Kerouac, Jean-Louis Lebris de 1922-1969
See Kerouac, Jack
See also AITN 1; CA 5-8R; 25-28R; CANR
26, 54; DA; DAB; DAC; DAM MST,
NOV, POET, POP; DA3; MTCW 1, 2;
WLC

Kerr, Jean 1923- .... **CLC 22**
See also CA 5-8R; CANR 7; INT CANR-7

Kerr, M. E. CLC 12, 35
See also Meaker, Marijane (Agnes)
See also AAYA 2, 23; CLR 29; SAAS 1

Kerr, Robert CLC 55

Kerrigan, (Thomas) Anthony 1918- .. **CLC 4, 6**
See also CA 49-52; CAAS 11; CANR 4

Kerry, Lois
See Duncan, Lois

Kesey, Ken (Elton) 1935- ..... **CLC 1, 3, 6, 11, 46, 64; DA; DAB; DAC; DAM MST, NOV, POP; WLC**
See also AAYA 25; CA 1-4R; CANR 22,
38, 66; CDALB 1968-1988; DA3; DLB
2, 16, 206; MTCW 1, 2; SATA 66

Kesselring, Joseph (Otto)
1902-1967 .... **CLC 45; DAM DRAM, MST**
See also CA 150

Kessler, Jascha (Frederick) 1929- ...... **CLC 4**
See also CA 17-20R; CANR 8, 48

Kettelkamp, Larry (Dale) 1933- .... **CLC 12**
See also CA 29-32R; CANR 16; SAAS 3;
SATA 2

Key, Ellen 1849-1926 .... **TCLC 65**

Keyber, Conny
See Fielding, Henry

Keyes, Daniel 1927- ...... **CLC 80; DA; DAC; DAM MST, NOV**
See also AAYA 23; CA 17-20R, 181; CAAE
181; CANR 10, 26, 54, 74; DA3; MTCW
2; SATA 37

Keynes, John Maynard
1883-1946 .... **TCLC 64**
See also CA 114; 162, 163; DLBD 10;
MTCW 2

Khanshendel, Chiron
See Rose, Wendy

Khayyam, Omar 1048-1131 .... **CMLC 11; DAM POET; PC 8**
See also DA3

Kherdian, David 1931- .... **CLC 6, 9**
See also CA 21-24R; CAAS 2; CANR 39,
78; CLR 24; JRDA; MAICYA; SATA 16,
74

Khlebnikov, Velimir TCLC 20
See also Khlebnikov, Viktor Vladimirovich

Khlebnikov, Viktor Vladimirovich 1885-1922
See Khlebnikov, Velimir
See also CA 117

Khodasevich, Vladislav (Felitsianovich)
1886-1939 .... **TCLC 15**
See also CA 115

Kielland, Alexander Lange
1849-1906 .... **TCLC 5**
See also CA 104

Kiely, Benedict 1919- .... **CLC 23, 43**
See also CA 1-4R; CANR 2, 84; DLB 15

Kienzle, William X(avier) 1928- ..... **CLC 25; DAM POP**
See also CA 93-96; CAAS 1; CANR 9, 31,
59; DA3; INT CANR-31; MTCW 1, 2

Kierkegaard, Soren 1813-1855 ..... **NCLC 34, 78**

Kieslowski, Krzysztof 1941-1996 .... **CLC 120**
See also CA 147; 151

Killens, John Oliver 1916-1987 .... **CLC 10**
See also BW 2; CA 77-80; 123; CAAS 2;
CANR 26; DLB 33

Killigrew, Anne 1660-1685 .... **LC 4**
See also DLB 131

Killigrew, Thomas 1612-1683 .... **LC 57**
See also DLB 58

Kim
See Simenon, Georges (Jacques Christian)

Kincaid, Jamaica 1949- .... **CLC 43, 68; BLC 2; DAM MULT, NOV**
See also AAYA 13; BW 2, 3; CA 125;
CANR 47, 59; CDALBS; CLR 63; DA3;
DLB 157, 227; MTCW 2

King, Francis (Henry) 1923- .... **CLC 8, 53; DAM NOV**
See also CA 1-4R; CANR 1, 33, 86; DLB
15, 139; MTCW 1

King, Kennedy
See Brown, George Douglas

King, Martin Luther, Jr.
1929-1968 .... **CLC 83; BLC 2; DA; DAB; DAC; DAM MST, MULT; WLCS**
See also BW 2, 3; CA 25-28; CANR 27,
44; CAP 2; DA3; MTCW 1, 2; SATA 14

King, Stephen (Edwin) 1947- .... **CLC 12, 26, 37, 61, 113; DAM NOV, POP; SSC 17**
See also AAYA 1, 17; BEST 90:1; CA 61-
64; CANR 1, 30, 52, 76; DA3; DLB 143;
DLBY 80; JRDA; MTCW 1, 2; SATA 9,
55

King, Steve
See King, Stephen (Edwin)

Larra (y Sanchez de Castro), Mariano Jose de 1809-1837 .... **NCLC 17**

Larsen, Eric 1941- .... **CLC 55**
See also CA 132

Larsen, Nella 1891-1964 .... **CLC 37; BLC 2; DAM MULT**
See also BW 1; CA 125; CANR 83; DLB 51

Larson, Charles R(aymond) 1938- ... **CLC 31**
See also CA 53-56; CANR 4

Larson, Jonathan 1961-1996 .... **CLC 99**
See also AAYA 28; CA 156

Las Casas, Bartolome de 1474-1566 ... **LC 31**

Lasch, Christopher 1932-1994 .... **CLC 102**
See also CA 73-76; 144; CANR 25; MTCW 1, 2

Lasker-Schueler, Else 1869-1945 ... **TCLC 57**
See also CA 183; DLB 66, 124

Laski, Harold 1893-1950 .... **TCLC 79**

Latham, Jean Lee 1902-1995 .... **CLC 12**
See also AITN 1; CA 5-8R; CANR 7, 84; CLR 50; MAICYA; SATA 2, 68

Latham, Mavis
See Clark, Mavis Thorpe

Lathen, Emma CLC 2
See also Hennissart, Martha; Latsis, Mary J(ane)

Lathrop, Francis
See Leiber, Fritz (Reuter, Jr.)

Latsis, Mary J(ane) 1927(?)-1997
See Lathen, Emma
See also CA 85-88; 162

Lattimore, Richmond (Alexander) 1906-1984 .... **CLC 3**
See also CA 1-4R; 112; CANR 1

Laughlin, James 1914-1997 .... **CLC 49**
See also CA 21-24R; 162; CAAS 22; CANR 9, 47; DLB 48; DLBY 96, 97

Laurence, (Jean) Margaret (Wemyss) 1926-1987 . **CLC 3, 6, 13, 50, 62; DAC; DAM MST; SSC 7**
See also CA 5-8R; 121; CANR 33; DLB 53; MTCW 1, 2; SATA-Obit 50

Laurent, Antoine 1952- .... **CLC 50**

Lauscher, Hermann
See Hesse, Hermann

Lautreamont, Comte de 1846-1870 .... **NCLC 12; SSC 14**

Laverty, Donald
See Blish, James (Benjamin)

Lavin, Mary 1912-1996 . **CLC 4, 18, 99; SSC 4**
See also CA 9-12R; 151; CANR 33; DLB 15; MTCW 1

Lavond, Paul Dennis
See Kornbluth, C(yril) M.; Pohl, Frederik

Lawler, Raymond Evenor 1922- .... **CLC 58**
See also CA 103

Lawrence, D(avid) H(erbert Richards) 1885-1930 .... **TCLC 2, 9, 16, 33, 48, 61, 93; DA; DAB; DAC; DAM MST, NOV, POET; SSC 4, 19; WLC**
See also CA 104; 121; CDBLB 1914-1945; DA3; DLB 10, 19, 36, 98, 162, 195; MTCW 1, 2

Lawrence, T(homas) E(dward) 1888-1935 .... **TCLC 18**
See also Dale, Colin
See also CA 115; 167; DLB 195

Lawrence of Arabia
See Lawrence, T(homas) E(dward)

Lawson, Henry (Archibald Hertzberg) 1867-1922 .... **TCLC 27; SSC 18**
See also CA 120; 181

Lawton, Dennis
See Faust, Frederick (Schiller)

Laxness, Halldor CLC 25
See also Gudjonsson, Halldor Kiljan

Layamon fl. c. 1200- .... **CMLC 10**
See also DLB 146

Laye, Camara 1928-1980 ... **CLC 4, 38; BLC 2; DAM MULT**
See also BW 1; CA 85-88; 97-100; CANR 25; MTCW 1, 2

Layton, Irving (Peter) 1912- .... **CLC 2, 15; DAC; DAM MST, POET**
See also CA 1-4R; CANR 2, 33, 43, 66; DLB 88; MTCW 1, 2

Lazarus, Emma 1849-1887 .... **NCLC 8**

Lazarus, Felix
See Cable, George Washington

Lazarus, Henry
See Slavitt, David R(ytman)

Lea, Joan
See Neufeld, John (Arthur)

Leacock, Stephen (Butler) 1869-1944 .... **TCLC 2; DAC; DAM MST; SSC 39**
See also CA 104; 141; CANR 80; DLB 92; MTCW 2

Lear, Edward 1812-1888 .... **NCLC 3**
See also CLR 1; DLB 32, 163, 166; MAICYA; SATA 18, 100

Lear, Norman (Milton) 1922- .... **CLC 12**
See also CA 73-76

Leautaud, Paul 1872-1956 .... **TCLC 83**
See also DLB 65

Leavis, F(rank) R(aymond) 1895-1978 .... **CLC 24**
See also CA 21-24R; 77-80; CANR 44; MTCW 1, 2

Leavitt, David 1961- ..... **CLC 34; DAM POP**
See also CA 116; 122; CANR 50, 62; DA3; DLB 130; INT 122; MTCW 2

Leblanc, Maurice (Marie Emile) 1864-1941 .... **TCLC 49**
See also CA 110

Lebowitz, Fran(ces Ann) 1951(?)- ... **CLC 11, 36**
See also CA 81-84; CANR 14, 60, 70; INT CANR-14; MTCW 1

Lebrecht, Peter
See Tieck, (Johann) Ludwig

le Carre, John CLC 3, 5, 9, 15, 28
See also Cornwell, David (John Moore)
See also BEST 89:4; CDBLB 1960 to Present; DLB 87; MTCW 2

Le Clezio, J(ean) M(arie) G(ustave) 1940- .... **CLC 31**
See also CA 116; 128; DLB 83

Leconte de Lisle, Charles-Marie-Rene 1818-1894 .... **NCLC 29**

Le Coq, Monsieur
See Simenon, Georges (Jacques Christian)

Leduc, Violette 1907-1972 .... **CLC 22**
See also CA 13-14; 33-36R; CANR 69; CAP 1

Ledwidge, Francis 1887(?)-1917 .... **TCLC 23**
See also CA 123; DLB 20

Lee, Andrea 1953- ... **CLC 36; BLC 2; DAM MULT**
See also BW 1, 3; CA 125; CANR 82

Lee, Andrew
See Auchincloss, Louis (Stanton)

Lee, Chang-rae 1965- .... **CLC 91**
See also CA 148; CANR 89

Lee, Don L. CLC 2
See also Madhubuti, Haki R.

Lee, George W(ashington) 1894-1976 .... **CLC 52; BLC 2; DAM MULT**
See also BW 1; CA 125; CANR 83; DLB 51

Lee, (Nelle) Harper 1926- . **CLC 12, 60; DA; DAB; DAC; DAM MST, NOV; WLC**
See also AAYA 13; CA 13-16R; CANR 51; CDALB 1941-1968; DA3; DLB 6; MTCW 1, 2; SATA 11

Lee, Helen Elaine 1959(?)- .... **CLC 86**
See also CA 148

Lee, Julian
See Latham, Jean Lee

Lee, Larry
See Lee, Lawrence

Lee, Laurie 1914-1997 .... **CLC 90; DAB; DAM POP**
See also CA 77-80; 158; CANR 33, 73; DLB 27; MTCW 1

Lee, Lawrence 1941-1990 .... **CLC 34**
See also CA 131; CANR 43

Lee, Li-Young 1957- .... **PC 24**
See also CA 153; DLB 165

Lee, Manfred B(ennington) 1905-1971 .... **CLC 11**
See also Queen, Ellery
See also CA 1-4R; 29-32R; CANR 2; DLB 137

Lee, Shelton Jackson 1957(?)- .... **CLC 105; BLCS; DAM MULT**
See also Lee, Spike
See also BW 2, 3; CA 125; CANR 42

Lee, Spike
See Lee, Shelton Jackson
See also AAYA 4, 29

Lee, Stan 1922- .... **CLC 17**
See also AAYA 5; CA 108; 111; INT 111

Lee, Tanith 1947- .... **CLC 46**
See also AAYA 15; CA 37-40R; CANR 53; SATA 8, 88

Lee, Vernon TCLC 5; SSC 33
See also Paget, Violet
See also DLB 57, 153, 156, 174, 178

Lee, William
See Burroughs, William S(eward)

Lee, Willy
See Burroughs, William S(eward)

Lee-Hamilton, Eugene (Jacob) 1845-1907 .... **TCLC 22**
See also CA 117

Leet, Judith 1935- .... **CLC 11**

Le Fanu, Joseph Sheridan 1814-1873 ..... **NCLC 9, 58; DAM POP; SSC 14**
See also DA3; DLB 21, 70, 159, 178

Leffland, Ella 1931- .... **CLC 19**
See also CA 29-32R; CANR 35, 78, 82; DLBY 84; INT CANR-35; SATA 65

Leger, Alexis
See Leger, (Marie-Rene Auguste) Alexis Saint-Leger

Leger, (Marie-Rene Auguste) Alexis Saint-Leger 1887-1975 .. **CLC 4, 11, 46; DAM POET; PC 23**
See also CA 13-16R; 61-64; CANR 43; MTCW 1

Leger, Saintleger
See Leger, (Marie-Rene Auguste) Alexis Saint-Leger

Le Guin, Ursula K(roeber) 1929- ..... **CLC 8, 13, 22, 45, 71; DAB; DAC; DAM MST, POP; SSC 12**
See also AAYA 9, 27; AITN 1; CA 21-24R; CANR 9, 32, 52, 74; CDALB 1968-1988; CLR 3, 28; DA3; DLB 8, 52; INT CANR-32; JRDA; MAICYA; MTCW 1, 2; SATA 4, 52, 99

Lehmann, Rosamond (Nina) 1901-1990 .... **CLC 5**
See also CA 77-80; 131; CANR 8, 73; DLB 15; MTCW 2

McCann, Arthur
   See Campbell, John W(ood, Jr.)
McCann, Edson
   See Pohl, Frederik
McCarthy, Charles, Jr. 1933-
   See McCarthy, Cormac
   See also CANR 42, 69; DAM POP; DA3;
     MTCW 2
McCarthy, Cormac 1933- ...... **CLC 4, 57, 59,**
    101
   See also McCarthy, Charles, Jr.
   See also DLB 6, 143; MTCW 2
McCarthy, Mary (Therese)
    1912-1989 .. **CLC 1, 3, 5, 14, 24, 39, 59;**
    SSC 24
   See also CA 5-8R; 129; CANR 16, 50, 64;
     DA3; DLB 2; DLBY 81; INT CANR-16;
     MTCW 1, 2
McCartney, (James) Paul 1942- . **CLC 12, 35**
   See also CA 146
McCauley, Stephen (D.) 1955- .... **CLC 50**
   See also CA 141
McClure, Michael (Thomas) 1932- ... **CLC 6,**
    10
   See also CA 21-24R; CANR 17, 46, 77;
     DLB 16
McCorkle, Jill (Collins) 1958- .... **CLC 51**
   See also CA 121; DLBY 87
McCourt, Frank 1930- .... **CLC 109**
   See also CA 157
McCourt, James 1941- .... **CLC 5**
   See also CA 57-60
McCourt, Malachy 1932- .... **CLC 119**
McCoy, Horace (Stanley)
    1897-1955 .... **TCLC 28**
   See also CA 108; 155; DLB 9
McCrae, John 1872-1918 .... **TCLC 12**
   See also CA 109; DLB 92
McCreigh, James
   See Pohl, Frederik
McCullers, (Lula) Carson (Smith)
    1917-1967 .... **CLC 1, 4, 10, 12, 48, 100;**
    DA; DAB; DAC; DAM MST, NOV;
    SSC 9, 24; WLC
   See also AAYA 21; CA 5-8R; 25-28R;
     CABS 1, 3; CANR 18; CDALB 1941-
     1968; DA3; DLB 2, 7, 173, 228; MTCW
     1, 2; SATA 27
McCulloch, John Tyler
   See Burroughs, Edgar Rice
McCullough, Colleen 1938(?)- .... **CLC 27,**
    107; DAM NOV, POP
   See also CA 81-84; CANR 17, 46, 67; DA3;
     MTCW 1, 2
McDermott, Alice 1953- .... **CLC 90**
   See also CA 109; CANR 40, 90
McElroy, Joseph 1930- .... **CLC 5, 47**
   See also CA 17-20R
McEwan, Ian (Russell) 1948- .... **CLC 13, 66;**
    DAM NOV
   See also BEST 90:4; CA 61-64; CANR 14,
     41, 69, 87; DLB 14, 194; MTCW 1, 2
McFadden, David 1940- .... **CLC 48**
   See also CA 104; DLB 60; INT 104
McFarland, Dennis 1950- .... **CLC 65**
   See also CA 165
McGahern, John 1934- ... **CLC 5, 9, 48; SSC**
    17
   See also CA 17-20R; CANR 29, 68; DLB
     14; MTCW 1
McGinley, Patrick (Anthony) 1937- . **CLC 41**
   See also CA 120; 127; CANR 56; INT 127
McGinley, Phyllis 1905-1978 .... **CLC 14**
   See also CA 9-12R; 77-80; CANR 19; DLB
     11, 48; SATA 2, 44; SATA-Obit 24
McGinniss, Joe 1942- .... **CLC 32**
   See also AITN 2; BEST 89:2; CA 25-28R;
     CANR 26, 70; DLB 185; INT CANR-26

McGivern, Maureen Daly
   See Daly, Maureen
McGrath, Patrick 1950- .... **CLC 55**
   See also CA 136; CANR 65
McGrath, Thomas (Matthew)
    1916-1990 ..... **CLC 28, 59; DAM POET**
   See also CA 9-12R; 132; CANR 6, 33;
     MTCW 1; SATA 41; SATA-Obit 66
McGuane, Thomas (Francis III)
    1939- .... **CLC 3, 7, 18, 45, 127**
   See also AITN 2; CA 49-52; CANR 5, 24,
     49; DLB 2, 212; DLBY 80; INT CANR-
     24; MTCW 1
McGuckian, Medbh 1950- .... **CLC 48; DAM**
    POET; PC 27
   See also CA 143; DLB 40
McHale, Tom 1942(?)-1982 .... **CLC 3, 5**
   See also AITN 1; CA 77-80; 106
McIlvanney, William 1936- .... **CLC 42**
   See also CA 25-28R; CANR 61; DLB 14,
     207
McIlwraith, Maureen Mollie Hunter
   See Hunter, Mollie
   See also SATA 2
McInerney, Jay 1955- .... **CLC 34, 112; DAM**
    POP
   See also AAYA 18; CA 116; 123; CANR
     45, 68; DA3; INT 123; MTCW 2
McIntyre, Vonda N(eel) 1948- .... **CLC 18**
   See also CA 81-84; CANR 17, 34, 69;
     MTCW 1
McKay, Claude **TCLC 7, 41; BLC 3; DAB;**
    PC 2
   See also McKay, Festus Claudius
   See also DLB 4, 45, 51, 117
McKay, Festus Claudius 1889-1948
   See McKay, Claude
   See also BW 1, 3; CA 104; 124; CANR 73;
     DA; DAC; DAM MST, MULT, NOV,
     POET; MTCW 1, 2; WLC
McKuen, Rod 1933- .... **CLC 1, 3**
   See also AITN 1; CA 41-44R; CANR 40
McLoughlin, R. B.
   See Mencken, H(enry) L(ouis)
McLuhan, (Herbert) Marshall
    1911-1980 .... **CLC 37, 83**
   See also CA 9-12R; 102; CANR 34, 61;
     DLB 88; INT CANR-12; MTCW 1, 2
McMillan, Terry (L.) 1951- .... **CLC 50, 61,**
    112; BLCS; DAM MULT, NOV, POP
   See also AAYA 21; BW 2, 3; CA 140;
     CANR 60; DA3; MTCW 2
McMurtry, Larry (Jeff) 1936- .. **CLC 2, 3, 7,**
    11, 27, 44, 127; DAM NOV, POP
   See also AAYA 15; AITN 2; BEST 89:2;
     CA 5-8R; CANR 19, 43, 64; CDALB
     1968-1988; DA3; DLB 2, 143; DLBY 80,
     87; MTCW 1, 2
McNally, T. M. 1961- .... **CLC 82**
McNally, Terrence 1939- ... **CLC 4, 7, 41, 91;**
    DAM DRAM
   See also CA 45-48; CANR 2, 56; DA3;
     DLB 7; MTCW 1, 2
McNamer, Deirdre 1950- .... **CLC 70**
McNeal, Tom **CLC 119**
McNeile, Herman Cyril 1888-1937
   See Sapper
   See also CA 184; DLB 77
McNickle, (William) D'Arcy
    1904-1977 .... **CLC 89; DAM MULT**
   See also CA 9-12R; 85-88; CANR 5, 45;
     DLB 175, 212; NNAL; SATA-Obit 22
McPhee, John (Angus) 1931- .... **CLC 36**
   See also BEST 90:1; CA 65-68; CANR 20,
     46, 64, 69; DLB 185; MTCW 1, 2
McPherson, James Alan 1943- .. **CLC 19, 77;**
    BLCS
   See also BW 1, 3; CA 25-28R; CAAS 17;
     CANR 24, 74; DLB 38; MTCW 1, 2

McPherson, William (Alexander)
    1933- .... **CLC 34**
   See also CA 69-72; CANR 28; INT
     CANR-28
Mead, George Herbert 1873-1958 . **TCLC 89**
Mead, Margaret 1901-1978 .... **CLC 37**
   See also AITN 1; CA 1-4R; 81-84; CANR
     4; DA3; MTCW 1, 2; SATA-Obit 20
Meaker, Marijane (Agnes) 1927-
   See Kerr, M. E.
   See also CA 107; CANR 37, 63; INT 107;
     JRDA; MAICYA; MTCW 1; SATA 20,
     61, 99; SATA-Essay 111
Medoff, Mark (Howard) 1940- ... **CLC 6, 23;**
    DAM DRAM
   See also AITN 1; CA 53-56; CANR 5; DLB
     7; INT CANR-5
Medvedev, P. N.
   See Bakhtin, Mikhail Mikhailovich
Meged, Aharon
   See Megged, Aharon
Meged, Aron
   See Megged, Aharon
Megged, Aharon 1920- .... **CLC 9**
   See also CA 49-52; CAAS 13; CANR 1
Mehta, Ved (Parkash) 1934- .... **CLC 37**
   See also CA 1-4R; CANR 2, 23, 69; MTCW
     1
Melanter
   See Blackmore, R(ichard) D(oddridge)
Melies, Georges 1861-1938 .... **TCLC 81**
Melikow, Loris
   See Hofmannsthal, Hugo von
Melmoth, Sebastian
   See Wilde, Oscar (Fingal O'Flahertie Wills)
Meltzer, Milton 1915- .... **CLC 26**
   See also AAYA 8; CA 13-16R; CANR 38,
     92; CLR 13; DLB 61; JRDA; MAICYA;
     SAAS 1; SATA 1, 50, 80
Melville, Herman 1819-1891 ..... **NCLC 3, 12,**
    29, 45, 49, 91; DA; DAB; DAC; DAM
    MST, NOV; SSC 1, 17; WLC
   See also AAYA 25; CDALB 1640-1865;
     DA3; DLB 3, 74; SATA 59
Menander c. 342B.C.-c. 292B.C. ... **CMLC 9;**
    DAM DRAM; DC 3
   See also DLB 176
Menchu, Rigoberta 1959-
   See also HLCS 2
Menchu, Rigoberta 1959-
   See also CA 175; HLCS 2
Mencken, H(enry) L(ouis)
    1880-1956 .... **TCLC 13**
   See also CA 105; 125; CDALB 1917-1929;
     DLB 11, 29, 63, 137; MTCW 1, 2
Mendelsohn, Jane 1965(?)- .... **CLC 99**
   See also CA 154
Mercer, David 1928-1980 .... **CLC 5; DAM**
    DRAM
   See also CA 9-12R; 102; CANR 23; DLB
     13; MTCW 1
Merchant, Paul
   See Ellison, Harlan (Jay)
Meredith, George 1828-1909 .. **TCLC 17, 43;**
    DAM POET
   See also CA 117; 153; CANR 80; CDBLB
     1832-1890; DLB 18, 35, 57, 159
Meredith, William (Morris) 1919- .... **CLC 4,**
    13, 22, 55; DAM POET; PC 28
   See also CA 9-12R; CAAS 14; CANR 6,
     40; DLB 5
Merezhkovsky, Dmitry Sergeyevich
    1865-1941 .... **TCLC 29**
   See also CA 169
Merimee, Prosper 1803-1870 ... **NCLC 6, 65;**
    SSC 7
   See also DLB 119, 192
Merkin, Daphne 1954- .... **CLC 44**
   See also CA 123

Merlin, Arthur
See Blish, James (Benjamin)

Merrill, James (Ingram) 1926-1995 .. **CLC 2, 3, 6, 8, 13, 18, 34, 91; DAM POET; PC 28**
See also CA 13-16R; 147; CANR 10, 49, 63; DA3; DLB 5, 165; DLBY 85; INT CANR-10; MTCW 1, 2

Merriman, Alex
See Silverberg, Robert

Merriman, Brian 1747-1805 .... **NCLC 70**

Merritt, E. B.
See Waddington, Miriam

Merton, Thomas 1915-1968 ..... **CLC 1, 3, 11, 34, 83; PC 10**
See also CA 5-8R; 25-28R; CANR 22, 53; DA3; DLB 48; DLBY 81; MTCW 1, 2

Merwin, W(illiam) S(tanley) 1927- ... **CLC 1, 2, 3, 5, 8, 13, 18, 45, 88; DAM POET**
See also CA 13-16R; CANR 15, 51; DA3; DLB 5, 169; INT CANR-15; MTCW 1, 2

Metcalf, John 1938- .... **CLC 37**
See also CA 113; DLB 60

Metcalf, Suzanne
See Baum, L(yman) Frank

Mew, Charlotte (Mary) 1870-1928 .. **TCLC 8**
See also CA 105; DLB 19, 135

Mewshaw, Michael 1943- .... **CLC 9**
See also CA 53-56; CANR 7, 47; DLBY 80

Meyer, Conrad Ferdinand
1825-1905 .... **NCLC 81**
See also DLB 129

Meyer, June
See Jordan, June

Meyer, Lynn
See Slavitt, David R(ytman)

Meyer-Meyrink, Gustav 1868-1932
See Meyrink, Gustav
See also CA 117

Meyers, Jeffrey 1939- .... **CLC 39**
See also CA 73-76; CAAE 186; CANR 54; DLB 111

Meynell, Alice (Christina Gertrude Thompson) 1847-1922 .... **TCLC 6**
See also CA 104; 177; DLB 19, 98

Meyrink, Gustav **TCLC 21**
See also Meyer-Meyrink, Gustav
See also DLB 81

Michaels, Leonard 1933- .... **CLC 6, 25; SSC 16**
See also CA 61-64; CANR 21, 62; DLB 130; MTCW 1

Michaux, Henri 1899-1984 .... **CLC 8, 19**
See also CA 85-88; 114

Micheaux, Oscar (Devereaux)
1884-1951 .... **TCLC 76**
See also BW 3; CA 174; DLB 50

Michelangelo 1475-1564 .... **LC 12**

Michelet, Jules 1798-1874 .... **NCLC 31**

Michels, Robert 1876-1936 .... **TCLC 88**

Michener, James A(lbert)
1907(?)-1997 .... **CLC 1, 5, 11, 29, 60, 109; DAM NOV, POP**
See also AAYA 27; AITN 1; BEST 90:1; CA 5-8R; 161; CANR 21, 45, 68; DA3; DLB 6; MTCW 1, 2

Mickiewicz, Adam 1798-1855 .... **NCLC 3**

Middleton, Christopher 1926- .... **CLC 13**
See also CA 13-16R; CANR 29, 54; DLB 40

Middleton, Richard (Barham)
1882-1911 .... **TCLC 56**
See also DLB 156

Middleton, Stanley 1919- .... **CLC 7, 38**
See also CA 25-28R; CAAS 23; CANR 21, 46, 81; DLB 14

Middleton, Thomas 1580-1627 .... **LC 33; DAM DRAM, MST; DC 5**
See also DLB 58

Migueis, Jose Rodrigues 1901- .... **CLC 10**

Mikszath, Kalman 1847-1910 .... **TCLC 31**
See also CA 170

Miles, Jack **CLC 100**

Miles, Josephine (Louise)
1911-1985 .. **CLC 1, 2, 14, 34, 39; DAM POET**
See also CA 1-4R; 116; CANR 2, 55; DLB 48

Militant
See Sandburg, Carl (August)

Mill, John Stuart 1806-1873 .... **NCLC 11, 58**
See also CDBLB 1832-1890; DLB 55, 190

Millar, Kenneth 1915-1983 ... **CLC 14; DAM POP**
See also Macdonald, Ross
See also CA 9-12R; 110; CANR 16, 63; DA3; DLB 2, 226; DLBD 6; DLBY 83; MTCW 1, 2

Millay, E. Vincent
See Millay, Edna St. Vincent

Millay, Edna St. Vincent
1892-1950 .... **TCLC 4, 49; DA; DAB; DAC; DAM MST, POET; PC 6; WLCS**
See also CA 104; 130; CDALB 1917-1929; DA3; DLB 45; MTCW 1, 2

Miller, Arthur 1915- ...... **CLC 1, 2, 6, 10, 15, 26, 47, 78; DA; DAB; DAC; DAM DRAM, MST; DC 1; WLC**
See also AAYA 15; AITN 1; CA 1-4R; CABS 3; CANR 2, 30, 54, 76; CDALB 1941-1968; DA3; DLB 7; MTCW 1, 2

Miller, Henry (Valentine)
1891-1980 .... **CLC 1, 2, 4, 9, 14, 43, 84; DA; DAB; DAC; DAM MST, NOV; WLC**
See also CA 9-12R; 97-100; CANR 33, 64; CDALB 1929-1941; DA3; DLB 4, 9; DLBY 80; MTCW 1, 2

Miller, Jason 1939(?)- .... **CLC 2**
See also AITN 1; CA 73-76; DLB 7

Miller, Sue 1943- .... **CLC 44; DAM POP**
See also BEST 90:3; CA 139; CANR 59, 91; DA3; DLB 143

Miller, Walter M(ichael, Jr.) 1923- ... **CLC 4, 30**
See also CA 85-88; DLB 8

Millett, Kate 1934- .... **CLC 67**
See also AITN 1; CA 73-76; CANR 32, 53, 76; DA3; MTCW 1, 2

Millhauser, Steven (Lewis) 1943- .... **CLC 21, 54, 109**
See also CA 110; 111; CANR 63; DA3; DLB 2; INT 111; MTCW 2

Millin, Sarah Gertrude 1889-1968 ... **CLC 49**
See also CA 102; 93-96; DLB 225

Milne, A(lan) A(lexander)
1882-1956 ..... **TCLC 6, 88; DAB; DAC; DAM MST**
See also CA 104; 133; CLR 1, 26; DA3; DLB 10, 77, 100, 160; MAICYA; MTCW 1, 2; SATA 100; YABC 1

Milner, Ron(ald) 1938- .... **CLC 56; BLC 3; DAM MULT**
See also AITN 1; BW 1; CA 73-76; CANR 24, 81; DLB 38; MTCW 1

Milnes, Richard Monckton
1809-1885 .... **NCLC 61**
See also DLB 32, 184

Milosz, Czeslaw 1911- ...... **CLC 5, 11, 22, 31, 56, 82; DAM MST, POET; PC 8; WLCS**
See also CA 81-84; CANR 23, 51, 91; DA3; MTCW 1, 2

Milton, John 1608-1674 .... **LC 9, 43; DA; DAB; DAC; DAM MST, POET; PC 19, 29; WLC**
See also CDBLB 1660-1789; DA3; DLB 131, 151

Min, Anchee 1957- .... **CLC 86**
See also CA 146

Minehaha, Cornelius
See Wedekind, (Benjamin) Frank(lin)

Miner, Valerie 1947- .... **CLC 40**
See also CA 97-100; CANR 59

Minimo, Duca
See D'Annunzio, Gabriele

Minot, Susan 1956- .... **CLC 44**
See also CA 134

Minus, Ed 1938- .... **CLC 39**
See also CA 185

Miranda, Javier
See Bioy Casares, Adolfo

Miranda, Javier
See Bioy Casares, Adolfo

Mirbeau, Octave 1848-1917 .... **TCLC 55**
See also DLB 123, 192

Miro (Ferrer), Gabriel (Francisco Victor)
1879-1930 .... **TCLC 5**
See also CA 104; 185

Mishima, Yukio 1925-1970 .... **CLC 2, 4, 6, 9, 27; DC 1; SSC 4**
See also Hiraoka, Kimitake
See also DLB 182; MTCW 2

Mistral, Frederic 1830-1914 .... **TCLC 51**
See also CA 122

Mistral, Gabriela **TCLC 2; HLC 2**
See also Godoy Alcayaga, Lucila
See also MTCW 2

Mistry, Rohinton 1952- .... **CLC 71; DAC**
See also CA 141; CANR 86

Mitchell, Clyde
See Ellison, Harlan (Jay); Silverberg, Robert

Mitchell, James Leslie 1901-1935
See Gibbon, Lewis Grassic
See also CA 104; DLB 15

Mitchell, Joni 1943- .... **CLC 12**
See also CA 112

Mitchell, Joseph (Quincy)
1908-1996 .... **CLC 98**
See also CA 77-80; 152; CANR 69; DLB 185; DLBY 96

Mitchell, Margaret (Munnerlyn)
1900-1949 . **TCLC 11; DAM NOV, POP**
See also AAYA 23; CA 109; 125; CANR 55; CDALBS; DA3; DLB 9; MTCW 1, 2

Mitchell, Peggy
See Mitchell, Margaret (Munnerlyn)

Mitchell, S(ilas) Weir 1829-1914 .... **TCLC 36**
See also CA 165; DLB 202

Mitchell, W(illiam) O(rmond)
1914-1998 .. **CLC 25; DAC; DAM MST**
See also CA 77-80; 165; CANR 15, 43; DLB 88

Mitchell, William 1879-1936 .... **TCLC 81**

Mitford, Mary Russell 1787-1855 ... **NCLC 4**
See also DLB 110, 116

Mitford, Nancy 1904-1973 .... **CLC 44**
See also CA 9-12R; DLB 191

Miyamoto, (Chujo) Yuriko
1899-1951 .... **TCLC 37**
See also CA 170, 174; DLB 180

Miyazawa, Kenji 1896-1933 .... **TCLC 76**
See also CA 157

Mizoguchi, Kenji 1898-1956 .... **TCLC 72**
See also CA 167

Mo, Timothy (Peter) 1950(?)- ... **CLC 46, 134**
See also CA 117; DLB 194; MTCW 1

Modarressi, Taghi (M.) 1931- .... **CLC 44**
See also CA 121; 134; INT 134

Modiano, Patrick (Jean) 1945- .... **CLC 18**
See also CA 85-88; CANR 17, 40; DLB 83

Moerck, Paal
    See Roelvaag, O(le) E(dvart)
Mofolo, Thomas (Mokopu)
        1875(?)-1948 .. **TCLC 22; BLC 3; DAM MULT**
    See also CA 121; 153; CANR 83; DLB 225; MTCW 2
Mohr, Nicholasa 1938- .... **CLC 12; DAM MULT; HLC 2**
    See also AAYA 8; CA 49-52; CANR 1, 32, 64; CLR 22; DLB 145; HW 1, 2; JRDA; SAAS 8; SATA 8, 97; SATA-Essay 113
Mojtabai, A(nn) G(race) 1938- ..... **CLC 5, 9, 15, 29**
    See also CA 85-88; CANR 88
Moliere 1622-1673 ..... **LC 10, 28; DA; DAB; DAC; DAM DRAM, MST; DC 13; WLC**
    See also DA3
Molin, Charles
    See Mayne, William (James Carter)
Molnar, Ferenc 1878-1952 .. **TCLC 20; DAM DRAM**
    See also CA 109; 153; CANR 83
Momaday, N(avarre) Scott 1934- ...... **CLC 2, 19, 85, 95; DA; DAB; DAC; DAM MST, MULT, NOV, POP; PC 25; WLCS**
    See also AAYA 11; CA 25-28R; CANR 14, 34, 68; CDALBS; DA3; DLB 143, 175; INT CANR-14; MTCW 1, 2; NNAL; SATA 48; SATA-Brief 30
Monette, Paul 1945-1995 .... **CLC 82**
    See also CA 139; 147
Monroe, Harriet 1860-1936 .... **TCLC 12**
    See also CA 109; DLB 54, 91
Monroe, Lyle
    See Heinlein, Robert A(nson)
Montagu, Elizabeth 1720-1800 .... **NCLC 7**
Montagu, Elizabeth 1917- .... **NCLC 7**
    See also CA 9-12R
Montagu, Mary (Pierrepont) Wortley
        1689-1762 .... **LC 9, 57; PC 16**
    See also DLB 95, 101
Montagu, W. H.
    See Coleridge, Samuel Taylor
Montague, John (Patrick) 1929- ..... **CLC 13, 46**
    See also CA 9-12R; CANR 9, 69; DLB 40; MTCW 1
Montaigne, Michel (Eyquem) de
        1533-1592 .... **LC 8; DA; DAB; DAC; DAM MST; WLC**
Montale, Eugenio 1896-1981 ... **CLC 7, 9, 18; PC 13**
    See also CA 17-20R; 104; CANR 30; DLB 114; MTCW 1
Montesquieu, Charles-Louis de Secondat
        1689-1755 .... **LC 7**
Montgomery, (Robert) Bruce 1921(?)-1978
    See Crispin, Edmund
    See also CA 179; 104
Montgomery, L(ucy) M(aud)
        1874-1942 .... **TCLC 51; DAC; DAM MST**
    See also AAYA 12; CA 108; 137; CLR 8; DA3; DLB 92; DLBD 14; JRDA; MAI-CYA; MTCW 2; SATA 100; YABC 1
Montgomery, Marion H., Jr. 1925- .... **CLC 7**
    See also AITN 1; CA 1-4R; CANR 3, 48; DLB 6
Montgomery, Max
    See Davenport, Guy (Mattison, Jr.)
Montherlant, Henry (Milon) de
        1896-1972 ..... **CLC 8, 19; DAM DRAM**
    See also CA 85-88; 37-40R; DLB 72; MTCW 1

Monty Python
    See Chapman, Graham; Cleese, John (Marwood); Gilliam, Terry (Vance); Idle, Eric; Jones, Terence Graham Parry; Palin, Michael (Edward)
    See also AAYA 7
Moodie, Susanna (Strickland)
        1803-1885 .... **NCLC 14**
    See also DLB 99
Mooney, Edward 1951-
    See Mooney, Ted
    See also CA 130
Mooney, Ted CLC 25
    See also Mooney, Edward
Moorcock, Michael (John) 1939- ...... **CLC 5, 27, 58**
    See also Bradbury, Edward P.
    See also AAYA 26; CA 45-48; CAAS 5; CANR 2, 17, 38, 64; DLB 14; MTCW 1, 2; SATA 93
Moore, Brian 1921-1999 ... **CLC 1, 3, 5, 7, 8, 19, 32, 90; DAB; DAC; DAM MST**
    See also CA 1-4R; 174; CANR 1, 25, 42, 63; MTCW 1, 2
Moore, Edward
    See Muir, Edwin
Moore, G. E. 1873-1958 .... **TCLC 89**
Moore, George Augustus
        1852-1933 .... **TCLC 7; SSC 19**
    See also CA 104; 177; DLB 10, 18, 57, 135
Moore, Lorrie CLC 39, 45, 68
    See also Moore, Marie Lorena
Moore, Marianne (Craig)
        1887-1972 .... **CLC 1, 2, 4, 8, 10, 13, 19, 47; DA; DAB; DAC; DAM MST, POET; PC 4; WLCS**
    See also CA 1-4R; 33-36R; CANR 3, 61; CDALB 1929-1941; DA3; DLB 45; DLBD 7; MTCW 1, 2; SATA 20
Moore, Marie Lorena 1957-
    See Moore, Lorrie
    See also CA 116; CANR 39, 83
Moore, Thomas 1779-1852 .... **NCLC 6**
    See also DLB 96, 144
Moorhouse, Frank 1938- .... **SSC 40**
    See also CA 118; CANR 92
Mora, Pat(ricia) 1942-
    See also CA 129; CANR 57, 81; CLR 58; DAM MULT; DLB 209; HLC 2; HW 1, 2; SATA 92
Moraga, Cherrie 1952- .... **CLC 126; DAM MULT**
    See also CA 131; CANR 66; DLB 82; HW 1, 2
Morand, Paul 1888-1976 .... **CLC 41; SSC 22**
    See also CA 184; 69-72; DLB 65
Morante, Elsa 1918-1985 .... **CLC 8, 47**
    See also CA 85-88; 117; CANR 35; DLB 177; MTCW 1, 2
Moravia, Alberto 1907-1990 .... **CLC 2, 7, 11, 27, 46; SSC 26**
    See also Pincherle, Alberto
    See also DLB 177; MTCW 2
More, Hannah 1745-1833 .... **NCLC 27**
    See also DLB 107, 109, 116, 158
More, Henry 1614-1687 .... **LC 9**
    See also DLB 126
More, Sir Thomas 1478-1535 .... **LC 10, 32**
Moreas, Jean TCLC 18
    See also Papadiamantopoulos, Johannes
Morgan, Berry 1919- .... **CLC 6**
    See also CA 49-52; DLB 6
Morgan, Claire
    See Highsmith, (Mary) Patricia
Morgan, Edwin (George) 1920- .... **CLC 31**
    See also CA 5-8R; CANR 3, 43, 90; DLB 27

Morgan, Harriet
    See Mencken, H(enry) L(ouis)
Morgan, Jane
    See Cooper, James Fenimore
Morgan, Janet 1945- .... **CLC 39**
    See also CA 65-68
Morgan, Lady 1776(?)-1859 .... **NCLC 29**
    See also DLB 116, 158
Morgan, Robin (Evonne) 1941- .... **CLC 2**
    See also CA 69-72; CANR 29, 68; MTCW 1; SATA 80
Morgan, Scott
    See Kuttner, Henry
Morgan, Seth 1949(?)-1990 .... **CLC 65**
    See also CA 185; 132
Morgenstern, Christian 1871-1914 .. **TCLC 8**
    See also CA 105
Morgenstern, S.
    See Goldman, William (W.)
Moricz, Zsigmond 1879-1942 .... **TCLC 33**
    See also CA 165
Morike, Eduard (Friedrich)
        1804-1875 .... **NCLC 10**
    See also DLB 133
Moritz, Karl Philipp 1756-1793 .... **LC 2**
    See also DLB 94
Morland, Peter Henry
    See Faust, Frederick (Schiller)
Morley, Christopher (Darlington)
        1890-1957 .... **TCLC 87**
    See also CA 112; DLB 9
Morren, Theophil
    See Hofmannsthal, Hugo von
Morris, Bill 1952- .... **CLC 76**
Morris, Julian
    See West, Morris L(anglo)
Morris, Steveland Judkins 1950(?)-
    See Wonder, Stevie
    See also CA 111
Morris, William 1834-1896 .... **NCLC 4**
    See also CDBLB 1832-1890; DLB 18, 35, 57, 156, 178, 184
Morris, Wright 1910-1998 .. **CLC 1, 3, 7, 18, 37**
    See also CA 9-12R; 167; CANR 21, 81; DLB 2, 206; DLBY 81; MTCW 1, 2
Morrison, Arthur 1863-1945 .... **TCLC 72; SSC 40**
    See also CA 120; 157; DLB 70, 135, 197
Morrison, Chloe Anthony Wofford
    See Morrison, Toni
Morrison, James Douglas 1943-1971
    See Morrison, Jim
    See also CA 73-76; CANR 40
Morrison, Jim CLC 17
    See also Morrison, James Douglas
Morrison, Toni 1931- . **CLC 4, 10, 22, 55, 81, 87; BLC 3; DA; DAB; DAC; DAM MST, MULT, NOV, POP**
    See also AAYA 1, 22; BW 2, 3; CA 29-32R; CANR 27, 42, 67; CDALB 1968-1988; DA3; DLB 6, 33, 143; DLBY 81; MTCW 1, 2; SATA 57
Morrison, Van 1945- .... **CLC 21**
    See also CA 116; 168
Morrissy, Mary 1958- .... **CLC 99**
Mortimer, John (Clifford) 1923- ..... **CLC 28, 43; DAM DRAM, POP**
    See also CA 13-16R; CANR 21, 69; CD-BLB 1960 to Present; DA3; DLB 13; INT CANR-21; MTCW 1, 2
Mortimer, Penelope (Ruth)
        1918-1999 .... **CLC 5**
    See also CA 57-60; CANR 45, 88
Morton, Anthony
    See Creasey, John

Mosca, Gaetano 1858-1941 .... **TCLC 75**
Mosher, Howard Frank 1943- .... **CLC 62**
    See also CA 139; CANR 65
Mosley, Nicholas 1923- .... **CLC 43, 70**
    See also CA 69-72; CANR 41, 60; DLB 14,
    207
Mosley, Walter 1952- .... **CLC 97; BLCS;
    DAM MULT, POP**
    See also AAYA 17; BW 2; CA 142; CANR
    57, 92; DA3; MTCW 2
Moss, Howard 1922-1987 ...... **CLC 7, 14, 45,
    50; DAM POET**
    See also CA 1-4R; 123; CANR 1, 44; DLB
    5
Mossgiel, Rab
    See Burns, Robert
Motion, Andrew (Peter) 1952- .... **CLC 47**
    See also CA 146; CANR 90; DLB 40
Motley, Willard (Francis)
    1909-1965 .... **CLC 18**
    See also BW 1; CA 117; 106; CANR 88;
    DLB 76, 143
Motoori, Norinaga 1730-1801 .... **NCLC 45**
Mott, Michael (Charles Alston)
    1930- .... **CLC 15, 34**
    See also CA 5-8R; CAAS 7; CANR 7, 29
Mountain Wolf Woman 1884-1960 .. **CLC 92**
    See also CA 144; CANR 90; NNAL
Moure, Erin 1955- .... **CLC 88**
    See also CA 113; DLB 60
Mowat, Farley (McGill) 1921- .... **CLC 26;
    DAC; DAM MST**
    See also AAYA 1; CA 1-4R; CANR 4, 24,
    42, 68; CLR 20; DLB 68; INT CANR-24;
    JRDA; MAICYA; MTCW 1, 2; SATA 3,
    55
Mowatt, Anna Cora 1819-1870 ..... **NCLC 74**
Moyers, Bill 1934- .... **CLC 74**
    See also AITN 2; CA 61-64; CANR 31, 52
Mphahlele, Es'kia
    See Mphahlele, Ezekiel
    See also DLB 125
Mphahlele, Ezekiel 1919- .... **CLC 25, 133;
    BLC 3; DAM MULT**
    See also Mphahlele, Es'kia
    See also BW 2, 3; CA 81-84; CANR 26,
    76; DA3; DLB 225; MTCW 2
Mqhayi, S(amuel) E(dward) K(rune Loliwe)
    1875-1945 ...... **TCLC 25; BLC 3; DAM
    MULT**
    See also CA 153; CANR 87
Mrozek, Slawomir 1930- .... **CLC 3, 13**
    See also CA 13-16R; CAAS 10; CANR 29;
    MTCW 1
Mrs. Belloc-Lowndes
    See Lowndes, Marie Adelaide (Belloc)
Mtwa, Percy (?)- .... **CLC 47**
Mueller, Lisel 1924- .... **CLC 13, 51**
    See also CA 93-96; DLB 105
Muir, Edwin 1887-1959 .... **TCLC 2, 87**
    See also CA 104; DLB 20, 100, 191
Muir, John 1838-1914 .... **TCLC 28**
    See also CA 165; DLB 186
Mujica Lainez, Manuel 1910-1984 ... **CLC 31**
    See Lainez, Manuel Mujica
    See also CA 81-84; 112; CANR 32; HW 1
Mukherjee, Bharati 1940- .... **CLC 53, 115;
    DAM NOV; SSC 38**
    See also BEST 89:2; CA 107; CANR 45,
    72; DLB 60; MTCW 1, 2
Muldoon, Paul 1951- .... **CLC 32, 72; DAM
    POET**
    See also CA 113; 129; CANR 52, 91; DLB
    40; INT 129
Mulisch, Harry 1927- .... **CLC 42**
    See also CA 9-12R; CANR 6, 26, 56

Mull, Martin 1943- .... **CLC 17**
    See also CA 105
Muller, Wilhelm **NCLC 73**
Mulock, Dinah Maria
    See Craik, Dinah Maria (Mulock)
Munford, Robert 1737(?)-1783 .... **LC 5**
    See also DLB 31
Mungo, Raymond 1946- .... **CLC 72**
    See also CA 49-52; CANR 2
Munro, Alice 1931- .... **CLC 6, 10, 19, 50, 95;
    DAC; DAM MST, NOV; SSC 3;
    WLCS**
    See also AITN 2; CA 33-36R; CANR 33,
    53, 75; DA3; DLB 53; MTCW 1, 2; SATA
    29
Munro, H(ector) H(ugh) 1870-1916
    See Saki
    See also CA 104; 130; CDBLB 1890-1914;
    DA; DAB; DAC; DAM MST, NOV; DA3;
    DLB 34, 162; MTCW 1, 2; WLC
Murdoch, (Jean) Iris 1919-1999 ... **CLC 1, 2,
    3, 4, 6, 8, 11, 15, 22, 31, 51; DAB;
    DAC; DAM MST, NOV**
    See also CA 13-16R; 179; CANR 8, 43, 68;
    CDBLB 1960 to Present; DA3; DLB 14,
    194; INT CANR-8; MTCW 1, 2
Murfree, Mary Noailles 1850-1922 ... **SSC 22**
    See also CA 122; 176; DLB 12, 74
Murnau, Friedrich Wilhelm
    See Plumpe, Friedrich Wilhelm
Murphy, Richard 1927- .... **CLC 41**
    See also CA 29-32R; DLB 40
Murphy, Sylvia 1937- .... **CLC 34**
    See also CA 121
Murphy, Thomas (Bernard) 1935- ... **CLC 51**
    See also CA 101
Murray, Albert L. 1916- .... **CLC 73**
    See also BW 2; CA 49-52; CANR 26, 52,
    78; DLB 38
Murray, Judith Sargent
    1751-1820 .... **NCLC 63**
    See also DLB 37, 200
Murray, Les(lie) A(llan) 1938- .... **CLC 40;
    DAM POET**
    See also CA 21-24R; CANR 11, 27, 56
Murry, J. Middleton
    See Murry, John Middleton
Murry, John Middleton
    1889-1957 .... **TCLC 16**
    See also CA 118; DLB 149
Musgrave, Susan 1951- .... **CLC 13, 54**
    See also CA 69-72; CANR 45, 84
Musil, Robert (Edler von)
    1880-1942 .... **TCLC 12, 68; SSC 18**
    See also CA 109; CANR 55, 84; DLB 81,
    124; MTCW 2
Muske, Carol 1945- .... **CLC 90**
    See also Muske-Dukes, Carol (Anne)
Muske-Dukes, Carol (Anne) 1945-
    See Muske, Carol
    See also CA 65-68; CANR 32, 70
Musset, (Louis Charles) Alfred de
    1810-1857 .... **NCLC 7**
    See also DLB 192
Mussolini, Benito (Amilcare Andrea)
    1883-1945 .... **TCLC 96**
    See also CA 116
My Brother's Brother
    See Chekhov, Anton (Pavlovich)
Myers, L(eopold) H(amilton)
    1881-1944 .... **TCLC 59**
    See also CA 157; DLB 15
Myers, Walter Dean 1937- ..... **CLC 35; BLC
    3; DAM MULT, NOV**
    See also AAYA 4, 23; BW 2; CA 33-36R;
    CANR 20, 42, 67; CLR 4, 16, 35; DLB
    33; INT CANR-20; JRDA; MAICYA;
    MTCW 2; SAAS 2; SATA 41, 71, 109;
    SATA-Brief 27

Myers, Walter M.
    See Myers, Walter Dean
Myles, Symon
    See Follett, Ken(neth Martin)
Nabokov, Vladimir (Vladimirovich)
    1899-1977 .... **CLC 1, 2, 3, 6, 8, 11, 15,
    23, 44, 46, 64; DA; DAB; DAC; DAM
    MST, NOV; SSC 11; WLC**
    See also CA 5-8R; 69-72; CANR 20;
    CDALB 1941-1968; DA3; DLB 2; DLBD
    3; DLBY 80, 91; MTCW 1, 2
Naevius c. 265B.C.-201B.C. .... **CMLC 37**
    See also DLB 211
Nagai Kafu 1879-1959 .... **TCLC 51**
    See also Nagai Sokichi
    See also DLB 180
Nagai Sokichi 1879-1959
    See Nagai Kafu
    See also CA 117
Nagy, Laszlo 1925-1978 .... **CLC 7**
    See also CA 129; 112
Naidu, Sarojini 1879-1943 .... **TCLC 80**
Naipaul, Shiva(dhar Srinivasa)
    1945-1985 .... **CLC 32, 39; DAM NOV**
    See also CA 110; 112; 116; CANR 33;
    DA3; DLB 157; DLBY 85; MTCW 1, 2
Naipaul, V(idiadhar) S(urajprasad)
    1932- .... **CLC 4, 7, 9, 13, 18, 37, 105;
    DAB; DAC; DAM MST, NOV; SSC 38**
    See also CA 1-4R; CANR 1, 33, 51, 91;
    CDBLB 1960 to Present; DA3; DLB 125,
    204, 206; DLBY 85; MTCW 1, 2
Nakos, Lilika 1899(?)- .... **CLC 29**
Narayan, R(asipuram) K(rishnaswami)
    1906- . **CLC 7, 28, 47, 121; DAM NOV;
    SSC 25**
    See also CA 81-84; CANR 33, 61; DA3;
    MTCW 1, 2; SATA 62
Nash, (Frediric) Ogden 1902-1971 . **CLC 23;
    DAM POET; PC 21**
    See also CA 13-14; 29-32R; CANR 34, 61;
    CAP 1; DLB 11; MAICYA; MTCW 1, 2;
    SATA 2, 46
Nashe, Thomas 1567-1601(?) .... **LC 41**
    See also DLB 167
Nashe, Thomas 1567-1601 .... **LC 41**
Nathan, Daniel
    See Dannay, Frederic
Nathan, George Jean 1882-1958 .... **TCLC 18**
    See also Hatteras, Owen
    See also CA 114; 169; DLB 137
Natsume, Kinnosuke 1867-1916
    See Natsume, Soseki
    See also CA 104
Natsume, Soseki 1867-1916 .... **TCLC 2, 10**
    See also Natsume, Kinnosuke
    See also DLB 180
Natti, (Mary) Lee 1919-
    See Kingman, Lee
    See also CA 5-8R; CANR 2
Naylor, Gloria 1950- .... **CLC 28, 52; BLC 3;
    DA; DAC; DAM MST, MULT, NOV,
    POP; WLCS**
    See also AAYA 6; BW 2, 3; CA 107; CANR
    27, 51, 74; DA3; DLB 173; MTCW 1, 2
Neihardt, John Gneisenau
    1881-1973 .... **CLC 32**
    See also CA 13-14; CANR 65; CAP 1; DLB
    9, 54
Nekrasov, Nikolai Alekseevich
    1821-1878 .... **NCLC 11**
Nelligan, Emile 1879-1941 .... **TCLC 14**
    See also CA 114; DLB 92
Nelson, Willie 1933- .... **CLC 17**
    See also CA 107

O'Brien, (William) Tim(othy) 1946- . **CLC 7, 19, 40, 103; DAM POP**
See also AAYA 16; CA 85-88; CANR 40, 58; CDALBS; DA3; DLB 152; DLBD 9; DLBY 80; MTCW 2

Obstfelder, Sigbjoern 1866-1900 .... **TCLC 23**
See also CA 123

O'Casey, Sean 1880-1964 .... **CLC 1, 5, 9, 11, 15, 88; DAB; DAC; DAM DRAM, MST; DC 12; WLCS**
See also CA 89-92; CANR 62; CDBLB 1914-1945; DA3; DLB 10; MTCW 1, 2

O'Cathasaigh, Sean
See O'Casey, Sean

Occom, Samson 1723-1792 .... **LC 60**
See also DLB 175; NNAL

Ochs, Phil(ip David) 1940-1976 .... **CLC 17**
See also CA 185; 65-68

O'Connor, Edwin (Greene)
1918-1968 .... **CLC 14**
See also CA 93-96; 25-28R

O'Connor, (Mary) Flannery
1925-1964 .... **CLC 1, 2, 3, 6, 10, 13, 15, 21, 66, 104; DA; DAB; DAC; DAM MST, NOV; SSC 1, 23; WLC**
See also AAYA 7; CA 1-4R; CANR 3, 41; CDALB 1941-1968; DA3; DLB 2, 152; DLBD 12; DLBY 80; MTCW 1, 2

O'Connor, Frank CLC 23; SSC 5
See also O'Donovan, Michael John
See also DLB 162

O'Dell, Scott 1898-1989 .... **CLC 30**
See also AAYA 3; CA 61-64; 129; CANR 12, 30; CLR 1, 16; DLB 52; JRDA; MAI-CYA; SATA 12, 60

Odets, Clifford 1906-1963 ..... **CLC 2, 28, 98; DAM DRAM; DC 6**
See also CA 85-88; CANR 62; DLB 7, 26; MTCW 1, 2

O'Doherty, Brian 1934- .... **CLC 76**
See also CA 105

O'Donnell, K. M.
See Malzberg, Barry N(athaniel)

O'Donnell, Lawrence
See Kuttner, Henry

O'Donovan, Michael John
1903-1966 .... **CLC 14**
See also O'Connor, Frank
See also CA 93-96; CANR 84

Oe, Kenzaburo 1935- .... **CLC 10, 36, 86; DAM NOV; SSC 20**
See also CA 97-100; CANR 36, 50, 74; DA3; DLB 182; DLBY 94; MTCW 1, 2

O'Faolain, Julia 1932- .... **CLC 6, 19, 47, 108**
See also CA 81-84; CAAS 2; CANR 12, 61; DLB 14; MTCW 1

O'Faolain, Sean 1900-1991 ...... **CLC 1, 7, 14, 32, 70; SSC 13**
See also CA 61-64; 134; CANR 12, 66; DLB 15, 162; MTCW 1, 2

O'Flaherty, Liam 1896-1984 .... **CLC 5, 34; SSC 6**
See also CA 101; 113; CANR 35; DLB 36, 162; DLBY 84; MTCW 1, 2

Ogilvy, Gavin
See Barrie, J(ames) M(atthew)

O'Grady, Standish (James)
1846-1928 .... **TCLC 5**
See also CA 104; 157

O'Grady, Timothy 1951- .... **CLC 59**
See also CA 138

O'Hara, Frank 1926-1966 .... **CLC 2, 5, 13, 78; DAM POET**
See also CA 9-12R; 25-28R; CANR 33; DA3; DLB 5, 16, 193; MTCW 1, 2

O'Hara, John (Henry) 1905-1970 . **CLC 1, 2, 3, 6, 11, 42; DAM NOV; SSC 15**
See also CA 5-8R; 25-28R; CANR 31, 60; CDALB 1929-1941; DLB 9, 86; DLBD 2; MTCW 1, 2

O Hehir, Diana 1922- .... **CLC 41**
See also CA 93-96

Ohiyesa
See Eastman, Charles A(lexander)

Okigbo, Christopher (Ifenayichukwu)
1932-1967 ... **CLC 25, 84; BLC 3; DAM MULT, POET; PC 7**
See also BW 1, 3; CA 77-80; CANR 74; DLB 125; MTCW 1, 2

Okri, Ben 1959- .... **CLC 87**
See also BW 2, 3; CA 130; 138; CANR 65; DLB 157; INT 138; MTCW 2

Olds, Sharon 1942- ... **CLC 32, 39, 85; DAM POET; PC 22**
See also CA 101; CANR 18, 41, 66; DLB 120; MTCW 2

Oldstyle, Jonathan
See Irving, Washington

Olesha, Yuri (Karlovich) 1899-1960 .. **CLC 8**
See also CA 85-88

Oliphant, Laurence 1829(?)-1888 .. **NCLC 47**
See also DLB 18, 166

Oliphant, Margaret (Oliphant Wilson)
1828-1897 .... **NCLC 11, 61; SSC 25**
See also DLB 18, 159, 190

Oliver, Mary 1935- .... **CLC 19, 34, 98**
See also CA 21-24R; CANR 9, 43, 84, 92; DLB 5, 193

Olivier, Laurence (Kerr) 1907-1989 . **CLC 20**
See also CA 111; 150; 129

Olsen, Tillie 1912- .... **CLC 4, 13, 114; DA; DAB; DAC; DAM MST; SSC 11**
See also CA 1-4R; CANR 1, 43, 74; CDALBS; DA3; DLB 28, 206; DLBY 80; MTCW 1, 2

Olson, Charles (John) 1910-1970 .. **CLC 1, 2, 5, 6, 9, 11, 29; DAM POET; PC 19**
See also CA 13-16; 25-28R; CABS 2; CANR 35, 61; CAP 1; DLB 5, 16, 193; MTCW 1, 2

Olson, Toby 1937- .... **CLC 28**
See also CA 65-68; CANR 9, 31, 84

Olyesha, Yuri
See Olesha, Yuri (Karlovich)

Ondaatje, (Philip) Michael 1943- .... **CLC 14, 29, 51, 76; DAB; DAC; DAM MST; PC 28**
See also CA 77-80; CANR 42, 74; DA3; DLB 60; MTCW 2

Oneal, Elizabeth 1934-
See Oneal, Zibby
See also CA 106; CANR 28, 84; MAICYA; SATA 30, 82

Oneal, Zibby CLC 30
See also Oneal, Elizabeth
See also AAYA 5; CLR 13; JRDA

O'Neill, Eugene (Gladstone)
1888-1953 .... **TCLC 1, 6, 27, 49; DA; DAB; DAC; DAM DRAM, MST; WLC**
See also AITN 1; CA 110; 132; CDALB 1929-1941; DA3; DLB 7; MTCW 1, 2

Onetti, Juan Carlos 1909-1994 .... **CLC 7, 10; DAM MULT, NOV; HLCS 2; SSC 23**
See also CA 85-88; 145; CANR 32, 63; DLB 113; HW 1, 2; MTCW 1, 2

O Nuallain, Brian 1911-1966
See O'Brien, Flann
See also CA 21-22; 25-28R; CAP 2

Ophuls, Max 1902-1957 .... **TCLC 79**
See also CA 113

Opie, Amelia 1769-1853 .... **NCLC 65**
See also DLB 116, 159

Oppen, George 1908-1984 ...... **CLC 7, 13, 34**
See also CA 13-16R; 113; CANR 8, 82; DLB 5, 165

Oppenheim, E(dward) Phillips
1866-1946 .... **TCLC 45**
See also CA 111; DLB 70

Opuls, Max
See Ophuls, Max

Origen c. 185-c. 254 .... **CMLC 19**

Orlovitz, Gil 1918-1973 .... **CLC 22**
See also CA 77-80; 45-48; DLB 2, 5

Orris
See Ingelow, Jean

Ortega y Gasset, Jose 1883-1955 ... **TCLC 9; DAM MULT; HLC 2**
See also CA 106; 130; HW 1, 2; MTCW 1, 2

Ortese, Anna Maria 1914- .... **CLC 89**
See also DLB 177

Ortiz, Simon J(oseph) 1941- . **CLC 45; DAM MULT, POET; PC 17**
See also CA 134; CANR 69; DLB 120, 175; NNAL

Orton, Joe CLC 4, 13, 43; DC 3
See also Orton, John Kingsley
See also CDBLB 1960 to Present; DLB 13; MTCW 2

Orton, John Kingsley 1933-1967
See Orton, Joe
See also CA 85-88; CANR 35, 66; DAM DRAM; MTCW 1, 2

Orwell, George -1950 ...... **TCLC 2, 6, 15, 31, 51; DAB; WLC**
See also Blair, Eric (Arthur)
See also CDBLB 1945-1960; DLB 15, 98, 195

Osborne, David
See Silverberg, Robert

Osborne, George
See Silverberg, Robert

Osborne, John (James) 1929-1994 .... **CLC 1, 2, 5, 11, 45; DA; DAB; DAC; DAM DRAM, MST; WLC**
See also CA 13-16R; 147; CANR 21, 56; CDBLB 1945-1960; DLB 13; MTCW 1, 2

Osborne, Lawrence 1958- .... **CLC 50**

Osbourne, Lloyd 1868-1947 .... **TCLC 93**

Oshima, Nagisa 1932- .... **CLC 20**
See also CA 116; 121; CANR 78

Oskison, John Milton 1874-1947 .. **TCLC 35; DAM MULT**
See also CA 144; CANR 84; DLB 175; NNAL

Ossian c. 3rd cent. - .... **CMLC 28**
See also Macpherson, James

Ossoli, Sarah Margaret (Fuller marchesa d')
1810-1850 .... **NCLC 5, 50**
See also Fuller, Margaret; Fuller, Sarah Margaret
See also CDALB 1640-1865; DLB 1, 59, 73, 83, 223; SATA 25

Ostriker, Alicia (Suskin) 1937- .... **CLC 132**
See also CA 25-28R; CAAS 24; CANR 10, 30, 62; DLB 120

Ostrovsky, Alexander 1823-1886 .. **NCLC 30, 57**

Otero, Blas de 1916-1979 .... **CLC 11**
See also CA 89-92; DLB 134

Otto, Rudolf 1869-1937 .... **TCLC 85**

Otto, Whitney 1955- .... **CLC 70**
See also CA 140

Ouida TCLC 43
See also De La Ramee, (Marie) Louise
See also DLB 18, 156

Ousmane, Sembene 1923- ... **CLC 66; BLC 3**
See also BW 1, 3; CA 117; 125; CANR 81; MTCW 1

Prevert, Jacques (Henri Marie)
1900-1977 .... **CLC 15**
See also CA 77-80; 69-72; CANR 29, 61;
MTCW 1; SATA-Obit 30

Prevost, Abbe (Antoine Francois)
1697-1763 .... **LC 1**

Price, (Edward) Reynolds 1933- ... **CLC 3, 6,
13, 43, 50, 63; DAM NOV; SSC 22**
See also CA 1-4R; CANR 1, 37, 57, 87;
DLB 2; INT CANR-37

Price, Richard 1949- .... **CLC 6, 12**
See also CA 49-52; CANR 3; DLBY 81

Prichard, Katharine Susannah
1883-1969 .... **CLC 46**
See also CA 11-12; CANR 33; CAP 1;
MTCW 1; SATA 66

Priestley, J(ohn) B(oynton)
1894-1984 .... **CLC 2, 5, 9, 34; DAM
DRAM, NOV**
See also CA 9-12R; 113; CANR 33; CD-
BLB 1914-1945; DA3; DLB 10, 34, 77,
100, 139; DLBY 84; MTCW 1, 2

Prince 1958(?)- .... **CLC 35**

Prince, F(rank) T(empleton) 1912- .. **CLC 22**
See also CA 101; CANR 43, 79; DLB 20

Prince Kropotkin
See Kropotkin, Peter (Aleksieevich)

Prior, Matthew 1664-1721 .... **LC 4**
See also DLB 95

Prishvin, Mikhail 1873-1954 .... **TCLC 75**

Pritchard, William H(arrison)
1932- .... **CLC 34**
See also CA 65-68; CANR 23; DLB 111

Pritchett, V(ictor) S(awdon)
1900-1997 ...... **CLC 5, 13, 15, 41; DAM
NOV; SSC 14**
See also CA 61-64; 157; CANR 31, 63;
DA3; DLB 15, 139; MTCW 1, 2

Private 19022
See Manning, Frederic

Probst, Mark 1925- .... **CLC 59**
See also CA 130

Prokosch, Frederic 1908-1989 ...... **CLC 4, 48**
See also CA 73-76; 128; CANR 82; DLB
48; MTCW 2

Propertius, Sextus c. 50B.C.-c.
16B.C. .... **CMLC 32**
See also DLB 211

Prophet, The
See Dreiser, Theodore (Herman Albert)

Prose, Francine 1947- .... **CLC 45**
See also CA 109; 112; CANR 46; SATA
101

Proudhon
See Cunha, Euclides (Rodrigues Pimenta)
da

Proulx, Annie
See Proulx, E(dna) Annie

Proulx, E(dna) Annie 1935- .. **CLC 81; DAM
POP**
See also CA 145; CANR 65; DA3; MTCW
2

**Proust, (Valentin-Louis-George-Eugene-)
Marcel** 1871-1922 .... **TCLC 7, 13, 33;
DA; DAB; DAC; DAM MST, NOV;
WLC**
See also CA 104; 120; DA3; DLB 65;
MTCW 1, 2

Prowler, Harley
See Masters, Edgar Lee

Prus, Boleslaw 1845-1912 .... **TCLC 48**

Pryor, Richard (Franklin Lenox Thomas)
1940- .... **CLC 26**
See also CA 122; 152

Przybyszewski, Stanislaw
1868-1927 .... **TCLC 36**
See also CA 160; DLB 66

Pteleon
See Grieve, C(hristopher) M(urray)
See also DAM POET

Puckett, Lute
See Masters, Edgar Lee

Puig, Manuel 1932-1990 .... **CLC 3, 5, 10, 28,
65, 133; DAM MULT; HLC 2**
See also CA 45-48; CANR 2, 32, 63; DA3;
DLB 113; HW 1, 2; MTCW 1, 2

Pulitzer, Joseph 1847-1911 .... **TCLC 76**
See also CA 114; DLB 23

Purdy, A(lfred) W(ellington) 1918- ... **CLC 3,
6, 14, 50; DAC; DAM MST, POET**
See also CA 81-84; CAAS 17; CANR 42,
66; DLB 88

Purdy, James (Amos) 1923- .... **CLC 2, 4, 10,
28, 52**
See also CA 33-36R; CAAS 1; CANR 19,
51; DLB 2; INT CANR-19; MTCW 1

Pure, Simon
See Swinnerton, Frank Arthur

Pushkin, Alexander (Sergeyevich)
1799-1837 . **NCLC 3, 27, 83; DA; DAB;
DAC; DAM DRAM, MST, POET; PC
10; SSC 27; WLC**
See also DA3; DLB 205; SATA 61

P'u Sung-ling 1640-1715 .... **LC 49; SSC 31**

Putnam, Arthur Lee
See Alger, Horatio Jr., Jr.

Puzo, Mario 1920-1999 ...... **CLC 1, 2, 6, 36,
107; DAM NOV, POP**
See also CA 65-68; 185; CANR 4, 42, 65;
DA3; DLB 6; MTCW 1, 2

Pygge, Edward
See Barnes, Julian (Patrick)

Pyle, Ernest Taylor 1900-1945
See Pyle, Ernie
See also CA 115; 160

Pyle, Ernie 1900-1945 .... **TCLC 75**
See also Pyle, Ernest Taylor
See also DLB 29; MTCW 2

Pyle, Howard 1853-1911 .... **TCLC 81**
See also CA 109; 137; CLR 22; DLB 42,
188; DLBD 13; MAICYA; SATA 16, 100

Pym, Barbara (Mary Crampton)
1913-1980 .... **CLC 13, 19, 37, 111**
See also CA 13-14; 97-100; CANR 13, 34;
CAP 1; DLB 14, 207; DLBY 87; MTCW
1, 2

Pynchon, Thomas (Ruggles, Jr.)
1937- ...... **CLC 2, 3, 6, 9, 11, 18, 33, 62,
72; DA; DAB; DAC; DAM MST, NOV,
POP; SSC 14; WLC**
See also BEST 90:2; CA 17-20R; CANR
22, 46, 73; DA3; DLB 2, 173; MTCW 1,
2

Pythagoras c. 570B.C.-c. 500B.C. . **CMLC 22**
See also DLB 176

Q
See Quiller-Couch, SirArthur (Thomas)

Qian Zhongshu
See Ch'ien Chung-shu

Qroll
See Dagerman, Stig (Halvard)

Quarrington, Paul (Lewis) 1953- ..... **CLC 65**
See also CA 129; CANR 62

Quasimodo, Salvatore 1901-1968 ..... **CLC 10**
See also CA 13-16; 25-28R; CAP 1; DLB
114; MTCW 1

Quay, Stephen 1947- .... **CLC 95**

Quay, Timothy 1947- .... **CLC 95**

Queen, Ellery **CLC 3, 11**
See also Dannay, Frederic; Davidson,
Avram (James); Lee, Manfred
B(ennington); Marlowe, Stephen; Stur-
geon, Theodore (Hamilton); Vance, John
Holbrook

Queen, Ellery, Jr.
See Dannay, Frederic; Lee, Manfred
B(ennington)

Queneau, Raymond 1903-1976 ..... **CLC 2, 5,
10, 42**
See also CA 77-80; 69-72; CANR 32; DLB
72; MTCW 1, 2

Quevedo, Francisco de 1580-1645 .... **LC 23**

Quiller-Couch, SirArthur (Thomas)
1863-1944 .... **TCLC 53**
See also CA 118; 166; DLB 135, 153, 190

Quin, Ann (Marie) 1936-1973 .... **CLC 6**
See also CA 9-12R; 45-48; DLB 14

Quinn, Martin
See Smith, Martin Cruz

Quinn, Peter 1947- .... **CLC 91**

Quinn, Simon
See Smith, Martin Cruz

Quintana, Leroy V. 1944-
See also CA 131; CANR 65; DAM MULT;
DLB 82; HLC 2; HW 1, 2

Quiroga, Horacio (Sylvestre)
1878-1937 .... **TCLC 20; DAM MULT;
HLC 2**
See also CA 117; 131; HW 1; MTCW 1

Quoirez, Francoise 1935- .... **CLC 9**
See also Sagan, Francoise
See also CA 49-52; CANR 6, 39, 73;
MTCW 1, 2

Raabe, Wilhelm (Karl) 1831-1910 . **TCLC 45**
See also CA 167; DLB 129

Rabe, David (William) 1940- .. **CLC 4, 8, 33;
DAM DRAM**
See also CA 85-88; CABS 3; CANR 59;
DLB 7, 228

Rabelais, Francois 1483-1553 .... **LC 5, 60;
DA; DAB; DAC; DAM MST; WLC**

Rabinovitch, Sholem 1859-1916
See Aleichem, Sholom
See also CA 104

Rabinyan, Dorit 1972- .... **CLC 119**
See also CA 170

Rachilde
See Vallette, Marguerite Eymery

Racine, Jean 1639-1699 . **LC 28; DAB; DAM
MST**
See also DA3

Radcliffe, Ann (Ward) 1764-1823 ... **NCLC 6,
55**
See also DLB 39, 178

Radiguet, Raymond 1903-1923 ...... **TCLC 29**
See also CA 162; DLB 65

Radnoti, Miklos 1909-1944 .... **TCLC 16**
See also CA 118

Rado, James 1939- .... **CLC 17**
See also CA 105

Radvanyi, Netty 1900-1983
See Seghers, Anna
See also CA 85-88; 110; CANR 82

Rae, Ben
See Griffiths, Trevor

Raeburn, John (Hay) 1941- .... **CLC 34**
See also CA 57-60

Ragni, Gerome 1942-1991 .... **CLC 17**
See also CA 105; 134

Rahv, Philip 1908-1973 .... **CLC 24**
See also Greenberg, Ivan
See also DLB 137

Raimund, Ferdinand Jakob
1790-1836 .... **NCLC 69**
See also DLB 90

Raine, Craig 1944- .... **CLC 32, 103**
See also CA 108; CANR 29, 51; DLB 40

Raine, Kathleen (Jessie) 1908- ..... **CLC 7, 45**
See also CA 85-88; CANR 46; DLB 20;
MTCW 1

Rainis, Janis 1865-1929 .... **TCLC 29**
See also CA 170; DLB 220

Rich, Adrienne (Cecile) 1929- ... **CLC 3, 6, 7, 11, 18, 36, 73, 76, 125; DAM POET; PC 5**
See also CA 9-12R; CANR 20, 53, 74; CDALBS; DA3; DLB 5, 67; MTCW 1, 2

Rich, Barbara
See Graves, Robert (von Ranke)

Rich, Robert
See Trumbo, Dalton

Richard, Keith CLC 17
See also Richards, Keith

Richards, David Adams 1950- .... **CLC 59; DAC**
See also CA 93-96; CANR 60; DLB 53

Richards, I(vor) A(rmstrong) 1893-1979 .... **CLC 14, 24**
See also CA 41-44R; 89-92; CANR 34, 74; DLB 27; MTCW 2

Richards, Keith 1943-
See Richard, Keith
See also CA 107; CANR 77

Richardson, Anne
See Roiphe, Anne (Richardson)

Richardson, Dorothy Miller 1873-1957 .... **TCLC 3**
See also CA 104; DLB 36

Richardson, Ethel Florence (Lindesay) 1870-1946
See Richardson, Henry Handel
See also CA 105

Richardson, Henry Handel TCLC 4
See also Richardson, Ethel Florence (Lindesay)
See also DLB 197

Richardson, John 1796-1852 .... **NCLC 55; DAC**
See also DLB 99

Richardson, Samuel 1689-1761 ...... **LC 1, 44; DA; DAB; DAC; DAM MST, NOV; WLC**
See also CDBLB 1660-1789; DLB 39

Richler, Mordecai 1931- ...... **CLC 3, 5, 9, 13, 18, 46, 70; DAC; DAM MST, NOV**
See also AITN 1; CA 65-68; CANR 31, 62; CLR 17; DLB 53; MAICYA; MTCW 1, 2; SATA 44, 98; SATA-Brief 27

Richter, Conrad (Michael) 1890-1968 .... **CLC 30**
See also AAYA 21; CA 5-8R; 25-28R; CANR 23; DLB 9, 212; MTCW 1, 2; SATA 3

Ricostranza, Tom
See Ellis, Trey

Riddell, Charlotte 1832-1906 .... **TCLC 40**
See also CA 165; DLB 156

Ridge, John Rollin 1827-1867 ...... **NCLC 82; DAM MULT**
See also CA 144; DLB 175; NNAL

Ridgway, Keith 1965- .... **CLC 119**
See also CA 172

Riding, Laura CLC 3, 7
See also Jackson, Laura (Riding)

Riefenstahl, Berta Helene Amalia 1902-
See Riefenstahl, Leni
See also CA 108

Riefenstahl, Leni CLC 16
See also Riefenstahl, Berta Helene Amalia

Riffe, Ernest
See Bergman, (Ernst) Ingmar

Riggs, (Rolla) Lynn 1899-1954 ..... **TCLC 56; DAM MULT**
See also CA 144; DLB 175; NNAL

Riis, Jacob A(ugust) 1849-1914 ..... **TCLC 80**
See also CA 113; 168; DLB 23

Riley, James Whitcomb 1849-1916 .... **TCLC 51; DAM POET**
See also CA 118; 137; MAICYA; SATA 17

Riley, Tex
See Creasey, John

Rilke, Rainer Maria 1875-1926 .. **TCLC 1, 6, 19; DAM POET; PC 2**
See also CA 104; 132; CANR 62; DA3; DLB 81; MTCW 1, 2

Rimbaud, (Jean Nicolas) Arthur 1854-1891 . **NCLC 4, 35, 82; DA; DAB; DAC; DAM MST, POET; PC 3; WLC**
See also DA3

Rinehart, Mary Roberts 1876-1958 .... **TCLC 52**
See also CA 108; 166

Ringmaster, The
See Mencken, H(enry) L(ouis)

Ringwood, Gwen(dolyn Margaret) Pharis 1910-1984 .... **CLC 48**
See also CA 148; 112; DLB 88

Rio, Michel 19(?)- .... **CLC 43**

Ritsos, Giannes
See Ritsos, Yannis

Ritsos, Yannis 1909-1990 .... **CLC 6, 13, 31**
See also CA 77-80; 133; CANR 39, 61; MTCW 1

Ritter, Erika 1948(?)- .... **CLC 52**

Rivera, Jose Eustasio 1889-1928 ... **TCLC 35**
See also CA 162; HW 1, 2

Rivera, Tomas 1935-1984
See also CA 49-52; CANR 32; DLB 82; HLCS 2; HW 1

Rivers, Conrad Kent 1933-1968 .... **CLC 1**
See also BW 1; CA 85-88; DLB 41

Rivers, Elfrida
See Bradley, Marion Zimmer

Riverside, John
See Heinlein, Robert A(nson)

Rizal, Jose 1861-1896 .... **NCLC 27**

Roa Bastos, Augusto (Antonio) 1917- .... **CLC 45; DAM MULT; HLC 2**
See also CA 131; DLB 113; HW 1

Robbe-Grillet, Alain 1922- .... **CLC 1, 2, 4, 6, 8, 10, 14, 43, 128**
See also CA 9-12R; CANR 33, 65; DLB 83; MTCW 1, 2

Robbins, Harold 1916-1997 .... **CLC 5; DAM NOV**
See also CA 73-76; 162; CANR 26, 54; DA3; MTCW 1, 2

Robbins, Thomas Eugene 1936-
See Robbins, Tom
See also CA 81-84; CANR 29, 59; DAM NOV, POP; DA3; MTCW 1, 2

Robbins, Tom CLC 9, 32, 64
See also Robbins, Thomas Eugene
See also AAYA 32; BEST 90:3; DLBY 80; MTCW 2

Robbins, Trina 1938- .... **CLC 21**
See also CA 128

Roberts, Charles G(eorge) D(ouglas) 1860-1943 .... **TCLC 8**
See also CA 105; CLR 33; DLB 92; SATA 88; SATA-Brief 29

Roberts, Elizabeth Madox 1886-1941 .... **TCLC 68**
See also CA 111; 166; DLB 9, 54, 102; SATA 33; SATA-Brief 27

Roberts, Kate 1891-1985 .... **CLC 15**
See also CA 107; 116

Roberts, Keith (John Kingston) 1935- .... **CLC 14**
See also CA 25-28R; CANR 46

Roberts, Kenneth (Lewis) 1885-1957 .... **TCLC 23**
See also CA 109; DLB 9

Roberts, Michele (B.) 1949- .... **CLC 48**
See also CA 115; CANR 58

Robertson, Ellis
See Ellison, Harlan (Jay); Silverberg, Robert

Robertson, Thomas William 1829-1871 .... **NCLC 35; DAM DRAM**

Robeson, Kenneth
See Dent, Lester

Robinson, Edwin Arlington 1869-1935 ... **TCLC 5; DA; DAC; DAM MST, POET; PC 1**
See also CA 104; 133; CDALB 1865-1917; DLB 54; MTCW 1, 2

Robinson, Henry Crabb 1775-1867 .... **NCLC 15**
See also DLB 107

Robinson, Jill 1936- .... **CLC 10**
See also CA 102; INT 102

Robinson, Kim Stanley 1952- .... **CLC 34**
See also AAYA 26; CA 126; SATA 109

Robinson, Lloyd
See Silverberg, Robert

Robinson, Marilynne 1944- .... **CLC 25**
See also CA 116; CANR 80; DLB 206

Robinson, Smokey CLC 21
See also Robinson, William, Jr.

Robinson, William, Jr. 1940-
See Robinson, Smokey
See also CA 116

Robison, Mary 1949- .... **CLC 42, 98**
See also CA 113; 116; CANR 87; DLB 130; INT 116

Rod, Edouard 1857-1910 .... **TCLC 52**

Roddenberry, Eugene Wesley 1921-1991
See Roddenberry, Gene
See also CA 110; 135; CANR 37; SATA 45; SATA-Obit 69

Roddenberry, Gene CLC 17
See also Roddenberry, Eugene Wesley
See also AAYA 5; SATA-Obit 69

Rodgers, Mary 1931- .... **CLC 12**
See also CA 49-52; CANR 8, 55, 90; CLR 20; INT CANR-8; JRDA; MAICYA; SATA 8

Rodgers, W(illiam) R(obert) 1909-1969 .... **CLC 7**
See also CA 85-88; DLB 20

Rodman, Eric
See Silverberg, Robert

Rodman, Howard 1920(?)-1985 .... **CLC 65**
See also CA 118

Rodman, Maia
See Wojciechowska, Maia (Teresa)

Rodo, Jose Enrique 1872(?)-1917
See also CA 178; HLCS 2; HW 2

Rodriguez, Claudio 1934- .... **CLC 10**
See also DLB 134

Rodriguez, Richard 1944-
See also CA 110; CANR 66; DAM MULT; DLB 82; HLC 2; HW 1, 2

Roelvaag, O(le) E(dvart) 1876-1931 .... **TCLC 17**
See also Rolvaag, O(le) E(dvart)
See also CA 117; 171; DLB 9

Roethke, Theodore (Huebner) 1908-1963 ..... **CLC 1, 3, 8, 11, 19, 46, 101; DAM POET; PC 15**
See also CA 81-84; CABS 2; CDALB 1941-1968; DA3; DLB 5, 206; MTCW 1, 2

Rogers, Samuel 1763-1855 .... **NCLC 69**
See also DLB 93

Rogers, Thomas Hunton 1927- .... **CLC 57**
See also CA 89-92; INT 89-92

Rogers, Will(iam Penn Adair) 1879-1935 .. **TCLC 8, 71; DAM MULT**
See also CA 105; 144; DA3; DLB 11; MTCW 2; NNAL

Rogin, Gilbert 1929- .... **CLC 18**
See also CA 65-68; CANR 15

Rohan, Koda
See Koda Shigeyuki

Satyremont
See Peret, Benjamin
Saul, John (W. III) 1942- ...... **CLC 46; DAM NOV, POP**
See also AAYA 10; BEST 90:4; CA 81-84; CANR 16, 40, 81; SATA 98
Saunders, Caleb
See Heinlein, Robert A(nson)
Saura (Atares), Carlos 1932- .... **CLC 20**
See also CA 114; 131; CANR 79; HW 1
Sauser-Hall, Frederic 1887-1961 ...... **CLC 18**
See also Cendrars, Blaise
See also CA 102; 93-96; CANR 36, 62; MTCW 1
Saussure, Ferdinand de 1857-1913 .... **TCLC 49**
Savage, Catharine
See Brosman, Catharine Savage
Savage, Thomas 1915- .... **CLC 40**
See also CA 126; 132; CAAS 15; INT 132
Savan, Glenn 19(?)- .... **CLC 50**
Sayers, Dorothy L(eigh) 1893-1957 .... **TCLC 2, 15; DAM POP**
See also CA 104; 119; CDBLB 1914-1945; DLB 10, 36, 77, 100; MTCW 1, 2
Sayers, Valerie 1952- .... **CLC 50, 122**
See also CA 134; CANR 61
Sayles, John (Thomas) 1950- . **CLC 7, 10, 14**
See also CA 57-60; CANR 41, 84; DLB 44
Scammell, Michael 1935- .... **CLC 34**
See also CA 156
Scannell, Vernon 1922- .... **CLC 49**
See also CA 5-8R; CANR 8, 24, 57; DLB 27; SATA 59
Scarlett, Susan
See Streatfeild, (Mary) Noel
Scarron
See Mikszath, Kalman
Schaeffer, Susan Fromberg 1941- ..... **CLC 6, 11, 22**
See also CA 49-52; CANR 18, 65; DLB 28; MTCW 1, 2; SATA 22
Schary, Jill
See Robinson, Jill
Schell, Jonathan 1943- .... **CLC 35**
See also CA 73-76; CANR 12
Schelling, Friedrich Wilhelm Joseph von 1775-1854 .... **NCLC 30**
See also DLB 90
Schendel, Arthur van 1874-1946 ... **TCLC 56**
Scherer, Jean-Marie Maurice 1920-
See Rohmer, Eric
See also CA 110
Schevill, James (Erwin) 1920- .... **CLC 7**
See also CA 5-8R; CAAS 12
Schiller, Friedrich 1759-1805 . **NCLC 39, 69; DAM DRAM; DC 12**
See also DLB 94
Schisgal, Murray (Joseph) 1926- .... **CLC 6**
See also CA 21-24R; CANR 48, 86
Schlee, Ann 1934- .... **CLC 35**
See also CA 101; CANR 29, 88; SATA 44; SATA-Brief 36
Schlegel, August Wilhelm von 1767-1845 .... **NCLC 15**
See also DLB 94
Schlegel, Friedrich 1772-1829 .... **NCLC 45**
See also DLB 90
Schlegel, Johann Elias (von) 1719(?)-1749 .... **LC 5**
Schlesinger, Arthur M(eier), Jr. 1917- .... **CLC 84**
See also AITN 1; CA 1-4R; CANR 1, 28, 58; DLB 17; INT CANR-28; MTCW 1, 2; SATA 61
Schmidt, Arno (Otto) 1914-1979 ...... **CLC 56**
See also CA 128; 109; DLB 69

Schmitz, Aron Hector 1861-1928
See Svevo, Italo
See also CA 104; 122; MTCW 1
Schnackenberg, Gjertrud 1953- .... **CLC 40**
See also CA 116; DLB 120
Schneider, Leonard Alfred 1925-1966
See Bruce, Lenny
See also CA 89-92
Schnitzler, Arthur 1862-1931 . **TCLC 4; SSC 15**
See also CA 104; DLB 81, 118
Schoenberg, Arnold 1874-1951 ...... **TCLC 75**
See also CA 109
Schonberg, Arnold
See Schoenberg, Arnold
Schopenhauer, Arthur 1788-1860 .. **NCLC 51**
See also DLB 90
Schor, Sandra (M.) 1932(?)-1990 ..... **CLC 65**
See also CA 132
Schorer, Mark 1908-1977 .... **CLC 9**
See also CA 5-8R; 73-76; CANR 7; DLB 103
Schrader, Paul (Joseph) 1946- .... **CLC 26**
See also CA 37-40R; CANR 41; DLB 44
Schreiner, Olive (Emilie Albertina) 1855-1920 .... **TCLC 9**
See also CA 105; 154; DLB 18, 156, 190, 225
Schulberg, Budd (Wilson) 1914- .. **CLC 7, 48**
See also CA 25-28R; CANR 19, 87; DLB 6, 26, 28; DLBY 81
Schulz, Bruno 1892-1942 .. **TCLC 5, 51; SSC 13**
See also CA 115; 123; CANR 86; MTCW 2
Schulz, Charles M(onroe) 1922-2000 .... **CLC 12**
See also CA 9-12R; CANR 6; INT CANR-6; SATA 10
Schumacher, E(rnst) F(riedrich) 1911-1977 .... **CLC 80**
See also CA 81-84; 73-76; CANR 34, 85
Schuyler, James Marcus 1923-1991 .. **CLC 5, 23; DAM POET**
See also CA 101; 134; DLB 5, 169; INT 101
Schwartz, Delmore (David) 1913-1966 ... **CLC 2, 4, 10, 45, 87; PC 8**
See also CA 17-18; 25-28R; CANR 35; CAP 2; DLB 28, 48; MTCW 1, 2
Schwartz, Ernst
See Ozu, Yasujiro
Schwartz, John Burnham 1965- .... **CLC 59**
See also CA 132
Schwartz, Lynne Sharon 1939- .... **CLC 31**
See also CA 103; CANR 44, 89; MTCW 2
Schwartz, Muriel A.
See Eliot, T(homas) S(tearns)
Schwarz-Bart, Andre 1928- .... **CLC 2, 4**
See also CA 89-92
Schwarz-Bart, Simone 1938- . **CLC 7; BLCS**
See also BW 2; CA 97-100
Schwitters, Kurt (Hermann Edward Karl Julius) 1887-1948 .... **TCLC 95**
See also CA 158
Schwob, Marcel (Mayer Andre) 1867-1905 .... **TCLC 20**
See also CA 117; 168; DLB 123
Sciascia, Leonardo 1921-1989 .. **CLC 8, 9, 41**
See also CA 85-88; 130; CANR 35; DLB 177; MTCW 1
Scoppettone, Sandra 1936- .... **CLC 26**
See also AAYA 11; CA 5-8R; CANR 41, 73; SATA 9, 92
Scorsese, Martin 1942- .... **CLC 20, 89**
See also CA 110; 114; CANR 46, 85
Scotland, Jay
See Jakes, John (William)

Scott, Duncan Campbell 1862-1947 .... **TCLC 6; DAC**
See also CA 104; 153; DLB 92
Scott, Evelyn 1893-1963 .... **CLC 43**
See also CA 104; 112; CANR 64; DLB 9, 48
Scott, F(rancis) R(eginald) 1899-1985 .... **CLC 22**
See also CA 101; 114; CANR 87; DLB 88; INT 101
Scott, Frank
See Scott, F(rancis) R(eginald)
Scott, Joanna 1960- .... **CLC 50**
See also CA 126; CANR 53, 92
Scott, Paul (Mark) 1920-1978 ...... **CLC 9, 60**
See also CA 81-84; 77-80; CANR 33; DLB 14, 207; MTCW 1
Scott, Sarah 1723-1795 .... **LC 44**
See also DLB 39
Scott, Walter 1771-1832 . **NCLC 15, 69; DA; DAB; DAC; DAM MST, NOV, POET; PC 13; SSC 32; WLC**
See also AAYA 22; CDBLB 1789-1832; DLB 93, 107, 116, 144, 159; YABC 2
Scribe, (Augustin) Eugene 1791-1861 ..... **NCLC 16; DAM DRAM; DC 5**
See also DLB 192
Scrum, R.
See Crumb, R(obert)
Scudery, Madeleine de 1607-1701 .. **LC 2, 58**
Scum
See Crumb, R(obert)
Scumbag, Little Bobby
See Crumb, R(obert)
Seabrook, John
See Hubbard, L(afayette) Ron(ald)
Sealy, I(rwin) Allan 1951- .... **CLC 55**
See also CA 136
Search, Alexander
See Pessoa, Fernando (Antonio Nogueira)
Sebastian, Lee
See Silverberg, Robert
Sebastian Owl
See Thompson, Hunter S(tockton)
Sebestyen, Ouida 1924- .... **CLC 30**
See also AAYA 8; CA 107; CANR 40; CLR 17; JRDA; MAICYA; SAAS 10; SATA 39
Secundus, H. Scriblerus
See Fielding, Henry
Sedges, John
See Buck, Pearl S(ydenstricker)
Sedgwick, Catharine Maria 1789-1867 .... **NCLC 19**
See also DLB 1, 74
Seelye, John (Douglas) 1931- .... **CLC 7**
See also CA 97-100; CANR 70; INT 97-100
Seferiades, Giorgos Stylianou 1900-1971
See Seferis, George
See also CA 5-8R; 33-36R; CANR 5, 36; MTCW 1
Seferis, George CLC 5, 11
See also Seferiades, Giorgos Stylianou
Segal, Erich (Wolf) 1937- . **CLC 3, 10; DAM POP**
See also BEST 89:1; CA 25-28R; CANR 20, 36, 65; DLBY 86; INT CANR-20; MTCW 1
Seger, Bob 1945- .... **CLC 35**
Seghers, Anna CLC 7
See also Radvanyi, Netty
See also DLB 69
Seidel, Frederick (Lewis) 1936- .... **CLC 18**
See also CA 13-16R; CANR 8; DLBY 84
Seifert, Jaroslav 1901-1986 .. **CLC 34, 44, 93**
See also CA 127; MTCW 1, 2

Smart, Elizabeth 1913-1986 .... **CLC 54**
See also CA 81-84; 118; DLB 88

Smiley, Jane (Graves) 1949- ...... **CLC 53, 76; DAM POP**
See also CA 104; CANR 30, 50, 74; DA3; DLB 227; INT CANR-30

Smith, A(rthur) J(ames) M(arshall) 1902-1980 .... **CLC 15; DAC**
See also CA 1-4R; 102; CANR 4; DLB 88

Smith, Adam 1723-1790 .... **LC 36**
See also DLB 104

Smith, Alexander 1829-1867 .... **NCLC 59**
See also DLB 32, 55

Smith, Anna Deavere 1950- .... **CLC 86**
See also CA 133

Smith, Betty (Wehner) 1896-1972 .... **CLC 19**
See also CA 5-8R; 33-36R; DLBY 82; SATA 6

Smith, Charlotte (Turner) 1749-1806 .... **NCLC 23**
See also DLB 39, 109

Smith, Clark Ashton 1893-1961 .... **CLC 43**
See also CA 143; CANR 81; MTCW 2

Smith, Dave **CLC 22, 42**
See also Smith, David (Jeddie)
See also CAAS 7; DLB 5

Smith, David (Jeddie) 1942-
See Smith, Dave
See also CA 49-52; CANR 1, 59; DAM POET

Smith, Florence Margaret 1902-1971
See Smith, Stevie
See also CA 17-18; 29-32R; CANR 35; CAP 2; DAM POET; MTCW 1, 2

Smith, Iain Crichton 1928-1998 .... **CLC 64**
See also CA 21-24R; 171; DLB 40, 139

Smith, John 1580(?)-1631 .... **LC 9**
See also DLB 24, 30

Smith, Johnston
See Crane, Stephen (Townley)

Smith, Joseph, Jr. 1805-1844 .... **NCLC 53**

Smith, Lee 1944- .... **CLC 25, 73**
See also CA 114; 119; CANR 46; DLB 143; DLBY 83; INT 119

Smith, Martin
See Smith, Martin Cruz

Smith, Martin Cruz 1942- .... **CLC 25; DAM MULT, POP**
See also BEST 89:4; CA 85-88; CANR 6, 23, 43, 65; INT CANR-23; MTCW 2; NNAL

Smith, Mary-Ann Tirone 1944- .... **CLC 39**
See also CA 118; 136

Smith, Patti 1946- .... **CLC 12**
See also CA 93-96; CANR 63

Smith, Pauline (Urmson) 1882-1959 .... **TCLC 25**
See also DLB 225

Smith, Rosamond
See Oates, Joyce Carol

Smith, Sheila Kaye
See Kaye-Smith, Sheila

Smith, Stevie **CLC 3, 8, 25, 44; PC 12**
See also Smith, Florence Margaret
See also DLB 20; MTCW 2

Smith, Wilbur (Addison) 1933- .... **CLC 33**
See also CA 13-16R; CANR 7, 46, 66; MTCW 1, 2

Smith, William Jay 1918- .... **CLC 6**
See also CA 5-8R; CANR 44; DLB 5; MAICYA; SAAS 22; SATA 2, 68

Smith, Woodrow Wilson
See Kuttner, Henry

Smolenskin, Peretz 1842-1885 .... **NCLC 30**

Smollett, Tobias (George) 1721-1771 .. **LC 2, 46**
See also CDBLB 1660-1789; DLB 39, 104

Snodgrass, W(illiam) D(e Witt) 1926- .... **CLC 2, 6, 10, 18, 68; DAM POET**
See also CA 1-4R; CANR 6, 36, 65, 85; DLB 5; MTCW 1, 2

Snow, C(harles) P(ercy) 1905-1980 ... **CLC 1, 4, 6, 9, 13, 19; DAM NOV**
See also CA 5-8R; 101; CANR 28; CDBLB 1945-1960; DLB 15, 77; DLBD 17; MTCW 1, 2

Snow, Frances Compton
See Adams, Henry (Brooks)

Snyder, Gary (Sherman) 1930- . **CLC 1, 2, 5, 9, 32, 120; DAM POET; PC 21**
See also CA 17-20R; CANR 30, 60; DA3; DLB 5, 16, 165, 212; MTCW 2

Snyder, Zilpha Keatley 1927- .... **CLC 17**
See also AAYA 15; CA 9-12R; CANR 38; CLR 31; JRDA; MAICYA; SAAS 2; SATA 1, 28, 75, 110; SATA-Essay 112

Soares, Bernardo
See Pessoa, Fernando (Antonio Nogueira)

Sobh, A.
See Shamlu, Ahmad

Sobol, Joshua **CLC 60**

Socrates 469B.C.-399B.C. .... **CMLC 27**

Soderberg, Hjalmar 1869-1941 ...... **TCLC 39**

Sodergran, Edith (Irene)
See Soedergran, Edith (Irene)

Soedergran, Edith (Irene) 1892-1923 .... **TCLC 31**

Softly, Edgar
See Lovecraft, H(oward) P(hillips)

Softly, Edward
See Lovecraft, H(oward) P(hillips)

Sokolov, Raymond 1941- .... **CLC 7**
See also CA 85-88

Solo, Jay
See Ellison, Harlan (Jay)

Sologub, Fyodor **TCLC 9**
See also Teternikov, Fyodor Kuzmich

Solomons, Ikey Esquir
See Thackeray, William Makepeace

Solomos, Dionysios 1798-1857 .... **NCLC 15**

Solwoska, Mara
See French, Marilyn

Solzhenitsyn, Aleksandr I(sayevich) 1918- .. **CLC 1, 2, 4, 7, 9, 10, 18, 26, 34, 78, 134; DA; DAB; DAC; DAM MST, NOV; SSC 32; WLC**
See also AITN 1; CA 69-72; CANR 40, 65; DA3; MTCW 1, 2

Somers, Jane
See Lessing, Doris (May)

Somerville, Edith 1858-1949 .... **TCLC 51**
See also DLB 135

Somerville & Ross
See Martin, Violet Florence; Somerville, Edith

Sommer, Scott 1951- .... **CLC 25**
See also CA 106

Sondheim, Stephen (Joshua) 1930- . **CLC 30, 39; DAM DRAM**
See also AAYA 11; CA 103; CANR 47, 68

Song, Cathy 1955- .... **PC 21**
See also CA 154; DLB 169

Sontag, Susan 1933- .... **CLC 1, 2, 10, 13, 31, 105; DAM POP**
See also CA 17-20R; CANR 25, 51, 74; DA3; DLB 2, 67; MTCW 1, 2

Sophocles 496(?)B.C.-406(?)B.C. ... **CMLC 2; DA; DAB; DAC; DAM DRAM, MST; DC 1; WLCS**
See also DA3; DLB 176

Sordello 1189-1269 .... **CMLC 15**

Sorel, Georges 1847-1922 .... **TCLC 91**
See also CA 118

Sorel, Julia
See Drexler, Rosalyn

Sorrentino, Gilbert 1929- .. **CLC 3, 7, 14, 22, 40**
See also CA 77-80; CANR 14, 33; DLB 5, 173; DLBY 80; INT CANR-14

Soto, Gary 1952- .... **CLC 32, 80; DAM MULT; HLC 2; PC 28**
See also AAYA 10; CA 119; 125; CANR 50, 74; CLR 38; DLB 82; HW 1, 2; INT 125; JRDA; MTCW 2; SATA 80

Soupault, Philippe 1897-1990 .... **CLC 68**
See also CA 116; 147; 131

Souster, (Holmes) Raymond 1921- .... **CLC 5, 14; DAC; DAM POET**
See also CA 13-16R; CAAS 14; CANR 13, 29, 53; DA3; DLB 88; SATA 63

Southern, Terry 1924(?)-1995 .... **CLC 7**
See also CA 1-4R; 150; CANR 1, 55; DLB 2

Southey, Robert 1774-1843 .... **NCLC 8**
See also DLB 93, 107, 142; SATA 54

Southworth, Emma Dorothy Eliza Nevitte 1819-1899 .... **NCLC 26**

Souza, Ernest
See Scott, Evelyn

Soyinka, Wole 1934- .... **CLC 3, 5, 14, 36, 44; BLC 3; DA; DAB; DAC; DAM DRAM, MST, MULT; DC 2; WLC**
See also BW 2, 3; CA 13-16R; CANR 27, 39, 82; DA3; DLB 125; MTCW 1, 2

Spackman, W(illiam) M(ode) 1905-1990 .... **CLC 46**
See also CA 81-84; 132

Spacks, Barry (Bernard) 1931- .... **CLC 14**
See also CA 154; CANR 33; DLB 105

Spanidou, Irini 1946- .... **CLC 44**
See also CA 185

Spark, Muriel (Sarah) 1918- ..... **CLC 2, 3, 5, 8, 13, 18, 40, 94; DAB; DAC; DAM MST, NOV; SSC 10**
See also CA 5-8R; CANR 12, 36, 76, 89; CDBLB 1945-1960; DA3; DLB 15, 139; INT CANR-12; MTCW 1, 2

Spaulding, Douglas
See Bradbury, Ray (Douglas)

Spaulding, Leonard
See Bradbury, Ray (Douglas)

Spence, J. A. D.
See Eliot, T(homas) S(tearns)

Spencer, Elizabeth 1921- .... **CLC 22**
See also CA 13-16R; CANR 32, 65, 87; DLB 6; MTCW 1; SATA 14

Spencer, Leonard G.
See Silverberg, Robert

Spencer, Scott 1945- .... **CLC 30**
See also CA 113; CANR 51; DLBY 86

Spender, Stephen (Harold) 1909-1995 .... **CLC 1, 2, 5, 10, 41, 91; DAM POET**
See also CA 9-12R; 149; CANR 31, 54; CDBLB 1945-1960; DA3; DLB 20; MTCW 1, 2

Spengler, Oswald (Arnold Gottfried) 1880-1936 .... **TCLC 25**
See also CA 118

Spenser, Edmund 1552(?)-1599 ..... **LC 5, 39; DA; DAB; DAC; DAM MST, POET; PC 8; WLC**
See also CDBLB Before 1660; DA3; DLB 167

Spicer, Jack 1925-1965 .... **CLC 8, 18, 72; DAM POET**
See also CA 85-88; DLB 5, 16, 193

Spiegelman, Art 1948- .... **CLC 76**
See also AAYA 10; CA 125; CANR 41, 55, 74; MTCW 2; SATA 109

Spielberg, Peter 1929- .... **CLC 6**
See also CA 5-8R; CANR 4, 48; DLBY 81

Stone, Robert (Anthony) 1937- ... **CLC 5, 23, 42**
See also CA 85-88; CANR 23, 66; DLB 152; INT CANR-23; MTCW 1

Stone, Zachary
See Follett, Ken(neth Martin)

Stoppard, Tom 1937- ... **CLC 1, 3, 4, 5, 8, 15, 29, 34, 63, 91; DA; DAB; DAC; DAM DRAM, MST; DC 6; WLC**
See also CA 81-84; CANR 39, 67; CDBLB 1960 to Present; DA3; DLB 13; DLBY 85; MTCW 1, 2

Storey, David (Malcolm) 1933- . **CLC 2, 4, 5, 8; DAM DRAM**
See also CA 81-84; CANR 36; DLB 13, 14, 207; MTCW 1

Storm, Hyemeyohsts 1935- ..... **CLC 3; DAM MULT**
See also CA 81-84; CANR 45; NNAL

Storm, Theodor 1817-1888 .... **SSC 27**

Storm, (Hans) Theodor (Woldsen) 1817-1888 .... **NCLC 1; SSC 27**
See also DLB 129

Storni, Alfonsina 1892-1938 . **TCLC 5; DAM MULT; HLC 2**
See also CA 104; 131; HW 1

Stoughton, William 1631-1701 .... **LC 38**
See also DLB 24

Stout, Rex (Todhunter) 1886-1975 ..... **CLC 3**
See also AITN 2; CA 61-64; CANR 71

Stow, (Julian) Randolph 1935- ... **CLC 23, 48**
See also CA 13-16R; CANR 33; MTCW 1

Stowe, Harriet (Elizabeth) Beecher 1811-1896 .... **NCLC 3, 50; DA; DAB; DAC; DAM MST, NOV; WLC**
See also CDALB 1865-1917; DA3; DLB 1, 12, 42, 74, 189; JRDA; MAICYA; YABC 1

Strabo c. 64B.C.-c. 25 .... **CMLC 37**
See also DLB 176

Strachey, (Giles) Lytton 1880-1932 .... **TCLC 12**
See also CA 110; 178; DLB 149; DLBD 10; MTCW 2

Strand, Mark 1934- .... **CLC 6, 18, 41, 71; DAM POET**
See also CA 21-24R; CANR 40, 65; DLB 5; SATA 41

Straub, Peter (Francis) 1943- . **CLC 28, 107; DAM POP**
See also BEST 89:1; CA 85-88; CANR 28, 65; DLBY 84; MTCW 1, 2

Strauss, Botho 1944- .... **CLC 22**
See also CA 157; DLB 124

Streatfeild, (Mary) Noel 1895(?)-1986 .... **CLC 21**
See also CA 81-84; 120; CANR 31; CLR 17; DLB 160; MAICYA; SATA 20; SATA-Obit 48

Stribling, T(homas) S(igismund) 1881-1965 .... **CLC 23**
See also CA 107; DLB 9

Strindberg, (Johan) August 1849-1912 .... **TCLC 1, 8, 21, 47; DA; DAB; DAC; DAM DRAM, MST; WLC**
See also CA 104; 135; DA3; MTCW 2

Stringer, Arthur 1874-1950 .... **TCLC 37**
See also CA 161; DLB 92

Stringer, David
See Roberts, Keith (John Kingston)

Stroheim, Erich von 1885-1957 ..... **TCLC 71**

Strugatskii, Arkadii (Natanovich) 1925-1991 .... **CLC 27**
See also CA 106; 135

Strugatskii, Boris (Natanovich) 1933- .... **CLC 27**
See also CA 106

Strummer, Joe 1953(?)- .... **CLC 30**

Strunk, William, Jr. 1869-1946 ...... **TCLC 92**
See also CA 118; 164

Stryk, Lucien 1924- .... **PC 27**
See also CA 13-16R; CANR 10, 28, 55

Stuart, Don A.
See Campbell, John W(ood, Jr.)

Stuart, Ian
See MacLean, Alistair (Stuart)

Stuart, Jesse (Hilton) 1906-1984 ... **CLC 1, 8, 11, 14, 34; SSC 31**
See also CA 5-8R; 112; CANR 31; DLB 9, 48, 102; DLBY 84; SATA 2; SATA-Obit 36

Sturgeon, Theodore (Hamilton) 1918-1985 .... **CLC 22, 39**
See also Queen, Ellery
See also CA 81-84; 116; CANR 32; DLB 8; DLBY 85; MTCW 1, 2

Sturges, Preston 1898-1959 .... **TCLC 48**
See also CA 114; 149; DLB 26

Styron, William 1925- .... **CLC 1, 3, 5, 11, 15, 60; DAM NOV, POP; SSC 25**
See also BEST 90:4; CA 5-8R; CANR 6, 33, 74; CDALB 1968-1988; DA3; DLB 2, 143; DLBY 80; INT CANR-6; MTCW 1, 2

Su, Chien 1884-1918
See Su Man-shu
See also CA 123

Suarez Lynch, B.
See Bioy Casares, Adolfo; Borges, Jorge Luis

Suassuna, Ariano Vilar 1927-
See also CA 178; HLCS 1; HW 2

Suckling, John 1609-1641 .... **PC 30**
See also DAM POET; DLB 58, 126

Suckow, Ruth 1892-1960 .... **SSC 18**
See also CA 113; DLB 9, 102

Sudermann, Hermann 1857-1928 .. **TCLC 15**
See also CA 107; DLB 118

Sue, Eugene 1804-1857 .... **NCLC 1**
See also DLB 119

Sueskind, Patrick 1949- .... **CLC 44**
See also Suskind, Patrick

Sukenick, Ronald 1932- .... **CLC 3, 4, 6, 48**
See also CA 25-28R; CAAS 8; CANR 32, 89; DLB 173; DLBY 81

Suknaski, Andrew 1942- .... **CLC 19**
See also CA 101; DLB 53

Sullivan, Vernon
See Vian, Boris

Sully Prudhomme 1839-1907 .... **TCLC 31**

Su Man-shu **TCLC 24**
See also Su, Chien

Summerforest, Ivy B.
See Kirkup, James

Summers, Andrew James 1942- .... **CLC 26**

Summers, Andy
See Summers, Andrew James

Summers, Hollis (Spurgeon, Jr.) 1916- .... **CLC 10**
See also CA 5-8R; CANR 3; DLB 6

Summers, (Alphonsus Joseph-Mary Augustus) Montague 1880-1948 .... **TCLC 16**
See also CA 118; 163

Sumner, Gordon Matthew CLC 26
See also Sting

Surtees, Robert Smith 1803-1864 .. **NCLC 14**
See also DLB 21

Susann, Jacqueline 1921-1974 .... **CLC 3**
See also AITN 1; CA 65-68; 53-56; MTCW 1, 2

Su Shih 1036-1101 .... **CMLC 15**

Suskind, Patrick
See Sueskind, Patrick
See also CA 145

Sutcliff, Rosemary 1920-1992 .... **CLC 26; DAB; DAC; DAM MST**
See also AAYA 10; CA 5-8R; 139; CANR 37; CLR 1, 37; JRDA; MAICYA; SATA 6, 44, 78; SATA-Obit 73

Sutro, Alfred 1863-1933 .... **TCLC 6**
See also CA 105; 185; DLB 10

Sutton, Henry
See Slavitt, David R(ytman)

Svevo, Italo 1861-1928 ...... **TCLC 2, 35; SSC 25**
See also Schmitz, Aron Hector

Swados, Elizabeth (A.) 1951- .... **CLC 12**
See also CA 97-100; CANR 49; INT 97-100

Swados, Harvey 1920-1972 .... **CLC 5**
See also CA 5-8R; 37-40R; CANR 6; DLB 2

Swan, Gladys 1934- .... **CLC 69**
See also CA 101; CANR 17, 39

Swanson, Logan
See Matheson, Richard Burton

Swarthout, Glendon (Fred) 1918-1992 .... **CLC 35**
See also CA 1-4R; 139; CANR 1, 47; SATA 26

Sweet, Sarah C.
See Jewett, (Theodora) Sarah Orne

Swenson, May 1919-1989 ...... **CLC 4, 14, 61, 106; DA; DAB; DAC; DAM MST, POET; PC 14**
See also CA 5-8R; 130; CANR 36, 61; DLB 5; MTCW 1, 2; SATA 15

Swift, Augustus
See Lovecraft, H(oward) P(hillips)

Swift, Graham (Colin) 1949- ...... **CLC 41, 88**
See also CA 117; 122; CANR 46, 71; DLB 194; MTCW 2

Swift, Jonathan 1667-1745 ..... **LC 1, 42; DA; DAB; DAC; DAM MST, NOV, POET; PC 9; WLC**
See also CDBLB 1660-1789; CLR 53; DA3; DLB 39, 95, 101; SATA 19

Swinburne, Algernon Charles 1837-1909 .... **TCLC 8, 36; DA; DAB; DAC; DAM MST, POET; PC 24; WLC**
See also CA 105; 140; CDBLB 1832-1890; DA3; DLB 35, 57

Swinfen, Ann CLC 34

Swinnerton, Frank Arthur 1884-1982 .... **CLC 31**
See also CA 108; DLB 34

Swithen, John
See King, Stephen (Edwin)

Sylvia
See Ashton-Warner, Sylvia (Constance)

Symmes, Robert Edward
See Duncan, Robert (Edward)

Symonds, John Addington 1840-1893 .... **NCLC 34**
See also DLB 57, 144

Symons, Arthur 1865-1945 .... **TCLC 11**
See also CA 107; DLB 19, 57, 149

Symons, Julian (Gustave) 1912-1994 .... **CLC 2, 14, 32**
See also CA 49-52; 147; CAAS 3; CANR 3, 33, 59; DLB 87, 155; DLBY 92; MTCW 1

Synge, (Edmund) J(ohn) M(illington) 1871-1909 . **TCLC 6, 37; DAM DRAM; DC 2**
See also CA 104; 141; CDBLB 1890-1914; DLB 10, 19

Syruc, J.
See Milosz, Czeslaw

Szirtes, George 1948- .... **CLC 46**
See also CA 109; CANR 27, 61

Thomas, M. Carey 1857-1935 .... **TCLC 89**
Thomas, Paul
  See Mann, (Paul) Thomas
Thomas, Piri 1928- .... **CLC 17; HLCS 2**
  See also CA 73-76; HW 1
Thomas, R(onald) S(tuart) 1913- .... **CLC 6,**
  13, 48; DAB; DAM POET
  See also CA 89-92; CAAS 4; CANR 30;
  CDBLB 1960 to Present; DLB 27; MTCW
  1
Thomas, Ross (Elmore) 1926-1995 .. **CLC 39**
  See also CA 33-36R; 150; CANR 22, 63
Thompson, Francis Clegg
  See Mencken, H(enry) L(ouis)
Thompson, Francis Joseph
  1859-1907 .... **TCLC 4**
  See also CA 104; CDBLB 1890-1914; DLB
  19
Thompson, Hunter S(tockton)
  1939- ... **CLC 9, 17, 40, 104; DAM POP**
  See also BEST 89:1; CA 17-20R; CANR
  23, 46, 74, 77; DA3; DLB 185; MTCW
  1, 2
Thompson, James Myers
  See Thompson, Jim (Myers)
Thompson, Jim (Myers)
  1906-1977(?) .... **CLC 69**
  See also CA 140; DLB 226
Thompson, Judith **CLC 39**
Thomson, James 1700-1748 ... **LC 16, 29, 40;**
  DAM POET
  See also DLB 95
Thomson, James 1834-1882 .... **NCLC 18;**
  DAM POET
  See also DLB 35
Thoreau, Henry David 1817-1862 .. **NCLC 7,**
  21, 61; DA; DAB; DAC; DAM MST;
  PC 30; WLC
  See also CDALB 1640-1865; DA3; DLB 1,
  223
Thornton, Hall
  See Silverberg, Robert
Thucydides c. 455B.C.-399B.C. ..... **CMLC 17**
  See also DLB 176
Thumboo, Edwin 1933- .... **PC 30**
Thurber, James (Grover)
  1894-1961 .... **CLC 5, 11, 25, 125; DA;**
  DAB; DAC; DAM DRAM, MST, NOV;
  SSC 1
  See also CA 73-76; CANR 17, 39; CDALB
  1929-1941; DA3; DLB 4, 11, 22, 102;
  MAICYA; MTCW 1, 2; SATA 13
Thurman, Wallace (Henry)
  1902-1934 .... **TCLC 6; BLC 3; DAM**
  MULT
  See also BW 1, 3; CA 104; 124; CANR 81;
  DLB 51
Tibullus, Albius c. 54B.C.-c.
  19B.C. .... **CMLC 36**
  See also DLB 211
Ticheburn, Cheviot
  See Ainsworth, William Harrison
Tieck, (Johann) Ludwig
  1773-1853 .... **NCLC 5, 46; SSC 31**
  See also DLB 90
Tiger, Derry
  See Ellison, Harlan (Jay)
Tilghman, Christopher 1948(?)- .... **CLC 65**
  See also CA 159
Tillich, Paul (Johannes)
  1886-1965 .... **CLC 131**
  See also CA 5-8R; 25-28R; CANR 33;
  MTCW 1, 2
Tillinghast, Richard (Williford)
  1940- .... **CLC 29**
  See also CA 29-32R; CAAS 23; CANR 26,
  51
Timrod, Henry 1828-1867 .... **NCLC 25**
  See also DLB 3

Tindall, Gillian (Elizabeth) 1938- ...... **CLC 7**
  See also CA 21-24R; CANR 11, 65
Tiptree, James, Jr. **CLC 48, 50**
  See also Sheldon, Alice Hastings Bradley
  See also DLB 8
Titmarsh, Michael Angelo
  See Thackeray, William Makepeace
Tocqueville, Alexis (Charles Henri Maurice
  Clerel, Comte) de 1805-1859 . **NCLC 7,**
  63
Tolkien, J(ohn) R(onald) R(euel)
  1892-1973 .. **CLC 1, 2, 3, 8, 12, 38; DA;**
  DAB; DAC; DAM MST, NOV, POP;
  WLC
  See also AAYA 10; AITN 1; CA 17-18; 45-
  48; CANR 36; CAP 2; CDBLB 1914-
  1945; CLR 56; DA3; DLB 15, 160;
  JRDA; MAICYA; MTCW 1, 2; SATA 2,
  32, 100; SATA-Obit 24
Toller, Ernst 1893-1939 .... **TCLC 10**
  See also CA 107; 186; DLB 124
Tolson, M. B.
  See Tolson, Melvin B(eaunorus)
Tolson, Melvin B(eaunorus)
  1898(?)-1966 .... **CLC 36, 105; BLC 3;**
  DAM MULT, POET
  See also BW 1, 3; CA 124; 89-92; CANR
  80; DLB 48, 76
Tolstoi, Aleksei Nikolaevich
  See Tolstoy, Alexey Nikolaevich
Tolstoy, Alexey Nikolaevich
  1882-1945 .... **TCLC 18**
  See also CA 107; 158
Tolstoy, Count Leo
  See Tolstoy, Leo (Nikolaevich)
Tolstoy, Leo (Nikolaevich)
  1828-1910 .. **TCLC 4, 11, 17, 28, 44, 79;**
  DA; DAB; DAC; DAM MST, NOV;
  SSC 9, 30; WLC
  See also CA 104; 123; DA3; SATA 26
Tomasi di Lampedusa, Giuseppe 1896-1957
  See Lampedusa, Giuseppe (Tomasi) di
  See also CA 111
Tomlin, Lily **CLC 17**
  See also Tomlin, Mary Jean
Tomlin, Mary Jean 1939(?)-
  See Tomlin, Lily
  See also CA 117
Tomlinson, (Alfred) Charles 1927- .... **CLC 2,**
  4, 6, 13, 45; DAM POET; PC 17
  See also CA 5-8R; CANR 33; DLB 40
Tomlinson, H(enry) M(ajor)
  1873-1958 .... **TCLC 71**
  See also CA 118; 161; DLB 36, 100, 195
Tonson, Jacob
  See Bennett, (Enoch) Arnold
Toole, John Kennedy 1937-1969 ..... **CLC 19,**
  64
  See also CA 104; DLBY 81; MTCW 2
Toomer, Jean 1894-1967 .... **CLC 1, 4, 13, 22;**
  BLC 3; DAM MULT; PC 7; SSC 1;
  WLCS
  See also BW 1; CA 85-88; CDALB 1917-
  1929; DA3; DLB 45, 51; MTCW 1, 2
Torley, Luke
  See Blish, James (Benjamin)
Tornimparte, Alessandra
  See Ginzburg, Natalia
Torre, Raoul della
  See Mencken, H(enry) L(ouis)
Torrence, Ridgely 1874-1950 .... **TCLC 97**
  See also DLB 54
Torrey, E(dwin) Fuller 1937- .... **CLC 34**
  See also CA 119; CANR 71
Torsvan, Ben Traven
  See Traven, B.
Torsvan, Benno Traven
  See Traven, B.

Torsvan, Berick Traven
  See Traven, B.
Torsvan, Berwick Traven
  See Traven, B.
Torsvan, Bruno Traven
  See Traven, B.
Torsvan, Traven
  See Traven, B.
Tournier, Michel (Edouard) 1924- .... **CLC 6,**
  23, 36, 95
  See also CA 49-52; CANR 3, 36, 74; DLB
  83; MTCW 1, 2; SATA 23
Tournimparte, Alessandra
  See Ginzburg, Natalia
Towers, Ivar
  See Kornbluth, C(yril) M.
Towne, Robert (Burton) 1936(?)- ..... **CLC 87**
  See also CA 108; DLB 44
Townsend, Sue **CLC 61**
  See also Townsend, Susan Elaine
  See also AAYA 28; SATA 55, 93; SATA-
  Brief 48
Townsend, Susan Elaine 1946-
  See Townsend, Sue
  See also CA 119; 127; CANR 65; DAB;
  DAC; DAM MST
Townshend, Peter (Dennis Blandford)
  1945- .... **CLC 17, 42**
  See also CA 107
Tozzi, Federigo 1883-1920 .... **TCLC 31**
  See also CA 160
Traill, Catharine Parr 1802-1899 .. **NCLC 31**
  See also DLB 99
Trakl, Georg 1887-1914 .... **TCLC 5; PC 20**
  See also CA 104; 165; MTCW 2
Transtroemer, Tomas (Goesta)
  1931- .... **CLC 52, 65; DAM POET**
  See also CA 117; 129; CAAS 17
Transtromer, Tomas Gosta
  See Transtroemer, Tomas (Goesta)
Traven, B. (?)-1969 .... **CLC 8, 11**
  See also CA 19-20; 25-28R; CAP 2; DLB
  9, 56; MTCW 1
Treitel, Jonathan 1959- .... **CLC 70**
Trelawny, Edward John
  1792-1881 .... **NCLC 85**
  See also DLB 110, 116, 144
Tremain, Rose 1943- .... **CLC 42**
  See also CA 97-100; CANR 44; DLB 14
Tremblay, Michel 1942- .... **CLC 29, 102;**
  DAC; DAM MST
  See also CA 116; 128; DLB 60; MTCW 1,
  2
Trevanian **CLC 29**
  See also Whitaker, Rod(ney)
Trevor, Glen
  See Hilton, James
Trevor, William 1928- .. **CLC 7, 9, 14, 25, 71,**
  116; SSC 21
  See also Cox, William Trevor
  See also DLB 14, 139; MTCW 2
Trifonov, Yuri (Valentinovich)
  1925-1981 .... **CLC 45**
  See also CA 126; 103; MTCW 1
Trilling, Diana (Rubin) 1905-1996 . **CLC 129**
  See also CA 5-8R; 154; CANR 10, 46; INT
  CANR-10; MTCW 1, 2
Trilling, Lionel 1905-1975 .... **CLC 9, 11, 24**
  See also CA 9-12R; 61-64; CANR 10; DLB
  28, 63; INT CANR-10; MTCW 1, 2
Trimball, W. H.
  See Mencken, H(enry) L(ouis)
Tristan
  See Gomez de la Serna, Ramon
Tristram
  See Housman, A(lfred) E(dward)

Trogdon, William (Lewis) 1939-
  See Heat-Moon, William Least
  See also CA 115; 119; CANR 47, 89; INT 119

Trollope, Anthony 1815-1882 ... NCLC 6, 33;
  DA; DAB; DAC; DAM MST, NOV; SSC 28; WLC
  See also CDBLB 1832-1890; DA3; DLB 21, 57, 159; SATA 22

Trollope, Frances 1779-1863 .... NCLC 30
  See also DLB 21, 166

Trotsky, Leon 1879-1940 .... TCLC 22
  See also CA 118; 167

Trotter (Cockburn), Catharine 1679-1749 .... LC 8
  See also DLB 84

Trotter, Wilfred 1872-1939 .... TCLC 97

Trout, Kilgore
  See Farmer, Philip Jose

Trow, George W. S. 1943- .... CLC 52
  See also CA 126; CANR 91

Troyat, Henri 1911- .... CLC 23
  See also CA 45-48; CANR 2, 33, 67; MTCW 1

Trudeau, G(arretson) B(eekman) 1948-
  See Trudeau, Garry B.
  See also CA 81-84; CANR 31; SATA 35

Trudeau, Garry B. CLC 12
  See Trudeau, G(arretson) B(eekman)
  See also AAYA 10; AITN 2

Truffaut, Francois 1932-1984 ... CLC 20, 101
  See also CA 81-84; 113; CANR 34

Trumbo, Dalton 1905-1976 .... CLC 19
  See also CA 21-24R; 69-72; CANR 10; DLB 26

Trumbull, John 1750-1831 .... NCLC 30
  See also DLB 31

Trundlett, Helen B.
  See Eliot, T(homas) S(tearns)

Tryon, Thomas 1926-1991 .... CLC 3, 11;
  DAM POP
  See also AITN 1; CA 29-32R; 135; CANR 32, 77; DA3; MTCW 1

Tryon, Tom
  See Tryon, Thomas

Ts'ao Hsueh-ch'in 1715(?)-1763 .... LC 1

Tsushima, Shuji 1909-1948
  See Dazai Osamu
  See also CA 107

Tsvetaeva (Efron), Marina (Ivanovna) 1892-1941 .... TCLC 7, 35; PC 14
  See also CA 104; 128; CANR 73; MTCW 1, 2

Tuck, Lily 1938- .... CLC 70
  See also CA 139; CANR 90

Tu Fu 712-770 .... PC 9
  See also DAM MULT

Tunis, John R(oberts) 1889-1975 ..... CLC 12
  See also CA 61-64; CANR 62; DLB 22, 171; JRDA; MAICYA; SATA 37; SATA-Brief 30

Tuohy, Frank CLC 37
  See also Tuohy, John Francis
  See also DLB 14, 139

Tuohy, John Francis 1925-
  See Tuohy, Frank
  See also CA 5-8R; 178; CANR 3, 47

Turco, Lewis (Putnam) 1934- ..... CLC 11, 63
  See also CA 13-16R; CAAS 22; CANR 24, 51; DLBY 84

Turgenev, Ivan 1818-1883 .... NCLC 21; DA;
  DAB; DAC; DAM MST, NOV; DC 7; SSC 7; WLC

Turgot, Anne-Robert-Jacques 1727-1781 .... LC 26

Turner, Frederick 1943- .... CLC 48
  See also CA 73-76; CAAS 10; CANR 12, 30, 56; DLB 40

Tutu, Desmond M(pilo) 1931- .... CLC 80;
  BLC 3; DAM MULT
  See also BW 1, 3; CA 125; CANR 67, 81

Tutuola, Amos 1920-1997 ...... CLC 5, 14, 29;
  BLC 3; DAM MULT
  See also BW 2, 3; CA 9-12R; 159; CANR 27, 66; DA3; DLB 125; MTCW 1, 2

Twain, Mark 1835-1910 ...... TCLC 6, 12, 19,
  36, 48, 59; SSC 34; WLC
  See also Clemens, Samuel Langhorne
  See also AAYA 20; CLR 58, 60, 66; DLB 11, 12, 23, 64, 74

20/1631
  See Upward, Allen

Tyler, Anne 1941- . CLC 7, 11, 18, 28, 44, 59,
  103; DAM NOV, POP
  See also AAYA 18; BEST 89:1; CA 9-12R; CANR 11, 33, 53; CDALBS; DLB 6, 143; DLBY 82; MTCW 1, 2; SATA 7, 90

Tyler, Royall 1757-1826 .... NCLC 3
  See also DLB 37

Tynan, Katharine 1861-1931 .... TCLC 3
  See also CA 104; 167; DLB 153

Tyutchev, Fyodor 1803-1873 .... NCLC 34

Tzara, Tristan 1896-1963 ...... CLC 47; DAM
  POET; PC 27
  See also CA 153; 89-92; MTCW 2

Uhry, Alfred 1936- .. CLC 55; DAM DRAM,
  POP
  See also CA 127; 133; DA3; INT 133

Ulf, Haerved
  See Strindberg, (Johan) August

Ulf, Harved
  See Strindberg, (Johan) August

Ulibarri, Sabine R(eyes) 1919- .... CLC 83;
  DAM MULT; HLCS 2
  See also CA 131; CANR 81; DLB 82; HW 1, 2

Unamuno (y Jugo), Miguel de 1864-1936 ..... TCLC 2, 9; DAM MULT,
  NOV; HLC 2; SSC 11
  See also CA 104; 131; CANR 81; DLB 108; HW 1, 2; MTCW 1, 2

Undercliffe, Errol
  See Campbell, (John) Ramsey

Underwood, Miles
  See Glassco, John

Undset, Sigrid 1882-1949 .... TCLC 3; DA;
  DAB; DAC; DAM MST, NOV; WLC
  See also CA 104; 129; DA3; MTCW 1, 2

Ungaretti, Giuseppe 1888-1970 ... CLC 7, 11,
  15
  See also CA 19-20; 25-28R; CAP 2; DLB 114

Unger, Douglas 1952- .... CLC 34
  See also CA 130

Unsworth, Barry (Forster) 1930- .... CLC 76,
  127
  See also CA 25-28R; CANR 30, 54; DLB 194

Updike, John (Hoyer) 1932- . CLC 1, 2, 3, 5,
  7, 9, 13, 15, 23, 34, 43, 70; DA; DAB; DAC; DAM MST, NOV, POET, POP; SSC 13, 27; WLC
  See also CA 1-4R; CABS 1; CANR 4, 33, 51; CDALB 1968-1988; DA3; DLB 2, 5, 143, 227; DLBD 3; DLBY 80, 82, 97; MTCW 1, 2

Upshaw, Margaret Mitchell
  See Mitchell, Margaret (Munnerlyn)

Upton, Mark
  See Sanders, Lawrence

Upward, Allen 1863-1926 .... TCLC 85
  See also CA 117; DLB 36

Urdang, Constance (Henriette) 1922- .... CLC 47
  See also CA 21-24R; CANR 9, 24

Uriel, Henry
  See Faust, Frederick (Schiller)

Uris, Leon (Marcus) 1924- .... CLC 7, 32;
  DAM NOV, POP
  See also AITN 1, 2; BEST 89:2; CA 1-4R; CANR 1, 40, 65; DA3; MTCW 1, 2; SATA 49

Urista, Alberto H. 1947-
  See Alurista
  See also CA 45-48, 182; CANR 2, 32; HLCS 1; HW 1

Urmuz
  See Codrescu, Andrei

Urquhart, Guy
  See McAlmon, Robert (Menzies)

Urquhart, Jane 1949- .... CLC 90; DAC
  See also CA 113; CANR 32, 68

Usigli, Rodolfo 1905-1979
  See also CA 131; HLCS 1; HW 1

Ustinov, Peter (Alexander) 1921- .... CLC 1
  See also AITN 1; CA 13-16R; CANR 25, 51; DLB 13; MTCW 2

U Tam'si, Gerald Felix Tchicaya
  See Tchicaya, Gerald Felix

U Tam'si, Tchicaya
  See Tchicaya, Gerald Felix

Vachss, Andrew (Henry) 1942- .... CLC 106
  See also CA 118; CANR 44

Vachss, Andrew H.
  See Vachss, Andrew (Henry)

Vaculik, Ludvik 1926- .... CLC 7
  See also CA 53-56; CANR 72

Vaihinger, Hans 1852-1933 .... TCLC 71
  See also CA 116; 166

Valdez, Luis (Miguel) 1940- .. CLC 84; DAM
  MULT; DC 10; HLC 2
  See also CA 101; CANR 32, 81; DLB 122; HW 1

Valenzuela, Luisa 1938- .... CLC 31, 104;
  DAM MULT; HLCS 2; SSC 14
  See also CA 101; CANR 32, 65; DLB 113; HW 1, 2

Valera y Alcala-Galiano, Juan 1824-1905 .... TCLC 10
  See also CA 106

Valery, (Ambroise) Paul (Toussaint Jules) 1871-1945 ... TCLC 4, 15; DAM POET;
  PC 9
  See also CA 104; 122; DA3; MTCW 1, 2

Valle-Inclan, Ramon (Maria) del 1866-1936 .... TCLC 5; DAM MULT;
  HLC 2
  See also CA 106; 153; CANR 80; DLB 134; HW 2

Vallejo, Antonio Buero
  See Buero Vallejo, Antonio

Vallejo, Cesar (Abraham) 1892-1938 .. TCLC 3, 56; DAM MULT;
  HLC 2
  See also CA 105; 153; HW 1

Valles, Jules 1832-1885 .... NCLC 71
  See also DLB 123

Vallette, Marguerite Eymery 1860-1953 .... TCLC 67
  See also CA 182; DLB 123, 192

Valle Y Pena, Ramon del
  See Valle-Inclan, Ramon (Maria) del

Van Ash, Cay 1918- .... CLC 34

Vanbrugh, Sir John 1664-1726 .... LC 21;
  DAM DRAM
  See also DLB 80

Van Campen, Karl
  See Campbell, John W(ood, Jr.)

Vance, Gerald
  See Silverberg, Robert

Vance, Jack CLC 35
  See also Vance, John Holbrook
  See also DLB 8

Vance, John Holbrook 1916-
See Queen, Ellery; Vance, Jack
See also CA 29-32R; CANR 17, 65; MTCW
1

Van Den Bogarde, Derek Jules Gaspard
Ulric Niven 1921-1999 .... **CLC 14**
See also CA 77-80; 179; DLB 19

Vandenburgh, Jane **CLC 59**
See also CA 168

Vanderhaeghe, Guy 1951- .... **CLC 41**
See also CA 113; CANR 72

van der Post, Laurens (Jan)
1906-1996 .... **CLC 5**
See also CA 5-8R; 155; CANR 35; DLB
204

van de Wetering, Janwillem 1931- ... **CLC 47**
See also CA 49-52; CANR 4, 62, 90

Van Dine, S. S. **TCLC 23**
See also Wright, Willard Huntington

Van Doren, Carl (Clinton)
1885-1950 .... **TCLC 18**
See also CA 111; 168

Van Doren, Mark 1894-1972 .... **CLC 6, 10**
See also CA 1-4R; 37-40R; CANR 3; DLB
45; MTCW 1, 2

Van Druten, John (William)
1901-1957 .... **TCLC 2**
See also CA 104; 161; DLB 10

Van Duyn, Mona (Jane) 1921- ...... **CLC 3, 7,
63, 116; DAM POET**
See also CA 9-12R; CANR 7, 38, 60; DLB
5

Van Dyne, Edith
See Baum, L(yman) Frank

van Itallie, Jean-Claude 1936- .... **CLC 3**
See also CA 45-48; CAAS 2; CANR 1, 48;
DLB 7

van Ostaijen, Paul 1896-1928 .... **TCLC 33**
See also CA 163

Van Peebles, Melvin 1932- .... **CLC 2, 20;
DAM MULT**
See also BW 2, 3; CA 85-88; CANR 27,
67, 82

Vansittart, Peter 1920- .... **CLC 42**
See also CA 1-4R; CANR 3, 49, 90

Van Vechten, Carl 1880-1964 .... **CLC 33**
See also CA 183; 89-92; DLB 4, 9, 51

Van Vogt, A(lfred) E(lton)
1912-2000 .... **CLC 1**
See also CA 21-24R; CANR 28; DLB 8;
SATA 14

Varda, Agnes 1928- .... **CLC 16**
See also CA 116; 122

Vargas Llosa, (Jorge) Mario (Pedro)
1936- .... **CLC 3, 6, 9, 10, 15, 31, 42, 85;
DA; DAB; DAC; DAM MST, MULT,
NOV; HLC 2**
See also CA 73-76; CANR 18, 32, 42, 67;
DA3; DLB 145; HW 1, 2; MTCW 1, 2

Vasiliu, Gheorghe 1881-1957
See Bacovia, George
See also CA 123; DLB 220

Vassa, Gustavus
See Equiano, Olaudah

Vassilikos, Vassilis 1933- .... **CLC 4, 8**
See also CA 81-84; CANR 75

Vaughan, Henry 1621-1695 .... **LC 27**
See also DLB 131

Vaughn, Stephanie **CLC 62**

Vazov, Ivan (Minchov) 1850-1921 . **TCLC 25**
See also CA 121; 167; DLB 147

Veblen, Thorstein B(unde)
1857-1929 .... **TCLC 31**
See also CA 115; 165

Vega, Lope de 1562-1635 .... **LC 23; HLCS 2**

Venison, Alfred
See Pound, Ezra (Weston Loomis)

Verdi, Marie de
See Mencken, H(enry) L(ouis)

Verdu, Matilde
See Cela, Camilo Jose

Verga, Giovanni (Carmelo)
1840-1922 .... **TCLC 3; SSC 21**
See also CA 104; 123

Vergil 70B.C.-19B.C. .... **CMLC 9, 40; DA;
DAB; DAC; DAM MST, POET; PC
12; WLCS**
See also Virgil
See also DA3; DLB 211

Verhaeren, Emile (Adolphe Gustave)
1855-1916 .... **TCLC 12**
See also CA 109

Verlaine, Paul (Marie) 1844-1896 .. **NCLC 2,
51; DAM POET; PC 2**

Verne, Jules (Gabriel) 1828-1905 ... **TCLC 6,
52**
See also AAYA 16; CA 110; 131; DA3;
DLB 123; JRDA; MAICYA; SATA 21

Very, Jones 1813-1880 .... **NCLC 9**
See also DLB 1

Vesaas, Tarjei 1897-1970 .... **CLC 48**
See also CA 29-32R

Vialis, Gaston
See Simenon, Georges (Jacques Christian)

Vian, Boris 1920-1959 .... **TCLC 9**
See also CA 106; 164; DLB 72; MTCW 2

Viaud, (Louis Marie) Julien 1850-1923
See Loti, Pierre
See also CA 107

Vicar, Henry
See Felsen, Henry Gregor

Vicker, Angus
See Felsen, Henry Gregor

Vidal, Gore 1925- ...... **CLC 2, 4, 6, 8, 10, 22,
33, 72; DAM NOV, POP**
See also AITN 1; BEST 90:2; CA 5-8R;
CANR 13, 45, 65; CDALBS; DA3; DLB
6, 152; INT CANR-13; MTCW 1, 2

Viereck, Peter (Robert Edwin)
1916- .... **CLC 4; PC 27**
See also CA 1-4R; CANR 1, 47; DLB 5

Vigny, Alfred (Victor) de
1797-1863 .. **NCLC 7; DAM POET; PC
26**
See also DLB 119, 192

Vilakazi, Benedict Wallet
1906-1947 .... **TCLC 37**
See also CA 168

Villa, Jose Garcia 1904-1997 .... **PC 22**
See also CA 25-28R; CANR 12

Villarreal, Jose Antonio 1924-
See also CA 133; DAM MULT; DLB 82;
HLC 2; HW 1

Villaurrutia, Xavier 1903-1950 ...... **TCLC 80**
See also HW 1

Villehardouin 1150(?)-1218(?) .... **CMLC 38**

Villiers de l'Isle Adam, Jean Marie Mathias
Philippe Auguste, Comte de
1838-1889 .... **NCLC 3; SSC 14**
See also DLB 123

Villon, Francois 1431-1463(?) .... **PC 13**
See also DLB 208

Vine, Barbara **CLC 50**
See also Rendell, Ruth (Barbara)
See also BEST 90:4

Vinge, Joan (Carol) D(ennison)
1948- .... **CLC 30; SSC 24**
See also AAYA 32; CA 93-96; CANR 72;
SATA 36, 113

Violis, G.
See Simenon, Georges (Jacques Christian)

Viramontes, Helena Maria 1954-
See also CA 159; DLB 122; HLCS 2; HW
2

Virgil 70B.C.-19B.C.
See Vergil

Visconti, Luchino 1906-1976 .... **CLC 16**
See also CA 81-84; 65-68; CANR 39

Vittorini, Elio 1908-1966 .... **CLC 6, 9, 14**
See also CA 133; 25-28R

Vivekananda, Swami 1863-1902 .... **TCLC 88**

Vizenor, Gerald Robert 1934- .... **CLC 103;
DAM MULT**
See also CA 13-16R; CAAS 22; CANR 5,
21, 44, 67; DLB 175, 227; MTCW 2;
NNAL

Vizinczey, Stephen 1933- .... **CLC 40**
See also CA 128; INT 128

Vliet, R(ussell) G(ordon)
1929-1984 .... **CLC 22**
See also CA 37-40R; 112; CANR 18

Vogau, Boris Andreyevich 1894-1937(?)
See Pilnyak, Boris
See also CA 123

Vogel, Paula A(nne) 1951- .... **CLC 76**
See also CA 108

Voigt, Cynthia 1942- .... **CLC 30**
See also AAYA 3, 30; CA 106; CANR 18,
37, 40; CLR 13, 48; INT CANR-18;
JRDA; MAICYA; SATA 48, 79, 116;
SATA-Brief 33

Voigt, Ellen Bryant 1943- .... **CLC 54**
See also CA 69-72; CANR 11, 29, 55; DLB
120

Voinovich, Vladimir (Nikolaevich)
1932- .... **CLC 10, 49**
See also CA 81-84; CAAS 12; CANR 33,
67; MTCW 1

Vollmann, William T. 1959- .. **CLC 89; DAM
NOV, POP**
See also CA 134; CANR 67; DA3; MTCW
2

Voloshinov, V. N.
See Bakhtin, Mikhail Mikhailovich

Voltaire 1694-1778 .... **LC 14; DA; DAB;
DAC; DAM DRAM, MST; SSC 12;
WLC**
See also DA3

von Aschendrof, BaronIgnatz
See Ford, Ford Madox

von Daeniken, Erich 1935- .... **CLC 30**
See also AITN 1; CA 37-40R; CANR 17,
44

von Daniken, Erich
See von Daeniken, Erich

von Hartmann, Eduard
1842-1906 .... **TCLC 96**

von Heidenstam, (Carl Gustaf) Verner
See Heidenstam, (Carl Gustaf) Verner von

von Heyse, Paul (Johann Ludwig)
See Heyse, Paul (Johann Ludwig von)

von Hofmannsthal, Hugo
See Hofmannsthal, Hugo von

von Horvath, Odon
See Horvath, Oedoen von

von Horvath, Oedoen -1938
See Horvath, Oedoen von
See also CA 184

von Liliencron, (Friedrich Adolf Axel)
Detlev
See Liliencron, (Friedrich Adolf Axel) De-
tlev von

Vonnegut, Kurt, Jr. 1922- . **CLC 1, 2, 3, 4, 5,
8, 12, 22, 40, 60, 111; DA; DAB; DAC;
DAM MST, NOV, POP; SSC 8; WLC**
See also AAYA 6; AITN 1; BEST 90:4; CA
1-4R; CANR 1, 25, 49, 75, 92; CDALB
1968-1988; DA3; DLB 2, 8, 152; DLBD
3; DLBY 80; MTCW 1, 2

Von Rachen, Kurt
See Hubbard, L(afayette) Ron(ald)

von Rezzori (d'Arezzo), Gregor
See Rezzori (d'Arezzo), Gregor von

von Sternberg, Josef
See Sternberg, Josef von

Wilson, Edmund 1895-1972 .. **CLC 1, 2, 3, 8, 24**
See also CA 1-4R; 37-40R; CANR 1, 46; DLB 63; MTCW 1, 2

Wilson, Ethel Davis (Bryant)
1888(?)-1980 .... **CLC 13; DAC; DAM POET**
See also CA 102; DLB 68; MTCW 1

Wilson, John 1785-1854 .... **NCLC 5**

Wilson, John (Anthony) Burgess 1917-1993
See Burgess, Anthony
See also CA 1-4R; 143; CANR 2, 46; DAC; DAM NOV; DA3; MTCW 1, 2

Wilson, Lanford 1937- .... **CLC 7, 14, 36; DAM DRAM**
See also CA 17-20R; CABS 3; CANR 45; DLB 7

Wilson, Robert M. 1944- .... **CLC 7, 9**
See also CA 49-52; CANR 2, 41; MTCW 1

Wilson, Robert McLiam 1964- .... **CLC 59**
See also CA 132

Wilson, Sloan 1920- .... **CLC 32**
See also CA 1-4R; CANR 1, 44

Wilson, Snoo 1948- .... **CLC 33**
See also CA 69-72

Wilson, William S(mith) 1932- .... **CLC 49**
See also CA 81-84

Wilson, (Thomas) Woodrow
1856-1924 .... **TCLC 79**
See also CA 166; DLB 47

Winchilsea, Anne (Kingsmill) Finch Counte
1661-1720
See Finch, Anne

Windham, Basil
See Wodehouse, P(elham) G(renville)

Wingrove, David (John) 1954- .... **CLC 68**
See also CA 133

Winnemucca, Sarah 1844-1891 ..... **NCLC 79**

Winstanley, Gerrard 1609-1676 .... **LC 52**

Wintergreen, Jane
See Duncan, Sara Jeannette

Winters, Janet Lewis CLC 41
See Lewis, Janet
See also DLBY 87

Winters, (Arthur) Yvor 1900-1968 .... **CLC 4, 8, 32**
See also CA 11-12; 25-28R; CAP 1; DLB 48; MTCW 1

Winterson, Jeanette 1959- .... **CLC 64; DAM POP**
See also CA 136; CANR 58; DA3; DLB 207; MTCW 2

Winthrop, John 1588-1649 .... **LC 31**
See also DLB 24, 30

Wirth, Louis 1897-1952 .... **TCLC 92**

Wiseman, Frederick 1930- .... **CLC 20**
See also CA 159

Wister, Owen 1860-1938 .... **TCLC 21**
See also CA 108; 162; DLB 9, 78, 186; SATA 62

Witkacy
See Witkiewicz, Stanislaw Ignacy

Witkiewicz, Stanislaw Ignacy
1885-1939 .... **TCLC 8**
See also CA 105; 162

Wittgenstein, Ludwig (Josef Johann)
1889-1951 .... **TCLC 59**
See also CA 113; 164; MTCW 2

Wittig, Monique 1935(?)- .... **CLC 22**
See also CA 116; 135; DLB 83

Wittlin, Jozef 1896-1976 .... **CLC 25**
See also CA 49-52; 65-68; CANR 3

Wodehouse, P(elham) G(renville)
1881-1975 .... **CLC 1, 2, 5, 10, 22; DAB; DAC; DAM NOV; SSC 2**
See also AITN 2; CA 45-48; 57-60; CANR 3, 33; CDBLB 1914-1945; DA3; DLB 34, 162; MTCW 1, 2; SATA 22

Woiwode, L.
See Woiwode, Larry (Alfred)

Woiwode, Larry (Alfred) 1941- ... **CLC 6, 10**
See also CA 73-76; CANR 16; DLB 6; INT CANR-16

Wojciechowska, Maia (Teresa)
1927- .... **CLC 26**
See also AAYA 8; CA 9-12R, 183; CAAE 183; CANR 4, 41; CLR 1; JRDA; MAICYA; SAAS 1; SATA 1, 28, 83; SATA-Essay 104

Wojtyla, Karol
See John Paul II, Pope

Wolf, Christa 1929- .... **CLC 14, 29, 58**
See also CA 85-88; CANR 45; DLB 75; MTCW 1

Wolfe, Gene (Rodman) 1931- .... **CLC 25; DAM POP**
See also CA 57-60; CAAS 9; CANR 6, 32, 60; DLB 8; MTCW 2

Wolfe, George C. 1954- .... **CLC 49; BLCS**
See also CA 149

Wolfe, Thomas (Clayton)
1900-1938 ...... **TCLC 4, 13, 29, 61; DA; DAB; DAC; DAM MST, NOV; SSC 33; WLC**
See also CA 104; 132; CDALB 1929-1941; DA3; DLB 9, 102; DLBD 2, 16; DLBY 85, 97; MTCW 1, 2

Wolfe, Thomas Kennerly, Jr. 1930-
See Wolfe, Tom
See also CA 13-16R; CANR 9, 33, 70; DAM POP; DA3; DLB 185; INT CANR-9; MTCW 1, 2

Wolfe, Tom CLC 1, 2, 9, 15, 35, 51
See also Wolfe, Thomas Kennerly, Jr.
See also AAYA 8; AITN 2; BEST 89:1; DLB 152

Wolff, Geoffrey (Ansell) 1937- .... **CLC 41**
See also CA 29-32R; CANR 29, 43, 78

Wolff, Sonia
See Levitin, Sonia (Wolff)

Wolff, Tobias (Jonathan Ansell)
1945- .... **CLC 39, 64**
See also AAYA 16; BEST 90:2; CA 114; 117; CAAS 22; CANR 54, 76; DA3; DLB 130; INT 117; MTCW 2

Wolfram von Eschenbach c. 1170-c.
1220 .... **CMLC 5**
See also DLB 138

Wolitzer, Hilma 1930- .... **CLC 17**
See also CA 65-68; CANR 18, 40; INT CANR-18; SATA 31

Wollstonecraft, Mary 1759-1797 ..... **LC 5, 50**
See also CDBLB 1789-1832; DLB 39, 104, 158

Wonder, Stevie CLC 12
See also Morris, Steveland Judkins

Wong, Jade Snow 1922- .... **CLC 17**
See also CA 109; CANR 91; SATA 112

Woodberry, George Edward
1855-1930 .... **TCLC 73**
See also CA 165; DLB 71, 103

Woodcott, Keith
See Brunner, John (Kilian Houston)

Woodruff, Robert W.
See Mencken, H(enry) L(ouis)

Woolf, (Adeline) Virginia
1882-1941 .. **TCLC 1, 5, 20, 43, 56; DA; DAB; DAC; DAM MST, NOV; SSC 7; WLC**
See also Woolf, Virginia Adeline
See also CA 104; 130; CANR 64; CDBLB 1914-1945; DA3; DLB 36, 100, 162; DLBD 10; MTCW 1

Woolf, Virginia Adeline
See Woolf, (Adeline) Virginia
See also MTCW 2

Woollcott, Alexander (Humphreys)
1887-1943 .... **TCLC 5**
See also CA 105; 161; DLB 29

Woolrich, Cornell 1903-1968 .... **CLC 77**
See also Hopley-Woolrich, Cornell George

Woolson, Constance Fenimore
1840-1894 .... **NCLC 82**
See also DLB 12, 74, 189, 221

Wordsworth, Dorothy 1771-1855 .. **NCLC 25**
See also DLB 107

Wordsworth, William 1770-1850 .. **NCLC 12, 38; DA; DAB; DAC; DAM MST, POET; PC 4; WLC**
See also CDBLB 1789-1832; DA3; DLB 93, 107

Wouk, Herman 1915- ... **CLC 1, 9, 38; DAM NOV, POP**
See also CA 5-8R; CANR 6, 33, 67; CDALBS; DA3; DLBY 82; INT CANR-6; MTCW 1, 2

Wright, Charles (Penzel, Jr.) 1935- .. **CLC 6, 13, 28, 119**
See also CA 29-32R; CAAS 7; CANR 23, 36, 62, 88; DLB 165; DLBY 82; MTCW 1, 2

Wright, Charles Stevenson 1932- ... **CLC 49; BLC 3; DAM MULT, POET**
See also BW 1; CA 9-12R; CANR 26; DLB 33

Wright, Frances 1795-1852 .... **NCLC 74**
See also DLB 73

Wright, Frank Lloyd 1867-1959 .... **TCLC 95**
See also AAYA 33; CA 174

Wright, Jack R.
See Harris, Mark

Wright, James (Arlington)
1927-1980 .... **CLC 3, 5, 10, 28; DAM POET**
See also AITN 2; CA 49-52; 97-100; CANR 4, 34, 64; CDALBS; DLB 5, 169; MTCW 1, 2

Wright, Judith (Arundell)
1915-2000 .... **CLC 11, 53; PC 14**
See also CA 13-16R; CANR 31, 76; MTCW 1, 2; SATA 14

Wright, L(aurali) R. 1939- .... **CLC 44**
See also CA 138

Wright, Richard (Nathaniel)
1908-1960 .... **CLC 1, 3, 4, 9, 14, 21, 48, 74; BLC 3; DA; DAB; DAC; DAM MST, MULT, NOV; SSC 2; WLC**
See also AAYA 5; BW 1; CA 108; CANR 64; CDALB 1929-1941; DA3; DLB 76, 102; DLBD 2; MTCW 1, 2

Wright, Richard B(ruce) 1937- .... **CLC 6**
See also CA 85-88; DLB 53

Wright, Rick 1945- .... **CLC 35**

Wright, Rowland
See Wells, Carolyn

Wright, Stephen 1946- .... **CLC 33**

Wright, Willard Huntington 1888-1939
See Van Dine, S. S.
See also CA 115; DLBD 16

Wright, William 1930- .... **CLC 44**
See also CA 53-56; CANR 7, 23

Wroth, LadyMary 1587-1653(?) .... **LC 30**
See also DLB 121

Wu Ch'eng-en 1500(?)-1582(?) .... **LC 7**

Wu Ching-tzu 1701-1754 .... **LC 2**

Wurlitzer, Rudolph 1938(?)- .... **CLC 2, 4, 15**
See also CA 85-88; DLB 173

Wyatt, Thomas c. 1503-1542 .... **PC 27**
See also DLB 132

Wycherley, William 1641-1715 ...... **LC 8, 21; DAM DRAM**
See also CDBLB 1660-1789; DLB 80

Wylie, Elinor (Morton Hoyt)
1885-1928 .... **TCLC 8; PC 23**
See also CA 105; 162; DLB 9, 45

Literary Criticism Series
Cumulative Topic Index

This index lists all topic entries in Gale's *Classical and Medieval Literature Criticism, Contemporary Literary Criticism, Literature Criticism from 1400 to 1800, Nineteenth-Century Literature Criticism,* and *Twentieth-Century Literary Criticism.*

Topic Index

CMLC Cumulative Nationality Index

CMLC Cumulative Title Index

     CLASSICAL AND MEDIEVAL LITERATURE CRITICISM

Title Index